# Lecture Notes in Computer Science 8731

Commenced Publication in 1973
Founding and Former Series Editors:
Gerhard Goos, Juris Hartmanis, and Jan van Leeuwen

T0224054

Lejla Batina    Matthew Robshaw (Eds.)

# Cryptographic Hardware and Embedded Systems – CHES 2014

16th International Workshop
Busan, South Korea, September 23-26, 2014
Proceedings

 Springer

Volume Editors

Lejla Batina
Radboud University Nijmegen
FNWI-iCIS/DS
P.O. Box 9010, 6500 GL Nijmegen, The Netherlands
E-mail: lejla@cs.ru.nl

Matthew Robshaw
Impinj, Inc.
701 N. 34th Street, Suite 300, Seattle, WA 98103, USA
E-mail: matt.robshaw@impinj.com

ISSN 0302-9743                          e-ISSN 1611-3349
ISBN 978-3-662-44708-6                   e-ISBN 978-3-662-44709-3
DOI 10.1007/978-3-662-44709-3
Springer Heidelberg New York Dordrecht London

Library of Congress Control Number: 2014947647

LNCS Sublibrary: SL 4 – Security and Cryptology

*Typesetting:* Camera-ready by author, data conversion by Scientific Publishing Services, Chennai, India

Printed on acid-free paper

Springer is part of Springer Science+Business Media (www.springer.com)

# Preface

The 16th International Workshop on Cryptographic Hardware and Embedded Systems was held in Busan, South Korea, during September 23–26, 2014. The workshop was sponsored by the International Association for Cryptologic Research.

CHES 2014 received 127 submissions from all parts of the globe. Each paper was reviewed by at least four independent reviewers, with papers from Program Committee members receiving five reviews in the first round of reviewing. The 43 members of the Program Committee were aided in this complex and time-consuming task by a further 203 external reviewers, providing striking testament to the size and robust health of the CHES community.

Out of the 127 submissions, 33 were chosen for presentation at the workshop. They represented all areas of research that are considered to sit under the CHES umbrella, and they reflected the particular blend of the theoretical and practical that makes CHES such an appealing (and successful) workshop.

We would like to thank the Program Committee and external reviewers for their expert views and spirited contributions to the review process. It was a tremendously difficult task to choose the program for CHES 2014; the standard of submissions was very high. It was even harder to identify a single best paper, but our congratulations go to Naofumi Homma, Yu-ichi Hayashi, Noriyuki Miura, Daisuke Fujimoto, Daichi Tanaka, Makoto Nagata, and Takafumi Aoki from Kobe and Tohoku Universities for the CHES 2014 Best Paper "EM Attack Is Non-Invasive? - Design Methodology and Validity Verification of EM Attack Sensor."

We were delighted that André Weimerskirch was able to accept our invitation to be the invited speaker at CHES 2014. His presentation "V2V Communication Security: A Privacy-Preserving Design for 300 Million Vehicles" cast a fascinating light on a new and far-reaching area of deployment. In addition, expert tutorials by Guido Bertoni and Viktor Fischer and a poster session chaired by Nele Mentens made CHES 2014 the complete workshop. Thank you all for your contributions.

We are, of course, indebted to the general chair, Prof. Kwangjo Kim, and the local Organizing Committee who together proved the ideal liaison for establishing the layout of the program and for supporting the speakers. Our job as program co-chairs was made much easier by the excellent tools developed by Shai Halevi and we offer our thanks to Thomas Eisenbarth, who maintained the CHES 2014 website; both Shai and Thomas were always available at short notice to answer our queries. On behalf of the CHES community we would like to thank the CHES 2014 sponsors. The interest of companies in supporting CHES is an excellent indication of the continued relevance and importance of the workshop.

Finally, we would like to thank all the authors who contributed their work to CHES 2014. Without you, the workshop would not exist.

July 2014

Lejla Batina
Matt Robshaw

# CHES 2014

## Workshop on Cryptographic Hardware and Embedded Systems

Busan, South Korea
September 23–26, 2014

Sponsored by the International Association for Cryptologic Research

## General Chair

Kwangjo Kim                  KAIST, South Korea

## Program Chairs

Lejla Batina                 Radboud University Nijmegen,
                             The Netherlands
Matt Robshaw                 Impinj, USA

## Program Committee

Onur Aciiçmez                Samsung Research America, USA
Dan Bernstein                University of Illinois at Chicago, USA, and
                             Technische Universiteit Eindhoven,
                             The Netherlands
Guido Bertoni                STMicroelectronics, Italy
Christophe Clavier           University of Limoges, France
Jean-Sebastien Coron         University of Luxembourg, Luxembourg
Thomas Eisenbarth            Worcester Polytechnic Institute, USA
Junfeng Fan                  Nationz Technologies, China
Wieland Fischer              Infineon Technologies, Germany
Pierre-Alain Fouque          Université Rennes 1 and Institut Universitaire
                             de France, France
Kris Gaj                     George Mason University, USA
Benedikt Gierlichs           KU Leuven, Belgium
Louis Goubin                 University of Versailles, France
Tim Güneysu                  Ruhr-Universität Bochum, Germany
Dong-Guk Han                 Kookmin University, South Korea
Helena Handschuh             Cryptography Research, USA, and KU Leuven,
                             Belgium
Michael Hutter               Graz University of Technology, Austria

## External Reviewers

François Durvaux
Barış Ege
Maria Eichlseder
Benoit Feix
Martin Feldhofer
Matthieu Finiasz
Robert FitzPatrick
Jean-Pierre Flori
Hamza Fraz
Steven Galbraith
Bayrak Ali Galip
Jean-François Gallais
Berndt Gammel
Lubos Gaspar
Laurie Genelle
Benoit Gerard
Nahid Farhady Ghalaty
Chris Gori
Hannes Gross
Vincent Grosso
Jorge Guajardo
Sylvain Guilley
Frank Gurkaynak
Benoit Gérard
Bilal Habib
Mike Hamburg
Neil Hanley
Christian Hanser
Nadia Heninger
Anthony Van Herrewege
Johann Heyszl
Markus Hinkelmann
Gesine Hinterwälder
Naofumi Homma
Ekawat Homsirikamol
Seokhie Hong
Philippe Hoogvorst
Siam Umar Hussain
Jong-Hyuk Im
Jong-Yeon Park
Pascal Junod
Stefan Katzenbeisser
Stéphanie Kerckhof
HeeSeok Kim
Hyunmin Kim

Tae Hyun Kim
Taewon Kim
Thomas Korak
Po-Chun Kuo
Sebastian Kutzner
Mario Lamberger
Tanja Lange
Martin Lauridsen
Moon Kyu Lee
Vincent van der Leest
Andrew Leiserson
Tancrède Lepoint
Liran Lerman
Yang Li
Zhe Liu
Patrick Longa
Robert Lorentz
Abhranil Maiti
Avradip Mandal
Stefan Mangard
Federica Maria Marino
Damien Marion
Mark Marson
Daniel Martin
Silvia Mella
Filippo Melzani
Florian Mendel
Bernd Meyer
Azalia Mirhoseini
Oliver Mischke
Noriyuki Miura
Amir Moradi
Nadia El Mrabet
Michael Muehlberghuber
Arslan Munir
Yumiko Murakami
Ruben Niederhagen
Eva Van Niekerk
Velickovic Nikola
Ivica Nikolić
Ventzislav Nikov
Svetla Nikova
Martin Novotny
Colin O'Flynn
Katsuyuki Okeya

David Oswald
Jing Pan
Roel Peeters
Pedro Peris-Lopez
John Pham
Thomas Plos
Joop van de Pol
Thomas Pöppelmann
Frank Quedenfeld
Michael Quisquater
Yamini Ravishankar
Christian Rechberger
Oscar Reparaz
Thomas Roche
Pankaj Rohatgi
Sondre Rønjom
Masoud Rostami
Sujoy Sinha Roy
Vladimir Rozic
Minoru Saeki
Gokay Saldamli
Ahmad Salman
Peter Samarin
Jacek Samotyja
Fabrizio De Santis
Pascal Sasdrich
Falk Schellenberg
Werner Schindler
Alexander Schloesser
Martin Schläffer
Tobias Schneider
Rabia Shahid
Aria Shahverdi
Malik Umar Sharif
Koichi Shimizu
Jeong Eun Song
Raphael Spreitzer
Albert Spruyt
François-Xavier
    Standaert
Marc Stoettinger
Daehyun Strobel
Takeshi Sugawara
Berk Sunar
Ruggero Susella

Pawel Swierczynski
Mostafa Taha
Yannick Teglia
Russ Tessier
Adrain Thillard
Mike Tunstall
Pim Tuyls
Kerem Varici
Rajesh Velegalati
Alexandre Venelli
Fre Vercauteren
Dennis Vermoen

Vincent Verneuil
Ivan Visconti
Marcin Wójcik
Megan Wachs
Christian Wachsmann
Erich Wenger
Carolyn Whitnall
Alexander Wild
Theodore Winograd
Christopher Wolf
Jasper van Woudenberg
Antoine Wurcker

Tolga Yalcin
Panasayya Yalla
Dai Yamamoto
Bohan Yang
Shang-Yi Yang
Gavin Xiaoxu Yao
Xin Ye
Meng-Day Yu
Christian Zenger
Ralf Zimmermann

## Local Organizers

Kwangjo Kim          KAIST, South Korea
Kyung Hyune Rhee     Pukyong National University, South Korea
Howon Kim            Pusan National University, South Korea
Daehyun Ryu          Hansei University, South Korea
Sanguk Shin          Pukyong National University, South Korea
Dongkuk Han          Kookmin University, South Korea
Dooho Choi           ETRI, South Korea
Byoungcheon Lee      Joongbu University, South Korea

# Table of Contents

## Algorithm Specific SCA

## ECC Implementations

## Implementations

## Hardware Implementations of Symmetric Cryptosystems

## PUFs

# RNGs and SCA Issues in Hardware

# EM Attack Is Non-invasive?
# - Design Methodology and Validity Verification
# of EM Attack Sensor

Naofumi Homma[1], Yu-ichi Hayashi[1], Noriyuki Miura[2], Daisuke Fujimoto[2],
Daichi Tanaka[2], Makoto Nagata[2], and Takafumi Aoki[1]

[1] Graduate School of Information Sciences, Tohoku University, Japan
homma@aoki.ecei.tohoku.ac.jp
[2] Graduate School of System Informatics, Kobe University, Japan
miura@cs.kobe-u.ac.jp

**Abstract.** This paper presents a standard-cell-based semi-automatic
design methodology of a new conceptual countermeasure against
electromagnetic (EM) analysis and fault-injection attacks. The countermeasure namely EM attack sensor utilizes LC oscillators which detect
variations in the EM field around a cryptographic LSI caused by a micro probe brought near the LSI. A dual-coil sensor architecture with
an LUT-programming-based digital calibration can prevent a variety of
microprobe-based EM attacks that cannot be thwarted by conventional
countermeasures. All components of the sensor core are semiautomati-
cally designed by standard EDA tools with a fully-digital standard cell
library and hence minimum design cost. This sensor can be therefore
scaled together with the cryptographic LSI to be protected. The sensor prototype is designed based on the proposed methodology together
with a 128bit-key composite AES processor in 0.18$\mu$m CMOS with overheads of only 2respectively. The validity against a variety of EM attack
scenarios has been verified successfully.

**Keywords:** EM analysis attack, EM fault injection attack, countermeasure, attack detection, micro EM probe.

## 1 Introduction

Side-channel attacks have become a source of major concern in the design and
evaluation of cryptographic LSIs. In such attacks, side-channel information, such
as power dissipation, electromagnetic (EM) radiation, and/or the timing of internal operations, are observed or manipulated. Two of the best known attacks developed thus far are simple power analysis (SPA) and differential power analysis
(DPA), both of which were proposed by Kocher et al. [1][2]. A variety of related
attacks and countermeasures have been reported [3]. EM analysis (EMA), which
exploits EM radiation from LSIs, is also known as a potentially more versatile
alternative of power analysis [4]-[6].

L. Batina and M. Robshaw (Eds.): CHES 2014, LNCS 8731, pp. 1–16, 2014.

One of the main characteristics of EMA is that it can perform the precise observation of information leakage from a specific part of the target LSI. Such locally observed EM radiation underlies the effectiveness of EMA [7]. In a semi-invasive context, it enables attacks to be performed at the surface of LSIs beyond the conventional security assumptions (i.e., power/EM models or attackers' capabilities). For example, the study on EMA in [8] showed that the use of micro magnetic field probing makes it possible to obtain more detailed information about an unpacked microcontroller. The authors of [8] first showed that the charge (low-to-high transition) and discharge (high-to-low transition) are distinguishable by EMA. The feasibility and effectiveness of localized EM fault injection exploiting this feature were also demonstrated in [9]. In general, such semi-invasive attacks are feasible since a plastic mold package device can be unpacked easily at low cost. Hereafter, we refer to the above sophisticated EM attack measuring and exploiting local information by micro scale probing as "microprobe-based EM attack."

More surprisingly, the possibility of exploiting leaks inside semi-custom ASICs by such microprobe-based EMA was shown in [10]. This impressive work showed current-path and internal-gate leaks in a standard cell, and geometric leaks in a memory macro were measurable by placing a micro magnetic field probe on its surface. This suggests that most of the conventional countermeasures become ineffective if such leaks are measured by attackers. For example, measuring current-path leaks circumvents conventional gate-level countermeasures involving WDDL [11], RSL [12], and MDPL [3]. Furthermore, measuring internal-gate leaks (e.g., from XOR gates) can be used to exploit, for example, XOR gates for unmasking operations. Conventional ROM-based countermeasures using dual-rail and pre-charge techniques can also be circumvented by measuring geometric leaks in a memory macro. These results still seem to be only in the realm of laboratory case studies. However, there is no doubt that microprobe-based EMA attacks on the surface of LSIs represent one of the most feasible types of attacks that operate by exploiting such critical leaks.

In order to reduce current-path and internal-gate leaks, a transistor-level countermeasure was also discussed in [10]. Such leaks can be reduced using transistor-level balancing (hiding). However, transistor-level countermeasures usually increase the design cost and significantly decrease the circuit performance. In the worst-case scenario, designers are required to prepare many balanced cells for every critical component and to perform the place and route with the utmost care. In addition, the literature does not provide any countermeasures against geometric leaks. Thus, the problem of designing effective countermeasures is still open, and the threat of microprobe-based EM attacks using such leaks is expected to increase in the future with the advancement of measurement instruments and techniques.

A natural approach to counteracting microprobe-based EM attacks is to prevent micro probes from approaching the LSI surface. The detection of package opening might be a possible solution [13], but such detection usually employs special packaging materials, which limits its applicability due to the substantial increase in manufacturing cost. In addition, tailored packaging cannot guarantee resistance against attacks from the reverse side of the chip. Another possibility is to install an active shield on or around the LSI to be protected [14]-[16]. However, the power needed to drive signals through the shield is non-trivial. A dynamic active shield surrounding an LSI was first presented in [16]. The new concept of 3D LSI integration is designed to counteract EM attacks exploiting all aspects of the LSI. However, such shielding countermeasures inevitably increase power consumption and implementation cost.

With the aim to address the above issues, this paper introduces a new countermeasure against such high-precision EM attacks using micro EM probes. The countermeasure is based on the physical law that any probe (i.e., a looped conductor) is electrically coupled with the measured object when they are placed close to each other. In other words, a probe cannot measure the original EM field without disturbing it. The proposed method detects the invasion by employing a sensor based on LC oscillators and therefore applies to any EM analysis and fault injection attack implemented with an EM probe placed near the target LSI. Such sensing is particularly resistant to attacks performed very near or on the surface of cryptographic cores, which are usually assumed for microprobe-based EM attacks, such as in [10]. In addition, the countermeasure uses a dual-coil sensor architecture and an LUT-programming-based digital sensor calibration in order to thwart a variety of microprobe-based EM attacks.

The original concept and the key sensor circuit block validation were presented in our previous report [17]. This paper proposes a standard-cell-based semi-automatic design methodology using conventional circuit design tools. A demonstrator LSI chip fully integrating a complete set of an AES processor and the sensor is brand-new designed by the proposed systematic design methodology. The sensor is composed of sensor coils and a sensor core integrated into the cryptographic LSI. It can be designed at the circuit level rather than at the transistor level since all components of the sensor, even including the coils, are semi-automatically designed by standard EDA tools with a fully-digital standard cell library, which minimizes the design cost. The validity and performance of the sensor designed based on the proposed methodology are demonstrated through experiments using a prototype integrating a 128bit-key composite AES processor in a 0.18$\mu$m CMOS process. We confirm that the prototype sensor successfully detects a variety of microprobe-based EM attacks with overheads of only 2% in area, 9% in power, and 0.2% in performance. Thus, the major contributions of the present paper are establishing a systematic design flow for the sensor using conventional circuit design tools, showing that the sensor can be developed at the circuit level, and demonstrating the validity and performance of the prototype sensor designed by using our design flow through a set of experiments for different attack scenarios.

The remainder of this paper is organized as follows. Section 2 introduces the concept of the countermeasure with the EM attack sensor. In Section 3, the semi-automatic design flow for the sensor is proposed. Section 4 shows the experimental results obtained using the prototype integrated into an AES processor

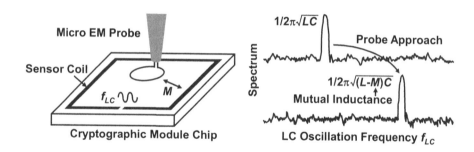

**Fig. 1.** Basic concept

and discusses its capabilities and limitations. Finally, Section 5 presents some concluding remarks.

## 2    EM Attack Sensor

Figure 1 illustrates the basic concept of the EM attack sensor. When a probe (i.e., a looped conductor) is brought close to an LSI (i.e., another electric object), mutual inductance increases. This is a physical law that is unavoidable in magnetic field measurement. Assuming current flowing through a coil (i.e., an LC circuit), its frequency shifts due to the mutual inductance $M$. The original frequency $f_{LC}$ and the shifted frequency $\tilde{f}_{LC}$ are approximately given by

$$f_{LC} \approx \frac{1}{2\pi\sqrt{LC}}, \tag{1}$$

$$\tilde{f}_{LC} \approx \frac{1}{2\pi\sqrt{(L-M)C}}, \tag{2}$$

respectively. Thus, it is possible to detect the presence of a probe that has been placed inside a common LSI package by detecting the frequency shift induced in an LC circuit. Note that the corresponding variation in electric field is also detectable in the equivalent principle by capacitive coupling.

The single-coil sensing scheme in Fig. 1 is simple and straightforward, but it requires a frequency reference generated either inside or outside the LSI for detecting frequency shifts. However, any external clock signal, including a system clock, may be manipulated by the attacker, and therefore cannot be used as a reliable frequency reference. In addition, an on-chip frequency reference requires area- and power-hungry analog circuitry, such as a bandgap reference circuit. These drawbacks of the single-coil scheme are overcome by using a dual- or multi-coil scheme.

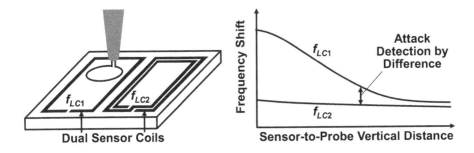

**Fig. 2.** Dual-coil sensor architecture

Figure 2 illustrates the concept of the dual-coil sensor architecture, where two coils are installed on the cryptographic core to be protected. Using two coils with different shape and number of turns, it is possible to detect an approaching probe by the difference of the oscillation frequencies of the two coils. This dual-coil sensor architecture avoids using any absolute frequency reference that is required in the single-coil scheme. The difference of frequencies is constant and remains detectable even if a frequency reference, such as a system clock, is tampered with. In addition, the difference of the frequencies of the two coils enables probe detection in a variety of probing scenarios (e.g., dual probing and cross-coil probing).

To enhance the attack detection accuracy, PVT (process, voltage, and temperature) variation in $f_{LC}$ should be suppressed. A ring oscillator can be utilized as a PVT monitor for calibrating $f_{LC}$ [17]. The abovementioned LC oscillators do not employ any varactor capacitance as they have a positive temperature coefficient ($k_{TC} > 0$). Instead, small MOS capacitors with low $k_{TC}$ are connected to the oscillator only for calibration. The $f_{LC}$ variation in this design is inversely proportional to the transconductance of a $g_m$ cell in the LC oscillator. As a result, the LC and the ring oscillators have a monotonic inverse dependence on PVT, and thus $f_{LC}$ can be digitally calibrated in one step with only two counters and a small lookup table (LUT) used for converting the difference of clock counts into capacitance values (i.e., the number of capacitors).

In the calibration, first we switch on both the LC and ring oscillators, after which we check the outputs of the counters attached to the oscillators, and finally increase or decrease the number of capacitors in accordance with the difference of counts. Here, a relative frequency difference is utilized, similarly to the attack detection concept. Such digital calibration setup is implemented in a compact and low-power manner since it does not require any analog circuitry for frequency reference. In principle, this calibration only handles $f_{LC}$ shift due to PVT variation, and the shift $\Delta f$ due to an approaching probe always remains after the calibration. Even if the probe is placed close to the chip before the power supply is switching on, the probe can be detected immediately after wake-up.

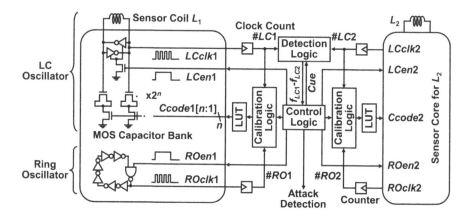

**Fig. 3.** Circuit diagram

## 3   Design Methodology

Figure 3 depicts a circuit diagram of the sensor core circuit. It consists of LC oscillators connected to sensor coils L1 and L2, ring oscillators, a detection logic circuit, two calibration logic circuits, and a control logic circuit. For the best compatibility with the standard digital design flow, standard digital cells are assigned to all the circuit components. The $g_m$ cell of the LC oscillator can be realized by using two gated CMOS inverter and the MOS capacitor bank is composed of $2^n$ sets of unit MOS capacitors with switch controlled by digital binary code Ccode. All other circuit components are of course realized by using the standard digital cell library. The sensor core performs detection of frequency difference, calibration of LC oscillator frequencies, and timing control of the sensor operation.

The detection logic circuit calculates the difference of LC oscillation frequencies by subtracting the clock counts of LCclk1 and LCclk2, which indicate the digitized values of the oscillation frequencies $f_{LC1}$ and $f_{LC2}$, respectively.

The two calibration logic circuits calculate the difference of clock counts of LCclk1 (LCclk2) and ROclk1 (ROclk2) obtained from the LC and ring oscillators, respectively. Here, note that we know both the frequencies of LC and ring oscillators in advance under typical PVT conditions. The difference is converted into the capacitance value Ccode1 (Ccode2) based on the lookup table (LUT) connected to the calibration logic circuit. The Ccode1 (Ccode2) switches the number of capacitors connected to the LC oscillator and consequently calibrates the LC oscillator frequency.

Figure 4 illustrates the process of calibration, where the LC and ring oscillators have a monotonic inverse dependence on the supply voltage and $\Delta C$ indicates the capacitance determined by the difference of LC and ring oscillation frequencies. Although Figure 4 illustrates a case when the supply voltage varies, this calibration method is applicable to variations in process and temperature.

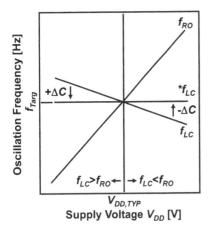

$f_{RO}$:  **Ring Oscillation Frequency**
$f_{LC}$:  **Natural LC Oscillation Frequency**

$$f_{LC} = \frac{1}{2\pi\sqrt{L(C \pm \Delta C)}}$$

$*f_{LC}$ : **Calibrated LC Oscillation Frequency**
$f_{Targ}$ : **Target Frequency after Calibration**
$\Delta C$ : **Capacitance Change for Calibration**
      **(Decided by $|f_{RO}\text{-}f_{LC}|$)**

**Fig. 4.** Calibration scheme

In order to suppress the $f_{LC}$ variation within $\pm1\%$, a 10-bit Ccode resolution is high enough. The LUT for this calibration is essentially a 10-bit subtracter whose gate count is only around 0.2k gates.

The control logic circuit provides the timings of detection and calibration operations, which are determined depending on the cryptographic operation to be protected. Calibration is performed once before the detection operation, which is performed in a timely fashion before and during cryptographic operation. If a frequency difference is detected, a signal to that effect is generated by the control logic circuit. The cryptographic operation is then changed in accordance with the detection signal.

As described above, all components of the sensor core are implemented as fully digital circuits available as standard cells (including transistor switches and capacitance cells), and therefore the sensor can be scaled together with the cryptographic LSI to be protected. The coil size is also scalable due to transistor performance improvement in device scaling. The sensor monitors for probe approach intermittently and periodically, which saves power and minimizes the performance overhead. In addition, the oscillators do not interfere with the cryptographic core since the sensor is usually activated while the cryptographic core is idle.

Figure 5 shows the proposed design methodology for the above sensor with conventional circuit design tools. The cryptographic and sensor cores are first described by a conventional hardware description language (e.g., Verilog-HDL) at the logic design step and synthesized by a logic synthesizer at the logic synthesis step. Logic synthesis is performed for each functional block since it is assumed that all functional blocks handling sensitive data are protected by sensor coils.

After the logic synthesis step, the sensor coils are designed in accordance with the above design. At the netlist generation step, a netlist of the sensor cores is generated for a SPICE simulation of the sensor core. In parallel, the external

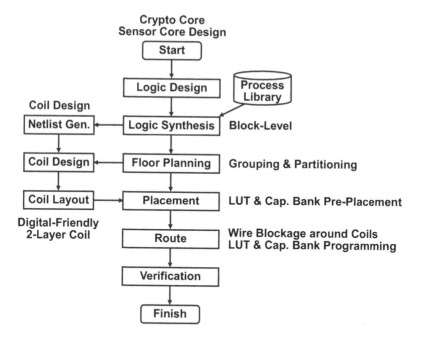

**Fig. 5.** Design flow

shape of the cryptographic and sensor cores is fixed at the floor planning step, which determines the overall coil size (i.e., length and width).

With the coil length and width fixed, at the coil design step, we determine the number of turns, which determines the oscillation frequency. The gap between the wires is also adjusted to fine-tune the oscillation frequency, and the wire width is adjusted to ensure stable oscillation. A wide wire reduces loss in the coil and hence meets the oscillation requirements, at the expense of using more resources to make the wire. Then, we perform a SPICE simulation with the coil parameters for a range of possible PVT conditions and determine the required capacitor bank structure (i.e., the range and step size of capacitance values). Unit capacitors with some margin are pre-arranged at the placement step, and then the actual bank structure is constructed at the following routing step by hard-wire programming between the capacitor bank and the LUT to convert the frequency difference to capacitance value for sensor calibration.

At the coil layout step, we design the coil layout according to the above parameters. Note here that we can utilize digital layout grids to provide the width and spacing of wires. A digital-friendly 2-layer coil layout style [18] is employing where coil is drawn by two different metal layers for orthogonal edges (Fig. 6). The coil can be hidden in the sea of logic interconnections as it only consumes several tens of logic interconnection tracks. Since a high Q factor is not required, it is also not necessary to have a thick upper layer of metal for the coil since phase noise (jitter) in the LC oscillator has no impact on detection

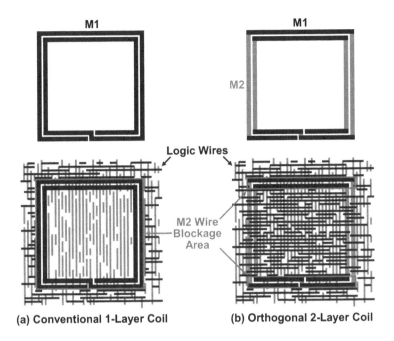

**Fig. 6.** Coil layout: (a) conventional one-layer coil, and (b) orthogonal two-layer coil

accuracy. Therefore, the coil can be fabricated by a standard digital process without any analog/RF options. Unlike analog LC oscillator such as for RF clock synthesizers, careful dedicated analog design is not necessary for this sensor coil and oscillator design, further lowering the design cost.

Based on the coil layout, at the placement and routing step, we place and route the components of the cryptographic and sensor cores, including the capacitor bank and LUT. The capacitor bank has n capacitors of different sizes, and therefore encodes $2^n - 1$ capacitance values for an n-bit input. Finally, we can verify the overall functionality with a digital verification tool at the verification step since the input and output of the sensor core are digital.

## 4   Validity Verification

The validity and performance of the proposed sensor were demonstrated through experiments with a newly fabricated chip designed on the basis of the proposed methodology. We assume here four attack scenarios with a single microprobe approaching during the sensing period, a larger micro probe approaching during the sensing period, a single micro probe approaching while the supply voltage was being changed, and a single micro probe approaching before the sensing period (i.e., during the sleep period). The first scenario assumed a conventional microprobe-based EM attack, such as that described in [8] and [10], where attackers move a microprobe close to the core surface while the sensor is working.

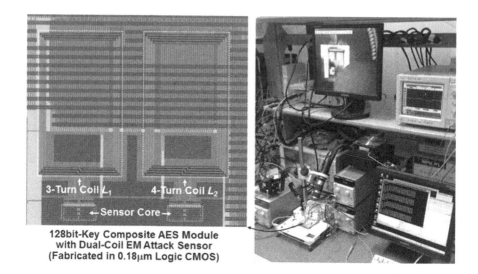

**Fig. 7.** Die photograph and measurement setup

The second scenario assumed an attempt to avoid detection by a larger probe crossing the two coils. This scenario is equivalent to EMA with two micro probes close to the two coils at the same time. The third scenario assumed that the attacker manipulate the PVT conditions to cheat the sensor. Finally, the fourth scenario assumed that the attacker can place a micro probe on the core surface in advance before the cryptographic and sensor cores are switched on, manipulating the PVT conditions.

The proposed sensor was implemented in a TSMC $0.18\mu m$ CMOS process by commercial CAD tools. More precisely, we used Design Compiler (G-2012.06-SP3), IC Compiler (vH-2013.03-SP2), and Virtuoso (6.1.4) for the logic synthesis, the P&R, and the coil design, respectively. Figure 7 shows a die photograph and the measurement setup. Two coils (a 4-turn coil (L1) and a 3-turn coil (L2)) were placed above an AES processor. The L1 (L2) coil had the resistance of $76\Omega$ ($55\Omega$), the capacitance of 68fF (64fF), and the inductance of 13.2nH (8.5nH) according to the EM field simulation with an equivalent circuit model. The AES processor was based on a common loop architecture operating at one round per clock cycle [19]. The test chip was mounted on a side-channel attack standard evaluation board (SASEBO R-II) [20]. A micro EM probe was fixed on a manipulator, and its position was controlled manually by monitoring through a microscope. We conducted successful microprobe-based EMA using EM waveforms observed in the experimental setup, where the EM signal from the probe was amplified by a 100 W +40 dB power amplifier.

Figure 8 shows the frequency spectra of L1 and L2 in the presence and absence of a micro probe. The oscillation frequency of each coil was clearly shifted by the probe, even at a distance of about $100\mu m$. The result indicates that

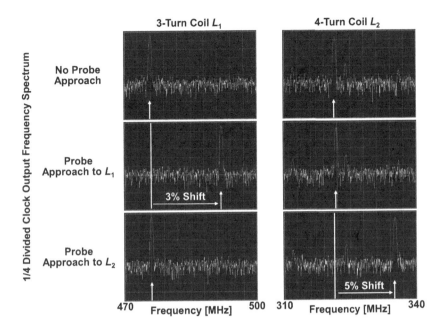

**Fig. 8.** Frequency shift caused by an approaching probe

microprobe-based EM attacks such as those assumed in the first scenario can be easily detected by the sensor.

Figure 9 shows the difference of the frequency shifts of L1 and L2 for different distances between the coils and the probe. The shift ratio of L1 was clearly different from that of L2 when the same probe was used. This suggests that the second scenario is also thwarted by our dual-coil detection scheme. Even if the attacker can observe the magnitude of the frequency shifts, they would still have substantial difficulty in matching the shifts, which are determined by many coil parameters, while performing high-density EM measurements. This result indicates that EM attacks with two micro probes are also detectable.

Figure 10 (a) presents the frequency shift dependence on the supply voltage VDD, where the left and right hands of the figure are the amount of frequency shifts before and after the calibration, respectively. The proposed one-step digital calibration suppresses the $f_{LC}$ variation to within $\pm 1\%$ over the temperature range of 0-60 °C at a VDD voltage of 1.6-2.0 V which corresponds to a variation greater than $\pm 10\%$ from the nominal VDD voltage of 1.8 V. This result shows that the proposed sensor is robust against PVT variation since the same calibration method is applicable for a range of possible PVT conditions.

Figure 10 (a) also shows that the sensor can thwart the fourth scenario. The frequency shift due to the approaching probe remains after calibration. The result indicates that even if the probe is brought close to the cryptographic core before its power supply is switched on, the probe can be detected immediately after wake-up. Figure 10 (b) presents the result for a sophisticated fourth

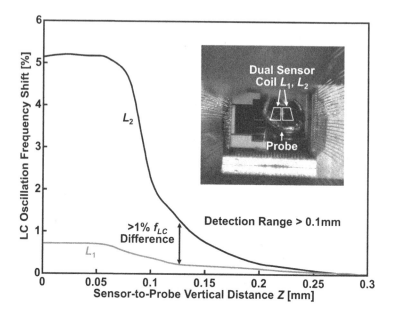

**Fig. 9.** Difference of frequency shifts of L1 and L2 for different distances

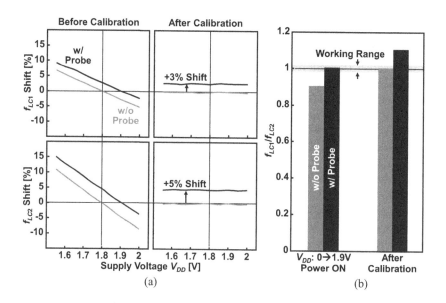

**Fig. 10.** Frequency shifts before and after calibration

scenario, where the attacker can manipulate the supply voltage and suppress $f_{LC}$ variation to within the working range ($\pm 1\%$) with a micro probe close to the core surface just after the power is switched on. It should be noted that such

**Table 1.** Overheads caused by sensor

|  | AES Core | Sensor | Total (Sensor Overhead) |
|---|---|---|---|
| 2NAND Gate Count | 24.3k | 0.3k | 24.6k (+1.2%) |
| Wire Resource | 0.40mm$^2$ | 0.05mm$^2$ | 0.45mm$^2$ (+11%) |
| Layout Area | 0.48mm$^2$ | 0.01mm$^2$ | 0.49mm$^2$ (+2%) |
| Performance | 125$\mu$s/Enc | 0.3$\mu$s/Sense | 125.3$\mu$s (-0.2%) |
| Power Consumption | 0.23mW | 0.02mW | 0.25mW (+9%) |

cheating was also thwarted by the calibration since the $f_{LC}$ variation is always corrected to within ±1% in the absence of a probe.

Table 1 summarizes the overheads caused by the sensor hardware. The time for a single detection operation (including calibration and sense operations) can be reduced to <1% of the time for one AES encryption operation, including data I/O. Note that the application considered here is a simple device with a few IO pins, such as smartcard, which can be mainly targeted by microprobe-based EMA. Such device usually equips serial IO and outputs the data at each time. This intermittent sensor operation at <1% duty cycle significantly reduces the power and performance overheads of the sensor. The power consumption was estimated from a calibration-and-sense operation before an AES encryption operation. With overheads of only 2% in area and 9% in power, the proposed sensor can be used as a countermeasure against microprobe-based EM attacks, filling a large security hole not covered by conventional countermeasures.

## 5   Discussion

The experimental results show that the proposed sensor is effective against micro-probe-based EM attacks which cannot be prevented by the conventional algorithmic- and circuit-level countermeasures. EM fault-injection attacks using a micro needle probe, such as that in [9], are also detected by the same principle. Using middle layers to draw sensor coils could also prevent attacks from the backside of the LSI since the magnetic sensing can work through interconnect, transistor and substrate layers. Thus, the proposed countermeasure can detect EM analysis and fault-injection attacks performed close to or on the LSI (front and back) surface in a robust manner.

The proposed sensor would also be invulnerable to frequency injection attacks. First, attackers must measure the original frequency very close to the coil surface but cannot measure it without disturbing the original one. Even if the frequency is known, a significant EM injection power is required to lock an oscillator since each coil is oscillating in a full swing manner. Such powerful EM injection must affect another oscillator. Note again that the oscillation frequencies are different for each other. If both oscillators are locked to the same frequency, the sensor detects it immediately. An attacker might attempt to attach a frequency-injection probe directly to an embedded coil, but it is hard to do it without affecting other wires.

One possible attack on the proposed setup would be to eliminate the difference between oscillation frequencies observed by the sensor by using two probes or similar alternatives. However, performing such a sophisticated attack is extremely difficult, even if the attacker can observe the frequency shifts shown in the above experiments. In addition, it is difficult to identify and disable the sensor prior to the attack since the coils and the sensor core are embedded in the sea of logic gates and wires. Reverse engineering to removing the sensor would also be a rather challenging task when the cryptographic core operation is linked with the sensor operation.

The detectable distance between the probe and the sensor is limited to a maximum of 0.1 mm in the experimental setup. The limited maximum detection distance means that conventional EMAs on the chip package such as DEMA and CEMA are still possible, even if the proposed sensor is installed over the cryptographic core. The extension of the maximum detection distance is an open issue that will be addressed in future work. For example, we could extend the detection distance using larger coils. Extending the maximum distance may enable the sensor to detect chip unpacking as well. On the other hand, the proposed sensor can be combined with any other conventional countermeasures due to the low area and performance overheads. In practice, a combination of conventional countermeasures and the proposed technique would work well in a complementary manner.

The power and performance overheads are further reduced by the optimization of intermittent sensor operation. The sensor should operate continuously during the cryptographic operations for increased security. However, intermittent operation would be sufficient for many applications. For example, one-time calibration and sensing before continuous cryptographic operations might be practical. Designers and users can determine the operation timing according to the target application and intended use. The post-detection operations (e.g., termination or dummy operations) should also be optimized depending on the application. Such optimizations will also be examined in future work.

## 6    Conclusion

This paper presented the design methodology and validity verification of a new countermeasure against microprobe-based EM analysis and fault-injection attacks. The proposed countermeasure detects variations in the EM field caused by a micro EM probe approaching the cryptographic LSI, and therefore thwarts microprobe-based EMA that cannot be prevented by conventional algorithmic- and circuit-level countermeasures. A dual-coil sensor architecture and an LUT-programming-based digital sensor calibration can prevent such EM attacks in a variety of scenarios where one or more micro EM probes are used under different PVT conditions. All components of the sensor core are implemented in a fully digital circuit and therefore can be scaled together with the cryptographic LSI to be protected.

The proposed systematic design flow for the sensor is based on standard digital circuit design tools. All the sensor circuit components, including the sensor coils, was semi-automatically designed by the synthesis and placement software once the coil parameters were fixed. The validity and performance of the sensor were demonstrated through experiments using a prototype integrated into an AES processor. The results show that our sensor successfully detects microscale EM probes approaching the AES processor for all assumed attack scenarios.

The sensor was designed based on the proposed design flow and integrated with overheads of only 2% in area, 9% in power, and 0.2% in performance, which are much lower than those of alternative active shield techniques. Such low overheads make it possible to implement the proposed technique together with conventional countermeasures developed for other types of attacks. Although the proposed countermeasure cannot thwart all types of EM attacks, it can significantly reduce the complexity and cost associated with conventional countermeasures against microprobe-based EMA. One direction of future work will be to find the most effective combination of the proposed and conventional countermeasures.

# References

1. Kocher, P.C.: Timing attacks on implementations of Diffie-Hellman, RSA, DSS, and other systems. In: Koblitz, N. (ed.) CRYPTO 1996. LNCS, vol. 1109, pp. 104–113. Springer, Heidelberg (1996)
2. Kocher, P.C., Jaffe, J., Jun, B.: Differential power analysis. In: Wiener, M. (ed.) CRYPTO 1999. LNCS, vol. 1666, pp. 388–397. Springer, Heidelberg (1999)
3. Mangard, S., Oswald, E., Popp, T.: Power Analysis Attacks - Revealing the Secrets of Smart Cards. Springer (2007)
4. Gandolfi, K., Mourtel, C., Olivier, F.: Electromagnetic analysis: Concrete results. In: Koç, Ç.K., Naccache, D., Paar, C. (eds.) CHES 2001. LNCS, vol. 2162, pp. 251–261. Springer, Heidelberg (2001)
5. Quisquater, J., Samyde, D.: Electromagnetic analysis (EMA): Measures and counter-measures for smart cards. In: Attali, S., Jensen, T. (eds.) E-smart 2001. LNCS, vol. 2140, pp. 200–210. Springer, Heidelberg (2001)
6. Agrawal, D., Archambeault, B., Rao, R., Rohatgi, P.: The EM side-channel(s). In: Kaliski Jr., B.S., Koç, Ç.K., Paar, C. (eds.) CHES 2002. LNCS, vol. 2523, pp. 29–45. Springer, Heidelberg (2003)
7. Réal, D., Valette, F., Drissi, M.: Enhancing Correlation Electromagnetic Attack Using Planar Near-Field Cartography. In: DATE 2009, pp. 628–633 (2009)
8. Peeters, E., Standaert, X., Quisquater, J.: Power and electromagnetic analysis: Improved model, consequences and comparisons. Integration, the VLSI Journal 40(1), 52–60 (2007)
9. Moro, N., Dehbaoui, A., Heydemann, K., Robisson, B., Encrenaz, E.: Electromagnetic fault injection: towards a fault model on a 32-bit microcontroller. In: FDTC 2013, pp. 77–88 (August 2013)
10. Sugawara, T., Suzuki, D., Saeki, M., Shiozaki, M., Fujino, T.: On Measurable Side-Channel Leaks Inside ASIC Design Primitives. In: Bertoni, G., Coron, J.-S. (eds.) CHES 2013. LNCS, vol. 8086, pp. 159–178. Springer, Heidelberg (2013)
11. Tiri, K., Hwang, D., Hodjat, A., Lai, B.-C., Yang, S., Schaumont, P., Verbauwhede, I.: Prototype IC with WDDL and differential routing – DPA resistance assessment. In: Rao, J.R., Sunar, B. (eds.) CHES 2005. LNCS, vol. 3659, pp. 354–365. Springer, Heidelberg (2005)

12. Suzuki, D., Saeki, M., Ichikawa, T.: Random Switching Logic: A Countermeasure against DPA based on Transition Probability, IACR Cryptology ePrint Archive 2004: 346 (2004)
13. Van Geloven, J.A.J., Wolters, R.A.M., Verhaegh, N.: Sensing circuit for devices with protective coating, United States Patent no. US 2010/0090714 Al (2010)
14. Beit-Grogger, A., Riegebauer, J.: Integrated circuit having an active shield. United States Patent no. 6,962,294 (2005)
15. Briais, S., Cioranesco, J.-M., Danger, J.-L., Guilley, S., Jourdan, J.-H., Milchior, A., Naccache, D., Porteboeuf, T.: Random Active Shield. In: FDTC 2012, pp. 103–113 (September 2012)
16. Briais, S., et al.: 3D Hardware Canaries. In: Prouff, E., Schaumont, P. (eds.) CHES 2012. LNCS, vol. 7428, pp. 1–22. Springer, Heidelberg (2012)
17. Miura, N., Fujimoto, D., Tanaka, D., Hayashi, Y., Homma, N., Aoki, T., Nagata, M.: A Local EM-Analysis Attack Resistant Cryptographic Engine with Fully-Digital Oscillator-Based Tamper-Access Sensor. In: 2014 Symposium on VLSI Circuits, Dig. Tech. Papers, pp. 172–173 (June 2014)
18. Saito, M., Kusaga, K., Takeya, T., Miura, N., Kuroda, T.: An Extended XY Coil for Noise Reduction in Inductive-coupling Link. A-SSCC Dig. Tech. Papers, pp. 305–308 (November 2009)
19. Cryptographic Hardware Project (August 2007),
    http://www.aoki.ecei.tohoku.ac.jp/crypto/
20. Side-channel Attack Standard Evaluation Board, SASEBO-RII (2012),
    http://www.risec.aist.go.jp/project/sasebo/

# A New Framework for Constraint-Based Probabilistic Template Side Channel Attacks

Yossef Oren[1], Ofir Weisse[2], and Avishai Wool[3]

[1] Network Security Lab, Columbia University, USA
[2] School of Computer Science, Tel-Aviv University, Israel
[3] School of Electrical Engineering, Tel-Aviv University, Israel
yos@cs.columbia.edu, ofirweisse@gmail.com, yash@eng.tau.ac.il

**Abstract.** The use of constraint solvers, such as SAT- or Pseudo-Boolean-solvers, allows the extraction of the secret key from one or two side-channel traces. However, to use such a solver the cipher must be represented at bit-level. For byte-oriented ciphers this produces very large and unwieldy instances, leading to unpredictable, and often very long, run times. In this paper we describe a specialized byte-oriented constraint solver for side channel cryptanalysis. The user only needs to supply code snippets for the native operations of the cipher, arranged in a flow graph that models the dependence between the side channel leaks. Our framework uses a soft decision mechanism which overcomes realistic measurement noise and decoder classification errors, through a novel method for reconciling multiple probability distributions. On the DPA v4 contest dataset our framework is able to extract the correct key from one or two power traces in under 9 seconds with a success rate of over 79%.

**Keywords:** Constraint solvers, power analysis, template attacks.

## 1 Introduction

In a constraint-based side-channel attack, the attacker is provided with a device under test (DUT) which performs a cryptographic operation (e.g., encryption). While performing this operation the device emits a data dependent side-channel leakage such as power consumption trace. As a result of the data dependence, a certain number of leaks are modulated into the trace together with some noise. In order to recover the secret key from a power trace the attacker performs the following steps:

*Profiling*: The DUT is analyzed in order to identify the position of the leaking operations in the traces, for instance by using classical side-channel attacks like CPA [4]. Then a decoding process is devised, that maps between a single power trace and a vector of leaks. A common output of the decoder is the Hamming weight of the processed data as in [22], but many other decoders are possible. An effective profiling method is a template attack, which was introduced in [5]. Profiling is an offline activity.

*Decoding*: After the profiling phase, the attacker is provided with a small number of power traces (typically, a single trace). The decoding process is applied

L. Batina and M. Robshaw (Eds.): CHES 2014, LNCS 8731, pp. 17–34, 2014.

to the power trace, and a vector of leaks is recovered. This vector of leaks may contain some errors, e.g., due to the effect of noise.

*Solving*: The leak vector, together with a description of the algorithm implemented in the DUT, and additional auxiliary information, is converted to a representation that is suitable to a constraint solver: e.g., a SAT-solver [21,22,28] or a Pseudo-Boolean solver [17,18]. The solver solves the problem instance, outputting the best candidates satisfying the constraints. However, previously used solvers require a bit-level representation which creates several challenges. In this paper we suggest a new solver which uses a byte-level representation.

**Related Work.** Side channel cryptanalysis was first suggested in [12] (cf. [13]). Template attacks were introduced in [5] and further explored in papers such as [24,20,7]. Algebraic side-channel attacks were introduced by Renauld et al. in [21,22], and first applied to the block ciphers PRESENT [3] and AES [15]. These works showed how keys can be recovered from a single measurement trace of these algorithms implemented in an 8-bit microcontroller, provided that the attacker can identify the Hamming weights of several intermediate computations during the encryption process. Already in these papers, it was observed that noise was the main limiting factor for algebraic attacks. To mitigate this issue, a heuristic solution was introduced in [22], and further elaborated in [28,14]. The main idea was to adapt the leakage model in order to trade some loss of information for more robustness, for example by grouping hard-to-distinguish Hamming weight values together into sets. An alternative proposal [17] suggested to include the imprecise Hamming weights in the equation set, and to deal with these imprecisions via the solver.

Despite their success, using generic SAT solvers or Pseudo-Boolean solvers still leaves room for improvement. The difficulties stem from the fact that in order to use them, the cipher representation has to be reduced to the bit-level. For byte-oriented ciphers this produces very large and complex instances, that are challenging to construct and debug. [16] notes that an AES equations instance may reach a size of 2.3 MB, depending on the methodology used to construct the equations. However, the most problematic aspect of bit-level solvers is their unpredictable, and often very long, run times. In [18] the authors report that run times vary over an order of magnitude between 8.2 hours to more than 143 hours on instances belonging to the same data set. The solver behavior is very sensitive to technical representation issues, and is controlled by a myriad of configuration parameters that are unrelated to the cryptographic task. Algebraic side-channel attacks which use local calculations were also considered in [26] and in [8].

**Contribution.** The focus of this work is a new *constraint solver*. Our solver embeds a model of the encryption process, accepts the known plain-text, and the output of the *decoder*, and outputs the highest probability keys with an estimation of their likelihood. However, unlike the algebraic attacks of [22] and [18], our constraint solver is not a general purpose Pseudo-Boolean or SAT-solver.

We wrote a special solver that is targeted at the unique types of constraints that occur in a side channel cryptanalysis of byte-oriented ciphers. Our solver is fundamentally probabilistic. It tracks the likelihoods of values in the secret key bytes, and updates them step by step through the encryption process, utilizing the probability distributions output by the decoder. A key ingredient in our framework is a novel method for reconciling multiple probability distributions for the same variable.

Applying our framework to a byte-oriented cipher with available side-channel information is quite natural and does not involve complex representation conversions into bit-level equations: the user needs to supply code snippets for the native byte-level operations of the cipher, arranged in a flow graph that embeds the functional dependence between the side channel leaks. Our framework uses a soft decision mechanism which overcomes realistic measurement noise and decoder classification errors.

As in previous solver-based attacks, our framework requires a *decoder*. The decoder accepts a single power trace, and outputs estimates of multiple intermediate values that are computed during the encryption and leaked by the side-channel. An estimate of a leaked value $X$ in our framework is not a single "hard decision" value. Rather, as in [18], it is a probability distribution over the possible values of $X$. The decoder is usually constructed as a template decoder [5]. As in [18] we do not assume a Hamming-weight model for the leaked values - the decoder may output any probability distribution over the leak values. Note further that we do not impose a particular noise model on the decoder - e.g., it is not required to output only a single Hamming-weight value (or set of $k$ values, as done by [28] and [18]).

We tested our framework on the DPA v4 contest dataset [2]. On this dataset, our framework is able to extract the correct key from one or two power traces with predictable and very short run times. Our results show a success rate of over 79% using just two measurements and typical run times are under 9 seconds. The source code can be downloaded from [27].

**Organization.** In the next section we introduce the probabilistic tools used in our solver. In Section 3 we describe the construction of the solver's flow graph. In Section 4 we show how we applied our method to AES. Section 5 includes the performance evaluation we conducted using the DPAv4 traces, and we conclude with Section 6.

# 2    Probabilistic Methodology

## 2.1    The Conflation Operator

A central part of our framework is a novel method of reconciling probability distributions. The basic scenario is as follows. Suppose we are trying to measure an unknown quantity $X$ via two experiments. The outcome of the first experiment $E_1$ is a probability distribution $P_{E_1}$ such that $P_{E_1}(X = i)$ is the likelihood that X has value $i$. The second experiment $E_2$ measures the value of $X$ using a different method, providing a second distribution $P_{E_2}$. We now wish to reconcile the results of these two experiments into a combined distribution $\hat{P}$. Intuitively, we want $\hat{P}$ to "strengthen" values on which $E_1$ and $E_2$ agree, and "weaken" values on which $E_1$ and $E_2$ differ. Thus, we want a probabilistic analogue to the logical "AND" operator. At one extreme, if $P_{E_1}(X = i) = 0$ (the value $i$ is impossible according to $E_1$) then we want $\hat{P}(X = i) = 0$. At another extreme, if $P_{E_2}(X = i) = \frac{1}{N}$ for all $N$ possible values of $X$ ($E_2$ provides no information about $X$) then we want $\hat{P} = P_{E_1}$.

This general question was tackled by [9,10,11,6]. In particular, Hill [9] suggests a method called *conflation*, which is essentially the point-product of the distributions. In the case of two experiments $E_1, E_2$ the conflated probability $\hat{P} = \&(P_{E_1}, P_{E_2}) = (\hat{p}_1, .., \hat{p}_N)$ is defined as

$$\hat{p}_i = \hat{P}(X = i) = \frac{1}{\gamma} \cdot P_{E_1}(X = i) \cdot P_{E_2}(X = i)$$

where $\gamma$ is a normalization factor to ensure $\sum_{i=1}^{N} \hat{p}_n = 1$. And in general, if multiple distributions $P^1, .., P^T$ are given then the conflated distribution is the normalized point product of all $T$ distributions: $\hat{P} = \&(P^1, .., P^T) = (\hat{p}_1, .., \hat{p}_N)$ such that $\hat{p}_i = \frac{1}{\gamma} \prod_{t=1}^{T} p_i^t$

Hill [9] thoroughly analyzes the properties of the *conflation* operator. The paper shows that conflation is the unique probability distribution that minimizes the loss of Shannon Information. Further, conflation automatically gives more weight to more accurate experiments with smaller standard deviation. Finally, as desired, conflation with the uniform distribution is an identity transformation (i.e., it is indifferent to experiments with no information), and if $P^t(X = i) = 0$ for some $i$ then $\hat{P}(X = i) = 0$ regardless of all other experiments. As we shall see, using conflation as the main probabilistic reconciliation method is extremely effective in our solver.

## 2.2   Conflating Probabilities of Single-Input Computation

In a byte-oriented cipher, many steps are transformations operating on a single byte. E.g., an XOR of a key byte $X$ and a (known) plaintext byte is such a transformation. Similarly an SBox operation takes a single input $X$ and produces $f(X)$. Suppose a template-based side channel oracle $E_1$ exists, that returns a probability distribution $P_{E_1}$ of the values of $X$, and a second oracle $E_2$ returns a probability distribution $P_{E_2}$ of the values of $f(X)$. Assuming the transformation $f(X)$ is deterministic and 1-1, then $P_{E_1}(X = a)$ should agree with $P_{E_2}(f(X) = f(a))$. Thus, we have two experiments measuring the value of $f(X)$: one is $E_2$, and the other is a permutation of the distribution $E_1$. Combining the experiment results via conflation gives us a more accurate distribution of $f(X)$ - and, equivalently, of values of $X$. Therefore, the reconciled probability for a single-input computation is defined to be:

$$\hat{P}(X = a) = \frac{1}{\gamma} P_{E_1}(X = a) \cdot P_{E_2}(f(X) = f(a)) \tag{1}$$

## 2.3 Conflating Probabilities of Dual-Input Computations

Suppose we have a function $f$ of two independent byte values that outputs a byte: $f(X, Y) = Z$. We have oracles providing the probability distributions $P_X, P_Y$ and $P_Z$ for $X, Y, Z$ respectively, and we wish to reconcile them. We first calculate the distribution $P_f$ of $f(X, Y)$ based on $P_X, P_Y$: assuming $X$ and $Y$ are independent we get $P_f(c) = P(f(X, Y) = c) = \sum_{k,l:f(k,l)=c} P_X(k) \cdot P_Y(l)$. Now $P_f$ and $P_Z$ are distributions from two experiments estimating the same value $Z$, which we can conflate as before: $\hat{P} = \&(P_f, P_Z)$ so $\hat{P}(c) = P_f(c) \cdot P_Z(c) \cdot \frac{1}{\gamma}$ (for some normalization constant $\gamma$). However, we want to assign the reconciled probabilities $\hat{P}()$ to the inputs $X$ and $Y$. Specifically, we want to split the probability $\hat{P}(c)$ among the pairs $(X = a, Y = b)$ for which $f(a, b) = c$ such that each pair will get its weighted share of $\hat{P}(c)$. Assume as before that $c = f(a, b)$, then the weighted split is:

$$\hat{P}(X = a, Y = b) = \hat{P}(c) \cdot \frac{P_X(a) \cdot P_Y(b)}{\sum_{k,l:f(k,l)=c} P_X(k) \cdot P_Y(l)} = \hat{P}(c) \cdot \frac{P_X(a) \cdot P_Y(b)}{P_f(c)} =$$
$$\frac{1}{\gamma} P_f(c) P_Z(c) \cdot \frac{P_X(a) \cdot P_Y(b)}{P_f(c)} = \frac{1}{\gamma} P_X(a) P_Y(b) P_Z(c) \tag{2}$$

Thus we arrive at the following reconciled probability for the pair $X = a, Y = b$:

$$\hat{P}(X = a, Y = b) = \frac{1}{\gamma} P_X(a) P_Y(b) P_Z(f(a, b)) \tag{3}$$

# 3   Building Blocks

Our constraint model is a directed graph which describes the flow of information in the encryption process, as it affects the side channel leaks. The direction of the graph is from the unknown input bytes (the key in our case) to the output bytes (the ciphertext or intermediate values). Each part of the graph represents one of the following three constraint types: single-input constraint, dual-input constraint or data-redundancy constraint. There are two types of nodes in the graph:

1. Registry nodes - used to store possible values of intermediate values and their corresponding probabilities.
2. Compute nodes - used to connect registry nodes containing possible input values to registry nodes which should contain possible output values. Each compute node contains a code snippet implementing some step of the cipher.

## 3.1 Single-Input Computation Constraint

Suppose one of the steps of the cipher is a single-input byte function $f(X)$. Suppose we have two oracles, $E_{in}, E_{out}$ providing the probability distributions of $X$ and $f(X)$, respectively. Let $\alpha_{b_n}^{in} = P_{E_{in}}(X = b_n)$, and let $\alpha_{f(b_n)}^{out} = P_{E_{out}}(f(X) = f(b_n))$. These are the estimated probabilities of the input and output values given by the side channel information.

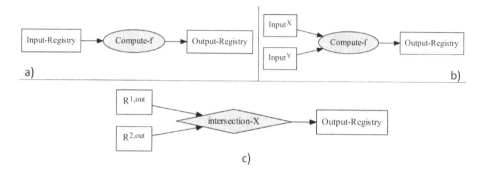

**Fig. 1.** Illustration of three types of constraints: a) single-input constraint, b) dual-input constraint, c) data-redundancy constraint

For a single input computation we define two registries: the *Input-Registry* contains the values $\{(b_n, \alpha_{b_n}^{in})\}$, and the *Output-Registry* contains the post-computation probabilities $\{(v_n, \alpha_{v_n})\}$ s.t $P(f(X) = v_n) = \alpha_{v_n}^{out}$.

We connect the input registry to the output registry via the *Compute-f* node (see Figure 1a), which contains a code snippet. The *Compute-f* node receives the tuples $\{(b_n, \alpha_{b_n}^{in})\}$ from the *Input-Registry*, computes the function $f$ for each tuple, and for every value $b_n$ outputs the tuple $(b_n, \alpha_{b_n}^{in}, f(b_n))$ to the *Output Registry*. Upon receiving the results from the compute function, the *Output-Registry* conflates $\alpha^{in}, \alpha^{out}$ as in Section 2.2: $\hat{\alpha}_n = \frac{1}{\gamma} P(X = b_n) \cdot P(f(X) = f(b_n)) = \alpha_{b_n}^{in} \cdot \alpha_{f(b_n)}^{out}$. After the computation is done the *Output-Registry* contains tuples of the form $(b_n, f(b_n), \hat{\alpha}_n)$.

## 3.2  Dual-Input Computation Constraint

Suppose a step in the cipher is a dual input byte-function $f(X, Y)$ such as an XOR of two intermediate values, and that side-channel information is available for $f(X, Y)$. In our constraint model we represent such a computation by two input registries entering a single compute node which includes the relevant code snippet (see Figure 1b). The compute node has to take into account all possible input combinations $\{b_n^X\} \times \{b_n^Y\}$. For every possible combination $(b_{n'}^X, b_{n''}^Y)$ the compute node outputs the tuple $(b_{n'}^X, b_{n''}^Y, \alpha_{n'}^{in,X}, \alpha_{n''}^{in,Y}, f(b_{n'}^X, b_{n''}^Y))$. The output registry now needs to compute the conflated probability for the combination $(b_{n'}^X, b_{n''}^Y, f(b_{n'}^X, b_{n''}^Y))$. As described in Section 2.3, the conflated probability in the output registry is computed by

$$\hat{\alpha}_{n',n''} = \frac{1}{\gamma} \cdot \alpha_n^{in,X} \cdot \alpha_n^{in,Y} \cdot P(f = f(b_{n'}^X, b_{n''}^Y))$$

for a normalization factor $\gamma$.

## 3.3  Pruning Records from a Registry

The output size of a dual-input compute node is the product of sizes of the input registries. In some cases storing this much information is not feasible. For example, when both input registries contain $256^2$ records the output registry will have to hold $256^4$ records, which is prohibitive. To avoid such a combinatorial explosion we can prune some of the records in the input registries by discarding all records with probabilities below a certain threshold $t$. Tuning the threshold is a trade off: selecting a tight threshold keeps combinatorial complexity low, but might cause pruning of records derived from the correct key bytes.

### 3.4   Data-Redundancy Constraint

We now deal with the case where some intermediate value $X$ is used as input to more than one function. In our graph notation it means that some registry $R^0$ was used as input to two or more compute nodes, $C^1, C^2$. Denote the output registries of these compute nodes $R^{1,out}, R^{2,out}$. Each record in these registries contains the relevant value of $X$ for that record. Enforcing a data-redundancy constraint over the value of X means that the records from $R^{1,out}, R^{2,out}$ should agree with each other probabilistically. For this purpose we introduce a special compute node which we call an *intersection* node (see Figure 1c). The records in $R^{1,out}, R^{2,out}$ are observations on the same value of $X$ thus we can conflate their probabilities as before. Note that unlike the single-input or dual-input constraints, for an intersection node we do not require a side channel oracle. Note also that if the input-probability of some value is 0 then the conflated probability for that value remains 0. This means that if the registries entering an intersection node were pruned, the intersection node's output-registry only includes combinations of the un-pruned values.

### 3.5   Constructing a Solver for a Cipher

The structure of the solver's flow graph follows the information flow in the cipher, as reflected by the side channel leaks. At the beginning of the flow are the first unknown values - the key bytes. We now follow the cipher's first computation which is done on those key bytes, and construct the *compute nodes* which perform that computation with their code snippet. The compute node is connected to its input and output registries as in Section 3.1. We continue to chain single-input constraints until we reach a dual-input computation. We then use the dual-input constraint (Section 3.2) to describe this flow of information in the algorithm. In the registries used as inputs for a dual-input constraint we may wish to impose pruning to prevent a combinatorial explosion in the output registry. Note that each record in a registry contains all intermediate values used in the computation for the specific value in the record. Thus, different registries in the same layer may share some intermediate values. In that case, it is useful to combine these registries via a data-redundancy constraint. At the end of the flow we have registries containing values of intermediate computations. Each record has its assigned conflated probability and contains the key bytes values which led to this intermediate value, and the framework automatically does everything else.

Thus we see that in order to instantiate the framework for a specific cipher, we need to construct a flow graph that mimics the flow of data through the cipher operations, with registries per side-channel leak. We need to supply code fragments for the compute nodes, select appropriate registries to prune and the pruning thresholds, and insert intersection nodes when possible.

# 4   Designing a Constraint Solver for AES

To evaluate our framework we built a constraint solver based on the side channel information from the first round of AES encryption, in a software implementation of the cipher. Our decoder extracted side channel information on:

1. 16 bytes of the output of AddRoundKey computation
2. 16 bytes of the output of SubBytes
3. 52 bytes from MixColumns computation:
   - 16 bytes of an XOR of 2 bytes, 4 in each column
   - 16 bytes of output of xtime computations , 4 in each column
   - 4 bytes of XOR of 4 bytes, 1 in each column
   - 16 bytes of output of the MixColumns computations

In total we have 84 intermediate byte values. For each leaked byte our decoder (see Section 5.2) produces a probability distribution over the 256 possible values.

Note that in the first round of AES the main diffusion operation is done by the MixColumns computation. MixColumns operates on groups of four bytes, thus a change of a single bit in the secret key can not affect more than four bytes of output (in the first round). This leads our constraint model to be a graph that can be divided into four connected components. Each connected component describes a constraint model for a single column. Each of the four components reflects the byte reordering done by the ShiftRows sub-rounds. This observation means that our solver actually works independently on each set of 4 key bytes.

## 4.1   Initialization and Single Input Computations

At the beginning of the computation for every key byte we consider all 256 values as possible. Since initially we do not have side channel information on the key bytes the probability for every value is 1/256. The AddRoundKey and SubBytes sub-rounds are single input computation. Note that no computation is done in the ShiftRows sub-round, thus it does not leak additional information and is not used in our constraint model. The left side of Figure 2 illustrates the single-input constraints for four key bytes.

## 4.2   Basic Computation of MixColumns

A common implementation of the MixColumns computation in software on an 8-bit microcontroller (cf. [23]) is to compute the following intermediate values:

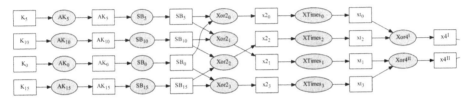

**Fig. 2.** Visual representation of the constraint solver tracking four key bytes up to the X4 computation in AES. Registry nodes are drawn as rectangles and compute nodes as ellipses. Abbreviations: AK-AddKey, SB-SubBytes

1. The XOR value of four column bytes:

$$x4 \leftarrow b_0 \oplus b_1 \oplus b_2 \oplus b_3$$

2. The XOR values of adjacent bytes:

$$x2_0 \leftarrow b_0 \oplus b_1$$
$$x2_1 \leftarrow b_1 \oplus b_2$$
$$x2_2 \leftarrow b_2 \oplus b_3$$
$$x2_3 \leftarrow b_3 \oplus b_0$$

3. The multiplication by 2 in Galois field $\mathbb{F}_{2^8}$ ("xtime") of the four values above:

$$xt_i \leftarrow 2 \cdot x2_i \mid_{\mathbb{F}_{2^8}} \text{ for } 0 \leq i \leq 3$$

Constructing the $x2_i$ constraints is done by using 4 dual-input compute nodes followed by a single-input constraint, for xtime (see Figure 2).

### 4.3   Pruning

Until the $x2_i$ registry, the AddKey and SubBytes registries contain 256 records for each of the 256 possible key bytes. Thus, the $x2_i$ registries and hence $xt_i$ registries contain $256^2$ records each. If we naively use the $xt_i$ registries as input for a dual-input constraint $X4$ to compute the XOR of four values - it means that $x4$ registry will contain $256^4$ records, which is prohibitive. We note that by the time we reach the $xt_i$ registry the probability assigned to each record is conflated over 6 side channel leaks: 2 AddRoundKey bytes, 2 SubBytes bytes, a single x2 byte and a single xtime byte. Therefore, the conflated probabilities of incorrect key bytes have dropped significantly. Hence, this is a good spot in our constraint model to perform pruning. We chose to prune all records with probability of less than $t = 10^{-25}$. This specific value keeps the correct records for 92% of the 600 traces we experimented with. On the other hand, this $t$ value leaves no more that 500 records (out of 65536) in each $xt_i$ registry, leading to low memory consumption and fast running times

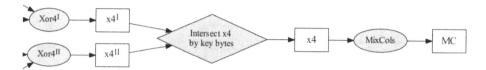

**Fig. 3.** Visual representation of the constraint solver tracking four key bytes, of column 0, from $x4$ to MixColumns computation. MC stands for MixColumns

### 4.4   Computing the Output of MixColumns

Each record in the $xt_i$ registry contains all the values involved in the computation path. That is: 2 plaintext bytes, 2 key bytes, 2 AddRoundKey bytes, 2 SubBytes output values, 1 value of XOR of 2 bytes and 1 value of the *xtime* operation on that XOR output. Here we can make a useful observation: We have leaks for $x4$ and also for $x2_0, x2_1, x2_2, x2_3$. But these leaked values need to be self-consistent regardless of how the implementation actually computes $x4$:

$$x4^I = x2_0 \oplus x2_2$$
$$x4^{II} = x2_1 \oplus x2_3$$

Thus we can compute (and conflate) the values of $x4$ in two ways. Since the $xt_i$ registries contain the corresponding values of $x2_i$ we can use these registries as inputs for two parallel dual-input Compute-$x4$ nodes. Figure 2 illustrates the constraint solver up to the $x4^I$, $x4^{II}$ registries.

Assuming we did not prune the records of the correct combination of key bytes, the quartet of the correct key bytes should appear in records of both $x4^I$ and $x4^{II}$ registries. Thus we now use a data-redundancy constraint (recall Section 3.4) to intersect records according to the 4 key bytes. The output of the data-redundancy node is inserted into a registry called $x4$. Each record of that registry contains all the byte values used for that specific record, that is: 4 plaintext bytes, 4 key bytes, 4 SubBytes outputs, 4 outputs of XOR of 2, 4 outputs of xtime computations, and 1 value of XOR of 4.

Each record in the $x4$ registry contains all the information required to compute the 4 output bytes of MixColumns. Since we use a single record to compute a tuple of 4 output bytes - we consider this computation as a single-input computation. As before let $\{\alpha^{in}\}$ denote the conflated probabilities of records in $x4$ registry. Since MixColumns has 4 output bytes - we have four leaks to conflate with, representing the separate side channel information on the four output bytes: $\{\alpha^{out,0}\}$, $\{\alpha^{out,1}\}$, $\{\alpha^{out,2}\}$, $\{\alpha^{out,3}\}$. The conflated probability is given by: $\hat{\alpha} = \alpha^{in} \cdot \alpha^{out,0} \cdot \alpha^{out,1} \cdot \alpha^{out,2} \cdot \alpha^{out,3}$. $\hat{\alpha}$ is then normalized so that all probabilities sum to 1. The final result is the MC registry. Figure 3 illustrates the constraint solver from $x4^I$, $x4^{II}$ registries to the MC registry.

### 4.5   Finding the Keys

We now have in each MC registry, for each "column", a set of records representing the possible computation paths and their corresponding probabilities. Recall that a "column" is defined at the entrance to MixColumns, so the key byte indices are reordered by the ShiftRows operation. Each registry record represents a candidate combination of 4 key bytes. Together all the MC registries contain possible combinations of 16 key bytes.

A naive way to iterate over the key candidates would be to sort the registries in decreasing probability order, to set some upper bound R, and to try all candidates from ranks $r_1, r_2, r_3, r_4$ s.t. $r_i \leq R$ (one per MC registry). This approach is bounded by $R^4$ key tries. However, using the method of [25], it is possible to iterate over these $R^4$ keys according to their probabilities, thus speeding up the key search. An alternative method for reducing the candidate keys is to run the constraint solver twice using different power traces and then intersect the groups of key candidates.

## 5   Performance Evaluation

### 5.1   Experimental Setup

We instantiated our framework for AES, and executed it on power traces extracted from a real implementation of an AES-256 variant. The implementation is the one presented in the DPA contest v4 [2]. This implementation contains a power-analysis counter measure called RSM described in [1]. The deviations from the classic AES are:

1. RSM-AES utilizes an arbitrary fixed 16-byte *Mask*. At the beginning of the encryption process a random *offset* between 0 to 15 is drawn. Let $o$ denote the *offset*, and let $m^o$ denote the cyclic rotation of *Mask* by offset $o$.
2. The 16 bytes of plaintext are XOR-ed with $m^o$. Let $pm$ be the result, i.e., $pm_i = p_i \oplus m_i^o$, $0 \leq i \leq 15$.
3. In the AddRoundKey sub-round the round key is XOR-ed with $pm$ instead of the plaintext.
4. RSM-AES uses different S-BOXs for every byte, which are derived from the value of the $m^o$.
5. The ShiftRows and MixColumns sub-rounds are unchanged.
6. An additional sub-round is added to extract the unmasked cipher text, but it is not relevant in our attack since the power traces only cover the first round.

### 5.2   Decoding

To profile the power consumption behavior of the RSM-AES implementation we used techniques similar to those of [19]. Our leak model is the Hamming-weight model. This model was chosen since our experiments showed high correlation with the Hamming weights of the intermediate values. Using the raw values, on the other hand, showed very low correlation. 100 classifiers were trained to classify the Hamming weights of 100 intermediate values. Of these, 84 intermediate values are those described in Section 4, and 16 values are the masked plaintext bytes of the RSM counter-measure (see $pm_i$ description in Section 5.1). We used

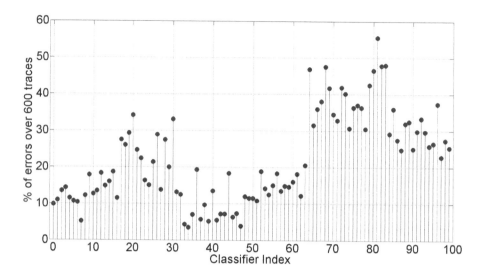

**Fig. 4.** Percent of classification errors per classifier, evaluated over 600 traces. Classifiers 0-15 are for Hamming-weights of $pm_i$, 16-31 are for AddKey outputs, 32-47 are for SubBytes, 48-63 are for $x2$, 64-79 are for $xt$, 80-83 are for $x4$ and 84-99 are for MixColumns outputs.

200 traces to train the classifiers and an additional 200 traces to evaluate the classifiers' performance, in order to select the best trace-samples to be used as inputs for each classifier. As described in [19] the classifiers were trained to identify Hamming weights 2-6 and were then extrapolated to classify all 9 possible Hamming weight values 0-8.

Let $C_l$ be the classifier for leak $l$, and let $C_l(hw)$ be the probability that classifier $C_l$ assigns to the event that the correct value has a Hamming-weight of $hw$ for $hw \in 0..8$. To evaluate the classifiers performance, we define a classification error to be when the Hamming-weight with the highest probability, as predicted by the classifier, is not the correct Hamming-weight. Our decoder is far from perfect: most classifiers have an average error rate of 10-20% and some have an error rate as poor as 55%. Some intermediate values are decoded with low error rates (e.g., SubBytes) while others are harder to decode (e.g., MixColumns). Specific classifiers' error rates are shown in Figure 4.

Note that in our framework a classifier failing to predict the exact Hamming-weight as the most likely value still conveys significant information: as long as the correct Hamming-weight has higher probability than other incorrect Hamming-weight classes, it helps the solver distinguish the correct values from the incorrect ones. As we will see, even with these far-from-perfect classifiers, our framework is able to find the correct keys.

**5.2.1 Overcoming the RSM Counter Measure.** As described above, we have 16 classifiers $C_i$, $0 \le i \le 15$, trained to estimate the probabilities of the

Hamming-weight values of $pm_i = p_i \oplus m_i^o$, where $m_i^o$ is the $i^{th}$ byte of the Mask rotated by offset $o$. For every possible value of $o \in 0..15$ we derive 16 mask bytes $m_i^o$ and compute $pm_i^o = p_i \oplus m_i^o$. Let $HW(x)$ denote the Hamming weight of $x$. Recall that for a given value $hw$, $C_i(hw)$ is the probability estimation of the decoder $C_i$ of $HW(pm_i)$, i.e $C_i(hw) = P(HW(pm_i) = hw)$. For every value of $o$, we compute the offset score: $S(o) = \prod_{i=0}^{15} C_i(HW(pm_i^o))$. The *offset* $o$ which gave the highest score $S(o)$ is declared the correct one. We experimented with this method on 600 traces (distinct from the 400 training traces) and measured an offset prediction success rate of 100%. Thus we see that the 4-bit side-channel counter-measure used in RSM-AES offers no protection against template based attacks, even without a constraint solver.

### 5.2.2 Probability Estimation for 256 Values.

Our constraint solver uses a soft-decision decoder: it requires as input a probability estimation for 256 possible values of every intermediate computation. We do not filter out the less likely Hamming weights: instead we split the 9-value distribution given by $C_l$ among the byte values $X$, according to their Hamming-weights. Let

$$S_{hw} = \|\{x \in \{0..255\}|HW(x) = hw\}\| \text{ for } 0 \leq hw \leq 8$$

be the number of values between 0-255 with Hamming weight $hw$. For every intermediate byte value $b_l$ among the 84 leaks $l \in 0..83$ and classier $C_l$ - we assign the probability for value $x \in 0..255$ to be $P(b_l = x) = \frac{C_l(HW(x))}{S_{HW(x)}}$. Note that $\sum_{x=0}^{255} P(b_l = x) = 1$.

## 5.3 Implementation of the Constraint Solver

The custom solver designed for AES as described in Sections 3 and 4 was implemented in Matlab R2013a. Our code consists of 6200 lines of code over 25 files. The implementation consists of general *registry* and *compute* blocks, and specialized compute classes to be used by the general compute blocks. Other than the 4 registries used for the intersection constraints, each registry is associated with a specific leak $l$ among the 84 leaks. They therefore receive an a-priori probability estimation for every value $X$ as explained in Section 5.2.2. These are the $\alpha^{out}$ values described in Section 3.1. The graph representing the full constraint solver is depicted in Figure 7.

## 5.4 Results and Discussion

We ran our solver on an Intel core i7 2.0 GHz PC running Ubuntu 13.04 64 bit, with 8 GB of RAM and a SSD hard drive. Over 600 traces the median running time of decoding + running the solver was 9 seconds. Solving of 98% of the experiments completed in under 30 seconds. The maximum running time was 85 seconds.

At the end of a run, each of the four MixColumns output registries contains records with 4-key-byte candidates. A full 16 byte key is constructed by taking

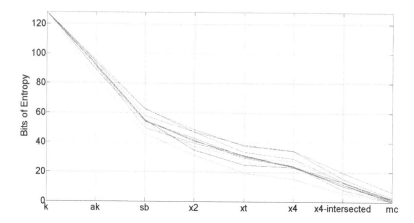

**Fig. 5.** Evolution of entropy of 16 key bytes at different solver phases, for 10 runs on randomly selected traces. Abbreviations: ak - AddKey, sb - SubBytes, x2 - XOR of 2 bytes, xt - xtime, x4 - XOR of 4 bytes, mc - MixColumns.

a record from each of the four MixColumns registries. The median number of 4-key-byte candidates (for a single column) was 43930, and the median number of full key candidates was $2^{61.2}$. To measure the solver's success, for each registry we look at the rank of the record containing the correct 4-key-byte combination. If the maximum rank of the correct key quartets in all four registries is lower than R, then exhaustive search for the correct key would require no more that $R^4$ tries. We found that in 38% out of 600 power traces, at least 3 key quartets were among the top 5 records. The correct key in over 50% of the traces can be found in less then $R^4 = 2^{30}$ attempts. We believe that using the optimized algorithm of [25] to iterate over key candidates according to probability would significantly decrease the number of tries before finding the correct key. We did not test the approach of [25] on our results. Instead, we opted to use a second power trace and intersect the candidate key-quartets (see below).

Figure 5 shows how the Shanon entropy of 16 key-bytes drops as the solver uses the side channel leaks. At the beginning of the flow each key byte has probability of $\frac{1}{256}$, giving $Entropy = 128$, as expected for 128 unknown bits of key. Figure 5 shows that the entropy dropped from 128 down to 0.2-6.6 bits. This means that although the solver outputs a median of $2^{61.2}$ key candidates, the probability mass is concentrated over very few candidates.

When more than one power trace is available for the attack, we can run the decoding + solver on each trace and intersect the candidate keys. The intersection is done separately on the 4-key-byte candidates for every column, and the probability distributions are conflated. To measure the performance of this approach we ran 250 experiments, each with independent traces. When the intersection was not empty, the median number of candidates per column was 4 and the median number of full key candidates was 315. Figure 6 shows how many power traces were required to yield the correct key as the first ranked

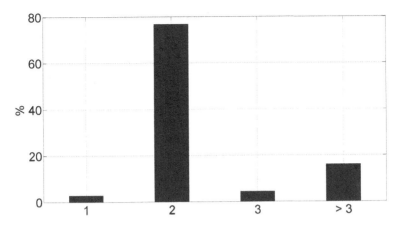

**Fig. 6.** Number of power traces needed to find the correct key.

candidate. It shows that with only 2 traces we can identify the correct key as the top candidate with success rate of 79.6%.

We submitted our solver to the DPA v4 contest. The formal evaluation process of the DPA contest is equivalent to a single experiment (in contrast to the 250 we performed). According to the above statistics, a single experiment has 20.4% chance of needing more than 2 traces - as actually happened. When more than 2 traces are used, our solver requires more time to perform the intersection between the possible key candidates. The DPA v4 hall of fame lists our contribution as requiring 5 traces and 55 seconds per trace to complete. As of the date of writing, our solver is one of the leading entries in the contest.

# 6   Conclusions and Future Work

In this paper we described a specialized byte-oriented constraint solver for side channel cryptanalysis. Instead of representing the cipher as a complex and un-wieldy set of bit-level equations, the user only needs to supply code snippets for the native operations of the cipher, arranged in a flow graph that models the de-pendence between the side channel leaks. Through extensive use of the conflation technique our solver is able to reconcile low-accuracy and noisy measurements into an accurate low-entropy probability distribution, with extremely low and very predictable run times. On the DPA v4 contest dataset our framework is able to extract the correct key from one or two power traces in under 9 seconds with a success rate of over 79%.

The technique is not dependent on the decoding method, does not assume a Hamming-weight model for the side channel, and does not impose any particular noise model. It can be applied as long as it is possible to decode the side-channel trace into a collection of probability distributions for the intermediate values. We believe it would be quite interesting to test our framework against other

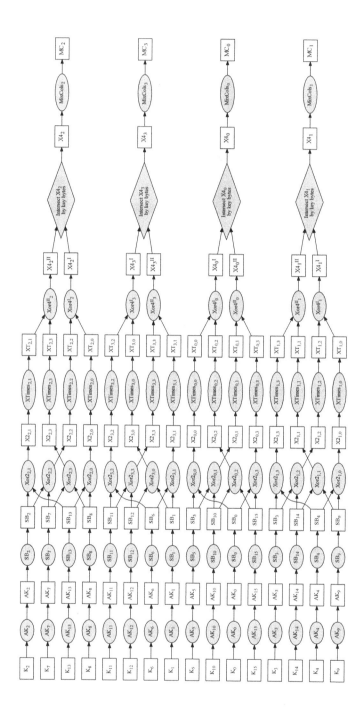

**Fig. 7.** Flow Graph of the Full AES Constraint Solver

implementations of AES, against other types of side-channel information, and against other byte-oriented ciphers.

## References

1. Description of the masked AES of the DPA contest v4, http://www.dpacontest.org/v4/data/rsm/aes-rsm.pdf
2. DPA contest v4, http://www.dpacontest.org/v4/
3. Bogdanov, A.A., Knudsen, L.R., Leander, G., Paar, C., Poschmann, A., Robshaw, M.J.B., Seurin, Y., Vikkelsoe, C.: PRESENT: An ultra-lightweight block cipher. In: Paillier, P., Verbauwhede, I. (eds.) CHES 2007. LNCS, vol. 4727, pp. 450–466. Springer, Heidelberg (2007)
4. Brier, E., Clavier, C., Olivier, F.: Correlation power analysis with a leakage model. In: Joye, M., Quisquater, J.-J. (eds.) CHES 2004. LNCS, vol. 3156, pp. 16–29. Springer, Heidelberg (2004)
5. Chari, S., Rao, J.R., Rohatgi, P.: Template attacks. In: Kaliski Jr., B.S., Koç, Ç.K., Paar, C. (eds.) CHES 2002. LNCS, vol. 2523, pp. 13–28. Springer, Heidelberg (2003)
6. Clemen, R.T., Winkler, R.L.: Combining probability distributions from experts in risk analysis. Risk Analysis 19(2), 187–203 (1999)
7. Elaabid, M.A., Guilley, S.: Practical improvements of profiled side-channel attacks on a hardware crypto-accelerator. In: Bernstein, D.J., Lange, T. (eds.) AFRICACRYPT 2010. LNCS, vol. 6055, pp. 243–260. Springer, Heidelberg (2010)
8. Guo, S., Zhao, X., Zhang, F., Wang, T., Shi, Z.J., Standaert, F., Ma, C.: Exploiting the incomplete diffusion feature: A specialized analytical side-channel attack against the aes and its application to microcontroller implementations. IEEE Transactions on Information Forensics and Security 9(6), 999–1014 (2014)
9. Hill, T.: Conflations of probability distributions. Transactions of the American Mathematical Society 363(6), 3351–3372 (2011)
10. Hinton, G.E.: Training products of experts by minimizing contrastive divergence. Neural Computation 14(8), 1771–1800 (2002)
11. Kahn, J.M.: A generative bayesian model for aggregating experts' probabilities. In: Proceedings of the 20th Conference on Uncertainty in Artificial Intelligence, pp. 301–308. AUAI Press (2004)
12. Kocher, P.C., Jaffe, J., Jun, B.: Differential power analysis. In: Wiener, M. (ed.) CRYPTO 1999. LNCS, vol. 1666, pp. 388–397. Springer, Heidelberg (1999)
13. Mangard, S., Oswald, E., Popp, T.: Power Analysis Attacks: Revealing the Secrets of Smart Cards (Advances in Information Security). Springer-Verlag New York, Inc., Secaucus (2007)
14. Mohamed, M.S.E., Bulygin, S., Zohner, M., Heuser, A., Walter, M., Buchmann, J.: Improved algebraic side-channel attack on AES. Journal of Cryptographic Engineering 3(3), 139–156 (2013)
15. Information Technology Laboratory (National Institute of Standards and Technology). Announcing the Advanced Encryption Standard (AES). Computer Security Division, Information Technology Laboratory, National Institute of Standards and Technology Gaithersburg, MD (2001)
16. Oren, Y.: Secure hardware - physical attacks and countermeasures. PhD thesis, Tel-Aviv University, Isreal (2013), https://www.iacr.org/phds/?p=detail&entry=893

17. Oren, Y., Kirschbaum, M., Popp, T., Wool, A.: Algebraic side-channel analysis in the presence of errors. In: Mangard, S., Standaert, F.-X. (eds.) CHES 2010. LNCS, vol. 6225, pp. 428–442. Springer, Heidelberg (2010)
18. Oren, Y., Renauld, M., Standaert, F.-X., Wool, A.: Algebraic side-channel attacks beyond the hamming weight leakage model. In: Prouff, E., Schaumont, P. (eds.) CHES 2012. LNCS, vol. 7428, pp. 140–154. Springer, Heidelberg (2012)
19. Oren, Y., Weisse, O., Wool, A.: Practical template-algebraic side channel attacks with extremely low data complexity. In: Proceedings of the 2nd International Workshop on Hardware and Architectural Support for Security and Privacy, p. 7. ACM (2013)
20. Oswald, D., Paar, C.: Improving side-channel analysis with optimal linear transforms. In: Mangard, S. (ed.) CARDIS 2012. LNCS, vol. 7771, pp. 219–233. Springer, Heidelberg (2013)
21. Renauld, M., Standaert, F.-X.: Algebraic side-channel attacks. In: Bao, F., Yung, M., Lin, D., Jing, J. (eds.) Inscrypt 2009. LNCS, vol. 6151, pp. 393–410. Springer, Heidelberg (2010)
22. Renauld, M., Standaert, F.-X., Veyrat-Charvillon, N.: Algebraic side-channel attacks on the AES: Why time also matters in DPA. In: Clavier, C., Gaj, K. (eds.) CHES 2009. LNCS, vol. 5747, pp. 97–111. Springer, Heidelberg (2009)
23. Stallings, W.: Cryptography and Network Security ch. 5, 6th edn. Pearson (2014)
24. Sugawara, T., Homma, N., Aoki, T., Satoh, A.: Profiling attack using multivariate regression analysis. IEICE Electronics Express 7(15), 1139–1144 (2010)
25. Veyrat-Charvillon, N., Gérard, B., Renauld, M., Standaert, F.-X.: An optimal key enumeration algorithm and its application to side-channel attacks. In: Knudsen, L.R., Wu, H. (eds.) SAC 2012. LNCS, vol. 7707, pp. 390–406. Springer, Heidelberg (2013)
26. Veyrat-Charvillon, N., Gérard, B., Standaert, F.-X.: Soft analytical side-channel attacks. Cryptology ePrint Archive, Report 2014/410 (2014), http://eprint.iacr.org/2014/410
27. Weisse, O.: Source code of our constraint solver as submitted to DPA v4 contest, http://www.ofirweisse.com see DPA v4
28. Zhao, X., Wang, T., Guo, S., Zhang, F., Shi, Z., Liu, H., Wu, K.: SAT based error tolerant algebraic side-channel attacks. In: 2011 Conference on Cryptographic Algorithms and Cryptographic Chips, CASC (2011)

# How to Estimate the Success Rate of Higher-Order Side-Channel Attacks

Victor Lomné[1], Emmanuel Prouff[1], Matthieu Rivain[2],
Thomas Roche[1], and Adrian Thillard[1]

[1] ANSSI, France
firstname.name@ssi.gouv.fr
[2] CryptoExperts
matthieu.rivain@cryptoexperts.com

**Abstract.** The resistance of a cryptographic implementation with regards to side-channel analysis is often quantified by measuring the success rate of a given attack. This approach cannot always be followed in practice, especially when the implementation includes some countermeasures that may render the attack too costly for an evaluation purpose, but not costly enough from a security point of view. An evaluator then faces the issue of estimating the success rate of an attack he cannot mount. The present paper addresses this issue by presenting a methodology to estimate the success rate of higher-order side-channel attacks targeting implementations protected by masking. Specifically, we generalize the approach initially proposed at SAC 2008 in the context of first-order side-channel attacks. The principle is to approximate the distribution of an attack's score vector by a multivariate Gaussian distribution, whose parameters are derived by profiling the leakage. One can then accurately compute the expected attack success rate with respect to the number of leakage measurements. We apply this methodology to higher-order side-channel attacks based on the widely used correlation and likelihood distinguishers. Moreover, we validate our approach with simulations and practical attack experiments against masked AES implementations running on two different microcontrollers.

## 1 Introduction

Estimating the success rate of a side-channel attack –that uses a given number of leakage observations– is a central issue regarding the physical security evaluation of a cryptographic implementation. The empirical way is to perform the attack a certain number of times and to record the average number of successes. However, this approach is prohibitive against implementations protected by effective countermeasures since the attacks may become too costly to be performed several times (or even once). This does not mean that the implementation is *secure* though; this only means that the implementation is secure beyond the means of the evaluator (which may not compete with the means of a motivated attacker). This situation is not satisfactory in practice where one desires that the computational cost of performing a security evaluation be fairly low and uncorrelated to the actual security of the target implementation.

L. Batina and M. Robshaw (Eds.): CHES 2014, LNCS 8731, pp. 35–54, 2014.

In this paper, we propose a methodology to estimate the success rate of higher-order side-channel attacks targeting implementations protected by masking. Our methodology is based on the approach proposed by Rivain in [13] in the context of first-order side-channel attacks. The principle of this approach is to study the multivariate distribution of the score vector resulting from an attack. Specifically, Rivain suggests to approximate this distribution by a multivariate Gaussian distribution, which is sound in the context of *additive distinguishers* such as the correlation and the likelihood. We generalize this approach to higher-order side-channel analysis and we show how to derive the distribution parameters with respect to the leakage parameters. We show that using this methodology makes it possible to accurately estimate the success rate of a higher-order side-channel attack based on a simple profiling of the leakage parameters. Moreover, we demonstrate the soundness of our methodology by comparing its results to various attack experiments against masked AES implementations running on two different microcontrollers.

**Related Works.** In [10] and [17], the success rate of first-order side-channel analysis based on the correlation distinguisher is evaluated using Fisher's transformation. The obtained formulas are simple and illustrative, but they lack of accuracy. Indeed, it has been observed in [18] that the estimated success rates using this approach do not well match to the experimental ones. As explained in [18], this is mainly due to the incorrect assumption that the scores for the wrong key guesses are independent of the score for the good key guess. That is why, one should rather focus on the joint distribution of all scores as initially suggested in [13]. In the latter work, the author provide accurate formulae for the success rate of first-order side-channel attacks based on the correlation and likelihood distinguishers. A more recent work [6] further focuses on the mono-bit difference-of-means distingusisher as originally described by Kocher *et al.* [9].

**Paper Organization.** In Section 2, we provide some preliminaries about probability theory and the (multivariate) Gaussian distribution. Then Section 3 introduces our theoretical model for higher-order side-channel attacks and Section 4 describes the general methodology for estimating the success rate of such attacks based on additive distinguishers. In Sections 5 and 6, we apply the methodology to the correlation and the likelihood distinguishers respectively, and we show how to compute the score vector distribution parameters. Eventually, some attack simulations and practical attack experiments are reported in Sections 7 and 8 that demonstrate the soundness of our approach.

## 2   Preliminaries

Calligraphic letters, like $\mathcal{X}$, are used to denote finite sets (*e.g.* $\mathbb{F}_2^n$). The corresponding large letter $X$ denotes a random variable over $\mathcal{X}$, while the lowercase letter $x$ a value over $\mathcal{X}$. The probability of an event $ev$ is denoted by $\mathrm{P}[ev]$. The expectation and the variance of a random variable $X$ are respectively denoted by $\mathrm{E}[X]$ and $\mathrm{Var}[X]$. The covariance between two random variables $X$ and $Y$ is denoted by $\mathrm{Cov}[X, Y]$.

The Gaussian distribution of dimension $T$ with $T$-size expectation vector $\boldsymbol{m}$ and $T \times T$ covariance matrix $\boldsymbol{\Sigma}$ is denoted by $\mathcal{N}(\boldsymbol{m}, \boldsymbol{\Sigma})$, and the corresponding probability density function (pdf) is denoted by $\phi_{\boldsymbol{m},\boldsymbol{\Sigma}}$. We recall that this pdf is defined for every $\boldsymbol{x} \in \mathbb{R}^T$ as

$$\phi_{\boldsymbol{m},\boldsymbol{\Sigma}}(\boldsymbol{x}) = \frac{1}{\sqrt{(2\pi)^T |\boldsymbol{\Sigma}|}} \exp\left(-\frac{1}{2}(\boldsymbol{x} - \boldsymbol{m})' \cdot \boldsymbol{\Sigma}^{-1} \cdot (\boldsymbol{x} - \boldsymbol{m})\right) , \qquad (1)$$

where $(\boldsymbol{x} - \boldsymbol{m})'$ denotes the transpose of the vector $(\boldsymbol{x} - \boldsymbol{m})$ and $|\boldsymbol{\Sigma}|$ denotes the determinant of the matrix $\boldsymbol{\Sigma}$. The corresponding cumulative distribution function (cdf) is denoted $\Phi_{\boldsymbol{m},\boldsymbol{\Sigma}}$ and is defined for a pair of vectors $\boldsymbol{a} = (a_1, a_2, \ldots, a_T)$ and $\boldsymbol{b} = (b_1, b_2, \ldots, b_T)$ over $(\mathbb{R} \cup \{-\infty, +\infty\})^T$ by

$$\Phi_{\boldsymbol{m},\boldsymbol{\Sigma}}(\boldsymbol{a}, \boldsymbol{b}) = \int_{a_1}^{b_1} \int_{a_2}^{b_2} \cdots \int_{a_T}^{b_T} \phi_{\boldsymbol{m},\boldsymbol{\Sigma}}(\boldsymbol{x}) \, d\boldsymbol{x} . \qquad (2)$$

If the dimension $T$ equals 1, then the Gaussian distribution is said to be *univariate* and its covariance matrix is reduced to the variance of the single coordinate denoted $\sigma^2$. If $T$ is greater than 1, the Gaussian distribution is said to be *multivariate*.

## 3   Higher-Order Side-Channel Model

We consider a cryptographic algorithm protected by *masking* and running on a leaking device. A (higher-order) side-channel attack exploits the leakage resulting from intermediate computations in order to recover (part of) the secret involved in the cryptographic algorithm. Let $s$ denote such an intermediate variable satisfying:

$$s = \varphi(x, k^*) , \qquad (3)$$

where $x$ is (part of) the public input of the algorithm, $k^*$ is (part of) the secret input of the algorithm, and $\varphi$ is some function from $\mathcal{X} \times \mathcal{K}$ to $\mathcal{S}$.

For an implementation protected with masking, such a variable $s$ is never stored nor handled in clear but in the form of several, say $d + 1$, *shares* $s_0$, $s_1$, ..., $s_d$ satisfying the relation

$$s_0 \oplus s_1 \oplus \cdots \oplus s_d = s \qquad (4)$$

for some operation $\oplus$. In the common case of Boolean masking this operation is the bitwise addition (or XOR), but it might be some other group addition law. One of the share, say $s_0$, is sometimes referred to as *masked variable* and the other shares, $s_1$, $s_2$, ..., $s_d$ as the *masks*. For masking approach to be sound, it is usually required that the masks are uniformly and independently generated. In that case, the $(d + 1)$-tuple of shares can be modeled as a random vector $(S_0, S_1, \ldots, S_d)$ where $S_0 = s \oplus \bigoplus_{j=1}^d S_j$ and, for $j \geqslant 1$, the $S_j$ are mutually independent random variables with uniform distribution over $\mathcal{S}$.

### 3.1   Leakage Model

During the execution of the algorithm, the processing of each share $S_j$ produces some leakage $L_j$ revealing some information about the share value. In what follows, we shall denote by $L$ the leakage tuple:

$$L = (L_0, L_1, \ldots, L_d) . \tag{5}$$

We shall sometimes use the alternative notation $L_s$ or $L_{x,k^*}$ to indicate that the leakage arises for the shared value $s = \varphi(x, k^*)$.

In this paper, we shall make the common assumption that given the values of the shares, the leakage has a Gaussian distribution. This assumption is referred here as the *Gaussian leakage assumption*, and it is formally stated by:

$$(L_j \mid S_j = s) \sim \mathcal{N}(m_{j,s}, \Sigma_{j,s}) , \tag{6}$$

for every $j \in \{0, 1, \ldots, d\}$ and for every $s \in \mathcal{S}$, where $m_{j,s}$ are expectation vectors defined over $\mathbb{R}^T$ and $\Sigma_{j,s}$ are (non-singular) covariance matrices defined over $\mathbb{R}^{T \times T}$. We shall further assume that the leakage $L_j$ can be viewed as a deterministic function of $S_j$ with an additive Gaussian noise:

$$L_j = f_j(S_j) + N_j . \tag{7}$$

This assumption, referred here as *Gaussian noise assumption*, is equivalent to the Gaussian leakage assumption with the additional requirement that the covariance matrices $\Sigma_{j,s}$ are all equal to some matrix $\Sigma_j$. We then have $f_j : s \mapsto m_{j,s}$ and $N_j \sim \mathcal{N}(0, \Sigma_j)$, where $0$ denotes the null vector.

As a final assumption, we consider that for any fixed values of the shares, the leakage components are independent. That is, for every $(s_0, s_1, \ldots, s_d) \in \mathcal{S}^{d+1}$, the random variables $(L_j \mid S_j = s_j)$ are mutually independent. Under the Gaussian noise assumption, this simply means that the noises $N_j$ are mutually independent, and that is why we shall refer to this assumption as the *independent noises assumption*.

*Remark 1.* For the sake of simplicity, we consider that all the leakages $L_j$ have the same dimension $T$. Note that our analysis could be easily extended to the general case where each leakage $L_j$ has its own dimension $T_j$.

### 3.2   Higher-Order Side-Channel Attacks

In a higher-order side-channel attack (HO-SCA), the adversary aims to extract information about $k^*$ by monitoring the leakage of the shares. Specifically, the adversary observes several samples $\ell_i \in \mathcal{L}$ of the leakage $L_{x_i,k^*}$, corresponding to some public input $x_i$ that he may either choose or just know. According to the above leakage model, the leakage space $\mathcal{L}$ is defined as $\mathcal{L} = \mathbb{R}^{T \times (d+1)}$ and each leakage sample can be written as

$$\ell_i = (\ell_{i,0}, \ell_{i,1}, \cdots, \ell_{i,d}) , \tag{8}$$

with $\ell_{i,j} \in \mathbb{R}^T$ for every $j$. Moreover, the Gaussian noise assumption implies that each leakage sample coordinate can be further written as

$$\ell_{i,j} = f_j(s_{i,j}) + n_{i,j} , \qquad (9)$$

where $s_{i,1}$, $s_{i,2}$, $\ldots$, $s_{i,d}$ are $d$ random mask values, where $s_{i,0} = \varphi(x_i, k^*) \oplus \bigoplus_{j=1}^{d} s_{i,j}$, and where $n_{i,0}$, $n_{i,1}$, $\ldots$, $n_{i,d}$ are samples of the Gaussian noises $N_0$, $N_1, \ldots, N_d$.

Once several, say $q$, leakage samples have been collected, the adversary makes use of a *distinguisher*, that is a function mapping the input-leakage samples $(x_1, \ell_1)$, $(x_2, \ell_2)$, $\ldots$, $(x_q, \ell_q)$ to some *score vector* $\mathbf{d} = (d_k)_{k \in \mathcal{K}} \in \mathbb{R}^{|\mathcal{K}|}$. If the distinguisher is sound and if the leakage brings enough information on the shares, then the equality

$$k^* = \underset{k \in \mathcal{K}}{\operatorname{argmax}} \, d_k$$

should hold with a probability substantially greater than $\frac{1}{|\mathcal{K}|}$.

In what follows, we shall consider a natural equivalence relation between distinguishers. We say that two score vectors are *rank-equivalent* if for every $n \in \{1, 2, \ldots, |\mathcal{K}|\}$, the $n$ coordinates with highest scores are the same for the two vectors. Two distinguishers d and d' are then said *equivalent*, denoted $\mathbf{d} \equiv \mathbf{d}'$ if for every $(x_i, \ell_i)_i \in (\mathcal{X} \times \mathcal{L})^q$, the score vectors $\mathbf{d}((x_i, \ell_i)_i)$ and $\mathbf{d}'((x_i, \ell_i)_i)$ are rank-equivalent.

In this paper, we focus on *additive distinguishers* which we formally define hereafter.

**Definition 1.** *A distinguisher* d *is additive if for every* $(x_1, x_2, \ldots, x_q) \in \mathcal{X}^q$, *there exists a family of functions* $\{g_{x,k} : \mathcal{L} \to \mathbb{R} \; ; \; (x, k) \in \mathcal{X} \times \mathcal{K}\}$ *such that for every* $(\ell_1, \ell_2, \ldots, \ell_q) \in \mathcal{L}^q$ *we have*

$$\mathsf{d}((x_i, \ell_i)_i) = (d_k)_{k \in \mathcal{K}} \quad with \quad d_k = \frac{1}{q} \sum_{i=1}^{q} g_{x_i, k}(\ell_i) \quad for \; every \; k \in \mathcal{K}.$$

*A distinguisher equivalent to an additive distinguisher as defined above is also said to be additive.*

It was shown in [13] that the widely used first-order correlation and likelihood distinguishers are both additive distinguishers in the sense of the above definition. We will show in Sections 5 and 6 that their higher-order counterparts are also additive.

## 4    Estimating the Success Rate

In this section, we generalize the methodology introduced in [13] to HO-SCA as modelled in the previous section. Namely, we show how to get a sound estimation of the attack success rate by studying the multivariate probability distribution of the score vector for the case of additive distinguishers.

The success rate of a HODPA, denoted $\mathsf{Succ}^{\mathsf{d}}_{x,k^*}$, is defined with respect to some input vector $x = (x_1, x_2, \ldots, x_q)$, some secret $k^*$, and some distinguisher d, as the probability:

$$P\left[k^* = \underset{k \in \mathcal{K}}{\mathrm{argmax}}\, d_k \;\middle|\; \ell_1 \xleftarrow{\$} \boldsymbol{L}_{x_1,k^*};\; \ldots;\; \ell_q \xleftarrow{\$} \boldsymbol{L}_{x_q,k^*};\; (d_k)_{k \in \mathcal{K}} = \mathsf{d}\big((x_i, \ell_i)_i\big)\right],$$

where $\ell_i \xleftarrow{\$} \boldsymbol{L}_{x_i,k^*}$ means randomly sampling $\ell_i$ according to the distribution of $\boldsymbol{L}_{x_i,k^*}$.

*Remark 2.* For the sake of generality, we chose to fix the input vector $x$ as a parameter of the attack so that we do not need to assume any specific strategy for the choice of the public inputs. However, we will investigate the particular setting where the $x_i$ are uniformly distributed.

According to Definition 1, the score vector $(d_k)_{k \in \mathcal{K}}$ resulting from an additive distinguisher satisfies

$$d_k = \frac{1}{q} \sum_{i=1}^{q} g_{x_i,k}(\ell_i) , \tag{10}$$

for some $g_{x,k} : \mathcal{L} \to \mathbb{R}$. Then a simple application of the central limit theorem yields the following result, where we define the *occurrence ratio* $\tau_x$ of an element $x \in \mathcal{X}$ in the input vector $(x_1, x_2, \ldots, x_q)$ as

$$\tau_x = \frac{|\{i;\; x_i = x\}|}{q} . \tag{11}$$

**Proposition 1.** *The distribution of the score vector $(d_k)_{k \in \mathcal{K}}$ tends toward a multivariate Gaussian distribution as $q$ grows, with expectation vector $(\mathrm{E}\,[d_k])_{k \in \mathcal{K}}$ satisfying*

$$\mathrm{E}\,[d_k] = \sum_{x \in \mathcal{X}} \tau_x\, \mathrm{E}\,[g_{x,k}(\boldsymbol{L}_{x,k^*})] \tag{12}$$

*for every $k \in \mathcal{K}$, and with covariance matrix $(\mathrm{Cov}\,[d_{k_1}, d_{k_2}])_{(k_1,k_2) \in \mathcal{K}^2}$ satisfying*

$$\mathrm{Cov}\,[d_{k_1}, d_{k_2}] = \frac{1}{q} \sum_{x \in \mathcal{X}} \tau_x\, \mathrm{Cov}\,[g_{x,k_1}(\boldsymbol{L}_{x,k^*}), g_{x,k_2}(\boldsymbol{L}_{x,k^*})] \tag{13}$$

*for every $(k_1, k_2) \in \mathcal{K}^2$.*

*Proof.* The first statement results by definition of additive distinguishers and the central limit theorem. Equations (12) and (13) directly holds by mutual independence between the leakage samples. □

The above proposition shows that for a sufficient number of leakage observations, the distribution of the score vector $d = (d_k)_{k \in \mathcal{K}}$ can be soundly estimated by a multivariate Gaussian. As in [13], we now define the *comparison vector* as the $(|\mathcal{K}| - 1)$-size vector $\mathbf{c} = (c_k)_{k \in \mathcal{K}/\{k^*\}}$ whose coordinates satisfy

$$c_k = d_{k^*} - d_k , \tag{14}$$

for every $k \in \mathcal{K}/\{k^*\}$. The comparison vector is a linear transformation of the score vector by a $((|\mathcal{K}| - 1) \times |\mathcal{K}|)$-matrix $P$ whose expression straightforwardly follows from (14). This implies that the distribution of the comparison vector can also be soundly estimated by a multivariate Gaussian distribution $\mathcal{N}(\mathbf{m_c}, \mathbf{\Sigma_c})$ where $\mathbf{m_c} = P \cdot \mathbf{m_d}$ and $\mathbf{\Sigma_c} = P \cdot \mathbf{\Sigma_d} \cdot P'$. Moreover, by definition of the comparison vector, an attack is successful (*i.e.* the correct secret $k^*$ is ranked first in the score vector) if and only if all the coordinates of the comparison vector are positive. We deduce that the success rate $\mathsf{Succ}^{\mathsf{d}}_{x,k^*}$ of a distinguisher d satisfies

$$\mathsf{Succ}^{\mathsf{d}}_{x,k^*} = \mathrm{P}[\mathbf{c} > \mathbf{0}] \approx \Phi_{\mathbf{m_c}, \mathbf{\Sigma_c}}(\mathbf{0}, \infty) \tag{15}$$

where $\Phi_{\mathbf{m}, \mathbf{\Sigma}}$ denotes the Gaussian cdf as defined in (2), $\mathbf{0}$ denotes the null vector, and $\infty$ denotes the vector $(\infty, \infty, \ldots, \infty)$.

*Remark 3.* In [16], the authors propose to extend the notion of success rate to different orders. The *o*-th order success rate of a side-channel attack is defined as the probability that the target secret $k^*$ is ranked among the *o* first key guesses by the score vector. The authors of [16] also suggest to consider the so-called *guessing entropy*, which is defined as the expected rank of the good key guess in the score vector [11,3]. As shown in [13], both the success rate of any order and the guessing entropy can be estimated using a similar approach as above.

**Methodology.** According to the above analysis, we propose the following methodology for an evaluator of some cryptographic algorithm to estimate the success rate of a HO-SCA against his masked implementation. We consider that the evaluator has access to the random masks generated during the computation, and is therefore able to predict the value of each share involved in the successive execution of the protected algorithm. The methodology is composed of three main steps:

1. Profile the leakage of every share using standard estimation techniques. Under the Gaussian leakage assumption, this estimation amounts to compute the sample means and the sample covariance matrices of the leakage $(L_i \mid S_i = s)$ for every share $S_i$ and every possible value $s \in \mathcal{S}$ based on a set of collected leakage samples.
2. Use Proposition 1 to compute the expectation vector and covariance matrix of the score vector with respect to the leakage parameters.
3. Deduce the parameters of the comparison vector distribution and evaluate the success rate according to (15).

The precision of the obtained estimation is impacted by two main factors:

- the accuracy of the leakage parameter estimations, and
- the tightness of the Gaussian approximation arising in Proposition 1.

The accurate estimation of leakage parameters has been a widely investigated issue and efficient techniques are known to deal with it (see for instance [4,15,1,7]). Basically, the more noisy the leakage, the more samples must be used to get an accurate estimation. Note that in our approach, the evaluator only has to estimate first-order leakage parameters with respect to the share values. Practical aspects of leakage parameter estimation are further discussed in Section 8.

On the other hand, the Gaussian approximation is the main issue in our approach. One can fairly expect that if the considered implementation is not too weak, the convergence toward the Gaussian distribution should be rather fast compared to the number of leakage observations required to succeed the HO-SCA. In order to validate this intuition, we provide in Section 7 an empirical validation of the Gaussian approximation.

## 5    Application to the Correlation Distinguisher

In this section, we apply the general methodology described in Section 4 when the linear correlation coefficient is used as distinguisher [2]. For two samples $\boldsymbol{x} = (x_1, x_2, \ldots, x_q) \in \mathbb{R}^q$ and $\boldsymbol{y} = (y_1, y_2, \ldots, y_q) \in \mathbb{R}^q$, the linear coefficient is defined by

$$\rho(\boldsymbol{x}, \boldsymbol{y}) = \frac{\frac{1}{q} \sum_{i=1}^{q} (x_i - \overline{\boldsymbol{x}}) \cdot (y_i - \overline{\boldsymbol{y}})}{\sqrt{\frac{1}{q} \sum_i (x_i - \overline{\boldsymbol{x}})^2} \cdot \sqrt{\frac{1}{q} \sum_i (y_i - \overline{\boldsymbol{y}})^2}} , \qquad (16)$$

where $\overline{\boldsymbol{x}}$ (resp. $\overline{\boldsymbol{y}}$) denotes the sample mean $q^{-1} \sum_i x_i$ (resp. $q^{-1} \sum_i y_i$).

In the context of HO-SCA, the correlation coefficient is used together with a *model function* $\mathtt{m} : \mathcal{X} \times \mathcal{K} \mapsto \mathbb{R}$ and a *combining function* $\mathtt{C} : \mathcal{L} \mapsto \mathbb{R}$ (see for instance [12]). The combining function is involved to map a leakage sample into a univariate sample combining the leakages of the different shares. On the other hand, the model function computes some expected value for the combined leakage with respect to some input $x$ and some guess $k$ on the target secret. The correlation distinguisher $\mathtt{d}_{\mathsf{cor}}$ is then defined as

$$\mathtt{d}_{\mathsf{cor}}\big((x_i, \boldsymbol{\ell}_i)_i\big) = \rho\big((\mathtt{m}(x_i, k))_i, (\mathtt{C}(\boldsymbol{\ell}_i))_i\big) . \qquad (17)$$

The following proposition extends the analysis conducted in [13] and states that the (higher-order) correlation distinguisher $\mathtt{d}_{\mathsf{cor}}$ is additive (see proof in appendix). This particularly implies that the methodology described in Section 4 can be applied to this distinguisher.

**Proposition 2.** *For any model function* $\mathtt{m} : \mathcal{X} \times \mathcal{K} \mapsto \mathbb{R}$ *and any combining function* $\mathtt{C} : \mathcal{L} \mapsto \mathbb{R}$, *the correlation distinguisher* $\mathtt{d}_{\mathsf{cor}}$ *is additive. Moreover,* $\mathtt{d}_{\mathsf{cor}}$ *is equivalent to the distinguisher* $\mathtt{d}'_{\mathsf{cor}}$ *defined for every* $(x_i, \boldsymbol{\ell}_i)_i \in (\mathcal{X} \times \mathcal{L})^q$ *by*

$$\mathtt{d}'_{\mathsf{cor}}\big((x_i, \boldsymbol{\ell}_i)_i\big) = \left(\frac{1}{q} \sum_{i=1}^{q} g_{x_i, k}(\boldsymbol{\ell}_i)\right)_{k \in \mathcal{K}} ,$$

*where the function $g_{x,k} : \mathcal{L} \to \mathbb{R}$ satisfies*

$$g_{x,k}(\boldsymbol{\ell}) = \frac{1}{s_k} \left( \mathbf{m}(x,k) - \overline{\mathbf{m}}_k \right) \cdot \mathbf{C}(\boldsymbol{\ell}) \ , \tag{18}$$

*for every $(x,k) \in \mathcal{X} \times \mathcal{K}$, with $\overline{\mathbf{m}}_k = \frac{1}{q} \sum_i \mathbf{m}(x_i,k)$ and $s_k = \sqrt{\frac{1}{q} \sum_i (\mathbf{m}(x_i,k) - \overline{\mathbf{m}}_k)^2}$.*

*Remark 4.* If we focus on the uniform setting where the input vector $\boldsymbol{x} = (x_1, x_2, \ldots, x_q)$ is balanced (meaning that each value $x \in \mathcal{X}$ have an occurrence ratio of $\tau_x = \frac{1}{|\mathcal{X}|}$), then $\overline{\mathbf{m}}_k$ and $s_k$ are constant with respect to $k$ and $\mathsf{d}_{\mathrm{cor}}$ is equivalent to another simpler distinguisher:

$$\mathsf{d}''_{\mathrm{cor}} : \left( (x_i, \boldsymbol{\ell}_i)_i \right) \mapsto \left( \frac{1}{q} \sum_i \mathbf{m}(x_i, k) \cdot \mathbf{C}(\boldsymbol{\ell}_i) \right)_{k \in \mathcal{K}} \ . \tag{19}$$

**Application to the Normalized Product Combining.** Let us now study the particular case of the higher-order correlation distinguisher based on the *centered product* combining function [12]. This combining function is defined for univariate share leakages (*i.e.* for $T = 1$ in the model of Section 3), namely its domain is $\mathcal{L} = \mathbb{R}^{d+1}$. For every $(\ell_0, \ell_1, \ldots, \ell_d) \in \mathcal{L}$, it is defined as

$$\mathbf{C}(\ell_0, \ell_1, \ldots, \ell_d) = \prod_{j=0}^{d} (\ell_j - \mu_j) \ , \tag{20}$$

where $\mu_j$ denotes the leakage expectation $\mathrm{E}\,[L_j]$.

Note that in practice, the adversary does not know the exact expectation $\mu_j$ but he can estimate it based on leakage samples. As argued in [12], the number of leakage samples required to succeed a HO-SCA is substantially greater than the number of leakage samples required to get precise estimations of the expectations $\mu_j$. Therefore, we can soundly assume that the $\mu_j$ in (20) are the exact expectations $\mathrm{E}\,[L_j]$.

We recall that, according to the leakage model presented in Section 3.1, the $j$th leakage component $L_j$ satisfies $L_j = f_j(S_j) + N_j$ where $f_j : s \mapsto m_{j,s}$ and $N_j \sim \mathcal{N}(0, \sigma_j^2)$. Since the noise $N_j$ is centered in 0, we have $\mathrm{E}\,[f_j(S_j)] = \mathrm{E}\,[L_j] = \mu_j$. Moreover, we shall denote $\nu_j = \mathrm{Var}\,[f_j(S_j)]$. By uniformity of $S_j$ over $\mathcal{S}$, we have:

$$\mu_j = \frac{1}{|\mathcal{S}|} \sum_{s \in \mathcal{S}} m_{j,s} \quad \text{and} \quad \nu_j = \frac{1}{|\mathcal{S}|} \sum_{s \in \mathcal{S}} (m_{j,s} - \mu_j)^2 \ . \tag{21}$$

In the following we shall further denote, for every $s \in \mathcal{S}$,

$$\alpha_s := \frac{1}{|\mathcal{S}|^d} \sum_{s_1 \in \mathcal{S}} \sum_{s_2 \in \mathcal{S}} \cdots \sum_{s_d \in \mathcal{S}} \prod_{j=0}^{d} (m_{j,s_j} - \mu_j) \tag{22}$$

and

$$\beta_s := \frac{1}{|\mathcal{S}|^d} \sum_{s_1 \in \mathcal{S}} \sum_{s_2 \in \mathcal{S}} \cdots \sum_{s_d \in \mathcal{S}} \prod_{j=0}^{d} (m_{j,s_j} - \mu_j)^2 \tag{23}$$

where $s_0 = s \oplus \bigoplus_{j=1}^{d} s_j$.

Note that both (22) and (23) can be expressed as a higher-order convolution product of the form

$$H(s) = \sum_{s_1} \sum_{s_2} \cdots \sum_{s_d} h_0(s \oplus s_1 \oplus s_2 \oplus \cdots \oplus s_d) \cdot h_1(s_1) \cdot h_2(s_2) \cdots h_d(s_d) . \quad (24)$$

We show in appendix how such a convolution can be efficiently computed for all values over $\mathcal{S}$ in $O(d \cdot |\mathcal{S}| \cdot \log |\mathcal{S}|)$ operations.

We then have the following corollary of Proposition 1 for the distinguisher $\mathsf{d}'_{\text{cor}}$ with centered product combining function (see proof in appendix).

**Corollary 1.** *Let $k^* \in \mathcal{K}$, let $(x_1, x_2, \ldots, x_q) \in \mathcal{X}^q$ and let $\ell_i \overset{\$}{\leftarrow} L_{x_i,k^*}$ for every $i \in \{1, 2, \ldots, q\}$. Then the distribution of the score vector $(d'_k)_{k \in \mathcal{K}} = \mathsf{d}'_{\text{cor}}\big((x_i, \ell_i)_i\big)$ with centered product combining function tends toward a multivariate Gaussian distribution with expectation vector $(\mathrm{E}\,[d'_k])_{k \in \mathcal{K}}$ satisfying*

$$\mathrm{E}\,[d'_k] = \sum_{x \in \mathcal{X}} \tau_x \, \mathsf{M}(x, k) \, \alpha_{\varphi(x,k^*)} \ , \quad (25)$$

*for every $k \in \mathcal{K}$, and with covariance matrix $(\mathrm{Cov}\,[d'_{k_1}, d'_{k_2}])_{(k_1,k_2) \in \mathcal{K}^2}$ satisfying*

$$\mathrm{Cov}\,[d'_{k_1}, d'_{k_2}] = \frac{1}{q} \sum_{x \in \mathcal{X}} \tau_x \, \mathsf{M}(x, k_1) \, \mathsf{M}(x, k_2)$$

$$\times \left( \beta_{\varphi(x,k^*)} - \alpha^2_{\varphi(x,k^*)} + \prod_{j=0}^{d}(\nu_j + \sigma_j^2) - \prod_{j=0}^{d} \nu_j \right) , \quad (26)$$

*for every $(k_1, k_2) \in \mathcal{K}^2$, where*

$$\mathsf{M} : (x, k) \mapsto \frac{\mathsf{m}(x, k) - \overline{\mathsf{m}}_k}{s_k} \ . \quad (27)$$

*Remark 5.* For the distinguisher $\mathsf{d}''_{\text{cor}}$ defined in (19) and which is equivalent to the correlation distinguisher in the uniform setting (see Remark 4), we have the same result as in Corollary 1 but the function $\mathsf{M}$ is simply defined as the model function $\mathsf{m}$.

According to Corollary 1, the methodology presented in Section 4 can be applied to estimate the success rate of a HO-SCA based on the correlation distinguisher with centered product combining. The first step of the methodology shall provide estimations of the leakage functions $f_j : s \mapsto m_{j,s}$ (and hence of the corresponding $\mu_j$ and $\nu_j$), while the second step shall simply consist in the evaluations of Formulae (25) and (26).

# 6    Application to the Likelihood Distinguisher

In this section, we apply the general methodology described in Section 4 when the likelihood is used as distinguisher [4]. The likelihood distinguisher, denoted $\mathsf{d_{lik}}$, is usually applied after a *profiling step* whose goal is to provide an estimation $\hat{\mathsf{p}}_s$ of the pdf of the random variable $\boldsymbol{L}_s$ for every $s \in \mathcal{S}$. Then, for every sample $(x_i, \boldsymbol{\ell_i})_i \in (\mathcal{X} \times \mathcal{L})^q$, the likelihood distinguisher is defined as

$$\mathsf{d_{lik}}\big((x_i, \boldsymbol{\ell_i})_i\big) = \prod_{i=1}^{q} \hat{\mathsf{p}}_{\varphi(x_i,k)}(\boldsymbol{\ell_i}) \ . \tag{28}$$

In practice, one often makes use of the equivalent (averaged) log-likelihood distinguisher $\mathsf{d'_{lik}}$ defined as

$$\mathsf{d'_{lik}}\big((x_i, \boldsymbol{\ell_i})_i\big) = \frac{1}{q} \log \mathsf{d_{lik}}\big((x_i, \boldsymbol{\ell_i})_i\big) = \frac{1}{q} \sum_{i=1}^{q} \log(\hat{\mathsf{p}}_{\varphi(x_i,k)}(\boldsymbol{\ell_i})) \ . \tag{29}$$

The log-likelihood distinguisher is usually preferred as it less susceptible to approximation errors than the likelihood. We straightforwardly get the following proposition.

**Proposition 3.** *The likelihood distinguisher $\mathsf{d_{lik}}$ is additive and equivalent to the log-likelihood distinguisher $\mathsf{d'_{lik}}$. Moreover, for every $(x_i, \boldsymbol{\ell_i})_i \in (\mathcal{X} \times \mathcal{L})^q$, $\mathsf{d'_{lik}}$ satisfies*

$$\mathsf{d'_{lik}}\big((x_i, \boldsymbol{\ell_i})_i\big) = \left(\frac{1}{q} \sum_{i=1}^{q} g_{x_i,k}(\boldsymbol{\ell_i})\right)_{k \in \mathcal{K}} \ , \tag{30}$$

*where the function $g_{x,k} : \mathcal{L} \to \mathbb{R}$ satisfies*

$$g_{x,k}(\boldsymbol{\ell}) = \log(\hat{\mathsf{p}}_{\varphi(x,k)}(\boldsymbol{\ell})) \ , \tag{31}$$

*for every $(x, k) \in \mathcal{X} \times \mathcal{K}$.*

Under the Gaussian leakage assumption, it can be checked that the variable $\boldsymbol{L}_s$ has a Gaussian mixture distribution, with pdf $\mathsf{p}_s$ satisfying

$$\mathsf{p}_s : (\ell_0, \ell_1, \ldots, \ell_d) \mapsto \frac{1}{|\mathcal{S}|^d} \sum_{s_1 \in \mathcal{S}} \sum_{s_2 \in \mathcal{S}} \cdots \sum_{s_d \in \mathcal{S}} \prod_{j=0}^{d} \phi_{m_{j,s_j}, \boldsymbol{\Sigma}_j}(\ell_j) \ , \tag{32}$$

where $s_0 = s \oplus \bigoplus_{j=1}^{d} s_j$. Note that for every $s \in \mathcal{S}$, the estimated pdf $\hat{\mathsf{p}}_s$ obtained from the profiling phase has a similar expression as $\mathsf{p}_s$ but with estimations $\hat{m}_{j,s_j}$ and $\hat{\boldsymbol{\Sigma}}_j$ for the leakage means and covariance matrices.

Here again, it can be seen from (32) that for a given $\boldsymbol{\ell} \in \mathcal{L}$ the probability $\mathsf{p}_s(\boldsymbol{\ell})$ is a higher-order convolution product as in (24). The set of probability values $\{\mathsf{p}_s(\boldsymbol{\ell}) \ ; \ s \in \mathcal{S}\}$ can then be computed in $O(d \cdot |\mathcal{S}| \cdot \log |\mathcal{S}|)$ operations (see details in appendix).

Let us now consider the two functions:

$$\lambda(s_1, s_2) := \int_{\ell \in \mathcal{L}} \log(\hat{\mathsf{p}}_{s_1}(\ell)) \, \mathsf{p}_{s_2}(\ell) \, d\ell \;, \tag{33}$$

and

$$\psi(s_1, s_2, s_3) := \int_{\ell \in \mathcal{L}} \log(\hat{\mathsf{p}}_{s_1}(\ell)) \, \log(\hat{\mathsf{p}}_{s_2}(\ell)) \, \mathsf{p}_{s_3}(\ell) \, d\ell \;. \tag{34}$$

Then, by definition, we have

$$\Lambda(x, k, k^*) := \lambda(\varphi(x, k), \varphi(x, k^*)) = \mathrm{E}\left[g_{x,k}(\boldsymbol{L}_{x,k^*})\right]$$

and

$$\Psi(x, k_1, k_2, k^*) := \psi(\varphi(x, k_1), \varphi(x, k_2), \varphi(x, k^*))$$
$$= \mathrm{E}\left[g_{x,k_1}(\boldsymbol{L}_{x,k^*}) \cdot g_{x,k_2}(\boldsymbol{L}_{x,k^*})\right] \;.$$

A direct application of Proposition 1 then yields the following corollary for the log-likelihood distinguisher.

**Corollary 2.** *Let $k^* \in \mathcal{K}$, let $(x_1, x_2, \ldots, x_q) \in \mathcal{X}^q$ and let $\ell_i \xleftarrow{\$} \boldsymbol{L}_{x_i,k^*}$ for every $i \in \{1, 2, \ldots, q\}$. Then the distribution of the score vector $(d'_k)_{k \in \mathcal{K}} = \mathsf{d}'_{\mathsf{lik}}((x_i, \ell_i)_i)$ tends toward a multivariate Gaussian distribution with expectation vector $(\mathrm{E}[d'_k])_{k \in \mathcal{K}}$ satisfying*

$$\mathrm{E}[d'_k] = \sum_{x \in \mathcal{X}} \tau_x \, \Lambda(x, k, k^*) \;, \tag{35}$$

*for every $k \in \mathcal{K}$, and with covariance matrix $(\mathrm{Cov}\left[d'_{k_1}, d'_{k_2}\right])_{(k_1,k_2) \in \mathcal{K}^2}$ satisfying*

$$\mathrm{Cov}\left[d'_{k_1}, d'_{k_2}\right] = \frac{1}{q} \sum_{x \in \mathcal{X}} \tau_x \left(\Psi(x, k_1, k_2, k^*) - \Lambda(x, k_1, k^*) \cdot \Lambda(x, k_2, k^*)\right) \;. \tag{36}$$

According to Corollary 2, the methodology presented in Section 4 can be applied to estimate the success rate of a HO-SCA based on the likelihood distinguisher.

## 7   Empirical Validation of the Gaussian Approximation

In Section 4, we have presented a methodology to estimate the success rate of higher-order side-channel attacks based on so-called additive distinguishers. The principle of this methodology is to approximate the distribution of the score vector by a multivariate Gaussian distribution whose parameters are derived from the leakage parameters. This Gaussian approximation is asymptotically sound by the central limit theorem. However, in the non-asymptotic context of a HO-SCA with a given number of leakage samples, it is fair to question whether this approximation is sound or not. In this section, we conduct an empirical study of the Gaussian approximation. For this purpose, we compare the success rates obtained from attack simulations, to the success rates obtained by applying the methodology of Section 4.

Since our purpose here is the sole validation of the Gaussian approximation, we do not focus on the leakage estimation issue, but we assume the exact leakage parameters $\{(m_{j,s}, \sigma_j^2) \; ; \; 0 \leqslant j \leqslant d, \; s \in \mathcal{S}\}$ are known (in a univariate setting). From these leakage parameters, and for a given HO-SCA based on some distinguisher $\mathsf{d} \in \{\mathsf{d}_{\mathsf{cor}}, \mathsf{d}_{\mathsf{lik}}\}$, we evaluate the success rate with the two following approaches:

- **Simulation success rate.** We perform several attack simulations and count the number of successes in order to get an estimation of the success rate. For each attack simulation, we randomly generate input-leakage samples $(x_1, \ell_1)$, $(x_2, \ell_2)$, ..., $(x_q, \ell_q)$. Specifically, for every $i$, $x_i$ is uniformly picked up and $\ell_i$ is randomly sampled from the variable $L_{x_i, k^*}$ according to the leakage parameters. Then we apply the distinguisher $\mathsf{d}$ to these samples, and we count a success whenever the good secret is ranked first.
- **Gaussian cdf evaluation.** We apply Corollaries 1 and 2 to compute the expectation vector and covariance matrix of the score vector with respect to the leakage parameters and taking $\tau_x = 1/|\mathcal{X}|$ as occurrence ratio for every $x \in \mathcal{X}$ (in accordance to the uniform distribution of the $x_i$). Then we compute the Gaussian cdf of the comparison vector to evaluate the success rate according to (15).

We plot hereafter the results obtained with these two approaches for different HO-SCA targeting an AES Sbox output:

$$\varphi(x, k^*) = \mathsf{SB}(x \oplus k^*) \, ,$$

where $\mathsf{SB}$ denote the AES Sbox function. For the leakage parameters, we used sample means and sample variances obtained by monitoring the leakage of two different devices running masked AES implementations (Device A and Device B, see Section 8 for details).

Figure 1 shows the results obtained for a second-order correlation attack with centered product combining function and Hamming weight model function (*i.e.* $\mathsf{m} = \mathsf{HW}$), for leakage parameters from Device A. Figure 2 plots the results of a second-order likelihood attack with the same leakage parameters, assuming a perfect profiling (*i.e.* $\hat{\mathsf{p}}_s = \mathsf{p}_s$ for every $s$) on the one hand and a slightly erroneous profiling on the other hand.[1] We observe that for both distinguishers, the experimental success rate curves and theoretical success rate curves clearly match. This validates the Gaussian approximation in these HO-SCA contexts.

In order to test the Gaussian approximation to higher orders, we also performed third-order and fourth-order attacks, with leakage parameters from Device B. The results of the correlation attacks (centered product combining function and Hamming weight model function) are presented in Figure 3 and Figure 4 respectively.

---

[1] Specifically, we introduce random errors in the $(m_{j,s})_{j,s}$ used in the estimated pdfs $\hat{\mathsf{p}}_s$.

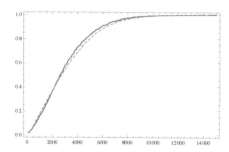

**Fig. 1.** Simulation SR (plain curve) *vs.* theoretical SR (dashed curve) for 2nd-order correlation attack

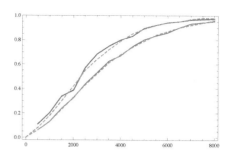

**Fig. 2.** Simulation SR (plain curves) *vs.* theoretical SR (dashed curves) for 2nd-order likelihood attacks

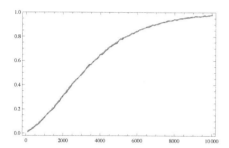

**Fig. 3.** Simulation SR (plain curve) *vs.* theoretical SR (dashed curve) for 3rd-order correlation attack

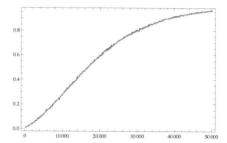

**Fig. 4.** Simulation SR (plain curve) *vs.* theoretical SR (dashed curve) for 4th-order correlation attack

The figures for the higher-order likelihood attacks are provided in the full version of the paper. We see that the curves perfectly match, which further validates the Gaussian approximation in these higher-order contexts.

## 8   Practical Experiments

In this section, we confront our methodology to practical attack experiments. We report the results of several higher-order correlation attacks against two different devices running masked AES implementations. We also apply our methodology to estimate the expected success rate of these attacks with respect to the inferred leakage parameters.

**Experimental Setup.** Practical experiments were performed on two microcontrollers made in different CMOS technologies (130 and 350 nanometer processes, respectively called devices A and device B in the sequel). The side-channel traces were obtained by measuring the electromagnetic (EM) radiations emitted by the device during a masked AES-128 encryption handling one byte at a time. To this aim, an EM sensor was used (made of several coils of copper with diameter of $500\mu m$), and was plugged into a low-noise amplifier. To sample the leakage measurements, a digital oscilloscope was used with a sampling rate of 10G samples per second for the device A and 2G samples per second for the device B, whereas microcontrollers were running at few dozen of MHz. As the microcontrollers clocks were not stable, we had to resynchronize the EM traces. This process is out of the scope of this work, but we would like to emphasize that resynchronization is always required in a practical context and it has a non negligible impact on the measurements noise.

In our attack context, the random values involved in the masking/sharing could be known by the evaluator and we used this ability to identify the time samples corresponding to the different manipulation of the different shares. This step allowed us to associate each share to a unique time sample (the one with maximal SNR) and to profile the leakage parameters.[2]

**Estimation of the Leakage Parameters.** To estimate the leakage functions $f_j : s \mapsto m_{j,s}$, we applied linear regression techniques on 200000 leakage samples. When applied on leakage samples $\ell_{1,j}, \ell_{2,j}, \ldots, \ell_{q,j}$, corresponding to successive share values $s_{1,j}, s_{2,j}, \ldots, s_{q,j}$, a linear regression *of degree t* returns an approximation of $f_j(s)$ as a degree-$t$ polynomial in the bits of $s$ (see [15,5] for more detail on linear regression in the context of side-channel attacks). We applied linear regression of degree 1 and 2 on Device A and B respectively. Once the $f_j$ function estimated, we could easily get an estimation for the variance $\sigma_j^2$ of the noise $N_j$ by computing the sample variance of $(\ell_{i,j} - f_j(s_{i,j}))_i$ for every $j$.

**Methodology *versus* Practice.** In order to validate our methodology in practice, we performed higher-order correlation attacks with centered product combining function (see Section 5) and Hamming weight model function (*i.e.* m = HW). On the other hand, the success rate was estimated using the methodology described in Sections 4 and 5 by computing the parameters of the multivariate Gaussian distribution arising for the correlation distinguisher with respect to the inferred leakage parameters.

Figures 5 and 6 plot the experimental success rates *versus* the theoretical success rates for the second-order correlation attacks against Device A and Device B. In order to validate our approach with respect to higher-order attacks in practice, we also compare the results obtained with our methodology to third-order and fourth-order attack results on Device B (see Figures 7 and 8). We observe a clear match between the experimental and theoretical success rate curves. These results demonstrate the soundness of the methodology in practice.

Further experiments are provided in the full version of the paper in order to observe the impact of the leakage profiling phase on our methodology.

---

[2] The knowledge of the masks was however not used in the attack phase itself.

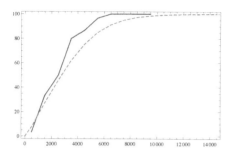

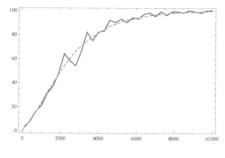

**Fig. 5.** Experimental SR (plain curve) *vs.* theoretical SR (dashed curve) for 2nd-order correlation attack on Device A

**Fig. 6.** Experimental SR (plain curve) *vs.* theoretical SR (dashed curve) for 2nd-order correlation attack on Device B

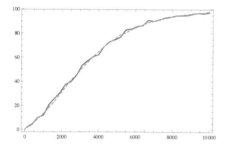

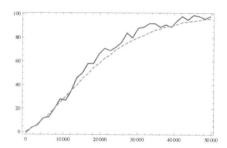

**Fig. 7.** Experimental SR (plain curve) *vs.* theoretical SR (dashed curve) for 3rd-order correlation attack on Device B

**Fig. 8.** Experimental SR (plain curve) *vs.* theoretical SR (dashed curve) for 4th-order correlation attack on Device B

## 9    Conclusion

In this work we have presented a methodology to evaluate the success rate of higher-order side-channel attacks. We have shown how to apply this methodology in the particular cases of attacks based on the correlation and likelihood distinguishers. The soundness of our approach has been validated by simulations and experiments performed on different microcontrollers. Using this methodology, an evaluator can estimate the side-channel resistance of his masked cryptographic implementation at the cost of inferring a few linear regression coefficients.

## References

1. Archambeau, C., Peeters, E., Standaert, F.-X., Quisquater, J.-J.: Template Attacks in Principal Subspaces. In: Goubin and Matsui [8], pp. 1–14
2. Brier, E., Clavier, C., Olivier, F.: Correlation power analysis with a leakage model. In: Joye, M., Quisquater, J.-J. (eds.) CHES 2004. LNCS, vol. 3156, pp. 16–29. Springer, Heidelberg (2004)

3. Cachin, C.: Entropy Measures and Unconditional Security in Cryptography. PhD thesis (1997)
4. Chari, S., Rao, J., Rohatgi, P.: Template attacks. In: Kaliski Jr., B.S., Koç, Ç.K., Paar, C. (eds.) CHES 2002. LNCS, vol. 2523, pp. 13–28. Springer, Heidelberg (2003)
5. Doget, J., Prouff, E., Rivain, M., Standaert, F.-X.: Univariate Side Channel Attacks and Leakage Modeling. Journal of Cryptographic Engineering 1(2), 123–144 (2011)
6. Fei, Y., Luo, Q., Ding, A.A.: A statistical model for DPA with novel algorithmic confusion analysis. In: Prouff, E., Schaumont, P. (eds.) CHES 2012. LNCS, vol. 7428, pp. 233–250. Springer, Heidelberg (2012)
7. Gierlichs, B., Lemke-Rust, K., Paar, C.: Templates vs. Stochastic Methods. In: Goubin and Matsui [8], pp. 15–29
8. Goubin, L., Matsui, M. (eds.): CHES 2006. LNCS, vol. 4249. Springer, Heidelberg (2006)
9. Kocher, P.C., Jaffe, J., Jun, B.: Differential power analysis. In: Wiener, M. (ed.) CRYPTO 1999. LNCS, vol. 1666, pp. 388–397. Springer, Heidelberg (1999)
10. Mangard, S.: Hardware countermeasures against DPA – A statistical analysis of their effectiveness. In: Okamoto, T. (ed.) CT-RSA 2004. LNCS, vol. 2964, pp. 222–235. Springer, Heidelberg (2004)
11. Massey, J.: Guessing and Entropy. In: IEEE International Symposium on Information Theory, p. 204 (1994)
12. Prouff, E., Rivain, M., Bévan, R.: Statistical Analysis of Second Order Di_er- ential Power Analysis. IEEE Transactions on Computers 58(6), 799–811 (2009)
13. Rivain, M.: On the exact success rate of side channel analysis in the gaussian model. In: Avanzi, R.M., Keliher, L., Sica, F. (eds.) SAC 2008. LNCS, vol. 5381, pp. 165–183. Springer, Heidelberg (2009)
14. Rivain, M., Prouff, E., Doget, J.: Higher-order Masking and Shu_ing for Software Implementations of Block Ciphers. Cryptology ePrint Archive (2009), http://eprint.iacr.org/
15. Schindler, W., Lemke, K., Paar, C.: A stochastic model for differential side channel cryptanalysis. In: Rao, J.R., Sunar, B. (eds.) CHES 2005. LNCS, vol. 3659, pp. 30–46. Springer, Heidelberg (2005)
16. Standaert, F.-X., Malkin, T.G., Yung, M.: A Formal Practice-Oriented Model For The Analysis of Side-Channel Attacks. Cryptology ePrint Archive, Report 2006/139 (2006)
17. Standaert, F.-X., Peeters, E., Rouvroy, G., Quisquater, J.-J.: An Overview of Power Analysis Attacks Against Field Programmable Gate Arrays. IEEE 94(2), 383–394 (2006)
18. Thillard, A., Prouff, E., Roche, T.: Success through confidence: Evaluating the effectiveness of a side-channel attack. In: Bertoni, G., Coron, J.-S. (eds.) CHES 2013. LNCS, vol. 8086, pp. 21–36. Springer, Heidelberg (2013)

# A    Proof of Proposition 2

*Proof.* Let $(d_k)_{k \in \mathcal{K}} = \mathsf{d}_{\mathsf{cor}}\big((x_i, \ell_i)_i\big)$ and $(d'_k)_{k \in \mathcal{K}} = \mathsf{d}'_{\mathsf{cor}}\big((x_i, \ell_i)_i\big)$ for some input-leakage samples $(x_i, \ell_i)_{i \leqslant q} \in (\mathcal{X} \times \mathcal{L})^q$. We have:

$$d_k = \frac{1}{s_\mathsf{C}} \frac{\sum_{i=1}^q (\mathsf{m}(x_i, k) - \overline{\mathsf{m}}_k)\mathsf{C}(\ell_i)}{s_k} = \frac{1}{s_\mathsf{C}} d'_k ,$$

where $s_\mathsf{C} = \sqrt{\frac{1}{q} \sum_i (\mathsf{C}(\ell_i) - \overline{\mathsf{C}})^2}$ with $\overline{\mathsf{C}} = \frac{1}{q} \sum_i \mathsf{C}(\ell_i)$.

Since $s_\mathsf{C}$ is strictly positive and constant with respect to the guess $k$, the score vectors $(d_k)_{k \in \mathcal{K}}$ and $(d'_k)_{k \in \mathcal{K}}$ are clearly rank-equivalent, implying that the distinguishers $\mathsf{d}_{\mathsf{cor}}$ and $\mathsf{d}'_{\mathsf{cor}}$ are equivalent. Moreover, after denoting by $g_{x,k}$ the function $\ell_i \mapsto s_k^{-1}(\mathsf{m}(x, k) - \overline{\mathsf{m}}_k)\mathsf{C}(\ell_i)$, we get $d'_k = \frac{1}{q} \sum_{i=1}^q g_{x_i, k}(\ell_i)$, which implies that $\mathsf{d}'_{\mathsf{cor}}$ is additive. $\qquad\square$

# B    Fast Evaluation of Higher-Order Convolution

**Proposition 4.** *Let $d$ be a positive integer, and let $(\mathcal{S}, \oplus)$ be a group of size $|\mathcal{S}| = 2^m$. Let $(h_j)_{0 \leq j \leq d}$ be a family of functions from $\mathcal{S}$ into $\mathbb{R}$, such that $h_j(s)$ can be efficiently evaluated for every $s \in \mathcal{S}$ in $o(1)$ operations (one typically has a look-up table for every $h_j$). Consider the function $H : \mathcal{S} \to \mathbb{R}$ defined as*

$$H : s \mapsto \sum_{s_1 \in \mathcal{S}} \sum_{s_2 \in \mathcal{S}} \cdots \sum_{s_d \in \mathcal{S}} h_0(s \oplus s_1 \oplus s_2 \oplus \cdots \oplus s_d) \cdot h_1(s_1) \cdot h_2(s_2) \cdots h_d(s_d) .$$

*Then, the whole set of outputs $\{H(s) ; \ s \in \mathcal{S}\}$ can be computed in $O(d \cdot 2^m \cdot m)$ operations.*

*Proof.* For every $s \in \mathcal{S}$, the function $H$ satisfies

$$H(s) = \sum_{s_d \in \mathcal{S}} h_d(s_d) \cdots \sum_{s_2 \in \mathcal{S}} h_2(s_2) \sum_{s_1 \in \mathcal{S}} h_1(s_1) \cdot h_0(s \oplus s_1 \oplus s_2 \oplus \cdots s_d) .$$

Consider the convolution product of the form

$$h_1 \otimes h_0 : s \mapsto \sum_{t \in \mathcal{S}} h_1(t) \cdot h_0(s \oplus t) .$$

We have

$$\mathcal{WH}(h_1 \otimes h_0) = 2^{\frac{m}{2}} \, \mathcal{WH}(h_1) \cdot \mathcal{WH}(h_0) ,$$

where $\mathcal{WH}$ is the (normalized) Walsh-Hadamard transform (WHT). This convolution product can hence be efficiently computed from three evaluations of fast WHT that each takes $O(2^m \cdot m)$ operations.[3]

---

[3] The WHT is involutive, hence we have $h_1 \otimes h_0 = 2^{\frac{m}{2}} \, \mathcal{WH}\big(\mathcal{WH}(h_1) \cdot \mathcal{WH}(h_0)\big)$.

One can check that the sequence of functions $(H_i)_{0 \leq i \leq d}$ defined as

$$\begin{cases} H_0 = h_0 \\ H_i = h_i \otimes H_{i-1} \quad \text{for every } i \geqslant 1 \end{cases}$$

is such that $H_d = H$. One can then sequentially compute the set of outputs of $H_1, H_2, \ldots, H_d = H$ by evaluating $d$ convolution products, which gives a total cost of $O(d \cdot 2^m \cdot m)$ operations. $\qquad \square$

## C    Proof of Corollary 1

To prove the corollary, we first introduce the following lemma.

**Lemma 1.** *The expectation and variance of the random variable* $C(L_{x,k^*})$ *respectively satisfy*

$$\mathrm{E}\left[C(L_{x,k^*})\right] = \alpha_{\varphi(x,k^*)} \tag{37}$$

*and*

$$\mathrm{Var}\left[C(L_{x,k^*})\right] = \beta_{\varphi(x,k^*)} - \alpha^2_{\varphi(x,k^*)} + \prod_{j=0}^{d}(\nu_j + \sigma_j^2) - \prod_{j=0}^{d}\nu_j \ . \tag{38}$$

*Proof.* Since the $N_j$ are independent and centered in 0, we have

$$\mathrm{E}\left[C(L_{x,k^*})\right] = \mathrm{E}\left[C\big(f_0(S_0), f_1(S_1), \ldots, f_d(S_d)\big)^2\right] = \alpha_{\varphi(x,k^*)} \ ,$$

On the other hand, by definition of the variance, we have

$$\mathrm{Var}\left[C(L_{x,k^*})\right] = \mathrm{E}\left[C(L_{x,k^*})^2\right] - \mathrm{E}\left[C(L_{x,k^*})\right]^2 = \mathrm{E}\left[C(L_{x,k^*})^2\right] - \alpha^2_{\varphi(x,k^*)} \ .$$

Then, we have

$$\mathrm{E}\left[C(L_{x,k^*})^2\right] = \mathrm{E}\left[\prod_{j=0}^{d}\left(f_j(S_j) + N_j - \mu_j\right)^2\right] = \mathrm{E}\left[\prod_{j=0}^{d}\left((f_j(S_j) - \mu_j)^2 + N_j^2\right)\right]$$

where the second holds since the $N_j$ have zero means and are mutually independent and independent of the $S_j$. By developing the product, we get a sum of monomials, such that each monomial involves random variables that are mutually independent, except for one single monomial which is $\prod_{j=0}^{d}(f_j(S_j) - \mu_j)^2$. We can then develop the above equation as

$$\mathrm{E}\left[C(L_{x,k^*})^2\right] = \prod_{j=0}^{d}\left(\mathrm{E}\left[(f_j(S_j) - \mu_j)^2\right] + \mathrm{E}\left[N_j^2\right]\right)$$

$$- \prod_{j=0}^{d}\mathrm{E}\left[(f_j(S_j) - \mu_j)^2\right] + \mathrm{E}\left[\prod_{j=0}^{d}(f_j(S_j) - \mu_j)^2\right] \ ,$$

which gives

$$E\left[C(L_{x,k^*})^2\right] = \prod_{j=0}^{d}(\nu_j + \sigma_j^2) - \prod_{j=0}^{d}\nu_j + \beta_{\varphi(x,k^*)}.$$

□

*Proof of Corollary 1.* Applying (12) and (13) to the functions $g_{x,k} : \ell \mapsto \frac{1}{s_k}\left(m(x,k) - \overline{m}_k\right) \cdot C(\ell)$ as defined in (18), we get

$$E\left[d_k'\right] = \frac{1}{s_k}\sum_{x \in \mathcal{X}} \tau_x \left(m(x,k) - \overline{m}_k\right) E\left[C(L_{x,k^*})\right] \ ,$$

and

$$\mathrm{Cov}\left[d_{k_1}', d_{k_2}'\right] = \frac{1}{q}\frac{1}{s_{k_1}s_{k_2}}\sum_{x \in \mathcal{X}} \tau_x \left(m(x,k_1) - \overline{m}_{k_1}\right)\left(m(x,k_2) - \overline{m}_{k_2}\right)\mathrm{Var}\left[C(L_{x,k^*})\right] \ ,$$

Then Lemma 1 directly yields the corollary statement.

□

# Good Is Not Good Enough
## Deriving Optimal Distinguishers from Communication Theory

Annelie Heuser[1][*], Olivier Rioul[1], and Sylvain Guilley[1,2]

[1] Télécom ParisTech, Institut Mines-Télécom, CNRS LTCI,
Department Comelec46 rue Barrault, 75 634 Paris Cedex 13, France
`firstname.lastname@telecom-paristech.fr`
[2] Secure-IC S.A.S.,
80 avenue des Buttes de Coësmes, 35 700 Rennes, France

**Abstract.** We find mathematically optimal side-channel distinguishers by looking at the side-channel as a communication channel. Our methodology can be adapted to any given scenario (device, signal-to-noise ratio, noise distribution, leakage model, etc.). When the model is known and the noise is Gaussian, the optimal distinguisher outperforms CPA and covariance. However, we show that CPA is optimal when the model is only known on a proportional scale. For non-Gaussian noise, we obtain different optimal distinguishers, one for each noise distribution. When the model is imperfectly known, we consider the scenario of a weighted sum of the sensitive variable bits where the weights are unknown and drawn from a normal law. In this case, our optimal distinguisher performs better than the classical linear regression analysis.

**Keywords:** Side-channel analysis, distinguisher, communication channel, maximum likelihood, correlation power analysis, uniform noise, Laplacian noise.

## 1 Introduction

Any embedded system that contains secrets, such as a cryptographic key $k^\star$, is prone to side-channel attacks, which proceed in two steps. First, a leakage (power consumption, electromagnetic radiations, time, etc.) is measured, which is a noisy signal dependent on internally manipulated data, some of which are sensitive, meaning that they depend on the secret key $k^\star$ and on some plaintext or cipher-text (denoted by $T$). A distinguisher is then used to quantify the similarity between the measured leakage and an assumed leakage model. The result is an estimation $\hat{k}$ of the secret key $k^\star$.

In the literature, side-channel distinguishers are customarily presented as statistical operators that confront the leakage and the sensitive variable, both seen

---

[*] Annelie Heuser is a Google European fellow in the field of privacy and is partially founded by this fellowship.

L. Batina and M. Robshaw (Eds.): CHES 2014, LNCS 8731, pp. 55–74, 2014.

as random variables, in order to extract the secret key. Different choices of distinguishers as statistical tools yield different performances, depending on the scenario (device, signal-to-noise ratio, noise distributions, leakage models, etc.)

There are certainly various ways to appreciate the quality of distinguishers. In this article, we focus on distinguishers that maximize the probability of revealing the correct key. In the field of side-channel analysis , somewhat paradoxically, most of the academic works have eluded the precise mathematical derivation of the best distinguisher given a precise attack scenario. Specifically, the community has introduced popular statistical tools (maximum likelihood (ML), difference of means (DoM), covariance, Pearson correlation coefficient (correlation power analysis (CPA)), Kolmogorov-Smirnov distance, etc.) and addressed two questions: *Q1: what distinguishes known distinguishers in terms of distinctive features?*, and *Q2: given a side-channel context what is the best distinguisher among all known ones?*

As for *Q1*, there have been some publications that attempt to highlight specificities of distinguishers. For instance, Doget et al. [4] show that some distinguishers seemingly have different expressions, but are in practice the same one fed with different variants of leakage models. Mangard et al. [11] argue that some distinguishers achieve success performance all the more similar as the noise variance increases; they conclude that only "statistical artifacts" can explain the difference of success probability between a class of selected distinguishers (notably maximum likelihood and correlation). Souissi et al. [20] note that the closer the noise is to a normal distribution (measured by a gaussianity metric), the better the correlation compared to other distinguishers. Besides, it was noticed by Prouff and Rivain [16] that the way a distinguisher is estimated seriously impacts its success rate. This is especially true for information-theoretic side-channel distinguishers, because probability density functions are to be estimated, which is a notoriously difficult problem. In contrast, Whitnall and Oswald [24] defined metrics (such as RDM, the relative distinguishing margin) to rank distinguishers according to exact values, independently of the way they are estimated (notably mutual information). However, the RDM has recently been found questionable in some situations [17]. All in one, it appears difficult to identify salient features that make one distinguisher in particular more appropriate than another.

Regarding question *Q2*, a usual practice is to estimate the success rate using enough simulations or experiments until an unambiguous ranking of the distinguishers can be carried out. In [21], Standaert et al. also consider the quality of the profiling stage when comparing distinguishers. But the fundamental shortcoming of this approach is that the pool of investigated distinguishers is always limited and does not necessarily contain the best possible distinguisher in every scenario.

**Contributions.** In this paper, we answer the ultimate version of *Q2*, which is also related to *Q1*, namely: *Q3: given a side-channel scenario what is the best distinguisher among all possible ones?* The *"best"* distinguisher is to be understood in terms of *success probability maximization*. Our analyses show that such an objective coincides with the one pursued in digital communication theory [5,23], where it is rather formulated as the minimization of the *error probability* (i.e., one minus the success probability). Interestingly, in this approach, it is not necessary to investigate how a distinguisher can be estimated as a stochastic tool, since our analysis already gives the optimal way of estimating the secret key from the measured data.

We show that, when the leakage model is perfectly known by the attacker (on a direct scale [25]), the optimal distinguisher depends only on the noise distribution, not necessarily Gaussian. Consideration of different noise models (Gaussian, uniform, Laplacian) shows that there is no "universal" distinguisher, only one best distinguisher per noise distribution type. Surprisingly, in the additive Gaussian noise case, we find that neither the DoM, nor the CPA are optimal: we exhibit the optimal distinguisher that slightly outperforms them all. The optimal distinguishers for uniform and Laplacian noise are different from Pearson correlation or covariance, and simulations show that they can be much more efficient. When the leakage model is only known on a proportional scale [25] (i.e., $ax + b$ where $a$ and $b$ are unknown) and when the noise is Gaussian, we show that the optimal expression leads exactly to Pearson correlation coefficient. This in particular explains optimality of CPA in this context.

When the model drifts away from Hamming weight (or Hamming distance) and is thus (at least partially) unknown to the attacker, we use a stochastic linear leakage model with unknown coefficients drawn from a normal distribution and derive an optimal distinguisher that outperforms the linear regression attack [4]. Our result has the merit of showing that a rigorous derivation of the optimal attack is possible and that it yields a new expression, which is interpretable in terms of *stochastic* vs. *epistemic* noise[1].

**Outline.** The remainder of the paper is organized as follows. We express the problem of side-channel analysis (SCA) as a communication problem in Sect. 2. The mathematical derivation of the optimal distinguishers in various scenarios is carried out in Sect. 3 when the leakage model is known. Section 4 derives the optimal distinguisher when the leakage model is partially known to the attacker. Then, Sect. 5 validates the results using simulations. Conclusions and perspectives are in Sect. 6.

## 2    Side-Channel Analysis as a Communication Problem

### 2.1    Notations

Calligraphic letters (e.g., $\mathcal{X}$) denote sets, capital letters (e.g., $X$) denote random variables taking values in these sets, and the corresponding lowercase letters (e.g., $x$) denote their realizations. We write $\mathbb{P}$ for probability distributions, $p$ for

---

[1] In our paper, we use the term *stochastic* for the independent noise $N$ added to the leakage model, and we resort to the term *epistemic* to characterize the distribution of the leakage model when it is not deterministically known.

densities, and let $p_X$ denote the density of $X$. Symbols in bold are vectors: $\mathbf{X}$ or $\mathbf{x}$; implicitly, the length of all vectors is $m$, which is the number of queries (i.e., $\mathbf{X} = (X_i)_{1 \le i \le m}$). We denote the average of $\mathbf{x}$ by $\overline{\mathbf{x}} = \frac{1}{m} \sum_{i=1}^{m} x_i$, and the scalar product between $\mathbf{x}$ and $\mathbf{y}$ by $\langle \mathbf{x} | \mathbf{y} \rangle = \sum_{i=1}^{m} x_i y_i$. The norms $1, 2, \ldots, q, \ldots, \infty$ are denoted as $\|\mathbf{x}\|_1 = \sum_{i=1}^{m} |x_i|$ (*Manhattan norm*), $\|\mathbf{x}\|_2 = \sqrt{\sum_{i=1}^{m} x_i^2}$ (*Euclidean norm*), $\ldots$, $\|\mathbf{x}\|_q = (\sum_{i=1}^{m} |x_i|^q)^{\frac{1}{q}}$ (*q-norm*) with $q \in \mathbb{R}$, $\ldots$, and $\|\mathbf{x}\|_\infty = \max_{i \in \llbracket 1, m \rrbracket} |x_i|$ (*uniform norm*), respectively. Let $k$ denote any possible key hypothesis from the keyspace $\mathcal{K}$, let $k^\star$ denote the secret secret cryptographic key, and let $T$ be the input or cipher text in the cryptographic algorithm.

### 2.2   Modeling through a Communication Channel

In this section, we rewrite the SCA problem as a communication channel problem (Fig. 1). Our setup resembles the one presented by Standaert et al. [22], but focuses specifically on key recovery.

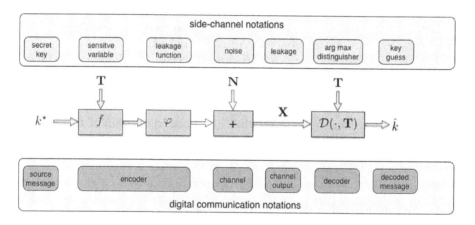

**Fig. 1.** Side-channel analysis as a communication channel

The *input message* is the secret key $k = k^\star$ (assumed uniformly distributed over $\mathbb{F}_2^n$ in a Bayesian approach). The key is most often recovered piece by piece (independently) using a divide-and-conquer strategy, so $n$ is typically equal to 8 (as in AES, a byte-oriented block cipher). The *encoder* can be any function $\varphi(f(k, \mathbf{T}))$. In SCA, the *sensitive variable* $f(\mathbf{T}, k)$ is normally assumed to be known, since it is part of the algorithm's specification. Depending on the scenario, the *leakage function* $\varphi : \mathbb{F}_2^n \to \mathbb{R}$ can be known (see Sect. 3) or partly unknown (see Sect. 4). Accordingly, $\varphi(f(k, \mathbf{T}))$ can be known or partly unknown. The *communication channel* is the side-channel, typically with *additive* noise $\mathbf{N}$. The decoder to be optimized maximizes the value of the distinguisher by taking its maximal argument over the keyspace[2]. The output of the decoder is then the

---
[2] Given a function $g(k)$, we use the notation $\arg\max_k g(k)$ to denote the value of $k$ that maximizes $g(k)$.

*decoded message* $\hat{k} = \mathcal{D}(\mathbf{X}, \mathbf{T})$, where $\mathcal{D}$ is the *optimal distinguishing rule*. Notice that we consider the distinguisher as a deterministic mapping, which allows us to rigorously derive optimal expressions. There is an additional *side information*[3] $\mathbf{T}$, which corresponds to the message or the ciphertext, which is assumed to be known both at the encoder and the decoder.

Capturing $m$ measurements means that the channel is used $m$ times. Specifically, the output of the encoder is an independent and identically distributed (i.i.d.) sequence ("codeword") $\varphi(f(k^\star, T_1)), \varphi(f(k^\star, T_2)), \ldots, \varphi(f(k^\star, T_m))$ depending on the i.i.d. sequence of side information $\mathbf{T} = (T_1, T_2, \ldots, T_m)$. The channel is assumed memoryless so that $\mathbf{X} = (X_1, X_2, \ldots, X_m)$ ("received noisy codeword") again forms an i.i.d. sequence; this implies in particular that the additive noise (if present) is white, and successive noise samples $\mathbf{N} = (N_1, N_2, \ldots, N_m)$ are i.i.d.

The problem is to determine the optimum distinguishing (or decoding) rule $\mathcal{D}$ so as to minimize the probability of error

$$\mathbb{P}_e = \mathbb{P}\{\hat{k} \neq k^\star\}, \tag{1}$$

or equivalently to maximize the success probability $\mathbb{P}_s = 1 - \mathbb{P}_e$, which is also referred to as the theoretical or exact success rate [18]).

**Theorem 1 (Optimal distinguishing rule).** *The optimal distinguishing rule is given by the* maximum a posteriori probability (MAP) *rule*

$$\mathcal{D}(\mathbf{x}, \mathbf{t}) = \arg\max_k \left( \mathbb{P}\{k\} \cdot p(\mathbf{x}|\mathbf{t}, k) \right). \tag{2}$$

*If the keys are assumed equiprobable, i.e.,* $\mathbb{P}\{k\} = 2^{-n}$, *Eq.* (2) *reduces to the* maximum likelihood (ML) *rule*

$$\mathcal{D}(\mathbf{x}, \mathbf{t}) = \arg\max_k p(\mathbf{x}|\mathbf{t}, k). \tag{3}$$

*Proof.* This is similar to a classical result in communication theory [23, Chap. 2] or [5, Chap. 8], except that one should take the side information into account. The optimal distinguishing rule maximizes

$$\mathbb{P}_s = 1 - \mathbb{P}_e = \mathbb{P}\{\hat{k} = k^\star\} = \mathbb{P}\{k^\star = \mathcal{D}(\mathbf{X}, \mathbf{T})\} \tag{4}$$

$$= \sum_{\mathbf{t}} \mathbb{P}\{\mathbf{t}\} \int p(\mathbf{x}|\mathbf{t}) \cdot \mathbb{P}\{k^\star = \mathcal{D}(\mathbf{x}, \mathbf{t})|\mathbf{x}, \mathbf{t}\} \, d\mathbf{x}. \tag{5}$$

Since $\mathbb{P}\{\mathbf{t}\} \geq 0$ and $p(\mathbf{x}|\mathbf{t}) \geq 0$, it suffices to maximize the *a posteriori* probability $\mathbb{P}\{k|\mathbf{x}, \mathbf{t}\}$ for every value of $(\mathbf{x}, \mathbf{t})$. Thus the optimal distinguishing rule is $\mathcal{D}(\mathbf{x}, \mathbf{t}) = \arg\max_k \mathbb{P}\{k|\mathbf{x}, \mathbf{t}\}$. To evaluate the latter distribution, we apply the Bayes' rule $\mathbb{P}\{k|\mathbf{x}, \mathbf{t}\} = \mathbb{P}\{k\} \cdot p(\mathbf{x}, \mathbf{t}|k)/p(\mathbf{x}, \mathbf{t})$. This gives the MAP optimal distinguishing rule $\mathcal{D}(\mathbf{x}, \mathbf{t}) = \arg\max_k \mathbb{P}\{k\} \cdot p(\mathbf{x}, \mathbf{t}|k)$. Furthermore, since

---

[3] This term, not to be confused with the side-channel, is used in communication theory to refer to a variable that is shared unaltered between the encoder and the decoder.

$\mathbf{T}$ is obviously key-independent, one can simplify $p(\mathbf{x}, \mathbf{t}|k) = \mathbb{P}\{\mathbf{t}|k\}p(\mathbf{x}|\mathbf{t}, k) = \mathbb{P}\{\mathbf{t}\}p(\mathbf{x}|\mathbf{t}, k)$ so that the MAP and ML rules become as stated. □

*Remark 1.* Distinguishing rule in Eq. (2) is useful if there is some a priori knowledge about the distribution of the secret key $k^\star$ (e.g., weak or semi-weak keys in DES [12]).

*Remark 2.* Provided $p(\mathbf{x}, \mathbf{t}|k)$ is known (for instance through a *profiling* stage), optimal distinguishing rules (2) and (3) can be readily used as an attack. They are known as *template attacks* [2], which are indeed optimal.

## 3   Optimal Attacks When the Leakage Model is Known

### 3.1   Derivation

We first consider the scenario of an attacker who knows precisely the leakage model of the device under attack on a "direct scale", in such a way that the *leakage prediction* $Y(k)$ coincides exactly with the deterministic part of the leakage. For example, in an AES software implementation, the device might leak in the Hamming weight (HW) model as $X = \mathsf{HW}[\mathsf{Sbox}[T \oplus k^\star]] + N$, where Sbox is the SubBytes transformation and $Y(k) = \mathsf{HW}[\mathsf{Sbox}[T \oplus k]]$ for all $k \in \mathcal{K}$.

**Proposition 2 (Maximum likelihood).** *When $f$ and $\varphi$ are known to the attacker and $\mathbf{Y}(k) = \varphi(f(k, \mathbf{T}))$, the optimal decision becomes*

$$\mathcal{D}(\mathbf{x}, \mathbf{t}) = \arg\max_k \Big( \mathbb{P}\{k\} \cdot p(\mathbf{x}|\mathbf{y}(k)) \Big). \qquad (6)$$

*For equiprobable keys this reduces to*

$$\mathcal{D}(\mathbf{x}, \mathbf{t}) = \arg\max_k \ p(\mathbf{x}|\mathbf{y}(k)). \qquad (7)$$

*Proof.* Since $(k, \mathbf{T}) \to \mathbf{Y}(k) \to \mathbf{X}$ forms a Markov chain, we have the identity $p(\mathbf{x}|\mathbf{t}, k) = p(\mathbf{x}|\mathbf{t}, k, \mathbf{y}(k)) = p(\mathbf{x}|\mathbf{y}(k))$. Apply Theorem 1. □

**Corollary 3.** *When the leakage arises from $\mathbf{X} = \mathbf{Y}(k^\star) + \mathbf{N}$,*

$$p(\mathbf{x}|\mathbf{y}(k)) = p_\mathbf{N}(\mathbf{x} - \mathbf{y}(k)) = \prod_{i=1}^{m} p_{N_i}(x_i - y_i(k)). \qquad (8)$$

*This expression, which can be substituted in Eq. (6) or (7), depends only on the noise probability distribution $p_\mathbf{N}$.*

*Proof.* Trivial, since $\mathbf{N}$ is independent of $\mathbf{Y}(k)$. □

Most publications [2, 13, 18] examine the scenario of Gaussian noise, which we consider next. However, this might not always be valid in practice. Due to other activities on the device, or to some sampling/quantization process for $\mathbf{X}$, or even due to countermeasures, the distribution of the noise might differ from Gaussian. This is addressed in SubSect. 3.3.

## 3.2   Gaussian Noise Assumption

**Theorem 4 (Optimal expression for Gaussian noise).** *When the noise is zero mean Gaussian, $N \sim \mathcal{N}(0, \sigma^2)$, the optimal distinguishing rule is*

$$\mathcal{D}_{opt}^{M,G}(\mathbf{x}, \mathbf{t}) = \arg\max_{k} \; \langle \mathbf{x} | \mathbf{y}(k) \rangle - \frac{1}{2} \| \mathbf{y}(k) \|_2^2. \tag{9}$$

*Proof.* Applying Corollary 3, a straightforward computation yields

$$\arg\max_{k} p(\mathbf{x} | \mathbf{y}(k)) = \arg\max_{k} \; \frac{1}{(\sigma\sqrt{2\pi})^m} e^{-\frac{\| \mathbf{x} - \mathbf{y}(k) \|_2^2}{2\sigma^2}}$$

$$= \arg\min_{k} \; \| \mathbf{x} - \mathbf{y}(k) \|_2^2 \tag{10}$$

$$= \arg\min_{k} \; \| \mathbf{x} \|_2^2 + \| \mathbf{y}(k) \|_2^2 - 2\langle \mathbf{x} | \mathbf{y}(k) \rangle. \tag{11}$$

Since $\| \mathbf{x} \|_2^2$ is not key dependent, we obtain Eq. (9).    □

*Remark 3.* Notice that the optimal distinguisher corresponding to the optimal distinguishing rule of Eq. (9) is $\mathbb{E}\left\{ X \cdot Y(k) - \frac{1}{2} Y(k)^2 \right\}$, which does not normally reduce to a covariance or correlation coefficient.

*Remark 4.* The scalar product $\langle \mathbf{x} | \mathbf{y}(k) \rangle$ can be negative, but the optimal expression in Eq. (9) does not involve absolute values. This would only be necessary if the sign of the model was unknown.

*Remark 5.* In the mono-bit case (i.e., $Y_i(k)$ takes two opposite values), the distinguisher simplifies to $\arg\max_{k} \langle \mathbf{x} | \mathbf{y}(k) \rangle$. However, somewhat surprisingly, this distinguisher is not the same as the usual DoM from the literature [3,8] and empirical results show that indeed our optimal distinguishing rule is slightly more efficient. This is detailed in Appendix A.

*Remark 6.* For a very large number of traces $\frac{1}{2} \| \mathbf{y}(k) \|_2^2$ becomes key independent[4]. However, as we will show in Sect. 5 this factor plays an important role, especially when the signal-to-noise ratio (SNR) is high and thus the number of traces needed to reveal the secret key is low. We insist that the expression in Eq. (9) is a deterministic value that can be computed from a series of $m$ sampled pairs of leakages and corresponding texts. As the second term $(-\frac{1}{2} \| \mathbf{y}(k) \|_2^2)$ becomes key independent when $m \to \infty$, this expression approximates to $\langle \mathbf{x} | \mathbf{y}(k) \rangle$ or even $\langle \mathbf{x} | \mathbf{y}(k) - \overline{\mathbf{y}}(k) \rangle$ (similar assumption as done in Footnote 4), which is an estimator of the covariance. This is why it can be claimed that when the leakage model is known, the noise is Gaussian and $m \to \infty$ the optimal distinguisher is very close to the covariance (or to the correlation, since the normalization factor of the Pearson correlation coefficient is also key-independent for large $m$).

---

[4] Informally, let us make the hypothesis that $T$ is uniformly distributed in $\mathbb{F}_2^n$ and that $Y(k)$ has the following expression $Y(k) = \varphi(f(T \oplus k))$; then, for large $m$, we have $\frac{1}{m}\sum_{i=1}^{m} \varphi(f(t_i \oplus k)) \approx \frac{1}{2^n}\sum_{t \in \mathbb{F}_2^n} \varphi(f(t \oplus k)) = \frac{1}{2^n}\sum_{t' \in \mathbb{F}_2^n} \varphi(f(t'))$ which clearly does not depend on $k$. See also the EIS (Equal Images under the Same key) assumption in [19].

*Remark 7.* As already mentioned in Remark 2, the best distinguisher when the model is known boils down to a template attack (ML). When the model is known and the noise is Gaussian, it specializes to an equivalent distinguisher which is all the closer to correlation as the SNR is low (by previous Remark 6). This is an independent proof of the main result of [11]. More precisely, the CPA is tolerant to any scaling of the leakage function, provided it is *positive*; otherwise, the attacker must resort to the absolute value of the Pearson correlation coefficient. It is known to be less efficient as depicted in our empirical results in Sect. 5 since there exists more rivals, and the soundness can even be impacted (e.g., if there exists a key $k^c \neq k^\star$ that satisfies $f(k^\star, t) = -f(k^c, t)$ for all $t \in \mathbb{F}_2^n$).

*Remark 8.* The expression in Eq. (9) can be computed only if the leakage model is known, including its scaling factor (denoted *direct scale* in [25]). In contrast, for CPA the relationship between $X$ and $Y(k)$ is only known up to some affine law (denoted *proportional scale* in [25]) such that $X = aY(k^\star) + b + N$, where $a$ and $b$ are unknown. These coefficients have to be estimated such as to maximize the attacker's performance, i.e., minimize $\|\mathbf{x} - a\mathbf{y}(k) - b\|_2$ in Eq. (10) so as to maximize the likelihood. The following theorem shows that this is equivalent to CPA.

**Theorem 5 (Correlation power analysis).** *When the leakage arises from* $X = aY(k^\star) + b + N$ *where* $N$ *is zero-mean Gaussian,* $\hat{k} = \arg\min_k \min_{a,b} \|\mathbf{x} - a\mathbf{y}(k) - b\|^2$, *is equivalent to maximizing the absolute value of the empirical Pearson's coefficient:*

$$\hat{k} = \arg\max_k |\hat{\rho}(k)| = |\widehat{\mathrm{Cov}}(\mathbf{x}, \mathbf{y}(k))| \Big/ \sqrt{\widehat{\mathrm{Var}}(\mathbf{x})\widehat{\mathrm{Var}}(\mathbf{y}(k))} \qquad (12)$$

*where the empirical (co)variances are defined by* $\widehat{\mathrm{Cov}}(\mathbf{x}, \mathbf{y}) = \sum_{i=1}^m (x_i - \bar{x})(y_i - \bar{y})$ *and* $\widehat{\mathrm{Var}}(\mathbf{x}) = \widehat{\mathrm{Cov}}(\mathbf{x}, \mathbf{x})$.

*Proof.* The minimization $\min_{a,b} \|\mathbf{x} - a\mathbf{y}(k) - b\|^2$ corresponds to the well-known linear regression analysis (ordinary least squares) [6]. The optimal values of $a$ and $b$ are $a^* = \widehat{\mathrm{Cov}}(\mathbf{x}, \mathbf{y})/\widehat{\mathrm{Var}}(\mathbf{y})$, $b^* = \bar{x} - a^*\bar{y}$, and the minimized mean-squared error takes the well-known expression $\min_{a,b} \|\mathbf{x} - a\mathbf{y} - b\|^2 = \widehat{\mathrm{Var}}(\mathbf{x}) \cdot (1 - \hat{\rho}^2)$ therefore minimizing $\min_{a,b} \|\mathbf{x} - a\mathbf{y} - b\|^2$ amounts to maximizing $|\hat{\rho}|$. □

### 3.3   Non-Gaussian Noise

The assumption of Gaussian noise may not always hold in practice. We first consider the case of uniform $\mathcal{U}(0, \sigma^2)$ and Laplacian noise distribution $\mathcal{L}(0, \sigma^2)$ as depicted in Fig. 2.

**Definition 6 (Noise distributions).** *Let* $N$ *be a zero-mean variable with variance* $\sigma^2$ *modeling the noise. Its distribution is:*

- *Uniform,* $N \sim \mathcal{U}(0, \sigma^2)$ *if* $p_N(n) = \begin{cases} \frac{1}{2\sigma\sqrt{3}} & \text{for } n \in [-\sqrt{3}\sigma, \sqrt{3}\sigma], \\ 0 & \text{otherwise.} \end{cases}$

- *Laplacian,* $N \sim \mathcal{L}(0, \sigma^2)$ *if* $p_N(n) = \frac{1}{\sqrt{2}\sigma} e^{-\frac{|n|}{\sigma/\sqrt{2}}}$.

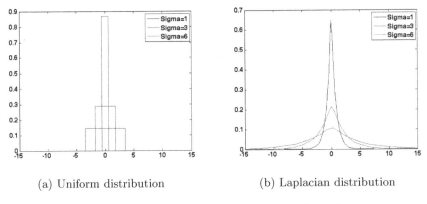

(a) Uniform distribution  (b) Laplacian distribution

**Fig. 2.** Probability distributions for $\sigma \in \{1,3,6\}$

For example, uniform noise can arise in side-channel analysis in the case where the only measurement error is the quantization noise. "Oscilloscopes" or most "digital sampling devices" use Analog-to-Digital Converters with only 8 bit resolution. Appendix B shows that Laplacian noise is a good approximation to the noise when combining multiplicatively two (or more) leakage samples.

**Theorem 7 (Optimal expression for uniform and Laplacian noises).**
*When $f$ and $\varphi$ are known such that $Y(k) = \varphi(f(k,T))$, and the leakage arises from $X = Y(k^\star) + N$ with $N \sim \mathcal{U}(0,\sigma^2)$ or $N \sim \mathcal{L}(0,\sigma^2)$, then the optimal distinguishing rule becomes*

- *Uniform noise distribution:* $\mathcal{D}_{opt}^{M,U}(\mathbf{x},\mathbf{t}) = \arg\max_k -\|\mathbf{x} - \mathbf{y}(k)\|_\infty$,
- *Laplace noise distribution:* $\mathcal{D}_{opt}^{M,L}(\mathbf{x},\mathbf{t}) = \arg\max_k -\|\mathbf{x} - \mathbf{y}(k)\|_1$.

*Proof.* In case of a uniform noise distribution $\mathcal{U}(0,\sigma^2)$ we have

$$p(\mathbf{x}|\mathbf{y}(k)) = p_N(\mathbf{x} - \mathbf{y}(k)) = \begin{cases} 0 \text{ if } \exists i \mid x_i - y_i(k) \notin [-\sqrt{3}\sigma, \sqrt{3}\sigma], \\ (2\sigma\sqrt{3})^{-m} \text{ otherwise.} \end{cases} \tag{13}$$

Hence, $\arg\max_k \ p_N(\mathbf{x}|\mathbf{y}(k)) = 0$ if and only if $\|\mathbf{x} - \mathbf{y}(k)\|_\infty > \sqrt{3}\sigma$, i.e., $\mathcal{D}_{opt}^{M,U}(\mathbf{x},\mathbf{t}) = \arg\min_k \|\mathbf{x} - \mathbf{y}(k)\|_\infty = \arg\max_k -\|\mathbf{x} - \mathbf{y}(k)\|_\infty$.

Assuming a Laplacian noise distribution $\mathcal{L}(0,\sigma^2)$ we have

$$\arg\max_k p(\mathbf{x}|\mathbf{y}(k)) = \arg\max_k \ (\sqrt{2}\sigma)^{-m} \cdot e^{-\frac{\|\mathbf{x}-\mathbf{y}(k)\|_1}{\sigma/\sqrt{2}}}, \tag{14}$$

which reduces to $\arg\max_k -\|\mathbf{x} - \mathbf{y}(k)\|_1$. $\qquad\square$

We can even be more general. Let $q \in \mathbb{R}$. Consider the *generalized Gaussian* noise distributions [14] of variance $\sigma^2$:

$$p(\mathbf{x}|\mathbf{y}(k)) = \left(\frac{q}{2\alpha}\Gamma\left(\frac{1}{q}\right)\right)^m e^{-\left(\frac{\|\mathbf{x}-\mathbf{y}(k)\|_q}{\alpha}\right)^q}, \tag{15}$$

where $\Gamma(\cdot)$ is the *Gamma function* and $\alpha = \sqrt{\frac{\Gamma(1/q)}{\Gamma(3/q)}}\,\sigma$. The optimal distinguishing rule becomes $\mathcal{D}_{opt}^{M,q}(\mathbf{x},\mathbf{t}) = \arg\max_k -\|\mathbf{x}-\mathbf{y}(k)\|_q^q = \arg\max_k -\|\mathbf{x}-\mathbf{y}(k)\|_q$. The Gaussian, Laplacian and uniform distributions are particular cases obtained for $q = 2, 1, \infty$, respectively.

## 4 Optimal Attacks When the Leakage Model Is Partially Unknown

For standard technologies, the leakage model is either predictable or can be profiled accurately, while being portable from one implementation to another. However, in some contexts, profiling is not possible (the key can neither be chosen nor varied), or changes from one device to the other because of the technological dispersion. Accordingly, the model might not be known exactly to the attacker yielding *epistemic noise*. We now extend our assumptions made in Sect. 3. We assume a linear leakage model as in [4,19,25] arising from a weighted sum of the bits of the sensitive variable and additive Gaussian noise $N$, i.e.,

$$X = \sum_{j=1}^{n} \alpha_j [f(T,k^\star)]_j + N, \tag{16}$$

where $[\cdot]_j : \mathbb{F}_2^n \to \mathbb{F}_2$ is the projection mapping onto the $j^{th}$ bit. But now, the attacker has no knowledge about $\boldsymbol{\alpha} = (\alpha_1, \cdots, \alpha_n)$ (except that $\boldsymbol{\alpha}$ is distributed according to a given law). This $\boldsymbol{\alpha}$ is unknown but fixed for the whole experiment (series of $m$ measurements). This setting is just one (stochastic) way of considering a leakage model that is not entirely known[5]. See e.g. [1] for a motivation of this scenario, and [4,24] for assuming and evaluating similar scenarios.

**Theorem 8 (Optimal expression for unknown weights).** *Let* $\mathbf{Y}_\alpha(k) = \sum_{j=1}^{n} \alpha_j [f(\mathbf{T},k)]_j$ *and* $\mathbf{Y}_j(k) = [f(\mathbf{T},k)]_j$, *where the weights are independently deviating normally from the Hamming weight model, i.e.,* $\forall j \in [\![1,8]\!], \alpha_j \sim \mathcal{N}(1,\sigma_\alpha^2)$. *Then the optimal distinguishing rule is*

$$\mathcal{D}_{opt}^{\alpha,G}(\mathbf{x},\mathbf{t}) = \arg\max_k \left(\gamma\langle\mathbf{x}|\mathbf{y}(k)\rangle + \mathbf{1}\right)^t \cdot \left(\gamma Z(k) + I\right)^{-1} \cdot \left(\gamma\langle\mathbf{x}|\mathbf{y}(k)\rangle + \mathbf{1}\right)$$
$$- \sigma_\alpha^2 \ln\det(\gamma Z(k) + I), \tag{17}$$

*where* $\gamma = \frac{\sigma_\alpha^2}{\sigma^2}$ *is the epistemic to stochastic noise ratio (ESNR),* $\langle\mathbf{x}|\mathbf{y}\rangle$ *is the vector with elements* $(\langle\mathbf{x}|\mathbf{y}(k)\rangle)_j = \langle\mathbf{x}|\mathbf{y}_j(k)\rangle$, $Z(k)$ *is the* $n \times n$ *Gram matrix with entries* $Z_{j,j'}(k) = \langle\mathbf{y}_j(k)|\mathbf{y}_{j'}(k)\rangle$, $\mathbf{1}$ *is the all-one vector, and* $I$ *is the identity matrix.*

---

[5] For example, diversion of bit loads due to routing, fanout gates, etc. are difficult to model; we used randomly weighted bit sums, randomization being due to technological dispersing (like for PUFS, analog characterization is highly device-dependent due to unpredictable manufacturing defects) and with the idea that the design is balanced (e.g., FPGA, full costume ASIC designs) so that $\alpha_j$'s have equal means.

*Proof.* Again we start from Eq. (7):

$$\mathcal{D}(\mathbf{x}, \mathbf{t}) = \arg\max_k \, p(\mathbf{x}|\mathbf{y_\alpha}(k)) = \arg\max_k \int_{\mathbb{R}^n} p(\mathbf{x}|\mathbf{y_\alpha}(k), \boldsymbol{\alpha}) \, p(\boldsymbol{\alpha}) \, d\boldsymbol{\alpha} \qquad (18)$$

$$= \arg\max_k \int_{\mathbb{R}^n} \frac{1}{(\sqrt{2\pi}\sigma)^m} e^{-\frac{1}{2\sigma}\|\mathbf{x}-\mathbf{y_\alpha}(k)\|_2^2} \frac{1}{(\sqrt{2\pi}\sigma_\alpha)^n} e^{-\frac{1}{2\sigma_\alpha}\|\boldsymbol{\alpha}-\mathbf{1}\|_2^2} \, d\boldsymbol{\alpha}$$

$$= \arg\max_k \int_{\mathbb{R}^n} \frac{1}{(\sqrt{2\pi}\sigma)^m} \exp\left(-\frac{1}{2\sigma^2}\|\mathbf{x} - \sum_{j=1}^n \alpha_j \mathbf{y}_j(k)\|^2\right) \times$$

$$\frac{1}{(\sqrt{2\pi}\sigma_\alpha)^n} \exp\left(-\frac{1}{2\sigma_\alpha^2}\sum_{j=1}^n (\alpha_j - 1)^2\right) \, d\boldsymbol{\alpha}. \qquad (19)$$

Now expanding the squares and dropping all multiplicative constants that are independent of $k$, the distinguishing rule takes the form

$$\arg\max_k \int_{\mathbb{R}^n} \exp\left(-R(\boldsymbol{\alpha})/2\right) d\boldsymbol{\alpha}, \qquad (20)$$

$$R(\boldsymbol{\alpha}) = \frac{1}{\sigma^2}\left(\|\sum_{j=1}^n \alpha_j \mathbf{y}_j\|^2 - 2\sum_{j=1}^n \alpha_j \langle \mathbf{x} \mid \mathbf{y}_j \rangle\right) + \frac{1}{\sigma_\alpha^2}\sum_{j=1}^n (\alpha_j^2 - 2\alpha_j) \qquad (21)$$

$$= \sum_{j,j'=1}^n \alpha_j \alpha_{j'}(\sigma^{-2}\langle \mathbf{y}_j(k) \mid \mathbf{y}_{j'}(k) \rangle + \sigma_\alpha^{-2}\delta_{j,j'}) - 2\sum_{j=1}^n \alpha_j (\sigma^{-2}\langle \mathbf{x}|\mathbf{y}_j(k) \rangle + \sigma_\alpha^{-2}).$$

Using an $n \times n$ matrix notation as $\boldsymbol{\alpha}^t Q \boldsymbol{\alpha} = \sum_{j,j'=1}^n \alpha_j \alpha_{j'} Q_{j,j'}$ and $\mathbf{a}^t \boldsymbol{\alpha} = \sum_{j=1}^n a_j \alpha_j$, Eq. (21) takes the form $\boldsymbol{\alpha}^t Q \boldsymbol{\alpha} - 2\mathbf{a}^t \boldsymbol{\alpha}$, where $Q = \sigma^{-2} Z(k) + \sigma_\alpha^{-2} I = \sigma_\alpha^{-2}(\gamma Z(k) + I)$, $\mathbf{a} = \sigma^{-2}\langle \mathbf{x}|\mathbf{y}(k) \rangle + \sigma_\alpha^{-2}\mathbf{1} = \sigma_\alpha^{-2}(\gamma \langle \mathbf{x}|\mathbf{y}(k) \rangle + \mathbf{1})$ and $I$ is the identity matrix, $Z$ is the Gram matrix with entries $Z_{j,j'}(k) = \langle \mathbf{y}_j(k)|\mathbf{y}_{j'}(k) \rangle$, $\mathbf{1}$ is the all-one vector, $\langle \mathbf{x}|\mathbf{y} \rangle$ is the vector with entries $(\langle \mathbf{x}|\mathbf{y} \rangle)_j = \langle \mathbf{x}|\mathbf{y}_j \rangle$. Now, $\boldsymbol{\alpha}^t Q \boldsymbol{\alpha} - 2\mathbf{a}^t \boldsymbol{\alpha} = (\boldsymbol{\alpha} - Q^{-1}\mathbf{a})^t Q (\boldsymbol{\alpha} - Q^{-1}\mathbf{a}) - \mathbf{a}^t Q^{-1}\mathbf{a}$. So,

$$\arg\max_k \int \exp\left(-\frac{1}{2}((\boldsymbol{\alpha} - Q^{-1}\mathbf{a})^t Q(\boldsymbol{\alpha} - Q^{-1}\mathbf{a}) - \mathbf{a}^t \cdot Q^{-1} \cdot \mathbf{a})\right) d\boldsymbol{\alpha} \qquad (22)$$

$$= \arg\max_k (2\pi)^{n/2} |\det Q|^{-1/2} \exp\left(\frac{1}{2}\mathbf{a}^t Q^{-1}\mathbf{a}\right) \qquad (23)$$

$$= \arg\max_k \frac{1}{2}\mathbf{a}^t \, Q^{-1}\mathbf{a} - \frac{1}{2}\ln \det Q. \qquad (24)$$

Finally, multiplying by $2\sigma_\alpha^2$ we achieve the optimal distinguishing rule. □

*Remark 9.* For Eq. (17) to work the ESNR $\gamma$ should be somehow known from some experiments (e.g., Pelgrom coefficients [15] for $\sigma_\alpha$ and platform noise for $\sigma$).

*Remark 10.* If the ESNR $\gamma$ is small, i.e., $\sigma_\alpha$ is small w.r.t. $\sigma$, expanding about $\gamma = 0$ and neglecting the term $\sigma_\alpha^2 \gamma$ in the expansion of the logarithm gives (at first order in $\gamma$):

$$(1 + \gamma\langle \mathbf{x}|\mathbf{y}(k) \rangle)^t (I + \gamma Z(k))^{-1}(1 + \gamma\langle \mathbf{x}|\mathbf{y}(k) \rangle) \qquad (25)$$

$$\approx n + 2\gamma \, \mathbf{1}^t \langle \mathbf{x}|\mathbf{y}(k) \rangle - \gamma \mathbf{1}^t Z(k) \cdot \mathbf{1}^t. \qquad (26)$$

Since $\mathbf{1}^t\mathbf{y}(k) = \sum_{j=1}^n y_j(k) = \mathsf{HW}[\mathbf{y}]$ and

$$\mathbf{1}^t Z(k)\mathbf{1}^t = \sum_{j,j'=1}^n \langle y_j(k)|y_{j'}(k)\rangle = \langle \sum_{j=1}^n y_j(k)| \sum_{j'=1}^n y_{j'}(k)\rangle = \|\mathsf{HW}[\mathbf{y}]\|_2^2, \qquad (27)$$

Eq. (26) boils down to maximizing $\langle\mathbf{x}|\mathsf{HW}[\mathbf{y}]\rangle - \frac{1}{2}\|\mathsf{HW}[\mathbf{y}]\|_2^2$. As expected, we recover the optimal distinguishing rule when the Hamming weight model is assumed to be known and $\alpha_j \approx 1$ (see SubSect. 3.2).

*Remark 11.* If ESNR $\gamma$ is large ($\sigma_\alpha$ is large w.r.t. $\sigma$), a similar calculation as done in Remark 10 shows that the optimal distinguishing rule becomes

$$\gamma\langle\mathbf{x}|\mathbf{y}(k)\rangle^t \cdot Z^{-1}(k) \cdot \langle\mathbf{x}|\mathbf{y}(k)\rangle - \sigma_\alpha^2 \ln\det(Z(k)), \qquad (28)$$

where $\det(Z(k)) = \|\mathbf{y}_1(k) \wedge \cdots \wedge \mathbf{y}_n(k)\|_2^2$ is the Gram determinant, the squared norm of the exterior product of the $\mathbf{y}_j(k)$'s . This simpler formula can be useful to be directly implemented for small stochastic noise.

*Remark 12.* Note that, in contrast to the linear regression attack (LRA) [4], $\mathcal{D}^{\alpha,G}$ does not require an estimation of $\boldsymbol{\alpha}$ explicitly; $\mathcal{D}^{\alpha,G}$ is already optimal given the *a priori* probability distribution of $\boldsymbol{\alpha}$. An empirical comparison is shown in Subsec 5.2.

# 5   Experimental Validation

## 5.1   Known Model: *Stochastic* Noise

As an application we choose $Y = \mathsf{HW}[\mathsf{Sbox}[T \oplus k]]$ and $X = Y(k^\star) + N$, where $\mathsf{Sbox}: \mathbb{F}_2^8 \to \mathbb{F}_2^8$ is the AES Substitution box and $T$ is uniformly distributed over $\mathbb{F}_2^8$. We simulated noise from several distributions $p_N$ and for $\sigma \in \{1,3,6\}$ resulting in an SNR of $\frac{Var(Y)}{Var(N)} = \frac{2}{\sigma^2} \in \{2, 0.222, 0.056\}$. Note that since the SNR is equivalent for all noise distributions, we can compare the performance of the distinguishers across different noise distributions. For reliability, we conducted 500 independent experiments in each setting with uniformly distributed $k^\star$ to compute the empirical success rate (noted $\hat{\mathbb{P}}_s$). Moreover, as suggested in [10], when plotting the empirical success rate, we highlight the standard deviation of the success rate by error bars. In particular, since $\hat{\mathbb{P}}_s$ follows a binomial distribution, we shaded the confidence interval $\left[\hat{\mathbb{P}}_s \pm \sqrt{\frac{\hat{\mathbb{P}}_s(1-\hat{\mathbb{P}}_s)}{n_{\exp}}}\right]$, where $n_{\exp} = 500$ is the number of experiments. If the error bars do not overlap, we can unambiguously conclude that one distinguisher is better than the other [10].

In the scenario where the model is known, we implemented the following distinguishers, where the labels for the figures are put within parentheses:

$$\mathcal{D}_{opt}^{M,G}(\mathbf{x}, \mathbf{t}) = \arg\max_k \ \langle \mathbf{x}|\mathbf{y}(k)\rangle - \frac{1}{2}\|\mathbf{y}(k)\|_2^2, \qquad \text{(Euclidean norm)} \quad (29)$$

$$\mathcal{D}_{opt\text{-}s}^{M,G}(\mathbf{x}, \mathbf{t}) = \arg\max_k \ \langle \mathbf{x}|\mathbf{y}(k)\rangle, \qquad \text{(Scalar product)} \quad (30)$$

$$\mathcal{D}_{opt}^{M,L}(\mathbf{x}, \mathbf{t}) = \arg\max_k \ -\|\mathbf{x} - \mathbf{y}(k)\|_1, \qquad \text{(Manhattan norm)} \quad (31)$$

$$\mathcal{D}_{opt}^{M,U}(\mathbf{x}, \mathbf{t}) = \arg\max_k \ -\|\mathbf{x} - \mathbf{y}(k)\|_\infty, \qquad \text{(Uniform norm)} \quad (32)$$

$$\mathcal{D}_{Cov}(\mathbf{x}, \mathbf{t}) = \arg\max_k \ |\langle \mathbf{x} - \overline{\mathbf{x}}|\mathbf{y}(k)\rangle|, \qquad \text{(Covariance)} \quad (33)$$

$$\mathcal{D}_{CPA}(\mathbf{x}, \mathbf{t}) = \arg\max_k \ \left| \frac{\langle \mathbf{x} - \overline{\mathbf{x}}|\mathbf{y}(k)\rangle}{\|\mathbf{x} - \overline{\mathbf{x}}\|_2 \cdot \|\mathbf{y}(k) - \overline{\mathbf{y}(k)}\|_2} \right|. \quad \text{(CPA)} \quad (34)$$

Figures 3a, 3c and 3e show empirical success rate curves for Gaussian noise. One can see that for all levels of SNR $\mathcal{D}_{opt}^{M,G}$ outperforms the other distinguishers, including CPA. As expected from Remark 6, scalar product, covariance, and correlation have poorer but comparable performance than $\mathcal{D}_{opt}^{M,G}$ for high noise.

Figures 3b, 3d and 3f show the empirical success rate curves for Laplacian noise. For low noise, $\mathcal{D}_{opt}^{M,L}$ is the most efficient and $\mathcal{D}_{opt}^{M,G}$ is the nearest rival, whereas $\mathcal{D}_{CPA}$ and $\mathcal{D}_{Cov}$ are less efficient. As the noise increases the difference becomes more significant. As expected, $\mathcal{D}_{CPA}$ and $\mathcal{D}_{Cov}$ become equivalent for high noise, and $\mathcal{D}_{opt}^{M,U}$ fails to distinguish.

In case of uniform noise (see Fig. 4) all optimal distinguishers behave similarly for $\sigma = 1$, whereas CPA, covariance and the scalar product are less efficient. When the noise increases, $\mathcal{D}_{opt}^{M,U}$ is the most efficient distinguisher. One can see that $\mathcal{D}_{opt}^{M,U}$ for uniform noise and $\mathcal{D}_{opt}^{M,L}$ for Laplacian noise require less traces to succeed than $\mathcal{D}_{opt}^{M,G}$ does for Gaussian noise. More precisely, for $\sigma = 6$, $\mathcal{D}_{opt}^{M,U}$ requires only 28 traces to reach $\hat{\mathbb{P}}_s \geq 90\%$, $\mathcal{D}_{opt}^{M,L}$ requires 200 traces, whereas $\mathcal{D}_{opt}^{M,G}$ in case of Gaussian noise needs 300 measurements. This is in keeping with the known information-theoretic fact that detection (or decoding) in Gaussian noise is harder than in any other type of noise.

## 5.2    Unknown Model: *Epistemic* and *Stochastic* Noise

To account for a partially unknown model, we choose $Y_j = [\mathtt{Sbox}[T \oplus k]]_j$ for $j = 1, \ldots, 8$ and $X = \sum_{j=1}^{8} \alpha_j Y_j(k^\star) + N$, where $\alpha_j \sim \mathcal{N}(1, \sigma_\alpha)$ are unknown and changing for each experiment. Note that in this scenario $\mathbf{Y}(k)$ is a *column* and not a value as in the previous subsection. Figure 5 shows typical values for $\sigma_\alpha \in \{2, 4\}$, showing that the assumption about $\boldsymbol{\alpha}$ is realistic (see e.g., [7]). We compare our new optimal distinguisher with the linear regression analysis (LRA) [4], which is a *non-profiling* variant of the stochastic approach [19] and the most efficient attack so far in the case where the model drifts away from the

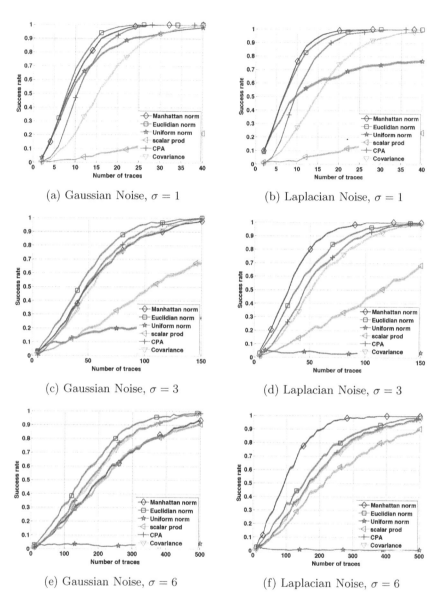

(a) Gaussian Noise, $\sigma = 1$   (b) Laplacian Noise, $\sigma = 1$

(c) Gaussian Noise, $\sigma = 3$   (d) Laplacian Noise, $\sigma = 3$

(e) Gaussian Noise, $\sigma = 6$   (f) Laplacian Noise, $\sigma = 6$

**Fig. 3.** Success rate for various $\sigma$, with a known model

Hamming weight model [4,9]. LRA is defined as

$$\mathcal{D}_{LRA}(\mathbf{x}, \mathbf{t}) = \arg\max_k \frac{\|\mathbf{x} - \mathbf{y}'(k) \cdot \boldsymbol{\beta}(k)\|_2^2}{\|\mathbf{x} - \overline{\mathbf{x}}\|_2^2}, \tag{35}$$

where $\mathbf{y}'(k) = (\mathbf{1}, \mathbf{y}_1(k), \mathbf{y}_2(k), \ldots, \mathbf{y}_8(k))$ is an $m \times 9$ matrix and $\boldsymbol{\beta}(k) = (\beta_1(k), \ldots, \beta_9(k))$ are the regression coefficients $\boldsymbol{\beta}(k) = (\mathbf{y}'(k)^t \cdot \mathbf{y}'(k))^{-1} \mathbf{y}'(k)^t \mathbf{x}$.

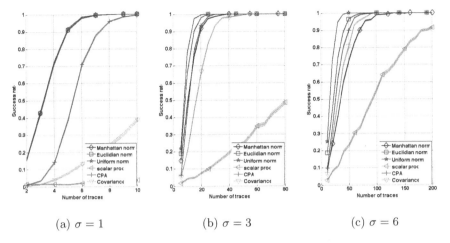

(a) $\sigma = 1$      (b) $\sigma = 3$      (c) $\sigma = 6$

**Fig. 4.** Success rate for a uniform noise distribution, with a known model

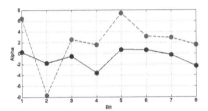

**Fig. 5.** Exemplary values of $\alpha$ for $\sigma_\alpha = 2$ (blue) and $\sigma_\alpha = 4$ (red dashed)

Criterion (35) is also known as the *coefficient of determination* [6]. We compared the optimal distinguisher to LRA and CPA, for which we used $Y = \mathsf{HW}[\mathsf{Sbox}[T \oplus k]]$. Apart from this we used the same experimental setup as above.

Figure 6 displays the success rate for $\sigma \in \{1, 3, 6\}$ and $\sigma_\alpha \in \{2, 4\}$. As expected CPA is performing worse than both other attacks. Remarkably, in all scenarios $\mathcal{D}_{opt}^{\alpha,G}$ (labeled Optimal dist alpha) is more efficient than LRA. This is perhaps not surprising as regression analysis involves mean squared minimization rather than direct success probability maximization as $\mathcal{D}_{opt}^{\alpha,G}$ does. As already observed in [4], LRA needs a large enough number of traces for estimation, that is why $\hat{\mathbb{P}}_s$ stays low until around 10 traces (Fig. 6a and 6b). One can observe that both distinguishers perform better for $\sigma_\alpha = 4$ (Figures 6b, 6d and 6f) than for $\sigma_\alpha = 2$ (Figures 6a, 6c and 6e). This can be explained by the improved distinguishability through the *distinct influence of each bit*. On the contrary, $\mathcal{D}_{CPA}$ becomes worse when $\sigma_\alpha$ increases, because the model drifts father away from the Hamming weight model.

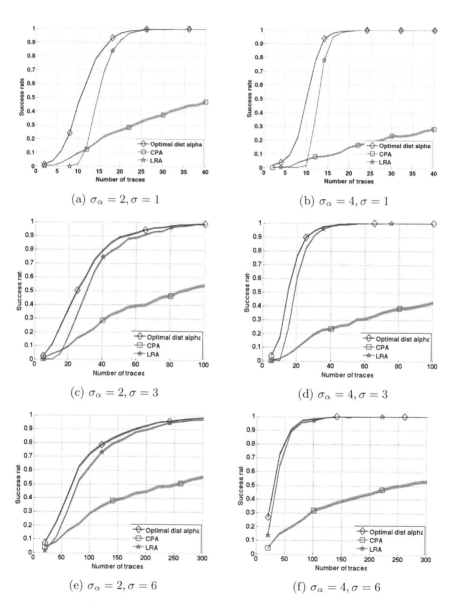

**Fig. 6.** Success rate for various ESNRs, unknown model

# 6 Conclusion

We examined the *key extraction* problem in *a side-channel context* as a *digital communication* problem. Following the reasoning used in digital communication theory, we derived the *optimal distinguisher* (called *optimal decoder* in digital communication theory). It is a formula that takes as input a multiplicity of pairs of side-channel leakage measurements and corresponding text chunks, and that returns the key guess that maximizes the success probability. The methodical derivation of distinguishers yields an estimator that can be directly computed from the measured data.

In the case where no information is known about the channel (Sect. 2.2), we recovered the template attack. When the leakage function is known (Sect. 3), the approach yields a different distinguisher for each noise distribution. For the classical case of additive Gaussian noise, the optimal distinguisher cannot be interpreted as a covariance nor as a correlation, albeit very close for low SNR. In addition, when the leakage model is known only on a proportional scale we recover CPA exactly. When the noise is non-Gaussian, the optimal distinguishers are very different from CPA or correlation and each optimal distinguisher is the most efficient in its scenario. When the leakage model is partially unknown (Sect. 4) and modeled as an unevenly weighted sum of bits with unknown weights, our method outperforms the non-profiled version of the stochastic approach (LRA).

This study suggests that a mathematical study of distinguishers should prevail in the field of side-channel analysis. As a perspective, our optimal distinguishers may be tested on real measurements. This should include a preliminary step to determine the underlying scenario as precisely and efficiently as possible in terms of the number of traces. Especially, the determination of the noise distribution is a notoriously difficult problem. Moreover, the extension of our work to higher-order attacks (when the noise distribution might differ from Gaussian) seems promising.

# References

1. Akkar, M.-L., Bévan, R., Dischamp, P., Moyart, D.: Power analysis, what is now possible... In: Okamoto, T. (ed.) ASIACRYPT 2000. LNCS, vol. 1976, pp. 489–502. Springer, Heidelberg (2000)
2. Chari, S., Rao, J.R., Rohatgi, P.: Template Attacks. In: Kaliski Jr., B.S., Koç, Ç.K., Paar, C. (eds.) CHES 2002. LNCS, vol. 2523, pp. 13–28. Springer, Heidelberg (2003)
3. Coron, J.-S., Kocher, P.C., Naccache, D.: Statistics and Secret Leakage. In: Frankel, Y. (ed.) FC 2000. LNCS, vol. 1962, pp. 157–173. Springer, Heidelberg (2001)
4. Doget, J., Prouff, E., Rivain, M., Standaert, F.-X.: Univariate side channel attacks and leakage modeling. J. Cryptographic Engineering 1(2), 123–144 (2011)
5. Gallager, R.G.: Information theory and reliable communication. Wiley (1968)
6. Kardaun, O.J.W.F.: Classical Methods of Statistics. Springer (2005)
7. Kasper, M., Schindler, W., Stöttinger, M.: A stochastic method for security evaluation of cryptographic FPGA implementations. In: Bian, J., Zhou, Q., Athanas, P., Ha, Y., Zhao, K. (eds.) FPT, pp. 146–153. IEEE (2010)

8. Kocher, P.C., Jaffe, J., Jun, B.: Differential Power Analysis. In: Wiener, M. (ed.) CRYPTO 1999. LNCS, vol. 1666, pp. 388–397. Springer, Heidelberg (1999)
9. Lomné, V., Prouff, E., Roche, T.: Behind the scene of side channel attacks. In: Sako, K., Sarkar, P. (eds.) ASIACRYPT 2013, Part I. LNCS, vol. 8269, pp. 506–525. Springer, Heidelberg (2013)
10. Maghrebi, H., Rioul, O., Guilley, S., Danger, J.-L.: Comparison between Side-Channel Analysis Distinguishers. In: Chim, T.W., Yuen, T.H. (eds.) ICICS 2012. LNCS, vol. 7618, pp. 331–340. Springer, Heidelberg (2012)
11. Mangard, S., Oswald, E., Standaert, F.-X.: One for All - All for One: Unifying Standard DPA Attacks. Information Security, IET 5(2), 100–111 (2011)
12. Moore, J.H., Simmons, G.J.: Cycle Structure of the DES with Weak and Semi-weak Keys. In: Odlyzko, A.M. (ed.) CRYPTO 1986. LNCS, vol. 263, pp. 9–32. Springer, Heidelberg (1987)
13. Moradi, A., Mousavi, N., Paar, C., Salmasizadeh, M.: A Comparative Study of Mutual Information Analysis under a Gaussian Assumption. In: Youm, H.Y., Yung, M. (eds.) WISA 2009. LNCS, vol. 5932, pp. 193–205. Springer, Heidelberg (2009)
14. Nadarajah, S.: A generalized normal distribution. Journal of Applied Statistics 32(7), 685–694 (2005)
15. Pelgrom, M.J.M., Duinmaijer, A.C.J., Welbers, A.P.G.: Matching properties of MOS transistors. IEEE Journal of Solid State Circuits 24(5), 1433–1439 (1989)
16. Prouff, E., Rivain, M.: Theoretical and practical aspects of mutual information-based side channel analysis. International Journal of Applied Cryptography (IJACT) 2(2), 121–138 (2010)
17. Reparaz, O., Gierlichs, B., Verbauwhede, I.: A note on the use of margins to compare distinguishers. In: COSADE, Paris, France, April 14-15. LNCS. Springer (to appear, 2014)
18. Rivain, M.: On the Exact Success Rate of Side Channel Analysis in the Gaussian Model. In: Avanzi, R.M., Keliher, L., Sica, F. (eds.) SAC 2008. LNCS, vol. 5381, pp. 165–183. Springer, Heidelberg (2009)
19. Schindler, W., Lemke, K., Paar, C.: A Stochastic Model for Differential Side Channel Cryptanalysis. In: Rao, J.R., Sunar, B. (eds.) CHES 2005. LNCS, vol. 3659, pp. 30–46. Springer, Heidelberg (2005)
20. Souissi, Y., Debande, N., Mekki, S., Guilley, S., Maalaoui, A., Danger, J.-L.: On the Optimality of Correlation Power Attack on Embedded Cryptographic Systems. In: Askoxylakis, I., Pöhls, H.C., Posegga, J. (eds.) WISTP 2012. LNCS, vol. 7322, pp. 169–178. Springer, Heidelberg (2012)
21. Standaert, F.-X., Koeune, F., Schindler, W.: How to Compare Profiled Side-Channel Attacks? In: Abdalla, M., Pointcheval, D., Fouque, P.-A., Vergnaud, D. (eds.) ACNS 2009. LNCS, vol. 5536, pp. 485–498. Springer, Heidelberg (2009)
22. Standaert, F.-X., Malkin, T.G., Yung, M.: A Unified Framework for the Analysis of Side-Channel Key Recovery Attacks. In: Joux, A. (ed.) EUROCRYPT 2009. LNCS, vol. 5479, pp. 443–461. Springer, Heidelberg (2009)
23. Viterbi, A.J., Omura, J.K.: Principles of digital communication and coding. McGraw-Hill series in electrical engineering (2007)
24. Whitnall, C., Oswald, E.: A Fair Evaluation Framework for Comparing Side-Channel Distinguishers. J. Cryptographic Engineering 1(2), 145–160 (2011)
25. Whitnall, C., Oswald, E., Standaert, F.-X.: The Myth of Generic DPA... and the Magic of Learning. In: Benaloh, J. (ed.) CT-RSA 2014. LNCS, vol. 8366, pp. 183–205. Springer, Heidelberg (2014)

# A  Optimal Mono-Bit Distinguisher for Known Model and Gaussian Noise

In the mono-bit case, every $Y_i(k)$ ($0 \leq i < m$) takes only two different values. W.l.o.g., let us assume $Y_i(k) = \pm 1$. Then, $\|\mathbf{y}(k)\|_2^2 = m$ and is thus independent on the key. Thus,

$$\mathcal{D}_{opt(1\ bit)}^{M,G}(\mathbf{x}, \mathbf{t}) = \arg\max_k \sum_{i|y_i(k)=1} x_i - \sum_{i|y_i(k)=-1} x_i. \tag{36}$$

Surprisingly, this distinguisher *is not* any variant of DoM presented in the seminal paper [8] by Kocher, Jaffe and Jun ($\mathcal{D}_{KJJ}^{M,G}$) nor in the alleged t-test improvement [3] by Coron, Kocher and Naccache ($\mathcal{D}_{CKN}^{M,G}$). In particular,

$$\mathcal{D}_{KJJ}^{M,G}(\mathbf{x}, \mathbf{t}) = \arg\max_k \overline{\mathbf{x}_{+1}} - \overline{\mathbf{x}_{-1}}, \tag{37}$$

$$\mathcal{D}_{CKN}^{M,G}(\mathbf{x}, \mathbf{t}) = \arg\max_k (\overline{\mathbf{x}_{+1}} - \overline{\mathbf{x}_{-1}}) / \sqrt{\frac{\sigma_{\mathbf{x}_{+1}}^2}{n_{+1}} + \frac{\sigma_{\mathbf{x}_{-1}}^2}{n_{-1}}}, \tag{38}$$

where $n_{\pm 1} = \sum_{i|y_i(k)=\pm 1} 1$, $\sigma_{\mathbf{x}_{\pm 1}}^2 = \frac{1}{n_{\pm 1}-1} \sum_{i|y_i(k)=\pm 1} (x_i - \overline{\mathbf{x}_{\pm 1}})^2$ and $\overline{\mathbf{x}_{\pm 1}} = \frac{1}{n_{\pm 1}} \sum_{i|y_i(k)=\pm 1} x_i$ . However, when $m$ is large, the two distinguishers $\mathcal{D}_{opt(1\ bit)}^{M,G}$ and $\mathcal{D}_{KJJ}^{M,G}$ become equivalent, as $n_{\pm 1} \approx m/2$ (independently of $k$, using an argument similar to that of Footnote 4). But even in this case, $\mathcal{D}_{CKN}^{M,G}$ is non-equivalent with them. We notice that the normalization $\mathcal{D}_{CKN}^{M,G}$ is useful when there are many samples, since it normalizes the difference between $Y(k) = -1$ and $Y(k) = +1$ (hence avoid ghost peaks), but this consideration is out of the scope of this paper.

The success rate of all three attacks for $\sigma = 1$ is displayed in Fig. 7 showing that the optimal distinguishing rule (Eq. (36)) is the most efficient to reach a empirical success rate $\hat{\mathbb{P}}_s = 90\%$. For $\sigma > 1$ all 3 distinguishers were found almost equivalent, which is reasonable. Those results highlight that *intuitive* distinguishers (such as $\mathcal{D}_{KJJ}^{M,G}$, that aims at showing a difference of leakage) or *classic* (such as $\mathcal{D}_{CKN}^{M,G}$, based on the well-established t-test) distinguishers are not necessarily the best.

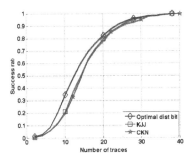

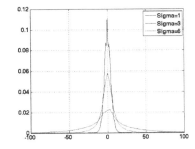

**Fig. 7.** Success rate for one-bit attacks    **Fig. 8.** Empirical distribution of $X_1 X_2$

# B    Noise Distribution Resulting from Multiplication

When combining two leakage samples multiplicatively in case of Gaussian noise, the noise distribution is no longer following a Gaussian distribution. More precisely, let us assume we have two leakages $X_1 = Y_1(k^\star)+N_1$ and $X_2 = Y_2(k^\star)+N_2$ that are multiplied, then

$$X_1X_2 = (Y_1(k^\star) + N_1) \cdot (Y_2(k^\star) + N_2) \tag{39}$$
$$= Y_1(k^\star) \cdot Y_2(k^\star) + Y_2(k^\star) \cdot N_2 + Y_2(k^\star) \cdot N_1 + N_1 \cdot N_2. \tag{40}$$

Due to the product, the distribution of $X_1X_2$ is no longer Gaussian. Figure 8 displays the empirical distribution in this case, which looks similar to a Laplacian distribution (compare to Fig. 2b).

# "Ooh Aah... Just a Little Bit" : A Small Amount of Side Channel Can Go a Long Way

Naomi Benger[1], Joop van de Pol[2], Nigel P. Smart[2], and Yuval Yarom[1]

[1] School of Computer Science, The University of Adelaide, Australia
mail.for.minnie@gmail.com, yval@cs.adelaide.edu.au
[2] Dept. Computer Science, University of Bristol, United Kingdom
joop.vandepol@bristol.ac.uk, nigel@cs.bris.ac.uk

**Abstract.** We apply the FLUSH+RELOAD side-channel attack based on cache hits/misses to extract a small amount of data from OpenSSL ECDSA signature requests. We then apply a "standard" lattice technique to extract the private key, but unlike previous attacks we are able to make use of the side-channel information from almost all of the observed executions. This means we obtain private key recovery by observing a relatively small number of executions, and by expending a relatively small amount of post-processing via lattice reduction. We demonstrate our analysis via experiments using the curve **secp256k1** used in the Bitcoin protocol. In particular we show that with as little as 200 signatures we are able to achieve a reasonable level of success in recovering the secret key for a 256-bit curve. This is significantly better than prior methods of applying lattice reduction techniques to similar side channel information.

## 1 Introduction

One important task of cryptographic research is to analyze cryptographic implementations for potential security flaws. This aspect has a long tradition, and the most well known of this line of research has been the understanding of side-channels obtained by power analysis, which followed from the initial work of Kocher and others [22]. More recently work in this area has shifted to looking at side-channels in software implementations, the most successful of which has been the exploitation of cache-timing attacks, introduced in 2002 [32]. In this work we examine the use of spy-processes on the OpenSSL implementation of the ECDSA algorithm.

OpenSSL [31] is an open source tool kit for the implementation of cryptographic protocols. The library of functions, implemented using C, is often used for the implementation of Secure Sockets Layer and Transport Layer Security protocols and has also been used to implement OpenPGP and other cryptographic standards. The library includes cryptographic functions for use in Elliptic Curve Cryptography (ECC), and in particular ECDSA. In particular we will examine the application of the FLUSH+RELOAD attack, first proposed by Yarom and Falkner [40], then adapted to the case of OpenSSL's implementation of ECDSA over binary fields by Yarom and Benger [39], running on X86 processor architecture. We exploit a property of the Intel implementation of the X86 and X86_64 processor architectures using the FLUSH+RELOAD cache side-channel attack [39, 40] to partially recover the ephemeral key used in ECDSA.

L. Batina and M. Robshaw (Eds.): CHES 2014, LNCS 8731, pp. 75–92, 2014.

In Yarom and Benger [39] the case of characteristic two fields was considered, but the algorithms used by OpenSSL in the characteristic two and prime characteristic cases are very different. In particular for the case of prime fields one needs to perform a post-processing of the side-channel information using cryptanalysis of lattices. We adopt a standard technique [21, 30] to perform this last step, but in a manner which enables us to recover the underlying secret with few protocol execution runs. This is achieved by using as much information obtained in the FLUSH+RELOAD step as possible in the subsequent lattice step.

We illustrate the effectiveness of the attack by recovering the secret key with a very high probability using only a small number of signatures. After this, we are able to forge unlimited signatures under the hidden secret key. The results of this attack are not limited to ECDSA but have implications for many other cryptographic protocols implemented using OpenSSL for which the scalar multiplication is performed using a sliding window and the scalar is intended to remain secret.

**Related Work.** Microarchitectural side-channel attacks have been used against a number of implementations of cryptosystems. These attacks often target the L1 cache level [1, 2, 5, 10, 13, 14, 37, 41] or the branch prediction buffer [3, 4]. The use of these components is limited to a single execution core. Consequently, the spy program and the victim must execute on the same execution core of the processor. Unlike these attacks, the FLUSH+RELOAD attack we use targets the last level cache (LLC). As the LLC is shared between cores, the attack can be mounted between different cores.

The attack used by Gullasch et al. [20] against AES, is very similar to FLUSH+RE-LOAD. The attack, however, requires the interleaving of spy and victim execution on the same processor core, which is achieved by relying on a scheduler bug to interrupt the victim and gain control of the core on which it executes. Furthermore, the Gullasch et al. attack results in a large number of false positives, requiring the use of a neural network to filter the results.

In [40], Yarom and Falkner first describe the FLUSH+RELOAD attack and use it to snoop on the square-and-multiply exponentiation in the GnuPG implementation of RSA and thus retrieve the RSA secret key from the GnuPG decryption step. The OpenSSL (characteristic two) implementation of ECDSA was also shown to be vulnerable to the FLUSH+RELOAD attack [39]; around 95% of the ephemeral private key was recovered when the Montgomery ladder was used for the scalar multiplication step. The full ephemeral private key was then recovered at very small cost using a Baby-Step-Giant-Step (BSGS) algorithm. Knowledge of the ephemeral private key leads to recovery of the signer's private key, thus fully breaking the ECDSA implementation using only one signature.

One issue hindering the extension of the attack to implementations using the sliding window method for scalar multiplications instead of the Montgomery ladder is that only a lower proportion of the bits of the ephemeral private key can be recovered so the BSGS reconstruction becomes infeasible. It is to extend the FLUSH+RELOAD attack to implementations which use sliding window exponentiation methods that this paper is addressed.

Suppose we take a single ECDLP instance, and we have obtained partial information about the discrete logarithm. In [19, 26, 36] techniques are presented which reduce the search space for the underlying discrete logarithm when various types of partial information is revealed. These methods work quite well when the information leaked is considerable for the single discrete logarithm instance; as for example evidenced by the side-channel attack of [39] on the Montgomery ladder. However, in our situation a different approach needs to be taken.

Similar to several past works, e.g. [10, 11, 27], we will exploit a well known property of ECDSA, that if a small amount of information about each ephemeral key in each signature leaks, for a number of signatures, then one can recover the underlying secret using a lattice based attack [21, 30]. The key question arises as to how many signatures are needed so as to be able to extract the necessary side channel information to enable the lattice based attack to work. The lattice attack works by constructing a lattice problem from the obtained digital signatures and side channel information, and then applying lattice reduction techniques such as LLL [23] or BKZ [35] to solve the lattice problem. Using this methodology Nguyen and Shparlinski [30], suggest that for an elliptic curve group of order around 160 bits, their probabilistic algorithm would obtain the secret key using an expected $23 \times 2^7$ signatures (assuming independent and uniformly at random selected messages) in polynomial time, using only seven consecutive least significant leaked bits of each ephemeral private key. A major issue of their attack in practice is that it seems hard to apply when only a few bits of the underlying ephemeral private key are determined.

**Our Contribution.** Through the FLUSH+RELOAD attack we are able to obtain a significant proportion of the ephemeral private key bit values, but they are not clustered but in positions spread through the length of the ephemeral private key. As a result, we only obtain for each signature a few (maybe only one) consecutive bits of the ECDSA ephemeral private key, and so the technique described in [30] does not appear at first sight to be instantly applicable. The main contribution of this work is to combine and adapt the FLUSH+RELOAD attack and the lattice techniques. The FLUSH+RELOAD attack is refined to optimise the proportion of information which can be obtained, then the lattice techniques are adapted to utilize the information in the acquired data in an optimal manner. The result is that we are able to reconstruct secret keys for 256 bit elliptic curves with high probability, and low work effort, after obtaining less than 256 signatures.

We illustrate the effectiveness of the attack by applying it to the OpenSSL implementation of ECDSA using a sliding window to compute scalar multiplication, recovering the victims's secret key for the elliptic curve **secp256k1** used in Bitcoin [28]. The implementation of the **secp256k1** curve in OpenSSL is interesting as it uses the wNAF method for exponentiation, as opposed to the GLV method [18], for which the curve was created. It would be an interesting research topic to see how to apply the FLUSH+RELOAD technique to an implementation which uses the GLV point multiplication method.

In terms of the application to Bitcoin an obvious mitigation against the attack is to limit the number of times a private key is used within the Bitcoin protocol. Each wallet corresponds to a public/private key pair, so this essentially limits the number of times one can spend from a given wallet. Thus, by creating a chain of wallets and transferring Bitcoins from one wallet to the next it is easy to limit the number of signing operations carried out by a single private key. See [9] for a discussion on the distribution of public keys currently used in the Bitcoin network.

The remainder of the paper is organised as follows: In 2 we present the background on ECDSA and the signed sliding window method (or wNAF representation) needed to understand our attack. Then in 3 we present our methodology for applying the FLUSH+ RELOAD attack on the OpenSSL implementation of the signed sliding window method of exponentiation. Then in 4 we use the information so obtained to create a lattice problem, and we demonstrate the success probability of our attack.

## 2 Mathematical Background

In this section we present the mathematical background to our work, by presenting the wNAF/signed window method of point multiplication which is used by OpenSSL to implement ECDSA in the case of curves defined over prime finite fields.

**Scalar Multiplication Using wNAF.** In OpenSSL the scalar multiplication in the signing algorithm is implemented using the wNAF algorithm. Suppose we wish to compute $[d]P$ for some integer value $d \in [0, \ldots, 2^\ell]$, the wNAF method utilizes a small amount of pre-processing on $P$ and the fact that addition and subtraction in the elliptic curve group have the same cost, so as to obtain a large performance improvement on the basic binary method of point multiplication. To define wNAF a window size $w$ is first chosen, which for OpenSSL, and the curve **secp256k1**, we have $w = 3$. Then $2^w - 2$ extra points are stored, with a precomputation cost of $2^{w-1} - 1$ point additions, and one point doubling. The values stored are the points $\{\pm G, \pm[3]G, \ldots, \pm[2^w - 1]G\}$.

The next task is to convert the integer $d$ into so called Non-Adjacent From (NAF). This is done by the method in Algorithm 1 which rewrites the integer $d$ as a sum $d = \sum_{i=0}^{\ell-1} d_i \cdot 2^i$, where $d_i \in \{\pm 1, \pm 3, \ldots, \pm(2^w - 1)\}$. The Non-Adjacent From is so named as for any $d$ written in NAF, the output values $d_0, \ldots, d_{\ell-1}$, are such that for every non-zero element $d_i$ there are at least $w + 1$ following zero values.

Once the integer $d$ has been re-coded into wNAF form, the point multiplication can be carried out by Algorithm 2. The occurrence of a non-zero $d_i$ controls when an addition is performed, with the precise value of $d_i$ determining which point from the list is added.

Before ending this section we note some aspects of the algorithm, and how these are exploited in our attack. A spy process, by monitoring the cache hits/misses, can determine when the code inside the **if–then** block in Algorithm 2 is performed. This happens when the element $d_i$ is non-zero, which reveals the fact that the following $w + 1$ values $d_{i+1}, \ldots, d_{i+w+1}$ are all zero. This reveals some information about the value $d$, but not enough to recover the value of $d$ itself.

Instead we focus on the last values of $d_i$ processed by Algorithm 2. We can determine precisely how many least significant bits of $d$ are zero, which means we can determine at least one bit of $d$, and with probability $1/2$ we determine two bits, with probability

---

**Input:** scalar $d$ and window width $w$
**Output:** $d$ in wNAF: $d_0, \ldots, d_{\ell-1}$
$\ell \leftarrow 0$
**while** $d > 0$ **do**
    **if** $d \bmod 2 = 1$ **then**
        $d_\ell \leftarrow d \bmod 2^{w+1}$
        **if** $d_\ell \geq 2^w$ **then**
            $d_\ell \leftarrow d_\ell - 2^{w+1}$
        **end**
        $d = d - d_\ell$
    **else**
        $d_\ell = 0$
    **end**
    $d = d/2$
    $\ell + = 1$
**end**

**Algorithm 1.** Conversion to Non-Adjacent Form

---

**Input:** scalar $d$ in wNAF $d_0, \ldots, d_{\ell-1}$ and precomputed points
$\{G, \pm[3]G, \pm[5]G, \ldots, \pm[2^w - 1]G\}$
**Output:** $[d]G$
$Q \leftarrow 1$
**for** $j$ *from* $\ell - 1$ *downto* 0 **do**
    $Q \leftarrow [2]Q$
    **if** $d_j \neq 0$ **then**
        $Q \leftarrow Q + [d_j]G$
    **end**
**end**

**Algorithm 2.** Computation of $kG$ using OpenSSL wNAF

---

$1/4$ we determine three bits and so on. Thus we not only extract information about whether the least significant bits are zero, but we also use the information obtained from the first non-zero bit.

In practice in the OpenSSL code the execution of scalar multiplication by the ephemeral key $k$ is slightly modified. Instead of computing $[k]G$, the code computes $[k + \lambda \cdot n]G$ where $\lambda \in \{1, 2\}$ is chosen such that $\lfloor \log_2(k + \lambda \cdot n) \rfloor = \lfloor \log_2(n) \rfloor + 1$. The fixed size scalar provides protection against the Brumley and Tuveri remote timing attack [11]. For the **secp256k1** curve, $n$ is $2^{256} - \varepsilon$ where $\varepsilon < 2^{129}$. The case $\lambda = 2$, therefore, only occurs for $k < \varepsilon$. As the probability of this case is less than $2^{-125}$, we can assume the wNAF algorithm is applied with $d = k + n$.

## 3   Attacking OpenSSL

In prior work the Montgomery ladder method of point multiplication was shown to be vulnerable to a FLUSH+RELOAD attack [39]. This section discusses the wNAF implementation of OpenSSL and demonstrates that it is also vulnerable. Unlike the side-channel in the Montgomery ladder implementation, which recovers enough bits to allow a direct recovery of the ephemeral private key [39], the side-channel in the wNAF implementation only leaks an average of two bits in each window. Consequently, a further algebraic attack is required to recover the private key. This section describes the FLUSH+RELOAD attack, and its application to the OpenSSL wNAF implementation. The next section completes the recovery of the secret key.

FLUSH+RELOAD is a cache side-channel attack that exploits a property of the Intel implementation of the X86 and X86_64 processor architectures, which allows processes to manipulate the cache of other processes [39, 40].

Using the attack, a spy program can trace or monitor memory read and execute access of a victim program to shared memory pages. The spy program only requires read access to the shared memory pages, hence pages containing binary code in executable files and in shared libraries are susceptible to the attack. Furthermore, pages shared through the use of memory de-duplication in virtualized environments [6, 38] are also susceptible and using them the attack can be applied between co-located virtual machines.

The spy program needs to execute on the same physical processor as the victim, however, unlike most cache-based side channel attacks, our spy monitors access to the last-level cache (LLC). As the LLC is shared between the processing cores of the processor, the spy does not need to execute on the same processing core as the victim. Consequently, the attack is applicable to multi-core processors and is not dependent on hyperthreading or on exploitable scheduler limitations like other published microarchitectural side-channel attacks.

---

**Input**: *adrs*—the probed address
**Output**: true if the address was accessed by the victim
**begin**
  evict(*adrs*)
  wait_a_bit()
  *time* ← current_time()
  *tmp* ← read(*adrs*)
  *readTime* ← current_time()-*time*
  **return** *readTime* < **threshold**
**end**

**Algorithm 3.** FLUSH+RELOAD Algorithm

---

To monitor access to memory, the spy repeatedly evicts the contents of the monitored memory from the LLC, waits for some time and then measures the time to read the contents of the monitored memory. See Algorithm 3 for a pseudo-code of the attack. As reading from the LLC is much faster than reading from memory, the spy can differentiate between these two cases. If, following the wait, the contents of the memory is retrieved from the cache, it indicates that another process has accessed the memory. Thus, by measuring the time to read the contents of the memory, the spy can decide whether the victim has accessed the monitored memory since the last time it was evicted.

Monitoring access to specific memory lines is one of the strengths of the FLUSH+RELOAD technique. Other cache-based tracing techniques monitor access to sets of memory lines that map to the same cache set. The use of specific memory lines reduces the chance of false positives. Capturing the access to the memory line, therefore, indicates that the victim executes and has accessed the line. Consequently, FLUSH+RELOAD does not require any external mechanism to synchronize with the victim.

We tested the attack on an HP Elite 8300 running Fedora 18. The machine features an Intel Core i5-3470 processor, with four execution cores and a 6MB LLC. As the OpenSSL package shipped with Fedora does not support ECC, we used our own build of OpenSSL 1.0.1e. For the experiment we used the curve **secp256k1** which is used by Bitcoin.

For the attack, we used the implementation of FLUSH+RELOAD from [40]. The spy program divides time into time slots of approximately 3,000 cycles (almost $1\mu s$). In each time slot the spy probes memory lines in the group add and double functions. (ec_GFp_simple_add and ec_GFp_simple_dbl, respectively.) The time slot length is chosen to ensure that there is an empty slot during the execution of each group operation. This allows the spy to correctly distinguish consecutive doubles.

The probes are placed on memory lines which contain calls to the field multiplication function. Memory lines containing call sites are accessed both when the function is called and when it returns. Hence, by probing these memory lines, we reduce the chance of missing accesses due to overlaps with the probes. See [40] for a discussion of overlaps.

To find the memory lines containing the call sites we built OpenSSL with debugging symbols. These symbols are not loaded at run time and do not affect the performance of the code. The debugging symbols are, typically, not available for attackers, however their absence would not present a major obstacle to a determined attacker who could use reverse engineering [16].

## 4  Lattice Attack Details

We applied the above process on the OpenSSL implementation of ECDSA for the curve **secp256k1**. We fixed a public key $Q = [\alpha]G$, and then monitored via the FLUSH+RELOAD spy process the generation of a set of $d$ signature pairs $(r_i, s_i)$ for $i = 1, \ldots, d$. For each signature pair there is a known hashed message value $h_i$ and an unknown ephemeral private key value $k_i$.

Using the FLUSH+RELOAD side-channel we also obtained, with very high probability, the sequence of point additions and doubling used when OpenSSL executes the operation $[k_i + n]G$. In particular, this means we learn values $c_i$ and $l_i$ such that

$$k_i + n \equiv c_i \pmod{2^{l_i}},$$

or equivalently

$$k_i \equiv c_i - n \pmod{2^{l_i}}.$$

Where $l_i$ denotes the number of known bits. We can also determine the length of the known run of zeroes in the least significant bits of $k_i + n$, which we will call $z_i$. In presenting the analysis we assume the $d$ signatures have been selected such that we already know that the value of $k_i + n$ is divisible by $2^Z$, for some value of Z, i.e. we pick signatures for which $z_i \geq Z$. In practice this means that to obtain $d$ such signatures we need to collect (on average) $d \cdot 2^Z$ signatures in total.

We write $a_i = c_i - n \pmod{2^{l_i}}$. For example, writing $A$ for an add, $D$ for a double and $X$ for a *don't know*, we can read off $c_i$, $l_i$ and $z_i$ from the least execution sequence obtained in the FLUSH+RELOAD analysis. In practice the FLUSH+RELOAD attack is so efficient that we are able to identify $A$'s and $D$'s with almost 100% certainty, with only $\varepsilon = 0.55\% - 0.65\%$ of the symbols turning out to be *don't knows*. To read off the values we use the following table (and its obvious extension), where we present the approximate probability of our attack revealing this sequence.

| Sequence | $c_i$ | $l_i$ | $z_i$ | Pr $\approx$ |
|---|---|---|---|---|
| $...X$ | 0 | 0.0 | 0 | $\varepsilon$ |
| $...A$ | 1 | 1.0 | 0 | $(1-\varepsilon)/2$ |
| $...XD$ | 0 | 1.0 | 1 | $\varepsilon \cdot (1-\varepsilon)/2$ |
| $...AD$ | 2 | 2.0 | 1 | $((1-\varepsilon)/2)^2$ |
| $...XDD$ | 0 | 2.0 | 2 | $\varepsilon \cdot ((1-\varepsilon)/2)^2$ |
| $...ADD$ | 4 | 3.0 | 2 | $((1-\varepsilon)/2)^3$ |

For a given execution of the FLUSH+RELOAD attack, from the table we can determine $c_i$ and $l_i$, and hence $a_i$. Then, using the standard analysis from [29, 30], we determine the following values

$$t_i = \lfloor r_i/(2^{l_i} \cdot s_i) \rfloor_n,$$
$$u_i = \lfloor (a_i - h_i/s_i)/2^{l_i} \rfloor_n + n/2^{l_i+1},$$

where $\lfloor \cdot \rfloor_n$ denotes reduction modulo $n$ into the range $[0, \ldots, n)$. We then have that

$$v_i = |\alpha \cdot t_i - u_i|_n < n/2^{l_i+1}, \tag{1}$$

where $|\cdot|_n$ denotes reduction by $n$, but into the range $(-n/2, \ldots, n/2)$. It is this latter equation which we exploit, via lattice basis reduction, so as to recover $d$. The key observation found in [29, 30] is that the value $v_i$ is smaller (by a factor of $2^{l_i+1}$) than a random integer. Unlike prior work in this area we do not (necessarily) need to just select those executions which give us a "large" value of $z_i$, say $z_i \geq 3$. Prior work fixes a minimum value of $z_i$ (or essentially equivalently $l_i$) and utilizes this single value in all equations such as (1). If we do this we would need to throw away all bar $1/2^{z_i+1}$ of the executions obtained. By maintaining full generality, i.e. a variable value of $z_i$ (subject to the constraint $z_i \geq Z$) in each instance of (1), we are able to utilize all information at our disposal and recover the secret key $\alpha$ with very little effort indeed.

The next task is to turn the equations from (1) into a lattice problem. Following [29, 30] we do this in one of two possible ways, which we now recap on.

*Attack via CVP:* We first consider the lattice $L(B)$ in $d+1$-dimensional real space, generated by the rows of the following matrix

$$B = \begin{pmatrix} 2^{l_1+1} \cdot n & & & \\ & \ddots & & \\ & & 2^{l_d+1} \cdot n & \\ 2^{l_1+1} \cdot t_1 & \cdots & 2^{l_d+1} \cdot t_d & 1 \end{pmatrix}.$$

From (1) we find that there are integers $(\lambda_1, \ldots, \lambda_d)$ such that if we set $\mathbf{x} = (\lambda_1, \ldots, \lambda_d, \alpha)$ and $\mathbf{y} = (2^{l_1+1} \cdot v_1, \ldots, 2^{l_d+1} \cdot v_d, \alpha)$ and $\mathbf{u} = (2^{l_1+1} \cdot u_1, \ldots, 2^{l_d+1} \cdot u_d, 0)$, then we have

$$\mathbf{x} \cdot B - \mathbf{u} = \mathbf{y}.$$

We note that the 2-norm of the vector $\mathbf{y}$ is about $\sqrt{d+1} \cdot n$, whereas the lattice determinant of $L(B)$ is $2^{d+\Sigma l_i} \cdot n^d$. Thus the vector $\mathbf{u}$ is a close vector to the lattice. Solving the Closest Vector Problem (CVP) with input $B$ and $\mathbf{u}$ therefore reveals $\mathbf{x}$ and hence the secret key $\alpha$.

*Attack via SVP:* It is often more effective in practice to solve the above CVP problem via the means of embedding the CVP into a Shortest Vector Problem (SVP) in a slightly bigger lattice. In particular we take the lattice $L(B')$ in $d+2$-dimensional real space generated by the rows of the matrix

$$B' = \begin{pmatrix} B & 0 \\ \mathbf{u} & n \end{pmatrix}.$$

This lattice has determinant $2^{d+\Sigma l_i} \cdot n^{(d+1)}$, by taking the lattice vector generated by $\mathbf{x}' = (\mathbf{x}, \alpha, -1)$ we obtain the lattice vector $\mathbf{y}' = \mathbf{x}' \cdot B' = (\mathbf{y}, -n)$. The 2-norm of this lattice vector is roughly $\sqrt{d+2} \cdot n$. We expect the second vector in a reduced basis to be of size $c \cdot n$, and so there is a "good" chance for a suitably strong lattice reduction to obtain a lattice basis whose second vector is equal to $\mathbf{y}'$. Note, the first basis vector is likely to be given by $(-t_1, \ldots, -t_d, n, 0) \cdot B' = (0, \ldots, 0, n, 0)$.

### 4.1 Experimental Results

To solve the SVP problem we used the BKZ algorithm [35] as implemented in fplll [12]. However, this implementation is only efficient for small block size (say less than 35), due to the fact that BKZ is an exponential algorithm in the block size. Thus for larger block size we implemented a variant of the BKZ-2.0 algorithm [15], however this algorithm is only effective for block sizes $\beta$ greater than 50. In tuning BKZ-2.0 we used the following strategy, at the end of every round we determined whether we had already solved for the private key, if not we continued, and then gave up after ten rounds. As stated above we applied our attack to the curve **secp256k1**.

We wished to determine what the optimal strategy was in terms of the minimum value of $Z$ we should take, the optimal lattice dimension, and the optimal lattice algorithm. Thus we performed a number of experiments which are reported on in Tables

2 and 3 in Appendix A; where we present our best results obtained for each $(d, Z)$ pair. We also present graphs to show how the different values of $\beta$ affected the success rate. For each lattice dimension, we measured the optimal parameters as the ones which minimized the value of lattice execution time divided by probability of success. The probability of success was measured by running the attack a number of times, and seeing in how many executions we managed to recover the underlying secret key. We used Time divided by Probability is a crude measure of success, but we note this hides other issues such as expected number of executions of the signature algorithm needed.

All executions were performed on an Intel Xeon CPU running at 2.40 GHz, on a machine with 4GB of RAM. The programs were run in a single thread, and so no advantages where made of the multiple cores on the processor. We ran experiments for the SVP attack using BKZ with block size ranging from 5 to 40 and with BKZ-2.0 with blocksize 50. With our crude measure of Time divided by Probability we find that BKZ with block size 15 or 20 is almost always the method of choice for the SVP method.

We see that the number of signatures needed is consistent with what theory would predict in the case of $Z = 1$ and $Z = 2$, i.e. the lattice reduction algorithm can extract from the side-channel the underlying secret key as soon as the expected number of leaked bits slightly exceeds the number of bits in the secret key. For $Z = 0$ this no longer holds, we conjecture that this is because the lattice algorithms are unable to reduce the basis well enough, in a short enough amount of time, to extract the small amount of information which is revealed by each signature. In other words the input basis for $Z = 0$ is too close to looking like a random basis, unless a large amount of signatures is used.

To solve the CVP problem variant we applied a pre-processing of either fp|l| or BKZ-2.0. When applying pre-processing of BKZ-2.0 we limited to only one round of execution. We then applied an enumeration technique, akin to the enumeration used in the enumeration sub-routine of BKZ, but centered around the target close vector as opposed to the origin. When a close vector was found this was checked to see whether it revealed the secret key, and if not the enumeration was continued. We restricted the number of nodes in the enumeration tree to $2^{29}$, so as to ensure the enumeration did not go on for an excessive amount of time in the cases where the solution vector is hard to find (this mainly affected the experiments in dimension greater than 150). See Tables 4 and 5, in Appendix A, for details of these experiments; again we present the best results for each $(d, Z)$ pair. The enumeration time is highly dependent on whether the close lattice vector is really close to the lattice, thus we see that when the expected number of bits revealed per signature times the number of signatures utilized in the lattice, gets close to the bit size of elliptic curve (256) the enumeration time drops. Again we see that extensive pre-processing of the basis with more complex lattice reduction techniques provides no real benefit.

The results of the SVP and CVP experiments (Appendix A) show that for fixed $Z$, increasing the dimension generally decreases the overall expected running time. In some sense, as the dimension increases more information is being added to the lattice and this makes the desired solution vector stand out more. The higher block sizes perform better in the lower dimensions, as the stronger reduction allows them to isolate the solution vector better. The lower block sizes perform better in the higher dimensions, as the high-dimensional lattices already contain much information and strong reduction is not required.

The one exception to this rule is the case of $Z = 2$ in the CVP experiments. In dimensions below 80 the CVP can be solved relatively quickly here, whereas in dimensions 80 up to 100 it takes more time. This can be explained as follows: in the low dimension the CVP-tree is not very big, but contains many solutions. This means that enumeration of the CVP-tree is very quick, but the solution vector is not unique. Thus, the probability of success is equal to the probability of finding the right vector. From dimension 80 upwards, we expect the solution vector to be unique, but the CVP-trees become much bigger on average. If we do not stop the enumeration after a fixed number of nodes, it will find the solution with high probability, but the enumeration takes much longer. Here, the probability of success is the probability of finding a solution at all.

We first note, for both our lattice variants, that there is a wide variation in the probability of success, if we ran a larger batch of tests we would presume this would stabilize. However, even with this caveat we notice a number of remarkable facts. Firstly, recall we are trying to break a 256 bit elliptic curve private key. The conventional wisdom has been that using a window style exponentiation method and a side-channel which only records a distinction between addition and doubling (i.e. does not identify which additions), one would need much more than 256 executions to recover the secret key. However, we see that we have a good chance of recovering the key with less than this. For example, Nguyen and Shparlinksi [30] estimated needing $23 \times 2^7 = 2944$ signatures to recover a 160 bit key, when seven consecutive zero bits of the ephemeral private key were detected. Namely they would use a lattice of dimension 23, but require 2944 signatures to enable to obtain 23 signatures for which they could determine the ones with seven consecutive digits of the ephemeral private key. Note that $23 \cdot 7 = 161 > 160$. Liu and Nguyen [24] extended this attack by using improved lattice algorithms, decreasing the number of signatures required. We are able to have a reasonable chance of success with as little as 200 signatures obtained against a 256 bit key.

In our modification of the lattice attack we not only utilize zero least significant bits, but also notice that the end of a run of zeros tells us that the next bit is one. In addition we utilize all of the run of zeros (say for example eight) and not just some fixed predetermined number (such as four). This explains our improved lattice analysis, and shows that one can recover the secret with relatively high probability with just a small number of measurements.

As a second note we see that strong lattice reduction, i.e. high block sizes in the BKZ algorithm, or even applying BKZ-2.0, does not seem to gain us very much. Indeed acquiring a few extra samples allows us to drop down to using BKZ with blocksize twenty in almost all cases. Note that in many of our experiments a smaller value of $\beta$ resulted in a much lower probability of success (often zero), whilst a higher value of $\beta$ resulted in a significantly increased run time.

Thirdly, we note that if one is unsuccessful on one run, one does not need to derive a whole new set of traces, simply by increasing the number of traces a little bit one can either take a new random sample of the traces one has, or increase the lattice dimension used.

We end by presenting in Table 1 the best variant of the lattice attack, measured in terms of the minimal value of Time divided by Probability of success, for the number of signatures obtained. We see that in a very short amount of time we can recover the secret key from 260 signatures, and with more effort we can even recover it from the FLUSH+RELOAD attack applied to as little at 200 signatures. We see that it is not clear whether the SVP or the CVP approach is the best strategy.

**Table 1.** Combined Results. The best lattice parameter choice for each number of signatures obtained (in steps of 20)

| Expected # Sigs | SVP/ SVP | $d$ | $Z = \min\{z_i\}$ | Pre-Processing and/or SVP Algorithm | Time (s) | Prob Success | $100\times$ Time/Prob |
|---|---|---|---|---|---|---|---|
| 200 | SVP | 100 | 1 | BKZ $(\beta = 30)$ | 611.13 | 3.5 | 17460 |
| 220 | SVP | 110 | 1 | BKZ $(\beta = 25)$ | 78.67 | 2.0 | 3933 |
| 240 | CVP | 60 | 2 | BKZ $(\beta = 25)$ | 2.68 | 0.5 | 536 |
| 260 | CVP | 65 | 2 | BKZ $(\beta = 10)$ | 2.26 | 5.5 | 41 |
| 280 | CVP | 70 | 2 | BKZ $(\beta = 15)$ | 4.46 | 29.5 | 15 |
| 300 | CVP | 75 | 2 | BKZ $(\beta = 20)$ | 13.54 | 53.0 | 26 |
| 320 | SVP | 80 | 2 | BKZ $(\beta = 20)$ | 6.67 | 22.5 | 29 |
| 340 | SVP | 85 | 2 | BKZ $(\beta = 20)$ | 9.15 | 37.0 | 24 |
| 360 | SVP | 90 | 2 | BKZ $(\beta = 15)$ | 6.24 | 23.5 | 26 |
| 380 | SVP | 95 | 2 | BKZ $(\beta = 15)$ | 6.82 | 36.0 | 19 |
| 400 | SVP | 100 | 2 | BKZ $(\beta = 15)$ | 7.22 | 33.5 | 21 |
| 420 | SVP | 105 | 2 | BKZ $(\beta = 15)$ | 7.74 | 43.0 | 18 |
| 440 | SVP | 110 | 2 | BKZ $(\beta = 15)$ | 8.16 | 49.0 | 16 |
| 460 | SVP | 115 | 2 | BKZ $(\beta = 15)$ | 8.32 | 52.0 | 16 |
| 480 | CVP | 120 | 2 | BKZ $(\beta = 10)$ | 11.55 | 87.0 | 13 |
| 500 | CVP | 125 | 2 | BKZ $(\beta = 10)$ | 10.74 | 93.5 | 12 |
| 520 | CVP | 130 | 2 | BKZ $(\beta = 10)$ | 10.50 | 96.0 | 11 |
| 540 | SVP | 135 | 2 | BKZ $(\beta = 10)$ | 7.44 | 55.0 | 13 |

## 5 Mitigation

As our attack requires capturing multiple signatures, one way of mitigating it is limiting the number of times a private key is used for signing. Bitcoin, which uses the **secp256k1** curve on which this work focuses, recommends using a new key for each transaction [28]. This recommendation, however, is not always followed [34], exposing users to the attack.

Another option to reduce the effectiveness of the FLUSH+RELOAD part of the attack would be to exploit the inherent properties of this "Koblitz" curve within the OpenSSL implementation; which would also have the positive side result of speeding up the scalar multiplication operation. The use of the *GLV method* [18] for point multiplication would not completely thwart the above attack, but, in theory, reduces its effectiveness. The GLV method is used to speed up the computation of point scalar multiplication when the elliptic curve has an efficiently computable endomorphism. This partial solution is only applicable to elliptic curves with easily computable automorphisms with sufficiently large automorphism group; such as the curve **secp256k1** which we used in our example.

The curve **secp256k1** is defined over a prime field of characteristic $p$ with $p \equiv 1$ mod 6. This means that $\mathbb{F}_p$ contains a primitive 6th root of unity $\zeta$ and if $(x,y)$ is in the group of points on $E$, then $(-\zeta x, y)$ is also. In fact, $(-\zeta x, y) = [\lambda](x,y)$ for some $\lambda^6 = 1 \mod n$. Since the computation of $(-\zeta x, y)$ from $(x,y)$ costs only one finite field multiplication (far less than computing $[\lambda](x,y)$) this can be used to speed up scalar multiplication: instead of computing $[k]G$, one computes $[k_0]G + [k_1]([\lambda]G)$ where $k_0, k_1$ are around the size of $k^{1/2}$. This is known to be one of the fastest methods of performing scalar multiplication [18]. The computation of $[k_0]G + [k_1]([\lambda]G)$ is not done using two scalar multiplications then a point addition, but uses the so called *Straus-Shamir* trick which used joint double and add operations [18, Alg 1] performing the two scalar multiplications and the addition simultaneously.

The GLV method alone would be vulnerable to simple side-channel analysis. It is necessary to re-code the scalars $k_0$ and $k_1$ and comb method as developed and assembled in [17] so that the execution is regular to thwart simple power analysis and timing attacks. Using the attack presented above we are able to recover around 2 bits of the secret key for each signature monitored. If the GLV method were used in conjunction with wNAF, the number of bits (on average) leaked per signature would be reduced to $4/3$. It is also possible to extend the GLV method to representations of $k$ in terms of higher degrees of $\lambda$, for example writing $k = k_0 + k_1 \lambda + \cdots + k_t \lambda^t \mod n$. For $t = 2$ the estimated rate of bit leakage would be $6/7$ bits per signature (though this extension is not possible for the example curve due to the order of the automorphism).

We see that using the GLV method can reduce the number of leaked bits but it is not sufficient to prevent the attack. A positive flip side of this and the attack of [39] is that implementing algorithms which will improve the efficiency of the scalar multiplication seem, at present, to reduce the effectiveness of the attacks.

Scalar blinding techniques [10,25] use arithmetic operations on the scalar to hide the value of the scalar from potential attackers. The method suggested by these works is to compute $[(k + m \cdots n + \bar{m})]G - [\bar{m}]G$ where $m$ and $\bar{m}$ are small (e.g. 32 bits) numbers. The random values used mask the bits of the scalar and prevent the spy from recovering the scalar from the leaked data.

The information leak in our attack originates from using the sliding window in the wNAF algorithm for scalar multiplication. Hence, an immediate fix for the problem is to use a fixed window algorithm for scalar multiplication. A naïve implementation of a fixed window algorithm may still be vulnerable to the PRIME+PROBE attack, e.g. by adapting the technique of [33]. To provide protection against the attack, the implementation must prevent any data flow from sensitive key data to memory access patterns. Methods for achieving this are used in NaCL [8], which ensures that the sequence of memory accesses it performs is not dependent on the private key. A similar solution is available in the implementation of modular exponentiation in OpenSSL, where the implementation attempts to access the same sequence of memory lines irrespective of the private key. However, this approach may leak information [7,37].

**Acknowledgements.** The first and fourth authors wish to thank Dr Katrina Falkner for her advice and support and the Defence Science and Technology Organisation (DSTO) Maritime Division, Australia, who partially funded their work. The second and third authors work has been supported in part by ERC Advanced Grant ERC-2010-AdG-267188-CRIPTO, by EPSRC via grant EP/I03126X, and by Defense Advanced Research Projects Agency (DARPA) and the Air Force Research Laboratory (AFRL) under agreement number FA8750-11-2-0079[1].

# References

1. Acıiçmez, O.: Yet another microarchitectural attack: exploiting I-Cache. In: Ning, P., Atluri, V. (eds.) Proceedings of the ACM Workshop on Computer Security Architecture, Fairfax, Virginia, United States, pp. 11–18 (November 2007)
2. Acıiçmez, O., Brumley, B.B., Grabher, P.: New results on instruction cache attacks. In: Mangard, S., Standaert, F.-X. (eds.) Proceedings of the Workshop on Cryptographic Hardware and Embedded Systems, Santa Barbara, California, United States, pp. 110–124 (August 2010)
3. Acıiçmez, O., Gueron, S., Seifert, J.-P.: New branch prediction vulnerabilities in OpenSSL and necessary software countermeasures. In: Galbraith, S.D. (ed.) Cryptography and Coding 2007. LNCS, vol. 4887, pp. 185–203. Springer, Heidelberg (2007)
4. Acıiçmez, O., Koç, Ç.K., Seifert, J.-P.: On the power of simple branch prediction analysis. In: Proceedings of the Second ACM Symposium on Information, Computer and Communication Security, Singapore, pp. 312–320 (2007)
5. Acıiçmez, O., Schindler, W.: A vulnerability in RSA implementations due to instruction cache analysis and its demonstration on OpenSSL. In: Malkin, T. (ed.) CT-RSA 2008. LNCS, vol. 4964, pp. 256–273. Springer, Heidelberg (2008)
6. Arcangeli, A., Eidus, I., Wright, C.: Increasing memory density by using KSM. In: Proceedings of the Linux Symposium, Montreal, Quebec, Canada, pp. 19–28 (July 2009)
7. Bernstein, D.J.: Cache-timing attacks on AES (April 2005),
   http://cr.yp.to/antiforgery/cachetiming-20050414.pdf
8. Bernstein, D.J., Lange, T., Schwabe, P.: The security impact of a new cryptographic library. In: Hevia, A., Neven, G. (eds.) LatinCrypt 2012. LNCS, vol. 7533, pp. 159–176. Springer, Heidelberg (2012)
9. Bos, J.W., Halderman, J.A., Heninger, N., Moore, J., Naehrig, M., Wustrow, E.: Elliptic curve cryptography in practice. Cryptology ePrint Archive, Report 2013/734 (2013), http://eprint.iacr.org/
10. Brumley, B.B., Hakala, R.M.: Cache-timing template attacks. In: Matsui, M. (ed.) ASIACRYPT 2009. LNCS, vol. 5912, pp. 667–684. Springer, Heidelberg (2009)
11. Brumley, B.B., Tuveri, N.: Remote timing attacks are still practical. In: Atluri, V., Diaz, C. (eds.) ESORICS 2011. LNCS, vol. 6879, pp. 355–371. Springer, Heidelberg (2011)
12. Cadé, D., Pujol, X., Stehlé, D.: Fplll-4.0.4 (2013),
    http://perso.ens-lyon.fr/damien.stehle/fplll/

---

[1] The US Government is authorized to reproduce and distribute reprints for Government purposes notwithstanding any copyright notation thereon. The views and conclusions contained herein are those of the authors and should not be interpreted as necessarily representing the official policies or endorsements, either expressed or implied, of Defense Advanced Research Projects Agency (DARPA) or the U.S. Government.

13. Canteaut, A., Lauradoux, C., Seznec, A.: Understanding cache attacks. Technical Report 5881, INRIA (April 2006)
14. Chen, C., Wang, T., Kou, Y., Chen, X., Li, X.: Improvement of trace-driven I-Cache timing attack on the RSA algorithm. The Journal of Systems and Software 86(1), 100–107 (2013)
15. Chen, Y., Nguyen, P.Q.: BKZ 2.0: Better lattice security estimates. In: Lee, D.H., Wang, X. (eds.) ASIACRYPT 2011. LNCS, vol. 7073, pp. 1–20. Springer, Heidelberg (2011)
16. Cipresso, T., Stamp, M.: Software reverse engineering. In: Stavroulakis, P., Stamp, M. (eds.) Handbook of Information and Communication Security, vol. 31, pp. 659–696. Springer (2010)
17. Faz-Hernandez, A., Longa, P., Sanchez, A.H.: Efficient and secure algorithms for GLV-based scalar multiplication and their implementation on GLV-GLS curves. Cryptology ePrint Archive, Report 2013/158 (2013), http://eprint.iacr.org/
18. Gallant, R.P., Lambert, R.J., Vanstone, S.A.: Faster point multiplication on elliptic curves with efficient endomorphisms. In: Kilian, J. (ed.) CRYPTO 2001. LNCS, vol. 2139, pp. 190–200. Springer, Heidelberg (2001)
19. Gopalakrishnan, K., Thériault, N., Yao, C.Z.: Solving discrete logarithms from partial knowledge of the key. In: Srinathan, K., Rangan, C.P., Yung, M. (eds.) INDOCRYPT 2007. LNCS, vol. 4859, pp. 224–237. Springer, Heidelberg (2007)
20. Gullasch, D., Bangerter, E., Krenn, S.: Cache games — bringing access-based cache attacks on AES to practice. In: Proceedings of the IEEE Symposium on Security and Privacy, Oakland, California, United States, pp. 490–595 (May 2011)
21. Howgrave-Graham, N., Smart, N.P.: Lattice attacks on digital signature schemes. Designs, Codes and Cryptography 23(3), 283–290 (2001)
22. Kocher, P.C., Jaffe, J., Jun, B.: Differential power analysis. In: Wiener, M. (ed.) CRYPTO 1999. LNCS, vol. 1666, pp. 388–397. Springer, Heidelberg (1999)
23. Lenstra, A.K., Lenstra Jr., H.W., Lovász, L.: Factoring polynomials with rational coefficients. Mathematische Annalen 261(4), 515–534 (1982)
24. Liu, M., Nguyen, P.Q.: Solving BDD by enumeration: An update. In: Dawson, E. (ed.) CT-RSA 2013. LNCS, vol. 7779, pp. 293–309. Springer, Heidelberg (2013)
25. Möller, B.: Parallelizable elliptic curve point multiplication method with resistance against side-channel attacks. In: Chan, A.H., Gligor, V.D. (eds.) ISC 2002. LNCS, vol. 2433, pp. 402–413. Springer, Heidelberg (2002)
26. Muir, J.A., Stinson, D.R.: On the low Hamming weight discrete logarithm problem for non-adjacent representations. Appl. Algebra Eng. Commun. Comput. 16(6), 461–472 (2006)
27. Naccache, D., Nguyên, P.Q., Tunstall, M., Whelan, C.: Experimenting with faults, lattices and the DSA. In: Vaudenay, S. (ed.) PKC 2005. LNCS, vol. 3386, pp. 16–28. Springer, Heidelberg (2005)
28. Nakamoto, S.: Bitcoin: A peer-to-peer electronic cash system, http://bitcoin.org/bitcoin.pdf
29. Nguyen, P.Q., Shparlinski, I.: The insecurity of the digital signature algorithm with partially known nonces. J. Cryptology 15(3), 151–176 (2002)
30. Nguyen, P.Q., Shparlinski, I.E.: The insecurity of the elliptic curve digital signature algorithm with partially known nonces. Designs, Codes and Cryptography 30(2), 201–217 (2003)
31. OpenSSL, http://www.openssl.org.
32. Page, D.: Theoretical use of cache memory as a cryptanalytic side-channel. IACR Cryptology ePrint Archive, 2002:169 (2002)
33. Percival, C.: Cache missing for fun and profit (2005), http://www.daemonology.net/papers/htt.pdf
34. Ron, D., Shamir, A.: Quantitative analysis of the full Bitcoin transaction graph. Cryptology ePrint Archive, Report 2012/584 (2012), http://eprint.iacr.org/

35. Schnorr, C.-P., Euchner, M.: Lattice basis reduction: Improved practical algorithms and solving subset sum problems. In: Budach, L. (ed.) FCT 1991. LNCS, vol. 529, pp. 68–85. Springer, Heidelberg (1991)

36. Stinson, D.R.: Some baby-step giant-step algorithms for the low Hamming weight discrete logarithm problem. Math. Comput. 71(237), 379–391 (2002)

37. Tromer, E., Osvik, D.A., Shamir, A.: Efficient cache attacks in AES, and countermeasures. Journal of Cryptology 23(2), 37–71 (2010)

38. Waldspurger, C.A.: Memory resource management in VMware ESX Server. In: Culler, D.E., Druschel, P. (eds.) Proceedings of the Fifth Symposium on Operating Systems Design and Implementation, Boston, Massachusetts, United States, pp. 181–194 (December 2002)

39. Yarom, Y., Benger, N.: Recovering OpenSSL ECDSA nonces using the Flush+Reload cache side-channel attack. Cryptology ePrint Archive, Report 2014/140 (2014), http://eprint.iacr.org/

40. Yarom, Y., Falkner, K.: FLUSH+RELOAD: a high resolution, low noise, L3 cache side-channel attack. In: Proceedings of the 23rd USENIX Security Symposium (to appear, 2014)

41. Zhang, Y., Jules, A., Reiter, M.K., Ristenpart, T.: Cross-VM side channels and their use to extract private keys. In: Yu, T., Danezis, G., Gligor, V.D. (eds.) Proceedings of the 19th ACM Conference on Computer and Communication Security, Raleigh, North Carolina, United States, pp. 305–316 (October 2012)

# A    Experimental Results

**Table 2.** SVP Analysis Experimental Results : $Z = \min z_i = 1$

| $d$ | Algorithm | Expected # Sigs | Lattice Time (s) | Prob.0 Success | 100× Time/Prob |
|---|---|---|---|---|---|
| 100 | BKZ ($\beta = 30$) | 200 | 611.13 | 3.5 | 17460 |
| 105 | BKZ ($\beta = 30$) | 210 | 702.67 | 7.5 | 9368 |
| 110 | BKZ ($\beta = 25$) | 220 | 78.67 | 2.0 | 3933 |
| 115 | BKZ ($\beta = 25$) | 230 | 71.18 | 3.5 | 2033 |
| 120 | BKZ ($\beta = 20$) | 240 | 14.78 | 1.0 | 1478 |
| 125 | BKZ ($\beta = 10$) | 250 | 6.81 | 1.0 | 681 |
| 130 | BKZ ($\beta = 20$) | 260 | 15.12 | 4.0 | 378 |
| 135 | BKZ ($\beta = 25$) | 270 | 57.83 | 20.0 | 289 |
| 140 | BKZ ($\beta = 20$) | 280 | 16.47 | 9.0 | 182 |
| 145 | BKZ ($\beta = 25$) | 290 | 57.63 | 29.5 | 195 |
| 150 | BKZ ($\beta = 20$) | 300 | 19.05 | 17.0 | 112 |
| 155 | BKZ ($\beta = 15$) | 310 | 13.14 | 13.5 | 97 |
| 160 | BKZ ($\beta = 15$) | 320 | 14.00 | 16.0 | 87 |
| 165 | BKZ ($\beta = 15$) | 330 | 15.75 | 17.5 | 90 |
| 170 | BKZ ($\beta = 15$) | 340 | 17.09 | 23.0 | 74 |
| 175 | BKZ ($\beta = 15$) | 350 | 18.14 | 23.0 | 78 |

**Table 3.** SVP Analysis Experimental Results : $Z = \min z_i = 2$

| $d$ | Algorithm | Expected # Sigs | Lattice Time (s) | Prob.0 Success | 100× Time/Prob |
|---|---|---|---|---|---|
| 65 | BKZ ($\beta = 25$) | 260 | 5.17 | 2.5 | 206 |
| 70 | BKZ ($\beta = 25$) | 280 | 7.93 | 13.5 | 58 |
| 75 | BKZ ($\beta = 25$) | 300 | 13.58 | 23.5 | 57 |
| 80 | BKZ ($\beta = 20$) | 320 | 6.67 | 22.5 | 29 |
| 85 | BKZ ($\beta = 20$) | 340 | 9.15 | 37.0 | 24 |
| 90 | BKZ ($\beta = 15$) | 360 | 6.24 | 23.5 | 26 |
| 95 | BKZ ($\beta = 15$) | 380 | 6.82 | 36.0 | 19 |
| 100 | BKZ ($\beta = 15$) | 400 | 7.22 | 33.5 | 21 |
| 105 | BKZ ($\beta = 15$) | 420 | 7.74 | 43.0 | 18 |
| 110 | BKZ ($\beta = 15$) | 440 | 8.16 | 49.0 | 16 |
| 115 | BKZ ($\beta = 15$) | 460 | 8.32 | 52.0 | 16 |
| 120 | BKZ ($\beta = 10$) | 480 | 6.49 | 44.0 | 14 |
| 125 | BKZ ($\beta = 10$) | 500 | 6.83 | 45.0 | 14 |
| 130 | BKZ ($\beta = 10$) | 520 | 7.06 | 48.0 | 14 |
| 135 | BKZ ($\beta = 10$) | 540 | 7.44 | 55.0 | 13 |

**Table 4.** CVP Analysis Experimental Results : $Z = \min z_i = 1$

| $d$ | Pre-Processing Algorithm | Expected # Sigs | Time (s) | Prob.0 Success | 100× Time/Prob |
|---|---|---|---|---|---|
| 150 | BKZ ($\beta = 15$) | 300 | 32.43 | 3.0 | 1081 |
| 155 | BKZ ($\beta = 15$) | 310 | 33.90 | 8.0 | 424 |
| 160 | BKZ ($\beta = 20$) | 320 | 48.26 | 13.5 | 357 |
| 165 | BKZ ($\beta = 20$) | 330 | 50.97 | 20.0 | 255 |
| 170 | BKZ ($\beta = 15$) | 340 | 39.58 | 22.0 | 180 |
| 175 | BKZ ($\beta = 15$) | 350 | 41.20 | 26.0 | 158 |
| 180 | BKZ ($\beta = 15$) | 360 | 43.50 | 31.5 | 138 |
| 185 | BKZ ($\beta = 15$) | 370 | 44.30 | 39.5 | 112 |
| 190 | BKZ ($\beta = 15$) | 380 | 45.98 | 42.0 | 109 |
| 195 | BKZ ($\beta = 15$) | 390 | 46.15 | 46.0 | 100 |
| 200 | BKZ ($\beta = 15$) | 400 | 45.41 | 60.5 | 75 |
| 205 | BKZ ($\beta = 15$) | 410 | 48.45 | 65.5 | 74 |
| 210 | BKZ ($\beta = 10$) | 420 | 41.89 | 59.5 | 70 |
| 215 | BKZ ($\beta = 15$) | 430 | 49.56 | 76.0 | 65 |
| 220 | BKZ ($\beta = 15$) | 440 | 49.88 | 86.0 | 58 |
| 225 | BKZ ($\beta = 10$) | 450 | 44.58 | 77.0 | 58 |
| 230 | BKZ ($\beta = 15$) | 460 | 53.23 | 92.0 | 58 |
| 235 | BKZ ($\beta = 10$) | 470 | 52.86 | 88.0 | 60 |
| 240 | BKZ ($\beta = 10$) | 480 | 48.37 | 90.5 | 53 |
| 245 | BKZ ($\beta = 10$) | 490 | 49.74 | 89.5 | 56 |

**Table 5.** CVP Analysis Experimental Results : $Z = \min z_i = 2$

| $d$ | Pre-Processing Algorithm | Expected # Sigs | Time (s) | Prob.0 Success | 100× Time/Prob |
|---|---|---|---|---|---|
| 60 | BKZ ($\beta = 25$) | 240 | 2.68 | 0.5 | 536 |
| 65 | BKZ ($\beta = 10$) | 260 | 2.26 | 5.5 | 41 |
| 70 | BKZ ($\beta = 15$) | 280 | 4.46 | 29.5 | 15 |
| 75 | BKZ ($\beta = 20$) | 300 | 13.54 | 53.0 | 26 |
| 80 | BKZ ($\beta = 20$) | 320 | 21.83 | 17.0 | 128 |
| 85 | BKZ ($\beta = 15$) | 340 | 20.08 | 25.5 | 130 |
| 90 | BKZ ($\beta = 20$) | 360 | 23.36 | 35.0 | 67 |
| 95 | BKZ ($\beta = 20$) | 380 | 22.40 | 52.5 | 43 |
| 100 | BKZ ($\beta = 20$) | 400 | 22.95 | 67.0 | 34 |
| 105 | BKZ ($\beta = 20$) | 420 | 21.76 | 77.0 | 28 |
| 110 | BKZ ($\beta = 15$) | 440 | 14.74 | 81.0 | 18 |
| 115 | BKZ ($\beta = 15$) | 460 | 14.82 | 86.5 | 17 |
| 120 | BKZ ($\beta = 10$) | 480 | 11.55 | 87.0 | 13 |
| 125 | BKZ ($\beta = 10$) | 500 | 10.74 | 93.5 | 12 |
| 130 | BKZ ($\beta = 10$) | 520 | 10.50 | 96.0 | 11 |

# Destroying Fault Invariant with Randomization
## A Countermeasure for AES Against Differential Fault Attacks

Harshal Tupsamudre, Shikha Bisht, and Debdeep Mukhopadhyay

Department of Computer Science and Engg.
IIT Kharagpur, India
{thanil, shikhab, debdeep}@cse.iitkgp.ernet.in

**Abstract.** Researchers have demonstrated the ineffectiveness of deterministic countermeasures and emphasized on the use of randomness for protecting cryptosystems against fault attacks. One such countermeasure for AES was proposed in LatinCrypt 2012, which masks the faulty output with secret values. However this countermeasure does not affect the erroneous byte in the faulty computation of the last AES round and is thus shown to be flawed in FDTC 2013. In this paper, we examine the Latin-Crypt 2012 countermeasure in detail and identify its additional flaws in order to develop a robust countermeasure. We bring out the major weakness in the infection mechanism of the LatinCrypt 2012 countermeasure which not only makes the attack of FDTC 2013 much more flexible, but also enables us to break this seemingly complex countermeasure using Piret & Quisquater's attack that requires only 8 pairs of correct and faulty ciphertexts. Finally, we combine all our observations and propose a countermeasure that employs randomness much more effectively to prevent state-of-the-art differential fault attacks against AES.

**Keywords:** Infection Countermeasure, AES, Randomness, Fault Attack.

## 1 Introduction

Ever since the demonstration of fault attacks by Dan Boneh *et.al* [1] on RSA cryptosystem, fault analysis has been extensively studied and cryptosystems such as DES and AES have been shown vulnerable to fault attacks. The purpose of fault attacks is to retrieve the secret key used in the cryptosystems. This is done by injecting a fault in a specific operation of the cipher and exploiting the erroneous result. With respect to AES, there are multiple flavors of fault attacks. While some of them exploit the relation between the faulty and fault free ciphertext [2,3,4,5], some attacks can succeed with the knowledge of faulty ciphertexts only [6]. There are attacks which require as many as 128 faults to recover the secret key [7] whereas there are also attacks which require as few as one random fault to retrieve the entire secret key of AES [8].

With so many variants of attacks introduced so far, it is now a well known fact that fault attacks are a serious threat to the cryptographic implementations

L. Batina and M. Robshaw (Eds.): CHES 2014, LNCS 8731, pp. 93–111, 2014.

and therefore, sound countermeasures are required to protect them. We focus our discussion on AES, for which many countermeasures have been suggested. These countermeasures can be broadly classified into two categories - detection and infection. The detection countermeasure is usually implemented by duplicating the computation and finally comparing the results of two computations. But in this countermeasure, the comparison step itself is prone to fault attacks. The infection countermeasure on the other hand, aims to destroy the fault invariant by diffusing the effect of a fault in such a way that it renders the faulty ciphertext unexploitable. Infection countermeasures are preferred to detection as they avoid the use of attack vulnerable operations such as comparison.

In FDTC 2012, Lomné *et.al* [9] showed that infection countermeasures which use deterministic diffusion to infect the intermediate output are not secure and emphasized on the need of randomness in these countermeasures. In LatinCrypt 2012, Gierlichs *et.al* [10] proposed an infection countermeasure for AES which infects the faulty computation with random values. Despite the use of randomness in the infection mechanism, the countermeasure for AES128 [10] was attacked by Battistello and Giraud in FDTC 2013 [11]. They observed that if a fault is injected in any byte of the last three rows of the $10^{th}$ round input, then the erroneous byte remains unaffected by the infection method and can be exploited to retrieve the corresponding key byte. This attack assumes a *constant byte fault model* to retrieve 12 bytes of AES128 key using 36 faults on average and recovers the remaining 4 key bytes corresponding to the top row using a brute-force search.

In this paper, we concern ourselves with the countermeasure proposed in [10], study its flaws in light of two different attacks and subsequently propose a modified countermeasure that prevents the differential fault attacks.

**Contribution.** The main objective of this paper is to develop an infection countermeasure for AES based upon the idea proposed by Gierlichs *et. al* [10]. For this purpose, we show that the infection method employed in the countermeasure [10] is not strong as we can remove the infection and obtain exploitable faulty ciphertext. Using this observation, we can attack the top row of the $10^{th}$ cipher round input, which makes the attack presented in [11] more flexible. Furthermore, we show that despite the presence of infection we can mount a more practical attack, i.e the Piret & Quisquater's attack [4] on this countermeasure, thus exposing its weakness against classical fault attacks. We finally present a modified algorithm that avoids all the pitfalls of the countermeasure [10] thereby thwarting state-of-the-art differential fault attacks.

**Organization.** The rest of this paper is organized as follows. Section 2 sets the background by briefly explaining the infection scheme proposed in [10], followed by the attack description [11]. In Section 3, we examine additional flaws in the scheme [10] which make the attack of [11] more flexible and finally demonstrate an efficient attack on [10]. Based on the observations in section 2 and 3, we present the modified countermeasure in section 4. Section 5 concludes the paper.

## 2   Preliminaries

In the rest of the discussion, we use the following notations:

**RoundFunction** - The round function of AES128 block cipher which operates on a 16 byte state matrix and 16 byte round key. In a *RoundFunction*, the SubByte, ShiftRow and MixColumn transformations are applied successively on the state matrix, followed by the KeyXor operation. AES128 has 10 rounds in addition to the initial Key Whitening step, which we refer to as the $0^{th}$ round.

**S** - The SubByte operation in the *RoundFunction*.

**SR** - The ShiftRow operation in the *RoundFunction*.

**MC** - The MixColumn operation in the *RoundFunction*.

**$\mathbf{I^i}$** - The 16 byte input to the $i^{th}$ round of AES128, where $i \in \{0, \ldots, 10\}$.

**K** - The 16 byte secret key used in AES128.

**$\mathbf{k^j}$** - The 16 byte matrix that represents $(j-1)^{th}$ round key, $j \in \{1, \ldots, 11\}$, derived from the main secret key $K$.

**$\beta$** - The 16 byte secret input to the dummy round.

**$\mathbf{k^0}$** - The 16 byte secret key used in the computation of dummy round.

The 16 bytes $(m_0 \ldots m_{15})$ of a matrix are arranged in $4 \times 4$ arrays and follow a column major order. We denote multiplication symbol by $\cdot$ , a bitwise logical AND operation by $\wedge$, a bitwise logical OR operation by $\vee$, a bitwise logical NOT operation by $\neg$ and a bitwise logical XOR operation by $\oplus$.

In this section, we begin by explaining the countermeasure for AES128 proposed in [10], followed by a brief description of the attack [11] mounted on it.

### 2.1   Infection Countermeasure

---

**Algorithm 1.** Infection Countermeasure [10]

---

Inputs : $P$, $k^j$ for $j \in \{1, \ldots, n\}$, $(\beta, k^0)$, $(n = 11)$ for AES128
Output : $C = \text{BlockCipher}(P, K)$

1. State $R_0 \leftarrow P$, Redundant state $R_1 \leftarrow P$, Dummy state $R_2 \leftarrow \beta$
2. $C_0 \leftarrow 0$, $C_1 \leftarrow 0$, $C_2 \leftarrow \beta$, $i \leftarrow 1$
3. while $i \leq 2n$ do
4.      $\lambda \leftarrow RandomBit()$    // $\lambda = 0$ implies a dummy round
5.      $\kappa \leftarrow (i \wedge \lambda) \oplus 2(\neg\lambda)$
6.      $\zeta \leftarrow \lambda \cdot \lceil i/2 \rceil$    // $\zeta$ is actual round counter, 0 for dummy
7.      $R_\kappa \leftarrow RoundFunction(R_\kappa, k^\zeta)$
8.      $C_\kappa \leftarrow R_\kappa \oplus C_2 \oplus \beta$    // infect $C_\kappa$ to propagate a fault
9.      $\epsilon \leftarrow \lambda(\neg(i \wedge 1)) \cdot SNLF(C_0 \oplus C_1)$    // check if $i$ is even
10.      $R_2 \leftarrow R_2 \oplus \epsilon$
11.      $R_0 \leftarrow R_0 \oplus \epsilon$
12.      $i \leftarrow i + \lambda$
13. end
14. $R_0 \leftarrow R_0 \oplus RoundFunction(R_2, k^0) \oplus \beta$
15. return($R_0$)

---

Algorithm 1 depicts the infection countermeasure proposed in [10] for AES128. At the beginning of this algorithm, plaintext $P$ is copied to both $R_0$ and $R_1$ and a secret value $\beta$ is copied to $R_2$. In this algorithm, every round of AES is executed twice. The redundant round which operates on $R_1$, occurs before the cipher round which operates on $R_0$. There are dummy rounds which occur randomly across the execution of this algorithm, in addition to one compulsory dummy round in step 14. The input to the dummy round is a secret value $\beta$ and a secret key $k^0$, which is chosen such that $RoundFunction(\beta, k^0) = \beta$. To prevent the information leakage through side channels *e.g. power analysis*, dummy SubByte, ShiftRow and MixColumn operations are added to the $0^{th}$ round and a dummy MixColumn operation is added to the $10^{th}$ round of AES128. The intermediate computation of cipher, redundant and dummy round is stored in $C_0$, $C_1$ and $C_2$ respectively. A random bit $\lambda$ decides the course of the algorithm as follows:

1. $\lambda = 0$, dummy round is executed.
2. $\lambda = 1$ and parity of $i$ is even, cipher round is executed.
3. $\lambda = 1$ and parity of $i$ is odd, redundant round is executed.

After the computation of every cipher round, the difference between $C_0$ and $C_1$ is transformed by Some Non Linear Function($SNLF$) which operates on each byte of the difference $(C_0 \oplus C_1)$. $SNLF$ maps all but zero byte to non-zero bytes and $SNLF(0) = 0$. Authors in [10] have suggested to use inversion in $GF(2^8)$ as $SNLF$. In case of fault injection in either cipher or redundant round, the difference $(C_0 \oplus C_1)$ is non-zero and the infection spreads in subsequent computations through $R_0$ and $R_2$ according to steps 9-11. Also, if the output of dummy round, $C_2$, is not $\beta$, the infection spreads in the subsequent computations through the steps 8-11. Finally in the step 14, the output of last cipher round is xored with the output of dummy round and $\beta$, and the resulting value is returned.

## 2.2   Attack on the Infection Countermeasure

In the absence of any side channel and with the countermeasure [10] in place, it seems difficult to identify whether a fault is injected in the target round by analysing the faulty ciphertext. For example, in the implementation of AES128 without countermeasure, if a fault is injected in the input of $9^{th}$ round, then the expected number of faulty ciphertext bytes which differ from the correct ciphertext is 4. In this countermeasure, the presence of compulsory dummy round ensures that the expected number of different bytes is 16 when the $9^{th}$ round computation is faulty. Moreover, the occurence of random dummy rounds makes it difficult to inject the same fault in both the branches of the computation.

Despite the strength of the countermeasure [10], authors in [11] showed how to attack it using a *constant byte fault model*. They observed that only one dummy round occurs after the $10^{th}$ cipher round of AES128, which limits the infection to only 4 bytes if the $10^{th}$ round's computation is faulty. The attack details are as follows:

Suppose a fault $f$ disturbs $I_1^{10}$, i.e. the first byte of second row in $10^{th}$ cipher round input $I^{10}$. The difference between the faulty and redundant intermediate state after the step 7 of Algorithm 1 is:

$$R_0 \oplus R_1 = \begin{pmatrix} 0 & 0 & 0 & 0 \\ 0 & 0 & 0 & \varepsilon \\ 0 & 0 & 0 & 0 \\ 0 & 0 & 0 & 0 \end{pmatrix}$$

where $\varepsilon = S[I_1^{10} \oplus f] \oplus S[I_1^{10}]$.

$R_2$ and $R_0$ are infected in steps 10 and 11. After the infection steps, we obtain:

$$R_0 \oplus R_1 = \begin{pmatrix} 0 & 0 & 0 & 0 \\ 0 & 0 & 0 & \varepsilon \oplus SNLF[\varepsilon] \\ 0 & 0 & 0 & 0 \\ 0 & 0 & 0 & 0 \end{pmatrix}$$

Finally, in the step 14, dummy round operates on infected $R_2$ which further infects $R_0$. But, the ShiftRow operation of dummy round shifts the infection to column 3 and leaves the faulty byte of $R_0$ in column 4 unmasked. The output of compulsory dummy round differs from $\beta$ in column 3 and therefore, the final difference between the correct ciphertext $C$ and faulty ciphertext $C^*$ is:

$$\therefore C \oplus C^* = \begin{pmatrix} 0 & 0 & \beta_8' \oplus \beta_8 & 0 \\ 0 & 0 & \beta_9' \oplus \beta_9 & \varepsilon \oplus SNLF[\varepsilon] \\ 0 & 0 & \beta_{10}' \oplus \beta_{10} & 0 \\ 0 & 0 & \beta_{11}' \oplus \beta_{11} & 0 \end{pmatrix} \tag{1}$$

where $\beta_8'$, $\beta_9'$, $\beta_{10}'$, $\beta_{11}'$ are the infected bytes of the compulsory dummy round output. Since the byte $C_{13}^*$ is unaffected by the infected output of dummy round, it is exploited to retrieve the byte $k_{13}^{11}$ of the $10^{th}$ round key using two more pairs of faulty and correct ciphertexts. Similarly, the remaining 11 key bytes corresponding to last three rows of $k^{11}$ can be retrieved. For details on attack procedure, the reader is referred to [11].

If a fault is injected in any byte of the last three rows of $I^{10}$, the resulting erroneous byte is left unmasked and hence is exploited in the attack. However, if a fault is injected in any byte of the top row, the erroneous byte is masked by the infected output of compulsory dummy round. *This attack does not target the remaining 4 key bytes that correspond to the top row and they are computed using a brute force search.*

*Observation 1:* Ideally, the countermeasure should infect the entire result if a fault is injected in any of the rounds. But Algorithm 1 fails to protect the last round and it is exploited in the attack. Moreover, in this algorithm, the last cipher round is always the penultimate round. Thus, using a side channel, one can always observe a posteriori whether a fault was injected in the last but one round.

In the next section, we present additional flaws in the countermeasure [10] which were considered while developing the countermeasure presented in section4.

# 3   Further Loop Holes in the Countermeasure: Attacking the Infection Technique

It might seem that if the output of compulsory dummy round infects the erroneous byte of $10^{th}$ round's output, then the attack [11] can be thwarted. However, in this section, we demonstrate that the infection caused by compulsory dummy round is ineffective and can be removed.

## 3.1   Infection Caused by Compulsory Dummy Round

In Algorithm 1, since the input as well as the output of dummy round is $\beta$, *i.e.* $RoundFunction(\beta, k^0) = \beta$, we can write:

$$MC(SR(S(\beta))) \oplus k^0 = \beta$$

Using this relation, the xor of $RoundFunction(R_2, k^0)$ and $\beta$ in step 14 of Algorithm 1 can now be expressed as:

$$\begin{aligned} RoundFunction(R_2, k^0) \oplus \beta &= MC(SR(S(R_2))) \oplus k^0 \oplus MC(SR(S(\beta))) \oplus k^0 \\ &= MC(SR(S(R_2))) \oplus MC(SR(S(\beta))) \end{aligned}$$

Since SubByte operation is the only non-linear operation in the above equation,

$$\therefore RoundFunction(R_2, k^0) \oplus \beta = MC(SR(S(R_2) \oplus S(\beta))) \qquad (2)$$

If $R_2 = \beta$ then the execution of compulsory dummy round in step 14 has no effect on the final output $R_0$, but if $R_2 \neq \beta$ then the output of compulsory dummy round infects the final output $R_0$. However, this infection can be removed using the above derived equation and the desired faulty ciphertext can be recovered. On the basis of equation (2), the xor of correct ciphertext $C$ and faulty ciphertext $C^*$ in equation (1) can now be expressed as:

$$C \oplus C^* = \begin{pmatrix} 0 & 0 & 3 \cdot x & 0 \\ 0 & 0 & 2 \cdot x & \varepsilon \oplus SNLF[\varepsilon] \\ 0 & 0 & 1 \cdot x & 0 \\ 0 & 0 & 1 \cdot x & 0 \end{pmatrix}$$

where $x = S[\beta_{13} \oplus SNLF[\varepsilon]] \oplus S[\beta_{13}]$ (for details refer Appendix A). Ideally, every byte of $C^*$ should be infected with an independent random value but here the compulsory dummy round in Algorithm 1 infects only column 3 of $C^*$ and that too, with interrelated values and leaves the rest of the bytes unmasked.

In the following discussion, we show the significance of this result, by attacking the top row of $I^{10}$, which was not shown in [11]. Subsequently, we show that the infection can be removed even if the fault is injected in the input of the $9^{th}$ cipher round. We prove this by mounting the classical Piret & Quisquater's attack [4] on the countermeasure [10].

## 3.2   Attacking the Top Row

We now demonstrate the attack on the top row of $I^{10}$ to retrieve the remaining 4 bytes of $k^{10}$.

Suppose a fault $f$ disturbs $I_0^{10}$ i.e. the first byte of $10^{th}$ cipher round input $I^{10}$. The difference between the faulty and redundant intermediate state after the step 7 of Algorithm 1 is:

$$R_0 \oplus R_1 = \begin{pmatrix} \varepsilon & 0 & 0 & 0 \\ 0 & 0 & 0 & 0 \\ 0 & 0 & 0 & 0 \\ 0 & 0 & 0 & 0 \end{pmatrix}$$

where $\varepsilon = S[I_0^{10} \oplus f] \oplus S[I_0^{10}]$.
$R_2$ and $R_0$ are infected in steps 10 and 11. After the infection steps, we obtain:

$$R_0 \oplus R_1 = \begin{pmatrix} \varepsilon \oplus SNLF[\varepsilon] & 0 & 0 & 0 \\ 0 & 0 & 0 & 0 \\ 0 & 0 & 0 & 0 \\ 0 & 0 & 0 & 0 \end{pmatrix}$$

Finally, in the step 14, dummy round operates on infected $R_2$ which further infects $R_0$. In this case, the ShiftRow operation of dummy round does not shift the infection and the erroneous byte of $R_0$ in column 1 is masked. The final difference between the correct ciphertext $C$ and faulty ciphertext $C^*$ is:

$$\therefore C \oplus C^* = \begin{pmatrix} \varepsilon \oplus SNLF[\varepsilon] \oplus \beta_0' \oplus \beta_0 & 0 & 0 & 0 \\ \beta_1' \oplus \beta_1 & 0 & 0 & 0 \\ \beta_2' \oplus \beta_2 & 0 & 0 & 0 \\ \beta_3' \oplus \beta_3 & 0 & 0 & 0 \end{pmatrix} \quad (3)$$

where $\beta_0', \beta_1', \beta_2', \beta_3'$ are the infected bytes of the compulsory dummy round output. and $\varepsilon = S[I_0^{10} \oplus f] \oplus S[I_0^{10}]$. Here, we cannot use the attack technique described in [11] directly, because the erroneous byte of $10^{th}$ cipher round has also been infected with the output of compulsory dummy round in step 14. *This is different from the case when fault is injected in any of the last three rows of $10^{th}$ cipher round input.* In order to carry out the attack [11], we need to remove the infection caused by the dummy round.
Now, we can use equation (2) to write the above matrix as:

$$C \oplus C^* = \begin{pmatrix} \varepsilon \oplus SNLF[\varepsilon] \oplus 2 \cdot y & 0 & 0 & 0 \\ 1 \cdot y & 0 & 0 & 0 \\ 1 \cdot y & 0 & 0 & 0 \\ 3 \cdot y & 0 & 0 & 0 \end{pmatrix} \quad (4)$$

where $y = S[\beta_0 \oplus SNLF[\varepsilon]] \oplus S[\beta_0]$ ( for details refer Appendix B). We can use the value of $1 \cdot y$ from $C \oplus C^*$ to remove the infection from $C^*$ and therefore unmask the erroneous byte. As a consequence, we can perform the attack suggested in

[11] to get the key byte $k_0^{11}$. *By attacking the top row, now the attacker has the flexibility to mount the attack on any of the 12 bytes of $10^{th}$ cipher round instead of always targeting the last three rows.*

*Observation 2:* It is quite evident from this attack that the infection mechanism used in the countermeasure [10] is not effective. The purpose of this infection countermeasure is defeated as we can easily remove the infection and recover the desired faulty ciphertext. This is a major flaw in this countermeasure as it makes even the $9^{th}$ round susceptible to the fault attack which we will illustrate in the following discussion.

### 3.3 Piret & Quisquater's Attack on the Countermeasure

The presence of compulsory dummy round in the countermeasure [10] ensures that a fault in the $9^{th}$ cipher round input of AES128 infects all 16 bytes in the output. Even though the countermeasure infects all the bytes of the resulting ciphertext, we show that we can again remove the infection caused by compulsory dummy round using equation (2) and obtain the desired faulty ciphertext. To mount this attack, we consider the following two facts:

1. The authors of [10] have mentioned that an attacker can affect the *RandomBit* function in the Algorithm 1, so that the random dummy round never occurs. To counteract this effect, they added a compulsory dummy round at the end of the algorithm which ensures that the faulty ciphertext is infected in such a way that no information is available to the attacker.
2. Also, because of performance issues, Algorithm 1 should terminate within a reasonable amount of time and hence, the number of random dummy rounds should be limited to a certain value.

First, we show that if random dummy rounds never occur in the while loop, then despite the presence of compulsory dummy round in step 14, we can mount the Piret & Quisquater's attack [4] on this countermeasure and *recover the entire key using only 8 faulty ciphertexts.* Subsequently, we show that even if the random dummy rounds occur, we can still mount this attack [4].

**Attack in the Absence of Random Dummy Rounds.** Consider the scenario where the attacker influences the *RandomBit* function so that no dummy round occurs except the compulsory dummy round in step 14. We observe that if a fault is injected in the $9^{th}$ cipher round, then the rest of the computation is infected thrice. Once, after the $9^{th}$ cipher round in step 11, then after the $10^{th}$ cipher round in step 11 and finally after the execution of compulsory dummy round in step 14. To be able to mount Piret & Quisquater's attack [4], we first analyze the faulty ciphertext and identify whether a fault was injected in the input of $9^{th}$ cipher round. After identifying such faulty ciphertexts, we remove the infection caused by the output of compulsory dummy round and $10^{th}$ cipher round. Once the infection is removed, we can proceed with the attack described in [4].

The attack procedure can be summarized as follows:

1. Suppose a random fault $f$ is injected in the first byte of the $9^{th}$ cipher round input. Before the execution of step 14, the output of faulty computation differs from the output of correct computation in 4 positions $viz.$ 0, 13, 10 and 7 which comprises a diagonal. But the execution of compulsory dummy round in step 14 infects all the 16 bytes of the faulty computation. Therefore, the resulting faulty ciphertext $T^*$ differs from the correct ciphertext $T$ in 16 bytes. We use equation (2) to represent this difference as:

$$T \oplus T^* = \begin{pmatrix} m_0 \oplus 2F_1 \oplus 1F_2 & 1F_3 & 3F_4 \oplus 1F_5 \oplus 1F_6 & 3F_7 \\ 1F_1 \oplus 3F_2 & 1F_3 & 2F_4 \oplus 3F_5 \oplus 1F_6 & m_1 \oplus 2F_7 \\ 1F_1 \oplus 2F_2 & 3F_3 & m_2 \oplus 1F_4 \oplus 2F_5 \oplus 3F_6 & 1F_7 \\ 3F_1 \oplus 1F_2 & m_3 \oplus 2F_3 & 1F_4 \oplus 1F_5 \oplus 2F_6 & 1F_7 \end{pmatrix}$$
$$(5)$$

where $F_i$, $i \in \{1, \ldots, 7\}$, represents the infection caused by the compulsory dummy round in step 14 and $m_j$, $j \in \{0,1,2,3\}$, represents the difference between the correct and faulty computation before the execution of step 14 in Algorithm 1 (for more details refer Appendix C). Now, we can deduce the values of $F_1$ and $F_2$ from column 1, $F_3$ from column 2, $F_4$, $F_5$ and $F_6$ from column 3 and $F_7$ from column 4 and thus remove the infection caused by the compulsory dummy round from $T^*$.

2. After removing the infection caused by compulsory dummy round, we get:

$$T \oplus T^* = \begin{pmatrix} m_0 & 0 & 0 & 0 \\ 0 & 0 & 0 & m_1 \\ 0 & 0 & m_2 & 0 \\ 0 & m_3 & 0 & 0 \end{pmatrix}$$

We can now remove the infection caused by the $10^{th}$ cipher round. Each $m_j$ can be written as $z_j \oplus SNLF[z_j]$, $j \in \{0,1,2,3\}$, where $SNLF[z_j]$ represents the infection caused in step 11 of Algorithm 1, after the execution of $10^{th}$ cipher round and $z_j$ represents the difference between the outputs of correct and faulty computations before step 11 (for more details refer Appendix C). If $SNLF$ is implemented as inversion in $GF(2^8)$, we get two solutions of $z_j$ for every $m_j$. Since the 4 equations represented by $m_j$ are independent, we obtain $2^4$ solutions for $T \oplus T^*$. Here, $T$ is known, therefore we have $2^4$ solutions for $T^*$ as well.

3. After removing the infection caused by $10^{th}$ cipher round, the attacker makes hypotheses on 4 bytes of the $10^{th}$ round key $k^{11}$ and uses the faulty and correct output of $9^{th}$ cipher round to verify the following relations:

$$2 \cdot f' \oplus SNLF[2 \cdot f'] = S^{-1}[T_0 \oplus k_0^{11}] \oplus S^{-1}[T_0^* \oplus k_0^{11}]$$
$$1 \cdot f' \oplus SNLF[1 \cdot f'] = S^{-1}[T_{13} \oplus k_{13}^{11}] \oplus S^{-1}[T_{13}^* \oplus k_{13}^{11}]$$
$$1 \cdot f' \oplus SNLF[1 \cdot f'] = S^{-1}[T_{10} \oplus k_{10}^{11}] \oplus S^{-1}[T_{10}^* \oplus k_{10}^{11}]$$
$$3 \cdot f' \oplus SNLF[3 \cdot f'] = S^{-1}[T_7 \oplus k_7^{11}] \oplus S^{-1}[T_7^* \oplus k_7^{11}]$$

where $SNLF[b \cdot f']$, $b \in \{1, 2, 3\}$ is the infection caused in step 11, after the execution of $9^{th}$ cipher round. The above set of equations is solved for all $2^4$ possible values of $T^*$ (for the complexity analysis of the attack, refer Appendix D).

**Identifying Desired Faulty Ciphertexts.** As done in [4], we call a ciphertext resulting from a fault injected in the input of $9^{th}$ round as desired faulty ciphertext, otherwise we call it undesired. It is not difficult to identify whether the given faulty ciphertext is desired or not. With the countermeasure [10] in place, if a fault affects a byte of column $i$ in the $9^{th}$ round input, where $i \in \{0,1,2,3\}$, we observed that the following relations hold in the xor of faulty and correct ciphertext:

$$
\begin{aligned}
(T \oplus T^*)_{(4 \cdot (i+1))\%16} &= (T \oplus T^*)_{(4 \cdot (i+1))\%16+1} \\
(T \oplus T^*)_{(4 \cdot (i+1))\%16+2} &= 3 \cdot (T \oplus T^*)_{(4 \cdot (i+1))\%16} \\
(T \oplus T^*)_{(4 \cdot (i+3))\%16+2} &= (T \oplus T^*)_{(4 \cdot (i+3))\%16+3} \\
(T \oplus T^*)_{(4 \cdot (i+3))\%16} &= 3 \cdot (T \oplus T^*)_{(4 \cdot (i+3))\%16+2}
\end{aligned}
\tag{6}
$$

where $(T \oplus T^*)_j$ represents the $j^{th}$ byte in matrix $T \oplus T^*$. One can see from equation (5), that the above relation arises because the compulsory dummy round uses the same value to mask more than one byte of the faulty computation.

**Attack Considering Random Dummy Rounds.** In the attack explained above, we assumed that the attacker influences the $RandomBit$ function in the countermeasure [10] so that the dummy rounds do not occur in the while loop. Now, we consider the case where the number of random dummy rounds occuring in every execution of Algorithm 1 is exactly $d^1$. Since $\lambda = 0$ corresponds to a dummy round and $\lambda = 1$ corresponds to an AES round, we can view the computation of Algorithm 1 as if decided by a binary string of length $(22 + d)$, where $(22 + d)^{th}$ $RoundFunction$ is always the $10^{th}$ cipher round. We choose to inject the fault in $(22 + d - 2)^{th}$ round as it can be a $9^{th}$ cipher or a $10^{th}$ redundant or a dummy round. This increases the probability of injecting the fault in $9^{th}$ cipher round.

Assuming that every string of length $(22 + d)$, consisting of exactly 22 1's and $d$ 0's, is equally likely, then the probability that $(22 + d - 2)^{th}$ $RoundFunction$ is a $9^{th}$ cipher round is the same as that of a binary string of length $(22 + d)$ that ends in '111'. Since the while loop in Algorithm 1 always terminates with the execution of $10^{th}$ cipher round, the binary string always ends with a 1. Therefore this probability is: $\frac{(19+d)!/((19)! \cdot (d)!)}{(21+d)!/((21)! \cdot (d)!)}$ (refer Appendix E). If $d = 20$ then the probability that $40^{th}$ $RoundFunction$ is a $9^{th}$ cipher round is nearly 0.26.

**Simulation Results.** We carried out Piret & Quisquater's attack [4] on Algorithm 1 using a random byte fault model with no control over fault local-

---

[1] If the value of $d$ varies across different executions, one can still compute a mean value of $d$ by observing the number of $RoundFunctions$ through a side channel.

ization. We implemented the Algorithm 1 in C and used the GNU Scientific Library(GSL) for *RandomBit* function. The simulation details are as follows:

1. The value of $d$ is kept constant and 1000 tests are performed.
2. Each test executes Algorithm 1 until 8 desired faulty ciphertexts are obtained. However, as the target $(22 + d - 2)^{th}$ *RoundFunction* can also be a dummy or $10^{th}$ redundant round, the undesired faulty ciphertexts obtained in such cases are discarded. The equation set (6) can be used to distinguish between desired and undesired faulty ciphertexts.
3. An average of the faulty encryptions over 1000 tests is taken, where number of faulty encryptions in a test = (8 desired faulty ciphertext + undesired faulty ciphertexts).
4. Subsequently, the value of $d$ is incremented by 5 and the above procedure is repeated.

The probability that the targeted *RoundFunction* is a $9^{th}$ cipher round decreases with higher values of $d$ but it still remains non-negligible. In other words, higher the value of $d$, more is the number of faulty encryptions required in a test as evident from Fig.1.

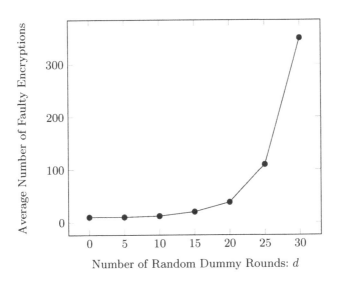

**Fig. 1.** Piret & Quisquater's Attack on Algorithm 1

*Observation 3:* The feasibility of Piret and Quisquater's attack shows that the infection method employed in the countermeasure [10] fails to protect against classical fault attacks.

## 4    Improved Countermeasure

In this section, we propose an improved countermeasure based upon the principles used in the Algorithm 1. The *observations* enumerated in this paper were used as a guideline for developing this countermeasure. As evident from the attacks explained earlier, the infection countermeasure for protecting AES against the differential fault attacks should have the following properties:

1. If a fault is injected in any of the cipher, redundant or dummy round, all bytes in the resulting ciphertext should be infected.
2. As shown in Section 3 of this paper, merely infecting all bytes in the output is not sufficient. Therefore, the infection technique should result in such a faulty ciphertext that any attempts to make hypothesis on the secret key used in AES are completely nullified.
3. The countermeasure itself should not leak any information related to the *RoundFunction* computations which can be exploited through a side channel.

Given below is an algorithm, which is designed to possess all the aforementioned properties. It uses cipher, redundant and dummy rounds along the lines of Algorithm 1 but exhibits a rather robust behaviour against fault attacks.

---

**Algorithm 2.** Improved Countermeasure

---

Inputs : $P$, $k^j$ for $j \in \{1, \dots, n\}$, $(\beta, k^0)$, $(n = 11)$ for AES128
Output : $C = BlockCipher(P, K)$

1. State $R_0 \leftarrow P$, Redundant state $R_1 \leftarrow P$, Dummy state $R_2 \leftarrow \beta$
2. $i \leftarrow 1$, $q \leftarrow 1$
3. $rstr \leftarrow \{0,1\}^t$      $// \#1(rstr) = 2n, \#0(rstr) = t - 2n$
4. while $q \le t$ do
5.        $\lambda \leftarrow rstr[q]$      $// \lambda = 0$ implies a dummy round
6.        $\kappa \leftarrow (i \wedge \lambda) \oplus 2(\neg\lambda)$
7.        $\zeta \leftarrow \lambda \cdot \lceil i/2 \rceil$      $// \zeta$ is actual round counter, 0 for dummy
8.        $R_\kappa \leftarrow RoundFunction(R_\kappa, k^\zeta)$
9.        $\gamma \leftarrow \lambda(\neg(i \wedge 1)) \cdot BLFN(R_0 \oplus R_1)$      $//$ check if $i$ is even
10.       $\delta \leftarrow (\neg\lambda) \cdot BLFN(R_2 \oplus \beta)$
11.       $R_0 \leftarrow (\neg(\gamma \vee \delta) \cdot R_0) \oplus ((\gamma \vee \delta) \cdot R_2)$
12.       $i \leftarrow i + \lambda$
13.       $q \leftarrow q + 1$
14. end
15. return($R_0$)

---

Following additional notations are used in this algorithm:

1. **rstr**: A '$t$' bit random binary string, consisting of $(2n)$ 1's corresponding to AES rounds and $(t - 2n)$ 0's corresponding to dummy rounds.
2. **BLFN**: A boolean function that maps a 128 bit value to a 1 bit value. Specifically, $BLFN(0) = 0$ and for nonzero input $BLFN$ evaluates to 1.
3. **$\gamma$**: A one bit comparison variable to detect fault injection in AES round.
4. **$\delta$**: A one bit comparison variable to identify a fault injection in dummy round.

Apart from these elements, Algorithm 2 exhibits the following features which makes it stronger than Algorithm 1:

1. In Algorithm 2, matrix $R_2$ represents the state of the dummy round and is initialized to a random value $\beta$. This state matrix $R_2$ bears no relation with any of the intermediate states or the round keys of AES. When a fault is induced in any of the rounds, Algorithm 2 outputs a matrix $R_2$. For fault analysis to succeed, the faulty output should contain some information about the key used in the cipher. However, the new countermeasure outputs matrix $R_2$ which is completely random and does not have any information about the key used in the AES, which makes the differential fault analysis impossible. Since in the case of fault injection, Algorithm 2 outputs dummy state $R_2$, the pair $(\beta, k^0)$ should be refreshed in every execution[2].
2. In Algorithm 2, more than one dummy round can occur after the execution of last cipher round and consequently the $10^{th}$ cipher round is not always the penultimate round.
3. Since the number of dummy rounds in Algorithm 2 is kept constant, the leakage of timing information through a side channel is also prevented.

For a clear illustration, Table 1 shows the functioning of Algorithm 2. If any of the

**Table 1.** Computation of Algorithm 2

| Step | Redundant Round | Cipher Round | Dummy Round |
|---|---|---|---|
| 5. | $\lambda = 1$, $i$ is odd | $\lambda = 1$, $i$ is even | $\lambda = 0$ |
| 6. | $\kappa \leftarrow 1$ | $\kappa \leftarrow 0$ | $\kappa \leftarrow 2$ |
| 7. | $\zeta \leftarrow \lceil i/2 \rceil$ | $\zeta \leftarrow \lceil i/2 \rceil$ | $\zeta \leftarrow 0$ |
| 8. | $R_1 \leftarrow RoundFunction(R_1, k^\zeta)$ | $R_0 \leftarrow RoundFunction(R_0, k^\zeta)$ | $R_2 \leftarrow RoundFunction(R_2, k^0)$ |
| 9. | $\gamma \leftarrow 0$ | $\gamma \leftarrow BLFN(R_0 \oplus R_1)$ | $\gamma \leftarrow 0$ |
| 10. | $\delta \leftarrow 0$ | $\delta \leftarrow 0$ | $\delta \leftarrow BLFN(R_2 \oplus \beta)$ |
| 11. | $R_0 \leftarrow R_0$ | $R_0 \leftarrow (\neg(\gamma) \cdot R_0) \oplus ((\gamma) \cdot R_2)$ | $R_0 \leftarrow (\neg(\delta) \cdot R_0) \oplus ((\delta) \cdot R_2)$ |
| 12. | $i \leftarrow i + 1$ | $i \leftarrow i + 1$ | $i \leftarrow i + 0$ |
| 13. | $q \leftarrow q + 1$ | $q \leftarrow q + 1$ | $q \leftarrow q + 1$ |

cipher or redundant round is disturbed, then during the computation of cipher round, $(R_0 \oplus R_1)$ is non-zero and BLFN$(R_0 \oplus R_1)$ updates the value of $\gamma$ to 1. As a result, $R_0$ is replaced by $R_2$ in step 11. Similarly, if the computation of dummy round is faulty, $(R_2 \oplus \beta)$ is non-zero and $\delta$ evaluates to 1. In this case too, $R_0$ is replaced by $R_2$. Also, if the state of comparison variables $\gamma$ and $\delta$ is 1 at the same time, then in step 11, $R_0$ is substituted by $R_2$ as this condition indicates fault in comparison variables themselves. In case of undisturbed execution, Algorithm 2 generates a correct ciphertext. Refer Appendix F for more details.

## 5    Conclusion

Recent works [6], [9] suggest the use of randomness to build sound countermeasures for protecting AES against the fault attacks. The infection countermeasure

---

[2] One should note that even a new pair of $(\beta, k^0)$ cannot protect Algorithm 1 against the attacks described in this paper.

in [10] introduces the element of randomness through the use of dummy round but is still ineffective against fault attacks which target the last and penultimate round. This is because the infection uses the same unknown value to mask the erroneous byte as well as the non-erroneous bytes. One can easily deduce the value of this unknown mask from the xor of correct and faulty output. Also in the case of erroneous computation of $10^{th}$ cipher round, the infection doesn't affect every byte in the faulty output. However, the modified countermeasure presented in this paper affects every erroneous as well as non-erroneous byte with independent random values irrespective of the round in which the fault is injected. Since these random values bear no relation with the intermediate output or the secret key, analysis of the resulting faulty ciphertext is a futile exercise for the attacker.

# References

1. Boneh, D., DeMillo, R.A., Lipton, R.J.: On the Importance of Checking Cryptographic Protocols for Faults. In: Fumy, W. (ed.) EUROCRYPT 1997. LNCS, vol. 1233, pp. 37–51. Springer, Heidelberg (1997)
2. Biham, E., Shamir, A.: Differential Fault Analysis of Secret Key Cryptosystems. In: Kaliski Jr., B.S. (ed.) CRYPTO 1997. LNCS, vol. 1294, pp. 513–525. Springer, Heidelberg (1997)
3. Giraud, C.: DFA on AES. In: Dobbertin, H., Rijmen, V., Sowa, A. (eds.) AES 2005. LNCS, vol. 3373, pp. 27–41. Springer, Heidelberg (2005)
4. Piret, G., Quisquater, J.-J.: A Differential Fault Attack Technique against SPN Structures, with Application to the AES and KHAZAD. In: Walter, C.D., Koç, Ç.K., Paar, C. (eds.) CHES 2003. LNCS, vol. 2779, pp. 77–88. Springer, Heidelberg (2003)
5. Mukhopadhyay, D.: An Improved Fault Based Attack of the Advanced Encryption Standard. In: Preneel, B. (ed.) AFRICACRYPT 2009. LNCS, vol. 5580, pp. 421–434. Springer, Heidelberg (2009)
6. Fuhr, T., Jaulmes, É., Lomné, V., Thillard, A.: Fault Attacks on AES with Faulty Ciphertexts Only. In: Fischer, W., Schmidt, J.-M. (eds.) Fault Diagnosis and Tolerance in Cryptography, FDTC 2013, pp. 108–118. IEEE Computer Society (2013)
7. Blömer, J., Seifert, J.-P.: Fault Based Cryptanalysis of the Advanced Encryption Standard (AES). In: Wright, R.N. (ed.) FC 2003. LNCS, vol. 2742, pp. 162–181. Springer, Heidelberg (2003)
8. Tunstall, M., Mukhopadhyay, D., Ali, S.: Differential Fault Analysis of the Advanced Encryption Standard Using a Single Fault. In: Ardagna, C.A., Zhou, J. (eds.) WISTP 2011. LNCS, vol. 6633, pp. 224–233. Springer, Heidelberg (2011)
9. Lomné, V., Roche, T., Thillard, A.: On the Need of Randomness in Fault Attack Countermeasures - Application to AES. In: Bertoni, G., Gierlichs, B. (eds.) Fault Diagnosis and Tolerance in Cryptography, FDTC 2012, pp. 85–94. IEEE Computer Society (2012)
10. Gierlichs, B., Schmidt, J.-M., Tunstall, M.: Infective Computation and Dummy Rounds: Fault Protection for Block Ciphers without Check-before-Output. In: Hevia, A., Neven, G. (eds.) LatinCrypt 2012. LNCS, vol. 7533, pp. 305–321. Springer, Heidelberg (2012)

11. Battistello, A., Giraud, C.: Fault Analysis of Infective AES Computations. In: Fischer, W., Schmidt, J.-M. (eds.) Fault Diagnosis and Tolerance in Cryptography, FDTC 2013, pp. 101–107. IEEE Computer Society (2013)

# A  Execution of Infected Compulsory Dummy Round: First Attack

After the execution of $10^{th}$ cipher round, a fault $f$ in $I_1^{10}$ infects the byte $\beta_{13}$ of $R_2$ in the step 10 of Algorithm 1:

$$R_2 = R_2 \oplus \epsilon = \begin{pmatrix} \beta_0 & \beta_4 & \beta_8 & \beta_{12} \\ \beta_1 & \beta_5 & \beta_9 & \beta_{13} \oplus SNLF[\varepsilon] \\ \beta_2 & \beta_6 & \beta_{10} & \beta_{14} \\ \beta_3 & \beta_7 & \beta_{11} & \beta_{15} \end{pmatrix}$$

where $\varepsilon = S[I_1^{10}] \oplus S[I_1^{10} \oplus f]$. Thus, the input $R_2$ of compulsory dummy round is infected. Execution of compulsory dummy round in step 14 on the infected $R_2$ is shown below.

After the ShiftRow and SubByte operation:

$$R_2 = \begin{pmatrix} S[\beta_0] & S[\beta_4] & S[\beta_8] & S[\beta_{12}] \\ S[\beta_5] & S[\beta_9] & S[\beta_{13} \oplus SNLF[\varepsilon]] & S[\beta_1] \\ S[\beta_{10}] & S[\beta_{14}] & S[\beta_2] & S[\beta_6] \\ S[\beta_{15}] & S[\beta_3] & S[\beta_7] & S[\beta_{11}] \end{pmatrix}$$

For clarity purpose, the output of MixColumn and KeyXor operations of only $3^{rd}$ column is shown:

$$\beta_8' = 2 \cdot S[\beta_8] \oplus 3 \cdot S[\beta_{13} \oplus SNLF[\varepsilon]] \oplus 1 \cdot S[\beta_2] \oplus 1 \cdot S[\beta_7] \oplus k_8^0$$
$$\beta_9' = 1 \cdot S[\beta_8] \oplus 2 \cdot S[\beta_{13} \oplus SNLF[\varepsilon]] \oplus 3 \cdot S[\beta_2] \oplus 1 \cdot S[\beta_7] \oplus k_9^0$$
$$\beta_{10}' = 1 \cdot S[\beta_8] \oplus 1 \cdot S[\beta_{13} \oplus SNLF[\varepsilon]] \oplus 2 \cdot S[\beta_2] \oplus 3 \cdot S[\beta_7] \oplus k_{10}^0$$
$$\beta_{11}' = 3 \cdot S[\beta_8] \oplus 1 \cdot S[\beta_{13} \oplus SNLF[\varepsilon]] \oplus 1 \cdot S[\beta_2] \oplus 2 \cdot S[\beta_7] \oplus k_{11}^0$$

Since $RoundFunction(\beta, k^0) = \beta$, we can write the $3^{rd}$ column of $\beta$ as:

$$\beta_8 = 2 \cdot S[\beta_8] \oplus 3 \cdot S[\beta_{13}] \oplus 1 \cdot S[\beta_2] \oplus 1 \cdot S[\beta_7] \oplus k_8^0$$
$$\beta_9 = 1 \cdot S[\beta_8] \oplus 2 \cdot S[\beta_{13}] \oplus 3 \cdot S[\beta_2] \oplus 1 \cdot S[\beta_7] \oplus k_9^0$$
$$\beta_{10} = 1 \cdot S[\beta_8] \oplus 1 \cdot S[\beta_{13}] \oplus 2 \cdot S[\beta_2] \oplus 3 \cdot S[\beta_7] \oplus k_{10}^0$$
$$\beta_{11} = 3 \cdot S[\beta_8] \oplus 1 \cdot S[\beta_{13}] \oplus 1 \cdot S[\beta_2] \oplus 2 \cdot S[\beta_7] \oplus k_{11}^0$$

The remaining columns in $\beta$ and in the output of dummy round are same. In step 14, the result of compulsory dummy round is xored with $\beta$.

$$\therefore RoundFunction(R_2, k^0) \oplus \beta = \begin{pmatrix} 0 & 0 & 3 \cdot S[\beta_{13} \oplus SNLF[\varepsilon]] \oplus 3 \cdot S[\beta_{13}] & 0 \\ 0 & 0 & 2 \cdot S[\beta_{13} \oplus SNLF[\varepsilon]] \oplus 2 \cdot S[\beta_{13}] & 0 \\ 0 & 0 & 1 \cdot S[\beta_{13} \oplus SNLF[\varepsilon]] \oplus 1 \cdot S[\beta_{13}] & 0 \\ 0 & 0 & 1 \cdot S[\beta_{13} \oplus SNLF[\varepsilon]] \oplus 1 \cdot S[\beta_{13}] & 0 \end{pmatrix}$$

## B  Execution of Infected Compulsory Dummy Round: Top Row Attack

After the execution of $10^{th}$ cipher round, a fault $f$ in $I_0^{10}$ infects the byte $\beta_0$ of $R_2$ in the step 10 of Algorithm 1:

$$R_2 = R_2 \oplus \epsilon = \begin{pmatrix} \beta_0 \oplus SNLF[\varepsilon] & \beta_4 & \beta_8 & \beta_{12} \\ \beta_1 & \beta_5 & \beta_9 & \beta_{13} \\ \beta_2 & \beta_6 & \beta_{10} & \beta_{14} \\ \beta_3 & \beta_7 & \beta_{11} & \beta_{15} \end{pmatrix}$$

where $\varepsilon = S[I_0^{10}] \oplus S[I_0^{10} \oplus f]$. Thus, the input $R_2$ of compulsory dummy round is infected. Execution of compulsory dummy round in step 14 on the infected $R_2$ is shown below.

After the ShiftRow and SubByte operation:

$$R_2 = \begin{pmatrix} S[\beta_0] \oplus SNLF[\varepsilon] & S[\beta_4] & S[\beta_8] & S[\beta_{12}] \\ S[\beta_5] & S[\beta_9] & S[\beta_{13}] & S[\beta_1] \\ S[\beta_{10}] & S[\beta_{14}] & S[\beta_2] & S[\beta_6] \\ S[\beta_{15}] & S[\beta_3] & S[\beta_7] & S[\beta_{11}] \end{pmatrix}$$

For clarity purpose, the output of MixColumn and KeyXor operations of only $3^{rd}$ column is shown:

$$\beta_0' = 2 \cdot S[\beta_0 \oplus SNLF[\varepsilon]] \oplus 3 \cdot S[\beta_5] \oplus 1 \cdot S[\beta_{10}] \oplus 1 \cdot S[\beta_{15}] \oplus k_0^0$$
$$\beta_1' = 1 \cdot S[\beta_0 \oplus SNLF[\varepsilon]] \oplus 2 \cdot S[\beta_5] \oplus 3 \cdot S[\beta_{10}] \oplus 1 \cdot S[\beta_{15}] \oplus k_1^0$$
$$\beta_2' = 1 \cdot S[\beta_0 \oplus SNLF[\varepsilon]] \oplus 1 \cdot S[\beta_5] \oplus 2 \cdot S[\beta_{10}] \oplus 3 \cdot S[\beta_{15}] \oplus k_2^0$$
$$\beta_3' = 3 \cdot S[\beta_0 \oplus SNLF[\varepsilon]] \oplus 1 \cdot S[\beta_5] \oplus 1 \cdot S[\beta_{10}] \oplus 2 \cdot S[\beta_{15}] \oplus k_3^0$$

Since $RoundFunction(\beta, k^0) = \beta$, we can write the $1^{st}$ column of $\beta$ as:

$$\beta_0' = 2 \cdot S[\beta_0] \oplus 3 \cdot S[\beta_5] \oplus 1 \cdot S[\beta_{10}] \oplus 1 \cdot S[\beta_{15}] \oplus k_0^0$$
$$\beta_1' = 1 \cdot S[\beta_0] \oplus 2 \cdot S[\beta_5] \oplus 3 \cdot S[\beta_{10}] \oplus 1 \cdot S[\beta_{15}] \oplus k_1^0$$
$$\beta_2' = 1 \cdot S[\beta_0] \oplus 1 \cdot S[\beta_5] \oplus 2 \cdot S[\beta_{10}] \oplus 3 \cdot S[\beta_{15}] \oplus k_2^0$$
$$\beta_3' = 3 * S[\beta_0] \oplus 1 \cdot S[\beta_5] \oplus 1 \cdot S[\beta_{10}] \oplus 2 \cdot S[\beta_{15}] \oplus k_3^0$$

The remaining columns in $\beta$ and in the output of dummy round are same. In step 14, the result of compulsory dummy round is xored with $\beta$.

$$\therefore RoundFunction(R_2, k^0) \oplus \beta = \begin{pmatrix} 2 \cdot S[\beta_0 \oplus SNLF[\varepsilon]] \oplus 2 \cdot S[\beta_0] & 0 & 0 & 0 \\ 1 \cdot S[\beta_0 \oplus SNLF[\varepsilon]] \oplus 1 \cdot S[\beta_0] & 0 & 0 & 0 \\ 1 \cdot S[\beta_0 \oplus SNLF[\varepsilon]] \oplus 1 \cdot S[\beta_0] & 0 & 0 & 0 \\ 3 \cdot S[\beta_0 \oplus SNLF[\varepsilon]] \oplus 3 \cdot S[\beta_0] & 0 & 0 & 0 \end{pmatrix}$$

## C  Diffusion of Fault and Infection in Piret & Quisquater's Attack

In this appendix, we explain how the fault diffuses and infects the computation of Algorithm 1, when a fault is injected in the input of $9^{th}$ cipher round. Let $I^9$ denote the input to the $9^{th}$ cipher round. Suppose a fault $f$ is injected in the first byte of $9^{th}$ cipher round input $I^9$.

$$I^9 = \begin{pmatrix} I_0^9 \oplus f & I_4^9 & I_8^9 & I_{12}^9 \\ I_1^9 & I_5^9 & I_9^9 & I_{13}^9 \\ I_2^9 & I_6^9 & I_{10}^9 & I_{14}^9 \\ I_3^9 & I_7^9 & I_{11}^9 & I_{15}^9 \end{pmatrix}$$

After the execution of $9^{th}$ cipher round in the step 7 of Algorithm 1, the difference between the faulty and redundant intermediate state is:

$$R_0 \oplus R_1 = \begin{pmatrix} A & 0 & 0 & 0 \\ B & 0 & 0 & 0 \\ C & 0 & 0 & 0 \\ D & 0 & 0 & 0 \end{pmatrix}$$

where $A = 2 * f'$, $B = 1 * f'$, $C = 1 * f'$ and $D = 3 * f'$.
After infection in step 11, this difference is:

$$R_0 \oplus R_1 = \begin{pmatrix} A \oplus SNLF[A] & 0 & 0 & 0 \\ B \oplus SNLF[B] & 0 & 0 & 0 \\ C \oplus SNLF[C] & 0 & 0 & 0 \\ D \oplus SNLF[D] & 0 & 0 & 0 \end{pmatrix}$$

In step 10, $R_2$ is also infected.

$$R_2 = \begin{pmatrix} \beta_0 \oplus SNLF[A] & \beta_4 & \beta_8 & \beta_{12} \\ \beta_1 \oplus SNLF[B] & \beta_5 & \beta_9 & \beta_{13} \\ \beta_2 \oplus SNLF[C] & \beta_6 & \beta_{10} & \beta_{14} \\ \beta_3 \oplus SNLF[D] & \beta_7 & \beta_{11} & \beta_{15} \end{pmatrix}$$

Since $10^{th}$ redundant round executes without any error, after the execution of $10^{th}$ cipher round in the step 7 of Algorithm 1, the difference between the faulty and redundant computation is:

$$R_0 \oplus R_1 = \begin{pmatrix} z_0 & 0 & 0 & 0 \\ 0 & 0 & 0 & z_1 \\ 0 & 0 & z_2 & 0 \\ 0 & z_3 & 0 & 0 \end{pmatrix}$$

where $z_0 = S[I_0^{10} \oplus A \oplus SNLF[A]] \oplus S[I_0^{10}]$, $z_1 = S[I_1^{10} \oplus B \oplus SNLF[B]] \oplus S[I_1^{10}]$, $z_2 = S[I_2^{10} \oplus C \oplus SNLF[C]] \oplus S[I_2^{10}]$, $z_3 = S[I_3^{10} \oplus D \oplus SNLF[D]] \oplus S[I_3^{10}]$.

In step 11, $R_0$ is further infected, therefore the difference between faulty and redundant computation at the end of the while loop is:

$$R_0 \oplus R_1 = \begin{pmatrix} m_0 & 0 & 0 & 0 \\ 0 & 0 & 0 & m_1 \\ 0 & 0 & m_2 & 0 \\ 0 & m_3 & 0 & 0 \end{pmatrix}$$

where $m_j = z_j \oplus SNLF[z_j]$, $j \in \{0, 1, 2, 3\}$.
$R_2$ is also infected in the step 10. After infection, $R_2$ is

$$\begin{pmatrix} \beta_0 \oplus SNLF[A] \oplus SNLF[z_0] & \beta_4 & \beta_8 & \beta_{12} \\ \beta_1 \oplus SNLF[B] & \beta_5 & \beta_9 & \beta_{13} \oplus SNLF[z_1] \\ \beta_2 \oplus SNLF[C] & \beta_6 & \beta_{10} \oplus SNLF[z_2] & \beta_{14} \\ \beta_3 \oplus SNLF[D] & \beta_7 \oplus SNLF[z_3] & \beta_{11} & \beta_{15} \end{pmatrix}$$

Thus, at the end of the while loop, 4 bytes of $R_0$ and 7 bytes of $R_2$ are infected.

In step 14, when compulsory dummy round operates on $R_2$, the infection in the input of $R_2$ spreads to all the 16 bytes. Using equation (2), we can write the final difference $T \oplus T^*$ as:

$$T \oplus T^* = \begin{pmatrix} m_0 \oplus 2F_1 \oplus 1F_2 & 1F_3 & 3F_4 \oplus 1F_5 \oplus 1F_6 & 3F_7 \\ 1F_1 \oplus 3F_2 & 1F_3 & 2F_4 \oplus 3F_5 \oplus 1F_6 & m_1 \oplus 2F_7 \\ 1F_1 \oplus 2F_2 & 3F_3 & m_2 \oplus 1F_4 \oplus 2F_5 \oplus 3F_6 & 1F_7 \\ 3F_1 \oplus 1F_2 & m_3 \oplus 2F_3 & 1F_4 \oplus 1F_5 \oplus 2F_6 & 1F_7 \end{pmatrix}$$

where $F_1 = S[\beta_0 \oplus SNLF[A] \oplus SNLF[z_0]] \oplus S[\beta_0]$, $F_2 = S[\beta_{10} \oplus SNLF[z_2]] \oplus S[\beta_{10}]$, $F_3 = S[\beta_3 \oplus SNLF[D]] \oplus S[\beta_3]$, $F_4 = S[\beta_{13} \oplus SNLF[z_1]] \oplus S[\beta_{13}]$, $F_5 = S[\beta_2 \oplus SNLF[C]] \oplus S[\beta_2]$, $F_6 = S[\beta_7 \oplus SNLF[z_3]] \oplus S[\beta_7]$, and $F_7 = S[\beta_1 \oplus SNLF[B]] \oplus S[\beta_1]$.

## D   Complexity Analysis

A random byte fault in the input of $9^{th}$ cipher round results in $2^4$ solutions for $T^*$. Every solution of $T^*$ gives 1036 candidate values for 4 bytes of the $10^{th}$ round key $k^{11}$ as described in [4]. Thus the expected number of candidate values for 4 bytes of $k^{11}$ is $2^4 * 1036 = 16576$. If we repeat this attack process on another pair of faulty and correct ciphertext we expect to get no more than 2 values for 4 bytes of $k^{11}$ [4]. Our experiments also reveal that we are left with at most 2 candidate values for every 4 bytes of $k^{11}$.

## E   Probability Computation

Consider a set $L = \{s \in \{0, 1\}^{n+d}: \#|1| = n \wedge \#|0| = d\}$.
The number of unique binary strings, consisting of exactly $n$ 1's and $d$ 0's, i.e. $|L|$ is $(n + d)!/(n! \cdot d!)$.

Thus, the number of unique binary string $(S_{total})$ consisting of $n = 21$ 1's and $d$ 0's $= (21 + d)!/(21! \cdot d!)$.

And the number of unique binary string $(S_{favourable})$ consisting of $n = 21$ 1's, $d$ 0's and ending with '11' $= (19 + d)!/(19! \cdot d!)$.

Therefore, the probability of uniformly selecting a binary string from the set $L$ with $n = 21$ and terminating with '11' $= \frac{S_{favourable}}{S_{total}}$.

## F    Values of Bit Variables During the Execution of Algorithm 2

Table 2. Status of Variables during Execution of Algorithm 2

| $i\%2$ | $\lambda$ | $\gamma$ | $\delta$ | comments |
|--------|-----------|----------|----------|----------|
| 1 | 1 | 0 | 0 | correct computation of redundant round |
| U | 1 | U | U | correct computation of cipher round |
| X | 0 | 0 | 0 | correct computation of dummy round |
| 0 | 1 | 1 | 0 | detection of fault in AES round |
| X | 0 | 0 | 1 | detection of a fault in dummy round |
| X | X | 1 | 1 | detection of fault in comparison bit variable |

# Reversing Stealthy Dopant-Level Circuits

Takeshi Sugawara[1], Daisuke Suzuki[1], Ryoichi Fujii[1], Shigeaki Tawa[1]
Ryohei Hori[2], Mitsuru Shiozaki[2], and Takeshi Fujino[2]

[1] Mitsubishi Electric Corporation, Japan
[2] Ritsumeikan University, Japan
sugawara.takeshi@bp.mitsubishielectric.co.jp

**Abstract.** A successful detection of the stealthy dopant-level circuit (trojan), proposed by Becker *et al.* at CHES 2013 [1], is reported. Contrary to an assumption made by Becker *et al.*, dopant types in active region are visible with either scanning electron microscopy (SEM) or focused ion beam (FIB) imaging. The successful measurement is explained by an LSI failure analysis technique called the passive voltage contrast [2]. The experiments are conducted by measuring a dedicated chip. The chip uses the diffusion programmable device [3]: an anti-reverse-engineering technique by the same principle as the stealthy dopant-level trojan. The chip is delayered down to the contact layer, and images are taken with (1) an optical microscope, (2) SEM, and (3) FIB. As a result, the four possible dopant-well combinations, namely (i) p+/n-well, (ii) p+/p-well, (iii) n+/n-well and (iv) n+/p-well are distinguishable in the SEM images. Partial but sufficient detection is also achieved with FIB. Although the stealthy dopant-level circuits are visible, however, they potentially make a detection harder. That is because the contact layer should be measured. We show that imaging the contact layer is at most 16-times expensive than that of a metal layer in terms of the number of images.

**Keywords:** Stealthy dopant-level trojan, Chip reverse engineering, LSI failure analysis, Passive voltage contrast.

## 1 Introduction

Chips are widely used as "roots of trust" in modern security systems. The trust originates from properties that chip internals are difficult to inspect and/or modify. Limitations and improvements of such properties have been studied over the last decades in the chip security community. Recently, two related threats to the properties are drawing attentions. They are (i) hardware trojan and (ii) chip reverse engineering.

Hardware trojans are malicious modifications or implantations to circuit systems. An attacker uses a trojan as a backdoor to compromise security of a chip. Threats of hardware trojans are emerging because of the globalization [1]. Nowadays, many parties (*e.g.*, IP vendors, design houses, foundries, assembly and testing companies, etc.) are commonly involved in a chip development. The parties are not always trustworthy.

L. Batina and M. Robshaw (Eds.): CHES 2014, LNCS 8731, pp. 112–126, 2014.

In chip reverse engineering, on the other hand, an attacker tries to recover a netlist (or ultimately its logical functionality) of a target chip. The attempt is made by investigating depackaged and delayered chips. The attacker is motivated, for examples, (i) to make fakes, (ii) to obtain trade secrets, or (iii) to get an embedded secret key, etc. Nohl *et al.* showed a successful recovery of a hidden cipher algorithm as a result of reverse-engineering an RFID chip [4]. Analysis techniques are catching up with shrinking CMOS process. Torrance and James [5] showed that even a chip fabricated by a modern processes can be reverse-engineered.

Two problems are related. They can be modeled as a game between two players:

- *Hider* who try to hide something in a chip,
- *Seeker* who try to find the hidden something.

Note that the players *Hider* and *Seeker* appear throughout this paper. The labels are used because roles of an attacker and a defender are interchanged between the contexts of the hardware trojan and reverse engineering.

Seemingly, *Hider* is now advantageous because of the stealthy dopant-level trojans proposed by Becker *et al.* at CHES 2013 [1]. In the stealthy dopant-level trojan, dopant types in active region is modified. The proposers assume that measuring dopant types should be difficult even with scanning electron microscopy (SEM). If the assumption is true, then *Seeker* cannot find the trojan. Becker *et al.* showed a proof-of-concept modification and some realistic attack scenarios, which attracted much attentions [6]. Such a modification in active region is realistic especially when the trojan is implanted by a malicious foundry.

Soon after the proposal by Becker *et al.*, an anti-reverse-engineering technique called the diffusion programmable device (DPD) was proposed by Shiozaki *et al.* [3]. DPD uses the same principle as the stealthy dopant-level trojan. Therefore, reverse engineering of DPD is as difficult as detecting the stealthy dopant-level trojan. Both (i) the stealthy dopant-level trojan and (ii) DPD are referred to as "stealthy dopant-level circuits" in this paper.

As a first contribution, validity of the assumption, on which the stealthy dopant-level circuits are based, is examined with concrete experiments. Specifically, a dedicated chip containing DPD is measured with (a) an optical microscope, (b) SEM and (c) focused ion beam (FIB). As a result, we show that the stealthy dopant-level circuit is detectable contrary to the assumption made by the proposers. All the four possible dopant-well configurations, namely (i) p+/n-well, (ii) p+/p-well, (iii) n+/n-well and (iv) n+/p-well are distinguishable with SEM imaging. In addition, partial success is achieved with FIB imaging. The reason is explained by a technique called the passive voltage contrast (PVC) [2] studied in the LSI failure analysis community [5] [7] [8].

Although the stealthy dopant-level circuits are visible, however, they potentially make the detection harder. That is because the contact layer should be measured for detection. As a second contribution, the cost is estimated in terms of the number of images. We show that imaging of the contact layer can be 16-times expensive than that of the first metal (M1) layer in our setup.

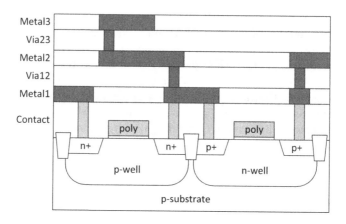

**Fig. 1.** Cross-sectional view of a CMOS circuit

# 2  Stealthy Dopant-Level Circuits

## 2.1  CMOS Circuit Fabrication

We firstly recall chip internals focusing on dopants. Fig. 1 shows a cross-sectional view of a common CMOS circuit. It has a layered structure. The layers are created through a series of processes summarized as [9]:

1. create n- and p-wells,
2. deposit and pattern polysilicon layer,
3. implant source and drain regions,
4. deposit and pattern metal layers.

Photo masks are used to determine shapes of circuits in the processes. A goal of circuit designers is to design layouts that is then converted to the photo masks.

In the stealthy dopant-level circuits, wells and dopants play important roles. At the process 1, wells are formed by implanting a moderate concentration of dopant on substrate. The implanted region is referred to as p- or n-wells depending on the types of dopants. Then, at the process 3, the source and drain junctions are formed by doping a high concentration of dopant (shown as n+ and p+) on the wells. Here, the p+/n+ regions are called active regions. Finally, contact plugs are formed. They connect between the p+/n+ regions and upper metal layers.

**Notation.** There are four possible dopant-well combinations. They are denoted as (i) p+/p-well, (ii) p+/n-well, (iii) n+/p-well and (iv) n+/n-well in this paper. Corresponding dopant types are summarized in Tab. 1. Two different junctions: the Ohmic and PN junctions are formed. The Ohmic and PN junctions form a resistor and diode, respectively.

**Table 1.** Notation

| name | source/drain dopant | well dopant | junction |
|------|---------------------|-------------|----------|
| (i) p+/p-well | p | p | Ohmic junction |
| (ii) p+/n-well | p | n | PN junction |
| (iii) n+/p-well | n | p | PN junction |
| (iv) n+/n-well | n | n | Ohmic junction |

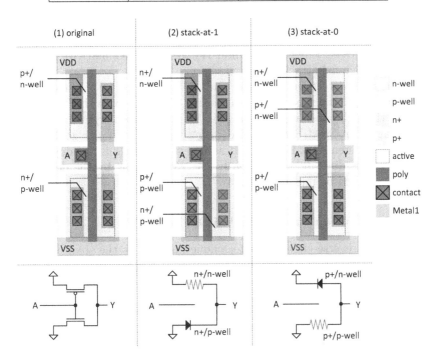

**Fig. 2.** Stealthy dopant trojan

## 2.2 Stealthy Dopant-Level Trojans

Becker *et al.* proposed a new hardware trojan at CHES 2013 [1]. Their idea is to make a trojan just by modifying dopant types in active region. They showed a proof-of-concept circuit modification to a CMOS inverter. If the modification is made, an output of the inverter is stuck to a constant.

Mechanism behind the modification is explained. Fig. 2 (1) shows an original CMOS inverter. Fig. 2 (2), (3) are modified ones. When the modification shown in Fig. 2 (2) is made, the output port $Y$ is tied to $V_{DD}$ through a resistor formed by the n+/n-well. The connection between the port $Y$ and GND is opened because of a diode formed by n+/p-well. Therefore, $V_{DD}$ and GND are safely insulated. As a result, the output of the inverter is always high, *i.e.*, it is stuck at 1. Stuck-at-0 fault is achieved by an alternative modification shown in Fig. 2 (3).

**Table 2.** Truth table of DPD-LE

| A | B | XOR | XNOR | BUF_B | INV_B | BUF_A | INV_A | OR | NOR | AND | NAND |
|---|---|-----|------|-------|-------|-------|-------|----|-----|-----|------|
| 0 | 0 | $S_1=0$ | $S_1=1$ | $S_1=0$ | $S_1=1$ | $S_1=0$ | $S_1=1$ | $S_1=0$ | $S_1=1$ | $S_1=0$ | $S_1=1$ |
| 0 | 1 | $S_2=1$ | $S_2=0$ | $S_2=1$ | $S_2=0$ | $S_2=0$ | $S_2=1$ | $S_2=1$ | $S_2=0$ | $S_2=0$ | $S_2=1$ |
| 1 | 0 | $S_3=1$ | $S_3=0$ | $S_3=0$ | $S_3=1$ | $S_3=1$ | $S_3=0$ | $S_3=1$ | $S_3=0$ | $S_3=0$ | $S_3=1$ |
| 1 | 1 | $S_4=0$ | $S_4=1$ | $S_4=1$ | $S_4=0$ | $S_4=1$ | $S_4=0$ | $S_4=1$ | $S_4=0$ | $S_4=1$ | $S_4=0$ |

Such a simple principle leads a variety of applications. Becker *et al.* showed example attack cases targeting (i) Intel Ivy Bridge RNG and (ii) iMDPL: a gate-level side-channel attack countermeasure.

An attempt to detect the trojan is made as follows [1] [11]. Firstly, a target chip is depackaged and a bare chip is exposed. Then, the bare chip is delayered one by one through polishing or etching [4] [5]. The exposed layers are measured with an imager *e.g.*, SEM. Secondly, the images are compared with golden images for a possible difference [1]. Becker *et al.* assume that distinguishing dopant types in such images is difficult. Consequently, the trojan made by the dopant-type modification should be undetectable.

### 2.3   DPD: Diffusion Programmable Device

DPD is an anti-reverse-engineering technique inspired by the stealthy dopant-level trojan [3]. The idea is to make a programmable look-up table (LUT), similar to that of an FPGA, but programmed by dopant (cf. SRAM in FPGA). There was a conventional dopant-based anti-reverse-engineering technique [11] [12] on which the work by Becker *et al.* is based. However, DPD is the first academic publication on the topic to the best of our knowledge.

Fig. 3 depicts a schematic diagram of a design unit called the DPD logic element (DPD-LE). DPD-LE implements a 2-input LUT. The two inputs $A$ and $B$ are used to select one out of four terminals. The terminals $S_1, \cdots, S_4$ are connected to the dopant-programmed ROM. The ROM is made with the stuck-at-0 and stuck-at-1 modifications shown in Fig. 2. Note that for the sake of performance, the ROM in DPD-LE is simplified from the ones shown in Fig. 2. DPD-LE can be configured to any 2-input gate. Tab. 2 shows a truth table of example configurations.

Layout of the DPD-LE is shown in Fig. 4 where programmable regions are indicated with rectangles. Similar to the stealthy dopant-level trojan, logic functions using DPD-LE are identical except for dopant types in the programmable regions.

An attempt of reverse-engineering is conducted as follows. Chip images are taken in the same manner as the trojan detection. Then, the images are analyzed with an image-processing tool [10] to extract standard cells and interconnections [10]. To reverse-engineer a circuit with DPD, *Seeker* needs revealing the ROM contents $S_1, \cdots, S_4$. However, that is as difficult as finding the stealthy-dopant trojan. Therefore, *Seeker* cannot recover a netlist from the images.

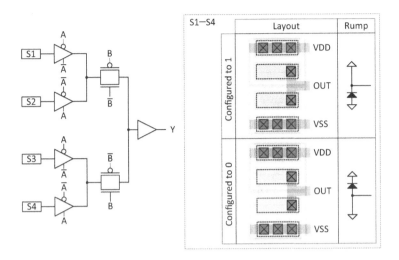

**Fig. 3.** Schematic of the DPD-LE

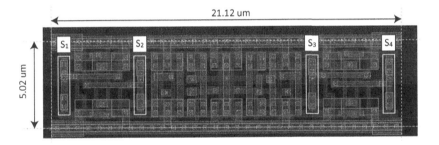

**Fig. 4.** Layout of DPD-LE configured to XOR

## 3 Measurement Principle

In this section, we firstly recall a measurement principle of SEM and FIB. Then, we explain a measurement technique called PVC [2] which potentially detects dopant types.

### 3.1 Measurement Using SEM/FIB

SEM is a common instrument for LSI failure analysis. FIB is another popular instrument for the same purpose. Although FIB is known for circuit modification (*e.g.*, micro surgery) [7], however, it can also be used as an imager based on the same principle as SEM.

SEM and FIB are advantageous in spatial resolution over optical microscopy. Resolution of optical microscopy is restricted by wave lengths of lights that are around 200 nm. That correspond to around 250–180 nm CMOS processes [4].

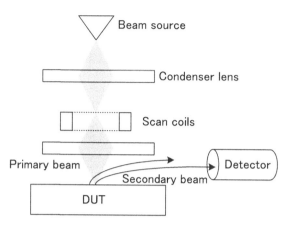

**Fig. 5.** SEM/FIB measurement system

Therefore, SEM or FIB is indispensable for imaging chips fabricated with modern CMOS processes.

A measurement system of SEM/FIB is shown in Fig. 5. Measurement is conducted as follows:

1. A primary beam (*i.e.*, accelerated electrons or ions) is injected onto sample surface.
2. As reaction to the primary beam, secondary electrons are emitted from the surface of the sample.
3. The number of secondary electrons is measured at the detector.
4. Iterate the above measurement by scanning the primary beam through magnetic field in the coils. Finally, a contrast image is complete.

The primary beam is different between SEM and FIB; electron and ions are used, respectively.

## 3.2   PVC: Passive Voltage Contrast

SEM/FIB can also be used to measure surface voltage of a sample. That is because a static field formed by the surface voltage interferes with secondary electrons. As a result, the number of secondary electrons caught at the detector is changed. Measurement based on the principle is called PVC. The method was developed in 90s and now widely used. We refer a paper by Rosenkranz as a good survey on the topic [2]. Voltage-contrast images of DRAM and SRAM are found in the paper by Rosenkranz [2] and one by Chen *et al.* [13], respectively.

The dopant configurations in Tab. 1 can be distinguished with PVC even when a chip is measured at power-off state. In the following description, we consider a case wherein contact plugs in Fig. 6 are measured with SEM.

When the primary beam is accelerated by a voltage around 0.7 kV, the total number of secondary electrons emitted from the plug exceeds that of the injected

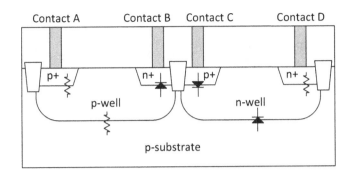

**Fig. 6.** Contacts and different dopant-well configurations

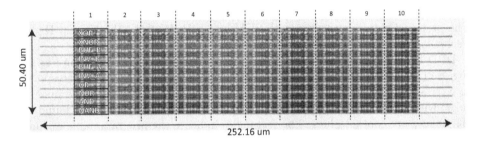

**Fig. 7.** An optical microscopy image of the DPD array in a delayered chip

primary electrons. As a result, the plug charges positively by lack of electrons. At the same time, external electrons are provided to the plug because of the voltage difference. In other words, the positive charges are shared by a whole conductive region from the plug. A resulting surface voltage, at stationary state, is determined by the mass of the region conducted to the contact plug. The mass depends on a dopant-well configuration. That attributes to diodes formed by PN junctions as shown in Fig. 6. For example, the contact B has the smallest conductive region (*i.e.*, the n+ region only) because of a reverse PN junction illustrated as a diode. On the other hand, the contact A has the largest conductive region involving the p-well, n-well, and p-substrate. As a result, the masses of the conductive regions are ordered as the contacts A > C ≈ D > B. When the resulting surface voltages are compared, they are ordered as the contacts A < D < C < B. Note that the difference between the contacts C and D is caused by the diffusion potential at the p+/n-well.

When the plug charges positively, secondary electrons are attracted back to the plug, and thus less is measured at the detector. Therefore, brightness of a corresponding pixel in a SEM image become darker as the plug voltage is higher (conversely, it become brighter as the voltage is lower). As a result, the brightnesses of the plugs are ordered as A > D > C > B, or equivalently (i) p+/p-well > (iv) n+/n-well > (ii) p+/n-well > (iii) n+/p-well. As a result, the configurations (i)–(iv) in Tab. 1 can be distinguished by looking at contacts in SEM images.

# 4    Experiment

## 4.1    Target Chip

Experiments are conducted using a chip implementing DPD. The chip is fabricated using the Rohm 180-nm CMOS process[1]. As a preparation, upper layers of the chip are removed with mechanical polishing and the contact layer is exposed.

Fig. 7 shows an optical-microscopy image of the prepared chip. The figure shows a DPD array containing $10 \times 10$ DPD-LEs configured to different 2-input logic gates. That are XOR, XNOR, BUF_B, INV_B, BUF_A, INV_A, OR, NOR, AND, and NAND gates as shown in Fig. 7.

## 4.2    Experiment 1: Distinguishing Dopant Types

The prepared chip is measured with SEM and FIB. We used the Hitachi High-Technologies S-5200 SEM and FB-2100 FIB.

DPD-LE configured to 2-input XOR is measured. Results are shown in Fig. 8. Fig. 8 (1) is the original layout. Regions shown in green and yellow correspond to $S_1, \cdots, S_4$ where $(S_1, S_2, S_3, S_4) = (0, 1, 1, 0)$. Fig. 8 (2), (3), (4) are images taken with (2) an optical microscope, (3) SEM, and (4) FIB. Many dots found in the images are contact plugs. The rectangles indicate the programmable regions (see Fig. 4).

Dopant types are undetectable by optical microscopy as shown in Fig. 8 (2). Meanwhile the contacts show different brightnesses in SEM/FIB images in Fig 8 (2) and (3). In the SEM image shown in Fig 8 (3), the brightnesses of the contacts are (p+/p-well, p+/n-well, n+/p-well, n+/n-well) = (white, dark grey, black, light grey), as expected in Sect. 3.2. Therefore, the four possible configurations are distinguishable. In the FIB image shown in Fig. 8 (4), on the other hand, (p+/p-well, p+/n-well, n+/p-well, n+/n-well) = (white, white, black, white). Only the n+/p-well is distinguishable from others with FIB.

The same experiment is repeated for other DPD-LEs configured to other logic gates. Results are shown in Fig. 9. We can observe different brightnesses depending on $S_1$–$S_4$ configurations. That correspond to the ROM contents $(S_1, S_2, S_3, S_4)$ summarized in Tab. 2. The results also indicate that measurements are well reproducible.

## 4.3    Experiment 2: Distinguishing Dopant Types under Various Measurement Conditions

The stealthy dopant-level circuits are visible. However, they potentially make a detection harder. That is because the contact layer should be measured in addition to metal layers. One metric to evaluate the cost of detection is the

---

[1] We used the 180-nm process because a good fabrication service is available. That does not mean PVC works only with old processes; PVC works with recent processes. For example, a successful PVC of a 65-nm SRAM is reported [15].

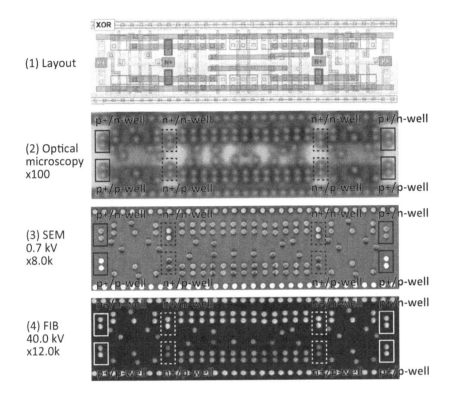

**Fig. 8.** Image of DPD-LE configured as XOR

number of images. That is because (i) usage of an instrument (e.g., SEM) is sometimes charged at an hour each [16], and (ii) a computational cost to process acquired images should depend on data size[2]. The relationship between the (i) number of images and (ii) gate counts are estimated in Appendix.

In order to estimate the cost, the chip is measured with different configurations: (i) acceleration voltage, (ii) scan speed, and (iii) magnification. Tab. 3 summarizes examined configurations and corresponding brightnesses of contacts. The acquired images are shown in Fig. 10.

Firstly, difficulty to detect non-dopant patterns is discussed. It is a common practice to use patterns in the M1 layer to identify types of standard cells [10] [14]. Therefore, the layer is desirable as a counterpart. Images Fig. 10 (2) and (3) are SEM images acquired at magnifications of x400 and x1.5k, respectively. The contacts are not visible in Fig. 10 (2). Therefore, the magnification of x1.5 is needed to image contacts. Patterns in the M1 layer, that lead standard-cell identifications, are in the similar dimension as contacts [14]. Therefore, we

---

[2] The cost to recover a netlist is not considered. That is an emerging research topic and is beyond the scope of this paper.

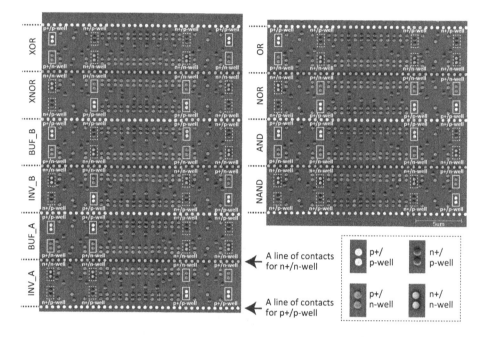

**Fig. 9.** SEM images of DPD-LE with various configurations

**Table 3.** Visibility of dopants with different measurement configurations

| Case | Inst. | Accele. | Scan | Magnification | (i) p+/p-well | (ii) p+/n-well | (iii) n+/p-well | (iv) n+/n-well |
|---|---|---|---|---|---|---|---|---|
| (1) | SEM | 0.7 kV | Fast | x1.5k, x3.0k | White | Grey | Grey | Grey |
| (2) | SEM | 0.7 kV | Slow | x100, x400, | — | — | — | — |
| (3) | SEM | 0.7 kV | Slow | x1.5k | Black | White | Black | Black |
| (4) | SEM | 0.7 kV | Slow | x3.0k | Grey | Grey | Grey | Grey |
| (5) | SEM | 0.7 kV | Slow | x6.0k, x8.0k, x10.0k, x15.0k, x30.0k | White | Grey (dark) | Black | Grey (bright) |
| (6) | SEM | 2.0 kV | Slow | x1.5k, x3.0k, x8.0k, x15.0k, | Grey | White | Grey | Grey |
| (7) | SEM | 5.0 kV | Slow | x8.0k | Grey | White | Grey | Grey |
| (8) | SEM | 30.0 kV | Slow | x8.0k | Grey | Grey | Grey | Grey |
| (9) | FIB | 40.0 kV | Slow | x2.5k, x5.0k, x12.0k, x25.0k | White | White | Black | White |

assume that the limit of magnification to measure the M1 layer is x1.5k in the following discussion.

If we want to distinguish the four dopant-well configurations, the case (5) in Tab. 3 is the only option. In that case, magnification should be at least x6.0k. Therefore, the number of images is 16 ($= (6.0k/1.5k)^2$) times larger than that

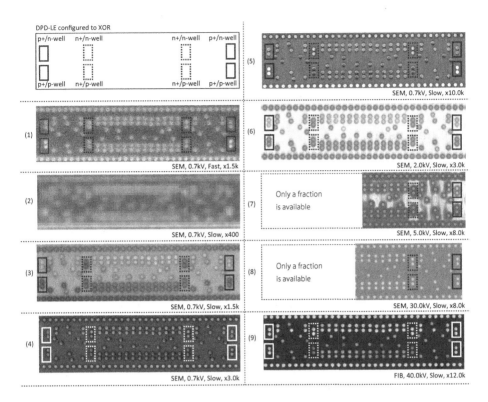

**Fig. 10.** Images with different configurations (the image numbers correspond to ones in Tab. 3)

of the M1 layer. In summary, the additional cost for *Seeker* to find the stealthy dopant-level circuits is the cost of imaging of one additional layer (*i.e.*, the contact layer). The layer is 16-times costly compared to the M1 layer.

On the other hand, distinguishing the four configurations is not necessary when the modifications in Fig. 2 are considered. That is because the dopant-well configurations appear in pairs. In other words, we can recover $S_1, \cdots, S_4$ if one out of the four dopant-well configurations is distinct from others. Such a detection succeeds in the cases (1), (3), (5), (6), (7), and (9). Therefore, the x1.5k magnification is sufficient. That is the same as the one required for the M1 layer. As a result, the additional cost for detecting these circuits are very limited i.e., the costs for imaging the contact layer at the same magnification as the M1 layer.

Finally, we discuss how to determine dopant-well configurations given images only. That is not trivial because the relationship between brightnesses and the dopant-well configurations is not consistent as shown in Tab. 3. One possible solution is to conduct a profiling using an open sample fabricated with the same CMOS process. Even without open samples, we can make an educated guess. That is because references are found everywhere in the chip. Important landmarks are the lines of contacts marked in Fig. 9. They are used to tie p/n-well voltages to $V_{DD}$/GND, thus they should be p+/p-well and n+/n-well. Since wells are regularly placed, contacts near the line of p+/p-well contacts should be either p+/p-well or n+/p-well. In that way, *Seeker* can efficiently find reference contacts for the four dopant-well configurations. Such a guess become easier if standard cells are found in the chip.

## 5    Conclusion

The assumption behind the stealthy dopant-level circuits (i.e., the stealthy dopant-level trojan and the diffusion programmable device) is examined with concrete experiments. As a result, it is shown that all the four possible dopant-well combinations are distinguishable with SEM. It is also shown that the stealthy dopant-level circuits are resistant against optical microscopy, however, that mean only a limited practical benefit because modern CMOS circuits are small beyond the limit of optical microscopy. To detect the stealthy dopant-level circuits, the contact layer should be measured. Additional experiments revealed that the layer can be 16-times more costly compared to the M1 layer in terms of the number of images. The results show that the assumption used in the previous works – dopant types are difficult to measure – was too optimistic.

An improved stealthy dopant-level circuit is opened for research. Since the measurement principle is known, thus we can possibly make a circuit that is invisible to the measurement. For example, the high contrast at p+/p-well could be reduced if p-well is isolated from substrate by a deep n-well that is available in a triple-well process. Meanwhile, the principle hints that a dopant modification is undetectable by PVC if modifications are limited to regions not connected to contact plugs. Making a meaningful circuit with the restriction is an interesting challenge. However, we stress that PVC is just one of many measurement techniques. Other options involve the active voltage contrast method and PVC combined with FIB circuit modifications [2]. Therefore, it would be more important to make a reasonable assumption considering these techniques, before rushing into studies of improved circuits/trojans. Knowledge in the LSI failure analysis community will help, because we will need to know state-of-the-art measurement techniques to make a reasonable assumption.

From the view point of trojan detection, cost will be a matter. That is because the detection becomes more expensive as chip size increases. It is estimated that we need 5.16 shots/kGE (see Appendix), but mega-gate chips are common now. One possible direction for settling the problem is to use a built-in testing instrument. The problem of finding a trojan in a chip may be reduced to a smaller problem of finding one in the testing instrument. However, Becker *et al.* already showed an example of bypassing a BIST (Built-in Self Test) without modifying the BIST itself. Building a sophisticated testing instrument will be an interesting research direction.

Another important viewpoint is a dilemma between goals of trojan detection and anti reverse engineering. We want *Hider* to win the game in reverse engineering and *Seeker* to win in trojan detection at the same time. A problem of finding a new technique that satisfies both requirements is opened. An important observation is that there are asymmetric capabilities between trojan attackers and circuit engineers. For example, the circuit engineers are allowed to modify metal layers while the (dopant-level) trojan attackers are not.

**Acknowledgement.** The authors would like to thank the anonymous reviewers at CHES 2014 for their valuable comments. The study was conducted as a part of the CREST Dependable VLSI Systems Project funded by the Japan Science and Technology Agency. The chip used in the paper was made in a fabrication program of the VLSI Design and Education Center at the University of Tokyo in collaboration with Rohm Corporation and Toppan Printing Corporation. The standard cell library used in the appendix was developed by the Tamaru and Onodera Laboratory at Kyoto University and released by the Kobayashi Laboratory at the Kyoto Institute of Technology.

# References

1. Becker, G.T., Regazzoni, F., Paar, C., Burleson, W.P.: Stealthy Dopant-Level Hardware Trojans. In: Bertoni, G., Coron, J.-S. (eds.) CHES 2013. LNCS, vol. 8086, pp. 197–214. Springer, Heidelberg (2013)
2. Rosenkranz, R.: Failure Localization with Active and Passive Voltage Contrast in FIB and SEM. Journal of Materials Science: Materials in Electronics 22(10), 1523–1535 (2011)
3. Shiozaki, M., Hori, R., Fujino, T.: Diffusion Programmable Device: The Device to Prevent Reverse Engineering. IACR Cryptology ePrint Archive 2014/109 (2014)
4. Nohl, K., Evans, D., Starbug, Plötz, H.: Reverse-Engineering a Cryptographic RFID Tag. In: Proceedings of the 17th USENIX Security Symposium (2008)
5. Torrance, R., James, D.: The State-of-the-Art in IC Reverse Engineering. In: Clavier, C., Gaj, K. (eds.) CHES 2009. LNCS, vol. 5747, pp. 363–381. Springer, Heidelberg (2009)
6. Slashdot, Stealthy Dopant-Level Hardware Trojans, http://hardware.slashdot.org/story/13/09/13/1228216/stealthy-dopant-level-hardware-trojans
7. Tarnovsky, C. (In)security of Commonly Found Smart Cards, Invited Talk II. In: CHES (2012)
8. Boit, C.: Security Risks Posed by Modern IC Debug and Diagnosis Tools, Keynote Talk I. In: 10th Workshop on Fault Diagnosis and Tolerance in Cryptography, FDTC 2013 (2013)
9. Kang, S.M., Leblebici, Y.: CMOS Digital Integrated Circuits Analysis & Design. McGraw-Hill (2002)
10. Reverse engineering integrated circuits with degate, http://www.degate.org/
11. Rajendran, J., Sam, M., Sinanoglu, O., Karri, R.: Security Analysis of Integrated Circuit Camouflaging. In: 2013 ACM SIGSAC Conference on Computer & Communications Security, pp. 709–720 (2013)
12. SypherMedia International. Circuit Camouflage Technology - SMI IP Protection and Anti-Tamper Technologies. White Paper Version 1.9.8j (March 2012)

13. Chen, H., Fan, R., Lou, H., Kuo, M., Huang, Y.: Mechanism and Application of NMOS Leakage with Intra-Well Isolation Breakdown by Voltage Contrast Detection. Journal of Semiconductor Technology and Science 13(4), 402–409 (2013)
14. Silicon zoo, Megamos chip XOR gate, http://www.siliconzoo.org/megamos.html
15. Yang, M., Liang, S., Wu, L., Lai, L., Su, J., Niou, C., Wen, Y., Zhu, Y.: Application of Passive Voltage Contrast Fault Isolation on 65nm SRAM Single Bit Failure. In: 16th IEEE International Symposium on the Physical and Failure Analysis of Integrated Circuits (2009)
16. Electron Microscope Lab. at UC Berkeley, Charges for training and use of EML facilities (November 2013), http://em-lab.berkeley.edu/EML/charge.php.
17. Cryptographic Hardware Project at Tohoku Univ., Aoki Lab, http://www.aoki.ecei.tohoku.ac.jp/crypto/web/cores.html.

# Appendix: Estimating the Number of Images per Gate

The relationship between (i) the number of gate elements, (ii) chip area, and (iii) the number of images is estimated.

As a target, we use an open-source AES core called AES_Comp [17]. The core is synthesized with the standard-cell library for the Rohm 180-nm process. The total cell area is 288,000 $\mu m^2$. The area corresponds to about 15 kGE. The utilization ratio after place and route is assumed to be 70 %. Then, the AES core uses about 411,000 $\mu m^2$ (=288,000/0.7).

In SEM imaging with x1.5k magnification, an area involved in a single image is about 5,000 $\mu m^2$ ($\approx$ 63 $\mu m$ × 84 $\mu m$). Therefore, we need about 77 ($\approx$ 411,000/5,000) shots to cover the AES core. If we normalize the number of shots by the gate counts, we get 5.16 shots/kGE.

# Constructing S-boxes for Lightweight Cryptography with Feistel Structure

Yongqiang Li and Mingsheng Wang

The State Key Laboratory of Information Security,
Institute of Information Engineering,
Chinese Academy of Sciences, Beijing, China
yongq.lee@gmail.com
wangmingsheng@iie.ac.cn

**Abstract.** Differential uniformity and nonlinearity are two basic properties of S-boxes, which measure the resistance of S-boxes to differential and linear attack respectively. Besides these two properties, the hardware cost of S-boxes is also an important property which should be considered primarily in a limited resource environment. By use of Feistel structure, we investigate the problem of constructing S-boxes with excellent cryptographic properties and low hardware implementation cost in the present paper. Feistel structure is a widely used structure in the design of block ciphers, and it can be implemented easily in hardware. Three-round Feistel structure has been used to construct S-boxes in symmetric algorithms, such as CS-CIPER, CRYPTON and ZUC. In the present paper, we investigate the bounds on differential uniformity and nonlinearity of S-boxes constructed with three-round Feistel structure. By choosing suitable round functions, we show that for odd $k$, differential 4-uniform S-boxes over $\mathbb{F}_{2^k}^2$ with the best known nonlinearity can be constructed via three-round Feistel structure. Some experiment results are also given which show that optimal 4-bit S-boxes can be constructed with 4 or 5 round unbalanced Feistel structure.

**Keywords:** lightweight cryptography, S-boxes, Feistel structure, differential uniformity, nonlinearity.

## 1  Introduction

S-box is an important component of symmetric cryptography algorithms since it provides "confusion" for algorithms and in most cases is the only nonlinear part of round functions. S-boxes used in cryptography should posses good properties to resist various attacks. As a nonlinear part, an S-box usually takes a relative high cost in hardware implementation. Thus the cost of hardware implementation of an S-box is also of significant importance in lightweight cryptography algorithms, which are aiming to provide security in a limited resource environment. With the rapid development of lightweight cryptography, it is of particular interest to investigate the problem of constructing S-boxes with excellent cryptographic properties and low cost hardware implementation.

L. Batina and M. Robshaw (Eds.): CHES 2014, LNCS 8731, pp. 127–146, 2014.

Feistel structure is a well-known and widely used structure in symmetric cryptography. There are too many block ciphers designed with the scheme, and the most famous one among them is Data Encryption Standard (DES). Feistel structure is also used for constructing components of block ciphers. For example, MISTY used three-round Feistel structure to construct its nonlinear part FI [20]. The S-boxes in CS-CIPER [24], CRYPTON [18] and ZUC [25] are also constructed with three-round Feistel structure.

In general, the cost of hardware implementation of nonlinear functions is in direct proportion to its input and output size. For example, the 8-bit S-box of AES cost around 200 gates [5], and optimal 4-bit S-boxes cost less than 40 gates [17]. Thus, implementing functions on $\mathbb{F}_{2^k}$ often cost much less area than implementing functions on $\mathbb{F}_{2^{2k}}$. An advantage of constructing S-boxes over $\mathbb{F}_{2^k}^2$ with Feistel structure is that it only need to implement round functions on $\mathbb{F}_{2^k}$. Therefore, comparing with $2k$-bit S-boxes constructed directly with permutation polynomials over $\mathbb{F}_{2^{2k}}$, S-boxes over $\mathbb{F}_{2^k}^2$ constructed via Feistel structure with round functions on $\mathbb{F}_{2^k}$ cost much less area in hardware implementation.

However, the best cryptographic performance of S-boxes constructed with Feistel structure is not known clearly. Differential uniformity and nonlinearity are two basic properties of S-boxes, which measure the resistance of S-boxes to differential and linear attack respectively. S-boxes with lower differential uniformity and higher nonlinearity posses better resistance to differential and linear attack. Then it is interesting to investigate the lower bound and upper bound of differential uniformity and nonlinearity of S-boxes constructed with Feistel structure respectively.

There are already some work on the provable security of Feistel structure, such as [19,21]. Based on the assumption that round keys are independent and uniformly random, it is proven that the average differential uniformity of all permutations constructed via $r$-round ($r \geq 3$) Feistel structure with round permutation $f$ and all possible round keys is less than or equal to $\Delta(f)^2$ [21]. Note that the bound is an average bound over all round keys, then for some fixed round keys, the differential uniformity of the corresponding permutation may larger than the above bound. This has been verified with experiment results in [1].

In the present paper, we mainly investigate the problem of constructing S-boxes with low differential uniformity, high nonlinearity and easy hardware implementation by use of Feistel structure. Without any statistical assumptions, we investigate the lower bound and upper bound of S-boxes constructed with three-round Feistel structure. We show that differential 4-uniform permutations with the best known nonlinearity can be constructed with three-round Feistel structure. It is also shown that optimal 4-bit S-boxes can be constructed with 4 and 5 round unbalanced Feistel structure.

The paper is organized as follows. In Sect. 2, some preliminaries are given. In Sect. 3, the bound on differential uniformity and nonlinearity of S-boxes constructed with three-round Feistel structure is characterized. In Sect. 4, a class of differential 4-uniform permutations with the best known nonlinearity over $\mathbb{F}_{2^{2k}}$ for odd $k$ is constructed via three-round Feistel structure. In Sect. 5, it is shown that optimal 4-bit S-boxes can be constructed with unbalanced Feistel structure. A conclusion is given in Sect. 6.

## 2    Preliminaries

An S-box with $n$-bit input and output can be represented by a polynomial on the finite field $\mathbb{F}_{2^n}$. First, we introduce the definitions of differential uniformity, nonlinearity and algebraic degree.

**Definition 1.** *[22] Let $F(x) \in \mathbb{F}_{2^n}[x]$. The differential uniformity of $F(x)$ is defined as*

$$\Delta(F) = \max\{|R_F(a,b)| : a \in \mathbb{F}_{2^n}^*, b \in \mathbb{F}_{2^n}\},$$

*where $R_F(a,b)$ means the set of solutions of equation $F(x) + F(x + a) = b$ in $\mathbb{F}_{2^n}$.*

$F(x)$ is called differential $\delta$-uniform when $\Delta(F) = \delta$. It is easy to see that the lower bound on differential uniformity of $F(x) \in \mathbb{F}_{2^n}[x]$ is 2. Differential 2-uniform functions are called almost perfect nonlinear (APN). The differential spectrum is the set $\{|R_F(a,b)| : a \in \mathbb{F}_{2^n}^*, b \in \mathbb{F}_{2^n}\}$.

**Definition 2.** *Let $F(x) \in \mathbb{F}_{2^n}[x]$. The minimum distance of the components of $F(x)$ and all affine Boolean functions on $n$ variables is called the nonlinearity of $F(x)$. It is denoted by $\mathcal{NL}(F)$ and can be computed as follows*

$$\mathcal{NL}(F) = 2^{n-1} - \frac{1}{2}\Lambda(F),$$

*where $\Lambda(F) = \max\{|\lambda_F(a,b)| : a \in \mathbb{F}_{2^n}, b \in \mathbb{F}_{2^n}^*\}$ and $\lambda_F(a,b) = \sum_{x \in \mathbb{F}_{2^n}} (-1)^{\mathrm{Tr}(bF(x)+ax)}$.*

For odd $n$ and $F(x) \in \mathbb{F}_{2^n}[x]$, it holds that $\mathcal{NL}(F) \le 2^{n-1} - 2^{\frac{n-1}{2}}$ [10]. For even $n$ and $F(x) \in \mathbb{F}_{2^n}[x]$, the upper bound on the nonlinearity of $F(x)$ is still open, and the best known nonlinearity is $2^{n-1} - 2^{\frac{n}{2}}$ [11].

**Definition 3.** *The algebraic degree of $G(x) = \sum_{j=0}^{2^n-1} c_j x^j \in \mathbb{F}_{2^n}[x]$, which is denoted by $d^{\circ}(G)$, equals the maximum hamming weight of binary expansion of $j$ with $c_j \ne 0$. In other words, $d^{\circ}(G) = \max_{j,c_j \ne 0}\{w_2(j)\}$, where $w_2(j)$ means the number of nonzero terms in the binary expansion of $j$.*

For other cryptographic properties of Boolean functions and vectorial Boolean functions, one can see [8,9] for more details.

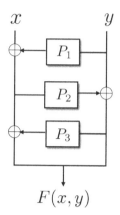

$$F(x,y)$$

**Fig. 1.** An S-box constructed with three-round Feistel structure

## 3 On Properties of S-boxes Constructed with Three-Round Feistel Structure

Throughout this section, we consider S-boxes constructed with three-round Feistel structure as in Figure 1. Let $P_i(x) \in \mathbb{F}_{2^k}[x], 1 \leq i \leq 3$. Then an S-box over $\mathbb{F}_{2^k}^2$ constructed as in Figure 1 can be characterized as

$$F(x,y) = (x + P_1(y) + P_3(y + P_2(x + P_1(y))), y + P_2(x + P_1(y))).$$

We also write $F(x,y)$ as $F_{P_1,P_2,P_3}(x,y)$ when the sequence of round transformations $P_1, P_2$ and $P_3$ is emphasized. It is easy to see that $F(x,y)$ is a permutation over $\mathbb{F}_{2^k}^2$ and

$$F_{P_1,P_2,P_3}(x,y)^{-1} = F_{P_3,P_2,P_1}(x,y),$$

where $F_{P_1,P_2,P_3}(x,y)^{-1}$ means the compositional inverse of $F_{P_1,P_2,P_3}(x,y)$.

This construction has been used in CS-CIPER [24], CRYPTON [18] and ZUC [25]. In this section, we mainly investigate the bound on differential uniformity and nonlinearity of $F(x,y)$.

First, it needs the following result. Remember that for $F(x) \in \mathbb{F}_{2^n}[x]$, $a \in \mathbb{F}_{2^n}^*$ and $b \in \mathbb{F}_{2^n}$, $R_F(a,b)$ means $\{y \in \mathbb{F}_{2^n} \mid F(y) + F(y+a) = b\}$.

**Lemma 1.** *[6,1] Suppose $P_i(x) \in \mathbb{F}_{2^k}[x], 1 \leq i \leq 3$, and $F(x,y)$ be the S-box constructed as in Figure 1. Then the following statements hold.*

*(1) Let $a,b,c \in \mathbb{F}_{2^k}$ and $(a,b) \neq (0,0)$. Then the equation $F(x,y) + F(x+a, y+b) = (c,0)$ has $|R_{P_1}(b, c + a)| \cdot |R_{P_2}(c, b)|$ roots in $\mathbb{F}_{2^k}^2$. Furthermore, these roots are $(z_i + P_1(y_j), y_j)$, where $y_j \in R_{P_1}(b, c + a)$ and $z_i \in R_{P_2}(c, b)$.*
*(2) Let $a, b \in \mathbb{F}_{2^k}$ and $c \in \mathbb{F}_{2^k}^*$. Then $\lambda_F((a,b),(0,c)) = \lambda_{P_1}(c + b, a)\lambda_{P_2}(a, c)$.*

**Theorem 1.** *Suppose $P_i(x) \in \mathbb{F}_{2^k}[x], 1 \leq i \leq 3$, and $F(x,y)$ be the S-box constructed as in Figure 1. Then the following statements hold.*

*(1)* If $P_2(x)$ is not a permutation over $\mathbb{F}_{2^k}$, then $\Delta(F) \geq 2^{k+1}$.
*(2)* If $P_2(x)$ is a permutation over $\mathbb{F}_{2^k}$, then $\Delta(F) \geq 2\Delta(P_2)$.

*Proof.* (1). Since $P_2(x)$ is not a permutation over $\mathbb{F}_{2^k}$, then there exists $a \in \mathbb{F}_{2^k}^*$ such that

$$P_2(x) + P_2(x + a) = 0$$

has at least 2 roots in $\mathbb{F}_{2^k}$, which means $|R_{P_2}(a, 0)| \geq 2$. Notice that $R_{P_1}(0, 0) = \mathbb{F}_{2^k}$, Then according to (1) of Lemma 1, $F(x, y) + F(x + a, y) = (a, 0)$ has at least

$$|R_{P_1}(0, 0)| \cdot |R_{P_2}(a, 0)| = 2^{k+1}$$

roots in $\mathbb{F}_{2^k}^2$, which implies $\Delta(F) \geq 2^{k+1}$.

(2). Firstly, we choose $b, c \in \mathbb{F}_{2^k}^*$, such that $|R_{P_2}(c, b)| = \Delta(P_2)$. Then we choose $a \in \mathbb{F}_{2^k}$, such that $R_{P_1}(b, c+a)$ is nonempty. This means $|R_{P_1}(b, c+a)| \geq 2$. Therefore, according to (1) of Lemma 1,

$$F(x, y) + F(x + a, y + b) = (c, 0)$$

has $2\Delta(P_2)$ roots in $\mathbb{F}_{2^k}$. Hence $\Delta(F) \geq 2\Delta(P_2)$.    □

Let

$$\lambda_k = \begin{cases} 2^{\frac{k+1}{2}} & k \text{ odd}, \\ 2^{\frac{k}{2}+1} & k \text{ even}. \end{cases}$$

For $F(x) \in \mathbb{F}_{2^k}[x]$, we assume it holds

$$\Lambda(F) \geq \lambda_k,$$

which is a bound accepted widely for $F(x) \in \mathbb{F}_{2^n}[x]$ with $n$ even, although it is not proven yet. Then we have the following result concerning the nonlinearity of $F(x, y)$.

**Theorem 2.** *Suppose $P_i(x) \in \mathbb{F}_{2^k}[x], 1 \leq i \leq 3$, and $F(x, y)$ be the S-box constructed as in Figure 1. If for any $a \in \mathbb{F}_{2^k}^*$, there exists $b \in \mathbb{F}_{2^k}^*$ such that $|\lambda_{P_2}(a, b)| \geq \lambda_k$, then $\mathcal{NL}(F(x, y)) \leq 2^{2k-1} - \frac{\lambda_k^2}{2}$.*

*Proof.* We only need to prove $\Lambda(F(x, y)) \geq \lambda_k^2$. Choose $a \in \mathbb{F}_{2^k}^*, c \in \mathbb{F}_{2^k}$ such that

$$|\lambda_{P_1}(c, a)| = \Lambda(P_1).$$

According to the condition of $P_2$, there exists $b \in \mathbb{F}_{2^k}^*$ such that $|\lambda_{P_2}(a, b)| \geq \lambda_k$. Then according to (2) of Lemma 1, it holds

$$\lambda_F((a, b + c), (0, b)) = \lambda_{P_1}(c, a)\lambda_{P_2}(a, b).$$

Note that

$$\Lambda(F(x, y)) = \max\{|\lambda_F((u_1, u_2), (v_1, v_2))| : (u_1, u_2), (v_1, v_2) \in \mathbb{F}_{2^k}^2, (v_1, v_2) \neq (0, 0)\},$$

**Table 1.** Properties of known 8-bit S-boxes constructed with three-round Feistel structure

| Algorithm/S-box | Differential uniformity | Nonlinearity | Algebraic degree |
|---|---|---|---|
| CS-CIPER/P | 16 | 96 | 5 |
| CRYPTON/$S_0, S_1$ | 8 | 96 | 5 |
| ZUC/$S_0$ | 8 | 96 | 5 |

then it holds

$$\Lambda(F(x,y)) \geq |\lambda_F((a, b+c),(0,b))|$$
$$= |\lambda_{P_1}(c,a)| \times |\lambda_{P_2}(a,b)|$$
$$\geq \Lambda(P_1)\lambda_k$$
$$\geq \lambda_k^2,$$

and we complete the proof.                                                                         □

As for 8-bit S-boxes, which are the most often usage size in real applications, we have the following result.

**Theorem 3.** *Suppose* $F_{P_1,P_2,P_3}(x,y)$ *is an S-box over* $\mathbb{F}_{2^4}^2$ *constructed by three-round Feistel structure with round functions* $P_i(x) \in \mathbb{F}_{2^4}[x]$, $1 \leq i \leq 3$. *Then the following statements hold.*

*(1)* $\Delta(F_{P_1,P_2,P_3}) \geq 8$.
*(2) If* $\Delta(F_{P_1,P_2,P_3}) = 8$, *then* $\mathcal{NL}(F_{P_1,P_2,P_3}) \leq 96$.

*Proof.* Notice that there are no APN permutations over $\mathbb{F}_{2^4}$ [16], then the differential uniformity of any permutation over $\mathbb{F}_{2^4}^2$ constructed with three-round Feistel structure is larger than or equal to 8.

If $\Delta(F_{P_1,P_2,P_3}) = 8$, then $P_2(x)$ is a differential 4-uniform permutation over $\mathbb{F}_{2^4}$ according to Theorem 1. By an exhaustive search, it can be checked that the condition of Theorem 2 is satisfied by all differential 4-uniform permutations over $\mathbb{F}_{2^4}$. Then according to Theorem 2, we have $\mathcal{NL}(F_{P_1,P_2,P_3}) \leq 96$.                    □

The permutation $P$ in CS-CIPER, S-boxes $S_0, S_1$ in CRYPTON and an S-box $S_0$ in ZUC are constructed by three-round Feistel structure. The properties of these 8-bit S-boxes are listed in Table 1.

The permutation $P$ in CS-CIPER is an involution over $\mathbb{F}_{2^4}^2$, which means $P(P(x,y)) = (x,y)$ for $(x,y) \in \mathbb{F}_{2^4}^2$. The differential uniformity of the permutation $P$ in CS-CIPER does not achieve the bound in Theorem 3. In Example 1, we give an involution over $\mathbb{F}_{2^4}^2$, which achieves the bound in Theorem 3 and has a better algebraic degree.

According to Theorem 3, the differential uniformity and nonlinearity of S-boxes in CRYPTON and ZUC can not be improved by choosing different round transformations. However, the following example shows that the algebraic degree of S-boxes constructed with three-round Feistel structure can be improved to 6.

*Example 1.* Let $P_1(x) = x^3, P_2(x) = x + g^6 x^{10} + g^3 x^{13}$, where $g$ is a root of $x^4 + x + 1 = 0$, and $P_3(x) = x^3 + (x^2 + x + 1)\mathrm{Tr}(x^3) = \sum\limits_{i=4}^{14} x^i$. $P_1(x)$ is a case of Gold function [12,22], which is an APN polynomial. $P_2(x)$ is a differential 4-uniform permutation over $\mathbb{F}_{2^4}$ got by computer searching. $P_3(x)$ is an APN polynomial which is CCZ-equivalent and EA-inequivalent to $P_1(x)$ [3].

It is easy to check that $F_{P_1,P_2,P_3}$ and $F_{P_3,P_2,P_3}$ are S-boxes over $\mathbb{F}_{2^4}^2$ with differential uniformity 8, nonlinearity 96 and algebraic degree 6. Furthermore, $F_{P_3,P_2,P_3}$ is an involution over $\mathbb{F}_{2^4}^2$.

# 4    Optimal S-boxes Constructed with Three Round Feistel Structure

When $k$ is odd, the upper bound on nonlinearity of $F(x, y)$ in Theorem 2 is $2^{2k-1} - 2^k$, which is the best known nonlinearity of functions on $\mathbb{F}_{2^k}^2$. Furthermore, there exist APN permutations over $\mathbb{F}_{2^k}$ with $k$ odd. Thus, it is possible to get differential 4-uniform permutations over $\mathbb{F}_{2^k}^2$ with the best known nonlinearity.

Suppose $k$ is an odd integer, $\gcd(i, k) = 1$. Then $x^{2^i+1}$ is an APN permutation over $\mathbb{F}_{2^k}$ and denote its compositional inverse by $x^{\frac{1}{2^i+1}}$. Let $F(x, y)$ be the S-box over $\mathbb{F}_{2^k}^2$ constructed by three-round Feistel structure with round functions $P_1(x) = P_3(x) = x^{2^i+1}$ and $P_2(x) = x^{\frac{1}{2^i+1}}$. Then

$$F(x, y) = (x + y^{2^i+1} + (y + (x + y^{2^i+1})^{\frac{1}{2^i+1}})^{2^i+1}, y + (x + y^{2^i+1})^{\frac{1}{2^i+1}})$$
$$= (y^{2^i+1} + y^{2^i}(x + y^{2^i+1})^{\frac{1}{2^i+1}} + y(x + y^{2^i+1})^{\frac{2^i}{2^i+1}}, y + (x + y^{2^i+1})^{\frac{1}{2^i+1}}).$$

In this section, we show that $F(x, y)$ constructed as above is a differential 4-uniform permutation over $\mathbb{F}_{2^k}^2$ with the best known nonlinearity.

In order to characterize the differential uniformity and nonlinearity of $F(x, y)$, we need the following lemmas firstly.

**Lemma 2.** *Suppose $k$ is an odd integer and $\gcd(i, k) = 1$. Then for any $(b, d) \in \mathbb{F}_{2^k}^2$ with $(b, d) \neq (0, 0)$, the following system of equations*

$$\begin{cases} dy^{2^i} + d^{2^i}y + b^{2^i}z + bz^{2^i} = 0, \\ by^{2^i} + b^{2^i}y + (b + d)z^{2^i} + (b + d)^{2^i}z = 0 \end{cases}$$

*has exactly 4 roots in $\mathbb{F}_{2^k}^2$. Furthermore, the following statements hold.*

*(1) If $bd(b + d) = 0$, then the 4 roots are $(0, 0), (0, \beta), (\beta, 0)$ and $(\beta, \beta)$, where $\beta \in \{b, d\}$ with $\beta \neq 0$.*
*(2) If $bd(b + d) \neq 0$, then the 4 roots are $(0, 0), (d, b), (b, b + d)$ and $(b + d, d)$.*

*Proof.* To solve the following system of equations

$$\begin{cases} dy^{2^i} + d^{2^i}y + b^{2^i}z + bz^{2^i} = 0, & (1) \\ by^{2^i} + b^{2^i}y + (b+d)^{2^i}z + (b+d)z^{2^i} = 0, & (2) \end{cases}$$

we have the following cases.

First, if $b = 0$, then $d \neq 0$ and the above system of equations becomes

$$\begin{cases} dy^{2^i} + d^{2^i}y = 0, \\ dz^{2^i} + d^{2^i}z = 0. \end{cases}$$

It is easy to see that the above systems of equations has exactly 4 roots in $\mathbb{F}_{2^k}^2$, which are

$$(0,0), (0,d), (d,0), (d,d).$$

This is because $\alpha x^{2^i} + \alpha^{2^i}x$ is a linear mapping on $\mathbb{F}_{2^k}$ with kernel $\{0, \alpha\}$ for any $\alpha \in \mathbb{F}_{2^k}^*$, since $\gcd(i,k) = 1$.

The case of $d = 0, b \neq 0$, and $b = d \in \mathbb{F}_{2^k}^*$ can be proved similarly.

Next, we prove the case of $bd(b+d) \neq 0$, which is equivalent to $b, d \in \mathbb{F}_{2^k}^*$ and $b \neq d$. Let

$$A = b^2 + bd + d^2,$$

and

$$B = b^{2^i}d + bd^{2^i}.$$

Notice that $k$ is odd, $\gcd(i,k) = 1$, $b, d \in \mathbb{F}_{2^k}^*$ and $b \neq d$, then $A \neq 0$ and $B \neq 0$. We add equation (1) multiplied by $b + d$ to equation (2) multiplied by $b$, from which we eliminate $z^{2^i}$ and get

$$z = \frac{1}{B}(Ay^{2^i} + (b^{2^i+1} + bd^{2^i} + d^{2^i+1})y).$$

Substitute the above equality to equation (1) and multiply both sides by $B^{2^i+1}$, then we have

$$\begin{aligned} 0 &= dB^{2^i+1}y^{2^i} + d^{2^i}B^{2^i+1}y + (bB)^{2^i}(Ay^{2^i} + (b^{2^i+1} + bd^{2^i} + d^{2^i+1})y) \\ &\quad + bB(Ay^{2^i} + (b^{2^i+1} + bd^{2^i} + d^{2^i+1})y)^{2^i} \\ &= bBA^{2^i}y^{2^{2i}} + (dB^{2^i+1} + (bB)^{2^i}A + bB(b^{2^i+1} + bd^{2^i} + d^{2^i+1})^{2^i})y^{2^i} \\ &\quad + (d^{2^i}B^{2^i+1} + (bB)^{2^i}(b^{2^i+1} + bd^{2^i} + d^{2^i+1}))y \\ &= bBA^{2^i}y^{2^{2i}} + bA^{2^i}(b^{2^{2i}}d + bd^{2^{2i}})y^{2^i} + bA^{2^i}B^{2^i}y, & (3) \end{aligned}$$

where the coefficients of $y^{2^i}$ and $y$ is computed as follows. First, we have

$$\begin{aligned} dB^{2^i+1} &= d(b^{2^i}d + bd^{2^i})^{2^i+1} \\ &= b^{2^{2i}+2^i}d^{2^i+2} + b^{2^{2i}+1}d^{2^{i+1}+1} + b^{2^i+1}d^{2^{2i}+2} + b^{2^i+1}d^{2^{2i}+2^i+1}, \end{aligned}$$

$$\begin{aligned} (bB)^{2^i}A &= (b^{2^{2i}+2^i}d^{2^i} + b^{2^{i+1}}d^{2^{2i}})(b^2 + bd + d^2) \\ &= b^{2^{2i}+2^i+2}d^{2^i} + b^{2^{2i}+2^i+1}d^{2^i+1} + b^{2^{2i}+2^i}d^{2^i+2} \\ &\quad + b^{2^{i+1}+2}d^{2^{2i}} + b^{2^{i+1}+1}d^{2^{2i}+1} + b^{2^{i+1}}d^{2^{2i}+2}, \end{aligned}$$

and

$$bB(b^{2^i+1} + bd^{2^i} + d^{2^i+1})^{2^i} = (b^{2^i+1}d + b^2d^{2^i})(b^{2^{2i}+2^i} + b^{2^i}d^{2^{2i}} + d^{2^{2i}+2^i})$$
$$= b^{2^{2i}+2^{i+1}+1}d + b^{2^{i+1}+1}d^{2^{2i}+1} + b^{2^i+1}d^{2^{2i}+2^i+1}$$
$$+ b^{2^{2i}+2^i+2}d^{2^i} + b^{2^i+2}d^{2^{2i}+2^i} + b^2d^{2^{2i}+2^{i+1}},$$

then it holds

$$dB^{2^i+1} + (bB)^{2^i}A + bB(b^{2^i+1} + bd^{2^i} + d^{2^i+1})^{2^i}$$
$$= b^{2^{2i}+1}d^{2^{i+1}+1} + b^{2^{2i}+2^i+1}d^{2^i+1} + b^{2^{i+1}+2}d^{2^{2i}}$$
$$+ b^{2^{2i}+2^{i+1}+1}d + b^{2^i+2}d^{2^{2i}+2^i} + b^2d^{2^{2i}+2^{i+1}}$$
$$= b(b^{2^{2i}}d(d^{2^{i+1}} + b^{2^i}d^{2^i} + b^{2^{i+1}}) + bd^{2^{2i}}(b^{2^{i+1}} + b^{2^i}d^{2^i} + d^{2^{i+1}}))$$
$$= bA^{2^i}(b^{2^{2i}}d + bd^{2^{2i}}).$$

The computation of the coefficient of $y$ is easy.

$$d^{2^i}B^{2^i+1} + (bB)^{2^i}(b^{2^i+1} + bd^{2^i} + d^{2^i+1})$$
$$= B^{2^i}(d^{2^i}(b^{2^i}d + bd^{2^i}) + b^{2^i}(b^{2^i+1} + bd^{2^i} + d^{2^i+1}))$$
$$= B^{2^i}(bd^{2^{i+1}} + b^{2^{i+1}+1} + b^{2^i+1}d^{2^i})$$
$$= bA^{2^i}B^{2^i}.$$

Note that $b \neq 0$ and $A \neq 0$, then equation (3) is equivalent to

$$0 = (b^{2^i}d + bd^{2^i})y^{2^{2i}} + (b^{2^{2i}}d + bd^{2^{2i}})y^{2^i} + (b^{2^{2i}}d^{2^i} + b^{2^i}d^{2^{2i}})y.$$

Divid both sides by $d^{2^{2i}+2^i+1}$, then we have

$$0 = (\frac{b}{d} + (\frac{b}{d})^{2^i})(\frac{y}{d})^{2^{2i}} + (\frac{b}{d} + (\frac{b}{d})^{2^{2i}})(\frac{y}{d})^{2^i} + ((\frac{b}{d})^{2^i} + (\frac{b}{d})^{2^{2i}})\frac{y}{d}$$
$$= (\frac{b}{d} + (\frac{b}{d})^{2^i})((\frac{y}{d})^{2^i} + (\frac{y}{d}))^{2^i} + ((\frac{b}{d}) + (\frac{b}{d})^{2^i})^{2^i}((\frac{y}{d})^{2^i} + \frac{y}{d}).$$

Notice that $\gcd(i,k) = 1$, then $\alpha x^{2^i} + \alpha^{2^i}x$ is a linear polynomial on $\mathbb{F}_{2^k}$ with kernel $\{0,\alpha\}$ for any $\alpha \in \mathbb{F}_{2^k}^*$. Note that $\frac{b}{d} + (\frac{b}{d})^{2^i} \neq 0$, since $b,d \in \mathbb{F}_{2^k}^*$ and $b \neq d$. Therefore, it holds

$$(\frac{y}{d})^{2^i} + \frac{y}{d} = 0$$

or

$$(\frac{y}{d})^{2^i} + \frac{y}{d} = \frac{b}{d} + (\frac{b}{d})^{2^i},$$

form which we get the roots of equation (3) are $y = 0, y = d$ and $y = b, b + d$ respectively.

Substitute the values of $y$ into equation (1) and equation (2), then one can solve and check that the roots of system of equation (1) and equation (2) are

$$(0,0), (d,b), (b,b+d), (b+d,d).$$

Then we complete the proof.     □

Let $a \in \mathbb{F}_{2^k}^*$, denote $L_a(x) = ax^{2^i} + a^{2^i}x$ and take $\alpha \cdot \beta = \text{Tr}(\alpha\beta)$ for inner product in $\mathbb{F}_{2^k}$, where $\text{Tr}(x)$ is the trace function from $\mathbb{F}_{2^k}$ to $\mathbb{F}_2$. The adjoint linear mapping of $L_a(x)$, which is denoted by $L_a^*(x)$, is a linear mapping such that

$$\text{Tr}(\beta L_a(\alpha)) = \text{Tr}(L_a^*(\beta)\alpha)$$

for all $\alpha, \beta \in \mathbb{F}_{2^k}$. It is easy to see that

$$L_a^*(x) = a^{2^i}x + (ax)^{2^{n-i}}.$$

Lemma 2 means that

$$\mathcal{L}(y, z) = (L_d(y) + L_b(z), L_b(y) + L_{b+d}(z))$$

is a linear mapping on $\mathbb{F}_{2^k}^2$ with kernel dimension equals 2. Take $(\alpha, \beta) \cdot (y, z) = \text{Tr}(\alpha y + \beta z)$ for inner product in $\mathbb{F}_{2^k}^2$, then we have

$$\begin{aligned}
(\alpha, \beta) \cdot \mathcal{L}(y, z) &= (\alpha, \beta) \cdot (L_d(y) + L_b(z), L_b(y) + L_{b+d}(z)) \\
&= \text{Tr}(\alpha L_d(y) + \alpha L_b(z) + \beta L_b(y) + \beta L_{b+d}(z)) \\
&= \text{Tr}(L_d^*(\alpha)y + L_b^*(\beta)y + L_b^*(\alpha)z + L_{b+d}^*(\beta)z) \\
&= (L_d^*(\alpha) + L_b^*(\beta), L_b^*(\alpha) + L_{b+d}^*(\beta)) \cdot (y, z).
\end{aligned}$$

Hence it holds

$$\mathcal{L}^*(y, z) = (L_d^*(y) + L_b^*(z), L_b^*(y) + L_{b+d}^*(z)),$$

where $\mathcal{L}^*$ is the adjoint mapping of $\mathcal{L}$. By an elementary knowledge of linear algebra, we have

$$\dim(\ker(\mathcal{L}^*)) = \dim(\ker(\mathcal{L})) = 2.$$

Then the following result holds.

**Lemma 3.** *Suppose $k$ is an odd integer and $\gcd(i, k) = 1$. Then for any $(b, d) \in \mathbb{F}_{2^k}^2$ with $(b, d) \neq (0, 0)$, the following system of equations*

$$\begin{cases}
d^{2^i}y + (dy)^{2^{n-i}} + b^{2^i}z + (bz)^{2^{n-i}} = 0, \\
b^{2^i}y + (by)^{2^{n-i}} + (b+d)^{2^i}z + ((b+d)z)^{2^{n-i}} = 0
\end{cases}$$

*has exactly 4 roots in $\mathbb{F}_{2^k}^2$.*

**Theorem 4.** *Suppose $k$ is odd and $\gcd(i, k) = 1$. Let $F(x, y)$ be the S-box over $\mathbb{F}_{2^k}^2$ constructed by three-round Feistel structure with round functions $P_1(x) = P_3(x) = x^{2^i+1}$ and $P_2(x) = x^{\frac{1}{2^i+1}}$. Then the differential uniformity of $F(x, y)$ equals 4. Furthermore, the differential spectrum of $F(x, y)$ is $\{0, 4\}$.*

*Proof.* Let $a, b, c, d \in \mathbb{F}_{2^k}$ and $(a, b) \neq (0, 0)$. Then we need to prove that

$$F(x, y) + F(x + a, y + b) = (c, d)$$

has 0 or 4 roots in $\mathbb{F}_{2^k}^2$.

First, it is easy to see that the above equation is equivalent to the following system of equations

$$\begin{cases} by^{2^i} + b^{2^i}y + F'(x,y) + F'(x+a,y+b) = b^{2^i+1} + c, & (4) \\ (x+y^{2^i+1})^{\frac{1}{2^i+1}} + (x+a+(y+b)^{2^i+1})^{\frac{1}{2^i+1}} = b + d, & (5) \end{cases}$$

where

$$F'(x) = y^{2^i}(x+y^{2^i+1})^{\frac{1}{2^i+1}} + y(x+y^{2^i+1})^{\frac{2^i}{2^i+1}}.$$

Let

$$z = (x+y^{2^i+1})^{\frac{1}{2^i+1}}.$$

Then according to equation (5), we have

$$(x+a+(y+b)^{2^i+1})^{\frac{1}{2^i+1}} = (x+y^{2^i+1})^{\frac{1}{2^i+1}} + b + d = z + b + d. \quad (6)$$

Raise both sides to the $(2^i+1)$th power, then we have

$$by^{2^i} + b^{2^i}y + (b+d)^{2^i}z + (b+d)z^{2^i} = a + b^{2^i+1} + (b+d)^{2^i+1}.$$

Furthermore, according to equality (6), it also holds

$$F'(x,y) + F'(x+a,y+b) = y^{2^i}z + yz^{2^i} + (y+b)^{2^i}(z+b+d) + (y+b)(z+b+d)^{2^i}$$
$$= (b+d)y^{2^i} + (b+d)^{2^i}y + b^{2^i}z + bz^{2^i} + b^{2^i}d + bd^{2^i}.$$

Thus equation (4) implies

$$dy^{2^i} + d^{2^i}y + bz^{2^i} + b^{2^i}z = b^{2^i+1} + b^{2^i}d + bd^{2^i} + c.$$

Therefore, $(x_0, y_0)$ is a root of equation

$$F(x,y) + F(x+a,y+b) = (c,d)$$

if and only if $(y_0, z_0)$, where $z_0 = (x_0 + y_0^{2^i+1})^{\frac{1}{2^i+1}}$, is a root of the following system of equations

$$\begin{cases} dy^{2^i} + d^{2^i}y + bz^{2^i} + b^{2^i}z = b^{2^i+1} + b^{2^i}d + bd^{2^i} + c, \\ by^{2^i} + b^{2^i}y + (b+d)^{2^i}z + (b+d)z^{2^i} = a + b^{2^i+1} + (b+d)^{2^i+1}. \end{cases}$$

Notice that $(a,b) \neq (0,0)$, then $a \neq 0$ when $b = 0$. Note that $x^{\frac{1}{2^i+1}}$ is a permutation over $\mathbb{F}_{2^k}$, then (5) does not has solutions on $\mathbb{F}_{2^k}^2$ when $(b,d) = (0,0)$. Therefore, we have $(b,d) \neq (0,0)$ when the system of equation (4) and equation (5) has solutions in $\mathbb{F}_{2^k}^2$.

Hence according to Lemma 2, the above system of equations has 0 or 4 root in $\mathbb{F}_{2^k}^2$. Then we complete the proof. $\qquad\square$

**Theorem 5.** *Suppose $k$ is odd and $\gcd(i,k) = 1$. Let $F(x,y)$ be the S-box over $\mathbb{F}_{2^k}^2$ constructed by three-round Feistel structure with round functions $P_1(x) = P_3(x) = x^{2^i+1}$ and $P_2(x) = x^{\frac{1}{2^i+1}}$. Then the nonlinearity of $F(x,y)$ equals $2^{2k-1} - 2^k$, which is the best known nonlinearity over $\mathbb{F}_{2^k}^2$. Furthermore, the Walsh spectrum of $F(x,y)$ is $\{0, \pm 2^{k+1}\}$.*

*Proof.* Let $a,b,c,d \in \mathbb{F}_{2^k}$, and $(c,d) \neq (0,0)$. Then we have

$$\lambda_F((a,b),(c,d))$$
$$= \sum_{x,y \in \mathbb{F}_{2^k}} (-1)^{\mathrm{Tr}(c(y^{2^i+1}+y^{2^i}(x+y^{2^i+1})^{\frac{1}{2^i+1}}+y(x+y^{2^i+1})^{\frac{2^i}{2^i+1}})+d(y+(x+y^{2^i+1})^{\frac{1}{2^i+1}})+ax+by)}.$$

Let $z = (x + y^{2^i+1})^{\frac{1}{2^i+1}}$. Then $x = y^{2^i+1} + z^{2^i+1}$ and $z$ runs over $\mathbb{F}_{2^k}$ when $x$ runs over $\mathbb{F}_{2^k}$. Therefore, we have

$$\lambda_F((a,b),(c,d)) = \sum_{y,z \in \mathbb{F}_{2^k}} (-1)^{\mathrm{Tr}(c(y^{2^i+1}+y^{2^i}z+yz^{2^i})+d(y+z)+a(y^{2^i+1}+z^{2^i+1})+by)}$$
$$= \sum_{y,z \in \mathbb{F}_{2^k}} (-1)^{f(y,z)},$$

where

$$f(y,z) = \mathrm{Tr}((a+c)y^{2^i+1} + az^{2^i+1} + c(y^{2^i}z + yz^{2^i}) + (b+d)y + dz).$$

Firstly, if $a = c = 0$, then $d \neq 0$ since $(c,d) \neq (0,0)$. Hence it holds

$$\lambda_F((0,b),(0,d)) = \sum_{y,z \in \mathbb{F}_{2^k}} (-1)^{\mathrm{Tr}((b+d)y+dz)}$$
$$= \sum_{y \in \mathbb{F}_{2^k}} (-1)^{\mathrm{Tr}((b+d)y)} \sum_{z \in \mathbb{F}_{2^k}} (-1)^{\mathrm{Tr}(dz)}$$
$$= 0.$$

Next, we suppose $(a,c) \neq (0,0)$. Note that

$$f(y,z) + f(y+u,z+v)$$
$$= \mathrm{Tr}((a+c)(y^{2^i+1} + (y+u)^{2^i+1}) + a(z^{2^i+1} + (z+v)^{2^i+1}))$$
$$\quad + \mathrm{Tr}(c(y^{2^i}z + yz^{2^i} + (y+u)^{2^i}(z+v) + (y+u)(z+v)^{2^i}) + (b+d)u + dv)$$
$$= \mathrm{Tr}((a+c)(u^{2^i}y + uy^{2^i} + u^{2^i+1}) + a(v^{2^i}z + vz^{2^i} + v^{2^i+1}))$$
$$\quad + \mathrm{Tr}(c(y^{2^i}v + u^{2^i}z + u^{2^i}v + yv^{2^i} + uz^{2^i} + uv^{2^i}) + (b+d)u + dv)$$
$$= \mathrm{Tr}(((a+c)u^{2^i} + (au+cu)^{2^{n-i}} + cv^{2^i} + (cv)^{2^{n-i}})y)$$
$$\quad + \mathrm{Tr}((av^{2^i} + (av)^{2^{n-i}} + cu^{2^i} + (cu)^{2^{n-i}})z) + f(u,v),$$

then it holds that

$$\lambda_F((a,b),(c,d))^2 = \sum_{y,z \in \mathbb{F}_{2^k}} (-1)^{f(y,z)} \times \sum_{u,v \in \mathbb{F}_{2^k}} (-1)^{f(y+u,z+v)}$$

$$= \sum_{y,z,u,v \in \mathbb{F}_{2^k}} (-1)^{f(y,z)+f(y+u,z+v)}$$

$$= \sum_{y \in \mathbb{F}_{2^k}} (-1)^{\mathrm{Tr}((cv^{2^i}+(cv)^{2^{n-i}}+(a+c)u^{2^i}+(au+cu)^{2^{n-i}})y)}$$

$$\times \sum_{z \in \mathbb{F}_{2^k}} (-1)^{\mathrm{Tr}((cu^{2^i}+(cu)^{2^{n-i}}+av^{2^i}+(av)^{2^{n-i}})z)}$$

$$\times \sum_{u,v \in \mathbb{F}_{2^k}} (-1)^{f(u,v)}$$

$$= 2^{2k} \sum_{u,v \in R(a,c)} (-1)^{f(u,v)},$$

where $R(a,c)$ is the solution set of the following system of equations with variables $u$ and $v$

$$\begin{cases} av^{2^i} + (av)^{2^{n-i}} + cu^{2^i} + (cu)^{2^{n-i}} = 0, \\ cv^{2^i} + (cv)^{2^{n-i}} + (a+c)u^{2^i} + (au+cu)^{2^{n-i}} = 0. \end{cases}$$

Note that $(a,c) \neq (0,0)$, then according to Lemma 3, the above system of equations has exactly 4 roots in $\mathbb{F}_{2^k}$. Denote

$$R(a,c) = \{(u_i,v_i) \mid 0 \leq i \leq 3\}.$$

Notice that $f(y,z)+f(y+u,z+v) = f(u,v)$ for $(u,v) \in R(a,c)$ and $(y,z) \in \mathbb{F}_{2^k}^2$, which means $f(u,v)$ is linear on $R(a,c)$. Therefore, $f(u,v)$ is a balanced function or a constant 0 on $R(a,c)$. Note that $(0,0) \in R(a,c)$, then it holds

$$\lambda_F((a,b),(c,d))^2 = \begin{cases} 2^{2k+2} & f(u_i,v_i) = 0 \text{ for all } 0 \leq i \leq 3, \\ 0 & \text{otherwise.} \end{cases}$$

Hence

$$\lambda_F((a,b),(c,d)) \in \{0, \pm 2^{k+1}\},$$

and we complete the proof.                                                    □

At the end of this section, we investigate the algebraic degree of $F(x,y)$. The following results are needed.

**Lemma 4.** [22] *Suppose $k$ is odd and $\gcd(i,k) = 1$. Then the compositional inverse of $x^{2^i+1}$ over $\mathbb{F}_{2^k}$ is $x^t$, where $t = \sum_{j=0}^{\frac{k-1}{2}} 2^{2ij} \bmod (2^k - 1)$. Its algebraic degree is $\frac{k+1}{2}$.*

**Lemma 5.** *[4,7] Suppose $F(x) \in \mathbb{F}_{2^n}[x]$. If $\lambda_F(a,b) \in \{0, \pm 2^{\frac{n+s}{2}}\}$ for all $b \in \mathbb{F}_{2^n}^*$ and $a \in \mathbb{F}_{2^n}$, then $d^\circ(F) \le \frac{n-s}{2} + 1$.*

**Theorem 6.** *Suppose $k$ is odd and $\gcd(i,k) = 1$. Let $F(x,y)$ be the S-box over $\mathbb{F}_{2^k}^2$ constructed by three-round Feistel structure with round functions $P_1(x) = P_3(x) = x^{2^i+1}$ and $P_2(x) = x^{\frac{1}{2^i+1}}$. Then the algebraic degree of $F(x,y)$ equals $k$.*

*Proof.* Firstly, according to Theorem 5 and Lemma 5, we have

$$d^\circ(F(x,y)) \le \frac{2k-2}{2} + 1 = k.$$

Next, let $S = \{2ij \bmod k \mid 0 \le j \le \frac{k-1}{2}\}$ and for $s \subseteq S$, define

$$2^s = \begin{cases} 0 & s = \emptyset, \\ \sum_{j \in s} 2^j \bmod (2^k - 1) & s \ne \emptyset. \end{cases}$$

Then according to Lemma 4, the compositional inverse of $x^{2^i+1}$ is $x^{2^S}$. Hence we have

$$\begin{aligned}
(x + y^{2^i+1})^{\frac{1}{2^i+1}} &= (x + y^{2^i+1})^{2^S} \\
&= \sum_{s_1 \subseteq S} x^{2^{s_1}} y^{(2^i+1)2^{S \setminus s_1}} \\
&= xy^{(2^i+1)\sum_{j=1}^{\frac{k-1}{2}} 2^{2ji} \bmod (2^k-1)} + \sum_{\{0\} \ne s_1 \subseteq S} x^{2^{s_1}} y^{(2^i+1)2^{S \setminus s_1}} \\
&= xy^{d_1} + F'(x,y),
\end{aligned}$$

where $F'(x,y) = \sum_{\{0\} \ne s_1 \subseteq S} x^{2^{s_1}} y^{(2^i+1)2^{S \setminus s_1}}$ and

$$d_1 = (2^i+1) \sum_{j=1}^{\frac{k-1}{2}} 2^{2ji} \bmod (2^k - 1) = \sum_{j=2}^{k} 2^{ji} \bmod (2^k - 1).$$

We claim that $\omega_2(d_1) = k - 1$. Otherwise there exist $2 \le j_1 < j_2 \le k$, such that $2^{ij_1} = 2^{ij_2} \bmod (2^k - 1)$. This is equivalent to $ij_1 = ij_2 \bmod k$, since for an integer $r \in \mathbb{Z}$, $2^r \bmod (2^k - 1) = 2^{r'}$, where $0 \le r' \le k - 1$ and $r' = r \bmod k$. Thus $k|i(j_2 - j_1)$. Note that $\gcd(i,k) = 1$, then $j_1 = j_2$, which is a contradiction. Therefore, it holds

$$\omega_2(d_1) = k - 1,$$

and hence

$$d^\circ(xy^{d_1}) = k.$$

Notice that $xy^{d_1}$ does not appear in the terms of $F'(x,y)$, then the algebraic degree of $y + (x + y^{2^i+1})^{\frac{1}{2^i+1}}$ equals $k$. This means $F(x,y)$ has a component function with algebraic degree $k$. Thus $d^\circ(F(x,y)) \ge k$. Then we complete the proof. $\qquad \square$

According to the above results, we have the following result.

**Theorem 7.** *Suppose $k$ is an odd integer and $\gcd(i, k) = 1$. Let*

$$F(x,y) = (x + y^{2^i+1} + (y + (x + y^{2^i+1})^{\frac{1}{2^i+1}})^{2^i+1}, y + (x + y^{2^i+1})^{\frac{1}{2^i+1}}),$$

*which is the S-box over $\mathbb{F}_{2^k}^2$ constructed by three-round Feistel structure with round functions $P_1 = P_3 = (x)^{2^i+1}$ and $P_2 = P_1(x)^{-1} = x^{\frac{1}{2^i+1}}$. Then the following statements hold.*

*(1) $F(x,y)$ is an involution over $\mathbb{F}_{2^k}^2$, which means $F(F(x,y)) = (x,y)$.*
*(2) The differential uniformity of $F(x,y)$ equals 4 and its differential spectrum is $\{0,4\}$.*
*(3) The nonlinearity of $F(x,y)$ equals $2^{2k-1} - 2^k$ and its Walsh spectrum is $\{0, \pm 2^{k+1}\}$.*
*(4) The algebraic degree of $F(x,y)$ equals $k$.*

*Remark 1.* When $k = 3$, $i = 1$, it can be checked that $F(x,y)$ in Theorem 7 is CCZ-equivalent to $x^5$. In general, we do not know whether $F(x,y)$ is CCZ-equivalent to the Gold type permutations over $\mathbb{F}_{2^{2k}}$, i.e., $x^{2^i+1}$ with $\gcd(i, 2k) = 2$. However, the permutations in Theorem 7 are still interesting due to their efficient hardware implementation.

The following result also holds, whose proof is similar to the proof of above results.

**Theorem 8.** *Suppose $k$ is an odd integer and $\gcd(i, k) = 1$, $\alpha, \beta, \gamma \in \mathbb{F}_{2^k}$. Let*

$$F(x,y) = (x + (y + \alpha)^{2^i+1} + (y + \gamma + (x + \beta + (y + \alpha)^{2^i+1})^{\frac{1}{2^i+1}})^{2^i+1}, y + (x + \beta + (y + \alpha)^{2^i+1})^{\frac{1}{2^i+1}}),$$

*which is the S-box over $\mathbb{F}_{2^k}^2$ constructed by three-round Feistel structure with round functions $P_1(x) = (x + \alpha)^{2^i+1}$, $P_2(x) = (x + \beta)^{\frac{1}{2^i+1}}$ and $P_3(x) = (x + \gamma)^{2^i+1}$. Then the following statements hold.*

*(1) $F(x,y)$ is an involution over $\mathbb{F}_{2^k}^2$ when $\alpha = \gamma$.*
*(2) The differential uniformity of $F(x,y)$ equals 4 and its differential spectrum is $\{0,4\}$.*
*(3) The nonlinearity of $F(x,y)$ equals $2^{2k-1} - 2^k$ and its Walsh spectrum is $\{0, \pm 2^{k+1}\}$.*
*(4) The algebraic degree of $F(x,y)$ equals $k$.*

*Remark 2.* "Characterizing the $F$-functions whose maximum differential probability with keys is small" is an open problem proposed in [1]. In that paper, the $i$-th round of Feistel structure is a transformation as $(L_i, R_i) \to (R_i, L_i + f(L_i + k_i))$. $F$-function means $f(x + k_i)$, where $f$ is a permutation and $k_i$ is the $i$-th round key. Theorem 8 means that for any fixed round keys, the three-round Feistel scheme with round functions $P_1 = P_3 = x^{2^i+1}$ and $P_2 = x^{\frac{1}{2^i+1}}$ always posses the best differential uniformity and nonlinearity.

# 5    Constructing Optimal 4-bit S-boxes with Unbalanced Feistel Structure

Four bit S-boxes are always chosen for lightweight cryptography because of their less hardware implementation cost. It has been shown that, the best differential uniformity and nonlinearity of 4-bit S-boxes both equal 4 [17]. These S-boxes are called optimal 4-bit S-boxes.

In order to reduce hardware implementation cost, a method of constructing recursive diffusion layers is proposed in PHONTON [14] and LED [15], and further studied in [26]. We use a similar idea to construct recursive S-boxes in this section. We show that some optimal 4-bit S-boxes can be constructed with 4 or 5 round unbalanced Feistel structure.

**Construction 1.** *Suppose $f$ is a nonlinear Boolean function with three variables, and $x_i \in \mathbb{F}_2, 1 \leq i \leq 4$. One round unbalanced Feistel structure is a transformation as follows*

$$P_f(x_1, x_2, x_3, x_4) = (x_2, x_3, x_4, x_1 + f(x_2, x_3, x_4)).$$

*Then an S-box over $\mathbb{F}_2^4$ can be constructed with $t$ round unbalanced Feistel structure as follows*

$$F(x_1, x_2, x_3, x_4) = P_f^t(x_1, x_2, x_3, x_4),$$

*where $t = 4$ or $5$, $P_f^j$ defined as $P_f(P_f^{j-1})$ for $j \geq 2$ and $P_f^1 = P_f$.*

It is easy to see that $P_f^t$ is a permutation over $\mathbb{F}_2^4$ for $t \geq 1$. In order to update every bit of the output of the S-boxes constructed as above, $t$ should larger than or equal to 4. Considering the efficiency of S-boxes, it is better to construct S-boxes with not too many rounds. Thus, we choose $t = 4$ or 5 in the above construction. $P_f^t$ can be implemented with nonlinear feedback register (NLFSR) as shown in Figure 2. It also can be implemented similarly as the implementation of S-boxes in Piccolo [23] and LS-design [13].

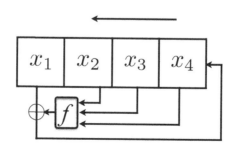

**Fig. 2.** Constructing S-box with NLFSR

**Table 2.** Boolean functions such that $P_f^4$ are optimal 4-bit S-boxes

| $f$ | Operations | $G_i$ | $f$ | Operations | $G_i$ |
|---|---|---|---|---|---|
| $x_2x_3$ | (1, 1, 0) | 8 | $x_2x_3 + 1$ | (1, 1, 1) | 8 |
| $x_3x_4$ | (1, 1, 0) | 8 | $x_3x_4 + 1$ | (1, 1, 1) | 8 |
| $(x_3 + 1)x_4$ | (1, 1, 1) | 8 | $(x_3 + 1)x_4 + 1^\star$ | (1, 1, 2) | 8 |
| $x_2(x_3 + 1)$ | (1, 1, 1) | 8 | $x_2(x_3 + 1) + 1^\star$ | (1, 1, 2) | 8 |
| $x_3(x_4 + 1)$ | (1, 1, 1) | 8 | $x_3(x_4 + 1) + 1^\star$ | (1, 1, 2) | 8 |
| $(x_2 + 1)x_3$ | (1, 1, 1) | 8 | $(x_2 + 1)x_3 + 1^\star$ | (1, 1, 2) | 8 |
| $(x_2 + 1)(x_3 + 1) + 1$ | (1, 1, 3) | 8 | $(x_2 + 1)(x_3 + 1)$ | (1, 1, 2) | 8 |
| $(x_3 + 1)(x_4 + 1) + 1$ | (1, 1, 3) | 8 | $(x_3 + 1)(x_4 + 1)$ | (1, 1, 2) | 8 |
| $x_2x_3 + x_4$ | (2, 1, 0) | 8 | $x_2x_3 + x_4 + 1^\star$ | (2, 1, 1) | 8 |
| $x_2 + x_3x_4$ | (2, 1, 0) | 8 | $x_2 + x_3x_4 + 1^\star$ | (2, 1, 1) | 8 |
| $x_2 + (x_3 + 1)x_4$ | (2, 1, 1) | 8 | $x_2 + (x_3 + 1)x_4 + 1$ | (2, 1, 2) | 8 |
| $(x_2 + 1)x_3 + x_4$ | (2, 1, 1) | 8 | $(x_2 + 1)x_3 + x_4 + 1$ | (2, 1, 2) | 8 |
| $x_2 + x_3(x_4 + 1)$ | (2, 1, 1) | 8 | $x_2 + x_3(x_4 + 1) + 1$ | (2, 1, 2) | 8 |
| $x_2(x_3 + 1) + x_4$ | (2, 1, 1) | 8 | $x_2(x_3 + 1) + x_4 + 1$ | (2, 1, 2) | 8 |
| $x_2 + (x_3 + 1)(x_4 + 1) + 1$ | (2, 1, 3) | 8 | $x_2 + (x_3 + 1)(x_4 + 1)^\star$ | (2, 1, 2) | 8 |
| $(x_2 + 1)(x_3 + 1) + x_4 + 1$ | (2, 1, 3) | 8 | $(x_2 + 1)(x_3 + 1) + x_4^\star$ | (2, 1, 2) | 8 |
| $x_2(x_3 + x_4) + x_3x_4$ | (3, 2, 0) | 1 | $x_2(x_3 + x_4) + x_3x_4 + 1$ | (3, 2, 1) | 1 |
| $x_2(x_4 + x_3 + 1) + (x_3 + 1)x_4$ | (3, 2, 1) | 1 | $x_2(x_4 + x_3 + 1) + (x_3 + 1)x_4 + 1$ | (3, 2, 2) | 1 |
| $x_2(x_3 + x_4 + 1) + x_3(x_4 + 1)$ | (3, 2, 1) | 1 | $x_2(x_3 + x_4 + 1) + x_3(x_4 + 1) + 1$ | (3, 2, 2) | 1 |
| $(x_2 + 1 + x_4)x_3 + (x_2 + 1)x_4$ | (3, 2, 1) | 1 | $(x_2 + 1 + x_4)x_3 + (x_2 + 1)x_4 + 1$ | (3, 2, 2) | 1 |

Let $Q_f(x_1, x_2, x_3, x_4) = (x_4 + f(x_1, x_2, x_3), x_1, x_2, x_3)$, which is also a transformation that can be implemented easily. Then it is easy to verify that

$$P(Q(x_1, x_2, x_3, x_4)) = (x_1, x_2, x_3, x_4).$$

Hence the compositional inverse of $P_f^t$ equals $Q_f^t$. It should be noticed $Q_f^t$ also can be implemented with nonlinear shift register.

By an exhaustive searching, we list all Boolean functions $f$ such that $P_f^4$, $P_f^5$ are optimal 4-bit S-boxes in Table 2 and Table 3 respectively. The cost of hardware implementation of one round transformations of $P_f^t$, i.e. $x_1 + f$, is estimated in the two tables. An element "$(r_1, r_2, r_3)$" in the "Operations" columns of the two tables means that the number of operations "+" (XOR), "$*$" (AND) and "+1" (NOT) in $x_1 + f$ is $r_1$, $r_2$ and $r_3$ respectively.

According to [17], there are exactly 16 classes of optimal 4-bit S-boxes up to affine equivalence. An element "$j$" in the columns "$G_i$" in Table 2 (resp. Table 3) means the $P_f^4$ (resp. $P_f^5$) is CCZ-equivalent to $G_j$ in [17]. It can be checked that the S-box used in PRESENT [2] is affine equivalent to $G_1$.

The functions with a "$\star$" in the superscript, such as "$f^\star$", in Table 2 (resp. Table 3) means that $P_f^4$ (resp. $P_f^5$) does not have fixed points. For other functions in the two tables, it can be checked that there always exists nonzero constant $(a_1, a_2, a_3, a_4) \in \mathbb{F}_2^4$, such that $P_f^4(x_1 + a_1, x_2 + a_2, x_3 + a_3, x_4 + a_4)$ (resp. $P_f^5(x_1 + a_1, x_2 + a_2, x_3 + a_3, x_4 + a_4)$) does not have fixed points. Note that adding a constant to input does not change the differential uniformity and nonlinearity, then for any function $f$ in the two tables, optimal 4-bit S-boxes with no fixed

**Table 3.** Boolean functions such that $P_f^5$ are optimal 4-bit S-boxes

| $f$ | Operations | $G_i$ | $f$ | Operations | $G_i$ |
|---|---|---|---|---|---|
| $x_2(x_3 + x_4) + 1$ | (2, 1, 1) | 7 | $(x_2 + x_4)x_3 + 1^*$ | (2, 1, 1) | 4 |
| $(x_2 + x_3)x_4 + 1$ | (2, 1, 1) | 7 | $(x_2 + x_4)(x_3 + 1) + 1^*$ | (2, 1, 2) | 4 |
| $(x_2 + x_3)(x_4 + 1) + 1$ | (2, 1, 2) | 7 | $(x_2 + 1)(x_3 + x_4) + 1$ | (2, 1, 2) | 7 |
| $x_2 x_3 + (x_2 + 1)x_4$ | (2, 2, 1) | 13 | $x_2(x_4 + 1) + x_3 x_4$ | (2, 2, 1) | 13 |
| $x_2 x_4 + x_3(x_4 + 1) + 1$ | (2, 2, 2) | 13 | $x_2(x_3 + 1) + x_3(x_4 + 1)$ | (2, 2, 2) | 4 |
| $(x_2 + 1)x_3 + x_2 x_4 + 1$ | (2, 2, 2) | 13 | $x_2 x_4 + (x_3 + 1)(x_4 + 1)^*$ | (2, 2, 2) | 13 |
| $x_2 x_3 + (x_2 + 1)(x_4 + 1)^*$ | (2, 2, 2) | 13 | $(x_2 + 1)(x_4 + 1) + x_3 x_4^*$ | (2, 2, 2) | 13 |
| $(x_2 + 1)(x_3 + 1) + x_2 x_4^*$ | (2, 2, 2) | 13 | $(x_2 + 1)x_3 + (x_3 + 1)x_4$ | (2, 2, 2) | 4 |
| $x_2((x_3 + 1)x_4 + 1) + x_3(x_4 + 1)$ | (2, 3, 3) | 11 | $(x_2(x_4 + 1) + 1)x_3 + (x_2 + 1)x_4$ | (2, 3, 3) | 11 |
| $(x_2 x_3 + 1)x_4 + (x_2 + 1)(x_3 + 1)$ | (2, 3, 3) | 11 | $x_2(x_3 x_4 + 1) + (x_3 + 1)(x_4 + 1)$ | (2, 3, 3) | 11 |
| $(x_2 x_3 + 1)x_4 + (x_2 + 1)(x_3 + 1) + 1$ | (2, 3, 4) | 11 | $(x_2 x_4 + 1)x_3 + (x_2 + 1)(x_4 + 1) + 1$ | (2, 3, 4) | 3 |
| $x_2(x_3 x_4 + 1) + (x_3 + 1)(x_4 + 1) + 1$ | (2, 3, 4) | 11 | $x_2(x_3(x_4 + 1) + 1) + (x_3 + 1)x_4 + 1$ | (2, 3, 4) | 3 |
| $(x_2(x_4 + 1) + 1)x_3 + (x_2 + 1)x_4 + 1$ | (2, 3, 4) | 11 | $x_2((x_3 + 1)x_4 + 1) + x_3(x_4 + 1) + 1$ | (2, 3, 4) | 11 |

points can also be constructed by adding a constant to the input. For example, let $f = x_2 x_3$, by adding $(1, 0, 1, 0)$ to the input of $P_f^4$, we have $P_f^4(x_1 + 1, x_2, x_3 + 1, x_4)$ is a optimal 4-bit S-boxes which does not have fixed points.

With the method in this section, it can only use 1 XOR, 1 AND and 2 NOT for one round transformation to construct an 4-bit optimal S-box with no fixed points by 4 round unbalanced Feistel structure, see Table 2.

# 6    Conclusion

In the present paper, we investigate cryptographic properties of S-boxes constructed with three-round Feistel structure. A class of differential 4-uniform S-boxes with the best known nonlinearity over $\mathbb{F}_{2^k}^2$ for $k$ odd is given. It is also shown that optimal 4-bit S-boxes can be constructed with unbalanced Feistel structure and some experiment results are given in the paper. The problem of constructing new, which means CCZ-inequivalent to known ones, differential 4-uniform permutations over $\mathbb{F}_{2^k}^2$ with the best known nonlinearity is an interesting problem that needs further study.

**Acknowledgements.** We are grateful to the anonymous reviewers for their valuable comments on this paper which have improved the presentation of the paper greatly. This work was supported by the 973 project under Grant (2013CB834203), by the National Science Foundation of China (No.61303255, No.61379142).

# References

1. Aoki, K.: On maximum non-averaged differential probability. In: Tavares, S., Meijer, H. (eds.) SAC 1998. LNCS, vol. 1556, pp. 118–130. Springer, Heidelberg (1999)

2. Bogdanov, A., Knudsen, L.R., Leander, G., Paar, C., Poschmann, A., Robshaw, M.J.B., Seurin, Y., Vikkelsoe, C.: PRESENT: An ultra-lightweight block cipher. In: Paillier, P., Verbauwhede, I. (eds.) CHES 2007. LNCS, vol. 4727, pp. 450–466. Springer, Heidelberg (2007)
3. Budaghyan, L., Carlet, C., Pott, A.: New classes of almost bent and almost perfect nonlinear polynomials. IEEE Trans. on Inform. Theory 52(3), 1141–1152 (2006)
4. Budaghyan, L., Pott, A.: On differential uniformity and nonlinearity of functions. Discrete Mathematics 309(2), 371–384 (2009)
5. Canright, D.: A Very Compact S-Box for AES. In: Rao, J.R., Sunar, B. (eds.) CHES 2005. LNCS, vol. 3659, pp. 441–455. Springer, Heidelberg (2005)
6. Canteaut, A.: Differential cryptanalysis of Feistel ciphers and differentially $\delta$-uniform mappings. In: Workshop on Selected Areas in Cryptography (SAC 1997), pp. 172–184 (1997)
7. Carlet, C., Charpin, P., Zinoviev, V.: Codes, bent functions and permutations sutiable for DES-like cryptosystems. Des. Codes Cryptogr. 15(2), 125–156 (1998)
8. Carlet, C.: Boolean Functions for Cryptography and Error Correcting Codes, Chapter of the monography. In: Crama, Y., Hammer, P.L. (eds.) Boolean Models and Methods in Mathematics, Computer Science, and Engineering, pp. 257–397. Cambridge University Press (2010)
9. Carlet, C.: Vectorial Boolean Functions for Cryptography, Chapter of the monography. In: Crama, Y., Hammer, P.L. (eds.) Boolean Models and Methods in Mathematics, Computer Science, and Engineering, pp. 398–469. Cambridge University Press (2010)
10. Chabaud, F., Vaudenay, S.: Links between differential and linear cryptanalysis. In: De Santis, A. (ed.) EUROCRYPT 1994. LNCS, vol. 950, pp. 356–365. Springer, Heidelberg (1995)
11. Dobbertin, H.: One-to-one highly nonlinear power functions on $GF(2^n)$. Appl. Algebra Engrg. Comm. Comput. 9(2), 139–152 (1998)
12. Gold, R.: Maximal recursive sequences with 3-valued recursive crosscorrelation functions. IEEE Trans. Inform. Theory 14, 154–156 (1968)
13. Grosso, V., Leurent, G., Standaert, F.-X., Varici, K.: LS-Designs: Bitslice Encryption for Efficient Masked Software Implementations. In: FSE 2014 (2014)
14. Guo, J., Peyrin, T., Poschmann, A.: The PHOTON Family of Lightweight Hash Functions. In: Rogaway, P. (ed.) CRYPTO 2011. LNCS, vol. 6841, pp. 222–239. Springer, Heidelberg (2011)
15. Guo, J., Peyrin, T., Poschmann, A., Robshaw, M.: The LED Block Cipher. In: Preneel, B., Takagi, T. (eds.) CHES 2011. LNCS, vol. 6917, pp. 326–341. Springer, Heidelberg (2011)
16. Hou, X.D.: Affinity of permutations of $\mathbb{F}_2^n$. Discrete Appl. Math. 154(2), 313–325 (2006)
17. Leander, G., Poschmann, A.: On the Classification of 4 Bit S-Boxes. In: Carlet, C., Sunar, B. (eds.) WAIFI 2007. LNCS, vol. 4547, pp. 159–176. Springer, Heidelberg (2007)
18. Lim, C.H.: CRYPTON: A new 128-bit block cipher. In: The First AES Candidate Conference. National Institute for Standards and Technology (1998)
19. Matsui, M.: New Structure of Block Ciphers with Provable Security against Differential and Linear Cryptanalysis. In: Gollmann, D. (ed.) FSE 1996. LNCS, vol. 1039, pp. 205–218. Springer, Heidelberg (1996)
20. Matsui, M.: New block encryption algorithm MISTY. In: Biham, E. (ed.) FSE 1997. LNCS, vol. 1267, pp. 54–68. Springer, Heidelberg (1997)

21. Nyberg, K., Knudsen, L.R.: Provable security against differential cryptanalysis. In: Brickell, E.F. (ed.) CRYPTO 1992. LNCS, vol. 740, pp. 566–574. Springer, Heidelberg (1993)
22. Nyberg, K.: Differentially uniform mappings for cryptography. In: Helleseth, T. (ed.) EUROCRYPT 1993. LNCS, vol. 765, pp. 55–64. Springer, Heidelberg (1994)
23. Shibutani, K., Isobe, T., Hiwatari, H., Mitsuda, A., Akishita, T., Shirai, T.: *Piccolo*: An Ultra-Lightweight Blockcipher. In: Preneel, B., Takagi, T. (eds.) CHES 2011. LNCS, vol. 6917, pp. 342–357. Springer, Heidelberg (2011)
24. Stern, J., Vaudenay, S.: CS-CIPHER. In: Vaudenay, S. (ed.) FSE 1998. LNCS, vol. 1372, pp. 189–204. Springer, Heidelberg (1998)
25. Specification of the 3GPP Confidentiality and Integrity Algorithms 128-EEA3 & 128-EIA3. Document 4: Design and Evaluation Report, version 1.3 (2011)
26. Wu, S., Wang, M., Wu, W.: Recursive Diffusion Layers for (Lightweight) Block Ciphers and Hash Functions. In: Knudsen, L.R., Wu, H. (eds.) SAC 2012. LNCS, vol. 7707, pp. 355–371. Springer, Heidelberg (2013)

# A Statistical Model for Higher Order DPA on Masked Devices

A. Adam Ding[1], Liwei Zhang[1], Yunsi Fei[2], and Pei Luo[2]

[1] Department of Mathematics, Northeastern University, Boston, MA 02115, USA
[2] Department of Electrical and Computer Engineering
Northeastern University, Boston, MA 02115, USA

**Abstract.** A popular effective countermeasure to protect block cipher implementations against differential power analysis (DPA) attacks is to mask the internal operations of the cryptographic algorithm with random numbers. While the masking technique resists against first-order (univariate) DPA attacks, higher-order (multivariate) attacks were able to break masked devices. In this paper, we formulate a statistical model for higher-order DPA attack. We derive an analytic success rate formula that distinctively shows the effects of algorithmic confusion property, signal-noise-ratio (SNR), and masking on leakage of masked devices. It further provides a formal proof for the centered product combination function being optimal for higher-order attacks in very noisy scenarios. We believe that the statistical model fully reveals how the higher-order attack works around masking, and would offer good insights for embedded system designers to implement masking techniques.

**Keywords:** Side-channel attack, differential power analysis, statistical model.

## 1 Introduction

Differential Power Analysis (DPA) and its variants, Correlation Power Attack (CPA) [1], Mutual Information Attack (MIA) [2], and template attacks [3,4], have been invented to successfully attack cryptographic implementations in many embedded systems [5]. Often these attacks exploit the correlation between the observed measurements and one intermediate data, so-called univariate or first-order attacks. Masking was proposed as an effective countermeasure to protect block cipher systems against first-order attacks. In masking, a random mask $M$ is generated for each execution of the cryptographic algorithm and applied to the internal operations. During the execution, any intermediate data $Z$ is replaced by its masked counterpart $f(Z, M)$ with a carefully designed masking function $f$. Various masking methods for AES have been investigated [6,7,8,9]. The boolean (exclusive OR) masking $f(Z, M) = Z \oplus M$ is the most commonly used one and will be considered in this paper.

Theoretically, the leakage at any time point of the execution on a boolean-masked device is independent of the secret key, and therefore cannot leak the

L. Batina and M. Robshaw (Eds.): CHES 2014, LNCS 8731, pp. 147–169, 2014.

key. The boolean masking protects cryptosystems against all first-order attacks that use only leakage measurements at one time point (or at multiple time points all related to the same intermediate data). However, higher-order attacks using leakages at more than one time points corresponding to multiple intermediate data are able to reveal the secret key. Particularly, let us consider the second-order attack that uses leakages $L(t_0)$ and $L(t_1)$ at two time points $t_0$ and $t_1$ on the device protected by a single mask variable $M$. A second-order attack can break the protected system by selecting the key $k_g$ that maximizes the correlation between the guessed intermediate data $Z^g$ (before the masking) and a combination function of the two leakages $L(t_0)$ and $L(t_1)$. Two combination functions are studied most in previous literatures. The absolute difference combination function $|L(t_0) - L(t_1)|$ was first proposed by Messerges [10] and analyzed mathematically by Joye et al. [11]. The centered product combination function $[L(t_0) - E(L(t_0))] \times [L(t_1) - E(L(t_1))]$ was proposed by Chari et al. [12] and analyzed by Schramm and Paar [13]. Gierlichs et al. analyzed the higher-order MIA attack using the centered combination function [14]. Oswald et al. compared several combination functions with simulation studies [15]. Prouff et al. provided a mathematical analysis of the second-order attack [16]. They showed that the centered product combination function is the best among product combination functions for CPA, and it is better than the absolute difference combination function in noisy situations. This analysis, however, does not tell if there exists other kinds of combination functions better than the product combination function. Standaert et al. applied the information theoretical framework to analyze second-order attacks [17]. They showed that when the noise increases, the information leakage of the centered product combination function gets close to the upper bound (the information leakage of the joint distribution), while for small noises, the information leakage of the absolute difference combination function gets close to the upper bound.

Recently, Prouff and Rivain [18] provided a formal security proof for a mask refresh scheme by a secure masking oracle as a leakage-resilient cryptographic primitive. Our work does not consider such sophisticated mask refreshing scheme, but attempts to bound the success rate of higher-order attack on standard and practical masking schemes. Previous side-channel modeling and analysis work [19] derives a simple success rate formula for first-order DPA attack on unmasked devices, which is explicitly dependent on the algorithmic confusion coefficients introduced in [20]. The formula shows the effect of both implementation-determined signal-to-noise-ratio (SNR) and algorithmic confusion properties. They demonstrated that the formula conforms with the empirical single-bit DPA attacks on DES and AES algorithms.

**Our Contributions.** In this paper, we adopt the algorithmic confusion analysis and apply it to higher-order attacks on masked devices and derive an explicit success rate formula. The analytical formula allows us to decouple and quantify the effect of the algorithmic confusion properties, SNR, and masking on the effectiveness of power analysis attacks, which will be useful to system designers when designing, implementing, and evaluating side-channel attack resistant cryptosystems. We will formally prove in this paper, for the first time, that the centered product combination function (CPCF) attack is the best possible combination function attack in noisy situations.

The rest of the paper is structured as follows. Section 2 presents some preliminaries on which our statistical model for higher-order DPA is based. Section 3 derives an analytical model for second-order DPAs and also extends to general higher-order attacks. We then use numerical studies on both real measurement data and synthetic data in Section 4 to validate the derived model. More discussions and conclusions are given in Section 5.

# 2    Preliminaries

## 2.1    Success Rate of Maximum Likelihood (ML) Attacks

SCA on a cryptographic system utilizes the correlation between the noisy physical leakage observation $L$ and a key-sensitive intermediate value $Z(X, k)$ to reveal the secret key $k$, where $X$ denotes a known input plaintext (or ciphertext). We denote $p(L|k)$ as the conditional probability density function (pdf) for $L$ given $k$ is the true key. With $n$ independent realizations of $L$, $l_1, ..., l_n$, the most powerful side-channel statistical test is the maximum likelihood (ML) test [21]:

$$\hat{k} = \underset{k_g \in S}{argmax} \frac{1}{n} \sum_{i=1}^{n} log[p(l_i|k_g)] \tag{1}$$

Here $k_g$ denotes a guessed key and $S = \{k_1, ..., k_{N_k}\}$ denotes the set of $N_k$ candidate keys. The secret key embedded in the system is denoted as $k_c$. We define:

$$\Delta(k_c, k_g) = \frac{1}{n} \sum_{i=1}^{n} [\log p(l_i|k_c) - \log p(l_i|k_g)] \tag{2}$$

as the difference between the two likelihoods for $k_c$ and $k_g$. With $(N_k - 1)$ incorrect keys, we have a $(N_k - 1)$-dimensional vector, $\tilde{\Delta}$, with an entry $\Delta(k_c, k_g)$ for each $k_g$. The ML attack (1) succeeds when $n$ is large enough to yield all the entries of $\tilde{\Delta}$ positive. We denote $\tilde{\Delta}_1$ as $\tilde{\Delta}$ with only one leakage observation $l_1$, and the mean and variance of $\tilde{\Delta}_1$ are a vector, $\boldsymbol{\mu}$, and a $(N_k - 1) \times (N_k - 1)$ matrix, $\boldsymbol{\Sigma}$, respectively. With $n$ independent realizations of $L$, $l_1, ..., l_n$, according to the Central Limit Theorem [22], $\tilde{\Delta}$ converges in law to the $(N_k - 1)$-dimensional Gaussian distribution, $N(\boldsymbol{\mu}, \boldsymbol{\Sigma}/n)$. The overall success rate of the ML attack, defined as the probability that $\tilde{\Delta}$ is a non-negative vector given $n$, is therefore:

$$SR = \Phi_{N_k - 1}(\sqrt{n}\boldsymbol{\Sigma}^{-1/2}\boldsymbol{\mu}) \tag{3}$$

where $\Phi_{N_k - 1}(\boldsymbol{x})$ is a known function, the cumulative distribution function (cdf) of the $(N_k - 1)$-dimensional standard Gaussian distribution. Equation (3) holds generally for most SCA, while the mean vector and variance matrix would vary for different attacks. We found that the entries in the mean vector $\boldsymbol{\mu}$ are in fact the conditional entropies similar to those defined in the seminal work of mutual information analysis [21]. However, the success rate formula in (3) considers not only the effect of the mean vector $\boldsymbol{\mu}$, but also the variance matrix $\boldsymbol{\Sigma}$ on SCAs. The mean $\boldsymbol{\mu}$ reflects the overall system side-channel signal and $\boldsymbol{\Sigma}$ reflects the system noise. The term $\boldsymbol{\Sigma}^{-1/2}\boldsymbol{\mu}$ can be taken as the system signal-to-noise ratio (SNR).

The higher-dimension Gaussian distribution $\Phi_{N_k-1}(\boldsymbol{x})$ in (3) is the asymptotic limit of ML-attack statistics coming from the Central Limit Theorem, and is independent of the actual noise distribution in the system leakage. Hence, formula (3) is general and does not require any assumption on the noise distribution. When assuming Gaussian power noise as in [3,23], the $\boldsymbol{\mu}$ and $\boldsymbol{\Sigma}$ can have analytic forms constituted by algorithmic properties as defined in [19,20] and side-channel SNR. In this paper, we also consider other noise distributions, like Laplace, in Section 4.3.

## 2.2   First-Order Power Leakage Model on Unmasked Devices

For a cryptographic device, a commonly used linear power leakage model is:

$$L = c + \varepsilon V + \sigma r \tag{4}$$

with $r$ as a standard Gaussian noise, $N(0,1)$, and $V = V(X, k_c)$ is the select function on the intermediate data $Z$ that depends on the known input $X$ and the secret key $k_c$. At a leakage time point corresponding to $Z$'s switching, $L$ is a univariate random variable. Here $c$ is a constant, representing the base level power consumption of the system, which is independent of both operations and data. The $\varepsilon$ reflects the side-channel signal strength and $\sigma$ is the standard deviation of power measurements, i.e., noise from both measurement and other parts of the device. The side channel signal-to-noise ratio (SNR) is defined as $\delta = \varepsilon/\sigma$. Under this model, the probability density function $p(L|k) = \phi(\frac{L-c-\varepsilon V(X,k)}{\sigma})$ with $\phi(\cdot)$ as the pdf of the standard Gaussian distribution. For a single-bit DPA, $V(X, k)$ is chosen as one bit of the non-linear SBox output $Z = SBox(X, k)$. The ML-attack with unknown parameters $(c, \varepsilon, \sigma)$ is equivalent to the distance-of-means (DoM) attack that selects the key $k_g$ to maximize the DoMs. For multi-bit CPA, often $V = H(Z)$ where $H(Z)$ is the Hamming weight (or distance) of the SBox output $Z$. The ML-attack with unknown parameters $(c, \varepsilon, \sigma)$ is equivalent to choosing the key $k_g$ that maximizes the Pearson's correlation between $L$ and $V^g = H(Z^g) = H[SBox(X, k_g)]$. That is, the Hamming weight power model results in the Correlation Power Attack (CPA).

## 2.3   First-Order DPA and CPA Models on Unmasked Devices with Confusion Coefficients

In general, the physical power leakage $L$ is affected by both the implementation and algorithm. To measure the effect of the algorithm, Luo and Fei [20] introduced the notion of confusion coefficients for single-bit DPA to reveal the distance between keys in terms of side-channel leakage. Let $S = \{k_1, ..., k_{N_k}\}$ denote the set of $N_k$ candidate keys. The *confusion coefficient* $\kappa$ over any two keys $(k_i, k_j)$ is defined as:

$$\kappa = \kappa(k_i, k_j) = \Pr\left[(V|k_i) \neq (V|k_j)\right] \tag{5}$$

Here $V$ is a chosen bit of the SBox output $Z = SBox(X, k)$.

Fei et al. [19] further showed that the success rate of the DoM attack follows (3) and the mean vector $\boldsymbol{\mu}$ and variance matrix $\boldsymbol{\Sigma}$ can be explicitly expressed in confusion coefficients and the SNR $\delta = \varepsilon/\sigma$ as:

$$\boldsymbol{\mu} = \frac{1}{2}\delta^2 \boldsymbol{\kappa}; \quad \boldsymbol{\Sigma} = \delta^2 \boldsymbol{K} + \frac{1}{4}\delta^4(\boldsymbol{K} - \boldsymbol{\kappa}\boldsymbol{\kappa}^T). \tag{6}$$

Here $\boldsymbol{\kappa}$ is a $(N_k - 1)$-dimensional *confusion vector* with elements $\kappa(k_c, k_{g_i})$, $i = 1, ..., N_k - 1$, defined in Equation (5), and $\boldsymbol{K}$ is a $(N_k - 1) \times (N_k - 1)$ *confusion matrix* that consists of three-way confusion coefficients:

$$\varkappa_{ij} = \kappa(k_c, k_{g_i}, k_{g_j}) = \Pr\left[V|k_{g_i} = V|k_{g_j}, V|k_{g_c} \neq V|k_c\right] = \tfrac{1}{2}[\kappa(k_c, k_{g_i}) + \kappa(k_c, k_{g_j}) - \kappa(k_{g_i}, k_{g_j})]. \tag{7}$$

The confusion analysis is extended to CPA in [24]. For first-order CPA that exploits leakage by multiple bits of an SBOX output, $V$ in (4) is the Hamming weight (or distance) of the SBox output $Z = SBox(X, k)$. The ML-attack's success rate also follows (3) but with:

$$\boldsymbol{\mu} = \frac{1}{2}\delta^2 \boldsymbol{\kappa}; \quad \boldsymbol{\Sigma} = \delta^2 \boldsymbol{K} + \frac{1}{4}\delta^4(\boldsymbol{K}^* - \boldsymbol{\kappa}\boldsymbol{\kappa}^T). \tag{8}$$

where the definition of *confusion vector* $\boldsymbol{\kappa}$ is the same as before. However, its element, confusion coefficient, is more general:

$$\kappa(k_c, k_{g_i}) = E[(V|k_c - V|k_{g_i})^2] \tag{9}$$

Here $\kappa(k_c, k_{g_i})$ is no longer $Pr(V|k_c \neq V|k_{g_i})$, because $V = H[SBox(X, k)]$ takes values among $\{0, 1, 2, \cdots, b\}$ for a $b$-bit SBox output. In the variance matrix, there are two $(N_k - 1) \times (N_k - 1)$ *confusion matrices*, $\boldsymbol{K}$ and $\boldsymbol{K}^*$, with elements:

$$\varkappa_{ij} = \kappa(k_c, k_{g_i}, k_{g_j}) = E[(V|k_c - V|k_{g_i})(V|k_c - V|k_{g_j})] = \tfrac{1}{2}[\kappa(k_c, k_{g_i}) + \kappa(k_c, k_{g_j}) - \kappa(k_{g_i}, k_{g_j})], \tag{10}$$

$$\varkappa_{ij}^* = \kappa^*(k_c, k_{g_i}, k_{g_j}) = E[(V|k_c - \frac{b}{2})^2 (V|k_c - V|k_{g_i})(V|k_c - V|k_{g_j})]. \tag{11}$$

When $b = 1$, these two matrices are the same, i.e., the first-order $\boldsymbol{K}$ with elements in (7) for single-bit DPA.

When $\delta$ is small, i.e., noisy situations, the higher-order $\delta^4$ term can be ignored and the variance in (8) can be simplified to $\boldsymbol{\Sigma} = \delta^2 \boldsymbol{K}$. Then the success rate becomes a simplified version as in [25]:

$$SR = \Phi_{N_k - 1}(\frac{\sqrt{n}\delta}{2} \boldsymbol{K}^{-1/2} \boldsymbol{\kappa}). \tag{12}$$

# 3  Statistical Model for Higher-Order DPA on Masked Devices

In this section, we first present the second-order power leakage model for masked devices. We then derive an approximation of the ML-test statistic under noisy situations to find the correspondingly equivalent optimal second-order DPA. Under the Hamming Weight leakage model, this turns out to be the centered product combination function (CPCF) attack. Finally, we derive the success rate formula for the optimal second-order DPA with explicit constituent terms of algorithmic properties and SNR. In the end, these derivations are generalized to higher $J$-th order masking models with $J$ random masks.

## 3.1  Second-Order Power Leakage Model on Masked Devices

We consider the boolean masking scheme where a secret intermediate data $Z$ is masked by one random mask $M$. The mask $M$ takes value uniformly in the set $\mathcal{M}$. Therefore, the masked variable $Z \oplus M$ follows a uniform distribution on $\mathcal{M}$, independent of $Z = Z(X, k_c)$, according to the property of the exclusive OR operation. Hence, the leakage at any selected time point only leaks the random $Z \oplus M$ and no longer leaks any key information, and therefore the first-order DPA will fail.

However, often the power consumption at another time point can leak the mask $M$, and can be combined with the leakage on the masked intermediate variable $Z \oplus M$ to break masked devices. We assume that $t_0$ and $t_1$ are the peak leakage time points for $V_0 = V_0(Z \oplus M)$ and $V_1 = V_1(M)$ respectively. Note here $V_0$ is key-sensitive and $V_1$ is key-independent. We denote $V_{M,0}^g = V_0(Z^g \oplus M)$ with $Z^g = Z(X, k_g)$ under key guess $k_g$. The ML-attack on the masked device is still of the same form as in (1) with the log-likelihood $\frac{1}{n} \sum_{i=1}^n \log p(l_i|k_g)$, taking a two-dimensional vector leakage input $l_i = (l_{i,0}, l_{i,1})$, rather than a scalar one as in univariate (first-order) ML attack. Assuming the leakages at the two time points are independent of each other, the log-likelihood becomes

$$\frac{1}{n} \sum_{i=1}^n \log[p(l_i|k_g)] = \frac{1}{n} \sum_{i=1}^n \log[\frac{1}{|\mathcal{M}|} \sum_{m \in \mathcal{M}} p_0(l_{i,0}|k_g, m) p_1(l_{i,1}|m)]. \qquad (13)$$

The above log-likelihood expression involves an iteration of $m$ over all possible mask values: $\frac{1}{|\mathcal{M}|} \sum_{m \in \mathcal{M}}$. We use the notation $E_m$ to denote such expectation over $M$. Hence we rewrite the ML-test statistic as:

$$T_{ML}^g = \frac{1}{n} \sum_{i=1}^n \log p(l_i|k_g) = \frac{1}{n} \sum_{i=1}^n \log\{E_m[p_0(l_{i,0}|k_g, m) p_1(l_{i,1}|m)]\}. \qquad (14)$$

The linear operation $E_m$ above prevents separating the factors inside the log into sums. This results in a mixture distribution density function, and is computationally intensive.

Under the commonly used leakage power model, the power consumptions at the two time points in a masked device are:

$$L_j = L(t_j) = c_j + \varepsilon_j V_j + \sigma_j r_j, \qquad j = 0, 1. \tag{15}$$

where the noises $r_0$ and $r_1$ are independent standard Gaussian noise, $N(0, 1)$. For $n$ executions of the cryptographic algorithm, each with a distinct input $x_i$ and a random mask $m_i$, $i = 1, ..., n$, we denote the $n$ realizations of $(Z, V_0, V_1, r_0, r_1, L_0, L_1)$ as $(Z_i, V_{i,0}, V_{i,1}, r_{i,0}, r_{i,1}, l_{i,0}, l_{i,1})$. Then under model (15), the ML-test statistic from Equation (14) results from the mixture distribution:

$$T_{ML}^g = \frac{1}{n} \sum_{i=1}^{n} \log\{E_m[\phi(r_{m,i,0}^g)\phi(r_{m,i,1})]\} \tag{16}$$

where $\phi(x) = e^{-x^2/2}/\sqrt{2\pi}$ is the pdf function of standard Gaussian distribution. $r_{m,i,0}^g = \frac{l_{i,0} - c_0 - \varepsilon_0 V_{m,i,0}^g}{\sigma_0} = r_{i,0} + \delta_0(V_{i,0} - V_{m,i,0}^g)$ is for time point $t_0$, where $V_{i,0} = V_0(Z_i^c \oplus m_i)$ is the correct select function at the point with the specific $m_i$, and $V_{m,i,0}^g = V_0(Z_i^g \oplus m)$ is the guessed one under $k_g$ given a random $m$. $r_{m,i,1} = \frac{l_{i,1} - c_1 - \varepsilon_1 V_{m,1}}{\sigma_1} = r_{i,1} + \delta_1(V_{i,1} - V_{m,1})$ is for time point $t_1$ (key-independent), where $V_{i,1}$ is the correct select function at the point with $m_i$ and $V_{m,1} = V_1(m)$ is the select function given a random $m$. $\delta_j = \varepsilon_j/\sigma_j$ denotes SNR for $j = 0, 1$.

The ML-attack select the key $k_g$ that maximizes the statistic $T_{ML}^g$ in (16). In contrast, the centered product combination function (CPCF) attack select the key $k_g$ that maximizes the statistic

$$\widetilde{T}^g = \frac{1}{n} \sum_{i=1}^{n} \widetilde{C}_i f(Z_i^g), \tag{17}$$

where $f(Z_i^g) = E_m(V_{m,i,0}^g V_{m,1})$, $\widetilde{C}_i = \tilde{l}_{i,0}\tilde{l}_{i,1}$ with centered leakage measurements at the two time points as

$$\tilde{l}_{i,j} = [l_{i,j} - E(L_{i,j})]/\sigma_j = r_{i,j} + \delta_j[V_{i,j} - E(V_{i,j})], \qquad \text{for} \qquad j = 0, 1. \tag{18}$$

Here $E(\cdot)$ denotes the unconditional expectation over all three sources of random variation in the leakage model (15): (a) the random mask $M$, (b) the random input $X$, and (c) the random noise vector $\boldsymbol{r} = (r_0, r_1)$. This is different from the $E_m(\cdot)$ operation defined earlier, which is in fact a conditional expectation integrating out the random variation from the first source (a) only.

In section 3.2, we prove the equivalence between the ML-attack (16) and the CPCF attack (17) in noisy situations, summarized in the following Theorem 1. Then under the Hamming Weight model, the prediction function $f(Z_i^g)$ can be simplified. We then derive an explicit success rate formula for the equivalent attack in terms of the confusion coefficients in section 3.3.

**Theorem 1** *Under the second-order leakage model (15), as the noises increase, $\delta \to 0$, the ML-attack is asymptotically equivalent to the CPCF attack.*

The main idea of the proof is to check the Taylor expansion of the $T_{ML}^g$ in (16) under noisy situations ($\delta \to 0$). Many leading terms in the expansion are in fact key-independent constants. The first leading key-dependent term turns out to be proportional to $\delta_0 \delta_1 \widetilde{T}^g$ in (17).

The previous work [26] also analyzes second-order ML attack, and approximates the Gaussian mixture density (16) by a bivariate Gaussian distribution using the techniques in [27]. They show that CPCF attack maximizes the likelihood for the best Gaussian approximation. However, there is no measure of the information lost in using such a Gaussian approximation. We prove formally that the CPCF attack approximation of ML-attack becomes exact in noisy situations ($\delta \to 0$), and would indeed provide the same security bound asymptotically.

### 3.2    Approximate ML-attack Statistic under Noisy Situations

While the ML-attack is the strongest statistical attack, the $E_m$ operation in calculating (16) is time-consuming with complexity $O(|\mathcal{M}|)$. Particularly, the complexity increases exponentially with the order $J$ of masking, as $O(|\mathcal{M}|^J)$. Hence, the exact ML-attack is computationally prohibitive in higher-order masking, say, $J = 8$. In practice, adversaries can use attacks based on some combination functions to avoid the $E_m$ operation. Since the $E_m$ of powers of $r_{m,i,0}^g$ and $r_{m,i,1}$ can be known with explicit forms, we wish to approximate the ML-attack statistic and therefore find practical but yet asymptotic equivalent attack to the ML-test. This is achieved by taking a Taylor expansion of (16).

We aim to extract the key-dependent components from the ML test statistic. We set the base of $T_{ML}^g$ as its value when the SNRs at both time points approach zero, which by model (15) becomes a key-independent constant:

$$T_0 = \frac{1}{n} \sum_{i=1}^n \log[\frac{1}{2\pi} e^{-\frac{r_{i,0}^2 + r_{i,1}^2}{2}}]$$

with the noises $r_{i,j} = (l_{i,j} - c_j)/\sigma_j$ for $j = 0, 1$. Removing this constant from (16), we get the rest key-sensitive part of the test statistic:

$$T_{ML}^g - T_0 = \frac{1}{n} \sum_{i=1}^n \log(S_i^g) = \frac{1}{n} \sum_{i=1}^n \log\{E_m[e^{R_{m,i}^g}]\} \tag{19}$$

where $S_i^g = E_m[e^{R_{m,i}^g}]$, $R_{m,i}^g = -\frac{1}{2}(A_{m,i}^g + A_{m,i,1}) = O(\delta)$ and $\delta = max(\delta_0, \delta_1)$ with

$$A_{m,i}^g = (r_{m,i,0}^g)^2 - r_{i,0}^2 = 2\delta_0(V_{i,0} - V_{m,i,0}^g)r_{i,0} + \delta_0^2(V_{i,0} - V_{m,i,0}^g)^2 = O(\delta_0);$$
$$A_{m,i,1} = r_{m,i,1}^2 - r_{i,1}^2 = 2\delta_1(V_{i,1} - V_{m,1})r_{i,1} + \delta_1^2(V_{i,1} - V_{m,1})^2 = O(\delta_1).$$
$$\tag{20}$$

When $\delta \to 0$, we have the Taylor expansion $S_i^g = E_m[e^{R_{m,i}^g}] = 1 + E_m(R_{m,i}^g) + O(\delta^2)$. However, this leading term $E_m(R_{m,i}^g) = E_m[-\frac{1}{2}(A_{m,i}^g + A_{m,i,1})]$ does not contribute to the key selection since it is a key-independent constant. This comes from a simple but very useful fact summarized as:

**Lemma 1** *For any statistic $S^g$ of the leakage measurements at a single time point, $E_m(S^g)$ is independent of key $k_g$.*

The above Lemma is due to the fact that, as $m$ iterates over the range $\mathcal{M}$, $Z^g \oplus m$ also iterates over $\mathcal{M}$. So the sum over the range $\mathcal{M}$ would be independent of the actual value of $Z^g$. Hence, after the $E_m(\cdot)$ operation, any statistic of $Z^g \oplus m$ becomes independent of $Z^g$ (hence independent of key $k_g$).

Lemma 1 implies that $E_m(R^g_{m,i})$ is key-independent which is the sum of two statistics on two different time points. We need to take in the next higher-order term in the Taylor expansion to find the leading key-sensitive term in the ML-attack statistic, $S^g_i = 1 + E_m[R^g_{m,i}] + \frac{1}{2}E_m[(R^g_{m,i})^2] + O(\delta^3)$. The key-sensitive part in $E_m[(R^g_{m,i})^2]$ is $(-1/2)^2 E_m[2A^g_{m,i}A_{m,i,1}]$ after applying Lemma 1 again. Combining this with $log(S^g_i) = (S^g_i - 1) - (S^g_i - 1)^2 + O(\delta^3)$, we have

$$log(S^g_i) = A_i + \frac{1}{4}E_m[A^g_{m,i}A_{m,i,1}] + O(\delta^3), \qquad (21)$$

with a key-independent constant $A_i$. From (21), we get:

$$T^g_{ML} = A + T^g + O(\delta^3), \text{ with } T^g = \frac{1}{4n}\sum_{i=1}^{n} E_m[A^g_{m,i}A_{m,i,1}], \qquad (22)$$

where $A$ is a constant, $A^g_{m,i}$ and $A_{m,i,1}$ are defined in (20). That is, *the ML-attack asymptotically (when $\delta \to 0$) is equivalent to selecting the key $k_g$ that maximizes the test statistic $T_g$ in (22).*

Remark 1: The error in the Taylor expansion of $e^{R^g_{m,i}}$ in (19) by $1 + R^g_{m,i} + (R^g_{m,i})^2/2$ is bounded by $\frac{max(1,e^{R^g_{m,i}})}{6}|R^g_{m,i}|^3$. From the definition of $R^g_{m,i}$ in (20), considering that $V$ is bounded and $R^g_{m,i}$ is linear in $r_i$, $E_m[\frac{max(1,e^{R^g_{m,i}})}{6}|R^g_{m,i}|^3]$ has finite moments for each $i$. By law of large numbers [28] there is a constant $Q$ such that, with probability one for large $n$,

$$\frac{1}{n}\sum_{i=1}^{n} E_m[\frac{max(1,e^{R^g_{m,i}})}{6}|R^g_{m,i}|^3] \leq Q\delta^3$$

uniformly for small enough $\delta$. Hence the above approximation (22) holds uniformly at the rate of $O(\delta^3)$ for small $\delta$ with probability one for large $n$.

Next we simplify the expression of test statistic $T^g$. We can rewrite (20) as

$$\begin{aligned} A^g_{m,i} &= A_{i,0} - 2\delta_0 \tilde{l}_{i,0} V^g_{m,i,0} + \delta^2_0 V^g_{m,i,0}[V^g_{m,i,0} - 2E(V_{i,0})]; \\ A_{m,i,1} &= A_{i,1} - 2\delta_1 \tilde{l}_{i,1} V_{m,1} + \delta^2_1 V_{m,1}[V_{m,1} - 2E(V_{i,1})], \end{aligned} \qquad (23)$$

where $A_{i,0}$ and $A_{i,1}$ are constants independent of guessed key $k_g$ and the random masks $m$. Using (23), we find the leading key-sensitive term in $E_m[A^g_{m,i}A_{m,i,1}]$ relates to the CPCF attack statistics (17),

$$E_m[(-2\delta_0 \tilde{l}_{i,0} V^g_{m,i,0})(-2\delta_j \tilde{l}_{i,j} V_{m,j})] = 4\delta_0 \delta_1 \tilde{C}_i f(Z^g_i) + O(\delta^3) = 4n\tilde{T}^g + O(\delta^3).$$

Plug this into (22), and the approximate ML-test statistic $T^g$ becomes $T^g = B + \delta_0 \delta_1 \widetilde{T}^g + O(\delta^3)$, with $B$ as another key-independent constant. Hence we establish the equivalence between (16) and (17), i.e., prove Theorem 1.

Given specific $V_0(\cdot)$ and $V_1(\cdot)$ functions, $f(Z_i^g) = E_m(V_{m,i,0}^g V_{m,1})$ is a deterministic function and $E_m$ operation can be skipped over using algebraic properties. We further simplify the test statistic $\widetilde{T}^g$ in (17), eliminating the iteration over $\mathcal{M}$ and finding an explicit formula for $f(Z_i^g)$ under the Hamming Weight power leakage model:

$$V_0(Z, M) = H(Z \oplus M) \quad \text{and} \quad V_1(M) = H(M). \tag{24}$$

By Lemma 21 in [16], for any $b$-bits random mask $M$, $E_m[H(Z \oplus M)H(M)|Z] = -\frac{1}{2}H(Z) + b/4$. Applying this formula to (24), we get

$$f(Z_i^g) = E_m(V_{m,i,0}^g V_{m,1}) = -\frac{1}{2}H(Z_i^g) + constant.$$

Therefore, under the Hamming Weight power leakage model, the CPCF attack maximizes

$$\widetilde{T}^g = -\frac{\delta_0 \delta_1}{2n} \sum_{i=1}^{n} \widetilde{C}_i H(Z_i^g). \tag{25}$$

Remark 2: The above derivations for approximate ML attacks assume that the system parameters $(c, \varepsilon, \sigma)$ are all known, and therefore the theoretically strongest attack can just plug these parameters into (18) with $E(L_{i,j}) = c_j + \varepsilon_j \frac{b}{2}$. The real applicable CPCF attack does not know these parameters and needs to estimate $E(L_{i,j}) = \sum_{i=1}^{n} l_{i,j}/n$ and $(c, \varepsilon, \sigma)$ just based on the power data. We therefore consider such two attacks: (a) the theoretical strongest approximate ML attack and (b) the real second-order attack. The real attack (b) should be less powerful due to parameter estimation using finite power data. Similar to the previous work on DPA and CPA modeling, the second-order approximate ML attack (a) provides a theoretical bound for the real CPCF attack (b). We will derive the success rate formula for (a) only in Section 3.3, and will compare these two attacks in Section 4.2.

### 3.3  The Explicit Asymptotic Success Rate Formula for Second-Order Attack

We now derive an explicit asymptotic success rate of the approximate second-order ML-attack, in terms of algorithm confusion coefficients and SNRs. For the test selecting $argmax_{k_g \in S} T^g$, the $\Delta(k_c, k_g)$ in Equation (2) becomes:

$$\Delta(k_c, k_g) = T^c - T^g = \frac{\delta_0 \delta_1}{n}(-\frac{1}{2}) \sum_{i=1}^{n} \widetilde{C}_i (H(Z_i^c) - H(Z_i^g)). \tag{26}$$

As explained in Section 2, the asymptotic success rate of the ML-attack is $\Phi_{N_k-1}(\sqrt{n}\Sigma^{-1/2}\mu)$ given in Equation (3). The mean $\mu$ and variance $\Sigma$ are for the $(N_k - 1)$-dimensional vector according to (26). Then $i$-th element in $\boldsymbol{\mu}$ is

$$\mu_i = (\frac{1}{2})^3 (\delta_0 \delta_1)^2 \kappa(k_c, k_{g_i}). \tag{27}$$

For the $ij$-th element of the covariance $\boldsymbol{\Sigma}$, we keep the leading term and simplify it as:

$$\sigma_{ij} = (\frac{1}{2})^2 (\delta_0 \delta_1)^2 \kappa(k_c, k_{g_i}, k_{g_j}). \tag{28}$$

The detailed calculations for (27) and (28) are provided in Appendix A.

Therefore, under the power leakage model (15) and (24) for masked devices, the asymptotic success rate for the second-order ML-attack is given by:

$$SR = \Phi_{N_k - 1}(\frac{\sqrt{n}\delta_0 \delta_1}{4} \boldsymbol{K}^{-1/2} \boldsymbol{\kappa}). \tag{29}$$

Here definitions of the confusion vector $\boldsymbol{\kappa}$ and the confusion matrix $\boldsymbol{K}$ are exactly the same as those for CPA attack on unmasked devices with elements given in (9) and (10). Compared to the simplified formula for CPA in (12), the second-order attack involves the same algorithmic confusion properties ($\boldsymbol{\kappa}$ and $\boldsymbol{K}$), and the product of two SNRs ($\frac{\delta_0}{2}$ and $\frac{\delta_1}{2}$ at the two time points) introduced by the masking.

The success rate formula (29) provides a good approximation of the true success rates when the noise is high. To also approximate well for moderate noises ($\delta \leq 1$), we keep all the terms in elements of the variance matrix $\boldsymbol{\Sigma}$ without approximation (in Appendix B) and get the complete theoretical model:

$$\boldsymbol{\mu} = \frac{1}{8}\delta_0^2 \delta_1^2 \boldsymbol{\kappa}; \quad \boldsymbol{\Sigma} = \frac{1}{4}\delta_0^2 \delta_1^2 (1 + \frac{b}{4}\delta_0^2)(1 + \frac{b}{4}\delta_1^2)\boldsymbol{K} + \frac{1}{64}\delta_0^4 \delta_1^4 (8\boldsymbol{K}^* - 2b\boldsymbol{K} - \boldsymbol{\kappa}\boldsymbol{\kappa}') \tag{30}$$

where $\boldsymbol{K}^*$ is the higher-order confusion matrix in (11) for CPA attack on unmasked devices. Then the general success rate $\Phi_{N_k - 1}(\sqrt{n}\boldsymbol{\Sigma}^{-1/2}\boldsymbol{\mu})$ in Equation (3) can be calculated with this full variance formula (30). Numerical results in next section show that this complete SR model is very accurate in moderate to high noise situations.

### 3.4 Extension to Higher-Order Masking Devices and Other Power Leakage Models

We now consider the $J$-th order masking scheme with $J$ shares of masking variables, $M_1, M_2, ..., M_J$. Each $M_j$ takes value uniformly in the set $\mathcal{M}$. The previous results can be extended to this general $J$-th order masking setting. The $(J+1)$-th order attack combines the leakage of $V_0 = V_0(Z \overset{J}{\underset{j=1}{\oplus}} M_j)$ at time $t_0$ and the leakage of $V_1 = V_1(M_1), ..., V_J = V_J(M_J)$ at other $J$ times points $t_1,...,t_J$, respectively. Denote $\boldsymbol{M} = (M_1, ..., M_J)$. The leakage vector is $\boldsymbol{l}_i = (l_{i,0}, l_{i,1}, ..., l_{i,J})$. The Gaussian leakage model is now:

$$L_j = L(t_j) = c_j + \varepsilon_j V_j + \sigma_j r_j, \qquad j = 0, ..., J. \tag{31}$$

To discover the first key-dependent term in the Taylor series, the number of $(J + 2)$ leading terms will be kept and the $(J + 1)$-th order ML attack can be shown again to be equivalent to the centered product combination attack. Furthermore, we can get the general formula for the success rate. The mean $\boldsymbol{\mu}$ and the simplified variance $\boldsymbol{\Sigma}$ of $\Delta(k_c, k_g)$ in (26) has elements

$$\mu_i = (\frac{1}{2})^{2J+1}(\prod_{j=0}^{J} \delta_j)^2 \kappa(k_c, k_{g_i}); \qquad \sigma_{ij} = (\frac{1}{2})^{2J}(\prod_{j=0}^{J} \delta_j)^2 \kappa(k_c, k_{g_i}, k_{g_j}). \tag{32}$$

Therefore the asymptotic success rate for $(J + 1)$-th order attack becomes:

$$SR = \Phi_{N_k-1}(\frac{\sqrt{n} \prod_{j=0}^{J} \delta_j}{2^{J+1}} \boldsymbol{K}^{-1/2} \boldsymbol{\kappa}). \tag{33}$$

The detailed analysis for the $(J + 1)$-th order attack is provided in Appendix A. Formula (33) shows that each time one more mask is applied, the entire system SNR (the factor inside function $\Phi_{N_k-1}$) changes by $\frac{\delta}{2}$ (normally lower than 1) and therefore the attack success rate reduces. Comparing a $J$-th order masked device to an unmasked device, we assume the first-order attack on the unmasked device requires $n$ measurement traces to achieve a certain success rate, then $(J + 1)$-th order attack on the $J$-th order masked device needs measurements in the order of $n(\frac{2}{\delta})^{2J}$ assuming all the $\delta_i$ are the same as $\delta$. It is clear from this expression that higher-order masking is more effective when the noise is high (small $\delta$).

We derived the results above under the Gaussian noise assumption (15) and Hamming Weight leakage model (24). Some extensions to other leakage models are possible. For non-Hamming Weight leakage, the CPCF attack (17) maximize the correlation with a function $f(Z_i^g)$ that may be different from $H(Z_i^g)$. However, the $f(Z_i^g)$ is still a deterministic function whose explicit formula can be calculated from the given leakage model. For example, recent work [26] does so for linear regression leakage model. For Non-Gaussian noise, the success rate formulas (29) and (33) still hold for CPCF attack. Some experimental results are presented in Section 4.3 with more discussions included in an extended version of the paper on eprint.iacr.org (#2014/433). Full extensions to other power leakage model and other masking schemes remains an open topic.

## 4    Numerical Results

In this section, we verify the derived statistical model for second-order DPA attacks on realistic measurement data, and also run numerical simulations on synthetic data for second-order and higher-order attacks.

### 4.1    Empirical Success Rates on Measurements from a Physical Implementation

We first verify the analytical results of Section 3 on real measurement data of a masked AES implementation on an SASEBO-GII board with a Virtex-5 FPGA.

The SASEBO board implements the boolean-masked AES algorithm according to the scheme described in [29]. A 128-bit random mask sequence is obtained from a set of linear shift registers [30], then XORed with the input plaintext before the AES AddRoundkey operation. The AES SBox module implementations are modified to keep all intermediate states masked. The overhead of such masking is large, with 50% more slices and 67% more power consumption than the unprotected AES implementation on the same FPGA board.

We collect $N = 1,400,000$ power traces with 3125 points for each one. The two leakage points are at the time points with the highest correlation between the power measurements and $H(M)$ and $H(Z \oplus M)$, respectively. The first leakage point leaks the Hamming Weight of the random mask $M$, while the second leakage point leaks the Hamming distance of the first byte of SBOX output in the last round of AES. We find them at the $581^{th}$ and $2873^{th}$ points, with their SNRs 0.0926 and 0.0955. To obtain the empirical success rate we repeatedly sample $n$ traces from the total number of $N = 1,400,000$ traces. We conduct the second-order DPA attack on the sampled $n$ traces with $1,000$ trials and calculate the empirical success rate for each selected $n$. We plot the empirical success rate versus number of traces in Fig. 1. To draw the theoretical success rate curve, we just use 10,000 traces to find the SNRs at the two points, and then plug them into formula (30) once, without complex experimental trials over millions of traces. Fig. 1 shows the two curves, *Empirical SR* and *Theoretical SR*, track each other very well, verifying that our theoretical success rate formula predicts the empirical success rates accurately. The analytical formula depicts the relation between the attack success rate and the number of traces, without collecting millions of traces and running statistical analysis to empirically calculate the SR. Such formula will be very useful for efficient countermeasure design evaluation before real implementation.

We also check the noise distribution in the measured power traces, and find that for the Virtex-5 FPGA chip on SASEBO-GII board under 65 nm technology, the power model is indeed linear. Fig. 2 shows the average power and distribution for each group of power traces (with different Hamming distances) at the two time points.

## 4.2   Success Rates on Synthetic Datasets

We further verify the analytic success rate formula on synthetic datasets generated from the Hamming weight model (15), to evaluate the effect of system parameters, SNRs, on side-channel attacks and validate our approximate ML-attacks with the centered-product attacks. For simplicity, we take $c_0 = c_1 = 1$ and signal strengths $\varepsilon_0 = \varepsilon_1 = 1$ in the simulation. The range of noises, standard deviations $\sigma_0$ and $\sigma_1$, is $\{1,5\}$. That is, the SNRs $\delta_0$ and $\delta_1$ take values in the range of $\{0.2, 1\}$. These settings are similar to those in previous work [16].

For each set of generated power leakages, we apply two attacks as discussed in Remark 2: (a) the theoretical strongest approximate ML-attack that assumes all the parameters $(c, \varepsilon, \sigma)$ known (as a system designer); (b) the real second-order attack with CPCF that only works on the power data (as an attacker).

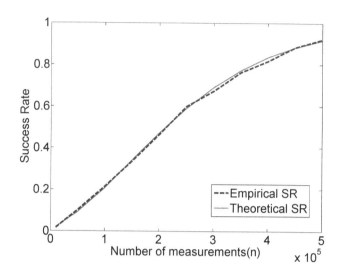

**Fig. 1.** Theoretical and empirical success rates of the second-order attack on a masked AES implementation

We plot the success rate versus number of measurements for different SNRs $\delta_0$ and $\delta_1$ values in Fig. 3, for the two attacks and the theoretical model. $10,000$ simulation trials were run to compute the empirical success rates of the attacks. We can see that the theoretical success rate curve fits the empirical results well when SNRs are small. In addition, attacks (a) and (b) match very well, showing the equivalence between our approximate second-order ML attack and the second-order attack based on the CPCF. In each graph of Fig. 3, when one SNR increases, the attack requires less measurements for the same success rate. When the SNRs are big, $\delta_0 = \delta_1 = 1$, the three curves diverge for small $n$ but still converge for large $n$ values. This confirms that our asymptotic analysis works for big sample size $n$ under very noisy situations (small SNRs). In reality, SNRs are small and would not be as high as 1.

Finding the success rate of an attack based on simulated power data can be as time-consuming as on real measurements, especially when the number of traces is large. For example, the $10,000$ simulations to create the success rate curve for $\delta_0 = \delta_1 = 0.2$ in Fig. 3 took about 11 hours on our workstation while the success rate curve using the explicit formula is produced within seconds. Hence, the analytic success rate formula would be very efficient and insightful for a secure system designer to evaluate any implementation.

The theoretical success rate model also helps us better understand the effect of masking on the security against SCAs. With masking, the number of measurements for the masked device should increase to be $(\frac{2}{\delta})^2$ times the number of measurements for the unmasked device to achieve the same success rate. For example, in noisy situations when $\delta = 0.1$, that is 400 times.

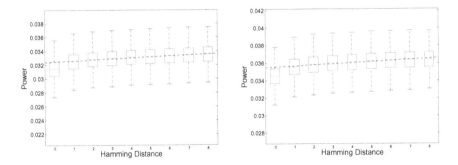

**Fig. 2.** The linear power model with Gaussian distribution noises at the two time points

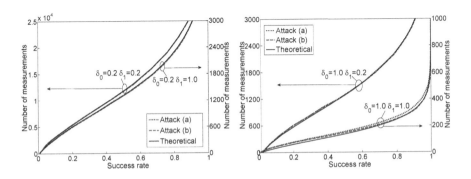

**Fig. 3.** The empirical and theoretical success rates of second order attacks (a) known parameter ML-attack and (b) the CPCF attack on masked AES SBox.

We see that while the second-order attack can break first-order masking, it is much harder to conduct due to significantly reduced information leakage. Moreover, the leakage reduction is much more pronounced in noisy situations with small SNRs. Hence the security benefit of masking is greater when it is combined with other countermeasures that aim to increase the noise and reduce the SNR.

### 4.3   Extension to Higher-Order Attacks and Other Power Models

The general formula for higher-order attacks is given in Section 3.4. As mentioned at the end of Section 3.4, the success rate formula also hold for other non-Gaussian noises. Here we numerically study these extended SR formula. Firstly, we generate power data from higher-order mask model (31) with $J = 2$ and SNRs $\delta_0 = \delta_1 = \delta_2 = 0.2$. Fig. 4 shows the success rates of the corresponding third-order approximate ML attack again fits the theoretical success rate formula very well. Compared to the second-order results in Fig. 3, the number

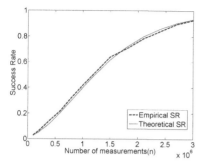
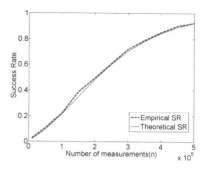

**Fig. 4.** The success rates of the third-order attack on simulated data with all three SNRs $\delta_0 = \delta_1 = \delta_2 = 0.2$.

**Fig. 5.** The success rates of the second-order attack on simulated data with noises from the Laplace distribution ($\delta_0 = 0.0955, \delta_1 = 0.0926$).

of measurements needed for the third-order attack increases to 100 times of that needed for the second-order attack to achieve the same success rate under the same SNRs ($\delta = 0.2$). Secondly, we generate synthetic power data from model (15) with Laplace noises instead. That is, the noises $r_0$ and $r_1$ both come from the probability density function $p(x) = e^{-\sqrt{2}|x|}/\sqrt{2}$. We set the SNRs $\delta_0 = 0.0955$ and $\delta_1 = 0.0926$ the same as the SNRs observed in our real measurements. The success rate curves for the second-order attack are shown in Fig. 5. We can see that the theoretical success rate formula fits the empirical success rates equally well for Laplace noises. The plot is very similar to the plot of success curves under Gaussian noises with the same SNRs.

# 5   Discussions and Conclusions

Various other combination functions have been proposed in literature. Joye et al. suggested raising the absolute difference combining to a power $\alpha$ in [11]. In [15], Oswald et al. proposed a combination function based on the sine function. There has not been any theoretical result indicating the optimal combination function. Prouff et al. proved in [16] that the CPCF is optimal among all attacks using the product combination functions in noisy situations. We prove for the first time that the most powerful SCA, ML-attack, is equivalent to the CPCF attack under very noisy situations. This gives a formal proof that the centered product combination function based attack is indeed optimal among all possible second-order and higher-order attacks on masked devices.

**Acknowledgments.** This work is supported in part by the National Science Foundation of United States under grants CNS-1314655 and CNS-1337854.

# References

1. Brier, E., Clavier, C., Olivier, F.: Correlation power analysis with a leakage model. In: Joye, M., Quisquater, J.-J. (eds.) CHES 2004. LNCS, vol. 3156, pp. 16–29. Springer, Heidelberg (2004)
2. Gierlichs, B., Batina, L., Tuyls, P., Preneel, B.: Mutual information analysis. In: Oswald, E., Rohatgi, P. (eds.) CHES 2008. LNCS, vol. 5154, pp. 426–442. Springer, Heidelberg (2008)
3. Chari, S., Rao, J., Rohatgi, P.: Template attacks. In: Kaliski Jr., B.S., Koç, Ç.K., Paar, C. (eds.) CHES 2002. LNCS, vol. 2523, pp. 13–28. Springer, Heidelberg (2003)
4. Gierlichs, B., Lemke-Rust, K., Paar, C.: Templates vs. stochastic methods: A performance analysis for side channel cryptanalysis. In: Goubin, L., Matsui, M. (eds.) CHES 2006. LNCS, vol. 4249, pp. 15–29. Springer, Heidelberg (2006)
5. Kocher, P.C., Jaffe, J., Jun, B.: Differential power analysis. In: Wiener, M. (ed.) CRYPTO 1999. LNCS, vol. 1666, pp. 388–397. Springer, Heidelberg (1999)
6. Chari, S., Jutla, C., Rao, J., Rohatgi, P.: A cautionary note regarding evaluation of AES candidates on smart-cards. In: Second Advanced Encryption Standard Candidate Conf., pp. 22–23 (1999)
7. Blömer, J., Guajardo, J., Krummel, V.: Provably secure masking of AES. In: Handschuh, H., Hasan, M.A. (eds.) SAC 2004. LNCS, vol. 3357, pp. 69–83. Springer, Heidelberg (2004)
8. Oswald, E., Mangard, S., Pramstaller, N., Rijmen, V.: A side-channel analysis resistant description of the AES S-box. In: Gilbert, H., Handschuh, H. (eds.) FSE 2005. LNCS, vol. 3557, pp. 413–423. Springer, Heidelberg (2005)
9. Canright, D., Batina, L.: A very compact "Perfectly masked" S-box for AES. In: Bellovin, S.M., Gennaro, R., Keromytis, A.D., Yung, M. (eds.) ACNS 2008. LNCS, vol. 5037, pp. 446–459. Springer, Heidelberg (2008)
10. Messerges, T.S.: Using second-order power analysis to attack DPA resistant software. In: Paar, C., Koç, Ç.K. (eds.) CHES 2000. LNCS, vol. 1965, pp. 238–251. Springer, Heidelberg (2000)
11. Joye, M., Paillier, P., Schoenmakers, B.: On second-order differential power analysis. In: Rao, J.R., Sunar, B. (eds.) CHES 2005. LNCS, vol. 3659, pp. 293–308. Springer, Heidelberg (2005)
12. Chari, S., Jutla, C.S., Rao, J.R., Rohatgi, P.: Towards sound approaches to counteract power-analysis attacks. In: Wiener, M. (ed.) CRYPTO 1999. LNCS, vol. 1666, pp. 398–412. Springer, Heidelberg (1999)
13. Schramm, K., Paar, C.: Higher order masking of the AES. In: Pointcheval, D. (ed.) CT-RSA 2006. LNCS, vol. 3860, pp. 208–225. Springer, Heidelberg (2006)
14. Gierlichs, B., Batina, L., Preneel, B., Verbauwhede, I.: Revisiting higher-order DPA attacks: In: Pieprzyk, J. (ed.) CT-RSA 2010. LNCS, vol. 5985, pp. 221–234. Springer, Heidelberg (2010)
15. Oswald, E., Mangard, S., Herbst, C., Tillich, S.: Practical second-order DPA attacks for masked smart card implementations of block ciphers. In: Pointcheval, D. (ed.) CT-RSA 2006. LNCS, vol. 3860, pp. 192–207. Springer, Heidelberg (2006)
16. Prouff, E., Rivain, M., Bevan, R.: Statistical analysis of second order differential power analysis. IEEE Trans. on Computers, 799–811 (2009)
17. Standaert, F.-X., Veyrat-Charvillon, N., Oswald, E., Gierlichs, B., Medwed, M., Kasper, M., Mangard, S.: The world is not enough: Another look on second-order DPA. In: Abe, M. (ed.) ASIACRYPT 2010. LNCS, vol. 6477, pp. 112–129. Springer, Heidelberg (2010)

18. Prouff, E., Rivain, M.: Masking against side-channel attacks: A formal security proof. In: Johansson, T., Nguyen, P.Q. (eds.) EUROCRYPT 2013. LNCS, vol. 7881, pp. 142–159. Springer, Heidelberg (2013)
19. Fei, Y., Luo, Q., Ding, A.A.: A statistical model for DPA with novel algorithmic confusion analysis. In: Prouff, E., Schaumont, P. (eds.) CHES 2012. LNCS, vol. 7428, pp. 233–250. Springer, Heidelberg (2012)
20. Luo, Q., Fei, Y.: Algorithmic collision analysis for evaluating cryptographic systems and side-channel attacks. In: IEEE Int. Symp. Hardware Oriented Security & Trust, pp. 75–80 (June 2011)
21. Standaert, F.-X., Malkin, T.G., Yung, M.: A unified framework for the analysis of side-channel key recovery attacks. In: Joux, A. (ed.) EUROCRYPT 2009. LNCS, vol. 5479, pp. 443–461. Springer, Heidelberg (2009)
22. Fischer, H.: A history of the Central Limit Theorem: From classical to modern probability theory. Springer (2011)
23. Rivain, M.: On the exact success rate of side channel analysis in the gaussian model. In: Avanzi, R.M., Keliher, L., Sica, F. (eds.) SAC 2008. LNCS, vol. 5381, pp. 165–183. Springer, Heidelberg (2009)
24. Fei, Y., Ding, A.A., Lao, J., Zhang, L.: A statistics-based fundamental model for side-channel attack analysis. Cryptology ePrint Archive, Report 2014/152 (2014), http://eprint.iacr.org/
25. Thillard, A., Prouff, E., Roche, T.: Success through confidence: Evaluating the effectiveness of a side-channel attack. In: Bertoni, G., Coron, J.-S. (eds.) CHES 2013. LNCS, vol. 8086, pp. 21–36. Springer, Heidelberg (2013)
26. Dabosville, G., Doget, J., Prouff, E.: A new second-order side channel attack based on linear regression. IEEE Transactions on Computers 62(8), 1629–1640 (2013)
27. Runnalls, A.: Kullback-leibler approach to gaussian mixture reduction. IEEE Transactions on Aerospace and Electronic Systems 43(3), 989–999 (2007)
28. Seneta, E.: A tricentenary history of the law of large numbers. Bernoulli 19(4), 1088–1121 (2013)
29. Akkar, M.-L., Giraud, C.: An implementation of DES and AES, secure against some attacks. In: Koç, Ç.K., Naccache, D., Paar, C. (eds.) CHES 2001. LNCS, vol. 2162, pp. 309–318. Springer, Heidelberg (2001)
30. Lewis, T.G., Payne, W.H.: Generalized feedback shift register pseudorandom number algorithm. Journal of the ACM (JACM) 20(3), 456–468 (1973)

## Appendix

# A    Derivations for the $(J+1)$-th order ML-attack on Masked Devices

For the $(J+1)$-th order ML-attack, the attack statistic from Equation (16) becomes

$$T_{ML}^g = \frac{1}{n} \sum_{i=1}^{n} \log\{E_{\boldsymbol{m}}[\phi(r_{\boldsymbol{m},i,0}^g) \prod_{j=1}^{J} \phi(r_{\boldsymbol{m},i,j})]\} \tag{34}$$

where $\boldsymbol{m} = (m_{(1)}, ..., m_{(J)})$, $r_{\boldsymbol{m},i,0}^g = \frac{l_{i,0}-c_0-\varepsilon_0 V_{\boldsymbol{m},i,0}^g}{\sigma_0} = r_{i,0} + \delta_0(V_{i,0} - V_{\boldsymbol{m},i,0}^g)$ and $r_{\boldsymbol{m},i,j} = \frac{l_{i,j}-c_j-\varepsilon_j V_{\boldsymbol{m},j}}{\sigma_j} = r_{i,j} + \delta_j(V_{i,j} - V_{\boldsymbol{m},j})$, $j = 0, ..., J$. Here $V_{\boldsymbol{m},i,0}^g =$

$V_0(Z_i^g \oplus_{j=1}^J m_{(j)})$, $V_{m,j} = V_j(m_{(j)})$, and $\delta_j = \varepsilon_j/\sigma_j$ denotes SNR for $j = 0, ..., J$. The $E_m$ takes expectation over all possible values of the vector $m = (m_{(1)}, ..., m_{(J)})$. That is, each element $m_{(j)}$ iterate over $\mathcal{M}$.

For the $(J+1)$-th order attack, we need to take $J+2$ terms in the Taylor expansion of (34). So the leading key-sensitive term (22) before becomes

$$T^g = \frac{1}{n}\sum_{i=1}^n B_i^g = \frac{1}{n}\sum_{i=1}^n (-\frac{1}{2})^{J+1} E_m[A_{m,i}^g \prod_{j=1}^J A_{m,i,j}], \qquad (35)$$

where $A_{m,i}^g$ and $A_{m,i,j}$ in (23) now become

$$\begin{aligned} A_{m,i}^g &= A_{i,0} - 2\delta_0 \tilde{l}_{i,0} V_{m,i,0}^g + \delta_0^2 V_{m,i,0}^g [V_{m,i,0}^g - E(V_{i,0})]; \\ A_{m,i,j} &= A_{i,j} - 2\delta_j \tilde{l}_{i,j} V_{m,j} + \delta_j^2 V_{m,j}[V_{m,j} - E(V_{i,j})] \qquad j = 1, ..., J, \end{aligned} \qquad (36)$$

Using (36), we find the leading key-sensitive term in $E_m[A_{m,i}^g \prod_{j=1}^J A_{m,i,j}]$ relates to the centered product combination as

$$E_m(\{-2\delta_0 \tilde{l}_{i,0} V_{m,i,0}^g\} \prod_{j=1}^J \{-2\delta_j \tilde{l}_{i,j} V_{m,j}\}) = (-2)^{J+1}(\prod_{j=0}^J \delta_j)\widetilde{C}_i f(Z_i^g).$$

Here $\widetilde{C}_i = \prod_{j=0}^J \tilde{l}_{i,j}$ and $f(Z_i^g) = E_m(V_{m,i,0}^g \prod_{j=1}^J V_{m,j})$. Plug this into (35),

$$T^g = B^* + \widetilde{T}^g + o(\prod_{j=0}^J \delta_j), \qquad \text{with } \widetilde{T}^g = \frac{(\prod_{j=0}^J \delta_j)}{n}\sum_{i=1}^n \widetilde{C}_i f(Z_i^g). \qquad (37)$$

The $f(Z_i^g)$ has an explicit formula as $E_m(V_{m,i,0}^g \prod_{j=1}^J V_{m,j})$ under the Hamming Weight power leakage model:

$$V_0(Z, M) = H(Z \overset{J}{\underset{j=1}{\oplus}} M_j) \qquad \text{and} \qquad V_j(M) = H(M_j), \qquad j = 1, ..., J. \quad (38)$$

By Lemma 21 in [16], for any $b$-bits random mask $M$, $E[H(Z \oplus M)H(M)|Z] = -\frac{1}{2}H(Z) + b/4$. Apply this formula once, we get

$$E_{m_{(1)}}(V_{m,i,0}^g V_{m,1}) = E_{m_{(1)}}[H(Z_i^g \overset{J}{\underset{j=1}{\oplus}} m_{(j)})H(m_{(1)})] = -\frac{1}{2}H(Z_i^g \overset{J}{\underset{j=2}{\oplus}} m_{(j)}) + b/4.$$

Repeatedly apply the formula another $J-1$ times, we get that

$$E_m(V_{m,i,0}^g \prod_{j=1}^J V_{m,j}) = (-\frac{1}{2})^J H(Z_i^g) + constant.$$

Hence under the Hamming Weight power leakage model, the centered product combination function attack maximizes

$$\widetilde{T}^g = (-\frac{1}{2})^J \frac{(\prod_{j=0}^J \delta_j)}{n}\sum_{i=1}^n \widetilde{C}_i H(Z_i^g). \qquad (39)$$

We now can calculate $\boldsymbol{u}$ and $\boldsymbol{\Sigma}$ in the success Rate (3) for the higher order attack. From (35), $\Delta(k_c, k_g) = T^c - T^g = \frac{1}{n}\sum_{i=1}^{n}(B_i^c - B_i^g)$. So as in Section 2, $\boldsymbol{u}$ and $\boldsymbol{\Sigma}$ are the mean and variance of $\tilde{\Delta}_1 = (B_1^c - B_1^{g_1}, \ldots, B_1^c - B_1^{g_{N_k-1}})^T$. Using (37) and (39), we get

$$B_1^c - B_1^g = (-\frac{1}{2})^J(\prod_{j=0}^{J}\delta_j)[\prod_{j=0}^{J}\tilde{l}_{1,j}][H(Z_1^c) - H(Z_1^g)]. \tag{40}$$

Recall $\tilde{l}_{1,j} = r_{1,j} + \delta_j[V_{1,j} - E(V_{1,j})]$. Since $E(r_{1,j}) = 0$ and $r_{1,j}$'s are independent of the $V_{i,j}$'s. We find

$$E(B_1^c - B_1^g) = (-\frac{1}{2})^J(\prod_{j=0}^{J}\delta_j)^2 E\{\prod_{j=0}^{J}[V_{1,j} - E(V_{1,j})][H(Z_1^c) - H(Z_1^g)]\}.$$

Recall that $V_{1,j} = H(m_{1,j})$'s are Hamming weights of the random masks for $j = 1, \ldots, J$. Using formula (46) in Appendix C, taking expectation over the masks, $E\{\prod_{j=0}^{J}[V_{1,j} - E(V_{1,j})][H(Z_1^c) - H(Z_1^g)]\} = E\{(-1/2)^J[H(Z_1^c) - b/2][H(Z_1^c) - H(Z_1^g)]\}$. Here $b$ is the bit length of $Z_1^c$. Since $E[H(Z_1^c) - H(Z_1^g)] = b/2 - b/2 = 0$, we get

$$
\begin{aligned}
E(B_1^c - B_1^g) &= (-\frac{1}{2})^{2J}(\prod_{j=0}^{J}\delta_j)^2 E\{H(Z_1^c)[H(Z_1^c) - H(Z_1^g)]\}\\
&= (\frac{1}{2})^{2J}(\prod_{j=0}^{J}\delta_j)^2 E\{[H(Z_1^c)]^2 - H(Z_1^c)H(Z_1^g)\}\\
&= (\frac{1}{2})^{2J}(\prod_{j=0}^{J}\delta_j)^2 \frac{1}{2}E\{[H(Z_1^c)]^2 + [H(Z_1^g)]^2 - 2H(Z_1^c)H(Z_1^g)\}\\
&= (\frac{1}{2})^{2J+1}(\prod_{j=0}^{J}\delta_j)^2 E\{[H(Z_1^g) - H(Z_1^c)]^2\}\\
&= (\frac{1}{2})^{2J+1}(\prod_{j=0}^{J}\delta_j)^2 \kappa(k_c, k_g).
\end{aligned}
$$

Here the confusion coefficient $\kappa(k_c, k_g)$ is exactly the same as the confusion coefficient for unmasked device defined in (9). Thus we arrive at the first formula in equation (32)

$$\mu_i = E[B_1^c - B_1^{g_i}] = (\frac{1}{2})^{2J+1}(\prod_{j=0}^{J}\delta_j)^2 \kappa(k_c, k_{g_i}).$$

The $ij$-th element in the variance $\boldsymbol{\Sigma} = Var(\tilde{\Delta}_1)$ is

$$\sigma_{ij} = Cov(B_1^c - B_1^{g_i}, B_1^c - B_1^{g_j}) = E[(B_1^c - B_1^{g_i})(B_1^c - B_1^{g_j})] - \mu_i\mu_j.$$

Since $E(r_{1,j}) = 0$ and $E(r_{1,j}^2) = 1$ for $j = 0, \ldots, J$, using equation (40), we have the leading term in $\sigma_{ij}$ as in the second formula in equation (32)

$$(-\frac{1}{2})^{2J}(\prod_{j=0}^{J}\delta_j)^2 E(\prod_{j=0}^{J}r_{1,j}^2)E\{[H(Z_1^{g_i}) - H(Z_1^c)][H(Z_1^{g_j}) - H(Z_1^c)]\} = (\frac{1}{2})^{2J}(\prod_{j=0}^{J}\delta_j)^2\kappa(k_c, k_{g_i}, k_{g_j}).$$

Here the three-way confusion coefficient $\kappa(k_c, k_{g_i}, k_{g_j})$ is exactly the same as those defined for unmasked device in (10).

Taking $J = 1$, (32) becomes (27) and (28).

# B   More Accurate Formula for the Covariance Matrix $\Sigma$ in the Second-Order ML Attack on Masked Devices

Equation (28) only calculate the leading term in $\sigma_{ij}$. We can calculate all the terms to get more accurate formula. Keeping all terms in $\tilde{l}_{1,0}$ and $\tilde{l}_{1,1}$ we have

$$B_1^c - B_1^g = -\frac{1}{2}\delta_0\delta_1[r_{1,0} + \delta_0(V_{1,0} - \frac{b}{2})][r_{1,1} + \delta_1(V_{1,1} - \frac{b}{2})][H(Z_1^c) - H(Z_1^g)].$$

Then, since $E(r_{1,0}) = E(r_{1,1}) = 0$ and $E(r_{1,0}^2) = E(r_{1,1}^2) = 1$, we have

$$
\begin{aligned}
\sigma_{ij} = {} & \tfrac{1}{4}\delta_0^2\delta_1^2 E\{[H(Z_1^{g_i}) - H(Z_1^c)][H(Z_1^{g_j}) - H(Z_1^c)]\} \\
& + \tfrac{1}{4}\delta_0^2\delta_1^4 E\{(V_{1,1} - \tfrac{b}{2})^2[H(Z_1^{g_i}) - H(Z_1^c)][H(Z_1^{g_j}) - H(Z_1^c)]\} \\
& + \tfrac{1}{4}\delta_0^4\delta_1^2 E\{(V_{1,0} - \tfrac{b}{2})^2[H(Z_1^{g_i}) - H(Z_1^c)][H(Z_1^{g_j}) - H(Z_1^c)]\} \\
& + \tfrac{1}{4}\delta_0^4\delta_1^4 E\{(V_{1,0} - \tfrac{b}{2})^2(V_{1,1} - \tfrac{b}{2})^2[H(Z_1^{g_i}) - H(Z_1^c)][H(Z_1^{g_j}) - H(Z_1^c)]\} - \mu_i\mu_j.
\end{aligned}
$$
(41)

Using (44) and (47) in Appendix C, this simplifies to

$$
\begin{aligned}
\sigma_{ij} = {} & \tfrac{1}{4}\delta_0^2\delta_1^2\kappa(k_c, k_{g_i}, k_{g_j}) + \tfrac{1}{4}\delta_0^2\delta_1^4\tfrac{b}{4}\kappa(k_c, k_{g_i}, k_{g_j}) + \tfrac{1}{4}\delta_0^4\delta_1^2\tfrac{b}{4}\kappa(k_c, k_{g_i}, k_{g_j}) \\
& + \tfrac{1}{4}\delta_0^4\delta_1^4[\tfrac{1}{2}\kappa^*(k_c, k_{g_i}, k_{g_j}) + \tfrac{b^2-2b}{16}\kappa(k_c, k_{g_i}, k_{g_j})] - \tfrac{1}{64}\delta_0^4\delta_1^4\kappa(k_c, k_{g_i})\kappa(k_c, k_{g_j}) \\
= {} & \tfrac{1}{4}\delta_0^2\delta_1^2(1 + \tfrac{b}{4}\delta_0^2)(1 + \tfrac{b}{4}\delta_1^2)\kappa(k_c, k_{g_i}, k_{g_j}) \\
& + \tfrac{1}{64}\delta_0^4\delta_1^4[8\kappa^*(k_c, k_{g_i}, k_{g_j}) - 2b\kappa(k_c, k_{g_i}, k_{g_j}) - \kappa(k_c, k_{g_i})\kappa(k_c, k_{g_j})].
\end{aligned}
$$
(42)

Here the three-way confusion coefficients $\kappa(k_c, k_{g_i}, k_{g_j})$ and $\kappa^*(k_c, k_{g_i}, k_{g_j})$ are the same as those defined for unmasked device in (10) and (11).

Thus we get the formula (30).

# C   Formulas for Eliminating $E_m$ with Hamming Weight Power Models on Masked Devices

Here we list some formulas used for calculation in the above derivations. We shall consider the $b$-bit mask $M$ similarly as in Prouff et al [16]. We are going to consider quantities involving $H(Z \oplus M)$ and $H(M)$ for a fixed $Z$. By Lemma 20 in [16],

$$E[H(M)] = \frac{b}{2}; \qquad E[H(M)^2] = \frac{b^2 + b}{4}. \tag{43}$$

Therefore,

$$E[(H(M) - \frac{b}{2})^2] = E[H(M)^2] - bE[H(M)] + \frac{b^2}{4} = \frac{b}{4}. \tag{44}$$

By Lemma 21 in [16],

$$E[H(M)H(Z \oplus M)|Z] = -\frac{1}{2}H(Z) + \frac{b^2 + b}{4}. \tag{45}$$

Combine (43) and (45), we arrive at

$$E\{[H(M) - \frac{b}{2}][H(Z \oplus M) - \frac{b}{2}]|Z\} = -\frac{1}{2}H(Z) + \frac{b^2+b}{4} - (\frac{b}{2})^2 = -\frac{1}{2}H(Z) + \frac{b}{4} = -\frac{1}{2}[H(Z) - \frac{b}{2}].$$

Hence for fixed $Z$ and $J$ random masks $M_1, ..., M_J$, we have

$$E\{[H(Z \underset{j=1}{\overset{J}{\oplus}} M_j) - \frac{b}{2}] \prod_{j=1}^{J}[H(M_j) - \frac{b}{2}]\} = -\frac{1}{2}E\{[H(Z \underset{j=1}{\overset{J-1}{\oplus}} M_j) - \frac{b}{2}] \prod_{j=1}^{J-1}[H(M_j) - \frac{b}{2}]\} = ... = (-\frac{1}{2})^J [H(Z) - \frac{b}{2}]$$

(46)

The last result required in earlier derivation is

$$E\{[H(Z \oplus M) - \frac{b}{2}]^2[H(M) - \frac{b}{2}]^2|Z\} = \frac{1}{2}[H(Z) - \frac{b}{2}]^2 + \frac{b^2 - 2b}{16}. \qquad (47)$$

This equation (47) follows from (43), (45) above, and (48), (49) below.

$$E[H(M)H(Z \oplus M)^2|Z] = E[H(M)^2 H(Z \oplus M)|Z] = -\frac{b}{2}H(Z) + \frac{b^2(b+3)}{8}; \quad (48)$$

$$E[H(M)^2 H(Z \oplus M)^2|Z] = \frac{1}{2}H(Z)^2 - \frac{b^2+b}{2}H(Z) + \frac{b(b^3 + 6b^2 + 3b - 2)}{16}. \quad (49)$$

Equations (48) and (49) come from straight calculation using formulas (43),(50), (57),(58), (59) and (60). The above calculation used the formulas below which are derived similar to those in in [16]. First, let $\wedge$ denote the bit-wise multiplication. Then the following formula is the property 2 in [16]:

$$H(Z \oplus M) = H(Z) + H(M) - 2H(Z \wedge M). \qquad (50)$$

Let $Z_{(i)}$ denotes the $i$th bit of $Z$. We derive the following formulas, using the fact that $E(M_{(i)}M_{(j)}) = E(M_{(i)}) = \frac{1}{2}$ when $i = j$ and $E(M_{(i)}M_{(j)}) = \frac{1}{4}$ by independence when $i \neq j$.

$$E[H(Z \wedge M)] = \frac{1}{2}H(Z), \qquad (51)$$

since $E[H(Z \wedge M)] = E[\sum_{i=1}^{b} Z_{(i)}M_{(i)}] = \sum_i Z_{(i)}\frac{1}{2}$.

$$E[H(M)H(Z \wedge M)] = \frac{b+1}{4}H(Z), \qquad (52)$$

since $E[H(M)H(Z \wedge M)] = \sum_{i=1}^{b} Z_{(i)} \sum_{j=1}^{b} E[M_{(i)}M_{(j)}] = \sum_i Z_{(i)}[\frac{1}{2} + (b-1)\frac{1}{4}]$.

$$E[H(Z \wedge M)H(Z^g \wedge M)] = \frac{1}{4}H(Z)H(Z^g) + \frac{1}{4}H(Z \wedge Z^g), \qquad (53)$$

since $E[H(Z \wedge M)H(Z^g \wedge M)] = \sum_{i,j} Z_{(i)}Z_{(j)}^g E[M_{(i)}M_{(j)}]$ which becomes

$$\sum_{i=j} Z_{(i)}Z_{(j)}^g \frac{1}{2} + \sum_{i \neq j} Z_{(i)}Z_{(j)}^g \frac{1}{4} = \sum_{i,j} Z_{(i)}Z_{(j)}^g \frac{1}{4} + \sum_i Z_{(i)}Z_{(i)}^g \frac{1}{4}.$$

We get the following two formulas similarly as (51), (52) and (53) above, with the detailed calculation omitted for space.

$$E[H(M)H(Z \wedge M)H(Z^g \wedge M)] = \frac{b+2}{8}H(Z)H(Z^g) + \frac{b}{8}H(Z \wedge Z^g), \quad (54)$$

$$E[(H(M))^2 H(Z \wedge M)H(Z^g \wedge M)] = \frac{b^2 + 5b + 2}{16}H(Z)H(Z^g) + \frac{b^2 + b - 2}{16}H(Z \wedge Z^g). \quad (55)$$

Taking $Z^g = Z$ in (54) and (55), we get

$$E[H(M)H(Z \wedge M)^2] = \frac{b+2}{8}H(Z)^2 + \frac{b}{8}H(Z), \quad (56)$$

$$E[(H(M))^2 H(Z \wedge M)^2] = \frac{b^2 + 5b + 2}{16}H(Z)^2 + \frac{b^2 + b - 2}{16}H(Z). \quad (57)$$

Taking $Z^g$ to have every bit equals to one in (54) and (55), we get

$$E[H(M)^2 H(Z \wedge M)] = \frac{b(b+3)}{8}H(Z), \quad (58)$$

$$E[(H(M))^3 H(Z \wedge M)] = \frac{b^3 + 6b^2 + 3b - 2}{16}H(Z). \quad (59)$$

Taking $Z$ to have every bit equals to one in (58) and (59), we get

$$E[H(M)]^3 = \frac{b^2(b+3)}{8}; \qquad E[H(M)]^4 = \frac{b(b^3 + 6b^2 + 3b - 2)}{16}. \quad (60)$$

# Fast Evaluation of Polynomials over Binary Finite Fields and Application to Side-Channel Countermeasures

Jean-Sébastien Coron[1], Arnab Roy[1,2], and Srinivas Vivek[1]

[1] University of Luxembourg, Luxembourg
{jean-sebastien.coron,srinivasvivek.venkatesh}@uni.lu
[2] Technical University of Denmark, Denmark
arroy@dtu.dk

**Abstract.** We describe a new technique for evaluating polynomials over binary finite fields. This is useful in the context of anti-DPA counter-measures when an S-box is expressed as a polynomial over a binary finite field. For $n$-bit S-boxes our new technique has heuristic complexity $\mathcal{O}(2^{n/2}/\sqrt{n})$ instead of $\mathcal{O}(2^{n/2})$ proven complexity for the Parity-Split method. We also prove a lower bound of $\Omega(2^{n/2}/\sqrt{n})$ on the complexity of any method to evaluate $n$-bit S-boxes; this shows that our method is asymptotically optimal. Here, complexity refers to the number of non-linear multiplications required to evaluate the polynomial corresponding to an S-box.

In practice we can evaluate any 8-bit S-box in 10 non-linear multiplications instead of 16 in the Roy-Vivek paper from CHES 2013, and the DES S-boxes in 4 non-linear multiplications instead of 7. We also evaluate any 4-bit S-box in 2 non-linear multiplications instead of 3. Hence our method achieves optimal complexity for the PRESENT S-box.

## 1 Introduction

The implementations of cryptographic algorithms on devices like PCs, micro-controllers, smart cards, etc. leak secret information to an adversary. Typical examples of such leakages are electro-magnetic emissions, power consumption and even acoustic emanations. An adversary can use this information to recover the secret key by applying different statistical techniques. Differential Power Analysis (DPA) – the most widely known and powerful technique – is based on statistical analysis of the power consumption of a device [KJJ99]. Other techniques including Template Attacks, Correlation Power Analysis Attacks (CPA), etc. were proposed in the past [CRR02, BCO04]. More recently, a side-channel attack on RSA was proposed using the acoustic emanations from a device [GST13].

**Masking.** A well known technique to protect implementations against power analysis based side-channel attacks is to mask internal *secret* variables. This is done by XORing any internal variable with a random variable $r$, for e.g., $x' = x \oplus$

L. Batina and M. Robshaw (Eds.): CHES 2014, LNCS 8731, pp. 170–187, 2014.

$r$. However, this will make the implementation secure against first-order attacks only. Second-order attacks against such counter-measures is proposed in [Mes00]. In this type of attack the adversary combines the information obtained from two internal variables. This will require more data (power consumption traces) in practice, which could make the attack infeasible in certain cases. In general the above masking technique can be extended to secure an implementation against higher-order attacks. This can be achieved by splitting an internal variable $x$ into $d$ shares, say, $x = \bigoplus_{i=1}^{d} x_i$. Using this idea it is easy to compute any linear/affine function $\ell$ in a secured way, since it is enough to compute $y_i = \ell(x_i)$ for $1 \leq i \leq d$. However, it is not obvious how to do this for non-linear functions. In practice, nearly every cryptographic primitive includes some non-linear function, e.g., S-box, modular addition, etc.

**Generic Higher-Order Masking.** The Rivain-Prouff masking scheme is the first provably secure higher-order masking technique for AES [RP10]. The main idea of this method is to perform secure monomial evaluation with $d$ shares of a secret variable using the previously known ISW scheme [ISW03]. Namely the (non-linear part of) AES S-box can be represented by the monomial $x^{254}$ over $\mathbb{F}_{2^8}$. Prouff and Rivain showed that this monomial can be evaluated securely using 4 non-linear multiplications and a few linear squarings. By using this scheme the AES S-box can be masked for any order $d$.

This method was extended to a generic technique for higher-order masking, in [CGP+12], by Carlet, Goubin, Prouff, Quisquater and Rivain (CGPQR). Any given $n$-bit S-box can be represented by a polynomial $\sum_{i=0}^{2^n-1} a_i x^i$ over $\mathbb{F}_{2^n}$ using Lagrange's interpolation theorem. Hence, any S-box can be masked by secure evaluation of this polynomial with $d$ shares of a secret variable. This is the first generic technique to mask any S-box for any order $d$. In this technique a polynomial evaluation in $\mathbb{F}_{2^n}$ is split into simple operations over $\mathbb{F}_{2^n}$: addition, multiplication by constant, and regular multiplication of two elements. Note that multiplication of two same elements (i.e. squaring) and multiplication by a constant – both are linear operations over $\mathbb{F}_{2^n}$, hence easy to mask. For performing a secure multiplication of two distinct elements, *i.e.* a non-linear multiplication, the CGPQR masking scheme uses the ISW method as in [RP10].

Asymptotically, the running time of the Rivain-Prouff and CGPQR masking schemes is dominated by the number of non-linear multiplications required to evaluate a polynomial over $\mathbb{F}_{2^n}$. Namely with $d$ shares, using the ISW method an affine function can be masked with only $\mathcal{O}(d)$ operations over $\mathbb{F}_{2^n}$, whereas a non-linear multiplication requires $\mathcal{O}(d^2)$ operations. Note that for achieving $d$-th order security the Rivain-Prouff scheme requires at least $2d+1$ shares.[1]

---

[1] Originally it was claimed in [RP10] that the scheme is secure against $d$-th order attack with $d+1$ shares. However, an attack of order $d/2$ was shown in [CPRR13] against the scheme. The authors of [CPRR13] also showed a $d$-th order secure scheme with $d+1$ shares for some subset of S-boxes.

**Efficient Polynomial Evaluation for Masking.** The CGPQR masking scheme can be made efficient by optimizing the number of multiplications required
for the polynomial evaluation in $\mathbb{F}_{2^n}$. In [CGP+12] two techniques – *Parity-Split*
and *Cyclotomic Class*, are used for optimizing the number of such non-linear
multiplications. For arbitrary $n$-bit S-box, or equivalently for evaluating any
polynomial over $\mathbb{F}_{2^n}$, the Parity-Split method has proven complexity $\mathcal{O}(2^{n/2})$.
Here complexity refers to the number of non-linear multiplications required to
evaluate the polynomial corresponding to an S-box. For the particular case of
monomials (e.g. AES S-box) the Cyclotomic Class method gives the optimal
number of multiplications in $\mathbb{F}_{2^n}$.

At CHES 2013, Roy and Vivek [RV13] adapted a generic method for improving
the efficiency of polynomial evaluation in $\mathbb{F}_{2^n}$. They demonstrated the technique
for the polynomials corresponding to several well known S-boxes including DES,
PRESENT and CLEFIA. In particular, the Roy-Vivek method reduces the number of non-linear multiplications for DES to 7 (from 10), for CLEFIA to 16 (from
22) and for CAMELLIA to 15 (from 22). This technique also achieves the optimal number of 4 multiplications for the monomial corresponding to the AES
S-box.

**Our Results.** In this article we propose an improved generic technique for
fast polynomial evaluation in $\mathbb{F}_{2^n}$. For arbitrary $n$-bit S-box our method has
heuristic complexity $\mathcal{O}(2^{n/2}/\sqrt{n})$, compared to the $\mathcal{O}(2^{n/2})$ proven complexity
for the Parity-Split method from [CGP+12].

Our method is as follows. We first generate a set $L$ of monomials $x^\alpha$, including
all the monomials from a cyclotomic class. We then randomly generate a fixed
set of "basis" polynomials $q_i(x)$, whose monomials are all in the precomputed
set $L$. Then given a polynomial $P(x)$ over $\mathbb{F}_{2^n}$ we try to write $P(x)$ as:

$$P(x) = \sum_{i=1}^{t-1} p_i(x) \cdot q_i(x) + p_t(x) \pmod{x^{2^n} + x}, \qquad (1)$$

where $p_i(x)$ are polynomials with monomials also in the set $L$, and $t$ is some
parameter. Since the $q_i(x)$ polynomials are fixed, the coefficients of the $p_i(x)$
polynomials can be obtained by solving a system of linear equations in $\mathbb{F}_{2^n}$.
Then to evaluate $P(x)$ one first evaluates all the monomials in the set $L$; the
polynomials $p_i(x)$ and $q_i(x)$ can then be evaluated without any further non-
linear multiplication. The polynomials $P(x)$ is then evaluated from (1) with
$t - 1$ additional non-linear multiplications.

The number of monomials in the set $L$ must be carefully chosen. Namely the
larger the basis set $L$ of monomials, the more degrees of freedom we have in
solving (1), with fewer polynomials $p_i(x)$ and therefore fewer additional non-
linear multiplications; however the number of non-linear multiplications to build
$L$ will increase. Therefore the number of monomials in the basis set $L$ must be
optimized to minimize the total number of non-linear multiplications, namely
the non-linear multiplications for building the set $L$, and the additional $t - 1$
non-linear multiplications for evaluating $P(x)$.

As a concrete application of our new method above, we show that for the generic higher-order masking of several well known S-boxes, e.g. DES, CLEFIA, PRESENT, etc., our method reduces the number of multiplications compared to the previously known methods [CGP+12, RV13]. In particular, using our method PRESENT can be masked with 2 multiplications (instead of 3), and DES with 4 multiplications (instead of 7), see Table 1. Our method achieves optimal complexity for the PRESENT S-box since it was proved in [RV13] that 2 non-linear multiplications are necessary to evaluate it.

**Table 1.** Number of non-linear multiplications required for the CGPQR generic higher-order masking scheme

| Methods | S-box | | | | |
|---|---|---|---|---|---|
| | DES | PRESENT | SERPENT | CAMELLIA | CLEFIA |
| Parity-Split [CGP+12] | 10 | 3 | 3 | 22 | 22 |
| Roy-Vivek [RV13] | 7 | 3 | 3 | 15 | 15,16 |
| **Our Method** (Sec. 4) | **4** | **2** | **2** | **10** | **10** |

We also prove a lower bound of $\Omega(2^{n/2}/\sqrt{n})$ for the complexity of any method to evaluate $n$-bit S-boxes, a.k.a. *masking complexity*; this shows that our method is asymptotically optimal. Our new lower bound significantly improves upon the previously known bound of $\Omega(\log_2 n)$ from [RV13].

# 2  Generic Polynomial Evaluation Technique

Before we describe our improved method to evaluate polynomials over $\mathbb{F}_{2^n}$, let us first recollect in Section 2.1 the method proposed by Roy and Vivek [RV13, Section 4] to evaluate the polynomials (over $\mathbb{F}_{2^6}$) corresponding to the DES S-boxes. Their method requires 7 non-linear multiplications. The method in [RV13] is based on the *Divide-and-Conquer* strategy, which is an adaptation of a polynomial evaluation technique by Paterson and Stockmeyer [PS73]. The technique consists in decomposing the polynomial to be evaluated in terms of polynomials having their monomials from a precomputed set. Our method is partly based on this idea.

## 2.1  The Roy-Vivek Method for DES S-boxes

Let $P_{DES}(x) \in \mathbb{F}_{2^6}[x]$ be the Lagrange interpolation polynomial corresponding to a DES S-box. Here the 4-bit output of a DES S-box is identified as a 6-bit output with two leading zeroes, and hence these bit strings are naturally identified with the elements of $\mathbb{F}_{2^6}$. Note that for all the DES S-boxes, $\deg(P_{DES}(x)) = 62$. Write

$$P_{DES}(x) = q(x) \cdot x^{36} + R(x),$$

where $\deg(R) \leq 35$ and $\deg(q) = 26$. Then divide the polynomial $R(x) - x^{27}$ by $q(x)$:

$$R(x) - x^{27} = c(x) \cdot q(x) + s(x),$$

where $\deg(c) \leq 9$ and $\deg(s) \leq 25$, which gives

$$P_{DES}(x) = \left(x^{36} + c(x)\right) \cdot q(x) + x^{27} + s(x).$$

Next decompose the polynomials $q(x)$ and $x^{27} + s(x)$ in a similar way but, instead, dividing first by $x^{18}$, and then using $x^9$ as the "correction term". One gets

$$q(x) = (x^{18} + c_1(x)) \cdot q_1(x) + x^9 + s_1(x),$$

$$x^{27} + s(x) = (x^{18} + c_2(x)) \cdot q_2(x) + x^9 + s_2(x)$$

where $\deg(q_1) = 8$, $\deg(c_1) \leq 9$, $\deg(s_1) \leq 7$, $\deg(q_2) = 9$, $\deg(c_2) \leq 8$, and $\deg(s_2) \leq 8$. Finally,

$$\begin{aligned} P_{DES}(x) =&(x^{36} + c(x)) \cdot \left( \left((x^{18} + c_1(x)) \cdot q_1(x)\right) + (x^9 + s_1(x)) \right) \\ &+ \left( (x^{18} + c_2(x)) \cdot q_2(x) + (x^9 + s_2(x)) \right). \end{aligned} \tag{2}$$

In [RV13], the monomials $x$, $x^2$, $x^3$, $x^4$, $x^5$, $x^6$, $x^7$, $x^8$, $x^9$, $x^{18}$, $x^{36}$ are first evaluated using 4 non-linear multiplications. Namely a non-linear multiplication is required for each of the monomials $x^3$, $x^5$, $x^7$ and $x^9$; the rest of the monomials can be evaluated using linear squarings only. Each of the individual polynomials in the above expression such as $x^{36} + c(x)$, $x^{18} + c_1(x)$, $q_1(x)$, and so on, can then be evaluated for free, that is without further non-linear multiplications. To evaluate $P_{DES}(x)$ from (2), 3 more non-linear multiplications are needed, and hence totally 7 non-linear multiplications are sufficient to evaluate a DES S-box.

To sum up, the basic idea behind the above technique is to precompute a set of monomials, and then obtain a decomposition of the required polynomial in terms of polynomials having their monomials only from the precomputed set. Note that the said decomposition is obtained in a "fixed" way that depends only on the degree of the polynomial, which is required to be of the form $k\left(2^p - 1\right) \pm c$, for some parameters $k$, $p$ and $c$; we refer to [RV13] for more details.

In the new method we propose next, we also precompute a set of monomials as above, but we also include every other monomial that can be computed for free by the squaring operation; that is we always generate the full cyclotomic class for any computed monomial. Then we try to decompose the polynomial as a sum of product of two polynomials having their monomials from the precomputed set. One of the two polynomials in every summand is randomly chosen, and we try to determine the other polynomial by solving (for unknown coefficients) the system of linear equations obtained by evaluating the polynomial at every point of the domain $\mathbb{F}_{2^n}$. This approach of determining the unknown coefficients of the polynomials is similar to the Lagrange interpolation technique.

## 2.2   Our New Generic Method

Let us first recollect the notion of cyclotomic class over $\mathbb{F}_{2^n}$ and introduce some notations. The cyclotomic class of $\alpha$ w.r.t. $n$ $(n \geq 1, 0 \leq \alpha \leq 2^n - 2)$, denoted by $C_\alpha$, is defined as the set of integers

$$C_\alpha = \left\{\alpha \cdot 2^i \ (\mathrm{mod}\ 2^n - 1)\ :\ i = 0, 1, \ldots, n - 1\right\}.$$

Intuitively, $C_\alpha$ corresponds to the exponents of all the monomials that can be computed from $x^\alpha \in \mathbb{F}_{2^n}[x]$ using only the squaring operations (modulo $x^{2^n} + x$). Since our goal is only to evaluate polynomials over $\mathbb{F}_{2^n}$, we will be actually working in the ring $\mathbb{F}_{2^n}[x]/(x^{2^n} + x)$, which is an abuse of the notation $\mathbb{F}_{2^n}[x]$. In other words, we treat any polynomial $P(x) \in \mathbb{F}_{2^n}[x]$ to be the same as $P(x)$ modulo $x^{2^n} + x$; hence $P(x)$ has degree at most $2^n - 1$.

By $d \stackrel{\$}{\leftarrow} D$ we denote an element $d$ chosen uniformly at random from a set $D$. For any subset $\Lambda \subseteq \{0, 1, \ldots, 2^n - 2\}$, $x^\Lambda$ denotes the set of monomials $x^\Lambda = \left\{x^i\ :\ i \in \Lambda\right\} \subseteq \mathbb{F}_{2^n}[x]$. Finally we denote by $\mathcal{P}(x^\Lambda)$ the set of all polynomials in $\mathbb{F}_{2^n}[x]$ whose monomials are only from the set $x^\Lambda$.

**Description.** Consider an $n$-bit to $n$-bit S-Box represented by a polynomial $P(x) \in \mathbb{F}_{2^n}[x]$. We consider a collection $\mathcal{S}$ of $\ell$ cyclotomic classes w.r.t. $n$:

$$\mathcal{S} = \{C_{\alpha_1=0}, C_{\alpha_2=1}, C_{\alpha_3}, \ldots, C_{\alpha_\ell}\}. \tag{3}$$

Also, define $L$ as the set of all integers in the cyclotomic classes of $\mathcal{S}$:

$$L = \bigcup_{C_i \in \mathcal{S}} C_i. \tag{4}$$

We choose the set $\mathcal{S}$ of $\ell$ cyclotomic classes in (3) so that the set of corresponding monomials $x^L$ from $\mathcal{S}$ can be computed using only $\ell - 2$ non-linear multiplications. We require that every monomial $x^0, x^1, \ldots, x^{2^n-1}$, can be written as product of some two monomials in $\mathcal{P}(x^L)$. Moreover, we try to choose only those cyclotomic classes with the maximum number of $n$ elements (except $C_0$ which has only a single element). This gives

$$|L| = 1 + n \cdot (\ell - 1). \tag{5}$$

Next, we generate $t - 1$ random polynomials $q_i(x) \stackrel{\$}{\leftarrow} \mathcal{P}(x^L)$ that have their monomials only in $x^L$. Suitable values for the parameters $t$ and $|L|$ will be determined later. Then, we try to find $t$ polynomials $p_i(x) \in \mathcal{P}(x^L)$ such that

$$P(x) = \sum_{i=1}^{t-1} p_i(x) \cdot q_i(x) + p_t(x). \tag{6}$$

It is easy to see that the coefficients of the $p_i(x)$ polynomials can be obtained by solving a system of linear equations in $\mathbb{F}_{2^n}$, as in the Lagrange interpolation theorem. More precisely, to find the polynomials $p_i(x)$, we solve the following system of linear equations over $\mathbb{F}_{2^n}$:

$$A \cdot c = b \tag{7}$$

where the matrix $A$ is obtained by evaluating the R.H.S. of (6) at every element of $\mathbb{F}_{2^n}$, and by treating the unknown coefficients of $p_i(x)$ as variables. This matrix has $2^n$ rows and $t \cdot |L|$ columns, since each of the $t$ polynomials $p_i(x)$ has $|L|$ unknown coefficients. The matrix $A$ can also be written as a block concatenation of smaller matrices:

$$A = (A_1|A_2|\dots|A_t), \tag{8}$$

where $A_i$ is a $2^n \times |L|$ matrix corresponding to the product $p_i(x) \cdot q_i(x)$. Let $a_j \in \mathbb{F}_{2^n}$ $(j = 0, 1, \dots, 2^n - 1)$ be all the field elements and $p_i(x)$ consists of the monomials $x^{k_1}, x^{k_2}, \dots, x^{k_{|L|}} \in x^L$. Then, the matrix $A_i$ has the following structure:

$$A_i = \begin{pmatrix} a_0^{k_1} \cdot q_i(a_0) & a_0^{k_2} \cdot q_i(a_0) & \dots & a_0^{k_{|L|}} \cdot q_i(a_0) \\ a_1^{k_1} \cdot q_i(a_1) & a_1^{k_2} \cdot q_i(a_1) & \dots & a_1^{k_{|L|}} \cdot q_i(a_1) \\ a_2^{k_1} \cdot q_i(a_2) & a_2^{k_2} \cdot q_i(a_2) & \dots & a_2^{k_{|L|}} \cdot q_i(a_2) \\ \vdots & \vdots & \dots & \vdots \\ a_{2^n-1}^{k_1} \cdot q_i(a_{2^n-1}) & a_{2^n-1}^{k_2} \cdot q_i(a_{2^n-1}) & \dots & a_{2^n-1}^{k_{|L|}} \cdot q_i(a_{2^n-1}) \end{pmatrix} \tag{9}$$

The unknown vector $c$ in (7) corresponds to the unknown coefficients of the polynomials $p_i(x)$. The vector $b$ is formed by evaluating $P(x)$ at every element of $\mathbb{F}_{2^n}$. Note that since $P(x)$ corresponds to an S-box, the vector $b$ can be directly obtained from the corresponding S-box lookup table.

If the matrix $A$ has rank $2^n$, then we are able to guarantee that the decomposition in (6) exists for every polynomial $P(x)$. To be of full rank $2^n$ the matrix must have a number of columns $\geq 2^n$. This gives us the necessary condition

$$t \cdot |L| \geq 2^n. \tag{10}$$

We stress that (10) is only a necessary condition. Namely we don't know how to prove that the matrix $A$ will be full rank when the previous condition is satisfied; this makes our algorithm heuristic. In practice for random polynomials $q_i(x)$ we almost always obtain a full rank matrix under condition (10).

From (5), we get the condition

$$t \cdot (1 + n \cdot (\ell - 1)) \geq 2^n \tag{11}$$

where $t$ is the number of polynomials $p_i(x)$ and $\ell$ the number of cyclotomic classes in the set $\mathcal{S}$, to evaluate a polynomial $P(x)$ over $\mathbb{F}_{2^n}$.

We summarize the above method in Algorithm 1 below. The number of non-linear multiplications required in the combining step (6) is $t - 1$. As mentioned earlier, we need $\ell - 2$ non-linear multiplications to precompute the set $x^L$. Hence the total number of non-linear multiplications required is then

$$N_{mult} = \ell - 2 + t - 1 = \ell + t - 3. \tag{12}$$

where $t$ is the number of polynomials $p_i(x)$ and $\ell$ the number of cyclotomic classes in the set $\mathcal{S}$.

---

**Algorithm 1.** New generic polynomial decomposition algorithm

**Input:** $P(x) \in \mathbb{F}_{2^n}[x]$.

**Output:** Polynomials $p_i(x), q_i(x)$ such that $P(x) = \sum_{i=1}^{t-1} p_i(x) \cdot q_i(x) + p_t(x)$.

1: Choose $\ell$ cyclotomic classes $C_{\alpha_i}$ :  $L \leftarrow \bigcup_{i=1}^{l} C_{\alpha_i}$, and the basis set $x^L$ can be computed using $\ell - 2$ non-linear multiplications.
2: Choose $t$ such that $t \cdot |L| \geq 2^n$.
3: For $1 \leq i \leq t$, choose $q_i(x) \xleftarrow{\$} \mathcal{P}(x^L)$.
4: Construct the matrix $A \leftarrow (A_1|A_2|\ldots|A_t)$, where each $A_i$ is the $2^n \times |L|$ matrix given by (9).
5: Solve the linear system $A \cdot c = b$, where $b$ is the evaluation of $P(x)$ at every element of $\mathbb{F}_{2^n}$.
6: Construct the polynomials $p_i(x)$ from the solution vector $c$.

---

**Remark 1.** If $A$ has rank $2^n$, then the same set of basis polynomials $q_i(x)$ will yield a decomposition as in (6) for any polynomial $P(x)$. That is, the matrix $A$ is independent from the polynomial $P(x)$ to be evaluated.

**Remark 2.** Our decomposition method is heuristic because for a given $n$ in $\mathbb{F}_{2^n}$ we do not know how to guarantee that the matrix $A$ has full rank $2^n$. However for typical values of $n$, say $n = 4, 6, 8$, we can definitely check that the matrix $A$ has full rank, for a particular choice of random polynomials $q_i(x)$. Then any polynomial $P(x)$ can be decomposed using these polynomials $q_i(x)$. In other words for a given $n$ we can once and for all generate the random polynomials $q_i(x)$ and check that the matrix $A$ has full rank $2^n$, which will prove that any polynomial $P(x) \in \mathbb{F}_{2^n}[x]$ can then be decomposed as above. In summary our method is heuristic for large values of $n$, but can be proven for small values of $n$. Such proof requires to compute the rank of a matrix with $2^n$ rows and a slightly larger number of columns, which takes $\mathcal{O}(2^{3n})$ time using Gaussian elimination.

**Asymptotic Analysis.** Substituting (12) in (11) to eliminate the parameter $\ell$, we get

$$t \cdot (1 + n \cdot (N_{mult} - t + 2)) \geq 2^n,$$

$$\implies N_{mult} \geq \frac{2^n}{n \cdot t} + t - \left(2 + \frac{1}{n}\right). \tag{13}$$

The R.H.S. of the above expression is minimized when $t \approx \sqrt{\frac{2^n}{n}}$, and hence we obtain

$$N_{mult} \geq 2 \cdot \sqrt{\frac{2^n}{n}} - \left(2 + \frac{1}{n}\right). \tag{14}$$

Hence, our heuristic method requires $\mathcal{O}(\sqrt{2^n/n})$ non-linear multiplications, which is asymptotically slightly better than the Parity-Split method [CGP+12], which has proven complexity $\mathcal{O}(\sqrt{2^n})$. If one has to rigorously establish the above bound for our method, then we may have to prove the following statements, which we leave as open problems:

- We can sample the collection $S$ of cyclotomic classes in (3), each having maximal length $n$ (other than $C_0$), using at most $\ell - 2$ non-linear multiplications.
- The condition $t \cdot |L| \geq 2^n$ suffices to ensure that the matrix $A$ has full rank $2^n$.

Table 2 lists the expected minimum number of non-linear multiplications, as determined by (14), for binary fields $\mathbb{F}_{2^n}$ of practical interest. It also lists the actual number of non-linear multiplications that suffices to evaluate any polynomial, for which we have verified that the matrix $A$ has full rank $2^n$, for a particular random choice of the $q_i(x)$ polynomials. We also provide a performance comparison of our method with that of the Cyclotomic Class and the Parity-Split methods from [CGP+12]. Here we do not compare with the results from [RV13] since that work is mainly concerned with the optimization of specific S-boxes and polynomials of specific degrees; however such comparison will be made for specific S-boxes in Section 4. In Appendix B, we list the specific choice of parameters $t$ and $L$ that we used in this experiment.

**Table 2.** Minimum values of $N_{mult}$

| $n$ | 4 | 5 | 6 | 7 | 8 | 9 | 10 |
|---|---|---|---|---|---|---|---|
| Cyclotomic Class method [CGP+12] | 3 | 5 | 11 | 17 | 33 | 53 | 105 |
| Parity-Split method [CGP+12] | 4 | 6 | 10 | 14 | 22 | 30 | 46 |
| Expected minimum value of $N_{mult}$ (cf. (14)) | 2 | 3 | 5 | 7 | 10 | 13 | 19 |
| **Achievable value of $N_{mult}$** | **2** | **4** | **5** | **7** | **10** | **14** | **19** |

**Counting the Linear Operations.** From (5) and (6), we get $(2t - 1) \cdot (|L| - 1) + (t - 1)$ as an upper-bound on the number of addition operations required to evaluate $P(x)$. This is because each of the $2t - 1$ polynomials $p_i(x)$ and $q_i(x)$ in (6) have (at most) $|L|$ terms, and there are $t$ summands in (6). From (10), we get:

$$(2t - 1) \cdot (|L| - 1) + (t - 1) \leq 2t\,|L| \approx 2 \cdot 2^n$$

Similarly, we get $(2t - 1) \cdot |L| \approx 2 \cdot 2^n$ as an estimate for the number of scalar multiplications. Since the squaring operations are used only to compute the list $L$, we need $|L| - \ell \leq |L| \approx \sqrt{n \cdot 2^n}$ many of them (cf. (13)).

## 3   New Lower Bound for Polynomial Evaluation

In this section, we show that our method from the previous section is asymptotically optimal. More precisely, we show that to evaluate any polynomial over $\mathbb{F}_{2^n}$, any algorithm must use at least $\mathcal{O}(\sqrt{2^n/n})$ non-linear multiplications. This improves the previously known bound of $\Omega(\log_2 n)$ from [RV13].

To establish our lower bound we first need a formal model that describes polynomial evaluation over $\mathbb{F}_{2^n}$. Such a model, the $\mathbb{F}_{2^n}$-*polynomial chain*, has been described in [RV13, Section 3]. For the sake of completeness, we briefly recollect the definition in Appendix A.

**Previous Result.** Let us recollect in slightly more details the previous lower bound of $\Omega(\log_2 n)$. The following proposition gives a lower bound on the number of non-linear multiplications necessary to evaluate a polynomial $P(x)$, a.k.a. *non-linear complexity* of $P(x)$, as the maximum of the quantity necessary to evaluate its monomials. Let $\mathcal{M}(P(x))$ denote the non-linear complexity of $P(x)$. If $P(x)$ corresponds to an $n$-bit S-box $S$, then $\mathcal{M}(P(x))$ is also called the *masking complexity* of $S$.

**Proposition 1.** [[RV13], Proposition 3] *Let* $P(x) := \sum_{i=0}^{2^n-1} a_i\, x^i$ *be a polynomial in* $\mathbb{F}_{2^n}[x]$. *Then*

$$\mathcal{M}(P(x)) \geq \max_{\substack{0 \leq i < 2^n - 1 \\ a_i \neq 0}} m_n(i),$$

*where $m_n(i)$ is the length of the shortest cyclotomic-class (CC) addition chain of $i$ w.r.t. $n$.*

The following result gives a lower bound on the value of $m_n(i)$ in terms of the Hamming weight of $i$.

**Proposition 2.** [[RV13], Proposition 1] $m_n(i) \geq \lceil \log_2(\nu(i)) \rceil$, *where $\nu(i)$ is the Hamming weight of the binary representation of $i$ $(0 \leq i \leq 2^n - 2)$.*

Since $\nu(2^n - 2) = n-1$, hence polynomials having the monomial $x^{2^n-2}$ will have non-linear complexity at least $\log_2(n-1)$. Hence $\Omega(\log_2 n)$ is a lower bound on the number of necessary non-linear multiplications required to evaluate polynomials over $\mathbb{F}_{2^n}$.

**New Lower Bound.** Our technique to prove the lower bound of $\Omega(\sqrt{2^n/n})$ on the non-linear complexity is similar to the one used in the proof of [PS73, Theorem 2]. But we would like to emphasize that their result is not applicable to our setting since they work over the integers and the cost model used there is different from the one used in our case.

**Proposition 3.** *There exists a polynomial $P(x) \in \mathbb{F}_{2^n}[x]$ such that $\mathcal{M}(P(x)) \geq$* $\sqrt{\dfrac{2^n}{n}} - 2$.

*Proof.* At a more abstract level, an $\mathbb{F}_{2^n}$-polynomial chain evaluating $P(x) \in \mathbb{F}_{2^n}[x]$ that uses $r$ non-linear multiplications ($r \geq 0$) can be equivalently described as a sequence $\mathcal{Z}$ of polynomials $z_{-1}, z_0, \ldots, z_r$, where

$$z_{-1} = 1,$$

$$z_0 = x,$$

$$z_k = \left( \beta_{k,-1} + \sum_{i=0}^{k-1}\sum_{j=0}^{n-1} \beta_{k,i,j}\, z_i^{2^j} \right) \cdot \left( \beta'_{k,-1} + \sum_{i=0}^{k-1}\sum_{j=0}^{n-1} \beta'_{k,i,j}\, z_i^{2^j} \right)$$
$$(\mathrm{mod}\ x^{2^n} + x), \quad (15)$$

where $k = 1, 2, \ldots, r$, $\beta_{k,-1}, \beta'_{k,-1}, \beta_{k,i,j}, \beta'_{k,i,j} \in \mathbb{F}_{2^n}$. Lastly,

$$P(x) = \beta_{r+1,-1} + \sum_{i=0}^{r}\sum_{j=0}^{n-1} \beta_{r+1,i,j}\, z_i^{2^j} \quad (\mathrm{mod}\ x^{2^n} + x), \quad (16)$$

where again $\beta_{r+1,-1}, \beta_{r+1,i,j} \in \mathbb{F}_{2^n}$. .

Since the squaring operation is $\mathbb{F}_2$-linear in $\mathbb{F}_{2^n}$, and that $x^{2^n} = x$ for all $x \in \mathbb{F}_{2^n}$, it is easy to see that any polynomial that can be evaluated using at most $t$ non-linear multiplications will be of the form as given in (16).

The number of parameters $\beta_{k,-1}$, $\beta'_{k,-1}$, $\beta_{k,i,j}$, $\beta'_{k,i,j}$ in (15) for a given value of $k$ ($k = 1, \ldots, r$) is $2 \cdot (k \cdot n + 1)$. In (16), the number of parameters $\beta_{r+1,-1}$, $\beta_{r+1,i,j}$ is $(r+1) \cdot n + 1$. Totally, the number of parameters are

$$(r+1)\,n + 1 + \sum_{k=1}^{r} 2\,(kn+1).$$

Since there are only $|\mathbb{F}_{2^n}|^{2^n}$ distinct polynomials in $\mathbb{F}_{2^n}[x]$ (i.e. up to evaluation), and a given set of values for the parameters enables to evaluate a single polynomial only, we get the following necessary condition to evaluate all polynomials over $\mathbb{F}_{2^n}[x]$

$$|\mathbb{F}_{2^n}|^{(r+1)n+1+\sum_{k=1}^{r} 2(kn+1)} \geq |\mathbb{F}_{2^n}|^{2^n},$$

$$\implies \quad (r+1)\,n + 1 + \sum_{k=1}^{r} 2\,(kn+1) \geq 2^n,$$

$$\implies \quad n \cdot r^2 + (2n+2) \cdot r - (2^n - n - 1) \geq 0,$$

$$\implies \quad r \geq \sqrt{\frac{2^n}{n}} - 2. \quad (17)$$

Hence there exists polynomials over $\mathbb{F}_{2^n}$ that require $\Omega(\sqrt{2^n/n})$ non-linear multiplications to evaluate them.                                                    □

The above proposition shows that our new method from Section 2.2 is asymptotically optimal.

**Concrete Lower Bound.** In Table 3 we compare, for various values of $n$, the previously known lower bound for non-linear complexity with the new lower bound as determined by (17).

**Table 3.** Lower bound for non-linear complexity in $\mathbb{F}_{2^n}$

| $n$ | 4 | 5 | 6 | 7 | 8 | 9 | 10 | 11 | 12 |
|---|---|---|---|---|---|---|---|---|---|
| Previous lower bound [CGP+12, RV13] | 2 | 2 | 3 | 3 | 4 | 4 | 4 | 4 | 4 |
| **Our lower bound** (cf. (17)) | 0 | 1 | 2 | 3 | 4 | 6 | 9 | 12 | 17 |

Note that there is still a gap between the lower bound from Table 3 and the achievable value of $N_{mult}$ for our method in Table 2. This is because in our method the decomposition of $P(x)$ as

$$P(x) = \sum_{i=1}^{t-1} p_i(x) \cdot q_i(x) + p_t(x) \tag{18}$$

is performed by first generating the polynomials $q_i(x)$ randomly and independently of $P(x)$, in order to have a linear system of equations over the coefficients of $p_i(x)$. Instead one could try to solve (18) for both the $p_i(x)$ and the $q_i(x)$ polynomials simultaneously; however this gives a quadratic system of equations, which is much harder to solve.

# 4    Application to Various S-boxes

In this section, we apply the generic method described in Section 2, to several well known S-boxes. Using our new method, we reduce the number of non-linear multiplications required in each case, resulting in an improvement over the previously known techniques.

We stress that in our method for an $n$-bit S-box, the maximum number of non-linear multiplications required is invariant of the choice of the S-box when $n$ is fixed. Hence, the number of non-linear multiplications obtained for a fixed $n$ actually provides an upper bound on the masking complexity of an S-box of size $n$.

## 4.1    CLEFIA and Other 8-bit S-boxes

The CLEFIA block cipher has two 8-bit S-boxes [SSA+07]. Let us denote the S-box lookup table for either of the S-boxes as $S_{\text{clefia}}$. We choose

$$L = C_0 \cup C_1 \cup C_3 \cup C_7 \cup C_{29} \cup C_{87} \cup C_{251}. \tag{19}$$

This implies that after choosing $t = 6$, and then 5 basis polynomials $q_i \overset{\$}{\leftarrow} \mathcal{P}(x^L)$ ($1 \le i \le 5$), the following system of equations is constructed in $\mathbb{F}_{2^8}$:

$$S_{\text{clefia}}[x_j] = \underbrace{\sum_{i=1}^{5} p_i(x_j) \cdot q_i(x_j)}_{Q} + p_6(x_j) \qquad j = 0, \ldots, 255. \tag{20}$$

We have checked that for some random choice of the polynomials $q_i(x)$ the corresponding matrix $A$ has full rank 256, and therefore we can determine the polynomials $p_i(x)$. Given the solution to the above system, the S-box evaluation is then the same as evaluating the polynomial $Q(x) + p_6(x)$. To evaluate all the monomials in $\{x, x^3, x^7, x^{29}, x^{87}, x^{251}\}$ we need 5 non-linear multiplications, implying that any monomial in $x^L$, any $q_i(x)$ (randomly chosen from $\mathcal{P}(x^L)$) and any $p_i(x)$ can all together be evaluated with 5 non-linear multiplications. Moreover the evaluation of $Q(x)$ requires 5 additional non-linear multiplications. Therefore the total number of non-linear multiplications required for evaluating the S-box is 10.

Note that it requires at least 4 non-linear multiplications to evaluate the polynomials corresponding to the two S-boxes of CLEFIA by any method. This is because these two polynomials over $\mathbb{F}_{2^8}$ have degrees 252 (S-box $S_0$) and 254 (S-box $S_1$), and the result follows from Proposition 1.

**Invariance.** If we choose some other 8-bit S-box, then the matrix corresponding to the resulting system remains the same. Hence, we will still get a solution to the system for the same set of polynomials $q_i(x)$. This implies that we can use the same set of basis polynomials to obtain polynomials $p_i(x)$ for any other 8-bit S-box. Hence, for any S-box of size 8, the number of non-linear multiplications is at most 10.

## 4.2    PRESENT and Other 4-bit S-boxes

For the 4-bit S-box of PRESENT [BKL+07], we choose $t = 2$ and $L = C_0 \cup C_1 \cup C_3$. By selecting $q_1 \overset{\$}{\leftarrow} \mathcal{P}(x^L)$, we construct the following linear system of equations:

$$S_{\text{present}}[x_j] = p_1(x_j) \cdot q_1(x_j) + p_2(x_j) \tag{21}$$

The monomials used to construct $q_1(x)$, $q_2(x)$ are $\{x, x^2, x^4, x^8, x^3, x^6, x^{12}, x^9\}$. All of these monomials can be evaluated with a single non-linear multiplication and to evaluate $p_1(x) \cdot q_1(x)$ we need only one more non-linear multiplication. Hence, the PRESENT S-box evaluation requires 2 multiplications. As in the case of 8-bit S-boxes, this proves that with the same $q_1(x)$ any 4-bit S-box can be evaluated with 2 multiplications. Table 4 gives the corresponding polynomials for the PRESENT S-box.

The polynomial corresponding to the PRESENT S-box has degree 14 and hence, from Proposition 1, its masking complexity is at least 2 [RV13]. This implies that our evaluation method achieves optimal complexity for the PRESENT S-box.

**Table 4.** Basis polynomial $q_1(x)$ for 4-bit S-boxes, and solutions $p_1(x), p_2(x)$ to PRESENT S-box. The irreducible polynomial is $a^4 + a + 1$ over $\mathbb{F}_2$.

| Basis Polynomial |
| --- |
| $q_1$ $\begin{array}{l}(a^3 + a^2 + 1) \cdot x^{12} + (a^3 + a^2 + a + 1) \cdot x^9 + a^2 \cdot x^8 + x^6 + (a^3 + a^2 + a) \cdot \\ x^4 + x^2 + (a^3 + a) \cdot x + a\end{array}$ |

| Solution to linear System |
| --- |
| $p_1$ $\begin{array}{l}(a^3 + a) \cdot x^{12} + x^9 + (a^3 + a^2) \cdot x^8 + (a^2 + 1) \cdot x^6 + (a^3 + a^2 + 1) \cdot x^4 + \\ (a^3 + a^2 + a + 1) \cdot x^3 + (a^2 + 1) \cdot x^2 + (a^2 + 1) \cdot x + a^2\end{array}$ |
| $p_2$ $(a^2 + 1) \cdot x^8 + (a^3 + a^2 + 1) \cdot x^6 + (a + 1) \cdot x^4 + a \cdot x^3 + x^2 + (a^3 + 1) \cdot x + a^2$ |

### 4.3  $(m, n)$-bit S-box: Application to DES

We now consider S-boxes whose output size $n$ is smaller than the input size $m$, as for the DES S-boxes with $m = 6$ and $n = 4$. We can view an $(m, n)$-bit S-box ($m > n$) as a mapping from $\mathbb{F}_{2^m}$ to $\mathbb{F}_{2^n}$. Given any such S-box table S, we want to construct a system of linear equations

$$S[x_j] = \underbrace{\sum_{i=1}^{t-1} p_i(x_j) \cdot q_i(x_j) + p_t(x_j)}_{G(x)} \tag{22}$$

Note that each $S[x_j]$ is an element of the smaller field $\mathbb{F}_{2^n}$, but each $G(x_j)$ is an element in the larger field $\mathbb{F}_{2^m}$. One trivial way to remove this inconsistency is to consider $S[x_j]$ as an element of the larger field $\mathbb{F}_{2^m}$, by padding the most significant bit of the S-box output with 0's. Then, we determine the polynomials $p_i(x)$ by solving the corresponding system $A \cdot c = S$, as described in Section 2.2. However intuitively this is not optimal, since we are creating an artificial constraint to be satisfied by the coefficients of the polynomials $p_i(x)$, namely that the $m - n$ most significant bits of $G(x)$ must be 0, while eventually these most significant bits will simply be discarded after the evaluation of $G(x)$, since to get $S(x)$ we only keep the $n$ least significant bits of $G(x)$.

Instead, we consider the representations of the unknown coefficients of the polynomials $p_i(x)$ in $\mathbb{F}_2$ instead of $\mathbb{F}_{2^m}$, and we transform the system of linear equations (22) over $\mathbb{F}_{2^m}$, into a system of linear equations over $\mathbb{F}_2$. By doing this, from each constraint $G(x_j)$, we generate $m$ equations over $\mathbb{F}_2$, instead of one equation over $\mathbb{F}_{2^m}$. Note that each of these $m$ equations will be an affine combination of the unknown bits of the coefficients of the polynomials $p_i(x)$. Only $n$ of these equations are actually necessary, since the output of the S-box is of size $n$ bits. By equating each of these equations to the corresponding output bit of the S-box, we get a transformed system of linear equations $B \cdot c = S$, where $B$ is an $(n \cdot 2^m) \times (t \cdot |L| \cdot m)$ matrix over $\mathbb{F}_2$ and $L$ is the set of elements from the chosen cyclotomic classes. By solving this transformed system over $\mathbb{F}_2$ we determine the polynomials $p_i(x)$.

**Example of DES.** The DES block cipher has 8 $(6, 4)$-bit S-boxes [oST93]. A DES S-box is a mapping from $\mathbb{F}_{2^6}$ to $\mathbb{F}_{2^4}$. In [RV13], the authors consider the S-boxes as a mapping from $\mathbb{F}_{2^6}$ to $\mathbb{F}_{2^6}$, where the two most significant bits of the output of S-box are fixed to 0, and as recalled in Section 2.1 the evaluation can be done with 7 non-linear multiplications. Also, for the same representation, there is a lower bound of 3 non-linear multiplications necessary to evaluate each DES S-box [RV13]. From Table 2, using our generic method over $\mathbb{F}_{2^6}$ we can perform the evaluation with 5 non-linear multiplications. Below we show that by working over $\mathbb{F}_2$ as explained above, only 4 non-linear multiplications are required.

We choose $L = C_0 \cup C_1 \cup C_3 \cup C_7$, $t = 3$, and $q_1(x), q_2(x) \overset{\$}{\leftarrow} \mathcal{P}(x^L)$. Then using our method we transform the following linear system of equations

$$S_{\mathsf{des}}[x_j] = \underbrace{\sum_{i=1}^{2} p_i(x_j) \cdot q_i(x_j)}_{Q(x)} + p_3(x_j) \tag{23}$$

to a system over $\mathbb{F}_2$. That is, instead of embedding $S_{\mathsf{des}}$ into $\mathbb{F}_{2^6}$, we write the system of equations over $\mathbb{F}_2$. This can be done by considering the binary representation of $x^\alpha$ evaluated at any given value in $\mathbb{F}_{2^6}$. This will give 6 equations over $\mathbb{F}_2$ for each equation $Q(x_j) + p_3(x_j)$. Out of these 6 equations only 4 will be necessary since the output of DES S-box has 4-bit values. By solving this new system of linear equations over $\mathbb{F}_2$ we can determine $p_i(x)$ for each $i$.

The number of multiplications required to evaluate $q_1(x), q_2(x)$ is 2, and $Q(x)$ can be evaluated with 2 additional multiplications. Hence, the total number of non-linear multiplications required is only 4. In Appendix C we give an example of basis polynomials $q_1(x), q_2(x)$ for DES and the solution polynomials $p_i(x)$ corresponding to the system of linear equations for the first DES S-box $S_1$.

As previously, once we obtain a full rank matrix for a set of randomly fixed $q_1(x), q_2(x)$, for any other $(6, 4)$-bit S-box we can use this basis to find the corresponding polynomials $p_i(x)$, since the matrix $A$ is independent from the S-box. Hence we can conclude that the masking complexity of any $(6, 4)$-bit S-box is at most 4.

# References

[BCO04]  Brier, E., Clavier, C., Olivier, F.: Correlation power analysis with a leakage model. In: Joye, M., Quisquater, J.-J. (eds.) CHES 2004. LNCS, vol. 3156, pp. 16–29. Springer, Heidelberg (2004)

[BKL+07]  Bogdanov, A., Knudsen, L.R., Leander, G., Paar, C., Poschmann, A., Robshaw, M.J.B., Seurin, Y., Vikkelsoe, C.: PRESENT: An ultra-lightweight block cipher. In: Paillier, P., Verbauwhede, I. (eds.) CHES 2007. LNCS, vol. 4727, pp. 450–466. Springer, Heidelberg (2007)

[CGP+12]  Carlet, C., Goubin, L., Prouff, E., Quisquater, M., Rivain, M.: Higher-order masking schemes for S-Boxes. In: Canteaut, A. (ed.) FSE 2012. LNCS, vol. 7549, pp. 366–384. Springer, Heidelberg (2012)

[CPRR13]   Coron, J.-S., Prouff, E., Rivain, M., Roche, T.: Higher-order side channel security and mask refreshing. In: Moriai, S. (ed.) FSE 2013. LNCS, vol. 8424, pp. 410–424. Springer, Heidelberg (2013)

[CRR02]   Chari, S., Rao, J.R., Rohatgi, P.: Template attacks. In: Kaliski Jr., B.S., Koç, Ç.K., Paar, C. (eds.) CHES 2002. LNCS, vol. 2523, pp. 13–28. Springer, Heidelberg (2003)

[GST13]   Genkin, D., Shamir, A., Tromer, E.: RSA key extraction via low-bandwidth acoustic cryptanalysis. IACR Cryptology ePrint Archive, 2013:857 (2013)

[ISW03]   Ishai, Y., Sahai, A., Wagner, D.: Private circuits: Securing hardware against probing attacks. In: Boneh, D. (ed.) CRYPTO 2003. LNCS, vol. 2729, pp. 463–481. Springer, Heidelberg (2003)

[KJJ99]   Kocher, P.C., Jaffe, J., Jun, B.: Differential power analysis. In: Wiener, M. (ed.) CRYPTO 1999. LNCS, vol. 1666, pp. 388–397. Springer, Heidelberg (1999)

[Mes00]   Messerges, T.S.: Using second-order power analysis to attack DPA resistant software. In: Paar, C., Koç, Ç.K. (eds.) CHES 2000. LNCS, vol. 1965, pp. 238–251. Springer, Heidelberg (2000)

[oST93]   National Institute of Standards and Technology. FIPS 46-3: Data Encryption Standard (March 1993), http://csrc.nist.gov

[PS73]   Paterson, M., Stockmeyer, L.J.: On the number of nonscalar multiplications necessary to evaluate polynomials. SIAM J. Comput. 2(1), 60–66 (1973)

[RP10]   Rivain, M., Prouff, E.: Provably secure higher-order masking of AES. In: Mangard, S., Standaert, F.-X. (eds.) CHES 2010. LNCS, vol. 6225, pp. 413–427. Springer, Heidelberg (2010)

[RV13]   Roy, A., Vivek, S.: Analysis and improvement of the generic higher-order masking scheme of FSE 2012. In: Bertoni, G., Coron, J.-S. (eds.) CHES 2013. LNCS, vol. 8086, pp. 417–434. Springer, Heidelberg (2013)

[SSA+07]   Shirai, T., Shibutani, K., Akishita, T., Moriai, S., Iwata, T.: The 128-bit blockcipher CLEFIA (extended abstract). In: Biryukov, A. (ed.) FSE 2007. LNCS, vol. 4593, pp. 181–195. Springer, Heidelberg (2007)

# A     $\mathbb{F}_{2^n}$-Polynomial Chain

**Definition 1.** [[RV13], Definition 4] *An $\mathbb{F}_{2^n}$-polynomial chain $S$ for a polynomial $P(x) \in \mathbb{F}_{2^n}[x]$ is defined as*

$$\lambda_{-1} = 1, \ \lambda_0 = x, \ \dots, \ \lambda_r = P(x) \tag{24}$$

*where*

$$\lambda_i = \begin{cases} \lambda_j + \lambda_k & -1 \leq j, k < i, \\ \lambda_j \cdot \lambda_k & -1 \leq j, k < i, \\ \alpha_i \odot \lambda_j & -1 \leq j < i, \ \alpha_i \ is \ a \ scalar, \\ \lambda_j^2 & -1 \leq j < i. \end{cases}$$

*Though $\cdot$ and $\odot$ both perform multiplication in $\mathbb{F}_{2^n}$, the operator "$\odot$" is reserved for the multiplication by a scalar. A step such as $\lambda_j \cdot \lambda_k$ denotes a non-linear multiplication. Let the number of non-linear multiplications involved in a chain $S$ be denoted as $\mathcal{N}(S)$. Then the* non-linear complexity *of $P(x)$, denoted by $\mathcal{M}(P(x))$, is defined as $\mathcal{M}(P(x)) = \min_S \mathcal{N}(S)$.*

# B     Heuristics for Choosing Parameters $t$ and $L$

| $n$ | $t$ | $L$ | $|L|$ |
|-----|-----|-----|-------|
| 4 | 2 | $C_0 \cup C_1 \cup C_3$ | 9 |
| 5 | 3 | $C_0 \cup C_1 \cup C_3 \cup C_7$ | 16 |
| 6 | 3 | $C_0 \cup C_1 \cup C_3 \cup C_7 \cup C_{11}$ | 25 |
| 7 | 4 | $C_0 \cup C_1 \cup C_3 \cup C_7 \cup C_{11} \cup C_{15}$ | 36 |
| 8 | 6 | $C_0 \cup C_1 \cup C_3 \cup C_7 \cup C_{29} \cup C_{87} \cup C_{251}$ | 49 |
| 9 | 8 | $C_0 \cup C_1 \cup C_3 \cup C_7 \cup C_{29} \cup C_{45} \cup C_{119} \cup C_{191} \cup C_{255}$ | 73 |
| 10 | 11 | $C_0 \cup C_1 \cup C_3 \cup C_7 \cup C_{29} \cup C_{45} \cup C_{119} \cup C_{191} \cup C_{155} \cup C_{255} \cup C_{339}$ | 101 |

# C     Evaluation Polynomials for DES S-boxes

In Table 5 we give an example of basis polynomials $q_1(x)$, $q_2(x)$ for DES and Table 6 shows the solution polynomials $p_i(x)$ corresponding to the system of linear equations for the first DES S-box $S_1$.

**Table 5.** Basis polynomials $q_1, q_2$ obtained from $\mathcal{P}(x^L)$, for DES

| | Basis Polynomials |
|---|---|
| $q_1$ | $(a^5 + a^4 + 1) \cdot x^{56} + (a^5 + 1) \cdot x^{49} + (a^2 + a) \cdot x^{48} + (a^4 + a^3) \cdot x^{35} + (a^5 + a^4 + a^2) \cdot x^{33} + (a^5 + a + 1) \cdot x^{32} + (a^3 + a) \cdot x^{28} + a^2 \cdot x^{24} + (a^5 + 1) \cdot x^{16} + (a^4 + a + 1) \cdot x^{14} + x^{12} + (a^4 + a^3 + a^2 + 1) \cdot x^8 + (a^5 + a^3 + a^2 + a + 1) \cdot x^7 + (a^5 + a^4 + a^3 + a^2 + 1) \cdot x^6 + (a^5 + a^4 + a^3 + 1) \cdot x^4 + (a^5 + a^2 + a + 1) \cdot x^3 + (a^3 + a^2 + a) \cdot x^2 + (a^4 + a^2 + a + 1) \cdot x + a^5 + a^4 + a^3 + a^2 + a$ |
| $q_2$ | $(a + 1) \cdot x^{56} + (a^5 + 1) \cdot x^{49} + (a + 1) \cdot x^{48} + a \cdot x^{35} + (a + 1) \cdot x^{33} + (a^4 + a^3 + a + 1) \cdot x^{32} + (a^3 + a^2 + a) \cdot x^{28} + (a^5 + a^3 + a + 1) \cdot x^{24} + (a^3 + 1) \cdot x^{16} + (a^4 + a^2 + 1) \cdot x^{14} + (a + 1) \cdot x^{12} + (a^5 + a^4 + 1) \cdot x^8 + (a^5 + a^4 + a^3 + a + 1) \cdot x^7 + (a^5 + a^4 + a^3) \cdot x^6 + (a + 1) \cdot x^4 + (a^5 + a^3 + a^2 + a) \cdot x^2 + a \cdot x + a^5 + a^4 + a^3 + a^2 + 1$ |

**Table 6.** Solution to the system of linear equations for DES S-box $(S_1)$. The irreducible polynomial is $a^6 + a + 1$ over $\mathbb{F}_2$.

| | Solution to linear system |
|---|---|
| $p_1$ | $(a^5 + a^4 + a^3 + a^2 + 1) \cdot x^{56} + (a^5 + a^2 + 1) \cdot x^{49} + a^4 \cdot x^{48} + (a^4 + a^3 + a) \cdot x^{35} + (a^5 + a^4 + a^2) \cdot x^{33} + (a^5 + 1) \cdot x^{32} + a \cdot x^{28} + (a^4 + a^2) \cdot x^{24} + (a^5 + a) \cdot x^{16} + (a^5 + a^2) \cdot x^{14} + (a^5 + a + 1) \cdot x^{12} + (a^5 + a^4 + a^3 + a) \cdot x^8 + (a^5 + a^4 + a^3 + a) \cdot x^7 + (a^5 + a^4 + a^3) \cdot x^6 + (a^2 + a + 1) \cdot x^4 + (a^5 + a^4 + a) \cdot x^2 + (a^5 + a^4 + 1) \cdot x + a^4 + a^3 + a^2$ |
| $p_2$ | $(a^5 + a^2) \cdot x^{49} + (a^3 + 1) \cdot x^{48} + (a^5 + a^3 + a + 1) \cdot x^{35} + (a^4 + a^2 + 1) \cdot x^{33} + (a^5 + a^4 + 1) \cdot x^{32} + (a^5 + a^4 + a^3 + a + 1) \cdot x^{28} + (a^3 + a^2) \cdot x^{24} + (a^2 + a + 1) \cdot x^{16} + (a^5 + a^4 + a^3) \cdot x^{14} + (a^4 + a^3 + a + 1) \cdot x^{12} + (a^4 + a^3) \cdot x^8 + (a^5 + a) \cdot x^7 + (a^5 + a^4) \cdot x^6 + (a^5 + a^4 + a^3 + a^2 + a + 1) \cdot x^4 + (a^5 + a^4 + a) \cdot x^3 + (a^5 + a^3 + a + 1) \cdot x^2 + (a^5 + a) \cdot x + a^5 + a^4 + a^2 + a$ |
| $p_3$ | $a \cdot x^7 + a \cdot x^6 + (a^4 + a + 1) \cdot x^4 + (a^5 + a^2 + a) \cdot x^3 + (a^5 + a^4 + a + 1) \cdot x^2 + (a^4 + a^2) \cdot x$ |

# Secure Conversion between Boolean and Arithmetic Masking of Any Order

Jean-Sébastien Coron, Johann Großschädl, and Praveen Kumar Vadnala

Laboratory of Algorithmics, Cryptology and Security (LACS),
University of Luxembourg, Luxembourg
{jean-sebastien.coron,johann.groszschaedl,praveen.vadnala}@uni.lu

**Abstract.** An effective countermeasure against side-channel attacks is to mask all sensitive intermediate variables with one (or more) random value(s). When a cryptographic algorithm involves both arithmetic and Boolean operations, it is necessary to convert from arithmetic masking to Boolean masking and vice versa. At CHES 2001, Goubin introduced two algorithms for secure conversion between arithmetic and Boolean masks, but his approach can only be applied to first-order masking. In this paper, we present and evaluate new conversion algorithms that are secure against attacks of any order. To convert masks of a size of $k$ bits securely against attacks of order $n$, the proposed algorithms have a time complexity of $\mathcal{O}(n^2 k)$ in both directions and are proven to be secure in the Ishai, Sahai, and Wagner (ISW) framework for private circuits. We evaluate our algorithms using HMAC-SHA-1 as example and report the execution times we achieved on a 32-bit AVR microcontroller.

**Keywords:** Side-channel analysis (SCA), higher-order SCA, arithmetic masking, Boolean masking, provably secure masking, HMAC-SHA-1.

## 1 Introduction

**Side-Channel Attacks.** Traditionally, cryptographic algorithms are designed under the premise that a system can only be attacked in a black-box way, even though in practice this assumption is not necessarily true. An attacker may be able to obtain some partial information about the secret key(s) through means that were originally not anticipated by the system designer. A typical example are the so-called side-channel attacks, which can be mounted by measuring the power consumption [14], EM radiations [8], or execution time [13] of a crypto-system, or by observing its response to fault injection [1]. It is widely accepted that these attacks are very powerful and can completely break a system.

Masking is a common countermeasure against side-channel attacks. Boolean masking, firstly suggested in [3,10], consists in splitting every sensitive variable $x$ in two shares $x'$ and $r$, where $x' = x \oplus r$ and $r$ is a randomly generated value [3]. The two shares are manipulated separately according to the cryptographic algorithm. Such modification is straightforward for linear functions, which can be computed separately on these two shares. For non-linear functions, such as

L. Batina and M. Robshaw (Eds.): CHES 2014, LNCS 8731, pp. 188–205, 2014.

SBOXes, the usual technique consists in pre-computing a randomized SBOX in RAM for every new execution of the algorithm [3].

First-order Boolean masking is vulnerable to a second-order attack in which the adversary combines information about the two shares $x'$ and $r$; such attacks are feasible in practice (see [18]). Boolean masking can actually be extended to any number of shares, e.g. when using $n$ shares, an implementation should be resistant against $t$-th order attacks, in which the adversary combines leakage information from $t < n$ variables. It was shown in [3] that, under a reasonable power leakage model, the overall number of executions required to recover the secret key grows exponentially with the number of shares.

At CHES 2010, Rivain and Prouff [20] proposed an algorithm to protect the AES against $t$-th order attacks, based on the Ishai-Sahai-Wagner construction [11]. Their basic idea is to write the AES round transformations as operations in the field $GF(2^8)$ and mask additions and multiplications. This approach can be extended to any SBOX by considering the polynomial representation of the SBOX, which can be computed using Lagrange polynomial interpolation over a finite field [2]. Rivain et al introduced in [19] a table re-computation method to protect any SBOX from second-order attacks. The classical randomized table countermeasure, secure against first-order attacks, has recently been extended to work against $t$-th order attacks [5].

**Security Model.** We definitely aim for countermeasures against side-channel attacks that can be proven secure in a reasonable model of side-channel leakage (i.e. we will not be satisfied with heuristic "ad-hoc" countermeasures). Perhaps the simplest such model is the probing attack model proposed by Ishai, Sahai and Wagner (ISW) at CRYPTO 2003 [11] (see Subsection 2.2). They initiated the theoretical study of securing circuits against an adversary who can probe its wires. In this model, the attacker is allowed to access at most $t$ wires of the circuit, but he should not be able to learn anything about the secret key. The authors show that any circuit $C$ can be transformed into a new circuit of size $\mathcal{O}(t^2 \cdot |C|)$ that is resistant against such an adversary. The approach is based on secret-sharing every variable $x$ into $n$ shares $x_i$ with $x = x_1 \oplus x_2 \cdots \oplus x_n$, and processing the shares in a way so that no information about the initial variable $x$ can be learned by any $t$-limited adversary, for $n \geq 2t + 1$.

In recent years, numerous papers on provable security against side-channel attacks have been published in the literature, forming the rapidly emerging field of leakage-resilient cryptography. Building upon the leakage model introduced by Micali and Reyzin [16] and on the bounded retrieval model [6,7], the leakage resilience model assumes that the adversary has the ability to repeatedly learn arbitrary functions of the secret key, as long as the total number of bits leaked to the adversary is bounded by some parameter $L$. This is a very strong security notion because an attacker can choose arbitrary leakage functions; only the amount of leaked information is bounded. In particular, it is more general than the ISW probing model [11], in which the attacker has only access to a limited number of physical bits computed in the circuit.

However, cryptosystems proven secure in the most general leakage-resilient model are often too inefficient for practical use. In practice, one typically has to design a countermeasure against side-channel attacks for an existing algorithm (such as AES or HMAC-SHA-1) instead of devising a completely new algorithm based on the principles of leakage-resilient cryptography. The main advantage of the ISW probing model is that it can potentially lead to relatively practical designs. Another benefit is its interplay with resistance against power analysis attacks. Namely, if a given algorithm is proven resistant against $t$ probes in the ISW model, then (at least) $t + 1$ measurements in a power acquisition must be combined to obtain the key. As shown in [3], the number of power acquisitions required to recover the key grows exponentially with $t$. This means that, even if a real probing attack would be physically impossible or too costly, it makes sense to obtain countermeasures with the largest possible value of $t$ since this translates into an (exponentially in $t$) increasing level of security against power attacks. In this paper, we mainly work in the ISW model.

Proving the resistance of a countermeasure against a single-probe attack (or a first-order attack) is usually straightforward since it suffices to show that all intermediate variables are uniformly distributed (or, at least, that their distribution is independent from the secret key) as in this case a single probe reveals no information to the attacker. To prove resistance against $t$ probes, one should a priori consider every possible $t$-tuple of variables and show that their joint distribution is independent from the secret key. This approach has been used to prove the security of algorithms against second-order attacks [19]. However, as the number of such $t$-tuples grows exponentially with $t$, this analysis becomes unfeasible, even for small values of $t$. To work around this problem, Ishai, Sahai and Wagner introduced in [11] a very practical simulation framework in which one shows how to simulate any set of $t$ wires probed by the adversary from a subset of the input shares of the transformed circuits. Since any proper subset of these input shares can be simulated without knowledge of the input values in the original circuit, a perfect simulation of the $t$ probed wires is possible. We follow the same approach in this paper.

**Boolean vs Arithmetic Masking.** Boolean masking is widely-used countermeasure for cryptographic algorithms that use only linear operations over the field $\mathbb{F}_2$ and non-linear SBOXes (e.g. DES and AES). However, if an algorithm includes arithmetic operations (such as IDEA [15], RC6 [4], and SHA-1 [17]), a masking scheme that is compatible with the arithmetic operation must be used [3]. For example, if $x_3 = x_1 + x_2$ must be computed securely, we can mask both $x_1$ and $x_2$ arithmetically by writing $x_1 = A_1 + r_1$ and $x_2 = A_2 + r_2$ for some random values $r_1$ and $r_2$. Then, instead of computing the sum $x_3$ directly, we can add the two shares separately, which results again in two arithmetic shares for $x_3 = (A_1 + A_2) + (r_1 + r_2)$. Note that throughout this paper all additions and subtractions are performed modulo $2^k$ for some $k$.

Besides IDEA, RC6 and SHA-1, there exist many other algorithms that execute both arithmetic (e.g. modular addition) and logical operations. Examples include ARX-based block ciphers like XTEA and Threefish, the SHA-3 finalists Blake and Skein, as well as all four stream ciphers from the e-Stream software portfolio. Hence, techniques to protect both kinds of operation are of practical importance. One approach to achieve this is to use appropriate masking (corresponding to the operation) and convert between the maskings whenever it is necessary. Of course, this requires that the mask conversion itself is also secure against first-order (resp. higher-order) attacks. Another idea is to use only one kind of masking (either Boolean or arithmetic) and employ secure algorithms to perform the needed operations directly on the shares. While there exist some papers about the first method, the second approach has, surprisingly, not been studied in detail. The decision whether to apply the conversion or not depends on the target cryptographic algorithm. For HMAC-SHA-1, the second method yields more efficient implementations, as we will show in this paper.

**Our Contribution.** Currently, there exists no practical conversion technique that works for masking of order two or higher. The present paper attempts to fill this gap. We introduce the first conversion algorithms between Boolean and arithmetic masking that are secure against $t$-th order attacks (instead of first-order only). We start with the problem of how to apply arithmetic operations directly on Boolean shares and present an algorithm for secure addition modulo $2^k$ with $n$ shares (where $n \geq 2t + 1$) that has a complexity of $\mathcal{O}(n^2 k)$. Then, we introduce algorithms to convert from Boolean to arithmetic masking and vice versa, again with a complexity of $\mathcal{O}(n^2 k)$ in both directions. These algorithms are proven secure in the Ishai, Sahai and Wagner (ISW) framework for private circuits [11].

We apply our countermeasures to protect HMAC-SHA-1 against second and third-order attacks. We implemented and evaluated all our masking schemes on a 32-bit AVR processor. Based on a detailed performance analysis, we identify the most efficient algorithms in practice for different levels of security.

## 2 Previous Work

### 2.1 First-Order Conversion: Goubin's Algorithms

In this section, we firstly recall Goubin's algorithm for conversion from Boolean to arithmetic masking and vice versa [9]. Goubin's conversion algorithms are proven secure against first-order attacks only; thus, we restrict our attention to first-order masking. For Boolean masking, we can write $x = x' \oplus r$, where $r$ is a randomly generated $k$-bit value, while for arithmetic masking, we can write $x = A + r \bmod 2^k$ (as mentioned previously, all additions and subtractions are performed modulo $2^k$ for some parameter $k$).

**Boolean to Arithmetic Conversion.** The Boolean to arithmetic conversion method of Goubin [9] is based on the following function $\Psi_{x'}(r) : \mathbb{F}_{2^k} \to \mathbb{F}_{2^k}$

$$\Psi_{x'}(r) = (x' \oplus r) - r$$

**Theorem 1 (Goubin [9]).** *The function $\Psi_{x'}(r)$ is affine over $\mathbb{F}_2$.*

Due to this affine property, the conversion from Boolean to arithmetic masking is fairly straightforward. Given $x'$ and $r$ so that $x = x' \oplus r$, we have to compute $A$ so that $x = A + r$, which can be done as follows:

$$A = (x' \oplus r) - r = \Psi_{x'}(r) = \Psi_{x'}(r \oplus r_2) \oplus (\Psi_{x'}(r_2) \oplus \Psi_{x'}(0))$$

where $r_2$ is a random element of $\mathbb{F}_{2^k}$. This conversion method is clearly secure against first-order attacks because the left term $\Psi_{x'}(r \oplus r_2)$ is independent from $r$ (and, therefore, independent from $x$), and the right term $\Psi_{x'}(r_2) \oplus \Psi_{x'}(0)$ is also independent from $r$ and $x$. Note that this technique is very efficient since it requires only a constant number of operations (independent of $k$).

**Arithmetic to Boolean Conversion.** Goubin also introduced a technique to convert from arithmetic to Boolean masking, secure against first-order attacks [9]. Unfortunately, his arithmetic-to-Boolean conversion is more costly than the conversion in the other direction since its time complexity is $\mathcal{O}(k)$ for registers of $k$ bits. It is based on the following theorem; we denote by $2x$ the multiplication of $x$ by 2 modulo $2^k$.

**Theorem 2 (Goubin [9]).** *If we denote $x' = (A + r) \oplus r$, we also have $x' = A \oplus u_{k-1}$, where $u_{k-1}$ is obtained from the following recursion formula:*

$$\begin{cases} u_0 = 0 \\ \forall i \geq 0, u_{i+1} = 2[u_i \wedge (A \oplus r) \oplus (A \wedge r)] \end{cases}$$

Since this iterative computation of $u_i$ contains only logical XOR and AND operations, it can be easily protected against first-order leakage. We refer to [9] for further details. Recently, Karroumi et al applied this method to obtain a first-order secure addition on Boolean shares directly [12].

## 2.2   The Ishai, Sahai and Wagner Framework

In this subsection we describe the framework of Ishai, Sahai and Wagner (ISW) [11] for proving the security against an adversary observing at most $t$ variables within a circuit. We will use this framework in Section 4 and in Appendix A to prove the security of our conversion algorithms.

A *stateless* circuit over $\mathbb{F}_2$ can be defined as a directed acyclic graph whose sources and sinks are input and output variables, respectively, while its vertices are Boolean gates [5]. Such a stateless circuit can be augmented with random-bit gates to form a *randomized circuit*. As stated in [11], a *random-bit gate* has no input and produces as output a uniformly random bit at each new invocation of the circuit. A $t$-limited adversary can probe up to $t$ wires in the circuit, and has unlimited computational power. Given a stateless circuit $C$, we must transform it into a new circuit $C'$ that can resist such an adversary. However, this is only possible if the inputs and outputs of the new circuit $C'$ are hidden since an input of $C$ might contain some secret-key bits and by probing these bits the adversary can obtain information about the secret key. Therefore, we allow the use of a randomized *input encoder* $I$ and *output decoder* $O$, whose wires can not be probed by the adversary. Both $I$ and $O$ should be independent from the circuit $C$ being transformed.

**Definition 1.** *Let $T$ be an efficiently computable, deterministic function mapping a stateless circuit $C$ to a stateless circuit $C'$, and let $I$, $O$ be input and output decoder, respectively. $(T, I, O)$ is said to be a t-private stateless transformer if it satisfies soundness and privacy, defined as follows:*

- *Soundness: $C$ and $O \circ C' \circ I$ have identical input-output functionality.*
- *Privacy: the values of any $t$ wires of $C'$ can be efficiently simulated without access to any wire of $C'$.*

In our conversion algorithms we will often work with $k$-bit variables (for some fixed parameter $k$) instead of single bits; in this case probing one such variable will automatically reveal its $k$-bit value instead of a single bit. Clearly, this can only make the adversary stronger.

The ISW framework also includes definitions for stateful circuits, i.e. circuits with memory gates. As shown in [11], achieving privacy for stateful circuits is easy once privacy has been achieved in the stateless model. Thus, we focus on the stateless model in our work. We recall the main theorem from [11] below.

**Theorem 3 (Ishai, Sahai, Wagner [11]).** *There exists a perfectly t-private stateless transformer $(T, I, O)$ such that $T$ maps any stateless circuit $C$ of size $|C|$ and depth $d$ to a randomized stateless circuit of size $\mathcal{O}(n^2 \cdot |C|)$ and depth $\mathcal{O}(d \log t)$, where $n = 2t + 1$.*

**Privacy for Stateless Circuits.** For an arbitrary circuit $C$ the corresponding circuit $C'$ is constructed by maintaining the following invariant: for each wire in the circuit $C$, there are $n$ wires in $C'$, which add up to the value on the wire in $C$. Without loss of generality, any circuit $C$ can be represented using NOT and AND gates only. Thus, if we can transform these two gates, the whole circuit is transformable. It is easy to transform a NOT gate using the following simple relation: If $x = x_1 \oplus x_2 \oplus \cdots \oplus x_n$ then $\text{NOT}(x) = \text{NOT}(x_1) \oplus x_2 \oplus \cdots \oplus x_n$. To transform AND gates, the authors present an elegant solution, which is shown in Algorithm 1.

# 3    Secure Addition on Boolean Shares

In this section, we describe algorithms that can be used to perform an addition (or a subtraction) on the Boolean shares directly, thereby eliminating the need to convert masks from one form to the other. Formally, given $n$ Boolean shares

---

**Algorithm 1. SecAnd**

---

**Input:** $(x_i)$ and $(y_i)$ for $1 \leq i \leq n$

**Output:** $(z_i)$ for $1 \leq i \leq n$, with $\bigoplus_{i=1}^{n} z_i = \bigoplus_{i=1}^{n} x_i \wedge \bigoplus_{i=1}^{n} y_i$

1: **for** $i = 1$ to $n$ **do**
2:     **for** $j = i + 1$ to $n$ **do**
3:         $r_{i,j} \leftarrow \mathsf{rand}(1)$
4:         $r_{j,i} \leftarrow (r_{i,j} \oplus (x_i \wedge y_j)) \oplus (x_j \wedge y_i)$
5:     **end for**
6: **end for**
7: **for** $i = 1$ to $n$ **do**
8:     $z_i = x_i \wedge y_i$
9:     **for** $j = 1$ to $n$ **do**
10:        **if** $i \neq j$ **then**
11:            $z_i \leftarrow z_i \oplus r_{i,j}$
12:        **end if**
13:    **end for**
14: **end for**

---

of $x = x_1 \oplus \cdots \oplus x_n$ and $y = y_1 \oplus \cdots \oplus y_n$, we need to compute $n$ Boolean shares of $z = z_1 \oplus \cdots \oplus z_n$ satisfying the relation $z = x + y$, i.e.

$$z_1 \oplus \cdots \oplus z_n = (x_1 \oplus \cdots \oplus x_n) + (y_1 \oplus \cdots \oplus y_n)$$

We propose two algorithms to solve this problem based on the ISW method.

### 3.1  First Variant

The first solution is obtained by transforming the $k$-bit addition circuit into a circuit of XOR and AND gates so that the the ISW technique can be applied directly [11]. A modular addition of two $k$-bit variables $x$ and $y$ can be defined recursively as $(x + y)^{(i)} = x^{(i)} \oplus y^{(i)} \oplus c^{(i)}$, where

$$\begin{cases} c^{(0)} = 0 \\ \forall i \geq 1, c^{(i)} = (x^{(i-1)} \wedge y^{(i-1)}) \oplus (x^{(i-1)} \wedge c^{(i-1)}) \oplus (c^{(i-1)} \wedge y^{(i-1)}) \end{cases} \quad (1)$$

Here, $x^{(i)}$ denotes the $i$-th bit of variable $x$, with $x^{(0)}$ being the least significant bit. Since this recursion formula involves solely XOR and AND operations, we can simply use the ISW approach from [11] to protect it against attacks of any order. The resulting algorithm is shown in Algorithm 2.

Initially, there will be no carry; therefore, we set all $n$ shares of the carry to zero (Step 1). Next, we compute the carries for the remaining bits through the formula given in Equation (1). The loop runs from 0 to $k - 2$ only, since the carry from the last bit does not need to be computed in a modular addition. In Step 8 we apply an XOR operation on the two inputs $x_i$, $y_i$ and the carry $c_i$ to obtain the $n$ shares corresponding to $x + y \bmod 2^k$. The algorithm SecAnd has a time complexity of $\mathcal{O}(n^2)$ and, as a consequence, the full algorithm has a time

---

**Algorithm 2.** SecAdd

---

**Input:** $(x_i)$ and $(y_i)$ for $1 \leq i \leq n$

**Output:** $(z_i)$ for $1 \leq i \leq n$, with $\bigoplus\limits_{i=1}^{n} z_i = \bigoplus\limits_{i=1}^{n} x_i + \bigoplus\limits_{i=1}^{n} y_i$

1:  $(c_i^{(0)})_{1 \leq i \leq n} \leftarrow 0$                                                                                        ▷ Initially carry is zero
2:  **for** $j = 0$ to $k - 2$ **do**                                                                         ▷ Compute carry bit by bit
3:      $(xy_i^{(j)})_{1 \leq i \leq n} \leftarrow \mathsf{SecAnd}((x_i^{(j)})_{1 \leq i \leq n}, (y_i^{(j)})_{1 \leq i \leq n})$                    ▷ $x^{(j)} \wedge y^{(j)}$
4:      $(xc_i^{(j)})_{1 \leq i \leq n} \leftarrow \mathsf{SecAnd}((x_i^{(j)})_{1 \leq i \leq n}, (c_i^{(j)})_{1 \leq i \leq n})$                    ▷ $x^{(j)} \wedge c^{(j)}$
5:      $(yc_i^{(j)})_{1 \leq i \leq n} \leftarrow \mathsf{SecAnd}((y_i^{(j)})_{1 \leq i \leq n}, (c_i^{(j)})_{1 \leq i \leq n})$                    ▷ $y^{(j)} \wedge c^{(j)}$
6:      $(c_i^{(j+1)})_{1 \leq i \leq n} \leftarrow (xy_i^{(j)})_{1 \leq i \leq n} \oplus (xc_i^{(j)})_{1 \leq i \leq n} \oplus (yc_i^{(j)})_{1 \leq i \leq n}$
7:  **end for**
8:  $(z_i)_{1 \leq i \leq n} \leftarrow (x_i)_{1 \leq i \leq n} \oplus (y_i)_{1 \leq i \leq n} \oplus (c_i)_{1 \leq i \leq n}$                        ▷ $z = x + y = x \oplus y \oplus c$
9:  **return** $(z_i)_{1 \leq i \leq n}$

---

complexity of $\mathcal{O}(n^2 k)$. Algorithm 2 has to perform AND and XOR operations only. Due to the ISW scheme, we already know that such a circuit is protected from attacks of order $t$, where $n \geq 2t + 1$. This proves the following theorem and shows the security of Algorithm 2 in the ISW model.

**Theorem 4.** *Let $(x_i)_{1 \leq i \leq n}$ and $(y_i)_{1 \leq i \leq n}$ be the input shares of Algorithm 2 and let $2t < n$. For any set of $t$ intermediate variables, there exists a subset $I \subset [1, n]$ of indices such that $|I| \leq n - 1$, whereby the shares $x_{|I}$ and $y_{|I}$ can perfectly simulate those $t$ intermediate variables as well as the output shares $z_{|I}$.*

### 3.2   Second Variant

The second approach is based on the recursion from Goubin's theorem (Theorem 2), which uses the relation $x + y = x \oplus y \oplus u_{k-1}$, where $u_{k-1}$ is obtained from the following recursion formula:

$$\begin{cases} u_0 = 0 \\ \forall i \geq 0, u_{i+1} = 2[u_i \wedge (x \oplus y) \oplus (x \wedge y)] \end{cases}$$

Algorithm 3 represents the solution based on Goubin's formula to compute the addition. Here, the function SecAnd is called with arguments of a size of $k$ bits instead of 1-bit arguments as in Algorithm 2. In this setting, the ISW scheme has to be adapted as follows: (i) all 1-bit variables defined over $\mathbb{F}_2$ are replaced by $k$-bit variables defined over $\mathbb{F}_{2^k}$; (ii) the 1-bit XOR operations are replaced by $k$-bit XOR operations; and (iii) the 1-bit AND operations are replaced by $k$-bit AND operations. This extension still preserves the security of the original scheme. Note that this method has been used before in the higher-order secure masking technique for AES proposed by Rivain and Prouff [20].[1]

---

[1] In the Rivain-Prouff masking scheme, the AND operations over $\mathbb{F}_2$ were replaced with multiplications over $\mathbb{F}_{2^k}$ instead of AND operations over $\mathbb{F}_{2^k}$.

---

**Algorithm 3.** SecAddGoubin

---

**Input:** $(x_i)$ and $(y_i)$ for $1 \leq i \leq n$

**Output:** $(z_i)$ for $1 \leq i \leq n$, with $\bigoplus_{i=1}^{n} z_i = \bigoplus_{i=1}^{n} x_i + \bigoplus_{i=1}^{n} y_i$

1: $(w_i)_{1 \leq i \leq n} \leftarrow \mathsf{SecAnd}((x_i)_{1 \leq i \leq n}, (y_i)_{1 \leq i \leq n})$      $\triangleright \, \omega = x \wedge y$
2: $(u_i)_{1 \leq i \leq n} \leftarrow 0$         $\triangleright$ Initialize shares of $u$ to zero
3: $(a_i)_{1 \leq i \leq n} \leftarrow (x_i)_{1 \leq i \leq n} \oplus (y_i)_{1 \leq i \leq n}$       $\triangleright \, a = x \oplus y$
4: **for** $j = 1$ to $k - 1$ **do**
5:   $(ua_i)_{1 \leq i \leq n} \leftarrow \mathsf{SecAnd}((u_i)_{1 \leq i \leq n}, (a_i)_{1 \leq i \leq n})$
6:   $(u_i)_{1 \leq i \leq n} \leftarrow (ua_i)_{1 \leq i \leq n} \oplus (w_i)_{1 \leq i \leq n}$
7:   $(u_i)_{1 \leq i \leq n} \leftarrow 2(u_i)_{1 \leq i \leq n}$      $\triangleright \, u \leftarrow 2(u \wedge a \oplus \omega)$
8: **end for**
9: $(z_i)_{1 \leq i \leq n} \leftarrow (x_i)_{1 \leq i \leq n} \oplus (y_i)_{1 \leq i \leq n} \oplus (u_i)_{1 \leq i \leq n}$   $\triangleright \, z = x + y = x \oplus y \oplus u$
10: **return** $(z_i)_{1 \leq i \leq n}$

---

The time complexity of Algorithm 3 is still $\mathcal{O}(n^2 k)$. However, in practice, this algorithm will be faster for two reasons: (i) the number of calls to the function SecAnd inside the loop is reduced from three to one, and (ii) all the operations are directly performed on the $k$-bit variables instead of single bits, thus there is no need to perform bit manipulations. Similar to Algorithm 2, it is easy to see that the security of Algorithm 3 follows from the original ISW scheme.

**Theorem 5.** *Let $(x_i)_{1 \leq i \leq n}$ and $(y_i)_{1 \leq i \leq n}$ be the input shares of Algorithm 3 and let $2t < n$. For any set of $t$ intermediate variables, there exists a subset $I \subset [1, n]$ of indices such that $|I| \leq n - 1$, whereby the shares $x_{|I}$ and $y_{|I}$ can perfectly simulate those $t$ intermediate variables as well as the output shares $z_{|I}$.*

# 4 Secure Arithmetic to Boolean Masking for Any Order

In this section, we describe two new algorithms for conversion from arithmetic to Boolean masking of any order. That is, given $n$ arithmetic shares with the property $x = A_1 + \cdots + A_n$, our algorithms output the corresponding Boolean shares satisfying $x = x_1 \oplus \cdots \oplus x_n$, secure against attacks of order $t$, where $2t \leq n - 1$. We describe in Section 5 the algorithm for secure conversion in the other direction, i.e. from Boolean to arithmetic masking.

We first present a straightforward algorithm with complexity $\mathcal{O}(n^3 k)$, where $n$ and $k$ are the number of shares and the register size, respectively. Then, we give an improved algorithm with a complexity of $\mathcal{O}(n^2 k)$. Internally, both algorithms use the secure addition function we described in Section 3. Though it is more efficient in practice to perform secure addition directly on Boolean shares (due to the overhead of converting between the masks twice), such conversion algorithms may still be useful, e.g. when the required number of conversions is lower than the required number of secure additions.[2]

---

[2] For HMAC-SHA-1, it is more efficient to perform secure addition directly on the Boolean shares, as we will show later.

## 4.1    A Simple Algorithm with Complexity $\mathcal{O}(n^3 k)$

We first describe a simple approach for converting from arithmetic to Boolean masking with complexity $\mathcal{O}(n^3 k)$. Assume that a sensitive variable $x$ is shared among $n$ arithmetic masks as follows:

$$x = A_1 + \cdots + A_n \tag{2}$$

We separately re-share each of the arithmetic shares $A_i$ $(1 \leq i \leq n)$ into $n$ random Boolean shares $x_{i,j}$ $(1 \leq j \leq n)$ so that $A_i = x_{i,1} \oplus \cdots \oplus x_{i,n}$. Hence, the sensitive variables $x$ is now given as:

$$x = (x_{1,1} \oplus \cdots \oplus x_{1,n}) + \cdots + (x_{n,1} \oplus \cdots \oplus x_{n,n}) \tag{3}$$

For each arithmetic share $A_i$ $(1 \leq i \leq n)$, such re-sharing can be accomplished by generating $x_{i,j}$ independently at random for $2 \leq j \leq n$ and letting $x_{i,1} = A_i \oplus x_{i,2} \oplus \cdots \oplus x_{i,n}$. We then sequentially add the $A_i$'s using their $n$-Boolean shared representation $A_i = \bigoplus_{j=1}^{n} x_{i,j}$. For this, we use either the SecAdd or the SecAddGoubin algorithm from Section 3. Eventually, we get the final result $x$ in Boolean form as

$$x = z_1 \oplus \cdots \oplus z_n \tag{4}$$

Since each of the $n - 1$ calls to SecAdd has a complexity of $\mathcal{O}(n^2 k)$, the overall complexity of the arithmetic to Boolean conversion is $\mathcal{O}(n^3 k)$.

**Theorem 6.** *Let $(A_i)_{1 \leq i \leq n}$ be the input shares of the previous algorithm and let $2t < n$. For any set of $t$ intermediate variables, there exists a subset $I \subset [1, n]$ of indices such that $|I| \leq 2t < n$, whereby the shares $A_{|I}$ can perfectly simulate those $t$ intermediate variables as well as the output shares $z_{|I}$.*

*Proof.* We show how to simulate any set of $t$ probes, for $2t < n$. We firstly consider the initial re-sharing of the arithmetic shares $A_i$ $(1 \leq i \leq n)$. At first, the set $I$ is empty. If there is a probe in the re-sharing of $A_i$, we add the index $i$ to $I$. Then, we consider the second part of the algorithm, starting from Equation (3) to the final result given by Equation (4). This second part is essentially an iteration of a circuit obtained through the ISW transform. Therefore, by applying the ISW methodology, we can simply continue with the construction of the subset $I$, so that any probe in this second part, and any of the output shares $z_{|I}$, can be perfectly simulated by knowing the inputs $x_{i,j}$ for $j \in I$ and for all $1 \leq i \leq n$; moreover, we know from the ISW methodology that $|I| \leq 2t < n$.

For any $i \notin I$, since the re-sharing of $A_i$ is not probed, we can perfectly simulate the $x_{i,j}$ for $j \in I$ without knowing $A_i$. Namely, since $|I| \leq 2t < n$, the $x_{i,j}$ for $j \in I$ form a proper subset of $n$ shares, and we can perfectly simulate such a subset without knowing $A_i$ by generating the values independently and uniformly at random. For $i \in I$, we can simulate the $x_{i,j}$ in the same way as in the "real" circuit because we know the input $A_i$. Therefore, as required, we can perfectly simulate the $x_{i,j}$ for $j \in I$ and all $1 \leq i \leq n$.

In summary, the $t$ probes as well as the output shares $z_{|I}$ can be perfectly simulated from the knowledge of the input shares $A_{|I}$, where $|I| \leq 2t < n$.    $\square$

It is easy to observe that one can improve the complexity of this algorithm by using fewer shares at the beginning. In particular, Equation (3) contains a total of $n^2$ shares, while only $n$ are necessary. Therefore, at the beginning, we use only two shares for every $A_i$ instead of $n$ shares. Then, we build a tree where at each layer the number of additive terms is divided by two, while the number of Boolean shares within an additive term is doubled. In this way, the overall number of shares remains $n$ or $2n$ at each level, and so the complexity becomes $\mathcal{O}(n^2 k)$ instead of $\mathcal{O}(n^3 k)$. We provide a complete description below.

## 4.2    Our New Arithmetic to Boolean Conversion Algorithm

In this section, we describe our new algorithm for converting from arithmetic to Boolean masking with a complexity of $\mathcal{O}(n^2 k)$. Our algorithm is best described recursively. Assume that we already found an algorithm $\mathcal{A}_{n/2}$ for converting a set of $n/2$ arithmetic shares $A_i$ into $n/2$ Boolean shares $x_i$ such that

$$A_1 + \cdots + A_{n/2} = x_1 \oplus \cdots \oplus x_{n/2}.$$

Now, given as input a variable $x$ represented with $n$ arithmetic shares $A_i$:

$$x = A_1 + \cdots + A_n$$

we can first apply algorithm $\mathcal{A}_{n/2}$ separately on the two halves to get

$$x = (A_1 + \cdots + A_{n/2}) + (A_{n/2+1} + \cdots + A_n)$$
$$= (x_1 \oplus \cdots \oplus x_{n/2}) + (y_1 \oplus \cdots \oplus y_{n/2})$$

We now apply a simple expansion step, in which the $n/2$ shares $x_i$ and $y_i$ are each expanded to $n$ shares. This can be done by randomly splitting every share $x_i$ into $x_i = x'_{2i-1} \oplus x'_{2i}$ and similarly for $y_i = y'_{2i-1} \oplus y'_{2i}$. We obtain:

$$x = (x'_1 \oplus \cdots \oplus x'_n) + (y'_1 \oplus \cdots \oplus y'_n)$$

Then, we apply the $n$-Boolean addition circuit SecAdd or SecAddGoubin from Section 3 to obtain $x$ represented with $n$ Boolean shares $x = z_1 \oplus \cdots \oplus z_n$ as required.

We now show that the algorithm has a complexity of $\mathcal{O}(n^2 k)$. For the sake of simplicity, we assume that $n$ is a power of two. Let $T_i$ be the execution time of $\mathcal{A}_i$, which takes $i$ arithmetic shares as input. We proceed by induction, based on the assumption that $T_i \leq c \cdot i^2$ for all $i \leq n/2$ and some constant $c$. When running algorithm $\mathcal{A}_n$ with $n$ shares, one first applies $\mathcal{A}_{n/2}$ on both halves, and then executes the expansion step (with $3n$ steps). Finally, the SecAdd algorithm is performed, which gives:

$$T_n \leq 2T_{n/2} + 3n + c' \cdot n^2 \leq 2c \cdot (n/2)^2 + 3n + c' \cdot n^2$$

for some constant $c'$, such that the execution time of SecAdd with $n$ shares is $\leq c' \cdot n^2$. We get:

$$T_n \leq (c/2 + 3 + c') \cdot n^2$$

## Algorithm 4. ConvertA→B

**Input:** $(A_i)$ for $1 \leq i \leq n$

**Output:** $(z_i)$ for $1 \leq i \leq n$, with $\bigoplus_{i=1}^{n} z_i = \sum_{i=1}^{n} A_i$

1: If $n = 1$ then **return** $A_1$

2: $(x_i)_{1 \leq i \leq n/2} \leftarrow$ ConvertA→B $\left( (A_i)_{1 \leq i \leq n/2} \right)$

3: $(x'_i)_{1 \leq i \leq n} \leftarrow$ Expand $\left( (x_i)_{1 \leq i \leq n/2} \right)$       ▷ $\bigoplus_{i=1}^{n} x'_i = \bigoplus_{i=1}^{n/2} x_i = \sum_{i=1}^{n/2} A_i$

4: $(y_i)_{1 \leq i \leq n/2} \leftarrow$ ConvertA→B $\left( (A_i)_{n/2+1 \leq i \leq n} \right)$

5: $(y'_i)_{1 \leq i \leq n} \leftarrow$ Expand $\left( (y_i)_{1 \leq i \leq n/2} \right)$       ▷ $\bigoplus_{i=1}^{n} y'_i = \bigoplus_{i=1}^{n/2} y_i = \sum_{i=n/2+1}^{n} A_i$

6: $(z_i)_{1 \leq i \leq n} \leftarrow$ SecAdd $((x'_i)_{1 \leq i \leq n}, (y'_i)_{1 \leq i \leq n})$

7: **return** $(z_i)_{1 \leq i \leq n}$       ▷ $\bigoplus_{i=1}^{n} z_i = \bigoplus_{i=1}^{n} x'_i + \bigoplus_{i=1}^{n} y'_i = \sum_{i=1}^{n} A_i$

## Algorithm 5. Expand

**Input:** $x_i$ for $1 \leq i \leq n$

**Output:** $y_i$ for $1 \leq i \leq 2n$ with $\bigoplus_{i=1}^{2n} y_i = \bigoplus_{i=1}^{n} x_i$

1: $(r_i)_{1 \leq i \leq n} \leftarrow$ Rand$(k)$

2: $(y_{2i})_{1 \leq i \leq n} \leftarrow (x_i \oplus r_i)_{1 \leq i \leq n}$

3: $(y_{2i+1})_{1 \leq i \leq n} \leftarrow (r_i)_{1 \leq i \leq n}$

4: **return** $(y_i)_{1 \leq i \leq 2n}$

Hence, it suffices to fix the constant $c$ so that $3 + c' \leq c/2$ to get $T_n \leq c \cdot n^2$ as required to prove the result. A formal description of our new conversion method can be found in Algorithm 4, which, in turn, uses the expansion step specified in Algorithm 5. The following theorem confirms that Algorithm 4 is secure in the ISW framework.

**Theorem 7.** *Let* $(A_i)_{1 \leq i \leq n}$ *be the input shares of Algorithm 4. For any set of* $t$ *intermediate variables and any* $k$ *output shares, there exists a subset* $I \subset [1, n]$ *of indices such that* $|I| \leq k + 2t$, *where the shares* $A_{|I}$ *can perfectly simulate those* $t$ *intermediate variables as well as the output shares* $x_{|I}$.

*Proof.* We first prove the following property of the Expand method.

**Lemma 1.** *In Algorithm 5, a set of* $k$ *outputs* $(k \leq 2n)$ *and* $t$ *probes* $(t \leq n)$ *can be perfectly simulated using at most* $\lfloor k/2 \rfloor + t$ *inputs.*

*Proof of Lemma 1.* We proceed by induction. When $n = 1$, the algorithm gets only $x$ as input and outputs $(x \oplus r, r)$ for a uniformly random $r$. Now, we have to distinguish between the following two cases: there is no probe $(t = 0)$, and there is at least one probe $(t \geq 1)$.

In the latter case, i.e. there is at least one probe (for $x$, or $r$, or $x \oplus r$), then $t \geq 1$ and the probe can be perfectly simulated by using the input $x$ and generating $r$ uniformly at random. This will also perfectly simulate both outputs.

As a consequence, for $t = 1$ and any $k$ with $0 \leq k \leq 2$, we can perfectly simulate the $t$ probes and the $k$ outputs using at most $1 \leq \lfloor k/2 \rfloor + t$ inputs.

We now assume that there are no probes ($t = 0$). If no output needs to be simulated (i.e. $k = 0$), then knowledge of the input $x$ is not required. If only a single output must be simulated ($k = 1$), where either $y_1 = x \oplus r$ or $y_2 = r$ has to be simulated, such output can be perfectly simulated by generating a random number uniformly, without knowing $x$. Finally, if $k = 2$, then one input is required. Therefore, for any $k$ with $0 \leq k \leq 2$, the number of required inputs is always at most $\lfloor k/2 \rfloor + t$.

For $n > 1$, let us consider the $i$-th sub-circuit and denote the number of outputs to be simulated by $k_i$ and the number of probes by $t_i$ for $1 \leq i \leq n$. Based on the above arguments, the total number of inputs needed for the simulation is then at most

$$\sum_{i=1}^{n} \lfloor k_i/2 \rfloor + t_i \leq \lfloor k/2 \rfloor + t,$$

which finally proves the Lemma.  □

The proof of Theorem 7 is obtained via induction on the number of shares $n$. We assume that the result holds for $n/2$ and prove that it holds for $n$. We distinguish among 5 sets of probes:

- The $t_A$ probes for the Secure Addition subroutine (Line 6 of Algorithm 4).
- The $t_{EL}$ and $t_{ER}$ probes for the left and right Expand circuit, respectively (lines 3 and 5 of Algorithm 4).
- The $t_{CL}$ and $t_{CR}$ probes for the left and right Arithmetic to Boolean conversion circuit, respectively (lines 2 and 4 of Algorithm 4).

From the security proof of the SecAnd algorithm given in [11], we know that a set of $k$ outputs and $t_A$ probes can be simulated using a subset of $k + 2t_A$ inputs in each of the two input shares $x'_i$ and $y'_i$. Therefore, the property also holds for the SecAdd algorithm.

According to Lemma 1, a set of $k + 2t_A$ outputs and $t_{EL}$ (resp. $t_{ER}$) probes can be simulated using at most $\lfloor (k + 2t_A)/2 \rfloor + t_{EL} = \lfloor k/2 \rfloor + t_A + t_{EL}$ inputs (resp. $\lfloor k/2 \rfloor + t_A + t_{ER}$ inputs). Since the result is assumed to hold for $n/2$, the $\lfloor k/2 \rfloor + t_A + t_{EL}$ outputs and the $t_{CL}$ probes of the left conversion can be simulated using at most $\lfloor k/2 \rfloor + t_A + t_{EL} + 2t_{CL}$ inputs. An upper bound of the number of inputs for the right conversion can be derived in the same way. As a consequence, the total number of required inputs is at most $k + 2t$ according to the following equation

$$\begin{aligned}
|I| &\leq \lfloor k/2 \rfloor + t_A + t_{EL} + 2t_{CL} + \lfloor k/2 \rfloor + t_A + t_{ER} + 2t_{CR} \\
&\leq k + 2(t_A + t_{EL} + t_{ER} + t_{CL} + t_{CR}) \\
&\leq k + 2t,
\end{aligned}$$

which proves Theorem 7.  □

# 5   From Boolean to Arithmetic Masking of Any Order

We now present a new algorithm for converting in the other direction, i.e. from Boolean to arithmetic masking, again with a complexity of $\mathcal{O}(n^2 k)$. Algorithm 6 specifies our arithmetic-to-Boolean conversion in detail.

---

**Algorithm 6.** Conversion from Boolean to Arithmetic Masking

**Input:** $(x_i)$ for $1 \leq i \leq n$

**Output:** $(A_i)$ for $1 \leq i \leq n$, with $\sum_{i=1}^{n} A_i = \bigoplus_{i=1}^{n} x_i$

1: $(A_i)_{1 \leq i \leq n-1} \leftarrow \mathsf{Rand}(k)$

2: $(A'_i)_{1 \leq i \leq n-1} \leftarrow (-A_i)_{1 \leq i \leq n-1}$, $A'_n \leftarrow 0$

3: $(y_i)_{1 \leq i \leq n} \leftarrow \mathsf{ConvertA \to B}\big((A'_i)_{1 \leq i \leq n}\big)$     $\triangleright \bigoplus_{i=1}^{n} y_i = \sum_{i=1}^{n} A'_i = -\sum_{i=1}^{n-1} A_i$

4: $(z_i)_{1 \leq i \leq n} \leftarrow \mathsf{SecAdd}\big((x_i)_{1 \leq i \leq n}, (y_i)_{1 \leq i \leq n}\big)$     $\triangleright \bigoplus_{i=1}^{n} z_i = \bigoplus_{i=1}^{n} x_i + \bigoplus_{i=1}^{n} y_i$

5: $A_n \leftarrow \mathsf{FullXor}\big((z_i)_{1 \leq i \leq n}\big)$     $\triangleright A_n = \bigoplus_{i=1}^{n} z_i = \bigoplus_{i=1}^{n} x_i - \sum_{i=1}^{n-1} A_i$

6: **return** $(A_i)_{1 \leq i \leq n}$.     $\triangleright \sum_{i=1}^{n} A_i = \bigoplus_{i=1}^{n} x_i$

---

We use the same randomized XOR method as in [5] to compute $A_n \leftarrow \bigoplus_{i=1}^{n} z_i$; we recall this method in Algorithm 7. The randomized XOR method, in turn, uses Algorithm 8 (which was first proposed by Rivain and Prouff [20]) to refresh the masks.

---

**Algorithm 7.** FullXor

**Input:** $y_1, \ldots, y_n$

**Output:** $y$ such that $y = y_1 \oplus \cdots \oplus y_n$

1: **for** $i = 1$ **to** $n$ **do** $(y_1, \ldots, y_n) \leftarrow \mathsf{RefreshMasks}(y_1, \ldots, y_n)$

2: **return** $y_1 \oplus \cdots \oplus y_n$

---

**Algorithm 8.** RefreshMasks

**Input:** $z_1, \ldots, z_n$ such that $z = z_1 \oplus \cdots \oplus z_n$

**Output:** $z_1, \ldots, z_n$ such that $z = z_1 \oplus \cdots \oplus z_n$

1: **for** $j = 2$ **to** $n$ **do**

2:     $tmp \leftarrow \mathsf{Rand}(k)$

3:     $z_1 \leftarrow z_1 \oplus tmp$

4:     $z_j \leftarrow z_j \oplus tmp$

5: **end for**

6: **return** $z_1, \ldots, z_n$

The following theorem proves the security of Algorithm 6 in the ISW model; the proof is provided in Appendix A.

**Theorem 8.** *Let $(x_i)_{1 \leq i \leq n}$ be the input shares of Algorithm 6. For any set of $t$ intermediate variables with $2t < n$, there exists a subset $I \subset [1, n]$ of indices such that $|I| \leq 2t$, whereby the shares $x_{|I}$ can perfectly simulate those $t$ intermediate variables as well as the output shares $A_{|I}$.*

# 6  Implementation Results

We have implemented all the solutions proposed in this paper on a 32-bit AVR microcontroller for security level $t = 2, 3$. We then applied all these techniques to HMAC-SHA-1 and compared the running time with respect to an unmasked implementation. Table 1 gives the running time of the addition and conversion algorithms along with the number of calls to the rand function for security level $t = 2, 3$. As expected, the addition algorithms using Goubin's theorem (i.e. the second variant presented in Section 3.2) outperform the first variant (given in Section 3.1). Therefore, we applied the second variant to implement the secure conversion algorithms.

**Table 1.** Execution times of all algorithms (in thousands of clock cycles) for $t = 2, 3$ and the number of calls to the rand function

| Algorithm | Time | rand |
|---|---|---|
| second-order addition | | |
| Algorithm 2 | 87 | 1240 |
| Algorithm 3 | 26 | 320 |
| second-order conversion | | |
| Algorithm 4 | 54 | 484 |
| Algorithm 6 | 81 | 822 |
| third-order addition | | |
| Algorithm 2 | 156 | 2604 |
| Algorithm 3 | 46 | 672 |
| third-order conversion | | |
| Algorithm 4 | 121 | 1288 |
| Algorithm 6 | 162 | 1997 |

**HMAC-SHA-1.** The hash function SHA-1 operates on blocks of 512 bits and produces a 160-bit message digest. Each message block is divided into 16 words of 32-bits each, which are extended to produce 64 further words (i.e. the total number of words is 80). The main loop contains 80 iterations corresponding to each of these 80 words. In order to protect HMAC-SHA-1 against side-channel attacks, we follow two different approaches, which are summarized below.

In the first approach, we use Boolean masking and perform secure addition on Boolean shares directly whenever required. Every iteration of the main loop requires four 32-bit additions, which amounts in a total of 320 additions for 80 iterations. Moreover, five additions have to be performed at the end to update the state. So, in total, 325 secure additions need to be carried out per message block.

In the other approach, we use Boolean masking and convert it to arithmetic masking wherever necessary. In this case, we need four Boolean to arithmetic conversions and one arithmetic to Boolean conversion per iteration, yielding a total of 400 conversions for 80 iterations. Additionally, we need 10 conversions to update the result, i.e. a total of 410 conversions per block are required. The execution times of both approaches are summarized in Table 2.

**Table 2.** Execution times of second and third-order secure masking (in thousands of clock cycles) and performance penalty compared to an unmasked implementation of HMAC-SHA-1

| Algorithm | Time | Penalty |
|---|---|---|
| HMAC-SHA-1 | 104 | 1 |
| second-order addition | | |
| Algorithm 2 | 57172 | 549 |
| Algorithm 3 | 17847 | 171 |
| second-order conversion | | |
| Algorithm 4, 6 | 62669 | 602 |
| third-order addition | | |
| Algorithm 2 | 106292 | 987 |
| Algorithm 3 | 31195 | 299 |
| third-order conversion | | |
| Algorithm 4, 6 | 127348 | 1224 |

# 7    Conclusions

In this paper, we addressed the problem of secure conversion between Boolean and arithmetic masking for any order. By applying the ISW framework and Goubin's results for first-order conversion, we developed two algorithms of the same asymptotic complexity to securely add Boolean shares. We then described novel conversion algorithms between Boolean and arithmetic masking that are provably secure at any order. Practical experiments based on HMAC-SHA-1 as case study show that, in the case of second and third-order security, using Boolean masking and performing secure addition on Boolean shares directly is more efficient than converting between Boolean and arithmetic masking. Even though the proposed algorithms entail a massive performance penalty, they can still be practically useful for applications like challenge-response authentication where only a single block of data needs to be encrypted.

# References

1. Boneh, D., DeMillo, R.A., Lipton, R.J.: On the importance of checking cryptographic protocols for faults. In: Fumy, W. (ed.) EUROCRYPT 1997. LNCS, vol. 1233, pp. 37–51. Springer, Heidelberg (1997)
2. Carlet, C., Goubin, L., Prouff, E., Quisquater, M., Rivain, M.: Higher-order masking schemes for S-boxes. In: Canteaut, A. (ed.) FSE 2012. LNCS, vol. 7549, pp. 366–384. Springer, Heidelberg (2012)
3. Chari, S., Jutla, C.S., Rao, J.R., Rohatgi, P.: Towards sound approaches to counteract power-analysis attacks. In: Wiener, M. (ed.) CRYPTO 1999. LNCS, vol. 1666, pp. 398–412. Springer, Heidelberg (1999)
4. Contini, S., Rivest, R.L., Robshaw, M.J.B., Yin, Y.L.: Improved analysis of some simplified variants of RC6. In: Knudsen, L.R. (ed.) FSE 1999. LNCS, vol. 1636, pp. 1–15. Springer, Heidelberg (1999)
5. Coron, J.-S.: Higher order masking of look-up tables. In: Nguyen, P.Q., Oswald, E. (eds.) EUROCRYPT 2014. LNCS, vol. 8441, pp. 441–458. Springer, Heidelberg (2014)
6. Di Crescenzo, G., Lipton, R.J., Walfish, S.: Perfectly secure password protocols in the bounded retrieval model. In: Halevi, S., Rabin, T. (eds.) TCC 2006. LNCS, vol. 3876, pp. 225–244. Springer, Heidelberg (2006)
7. Dziembowski, S.: Intrusion-resilience via the bounded-storage model. In: Halevi, S., Rabin, T. (eds.) TCC 2006. LNCS, vol. 3876, pp. 207–224. Springer, Heidelberg (2006)
8. Gandolfi, K., Mourtel, C., Olivier, F.: Electromagnetic analysis: Concrete results. In: Koç, Ç.K., Naccache, D., Paar, C. (eds.) CHES 2001. LNCS, vol. 2162, pp. 251–261. Springer, Heidelberg (2001)
9. Goubin, L.: A sound method for switching between Boolean and arithmetic masking. In: Koç, Ç.K., Naccache, D., Paar, C. (eds.) CHES 2001. LNCS, vol. 2162, pp. 3–15. Springer, Heidelberg (2001)
10. Goubin, L., Patarin, J.: DES and differential power analysis (the "duplication" method). In: Koç, Ç.K., Paar, C. (eds.) CHES 1999. LNCS, vol. 1717, pp. 158–172. Springer, Heidelberg (1999)
11. Ishai, Y., Sahai, A., Wagner, D.: Private circuits: Securing hardware against probing attacks. In: Boneh, D. (ed.) CRYPTO 2003. LNCS, vol. 2729, pp. 463–481. Springer, Heidelberg (2003)
12. Karroumi, M., Richard, B., Joye, M.: Addition with blinded operands. In: COSADE (2014)
13. Kocher, P.C.: Timing attacks on implementations of Diffie-Hellman, RSA, DSS, and other systems. In: Koblitz, N. (ed.) CRYPTO 1996. LNCS, vol. 1109, pp. 104–113. Springer, Heidelberg (1996)
14. Kocher, P.C., Jaffe, J., Jun, B.: Differential power analysis. In: Wiener, M. (ed.) CRYPTO 1999. LNCS, vol. 1666, pp. 388–397. Springer, Heidelberg (1999)
15. Lai, X., Massey, J.L.: A proposal for a new block encryption standard. In: Damgård, I.B. (ed.) EUROCRYPT 1990. LNCS, vol. 473, pp. 389–404. Springer, Heidelberg (1991)
16. Micali, S., Reyzin, L.: Physically observable cryptography (extended abstract). In: Naor, M. (ed.) TCC 2004. LNCS, vol. 2951, pp. 278–296. Springer, Heidelberg (2004)
17. NIST. Secure hash standard. In Federal Information Processing Standard, FIPA-180-1 (1995)

18. Oswald, E., Mangard, S., Herbst, C., Tillich, S.: Practical second-order DPA attacks for masked smart card implementations of block ciphers. In: Pointcheval, D. (ed.) CT-RSA 2006. LNCS, vol. 3860, pp. 192–207. Springer, Heidelberg (2006)
19. Rivain, M., Dottax, E., Prouff, E.: Block ciphers implementations provably secure against second order side channel analysis. In: Nyberg, K. (ed.) FSE 2008. LNCS, vol. 5086, pp. 127–143. Springer, Heidelberg (2008)
20. Rivain, M., Prouff, E.: Provably secure higher-order masking of AES. In: Mangard, S., Standaert, F.-X. (eds.) CHES 2010. LNCS, vol. 6225, pp. 413–427. Springer, Heidelberg (2010)

# A    Proof of Theorem 8

We recall the following Lemma from [5] (with $|I| \leq t$ instead of $|I| \leq 2t$) and its proof.

**Lemma 2.** *Let $(y_i)_{1 \leq i \leq n}$ be the input shares of the FullXor algorithm. For any set of $t$ intermediate variables, there exists a subset $I \subset [1, n]$ of indices such that $|I| \leq t$ and the distribution of those $t$ variables can be perfectly simulated from $y_{|I}$ and $y = y_1 \oplus \cdots \oplus y_n$.*

*Proof of Lemma 2.* We first consider the series of $n$ RefreshMasks. If any variable $y_j$ is probed inside any of the RefreshMasks, we add $j$ to $I$.

Moreover since $t < n$, there must be at least one RefreshMasks that is not probed at all; let $i^*$ be the index of this RefreshMasks. Since we know $y = y_1 \oplus \cdots \oplus y_n$, we can perfectly simulate all the shares $(y_i)_{1 \leq i \leq n}$ after this $i^*$-th RefreshMasks. Therefore we can perfectly simulate all $y_i$'s until the last RefreshMasks, and all intermediate variables for computing $y = y_1 \oplus \cdots \oplus y_n$.

In summary before the $i^*$ RefreshMasks, with the knowledge of the input shares $y_{|I}$, we can perfectly simulate all intermediate variables $y_j$ for $j \in I$, and after the $i^*$ RefreshMasks we can perfectly simulate all intermediate variables. Finally the $tmp$ variables are simulated as in the real circuit. This proves Lemma 2.    □

From Lemma 2, the set of $t_1$ probes in the FullXor circuit computing $A_n = \bigoplus_{i=1}^n z_i$ can be simulated from $A_n$ and at most $t_1$ inputs $z_i$. From the previous lemmas, those $t_1$ inputs $z_i$ and the $t_2$ probes in the remaining circuit can be perfectly simulated using $x_{|I}$, for $I \subset [1, n]$, where $|I| \leq t_1 + 2t_2$. If $t_1 > 0$ we add $n$ to $I$; we still have $|I| \leq 2t$ where $t = t_1 + t_2$.

It remains to show how we can simulate $A_n$, as this is required for the simulation in Lemma 2 if $t_1 > 0$, or if $t_1 = 0$ and $n \in I$, since we must simulate all outputs $A_{|I}$. We select an arbitrary $i_0 \notin I$ such that $i_0 \neq n$; this is possible since in both cases we have $n \in I$ and $|I| \leq 2t < n$. We have:

$$A_n = \left( x - \sum_{\substack{i=1 \\ i \neq i_0}}^{n-1} A_i \right) - A_{i_0}$$

Since $i_0 \notin I$ the variable $A_{i_0}$ does not enter in any computation of the simulation. Since in the real circuit $A_{i_0}$ is generated uniformly at random, we can simulate $A_n$ by generating a uniform random value. This proves Theorem 8.

# Making RSA–PSS Provably Secure against Non-random Faults

Gilles Barthe[1], François Dupressoir[1], Pierre-Alain Fouque[2],
Benjamin Grégoire[4], Mehdi Tibouchi[3], and Jean-Christophe Zapalowicz[4]

[1] IMDEA Software Institute, Madrid, Spain
{gilles.barthe,francois.dupressoir}@imdea.org
[2] Université de Rennes 1 and Institut universitaire de France, France
pierre-alain.fouque@ens.fr
[3] NTT Secure Platform Laboratories, Japan
tibouchi.mehdi@lab.ntt.co.jp
[4] INRIA, France
{benjamin.gregoire,jean-christophe.zapalowicz}@inria.fr

**Abstract.** RSA–CRT is the most widely used implementation for RSA signatures. However, deterministic and many probabilistic RSA signatures based on CRT are vulnerable to fault attacks. Nevertheless, Coron and Mandal (Asiacrypt 2009) show that the randomized PSS padding protects RSA signatures against *random faults*. In contrast, Fouque et al. (CHES 2012) show that PSS padding does not protect against certain *non-random faults* that can be injected in widely used implementations based on the Montgomery modular multiplication.

In this paper, we prove the security of an infective countermeasure against a large class of non-random faults; the proof extends Coron and Mandal's result to a strong model where the adversary can choose the value of the faulty signatures modulo one of the prime factors of the RSA modulus. This fault model is clearly strictly more general than Coron and Mandal's, and it captures most of the non-random faults of Fouque et al. Such non-random faults induce, together with the infective countermeasure, more complex probability distributions than in the original proof; we analyze them using careful estimates of character sums over finite fields. The security proof is formally verified using appropriate extensions of EasyCrypt, and provides the first application of formal verification to provable (i.e. reductionist) security in the context of fault attacks.

**Keywords:** Fault Attacks, PSS, RSA–CRT, Infective countermeasure, Formal Verification, EasyCrypt.

## 1  Introduction

Signature schemes are among the most widely used constructions in cryptography. Although there is much interest in signature schemes based on elliptic curves, RSA signatures are still widely used. Moreover, many implementations

L. Batina and M. Robshaw (Eds.): CHES 2014, LNCS 8731, pp. 206–222, 2014.

of RSA, including OpenSSL and implementations for embedded devices such as smartcards, use the well-known Chinese Remainder Theorem (CRT) technique for computing modular exponentiations more efficiently: exponentiations using the CRT can be expected to be 4 times faster than those using full-size exponents. However, when unprotected, RSA–CRT is vulnerable to the so-called Bellcore attack, first introduced by Boneh, DeMillo and Lipton [7], and later refined [3,29,9]. An adversary who knows the padded message and can inject a fault in one of the half exponentiations can efficiently factor the public modulus using a single faulty signature and a GCD computation.

Many countermeasures have been proposed to mitigate this vulnerability, including extra computations and sanity checks of intermediate and final results (see [25]). The simplest such protection is to verify the signature before releasing it. This is reasonably cheap since the public exponent $e$ is usually small. Another approach is to use an extended modulus, as in Shamir's trick [26] and its later refinements which also protect CRT recombination using Garner's formula [6,12,28,13]. Finally, redundant exponentiation algorithms [19,25] such as the Montgomery Ladder can be used. Regardless of the approach, RSA–CRT fault countermeasures tend to be rather costly: for example, Rivain's countermeasure [25,20] has a stated overhead of 10% compared to an unprotected implementation, and is purportedly more efficient than previous works [19,28,20].

Boneh et al.'s original fault attack does not apply to RSA signatures with probabilistic encoding functions, but some extensions of it were proposed to attack randomized ad-hoc padding schemes such as ISO 9796-2 and EMV [14,17]. At Asiacrypt 2009, Coron and Mandal [15] paved the way of provable security against side-channel attack in a practical setting by proving that RSA–PSS is secure against *random* faults in the random oracle model. Injecting a fault on the half-exponentiation modulo the second factor $q$ of $N$ produces a result that can be modeled as uniformly distributed modulo $q$, and the result of such a fault cannot be used to break RSA–PSS signatures. It is tempting to conclude that using RSA–PSS should enable signers to dispense with costly RSA–CRT countermeasures. However, Fouque et al. [18] show that it is possible to break RSA–PSS using certain *non-random* faults if the result is not checked. Indeed, they obtain a key recovery attack with a few faulty signatures on CRT implementations of RSA–PSS that use the state-of-the-art modular multiplication algorithm of Montgomery [22]. Thus, even with PSS, it remains important to check the signature before releasing it.

**Infective Countermeasures.** Checking results before release is a simple and practical security measure, but it is not sufficient by itself, since simple tests can be easily bypassed by flipping the outcome of a comparison [2,27]. Infective countermeasures are an alternate approach in which results are released all the time, but become gibberish when faulty computations occur: a fault (usually not controlled by the adversary) results in a random value, which consequently makes the faulty signature random. From a security point of view, since faults may not be random, we may not be able to prove that the faulty output is fully random. However, one may ask that the output be independent of secret information even in the presence of non-random faults. Infective countermeasures have been used before by Canetti and Goldwasser [10] to deal with fault-injecting adversaries when decrypting ciphertexts in a distributed manner. One such countermeasure for RSA–CRT was proposed by Boscher, Handschuh and Trichina [8]. In their technique, the signer computes the signature $S$ and recomputes $y' = S^e \bmod N$ to check the signature against the padded message $y$, before returning $S + y'_p - (y \bmod p) + y'_q - (y \bmod q)$ if $y' = y$, and an error otherwise. Even if the adversary bypasses the verification $y' = y$, the output signature mixes the fault and correct signature in a non-trivial way. Still, this countermeasure was later attacked by Trichina and Korkikyan [27] for deterministic padding schemes. We tackle the problem of masking faulty signatures so as to prevent the exploitation of faults and protect validity checks.

**Our Contributions.** In this paper we generalize the fault model from [16] and consider a very powerful adversary able to inject *non-random* faults. More precisely, we let the adversary set the value modulo $q$ of the computed signatures to an arbitrary value of his choice. Clearly, since he could choose that value randomly, the model is strictly more powerful than the one considered by Coron and Mandal. In addition, it captures many other types of faults, such as the "null faults" and "constant faults" introduced by Fouque et al. [18]. If such a signatures is directly returned to the adversary, he can clearly factor the modulus, but we consider a simple countermeasure to avoid that problem. The countermeasure, described in Fig. 1, uses infective techniques, mixing additional randomness into faulty signatures in a *provably secure way*. In practice, we show that our random infection masks faulty signatures enough for us to prove the security of RSA–PSS under the RSA assumption in the random oracle model if enough additional randomness is provided. Concretely, we sample a random value $r'$ and add $r' \cdot (y - y')$ to the signature mod $N$, where $y$ is the original padded message and $y'$ is the padded message recovered from the signature. When the signature is computed correctly, $(y - y')$ is zero and the correct signature is returned. If the signature is faulty, we show that the masked output is statistically close to uniform and hence leaks no secret information. We prove such results in two key lemmas corresponding to [15, Lemmas 1, 2]. Since our faults are non-random, the probability distributions are more complex; we use careful estimates of exponential sums attached to corresponding rational functions to establish their regularity. We only analyze this countermeasure when the validity check is performed in the standard way (by computing the public permutation), but our random infection might also be used to protect other checks such as Rivain's [25,20]. A discussion of the faults we model can be found in Section 2.

The second contribution of the paper is a formal proof of security of the countermeasure using EasyCrypt[1], a computer-aided framework that has previously been used to reason about the security of cryptographic constructions—but was never applied to fault attacks and countermeasures. Our proof is the first application of formal verification to provable security against fault attacks, as other works [11,23,24] applying formal verification to fault attacks are focused on prov-

---

[1] https://www.easycrypt.info

**Figure 1.** Protected signing algorithm

| | |
|---|---|
| 1: **function** SIGN($sk, pk, m$) | ▷ $sk = (d_p, d_q, \alpha_p, \alpha_q, N)$, $pk = (e, N)$ |
| 2:   $r \leftarrow \{0,1\}^{k_0}$ | ▷ Start of PSS padding |
| 3:   $\omega \leftarrow \mathcal{H}(m, r)$ | |
| 4:   $st \leftarrow \mathcal{G}(\omega) \oplus (r \,\|\, 0^{k_g - k_0})$ | |
| 5:   $y \leftarrow \mathsf{os2ip}(0 \,\|\, \omega \,\|\, st)$ | |
| 6:   $\sigma_p \leftarrow y^{d_p} \bmod p$ | ▷ Signature computation |
| 7:   $\sigma_q \leftarrow y^{d_q} \bmod q$ | |
| 8:   $\sigma \leftarrow (\alpha_p \cdot \sigma_p + \alpha_q \cdot \sigma_q) \bmod N$ | ▷ $\alpha_p = q \cdot (q^{-1} \bmod p)$ and similarly for $\alpha_q$ |
| 9:   $y' \leftarrow \sigma^e \bmod N$ | |
| 10:   $r' \leftarrow \{0,1\}^{\rho} \backslash \{0\}$ | ▷ Infective countermeasure |
| 11:   $\sigma' \leftarrow \sigma + r' \cdot (y - y') \bmod N$ | |
| 12:   **return** $\mathsf{i2osp}(\sigma')$ | |

ing the correctness of the countermeasures (that is, that the protected program either returns the same result as the original program, or fails), but do not provide any provable security guarantees. Apart from increasing our confidence in the effectiveness of the countermeasure, our formal proof reveals a glitch in the proof of Coron and Mandal [15], and also paves the way for formally verifying the effectiveness of the countermeasures on standard implementations of PKCS probabilistic signing, in the same way that [1] uses an older prototype of EasyCrypt [5] to prove security of an implementation of PKCS encryption.

**Related work.** Christofi et al. [11] use a combination of program transformation and verification techniques for proving Vigilant's countermeasure for CRT-RSA. They take a source program $p$ and output a program $\hat{p}$ that contains all possible faulty behaviors of $p$. Then, they show that the program $\hat{p}$ either returns a value that matches the value returned by $p$ on the same input, or else returns an error, they conclude that the program is correct for all faults. While it is a natural guarantee to seek, their theorem does not constitute a proof of security in the sense of provable security, but rather a heuristic to validate a countermeasure implementation.

Rauzy and Guilley [24] develop symbolic methods to analyze fault attacks against RSA–CRT implementations. They model arithmetic computations as algebraic expressions, and define a simplification procedure for expressions. Given an expression $e$ (representing the algorithm to be attacked), their tool tests for all possible faulty variants $\hat{e}$ of $e$ if the expression $\gcd(N, e - \hat{e})$ simplifies to a prime factor of the RSA modulus. If some expression $\hat{e}$ is found, then the algorithm is considered insecure. Their tool is useful to find fault attacks on an algorithm, but only provides guarantees of security against a restricted class of attackers. Moreover, it is specialized to deterministic signature schemes and cannot deal with randomized paddings like PSS.

Moro et al. [23] focus on the specific class of instruction skip attacks, in which an adversary forces to skip the execution of a targeted instruction. To protect against skip attacks, they transform a program $p$ into a fault-tolerant program $\hat{p}$, by providing for each instruction a possible replacement for execution in the presence of instruction skip faults. Using a model checker, they establish the equivalence between executing the instruction without faults and executing the replacement sequence of instructions with instruction skip faults. Their approach is general, and significantly improves resistance against instruction skip attacks. However, it is not suitable for obtaining the strong guarantees required by provable security.

## 2  Our Results

Instead of considering the many possible faults an adversary could inject in Fig. 1, we give the adversary access to two distinct oracles (Fig. 2) that compute valid signatures (oracle $S$) and generalize faulty signatures (oracle $\mathcal{F}$), as justified in Section 2. As discussed, our fault model is independent of the algorithm used to compute modular exponentiation. We therefore use simpler definitions for public and secret key, where a public key $pk$ is composed of a public exponent $e$ and a modulus $N$, and a secret key $sk$ is composed of a private exponent $d$ and a modulus $N$.

Throughout the security proof, we consider a fixed $k$ that serves as the size of the modulus and signatures. In particular, we assume that the modulus is balanced, that is $N = p \cdot q$ is such that $2^{k-1} \leq N < 2^k$ and $2^{k/2-1} \leq p < q < 2^{k/2}$. PSS padding is computed using two hash functions $\mathcal{H}$, outputting bitstrings of length $k_h$, and $\mathcal{G}$, producing bitstrings of length $k_g$, where $k_h + k_g + 1 = k$. In addition, the padding scheme uses a random salt of length $k_0 < k_g$. For simplicity, we model $\mathcal{H}$ as a function from $\{0,1\}^* \times \{0,1\}^{k_0}$ to $\{0,1\}^{k_h}$, and $\mathcal{G}$ as a function from $\{0,1\}^{k_h}$ to $\{0,1\}^{k_g}$. This is done without loss of generality. In algorithm

---

**Figure 2.** Oracles in our fault model

---

1: **oracle** $S(m)$
2:    $r \leftarrow \{0,1\}^{k_0}$
3:    $\omega \leftarrow \mathcal{H}(m, r)$
4:    $st \leftarrow \mathcal{G}(\omega) \oplus (r \,||\, 0^{k_g - k_0})$
5:    $y \leftarrow \mathsf{os2ip}(0 \,||\, \omega \,||\, st)$
6:    $\sigma \leftarrow y^d \bmod N$
7:    **return** $\mathsf{i2osp}(\sigma)$

1: **oracle** $\mathcal{V}(m, \sigma)$
2:    $r \leftarrow \perp$
3:    $s \leftarrow \mathsf{os2ip}(\sigma)$
4:    **if** $0 < s < N$ **then**
5:       $y \leftarrow s^e \bmod N$
6:       $b \,||\, \omega \,||\, st \leftarrow \mathsf{i2osp}(y)$
7:       $r \,||\, \gamma \leftarrow st \oplus \mathcal{G}(\omega)$
8:       $\omega' \leftarrow \mathcal{H}(m, r)$
9:       $r = b = 0 \wedge \omega = \omega' \wedge \gamma = 0^{k_g - k_0}$
10:   **return** $r$

1: **oracle** $\mathcal{F}(m, a)$
2:    $r \leftarrow \{0,1\}^{k_0}$
3:    $\omega \leftarrow \mathcal{H}(m, r)$
4:    $st \leftarrow \mathcal{G}(\omega) \oplus (r \,||\, 0^{k_g - k_0})$
5:    $y \leftarrow \mathsf{os2ip}(0 \,||\, \omega \,||\, st)$
6:    $\sigma \leftarrow y^d \bmod N$
7:    $r' \leftarrow \{0,1\}^\rho \backslash \{0\}$
8:    $\sigma' \leftarrow y^d \cdot \alpha_p + (a + r' \cdot (y - a^e)) \cdot \alpha_q$
9:    **return** $\mathsf{i2osp}(\sigma')$

and game descriptions, we denote with i2osp and os2ip the conversions between integers and their binary representations. For simplicity, i2osp always produces a bitstring of length $k$.

Under the Generalized Riemann Hypothesis, we reduce the $\mathcal{UF}$-$\mathcal{CMA}$ security of the faulty signature scheme presented in Fig. 2, where the adversary is given access to the faulty signature oracle along with the valid signature oracle and the random oracles $\mathcal{H}$ and $\mathcal{G}$, to the one-way security of RSA. We consider a forgery valid even if it was produced by the faulty signature oracle. In the rest of this paper, we use $\mathcal{S}$ to denote the valid signature oracle, $\mathcal{F}$ to denote the faulty signature oracle, $\mathcal{K}$ to denote the RSA key generation algorithm, and $\mathcal{V}$ for the PSS verification algorithm. Subscripts identify the game in which a particular oracle appears. We denote with $Q^{\mathcal{X}}$ the set of query-response pairs for queries made to oracle $\mathcal{X}$ so far.

---

**Figure 3.** Initial and Final Games

| | |
|---|---|
| 1: **game** $\mathcal{UF}$-$\mathcal{CMA}$ | 1: **game** $\mathcal{OW}$-$\mathcal{RSA}$ |
| 2:    $(e, d, N) \leftarrow \mathcal{K}()$ | 2:    $(e, d, N) \leftarrow \mathcal{K}()$ |
| 3:    $(m, s) \leftarrow \mathcal{A}^{\mathcal{S}, \mathcal{F}, \mathcal{H}, \mathcal{G}}(e, N)$ | 3:    $x^* \leftarrow [0..N)$ |
| 4:    $b \leftarrow \mathcal{V}(m, s)$ | 4:    $y^* \leftarrow x^{* e} \bmod N$ |
| 5:    $win \leftarrow b \wedge (m, s) \notin Q^{\mathcal{S}}$ | 5:    $x \leftarrow \mathcal{I}(e, N, y^*)$ |
| 6:    **return** $win$ | 6:    **return** $x = x^*$ |

---

**Theorem 1 ($\mathcal{UF}$-$\mathcal{CMA}$ security of protected PSS in the presence of faults).** *Assume that the Generalized Riemann Hypothesis holds. For all $\delta > 0$, there exists a constant $\kappa_\delta > 0$ depending only on $\delta$ such that given a CMA adversary $\mathcal{A}$ against the faulty signature scheme $(\mathcal{K}, \mathcal{S}, \mathcal{F}, \mathcal{V})$ that makes at most $q_{\mathcal{H}}$ queries to $\mathcal{H}$, $q_{\mathcal{G}}$ queries to $\mathcal{G}$, $q_{\mathcal{S}}$ queries to $\mathcal{S}$ and $q_{\mathcal{F}}$ queries to $\mathcal{F}$, we build a one-way inverter $\mathcal{I}$ such that*

$$\Pr[\mathcal{UF}\text{-}\mathcal{CMA} : win] \leq \Pr[\mathcal{OW}\text{-}\mathcal{RSA} : x = x^*] + \epsilon_0$$

*with*

$$\epsilon_0 = \frac{(q_{\mathcal{H}} + q_{\mathcal{S}} + q_{\mathcal{F}}) \cdot (q_{\mathcal{H}} + q_{\mathcal{G}} + q_{\mathcal{S}} + q_{\mathcal{F}}) + q_{\mathcal{G}} \cdot q_{\mathcal{F}} \cdot 3 + 1}{2^{k_h}} +$$
$$\frac{(q_{\mathcal{S}} + q_{\mathcal{F}}) \cdot (2 \cdot q_{\mathcal{H}} + q_{\mathcal{S}} + q_{\mathcal{F}}) + q_{\mathcal{H}} + q_{\mathcal{S}}}{2^{k_0}} + \frac{1}{2^{\frac{k}{2}-1}} + q_{\mathcal{F}} \cdot 2\kappa_\delta \cdot 2^{\frac{k\delta - \rho}{2}}$$

*Remark 1.* The constant $\kappa_\delta$ is as in Lemma 1. As observed in Remark 2, for large enough $N$, it suffices to take $\rho$ slightly larger than a given $m$ to bound the final term by $2^{-m}$. In addition, as mentioned in Remark 3, we assume that $\rho$ is chosen slightly larger than $k_h$ so that the assumptions of Lemma 3 are satisfied.

**Fault Model Justification.** In this section, we justify our fault model, described by oracle $\mathcal{F}(m,a)$ in Fig. 2. Our faulty signature oracle computes the correct padded message $y$, samples $r'$ and returns $\sigma' = y^d \cdot \alpha_p + (a + r'(y - a^e)) \cdot \alpha_q$ with $a \in \mathbb{Z}/q\mathbb{Z}$ chosen by the adversary.

We allow multiple faults to be injected, but only during the RSA–CRT computation (lines 6-7 of the protected signing Fig. 1). More precisely, we consider a scenario where the computation modulo $p$ is correct whereas those modulo $q$ is faulted to result in a constant $a$ chosen by the adversary, *i.e.* $\sigma_f = (y^d \bmod p, a) \in \mathbb{Z}/p\mathbb{Z} \times \mathbb{Z}$. Then, using our countermeasure we obtain:

$$\sigma' = \sigma_f + r'(y - \sigma_f^e)$$
$$= y^d \alpha_p + \alpha_q a + r'(y - (y^d \alpha_p + \alpha_q a)^e)$$
$$= y^d \alpha_p + (a + r'(y - a^e))\alpha_q.$$

Our fault model leverages the results of Coron and Mandal in [15] who treated the case of random faults against PSS scheme, and those of Fouque et al. [18] who proposed various faults: "null faults" (forcing a small register to 0), "constant faults" (forcing a small register to a constant) and "zero high-order bits faults" (forcing part of a small register to 0). When applied during the RSA–CRT computations using Montgomery multiplication, Fouque et al. showed that both "null faults" and "constant faults" result in a chosen, fixed value for the the signature modulo $q$, and those highly non-random faults are thus captured by our model together with the random faults of Coron and Mandal.

## 3    Statistical Lemmas

We need several results on the regularity of the probability distributions related to the infective countermeasure. Recall that the *statistical distance* between a random variable $X$ on a finite set $S$ and the uniform distribution is defined as:

$$\Delta_1(X) = \frac{1}{2} \cdot \sum_{s \in S} \left| \Pr[X = s] - \frac{1}{|S|} \right|.$$

We say that $X$ is $\delta$-*statistically close to uniform* when $\Delta_1(X) \le \delta$.

Our proofs rely on character sums over $\mathbb{Z}/q\mathbb{Z}$. We refer to [21] or the full version of this paper [4] for basic properties of Dirichlet characters and character sums. The main statistical result can be stated as follows.

**Lemma 1.** *Consider integer intervals* $\mathcal{X} = [1, X]$, $\mathcal{W} = [w_0, w_0 + W)$ *whose lengths* $X, W$ *satisfy* $X, W < q$, *and for all* $t \in \mathbb{Z}/q\mathbb{Z}$, *denote by* $T(\mathcal{X}, \mathcal{W}; t) = \frac{XW}{q} \cdot (1 + V(\mathcal{X}, \mathcal{W}; t))$ *the number of solutions* $(x, w) \in \mathcal{X} \times \mathcal{W}$ *of the congruence* $xw \equiv t \pmod{q}$. *Assuming that the Generalized Riemann Hypothesis holds, then for all* $\delta > 0$, *there exists a constant* $\kappa_\delta > 0$ *depending only on* $\delta$ *(and not* $q, \mathcal{X}, \mathcal{W}$*) such that:*

$$\sum_{t \in \mathbb{Z}/q\mathbb{Z}} |V(\mathcal{X}, \mathcal{W}; t)| \le \frac{\kappa_\delta q^{3/2 + \delta}}{\sqrt{XW}}.$$

*In particular, the distribution of the products $xw \bmod q$ is statistically close to uniform in $\mathbb{Z}/q\mathbb{Z}$ whenever $XW \gg q^{1+3\delta}$.*

*Proof.* Note first that all elements of $\mathcal{X}$ are invertible modulo $q$, whereas at most one element of $\mathcal{W}$ is divisible by $q$. Denote by $W^*$ the number of elements of $\mathcal{W}$ which are invertible modulo $q$, which is thus equal to $W$ or $W - 1$. We then have:

$$T(\mathcal{X}, \mathcal{W}; 0) = X \cdot (W - W^*) \leq X \quad \text{and hence} \quad |V(\mathcal{X}, \mathcal{W}; 0)| \leq \frac{q}{W}.$$

On the other hand, for $t \neq 0$, we can express $T(\mathcal{X}, \mathcal{W}; t)$ as a sum over the multiplicative characters modulo $q$. Indeed, the orthogonality of characters ensures that, for all $x, w$, we have $\sum_\chi \chi(xw)\overline{\chi(t)} = q - 1$ if $xw \equiv t \pmod{q}$ and $0$ otherwise. Hence:

$$\begin{aligned}
T(\mathcal{X}, \mathcal{W}; t) &= \frac{1}{q-1} \sum_\chi \sum_{(x,w) \in \mathcal{X} \times \mathcal{W}} \chi(xw)\overline{\chi(t)} \\
&= \frac{XW^*}{q-1} + \frac{1}{q-1} \sum_{\chi \neq \chi_0} \sum_{(x,w) \in \mathcal{X} \times \mathcal{W}} \chi(xw)\overline{\chi(t)},
\end{aligned}$$

by putting aside the contribution of the trivial character $\chi_0$. Write that equality as $T(\mathcal{X}, \mathcal{W}; t) = \frac{XW^*}{q-1} \cdot \left(1 + V^*(t)\right)$. We then have:

$$V^*(t) = \frac{1}{XW^*} \sum_{\chi \neq \chi_0} \sum_{(x,w) \in \mathcal{X} \times \mathcal{W}} \chi(xw)\overline{\chi(t)},$$

and we can express the sum of the squared deviations $|V^*(t)|^2$ as:

$$\sum_{t \neq 0} |V^*(t)|^2 = \frac{1}{(XW^*)^2} \sum_{\chi, \chi' \neq \chi_0} \sum_{x,w,x',w'} \chi(xw)\overline{\chi'(x'w')} \sum_{t \neq 0} (\chi\overline{\chi'})(t).$$

The sum over $t$ on the right-hand side is equal to $q - 1$ if $\chi = \chi'$ and vanishes otherwise, so that:

$$\sum_{t \neq 0} |V^*(t)|^2 = \frac{q-1}{(XW^*)^2} \sum_{\chi \neq \chi_0} \sum_{x,w,x',w'} \chi(xw)\overline{\chi'(xw)} = \frac{q-1}{(XW^*)^2} \sum_{\chi \neq \chi_0} |S(\chi)|^2,$$

where $S(\chi) = \sum_{x \in \mathcal{X}} \chi(x) \sum_{w \in \mathcal{W}} \chi(w)$. Now since $\mathcal{X}$ is an interval of the form $[1, X]$, it is classical that GRH implies, for any $\delta > 0$, $\left|\sum_{x \in \mathcal{X}} \chi(x)\right| \leq c_\delta X^{1/2} q^\delta$ for some constant $c_\delta > 0$ (see e.g. [21, Eq. (13.2)]). Hence:

$$\sum_{t \neq 0} |V^*(t)|^2 \leq \frac{q-1}{(XW^*)^2} \cdot c_\delta^2 X q^{2\delta} \cdot \sum_\chi \sum_{(w,w') \in \mathcal{W}^2} \chi(w)\overline{\chi(w')} \leq \frac{c_\delta^2 q^{2\delta}(q-1)^2}{XW^*}$$

by using orthogonality again. Then, the Cauchy–Schwarz inequility yields:

$$\sum_{t \neq 0} |V^*(t)| \leq \sqrt{\frac{c_\delta^2 q^{2+2\delta}}{XW^*}} \cdot \sqrt{q-1} \leq \frac{c_\delta q^\delta (q-1)^{3/2}}{\sqrt{XW}}.$$

Finally, observe that for $t \neq 0$, we have:

$$V(\mathcal{X}, \mathcal{W}; t) = \frac{q}{XW} T(\mathcal{X}, \mathcal{W}; t) - 1 = \frac{q}{XW} \cdot \frac{XW^*}{q-1} \cdot \left(1 + V^*(t)\right) - 1$$

$$= \frac{qW^*}{(q-1)W} V^*(t) - \frac{W - q(W - W^*)}{(q-1)W}.$$

On the last line, the first term is bounded in absolute value by $\frac{q}{q-1}\left|V^*(t)\right|$, and the second term by $\frac{q}{q-1}W$. As a result, we get:

$$\sum_{t \in \mathbb{Z}/q\mathbb{Z}} \left|V(\mathcal{X}, \mathcal{W}; t)\right| \leq \frac{q}{q-1} \sum_{t \neq 0} \left|V^*(t)\right| + \frac{q}{W} + \left|V(0)\right| \leq \frac{c_\delta q^{3/2+\delta}}{\sqrt{XW}} + \frac{2q}{W}$$

which yields the stated result for $\kappa_\delta = c_\delta + 2$, say (as a coarse upper bound). □

We now discuss our key statistical lemmas. The first one ensures that the faulty signature $\sigma' = y^d \cdot \alpha_p + \left(a + r'(y - a^e)\right) \cdot \alpha_q$ is indistinguishable from a uniform random element in $\mathbb{Z}/N\mathbb{Z}$ if the nonce $r'$ is large enough. We write $x$ instead of $r'$ in the rest of this section.

**Lemma 2.** *Let $N = pq$ be a $k$-bit balanced RSA modulus and $e$ the public exponent, $0 \leq y < 2^{k-1}$ a random integer and $x$ a random nonzero $\rho$-bit integer. Fix an arbitrary integer $a$. Assuming that the Generalized Riemann Hypothesis holds, the statistical distance between the distribution of $\sigma' = y^d \cdot \alpha_p + \left(a + x(y - a^e)\right) \cdot \alpha_q \bmod N$ and the uniform distribution modulo $N$ is bounded as:*

$$\Delta_1(\sigma') \leq \kappa_\delta q^\delta \sqrt{\frac{N}{XY}} \leq 2\kappa_\delta \cdot 2^{(\delta k - \rho)/2}$$

*for any $\delta > 0$, with $\kappa_\delta$ as in Lemma 1.*

*Proof.* The statistical distance between the distribution of $\sigma'$ and the uniform distribution can be written as:

$$\Delta_1(\sigma') = \frac{1}{2} \sum_{(s,t) \in \mathbb{Z}/p\mathbb{Z} \times \mathbb{Z}/q\mathbb{Z}} \left| \Pr_{(x,y) \in \mathcal{X} \times \mathcal{Y}} \left[ \begin{matrix} \sigma' \equiv s \pmod{p} \\ \sigma' \equiv t \pmod{q} \end{matrix} \right] - \frac{1}{N} \right|$$

where $\mathcal{X}$ and $\mathcal{Y}$ are the integer intervals $[1, X]$ and $[0, Y)$ with $X = 2^\rho - 1$ and $Y = 2^{k-1}$ respectively. Let us estimate the probability

$$P(s,t) = \Pr_{(x,y) \in \mathcal{X} \times \mathcal{Y}} \left[ \begin{matrix} \sigma' \equiv s \pmod{p} \\ \sigma' \equiv t \pmod{q} \end{matrix} \right]$$

appearing in that equation for some fixed $(s,t) \in \mathbb{Z}/p\mathbb{Z} \times \mathbb{Z}/q\mathbb{Z}$.

We have $\sigma' \equiv s \pmod{p}$ if and only if $y^d \equiv s \bmod p$, i.e. $y \equiv s^e \bmod p$. Hence, the solutions of the first congruence are of the form $y = (s^e \bmod p) + pw$ for $w$ in the integer interval $[0, W_s)$, $W_s = \lceil \frac{Y - (s^e \bmod p)}{p} \rceil$. Then, the second equation, which is equivalent to $a + x(y - a^e) \equiv t \pmod{q}$, becomes $x(pw + (s^e \bmod p) - a^e) \equiv t - a \pmod{q}$. This can be written in the form $x(w + w_0) = t_0$ $\pmod{q}$, with $w_0 = \frac{(s^e \bmod p) - a^e}{p} \bmod q$ and $t_0 = \frac{t - a}{p} \bmod q$. The number of solutions $(x, w)$ is thus $T(\mathcal{X}, \mathcal{W}_s; t_0)$, with $\mathcal{W}_s = [w_0, w_0 + W_s)$. Hence:

$$P(s, t) = \frac{1}{XY} T(\mathcal{X}, \mathcal{W}_s; t_0) = \frac{W_s}{qY} + \frac{W_s}{qY} V(\mathcal{X}, \mathcal{W}_s; t_0).$$

Note that $\mathcal{W}_s$ depends only on $s$ (not on $t$), and that $t \mapsto t_0$ is a permutation of $\mathbb{Z}/q\mathbb{Z}$. Thus, for fixed $s$, we can sum the previous equation over $t \in \mathbb{Z}/q\mathbb{Z}$, which gives:

$$\sum_{t \in \mathbb{Z}/q\mathbb{Z}} \left| P(s, t) - \frac{1}{N} \right| \leq q \cdot \left| \frac{W_s}{qY} - \frac{1}{N} \right| + \frac{W_s}{qY} \sum_{t \in \mathbb{Z}/q\mathbb{Z}} |V(\mathcal{X}, \mathcal{W}_s; t)|.$$

Now $Y/p - 1 \leq W_s \leq Y/p + 1$, so that the first term on the right-hand side is bounded by $1/Y$. Thus, Lemma 1 yields:

$$\sum_{t \in \mathbb{Z}/q\mathbb{Z}} \left| P(s, t) - \frac{1}{N} \right| \leq \frac{1}{Y} + \frac{W_s}{qY} \cdot \frac{\kappa_\delta q^{3/2+\delta}}{\sqrt{XW_s}} = \frac{\kappa_\delta q^{1/2+\delta}}{\sqrt{XY \cdot p/2}}$$

using the coarse upper bound $W_s/Y \leq 2/p$. Summing further over $s$, we finally obtain:

$$\sum_{s,t} \left| P(s, t) - \frac{1}{N} \right| \leq \frac{p}{Y} + \kappa_\delta q^\delta \sqrt{\frac{2N}{XY}}$$

and hence the desired result, since $p \leq \sqrt{N}$ and $Y > X$. □

*Remark 2.* Concretely, this result means that, for large enough $N$, it suffices to take $\rho$ slightly larger than $m$ to obtain a statistical distance of $2^{-m}$.

If we do not want to rely on the Riemann Hypothesis, we can obtain an unconditional bound by replacing the use of GRH in Lemma 1 by the Pólya–Vinogradov inequality (or the Burgess bound). However, statistical indistinguishability from uniform then requires somewhat larger values of $\rho$: at least $k/4 + m + o(1)$ with Pólya–Vinogradov or $k/8 + m + o(1)$ with the Burgess bound.

The security proof requires another statistical lemma which ensures that the adversary has a negligible probability of querying the correct value $\omega \leftarrow \mathcal{H}(M, r)$ given a faulty signature. The proof, which uses Lemma 1 in a very similar way as the proof of Lemma 2 (simply replacing the interval $\mathcal{Y}$ by a subinterval $\mathcal{Y}_\omega$), is given in the full version of this paper [4].

**Lemma 3.** *Let $N, e, a, \delta, \kappa_\delta$ be as in Lemma 2. Assume that $\rho \geq k_h + \delta k + \log_2(4\kappa_\delta)$. For any choice of $\sigma' \in \mathbb{Z}/N\mathbb{Z}$ and any $k_h$-bit value $\omega'$, the probability that a solution $(x, y) \in [1, 2^\rho) \times [0, 2^{k-1})$ of the equation $\sigma' \equiv y^d \cdot \alpha_p + (a + x(y -$*

$a^e$)) $\cdot \alpha_q$ (mod $N$) satisfies that the most significant $k_h$ bits $\omega \in [0, 2^{k_h})$ of $y$ coincides with $\omega'$ is bounded as:

$$\Pr \left[ \omega = \omega' | \sigma' \right] \leq \frac{3}{2^{k_h}}.$$

*Remark 3.* Concretely, this result means that we must choose $\rho$ larger than $k_h$.

# 4   Security Proof

The sequence of games presented in this Section and formal justifications for all transitions between games are formalized in EasyCrypt. However, Lemmas 2 and 3 are stated as axioms of the formalization. Formally proving these lemmas is outside the scope of this work, as it would first require to formalize at least those properties of additive characters used in our proof.

The hash functions $\mathcal{G}$ and $\mathcal{H}$ are modelled as random oracles. For clarity, we display the initial definition of $\mathcal{H}$ on the left in Fig. 4. The initial definition of $\mathcal{G}$ is similar. We assume two global maps $h$ and $g$ are used to build the random oracles. Our proof works mostly by transforming the random oracle $\mathcal{H}$. We therefore display the code for $\mathcal{H}$ for each transition, only displaying other oracles when they suffer non-trivial changes.

*Game 0.* We initially transform both random oracles to keep track of the first caller to make a particular query. It can be either the adversary (Adv), the signature oracle (Sig), or the faulty signature oracle (FSig). Calls made by the experiment when checking the validity of the forgery do not need to tag their query as they are the last queries made to the random oracles and do not need to update its state. We also extend the internal state of $\mathcal{H}$ with an additional field for use later in the proof, and currently set to a default value $\perp$.

---

**Figure 4.** Initial transition: extending state

| | |
|---|---|
| 1: **oracle** $\mathcal{H}(m, r)$ | 1: **oracle** $\mathcal{H}_0(m, r)$ |
| 2:　　**if** $(m, r) \notin \mathsf{dom}(h)$ **then** | 2:　　**if** $(m, r) \notin \mathsf{dom}(h)$ **then** |
| 3:　　　　$h[m, r] \leftarrow \{0, 1\}^{k_h}$ | 3:　　　　$\omega \leftarrow \{0, 1\}^{k_h}$ |
| 4:　　**return** $h[m, r]$ | 4:　　　　$h[m, r] \leftarrow (\omega, c, \perp)$ |
| | 5:　　**return** $\pi_1(h[m, r])$ |

$$\Pr[\mathcal{UF\text{-}CMA}^{\mathcal{A}, \mathcal{K}, \mathcal{S}, \mathcal{F}, \mathcal{V}} : win] = \Pr[\mathit{Game0} : win]$$

---

*Games 1 and 2.* In Game 1, we anticipate a call to $\mathcal{G}$ on the output of $\mathcal{H}$ every time $\mathcal{H}$ is called. When $\mathcal{H}$ is called by either one of the signing oracles, we return the result of that call to $\mathcal{G}$ as well as the result of the current $\mathcal{H}$ query,

**Figure 5.** Games 1 and 2: anticipating calls to $\mathcal{G}$ and removing signing collisions

1: **oracle** $\mathcal{H}_1(c, m, r)$
2:   **if** $(m, r) \notin \mathrm{dom}(h)$ **then**
3:     $\omega \leftarrow \{0, 1\}^{k_h}$
4:     $h[m, r] \leftarrow (\omega, c, \perp)$
5:     $st \leftarrow \mathcal{G}(c, \omega)$
6:   **else**
7:     $\omega \leftarrow \pi_1(h[m, r])$
8:     **if** $c = \mathsf{Adv}$ **then**
9:       $st \leftarrow \perp$
10:    **else**
11:      $st \leftarrow \mathcal{G}(c, \omega)$
12:  **return** $(\omega, st)$

1: **oracle** $\mathcal{H}_2(c, m, r)$
2:   **if** $\begin{array}{l}(m, r) \notin \mathrm{dom}(h) \vee c = \mathsf{FSig} \vee \\ (c = \mathsf{Sig} \wedge \pi_2(h[m, r]) = \mathsf{FSig})\end{array}$
   **then**
3:     $\omega \leftarrow \{0, 1\}^{k_h}$
4:     $st \leftarrow \{0, 1\}^{k_g}$
5:     **if** $c \neq \mathsf{FSig} \vee (m, r) \notin \mathrm{dom}(h)$
   **then**
6:       $h[m, r] \leftarrow (\omega, c, \perp)$
7:     **if** $c \neq \mathsf{FSig} \vee \omega \notin \mathrm{dom}(g)$ **then**
8:       $g[\omega] \leftarrow (st \oplus (r \,\|\, 0^{k_g - k_0}), c)$
9:   **else**
10:    $\omega \leftarrow \pi_1(h[m, r])$
11:    **if** $c = \mathsf{Adv}$ **then**
12:      $st \leftarrow \perp$
13:    **else**
14:      $(\omega, st) \leftarrow \perp$
15:  **return** $(\omega, st)$

$$\Pr[\mathit{Game0} : \mathit{win}] \leq \Pr[\mathit{Game2} : \mathit{win}] + (q_\mathcal{H} + q_S + q_\mathcal{F}) \cdot \left( \frac{q_S + q_\mathcal{F}}{2^{k_0}} + \frac{q_\mathcal{G} + q_\mathcal{H} + q_S + q_\mathcal{F}}{2^{k_h}} \right)$$

allowing broad simplifications to the signing oracles. In Game 2, we deal with collisions on $r$ and $\omega$ values in the signing oracles. In later steps of the proof, we will need the control-flow of the faulty signature oracle to be completely independent from both $r$ and $\omega$, and we modify the oracle to allow these later transformations. Fresh queries are treated normally. Non-fresh queries made by the signing oracles are resampled as fresh if the previous query had been made by the faulty signature oracle. Non-fresh queries made by the faulty signature oracle are resampled, but not stored into the state. Game 1 is perfectly indistinguishable from Game 0, and Game 2 can be distinguished from Game 1 if either  i. (lines 2, 5 and 6) the fresh $r$ used in $\mathcal{H}$-queries made by the signing oracles collides with a previously used $r$ (with probability at most $(q_S + q_\mathcal{F}) \cdot (q_\mathcal{H} + q_S + q_\mathcal{F}) \cdot 2^{-k_0}$); ii. (lines 4, 7 and 8) or the fresh $\omega$ used in $\mathcal{G}$-queries made by the signing oracles collides with a previously used $\omega$ (with probability at most $(q_\mathcal{H} + q_S + q_\mathcal{F}) \cdot (q_\mathcal{G} + q_\mathcal{H} + q_S + q_\mathcal{F}) \cdot 2^{-k_h}$). Note that the value stored in $g[\omega]$ at line 8 in $\mathcal{H}_2$ is uniformly distributed since $st$ is.

*Game 3.* Given that $\mathcal{H}$ now samples both bitstrings that compose the final padded message, we compute the entire signature in $\mathcal{H}$ when called by either one of the signing oracles. We transform the experiment to sample an integer $x^*$ and compute $y^* = x^{*e} \bmod N$ to serve as one-way challenge. We embed it in the state when replying to $\mathcal{H}$ queries made by the adversary. Everything up to this point has been set up so that the signing oracles can simply use $\pi_3(h[m, r])$

as the padded message for $m$ with salt $r$. Game 3 includes this simplification. We introduce additional notation for clarity in the rest of the proof. Consider the function:

$$f_{(e,N),y^*,c} : \sigma \mapsto \begin{cases} y^* \cdot \sigma^e \bmod N & \text{if } c = \mathsf{Adv} \\ \sigma^e \bmod N & \text{otherwise} \end{cases}$$

For a set $X \subseteq \mathbb{Z}/N\mathbb{Z}$, we denote by $\mathsf{pim}_{(e,N),y^*,c}(X)$ the uniform distribution on the set $S = \{\sigma \in \mathbb{Z}/N\mathbb{Z} \mid f_{(e,N),y^*,c}(\sigma) \in X\}$.

Game 3 is indistinguishable from Game 2 exactly when $x^*$ is invertible. Therefore, the probability that the adversary distinguishes the two games is exactly $\frac{p+q-1}{p \cdot q}$. We have $p + q - 1 \le 2^{\frac{k}{2}+1}$ and $2^{k-1} \le p \cdot q$ and we can therefore bound the probability of this simulation failing by $2^{-\frac{k}{2}+2}$. Since the invertibility of $x^*$ is important in some later steps, we in fact let $\mathcal{H}$ compute a response only when $x^*$ is invertible. In the inverter, since $x^*$ is not public, we instead check the invertibility of $y^*$, which is equivalent. For simplicity, we omit discussions regarding this detail in the rest of this section.

---

**Figure 6.** Games 3 and 4: Embedding one-way challenge and oracle queries in $\mathcal{F}$

| | |
|---|---|
| 1: **oracle** $\mathcal{H}_3(c, m, r)$ | 1: **oracle** $\mathcal{H}_4(c, m, r)$ |
| 2:    **if** $(m,r) \notin \mathsf{dom}(h) \vee c = \mathsf{FSig} \vee$ $(c = \mathsf{Sig} \wedge \pi_2(h[m,r]) = \mathsf{FSig})$ **then** | 2:    **if** $(m,r) \notin \mathsf{dom}(h) \vee c = \mathsf{FSig}$ **then** |
| | 3:      $\sigma \leftarrow \mathsf{pim}_{(e,N),y^*,c}\left([0..2^{k-1})\right)$ |
| 3:      $\sigma \leftarrow \mathsf{pim}_{(e,N),y^*,c}\left([0..2^{k-1})\right)$ | 4:      $y \leftarrow f_{(e,N),y^*,c}(\sigma)$ |
| 4:      $y \leftarrow f_{(e,N),y^*,c}(\sigma)$ | 5:      $b \,\|\, \omega \,\|\, st \leftarrow \mathsf{i2osp}(y)$ |
| 5:      $b \,\|\, \omega \,\|\, st \leftarrow \mathsf{i2osp}(y)$ | 6:      **if** $c \ne \mathsf{FSig}$ **then** |
| 6:      **if** $c \ne \mathsf{FSig} \vee (m,r) \notin \mathsf{dom}(h)$ **then** | 7:        $h[m,r] \leftarrow (\omega, c, \sigma)$ |
| 7:        $h[m,r] \leftarrow (\omega, c, \sigma)$ | 8:        $g[\omega] \leftarrow (st \oplus (r \,\|\, 0^{k_g - k_0}), c)$ |
| 8:      **if** $c \ne \mathsf{FSig} \vee \omega \notin \mathsf{dom}(g)$ **then** | 9:    **else** |
| 9:        $g[\omega] \leftarrow (st \oplus (r \,\|\, 0^{k_g - k_0}), c)$ | 10:      $\omega \leftarrow \pi_1(h[m,r])$ |
| 10:    **else** | 11:      **if** $c = \mathsf{Adv}$ **then** |
| 11:      $\omega \leftarrow \pi_1(h[m,r])$ | 12:        $st \leftarrow \bot$ |
| 12:      **if** $c = \mathsf{Adv}$ **then** | 13:      **else** |
| 13:        $st \leftarrow \bot$ | 14:        $(\omega, st) \leftarrow \bot$ |
| 14:      **else** | 15:    **return** $(\omega, st)$ |
| 15:        $(\omega, st) \leftarrow \bot$ | |
| 16:    **return** $(\omega, st)$ | |

$$\Pr[\mathcal{G}ame2 : win] \le \Pr[\mathcal{G}ame3 : win] + 2^{-\frac{k}{2}+2}$$

$$\Pr[\mathcal{G}ame3 : win] \le \Pr[\mathcal{G}ame4 : win] + \frac{q_{\mathcal{H}} \cdot q_S}{2^{k_0}} + \frac{q_{\mathcal{G}} \cdot q_{\mathcal{F}} \cdot 3}{2^{k_h}}$$

*Game 4.* In this game, we stop keeping track of the random oracle queries made by the faulty signature oracle. This is an important step towards being able to apply Lemma 2, which only discusses the statistical distance between two distributions on $\sigma'$, rather than $(\omega, \sigma')$. Note that, in Coron and Mandal's proof, Lemma 2 is applied before this transition, in a context in which its premises are not fulfilled. By removing data about random oracle queries, we introduce observable changes in the game's behaviour whenever the adversary queries $\mathcal{H}$ with an $r$ that was used previously in a faulty signature query, or whenever the adversary queries $\mathcal{G}$ with an $\omega$ that was used previously in a faulty signature query. We bound the probability of the adversary guessing an $\omega$ value using Lemma 3. Since the view of the adversary does not depend on $r$ values sampled by the faulty signature oracle (see Fig. 7), the probability of the adversary guessing an $r$ value used in generating a faulty signature is easily bounded.

*Game 5.* Our main goal at this stage is to show that faulty signatures are in fact indistinguishable from uniform randomness and can be simulated without using the random oracles. Once this is done, we will be able to resume the proof of security following more standard PSS proofs.

We now use Lemma 2 to completely simulate faulty signature oracle queries. We focus on the faulty signature oracle, inlining and simplifying $\mathcal{H}$ knowing that $c = \mathsf{FSig}$. On the left, we display the simplified faulty signature oracle from Game 4 for reference. We make use of elementary properties of the statistical

---

**Figure 7.** Game 5: sampling faulty signatures

| | |
|---|---|
| 1: **oracle** $\mathcal{F}_4(m, \epsilon, a)$ | 1: **oracle** $\mathcal{F}_5(m, \epsilon, a)$ |
| 2:     $r \leftarrow \{0,1\}^{k_0}$ | 2:     $r \leftarrow \{0,1\}^{k_0}$ |
| 3:     $\sigma \leftarrow \mathsf{pim}_{(e,N),y^*,c}\left([0..2^{k-1}]\right)$ | 3:     $\sigma' \leftarrow [0..N]$ |
| 4:     $y \leftarrow \sigma^e \bmod N$ | 4:     **return** $\mathsf{i2osp}(\sigma')$ |
| 5:     $r' \leftarrow \{0,1\}^\rho \setminus 0$ | |
| 6:     $\sigma' \leftarrow y^d * \alpha_p + (a + (y - a^e)) * \alpha_q$ | |
| 7:     **return** $\mathsf{i2osp}(\sigma')$ | |

$$\Pr[\mathit{Game4} : win] \leq \Pr[\mathit{Game5} : win] + q_{\mathcal{F}} \cdot 2 \cdot \kappa_\delta \cdot 2^{\frac{\delta k - \rho}{2}}$$

---

distance and Lemma 2 to bound the probability of distinguishing Games 5 and 6. Note that sampling $\sigma$ in $\mathsf{pim}_{(e,N),y^*,c}\left([0..2^{k-1}]\right)$ and applying the public RSA permutation to obtain $y$ is perfectly equivalent to sampling $y$ in $[0..2^{k-1})$. In the bound, the $\delta$ and $\kappa_\delta$ are as in Lemma 1.

*Game 6.* With the faulty signature oracle simplified away, we can now focus on simulating the signature oracle. From now on, the $c$ argument to $\mathcal{H}$ can no longer be $\mathsf{FSig}$. More generally, it is impossible for any entry in $h$ or $g$ to be tagged with $\mathsf{FSig}$. The signature oracle we have defined at this point is not a valid simulator as it does not run in polynomial time. To ensure that it does, we replace the sampling operation at line 3 in Fig. 6 (right) with the loop displayed on the left of Fig. 8 to sample $\sigma$. The adversary can distinguish the two games whenever the loop finishes in a state where $y$ does not start with a 0 bit. At

---

**Figure 8.** Game 6 and inverter: sampling $\sigma$ in polynomial time

1: **while** $(!0 \leq y < 2^{k-1}) \wedge i < k_0$ **do**      1: **oracle** $\mathcal{I}(e, N, y^*)$
2:      $\sigma \leftarrow [0..N)$                                        2:      $(m, s) \leftarrow \mathcal{A}^{\mathcal{H}_7, \mathcal{G}_7, \mathcal{S}_7, \mathcal{F}_7}(e, N)$
3:      $y \leftarrow f_{(e,N),y^*,c}(\sigma)$                       3:      $\sigma \leftarrow \mathsf{os2ip}(s)$
4:      $i \leftarrow i + 1$                                            4:      $y \leftarrow \sigma^e \bmod N$
                                                                          5:      $b \,\|\, \omega \,\|\, st \leftarrow \mathsf{i2osp}(y)$
                                                                          6:      $r \,\|\, \gamma \leftarrow st \oplus g[\omega]$
                                                                          7:      $(\omega', \mathsf{Adv}, u) \leftarrow h[m, r]$
                                                                          8:      **return** $\sigma \cdot u^{-1}$

$$\Pr[\mathit{Game5} : win] \leq \Pr[\mathit{Game6} : win] + \frac{q_{\mathcal{H}} + q_S}{2^{k_0}} \qquad \begin{array}{l} \Pr[\mathit{Game6} : win] \leq \\ \Pr[\mathit{OW\text{-}RSA}^{\mathcal{I}} : x = x^*] + \frac{1}{2^{k_h}} + \frac{q_{\mathcal{H}}}{2^{\frac{k}{2}-1}} \end{array}$$

---

each iteration of the loop, the $\sigma$ sampled is invalid with probability at most $\frac{1}{2}$. The probability that *all* iterations produce an invalid $\sigma$ is therefore bounded by $\frac{1}{2^{k_0}}$, since all samples are independent. $\mathcal{H}_7$ may now be queried $q_{\mathcal{H}} + q_S$ times, allowing us to conclude.

*Reduction* All the oracles are simulated without using any secret data. We now focus on building an inverter. The adversary can win in two disjoint cases:

- either the $\mathcal{H}$-query made by the verification algorithm is fresh (this occurs with probability at most $2^{-k_h}$),
- or the $\mathcal{H}$-query made by the verification algorithm was previously made by the adversary. If the query was made by the signature oracle, the forgery cannot be fresh and the adversary cannot win.

In the latter case, the one-way challenge can then be recovered by the inverter shown on the right of Fig. 8. The key observation is that, in case of a successful forgery, we have $y = \sigma^e \bmod N$ (line 4) and $y = y^* \cdot u^e \bmod N$ (by invariant on $h$). By definition of $y^*$ and the morphism and injectivity properties of RSA, we therefore have $\sigma = x^* \cdot u$. We need to also consider the case where a value $u$ stored in the $h$ map by the adversary is not invertible, which occurs with probability at most $q_{\mathcal{H}} \cdot 2^{-k/2+1}$.

The final bound is obtained by transitively using the individual transition bounds.

# References

1. Almeida, J.B., Barbosa, M., Barthe, G., Dupressoir, F.: Certified computer-aided cryptography: efficient provably secure machine code from high-level implementations. In: Sadeghi, A.-R., Gligor, V.D., Yung, M. (eds.) ACM CCS 2013, Berlin, Germany, November 4–8, pp. 1217–1230. ACM Press (2013)
2. Anderson, R.J., Kuhn, M.G.: Low cost attacks on tamper resistant devices. In: Christianson, B., Crispo, B., Lomas, M., Roe, M. (eds.) Security Protocols 1997. LNCS, vol. 1361, pp. 125–136. Springer, Heidelberg (1998)
3. Aumüller, C., Bier, P., Fischer, W., Hofreiter, P., Seifert, J.-P.: Fault attacks on RSA with CRT: Concrete results and practical countermeasures. In: Kaliski Jr., B.S., Koç, Ç.K., Paar, C. (eds.) CHES 2002. LNCS, vol. 2523, pp. 260–275. Springer, Heidelberg (2003)
4. Barthe, G., Dupressoir, F., Fouque, P.-A., Grégoire, B., Tibouchi, M., Zapalowicz, J.-C.: Making RSA-PSS provably secure against non-random faults. Cryptology eprint Archive, Report 2014/252 (2014), http://eprint.iacr.org/
5. Barthe, G., Grégoire, B., Heraud, S., Béguelin, S.Z.: Computer-aided security proofs for the working cryptographer. In: Rogaway, P. (ed.) CRYPTO 2011. LNCS, vol. 6841, pp. 71–90. Springer, Heidelberg (2011)
6. Blömer, J., Otto, M., Seifert, J.-P.: A new CRT-RSA algorithm secure against Bellcore attacks. In: ACM Conference on Computer and Communications Security, pp. 311–320 (2003)
7. Boneh, D., DeMillo, R.A., Lipton, R.J.: On the importance of eliminating errors in cryptographic computations. Journal of Cryptology 14(2), 101–119 (2001)
8. Boscher, A., Handschuh, H., Trichina, E.: Fault resistant RSA signatures: Chinese remaindering in both directions. IACR Cryptology eprint Archive, 2010:38 (2010)
9. Brier, É., Naccache, D., Nguyen, P.Q., Tibouchi, M.: Modulus fault attacks against RSA-CRT signatures. In: Preneel, B., Takagi, T. (eds.) CHES 2011. LNCS, vol. 6917, pp. 192–206. Springer, Heidelberg (2011)
10. Canetti, R., Goldwasser, S.: An efficient *threshold* public key cryptosystem secure against adaptive chosen ciphertext attack. In: Stern, J. (ed.) EUROCRYPT 1999. LNCS, vol. 1592, pp. 90–106. Springer, Heidelberg (1999)
11. Christofi, M., Chetali, B., Goubin, L., Vigilant, D.: Formal verification of a CRT-RSA implementation against fault attacks. J. Cryptographic Engineering 3(3), 157–167 (2013)
12. Ciet, M., Joye, M.: Practical fault countermeasures for Chinese remaindering based cryptosystems. In: Breveglieri, L., Koren, I. (eds.) FDTC, pp. 124–131 (2005)
13. Coron, J.-S., Giraud, C., Morin, N., Piret, G., Vigilant, D.: Fault attacks and countermeasures on Vigilant's RSA-CRT algorithm. In: FDTC, pp. 89–96 (2010)
14. Coron, J.-S., Joux, A., Kizhvatov, I., Naccache, D., Paillier, P.: Fault attacks on RSA signatures with partially unknown messages. In: Clavier, C., Gaj, K. (eds.) CHES 2009. LNCS, vol. 5747, pp. 444–456. Springer, Heidelberg (2009)
15. Coron, J.-S., Mandal, A.: PSS is secure against random fault attacks. In: Matsui, M. (ed.) ASIACRYPT 2009. LNCS, vol. 5912, pp. 653–666. Springer, Heidelberg (2009)
16. Coron, J.-S., Mandal, A.: PSS is secure against random fault attacks. In: Matsui, M. (ed.) ASIACRYPT 2009. LNCS, vol. 5912, pp. 653–666. Springer, Heidelberg (2009)
17. Coron, J.-S., Naccache, D., Tibouchi, M.: Fault attacks against EMV signatures. In: Pieprzyk, J. (ed.) CT-RSA 2010. LNCS, vol. 5985, pp. 208–220. Springer, Heidelberg (2010)

18. Fouque, P.-A., Guillermin, N., Leresteux, D., Tibouchi, M., Zapalowicz, J.-C.: Attacking RSA-CRT signatures with faults on Montgomery multiplication. J. Cryptographic Engineering 3(1), 59–72 (2013)

19. Giraud, C.: An RSA implementation resistant to fault attacks and to simple power analysis. IEEE Trans. Computers 55(9), 1116–1120 (2006)

20. Le, D.-P., Rivain, M., Tan, C.H.: On double exponentiation for securing RSA against fault analysis. In: Benaloh, J. (ed.) CT-RSA 2014. LNCS, vol. 8366, pp. 152–168. Springer, Heidelberg (2014)

21. Montgomery, H.L.: Topics in multiplicative number theory. Springer (1971)

22. Montgomery, P.L.: Modular multiplication without trial division. Mathematics of Computation 44, 519–521 (1985)

23. Moro, N., Heydemann, K., Encrenaz, E., Robisson, B.: Formal verification of a software countermeasure against instruction skip attacks. Journal of Cryptographic Engineering, 1–12 (2014)

24. Rauzy, P., Guilley, S.: A formal proof of countermeasures against fault injection attacks on CRT-RSA. Journal of Cryptographic Engineering, 1–13 (2013)

25. Rivain, M.: Securing RSA against fault analysis by double addition chain exponentiation. In: Fischlin, M. (ed.) CT-RSA 2009. LNCS, vol. 5473, pp. 459–480. Springer, Heidelberg (2009)

26. Shamir, A.: Improved method and apparatus for protecting public key schemes from timing and fault attacks. Patent Application, WO 1998/052319 A1 (1998)

27. Trichina, E., Korkikyan, R.: Multi fault laser attacks on protected CRT-RSA. In: Breveglieri, L., Joye, M., Koren, I., Naccache, D., Verbauwhede, I. (eds.) FDTC, pp. 75–86. IEEE Computer Society (2010)

28. Vigilant, D.: RSA with CRT: A new cost-effective solution to thwart fault attacks. In: Oswald, E., Rohatgi, P. (eds.) CHES 2008. LNCS, vol. 5154, pp. 130–145. Springer, Heidelberg (2008)

29. Yen, S.-M., Moon, S.-J., Ha, J.: Permanent fault attack on the parameters of RSA with CRT. In: Safavi-Naini, R., Seberry, J. (eds.) ACISP 2003. LNCS, vol. 2727, pp. 285–296. Springer, Heidelberg (2003)

# Side-Channel Attack against RSA Key Generation Algorithms

Aurélie Bauer, Eliane Jaulmes, Victor Lomné,
Emmanuel Prouff, and Thomas Roche

ANSSI,
51, Bd de la Tour-Maubourg, 75700 Paris 07 SP, France
{firstname.lastname}@ssi.gouv.fr

**Abstract.** Many applications of embedded devices require the generation of cryptographic secret parameters during the life cycle of the product. In such an unsafe context, several papers have shown that key generation algorithms are vulnerable to side-channel attacks. This is in particular the case of the generation of the secret prime factors in RSA. Until now, the threat has been demonstrated against naive implementations whose operations' flow depends on secret data, and a simple countermeasure is to avoid such kind of dependency. In this paper, we propose a new attack that renders this defence strategy ineffective. It is in particular able to break secure implementations recommended by the ANSI X9.31 and FIPS 186-4 standards. We analyse its efficiency for various realistic attack contexts and we demonstrate its practicality through experiments against a smart-card implementation. Possible countermeasures are eventually proposed, drawing the following main conclusion: prime generation algorithms should avoid the use of a prime sieve combined with a deterministic process to generate the prime candidates from a random seed.

## 1 Introduction

When signing or decrypting with RSA it is nowadays well-known that the modular exponentiation must be implemented with care to defeat Side-Channel Attacks (SCA). The use of the secret exponent indeed induces some vulnerabilities and a wide number of studies have been dedicated to this specific operation [4,7,12,20,23,27]. However this is not the unique vulnerable step of RSA cryptosystem implementations. The prime generation algorithm aiming at finding two large prime factors $p$ and $q$ to build the RSA modulus can also be threatened by SCA. Until recent years, this computation was solely performed during the device personalisation (when the device is uniquely associated to a device holder) and, for this reason, SCA was considered to be out-of-scope. This is no longer the case: the arrival of new security services (mobile payment, e-ticketing, OTP generations, and so on) has raised the need for devices able to perform key generations during their life cycle. The RSA key generation has then left the safe context of production firms for an hostile environment. This assessment has

L. Batina and M. Robshaw (Eds.): CHES 2014, LNCS 8731, pp. 223–241, 2014.

been highlighted in several papers [8,16,28] which show that the key generation security must be taken into account for today *open* platforms.

*Prime Generation Algorithms.* A straightforward method to generate a large prime number is to start from a random value, to perform a *provable primality* test, and in case of an invalid answer, to repeat the process with another random data until a prime is found. This procedure obviously leads to a valid solution, but also provides very costly prime generations. In fact, *provable prime* generations are considered to be less efficient, in time and memory usage, than *probable prime* ones [6]. Indeed, using the latter consists in replacing the costly primality proof of the selected candidate by a series of relatively efficient probabilistic tests [21]. When correctly parametrised, this probabilistic approach provides a satisfying confidence level in the primality of the generated value. Still this technique may remain costly, especially for embedded systems, since almost all probabilistic primality tests are based on non trivial arithmetic operations over large integer rings. For this reason, probable prime generation algorithms are often implemented together with a *prime sieve* [6,21]. That way, each new prime candidate is first checked for small factors (up to a fixed bound) by successive divisibility tests, and can thus be possibly eliminated without having to go through the probabilistic primality tests.

Whereas the implementations discussed previously enable to check whether candidates are prime or not at moderate cost, the overall efficiency of the algorithm can still remain poor if no particular attention is paid to the "generation" phase. In particular, randomly generating each new candidate until a probable prime is found turns out to be hardly practical. This is especially true when the access to the random number generator is expensive, which is usually the case on embedded devices. A more efficient technique consists in calling the random generator only once and in using the obtained value as a seed to generate a succession of prime candidates in a deterministic way. Usually the seed is simply chosen to be odd and incremented by an even constant iteratively [6,5], but any other kind of deterministic process can be devised. Early studies on the probable prime generations implemented with a prime sieve and an incremental generation of candidates [6,5] exhibit efficient optimisations and show that the entropy of the generated primes is close to the maximum. Therefore, even though recent work have proposed interesting alternatives [11] or discussed the relevance of the entropy evaluation [18], the approach with a prime sieve and deterministic candidates generation turns out to be nowadays the most common procedure in constrained environments. It is actually recommended by international standards like ANSI X9.31 [1] and FIPS 186-4 [17].

*Attacking the Sieving Process.* In [16], Finke *et al.* observe that using a deterministic process to generate the sequence of candidates from a random seed, combined with a naive implementation of the prime sieve, is threatened by a Simple Power Analysis (SPA for short). Roughly, if a side-channel attacker is able to identify each divisibility test on a leakage trace and if the sieving process abort as soon as a small factor is found, then a simple equation system can be obtained, whose resolution brings information on the generated prime (see [16] for more details). The type of weakness identified in [16] can potentially be found in any algorithm processing a prime sieve whose flow of operations is data dependent (which is for instance the case of naive implementations of the X9.31 standard [1]). To avoid it, a simple (and usually fairly efficient) countermeasure hence amounts to balance the conditional branches in the implementation. One way to do so is to apply the prime sieve entirely even if, at some point, the algorithm highlights a divisibility (in other words, the prime sieve should not be stopped once a divider is found). It must be observed that this implementation choice does not only prevent the state-of-the-art attacks but, as discussed in [6], also leads to a significant efficiency gain.

*Results.* This paper focuses on the security of the probable prime generation algorithms discussed previously (with prime sieve and deterministic candidates generation). For such algorithms, which, to the best of our knowledge, correspond to the most efficient and up-to-date implementations met on embedded devices, we exhibit an *Advanced Side-Channel Analysis* on the sieving process even when the latter is implemented to defeat the state-of-the-art attacks [16]. Contrary to [28], our attack does not target the probable prime tests but the prime sieve which was believed to be safe if implemented in a regular way. We show how useful information can be extracted from the divisibility phase and how this could finally lead, for practical implementations, to the recovery of more than half bits of information on the prime number generated. Combined with a well-known lattice reduction technique due to Coppersmith [14,3], we show that the attack leads to the recovery of a 1024-bit RSA modulus. Moreover it severely undermines the security of larger moduli. Additionally to the theoretical analysis, we provide experimental results from the analysis of the side-channel leakage on a real device. The success of these experimentations highlights the practicality of our attack and, as a side effect, shows that countermeasures against SPA attacks are not sufficient to ensure security. Our work also shows that the use of a deterministic process to build a sequence of candidates from a random seed represents a serious weakness. In view of this, the non-deterministic candidates generation proposed by Fouque and Tibouchi [18] seems to be a good alternative. As argued by the authors, it would moreover increase the entropy of the generated probable primes. Another possibility could be to implement the provable prime generation algorithm proposed recently in [11].

## 2 On a Standard Prime Generation Implementation

This section aims at describing the design of a standard RSA prime generation algorithm, such as recommended by the norms ANSI X9.31 [1, Annexes B and E] and FIPS 186-4 [17, Annex C]. This description is completed with implementation details that must be considered when embedding such algorithms on constrained devices. Implementation choices are also made and strengthened by efficiency rationales. Eventually, the section ends with an implementation of a probable prime generation algorithm which is very close to what can be found in todays' industry of embedded devices.

## 2.1    A Prime Generation Algorithm for Constrained Environments

The purpose of probable prime generation algorithms is to return a number which satisfies a series of probabilistic tests and is indistinguishable from a random prime. The latter property is ensured by randomly generating the candidates on which the probabilistic tests are passed. For efficiency reasons however, the implementations discussed here (and recommended in ANSI X9.31 [1, Annexes B and E] and FIPS 186-4 [17, Annex C]) do not generate all the candidates at random but deduce them from a common random seed through a deterministic process. In the following, we assume that the latter simply consists in adding a multiple of a constant, but our analysis would hold for any other deterministic process. Eventually, to spare the use of the costly probabilistic tests, a prime sieve is applied to directly eliminate candidates with small prime factors. More details about these two steps are given hereafter.

*Probabilistic primality tests.* Testing the primality of a candidate is usually done using Miller-Rabin and Lucas probabilistic tests. The reader can refer to [22] for their description. Actually, the only important fact to mention is that Miller-Rabin test performs several dozens of exponentiations of the form $a^{t \cdot 2^s} \bmod v$, for $a$ a random number and $v$ the tested candidate[1]. As $v$ is large, such exponentiations are very costly and are usually performed thanks to a modular arithmetic co-processor.

*Prime sieve.* The purpose of the prime sieve is to reduce the number of Miller-Rabin's tests. It precedes them and eliminates the candidates having small factors. It consists in a divisibility test w.r.t. all primes lower than some bound $r$. For efficiency reasons, a classical choice is to select only primes lower than 256 (there are 53 such primes). This choice indeed has both the advantage to limit the size of the array containing the sieve elements and to get efficient divisions even for an 8-bit architecture with limited instructions set. By Mertens' Theorem[2] [25], one can prove that choosing $r$ as 256 enables to eliminate around 87.5% of the tested integers without executing the probabilistic tests. On the other hand increasing $r$ to 9-bit long primes, "only" allows to exclude an additional 1.4% of the integers. Together with the efficiency reasons, this poor discrimination gain explains why the choice $r = 256$ is sound for prime sieves in constrained environments.

Summing-up all these steps leads to a full implementation of a standard prime generation algorithm on constrained environment, see Algorithm 1.

---

[1] In these relations, the parameters $s$ and $t$ satisfy $v - 1 = 2^s \cdot t$ and $t$ is odd.
[2] The probability that a random integer is not divisible by a number smaller than $r$ is well approximated by $1/\log(r)$.

---

**Algorithm 1.** Prime Generation Algorithm (for constrained environments)

**Input** : A bit-length $\ell$, an even constant $\tau$, the set $\mathcal{S} = \{s_0, \cdots, s_{52}\}$ of all odd primes
lower than 256 (stored in ROM), a number $t$ of Miller-Rabin tests to perform
**Output:** A probable prime $p$

  /* Generate a seed                                                      */
1  Randomly generate an odd $\ell$-bit integer $v_0$

  /* Prime Sieve                                                          */
2  $v \leftarrow v_0$
3  $s \leftarrow s_0$
4  $i = 0$
5  **while** $(v \mod s \neq 0)$ and $(i < 53)$ **do**
6  $\quad\lfloor \quad i = i + 1$
7  $\qquad s \leftarrow s_i$

8  **if** $(i \neq 53)$ **then**
9  $\quad\lfloor \quad v = v + \tau$
10 $\qquad$ **goto** Step 3

   /* Probabilistic primality tests                                       */
11 **else**
12 $\quad\lvert \quad i = 0$
   $\qquad$ /* Process $t$ Miller-Rabin's tests (stop if one fails)          */
13 $\quad\lvert \quad$ **while** $(\textit{Miller-Rabin}(v) = ok)$ and $(i < t)$ **do**
14 $\quad\lvert \qquad\lfloor \quad i = i + 1$

   /* Process 1 Lucas' test[a]                                            */
15 **if** $(i = t)$ and $(\textit{Lucas}(v) = ok)$ **then**
16 $\quad\lfloor \quad$ **return** $v$

17 **else**
18 $\quad\lvert \quad v = v + \tau$
19 $\quad\lfloor \quad$ **goto** Step 3

---

[a] Miller-Rabin's tests are followed by one Lucas' test because there is no known composite integer $n$ for which they are both reporting that $n$ is probably prime.

## 2.2 Algorithm's Improvement: An Up-to-Date Version

In practice, implementations of Algorithm 1 are often improved further by exploiting the fact that the sieve elements $s_j$ are very small compared to the prime candidate $v$. The idea, mentioned in ANSI X9.31 [1] and by Brandt *et al.* in [6], is to replace costly modular reductions over $\ell$-bit integers by fast reductions over 8-bit integers[3]. Indeed, by construction, the reduction $v \mod s$ at Step 5 for the $(i + 1)^{\text{th}}$ prime candidate may indeed be rewritten as $v_0 + i \cdot \tau \mod s_j$, for $s_j$ a prime in the sieve. Written differently, this relation can also be expressed as $(v_0 \mod s_j) + i \cdot \tau \mod s_j$. As a consequence, one can start by computing all the remainders $r_{0j} = (v_0 \mod s_j)$ and by storing them in a RAM table $R$ (containing 53 bytes). Then, the prime sieve for the next candidate $v_1$ is simply done by updating $R$ such that $R[j] = R[j] + \tau \mod s_j$ for any $j < 53$. After this step, which only processes 8-bit values as long as $\tau$ is small enough[4], $R$ contains all

---

[3] The choice of 8-bit integers here comes from an efficiency argument and is not related to the architecture of the device (see Section 2.1).

[4] If $\tau = 2$, since the greatest sieve element in our implementation is strictly lower than $256 - 2$, the value $R[j] + \tau$ can always be stored in a byte.

the remainders $r_{1j} = v_1 \mod s_j$. More generally, this idea can be applied recursively to efficiently deduce the remainders related to the candidate $v_i$ from those related to the previous one $v_{i-1}$. Eventually, after each update of $R$, the result of the prime sieve for a candidate is obtained by checking whether $R$ contains a null remainder or not.

The efficiency improvement described above leads to replace Steps 2-10 in Algorithm 1 (before the probabilistic tests) by the ones provided by Algorithm 2.

---

**Algorithm 2.** Improved Prime Sieve

---

/* Prime Sieve for $v_0$                                                   */
1  **for** $j = 0$ **to** 52 **do**
2  $\quad$ $R[j] \leftarrow v_0 \mod s_j$            /* costly modular reduction over $\ell$-bit integers */
3

/* Prime Sieve for $v_i$ with $i > 0$                                      */
4  $v \leftarrow v_0$
5  **while** *(R contains a null remainder)* **do**
6  $\quad$ $v = v + \tau$
7  $\quad$ **for** $j = 0$ **to** 52 **do**
8  $\quad\quad$ $R[j] \leftarrow R[j] + \tau \mod s_j$       /* efficient modular reduction over 8-bit integers */
9

---

*Remark 1.* Usually, reductions at Step 2 of Algorithm 2 are performed by calling the arithmetic coprocessor whereas those at Step 8 are done with standard CPU instructions[4]. For instance, in a 8051 architecture the instruction DIV may be used to compute the remainder.

In addition to its efficiency, Algorithm 2 has a side advantage: the prime sieve is regular[5] which renders Finke *et al.* 's attack [16] ineffective. The gain in efficiency and in security explains why an up-to-date implementation of Algorithm 1 must involve the improved prime sieve described in Algorithm 2. For this reason, our attack in the next section is described against such an implementation. It must however be mentioned that it can also be applied against a straightforward implementation of Algorithm 1, in addition to Finke *et al.* 's attack.

# 3   A New Attack

## 3.1   Core Idea

The attack developed in this section aims at recovering information on a probable prime $p$ generated by Algorithm 1, implemented with the improvements described in Algorithm 2. For this purpose, let us focus on this algorithm when the prime sieve is applied to test whether the $(i + 1)^{\text{th}}$ candidate $v_i$ has small factors. During this process, the following remainders are computed for every $s$ in the sieve set $\mathcal{S}$:

$$r_i = v_i \mod s \ . \tag{1}$$

---

[5] Assuming that testing whether the elements of $R$ are non-zero is done with caution.

Knowing that $v_i$ has been generated deterministically from a seed $v_0$ by an iterative increment of $\tau$, Equation (1) can be rewritten as: $r_i = v_0 + i \cdot \tau \mod s$. Moreover, if $n$ denotes the number of tested candidates, the probabilistic prime $p$ returned by Algorithm 1 satisfies the following equation: $p = v_0 + (n-1)\tau$. Eventually combining the two previous relations shows that the secret prime $p$ and the remainders $r_i$ are linked through the following equation:

$$r_i \equiv p - (n - i - 1) \cdot \tau \pmod{s} .\tag{2}$$

When the value $n$ is made public, the remainder $r_i$ is a function of both the secret $p$ and a known value $(n - i - 1)\tau$ (recalling that $\tau$ is public as part of the algorithm specification). From that point, if we denote by $\ell_i$ the measured device activity (e.g. power consumption or electromagnetic emanations) coming from the manipulation of $r_i$, then an SCA can straightforwardly be defined assuming that an attacker is able to isolate the trace $\ell_i$ for all $i < n$. Indeed, the sample $\{\ell_i; i < n\}$ can be compared with the predictions deduced from both the values $\{(n - i - 1) \cdot \tau; i < n\}$ and an hypothesis on $p \mod s$. This type of SCA, where a single algorithm execution is observed, is called horizontal in [2,9]. When $n$ is large enough, this attack leads to the recovery of $p$ modulo $s$ (i.e. brings $\log_2(s)$ bits of information on $p$).

Eventually, the attack is applied for every prime $s$ in the set sieve $\mathcal{S}$ and all results $p \mod s$ are combined through the Chinese Remainder Theorem to reconstruct $p$ modulo $\prod_{s \in \mathcal{S}} s$. This leads to the recovery of $\log_2(\prod_{s \in \mathcal{S}} s)$ bits of information on $p$. Of course, this situation corresponds to a perfect attack scenario where each SCA against $p \mod s$ succeeds. In practice, some of them will likely fail, which reduces the amount of recovered information.

The practical soundness of the assumption that $n$ is known by the adversary and that he/she is able to isolate the leakage traces $\ell_i$ (which are prerequisites for our attack to be applicable) is studied in Section 4.1.

## 3.2   Full Description

In this section, we denote by $r_{ij}$ the remainder corresponding to the division of the $(i+1)^{\text{th}}$ candidate $v_i$ by the $(j+1)^{\text{th}}$ sieve element $s_j$. Moreover, we use the notation $\ell_{ij}$ to refer to the measured device activity[6] during the processing of $r_{ij}$. Once all the measurements have been obtained, the adversary splits them into different samples $(\ell_{ij})_i$, one for each sieve element $s_j$. Each sample can thus be viewed as a set of noisy observations of the remainders $(r_{ij})_i$ satisfying (2) for $s = s_j$. Assuming that the prime generation algorithm outputs the $n^{\text{th}}$ tested candidate[7], then the size of each sample $(\ell_{ij})_i$ is $n$. To sum up, we have the following relation:

---

[6] Each $\ell_{ij}$ can be viewed as a vector of real values whose size depends on the sampling rate of the oscilloscope used for the measurements and the manipulation time of $r_{ij}$ by the device.

[7] Which means that the candidate $v_{n-1}$ is the first that has successfully passed all the primality tests

$$\ell_{ij} \hookleftarrow r_{ij} = p - (n - i - 1) \cdot \tau \bmod s_j \ , \tag{3}$$

where $\hookleftarrow$ denotes a noisy observation. With these different samples $(\ell_{ij})_i$ in hand, the adversary is now able to target each sieve element independently. Namely, for each $j$, the adversary will try to recover $p \bmod s_j$ by exhaustively testing all possible values that can be reached by this expression[8]. The test of each hypothesis, say $h$, on $p \bmod s_j$ is simply done by following the classical outlines of an SCA attack:

- use a leakage model $\mathbf{m}$ to deduce a set of predictions $\{\mathbf{m}(h - (n - i - 1)\tau \bmod s_j); i < n\}$. A possible choice for $\mathbf{m}$ is the Hamming weight function HW (as done in Section 3.3) but, if needed, more accurate models can be built by performing analyses based on *Linear Regression* [15,24];
- apply an SCA distinguisher $\Delta$ (*e.g.* a correlation coefficient) to compare the predictions with the measurements and to validate or invalidate the hypothesis.

In other words, a classical horizontal SCA as in [2,9,10] is performed against each secret $(p \bmod s_j)$, using the fact that this value is manipulated several times, combined with a known value of the form $(n - i - 1)\tau \bmod s_j$ with $i < n$. Each such attack, that will be called partial in the sequel, outputs a most likely candidate for $(p \bmod s_j)$. In case of success, it brings $\log_2(s_j)$ bits of information on $p$. We sum-up in Algorithm 3 the different steps of the full attack. The size of the sieve set $\mathcal{S}$ is denoted by $\lambda$ (we remind that it equals 53 in the standard implementation detailed in Section 2).

---

**Algorithm 3.** Attack Against Prime Generation Algorithm

```
/* Measurements Phase                                              */
1 for i = 0 to n − 1 do
2 │   for j = 0 to λ − 1 do
3 │   └   measure ℓ_ij

  /* Attack Phase:                                                 */
  /* for each sieve, perform a partial SCA                         */
4 for j = 0 to λ − 1 do
  │   /* ... test each possible candidate ...                      */
5 │   for h = 1 to s_j − 1 do
  │   │   /* ... by processing predictions ...                     */
6 │   │   for i = 0 to n − 1 do
7 │   │   └   m_ij = m(h − (n − i − 1)τ  mod s_j)
  │   │   /* ... and applying a statistical distinguisher ...      */
8 │   └   score[h] = Δ((m_ij)_i, (ℓ_ij)_i)
  │   /* ... then select the most likely candidate ...             */
9 └   candidate[j] = argmax_h (score[h])

  /* Apply the Chinese Remainder Theorem (CRT)                     */
10 p̂ = CRT (candidate[0]  mod s_0, ··· , candidate[λ − 1]  mod s_{λ−1})
11 return p̂
```

---

[8] Which excludes 0 since $p$ is prime.

Note that the attack described in Algorithm 3 could also be adapted to target straightforward implementations of Algorithm 1. The only difference is that the adversary will not have the same number of observations for each sieve element. Indeed, as the prime sieve is stopped each time a divisor is found, the probability that $r_{ij}$ is processed (and thus observed) decreases with respect to $j$. As we think that such a straightforward implementation of Algorithm 1 is unlikely to be implemented in secure devices (because it is not efficient and vulnerable to Finke *et al.* 's attack – see Section 2–), we decided not to detail it in this paper.

### 3.3   Attack Analysis

In this section we first study, for typical bit-lengths $\ell \in \{256, 512, 1024\}$, the number $n$ of prime sieve processings that can be observed by an attacker during the generation of a probable prime of size $\ell$. Then, we focus on the success rate of the attack (*i.e.* its ability to completely recover $p$) under different hypotheses on $n$. For simplicity and because this is a common choice in practice, we choose to focus on the case $\tau = 2$.

*About the number of prime sieve processings.* The effectiveness of our attack strongly depends on the number $n$ of leakage values that can be retrieved for each sieve element. This value, which is also the number of prime sieve processings, depends on the seed $v_0$; thus, contrary to what happens in classical SCA, it cannot be *a priori* chosen by the adversary[9].

On Figure 1, several estimations of the *complementary cumulative distribution function* (ccdf) $\overline{F}_n(x)$ of $n$, viewed as a random variable, are plotted. Namely, each curve corresponds to an estimation[10] of the probability $\overline{F}_n(x)$ (in ordinate) that $n$ is greater than or equal to some value $x$ (in abscissa). The three plotted curves correspond to prime generations for a bit-length $\ell$ equal to 256, 512 and 1024 respectively. In the sequel, we focus on the 512-bit case (even if the outlines of our approach could also be followed to study the two other cases) since generating primes of that size is for instance required when constructing a 1024-bit RSA modulus (*e.g.* for some banking applications) or when generating strong primes according to the ANSI X9.31 standard [1]. For a 512-bit prime, the *median* of the distribution of $n$ as well as the first and third *complementary quartiles*[11], are respectively equal to 53, 126 and 246. The quartiles $Q_1$, $Q_2$ and $Q_3$ related to 75%, 50% and 25% are represented by horizontal lines in Figure 1.

*Attack Effectiveness.* Let us now focus on the ability of our attack to recover $x$ bits of information on $p$ by combining the results of the partial CPA attacks

---

[9]  In classical SCA, the number of observations is chosen and increased until the attack achieves some success rate.

[10]  Estimations have been done over 2000 observations of $n$, namely for 2000 prime generations.

[11]  We recall that the median of a random variable $X$ is the value $Q_2$ such that $\Pr(X \leq Q_2) = 0.5$. Similarly, the first (resp. the third) complementary quartile of $X$ is the value $Q_1$ (resp. $Q_3$) s.t. $\Pr(X > Q_1) = 0.75$ (resp. $\Pr(X > Q_3) = 0.25$).

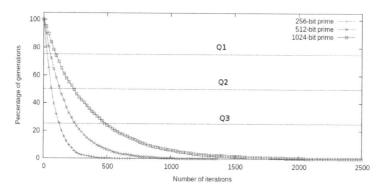

**Fig. 1.** Cumulative distribution function of $n$ for different prime bit-lengths $\ell$

against the remainders $p \bmod s_j$. We here assume that the attacker is able to detect when a partial CPA returns a correct result. It may first be noticed that a correct guess on all these remainders provides 333 bits of information on $p$ (assuming that $\mathcal{S}$ contains the 53 smallest primes). As argued in the next paragraph, this upper bound[12] limits the size of the prime numbers which can be successfully recovered with our attack. In Figure 2, we plot the probability (in ordinate) that our attack recovers at least $x$ bits of information on $p$. As done for the previous figure, the probabilities have been computed from simulations in three different contexts depending on whether the number $n$ of leakage values per CPA equals the first complementary quartile $Q_1 = 53$, the median $Q_2 = 126$ or the third complementary quartile $Q_3 = 246$. Several results are moreover presented, corresponding to different amounts of noise in the observations. For each quartile, the success rates have been estimated with 2000 attacks.

Before analysing the simulation results in Figure 2, it remains to define when our attack is considered to succeed. For this purpose, we recall that the generated prime $p$ is assumed to be afterwards used to define an RSA modulus. In such a context, a well-known technique introduced by Coppersmith [13,14] may be applied to reconstruct $p$ from approximately half of its bits[13]. This technique works by translating the problem of recovering the unknown part of $p$ into that of finding a small root on a bivariate polynomial equation. Such an issue can then be solved by performing a lattice reduction on a well-chosen basis. In our context, the number of bits that have to be retrieved to lead to the full recovery of a prime $p$ with bit-length 512 is $256 = 512/2$. We are aware that this bound is theoretical since it can only be achieved when reducing a lattice of infinite

---

[12] Since the upper bound increases with the number of primes involved in the sieving, the same holds for the size of the probable primes concerned by our attack.

[13] To be more accurate, Coppersmith's original technique aims at recovering $p$ knowing the half most (or least) significant bits. In our context, one gets a relation of the form $p \equiv p_0 \bmod \prod_{s_j \in \mathcal{S}} s_j$ with a known value $p_0$. This case can be handled using a slight generalisation of the original method, under the condition that $\prod_{s_j \in \mathcal{S}} s_j$ is approximately half the bit length of $p$ (see Corollary 2.2 in [3]).

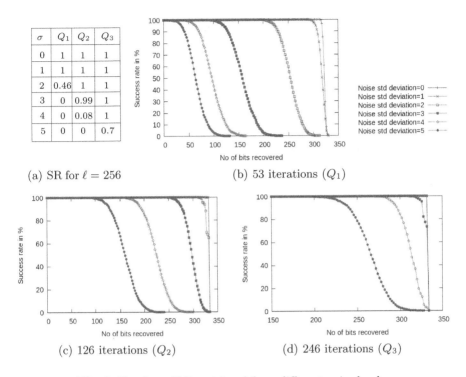

| $\sigma$ | $Q_1$ | $Q_2$ | $Q_3$ |
|---|---|---|---|
| 0 | 1 | 1 | 1 |
| 1 | 1 | 1 | 1 |
| 2 | 0.46 | 1 | 1 |
| 3 | 0 | 0.99 | 1 |
| 4 | 0 | 0.08 | 1 |
| 5 | 0 | 0 | 0.7 |

(a) SR for $\ell = 256$

(b) 53 iterations ($Q_1$)

(c) 126 iterations ($Q_2$)

(d) 246 iterations ($Q_3$)

**Fig. 2.** Number of bits retrieved from different noise levels

dimension. In practice, several additional bits are required for Coppersmith's method to work[14]. Nevertheless, the problem can be circumvented (even if the exact bound of "256 bits" can never be achieved in practice) at the price of an exhaustive search on the missing values, thus making the overall complexity of the attack increase. In our case, since we use Coppersmith's method as a black-box, we choose to define a successful attack as recovering 256 bits on $p$ (this bound thus corresponds to an "ideal" scenario) .

The results are summed up in Figure 2(a). Not surprisingly, the attack works better and recovers more bits on $p$ when the number of tested candidates $n$ increases (we indeed have more observations to recover each sensitive remainder). In the case where there is a lot of noise or few iterations, the expected number of bits correctly guessed on $p$ drops. These results can be exploited to obtain a lower bound on the overall success rate (SR for short) of our attack:

– [For $\sigma = 1$]: the attack recovers 256 bits of information on $p$ with probability 1 for $n = Q_1$, $Q_2$ and $Q_3$. In other terms, our attack succeeds for all the prime generations where $n$ reaches the first quartile, that is for 75% of the generations. We can thus estimate the lower bound for our success probability in this case by $p_{\sigma=1} \geq 0.75$.

---

[14] See [16] for heuristic results with respect to various numbers of retrieved bits.

- [For $\sigma = 2$]: the attack recovers 256 bits of information on $p$ with probability 1 for $n = Q_2$ and $Q_3$ and with probability 0.46 for $n = Q_1$. We can thus estimate the lower bound for our success probability in this case by $p_{\sigma=2} \geq (0.46 + 1 + 1)/4 = 0.615$.
- [For $\sigma \geq 3$]: we can estimate similarly the lower bound for our success probability in the remaining cases by $p_{\sigma=3} \geq 0.4975$, $p_{\sigma=4} \geq 0.27$ and $p_{\sigma=5} \geq 0.175$ respectively.

## 4    Attack Flow in Practice

### 4.1    Discussion on the Measurements Phase

In this section, we come back to the attack hypotheses made in Section 3 and we argue about their relevance. Namely, we study the practical soundness of the assumption that the number of tested candidates $n$ is known by the adversary and that he/she is able to isolate the leakage traces $\ell_{ij}$ defined as in Equation (3). For this purpose, we consider here an implementation of a 512-bit prime number generation, computed on a smart-card micro-controller equipped with an 8-bit CPU and a modular arithmetic co-processor, both running at several dozens of MHz. This implementation corresponds to an off-the-shelf smart-card. To simplify the analysis, we directly focus on the case where the attack described in Section 3 is effective with high probability. For this reason, we developed our argumentation under the hypothesis that the number of tested candidates $n$ is at least 250 (which happens with probability 25% – see Figure 1 –).

Let us now evaluate the time required by the platform to process a prime number generation as specified in the previous paragraph. Thanks to the sieving pre-processing, a probabilistic primality test (here a sequence of Miller-Rabin tests) is performed for 1 candidate over 10 in average (see Mertens' theorem [25]). Let $t$ be the maximum number of Miller-Rabin tests that must be passed by a candidate. Observing that each test takes 10ms on the considered platform, then the full processing time of the algorithm is upper bounded by $250t$ms. For instance, when $t = 10$, which is a reasonable value to ensure the primality of a number with satisfying probability, the full processing time is 2.5s. Note that this approximation does not take into account the time spent in the 250 efficient prime sieves, since this is negligible in comparison to the rest of the algorithm (see Section 2.2). For this (practical) attack scenario, several issues arise during the measurements phase (where we denote by $i$ the number of tested candidates):

1. how to record the long side-channel trace corresponding to the full prime number generation computation, or at least to the $i$ efficient prime sieve tests[15];
2. how to recognize and extract the patterns corresponding to the $i$ prime sieve tests and how to convert them into $i$ smaller side-channel traces;
3. in each small side-channel trace previously created, how to precisely align the sub-patterns corresponding to the trial divisions (Step 8 in Algorithm 2).

---

[15] Meaning $i$ iterations of the while loop in Algorithm 2.

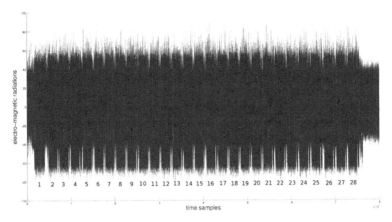

**Fig. 3.** Electro-magnetic radiations measured during a prime number generation computation on a commercial smartcard. Pattern 1 corresponds to the initial costly prime sieve, whereas patterns 2 to 28 correspond to Miller-Rabin tests.

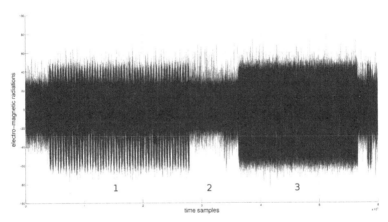

**Fig. 4.** Zoom on the two first patterns of Figure 3. Pattern 1 corresponds to the initial costly prime sieve, whereas pattern 3 corresponds to the first Miller-Rabin test. First efficient prime sieves (with small integer divisions) are located inside pattern 2.

Solving the first issue depends on the specifications of the oscilloscope used to record the long side-channel trace. More precisely, it depends on its channel memory depth, *i.e.* the number of samples the oscilloscope can record per channel during one single acquisition. To record 250 iterations with a sampling rate of 100MSamples per second (which is a minimum on such platforms to perform a CPA), then the channel memory depth must be at least of 250MSamples, which is available on high-end oscilloscopes. The oscilloscope trigger can moreover be set-up to skip the recording of the first prime sieve computation (Step 1-3 of Algorithm 2), as it is not used in our attack. This amounts to skip the step corresponding to the pattern 1 in Figures 3 and 4.

Once the long side-channel trace has been acquired, the second issue consists in recognizing patterns corresponding to the efficient prime sieve computations. Such patterns are located between those corresponding to probabilistic primality tests, which have a particular side-channel signature due to the use of the modular arithmetic co-processor. The Miller-Rabin tests correspond to patterns 2 to 28 on Figure 3, and to pattern 3 on Figure 4. Thanks to this patterns identification phase, one can then deduce that several prime sieve computations are located inside Pattern 2 of Figure 4. Once such patterns have been found, classical automated pattern matching techniques can eventually be used to extract the other ones in the rest of the long side-channel trace.

Finally, the third issue should be solved thanks to peak extraction techniques classically used in SCA. This would enable to align the patterns corresponding to the trial divisions in each small side-channel trace. On the traces we acquired (Figures 3 and 4), the signal is too noisy for such alignment. In the following we continue our practical analysis on a toy implementation of the prime sieve running on a different architecture than that used in this sub-section.

### 4.2   Experiments on a Toy Implementation

To confirm the analyses conducted in Section 3.3 and to validate our assumptions in practice, the new attack has been tested against a toy implementation embedded on an 8-bit ATMega128 micro-controller running at 8MHz. For simplicity reasons, we did not implement the full probabilistic prime generation described in Algorithm 1 but only 300 iterations of the loop corresponding to steps 5-9 in Algorithm 2 parametrised with a random seed $v_0$. As our attack only targets the prime sieve and not the probabilistic tests, this choice does not impact the soundness of the conclusions we are going to draw from the experimentations reported below.

The electro-magnetic activity of the device during the processing of the 300 prime sieve tests has been measured with a sampling rate of 1GSamples per second. $300 \times 53$ patterns have then been extracted. These patterns correspond to the trial divisions of the 300 prime candidates $v_i = v_0 + 2i$ by the 53 prime sieve elements $s_j$ (Steps 5-9 in Algorithm 2). Afterwards, the attack described in Algorithm 3 has been performed with the Pearson correlation coefficient as statistical distinguisher $\Delta$. The overall experiment (including the acquisition phase) has been repeated 200 times. Following the same approach as in Section 3.3, the effectiveness of our attack has then been studied under the assumption that the targeted prime value $p$ was known for each experiment. This assumption makes it possible to decide whether each partial attack on $p \bmod s_j$ succeeded or not, and hence allowed us to apply the Chinese Remainder Theorem only with the correct guesses. The results are reported in Figures 5(a) and 5(b). They correspond to attack scenarios where the number of exploited prime sieve observations (among the 300 ones) was respectively limited to 10, 50, 250 and 300. Figure 5(b) must be viewed as the experimental equivalent of the simulations described in Figure 2.

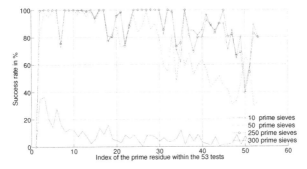

(a) Success rates for each prime sieve elements (over 200 attack experiments)

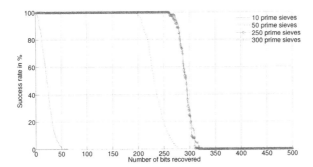

(b) Success rates for recovering $x$ bits of information on the generated prime

**Fig. 5.** Success rates in practice

Even if the experimental success rates are slightly below those obtained for our attack simulations[16] (see Section 3.3 for a theoretical analysis), the general trends are the same. In particular, our attack succeeds in recovering more than 256 bits of information with success probability 0.9 as long as the number $n$ of observed prime sieve tests is at least equal to 250 (which happens with probability 0.25 when the prime length $\ell$ equals 512, see Section 3.3). This not only confirms the soundness of the analysis in Section 3.3 but also demonstrates the practicality of our attack.

Let us now focus on a real attack context where the assumption "the target prime $p$ is known" has been relaxed. In this scenario, the adversary loses his ability to decide for each partial SCA (against the remainder of $p$ modulo a prime sieve element) whether it has succeeded or not. Consequently, he cannot select which remainders to keep for the recombining phase and must hence apply the

---

[16] This can easily be explained by the higher noise encountered during the practical experiments and the fact that the Hamming weight leakage model used in the CPA does not perfectly fit the real leakage function.

Chinese Remainder Theorem (CRT) on all the partial SCA results (as described in Step 10 of Algorithm 3). This attack will thus only work if all the retrieved remainders are correct, which occurs with a probability that can be approximated by the product of the 53 success rates plotted in Figure 5(a). Even for $n = 300$, it can be checked that this probability is very small. Fortunately, several strategies can be applied to significantly improve this success rate.

### 4.3   Avenues of Improvement

*Larger primes generation.* Our attack would not work for primes beyond 666 bits, since the 53 prime sieve elements $s_j$ only permit to retrieve a maximum of 333 bits on $p$. However the analysis can easily be adapted to 1024-bit primes, when the prime generation algorithm uses a larger sieve set $\mathcal{S}$ (requiring a product of its elements larger than 1024 bits).

*Case of RSA modulus.* For RSA key generation, the adversary may attack the two prime factors $p$ and $q$ independently. Then, the public relation $N = pq$ can be used to compare the remainder hypotheses returned by the partial SCA of each attack. Such a procedure is thoroughly described in [16]. The attacker can also gain some information about the secret exponent $d$ through the analysis of the equation $e \cdot d = k(N - (p+q) + 1) + 1$. When $e$ is small, implying $k$ small too, one can deduce information about $d \bmod s_j$, knowing $p \bmod s_j$ and $q \bmod s_j$.

*Key Enumeration Approach.* Instead of selecting only the remainder that maximizes the distinguisher value (as presented in Step 9 of Algorithm 3), one could choose to record the scores associated to any remainder hypothesis $h$ for any prime sieve element $s_j$. Then, instead of applying the CRT recombining to only one 53-tuple (as in Step 10 of Algorithm 3), we can do it for all the 53-tuples of hypotheses from the most to the least likely, until the correct $p$ is recovered (after applying Coppersmith technique, it should factor the RSA public modulus). A straightforward application of this strategy is clearly inefficient if the correct guess is not reconstructed after few steps. To optimise this phase, it is recommended to use a so-called *key-enumeration algorithm* (KEA) (see Appendix A for an efficient algorithm proposed by Veyrat-Charvillon *et al.* [26]).

*Initial Prime Sieve.* Additional information may be retrieved during the initial *expensive* prime sieve. Such information however is likely to be very different (in nature) than the information retrieved by the following sieves (since the operations are probably handled by different part of the hardware) and then should not be used directly during the CPA attack.

## 5   Conclusion and Countermeasures Proposal

In this paper, we have described an attack against prime number generation. Compared to the existing attack of [28], this attack defeats a protected implementation of the probable prime tests with a regular prime sieve. Our attack exploits two features of a prime generation algorithm: the use of a prime sieve and a deterministic candidates generation. Such algorithms are for example described in the well-known norms ANSI X9.31 and FIPS 186-4 [1,17]. We gave an analysis of the efficiency of our attack and demonstrated its practicality against a smart-card toy implementation (which confirms our analyses).

Several approaches can be followed to thwart our attack. A first one is to randomly add dummy trial divisions in each prime sieve computation. Another one is to perform each prime sieve computation in a pseudo-random order. Both countermeasures have the effect to misalign trial divisions, and then to increase the noise in the measurements. A different approach would be to choose a prime generation algorithm without the two features required in our attack. For example, Fouque and Tibouchi [18] propose a prime generation with a non-deterministic generation of prime candidates. Another recent proposal is the efficient provable prime generation algorithm of Clavier et al. [11].

**Acknowledgement.** Aurélie Bauer's research was supported in part by the French ANR-12-JS02-0004 ROMAnTIC Project.

# References

1. ANSI X9.31. Digital Signature Using Reversible Public Key Cryptography for the Financial Services Industry. American National Standards Institute (1998)
2. Bauer, A., Jaulmes, E., Prouff, E., Wild, J.: Horizontal and Vertical Side-Channel Attacks against Secure RSA Implementations. In: Dawson, E. (ed.) CT-RSA 2013. LNCS, vol. 7779, pp. 1–17. Springer, Heidelberg (2013)
3. Boneh, D., Durfee, G., Frankel, Y.: An Attack on RSA Given a Small Fraction of the Private Key Bits. In: Ohta, K., Pei, D. (eds.) ASIACRYPT 1998. LNCS, vol. 1514, pp. 25–34. Springer, Heidelberg (1998)
4. Boscher, A., Naciri, R., Prouff, E.: CRT RSA Algorithm Protected Against Fault Attacks. In: Sauveron, D., Markantonakis, K., Bilas, A., Quisquater, J.-J. (eds.) WISTP 2007. LNCS, vol. 4462, pp. 229–243. Springer, Heidelberg (2007)
5. Brandt, J., Damgård, I.B.: On Generation of Probable Primes by Incremental Search. In: Brickell, E.F. (ed.) CRYPTO 1992. LNCS, vol. 740, pp. 358–370. Springer, Heidelberg (1993)
6. Brandt, J., Damgård, I., Landrock, P.: Speeding Up Prime Number Generation. In: Imai, H., Rivest, R.L., Matsumoto, T. (eds.) ASIACRYPT 1991. LNCS, vol. 739, pp. 440–449. Springer, Heidelberg (1993)
7. Chevallier-Mames, B., Ciet, M., Joye, M.: Low-cost Solutions for Preventing Simple Side-Channel Analysis: Side-Channel Atomicity. IEEE Transactions on Computers 53(6), 760–768 (2004)
8. Clavier, C., Coron, J.-S.: On the Implementation of a Fast Prime Generation Algorithm. In: Paillier, P., Verbauwhede, I. (eds.) CHES 2007. LNCS, vol. 4727, pp. 443–449. Springer, Heidelberg (2007)
9. Clavier, C., Feix, B., Gagnerot, G., Giraud, C., Roussellet, M., Verneuil, V.: ROSETTA for Single Trace Analysis – Recovery of Secret Exponent by Triangular Trace Analysis. In: Galbraith, S., Nandi, M. (eds.) INDOCRYPT 2012. LNCS, vol. 7668, pp. 140–155. Springer, Heidelberg (2012)

10. Clavier, C., Feix, B., Gagnerot, G., Roussellet, M., Verneuil, V.: Horizontal Correlation Analysis on Exponentiation. In: Soriano, M., Qing, S., López, J. (eds.) ICICS 2010. LNCS, vol. 6476, pp. 46–61. Springer, Heidelberg (2010)
11. Clavier, C., Feix, B., Thierry, L., Paillier, P.: Generating Provable Primes Efficiently on Embedded Devices. In: Fischlin, M., Buchmann, J., Manulis, M. (eds.) PKC 2012. LNCS, vol. 7293, pp. 372–389. Springer, Heidelberg (2012)
12. Clavier, C., Joye, M.: Universal Exponentiation Algorithm – A First Step towards Provable SPA-Resistance. In: Koç, Ç.K., Naccache, D., Paar, C. (eds.) CHES 2001. LNCS, vol. 2162, pp. 300–308. Springer, Heidelberg (2001)
13. Coppersmith, D.: Finding a Small Root of a Bivariate Integer Equation; Factoring with High Bits Known. In: Maurer, U.M. (ed.) EUROCRYPT 1996. LNCS, vol. 1070, pp. 178–189. Springer, Heidelberg (1996)
14. Coppersmith, D.: Small Solutions to Polynomial Equations, and Low Exponent RSA Vulnerabilities. Journal of Cryptology 10(4), 233–260 (1997)
15. Doget, J., Prouff, E., Rivain, M., Standaert, F.-X.: Univariate Side Channel Attacks and Leakage Modeling. Journal of Cryptographic Engineering 1(2), 123–144 (2011)
16. Finke, T., Gebhardt, M., Schindler, W.: A New Side-Channel Attack on RSA Prime Generation. In: Clavier, C., Gaj, K. (eds.) CHES 2009. LNCS, vol. 5747, pp. 141–155. Springer, Heidelberg (2009)
17. FIPS PUB 186-4. Digital Signature Standard (DSS). Federal Information Processing Standards Publication (July 2013)
18. Fouque, P.-A., Tibouchi, M.: Close to Uniform Prime Number Generation With Fewer Random Bits. IACR Cryptology ePrint Archive, 2011:481 (2011)
19. Gérard, B., Standaert, F.-X.: Unified and Optimized Linear Collision Attacks and Their Application in a Non-profiled Setting. In: Prouff, E., Schaumont, P. (eds.) CHES 2012. LNCS, vol. 7428, pp. 175–192. Springer, Heidelberg (2012)
20. Giraud, C.: An RSA Implementation Resistant to Fault Attacks and to Simple Power Analysis. IEEE Transactions on Computers 55(9), 1116–1120 (2006)
21. Gordon, J.: Strong Primes are Easy to Find. In: Beth, T., Cot, N., Ingemarsson, I. (eds.) EUROCRYPT 1984. LNCS, vol. 209, pp. 216–223. Springer, Heidelberg (1985)
22. Menezes, A.J., van Oorschot, P.C., Vanstone, S.A.: Handbook of Applied Cryptography. CRC Press (1997)
23. Moreno, C., Hasan, M.A.: SPA-Resistant Binary Exponentiation with Optimal Execution Time. Journal of Cryptographic Engineering 1(2), 87–99 (2011)
24. Schindler, W.: Advanced Stochastic Methods in Side Channel Analysis on Block Ciphers in the Presence of Masking. Journal of Mathematical Cryptology 2, 291–310 (2008)
25. Forschungszentrum Graz. Mathematisch-Statistische Sektion. Berichte Der Mathematisch-Statistischen Sektion Im Forschungszentrum Graz (1973)
26. Veyrat-Charvillon, N., Gérard, B., Renauld, M., Standaert, F.-X.: An Optimal Key Enumeration Algorithm and Its Application to Side-Channel Attacks. In: Knudsen, L.R., Wu, H. (eds.) SAC 2012. LNCS, vol. 7707, pp. 390–406. Springer, Heidelberg (2013)
27. Vigilant, D.: RSA with CRT: A New Cost-Effective Solution to Thwart Fault Attacks. In: Oswald, E., Rohatgi, P. (eds.) CHES 2008. LNCS, vol. 5154, pp. 130–145. Springer, Heidelberg (2008)
28. Vuillaume, C., Endo, T., Wooderson, P.: RSA Key Generation: New Attacks. In: Schindler, W., Huss, S.A. (eds.) COSADE 2012. LNCS, vol. 7275, pp. 105–119. Springer, Heidelberg (2012)

# A  Key Enumeration Algorithm

The idea developed by the authors of [26] is to produce, one after another, the 16-byte hypotheses on the AES master key. The 8-bit sub-keys of each hypothesis are returned independently from 16 different SCA attacks and then concatenated together in order to be tested as the cipher secret key. This set-up is in fact very similar to ours: instead of 16 bytes, we consider 53 independent secret of different lengths. From these secret hypotheses, a part of the secret prime is recovered through CRT recombining and then used to recover the whole secret prime. Similarly to the work of Gérard and Standaert in [19], a Bayesian extension can be computed over the correlation coefficient values for each of the 53 independent attacks. Hence, to each small prime $s_j$, and each remainder hypothesis $h$ in the set $(\mathbb{Z}/s_j\mathbb{Z})^*$ is associated the following probability $\Pr[h = p \bmod s_j \mid \{\ell_{ij}\}_i]$, where the set of consumption traces $\{\ell_{ij}\}_{i,j}$ is defined as in Equation (3).

Once the latter probability has been computed for any value $h$ and any $s_j$, the recursive algorithm proposed in [26] can be straightforwardly applied to provide the list of 53-tuples of remainder hypotheses ordered from the most to the less likely hypothesis. We do not recall the algorithm here (a detailed description can be found in [26]).

*Further Improvements.* For the complete attack to be successful (*e.g.* factoring an RSA modulus), it is not necessary to recover all the 53 remainders of $p$ but only a sufficient number of them s.t. their product gives 256 bits of information (instead of the 333 bits given by the product of all the 53 first small primes). In view of this, the attacker goal is no longer to recover all the remainders $p \bmod s_j$ such that $s_j$ in $\mathcal{S}$ but a subset of them which brings 256 bits of information. Let us denote by $\{\mathcal{S}_1, ..., \mathcal{S}_m\}$ a family of $m$ subsets satisfying the latter property. The KEA algorithm recalled previously can now be applied to each subset independently (taking into account the corresponding CPA attacks). The brute-force processing then takes simultaneously the $m$ sets of attack results and, at each step, the most likely hypothesis is chosen among the most likely hypothesis of each set. The respective KEA instance is afterwards advanced to the next best solution. Such multi-set approach would definitely improve the attack efficiency.

# Get Your Hands Off My Laptop: Physical Side-Channel Key-Extraction Attacks on PCs

Daniel Genkin[1,2], Itamar Pipman[2], and Eran Tromer[2]

[1] Technion, Israel
danielg3@cs.technion.ac.il
[2] Tel Aviv University, Israel
{itamarpi,tromer}@tau.ac.il

**Abstract.** We demonstrate physical side-channel attacks on a popular software implementation of RSA and ElGamal, running on laptop computers. Our attacks use novel side channels, based on the observation that the "ground" electric potential, in many computers, fluctuates in a computation-dependent way. An attacker can measure this signal by touching exposed metal on the computer's chassis with a plain wire, or even with a bare hand. The signal can also be measured at the remote end of Ethernet, VGA or USB cables.

Through suitable cryptanalysis and signal processing, we have extracted 4096-bit RSA keys and 3072-bit ElGamal keys from laptops, via each of these channels, as well as via power analysis and electromagnetic probing. Despite the GHz-scale clock rate of the laptops and numerous noise sources, the full attacks require a few seconds of measurements using Medium Frequency signals (around 2 MHz), or one hour using Low Frequency signals (up to 40 kHz).

## 1 Introduction

### 1.1 Background

Side-channel attacks that exploit unintentional, abstraction-defying information leakage from physical computing devices have proven effective in breaking the security of numerous cryptographic implementations. However, most research attention has been focused on small devices: smartcards, RFID tags, FPGAs, microcontrollers, and simple embedded devices. The "PC" class of devices (commodity laptop/desktop/server computers) has been studied from the perspective of side channels measured by resident software (see [13] and subsequent works) and from peripherals (e.g., [17]).

PCs, however, have received little academic attention with regard to physical emanations from cryptographic computations, presumably due to three main barriers. First, PCs have highly complicated system architecture and CPU micro architecture, with many noise sources and asynchronous events. Fine low-level events are thus difficult to model and measure. Second, most physical

L. Batina and M. Robshaw (Eds.): CHES 2014, LNCS 8731, pp. 242–260, 2014.

side-channel cryptanalysis approaches require the leakage signal to be acquired at rates well beyond the device's clock rate; for multi-GHz CPUs, the requisite equipment is expensive, and the signals are difficult to probe. Finally, attack scenarios differ: the aforementioned small devices are often deployed into potentially-malicious hands, where they could be subjected to lengthy or invasive attacks; but for PCs, the typical scenario (short of theft) is where a physical attacker gains physical proximity for a restricted amount of time, and must operate surreptitiously.

Recently, a key extraction attack on PCs was demonstrated using the acoustic side channel, addressing all three barriers: using a chosen-ciphertext attack, the sound emanations of interest are made very robust, brought down to very low frequencies (tens or hundreds of kHz), and extended to long durations (hundreds of milliseconds), making it possible to record the leakage surreptitiously and non-invasively, by a cellphone microphone or from many meters away [12].

We thus study the question: *what other physical, non-invasive, cryptanalytic side-channel attacks can be effectively conducted on full-blown PC computers?*

## 1.2   Our Results

We demonstrate key extraction of 4096-bit RSA and 3072-bit ElGamal keys from laptop computers of various models. The attacked software implementation is GnuPG [2], a popular open source implementation of the OpenPGP standard. The attacks exploit several side channels, enumerated below:

1. **Chassis potential.** We identify a new side channel: fluctuations of the electric potential on the chassis of laptop computers, in reference to the mains earth ground. This potential can be measured by a simple wire, non-invasively touching a conductive part of the laptop, and connected to a suitable amplifier and digitizer. (This, essentially, creates a ground loop through the laptop and measures its voltage.) The chassis potential, thus measured, is affected by ongoing computation, and our attacks exploit this for extracting RSA and ElGamal keys, within a few seconds.

   *Scenarios*: The wire can be fixed in advance where the target laptop will be placed (e.g., a cluttered desk), or put in contact with the laptop by a passerby.

2. **Far end of cable.** The chassis potential can also be observed from afar, through any cable with a conductive shield that is attached to an I/O port on the laptop. For example, we demonstrated key recovery through a 10-meter long Ethernet cable, by tapping the cable shield at the remote Ethernet switch (see Figure 4(a)). Similar observations apply to USB, VGA, HDMI, etc. Since only the shield potential is used, the attack is oblivious to the data passing through the cable, and works even if the port is disabled.

   *Scenarios*: While many users are careful about connecting suspicious devices (such as USB sticks) to the physical ports of their machines, they will routinely connect VGA display cables and Ethernet network cables to their laptops. However, a simple voltage measurement device, perhaps located in the cabinet or server room to which the cable leads, could be capturing the leakage. This is hard to check, since Ethernet wiring and projectors' VGA cables are often hidden out of sight and cannot easily be tracked by the user.

3. **Human touch.** Surprisingly, the requisite signal can be measured, with sufficient fidelity, even through a human body. An attacker merely needs to touch the target with his bare hand, while his body potential is measured.

*Scenarios*: The attacker positions himself in physical proximity to the target laptop and touches it with his bare hand or a conducting pen (see Figures 4(b))–4(c)). Surreptitiously, the attacker carries the requisite equipment for measuring his body potential relative to some nearby grounded object. In the non-adaptive attack (see below), a few seconds' contact will suffice; in the adaptive attack, 1 key bit can be extracted approximately every 4 seconds.

Note that the above attacks all rely on fluctuations in the PC's ground (relative to the mains earth ground). This makes mitigation difficult: the usual method for preventing voltage fluctuations, using bypass capacitors to shunt stray AC currents into the device's ground, does not apply to the device ground itself.

We also revisit two traditional physical side channels, and demonstrate their applicability to software running on PCs:

4. **Electromagnetic (EM).** We performed key extraction by measuring the induced EM emanations, using a near-field probe placed next to the laptop.

*Scenarios*: Electromagnetic probes are easily hidden in nearby objects. A glove, containing a concealed probe loop and hovering over the target laptop, would unveil its key within seconds.

5. **Power.** Likewise, we extracted keys by measuring the current draw on the laptop's power supply. Our attack works even though PCs use complex switching power supplies, which partially decouple the power source from the CPU load,[1] and moreover employ large capacitors, chokes, and shields for electromagnetic compatibility (EMC) compliance — all of which attenuate and disrupt the signals sought in traditional power analysis.

*Scenarios*: A public charging station can be easily augmented with a current meter, logger, and transmitter. Even a regular power supply "brick" can be similarly augmented.

Our attacks require very low bandwidth, well below the laptop CPU's GHz-scale clock rate. We use two cryptanalytic approaches, based on known techniques and adapted to the target software:

**Fast, Non-adaptive MF Attack.** For both RSA and ElGamal key extraction, we can exploit signals circa 2 MHz (Medium Frequency band), using the "$n - 1$" non-adaptive chosen-ciphertext simple-power-analysis attack of Yen et al. [26]. Key extraction then requires a few seconds of measurements.

**Slow, Adaptive VLF/LF Attack.** For RSA key extraction, we can exploit signals of about 15–40 kHz (Very Low / Low Frequency bands), using

---

[1] In the realm of small devices, such similar decoupling has been proposed as an intentional countermeasure against power analysis [23].

the adaptive chosen-ciphertext attack of [12]. Full 4096-bit RSA key extraction then takes approximately one hour, but is very robust to low signal-to-noise ratio.

Our results require careful choice and tuning of the signal acquisition equipment, to attain usable signal-to-noise ratio in the presence of abundant noise, delicate grounding, and impedance-matching considerations. We report these choices in detail and describe the requisite signal processing. We also analyze the code of GnuPG's mathematical library, showing why the specific chosen ciphertext creates exploitable, key-dependent leakage in this implementation.

## 1.3  Vulnerable Software and Hardware

**Hardware.** We have tested various laptop computers, of different models, by various vendors. The signal quality varied dramatically, as did the relative quality between channels, the carrier frequencies of interest, the best placement of the probes or human hand, and the optimal grounding connection. Thus, manual calibration and experimentation were required. Generally, instruction-dependent leakage occurs on most laptops; key extraction is possible on many laptops, but the requisite signal-to-noise is not always present.

**GnuPG.** For this case study, we focused on GnuPG version 1.4.15, running on Windows XP and compiled with the MinGW GCC version 4.6.2. This version of GnuPG was the most recent when our research was publicly announced. Following the practice of responsible disclosure, we worked with the authors of GnuPG to suggest several countermeasures and verify their effectiveness against our attacks (including those in [12]; see discussion therein as well as CVE-2013-4576 [19]). GnuPG 1.4.16, released concurrently with the announcement of our results, contains these countermeasures.

**Chosen Ciphertext Injection.** Our key extraction attacks require chosen ciphertexts (either adaptive or non-adaptive, depending on the attack). As observed in [12], one way to remotely inject such ciphertexts into GnuPG is to send them as a PGP/MIME-encoded e-mail, to be automatically decrypted by the Enigmail [9] plugin for the Mozilla Thunderbird e-mail client. In the case of the non-adaptive attack, the attacker can provide the chosen ciphertext files to the victim (by any means or guise), and merely needs to conduct the measurement, for a few seconds, when those files are decrypted.

## 1.4  Related Work

Simple and differential power analysis attacks were introduced by Kocher et al. [15], and applied to both symmetric and asymmetric ciphers, implemented on hardware such as smartcards, microcontrollers and FPGAs (see [4,16,18] and the references therein).

Clark et al. [6] observed that is it possible to use power analysis to identify, with high probability, the web pages loaded by a web browser on the target

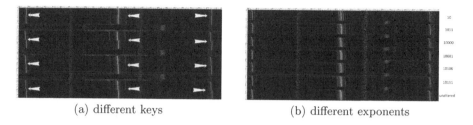

(a) different keys                          (b) different exponents

**Fig. 1.** Chassis measurement (1.7 sec, 1.9–2.6 MHz) of a Lenovo 3000 N200. (a) Four GnuPG RSA signatures. The transitions between $p$ and $q$ are marked with yellow arrows. (b) Seven GnuPG RSA decryptions. In the first 6 cases, exponents ($d_p$ and $d_q$) are both overridden to be the 2048-bit number obtained by repeating the pattern written to the right. In the last case, the exponent is unaltered. In all cases, the moduli $p$ and $q$ are the same and the ciphertext is set to $n - 1$.

machine, by tapping the AC outlet to which the target is connected. Oren and Shamir [20] observed that the power line voltage on USB ports exhibits a distinct signature when OpenSSL RSA decryption executes, even when the port is disabled; this property is shared by our "far end of cable" channel. Schmidt et al. [22] observed leakage through voltage variations on the I/O pins of embedded devices. Basic multiplication instructions were shown to have operand-specific leakage, in simulation [24] and embedded devices [8] (though this was not demonstrated or exploited on PCs).

The electromagnetic side channel has been studied and exploited for smartcards and FPGA's (e.g., [3, 10, 21]), including for RSA. More recently, Zajic and Prvulovic [27] observed electromagnetic leakage from laptop and desktop computers (but did not show cryptographic applications). Cache attacks were applied to GnuPG's RSA implementation [25].

# 2    Computation-Dependent Chassis-Potential Leakage

The electric potential on a laptop computer's chassis (metal panels, shields and ports) is ideally equal to that of the mains earth ground potential, but in reality it fluctuates greatly. Even when the laptop is grounded (via its power supply or via shielded cables such as Ethernet, USB or VGA), there is non-negligible impedance between the grounding point(s) and other points in the chassis. Voltage, often 10mV RMS or more,[2] develops across this impedance, in part due to currents and electromagnetic fields inside the computer. A natural question is whether information about the ongoing computation can be learned by measuring the chassis potential.

In this section, we show a very simple (yet already troubling) form of leaked information: determining which of several randomly-generated secret keys was

---

[2] After filtering out the strong, but cryptanalytically useless, 50 or 60 Hz components.

used by the target machine, for a signing or decryption operation. For brevity, in the remainder of this section we discuss chassis potential measurements; similar effects are also present when using the EM side channel.

Figure 1(a) depicts the spectrogram of four GnuPG RSA signing operations, using different 4096-bit random keys (generated beforehand), on a fixed message. Each signing operation is preceded by a short CPU sleep (for visual separation).

The different signing keys can be clearly distinguished by their subtly different spectral signatures (which may itself be of practical interest). Another telling detail is visible: halfway through each signing operation, a transition appears at several frequency bands (marked with yellow arrows). This corresponds to the transition between exponentiation modulo the secret $p$ to exponentiation modulo the secret $q$, in the RSA decryption implementation of GnuPG, which is based on the Chinese Remainder Theorem. We can thus spectrally observe internal, secret-dependent information within the signing operation.

Next, Figure 1(b) demonstrates seven RSA signing operations using different secret exponents which can also be easily distinguished. Finally, similar results are observed for ElGamal decryption, though the exponentiation is shorter and thus its frequency spectrum can be characterized less accurately.

# 3 Non-adaptive Attack

We proceed to describe our cryptanalytic attack techniques (whose applicability will be shown in Section 5). The first technique is a non-adaptive chosen ciphertext attack using very few traces, following the simple power analysis of RSA (see the surveys [4,16,18], and the references therein). We begin by reviewing the high-level modular exponentiation algorithm in GnuPG (Section 3.1), describe our attack (Section 3.2) exploiting this algorithm, and then analyze its success by recalling the inner squaring routines used by GnuPG (Section 3.3) and their behavior under the attack (Section 3.4).

## 3.1 GnuPG's Modular Exponentiation Routine

To perform arithmetic on the large integers occurring in RSA and ElGamal, GnuPG uses an internal mathematical library called MPI (based on GMP [1]). MPI stores large integers as arrays of *limbs*, i.e., 32-bit words (on x86).

We now review the modular exponentiation routine of GnuPG (as introduced in GnuPG v1.4.14), which is used for both RSA and ElGamal. GnuPG uses a variant of the square-and-multiply modular exponentiation algorithm, processing the bits of the exponent from the most significant bit to the least significant one. To mitigate a cache side-channel attack [25], GnuPG now always performs the multiplication operation in every loop iteration regardless of the exponent's bits (but only uses the result as needed). The pseudocode is given in Algorithm 1. This top-level exponentiation routine suffices for the high-level description of our attack. For details about GnuPG's underlying squaring routines, necessary for understanding the attack's success, see Sections 3.3 and 3.4.

---

**Algorithm 1.** GnuPG's modular exponentiation (see function mpi_powm in mpi/mpi-pow.c).

---

1: **procedure** MODULAR_EXPONENTIATION($a, b, p$)           ▷ returns $a^b$ mod $p$
2:     **if** SIZE_IN_LIMBS($a$) > SIZE_IN_LIMBS($p$) **then**
3:         $a \leftarrow a$ mod $p$
4:     $m \leftarrow 1$
5:     **for** $i \leftarrow 1$ **to** n **do**
6:         $m \leftarrow m^2$ mod $p$                     ▷ Karatsuba or grade-school squaring
7:         $t \leftarrow m \cdot a$ mod $p$               ▷ Karatsuba or grade-school multiplication
8:         **if** $b_i = 1$ **then**                      ▷ where $b = b_1 \cdots b_n$
9:             $m \leftarrow t$
10:    **return** $m$

---

## 3.2   The Attack Algorithm

Since GnuPG 1.4.15 attempts to avoid correlation between the bits of the exponent and *high-level* operations (such as multiplication), we use a chosen ciphertext attack in order to create correlations between these bits and intermediate
values computed inside the *low-level* operations inside GnuPG's modular exponentiation routine. Moreover, the chosen ciphertext will have an amplification
effect, whereby numerous recursive calls will be similarly affected, resulting in a
distinct leakage signal over a long time period. This is the key to conducting a
MHz-scale attack on a GHz-scale computation.

Following Yen et al. [26] we choose a ciphertext $c$ such that $a \equiv -1 \pmod{p}$
during the execution MODULAR_EXPONENTIATION. Within GnuPG, this creates
a correlation between the bits of the secret exponent $b$ and the number of zero
limbs of $m$, as described next. As we will analyze in Sections 3.3 and 3.4, the
number of zero limbs inside $m$ affects the control flow inside the GnuPG basic
squaring routine,thus creating discernible differences in the physical leakage.

Note that, for $a \equiv -1 \pmod{p}$, the value $m$ during the execution of MOD-
ULAR_EXPONENTIATION is always either 1 or $-1$ modulo $p$. Thus, the value of
$m$ in line 7 does not depend on the bits of $b$, and is always 1 modulo $p$ (since
$-1^2 \equiv 1^2 \equiv 1 \pmod{p}$). Consequently, the following correlation holds between
the value of $m$ at the start of the $i$-th iteration of the loop in line 5 and $b_{i-1}$.

- **$b_{i-1} = 0$.** In this case the branch on line 8 was not taken; thus, the value of $m$
  at the start of the $i$-th iteration of the loop in line 5 is also $m = 1$ mod $p = 1$.
  Next, since GnuPG's internal representation does not truncate leading zeros,
  it holds that the value $m$ sent to the squaring routine during the $i$-th iteration
  contains many zero limbs.

- **$b_{i-1} = 1$.** In this case the branch on line 8 was taken, so the value of $m$ at
  the start of the $i$-th iteration of the loop in line 5 is $m = -1$ mod $p = p - 1$.
  Since $p$ is a random large prime, the value $m$ sent to the squaring routine
  during the $i$-th iteration contains very few zero limbs.

**Algorithm 2.** GnuPG's basic squaring code (see function sqr_n_basecase in mpi/mpih-mul.c).

---

1: **procedure** SQR_BASECASE($a$)                                    ▷ returns $a^2$
2:   **if** $a_1 \leq 1$ **then**                                      ▷ where $a = a_k \cdots a_1$
3:     **if** $a_1 = 1$ **then**
4:       $p \leftarrow a$
5:     **else**                                                        ▷ $a_i = 0$
6:       $p \leftarrow 0$
7:   **else**
8:     $p \leftarrow$ MUL_BY_SINGLE_LIMB($a, a_1$)                     ▷ $p \leftarrow a \cdot a_1$
9:   **for** $i \leftarrow 2$ **to** n **do**
10:    **if** $a_i \leq 1$ **then**
11:      **if** $a_i = 1$ **then**                                     ▷ (and if $a_i = 0$ do nothing)
12:        $p \leftarrow$ ADD_WITH_OFFSET($p, a, i$)                   ▷ $p \leftarrow p + a \cdot 2^{32 \cdot i}$
13:    **else**
14:      $p \leftarrow$ MUL_AND_ADD_WITH_OFFSET($p, a, a_i, i$)        ▷ $p \leftarrow p + a \cdot a_i \cdot 2^{32 \cdot i}$
15:    **return** $p$

---

We now proceed to describe the specific ciphertext choices required for our attack for both the RSA and ElGamal case.

**Ciphertext Choice for RSA-CRT.** Recall that in the case of RSA decryption, GnuPG first computes $c^{d_p} \bmod p$ and $c^{d_q} \bmod q$, and then combines these via the Chinese Remainder Theorem. By choosing $c = n - 1$ where $n = pq$ is the public RSA modulus, the modular reduction in line 3 is always triggered, causing the value of $a$ in line 5 to be $p - 1$ (i.e., $-1$ modulo $p$ as desired).

**Ciphertext Choice for ElGamal.** For ElGamal encryption, the prime modulus $p$ is part of the public key, so we directly choose the ciphertext to be $p - 1$.

### 3.3  GnuPG's Squaring Routine

GnuPG's large-integer squaring routine combines two squaring algorithms: a basic quadratic-complexity squaring routine, and a variant based on a recursive Karatsuba multiplication algorithm [14]. The chosen combination of algorithms is based on the size of the operands, measured in whole limbs. We will first discuss the basic squaring algorithm and its key-dependent behavior, and then show how this behavior is preserved by the Karatsuba squaring.

**GnuPG's Basic Squaring Routine.** The core side-channel weakness we exploit in GnuPG's code lies inside the basic squaring routine. The basic squaring routine used by GnuPG is a quadratic-complexity "grade school" squaring, with optimizations for multiplication by limbs equal to 0 or 1, depicted in Algorithm 2.

Note how SQR_BASECASE handles zero limbs of $a$. When a zero limb of $a$ is encountered, none of the operations MUL_BY_SINGLE_LIMB, ADD_WITH_OFFSET and MUL_AND_ADD_WITH_OFFSET are performed and the loop in line 9 continues to the next limb of $a$. Our attack exploits this, by causing the number of such zero limbs to depend on the current bit of the secret exponent, thus affecting the control flow in lines 3 and 11, and thereby the side-channel emanations.

**GnuPG's Karatsuba Squaring Routine.** The basic squaring routine described above is invoked via two code paths: directly by the modular exponentiation routine (Section 3.1) when the operand is small, and also as the base-case by the Karatsuba squaring routine. The latter is a variant of the Karatsuba multiplication algorithm [14], relying on the following identity:

$$a^2 = \begin{cases} (2^{2n} + 2^n)a_H^2 - 2^n(a_H - a_L)^2 + (2^n + 1)a_L^2 & \text{if } a_H > a_L \\ (2^{2n} + 2^n)a_H^2 - 2^n(a_L - a_H)^2 + (2^n + 1)a_L^2 & \text{otherwise} \end{cases} , \quad (1)$$

where $a_H, a_L$ are the most and least significant halves of $a$, respectively.

### 3.4    Attack Analysis

In this section we analyze the effects of our attack on SQR_BASECASE (Algorithm 2). Recall that in Section 3.2 we created a correlation between the $i$-th bit of the secret exponent $b_i$ and the number of zero limbs in the operand $m$ of the squaring routine during iteration $i + 1$ of the main loop of the modular exponentiation routine. Concretely, for the case where $b_i = 1$, we have that $m = -1 \mod p = p - 1$ is a random-looking number containing several thousand bits (2048 bits for the case of RSA and 3072 bits for the case of ElGamal). Conversely, for the case where $b_i = 0$, we have that $m = 1 \mod p = 1$ and, since GnuPG does not truncate leading zeros, the representation of $m$ is a large number (2048 bits for the case of RSA and 3072 bits for ElGamal), all of whose limbs are 0 (except for the least significant).

The code of GnuPG passes $m$ to the Karatsuba squaring routine. For the case where $b_i = 1$, since $m$ is a random-looking number, this property of $m$ will be preserved in all 3 recursive calls (computing the three squaring operations in Equation 1). Similarly, for $b_i = 0$, we have that $m = 1$, meaning $m_H = 0$ and $m_L = 1$. Thus, the second case of Equation 1 will always be taken, again preserving the structure of $m$ as having mostly zero limbs, in all 3 recursive calls.

When reaching the recursion's base case, we have the following dependence on $b_i$. If $b_i = 0$, then the values of the operand of SQR_BASECASE during iteration $i + 1$ of the main loop of MODULAR_EXPONENTIATION (in all branches of the recursion) will have almost all of their limbs equal to zero. Conversely, if $b_i = 1$, then the values of the operand of SQR_BASECASE during iteration $i + 1$ of the main loop of MODULAR_EXPONENTIATION in all branches of the recursion will be random-looking.

Next, recall the effect of zero limbs in the operand on the code of SQR_BASECASE. Note that the control flow in SQR_BASECASE depends on the number of non-zero limbs in its operand. The drastic change in the number of zero limbs in the operand of SQR_BASECASE is detectable by our side-channel measurements. Thus, we are able to leak the bits of the secret exponent by creating the correlation between its bits and the number of zero limbs in the operand of SQR_BASECASE, using our carefully chosen cipher text.

# 4   Adaptive Attack

Our other cryptanalytic technique is an adaptive chosen-ciphertext side-channel attack, which extracts, bit by bit, the prime modulus used during the CRT-based RSA modular exponentiation routine. Our attack on GnuPG was introduced in [12] (following [5]) for the GnuPG acoustic side channel. For self-containment, we give an overview of the attack here. (This attack is not applicable to ElGamal, since the prime modulus $p$ is public.)

The attack recovers the bits of $p = p_1 \cdots p_k$ iteratively, starting with the MSB $p_1$. Once we learn all of $p$, we know the factorization of $n$. Moreover, after recovering just the top half of the bits of $p$, it is possible to use Coppersmith's attack [7] to recover the remaining bits.

**Ciphertext Choice for RSA.** In GnuPG, the MSB is always set, i.e., $p_k = 1$. Assume that we have already recovered the topmost $i-1$ bits of $p$. To extract the next bit $p_i$, we check the two hypotheses about its value, by requesting decryption of an adaptively chosen ciphertext $g^{i,0} + n$, where $g^{i,0} = p_1 \cdots p_{i-1} 1 0 \cdots 0$ ($k$ bits in total). Let $n = pq$ be the public RSA modulus. Consider the RSA decryption of $g^{i,0} + n$. Two cases are possible, depending on $p_i$.

- $p_i = 1$.   Then $g^{i,0} < p$. The ciphertext $g^{i,0} + n$ is passed as the variable $a$ to Algorithm 1. Since $n = pg$ we have that $g^{i,0} + n$ has a larger limb count than $p$. This triggers the modular reduction of $a$ in line 3 of Algorithm 1, which returns $g^{i,0}$, resulting in $a$ being a $k$-bit number having mostly zero limbs. Next, $a$ is passed to the multiplication routine in line 7.

- $p_i = 0$.   Then $p < g^{i,0}$ and as in the previous case, $g^{i,0} + n$ is passed as the variable $a$ to Algorithm 1 triggering the modular reduction of $a$ in line 3. Since $g^{i,0}$ and $p$ share the same topmost $i - 1$ bits, we have that $g^{i,0} < 2p$, and the reduction results in $a = g^{i,0} - q$, which is a $(k - i)$-bit random-looking number. This is then passed to the multiplication routine in line 7.

**Code Analysis.** We now present a high-level analysis of how our bit-by-bit chosen ciphertext attack affects the code of GnuPG. Using the above described ciphertexts, the second operand of the multiplication routine during the entire execution of the main loop of the modular exponentiation routine, will be either full-size and repetitive or shorter and random-looking (depending on $p_i$).

GnuPG's uses two algorithms for large integer multiplication: the Karatsuba-based multiplication algorithm and the grade-school (quadratic time) multiplication algorithm. GnuPG's variant of Karatsuba recursive multiplication relies on the identity $ab = (2^{2n} + 2^n)a_H b_H + 2^n (a_H - a_L)(b_L - b_H) + (2^n + 1)a_L b_L$, where $a_H, b_H$ and $a_L, b_L$ are the most and least significant halves of $a$ and $b$, respectively. We thus see that GnuPG's Karatsuba multiplication preserves the structure of $a$ as being either random-looking or containing many zero limbs. That is, if $a$ is random-looking, then $a_H b_H$, $(a_H - a_L)(b_L - b_H)$ and $a_L b_L$ are random-looking as well. Conversely, if $a$ contains mostly zero limbs, the values of $a_H b_H$, $(a_H - a_L)(b_L - b_H)$ and $a_L b_L$ also contain mostly zero limbs.

Next, when the recursion reaches its base case , GnuPG passes $a$ to the basic multiplication routine which is implemented similarly to Algorithm 2. In particular, it includes optimizations for zero limbs similar to lines 3 and 11. Thus, we are able to leak the bits of $p$, one bit at a time, by creating a correlation between the current bit of $p$ and the number of zero limbs in the second operand of GnuPG's basic multiplication routine using our chosen ciphertexts.

The above is a high-level description of the adaptive attack. In order to achieve full RSA key extraction, improvements are required to the basic attack algorithm. See [12] for details.

# 5    Empirical Key-Extraction Results

## 5.1    Chassis-Potential Attack

### 5.1.1    Setup
As discussed in Section 2, there are computation-dependent fluctuations of the electric potential on the chassis of laptop computers. We measured the electric potential of the laptop's chassis by touching it with the simplest possible probe: a plain wire, 80 cm long. The wire is pressed against the chassis by hand, or (for longer attacks) using an alligator clip. The wire's potential is then measured through an amplifier, filters, and a digitizer.

**Grounding.** The attack measures the voltage between the room's mains earth ground potential and the target computer's chassis potential. Put otherwise, we create a ground loop which includes the laptop chassis and the amplifier, and then measure the voltage across the amplifier's input impedance (and thus its complement: the voltage across the laptop chassis). Thus, correct grounding is essential to maximizing the signal-to-noise ratio. The measurement is done in single-ended mode, in reference to the mains earth ground potential, using low-impedance ground connection to the amplifier and digitizer. The target laptop is grounded through one of its shielded I/O ports (we used a VGA cable to a grounded screen, or a USB cable to a grounded printer). If the target laptop's grounding is removed, but the laptop is still connected to 3-prong (grounded) AC-DC power supply, the signal-to-noise ratio typically degrades. With a 2-prong (ungrounded) power supply and no other ground connections, the signal-to-noise ratio is very low and our attacks do not work.

**Chassis Probe Placement.** The chassis of modern laptops, while made mostly of metal (for EMI shielding), is typically covered with non-conductive plastic. However, many IO ports, such as USB, Ethernet, VGA and HDMI, typically have metal shielding which is connected to the chassis or PCB ground, and thus can be probed by the attacker. Also, metal heatsink fins are often easily reachable through the exhaust fan grill. Heuristically, the best results are achieved when the chassis is probed close to the CPU and its associated voltage regulator circuitry, and if the laptop's ground connection is distant from the probing point.

**Chassis Potential or EM?**    To ascertain that we were indeed measuring chassis potential rather than stray electromagnetic fields, we broke the direct galvanic connection between the probe wire and the laptop's chassis, by inserting a sheet of paper in-between. This always resulted in severe signal attenuation.

### 5.1.2    Non-adaptive Chassis-Potential Attack

**MF Measurement Equipment.**    The non-adaptive attack exploits signals in the Medium Frequency (MF) frequency band, on the order of 2 MHz. To measure these signals, we connected the probe wire to a 16 kHz high-pass filter, followed by a high-input-impedance low-noise amplifier (Femto HVA-200M-40-F, 40 dB gain). The amplified signal was then low-pass filtered at 5 MHz and digitized at 12 bits and 10 Msample/sec (National Instruments PCI 6115).

**Analyzing the Signal.**    The signals presented in Figure 1(b) provide the first indication as to how the different exponents might be distinguished. For periodic exponents, the leakage signal spectrum takes the form of small, distinct side lobes centered around a dominant frequency peak. This indicates that the bits of the exponents manifest themselves as modulations on a central sinusoidal carrier wave. Further analysis reveals that the carrier is frequency-modulated, meaning that its instantaneous frequency changes slightly in accordance with the current bit of the exponent. Thus, in order to recover these bits, we obtain the dominant instantaneous frequency as a function of time, by applying FM demodulation digitally. The signal is first filtered using a 30 kHz band-pass filter centered at the carrier frequency. Next, the signal is demodulated using a Discrete Hilbert Transform. Additional filtering is then performed on the demodulated signal, to suppress high frequency noise and to compensate for a slow frequency drift of the carrier wave. Figure 2(a) shows an example of a fully demodulated leakage signal; the correlation with the secret key bits can clearly be seen.

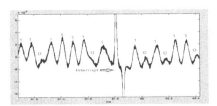
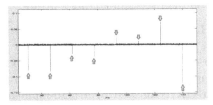

(a) A segment of the demodulated sig-     (b) Demodulation of the entire signal.
nal. Note the correlation between the sig-     The interrupts, occurring every 15 ms,
nal and the secret key bits.     are marked by green arrows.

**Fig. 2.** Frequency demodulation of the leakage signal during a decryption operation using a randomly generated 4096-bit RSA key

**Key Extraction.** Theoretically, it should be possible to extract the entire secret key from a single demodulated trace, provided the measurement is robust and has a high signal-to-noise ratio. However, we observed a periodic interrupt (marked in Figure 2(a)), which disrupted the key extraction. The interrupt manifests as a large frequency fluctuation in the carrier every 15 milliseconds (Figure 2(b)), corresponding to the 64 Hz timer interrupt frequency on the target laptop. These interrupts systematically occur at the same time during the decryption process, and thus disrupt similar bit offsets in repeated decryptions. Fortunately, the inherent jitter is sufficient so that, over a few measurements, every bit is (with high probability) undisturbed in some sample. Conversely, jitter creates a difficulty in aligning the multiple traces. We thus break each trace, post-modulation, into multiple time segments. The segments are then aligned via correlation, and averaged. This results in an interrupt-free aggregate trace, with very high SNR. The bits are then extracted using a peak detection algorithm.

**Non-adaptive RSA Key Extraction.** Applying our non-adaptive attack on a randomly generated 4096-bit RSA key while measuring the chassis potential of a Lenovo 3000 N200 laptop during 6 decryption operations, each lasting 0.35 sec, we have directly extracted 2044 out of 2048 bits of $d_p$ thereby extracting the key. The laptop was powered by a 3-prong AC-DC power supply (Lenovo, 90W, model 42T4428), without additional connections.

**Non-adaptive ElGamal Key Extraction.** Attacking the exponentiation in ElGamal decryption, and applying similar cryptanalytic and signal analysis, we extracted all but 2 of the bits of the secret exponent from a randomly generated 3072-bit ElGamal key by measuring the chassis potential of a Lenovo 3000 N200 laptop during 9 decryption operations, each lasting 0.1 sec

### 5.1.3   Adaptive Chassis-Potential Attack

We now discuss results obtained using the adaptive attack described in Section 4. While this attack requires more decryption operations in order to recover the key, it utilizes lower frequency signals and requires much lower signal-to-noise ratio than the non-adaptive attack.

**VLF/LF Measurement Equipment.** The adaptive attack can exploit very low bandwidth signals, in the VLF and LF frequency bands: in the order of 15–40 kHz (depending on the laptop model). To measure these signals, we used a more compact, higher dynamic range, measurement chain. The probe was directly connected to a high-input-impedance low-noise amplifier (customized Brüel&Kjær 5935, usually set to 40 dB gain). The amplified signal was high-pass filtered at 10 kHz, and digitized at 16 bits and 200 Ksample/sec (National Instruments MyDAQ).

**Analyzing the Leakage Signal.** Recall that GnuPG's RSA code performs modular exponentiation modulo $p$ followed by a modular exponentiation modulo $q$. Figure 3(a) shows a typical recording of RSA decryption when the value of the attacked bit of $q$ is 0, and Figure 3(b) shows a recording of RSA decryption

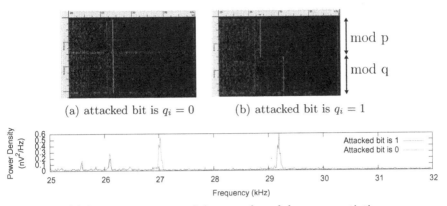

(a) attacked bit is $q_i = 0$      (b) attacked bit is $q_i = 1$

(c) Frequency spectra of the second modular exponentiation

**Fig. 3.** Chassis measurement of RSA decryption for various values of the attacked bit executed on a Lenovo ThinkPad T60

(a)   Measuring shield   potential at the far side of an Ethernet cable (probed   at   the Ethernet switch).

(b)   Non-adaptive   "human touch" attack through a metal pen touching the heatsink fins. The wristband is connected to the probe wire.

(c) Adaptive "human touch" attack by bare hand. The wristband is connected to the probe wire.

**Fig. 4.** "Far end of cable" and "human touch" attacks

when the value of the attacked bit of $q$ is 1. Several effects are shown in the figures. As in figure 1(a), the transition between $p$ and $q$ is clearly visible. Note, then, that the signatures of the modular exponentiation using the prime $q$ (the second exponentiation) are quite different in Figures 3(a) vs. 3(b). This can be seen more clearly in Figure 3(c), which summarizes the aforementioned spectral signatures by taking the median, over time, for each. This clear difference is used to extract the bits of $q$, as explained in Section 4.

**Adaptive RSA Key Extraction.** By connecting the VLF/LF measurement setup to a Lenovo ThinkPad T60, powered by the 3-prong AC-DC power supply without additional connections,[3] we directly extracted the 1024 most significant

---

[3] Grounding the laptop to mains earth, via some port, would improve the signal quality (see Section 5.1.1); but the adaptive attack is sufficiently robust to not require this.

bits of the secret prime $q$ of a randomly-generated 4096-bit RSA key in approximately 1 hour. By Coppersmith's technique, this results in full key extraction. (Alternately, it is possible to continue the attack and recover remaining bits.)

## 5.2  "Far End of Cable" Attack

The electric potential on a laptop's chassis and external ports can measured from far away. When a cable is plugged into one of the laptop's IO ports (such as USB, Ethernet and VGA), the port's shield typically contacts a plug shield, which in turn is connected to a conductive cable shield running the length of the cable. Thus, one can measure the chassis potential from the *far* side of cables connected to the aforementioned ports. Ethernet cables, for examples, often span long distances, across and between building floors. An attacker who gains access to the far side of the cable (see Figure 4(a)), or taps the shield along the way, can measure the approximate chassis potential.

The attack does not utilize data transmitted over the cable, and is oblivious to whether the port is even enabled.

We conducted the attacks by connecting the target laptop, through a 10-meter long shielded CAT5e Ethernet cable, to an Ethernet switch (EDIMAX ES-3308P). We attached a plain wire to the cable shield via a clip, on the switch side (see Figure 4(a)) and measured its potential.

**Non-adaptive RSA Key Extraction.** Using the MF measurement setup (see Section 5.1.2), we measured the chassis potential of a Lenovo 3000 N200 laptop through the shield of the Ethernet cable. The laptop was powered by the 3-prong AC-DC power supply, and was also connected via a shielded VGA cable to a grounded monitor (Dell 2412M). We directly extracted 2042 out of 2048 bits of $d_p$, by observing the shield's potential during 5 decryption operations (each lasting 0.35 sec). Similar results were obtained at the far side of a USB cable.

**Non-adaptive ElGamal Key Extraction.** Applying a similar attack to ElGamal decryption, we extracted all but 3 of the bits of the secret exponent, from a randomly-generated 3072-bit ElGamal key, by observing the shield's potential during 4 decryption operations (each lasting 0.1 sec).

**Adaptive RSA Key Extraction.** We attacked a Lenovo ThinkPad T60 laptop, through an Ethernetor USB cable, whose shield potential was measured using the VLF/LF measurement equipment (see Section 5.1.3). The laptop was powered by the 3-prong AC-DC power supply, without additional connections. In this setting, we extracted the 1024 most significant bits of the secret prime $q$ (and thus, by Coppersmith's technique, full key extraction) in 1 hour.

## 5.3  "Human Touch" Attack

On many laptops, the chassis potential can be sensed indirectly through a human body. An attacker can sense the chassis potential by merely *touching* a conductive part of the laptop chassis with his hand. This affects the electric potential of the attacker's body (assuming suitable insulation, e.g., nonconductive floor or shoes). Surreptitiously, the attacker can measure the electric potential induced on his own body, using a concealed probe, in reference to some nearby conductive grounded surface in the room. Even this circuitous measurement, through an ill-characterized, high-impedance path, can suffice for key extraction.

**Non-adaptive RSA Key Extraction.** Using the MF measurement setup (see Section 5.1.2), we measured the chassis potential of a Lenovo 3000 N200 laptop indirectly, though the body of a volunteer (one of the authors). The volunteer held a paperclip or a metal pen in his hand, and briefly touched it to the laptop's heatsink fins, which are easily reachable through the exhaust vent. Concurrently, the volunteer's body potential was measured using the MF measurement equipment (see Section 5.1.2), via a probe wire attached to a conductive wristband on his other wrist (see Figure 4(b)).

The laptop was powered by the 3-prong AC-DC power supply, with no further connection. Applying our non-adaptive attack and the signal analysis techniques from Section 5.1.2 on a randomly generated 4096-bit RSA key, we directly extracted 2042 out of 2048 bits of $d_p$ by observing the volunteer's body potential (while holding the paperclip against the laptop's heatsink) during 6 decryption operations, each lasting 0.35 sec.

**Non-adaptive ElGamal Key Extraction.** Applying our non-adaptive attack and the signal analysis techniques from Section 5.1.2 on a randomly generated 3072-bit ElGamal key, we were able to extract all but 3 of the bits of the secret exponent by observing the volunteer's body potential (while holding the paperclip against the laptop's heatsink) during 16 decryptions, each lasting 0.1 sec.

**Adaptive RSA Key Extraction.** The adaptive attack, being more robust (due to relying on lower-frequency, longer-duration signals), succeeded with unaided finger touch. A patient volunteer touched the chassis (specifically, VGA connector shield) of a Lenovo ThinkPad T61 with his fingers. The volunteer's body potential was measured using the VLF/LF measurement equipment (see Section 5.1.3), through the aforementioned wristband, and the laptop was connected as above. On some ThinkPad models, this attack can even be mounted by simply touching the rubber-coated LCD cover (see Figure 4(c)).

In this setting, we directly extracted the topmost 1024 bits of the prime $q$ of a randomly generated 4096-bit RSA key from in 1 hour, thereby (via Coppersmith's technique) completely extracting the key.

## 5.4  Electromagnetic (EM) Attack

Next, we studied EM emanations from laptop computers, in the MF band (approximately 2 MHz). We used a near-field magnetic probe (Rohde&Schwarz 7405901, 6 cm diameter, 50 Ω). The signal was low-pass filtered at 5 MHz and amplified using a low-noise amplifier (a customized Mini-Circuits ZPUL-30P). This is digitized at 12 bits and 10 Msample/sec (NI PCI 6115).

**EM Probe Placement.** The placement of the EM probe greatly influences the measured signal and noise. We wish to measure EM emanations close to the CPU's voltage regular, located on the laptop's motherboard, yet without mechanical intrusion. Concretely, the rear-left corner often yields the best signal.

**Non-adaptive RSA Key Extraction.** Applying our non-adaptive attack to a 4096-bit RSA key, we directly extracted 2046 out of 2048 bits of $d_p$, by measuring the EM emanations from a Lenovo 3000 N200 laptop during 5 decryption operations, each lasting about 0.35 sec.

**Non-adaptive ElGamal Key Extraction.** Using the same experimental setup and applying our non-adaptive attack to a randomly generated 3072-bit ElGamal key, we were able to extract all but 3 of the bits of the secret exponent by measuring the EM emanations from a Lenovo 3000 N200 laptop during 16 decryption operations, each lasting about 0.1 sec.

### 5.5   Power Analysis Attack

Finally, we revisited the classic power analysis channel, and analyzed the current draw fluctuations on the power supply of the target laptop in the VLF/LF frequency bands. Specifically, we placed a $0.5\Omega$ resistor in series with the laptop's power supply, on the low ("ground") supply rail.

**Adaptive RSA Key Extraction.** We measured the voltage on the resistor using a National Instruments MyDAQ device though a 150 kHz low-pass filter. We directly extracted the topmost 1024 bits of the prime $q$ of a randomly generated 4096-bit RSA key, from a Lenovo ThinkPad T61, in one hour.

## 6   Conclusion

While physical side-channel attacks have proven very effective at breaking cryptosystems, most research attention has focused on small and relatively simple devices. This paper demonstrated that PC systems too are vulnerable, despite their complexity, noise, and challenging electrical characteristics. Moreover, PCs can be attacked by mere touch or from afar by almost any wired connection.

Following our observations, several software countermeasures were proposed and incorporated into GnuPG 1.4.16 and libgcrypt 1.6. While these countermeasures indeed foil the attacks presented in this paper, the key distinguishing attack is unaffected and still present in the latest versions of GnuPG; mitigating it in software, without a large overhead, remains an open problem.

Physical mitigation techniques include Faraday cages (against EM attacks), insulating enclosures (against chassis and touch attacks), and photoelectric decoupling or fiberoptic connections (against "far end of cable" attacks). However, inexpensive protection of PCs appears difficult, especially for the chassis channel. The common method for filtering conducted emanations on power supply lines is to use bypass capacitors to shunt stray AC currents into the ground, but this obviously does not apply to the ground line itself. Robust low-impedance grounding and shielding, with careful attention to current paths, should reduce voltages across the ground and chassis (at costs in engineering effort and portability). We conjecture that prudent design of switching power supplies can reduce computation-dependent leakage without significantly hampering efficiency.

·**Acknowledgments.** We are indebted to Adi Shamir for insightful discussions and suggestions, and to Lev Pachmanov for writing much of the software setup used in our experiments. Ezra Shaked assisted in constructing and configuring the experimental setup. Assa Naveh assisted in various experiments, and offered valuable suggestions. Sharon Kessler provided copious editorial advice.

This work was sponsored by the Check Point Institute for Information Security; by European Union's Tenth Framework Programme (FP10/2010-2016) under grant agreement 259426 ERC-CaC, by the the Leona M. & Harry B. Helmsley Charitable Trust; by the Israeli Ministry of Science and Technology; by the Israeli Centers of Research Excellence I-CORE program (center 4/11); and by NATO's Public Diplomacy Division in the Framework of "Science for Peace".

# References

1. GNU multiple precision arithmetic library, http://gmplib.org/
2. The GNU Privacy Guard, http://www.gnupg.org
3. Agrawal, D., Archambeault, B., Rao, J.R., Rohatgi, P.: The EM side-channel(s). In: Kaliski Jr., B.S., Koç, Ç.K., Paar, C. (eds.) CHES 2002. LNCS, vol. 2523, pp. 29–45. Springer, Heidelberg (2003)
4. Anderson, R.J.: Security engineering — a guide to building dependable distributed systems, 2nd edn. Wiley (2008)
5. Brumley, D., Boneh, D.: Remote timing attacks are practical. Computer Networks 48(5), 701–716 (2005)
6. Clark, S.S., Mustafa, H., Ransford, B., Sorber, J., Fu, K., Xu, W.: Current events: Identifying webpages by tapping the electrical outlet. In: Crampton, J., Jajodia, S., Mayes, K. (eds.) ESORICS 2013. LNCS, vol. 8134, pp. 700–717. Springer, Heidelberg (2013)
7. Coppersmith, D.: Small solutions to polynomial equations, and low exponent RSA vulnerabilities. J. Cryptology 10(4), 233–260 (1997)
8. Courrège, J.-C., Feix, B., Roussellet, M.: Simple power analysis on exponentiation revisited. In: Gollmann, D., Lanet, J.-L., Iguchi-Cartigny, J. (eds.) CARDIS 2010. LNCS, vol. 6035, pp. 65–79. Springer, Heidelberg (2010)
9. Enigmail Project, T.: Enigmail: A simple interface for OpenPGP email security, https://www.enigmail.net
10. Gandolfi, K., Mourtel, C., Olivier, F.: Electromagnetic analysis: Concrete results. In: Koç, Ç.K., Naccache, D., Paar, C. (eds.) CHES 2001. LNCS, vol. 2162, pp. 251–261. Springer, Heidelberg (2001)
11. Genkin, D., Shamir, A., Tromer, E.: RSA key extraction via low-bandwidth acoustic cryptanalysis (extended version). IACR Cryptology ePrint Archive 2013, 857 (2013), extended version of [12]
12. Genkin, D., Shamir, A., Tromer, E.: RSA key extraction via low-bandwidth acoustic cryptanalysis. In: Garay, J.A., Gennaro, R. (eds.) CRYPTO 2014, Part I. LNCS, vol. 8616, pp. 444–461. Springer, Heidelberg (2014), See [11] for extended version

13. Hu, W.M.: Lattice scheduling and covert channels. In: Proceedings of the IEEE Symposium on Security and Privacy, pp. 52–61 (1992)
14. Karatsuba, A., Ofman, Y.: Multiplication of Many-Digital Numbers by Automatic Computers. Proceedings of the USSR Academy of Sciences 145, 293–294 (1962)
15. Kocher, P., Jaffe, J., Jun, B.: Differential power analysis. In: Wiener, M. (ed.) CRYPTO 1999. LNCS, vol. 1666, pp. 388–397. Springer, Heidelberg (1999)
16. Kocher, P., Jaffe, J., Jun, B., Rohatgi, P.: Introduction to differential power analysis. Journal of Cryptographic Engineering 1(1), 5–27 (2011)
17. Kuhn, M.G.: Compromising emanations: Eavesdropping risks of computer displays. PhD dissertation (2003)
18. Mangard, S., Oswald, E., Popp, T.: Power analysis attacks — revealing the secrets of smart cards. Springer (2007)
19. MITRE: Common vulnerabilities and exposures list, entry CVE-2013-4576 (2013), http://cve.mitre.org/cgi-bin/cvename.cgi?name=CVE-2013-4576
20. Oren, Y., Shamir, A.: How not to protect PCs from power analysis (2006), http://iss.oy.ne.ro/HowNotToProtectPCsFromPowerAnalysis, CRYPTO rump session
21. Quisquater, J.J., Samyde, D.: Electromagnetic analysis (EMA): Measures and counter-measures for smart cards. In: E-smart 2001, pp. 200–210 (2001)
22. Schmidt, J.-M., Plos, T., Kirschbaum, M., Hutter, M., Medwed, M., Herbst, C.: Side-channel leakage across borders. In: Gollmann, D., Lanet, J.-L., Iguchi-Cartigny, J. (eds.) CARDIS 2010. LNCS, vol. 6035, pp. 36–48. Springer, Heidelberg (2010)
23. Tokunaga, C., Blaauw, D.: Securing encryption systems with a switched capacitor current equalizer. IEEE Journal of Solid-State Circuits 45(1), 23–31 (2010)
24. Walter, C.D., Samyde, D.: Data dependent power use in multipliers. In: IEEE Symposium on Computer Arithmetic, pp. 4–12 (2005)
25. Yarom, Y., Falkner, K.E.: Flush+reload: a high resolution, low noise, L3 cache side-channel attack. IACR Cryptology ePrint Archive 2013, 448 (2013)
26. Yen, S.-M., Lien, W.-C., Moon, S.-J., Ha, J.: Power analysis by exploiting chosen message and internal collisions – vulnerability of checking mechanism for RSA-decryption. In: Dawson, E., Vaudenay, S. (eds.) Mycrypt 2005. LNCS, vol. 3715, pp. 183–195. Springer, Heidelberg (2005)
27. Zajic, A., Prvulovic, M.: Experimental demonstration of electromagnetic information leakage from modern processor-memory systems. IEEE Transactions on Electromagnetic Compatibility (to appear)

# RSA Meets DPA: Recovering RSA Secret Keys from Noisy Analog Data

Noboru Kunihiro and Junya Honda

The University of Tokyo, Japan
kunihiro@k.u-tokyo.ac.jp

**Abstract.** We discuss how to recover RSA secret keys from noisy analog data obtained through physical attacks such as cold boot and side channel attacks. Many studies have focused on recovering correct secret keys from noisy binary data. Obtaining noisy binary keys typically involves first observing the analog data and then obtaining the binary data through quantization process that discards much information pertaining to the correct keys. In this paper, we propose two algorithms for recovering correct secret keys from noisy analog data, which are generalized variants of Paterson et al.'s algorithm. Our algorithms fully exploit the analog information. More precisely, consider observed data which follows the Gaussian distribution with mean $(-1)^b$ and variance $\sigma^2$ for a secret key bit $b$. We propose a polynomial time algorithm based on the maximum likelihood approach and show that it can recover secret keys if $\sigma < 1.767$. The first algorithm works only if the noise distribution is explicitly known. The second algorithm does not need to know the explicit form of the noise distribution. We implement the first algorithm and verify its effectiveness.

**Keywords:** RSA, Key-Recovery, Cold Boot Attack, Side Channel Attack, Maximum Likelihood.

## 1 Introduction

### 1.1 Background and Motivation

Side channel attacks are important concerns for security analysis in the both of public key cryptography and symmetric cryptography. In the typical scenario of the side channel attacks, an attacker tries to recover the full secret key when he can measure some kind of leaked information from cryptographic devices. From the proposal of *Differential Power Analysis (DPA)* by Kocher et al. [6], many studies have been intensively made on the side channel attacks.

We focus on the side channel attacks on RSA cryptosystem. In the RSA cryptosystem [11], a public modulus $N$ is chosen as the product of two distinct primes $p$ and $q$. The key-pair $(e, d) \in \mathbb{Z}^2$ satisfies $ed \equiv 1 \pmod{(p-1)(q-1)}$. The encryption keys are $(N, e)$ and the decryption keys are $(N, d)$. The PKCS#1 standard [10] specifies that the RSA secret key includes $(p, q, d, d_p, d_q, q^{-1} \bmod p)$

L. Batina and M. Robshaw (Eds.): CHES 2014, LNCS 8731, pp. 261–278, 2014.

in addition to $d$, which allows for fast decryption using the Chinese Remainder Theorem. It is important to analyze its security as well as the original RSA.

Recently, the cold boot attack was proposed by Halderman et al. [3] at USENIX Security 2008. They demonstrated that DRAM remanence effects make possible practical, nondestructive attacks that recover a *noisy version of secret keys* stored in a computer's memory. They showed how to reconstruct the full of secret key from the noisy variants for some encryption schemes: DES, AES, tweakable encryption modes, and RSA. How can we recover the correct secret key from a noisy version of the secret key? This is an important question concerning the cold boot attack situation.

Inspired by cold boot attacks [3], much research has been carried on recovering an RSA secret key from a noisy version of the secret key. At Crypto 2009, Heninger and Shacham [5] proposed an algorithm that efficiently recovers secret keys $(p, q, d, d_p, d_q)$ given a random fraction of their bits. Concretely, they showed that if more than 27% of the secret key bits is leaked at random, the full secret key can be recovered. Conversely, this means that even if 73% of the correct secret bits is erased, the key can be recover. As opposed to the Heninger-Shacham algorithm for correcting erasures, Henecka et al. [4] proposed an algorithm for correcting error bits of secret keys at Crypto 2010. They showed that the secret key $(p, q, d, d_p, d_q)$ can be fully recovered if the error probability is less than 0.237. They also showed that the bound for the error probability is given by 0.084 if the associated secret key is $(p, q)$. Paterson et al. proposed an algorithm correcting error bits that occurs asymmetrically at Asiacrypt 2012 [9]. They adopted a coding theoretic approach for designing a new algorithm and analyzing its performance. Sarkar and Maitra [12] revisited the result of [4] and applied the Henecka et al.'s algorithm to break a Chinese Remainder Theorem type implementation of RSA with low weight decryption exponents. Kunihiro et al. [7] proposed an algorithm that generalized the work of [4,5], and which considered a combined erasure and error setting.

**Motivation: Key-Recovery from Noisy Analog Data.** The previous works [4,5,7,9] considered an erasure and/or error setting, where each bit of the secret key is either erased or flipped. Thus, the noisy version of the secret key is composed of discrete symbols, that is, $\{0, 1\}$ and the erasure symbol "?". However, such discrete data is not always obtained directly and analog data is more natural as observed data obtained through the actual physical attacks such as the cold boot and side channel attacks. We further assume that the observed data follows some fixed probability distributions. It is frequently considered and verified in the practice of side channel attacks (for details, see [8]). Thus, our leakage model is more realistic. Our goal is to propose efficient algorithms that can recover an RSA secret key from noisy analog data.

Paterson et al. [9] concluded that it is an open problem to generalize their approach to the case where soft information (that is, analog data) about the secret bits is available. This is the problem we address in this paper.

## 1.2    Our Contributions

This paper discusses secret key recovery from a noisy analog data sequence. In our leakage model, the observed value is output according to some fixed probability distribution depending on the corresponding correct secret key bit. Although we cannot directly obtain the true secret key bit, we can observe the noisy and analog variants of the secret key through a side channel or cold boot attack. If the noise is sufficiently small, key recovery from the noisy data is fairly easy in general. However, if the noise is large, the task of recovering the secret key becomes more difficult. Our challenge is to propose an efficient algorithm that recovers the RSA secret key even in the presence of large noise. For this purpose, we adopt a maximum likelihood-based approach.

First, we modify the algorithm of Paterson et al. [9] to adapt an analog data; while their algorithm takes a (noisy) binary bit sequence as input. For the modification, we introduce the concept of *score*; a node with a low score will be discarded, whereas a node with the highest score will be kept and generate a subtree of depth $t$ with $2^t$ leaf nodes. The score function is calculated from a candidate of the secret key in $\{0,1\}^{5t}$ and the corresponding observed data in $\mathbb{R}^{5t}$. The choice of score function is crucial for our modification.

We propose an algorithm whose score function is constructed from the likelihood ratio and in which the node with the maximal value is regarded as the correct node. We then prove that our algorithm recovers the correct secret key in polynomial time if the noise distribution satisfies a certain condition (Theorem 1). Note that the condition is represented by symmetric capacity. In particular, under the condition that the noise distribution is Gaussian with mean $(-1)^b$ and variance $\sigma^2$ for a secret key bit $b$, we show that we can recover the secret key if $\sigma < 1.767$ (Corollary 2).

The main drawback of the first algorithm is that we need to know the noise distribution exactly; indeed, without this knowledge it does not work. We also propose another algorithm that does not require any knowledge of noise distribution. The score function in the second algorithm is given as a difference between sums of the observed data when the candidate bits are 0 and that when the candidate bits are 1. This score is similar to that of differential power analysis (DPA) [6]. We also prove that the algorithm recovers the correct secret key with high probability if the noise distribution satisfies the certain condition (Theorems 2). Owing to the lack of knowledge of the noise distribution, the condition is slightly worse than that in the first algorithm. However, if the noise follows the Gaussian distribution, the algorithm achieves the same bound as the first one.

We then verify the effectiveness of our algorithm by numerical experiments in the case of Gaussian noise. Our experimental results show that the first algorithm recovers the RSA secret key with significant probability if $\sigma \leq 1.7$, which matches with theoretically predicted bound.

# 2    Preliminaries

This section presents an overview of the methods [4,5,9] using binary trees to recover the secret key of the RSA cryptosystem. We use similar notations to those in [4]. For an $n$-bit sequence $\mathbf{x} = (x_{n-1}, \ldots, x_0) \in \{0,1\}^n$, we denote the $i$-th bit of $\mathbf{x}$ by $x[i] = x_i$, where $x[0]$ is the least significant bit of $\mathbf{x}$. Let $\tau(M)$ denote the largest exponent such that $2^{\tau(M)} | M$. We denote by $\ln n$ the natural logarithm of $n$ to the base e and by $\log n$ the logarithm of $n$ to the base 2. We denote the expectation of random variable $X$ by $E[X]$.

## 2.1    Our Problem: RSA Key-Recovery from Analog Observed Data

Our problem is formulated as follows. We denote the correct secret key by $\mathbf{sk}$. For each bit in $\mathbf{sk}$, a value is observed from the probability distribution depending on the bit value, which means that the analog data are observed according to the leakage model. We denote the observed analog data sequence by $\bar{\mathbf{sk}}$. Our goal is to recover $\mathbf{sk}$ from $\bar{\mathbf{sk}}$.

We will give a more detailed explanation. Suppose that the probability distribution $F_x$ of the observed data is Gaussian with mean $(-1)^x$ and variance $\sigma^2$ for $x \in \{0,1\}$. The SNR is commonly used to evaluate the strength of noise is defined by (variance of signal)/(variance of noise). In our leakage model, the variance of the noise is given by $\sigma^2$ and that of signal is given by 1. Then, the SNR is given by $1/\sigma^2$. A greater SNR means that the signal is stronger and we can extract information with fewer errors. In this paper, we consider the standard deviation $\sigma$ for the strength of the noise.

Consider the case that noise level $\sigma$ is larger. In this case, key-recovery is difficult. In fact, if the noise is extremely large, we cannot recover the secret key, as is discussed in Section 6. Conversely, consider a smaller noise level. In this case, key recovery is relatively easy. Thus, it is important to make a detailed analysis for the value $\sigma$.

## 2.2    Recovering the RSA Secret Key Using a Binary Tree

The first half of explanation of this section is almost the same as previous works [4,5,7,9]. Making this paper self-contained, we give details. We review the key setting of the RSA cryptosystem [11], particular for the PKCS #1 standard [10]. Let $(N, e)$ be the RSA public key, where $N$ is an $n$-bit RSA modulus and $\mathbf{sk} = (p, q, d, d_p, d_q, q^{-1} \bmod p)$ be the RSA secret key. As in the previous works, we ignore the last component $q^{-1} \bmod p$ in the secret key. The public and secret keys have the following four equations:

$$N = pq, \ ed \equiv 1 \pmod{(p-1)(q-1)}, \ ed_p \equiv 1 \pmod{p-1}, \ ed_q \equiv 1 \pmod{q-1}.$$

There exist integers $k, k_p$ and $k_q$ such that

$$N = pq, \ ed = 1 + k(p-1)(q-1), \ ed_p = 1 + k_p(p-1), \ ed_q = 1 + k_q(q-1). \quad (1)$$

Suppose that we know the exact values of $k, k_p$ and $k_q$, then there are five unknowns $(p, q, d, d_p, d_q)$ in the four equations in Eq. (1).

A small public exponent $e$ is usually used in practical applications [15], so we suppose that $e$ is small enough such that $e = 2^{16} + 1$ as is the case in [4,5,7,9]. See [4] for how to compute $k, k_p$ and $k_q$.

In the previous methods and our new methods, a secret key **sk** is recovered by using a binary-tree-based technique. Here we explain how to recover secret keys, considering **sk** $= (p, q, d, d_p, d_q)$ as an example.

First we discuss the generation of the tree. Since $p$ and $q$ are $n/2$-bit prime numbers, there exist at most $2^{n/2}$ candidates for each secret key in $(p, q, d, d_p, d_q)$.

Heninger and Shacham [5] introduced the concept of *slice*. We define the $i$-th bit slice for each bit index $i$ as

$$\textbf{slice}(i) := (p[i], q[i], d[i + \tau(k)], d_p[i + \tau(k_p)], d_q[i + \tau(k_q)]).$$

Assume that we have computed a partial solution **sk**$' = (p', q', d', d_p', d_q')$ up to **slice**$(i - 1)$. Heninger and Shacham [5] applied Hensel's lemma to Eq. (1) and obtained the following equations

$$p[i] + q[i] = (N - p'q')[i] \bmod 2,$$
$$d[i + \tau(k)] + p[i] + q[i] = (k(N + 1) + 1 - k(p' + q') - ed')[i + \tau(k)] \bmod 2,$$
$$d_p[i + \tau(k_p)] + p[i] = (k_p(p' - 1) + 1 - ed_p')[i + \tau(k_p)] \bmod 2,$$
$$d_q[i + \tau(k_q)] + q[i] = (k_q(q' - 1) + 1 - ed_q')[i + \tau(k_q)] \bmod 2.$$

We can easily see that $p[i], q[i], d[i + \tau(k)], d_p[i + \tau(k_p)]$, and $d_q[i + \tau(k_q)]$ are not independent. Each Hensel lift, therefore, yields exactly two candidate solutions. Thus, the total number of candidates is given by $2^{n/2}$.

Henecka et al.'s algorithm (in short, the HMM algorithm) [4] and Paterson et al.'s algorithm (in short, the PPS algorithm) [9] perform $t$ Hensel lifts for some fixed parameter $t$. For each surviving candidate solution on **slice**(0) to **slice**$(it - 1)$, a tree with depth $t$ and whose $2^t$ leaf nodes represent candidate solutions on **slice**$(it)$ to **slice**$((i + 1)t - 1)$, is generated. This involves $5t$ new bits.

For each new node generated, a pruning phase is carried out. A solution is kept for the next iteration if the Hamming distance between the $5t$ new bits and the corresponding noisy variants of the secret key is less than some threshold as for the HMM algorithm or if the likelihood of the corresponding noisy variants of the secret key for the $5t$ new bits is the highest (or in the highest $L$ nodes) of the $2^t$ (or $L2^t$) nodes as for the PPS algorithm [9].

The main difference between the HMM and PPS algorithms is how to set the criterion determining whether a certain node is kept or discarded. We adopt a similar approach to the PPS algorithm [9] rather than the HMM algorithm [4]. In other words, we keep the top $L$ nodes with the highest likelihood rather than of the nodes with a lower Hamming distance than the fixed threshold.

# 3   Maximum Likelihood-Based Approach

## 3.1   Notation and Settings

We denote by $m$ the number of associated secret keys. For example, $m = 5$ if $\mathbf{sk} = (p, q, d, d_p, d_q)$, $m = 3$ if $\mathbf{sk} = (p, q, d)$, and $m = 2$ if $\mathbf{sk} = (p, q)$.

Let $\boldsymbol{x}_{1,a} \in \{0, 1\}^m$, $a \in \{1, 2\}$, be the $a$-th candidate of the first slice slice(0). We write the two candidates of the first $(i + 1)$ slices when the first $i$ slices are $\boldsymbol{x}_{i,a} = (\text{slice}(0), \cdots, \text{slice}(i-1))$ by $\boldsymbol{x}_{i+1,2a-1}$, $\boldsymbol{x}_{i+1,2a} \in \{0, 1\}^{m(i+1)}$.

For notational simplicity we write the $j$-th slice by $\boldsymbol{x}_{i,a}[j] \in \{0, 1\}^m$ and its $m$ elements are denoted by $\boldsymbol{x}_{i,a}[j][1], \boldsymbol{x}_{i,a}[j][2], \cdots, \boldsymbol{x}_{i,a}[j][m] \in \{0, 1\}$. Similarly, for a secret key sequence $\boldsymbol{x}_{i,a}$, the observed sequence is denoted by $\boldsymbol{y}_i \in \mathbb{R}^{mi}$ and its element corresponding to $\boldsymbol{x}_{i,a}[j][k]$ is denoted by $\boldsymbol{y}[j][k] \in \mathbb{R}$. We write the sequence of $j, j+1, \cdots, j'$-th elements of a vector $\boldsymbol{x}$ by $\boldsymbol{x}[j : j'] \in \{0, 1\}^{m(j'-j+1)}$ for $j' \geq j$. Therefore we have

$$\boldsymbol{x}_{i-1,a} = \boldsymbol{x}_{i,2a-1}[1 : i-1] = \boldsymbol{x}_{i,2a}[1 : i-1]. \tag{2}$$

Define $B_l(a) = \lceil a/2^l \rceil$. When we regard $\boldsymbol{x}_{i,a}$ as a node at depth $i$ of the binary tree, the node $\boldsymbol{x}_{i-l,B_l(a)}$ corresponds to the ancestor of $\boldsymbol{x}_{i,a}$ at depth $i - l$. Thus, the relation (2) is generalized to

$$\boldsymbol{x}_{i-l,B_l(a)} = \boldsymbol{x}_{i,a}[1 : i-l] = \boldsymbol{x}_{i,a'}[1 : i-l] \qquad \text{if } B_l(a) = B_l(a'). \tag{3}$$

We also write $\boldsymbol{x}^l$ for the last $l$ elements of a sequence $\boldsymbol{x}$, that is, we write $\boldsymbol{x}^l = \boldsymbol{x}[i - l + 1 : i]$ for $\boldsymbol{x} \in \{0, 1\}^{mi}$.

Now we introduce the assumption on the secret key.

**Assumption 1**

(i) Each $\boldsymbol{x}_{i,a}$ is a realization of a random variable $\boldsymbol{X}_{i,a}$ which is (marginally) distributed uniformly over $\{0, 1\}^{im}$.

(ii) There exists $c \geq 1$ satisfying the following: for any $i, l, a, a' \in \mathbb{Z}$ such that $c \leq l \leq i$ and $B_l(a) \neq B_l(a')$, a pair of two random variables $(\boldsymbol{X}_{i,a}^{l-c}, \boldsymbol{X}_{i,a'}^{l-c})$ is uniformly distributed over $\{0, 1\}^{2m(l-c)}$.

(iii) $\boldsymbol{X}_{i,2a-1}^1 \neq \boldsymbol{X}_{i,2a}^1$ holds almost surely for any $a$.

Assumptions (i) and (ii) correspond to *weak randomness assumption* considered in [9]. Assumption (iii) asserts that any pair of candidates of the key is not identical.

## 3.2   Generalized PPS Algorithm

Let $F_0$ and $F_1$ be probability distributions of an observed symbol when the correct secret key bits are 0 and 1, respectively. In the following algorithms we compare likelihood of each candidate of the secret key. We call a criterion for choice of candidates *score*. As the score we use the log-likelihood ratio given by

$$R_i(\boldsymbol{x};\boldsymbol{y}) = \sum_{j=1}^{i}\sum_{k=1}^{m} R(\boldsymbol{x}[j][k];\boldsymbol{y}[j][k]), \qquad \boldsymbol{x}\in\{0,1\}^{mi}, \boldsymbol{y}\in\mathbb{R}^{mi}$$

for a single-letter log-likelihood ratio

$$R(x;y) = \log\frac{\mathrm{d}F_x}{\mathrm{d}G}(y), \qquad x\in\{0,1\}, y\in\mathbb{R}, \tag{4}$$

where $G$ is the mixture distribution $(F_0 + F_1)/2$ and $\mathrm{d}F_x/\mathrm{d}G$ is the Radon-Nikodym's derivative. When $F_0$ and $F_1$ have probability densities $f_0$ and $f_1$, respectively, (4) is simply rewritten as

$$R(x;y) = \log\frac{f_x(y)}{g(y)}, \qquad x\in\{0,1\}, y\in\mathbb{R}, \tag{5}$$

where $g(y) = (f_0(y) + f_1(y))/2$. We use (4) for a definition of a score since (4) always exists even in the case of discrete noises, which are considered in preceding researches [4,5,7,9].

Let $X\in\{0,1\}$ be a random variable uniformly distributed over $\{0,1\}$. We define $Y\in\mathbb{R}$ as a random variable which follows distribution $F_X$ given $X$. The mutual information between $X$ and $Y$ is denoted by

$$I(X;Y) = \mathrm{E}[R(X;Y)].$$

*Remark 1.* $I(X;Y)$ is called a *symmetric capacity* for a channel $F_x$ and is generally smaller than the channel capacity for asymmetric cases. We show in Theorem 1 that $I(X;Y)$, rather than the channel capacity, appears in the asymptotic bound. This corresponds to the fact that in our problem the distribution of the input symbol (i.e., the secret key) is fixed to be uniform and cannot be designed freely.

Now we discuss the following algorithm, which is generalized variant of PPS algorithm proposed in [9]. Note that the original PPS algorithm deals with only discrete noises; while the generalized variant can deal with continuous noises. This algorithm maintains a list $\mathcal{L}_r$, $|\mathcal{L}_r| \le L$, of candidates of the first $tr$ bits of the secret key. We say that the recovery error occurred if the output $\mathcal{L}_{n/2t}$ does not contain the correct secret key. By abuse of notation each element of $\mathcal{L}_r$ denotes both a subsequence $\boldsymbol{x}_{tr,a}$ and its index $a$.

Now we bound the error probability of generalized PPS algorithm from above by the following theorem.

**Theorem 1.** Assume that

$$1/m < I(X;Y). \tag{6}$$

**Algorithm 1.** Generalized PPS Algorithm

**Input:** Public keys $(N, e)$, observed data sequences $\bar{\mathbf{s}\mathbf{k}}$
**Output:** Secret keys $\mathbf{sk}$.
**Parameter:** $t, L \in \mathbb{N}$.
**Initialization:** Set $\mathcal{L}_0 := \{1\}$.
**Loop:** For $r = 1, 2, \cdots, n/2t$ do the following.

1. **Expansion Phase** Generate list $\mathcal{L}'_r$ of all ancestors with depth $t$ from nodes in $\mathcal{L}_{r-1}$, that is,

$$\mathcal{L}'_r := \bigcup_{a \in \mathcal{L}_{r-1}} \{(a-1)2^t + 1, \ (a-1)2^t + 2, \cdots, a2^t\}.$$

2. **Pruning Phase** If $2^{tr} \leq L$ then set $\mathcal{L}_r := \mathcal{L}'_r$. Otherwise, set $\mathcal{L}_r$ to a subset of $\mathcal{L}'_r$ with size $L$ such that $R_{rt}(\mathbf{x}_{rt,a}; \mathbf{y}_{rt})$ are the largest so that for any $a \in \mathcal{L}_r$ and $a' \in \mathcal{L}'_r \setminus \mathcal{L}_r$

$$R_{rt}(\mathbf{x}_{rt,a}; \mathbf{y}_{rt}) \geq R_{rt}(\mathbf{x}_{rt,a'}; \mathbf{y}_{rt}).$$

Here the tie-breaking rule is arbitrary.

**Output of Loop:** List of candidates $\mathcal{L}_{n/2t}$.
**Finalization:** For each candidate in $\mathcal{L}_{n/2t}$, check whether the candidate is indeed a valid secret key with the help of public information.

Then, under generalized PPS algorithm it holds for any index $a$ and parameters $(t, L)$ that

$$\Pr[\mathbf{X}_{n/2,a} \notin \mathcal{L}_{n/2t} | \mathbf{X}_{n/2,a} \text{ is the correct secret key}] \leq \frac{n}{2t} \rho_1 L^{-\rho_2}. \tag{7}$$

for some $\rho_1, \rho_2 > 0$ which only depend on $c$, $m$ and $F_x$. Consequently, the error probability converges to zero as $L \to \infty$ for any $t > 0$.

The proof of Theorem 1 are given in the full version.

We evaluate the computational cost of generalized PPS algorithm. The costs of Expansion and Pruning phases in each loop are evaluated by $2L(2^t - 1)$ and $L2^t$. Since each phase is repeated $n/2t$ times, the whole cost of the Expansion phase and Pruning phase are given by $nL(2^t - 1)/t$ and $nL2^t/(2t)$, respectively.

This theorem shows that the error probability is bounded polynomially by $L$ and $t$. Here note that the RHS of (7) cannot go to to zero for fixed $L$ since $t \leq n/2$ is required, whereas it goes to zero[1] for any fixed $t$ as $L \to \infty$. Furthermore, the complexity grows exponentially in $t$ whereas it is linear in $L$. From these observations we can expect that the generalized PPS algorithm performs well for small $t$ and large $L$.

---

[1] In the theoretical analysis in [9], it seems to be implicitly assumed that the score of the first $mt(r-1)$ bits is discarded at each $r$-th loop, that is $R_{mt}(\mathbf{X}^t_{tr,i}; \mathbf{y}^t_{tr})$ is considered instead of $R_{mtr}(\mathbf{X}_{tr,i}; \mathbf{y}_{tr})$. In this case we require $t \to \infty$ to assure that the error probability approaches zero.

*Remark 2.* It is claimed in [9] for the case of binary observations that the error probability of PPS algorithm goes to zero as $t \to \infty$ for any fixed $L$ oppositely to the above argument. This gap does not mean that the bound (7) is loose but comes from an inappropriate argument in [9]. In fact, we can prove that the error probability never vanishes for any fixed $L$ as shown in Appendix A.

### 3.3 Implications: Continuous Distributions

Informally, Theorem 1 states that we can recover the secret key with high probability if $I(X;Y) > 1/m$. The actual values of $I(X;Y)$ depends on the distribution $F_x$. We evaluate the value of $I(X;Y)$ for some continuous distribution $F_x$ which has density $f_x(y)$.

First, we introduce a differential entropy.

**Definition 1.** The differential entropy $h(f)$ of a probability density function $f$ is defined as

$$h(f) = -\int_{-\infty}^{\infty} f(y) \log f(y) dy.$$

We give some properties of the differential entropy [1]. Let $f$ be an arbitrary probability density with mean $\mu$ and variance $\sigma^2$. Then it is shown in [1, Theorem 8.6.5] that

$$h(f) \leq h(\mathcal{N}(\mu, \sigma^2)) = \log \sqrt{2\pi e \sigma^2}, \tag{8}$$

where $\mathcal{N}(\mu, \sigma^2)$ is the density of Gaussian distribution with mean $\mu$ and variance $\sigma^2$.

The symmetric capacity $I(X;Y)$ can be expressed as $h(g) - (h(f_0) + h(f_1))/2$ for $g(y) = (f_0(y) + f_1(y))/2$ since

$$I(X;Y) = \sum_{x \in \{0,1\}} \int \frac{f_x(y)}{2} \log \frac{f_x(y)}{\sum_{x' \in \{0,1\}} \frac{f_{x'}(y)}{2}} dy = \sum_{x \in \{0,1\}} \int \frac{f_x(y)}{2} \log \frac{f_x(y)}{g(y)} dy$$

$$= \sum_{x \in \{0,1\}} \int \frac{f_x(y)}{2} \log f_x(y) dy - \int g(y) \log g(y) dy = h(g) - \frac{h(f_0) + h(f_1)}{2}.$$

Next, we further assume that the distributions are symmetric: $f_1(y) = f_0(\alpha - y)$ for some $\alpha$. Since the differential entropy is invariant under translation, we have $h(f_1) = h(f_0)$ and thus $I(X;Y) = h(g) - h(f_0)$ if the distributions are symmetric. A typical example of the symmetric distribution is *symmetric additive noise*: the sample can be written as the sum of a deterministic part and a symmetric random noise part.

Summing up the above discussion, we have the following corollary.

**Corollary 1.** Assume that $F_x$ has a probability density $f_x$. Then the error probability of generalized PPS algorithm converges to zero as $L \to \infty$ if

$$h(g) - \frac{h(f_0) + h(f_1)}{2} > \frac{1}{m}.$$

Further assume that the $f_0(y)$ and $f_1(y)$ are symmetric. In this case, the condition is expressed as $h(g) - h(f_0) > 1/m$.

**Gaussian Distribution.** We remind readers of the Gaussian distribution $\mathcal{N}(\mu, \sigma^2)$. The density function of this distribution is $f(x) = \frac{1}{\sqrt{2\pi\sigma^2}}$ $\exp\left(-\frac{(x-\mu)^2}{2\sigma^2}\right)$, where $\mu$ and $\sigma^2$ are the mean and variance of the distribution, respectively.

The most standard setting of a continuous noise is an additive white Gaussian noise (AWGN): the density $f_x$ of distribution $F_x$ is represented by

$$f_x(y) = \frac{1}{\sqrt{2\pi\sigma^2}} \exp\left(-\frac{(y-(-1)^x)^2}{2\sigma^2}\right). \tag{9}$$

Note that the expectation of $f_0(x)$ and $f_1(x)$ are $+1$ and $-1$, respectively. In this case the score is represented by

$$R_i(\boldsymbol{x}; \boldsymbol{y}) = \sum_{j=1}^{i} \sum_{k=1}^{m} \frac{(-1)^{\boldsymbol{x}[j][k]} \boldsymbol{y}[j][k]}{2(\ln 2)\sigma^2}$$

$$- \sum_{j=1}^{i} \sum_{k=1}^{m} \left( \frac{\boldsymbol{y}[j][k]^2 + 1}{2(\ln 2)\sigma^2} + \log \frac{\exp(-\frac{(\boldsymbol{y}[j][k]-1)^2}{2\sigma^2}) + \exp(-\frac{(\boldsymbol{y}[j][k]+1)^2}{2\sigma^2})}{2} \right). \tag{10}$$

The symmetric capacity for $F_x$ is given by

$$I(X; Y) - h(g) - h(f_0) = h(g) - \log\sqrt{2\pi e\sigma^2}. \tag{11}$$

It is equivalent to use a score

$$\sum_{j=1}^{i} \sum_{k=1}^{m} (-1)^{\boldsymbol{x}[j][k]} \boldsymbol{y}[j][k] \tag{12}$$

instead of (10) in generalized PPS algorithm since the factor $(2(\ln 2)\sigma^2)^{-1}$ and the second term of (10) are common to all candidates $\boldsymbol{x}_{i,a}$.

The following corollary is straightforward from the computation of $I(X; Y)$ for the Gaussian case.

**Corollary 2.** Assume that $f_x$ is the Gaussian distribution given in Eq. (9). Then the error probability of generalized PPS algorithm converges to zero as $L \to \infty$ if $\sigma < 1.767$ when $m = 5$ and if $\sigma < 1.297$ when $m = 3$ and if $\sigma < 0.979$ when $m = 2$.

*Proof.* Regarding $h(f)$, we have $h(f) = \log\sqrt{2\pi e\sigma^2}$ from (8). The differential entropy $h(g)$ of the mixture distribution $g$ is not given in explicit form but numerical calculation shows that $h(g) - h(f) = 1/5, 1/3, 1/2$ for $\sigma = 1.767, 1.297, 0.979$, respectively. Thus the corollary follows immediately from (11) and Theorem 1.

$\square$

### 3.4    Implications: Discrete Distribution

Next, we discuss the discrete distribution cases. As an example, we consider the binary symmetric error. In the case that $F_x$ is a discrete distribution on $\{0, 1\}$ such that

$$
\begin{cases}
F_0(\{0\}) = F_1(\{1\}) = 1 - p\,, \\
F_0(\{1\}) = F_1(\{0\}) = p\,,
\end{cases}
$$

for some $0 < p < 1/2$, we have

$$
R_i(\boldsymbol{x}; \boldsymbol{y}) = mi \log(2(1-p)) + d_{\mathrm{H}}(\boldsymbol{x}, \boldsymbol{y}) \log \frac{p}{1-p}\,, \boldsymbol{x} \in \{0, 1\}^{mi}, \boldsymbol{y} \in \mathbb{R}^{mi}\,, \quad (13)
$$

where $d_{\mathrm{H}}(\boldsymbol{x}, \boldsymbol{y})$ is the Hamming distance between $\boldsymbol{x}$ and $\boldsymbol{y}$. Note that it is equivalent to use a score $d_{\mathrm{H}}(\boldsymbol{x}; \boldsymbol{y})$ instead of (13) in generalized PPS algorithm since the factor $mi \log(p/(1-p))$ and the constant $\log(2(1-p))$ are common to all candidates $\boldsymbol{x}_{i,a}$ and do not change the order of scores.

In this case the capacity is given by $I(X; Y) = 1 - h_2(p)$ for the binary entropy function $h_2(p) = -p \log p - (1-p) \log(1-p)$.

### 3.5    Discussion: Comparison with Quantization-Based Approach

The simplest algorithm for our key-recovery problem would be a quantization-based algorithm. Here, we focus on the AWGN setting introduced in Section 3.3. First, we consider the following simple quantization. If the observed value is positive, its corresponding bit is converted to 0 and if it is negative, it is converted to 1. Then, the binary sequence of the secret key with error is obtained by quantization. The HMM algorithm [4] is applied to the obtained noisy secret key sequences. A simple calculation shows that we can recover the secret key if the noise follows the Gaussian distribution and $\sigma < 1.397$ when $m = 5$.

Next, we consider a more clever quantization rule, which uses the "erasure symbol". Let $D$ be a positive threshold; then the quantization rule is given as follows. The corresponding is converted to 0 if $x \geq D$; 1 if $x < -D$; "?" if $-D \leq x < D$. The binary sequence of the secret key with error and erasure is obtained by quantization. Kunihiro et al.'s algorithm [7] is applied to the obtained noisy secret key sequences. A simple calculation shows that we can recover the secret key if the noise follows the Gaussian distribution and $\sigma < 1.533$ when $m = 5$ under optimally chosen $D$.

As shown in Corollary 2, our proposed algorithm works well if $\sigma < 1.767$ when $m = 5$ and is significantly superior to the quantization-based algorithms. The reason for this is that generalized PPS algorithm uses all the information of the observed data whereas the quantization-based algorithms ignore the value of observed data after quantization and thus suffer from quantization errors. A consequence is that we can improve the bound of $\sigma$.

# 4    DPA-Like Algorithm: Unknown Distribution Case

The generalized PPS algorithm works only if the explicit form of $F_x$ is known since it is needed in the calculation of $R_{rt}(x_{rt,a}; y_{rt})$. However, in many actual attack situations, the explicit form of noise distribution is not known. In this section, we propose an effective algorithm that works well even if these explicit forms are unknown.

## 4.1    DPA-Like Algorithm

Consider the case that we only know the expectation of $F_0$ and $F_1$, which we assume without loss of generality to be $+1$ and $-1$, respectively. In this case it is natural to use (12) as a score from the viewpoint of DPA analysis [6] instead of $R_{mi}(x, y)$ itself. We define DPA function as follows.

$$\mathbf{DPA}_{mi}(x; y) := \sum_{j=1}^{i} \sum_{k=1}^{m} (-1)^{x[j][k]} y[j][k]. \tag{14}$$

Note that this score can be calculated without knowledge of the specific form of the noise distribution. In the case that $\mathbf{DPA}_{mi}$ is used as a score, the bound in Theorem 1 is no more achievable for distributions other than Gaussians but a similar bound can still be established.

**Theorem 2.** Assume that $F_x$ has a probability density $f_x$. Under generalized PPS algorithm with score function (14) the error probability converges to zero as $L \to \infty$ if

$$\frac{1}{m} < h(g) - \log \sqrt{\pi e(\sigma_0^2 + \sigma_1^2)},$$

where $g(y) = (f_0(y) + f_1(y))/2$ and $\sigma_x^2 = \mathrm{Var}(f_x)$ is the variance of distribution $f_x$.

The proof of Theorem 2 is almost the same as that of Theorem 1 and given in the full version.

Note that $I(X; Y)$ can be expressed as $h(g) - (h(f_0) + h(f_1))/2$. Thus, in view of Theorems 1 and 2, information loss of the score (14) can be expressed as $\log \sqrt{\pi e(\sigma_0^2 + \sigma_1^2)} - (h(f_0) + h(f_1))/2$, which is always nonnegative since

$$\log \sqrt{\pi e(\sigma_0^2 + \sigma_1^2)} - \frac{h(f_0) + h(f_1)}{2} \geq \log \sqrt{\pi e(\sigma_0^2 + \sigma_1^2)} - \frac{\log \sqrt{2\pi e\sigma_0^2} + \log \sqrt{2\pi e\sigma_1^2}}{2}$$

$$\geq 0,$$

where the first and second inequalities follow from (8) and from the concavity of the log function, respectively. This loss becomes zero if and only if $f_0$ and $f_1$ are Gaussians with the same variances.

Further assume that $f_0$ and $f_1$ are symmetric. In this case, it holds that $\sigma_1^2 = \sigma_0^2$ and $h(f_1) = h(f_0)$. Thus information loss of the score (14) can be expressed as $\log \sqrt{2\pi e\sigma_0^2} - h(f_0) = h(\mathcal{N}(0, \sigma_0^2)) - h(f_0)$, which increases as the true noise distribution deviates from Gaussian.

*Remark 3.* We need not to know the expectation of $F_0$ and $F_1$ in practice. To proceed the argument in this section it is sufficient to know the intermediate value of these expectations, that is, the expectation of $G = (F_0 + F_1)/2$. Since it is the expectation of the observed values, we can estimated it accurately by averaging all the elements of the observation $y$.

## 4.2   Connection to DPA

We briefly review DPA. It was proposed as a side channel attack against DES by Kocher et al. [6] and was then generalized to other common secret key encryption. It derives the secret key from many physically measured waveforms of power consumption. They introduced the DPA selection function whose input includes a guessed secret key. In attacking phase, an attacker guesses the secret key and calculate the difference between the average of the waveforms of power consumption for which the value of the DPA selection function is one and it is zero. If the guess is incorrect, the waveforms are cancelled since they are uncorrelated. Then, the resulting waveform becomes flat. However, if the guess is correct, they are correlated and the resulting waveform has spikes. By observing the difference, we can find the correct key.

We introduce two sets: $\mathcal{S}_1 = \{(j,k)|x[j][k] = 1\}$ and $\mathcal{S}_0 = \{(j,k)|x[j][k] = 0\}$. The function **DPA** can be transformed as follows:

$$\mathbf{DPA}_{mi}(x; y) = \sum_{(j,k)\in\mathcal{S}_0} y[j][k] - \sum_{(j,k)\in\mathcal{S}_1} y[j][k],$$

which is similar to the DPA selection function used in DPA [6].

We give an intuitive explanation of how the algorithm works. Without loss of generality, we assume that $\mathrm{E}(f_0) = +1$ and $\mathrm{E}(f_1) = -1$. We consider two cases that the candidate solution is correct and incorrect in the following. First, assume that the candidate solution is correct. If the bit in the candidate solution is 0, the observed value follows $f_0(y)$; if it is 1, the observed value follows $f_1(y)$ and then the negative of the observed value can be seen to be output according to $f_1(-y)$. The means of both $f_0(y)$ and $f_1(-y)$ are $+1$. Hence, the expectation of Eq. (14) is $mi$ if the candidate solution is correct. Hence, the score calculated by Eq. (14) is close to $mi$ with high probability. Second, Next, assume that the candidate solution is incorrect. In this case, the observed value is output according to the mixture distribution $g(y) = (f_1(y) + f_0(y))/2$ which has zero mean. Hence, the expectation of Eq. (14) is 0 if the the candidate solution is incorrect and the score calculated by Eq. (14) is close to 0 with high probability. Thus, if the score is high enough (that is, the score is around $mi$), the estimation is correct, whereas if the score is low enough (that is, the score is around 0), the estimation is incorrect and such a node will be discarded. We give a toy example on the function **DPA** in Appendix B for a better understanding.

## 4.3   Connection to Communication Theory

The problem of RSA secret key recovery is strongly related to the communication theory. Each candidate of the secret key corresponds to a codeword of a message and the attacker corresponds to the receiver trying to estimate the message from the sent codeword distorted by noise. The key estimation after quantization process in [4,5,7,9] is called a hard-decision decoding and the proposed algorithm exploiting full information of the observed data is called a soft-decision decoding.

The structure of the secret key characterized by Hensel lift can be regarded as a convolutional code with infinite constraint length. It is known that Viterbi algorithm works successfully for convolutional codes with small constraint length and many algorithms such as Fano algorithm and stack algorithm have been proposed for codes with large constraint length [13,14]. Thus one can expect that these algorithms for large constraint length perform well also for the problem of secret key recovery.

However there also exists a gap between the settings of the secret key recovery and the communication theory. In the case of message transmission, the noise ratio is set to be relatively small because the error probability has to be negligibly small value, say, e.g., $10^{-8}$. On the other hand when we consider security of the secret key, 10% success rate of the recovery is critical and we have to consider the success probability under large noise ratio. For this gap it is not obvious whether the above algorithms work successfully for the secret key recovery.

## 5    Implementation and Experiments

We have implemented generalized PPS algorithm. In our experiments on $1024, 2048$-bit RSA, we prepared 100 (or 200 if the success rate is less than 0.1) different tuples of secret keys $\mathbf{sk}$, e.g., $\mathbf{sk} = (p, q, d, d_p, d_q)$. We generated the Gaussian noisy output $\overline{\mathbf{sk}}$ for each $\mathbf{sk}$. In our experiments, the incorrect candidate solution is randomly generated based on Assumption 1 with $c = 1$.

The experimental results for $n = 1024$ and $\mathbf{sk} = (p, q, d, d_p, d_q)$ are shown in Figure 1. We set $(t, L) = (1, 2^{11}), (2, 2^{11}), (4, 2^{10}), (8, 2^7), (16, 2^0)$, which makes the computational cost for Pruning phase to be equal: $2^{21}$.

As can be seen in Figure 1, if $\sigma \leq 1.3$, the success rate for small $t$ (say, $t = 1, 2, 4$) is almost 1. Generalized PPS algorithm can succeed to recover the correct secret key with probability larger than 0.1 for $\sigma \leq 1.7$; while it almost fails to recover the key for $\sigma \geq 1.8$. This results match with theoretically predicted bound $\sigma = 1.767$. Figure 1 also shows generalized PPS algorithm fails with high probability if we use a small $L$, (say $L = 1$); while the computational cost is almost the same as the setting $(t, L) = (1, 2^{11})$. This fact is reinforced by Theorem 3 shown in Appendix A.

Figure 1 suggests that the setting $t = 1$ is enough for gaining high success rates. We then present experimental results for $t = 1$ and $n = 1024, 2048$ in Figures 2 and 3. Figures 2 and 3 show that the success rates for any $n$ and $\sigma$ will significantly increase if we use a larger list size $L$. For each bit size $n$, generalized PPS algorithm almost always succeed to find the secret key if $\sigma \leq 1.3$. The generalized PPS algorithm still has a non-zero success rate for $\sigma$ as large as 1.7.

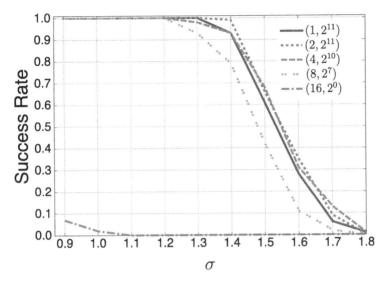

**Fig. 1.** Experiments for $\mathbf{sk} = (p, q, d, d_p, d_q)$, $n = 1024$

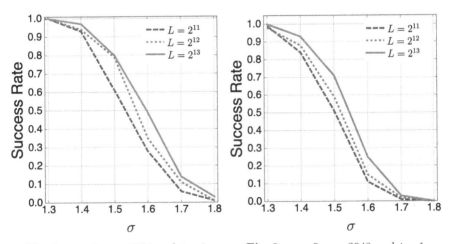

**Fig. 2.** $m = 5$, $n = 1024$ and $t = 1$      **Fig. 3.** $m = 5$, $n = 2048$ and $t = 1$

In communication theory, there are many techniques such as stack algorithm [13]. We do not implement such techniques in our experiments. It is possible to increase the success rate if we implement them together in our algorithm.

# 6 Concluding Remarks

In this paper, we showed that we can recover the secret key if Eq. (6) holds; the symmetric capacity $I(X;Y)$ is larger than $1/m$. As mentioned in [9], the success condition for key-recovery from noisy secret keys has a strong connection to channel capacity. As explained in Remark 1, symmetric capacity is less than channel capacity for asymmetric distribution cases. Hence, one might wonder if the condition can be improved. Unfortunately, it is hopeless to improve the bound since the distribution of input symbol (i.e., the correct secret key) is fixed to uniform in our problem whereas the input distribution is optimized to achieve the channel capacity in coding theory. Then, from the coding theoretic viewpoint, the condition $I(X;Y) > 1/m$ is optimal for our problem.

**Acknowledgement.** The first author was supported by JSPS Grant Number KAKENHI 25280001.

# References

1. Cover, C.M., Thomas, J.A.: Elements of Information Theory, 2nd edn. Wiley-Interscience (2006)
2. Dembo, A., Zeitouni, O.: Large deviations techniques and applications, 2nd edn. Applications of Mathematics, vol. 38. Springer, New York (1998)
3. Halderman, J.A., Schoen, S.D., Heninger, N., Clarkson, W., Paul, W., Calandrino, J.A., Feldman, A.J., Appelbaum, J., Felten, E.W.: Lest We Remember: Cold Boot Attacks on Encryption Keys. In: Proc. of USENIX Security Symposium 2008, pp. 45–60 (2008)
4. Henecka, W., May, A., Meurer, A.: Correcting Errors in RSA Private Keys. In: Rabin, T. (ed.) CRYPTO 2010. LNCS, vol. 6223, pp. 351–369. Springer, Heidelberg (2010)
5. Heninger, N., Shacham, H.: Reconstructing RSA Private Keys from Random Key Bits. In: Halevi, S. (ed.) CRYPTO 2009. LNCS, vol. 5677, pp. 1–17. Springer, Heidelberg (2009)
6. Kocher, P., Jaffe, J., Jun, B.: Differential Power Analysis. In: Wiener, M. (ed.) CRYPTO 1999. LNCS, vol. 1666, pp. 388–397. Springer, Heidelberg (1999)
7. Kunihiro, N., Shinohara, N., Izu, T.: Recovering RSA Secret Keys from Noisy Key Bits with Erasures and Errors. In: Kurosawa, K., Hanaoka, G. (eds.) PKC 2013. LNCS, vol. 7778, pp. 180–197. Springer, Heidelberg (2013)
8. Mangard, S., Oswald, E., Standaert, F.-X.: One for all - all for one: unifying standard differential power analysis attacks. IET Information Security 5(2), 100–110 (2011)
9. Paterson, K.G., Polychroniadou, A., Sibborn, D.L.: A Coding-Theoretic Approach to Recovering Noisy RSA Keys. In: Wang, X., Sako, K. (eds.) ASIACRYPT 2012. LNCS, vol. 7658, pp. 386–403. Springer, Heidelberg (2012)
10. PKCS #1 Standard for RSA, http://www.rsa.com/rsalabs/node.asp?id=2125
11. Rivest, R., Shamir, A., Adleman, L.: A Method for Obtaining Digital Signatures and Public-Key Cryptosystems. Communications of the ACM 21(2), 120–126 (1978)
12. Sarkar, S., Maitra, S.: Side Channel Attack to Actual Cryptanalysis: Breaking CRT-RSA with Low Weight Decryption Exponents. In: Prouff, E., Schaumont, P. (eds.) CHES 2012. LNCS, vol. 7428, pp. 476–493. Springer, Heidelberg (2012)
13. Schlegel, C., Perez, L.: Trellis and Turbo Codes. Wiley-IEEE Press (2004)

14. Sklar, B.: Digital Communications: Fundamentals and Applications, 2nd edn. Prentice Hall (2001)
15. Yilek, S., Rescorla, E., Shacham, H., Enright, B., Savage, S.: When Private Keys are Public: Results from the 2008 Debian OpenSSL Vulnerability. In: IMC 2009, pp. 15–27. ACM Press (2009)

# A    Lower Bound on Error Probability of Generalized PPS Algorithm

As mentioned in Remark 2, the upper bound (7) on the error probability of PPS algorithm cannot go to zero for fixed $L$ even though it is claimed in [9] that the error probability vanishes as $t$ increases for any fixed $L$. We show in this appendix that $L \to \infty$ is actually necessary to achieve an arbitrary small error probability.

Let $p_e = \Pr[R(1 - X; Y) > R(X; Y)]$ be the single-letter error probability under decoding $\hat{X} := \mathrm{argmax}_{x \in \{0,1\}}\{R(x; Y)\}$. Note that $p_e = 0$ is a degraded case in which each bit $X$ can be recovered from $Y$ without error by the above decoding rule. We can bound the error probability of PPS algorithm from below in a simple form by using $p_e$.

**Theorem 3.** Under generalized PPS algorithm it holds for any index $a$ and parameters $(t, L)$ that

$$\Pr[\boldsymbol{X}_{n/2,a} \notin \mathcal{L}_{n/2t} | \boldsymbol{X}_{n/2,a} \text{ is the correct secret key}] \geq p_e^{m(1+\log L)} . \quad (15)$$

Consequently, the error probability does not go to zero as $t \to \infty$ with a fixed $L$ if $p_e > 0$.

We can easily see that the error probability does not vanish for a fixed $L$ by the following argument. For simplicity let us consider the case that the correct secret key is $\boldsymbol{X}_{n/2,1}$. Then the candidate $\boldsymbol{X}_{n/2,2}$ is identical to the correct key except for the last $m$ bits. Similarly, $\boldsymbol{X}_{n/2,3}$ and $\boldsymbol{X}_{n/2,4}$ are identical to the correct key except for the last $2m$ bits. Thus, once the last $2m$ observed symbols $\boldsymbol{y}_{n/2}^2$ become very noisy (the probability of this event does not depend on $t$) then the likelihood of $\boldsymbol{X}_{n/2,b}$ for $b = 2, 3, 4$ exceeds that of the correct key $\boldsymbol{X}_{n/2,1}$, and the recovery error occurs when the list size is $L \leq 3$. This argument always holds when the list size $L$ is fixed and we see that the error probability heavily depends on $L$.

*Proof of Theorem 3.* Recall that $l_t = \lfloor (\log L)/t \rfloor + 1$. Since $\boldsymbol{X}_{n/2,1} \in \mathcal{L}_{n/2t}$ implies $\boldsymbol{X}_{n/2,1}[1 : tl_t] = \boldsymbol{X}_{tl_t,1} \in \mathcal{L}_{l_t}$, we have

$$\Pr[\boldsymbol{X}_{n/2,1} \notin \mathcal{L}_{n/2t}] \geq \Pr[\boldsymbol{X}_{tl_t,1} \notin \mathcal{L}_{l_t}]$$

$$\geq \Pr\left[\sum_{a=2}^{2^{tl_t}} \mathbf{1}\left[R_{tl_t}(\boldsymbol{X}_{tl_t,a}; \boldsymbol{Y}_{tl_t}) > R_{tl_t}(\boldsymbol{X}_{tl_t,1}; \boldsymbol{Y}_{tl_t})\right] \geq L\right] .$$

For $\bar{l} = \lfloor \log L \rfloor + 1$, we have $\bar{l} \le tl_t$ and

$$\Pr[X_{n/2,1} \notin \mathcal{L}_{n/2t}] \ge \Pr\left[\sum_{a=2}^{2^{\bar{l}}} \mathbf{1}\,[R_{tl_t}(X_{tl_t,a}; Y_{tl_t}) > R_{tl_t}(X_{tl_t,1}; Y_{tl_t})] \ge L\right]$$

$$= \Pr\left[\sum_{a=2}^{2^{\bar{l}}} \mathbf{1}\left[R_{\bar{l}}(X_{tl_t,a}^{\bar{l}}; Y_{tl_t}^{\bar{l}}) > R_{tl_t}(X_{tl_t,1}^{\bar{l}}; Y_{tl_t}^{\bar{l}})\right] \ge L\right] \qquad \text{(by (3))}$$

$$\ge \Pr\left[\sum_{a=2}^{2^{\bar{l}}} \mathbf{1}\left[R_{\bar{l}}(X_{tl_t,a}^{\bar{l}}; Y_{tl_t}^{\bar{l}}) > R_{tl_t}(X_{tl_t,1}^{\bar{l}}; Y_{tl_t}^{\bar{l}})\right] = 2^{\bar{l}} - 1\right] . \quad (16)$$

Now consider the case that $R(1 - X_{tl_t,1}[j][k]; Y_{tl_t}[j][k]) > R(X_{tl_t,1}[j][k]; Y_{tl_t}[j][k])$ for all $j = tl_t - \bar{l} + 1, \cdots, tl_t$ and $k = 1, \cdots, m$. Then $R_{\bar{l}}(x; Y_{tl_t}^{\bar{l}}) > R_{\bar{l}}(X_{tl_t,1}^{\bar{l}}; Y_{tl_t}^{\bar{l}})$ for all $x \ne X_{tl_t,1}^{\bar{l}}$. As a result, (16) is bounded as

$$\Pr[X_{n/2,1} \notin \mathcal{L}_{n/2t}]$$

$$\ge \Pr\left[\bigcap_{j=tl_t-\bar{l}+1}^{tl_t} \bigcap_{k=1}^{m} \{R(1 - X_{tl_t,1}[j][k]; Y_{tl_t}[j][k]) > R(X_{tl_t,1}[j][k]; Y_{tl_t}[j][k])\}\right]$$

$$= p_{\mathrm{e}}^{m\bar{l}} \ge p_{\mathrm{e}}^{m(1+\log L)} .$$

and we complete the proof.

*Remark 4.* In the theoretical analysis of Peterson et al. [9], they compared scores between the correct secret key and a subset of $\mathcal{L}'_r$ with size $L$ randomly chosen from $\mathcal{L}'$. However, in the actual algorithm all elements of $\mathcal{L}'_r$ are scanned and such an analysis based on the random choice does not have validity, which led to the conclusion contradicting Theorem 3.

# B    A Toy Example for Generalized PPS Algorithm with (14)

To better understand the algorithm, we present a toy example. Suppose that the correct solution is 1100010011 and that we observed the data sequence as $y = (-3, -2, +2, +3, +3, -3, +1, +4, -3, -2)$. Attackers know the observed data; but, do not know the correct solution. Assume that we know $\mathrm{E}(f_0) = 3$ and $\mathrm{E}(f_1) = -3$. Suppose that we have three candidate sequences: $x_1 = (1100010011)$, $x_2 = (1001110010)$ and $x_3 = (0101011001)$.

The score for $x_1 = (110001001)$ is given by $\mathbf{DPA}(x_1; y) = 3 + 2 + 2 + 3 + 3 + 3 + 1 + 4 + 3 + 2 = 26$. Since the value 26 is close to $3 \times 10 = 30$, the candidate seems to be correct.

The score for $x_2 = (1001110010)$ is given by $\mathbf{DPA}(x_2; y) = 3 - 2 + 2 - 3 - 3 + 3 + 1 + 4 + 3 - 2 = 6$. The value 6 is close to 0. The score for $x_3 = (0101011001)$ is given by $\mathbf{DPA}(x_3; y) = -3 + 2 + 2 - 3 + 3 + 3 - 1 + 4 - 3 + 2 = 2$. The value 2 is close to 0. Thus these candidates seem to be incorrect.

# Simple Power Analysis on AES
# Key Expansion Revisited

Christophe Clavier, Damien Marion, and Antoine Wurcker

Université de Limoges, XLIM-CNRS
Limoges, France
{christophe.clavier,damien.marion}@unilim.fr,
antoine.wurcker@xlim.fr

**Abstract.** We consider a simple power analysis on an 8-bit software implementation of the AES key expansion. Assuming that an attacker is able to observe the Hamming weights of the key bytes generated by the key expansion, previous works from Mangard and from VanLaven et al. showed how to exploit this information to recover the key from unprotected implementations.

Our contribution considers several possible countermeasures that are commonly used to protect the encryption process and may well be adopted to protect the computation and/or the manipulation of round keys from this attack. We study two different Boolean masking countermeasures and present efficient attacks against both of them. We also study a third countermeasure based on the computation of the key expansion in a shuffled order. We show that it is also possible to attack this countermeasure by exploiting the side-channel leakage only. As this last attack requires a not negligible computation effort, we also propose a passive and active combined attack (PACA) where faults injected during the key expansion are analyzed to derive information that render the side-channel analysis more efficient. These results put a new light on the (in-)security of implementations of the key expansion with respect to SPA.

As a side contribution of this paper, we also investigate the open question whether two different ciphering keys may be undistinguishable in the sense that they have exactly the same set of expanded key bytes Hamming weights. We think that this problem is of theoretical interest as being related to the quality of the diffusion process in the AES key expansion. We answer positively to this open question by devising a constructive method that exhibits many examples of such ambiguous observations.

**Keywords:** side-channel analysis, simple power analysis, passive and active combined attacks, AES key expansion.

## 1 Introduction

Side channel analysis is an effective means to derive secrets stored in a security device like a smart card from measurements of a leaking physical signal

L. Batina and M. Robshaw (Eds.): CHES 2014, LNCS 8731, pp. 279–297, 2014.

such as the execution duration, the power consumption or the electromagnetic emanation. Since the first publication of a timing attack by Kocher [6] many side-channel analysis methods have been presented that exploit a large number of leakage traces by a statistical method: Differential Power Analysis [7], Correlation Power Analysis [2], Mutual Information Analysis [4] and Template Analysis [3] are few such well known methods.

Simple Power Analysis (SPA) also permits to infer information in a more direct manner by "visually" inspecting a single (in the most favorable cases) trace. Two kinds of information can be retrieved by SPA. At a high level it allows to recognize different instructions or blocks of instructions that are executed on the device. This capability is typically exploited either to recover a sequence of arithmetic operations of a modular exponentiation used in public key cryptography, or for a rough reverse engineering and/or a first characterization phase of an implementation or of the leakage behavior of the device. At a lower level SPA informs about the values of the operands involved in each elementary instruction particularly for load and store operations when this data is read from or written to the bus. The dependency between the value of a data and that of the power consumption that leaks when it is manipulated has early been studied [11,9,10] and in the classical models the power consumption is tightly linked either with the Hamming weight of the data or with the Hamming distance between this data and the value it replaces on the bus.

In this paper we consider an attacker that is able to infer the Hamming weights of the data manipulated by targeted instructions of a software AES implementation on an 8-bit microprocessor. Specifically the targeted data are the different bytes of the different round keys, while the targeted instructions may be located either in the AES key expansion process which computes these round keys, or in the AddRoundKey function which XOR the round keys with the current state of the encryption process. While the problem of inferring an AES key from the Hamming weights and the expanded key bytes has first been mentioned in [1], Mangard [8] was the first to describe such an attack which has later been improved by VanLaven et al. [13]. While the SPA on the AES key expansion described in these works only apply on naive unprotected implementations, we study in this paper to which extent this attack may be adapted to implementations featuring side-channel countermeasures. We consider three different scenarios where either a Boolean masking is applied to the round keys or the order of computation of the expanded key bytes is randomly shuffled. The masking countermeasure prevents the attacker from obtaining the Hamming weight of actual key bytes, while the shuffling countermeasure prevents him to precisely know to which key byte an observation is related.

The paper is organized as follows: The problem statement and a background on the related previous works are presented in Sect. 2. This section also considers the open problem whether two expanded keys may have the same of Hamming weights. Section 3 presents our main contribution where we describe attacks on three countermeasures. In the light of these results we give implementation recommendations in Sect. 4 while Sect. 5 concludes this work.

## 2    Problem Statement and Previous Work

Given a 16-byte ciphering key $K$, the AES key expansion derives eleven 16-byte round keys $K_r$ $(r = 0, \ldots, 10)$ with $K_0 = K$ and where individual bytes of $K_r$ are denoted $k_{r,i}$ $(i = 0, \ldots, 15)$.

The expanded key $\overline{K} = \{K_0, \ldots, K_{10}\}$ is computed column by column by means of two types – a linear and a non-linear – of relations:

$$k_{r,i} = k_{r-1,i} \oplus k_{r,i-4} \quad \text{(for } i = 4, \ldots, 15\text{)} \tag{1}$$

$$k_{r,i} = k_{r-1,i} \oplus \mathrm{S}(k_{r-1,12+((i+1) \bmod 4)}) \oplus c'_r \quad \text{(for } i = 0, \ldots, 3\text{)} \tag{2}$$

where S is the S-Box substitution and $c'_r$ is a round specific constant equal to $\{02\}^{r-1}$ if $i = 0$ and equal to 0 if $i \in \{1, 2, 3\}$. We refer the interesting reader to the AES specifications [12] for further details on the AES ciphering process.

The problem considered in this paper is how to identify the ciphering key $K$ based on a set $\{\mathrm{HW}(k_{r,i})\}_{r,i}$ of part or all Hamming weights of the expanded key bytes.

Mangard [8] was the first to give a solution to this problem. He proposed to build lists of values of 5-byte key parts which are both compatible with the observed Hamming weights of these bytes, and also compatible with the Hamming weights of 9 other key bytes (and several other intermediate bytes) that can be computed from the 5-tuple.

In [13] VanLaven et al. also consider the same problem and give an elegant analysis of the key byte links which allows them to derive an efficient guess-compute-and-backtrack algorithm where a sequence of key bytes are successively guessed in an optimal order that maximizes the number of other bytes that can be computed and checked with respect to their Hamming weight. Once an inconsistency with respect to the observations is found the algorithm considers the next possible value for the current guessed byte and eventually backtracks one level back in the sequence of key bytes when all values for the current guessed byte have been considered. Interestingly the last contribution of this work shows that their algorithm can cope with (slightly) erroneous observation at the price of a more demanding computational work in the key space exploration process.

**Undistinguishable Keys.** We study the open question whether there exist key pairs – or more generally key sets – which are undistinguishable for having the same Hamming weights signatures[1]. We are thus concerned by the existence or non-existence of two different keys $K$ and $K'$ such that $\overline{K}$ and $\overline{K'}$ have exactly the same 176 Hamming weights.

If the AES key expansion was deriving round keys $K_1$ to $K_{10}$ with an ideal random behavior, the probability that there exist two keys having the same signature would be overwhelming low. Indeed the probability that two random bytes have same Hamming weight is $p = 2^{-2.348}$ so that the probability that the

---

[1] By *Hamming weights signature* of a key $K$ we mean the set of all the Hamming weights of its expanded key $\overline{K}$.

signatures of two random keys are the same is $q = p^{176} \simeq 2^{-413.3}$. It follows that the probability that at least one collision of signatures occurs among the whole key space is about $1 - e^{-\frac{q}{2} \cdot 2^{2*128}} \simeq 2^{-158.3}$.

While the AES key expansion is far from having a random behavior, it was considered in [8] that so-called twin keys probably do not exist or should be very rare[2]. We show in this paper that this belief is wrong by proposing a constructive method that can easily generate millions of them. We refer the reader to Appendix A for the description of this method and just provide here an example of such key pair:

$$\begin{cases} K\ = \text{B3 65 58 9D B4 EB 57 72 1F 51 F7 58 02 0C 00 17} \\ K'\ = \text{F2 65 19 DC B4 EB 57 33 5E 51 F7 19 02 0C 00 56} \end{cases}$$

Note that the existence of twin keys is of theoretical interest as it gives a new demonstration of the quite non-ideal behavior of the diffusion process of the AES key expansion. Nevertheless, it has no practical impact on the attacks considered in this paper since the only consequence is that when attacking a key belonging to such pair, the attack process ends with two possible keys instead of a unique one. The correct key can then be identified thanks to a known plaintext/ciphertext pair.

# 3    Key Recovery on Protected Implementations

In this section we study three different countermeasures that may be implemented to protect the key expansion function against simple power analysis.

The first two countermeasures are natural ways to apply a Boolean masking on the expanded key. They make use of 11-byte and 16-byte masks respectively in order to cope with limited RAM resources and/or small random entropy generation capacity that usually prevail on embedded devices. The third countermeasure is a columnwise shuffling of the expanded key computation.

## 3.1    11-byte Entropy Boolean Masking

We consider here that at each execution all round keys are masked by 11 specific random bytes $m_r$ so that the attacker has no longer access to the leakages of individual bytes $k_{r,i}$ of each $K_r$ but rather to those of masked versions $K'_r = (k'_{r,i})_i$ with $k'_{r,i} = k_{r,i} \oplus m_r$. Figure 1 depicts the mask pattern that applies on the expanded key bytes.

The basic attack does not apply directly since the measured Hamming weights are related to masked bytes that do not verify neither linear nor non-linear links of the key expansion process.

In order to apply the guess-compute-and-backtrack strategy of the basic attack we now have to make also guesses about the values of the masks of all key

---

[2] The exact sentence of the author was: *The high diffusion of the AES key expansion suggests that there are only very few keys of this kind, if there are such keys at all.*

| $K_0$ | | | | $K_1$ | | | | $K_2$ | | | |
|---|---|---|---|---|---|---|---|---|---|---|---|
| $m_0$ | $m_0$ | $m_0$ | $m_0$ | $m_1$ | $m_1$ | $m_1$ | $m_1$ | $m_2$ | $m_2$ | $m_2$ | $m_2$ |
| $m_0$ | $m_0$ | $m_0$ | $m_0$ | $m_1$ | $m_1$ | $m_1$ | $m_1$ | $m_2$ | $m_2$ | $m_2$ | $m_2$ |
| $m_0$ | $m_0$ | $m_0$ | $m_0$ | $m_1$ | $m_1$ | $m_1$ | $m_1$ | $m_2$ | $m_2$ | $m_2$ | $m_2$ |
| $m_0$ | $m_0$ | $m_0$ | $m_0$ | $m_1$ | $m_1$ | $m_1$ | $m_1$ | $m_2$ | $m_2$ | $m_2$ | $m_2$ |

$\cdots$

**Fig. 1.** Part of the 8-byte masking scheme

bytes involved in the key search. As each extra mask that must be guessed induces a multiplication by $2^8$ of the searched space, we use two tricks to contain the necessary computing work factor.

The first idea is to exploit some extra information that can be inferred about the key bytes $k_{r,i}$ by considering measured Hamming weights from multiple traces. More precisely, consider two bytes $x$ and $y$ masked by the same random value $m$. The respective Hamming weights of the masked bytes $x' = x \oplus m$ and $y' = y \oplus m$ verify the two following properties:

$$|\,\mathrm{HW}(x') - \mathrm{HW}(y')\,| \leqslant \mathrm{HD}(x,y) \leqslant \min(8, \mathrm{HW}(x') + \mathrm{HW}(y')) \qquad (3)$$
$$\mathrm{HD}(x,y) \equiv \mathrm{HW}(x') + \mathrm{HW}(y') \pmod 2 \qquad (4)$$

Both equations give information about the Hamming distance between unmasked values $x$ and $y$. For example, suppose that $x = 30$ and $y = 121$ (i.e. $\mathrm{HD}(x,y) = 5$). With a first trace for which $m = 70$, we measure $\mathrm{HW}(x') = \mathrm{HW}(30 \oplus 70) = 3$ and $\mathrm{HW}(y') = \mathrm{HW}(121 \oplus 70) = 6$. From Eq. (3) we infer that $3 \leqslant \mathrm{HD}(x,y) \leqslant 8$, and due to the odd parity given by Eq. (4) we learn that $\mathrm{HD}(x,y) \in \{3,5,7\}$. With a second trace for which $m = 24$, we measure $\mathrm{HW}(x') = \mathrm{HW}(30 \oplus 24) = 2$ and $\mathrm{HW}(y') = \mathrm{HW}(121 \oplus 24) = 3$. This second measure allows to further constrain $\mathrm{HD}(x,y)$ which now belongs to $\{3,5\}$. By exploiting more and more traces we can decrease the number of possible candidates and ultimately expect to identify the Hamming distance between the unmasked bytes. Interestingly we notice that the parity equation may be used to detect erroneous measurements. For example, if the measurements from ten traces give an odd parity for $\mathrm{HW}(x') + \mathrm{HW}(y')$ eight times and an even parity only twice, then one may conclude that either $\mathrm{HW}(x')$ or $\mathrm{HW}(y')$ has not been correctly measured on these two last traces.

In a first phase of the attack, multiple traces are analysed in order to get as much possible information about the Hamming distance $\mathrm{HD}(k_{r,i}, k_{r,i'})$ of each couple of bytes belonging to the same round key. Then in a second phase a smart exploration of the key space is performed based on the Hamming weights measured from a unique trace, and on the Hamming distances constraints obtained in the first phase.

The second idea to reduce to computational effort is to limit the process of guessing and computing key bytes to only two adjacent round keys $K_r$ and $K_{r+1}$. That way we have to guess only two mask bytes. For each $(m_r, m_{r+1})$ candidate we perform a key search where we guess successive bytes of $K_r$ and derive the values of successive bytes of $K_{r+1}$. For example, consider that we start the search by guessing $k_{r,12}$ (equivalently we could start at positions 13, 14 or 15). In a first step we guess $k_{r,3}$ and compute $k_{r+1,3}$. In a second step we guess $k_{r,7}$ and compute $k_{r+1,7}$. Then we guess $k_{r,11}$ and compute $k_{r+1,11}$, and so on. Figure 2 shows the order in which successive bytes of $K_r$ and $K_{r+1}$ are respectively guessed and computed. As in the basic attack, each time a key byte is guessed or computed we check the consistency with the measured Hamming weights of its masked values. A more efficient consistency check consists in verifying that each newly guessed or computed byte has compatible Hamming distances with all already known key bytes belonging to the same round key. For example, when $k_{r,11}$ is guessed in the third step four constraints on $\mathrm{HW}(k_{r,11} \oplus m_r)$, $\mathrm{HD}(k_{r,11}, k_{r,7})$, $\mathrm{HD}(k_{r,11}, k_{r,3})$ and $\mathrm{HD}(k_{r,11}, k_{r,12})$ are verified, and when $k_{r+1,11}$ is computed three checks imply $\mathrm{HW}(k_{r+1,11} \oplus m_{r+1})$, $\mathrm{HD}(k_{r+1,11}, k_{r+1,7})$ and $\mathrm{HD}(k_{r+1,11}, k_{r+1,3})$. As we can see, the more deeper we are in the exploration process, the more opportunities we have to invalidate wrong guess sequences and backtrack.

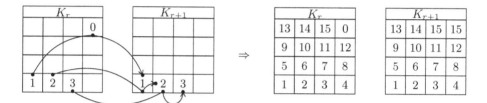

**Fig. 2.** Guess order of the 11-byte masking scheme

We have extensively simulated our attack by generating perfect measurement sets of Hamming weights. For different numbers $T$ of exploited traces ($T \in \{5, 10, 15, 20, 30\}$) – this number influences the tightness of the bounds derived for the Hamming distances – we ran $N$ simulations ($N = 1000$ in most cases) of the attack. For each run we picked a key at random, and for each $T$ executions we computed a masked expanded key based on an execution specific set of masks $(m_0, \ldots, m_{10})$, from which we derived the set of Hamming weights assumed to be available to the attacker. Given a round $r$ we computed the sets of possible Hamming distances between each couple $(k_{r,i}, k_{r,i'})$ and $(k_{r+1,i}, k_{r+1,i'})$. Then we choose one particular trace (actually a set of Hamming weights) among the $T$ available ones and a starting position of the guess sequence[3], and executed the second phase of the attack (exploration process).

Table 1 shows the simulation results obtained on a classical PC equipped with an 2.4 MHz I5 core processor and 4 GB of RAM. For each number of exploited traces we give the average computation time as well as the average

---

[3] Note that an attacker can freely choose both the trace which is exploited for the key search, the round $r$ from 0 to 9 and the starting position from 12 to 15. We took this opportunity to select those parameters that minimize the number of possible values of the starting triplet – i.e. $(k_{r,12}, k_{r,3}, k_{r+1,3})$ in the example above – that are compatible with the measured Hamming weights.

residual entropy of the key (the $\log_2$ of the number of compatible keys returned by the attack). Because of a large variance in the attack computation time, we choose to limit the exploration with a given timeout. The value of this timeout as well as the percentage of simulations that terminated within this limit are also presented. Note that the average figures in the second and third columns are computed over the set of terminating simulations.

**Table 1.** Simulation results of the attack on the 11-byte masking countermeasure

| Number of traces ($T$) | Average time (s) | Average residual entropy (bits) | Simulation timeout (s) | Percentage of terminating runs | Number of runs ($N$) |
|---|---|---|---|---|---|
| 5 | 398 | 5.9 | 1800 | 47.0 | 83 |
| 10 | 40.6 | 0.66 | 300 | 93.4 | 500 |
| 15 | 10.0 | 0.29 | 60 | 94.7 | 1000 |
| 20 | 5.9 | 0.24 | 60 | 98.2 | 1000 |
| 30 | 3.0 | 0.24 | 60 | 100.0 | 1000 |

The proposed attack is quite efficient, even for a number of exploited traces reduced to five. In this case about 45% of runs terminate in less than 30 minutes and the average entropy of the key set that remains to exhaust is only about five bits.

*Remark 1.* From a practical point of view related to the ability for the attacker to infer Hamming weight from the leakage traces, we notice that in this attack not all 176 Hamming weights are needed per trace but only 32 ones. Also, the opportunity that the attacker has to choose which round key he wants to attack may be exploited to select the portion of the traces where he is the more confident about the measured Hamming weights.

## 3.2    16-byte Entropy Boolean Masking

The second countermeasure that we consider consists in masking all bytes of a round key with a different random byte, while repeating these 16 masks for all round keys. Precisely, each masked round key is defined as $K'_r = (k'_{r,i})_i$ with $k'_{r,i} = k_{r,i} \oplus m_i$ ($i = 0, \ldots, 15$). Figure 3 depicts the mask pattern that applies on the expanded key bytes.

As in the attack on the 11-byte masking scheme, we will first exploit several traces in order to obtain information on Hamming distances between key bytes sharing a same mask. We also want to limit to two the number of mask values that must be simultaneously guessed in the most explosive (less constrained) part of the key space exploration. It follows from this that the sequence of guesses should extend horizontally on a same byte position $i$ rather than on a same round key $r$.

| $K_0$ | | | | $K_1$ | | | | $K_2$ | | | |
|---|---|---|---|---|---|---|---|---|---|---|---|
| $m_{00}$ | $m_{04}$ | $m_{08}$ | $m_{12}$ | $m_{00}$ | $m_{04}$ | $m_{08}$ | $m_{12}$ | $m_{00}$ | $m_{04}$ | $m_{08}$ | $m_{12}$ |
| $m_{01}$ | $m_{05}$ | $m_{09}$ | $m_{13}$ | $m_{01}$ | $m_{05}$ | $m_{09}$ | $m_{13}$ | $m_{01}$ | $m_{05}$ | $m_{09}$ | $m_{13}$ |
| $m_{02}$ | $m_{06}$ | $m_{10}$ | $m_{14}$ | $m_{02}$ | $m_{06}$ | $m_{10}$ | $m_{14}$ | $m_{02}$ | $m_{06}$ | $m_{10}$ | $m_{14}$ |
| $m_{03}$ | $m_{07}$ | $m_{11}$ | $m_{15}$ | $m_{03}$ | $m_{07}$ | $m_{11}$ | $m_{15}$ | $m_{03}$ | $m_{07}$ | $m_{11}$ | $m_{15}$ |

$\cdots$

**Fig. 3.** Part of the 16-byte masking scheme

Given a starting position $a \in \{0, 1, 2, 3\}$, we define the related position $b = 12 + ((a+1) \bmod 4)$. For each guess on the couple of masks $(m_a, m_b)$, we perform an exploration of the key space as follows. First we guess $k_{0,a}$. Then repeatedly for $r = 0, \ldots, 9$ we guess $k_{r,b}$ and derive $k_{r+1,a}$. As in the attack described in Sect. 3.1, each newly guessed or computed key byte is checked against available information about the Hamming weight of its masked value and the Hamming distances with other already known bytes at the same position. We have now performed the most demanding part of the exploration since we had to make a new guess for each byte $k_{r,b}$. At this point we have a reasonably small number of compatible key candidates for which we know all key bytes at positions $a$ and $b$ except $k_{10,b}$. We now guess $k_{10,b}$ which is quite constrained by the Hamming distances at position $b$ and so does not increase much the exploration size. Knowing $k_{10,b}$, we can now successively compute key bytes at position $c = b - 4$ backward from $k_{10,c}$ to $k_{1,c}$. Note that $m_c$ is the only value that we must guess to compute this line up to $k_{1,c}$. We terminate the line $c$ by guessing the quite constrained last byte $k_{0,c}$. Now, guessing the mask $m_d$ at position $d = c - 4$ we can compute in the same way all the line $d$ from $k_{10,d}$ to $k_{1,d}$, and terminate the line by guessing $k_{0,d}$. We can pursue the same process with one more line at position $e = d - 4$ and then the next line is located at position $f = 12 + ((b+1) \bmod 4)$ and is computed forward from $k_{0,f}$ to $k_{9,f}$ terminating with a guess on $k_{10,f}$. Successively we determine all the expanded key, line after line, at positions whose sequence $a, b, c, \ldots$ is presented on Fig. 4.

Interestingly, we can notice a property that stands for the first line $a$ and which allows to dramatically speed up the attack. For each solution found on

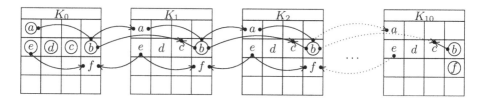

**Fig. 4.** Guess order of the 16-byte masking scheme

lines $a$ and $b$ by assuming the couple of masks $(m_a, m_b)$ we would have found a companion solution with any other value $m'_a$ where all $k_{r,b}$ are the same and where each $k_{r,a}$ is replaced by $k_{r,a} \oplus (m_a \oplus m'_a)$. As key bytes at position $a$ do not influence those recovered on the successive lines $b, c, d, \ldots$ we do not have to know the exact value of $m_a$ and can fix it arbitrary. At the end of the attack we are able to compute the correct value of the line $a$ by inferring the error made on $m_a$ based for example on the difference between the assumed value of $k_{10,a}$ and its exact value which can be computed as $k_{9,p} \oplus k_{10,p}$ where $p = a + 4$. Doing so, the first part of the exploration, which results in knowing values at positions $a$ and $b$, can be done by guessing virtually only one mask byte $(m_b)$. A speed-up factor of $2^8$ is achieved which results in a particularly efficient attack.

Table 2 presents simulation results for this attack in a similar manner than in Sect. 3.1. Surprisingly, the key recovery in the presence of a 16-byte masking is much more efficient than with the 11-byte masking despite the higher mask entropy. For example the key is recovered within 1 second on average when 10 traces are exploited against 40 seconds for the 11-byte masking. Also, it is possible to use only 3 traces with still small computation time and residual key entropy in a significant proportion of cases.

**Table 2.** Simulation results of the attack on the 16-byte masking countermeasure

| Number of traces ($T$) | Average time (s) | Average residual entropy (bits) | Simulation timeout (s) | Percentage of terminating runs | Number of runs ($N$) |
|---|---|---|---|---|---|
| 3 | 77.3 | 7.3 | 600 | 60.7 | 28 |
| 5 | 25.3 | 4.2 | 300 | 88.5 | 1000 |
| 10 | 1.09 | 1.7 | 60 | 100.0 | 1000 |
| 15 | 0.24 | 0.93 | 60 | 100.0 | 1000 |
| 20 | 0.12 | 0.55 | 60 | 100.0 | 1000 |
| 30 | 0.07 | 0.24 | 60 | 100.0 | 1000 |

### 3.3   Column-Wise Random Order Countermeasure

The third countermeasure consists in calculating independent bytes in a random order. Due to the column based structure of the key schedule the four bytes of each column can be calculated independently. Figure 5 gives an example of a possible sequence of permutation.

This countermeasure is hiding a part of information. We still assume that the attacker is able to correctly identify all 176 Hamming weights but for every column he only obtains a non-ordered set of 4 values. For example, given the example key represented in Figure 6 where key bytes Hamming weights are indicated in the corner, the information that an attacker has access to is shown on Figure 7. The key bytes of each column have been involved in a random order so that the attacker can only infer non-ordered quadruplets of Hamming weights.

| $K_0$ | | | | $K_1$ | | | | $K_2$ | | | |
|---|---|---|---|---|---|---|---|---|---|---|---|
| $k_{0,2}$ | $k_{0,4}$ | $k_{0,9}$ | $k_{0,14}$ | $k_{1,0}$ | $k_{1,7}$ | $k_{1,11}$ | $k_{1,15}$ | $k_{2,3}$ | $k_{2,7}$ | $k_{2,8}$ | $k_{2,13}$ |
| $k_{0,3}$ | $k_{0,6}$ | $k_{0,11}$ | $k_{0,12}$ | $k_{1,1}$ | $k_{1,6}$ | $k_{1,10}$ | $k_{1,14}$ | $k_{2,2}$ | $k_{2,5}$ | $k_{2,9}$ | $k_{2,15}$ |
| $k_{0,1}$ | $k_{0,5}$ | $k_{0,10}$ | $k_{0,13}$ | $k_{1,3}$ | $k_{1,5}$ | $k_{1,9}$ | $k_{1,12}$ | $k_{2,0}$ | $k_{2,6}$ | $k_{2,11}$ | $k_{2,14}$ |
| $k_{0,0}$ | $k_{0,7}$ | $k_{0,8}$ | $k_{0,15}$ | $k_{1,2}$ | $k_{1,4}$ | $k_{1,8}$ | $k_{1,13}$ | $k_{2,1}$ | $k_{2,4}$ | $k_{2,10}$ | $k_{2,12}$ |

Fig. 5. Part of an example of effect of random order countermeasure

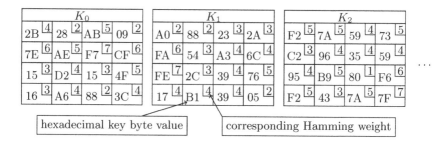

Fig. 6. Three first round keys derived from an example key with their corresponding Hamming weights

Since all 24 permutations on the quadruplet can be considered as valid a priori[4], the computational effort for considering every permutation on each column makes the key search computationally unfeasible. In order to reduce the exploration cost we use what we call a booking system. During our attack we will book Hamming weights at fixed positions, either by choice when the byte value is guessed, or by constraint when it is computed from a key byte relation. Once it is booked a Hamming weight is no more available in its column until a backtrack releases it due to a modification of the last guessed byte.

For instance, when we have to guess a value for $k_{1,15}$ we first guess its Hamming weight among the list $\{2,3,4,5\}$ of available Hamming weights. If we guess that $\mathrm{HW}(k_{1,15}) = 4$, then the guess on $k_{1,15}$ itself ranges over all values having an Hamming weight equal to 4, and the list of available Hamming weights for that column is now reduced to $\{2,3,5\}$. When another byte of the same column will be also guessed (or computed) at a deeper step of the exploration process its Hamming weight will necessarily have to belong to this reduced set. If at some point a backtrack occurs on $k_{1,15}$ then the Hamming weight value 4 is released and will be possibly available for other bytes of this column.

We describe here two versions of this attack, one using information given by one acquisition, which can take non-negligible time, and faster version which exploits faulty executions in order to gather more information.

---

[4] Due to possible Hamming weight duplicates, some columns may have a reduced number of possible permutations.

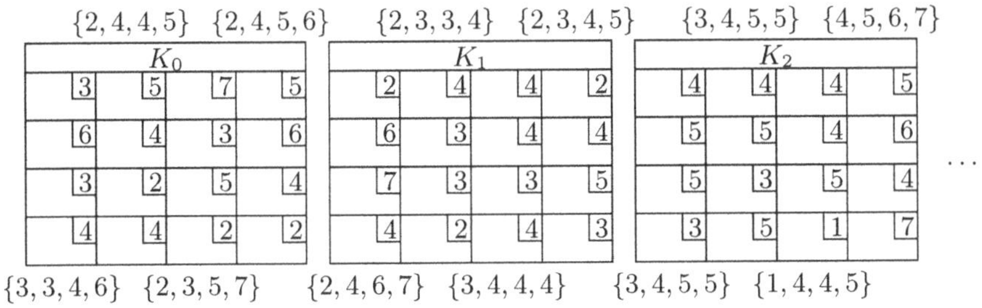

$\{2,4,4,5\}$  $\{2,4,5,6\}$    $\{2,3,3,4\}$  $\{2,3,4,5\}$    $\{3,4,5,5\}$  $\{4,5,6,7\}$

| $K_0$ | | | | | $K_1$ | | | | | $K_2$ | | | |
|---|---|---|---|---|---|---|---|---|---|---|---|---|---|
| 3 | 5 | 7 | 5 | | 2 | 4 | 4 | 2 | | 4 | 4 | 4 | 5 |
| 6 | 4 | 3 | 6 | | 6 | 3 | 4 | 4 | | 5 | 5 | 4 | 6 |
| 3 | 2 | 5 | 4 | | 7 | 3 | 3 | 5 | | 5 | 3 | 5 | 4 |
| 4 | 4 | 2 | 2 | | 4 | 2 | 4 | 3 | | 3 | 5 | 1 | 7 |

· · ·

$\{3,3,4,6\}$  $\{2,3,5,7\}$    $\{2,4,6,7\}$  $\{3,4,4,4\}$    $\{3,4,5,5\}$  $\{1,4,4,5\}$

**Fig. 7.** Information gained by the attacker reduces to quadruplets of Hamming weights of each column

**Basic Attack.** In a basic version of our attack we follow an equivalent exploration pattern than the one used in [13] for a non-protected implementation. The only difference is that the guess may have different possible Hamming weights. As explained above, before guessing a byte value at a current position we have to guess which un-booked Hamming weight value will be used at this position and book it while it's corresponding values are exhausted. When we have guessed bytes at enough positions to compute key bytes from others we check that the Hamming weight of the computed values are available for their columns and we book these Hamming weights also. If the Hamming weight of a computed byte is not available then this solution is not valid and we backtrack from the previous guessed byte. Note that if a same Hamming weight value is available $n$ times in a column it can be booked $n$ times too.

We simulated this attack by considering random keys and corresponding non-ordered quadruplets for each column. Table 3 presents the number of executions over 100 runs that ended before a time limit which ranges from 30 minutes to 6 hours. As it can take undefined long time we choose to interrupt a run if it takes more than 6 hours (27 % of cases). Note that the average time for the non-interrupted executions is about 2 hours, so that average time over all executions could possibly be quite larger.

**Faulting Attack.** We describe here a more efficient version of the attack which uses fault injections in order to significantly reduce the execution time of the key search.

We assume that the attacker can induce a fault in a random byte of a chosen column, and we take the example of the first column in the following explanations. The fault model assumes a random modification of the faulted byte value.

**Table 3.** Results of non-faulted attack against random order counter-measure

| Time Elapsed | $\leqslant$ 30 min | $\leqslant$ 1h | $\leqslant$ 2h | $\leqslant$ 3h | $\leqslant$ 4h | $\leqslant$ 5h | $\leqslant$ 6h | + 6h |
|---|---|---|---|---|---|---|---|---|
| # over 100 runs | 6 | 25 | 41 | 55 | 66 | 71 | 73 | 27 |

The key observation used in this attack is that a differential induced at some key byte of the first column propagates following a fixed pattern of active bytes. For example, if the fault modifies the value of $k_{0,0}$ then Figure 8 shows the positions of all active bytes in the first three round keys[5]. Due to the shuffling counter-measure, the attacker does not know which of $k_{0,0}$, $k_{0,1}$, $k_{0,2}$ or $k_{0,3}$ has been modified by the fault, but what is important is that the vertical relative positions of the active bytes are fixed (given by the pattern of Figure 8) and known from the attacker.

| $K_0$ | | | | $K_1$ | | | | $K_2$ | | | |
|---|---|---|---|---|---|---|---|---|---|---|---|
| $k_{0,0}$ | $k_{0,4}$ | $k_{0,8}$ | $k_{0,12}$ | $k_{1,0}$ | $k_{1,4}$ | $k_{1,8}$ | $k_{1,12}$ | $k_{2,0}$ | $k_{2,4}$ | $k_{2,8}$ | $k_{2,12}$ |
| $k_{0,1}$ | $k_{0,5}$ | $k_{0,9}$ | $k_{0,13}$ | $k_{1,1}$ | $k_{1,5}$ | $k_{1,9}$ | $k_{1,13}$ | $k_{2,1}$ | $k_{2,5}$ | $k_{2,9}$ | $k_{2,13}$ |
| $k_{0,2}$ | $k_{0,6}$ | $k_{0,10}$ | $k_{0,14}$ | $k_{1,2}$ | $k_{1,6}$ | $k_{1,10}$ | $k_{1,14}$ | $k_{2,2}$ | $k_{2,6}$ | $k_{2,10}$ | $k_{2,14}$ |
| $k_{0,3}$ | $k_{0,7}$ | $k_{0,11}$ | $k_{0,15}$ | $k_{1,3}$ | $k_{1,7}$ | $k_{1,11}$ | $k_{1,15}$ | $k_{2,3}$ | $k_{2,7}$ | $k_{2,11}$ | $k_{2,15}$ |

$\cdots$

**Fig. 8.** Part of the pattern induced by a fault on first byte of first column of $K_0$

As in the basic attack described above, the attacker can exploit a non-faulted execution to infer the reference quadruplets of Hamming weights for each column.

When exploiting a faulted execution, the attacker can compare, for each column, the possibly modified quadruplet of Hamming weights with the original one. He is thus able to identify which Hamming weights have been modified and thus concern active bytes. Let's consider an example where the faulted byte is $k_{0,2}$ which value has been modified from 0x15 to 0xB1. This example case is depicted on Figure 9 where one can see all subsequent active bytes. Note that in this example, some active bytes ($k_{2,5}$, $k_{2,9}$ and $k_{2,13}$) have been modified while their Hamming weights remained unchanged.

Due to the shuffling counter-measure, the attacker faces round keys where each column has been shuffled as shown on Figure 10. Remind that the attacker does not know neither the byte values nor the active bytes positions (colored in red on the figure), but only the quadruplets of Hamming weights. Comparing for example the original ($\{2,4,6,7\}$ on Figure 7) and faulted ($\{2,4,4,6\}$ on Figure 10) quadruplets of column 4, he can infer that 7 is the Hamming weight of the only active cell in this column. Similarly, he can also infer that the Hamming weight of the only active cell in the column 7 is 5. Considering column 10, the attacker infers the partial information that one of the two active bytes Hamming weights is equal to 1.

Even if the information retrieved about the Hamming weights of the active bytes of each column is only partial, we can nevertheless exploit them in the key search algorithm. For example, in the guess-compute-and-backtrack process, when one guesses that the value of e.g. $k_{1,3}$ has an Hamming weight of 7 (so that

---

[5] Obviously, the pattern is not limited to the three round keys, it extends on all 11 round keys.

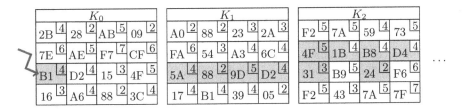

**Fig. 9.** Details of fault effect without considering countermeasure Red/darkgrey Active, green/lightgrey Active but remains unchanged

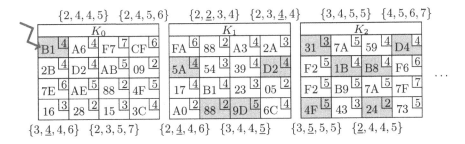

**Fig. 10.** Attacker point of view of faulted execution, underlined values in sets are thoses detected by the attacker as modified by the fault

$k_{1,3}$ would be an active byte), then in column 7 the active byte is necessarily located in the bottom cell also (cf. the active bytes pattern of Figure 8), so that we know that $HW(k_{1,15}) = 5$.

As one can see, the principle of the faulting attack is to exploit in the key search phase information about Hamming weights of active bytes (whose relative vertical positions is fixed) which have been acquired by comparing Hamming weight quadruplets of faulted executions from original ones. While the detailed explanations are quite intricate, it is though possible to infer more information from successive faulty executions to further reduce the execution time of the key search.

We have simulated the faulting attack by exploiting as much information given by faults as possible. We give in Table 4 average execution times of the key search phase as a function of the number of exploited faulty executions. Note that even with only one faulty execution the average attack time is dramatically reduced from several hours to only 20 minutes.

**Table 4.** Results of faulted attack against random order counter-measure

| fault number | time (min) |
|---|---|
| 1 | 20 |
| 5 | 5 |
| 10 | 3 |
| 20 | 2 |
| 30 | 2 |

*Remark 2.* It is interesting to notice that if the fault did not occur in the first column then the attack is still possible while possibly less efficient. Indeed the pattern of active bytes induced by a fault in any column is always a subset of the pattern induced by a fault in the first column. Consequently this shorter pattern has the same shape as the pattern starting from the first column and can then be exploited in the same way but will provide information only for rightmost columns. This allows to perform this attack even when the attacker do not have a precise control on the timing of the fault.

## 4 Recommendations for Secure Implementations

Considering the problem of recovering a key by analysing the Hamming weights of the key bytes computed during the key expansion process, several counter-measures are proposed in the seminal contribution [8] among which the Boolean masking of the key expansion. We showed that two versions of this countermeasure with 11 and 16 bytes of mask entropy are not sufficient to prevent the key recovery when the attacker can precisely infer the Hamming weights. Our attacks on the Boolean masking also apply if the expanded key is computed once for all and there is no key expansion process computed by the device. In that case the Hamming weights can still be measured, not while the key bytes are computed but rather when they are transferred into RAM and/or used in the AddRoundKey function.

Using an hardware or an 16- or 32-bit AES implementation prevents our attacks which only apply on 8-bit software implementations. On these later devices we recommend either to implement (if ever possible) a full 176-byte key masking where all key bytes are masked by independent random values, or to combine a weaker masking with other countermeasures that reinforce its security. For example, combining one of the two masking methods considered in this paper together with the column-wise shuffling should be sufficient to prevent the attacker from obtaining enough exploitable information from the computation of the round keys itself. As for the manipulation of the key bytes in the encryption process, the combination of masking and shuffling should also be sufficient with the advantage here that the entropy of the shuffling is higher in this later case since all 16 bytes may be shuffled together instead of per chunks of four bytes. Obviously, on top of these fundamental countermeasures, any means to make it difficult to find the relevant points of interest on the side-channel trace – e.g. random delays – or to interpret the leakage in terms of Hamming weight – added signal noise – would add extra security to the AES implementation.

## 5 Conclusion

In this paper we have revisited a simple power analysis on the AES key expansion. While previous works only apply on unprotected implementations, we have considered three different countermeasures and presented efficient attacks in each scenario. In two Boolean masking cases (11-byte and 16-byte mask entropy) our attacks recover the key in a matter of seconds when a few power traces are exploited. In the case of a column-wise shuffling of the key expansion process, we have devised an attack which takes several hours on average and proposed an improved version that takes advantage of extra information provided by fault analysis so that the computation time is reduced to a few minutes.

Our attacks assume that the attacker is able to obtain correct values of the Hamming weights of the key bytes. As a future work it may be interesting to study how more difficult it would be to cope with erroneous observations.

**Acknowledgments.** Simulations presented in this paper have been partly performed on the CALI computing cluster of university of Limoges, funded by the Limousin region, XLIM, IPAM and GEIST institutes, as well as the university of Limoges.

# References

1. Biham, E., Shamir, A.: Power Analysis of the Key Scheduling of the AES Candidates. In: Second AES Candidate Conference – AES2, Rome, Italy (1999)
2. Brier, E., Clavier, C., Olivier, F.: Correlation Power Analysis with a Leakage Model. In: Joye, M., Quisquater, J.-J. (eds.) CHES 2004. LNCS, vol. 3156, pp. 16–29. Springer, Heidelberg (2004)
3. Chari, S., Rao, J.R., Rohatgi, P.: Template attacks. In: Kaliski Jr., B.S., Koç, Ç.K., Paar, C. (eds.) CHES 2002. LNCS, vol. 2523, pp. 13–28. Springer, Heidelberg (2003)
4. Gierlichs, B., Batina, L., Tuyls, P., Preneel, B.: Mutual Information Analysis. In: Oswald, E., Rohatgi, P. (eds.) CHES 2008. LNCS, vol. 5154, pp. 426–442. Springer, Heidelberg (2008)
5. Koç, Ç.K., Paar, C.: CHES 2000. LNCS, vol. 1965. Springer, Heidelberg (2000)
6. Kocher, P.C.: Timing Attacks on Implementations of Diffie-Hellman, RSA, DSS, and Other Systems. In: Koblitz, N. (ed.) CRYPTO 1996. LNCS, vol. 1109, pp. 104–113. Springer, Heidelberg (1996)
7. Kocher, P.C., Jaffe, J., Jun, B.: Differential Power Analysis. In: Wiener, M. (ed.) CRYPTO 1999. LNCS, vol. 1666, pp. 388–397. Springer, Heidelberg (1999)
8. Mangard, S.: A Simple Power-Analysis (SPA) Attackon Implementations of the AES Key Expansion. In: Lee, P.J., Lim, C.H. (eds.) ICISC 2002. LNCS, vol. 2587, pp. 343–358. Springer, Heidelberg (2003)
9. Mayer-Sommer, R.: Smartly analyzing the simplicity and the power of simple power analysis on smartcards. In: Koç, Paar (eds.) [5], pp. 78–92
10. Messerges, T.S.: Using Second-Order Power Analysis to Attack DPA Resistant Software. In: Koç, Paar (eds.) [5], pp. 238–251
11. Messerges, T.S., Dabbish, E.A., Sloan, R.H.: Investigations of Power Analysis Attacks on Smartcards. In: WOST 1999: Proceedings of the USENIX Workshop on Smartcard Technology, pp. 151–162. USENIX Association, Berkeley (1999)
12. National Institute of Standards and Technology. Advanced Encryption Standard (AES). Federal Information Processing Standard #197 (2001)
13. VanLaven, J., Brehob, M., Compton, K.J.: Side Channel Analysis, Fault Injection and Applications - A Computationally Feasible SPA Attack on AES via Optimized Search. In: Sasaki, R., Qing, S., Okamoto, E., Yoshiura, H. (eds.) SEC 2005. IFIP AICT, vol. 181, pp. 577–588. Springer, Heidelberg (2005)

# A  Generating Undistinguishable Keys Pairs

The core idea of our method comes from the observation that given a permutation $\tau$ of $\{0, \ldots, 7\}$ and the byte transformation $\pi : b = (b_7 \ldots b_0) \mapsto \pi(b) = (b_{\tau(7)} \ldots b_{\tau(0)})$ we have $\mathrm{HW}(\pi(b)) = \mathrm{HW}(b)$. Thus, a sufficient condition for $K$ and $K'$ to form a twin pair is that $k_j' = \pi(k_j)$ for all $j = 0, \ldots, 175$. Our goal is to find $K$ such that defining $K'$ by $k_{0,i}' = \pi(k_{0,i}), i = 0, \ldots, 15$ the sufficient condition propagates up to (near) the end of the expansion. As $\pi$ is linear the sufficient condition propagates well on all linear relations. The only difficult task is to ensure the propagation of the condition also for non-linear relations. Denoting $c_r = \{02\}^{r-1}$ the constant involved in the first non-linear relation at round $r = 1, \ldots, 10$, and assuming that the sufficient conditions hold up to round key $K_{r-1}$, they propagate to $K_r$ provided that:

$$k_{r,0}' = \pi(k_{r,0}) \Leftrightarrow \mathrm{S}(\pi(k_{r-1,13})) \oplus c_r = \pi(\mathrm{S}(k_{r-1,13})) \oplus \pi(c_r) \tag{5}$$

$$k_{r,1}' = \pi(k_{r,1}) \Leftrightarrow \mathrm{S}(\pi(k_{r-1,14})) = \pi(\mathrm{S}(k_{r-1,14})) \tag{6}$$

$$k_{r,2}' = \pi(k_{r,2}) \Leftrightarrow \mathrm{S}(\pi(k_{r-1,15})) = \pi(\mathrm{S}(k_{r-1,15})) \tag{7}$$

$$k_{r,3}' = \pi(k_{r,3}) \Leftrightarrow \mathrm{S}(\pi(k_{r-1,12})) = \pi(\mathrm{S}(k_{r-1,12})) \tag{8}$$

The first task is to find a suitable bit permutation which maximizes the probability that these conditions hold by chance. Interestingly the probability that any condition (6) to (8) holds is as large as about $\frac{1}{4}$ when $\tau$ permutes only 2 bits[6]. This is due to the fact that $\mathrm{S}(\pi(x)) = \pi(\mathrm{S}(x))$ as soon as $\pi(x) = x$ and $\pi(y) = y$ for $y = \mathrm{S}(x)$ where both fixed-point conditions hold with probability $\frac{1}{2}$. Finding a twin pair only necessitates that all $k_{r-1,i}$ ($r = 1, \ldots 10$ and $i = 12, \ldots, 15$) belong the following sets:

$$\Omega_r = \{x : \mathrm{S}(\pi(x)) \oplus c_r = \pi(\mathrm{S}(x)) \oplus \pi(c_r)\} \quad \text{(for } i = 13)$$

$$\Omega = \{x : \mathrm{S}(\pi(x)) = \pi(\mathrm{S}(x))\} \quad \text{(for } i \in \{12, 14, 15\})$$

It is important that either $\Omega$ or $\Omega_1$ contains some value $x$ which satisfies the condition without being a fixed point for $\pi$ otherwise $K'$ would be equal to $K$. We have chosen $\tau$ which permutes bits 0 and 6. Note that it is the only bit transposition having a non fixed point for $\Omega$.

The second task is to generate many key candidates which verify by construction as many sufficient conditions as possible. We devised a method that efficiently generates a large number of candidates that systematically fulfill sufficient conditions for all $r \leqslant 5$. First we make vary the twelve key bytes $k_{1,12+n}$, $k_{2,12+n}$ and $k_{3,12+n}$ ($n = 0, \ldots, 3$) which are free except that they must all belong

---

[6] This is also true for condition (5) for a similar reason.

to their respective relevant $\Omega$, $\Omega_2$, $\Omega_3$ or $\Omega_4$ set. Due to the previous remark the number of possible choices for these bytes is lower bounded by $(256/4)^{12} = 2^{72}$. We also make use of the following relations among the key bytes

$$k_{4,12+n} = k_{0,12+n} \oplus S(k_{3,12+(n+1) \bmod 4}) \oplus c'_4 \tag{9}$$

$$k_{0,8+n} = k_{0,12+n} \oplus S(k_{2,12+(n+1) \bmod 4}) \oplus c'_3 \oplus k_{3,12+n} \tag{10}$$

$$k_{0,4+n} = k_{0,8+n} \oplus S(k_{1,12+(n+1) \bmod 4}) \oplus c'_2 \oplus k_{2,12+n} \oplus S(k_{2,12+(n+1) \bmod 4}) \oplus c'_3 \oplus k_{3,12+n} \tag{11}$$

$$k_{0,0+n} = k_{0,8+n} \oplus S(k_{0,12+(n+1) \bmod 4}) \oplus c'_1 \oplus k_{1,12+n} \oplus S(k_{1,12+(n+1) \bmod 4}) \oplus c'_2 \oplus k_{2,12+n} \tag{12}$$

where $c'_r$ is defined to be $c_r$ if $n = 0$ and 0 otherwise. The proofs of these relations are provided in Appendix B. Considering equation (9), and knowing that $k_{3,12...15}$ have been chosen in their respective $\Omega$ set, one can choose values for $k_{0,12+n}$ that belong to its $\Omega$ set such that $k_{4,12+n}$ also belongs to its own $\Omega$ set. For example, given $k_{3,14} \in \Omega$ one can find two values $k_{0,13}$ and $k_{4,13}$ which respectively belong to $\Omega_1$ and $\Omega_5$. There always exists several such choices that we have tabulated though only one choice was sufficient in our implementation. Choosing $k_{0,12+n}$ this way ensures that the sufficient conditions will be verified even for the non-linear relations involved in the computation of $K_5$.

The process to generate the key candidates resumes as follow: choose arbitrary value for $k_{1,12+n}$, $k_{2,12+n}$ and $k_{3,12+n}$ $(n = 0, \ldots, 3)$ that belong to their respective relevant $\Omega$ set, then choose values for $k_{0,12+n}$ as explain above, and terminate the valuation of $K = K_0$ by using equations (10) to (12) successively. For each such key $K$ we compute $K'$ by applying the bit transposition $\pi$ to all its bytes. Our construction method ensures that $k'_{r,i} = \pi(k_{r,i})$ – and so $\mathrm{HW}(k'_{r,i}) = \mathrm{HW}(k_{r,i})$ – for all $r = 0, \ldots, 5$.

Generating sufficiently many key candidates, one can expect to find one for which the sufficient conditions propagate by chance over the non-linear relations up to the end of the expansion.

After having found a first winning key pair – the one given in Sect. 2 – we explored in its neighborhood and we surprisingly generated many other undistinguishable pairs much more easily that it was to find the first one. For example, keeping the values of $k_{1,13}$, $k_{1,14}$, $k_{2,12}$ and $k_{2,13}$ involved in the first key pair, we have been able to generate more than 23 millions of other undistinguishable key pairs in a few days of computation. This tend to demonstrate that pairs of keys having same Hamming weight signatures are far from being uniformly distributed, but we have not studied this behavior in more detail.

# B    Proofs of Equations (9) to (12)

## B.1    Equation (9)

*Proof.*

$$
\begin{aligned}
k_{4,12+n} &= k_{4,8+n} \oplus k_{3,12+n} \\
&= k_{4,4+n} \oplus k_{3,12+n} \oplus k_{3,8+n} \\
&= k_{4,0+n} \oplus k_{3,12+n} \oplus k_{3,8+n} \oplus k_{3,4+n} \\
&= S(k_{3,12+(n+1)\bmod 4}) \oplus c'_4 \oplus k_{3,12+n} \oplus k_{3,8+n} \oplus k_{3,4+n} \oplus k_{3,0+n} \\
&= S(k_{3,12+(n+1)\bmod 4}) \oplus c'_4 \oplus k_{3,4+n} \oplus k_{3,0+n} \oplus k_{2,12+n} \\
&= S(k_{3,12+(n+1)\bmod 4}) \oplus c'_4 \oplus k_{2,12+n} \oplus k_{2,4+n} \\
&= S(k_{3,12+(n+1)\bmod 4}) \oplus c'_4 \oplus k_{2,8+n} \oplus k_{2,4+n} \oplus k_{1,12+n} \\
&= S(k_{3,12+(n+1)\bmod 4}) \oplus c'_4 \oplus k_{1,12+n} \oplus k_{1,8+n} \\
&= S(k_{3,12+(n+1)\bmod 4}) \oplus c'_4 \oplus k_{0,12+n}
\end{aligned}
$$

$\square$

## B.2    Equation (10)

*Proof.*

$$
\begin{aligned}
k_{3,12+n} &= k_{3,8+n} \oplus k_{2,12+n} \\
&= k_{3,4+n} \oplus k_{2,12+n} \oplus k_{2,8+n} \\
&= k_{3,0+n} \oplus k_{2,12+n} \oplus k_{2,8+n} \oplus k_{2,4+n} \\
&= S(k_{2,12+(n+1)\bmod 4}) \oplus c'_3 \oplus k_{2,12+n} \oplus k_{2,8+n} \oplus k_{2,4+n} \oplus k_{2,0+n} \\
&= S(k_{2,12+(n+1)\bmod 4}) \oplus c'_3 \oplus k_{2,4+n} \oplus k_{2,0+n} \oplus k_{1,12+n} \\
&= S(k_{2,12+(n+1)\bmod 4}) \oplus c'_3 \oplus k_{1,12+n} \oplus k_{1,4+n} \\
&= S(k_{2,12+(n+1)\bmod 4}) \oplus c'_3 \oplus k_{1,8+n} \oplus k_{1,4+n} \oplus k_{0,12+n} \\
&= S(k_{2,12+(n+1)\bmod 4}) \oplus c'_3 \oplus k_{0,12+n} \oplus k_{0,8+n}
\end{aligned}
$$

$\square$

## B.3    Equation (11)

*Proof.*

$$
\begin{aligned}
k_{3,12+n} &= k_{3,8+n} \oplus k_{2,12+n} \\
&= k_{3,4+n} \oplus k_{2,12+n} \oplus k_{2,8+n} \\
&= k_{3,0+n} \oplus k_{2,12+n} \oplus k_{2,8+n} \oplus k_{2,4+n} \\
&= S(k_{2,12+(n+1)\bmod 4}) \oplus c'_3 \oplus k_{2,12+n} \oplus k_{2,8+n} \oplus k_{2,4+n} \oplus k_{2,0+n} \\
&= S(k_{2,12+(n+1)\bmod 4}) \oplus c'_3 \oplus k_{2,12+n} \oplus k_{2,0+n} \oplus k_{1,8+n} \\
&= S(k_{2,12+(n+1)\bmod 4}) \oplus c'_3 \oplus k_{2,12+n} \oplus S(k_{1,12+(n+1)\bmod 4}) \oplus c'_2 \oplus k_{1,8+n} \oplus k_{1,0+n} \\
&= S(k_{2,12+(n+1)\bmod 4}) \oplus c'_3 \oplus k_{2,12+n} \oplus S(k_{1,12+(n+1)\bmod 4}) \oplus c'_2 \oplus k_{1,4+n} \oplus k_{1,0+n} \oplus k_{0,8+n} \\
&= S(k_{2,12+(n+1)\bmod 4}) \oplus c'_3 \oplus k_{2,12+n} \oplus S(k_{1,12+(n+1)\bmod 4}) \oplus c'_2 \oplus k_{0,8+n} \oplus k_{0,4+n}
\end{aligned}
$$

$\square$

## B.4    Equation (12)

*Proof.*

$$
\begin{aligned}
k_{2,12+n} &= k_{2,8+n} \oplus k_{1,12+n} \\
&= k_{2,4+n} \oplus k_{1,12+n} \oplus k_{1,8+n} \\
&= k_{2,0+n} \oplus k_{1,12+n} \oplus k_{1,8+n} \oplus k_{1,4+n} \\
&= S(k_{1,12+(n+1) \bmod 4}) \oplus c'_2 \oplus k_{1,12+n} \oplus k_{1,8+n} \oplus k_{1,4+n} \oplus k_{1,0+n} \\
&= S(k_{1,12+(n+1) \bmod 4}) \oplus c'_2 \oplus k_{1,12+n} \oplus k_{1,0+n} \oplus k_{0,8+n} \\
&= S(k_{1,12+(n+1) \bmod 4}) \oplus c'_2 \oplus k_{1,12+n} \oplus S(k_{0,12+(n+1) \bmod 4}) \oplus c'_1 \oplus k_{0,8+n} \oplus k_{0,0+n}
\end{aligned}
$$

□

# Efficient Pairings and ECC
# for Embedded Systems

Thomas Unterluggauer and Erich Wenger

Institute for Applied Information Processing and Communications,
Graz University of Technology,
Inffeldgasse 16a, 8010 Graz, Austria
{Thomas.Unterluggauer,Erich.Wenger}@iaik.tugraz.at

**Abstract.** The research on pairing-based cryptography brought forth
a wide range of protocols interesting for future embedded applications.
One significant obstacle for the widespread deployment of pairing-based
cryptography are its tremendous hardware and software requirements.
In this paper we present three side-channel protected hardware/software
designs for pairing-based cryptography yet small and practically fast:
our plain ARM Cortex-M0+-based design computes a pairing in less
than one second. The utilization of a multiply-accumulate instruction-
set extension or a light-weight drop-in hardware accelerator that is placed
between CPU and data memory improves runtime up to six times. With
a 10.1 kGE large drop-in module and a 49 kGE large platform, our design
is one of the smallest pairing designs available. Its very practical runtime
of 162 ms for one pairing on a 254-bit BN curve and its reusability for
other elliptic-curve based crypto systems offer a great solution for every
microprocessor-based embedded application.

**Keywords:** optimal-ate pairing, elliptic-curve cryptography, embedded
computing, hardware/software co-design.

## 1 Introduction

The field of pairing-based cryptography has become the key enabler for novel
protocols and algorithms: privacy-aware group-signature schemes [9,22], identity-
based encryption schemes [7,23], and since recently even provable leakage-
resilient protocols [25] rely on pairing operations. The practical advantages of
those protocols motivate their use in the very competitive markets of embedded
microprocessors and smart cards.

The biggest implementation challenges of pairing-based cryptography are
related to its tremendous resource and runtime requirements. Therefore, researchers started to implement optimized pairing operations for desktop computers [1,6], for smart phones [20,31], and as dedicated hardware modules [16,24].
Cost-sensitive embedded applications however simply do not have the budget
for such powerful application processors or 130-180 kGE of dedicated hardware.

L. Batina and M. Robshaw (Eds.): CHES 2014, LNCS 8731, pp. 298–315, 2014.

For these embedded scenarios, implementations on light-weight RISC processors have been done. For example, Szczechowiak *et al.* [33] need 17.9 seconds for a pairing on an ATmega microprocessor, Gouvêa *et al.* [18] need 1.9 seconds on an MSP430X microprocessor, and Devegili *et al.* [15] need 2.5 seconds on a Philips HiPerSmart™ MIPS microprocessor. Unfortunately, such runtimes are not very promising for real-world, interactive applications as pairing-based protocols like group-signature schemes often happen to rely on several pairing and group operations. The resulting overall runtimes of several seconds would be considerably too slow. Additionally, it is unclear to which degree timing-analysis, power-analysis, or fault-analysis attacks have been considered in all those implementations.

These limitations motivated us to be the first to implement constant-runtime, side-channel protected optimal-Ate pairings using Barreto-Naehrig (BN) curves [4] on an ARM Cortex-M0+ [2,3] microprocessor. The respective pairing runtime of 993 ms seems very promising as it is several times faster than related work[1], but might be insufficient for interactive protocols as well. Therefore, it was a necessity to improve performance by adding dedicated hardware.

In this paper, we present three reusable pairing platforms which offer runtimes of down to 162 ms requiring 10.1 kGE of dedicated hardware at most – significantly less than similarly fast hardware implementations by related work. Our rigorous hardware/software co-design approach equipped one platform with a multiply-accumulate instruction-set extension and another platform with a drop-in accelerator[2] [35]. By building a flexible, specially crafted drop-in module with several novel design ideas, we were able to improve the runtime of pairing and group operations up to ten times. This concept platform consisting of CPU, RAM, ROM, and drop-in module consumes merely 49 kGE of hardware in total with 10.1 kGE of those being spent for the drop-in accelerator. The practicability of this platform is evaluated for several high-level pairing protocols [7,8,22] – each operating in significantly less than one second. Its reusability for Elliptic-Curve Cryptography (ECC) is further verified for secp160r1, secp256r1 [11,29], and Curve25519 [5], requiring 11.9-36.8 ms for a side-channel protected point multiplication. Those results make the drop-in based platform highly suitable for embedded computing, smart cards, wireless sensor nodes, near-field communication, and the Internet of Things.

The paper is structured as follows: Section 2 gives an overview on pairings and Section 3 covers the implementation aspects of the high-level pairing arithmetic. In Section 4, the architectural options to build suitable pairing platforms are presented. The respective platforms are evaluated in Section 5 and compared with related work in Section 6. The (re-)usability of our drop-in platform is content of Section 7. A conclusion is finally done in Section 8.

---

[1] Not considering the different underlying microprocessor architectures.
[2] Wenger [35] applied the concept to binary-field based elliptic-curve cryptography while we apply the concept to prime-field based elliptic-curve cryptography.

# 2    Background on Pairings

The wide range of cryptographic protocols in pairing-based cryptography is based on three cyclic order-$n$ groups $\mathbb{G}_1$, $\mathbb{G}_2$, $\mathbb{G}_T$ and a bilinear pairing operation. A bilinear pairing $e : \mathbb{G}_1 \times \mathbb{G}_2 \to \mathbb{G}_T$ accepts an element of the two additive groups $\mathbb{G}_1$ and $\mathbb{G}_2$, respectively, maps these to the multiplicative group $\mathbb{G}_T$, and hereby fulfills several properties:

1. Bilinearity: $e(aP, bQ) = e(P, Q)^{ab} \; \forall P \in \mathbb{G}_1, \; Q \in \mathbb{G}_2, \; a, b \in \mathbb{Z}$.
2. Non-degeneracy: $\forall P \in \mathbb{G}_1 \setminus \{\mathcal{O}\} \; \exists \, Q \in \mathbb{G}_2 : e(P, Q) \neq 1$.
3. Computability: $e(P, Q)$ can be computed efficiently.

The groups $\mathbb{G}_1$, $\mathbb{G}_2$ are typically groups over elliptic curves and $\mathbb{G}_T$ is the subgroup of a large extension field. However, only certain elliptic curves allow the definition of $\mathbb{G}_1$, $\mathbb{G}_2$, $\mathbb{G}_T$ with an admissible bilinear pairing, e.g., [4,27]. In this paper, we focus on the pairing-friendly elliptic curves by Barreto and Naehrig [4] of the form $E : y^2 = x^3 + b$ with $b \neq 0$ (*BN curves*). Ate pairings $a(Q, P)$ based on these curves can be described as follows:

$$a \colon \mathbb{G}_2 \times \mathbb{G}_1 \to \mathbb{G}_T \; : \; E(\mathbb{F}_{p^{12}}) \times E(\mathbb{F}_p) \to \mathbb{F}_{p^{12}}^* . \tag{1}$$

Note that for $\mathbb{G}_1$, $\mathbb{G}_2$ and $\mathbb{G}_T$ to have the same prime order $n$, $\mathbb{G}_2$ and $\mathbb{G}_T$ need to be subgroups of $E(\mathbb{F}_{p^{12}})$ and $\mathbb{F}_{p^{12}}^*$, respectively. The BN curves use a parameter $u$ such that a desired security level is achieved. This allows the computation of the prime $p$ and the prime group order $n$ in dependence of $u$:

$$p(u) = 36u^4 + 36u^3 + 24u^2 + 6u + 1$$
$$n(u) = 36u^4 + 36u^3 + 18u^2 + 6u + 1 .$$

As another benefit, BN curves possess an efficiently computable group homomorphism that exploits the curve's sextic twist $E'$. Utilization of this homomorphism allows the compression of the elements in $\mathbb{G}_2$, which leads to a more efficient definition of the Ate pairing, namely

$$a \colon \mathbb{G}_2 \times \mathbb{G}_1 \to \mathbb{G}_T \; : \; E'(\mathbb{F}_{p^2}) \times E(\mathbb{F}_p) \to \mathbb{F}_{p^{12}}^* . \tag{2}$$

The pairing $a$ itself consists of the evaluation of a rational function $f_{\lambda,Q}$ and a final exponentiation that maps all cosets to the same unique representative:

$$a = f_{\lambda,Q}(P)^{(p^{12}-1)/n} .$$

Owing to the Frobenius homomorphism, the final exponentiation by $(p^{12} - 1)/n$ can be split into an easy part $(p^6 - 1)(p^2 + 1)$ and a hard part $(p^4 - p^2 + 1)/n$. The function $f_{\lambda,Q}$ can in general not be evaluated directly. However, Miller [26] described an important property of rational functions, namely

$$f_{i+j,P} = f_{i,P} f_{j,P} \frac{\ell_{[i]P,[j]P}}{\nu_{[i+j]P}} .$$

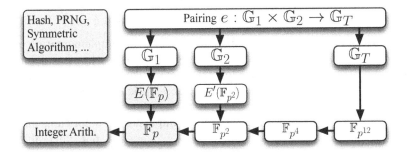

**Fig. 1.** Arithmetic required for pairings over Barreto-Naehrig curves

The property allows the computation of $f_{\lambda,Q}$ in polynomial time by merely evaluating vertical ($\nu$) and straight ($\ell$) lines in elliptic curve points using a double-and-add approach. Values of $\lambda$ with low Hamming weight result in a particularly fast computation of $f_{\lambda,Q}$, the pairing becomes optimal. In this work, we used the efficient optimal-Ate pairing by Vercauteren [34].

# 3 High-Level Arithmetic

The computation of bilinear pairings over BN curves requires several layers of arithmetic. As illustrated in Figure 1, all arithmetic is based on a multi-precision integer arithmetic layer. On top of that, prime-field arithmetic and a tower of extension fields are built upon. The elliptic curve groups used as $\mathbb{G}_1$ and $\mathbb{G}_2$ utilize the prime field and its quadratic extension field, respectively. The largest extension field $\mathbb{F}_{p^{12}}$ is used by $\mathbb{G}_T$. The pairing computation itself is based on the groups $\mathbb{G}_1$, $\mathbb{G}_2$, $\mathbb{G}_T$, and their underlying field arithmetic.

**Methodology.** Our state-of-the-art implementations are based on the techniques used by Beuchat et al. [6] and Devegili et al. [14]. The pairing implementation uses the fast formulas by Costello et al. [13], the inversion trick by Aranha et al. [1], a lazy reduction technique in $\mathbb{F}_{p^2}$ [6,31], and a slightly modified variant of the final exponentiation by Fuentes-Castañeda et al. [17] that requires less memory (see Appendix A.1). The prime-field inversion using Fermat's little theorem is optimized according to Appendix A.2. Since operations in $\mathbb{G}_T$ and in the hard part of the final exponentiation take place in the cyclotomic subgroup of $\mathbb{F}_{p^{12}}^*$, dedicated squaring formulas are utilized [19]. The point multiplications in both elliptic curve groups use Montgomery ladders that are based on fast formulas [21] in homogeneous projective co-Z coordinates.

**Parameters.** As this work aims to offer a certain degree of flexibility, both the 80-bit and the 128-bit security level are supported. The two elliptic curves BN158 [18] ($u = 40\,00800023_h$) and BN254 [30] ($u = -40800000\,00000001_h$) of the form $y^2 = x^3 + 2$ were chosen. Those lead to particularly fast execution times as the respective constants $\lambda$ of $f_{\lambda,Q}$ have low Hamming weights. The extension field $\mathbb{F}_{p^2}$ is represented as $\mathbb{F}_p[i]/(i^2 - \beta)$ with $\beta = -1$. The extension field $\mathbb{F}_{p^{12}}$ is built as $\mathbb{F}_{p^2}[z]/(z^6 - \zeta)$, with $\zeta = (1 + i)$ for BN254 and $\zeta = \frac{1}{1+i}$ for BN158.

**Implementation Attacks.** An important aspect in the implementation of pairings and group arithmetic for embedded applications is the consideration of side-channel attacks. While scalar factors or exponents are typically the secret operands for operations in $\mathbb{G}_1$, $\mathbb{G}_2$ and $\mathbb{G}_T$, an elliptic curve point may have to be protected in the case of pairing operations.

As a countermeasure to timing attacks, all implemented algorithms have constant, data-independent runtime. Therefore, e.g., some fast but vulnerable point multiplication algorithms are not used. Both the point multiplications in $\mathbb{G}_1$, $\mathbb{G}_2$ and the exponentiations in $\mathbb{G}_T$ hence use Montgomery ladders. The implementation's countermeasures against first-order Differential Power Analysis (DPA) attacks comprise Randomized Projective Coordinates (RPC) [12] in both the pairing computation and the point multiplications in $\mathbb{G}_1$ and $\mathbb{G}_2$. To detect fault attacks on data, point multiplications in $\mathbb{G}_1$ and $\mathbb{G}_2$ include several point verifications. DPA and fault attacks on exponentiations in $\mathbb{G}_T$ as well as fault attacks on pairings were also taken into consideration, but can better be handled on the protocol layer using randomization.

# 4    Hardware Architectures

To meet the high requirements of pairing-based cryptography in embedded devices, our goal was to equip a stand-alone microprocessor, designated for embedded applications, with a dedicated hardware unit such that: (i) Pairing computations are usable within interactive (e.g., authentication) protocols. (ii) A pre-existing microprocessor platform is modified only minimally. (iii) The overall hardware requirements, i.e., the costs, are kept small and considerably below 100 kGE needed in related work [16,24]. (iv) Embedded applications such as wireless sensor nodes and NFC should be practically feasible.

Figure 2 summarizes potential architectures that can be used to attain such goals. The straightforward solution *(a)*, a sole off-the-shelf microprocessor, requires minimal hardware-development time, however potentially delivers insufficient performance. The runtimes desirable for interactive protocols can only be achieved by either adding powerful, dedicated instructions *(b)*, or by adding dedicated co-processors. Contrary to a dedicated hardware module *(c)*, a drop-in module *(d)* is memoryless and requires neither a Direct Memory Access (DMA) controller nor a multi-master bus. Wenger [35] showed the advantages of the drop-in concept in comparison to a dedicated hardware module for binary-field ECC. However, the applicability of this technique for prime-field based pairings is still an open question.

Following up the potential architectures, we consecutively evaluate the practicability of a plain microprocessor design *(a)*, a multiply-accumulate instruction-set extension *(b)*, and a dedicated drop-in module *(d)*.

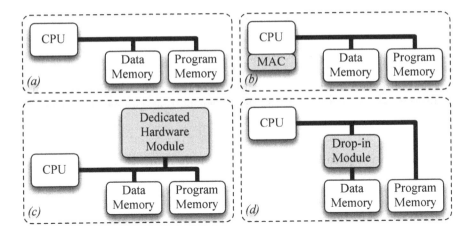

**Fig. 2.** Architectural options for fast and flexible pairing designs

### 4.1 The Used Microprocessor

The accomplishment of the initially set goals highly, depends on the used microprocessor. As the runtime figures by Szczechowiak *et al.* [32] and Gouvêa *et al.* [18] discourage the use of an 8-bit or 16-bit microprocessor, a 32-bit microprocessor is preferred as a basis. Moreover, the bottleneck between computation unit and RAM is less of an issue if 32-bit interfaces are used. We hence decided to utilize a self-built processor functionally equivalent to the ARM Cortex-M0+ [2], because the Cortex-M0+ was especially designed for embedded applications and currently is one of the smallest 32-bit processors in production. The Cortex-M0+ has 16 32-bit general-purpose registers of which 8 are efficiently usable. It comes with a mixed 16/32-bit Thumb/Thumb-2 instruction set and optionally either a 32-cycle or single-cycle 32-bit multiplier. In its minimum configuration, ARM specifies its Cortex-M0+ to require only 12 kGE in a 90 nm process technology.

### 4.2 The Software Framework

The biggest advantage of an off-the-shelf microprocessor are the vast (open-source) toolchains. Thus a high-level framework capable of pairing-based cryptography using BN curves was created in C. It provides extension field arithmetic, elliptic curve operations, and bilinear pairings. The framework focuses on both good performance and low memory consumption. To achieve the latter, several optimizations were incorporated into the framework. First, virtually all of the memory is allocated on the stack. As stack variables are discarded at the end of each function, stack allocation facilitates the reduction of required memory by separating code into different functions. Second, allocated memory is reutilized where possible. Third, memory-optimized algorithms are used, e.g., for the final exponentiation as in Appendix A.1. Last, compiler optimizations are used to decrease the program size. Therefore, the compiler options `-ffunction-sections`,

-fdata-sections and the linker options -gc-sections, --specs=nano.specs
are passed to the bare-metal ARM GNU toolchain (version 4.7.4).

The high-level pairing framework is common to all three evaluated platforms.
The main difference between these platforms is the implemented finite-field arithmetic. While *(a)* and *(b)* control the whole finite field arithmetic in software, *(d)*
relies on finite-state machines to perform additions, subtractions and multiplications in $\mathbb{F}_p$ and $\mathbb{F}_{p^2}$. Nevertheless, all implementation options ensure constant
runtime and consider side-channel attacks.

### 4.3    Assembly-Optimized Software Implementation *(a)*

The plain microprocessor platform *(a)* is based on a Cortex-M0+ with a single-
cycle multiplier. Its hand-crafted assembly routines for optimized prime-field
arithmetic always perform a reduction step to ensure constant runtime. This is
accomplished by storing the reduction result either to the target or a dummy
memory location via masking of the operand addresses. The crucial prime-field
multiplication utilizes an unrolled Separated Product Scanning (SPS) method of
the Montgomery multiplication [28] that is derived from [10]. The SPS variant
is chosen because of the particular $\mathbb{F}_{p^2}$-multiplication technique [6,31] we use,
which performs the required three multiplications and two reductions separately.
Product scanning can further be efficiently implemented on the processor if three
registers are used as an accumulator, as presented in [36]. The reduction step
for the curve BN254 is further optimized as several multiply-accumulates can be
skipped due to the sparse prime [18].

### 4.4    Multiply-Accumulate Hardware Extensions *(b)*

The performance of the prime-field multiplication significantly suffers from the
$32 \times 32 \rightarrow 32$ bit multiplier of the Cortex-M0+, which results in 80% of a pairing's runtime being spent in $\mathbb{F}_p$ multiplications. To improve this, the processor
core is equipped in *(b)* with a multiply-accumulate extension similar to [36].
It adds the result of a full $32 \times 32 \rightarrow 64$ bit multiplication to three accumulation registers in a single cycle. In order to avoid a modification of the compiler
toolchain, the TST instruction, which is not required for prime-field multiplication, is reinterpreted as a multiply-accumulate instruction if a certain bit in
the control register is set. The control register is manipulated accordingly at
the beginning and the end of a prime-field multiplication. Besides accelerated
multiply-accumulate operations, the prime-field multiplication requires less registers for temporary variables, which we exploit by caching some of the operand
words in the product scanning routine.

### 4.5    The Drop-in Module *(d)*

As a consequence of the high-level runtime and area goals, it is of utmost importance to maximize the utilization of the invested chip hardware. To achieve this,

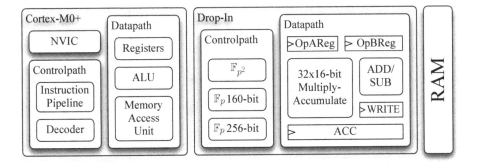

**Fig. 3.** High-level representation of architecture *(d)* (without program memory). Note that the sizes of the blocks are not proportional to their respective hardware footprints

a lightweight hardware drop-in accelerator is placed between processor and data memory. The respective design, which is shown in Figure 3, uses a Cortex-M0+, but any other processor is equally suitable.

The drop-in module provides unrolled state machines and an appropriate arithmetic unit for 160-bit and 256-bit $\mathbb{F}_p$ multiplication, $\mathbb{F}_p$ addition and $\mathbb{F}_p$ subtraction. It further encompasses state machines to control $\mathbb{F}_{p^2}$ addition, $\mathbb{F}_{p^2}$ subtraction, $\mathbb{F}_{p^2}$ multiplication and $\mathbb{F}_{p^2}$ squaring. Several memory-mapped registers are used to control the drop-in module. A lightweight arbiter is built in which always gives preference to the CPU when the CPU wants to access the data memory. In such case, the drop-in module is prepared to stall its operation.

The core element of our drop-in module is a multiply-accumulate unit that is used to perform a Finely Integrated Product Scanning (FIPS) [10] Montgomery multiplication. Within this algorithm approximately $2N^2 + N$, with $N = \lceil \frac{\mathrm{ld}(p)}{W} \rceil$, $W$-bit integer multiplications are performed that require approximately $4N^2$ load operations. Instead of using a dual-port memory, we attain a perfectly utilized bus and a perfectly utilized multiplier by using a two-cycle multiply-accumulate unit that is based on a $W \times W/2$-bit multiplier. This saves $3\,\mathrm{kGE}$ for $W = 32$ in an 130 nm process compared to a traditional $W \times W$-bit multiplier.

A finite-field operation is started by writing three memory pointer registers (OpA, OpB, and RES) and a control register. As those registers are mapped at consecutive addresses, the store-multiple instruction (STM) of the Cortex-M0+ can be used to efficiently start an operation. A started finite-field multiplication is performed using the following hardware components: a $W \times W/2 = 32 \times 16$-bit multiplier, a $\lceil \mathrm{ld}(2N) \rceil + 2W = 68$-bit ACCumulator, a $W = 32$-bit register for operand A (OpAReg), a $3W/2 = 48$-bit register for operand B (OpBReg), and a $W = 32$-bit WRITE register. In OpBReg, the top 32 bits are always written by the bus and the lowest 16 bits are used as an operand of the multiplier. Therefore, a sequence of shift/rotate operations is necessary to actually multiply the loaded operands. Table 1 visualizes the dataflow within the drop-in module. For a single multiply-accumulate operation five clock cycles are necessary. As the drop-in

**Table 1.** Propagation of data within the pipelined drop-in module

| Bus | OpBReg | OpAReg | Mult. | Accum. |
|---|---|---|---|---|
| LD OpB+0 | | | | |
| LD OpA+0 | WR | | | |
| LD OpB+0 | SH | WR | | |
| LD OpA+1 | WRSH | | MUL1 | |
| LD OpB+1 | SH | WR | MUL2 | SHIFT |
| LD OpA+0 | WRSH | | MUL1 | |
| LD OpB+2 | SH | WR | MUL2 | |
| ST RES+0 | WRSH | | MUL1 | |
| LD OpB+1 | SH | | MUL2 | SHIFT |
| LD OpA+1 | WRSH | | MUL1 | |
| LD OpB+0 | SH | WR | MUL2 | |

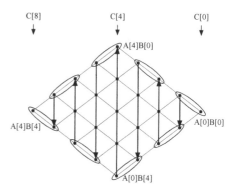

**Fig. 4.** 5 × 5-word zig-zag product scanning multi-precision multiplication method

module heavily relies on pipelining, practically only two cycles are needed. The following steps are performed: (i) OpB+i is applied to the bus. (ii) OpB+i is WRitten to OpBReg and OpA+j is applied to the bus. (iii) OpAReg is WRitten and OpBReg is SHifted by 16 bits. (iv) The first multiplication cycle (MUL1) multiplies the lower 16 bits of OpB+i with OpA+j and OpBReg is shifted again. (v) During the second multiplication cycle (MUL2) the accumulator is optionally SHIFTed. When shifted, the lowest 32-bit of the accumulator are stored in the WRITE register. This data is later written to the address RES+i+j, when the bus is not utilized.

As the fully utilized bus needs some free cycles to write the result, we use a zig-zag product scanning technique (cf. Figure 4) [37]. In this technique, consecutive columns are traversed in different order, which allows caching of a single operand from one column to the next. This frees the bus for $2N$ cycles, which are exactly the $2N$ cycles required to store the computed results.

Although the implemented FIPS multiplication is quite complex, the software running on the CPU is completely independent of the methodology used to perform finite-field arithmetic within the drop-in module. However, there are two implementation guidelines the software has to deal with. First, constant variables have to be temporarily copied to the data memory when being used. Second, there are two techniques to wait for the drop-in module to finish. A function delegating an operation to the drop-in module can either start an operation and wait for it to finish, or wait for a previously started operation to finish and only then start a new operation. The latter case is more performant because the CPU and the drop-in module potentially work in parallel, i.e., the control flow operations involved in the invocation of the routines that call the drop-in module are done while the drop-in module is computing. However, temporary variables on the stack are freed once a function finishes, which requires adding additional wait statements within the extension-field arithmetic to prevent the drop-in from accessing reallocated memory locations. Nevertheless, the utilization of the

**Table 2.** Performance of various operations on architectures *(a)*, *(b)*, and *(d)*

| Design | $\mathbb{F}_p$ Add [Cycles] | $\mathbb{F}_p$ Mul [Cycles] | $\mathbb{F}_p$ Inv [kCycles] | $\mathbb{G}_1$ Mul [kCycles] | $\mathbb{G}_2$ Mul [kCycles] | $\mathbb{G}_T$ Exp [kCycles] | $\mathbb{G}_1 \times \mathbb{G}_2$ Pairing [kCycles] | RAM [Byte] | ROM [Byte] |
|---|---|---|---|---|---|---|---|---|---|
| **BN158** | | | | | | | | | |
| Cortex-M0+ | 112 | 1,800 | 331 | 4,828 | 11,775 | 22,871 | 17,389 | 1,856 | 13,980 |
| MAC | 112 | 361 | 72 | 1,129 | 4,042 | 10,736 | 7,828 | 1,796 | 11,232 |
| Drop-in | 56 | 161 | 29 | 493 | 1,577 | 4,322 | 3,182 | 1,876 | 10,364 |
| **BN254** | | | | | | | | | |
| Cortex-M0+ | 166 | 3,782 | 1,122 | 16,071 | 38,277 | 72,459 | 47,643 | 2,828 | 18,116 |
| MAC | 166 | 934 | 285 | 4,323 | 11,449 | 27,460 | 17,960 | 2,836 | 12,572 |
| Drop-in | 75 | 335 | 97 | 1,566 | 4,858 | 12,076 | 7,763 | 2,880 | 10,764 |

drop-in is increased from 77.6% to 85.1% when the function first waits for previous operations to finish. Similarly, the utilization of the RAM is raised from 75.7% to 80.1% (cf. 34.6% in *(b)*, 17.0% in *(a)*).

# 5   Implementation Results

To verify the achievement of the area and performance goals initially set, the three microprocessor-based platforms *(a)*, *(b)* and *(d)* were evaluated with respect to hard- and software. Regarding the overall hardware platforms, runtime, area, power, and energy consumption are distinctive. Regarding the software part, the evaluation focuses on the runtimes of the underlying finite-field arithmetic and the most expensive operations used within protocols: the point multiplications in $\mathbb{G}_1$ and $\mathbb{G}_2$, the exponentiation in $\mathbb{G}_T$, and the pairing operation.

The results in Table 2 show that the multiply-accumulate extension speeds up the prime-field multiplications by factors of 4.0-5.0[3], but leaves the prime-field additions unaffected. The same speed-ups are observed for prime-field inversions and point multiplications in $\mathbb{G}_1$. However, the impact of the multiply-accumulate extension on the performance of both pairings and operations in $\mathbb{G}_2$, $\mathbb{G}_T$ is lower and lies between a factor of 2.1 and 3.3. Considering the performance of the drop-in module, an even greater speed-up is observed compared to the plain software implementation. In this case, prime-field multiplications, inversions and point multiplications in $\mathbb{G}_1$ are up to 11.3 times faster, which eventually results in an up to 6.1 times faster computation of pairings. On average, operations using BN158 are 3.0 times faster than operations using BN254.

Throughout all implementations, the demand for data memory is kept relatively low, with a maximum of 1,876 bytes and 2,880 bytes for BN158 and BN254, respectively. Similarly, the program sizes are kept small, e.g., 18 KB for BN254. Given a typical clock frequency of 48 Mhz, the performance results of the point multiplications in $\mathbb{G}_1$, $\mathbb{G}_2$, the exponentiation in $\mathbb{G}_T$, and the pairing operation are illustrated in Figure 5. The respective runtimes support our choice of a

---

[3] The implementation for BN158 with multiply-accumulate extension utilizes the FIPS method and discards lazy reduction in $\mathbb{F}_{p^2}$ [6,31] as it yields better performance.

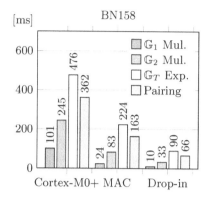

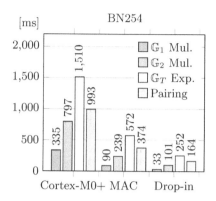

**Fig. 5.** Group operations at 48 MHz

32-bit architecture: providing 128-bit security, the drop-in based platform does pairing computations in highly practical 164 ms. The pure *embedded* software implementation performs the same computation in 993 ms.

While Table 2 focuses on the software part, the most important hardware characteristics are visualized in Table 3. The runtime is given for a single pairing computation. Both area and power measurements were determined for an 130 nm low-leakage UMC technology. The area results in a 90 nm UMC technology are explicitly marked. The designs were synthesized and their power and runtime evaluated for a clock frequency of 48 MHz. Both data and program memory were realized using RAM and ROM macros of appropriate sizes. The program memory encompasses all routines required to implement pairing-based protocols, i.e., pairings, operations in $\mathbb{G}_1$, $\mathbb{G}_2$, and $\mathbb{G}_T$. These platforms are hence ready-to-use for future applications based on pairings over BN curves.

According to Table 3, BN254 pairing computations with reasonable performance are available at the cost of 57.7 kGE in an 130 nm process technology. Switching to the more advanced 90 nm process technology shrinks the design to 49.0 kGE, constituting one of the smallest available hardware designs for pairings with practical relevance. In terms of power consumption, the plain microprocessor design is, as expected, the most economical. The multiply-accumulate extension and the drop-in module increase power consumption by 25% and 70%, respectively. Due to their increased performance, these platforms are more energy-efficient though. Their respective demand for energy is 2.1 and 3.5 times lower.

# 6 Comparison with Related Work

As a consequence of our hardware/software co-design approach, comparison with related work focuses on two aspects. On the one hand, the pure software implementation on the Cortex-M0+ is brought into relation to other software

**Table 3.** Implementation characteristics for 130 nm and 90 nm process technologies

| Platform | RAM [kGE] | ROM [kGE] | CPU [kGE] | Area Dedicated [kGE] | Total [kGE] | Power [mW] | Runtime [ms] | Energy [mJ] |
|---|---|---|---|---|---|---|---|---|
| | | | | BN158 | | | | |
| Cortex-M0+ | 11.4 | 15.6 | 18.4 | - | 45.4 | 5.92 | 362 | 2.14 |
| MAC | 11.1 | 13.8 | 27.1 | - | 52.0 | 7.38 | 163 | 1.20 |
| Drop-in | 11.4 | 13.8 | $17.0^a$ | 10.8 | 52.9 | 10.25 | 66 | **0.68** |
| Drop-in 90nm | 10.5 | 12.0 | $12.6^a$ | **10.1** | **45.2** | - | 66 | - |
| | | | | BN254 | | | | |
| Cortex-M0+ | 16.0 | 19.3 | 18.4 | - | 53.7 | 5.80 | 993 | 5.76 |
| MAC | 16.0 | 15.6 | 27.1 | - | 58.8 | 7.33 | 374 | 2.74 |
| Drop-in | 16.2 | 13.8 | $17.0^a$ | 10.8 | 57.7 | 9.96 | 162 | **1.61** |
| Drop-in 90nm | 14.3 | 12.0 | $12.6^a$ | **10.1** | **49.0** | - | 162 | - |

$^a$ Bit-serial multiplier.

implementations on low-resource hardware. On the other hand, the resulting hardware design is compared with other dedicated pairing hardware implementations.

The comparison of our software implementation with related implementations of Ate pairings over BN curves providing approximately 128-bit security is summarized in Table 4. Gouvêa et al. [18] provide highly optimized software implementations for the 16-bit microcontroller MSP430 and a variant of its successor MSP430X, which is equipped with a 32-bit multiplier (MPY32). The implementation by Devegili et al. [15] is evaluated on a 32-bit Philips HiPerSmart™ smart card, which has a SmartMIPS architecture and clearly is a direct competitor of Cortex-M0+-based smart cards. However, it is unclear to which extent side-channel resistance is considered by either of them.

As both the MSP430 and the Cortex-M0+ use a 16-bit instruction-set, it is important to highlight the exceptionally low program and data memory footprint of our implementations. It is however hard to compare the quality of an implementation when different frameworks and different microprocessors are involved.

Other pairing implementations for 32-bit ARM processors are limited to the Cortex-A series, such as in [20]. However, their pairing's runtime of 9.9 ms on a 1.2 GHz Cortex-A9 is as well hardly comparable with our pairing's runtime

**Table 4.** Related software implementations of Ate pairings over BN curves

| | Platform | RAM [Byte] | ROM [Byte] | Runtime [kCycles] | Frequ. [MHz] | Runtime [ms] |
|---|---|---|---|---|---|---|
| Gouvêa [18] | MSP430 | 6,500 | 36,000 | 79,440 | 8 | 9,930 |
| Devegili [15] | Philips HiPerSmart™ | <16,000 | - | 90,462 | 36 | 2,513 |
| Gouvêa [18] | MSP430X/MPY32 | 6,500 | 34,400 | 47,736 | 25 | 1,909 |
| **Ours** | Cortex-M0+ | **2,828** | **18,116** | **47,643** | 48 | **993** |

**Table 5.** Related hardware platforms (130 nm)

|  | Area | | Time |
|---|---|---|---|
|  | Ded. [kGE] | Total [kGE] | [kCycles] |
| Fan [16] | 183 | 183 | **593** |
| Kammler [24] | 71$^a$ | 164 | 5,340 |
| Kammler [24] | 67$^a$ | 145 | 6,490 |
| Kammler [24] | 53$^a$ | 130 | 10,816 |
| **Ours** (Drop-in) | 11$^b$ | 58 | 7,763 |

$^a$ Core excl. 26 kGE of original RISC
$^b$ Drop-in module.

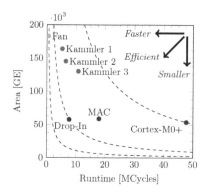

**Fig. 6.** Characteristics of related hardware

on the Cortex-M0+ since the multi-core Cortex-A processors provide massively higher clock frequencies along with a more powerful instruction set.

Regarding related hardware platforms, Table 5 covers hardware implementations of pairings providing roughly 128-bit security. Fan et al. [16] proposed a dedicated pairing cryptoprocessor with parallelized, full-precision $\mathbb{F}_p$ arithmetic. Its centerpiece is a hardware implementation of a hybrid modular multiplication algorithm that performs both polynomial and coefficient reduction. Their area figures, however, exclude the required RAM. Kammler et al. [24] extended a 5-stage 32-bit RISC core with instructions for $\mathbb{F}_p$ arithmetic. Their Application-Specific Instruction-set Processor (ASIP) uses a Montgomery multiplier structure that can be synthesized in different configurations and sizes. Unfortunately, their area figures do not contain the program memory.

In comparison to [16] and [24], our drop-in-based platform is 2.2-3.1 times smaller with regard to total area consumption. In both [24] and our case the CPU and the data memory can be reused for other applications. In terms of dedicated hardware, our drop-in-based platform is 16.6 times smaller than the work of Fan et al. In exchange, their design is faster and provides the best area-runtime product according to Figure 6. However, it depends on the application how much hardware area is actually acceptable to be spent on a dedicated pairing accelerator.

# 7    Re-usability of Our Drop-in Architecture

To emphasize the practicability of our low-area platforms for deploying cryptography to embedded environments, several protocols that are relevant in such context have been assessed in terms of the performance to expect.

**Table 6.** Performance of pairing-based protocols on the drop-in platform

| | $G_1$ Mul | $G_2$ Mul | $G_T$ Exp | $G_1 \times G_2$ Pairing | BN158 [ms] | BN254 [ms] |
|---|---|---|---|---|---|---|
| **Leakage Resilient KEM [25]** | | | | | | |
| Encaps. | 0 | 1 | 1 | 0 | 123 | 353 |
| Decaps. | 2 | 0 | 0 | 2 | 153 | 389 |
| **Identity-Based Encryption KEM [7,23]** | | | | | | |
| Encaps. | 3 | 0 | 1 | 0 | 121 | 349 |
| Decaps. | 0 | 0 | 0 | $1.5^a$ | 99 | 243 |

| | $G_1$ Mul | $G_2$ Mul | $G_T$ Exp | $G_1 \times G_2$ Pairing | BN158 [ms] | BN254 [ms] |
|---|---|---|---|---|---|---|
| **Short Signatures [8]** | | | | | | |
| Sign | 1 | 0 | 0 | 0 | 10 | 33 |
| Verify | 0 | 2 | 0 | 1 | 132 | 364 |
| **Short Group Signatures [22]** | | | | | | |
| Sign | 9 | 2 | 0 | $1.5^a$ | 258 | 739 |
| Verify | 9 | 2 | 0 | 3 | 357 | 981 |
| Link | 0 | 0 | 0 | 3 | 199 | 485 |

[a] Ratios and products of pairings are counted as 1.5 pairing computations.

**Using the Drop-in Module for Pairing-Based Protocols.** The short signature scheme by Boneh et al. [8] is interesting for constrained signature devices as it aids to reduce communication. As a representative of group signatures, which help to provide anonymous authentication, the scheme by Hwang et al. [22] was chosen. To be able to establish a random session key without the necessity of verifying public keys, the identity-based encryption scheme by Boneh et al. [7] in its Key Encapsulation Mechanism (KEM) variant was evaluated as it combines good performance with small parameters. Additionally, the leakage resilient bilinear ElGamal KEM by Kiltz and Pietrzak [25] is taken into consideration because it is proven to have bounded side-channel leakage.

The number of computationally expensive operations and the expected overall runtime of each of the aforementioned protocols are presented in Table 6. The runtimes are given for the drop-in module based platform. As the figures suggest, all of the protocols may be performed on the device with user interaction as response times lie noticeably below one second.

**Using the Drop-in Module for ECC.** In order to emphasize the re-usability of our drop-in module based design, we also evaluated the performance of the standardized curves [11,29] secp160r1 and secp256r1 and the performance of Curve25519 by Bernstein [5], which many people fancy as replacement curve of standardized NIST curves. Again, we follow the point multiplication methodology from [36], which relies on Montgomery ladders, randomized projective coordinates and multiple point validation checks. All implementations have similar hardware footprints and require 4.1 kGE (500 bytes) for RAM, 6.2 kGE (3,200 bytes) for ROM, 10.1 kGE for the drop-in module, 12.6 kGE for the Cortex-M0+, and 33 kGE in total (in a 90 nm UMC technology). Point multiplications for secp160r1, secp256r1, and Curve25519 need 570 kcycles, 1,765 kcycles, and 1,110 kcycles, respectively. Note that we do not take advantage of the special form of the underlying primes. However, with runtimes of 11.9-36.8 ms (at 48 MHz) the drop-in concept is clearly an enabler of elliptic-curve based interactive protocols.

# 8    Conclusion

According to our evaluations of three microprocessor-based hardware designs, the utilization of a compact 32-bit microprocessor results in notably small pairing implementations. Requiring merely 45.2-49.0 kGE of chip area, we provided one of the smallest available hardware designs capable of bilinear pairings. The most prominent platform was however obtained by the construction of a dedicated drop-in hardware module for prime-field arithmetic. Its low area requirements and highly practical runtime facilitate pairing-based cryptography in interactive embedded applications.

**Acknowledgments.** This work has been supported in part by the Austrian Government through the research program FIT-IT under the project number 835917 (project NewP@ss) and by the European Commission through the FP7 program under project number 610436 (project MATTHEW).

# References

1. Aranha, D.F., Karabina, K., Longa, P., Gebotys, C.H., López, J.: Faster Explicit Formulas for Computing Pairings over Ordinary Curves. In: Paterson, K.G. (ed.) EUROCRYPT 2011. LNCS, vol. 6632, pp. 48–68. Springer, Heidelberg (2011)
2. ARM Ltd.: Cortex-M0+ Processor (September 2013),
   http://www.arm.com/products/processors/cortex-m/cortex-m0plus.php
3. Atmel Corporation: Atmel SAM D20 ARM-based Microcontroller Datasheet (December 2013),
   http://www.atmel.com/Images/Atmel-42129-SAM-D20_Summary.pdf
4. Barreto, P.S.L.M., Naehrig, M.: Pairing-Friendly Elliptic Curves of Prime Order. In: Preneel, B., Tavares, S. (eds.) SAC 2005. LNCS, vol. 3897, pp. 319–331. Springer, Heidelberg (2006)
5. Bernstein, D.J.: Curve25519: New Diffie-Hellman Speed Records. In: Yung, M., Dodis, Y., Kiayias, A., Malkin, T. (eds.) PKC 2006. LNCS, vol. 3958, pp. 207–228. Springer, Heidelberg (2006)
6. Beuchat, J.-L., González-Díaz, J.E., Mitsunari, S., Okamoto, E., Rodríguez-Henríquez, F., Teruya, T.: High-Speed Software Implementation of the Optimal Ate Pairing over Barreto–Naehrig Curves. In: Joye, M., Miyaji, A., Otsuka, A. (eds.) Pairing 2010. LNCS, vol. 6487, pp. 21–39. Springer, Heidelberg (2010)
7. Boneh, D., Boyen, X.: Secure Identity Based Encryption Without Random Oracles. In: Franklin, M. (ed.) CRYPTO 2004. LNCS, vol. 3152, pp. 443–459. Springer, Heidelberg (2004)
8. Boneh, D., Boyen, X.: Short Signatures Without Random Oracles and the SDH Assumption in Bilinear Groups. Journal of Cryptology 21(2), 149–177 (2008)
9. Boneh, D., Boyen, X., Shacham, H.: Short Group Signatures. In: Franklin, M. (ed.) CRYPTO 2004. LNCS, vol. 3152, pp. 41–55. Springer, Heidelberg (2004)
10. Koç, Ç.K., Acar, T., Kaliski Jr., B.S.: Analyzing and Comparing Montgomery Multiplication Algorithms. IEEE Micro 16(3), 26–33 (1996)
11. Certicom Research: Standards for Efficient Cryptography, SEC 2: Recommended Elliptic Curve Domain Parameters, Version 1.0 (September 2000),
    http://www.secg.org/

12. Coron, J.-S.: Resistance against Differential Power Analysis for Elliptic Curve Cryptosystems. In: Koç, Ç.K., Paar, C. (eds.) CHES 1999. LNCS, vol. 1717, pp. 292–302. Springer, Heidelberg (1999)
13. Costello, C., Lange, T., Naehrig, M.: Faster Pairing Computations on Curves with High-Degree Twists. In: Nguyen, P.Q., Pointcheval, D. (eds.) PKC 2010. LNCS, vol. 6056, pp. 224–242. Springer, Heidelberg (2010)
14. Devegili, A.J., hÉigeartaigh, C.O., Scott, M., Dahab, R.: Multiplication and Squaring on Pairing-Friendly Fields. Cryptology ePrint Archive, Report 2006/471 (2006)
15. Devegili, A.J., Scott, M., Dahab, R.: Implementing Cryptographic Pairings over Barreto-Naehrig Curves. In: Takagi, T., Okamoto, T., Okamoto, E., Okamoto, T. (eds.) Pairing 2007. LNCS, vol. 4575, pp. 197–207. Springer, Heidelberg (2007)
16. Fan, J., Vercauteren, F., Verbauwhede, I.: Faster $\mathbb{F}_p$-Arithmetic for Cryptographic Pairings on Barreto-Naehrig Curves. In: Clavier, C., Gaj, K. (eds.) CHES 2009. LNCS, vol. 5747, pp. 240–253. Springer, Heidelberg (2009)
17. Fuentes-Castañeda, L., Knapp, E., Rodríguez-Henríquez, F.: Faster hashing to $\mathbb{G}_2$. In: Miri, A., Vaudenay, S. (eds.) SAC 2011. LNCS, vol. 7118, pp. 412–430. Springer, Heidelberg (2012)
18. Gouvêa, C., Oliveira, L., López, J.: Efficient Software Implementation of Public-Key Cryptography on Sensor Networks Using the MSP430X Microcontroller. Journal of Cryptographic Engineering 2(1), 19–29 (2012)
19. Granger, R., Scott, M.: Faster Squaring in the Cyclotomic Subgroup of Sixth Degree Extensions. In: Nguyen, P.Q., Pointcheval, D. (eds.) PKC 2010. LNCS, vol. 6056, pp. 209–223. Springer, Heidelberg (2010)
20. Grewal, G., Azarderakhsh, R., Longa, P., Hu, S., Jao, D.: Efficient Implementation of Bilinear Pairings on ARM Processors. In: Knudsen, L.R., Wu, H. (eds.) SAC 2012. LNCS, vol. 7707, pp. 149–165. Springer, Heidelberg (2013)
21. Hutter, M., Joye, M., Sierra, Y.: Memory-Constrained Implementations of Elliptic Curve Cryptography in Co-$Z$ Coordinate Representation. In: Nitaj, A., Pointcheval, D. (eds.) AFRICACRYPT 2011. LNCS, vol. 6737, pp. 170–187. Springer, Heidelberg (2011)
22. Hwang, J.Y., Lee, S., Chung, B.H., Cho, H.S., Nyang, D.: Short Group Signatures with Controllable Linkability. In: LIGHTSEC 2011, pp. 44–52. IEEE Computer Society, Washington, DC (2011)
23. IEEE: P1363.3TM/D1 Draft Standard for Identity-based Public-key Cryptography Using Pairings (2008)
24. Kammler, D., Zhang, D., Schwabe, P., Scharwaechter, H., Langenberg, M., Auras, D., Ascheid, G., Mathar, R.: Designing an ASIP for Cryptographic Pairings over Barreto-Naehrig Curves. In: Clavier, C., Gaj, K. (eds.) CHES 2009. LNCS, vol. 5747, pp. 254–271. Springer, Heidelberg (2009)
25. Kiltz, E., Pietrzak, K.: Leakage Resilient ElGamal Encryption. In: Abe, M. (ed.) ASIACRYPT 2010. LNCS, vol. 6477, pp. 595–612. Springer, Heidelberg (2010)
26. Miller, V.S.: The Weil Pairing, and Its Efficient Calculation. Journal of Cryptology 17(4), 235–261 (2004)
27. Miyaji, A., Nakabayashi, M., Takano, S.: New Explicit Conditions of Elliptic Curve Traces for FR-Reduction (2001)
28. Montgomery, P.L.: Modular Multiplication without Trial Division. Mathematics of Computation 44, 519–521 (1985)
29. National Institute of Standards and Technology (NIST): FIPS-186-3: Digital Signature Standard (DSS) (2009), http://csrc.nist.gov/publications/fips/fips186-3/fips_186-3.pdf

30. Nogami, Y., Akane, M., Sakemi, Y., Kato, H., Morikawa, Y.: Integer Variable $\chi$-Based Ate Pairing. In: Galbraith, S.D., Paterson, K.G. (eds.) Pairing 2008. LNCS, vol. 5209, pp. 178–191. Springer, Heidelberg (2008)
31. Sánchez, A.H., Rodríguez-Henríquez, F.: NEON Implementation of an Attribute-Based Encryption Scheme. In: Jacobson, M., Locasto, M., Mohassel, P., Safavi-Naini, R. (eds.) ACNS 2013. LNCS, vol. 7954, pp. 322–338. Springer, Heidelberg (2013)
32. Szczechowiak, P., Kargl, A., Scott, M., Collier, M.: On the Application of Pairing Based Cryptography to Wireless Sensor Networks. In: Basin, D.A., Capkun, S., Lee, W. (eds.) WISEC 2009, pp. 1–12. ACM (2009)
33. Szczechowiak, P., Oliveira, L.B., Scott, M., Collier, M., Dahab, R.: NanoECC: Testing the Limits of Elliptic Curve Cryptography in Sensor Networks. In: Verdone, R. (ed.) EWSN 2008. LNCS, vol. 4913, pp. 305–320. Springer, Heidelberg (2008)
34. Vercauteren, F.: Optimal Pairings. IEEE Transactions on Information Theory 56(1), 455–461 (2010)
35. Wenger, E.: Hardware Architectures for MSP430-Based Wireless Sensor Nodes Performing Elliptic Curve Cryptography. In: Jacobson, M., Locasto, M., Mohassel, P., Safavi-Naini, R. (eds.) ACNS 2013. LNCS, vol. 7954, pp. 290–306. Springer, Heidelberg (2013)
36. Wenger, E., Unterluggauer, T., Werner, M.: 8/16/32 Shades of Elliptic Curve Cryptography on Embedded Processors. In: Paul, G., Vaudenay, S. (eds.) INDOCRYPT 2013. LNCS, vol. 8250, pp. 244–261. Springer, Heidelberg (2013)
37. Wenger, E., Werner, M.: Evaluating 16-Bit Processors for Elliptic Curve Cryptography. In: Prouff, E. (ed.) CARDIS 2011. LNCS, vol. 7079, pp. 166–181. Springer, Heidelberg (2011)

# A    Optimizations

## A.1    Final Exponentiation

The hard part of the final exponentiation by Fuentes-Castañeda *et al.* [17] yields fast execution by reducing the number of multiplications and exponentiations in $\mathbb{F}_{p^{12}}$. As a drawback, it requires four large temporary variables in $\mathbb{F}_{p^{12}}$. In order to attain a low-memory implementation, we decreased the number of temporary variables by adapting their formulas without noticeably degrading performance. Therefore, we initially set $t_0 = f^p$ and compute the chain

$$f^u \to f^{2u} \to f^{4u} \to f^{6u} \to f^{6u^2} \to f^{12u^2} \to f^{12u^3} .$$

Following, $a$ and $b$ are set to $a = f^{6u} \cdot f^{6u^2} \cdot f^{12u^3}$ and $b = a \cdot (f^{2u} \cdot f)^{-1}$. The computation of the result, namely

$$f = f^{6u^2} \cdot f \cdot f^p ,$$
$$f = [f \cdot a][b]^p [a]^{p^2} [b]^{p^3} ,$$

requires one more multiplication and one more Frobenius action than originally. However, the respective implementation in Algorithm 1 requires three temporary

**Algorithm 1.** Memory-optimized hard part of the final exponentiation for pairings over BN curves

**Input:** $f \in \mathbb{F}_{p^{12}}$
**Output:** $f^{\phi_{12}(p)/n} \in \mathbb{F}_{p^{12}}$
1: $t_0 \leftarrow f^p$
2: $b \leftarrow f^u$
3: **if** $u < 0$ **then** $b \leftarrow \bar{b}$ ▷ Conjugate
4: $b \leftarrow b^2$
5: $a \leftarrow b^2$
6: $a \leftarrow a \cdot b$
7: $b \leftarrow b \cdot f$
8: $b \leftarrow \bar{b}$
9: $f \leftarrow f \cdot t_0$
10: $t_0 \leftarrow a^u$
11: **if** $u < 0$ **then** $t_0 \leftarrow \bar{t_0}$

12: $f \leftarrow f \cdot t_0$
13: $a \leftarrow a \cdot t_0$
14: $t_0 \leftarrow t_0^2$
15: **if** $u < 0$ **then** $t_0 \leftarrow \bar{t_0}$
16: $a \leftarrow a \cdot t_0^u$ ▷ Interleaved
17: $b \leftarrow b \cdot a$
18: $t_0 \leftarrow b^p$
19: $t_0 \leftarrow t_0 \cdot a$
20: $t_0 \leftarrow t_0^p$
21: $t_0 \leftarrow t_0 \cdot b$
22: $t_0 \leftarrow t_0^p$
23: $t_0 \leftarrow t_0 \cdot f$
24: $f \leftarrow t_0 \cdot a$
25: **return** $f$

variables instead of four when the exponentiation and the multiplication on Line 16 are done simultaneously using a dedicated function. Since variables in $\mathbb{F}_{p^{12}}$ are large and RAM is more expensive than ROM, this approach aids to keep chip area low.

## A.2  Prime-Field Inversion

The parameterized prime $p(u)$ facilitates an optimized exponentiation-based prime-field inversion for positive $u$ that have low Hamming weight. In such cases, the inverse $a^{-1} \in \mathbb{F}_p$ can be expressed as

$$a^{-1} \bmod p = a^{p-2} \bmod p = a^{36u^4+36u^3+24u^2+6u-1} \bmod p$$
$$= a^{6u(4u+6u^2(1+u))} \cdot a^{6u-1} \bmod p \,.$$

Precomputation of the constant $6u - 1$ and the chain of computations

$$a^{6u-1} \rightarrow a^{6u} \rightarrow a^{12u^2} \rightarrow a^{24u^2} \rightarrow a^{36u^2} \rightarrow a^{36u^3} \rightarrow a^{36u^4}$$

enables the computation of the inverse as

$$a^{-1} \bmod p = a^{6u-1} \cdot a^{24u^2} \cdot a^{36u^3} \cdot a^{36u^4} \bmod p \,.$$

Consequently, prime field inversion is done using three fast exponentiations by $u$, one exponentiation by $6u-1$, five multiplications and two squarings. Since the exponents are fixed and publicly known, Montgomery ladders are not required and runtime thus remarkably benefits from the low Hamming weight of $u$.

# Curve41417: Karatsuba Revisited

Daniel J. Bernstein[1,2], Chitchanok Chuengsatiansup[2], and Tanja Lange[2]

[1] Department of Computer Science
University of Illinois at Chicago
Chicago, IL 60607–7045, USA
djb@cr.yp.to
[2] Department of Mathematics and Computer Science
Technische Universiteit Eindhoven
P.O. Box 513, 5600 MB Eindhoven, The Netherlands
c.chuengsatiansup@tue.nl, tanja@hyperelliptic.org

**Abstract.** This paper introduces constant-time ARM Cortex-A8 ECDH software that (1) is faster than the fastest ECDH option in the latest version of OpenSSL but (2) achieves a security level above $2^{200}$ using a prime above $2^{400}$. For comparison, this OpenSSL ECDH option is not constant-time and has a security level of only $2^{80}$. The new speeds are achieved in a quite different way from typical prime-field ECC software: they rely on a synergy between Karatsuba's method and choices of radix smaller than the CPU word size.

**Keywords:** performance, Karatsuba, refined Karatsuba, reduced refined Karatsuba, radix choices, vectorization, Edwards curves, Curve41417.

## 1   Introduction

This paper introduces new ECDH software for a standard ARM Cortex-A8 CPU. This software is faster than the fastest ECDH option (secp160r1) in the latest version of OpenSSL (version 1.0.2-beta1, released 24 February 2014).

This performance bar was already reached in one previous paper, "NEON crypto" (CHES 2012) by Bernstein and Schwabe [11], implementing Bernstein's Curve25519 [2] elliptic curve. The difference is that we now reach the same performance bar at a much higher security level, implementing a very strong new "Curve41417" elliptic curve introduced informally by Bernstein and Lange in [7, page 12] and introduced formally in this paper.

We are not saying that Curve41417 is as fast as Curve25519. We are saying that it is fast enough for applications and provides a much higher security level than Curve25519. This paper addresses the scalability challenges that appear at higher security levels.

This work was supported by the National Science Foundation under grant 1018836 and by the Netherlands Organisation for Scientific Research (NWO) under grants 639.073.005 and 613.001.011. Permanent ID of this document: 8302181bad3a3e2fcf91ee3e72b49edd. Date: 2014.06.17.

L. Batina and M. Robshaw (Eds.): CHES 2014, LNCS 8731, pp. 316–334, 2014.

Hyperelliptic-curve DH has also recently reached this performance bar for the Cortex-A8: the HECDH implementation in [4] is even faster than Curve25519. However, the performance benefits of hyperelliptic curves are specific to DH, as admitted in [4], while elliptic curves are easily adapted to other important applications such as signatures. More importantly, the 128-bit hyperelliptic curve used in [4] came from a massive computation by Gaudry and Schost in [20], using more than 1000000 hours of CPU time. Finding a similar curve at a higher security level would be extraordinarily difficult.

**1.1. Karatsuba's Method in Prime-Field ECC Software.** The Cortex-A8 contains a large integer-multiplication unit that multiplies 32-bit words to produce 64-bit results. Of course, there are CPUs with even larger multipliers, and CPUs (and FPGAs) with smaller multipliers, but 32-bit multipliers have been a popular choice for many years and seem likely to remain in widespread use in embedded systems for many years to come. We focus on the Cortex-A8 for the same reasons as [11] and [4, Section 5].

The conventional approach in ECC software is to take advantage of 32-bit multipliers by splitting, e.g., 160-bit prime-field elements into 5 words to be multiplied, or 256-bit prime-field elements into 8 words to be multiplied. Karatsuba's method [29, Theorem 2] is well known to be useful for binary fields, and is occasionally also considered for prime-field ECC software, but is practically always dismissed as having too much overhead: one Karatsuba level saves 25% of the integer-multiply instructions, but this is outweighed by the cost of many extra additions. (Of course, this comparison is biased by the availability of a large multiplier and relatively little area spent on adders, but this is how mass-market CPUs have always been designed.)

It should be obvious that scaling to larger and larger input sizes will eventually reach a cutoff where one Karatsuba level is useful: the overhead is linear in the size, while the 25% savings is quadratic in the size. But the conventional wisdom is that this cutoff is far beyond ECC sizes, so one would not expect that aiming for high-security ECC would reach this cutoff. The heavily optimized GMP multiprecision library [22], which includes automated searches for optimal cutoffs, does not switch over from schoolbook multiplication to one Karatsuba level on the Cortex-A8 until it reaches 832-bit inputs. A recent RSA performance analysis by Bos, Montgomery, Shumow, and Zaverucha [15] avoided all use of Karatsuba's method even for 1024-bit modular multiplication.

We use *two* Karatsuba levels. There is a synergy between two design choices here: (1) we use Karatsuba's method; (2) we use a radix smaller than the CPU word size.

The conventional choice for $b$-bit CPUs is to use radix $2^b$, minimizing the number of words that need to be multiplied. See, for example, the recent DH software from [24], [32], [13], [19], and [16]. However, a corner of the DH literature uses a smaller radix, with the goal of delaying carries, the same way that hardware multipliers typically use carry-save adders. See, for example, [11] and [4].

This corner of the literature does not seem to have exploited the fact that Karatsuba's method benefits heavily from a smaller radix. With radix $2^b$, the extra additions in Karatsuba's method are add-with-carry chains. With a smaller radix, the extra additions in Karatsuba's method are independent additions without carries. Even on CPUs where add-with-carry is as cheap as add, having independent operations creates tremendous extra flexibility in register allocation, instruction scheduling, and vectorization.

Conversely, a smaller radix benefits from Karatsuba's method, especially as the security level increases. Reducing a radix from, e.g., $2^{32}$ to $2^{26}$ means that instead of $w$ words one now needs $(32/26)w$ words and thus, without Karatsuba's method, $(32/26)^2w^2 \approx 1.5w^2$ multiplications instead of $w^2$ multiplications; this means that the benefits of eliminating carries have to be compared to the loss of $0.5w^2$ multiplications. Karatsuba's method moves the number of multiplications down to a smaller scale, improving this tradeoff.

**1.2. Choice of Prime and Choice of Curve.** The standard NIST elliptic curves [34] use primes $p$ designed to allow easy computation of $x \bmod p$ in radix $2^{32}$. For example, the popular NIST P-256 curve uses $p = 2^{256} - 2^{224} + 2^{192} + 2^{96} - 1$, and at a higher security level NIST P-384 uses $p = 2^{384} - 2^{128} - 2^{96} + 2^{32} - 1$.

We leave a gap between our radix and $2^{32}$ to speed up multiplications, as explained above, but this makes computation of $x \bmod p$ quite painful for the NIST primes $p$. The NIST primes are also suitable for a much smaller radix, namely $2^{16}$, but that radix would make our multiplications considerably slower.

The Curve25519 prime, $2^{255} - 19$, is much less sensitive to the choice of radix, but our objective is to provide as much security as possible subject to a specified performance requirement, and in particular more security than Curve25519. An initial performance estimate indicated that a carefully designed curve of 384 bits or larger could meet our performance requirement, but we found very few 384-bit curves in the literature, and all of them have obvious performance problems.

We therefore designed a prime and curve from scratch. This also allowed us to take advantage of state-of-the-art curve shapes, while meeting stringent security criteria that are flunked by the NIST curves. See Section 2.

The prime we ended up with, namely $p = 2^{414} - 17$, has many attractive features from a performance perspective. It is extremely close to a power of 2. The difference 17 has just two bits set, allowing $2^{414}x \bmod p$ to be computed as $16x + x$ with a single shift-and-add operation. The exponent 414 is divisible by $9, 18, 23, 46$ and the exponent 416 (for $4p$) is divisible by $8, 13, 16, 26, 32, 52$, allowing easy choices of integer radix suitable with low overhead for practically any size of multiplier. A field element is easily transmitted in 32-bit words with under 1% wasted space ($13 \cdot 32 = 416$), while still allowing two extra bits for extensions, such as a bit typically used in encoding a compressed curve point.

For our software we decided to use a slightly harder, but slightly more efficient, non-integer radix, namely $2^{414/16} = 2^{25.875}$. We split 414-bit prime-field elements into 16 words, use one Karatsuba level to reduce 16-word multiplication to three 8-word multiplications, and use another Karatsuba level to reduce each 8-word multiplication to three 4-word multiplications. See Section 4 for details

**Table 1.** Prime-field ECC timings from `openssl speed ecdh` on two Cortex-A8 devices. Warning: `openssl speed ecdh` reports "operations per second" as the reciprocal of average seconds per operation without indicating standard deviation or other stability metrics. "i.MX515 op/s" column is reported by OpenSSL 1.0.2-beta1 compiled with gcc 4.4.3 on a Hercules eCafe laptop (`h4mx515e`) with a 2009 Freescale i.MX515 CPU running at 800MHz. "Sitara op/s" column is reported by OpenSSL 1.0.2-beta1 compiled with gcc 4.7.3 on a BeagleBone Black development board (`bblack`) with a 2012 TI Sitara XAM3359AZCZ100 CPU running at 1000MHz. The "cycles" columns translate "op/s" into CPU cycles per operation.

| curve | i.MX515 op/s | cycles | Sitara op/s | cycles |
|---|---|---|---|---|
| `secp160r1` | 379.2 | ≈2.1 million | 468.1 | ≈2.1 million |
| `nistp192` | 274.3 | ≈2.9 million | 350.9 | ≈2.8 million |
| `nistp224` | 200.4 | ≈4.0 million | 257.6 | ≈3.9 million |
| `nistp256` | 201.1 | ≈4.0 million | 258.7 | ≈3.9 million |
| `nistp384` | 60.1 | ≈13.3 million | 75.9 | ≈13.2 million |
| `nistp521` | 26.9 | ≈29.7 million | 33.7 | ≈29.7 million |

of our multiplication strategy, and Section 5 for the extra challenges created by vectorization.

**1.3. Expected Scalability.** As a measurement of the conventional scaling of ECC performance to higher security levels, we compiled OpenSSL 1.0.2-beta1 on two Cortex-A8 devices and ran `openssl speed ecdh`. The prime-field results are shown in Table 1. We also checked that (as expected) the prime-field results were faster than the binary-field results at each security level; the binary-field results are not shown here. The fastest OpenSSL cycle count was 2.1 million cycles for `secp160r1` ($2^{80}$ security).

The following back-of-the-envelope calculation suggests that moving from 256 bits to 384 bits increases costs by a factor of $1.5^3 = 3.375$: each multiplication input is longer by a factor of 1.5, increasing the multiplication cost by a factor of $1.5^2$; and the scalar in ECDH is $1.5\times$ longer. The actual ratios between `nistp256` and `nistp384` in the table are close to this. The slowdown factor for `nistp521` is about 7.5, noticeably better than $(521/256)^3 \approx 8.4$, presumably because of the simpler prime shape used in P-521. The speedup factor for smaller curves is considerably worse than this calculation would suggest; presumably this reflects OpenSSL function-call overheads that become troublesome for smaller integers.

We also checked the eBACS [8] benchmarking site for Cortex-A8 results. The only results faster than 2.1 million cycles were 0.46 million cycles (i.MX515) and 0.50 million cycles (Sitara) for the Curve25519 ($2^{125}$ security) implementation from [11]. The paper [4] reports better speeds, just 0.27 million Cortex-A8 cycles for HECDH; but scaling HECDH to higher security levels is very difficult, as mentioned earlier. The paper [14] reports 0.77 million Cortex-A8 cycles for $2^{103}$ security using a different type of curve, evidently not competitive.

The same type of back-of-the-envelope calculation suggests that moving from Curve25519 up to Curve41417 would cost a factor of 4.3, increasing 0.50 million

Sitara Cortex-A8 cycles to 2.15 million cycles. We do considerably better than this; see below.

**1.4. Performance Results.** We tried our Curve41417 software on the same two Cortex-A8 machines shown in Table 1. On the Freescale i.MX515 (h4mx515e) our software uses just 1829903 cycles. On the TI Sitara (bblack) our software uses just 1964334 cycles. These figures are for a complete scalar-multiplication operation, including unpacking a point from network format, precomputation, main computation, final inversion, and converting the result back to network format. We emphasize that our curve choice has security level above $2^{200}$, and that the software is free of data-dependent branches and data-dependent array indices.

These speeds are, despite their very high security level, considerably faster than the 2.1 million cycles for the fastest ECDH in OpenSSL. These speeds are also considerably faster than the 2.15 million cycles predicted above by extrapolation from Curve25519. This paper explains the design and implementation choices that led to this performance.

As a followup to our initial Curve41417 announcement, Hamburg announced a similar, slightly larger, curve "Ed448-Goldilocks". Hamburg's most recent performance report [25] says 3.6 million Cortex-A9 cycles for Ed448-Goldilocks, compared to 4.4 million Cortex-A9 cycles for the implementation of NIST P-256 in OpenSSL 1.0.1. There are several reasons that it is difficult to extrapolate from these results: the Cortex-A9 is not the same as the Cortex-A8; Hamburg's Ed448-Goldilocks software is not vectorized; and OpenSSL 1.0.1 was missing some NIST P-256 speedups that appear in the most recent version of OpenSSL.

**1.5. Is High Security Useful?** Most papers today consider security levels between $2^{80}$ and $2^{128}$. The adequacy of $2^{80}$ is frequently a subject of dispute. There is general consensus that well-funded attackers and botnets can already perform $2^{80}$ operations; most HTTPS web sites have now switched from RSA-1024 ($2^{80}$ security) to RSA-2048 ($2^{112}$ security) or 256-bit ECC ($2^{128}$ security). On the other hand, there are also many papers continuing to study $2^{80}$ security and stating that $2^{80}$ is ample protection for low-value targets.

The adequacy of $2^{128}$ is rarely a subject of dispute. It is easy to see that $2^{128}$ is far beyond any computation feasible today. Choosing $2^{128}$ is so common in the current literature that papers studying a $2^{128}$ security level rarely bother to justify this choice.

One can therefore reasonably ask whether there is any reason to go beyond $2^{128}$ security, and in particular whether we are accomplishing anything useful by going beyond $2^{200}$ security. We give five answers to this question, in what we consider to be increasing order of importance.

First, cryptographic primitives need time to be reviewed before they are standardized and deployed in embedded systems, so designers of cryptographic primitives today should be considering embedded systems designed at least 10 years from now. Some of those systems will have a lifetime of 30 years, and at the end of that lifetime could still be encrypting data that — even if recorded by an attacker — should remain confidential for another 30 years, i.e., 70 years from now.

Today's mass-market GPUs perform approximately $2^{58}$ floating-point operations per year per watt. If computation becomes a factor of 10 more efficient each decade then mass-market chips in 70 years will perform approximately $2^{81}$ floating-point operations per year per watt. Carrying out a 1-year computation on the same scale as $2^{128}$ floating-point operations will thus require just $2^{47}$ watts. For comparison, the Earth's surface receives $2^{56}$ watts from the Sun.

We do not mean to suggest that typical cryptographic applications should worry about such large attacks. But we also see value in designing cryptographic systems that are not broken by such large attacks.

Second, even though many researchers have studied the security of ECC and expressed confidence in the security of prime-field ECC, there is still the possibility of an algorithmic breakthrough that considerably reduces the amount of computation required to break ECC. By moving to a much higher security level we are providing a security margin against unexpected attack improvements.

For comparison, over the past 18 months the security of small-characteristic multiplicative-group discrete logarithms has dropped dramatically. A very recent paper [21] reports $2^{59}$ security for a system previously thought to provide $2^{128}$ security. We do not mean to suggest that this is a threat to prime-field ECC (there are clear barriers between small characteristic and prime fields, and more importantly between multiplicative groups and ECC) but it does illustrate the general principle that attack cost can suddenly drop.

Third, sometimes cryptographic protocols are not as secure as the underlying cryptographic primitives. Often there is a security proof putting a bound on the gap, but usually the security proofs are not "tight". In particular, many ECC protocols are not guaranteed to provide $2^{128}$ security using 256-bit curves, even assuming the standard security conjectures for ECDLP on those curves. Achieving a $2^{128}$ guarantee requires taking larger curves. We thank an anonymous referee for pointing out this argument.

Fourth, we suggest that the right question is not how efficiently a particular security level can be achieved, but rather how much security can be provided subject to the performance requirements set by the users. Of course, a typical cryptographic system also relies on block ciphers, hash functions, etc., and if those are breakable in time $2^{128}$ then the attacker does not have to bother breaking a 414-bit elliptic curve; but AES-256 costs only 40% more than AES-128, and standard hashes also provide high-security options. It is natural for research into high-performance ECC to similarly provide high-security options for users who can afford those options.

The normal reason for users to reject high-security options is not that the users dislike high security, but rather that the high-security options are too slow. If a user rejects OpenSSL's `nistp384` in favor of `secp160r1`, probably the reason is that the user's performance budget does not allow 13.3 million cycles, while it does allow 2.1 million cycles. Unless there are severe bandwidth constraints, the user will be happier with Curve41417, which provides much higher security within the same performance budget.

Fifth, there are at least some users already demanding cryptography beyond a $2^{128}$ security level. For example, NSA's Suite B allows NIST P-256 for Secret information, but for Top Secret information it requires NIST P-384, SHA-384, and AES-256. This project began when Silent Circle requested a non-NIST curve to replace NIST P-384; we realized that we could design a curve that simultaneously provided better performance and better security. Silent Circle is now using Curve41417 by default.

## 2 Design of Curve41417

The IEEE standard P1363 [27] and the Brainpool recommendations [17] specify procedures to generate secure elliptic curves. Research has identified several other properties a secure curve should satisfy. A recent collection of these properties is provided by Bernstein and Lange in the "SafeCurves" web site [10].

**2.1. Standard Security Criteria.** There are several standard criteria on which all methods cited on [10] agree. The elliptic curve $E$ must be defined over a prime field $\mathbf{F}_p$ or a binary field $\mathbf{F}_{2^p}$, for $p$ a prime; its group order must be divisible by a large prime $\ell$; this prime must not match the field characteristic; and the embedding degree must be large. Over a prime field $\mathbf{F}_p$ the embedding degree is defined as the smallest positive integer $k$ so that $\ell$ divides $p^k - 1$. Brainpool requires $k \geq (\ell - 1)/100$, and P1363 imposes a weaker requirement.

For efficiency and security reasons we focus on prime fields, a recommendation supported by Brainpool and the more recent NIST/NSA documents [35].

**2.2. Additional Security Criteria.** SafeCurves imposes several further requirements to avoid "conflicts between simplicity, efficiency, and security". Specifically, it requires curves to support "simple, fast, complete, constant-time" algorithms for single-coordinate single-scalar multiplication and for multi-scalar multiplication. Montgomery curves [33] meet the single-coordinate single-scalar requirement; Edwards curves [18], when chosen to be complete [6], meet all of the requirements. Compared to Weierstrass curves, these curves make it easier to implement the curve arithmetic correctly: scalar multiplication is a very regular operation without exceptional cases that require special handling and that could reveal information about the scalar. The NIST curves do not meet these requirements.

SafeCurves also requires curves to be twist-secure. Twist-security means that the order of the twist, namely $2p + 2 - \#E(\mathbf{F}_p)$, is nearly prime. This criterion eliminates security problems caused by single-coordinate single-scalar multiplication algorithms that do not take extra effort to validate their inputs: for example, when a curve is given in Montgomery form and only the $x$-coordinate is transmitted and used, twist-security eliminates the need to check that the incoming $x$-coordinate is on the curve.

The NIST curve constants are not explained: in the SafeCurves terminology, the NIST curve choice is not "rigid". This has led to speculation about how the

NIST curves were designed and about whether the NSA has implemented a back door in the choice of the curves. Our curve is "fully rigid": the prime and all curve constants are fully explained here.

**2.3. Choice of Prime Field.** Our target in designing the new curve was to generate an elliptic curve at a security level larger than $2^{192}$ that meets the SafeCurves requirements and that supports efficient implementations. To this aim we start with finding a prime for which field elements can be efficiently represented and modulo which reductions are efficient. Prime numbers of the form $2^j - c$ for $12 \cdot 32 < j < 13 \cdot 32$ and $0 < c < 32$ are rare: the only possibilities are $2^{389} - 21$, $2^{401} - 31$, $2^{413} - 21$, and $2^{414} - 17$. We selected $p = 2^{414} - 17$ because 17 is the smallest $c$ in this list; it also has the lowest Hamming weight. Section 4 explains how we perform arithmetic in $\mathbf{F}_p$; this prime also leaves enough space in the limbs when we represent field elements as 16 words of 32 bits that carries between the limbs and reductions modulo $p$ can be delayed for long enough to be useful in the curve arithmetic. The next larger candidate prime would be $2^{444} - 17$ which does not have this feature; our $p$ is already very large for our security needs.

**2.4. Choice of Curve Shape.** For efficient and secure arithmetic in Diffie–Hellman key exchange and digital signature applications we insist on a curve in Edwards form. Note that each curve in Edwards form is birationally equivalent to one in Montgomery form, so there is no need to choose one over the other. The coefficient $d$ in the Edwards curve $x^2 + y^2 = 1 + dx^2y^2$ appears as a factor in the addition formulas, so choosing $d$ to be small in absolute value is good for efficiency. For security we chose a complete Edwards curve ($d$ is not a square in $\mathbf{F}_p$) and insisted on the same level of twist-security as Curve25519—the cofactors of the curve and its twist are in $\{4, 8\}$.

**2.5. A Safe Curve.** Curve41417 (named after the prime field) is defined as

$$x^2 + y^2 = 1 + 3617x^2y^2 \text{ over } \mathbf{F}_p, \qquad p = 2^{414} - 17.$$

Its order is $8\ell$, where
$\ell = 2^{411} - 33364140863755142520810177694098385178984727200411208589594 75$.
The order of the twist is also 8 times a prime. The value $d = 3617$ is the smallest integer in absolute value meeting the above security requirements.

# 3  ECC Arithmetic

Our featured application is static Diffie–Hellman in which a user Alice computes her private key $a$ and her public key $P_A = aP$ once and then publishes $P_A$. If Alice wants to communicate with user Bob she looks up Bob's public key $P_B$ and computes $aP_B$. This means that the computations use variable base points. The computations involve the long-term secret key $a$ and need to be protected against side-channel attacks by attackers sitting on the same device or having a connection to it. This means in particular that the scalar multiplication should run in constant time, independent of the scalar $a$, and that there should be no data-dependent branches or table lookups involving $a$.

We use a windowing method with fixed window width for constant-time single-scalar multiplication on Curve41417 in Edwards form. Our analysis also allows good estimates of, e.g., the cost of signature verification using Curve41417. Another option for single-scalar multiplication is the Montgomery ladder for the Montgomery form of Curve41417; this is not quite as fast as the Edwards form but has the advantage of fitting the computation into less SRAM.

**3.1. Coordinate Systems.** The fastest doubling formulas in the EFD [9] for curves in Edwards form are in projective coordinates $X, Y, Z$ with $x = X/Z, y = Y/Z$ for $Z \neq 0$. These take $3\mathbf{M} + 4\mathbf{S}$ per doubling where $\mathbf{M}$ and $\mathbf{S}$ denote field multiplication and field squaring respectively. See Appendix A for the formulas used in this paper.

The fastest addition formulas are in extended coordinates $X, Y, Z, T$ with $x = X/Z, y = Y/Z$, and $xy = T/Z$ for $Z \neq 0$. These take $9\mathbf{M} + 1\mathbf{M}_d$. Here $\mathbf{M}_d$ is a multiplication by curve constant $d$; for us $d = 3617$, which is significantly smaller than $p$, so this multiplication $\mathbf{M}_d$ is cheaper than general multiplications $\mathbf{M}$. (The curve $-x^2 + y^2 = 1 - dx^2y^2$ allows faster additions, saving $1\mathbf{M}$ in each addition. If $-1$ were a square in $\mathbf{F}_p$ then we could apply an isomorphism to that curve. However, $-1$ is not a square in $\mathbf{F}_p$, so that curve is not complete.)

Achieving the best performance requires combining these two coordinate systems: computing the extra $T$ coordinate for a doubling output that will be used for addition, and skipping the extra $T$ coordinate for an addition output that will be used only for doubling. This suggestion was made in [26], the paper introducing extended coordinates.

**3.2. Scalar Multiplication.** Constant-time sliding windows are difficult so we use fixed windows. We analyzed operation counts for signed fixed windows for window widths $w = 4$, $w = 5$, and $w = 6$, and concluded that $w = 5$ is optimal. We therefore precompute $0P_B = (0, 1), P_B, 2P_B, \ldots, 16P_B$ and store the results in a table. We do table lookups in constant time using the same technique as in, e.g., [5]: we load the entire table into registers and perform the selection via arithmetic.

Precomputation is done as follows. We double $P_B$ to obtain $2P_B$; add $P_B$ to obtain $3P_B$; double $2P_B$ to obtain $4P_B$; add $P_B$ to obtain $5P_B$; double $3P_B$ to obtain $6P_B$; add $P_B$ to obtain $7P_B$; and so on through $16P_B$. We also multiply each resulting $T$ coordinate by $d = 3617$, eliminating the multiplications by $d$ in the main computation.

In total 8 doublings, 7 additions, and 16 multiplications by $d$ are required. Note that these doublings are followed by additions and thus need one extra $\mathbf{M}$ for the $T$ coordinate in the transition to extended coordinates. Note also that we have to compute $T$ for $P_B$ which costs $1\mathbf{M}$. For the first doubling, $(X, Y, Z, T)$ is $(x, y, 1, xy)$. We save $1\mathbf{S}$ by not having to compute $Z^2$ since $Z = 1$; we save another $1\mathbf{S}$ by not having to compute $(x + y)^2$ but using the equality $(x+y)^2 - x^2 - y^2 = 2xy = 2T$; and we use $Z = 1$ again for an $\mathbf{S} - \mathbf{M}$ tradeoff. The overall cost for the first doubling is $3\mathbf{M} + 3\mathbf{S}$ while for the rest it is $4\mathbf{M} + 4\mathbf{S}$. Note that all additions in precomputation are adding $P_B$ which has $Z = 1$. We thus use mixed addition which saves $1\mathbf{M}$. This results in the total cost for precomputation of $1\mathbf{M} + (3\mathbf{M} + 3\mathbf{S}) + 7(4\mathbf{M} + 4\mathbf{S}) + 7(8\mathbf{M}) + 16\mathbf{M}_d = 88\mathbf{M} + 31\mathbf{S} + 16\mathbf{M}_d$.

The main computation uses a fixed pattern of five doublings followed by one addition. Four regular doublings in a block of five take $3\mathbf{M} + 4\mathbf{S}$ each. The fifth doubling in a block requires 1 more $\mathbf{M}$ to calculate $T$ for the following addition. On the other hand, addition does not need to compute $T$ since the following doubling is in projective coordinates. Furthermore, $dT$ was precomputed for each $T$ in the table. Therefore the addition takes only $8\mathbf{M}$. In total the five doublings and one addition take only $4(3\mathbf{M} + 4\mathbf{S}) + (4\mathbf{M} + 4\mathbf{S}) + (8\mathbf{M}) = 24\mathbf{M} + 20\mathbf{S}$.

Note that, since the Edwards addition law is complete, no special handling is required for the neutral element $0P_B$. An addition when the coefficient of the scalar happens to be 0 is handled the same way as any other addition.

A scalar between 0 and $2^{414} - 1$ uses 82 signed windows of width 5, after an initial selection from $0P_B, 1P_B, \ldots, 16P_B$. The total cost for scalar multiplication including precomputation is $(88\mathbf{M} + 31\mathbf{S} + 16\mathbf{M}_d) + 82(24\mathbf{M} + 20\mathbf{S}) = 2056\mathbf{M} + 1671\mathbf{S} + 16\mathbf{M}_d$, plus 1 inversion and $2\mathbf{M}$ to convert to $X/Z, Y/Z$ for output.

# 4    Karatsuba Multiplication

Karatsuba, Toom, and the FFT are polynomial-multiplication methods that are asymptotically faster than schoolbook multiplication. However, for small input sizes the speedups are outweighed by the expense of more additions and subtractions, which in turn require more carries. These effects are particularly noticeable for polynomials of low degree — or equivalently for integers occupying just a few words. In software implementations of cryptography we rarely find integers large enough to justify use of FFT or Toom, and even Karatsuba's method is commonly only used in implementations of RSA and not ECC.

In this section we explain how to reduce the cost of carries by working with multiple levels of redundancy in the representation and thereby delaying carries. We also introduce "reduced refined Karatsuba", a new variant of the "refined Karatsuba" method; this variant eliminates some additions by merging Karatsuba multiplication with a subsequent modular reduction.

**4.1. Redundant Number Representation.** We decompose an integer $f$ modulo $2^{414} - 17$ into 16 integer pieces in radix $2^{414/16} = 2^{25.875}$, i.e., we write $f$ as $f_0 + 2^{26} f_1 + 2^{52} f_2 + 2^{78} f_3 + 2^{104} f_4 + 2^{130} f_5 + 2^{156} f_6 + 2^{182} f_7 + 2^{207} f_8 + 2^{233} f_9 + 2^{259} f_{10} + 2^{285} f_{11} + 2^{311} f_{12} + 2^{337} f_{13} + 2^{363} f_{14} + 2^{389} f_{15}$. With this decomposition, each limb $f_0, f_1, \ldots, f_{14}, f_{15}$ is small enough to fit into a 32-bit integer and to still have space to delay carries occurring when adding these pieces. The results of the 32-bit-by-32-bit multiplications fit into 64-bit words, and we can add thousands of them together before causing an overflow.

Note that $f_7$ is multiplied by $2^{207}$, not $2^{208}$. Having $f_7$ and $f_{15}$ contain 25 bits makes $f_0, \ldots, f_7$ symmetric to $f_8, \ldots, f_{15}$, aiding vectorization. We considered using fewer limbs, but the advantage of saving multiplications is outweighed by the disadvantages of (1) extra carries and (2) extra vectorization overhead.

**4.2. Two-Level Karatsuba: Decomposition Strategy.** As mentioned in Section 1, we use 2 Karatsuba levels. This fits nicely into the 128-bit Cortex-A8 vector units, and uses less arithmetic than 3 or 1 (or 0) Karatsuba levels.

We start with what Bernstein in [3] calls the "refined Karatsuba identity"

$$(F_0 + t^n F_1)(G_0 + t^n G_1) = (1 - t^n)(F_0 G_0 - t^n F_1 G_1) + t^n (F_0 + F_1)(G_0 + G_1).$$

This uses fewer additions than the original Karatsuba identity from [29].

For the *first* level of Karatsuba, we split one 16-limb integer $f$ into two 8-limb integers $F_0$ and $F_1$ with $f = F_0 + 2^{207} F_1$ as:

$$F_0 = f_0 + 2^{26} f_1 + 2^{52} f_2 + 2^{78} f_3 + 2^{104} f_4 + 2^{130} f_5 + 2^{156} f_6 + 2^{182} f_7 ;$$
$$F_1 = f_8 + 2^{26} f_9 + 2^{52} f_{10} + 2^{78} f_{11} + 2^{104} f_{12} + 2^{130} f_{13} + 2^{156} f_{14} + 2^{182} f_{15}.$$

We also decompose another integer $g$ similarly to $f$. Then, we have

$$fg = (1 - 2^{207})(F_0 G_0 - 2^{207} F_1 G_1) + 2^{207}(F_0 + F_1)(G_0 + G_1).$$

For the *second* level of Karatsuba, we further split the 8 limbs of $F_0$ (and those of $F_1$) into two 4-limb integers $F_{00}$, $F_{01}$ (and $F_{10}$, $F_{11}$) with $F_0 = F_{00} + 2^{104} F_{01}$ (and $F_1 = F_{10} + 2^{104} F_{11}$) as:

$$F_{00} = f_0 + 2^{26} f_1 + 2^{52} f_2 + 2^{78} f_3 ; \qquad F_{01} = f_4 + 2^{26} f_5 + 2^{52} f_6 + 2^{78} f_7;$$
$$F_{10} = f_8 + 2^{26} f_9 + 2^{52} f_{10} + 2^{78} f_{11}; \qquad F_{11} = f_{12} + 2^{26} f_{13} + 2^{52} f_{14} + 2^{78} f_{15}.$$

We similarly split $G_0$ and $G_1$ to obtain $G_{00}$, $G_{01}$, $G_{10}$, and $G_{11}$. Then

$$F_0 G_0 = (1 - 2^{104})(F_{00} G_{00} - 2^{104} F_{01} G_{01}) + 2^{104}(F_{00} + F_{01})(G_{00} + G_{01});$$
$$F_1 G_1 = (1 - 2^{104})(F_{10} G_{10} - 2^{104} F_{11} G_{11}) + 2^{104}(F_{10} + F_{11})(G_{10} + G_{11}).$$

To compute $(F_0+F_1)(G_0+G_1)$ we first compute $F_0+F_1$ and $G_0+G_1$ without carries and then apply the same type of decomposition. For example, we split $F_0 + F_1$ into two 4-limb integers, namely $F_{00} + F_{10}$ and $F_{01} + F_{11}$.

**4.3. Lowest-Level Multiplication.** On the lowest level we need to multiply two 4-limb integers; we do this by schoolbook multiplication. For $F_{00} G_{00}$ this works as follows:

$$h_0 = f_0 g_0,$$
$$h_1 = f_0 g_1 + f_1 g_0, \qquad\qquad\qquad h_4 = f_1 g_3 + f_2 g_2 + f_3 g_1,$$
$$h_2 = f_0 g_2 + f_1 g_1 + f_2 g_0, \qquad\qquad h_5 = f_2 g_3 + f_3 g_2,$$
$$h_3 = f_0 g_3 + f_1 g_2 + f_2 g_1 + f_3 g_0, \qquad h_6 = f_3 g_3.$$

We store each input limb $f_i$ and $g_i$ in a word of 32 bits and use the processor's multiplication and addition units to compute each $h_i$. This takes 16 32-bit-by-32-bit multiplications and 9 64-bit additions. Each of the initial limbs has at most 26 bits and each of the $h_i$ fits into 64 bits. The values $h_4, h_5$, and $h_6$ belong to the powers $2^{104}, 2^{130}$, and $2^{156}$, i.e., they are implicitly multiplied by $2^{104}$.

**4.4. Middle-Level Recombination.** After computing the three lowest-level products $F_{00}G_{00}, F_{01}G_{01}$ and $(F_{00} + F_{01})(G_{00} + G_{01})$, we obtain $F_0G_0$ as follows.

*Step 1.1: Compute $F_{00}G_{00} - 2^{104}F_{01}G_{01}$.* We merge $F_{01}G_{01}$ to $F_{00}G_{00}$ at the $2^{104}$ boundary using 3 subtractions of 64-bit words. In other words, we align the 5th limb of $F_{00}G_{00}$ with the 1st limb of $F_{01}G_{01}$ as shown in the following diagram. The result is thus 11 limbs long. The top limbs are not actually subtracted from 0; they are tracked as being implicitly negated.

$F_{00}G_{00}$

$F_{01}G_{01}$

subtract

*Step 1.2: Compute $(1 - 2^{104})(F_{00}G_{00} - 2^{104}F_{01}G_{01})$.* This is equivalent to merging $F_{00}G_{00} - 2^{104}F_{01}G_{01}$ to itself at the $2^{104}$ boundary. We conduct this merge similarly to Step 1.1: we align the 5th limb of $F_{00}G_{00} - 2^{104}F_{01}G_{01}$ with the 1st limb and subtract. The following diagram depicts this step. This merge requires 7 subtractions of 64-bit words, and the result is 15 limbs long.

$F_{00}G_{00}$ - $2^{104}F_{01}G_{01}$

$F_{00}G_{00}$ - $2^{104}F_{01}G_{01}$

subtract

*Step 1.3: Compute $F_0G_0$.* We finish this level of computation by adding $2^{104}(F_{00} + F_{01})(G_{00} + G_{01})$ to $(1 - 2^{104})(F_{00}G_{00} - 2^{104}F_{01}G_{01})$. This is done by merging the former to the latter at the $2^{104}$ boundary, i.e., the 5th limb of the former is aligned with the 1st limb of the latter as shown in the following diagram. Note that this merge requires 7 additions of 64-bit words, and the result remains 15 limbs long.

$(1-2^{104})(F_{00}G_{00}$ - $2^{104}F_{01}G_{01})$

$(F_{00}+F_{01})(G_{00}+G_{01})$

subtract

When combining the results we need to pay attention to the 9th through 15th limbs. Those limbs are implicitly multiplied by $2^{207}$. However, during the above computation they appear naturally as multiples of $2^{208}$ instead of $2^{207}$. We therefore shift those seven limbs by one bit.

To summarize, the computation of the product $F_0G_0$ consists of

- $2 \times 4$ 32-bit additions for $F_{00} + F_{01}$ and $G_{00} + G_{01}$;
- $3 \times 16$ 32-bit-by-32-bit-producing-64-bit multiplications for $F_{00}G_{00}, F_{01}G_{01}$, and $(F_{00} + F_{01})(G_{00} + G_{01})$;

- $3 \times 9$ 64-bit additions for computing the $h_i$;
- $1 \times 3$ 64-bit subtractions for computing Step 1.1;
- $1 \times 7$ 64-bit subtractions for computing Step 1.2;
- $1 \times 7$ 64-bit additions for computing Step 1.3;
- $1 \times 7$ 64-bit shifts for handling $2^{207}$ and $2^{208}$.

The total is 8 32-bit additions (counting subtractions as additions), 48 32-bit-by-32-bit multiplications, 44 64-bit additions, and 7 64-bit shifts.

We compute products $F_1G_1$ and $(F_0+F_1)(G_0+G_1)$ in the same way as $F_0G_0$. The total cost for these three products is 24 32-bit additions, 144 32-bit-by-32-bit multiplications, 132 64-bit additions, and 21 64-bit shifts.

**4.5. Top-Level Recombination and Reduction.** After computing $F_0G_0$ etc., we compute $fg = (1-2^{207})(F_0G_0-2^{207}F_1G_1)+2^{207}(F_0+F_1)(G_0+G_1)$ as follows. This top-level recombination is immediately followed by a reduction, and we save some additions by interleaving the reduction into the refined-Karatsuba computation, a technique that we call "reduced refined Karatsuba". What is important here is that we reduce $F_0G_0-2^{207}F_1G_1$ before multiplying by $1-2^{207}$.

*Step 2.1: Compute $F_0G_0 - 2^{207}F_1G_1$.* This is similar to Step 1.1 but includes an extra reduction. The merge of $F_1G_1$ to $F_0G_0$ is at the $2^{207}$ boundary and uses 7 subtractions of 64-bit words; the 9th limb of $F_0G_0$ is aligned with the 1st limb of $F_1G_1$. The intermediate result is 23 limbs long. Then we reduce modulo $2^{414} - 17$: we multiply the 17th through 23rd limbs by 17 (using shifts and additions) and add to the 1st through 7th limbs. This requires another 7 shifts and 14 additions of 64-bit words. The result is thus only 16 limbs long, as indicated in the following diagram.

*Step 2.2: Compute $(1 - 2^{207})(F_0G_0 - 2^{207}F_1G_1)$.* This is similar to Step 1.2. The earlier reduction in Step 2.1 means that Step 2.2 uses only 8 subtractions of 64-bit words. The result is 24 limbs long as shown in the following diagram. We do *not* perform an extra reduction here: by keeping this long result of 24 limbs, we save 8 shifts and 16 additions.

*Step 2.3: Compute $fg$.* We finish by adding 15-limb $2^{207}(F_0+F_1)(G_0+G_1)$ to 24-limb $(1-2^{207})(F_0G_0-2^{207}F_1G_1)$. This is done by merging the former to the latter at the $2^{207}$ boundary: i.e., the 9th limb of $(1-2^{207})(F_0G_0-2^{207}F_1G_1)$ is aligned with the 1st limb of $(F_0+F_1)(G_0+G_1)$. This merge requires 15 additions of 64-bit words and results in 24 limbs. We do another reduction similar to Step 2.1 to bring the result back to 16 limbs; this requires another 8 shifts and 16 additions of 64-bit words. The following diagram illustrates this step.

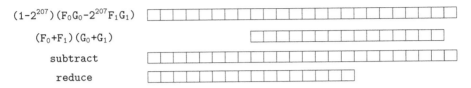

To summarize, computing $fg$ from $F_0G_0$, $F_1G_1$ and $(F_0 + F_1)(G_0 + G_1)$ uses

- 7 64-bit subtractions for computing Step 2.1;
- 7 64-bit shift instructions for reduction in Step 2.1;
- 14 64-bit additions for reduction in Step 2.1;
- 8 64-bit subtractions for computing Step 2.2;
- 15 64-bit additions for computing Step 2.3;
- 8 64-bit shift instructions for reduction in Step 2.3;
- 16 64-bit additions for reduction in Step 2.3.

This sums up to 60 64-bit additions and 15 64-bit shift instructions. Therefore, the total cost for computing $fg$ is 24 32-bit additions, 144 32-bit-by-32-bit multiplications, $132 + 60 = 192$ 64-bit additions, and $21 + 15 = 36$ 64-bit shifts.

**4.6. Principles Behind Reduced Refined Karatsuba.** Our elimination of some additions can be viewed as following the general strategy of reducing *inputs* to a multiplication rather than *outputs* of a multiplication. Specifically, we reduce $F_0G_0 - 2^{207}F_1G_1$ before multiplying it by $1 - 2^{207}$; we do not reduce the product until after adding it to $(F_0 + F_1)(G_0 + G_1)$; if $fg$ were being added to other products then we would similarly delay the reduction until after the addition. What is new here is seeing the multiplication by $1 - t^n$ inside refined Karatsuba as a useful target of the general strategy, despite the sparsity of $1 - t^n$.

# 5   Vectorization

The "NEON" vector unit in each Cortex-A8 core can compute a vector of two 64-bit products $ac$ and $bd$ in just 2 cycles given 32-bit inputs $a, b, c, d$. It can compute a vector of two 64-bit sums or four 32-bit sums in just 1 cycle. The latencies of these operations are actually higher, up to 7 cycles, but throughput is improved by pipelining. Taking advantage of this computational power requires that at every moment there are 2 or 4 identical computations to perform, and on top of this enough independent computations to hide latencies.

**5.1. Karatsuba Vectorization.** Most of the computations in Section 4 are suitable for vectorization. For example, $F_{01}G_{01}$ takes $f_4, f_5, f_6, f_7, g_4, g_5, g_6, g_7$ as input; $F_{10}G_{10}$ takes $f_8, f_9, f_{10}, f_{11}, g_8, g_9, g_{10}, g_{11}$. There are no dependencies between these two identical sets of multiplications. Similar comments apply to

$F_{00}G_{00}$ and $F_{11}G_{11}$; $(F_{00} + F_{10})(G_{00} + G_{10})$ and $(F_{01} + F_{11})(G_{01} + G_{11})$; and $(F_{00} + F_{01})(G_{00} + G_{01})$ and $(F_{10} + F_{11})(G_{10} + G_{11})$. The remaining multiplication consists of 16 32-bit products, which we partition into 8 vectorized products at the cost of some shuffling. Similarly, we vectorize between combining $F_0 G_0$ and combining $F_1 G_1$, and at the cost of some shuffling we vectorize within the computation of $(F_0 + F_1)(G_0 + G_1)$. NEON also supports a multiply-accumulate instruction, allowing us to eliminate many addition instructions.

**5.2. Carry Vectorization.** At the end of the Karatsuba computation, reduction modulo $p$ produces a product of the form $\sum_{i=0}^{7} m_i 2^{26i} + 2^{207} \sum_{i=0}^{7} m_{i+8} 2^{26i}$. We then use a sequence of carries to bring each limb down to 26 (or in some cases 25) bits. We vectorize between a carry $m_0 \to m_1$ and a carry $m_8 \to m_9$, between a carry $m_1 \to m_2$ and a carry $m_9 \to m_{10}$, etc.

Each carry has very high latency, so we perform four carry chains in parallel. Specifically, we vectorize between a carry $m_0 \to m_1$ and a carry $m_8 \to m_9$, and in parallel vectorize between a carry $m_4 \to m_5$ and a carry $m_{12} \to m_{13}$; we then vectorize between a carry $m_1 \to m_2$ and a carry $m_9 \to m_{10}$, and in parallel vectorize between a carry $m_5 \to m_6$ and a carry $m_{13} \to m_{14}$; and so on. This hides almost all latency.

**5.3. Performance.** See Section 1.4 for our Cortex-A8 performance results.

# References

[1] Benaloh, J. (ed.): Topics in cryptology — CT-RSA 2014 — The cryptographer's track at the RSA conference 2014, San Francisco, CA, USA, February 25–28, 2014, proceedings. LNCS, vol. 8366. Springer (2014). ISBN 978-3-319-04851-2. See [19]

[2] Bernstein, D.J.: Curve25519: new Diffie-Hellman speed records. In: PKC 2006 [41], pp. 207–228 (2006). http://cr.yp.to/papers.html#curve25519. Citations in this document: §1

[3] Bernstein, D.J.: Batch binary Edwards. In: Crypto 2009 [23], pp. 317–336 (2009). http://cr.yp.to/papers.html#bbe. Citations in this document: §4.2

[4] Bernstein, D.J., Chuengsatiansup, C., Lange, T., Schwabe, P.: Kummer strikes back: new DH speed records (2014). https://eprint.iacr.org/2014/134. Citations in this document: §1, §1, §1, §1.1, §1.1, §1.3

[5] Bernstein, D.J., Duif, N., Lange, T., Schwabe, P., Yang, B.-Y.: High-speed high-security signatures. In: CHES 2011 [38] (2011). http://eprint.iacr.org/2011/368. Citations in this document: §3.2

[6] Bernstein, D.J., Lange, T.: Faster addition and doubling on elliptic curves. In: Asiacrypt 2007 [30], pp. 29–50 (2007). http://eprint.iacr.org/2007/286. Citations in this document: §2.2

[7] Bernstein, D.J., Lange, T.: Security dangers of the NIST curves (2013). http://cr.yp.to/talks/2013.09.16/slides-djb-20130916-a4.pdf. Citations in this document: §1

[8] Bernstein, D.J., Lange, T. (eds.): eBACS: ECRYPT Benchmarking of Cryptographic Systems, accessed 13 June 2014 (2014). http://bench.cr.yp.to. Citations in this document: §1.3

[9] Bernstein, D.J., Lange, T. (eds.): Explicit Formulas Database, accessed 13 June 2014 (2014). http://hyperelliptic.org/EFD. Citations in this document: §3.1, §A

[10] Bernstein, D.J., Lange, T.: SafeCurves: choosing safe curves for elliptic-curve cryptography, accessed 13 June 2014 (2014). http://safecurves.cr.yp.to. Citations in this document: §2, §2.1

[11] Bernstein, D.J., Schwabe, P.: NEON crypto. In: CHES 2012 [39], pp. 320–339 (2012). http://cr.yp.to/papers.html#neoncrypto. Citations in this document: §1, §1.1, §1.1, §1.3

[12] Bertoni, G., Coron, J.-S. (eds.): Cryptographic hardware and embedded systems — CHES 2013 — 15th international workshop, Santa Barbara, CA, USA, August 20–23, 2013, proceedings. LNCS, vol. 8086. Springer (2013). ISBN 978-3-642-40348-4. See [14]

[13] Bos, J.W., Costello, C., Hisil, H., Lauter, K.: Fast cryptography in genus 2. In: Eurocrypt 2013 [28], pp. 194–210 (2013). http://eprint.iacr.org/2012/670. Citations in this document: §1.1

[14] Bos, J.W., Costello, C., Hisil, H., Lauter, K.: High-performance scalar multiplication using 8-dimensional GLV/GLS decomposition. In: CHES 2013 [12], pp. 331–348 (2013). http://eprint.iacr.org/2013/146. Citations in this document: §1.3

[15] Bos, J.W., Montgomery, P.L., Shumow, D., Zaverucha, G.M.: Montgomery multiplication using vector instructions. In: SAC 2013 [31], pp. 471–489 (2014). http://eprint.iacr.org/2013/519. Citations in this document: §1.1

[16] Costello, C., Hisil, H., Smith, B.: Faster compact Diffie–Hellman: endomorphisms on the x-line. In: Eurocrypt 2014 [36], pp. 183–200 (2014). http://eprint.iacr.org/2013/692. Citations in this document: §1.1

[17] ECC Brainpool: ECC Brainpool standard curves and curve generation (2005). http://www.ecc-brainpool.org/download/Domain-parameters.pdf. Citations in this document: §2

[18] Edwards, H.M.: A normal form for elliptic curves. Bulletin of the American Mathematical Society 44, 393–422 (2007). http://www.ams.org/bull/2007-44-03/S0273-0979-07-01153-6/home.html. Citations in this document: §2.2

[19] Faz-Hernández, A., Longa, P., Sánchez, A.H.: Efficient and secure algorithms for GLV-based scalar multiplication and their implementation on GLV-GLS curves. In: CT-RSA 2014 [1], pp. 1–27 (2014). http://eprint.iacr.org/2013/158. Citations in this document: §1.1

[20] Gaudry, P., Schost, É.: Genus 2 point counting over prime fields. Journal of Symbolic Computation 47, 368–400 (2012). http://www.csd.uwo.ca/~eschost/publications/countg2.pdf. Citations in this document: §1

[21] Granger, R., Kleinjung, T., Zumbrägel, J.: Breaking "128-bit secure" supersingular binary curves (or how to solve discrete logarithms in $\mathbf{F}_{2^{4 \cdot 1223}}$ and $\mathbf{F}_{2^{12 \cdot 367}}$). In: Crypto 2014, to appear (2014). http://eprint.iacr.org/2014/119. Citations in this document: §1.5

[22] Granlund, T. (ed.): GMP 5.1.3: GNU multiple precision arithmetic library (2014). http://gmplib.org. Citations in this document: §1.1

[23] Halevi, S. (ed.): Advances in cryptology — CRYPTO 2009, 29th annual international cryptology conference, Santa Barbara, CA, USA, August 16–20, 2009, proceedings. LNCS, vol. 5677. Springer (2009). See [3]

[24] Hamburg, M.: Fast and compact elliptic-curve cryptography (2012). http://eprint.iacr.org/2012/309. Citations in this document: §1.1

[25] Hamburg, M.: New Ed448-Goldilocks release (2014). https://moderncrypto.org/mail-archive/curves/2014/000101.html. Citations in this document: §1.4

[26] Hisil, H., Wong, K.K.-H., Carter, G., Dawson, E.: Twisted Edwards curves revisited. In: Asiacrypt 2008 [37], pp. 326–343 (2008). http://eprint.iacr.org/2008/522. Citations in this document: §3.1

[27] Institute of Electrical and Electronics Engineers: IEEE 1363-2000: Standard specifications for public key cryptography, Preliminary draft at (2000). http://grouper.ieee.org/groups/1363/P1363/draft.html. Citations in this document: §2

[28] Johansson, T., Nguyen, P.Q. (eds.): Advances in cryptology — EUROCRYPT 2013, 32nd annual international conference on the theory and applications of cryptographic techniques, Athens, Greece, May 26–30, 2013, proceedings. LNCS, vol. 7881. Springer (2013). ISBN 978-3-642-38347-2. See [13]

[29] Karatsuba, A.A., Ofman, Y.: Multiplication of multidigit numbers on automata. Soviet Physics Doklady 7, 595–596 (1963). ISSN 0038-5689. Citations in this document: §1.1, §4.2

[30] Kurosawa, K. (ed.): Advances in cryptology — ASIACRYPT 2007, 13th international conference on the theory and application of cryptology and information security, Kuching, Malaysia, December 2–6, 2007, proceedings. LNCS, vol. 4833. Springer (2007). ISBN 978-3-540-76899-9. See [6]

[31] Lange, T., Lauter, K., Lisonek, P. (eds.): Selected areas in cryptography — SAC 2013 — 20th international conference, Burnaby, BC, Canada, August 14–16, 2013, revised selected papers. LNCS, vol. 8282. Springer (2014). ISBN 978-3-662-43413-0. See [15]

[32] Longa, P., Sica, F.: Four-dimensional Gallant–Lambert–Vanstone scalar multiplication. In: Asiacrypt 2012 [40], pp. 718–739 (2012). http://eprint.iacr.org/2011/608. Citations in this document: §1.1

[33] Montgomery, P.L.: Speeding the Pollard and elliptic curve methods of factorization. Mathematics of Computation 48, 243–264 (1987). ISSN 0025-5718. MR 88e:11130. http://links.jstor.org/sici?sici=0025-5718(198701)48:177<243:STPAEC>2.0.CO;2-3. Citations in this document: §2.2

[34] National Institute for Standards and Technology: Digital signature standard. Federal Information Processing Standards Publication 186-2 (2000). http://csrc.nist.gov/publications/fips/archive/fips186-2/fips186-2.pdf. Citations in this document: §1.2

[35] National Security Agency: Suite B Cryptography / Cryptographic Interoperability (2009). http://www.nsa.gov/ia/programs/suiteb_cryptography/. Citations in this document: §2.1

[36] Nguyen, P.L., Oswald, E. (eds.): Advances in cryptology — EUROCRYPT 2014 — 33rd annual international conference on the theory and applications of cryptographic techniques, Copenhagen, Denmark, May 11–15, 2014, proceedings. LNCS, vol. 8441. Springer (2014). ISBN 978-3-642-55219-9. See [16]

[37] Pieprzyk, J. (ed.): Advances in cryptology — ASIACRYPT 2008, 14th international conference on the theory and application of cryptology and information security, Melbourne, Australia, December 7–11, 2008. LNCS, vol. 5350 (2008). ISBN 978-3-540-89254-0. See [26]

[38] Preneel, B., Takagi, T. (eds.): Cryptographic hardware and embedded systems — CHES 2011, 13th international workshop, Nara, Japan, September 28–October 1, 2011, proceedings. LNCS, vol. 6917. Springer (2011). ISBN 978-3-642-23950-2. See [5]

[39] Prouff, E., Schaumont, P. (eds.): Cryptographic hardware and embedded systems — CHES 2012 — 14th international workshop, Leuven, Belgium, September 9–12, 2012, proceedings. LNCS, vol. 7428. Springer (2012). ISBN 978-3-642-33026-1. See [11]

[40] Wang, X., Sako, K. (eds.): Advances in cryptology — ASIACRYPT 2012, 18th international conference on the theory and application of cryptology and information security, Beijing, China, December 2–6, 2012, proceedings. LNCS, vol. 7658. Springer (2012). ISBN 978-3-642-34960-7. See [32]

[41] Yung, M., Dodis, Y., Kiayias, A., Malkin, T. (eds.): Public key cryptography — 9th international conference on theory and practice in public-key cryptography, New York, NY, USA, April 24–26, 2006, proceedings. LNCS, vol. 3958. Springer (2006). ISBN 978-3-540-33851-2. See [2]

# A    Point Arithmetic Formulas

This appendix presents the formulas that we use for doubling and addition of curve points. Most of these formulas are taken from the EFD [9]. To simplify the cost statements we count only field multiplications and squarings, not additions and subtractions.

## A.1    Formulas for Doubling

We use three different formulas for point doubling. The slowest formulas are the following:

Input:    $X_1, Y_1, Z_1$
Output: $X_3, Y_3, Z_3, T_3$
Cost:    $4\mathbf{M} + 4\mathbf{S}$

$$A = X_1^2, \qquad G = A + B, \qquad X_3 = EF,$$
$$B = Y_1^2, \qquad F = G - C, \qquad Y_3 = GH,$$
$$C = 2Z_1^2, \qquad H = A - B, \qquad Z_3 = FG,$$
$$E = (X_1 + Y_1)^2 - A - B, \qquad\qquad T_3 = EH.$$

We use these formulas once in each five-doubling window, specifically for the last doubling before point addition. Each of the other four doublings costs just $3\mathbf{M} + 4\mathbf{S}$: we save $1\mathbf{M}$ by skipping the computation of $T_3$.

For the first doubling in the precomputation we use the following faster formulas.

Input: $X_1, Y_1, T_1$ where $Z_1 = 1$
Output: $X_3, Y_3, Z_3, T_3$
Cost: $3\mathbf{M} + 3\mathbf{S}$

$$
\begin{aligned}
A &= X_1^2, & G &= A + B, & X_3 &= EF, \\
B &= Y_1^2, & F &= G - 2, & Y_3 &= GH, \\
E &= 2T_1, & H &= A - B, & Z_3 &= G^2 - 2G, \\
& & & & T_3 &= EH.
\end{aligned}
$$

## A.2    Formulas for Addition

All additions in the precomputation use the following formulas. These formulas save $1\mathbf{M}$ using $Z_2 = 1$.

Input: $X_1, Y_1, Z_1, T_1, X_2, Y_2, dT_2$ where $Z_2 = 1$
Output: $X_3, Y_3, Z_3, T_3$
Cost: $8\mathbf{M}$

$$
\begin{aligned}
A &= X_1 X_2, & F &= Z_1 - C, & X_3 &= EF, \\
B &= Y_1 Y_2, & G &= Z_1 + C, & Y_3 &= GH, \\
C &= T_1 dT_2, & H &= B - A, & Z_3 &= FG, \\
E &= (X_1 + Y_1)(X_2 + Y_2) - A - B, & & & T_3 &= EH.
\end{aligned}
$$

All additions in the main computation use the following formulas. These formulas save $1\mathbf{M}$ by skipping the computation of $T_3$; the next operation is doubling, which does not use $T$.

Input: $X_1, Y_1, Z_1, T_1, X_2, Y_2, Z_2, dT_2$
Output: $X_3, Y_3, Z_3$
Cost: $8\mathbf{M}$

$$
\begin{aligned}
A &= X_1 X_2, & E &= (X_1 + Y_1)(X_2 + Y_2) - A - B, & & \\
B &= Y_1 Y_2, & F &= D - C, & X_3 &= EF, \\
C &= T_1 dT_2, & G &= D + C, & Y_3 &= GH, \\
D &= Z_1 Z_2, & H &= B - A, & Z_3 &= FG.
\end{aligned}
$$

# Cofactorization on Graphics Processing Units

Andrea Miele[1], Joppe W. Bos[2,*], Thorsten Kleinjung[1], and Arjen K. Lenstra[1]

[1] LACAL, EPFL, Lausanne, Switzerland
[2] NXP Semiconductors, Leuven, Belgium

**Abstract.** We show how the cofactorization step, a compute-intensive part of the relation collection phase of the number field sieve (NFS), can be farmed out to a graphics processing unit. Our implementation on a GTX 580 GPU, which is integrated with a state-of-the-art NFS implementation, can serve as a *cryptanalytic co-processor* for several Intel i7-3770K quad-core CPUs simultaneously. This allows those processors to focus on the memory-intensive sieving and results in more useful NFS-relations found in less time.

**Keywords:** Cofactorization, Graphics Processing Unit, Number Field Sieve.

## 1 Introduction

Today, the asymptotically fastest publicly known integer factorization method is the number field sieve (NFS, [47,30]). It has been used to set several integer factorization records, most recently a 768-bit RSA modulus as described in [27]. In the first of its two main steps, pairs of integers called *relations* are collected. This is done by iterating a two-stage approach: *sieving* to collect a large batch of promising pairs, followed by the identification of the relatively few relations among them. Sieving requires a lot of memory and is commonly done on CPUs. The follow-up stage requires little memory and can be parallelized in multiple ways. It may therefore be cost-effective to offload this follow-up stage to a coprocessor. Most previous work in this direction focussed on offloading the elliptic curve integer factoring (ECM, [31]), which is only part of this follow-up stage. For graphics processing units (GPUs) this is considered in [7,5,10] and for reconfigurable hardware such as field-programmable gate arrays in [54,46,17,14,19,32,59]. To allow the CPUs to keep sieving, thus optimally using their memory, in this paper the possibility is explored to offload the *entire* follow-up stage to GPUs. We describe our approach, with a focus on modular and elliptic curve arithmetic, to do so on the many-core, memory-constrained GPU platform. Our results demonstrate that GPUs can be used as an efficient *high-throughput co-processor* for this application.

Our design strategy exploits the inherent task parallelism of the stage that follows the actual sieving, namely the fact that collected pairs can be processed independently in parallel. Because the integers involved are relatively small (at

---

* Part of this work has been performed while the second author was working for Microsoft Research, WA, USA.

L. Batina and M. Robshaw (Eds.): CHES 2014, LNCS 8731, pp. 335–352, 2014.

most 384 bits for our target number), we have chosen not to parallelize the integer arithmetic, thereby avoiding performance penalties due to inter-thread synchronization while maximizing the compute-to-memory-access ratio [5]. We use a single thread to process a single pair from the input batch, aiming to maximize the number of pairs processed per second. Because this requires a large number of registers per thread and potentially reduces the GPU utilization, we use integer arithmetic algorithms that minimize register usage and apply native multiply-and-add instructions wherever possible.

For each pair the follow-up stage consists of checking if two integer values, obtained by evaluating two bivariate integer polynomials at the point determined by the pair, are both smooth, i.e., divisible by primes up to certain bounds. This is done sequentially: a first kernel filters the pairs for which the first polynomial value is smooth, once enough pairs have been collected a second kernel does the same for the second polynomial value, and pairs that pass both filters correspond to relations. Each kernel first computes the relevant polynomial value and then subjects it to a sequence of occasional compositeness tests and factorization attempts aimed at finding small factors.

We have determined good parameters for two different approaches: to find as many relations as possible ($\approx 99\%$ in a batch) and a faster one to find most relations ($\approx 95\%$ in a batch). The effectiveness of these approaches is demonstrated by integrating the GPU software with state-of-the-art NFS software [16] tuned for the factorization of the 768-bit modulus from [27]. A single GTX 580 GPU can serve between 3 and 10 Intel i7-3770K *quad-core* CPUs.

Cryptologic applications of GPUs have been considered before: symmetric cryptography in [33,20,57,21,45,11,18], asymmetric cryptography in [40,55,22] for RSA and in [55,1,9] for ECC, and enhancing symmetric [8] and asymmetric [7,5,6,10] cryptanalysis.

Our source code will be made available.

## 2 Preliminaries

**The Number Field Sieve.** For details on how NFS works, see [30,51]. Its major steps are polynomial selection, relation collection, and the matrix step. For this paper, an operational description of relation collection for numbers in the current range of interest suffices. For those numbers relation collection is responsible for about 90% of the computational effort.

Here we call an integer $B$-smooth if there is no prime-power larger than $B$ that divides it (elsewhere such numbers are called $B$-powersmooth). Relation collection uses smoothness bounds $B_r, B_a \in \mathbf{Z}_{>0}$ and polynomials $f_r(X), f_a(X) \in \mathbf{Z}[X]$ such that $f_r$ is of degree one, $f_a$ is irreducible of (small) degree $d > 1$, and $f_r$ and $f_a$ have a common root modulo the number to be factored. The polynomials $f_r$ and $f_a$ are commonly referred to as the *rational* and the *algebraic* polynomial, respectively. A relation is a pair of coprime integers $(a, b)$ with $b > 0$ such that $bf_r(a/b)$ is $B_r$-smooth and $b^d f_a(a/b)$ is $B_a$-smooth.

Relations are determined by successively processing relatively large *special primes* until sufficiently many relations have been found. A special prime $q$ defines an index-$q$ sublattice in $\mathbf{Z}^2$ of pairs $(a, b)$ such that $q$ divides $bf_{\mathrm{r}}(a/b)b^d f_{\mathrm{a}}(a/b)$. Sieving in the sublattice results in a collection of pairs for which $bf_{\mathrm{r}}(a/b)$ and $b^d f_{\mathrm{a}}(a/b)$ have relatively many small factors. To identify the relations, for all collected pairs the values $bf_{\mathrm{r}}(a/b)$ and $b^d f_{\mathrm{a}}(a/b)$ are further inspected. This can be done by first simultaneously *resieving* the $bf_{\mathrm{r}}(a/b)$-values to remove their small factors, then doing the same for the $b^d f_{\mathrm{a}}(a/b)$-values, after which any cofactors are dealt with on a pair-by-pair basis. Alternatively, cofactoring can be preceded by a pair-by-pair search for the small factors in $bf_{\mathrm{r}}(a/b)$ and $b^d f_{\mathrm{a}}(a/b)$, thus simplifying the sieving step. The latter approach is adopted here, to offload as much as possible from the regular CPU cores, including the calculation of the relevant $bf_{\mathrm{r}}(a/b)$- and $b^d f_{\mathrm{a}}(a/b)$-values. The steps involved in this extended (and thus somewhat misnomered) cofactoring are described in Section 3.

**Montgomery Arithmetic.** For arithmetic modulo a fixed odd modulus $m$ *Montgomery arithmetic* [36] may be used because it avoids trials during the divisions and allows simple coding. Let $r$ be the machine radix (here $r = 2^{32}$), let $k \in \mathbf{Z}_{>0}$ be minimal such that $r^k > m$, and let $\mu = -m^{-1} \bmod r$. The *Montgomery representation* of an integer $x \in \mathbf{Z}/m\mathbf{Z}$ is defined as $\tilde{x} = xr^k \bmod m$. Given Montgomery representations $\tilde{x}, \tilde{y}$ of $x, y \in \mathbf{Z}/m\mathbf{Z}$, it follows that $\tilde{t}$ such that $t = (x \pm y) \bmod m$ is calculated as $\tilde{t} = (\tilde{x} \pm \tilde{y}) \bmod m$, and that $\tilde{s}$ such that $s = xy \bmod m$ satisfies $\tilde{s} = \tilde{x}\tilde{y}r^{-k} \bmod m$. This Montgomery product $\tilde{s}$ can be computed by first calculating the ordinary integer product $u = \tilde{x}\tilde{y}$, and by next performing *Montgomery reduction*: modulo $m$ divide $u$ by $r^k$ by replacing $k$ times in succession $u$ by $(u + [((u \bmod r)\mu) \bmod r]m)/r$, then $\tilde{s} = u - m$ if $u \ge m$ and $\tilde{s} = u$ otherwise. If $0 \le \tilde{x}, \tilde{y} < m$, then the same bound hold for $\tilde{s}$.

**Jebelean's Exact Division.** If $n$ is known to be an integer multiple of an odd integer $p$, the quotient $\frac{n}{p}$ can be computed using an iteration very similar to Montgomery reduction: let $\mu = -p^{-1} \bmod r$, then $v = ((n \bmod r)(r - \mu)) \bmod r$ equals the least significant radix-$r$ block $\frac{n}{p} \bmod r$ of $\frac{n}{p}$, after which $n$ is replaced by $(n - vp)/r$ and the other radix-$r$ blocks of $\frac{n}{p}$ are iteratively computed in the same way. This is known as *Jebelean's exact division method* [24].

# 3 Cofactoring Steps

This section lists the steps used to identify the relations among a collection of pairs of integers $(a, b)$ that results from NFS sieving for one or more special primes. See [26] for related previous work. The notation is as in Section 2.

For all collected pairs $(a, b)$ the values $bf_{\mathrm{r}}(a/b)$ and $b^d f_{\mathrm{a}}(a/b)$ can be calculated by observing that $b^k f(a/b) = \sum_{i=0}^{k} f_i a^i b^{k-i}$ for $f(X) = \sum_{i=0}^{k} f_i X^i \in \mathbf{Z}[X]$. The value $z = b^k f(a/b)$ is trivially calculated in $k(k-1)$ multiplications by initializing $z$ as 0, and by replacing, for $i = 0, 1, \ldots, k$ in succession, $z$ by $z + f_i a^i b^{k-i}$, or, at the cost of an additional memory location, in $3k - 1$ multiplications by initializing $z = f_0$ and $t = a$ and by replacing, for $i = 1, 2, \ldots, k$ in succession,

$z$ by $zb + f_i t$ and, if $i < k$, $t$ by $ta$. Even with the most naive approach (as opposed to asymptotically faster methods), this is a negligible part of the overall calculation. The resulting values need to be tested for smoothness, with bound $B_r$ for the $bf_r(a/b)$-values and bound $B_a$ for the $b^d f_a(a/b)$-values.

For all pairs $(a, b)$ both $bf_r(a/b)$ and $b^d f_a(a/b)$ have relatively many small factors (because the pairs are collected during NFS sieving). After shifting out all factors of two, other very small factors may be found using trial division, somewhat larger ones by Pollard $p-1$ [48], and the largest ones using ECM [31]. These three methods are further described below. In our experiment (cf. 5.2) it turned out to be best to skip trial division for $bf_r(a/b)$ and let Pollard $p-1$ and ECM take care of the very small factors as well. Based on the findings reported in [28] or their GPU-incompatibility, other integer factorization methods like Pollard rho [49] or quadratic sieve [50] are not considered. It is occasionally useful to make sure that remaining cofactors are composite. An appropriate compositeness test is therefore described first.

**Compositeness Test.** Let $m - 1 = 2^t u$ for $t \in \mathbf{Z}_{\geq 0}$ and odd $u \in \mathbf{Z}$. If for some $a \in (\mathbf{Z}/m\mathbf{Z})^*$ it is the case that $a^u \not\equiv 1 \bmod m$ and $a^{u2^i} \not\equiv -1 \bmod m$ for $0 \leq i < t$, then $m$ is composite and $a$ is a *witness* to $m$'s compositeness. As shown in [35,52], for composite $m$ more than 75% of the integers in $\{1, 2, \ldots, m-1\}$ are witnesses to $m$'s compositeness.

This test is used as follows to process an $m$-value that is found as an as yet unfactored part of a polynomial value $bf_r(a/b)$ or $b^d f_a(a/b)$. If 2 is a witness to $m$'s compositeness, then $m$ is subjected to further factoring attempts; if not, the polynomial value is declared fully factored and the corresponding pair $(a, b)$ is cast aside if $m > B_r$ for $m \mid bf_r(a/b)$ or $m > B_a$ for $m \mid b^d f_a(a/b)$. This carries the risk that a non-prime factor may appear in a supposedly fully factored polynomial value, or that a pair $(a, b)$ is wrongly discarded. With a small probability to occur, either type of failure is of no concern in our cryptanalytic context.

**Trial Division.** Given an odd integer $n$, all its prime factors up to some small trial division bound are removed using trial division. For each small odd prime $p$ (possibly tabulated, if memory is available) first $\pi = (-p)^{-1} \bmod r$ is calculated (per thread, at negligible overhead), with $r = 2^{32}$ as in Section 2. Next, $n$ is tested for divisibility by $p$: with $u$ initialized as $n$ and $k$ the least integer such that $u < r^k$, the integer $u$ is modulo $p$ divided by $r^k$ (using Montgomery reduction, with $p$ and $\pi$ in the roles of $m$ and $\mu$, respectively). If the resulting 32-bit value $u$ satisfies $u \bmod p \equiv 0$, then $n$ is divisible by $p$ and the divisibility test is repeated with $n$ replaced by $\frac{n}{p}$ (computed using Jebelean's method).

**Pollard $p - 1$.** The prime factors $p$ of $n$ for which $p - 1$ is $B_1$-smooth can be found at a cost of $O(B_1)$ multiplications modulo $n$ by means of "stage 1" of Pollard's $p - 1$ method [48]: with $t = a^k \bmod n$, for some $a \not\equiv \pm 1 \bmod n$, $a \not\equiv 0 \bmod n$ and $k$ the product of all prime powers $\leq B_1$, the product of all such $p$ divides $\gcd(t - 1, n)$. In practice the value $a = 2$ is used for efficiency reasons. If the order modulo $n$ of $t$ is at most $B_2$, for some bound $B_2 > B_1$, this can be exploited in "stage 2" [37], thereby allowing in $p - 1$ one additional prime factor between $B_1$ and $B_2$. Naively, $\gcd(t^\ell - 1, n)$ could be computed for all primes $\ell$ in $(B_1, B_2]$. A much faster but memory-consuming method uses the fast Fourier transform (cf. [39]). On GPUs a baby-step giant-step approach is more suitable and is used here. It follows from the description below and the optimizations described in [37].

**Elliptic Curve Method.** Stage 1 of Pollard's $p - 1$ method uses $O(B_1)$ multiplications modulo $n$ to find prime factors $p$ of $n$ for which the groups $(\mathbf{Z}/p\mathbf{Z})^*$ have $B_1$-smooth order. Thus, $p$ can be found in time mostly linear in the largest prime factor of $p - 1$. The elliptic curve method (ECM) for integer factorization [31] works analogously but replaces the fixed group $(\mathbf{Z}/p\mathbf{Z})^*$ of order $p - 1$ by a number of groups with orders behaving like random integers *close to* $p$: given one such group with $B_1$-smooth order, $p$ can be found in $O(B_1)$ multiplications and additions modulo $n$. Trading off the number of groups attempted and the smoothness bound, finding $p$ can heuristically be argued to take $\exp((\sqrt{2} + o(1))(\sqrt{\log p \log \log p}))$ elementary operations modulo $n$, where $p \to \infty$.

Like Pollard's $p - 1$ method, each ECM attempt operates on a group element and the product $k$ of all prime powers $\leq B_1$, mimics the "mod $p$" operations by doing them "mod $n$", and hopes to run into the identity element mod $p$ but not mod $n$, if not in stage 1 then in stage 2. Where Pollard's method is based on arithmetic in the group of integers modulo the composite multiple $n$ of $p$, ECM is based on arithmetic with "points" belonging to groups associated with elliptic curves over prime fields, mimicking those operations by doing them modulo the composite multiple $n$ of those primes. Because the operations may not be well-defined, they may fail, thereby revealing a factor of $n$.

The current best approach to implement ECM, as used here, is "$a = -1$" *twisted Edwards curves* (based on [15,4,23,3]) with extended twisted Edwards coordinates (improving on *Montgomery curves* [37] and methods from [58]). Below points are represented as pairs of projective points $((x : z), (y : t))$ for $x, z, y, t \in \mathbf{Z}/n\mathbf{Z}$, with *zero point* $((0 : 1), (1 : 1))$. Applying the additively written "group operation" requires a total of eight multiplications and squarings in $\mathbf{Z}/n\mathbf{Z}$. With initial point $P$ the point $kP$ can thus be calculated in $O(B_1)$ multiplications in $\mathbf{Z}/n\mathbf{Z}$, after which the gcd of $n$ and the $x$-coordinate of $kP$ is computed. Because the same $k$ is often used, good addition-subtraction chains can be prepared (cf. [10]): for $B_1 = 256$, the point $kP$ can be computed in 1400 multiplications and 1444 squarings modulo $n$. Due to the significant memory reduction this approach is particularly efficient for memory constrained devices like GPUs. We also select curves for which 16 divides the group order, further enhancing the success probability of ECM (cf. [2, Thm. 3.4 and 3.6] and [3]). More specifically we use "$a = -1$" twisted Edwards curve $(E : -x^2 + y^2 = 1 + dx^2 y^2)$ over $\mathbf{Q}$ with $d = -((g - 1/g)/2)^4$ such that $d(d + 1) \neq 0$ and $g \in \mathbf{Q} \setminus \{\pm 1, 0\}$.

Related work on stage 1 of ECM for cofactoring on constrained devices can be found in [54,46,17,14,19,32,59,7,5,10]. Unlike these publications, the GPU-implementation presented here includes stage 2 of ECM, as it significantly improves the performance of ECM.

**ECM Stage 2 on GPUs.** The fastest known methods to implement stage 2 of ECM are FFT-based [12,37,38] and rather memory-hungry, which may explain why earlier constrained device ECM-cofactoring work did not consider stage 2. These methods are also incompatible with the memory restrictions of current GPUs. Below a baby-step giant-step approach [53] to stage 2 is described that is suitable for GPUs. Let $Q = kP$ be as above. Similar to the naive approach to stage 2 of Pollard's $p - 1$ method, the points $\ell Q$ for the primes $\ell$ in $(B_1, B_2]$ can be computed and be compared to the zero point modulo a prime dividing $p$ but not modulo $n$. The latter amounts to computing the gcd of $n$ and the product of the $x$-coordinates of the points $\ell Q$. With $N$ primes $\ell$, computing all points requires about $8N$ multiplications in $\mathbf{Z}/n\mathbf{Z}$, assuming a few precomputed small even multiples of $Q$. Balancing the computational efforts of the two stages with $B_1 = 256$ as above, leads to $B_2 = 2803$ (and $N = 354$).

The baby-step giant step approach from [37] speeds up the calculation at the cost of more memory, while also exploiting that for Edwards curves and any point $P$ it is the case that

$$\frac{y(P)}{t(P)} = \frac{y(-P)}{t(-P)}, \tag{1}$$

with $y(P)$ and $t(P)$ the $y$- and $t$-coordinate, respectively, of $P$.

For a giant-step value $w < B_1$, any $\ell$ as above can be written as $vw \pm u$ where $u \in U = \left\{ u \in \mathbf{Z} : 1 \le u \le \frac{w}{2}, \gcd(u,w) = 1 \right\}$, and $v \in V = \left\{ v \in \mathbf{Z} : \left\lceil \frac{B_1}{w} - \frac{1}{2} \right\rceil \le v \le \left\lfloor \frac{B_2}{w} + \frac{1}{2} \right\rfloor \right\}$. Comparing $(vw - u)Q$ to the zero point modulo $p$ but not modulo $n$ amounts to checking if $\gcd(t(uQ)y(vwQ) - t(vwQ)y(uQ), n) \ne 1$. Because of (1), this compares $(vw + u)Q$ to the zero point as well. Hence, computation of $\gcd(m, n)$ for $m = \prod_{v \in V} \prod_{u \in U} (t(uQ)y(vwQ) - t(vwQ)y(uQ))$ suffices to check if $Q$ has prime order in $(B_1, B_2]$. Optimal parameters balance the costs of the preparation of the $\frac{\varphi(w)}{2}$ tabulated baby-step values $(y(uQ) : t(uQ))$ (where $\varphi$ is Euler's totient function) and on the fly computation of the giant-step values $(y(vwQ) : t(vwQ))$. Suboptimal, smaller $w$-values may be used to reduce storage requirements. For instance, the choice $w = 2 \cdot 3 \cdot 5 \cdot 7$ and $B_2 = 7770$ leads to 24 tabulated values and a total of 2904 multiplications and squarings modulo $n$, which matches the computational effort of stage 1 with $B_1 = 256$. Although $\gcd(u, w) = 1$ already avoids easy composites, the product can be restricted to those $u, v$ for which one of $vw \pm u$ is prime if storage for about $\frac{B_2 - B_1}{w} \times \frac{\varphi(w)}{2}$ bits is available. With $w$ and tabulated baby-step values as above, this increases $B_2$ to 8925 for a similar computational effort, but requires about 125 bytes of storage. A more substantial improvement is to define

$$y_v = \left( \prod_{\tilde{v} \in V - \{v\}} t(\tilde{v}wQ) \right) \left( \prod_{\tilde{u} \in U} t(\tilde{u}Q) \right) y(vwQ)$$

and

$$y_u = \left( \prod_{\tilde{u} \in U - \{u\}} t(\tilde{u}Q) \right) \left( \prod_{\tilde{v} \in V} t(\tilde{v}wQ) \right) y(uQ),$$

and to replace $m$ by $\prod_{v \in V} \prod_{u \in U} (y_v - y_u)$. This saves $2|V||U|$ of the $3|V||U|$ multiplications in the calculation of $m$ at a cost that is linear in $|U| + |V|$ to tabulate the $y_v$ and $y_u$ values. For instance, it allows usage of $B_2 = 16\,384$ at an effort of 3368 modular multiplications.

# 4  GPU Implementation Details

In this section we outline our approach to implement the algorithms from Section 3 with a focus on the many-core GPU architecture. We used a quad-core Intel i7-3770K CPU running at 3.5 GHz with 16 GB of memory and an NVIDIA GeForce GTX 580 GPU, with 512 CUDA cores running at 1544 MHz and 1.5 GB of global memory, as further described below.

## 4.1  Compute Unified Device Architecture

We focus on the GeForce $x$-series families for $x \in \{8, 9, 100, 200, 400, 500, 600, 700\}$, of the NVIDIA GPU architecture with the compute unified device architecture (CUDA) [42]. Our NVIDIA GeForce GTX 580 GPU belongs to the GeForce 400- and 500-series ([41]) of the Fermi architecture family. These GPUs support $32 \times 32 \rightarrow 32$-bit multiplication instructions, for both the least and most significant 32 bits of the result.

Each GPU contains a number of streaming multiprocessors (SMs), with each SM consisting of multiple scalar processor cores (SP). On a Fermi architecture GPU there are typically about 16 SMs and 32 SPs per SM, but numbers vary per model. C for CUDA is an extension to the C language that employs the *single-instruction multiple-thread* (SIMT) model of massively parallel programming. The programmer defines *kernel functions*, which are compiled for and executed in parallel on the SPs such that each light-weight thread executes the same instructions but on its own data. A number of threads is grouped into a *thread block* which is scheduled on a single SM, the threads of which time-share the SPs.

Threads inside a thread block are executed in groups of 32 called *warps*. On Fermi architecture GPUs each SM has two warp schedulers and two instruction dispatch units. This means that two instructions, from separate warps, can be scheduled and dispatched at the same time. Switching between warps, filling the pipeline as much as possible, a high throughput rate can be sustained. The distinct possibilities of a conditional branch are executed serially by the threads inside a warp, with threads active only when their branch is executed. Multiple execution paths within a warp are thus best avoided.

Threads in the same block can communicate via on-chip shared memory and may synchronize their execution using barriers (a synchronization method which makes threads wait until all reach a certain point). There is a large but relatively slow amount of global memory that is accessible to all threads. Fermi architecture GPUs have an L1-cache for each SM, and a unified L2-cache together with fast constant (read-only) memory initialized by the CPU.

## 4.2   Modular Arithmetic on GPUs

We used the parallel thread execution (PTX) instruction set and inline assembly wherever possible to simplify (cf. carry-handling) and speed-up (cf. multiply-and-add) our code; Table 7 in the Appendix lists the arithmetic assembly routines used. "Warp divergent" code was reduced to a minimum by converting most branches into *straight line code* to avoid different execution paths within a warp: branch-free code that executes both branches and uses a bit-mask to select the correct value was often found to be more efficient than "if-else" statements.

**Practical Performance.** Our decision not to use parallel integer arithmetic dictates the use of algorithms with minimal register usage. For Montgomery multiplication, the most critical operation, we therefore preferred the plain interleaved schoolbook method to Karatsuba [25]; the CUDA pseudo-code for moduli of at least 96 bits is given in the full version of this paper [34].

Table 1 compares our results both with the state-of-the-art implementation from [29] benchmarked on an NVIDIA GTX 480 card (480 cores, 1401Mhz) and with the ideal peak throughput attainable on our GTX 580 GPU. Compared to [29] our throughput is up to twice better, especially for smaller (128-bit) moduli, even after the figures from [29] are scaled by a factor of $\frac{512}{480} \cdot \frac{1544}{1401}$ to account for our larger number of cores (512) and higher frequency (1544 MHz). For $32\ell$-bit moduli, with $\ell \in [3, 12]$ (i.e. moduli ranging from 96 to 384 bits), we counted the total number of multiplication and multiply-and-add instructions required by Montgomery multiplication. The throughput of those instructions on our GPU is 0.5 per clock cycle per core, whereas the throughput of the addition instructions is 1 per clock cycle per core. Since we use fewer addition than multiplication instructions, our throughput count considers only the latter. In our benchmarks we transfer to the GPU two (distinct) operands and a modulus for each thread, and then compute one million Montgomery multiplications (using each output as one of the next inputs) before transferring the results back to the CPU. Our throughput turns out to be very close to the peak value.

## 4.3   Elliptic Curve Arithmetic on GPUs

When running stage 1 of ECM on memory constrained devices like GPUs, the large number of precomputed points required for windowing methods cannot be stored in fast memory. Thus, one is forced to settle for a (much) smaller window size, thereby reducing the advantage of using twisted Edwards curves. For example, in [7] windowing is not used at all because, citing [7], "Besides the base point, we cannot cache any other points". Memory is also a problem in [5], where the faster curve arithmetic from Hisil et al. [23] is not used since this requires storing a fourth coordinate per point. These concerns were the motivation behind [10], the approach we adopted for stage 1 of ECM (as indicated in Section 3). For stage 2 we use the baby-step giant-step approach, optimized as described at the end of Section 3 for $B_2 \leq 32768$. Using bounds that balance

**Table 1.** Benchmark results for the NVIDIA GTX 580 GPU for numbers of Montgomery multiplications and ECM trials per second for various modulus sizes, with the results from [29] scaled as explained in the text. The estimated peak throughput based on an instruction count is also included together with the total number of dispatched threads. ECM used bounds $B_1 = 256$ and $B_2 = 16384$ (for a total of $2844+3368 = 6212$ Montgomery multiplications per trial).

| moduli bitsize | Leboeuf [29] Montgomery muls measured (scaled, $10^6$) | this work |||||
|---|---|---|---|---|---|---|
| | | Montgomery muls |  | | ECM (8192 threads for all sizes) ||
| | | measured ($10^6$) | peak | #threads | trials ($10^3$) | Montgomery muls measured ($10^6$) |
| 96 | | 10119 | 10135 | 16384 | 1078 | 6697 |
| 128 | 2799 | 5805 | 5813 | 16384 | 674 | 4187 |
| 160 | 2261 | 3760 | 3764 | 16384 | 453 | 2814 |
| 192 | 1837 | 2631 | 2635 | 16384 | 309 | 1920 |
| 224 | 1507 | 1943 | 1947 | 15360 | 243 | 1510 |
| 256 | 1212 | 1493 | 1497 | 10240 | 180 | 1118 |
| 320 | 828 | 962 | 964 | 10240 | 107 | 665 |
| 384 | 600 | 671 | 672 | 9216 | 86 | 534 |

the number of stage 1 and  2 multiplications does not necessarily balance the GPU running time of the two stages (this varies with the modulus size), but it is a good starting point for further optimization.

Table 1 lists the resulting performance figures, in terms of thousands of trials per second for various modulus sizes. Two jobs each consisting of 8192 threads were launched simultaneously, with each job per thread doing an ECM trial with the bounds as indicated, and with at the start a unique modulus per thread transferred to the GPU. The relatively high register usage of ECM reduces the number of threads that can be launched per SM before running out of registers. Nevertheless, and despite its large number of modular additions and subtractions, ECM manages to sustain a high Montgomery multiplication throughput. Except for the comparison to the work reported in [29], we have not been able to put our results in further perspective because we did not have access to other multiplication or ECM results or implementations in a comparable context.

## 5    Cofactorization on GPUs

This section describes our GPU approach to cofactoring, i.e., recognizing among the pairs $(a, b)$ resulting from NFS sieving those pairs for which $bf_r(a/b)$ is $B_r$-smooth and $b^d f_a(a/b)$ is $B_a$-smooth. Approaches common on regular cores (resieving followed by sequential processing of the remaining candidates) allow pair-by-pair optimization with respect to the highest overall yield or yield per second while exploiting the available memory, but are incompatible with the memory and SIMT restrictions of current GPUs.

## 5.1  Cofactorization Overview

Given our application, where throughput is important but latency almost irrelevant, it is a natural choice to process each pair in a single thread, eliminating the need for inter-thread communication, minimizing synchronization overhead, and allowing the scheduler to maximize pipelining by interleaving instructions from different warps. On the negative side, the large memory footprint per thread reduces the number of simultaneously active threads per SM.

The cofactorization stage is split into two GPU kernel functions that receive pairs $(a, b)$ as input: the rational kernel outputs pairs for which $bf_r(a/b)$ is $B_r$-smooth to the algebraic kernel that outputs those pairs for which $b^d f_a(a/b)$ is $B_a$-smooth as well. The two kernels have the same code structure: all that distinguishes them is that the algebraic one usually has to handle larger values and a higher degree polynomial. To make our implementation flexible with respect to the polynomial selection, the maximum size of the polynomial values is a kernel parameter that is fixed at compile time and that can easily be changed together with the polynomial degree and coefficient size and the size of the inputs.

**Kernel Structure.** Given a pair $(a, b)$, a kernel-thread first evaluates the relevant polynomial, storing the odd part $n$ of the resulting value along with identifying information $i$ as a pair $(i, n)$; if applicable the special prime is removed from $n$. The value $n$ is then updated in the following sequence of steps, with all parameters set at run-time using a configuration file. First trial division may be applied up to a small bound. The resulting pairs $(i, n)$ are regrouped depending on their radix-$2^{32}$ sizes. The cost of the resulting inter-thread communication and synchronization is outweighed by the advantage of being able to run size-specific versions of the other steps. All threads in a warp then grab a pair $(i, n)$ of the same size and each thread attempts to factor its $n$-value using Pollard's $p - 1$ method or ECM. If the resulting $n$ is at most the smoothness bound, the kernel outputs the $i$th pair $(a, b)$. If $n$'s compositeness cannot be established or if $n$ is larger than some user-defined threshold, the $i$th pair $(a, b)$ is discarded. Pairs $(i, n)$ with small enough composite $n$ are regrouped and reprocessed.

This approach treats every pair $(i, n)$ in the same group in the same way, which makes it attractive for GPUs. However, unnecessary computations may be performed: for instance, if a factoring attempt fails, compositeness does not need to be reascertained. Avoiding this requires divergent code which, as it turned out, degrades the performance. Also, factoring attempts may chance upon a factor larger than the smoothness bound, an event that goes by unnoticed as only the unfactored part is reported back. We have verified that the CPU easily discards such mishaps at negligible overhead.

**Interaction between CPU and GPU.** The CPU uses two programs to interact with the GPU. The first one adds batches of $(a, b)$ pairs produced by the siever (which may be running on the CPU too) to a FIFO buffer and keeps track of special primes. The second program controls the GPU by iterating the following steps (where the roles of the kernels may be reversed and the batch sizes depend on the GPU memory constraints and the kernel):

**Table 2.** Time in seconds to process a single special prime on all cores of a quad-core Intel i7-3770K CPU

| large primes | number of pairs after sieving | relations found | sieving time | cofactoring time | total time | % of time spent on cofactoring | relations per second |
|---|---|---|---|---|---|---|---|
| 3 | $\approx 5 \cdot 10^5$ | 125 | 25.6 | 4.0 | 29.6 | 13.5 | 4.22 |
| 4 | $\approx 10^6$ | 137 | 25.9 | 6.1 | 32.0 | 19.1 | 4.28 |

**Table 3.** Parameters choices for cofactoring. Later ECM attempts use larger bounds in the specified ranges.

| desired yield | algorithm | rational kernel | | | algebraic kernel | | |
|---|---|---|---|---|---|---|---|
| | | attempts | $B_1$ | $B_2$ | attempts | $B_1$ | $B_2$ |
| 95% | Pollard $p-1$ | 1 | $[2^8, 2^{11}]$ | $[2^{13}, 2^{14}]$ | 1 | $[2^8, 2^{12}]$ | $[2^{14}, 2^{15}]$ |
| | ECM | $[5, 10]$ | $2^8$ | $[2^{12}, 2^{13}]$ | 10 | $[2^8, 2^9]$ | $[2^{12}, 2^{15}]$ |
| 99% | Pollard $p-1$ | 1 | $[2^{10}, 2^{12}]$ | $[2^{13}, 2^{15}]$ | 1 | $[2^8, 2^{11}]$ | $[2^{13}, 2^{14}]$ |
| | ECM | $[10, 12]$ | $[2^8, 2^9]$ | $[2^{12}, 2^{15}]$ | $[10, 20]$ | $[2^8, 2^9]$ | $[2^{12}, 2^{15}]$ |

1. copy a batch from the FIFO buffer to the GPU;
2. launch the rational kernel on the GPU;
3. store the pairs output by the rational kernel in an intermediate buffer;
4. if the intermediate buffer does not contain enough pairs, return to Step 1;
5. copy a batch from the intermediate buffer to the GPU;
6. launch the algebraic kernel on the GPU (providing it with the proper special primes);
7. store the pairs output by the algebraic kernel in a file and return to Step 1.

**Exploiting the GPU Memory Hierarchy.** GPU performance strongly depends on where intermediate values are stored. We use constant memory for fixed data precomputed by the CPU and accessed by *all threads at the same time*: primes for trial division, polynomial coefficients, and baby-step giant-step table-indices for the second stages of factoring attempts. To lower register pressure, the fast shared memory per SM acts as a "user-defined cache" for the values most frequently accessed, such as the moduli $n$ to be factored and the values $-n^{-1} \bmod 2^{32}$. The slower but much larger global memory stores the batch of $(a, b)$ pairs along with their current $n$-values. To reduce memory overhead, the $n$-values are moved back and forth to shared memory after regrouping.

### 5.2    Parameter Selection

For our experiments we applied the CPU NFS siever from [16] (obviously, with multi-threading enabled) to produce relations for the 768-bit number from [27]. Except for the special prime, three so-called *large primes* (i.e., primes not used for sieving but bounded by the applicable smoothness bound) are allowed in the rational polynomial value, whereas on the algebraic side the number of large primes is limited to three or four. Table 2 lists typical figures obtained when

TIME, B1 B2 POLLARD P-1 RATIONAL SIDE (95% YIELD)

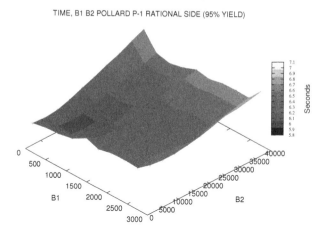

**Fig. 1.** Rational kernel cofactoring run times as a function of the Pollard $p-1$ bounds with desired yield 95%

processing a single special prime in either setting; the percentages are indicative for NFS factorizations in general. The relatively small amount of time spent by the CPU on cofactoring suggests various ways to select optimal GPU parameters. One approach is aiming for as many relations per second as possible. Another approach is to aim for a certain fixed percentage of the relations among the pairs produced by NFS sieving, and then to select parameters that minimize the GPU time (thus maximizing the number of CPUs that can be served by a GPU). Although in general a fixed percentage cannot be ascertained, it can be done for experimental runs covering a fixed set of special prime ranges, and the resulting parameters can be used for production runs covering all special primes. Here we report on this latter approach in two settings: aiming for all (denoted by "99%") or for 95% of all relations.

**Experiments.** For a fixed set of special prime ranges and both large prime settings we determined all $(a, b)$ pairs generated by NFS sieving and counted all relations resulting from those $(a, b)$ pairs. Next, we processed the $(a, b)$ pairs for either setting using our GPU cofactoring program, while widely varying all possible choices and aiming for 95% or 99% of all relations. This led to the observations below. Although other input numbers (than our 768-bit modulus) may lead to other choices our results are indicative for generic large composites.

We found that the rational kernel should be executed first, that it is best to skip trial division in the rational kernel, and that a small trial division bound (say, 200) in the algebraic kernel leads to a slight speed-up compared to not using algebraic trial division. For all other steps the two kernels behave similarly, though with somewhat different parameters that also depend on the desired yield (but not on the large prime setting). The details are listed in Table 3. Not shown there are the discarding thresholds that slightly decrease with the number of ECM attempts. Actual run times of the cofactoring steps are given in Table 4.

**Table 4.** Approximate timings in seconds of cofactoring steps to process approximately 50 million $(a, b)$ pairs, measured using the CUDA `clock64` instruction. The wall clock time (measured with the unix `time` utility) includes the kernel launch overhead the CPU/GPU memory transfer and all CPU book-keeping operations. We measured both kernels (K): algebraic (a) and rational (r).

| # of large primes | desired yield | K | polynomial evaluation | trial division | Pollard $p-1$ | ECM | regrouping | total | wall clock |
|---|---|---|---|---|---|---|---|---|---|
| 3 | 95% | r | 0.05 | - | 56.42 | 149.49 | 5.97 | 211.94 | 263 |
| | | a | 0.10 | 0.36 | 6.21 | 39.05 | 0.44 | 46.16 | |
| | 99% | r | 0.05 | - | 79.19 | 213.15 | 7.75 | 300.16 | 367 |
| | | a | 0.10 | 0.36 | 10.84 | 48.93 | 0.68 | 60.91 | |
| 4 | 95% | r | 0.06 | - | 57.50 | 122.66 | 7.22 | 187.45 | 324 |
| | | a | 0.18 | 0.88 | 15.75 | 110.75 | 1.11 | 128.68 | |
| | 99% | r | 0.06 | - | 57.48 | 158.49 | 8.53 | 224.57 | 479 |
| | | a | 0.18 | 0.89 | 27.47 | 212.47 | 1.79 | 242.80 | |

Rational batches contain 3.5 times more pairs than algebraic ones (because the algebraic kernel has to handle larger values). For 3 large primes the rational kernel is called 5 times more often than the algebraic one, for 4 large primes 2.2 times more often.

Varying the bounds of the Pollard $p-1$ factoring attempt on the rational side within reasonable ranges does not noticeably affect the yield because almost all missed prime factors are found by the subsequent ECM attempts. However, early removal of small primes may reduce the sizes, thus reducing the ECM run time and, if not too much time is spent on Pollard $p-1$, also the overall run time. This is depicted in Figure 1. Note that in record breaking ECM work the number of trials is much larger; however, according to [56] the empirically determined numbers reported in Table 3 are in the theoretically optimal range.

### 5.3  Performance Results

Table 5 summarizes the results when the same special prime as in Table 2 is processed, but now with GPU-assistance. The figures clearly show that farming out cofactoring to a GPU is advantageous from an overall run time point

**Table 5.** GPU cofactoring for a single special prime. The number of quad-core CPUs that can be served by a single GPU is given in the second to last column.

| large primes | number of pairs after sieving | desired yield | seconds | CPU/GPU ratio | relations found |
|---|---|---|---|---|---|
| 3 | $\approx 5 \cdot 10^5$ | 95% | 2.6 | 9.8 | 132 |
| | | 99% | 3.7 | 6.9 | 136 |
| 4 | $\approx 10^6$ | 95% | 6.5 | 4.0 | 159 |
| | | 99% | 9.6 | 2.7 | 165 |

**Table 6.** Processing multiple special primes with desired yield 99%

| large primes | special primes | number of pairs after sieving | setting | total seconds | relations found | relations per second |
|---|---|---|---|---|---|---|
| 3 | 100 | $\approx 5 \cdot 10^7$ | CPU only | 2961 | 12523 | 4.23 |
|   |     |                       | CPU and GPU | 2564 | 13761 | 5.37 |
| 4 | 50  | $\approx 5 \cdot 10^7$ | CPU only | 1602 | 6855 | 4.28 |
|   |     |                       | CPU and GPU | 1300 | 8302 | 6.39 |

of view and that, depending on the yield desired, a single GPU can keep up with multiple quad-core CPUs. Remarkably, more relations may be found given the same collection of $(a, b)$ pairs: with an adequate number of GPUs each special prime can be processed faster and produces more relations. Based on more extensive experiments the overall performance gain measured in "relations per second" found with and without GPU assistance is 27% in the 3 large primes case and 50% in the 4 large primes case (cf. Table 6).

Including equipment and power expenses in the analysis is much harder, as illustrated by (unrelated) experiments in [44]. Relative power and purchase costs vary constantly, and the power consumption of a GPU running CUDA applications depends on the configuration and the operations performed [13]. For instance, global memory accesses account for a large fraction of the power consumption and the effect on the power consumption of arithmetic instructions depends more on their throughput than on their type. We have not carried out actual power consumption measurements comparing the settings from Table 6.

# 6    Conclusion

It was shown that modern GPUs can be used to accelerate a compute-intensive part of the relation collection step of the number field sieve integer factorization method. Strategies were outlined to perform the entire cofactorization stage on a GPU. Integration with state-of-the-art lattice siever software indicates that a performance gain of up to 50% can be expected for the relation collection step of factorization of numbers in the current range of interest, if a single GPU can assist a regular multi-core CPU. Because relation collection for such numbers is responsible for about 90% of the total factoring effort the overall gain may be close to 45%; we have no experience with other sizes yet.

It is a subject of further research if a speed-up can be obtained using other types of graphic cards (to which we did not have access). In particular it would be interesting to explore if and how lower-end CUDA enabled GPUs can still be used for the present application and if the larger memory of more recent cards such as the GeForce GTX 780 Ti or GeForce GTX Titan can be exploited. Given our results we consider it unlikely that it would be advantageous to combine multiple GPUs using NVIDIA's scalable link interface.

**Acknowledgements.** This work was supported by the Swiss National Science Foundation under grant number 200020-132160. We gratefully acknowledge comments by the anonymous referees.

# References

1. Antao, S., Bajard, J.-C., Sousa, L.: Elliptic curve point multiplication on GPUs. In: 2010 21st IEEE International Conference on Application-specific Systems Architectures and Processors (ASAP), pp. 192–199 (2010)
2. Barbulescu, R., Bos, J.W., Bouvier, C., Kleinjung, T., Montgomery, P.L.: Finding ECM-friendly curves through a study of Galois properties. In: Howe, E.W., Kedlaya, K.S. (eds.) ANTS 2012. The Open Book Series, vol. 1, pp. 63–86. Mathematical Sciences Publishers (2013)
3. Bernstein, D.J., Birkner, P., Lange, T.: Starfish on strike. In: Abdalla, M., Barreto, P.S.L.M. (eds.) LATINCRYPT 2010. LNCS, vol. 6212, pp. 61–80. Springer, Heidelberg (2010)
4. Bernstein, D.J., Birkner, P., Lange, T., Peters, C.: ECM using Edwards curves. Mathematics of Computation 82(282), 1139–1179 (2013)
5. Bernstein, D.J., Chen, H.-C., Chen, M.-S., Cheng, C.-M., Hsiao, C.-H., Lange, T., Lin, Z.-C., Yang, B.-Y.: The billion-mulmod-per-second PC. In: Special-purpose Hardware for Attacking Cryptographic Systems – SHARCS 2009, pp. 131–144 (2009)
6. Bernstein, D.J., Chen, H.-C., Cheng, C.-M., Lange, T., Niederhagen, R., Schwabe, P., Yang, B.-Y.: ECC2K-130 on NVIDIA gPUs. In: Gong, G., Gupta, K.C. (eds.) INDOCRYPT 2010. LNCS, vol. 6498, pp. 328–346. Springer, Heidelberg (2010)
7. Bernstein, D.J., Chen, T.-R., Cheng, C.-M., Lange, T., Yang, B.-Y.: ECM on graphics cards. In: Joux, A. (ed.) EUROCRYPT 2009. LNCS, vol. 5479, pp. 483–501. Springer, Heidelberg (2009)
8. Bevand, M.: MD5 Chosen-Prefix Collisions on GPUs. Black Hat (2009); Whitepaper
9. Bos, J.W.: Low-latency elliptic curve scalar multiplication. International Journal of Parallel Programming 40(5), 532–550 (2012)
10. Bos, J.W., Kleinjung, T.: ECM at work. In: Wang, X., Sako, K. (eds.) ASIACRYPT 2012. LNCS, vol. 7658, pp. 467 484. Springer, Heidelberg (2012)
11. Bos, J.W., Stefan, D.: Performance analysis of the SHA-3 candidates on exotic multi-core architectures. In: Mangard, S., Standaert, F.-X. (eds.) CHES 2010. LNCS, vol. 6225, pp. 279–293. Springer, Heidelberg (2010)
12. Brent, R.P.: Some integer factorization algorithms using elliptic curves. Australian Computer Science Communications 8, 149–163 (1986)
13. Collange, S., Defour, D., Tisserand, A.: Power consumption of gPUs from a software perspective. In: Allen, G., Nabrzyski, J., Seidel, E., van Albada, G.D., Dongarra, J., Sloot, P.M.A. (eds.) ICCS 2009, Part I. LNCS, vol. 5544, pp. 914–923. Springer, Heidelberg (2009)
14. de Meulenaer, G., Gosset, F., de Dormale, G.M., Quisquater, J.-J.: Integer factorization based on elliptic curve method: Towards better exploitation of reconfigurable hardware. In: Field-Programmable Custom Computing Machines – FCCM 2007, pp. 197–206. IEEE Computer Society (2007)
15. Edwards, H.M.: A normal form for elliptic curves. Bulletin of the American Mathematical Society 44, 393–422 (2007)

16. Franke, J., Kleinjung, T.: GNFS for linux. Software (2012)
17. Gaj, K., Kwon, S., Baier, P., Kohlbrenner, P., Le, H., Khaleeluddin, M., Bachimanchi, R.: Implementing the elliptic curve method of factoring in reconfigurable hardware. In: Goubin, L., Matsui, M. (eds.) CHES 2006. LNCS, vol. 4249, pp. 119–133. Springer, Heidelberg (2006)
18. Gilger, J., Barnickel, J., Meyer, U.: GPU-acceleration of block ciphers in the openssl cryptographic library. In: Gollmann, D., Freiling, F.C. (eds.) ISC 2012. LNCS, vol. 7483, pp. 338–353. Springer, Heidelberg (2012)
19. Güneysu, T., Kasper, T., Novotny, M., Paar, C., Rupp, A.: Cryptanalysis with COPACOBANA. IEEE Transactions on Computers 57, 1498–1513 (2008)
20. Harrison, O., Waldron, J.: AES encryption implementation and analysis on commodity graphics processing units. In: Paillier, P., Verbauwhede, I. (eds.) CHES 2007. LNCS, vol. 4727, pp. 209–226. Springer, Heidelberg (2007)
21. Harrison, O., Waldron, J.: Practical symmetric key cryptography on modern graphics hardware. In: Proceedings of the 17th Conference on Security Symposium, pp. 195–209. USENIX Association (2008)
22. Harrison, O., Waldron, J.: Efficient acceleration of asymmetric cryptography on graphics hardware. In: Preneel, B. (ed.) AFRICACRYPT 2009. LNCS, vol. 5580, pp. 350–367. Springer, Heidelberg (2009)
23. Hisil, H., Wong, K.K.-H., Carter, G., Dawson, E.: Twisted edwards curves revisited. In: Pieprzyk, J. (ed.) ASIACRYPT 2008. LNCS, vol. 5350, pp. 326–343. Springer, Heidelberg (2008)
24. Jebelean, T.: An algorithm for exact division. Journal of Symbolic Computation 15(2), 169–180 (1993)
25. Karatsuba, A.A., Ofman, Y.: Multiplication of many-digital numbers by automatic computers. In: Number 145 in Proceedings of the USSR Academy of Science, pp. 293–294 (1962)
26. Kleinjung, T.: Cofactorisation strategies for the number field sieve and an estimate for the sieving step for factoring 1024-bit integers. In: Special-purpose Hardware for Attacking Cryptographic Systems – SHARCS 2006 (2006)
27. Kleinjung, T., Aoki, K., Franke, J., Lenstra, A.K., Thomé, E., Bos, J.W., Gaudry, P., Kruppa, A., Montgomery, P.L., Osvik, D.A., te Riele, H., Timofeev, A., Zimmermann, P.: Factorization of a 768-bit RSA modulus. In: Rabin, T. (ed.) CRYPTO 2010. LNCS, vol. 6223, pp. 333–350. Springer, Heidelberg (2010)
28. Kruppa, A.: A software implementation of ECM for NFS. Research Report RR-7041, INRIA (2009), http://hal.inria.fr/inria-00419094/PDF/RR-7041.pdf
29. Leboeuf, K., Muscedere, R., Ahmadi, M.: A GPU implementation of the Montgomery multiplication algorithm for elliptic curve cryptography. In: IEEE International Symposium on Circuits and Systems (ISCAS), pp. 2593–2596 (2013)
30. Lenstra, A.K., Lenstra Jr., H.W.: The Development of the Number Field Sieve. Lecture Notes in Mathematics, vol. 1554. Springer, Heidelberg (1993)
31. Lenstra Jr., H.W.: Factoring integers with elliptic curves. Annals of Mathematics 126(3), 649–673 (1987)
32. Loebenberger, D., Putzka, J.: Optimization strategies for hardware-based cofactorization. In: Jacobson Jr., M.J., Rijmen, V., Safavi-Naini, R. (eds.) SAC 2009. LNCS, vol. 5867, pp. 170–181. Springer, Heidelberg (2009)
33. Manavski, S.: CUDA compatible GPU as an efficient hardware accelerator for AES cryptography. In: IEEE International Conference on Signal Processing and Communications, ICSPC 2007, pp. 65–68 (2007)

34. Miele, A., Bos, J.W., Kleinjung, T., Lenstra, A.K.: Cofactorization on graphics processing units. Cryptology ePrint Archive, Report 2014/397 (2014), http://eprint.iacr.org/
35. Miller, G.L.: Riemann's hypothesis and tests for primality. In: Proceedings of Seventh Annual ACM Symposium on Theory of Computing, STOC 1975, pp. 234–239. ACM (1975)
36. Montgomery, P.L.: Modular multiplication without trial division. Mathematics of Computation 44(170), 519–521 (1985)
37. Montgomery, P.L.: Speeding the Pollard and elliptic curve methods of factorization. Mathematics of Computation 48(177), 243–264 (1987)
38. Montgomery, P.L.: An FFT extension of the elliptic curve method of factorization. PhD thesis, University of California (1992)
39. Montgomery, P.L., Silverman, R.D.: An FFT extension to the p-1 factoring algorithm. Mathematics of Computation 54(190), 839–854 (1990)
40. Moss, A., Page, D., Smart, N.P.: Toward acceleration of RSA using 3D graphics hardware. In: Galbraith, S.D. (ed.) Cryptography and Coding 2007. LNCS, vol. 4887, pp. 364–383. Springer, Heidelberg (2007)
41. NVIDIA. Fermi architecture whitepaper (2010), http://www.nvidia.com/content/PDF/fermi_white_papers/ NVIDIA_Fermi_Compute_Architecture_Whitepaper.pdf
42. NVIDIA. Cuda programming guide 5 (2013), http://docs.nvidia.com/cuda/cuda-c-programming-guide/index.html
43. NVIDIA. Parallel thread execution isa version 3.2 (2013), http://docs.nvidia.com/cuda/parallel-thread-execution/index.html
44. NVIDIA Developer Zone (2011), https://devtalk.nvidia.com/default/topic/ 491799/gtx-590-cuda-power-tests/
45. Osvik, D.A., Bos, J.W., Stefan, D., Canright, D.: Fast software AES encryption. In: Hong, S., Iwata, T. (eds.) FSE 2010. LNCS, vol. 6147, pp. 75–93. Springer, Heidelberg (2010)
46. Pelzl, J., Šimka, M., Kleinjung, T., Franke, J., Priplata, C., Stahlke, C., Drutarovský, M., Fischer, V., Paar, C.: Area-time efficient hardware architecture for factoring integers with the elliptic curve method. IEE Proceedings on Information Security 152(1), 67–78 (2005)
47. Pollard, J.M.: The lattice sieve. pp. 43–49 in [30]
48. Pollard, J.M.: Theorems on factorization and primality testing. Proceedings of the Cambridge Philosophical Society 76, 521–528 (1974)
49. Pollard, J.M.: A Monte Carlo method for factorization. BIT Numerical Mathematics 15(3), 331–334 (1975)
50. Pomerance, C.: The quadratic sieve factoring algorithm. In: Beth, T., Cot, N., Ingemarsson, I. (eds.) EUROCRYPT 1984. LNCS, vol. 209, pp. 169–182. Springer, Heidelberg (1985)
51. Pomerance, C.: A tale of two sieves. Biscuits of Number Theory 85 (2008)
52. Rabin, M.O.: Probabilistic algorithm for testing primality. Journal of Number Theory 12(1), 128–138 (1980)
53. Shanks, D.: Class number, a theory of factorization, and genera. In: Lewis, D.J. (ed.) Symposia in Pure Mathematics, vol. 20, pp. 415–440. American Mathematical Society (1971)
54. Šimka, M., Pelzl, J., Kleinjung, T., Franke, J., Priplata, C., Stahlke, C., Drutarovský, M., Fischer, V.: Hardware factorization based on elliptic curve method. In: Field-Programmable Custom Computing Machines – FCCM 2005, pp. 107–116. IEEE Computer Society (2005)

55. Szerwinski, R., Güneysu, T.: Exploiting the power of gpus for asymmetric cryptography. In: Oswald, E., Rohatgi, P. (eds.) CHES 2008. LNCS, vol. 5154, pp. 79–99. Springer, Heidelberg (2008)
56. Xin, G.: Fast smoothness test. Semester project report (June 2013)
57. Yang, J., Goodman, J.: Symmetric key cryptography on modern graphics hardware. In: Kurosawa, K. (ed.) ASIACRYPT 2007. LNCS, vol. 4833, pp. 249–264. Springer, Heidelberg (2007)
58. Zimmermann, P., Dodson, B.: 20 years of ECM. In: Hess, F., Pauli, S., Pohst, M. (eds.) ANTS 2006. LNCS, vol. 4076, pp. 525–542. Springer, Heidelberg (2006)
59. Zimmermann, R., Güneysu, T., Paar, C.: High-performance integer factoring with reconfigurable devices. In: Field Programmable Logic and Applications – FPL 2010, pp. 83–88. IEEE (2010)

# Appendix

Let $r = 2^{32}$.

**Table 7.** Pseudo-code notation for CUDA PTX assembly instructions [43] used in our implementation. Function parameters are 32-bit unsigned integers and the suffixes are analogous to the actual CUDA PTX suffixes. We denote by $f$ the single-bit carry flag set by instructions with suffix ".cc".

| Pseudo-code notation | Operation | Carry flag effect |
|---|---|---|
| $\mathrm{addc}(c, a, b)$ | $c \leftarrow a + b + f \bmod r$ | |
| $\mathrm{addc.cc}(c, a, b)$ | $c \leftarrow a + b + f \bmod r$ | $f \leftarrow \lfloor (a + b + f)/r \rfloor$ |
| $\mathrm{subc}(c, a, b)$ | $c \leftarrow a - b - f \bmod r$ | |
| $\mathrm{subc.cc}(c, a, b)$ | $c \leftarrow a - b - f \bmod r$ | $f \leftarrow \lfloor (a - b - f)/r \rfloor$ |
| $\mathrm{mul.lo}(c, a, b)$ | $c \leftarrow a \cdot b \bmod r$ | |
| $\mathrm{mul.hi}(c, a, b)$ | $c \leftarrow \lfloor (a \cdot b)/r \rfloor$ | |
| $\mathrm{mad.lo.cc}(d, a, b, c)$ | $d \leftarrow a \cdot b + c \bmod r$ | $f \leftarrow \lfloor ((a \cdot b) \bmod r + c)/r \rfloor$ |
| $\mathrm{madc.lo.cc}(d, a, b, c)$ | $d \leftarrow a \cdot b + c + f \bmod r$ | $f \leftarrow \lfloor ((a \cdot b) \bmod r + c + f)/r \rfloor$ |
| $\mathrm{mad.hi.cc}(d, a, b, c)$ | $d \leftarrow (\lfloor (a \cdot b)/r \rfloor + c) \bmod r$ | $f \leftarrow \lfloor (\lfloor (a \cdot b)/r \rfloor + c)/r \rfloor$ |
| $\mathrm{madc.hi.cc}(d, a, b, c)$ | $d \leftarrow (\lfloor (a \cdot b)/r \rfloor + c + f) \bmod r$ | $f \leftarrow \lfloor (\lfloor (a \cdot b)/r \rfloor + c + f)/r \rfloor$ |

# Enhanced Lattice-Based Signatures on Reconfigurable Hardware

Thomas Pöppelmann[1], Léo Ducas[2], and Tim Güneysu[1]

[1] Horst Görtz Institute for IT-Security, Ruhr-University Bochum, Germany
thomas.poeppelmann@rub.de, tim.gueneysu@rub.de
[2] University of California, San-Diego, USA
lducas@eng.ucsd.edu

**Abstract.** The recent Bimodal Lattice Signature Scheme (BLISS) showed that lattice-based constructions have evolved to practical alternatives to RSA or ECC. Besides reasonably small signatures with 5600 bits for a 128-bit level of security, BLISS enables extremely fast signing and signature verification in software. However, due to the complex sampling of Gaussian noise with high precision, it is not clear whether this scheme can be mapped efficiently to embedded devices. Even though the authors of BLISS also proposed a new sampling algorithm using Bernoulli variables this approach is more complex than previous methods using large precomputed tables. The clear disadvantage of using large tables for high performance is that they cannot be used on constrained computing environments, such as FPGAs, with limited memory. In this work we thus present techniques for an efficient Cumulative Distribution Table (CDT) based Gaussian sampler on reconfigurable hardware involving Peikert's convolution lemma and the Kullback-Leibler divergence. Based on our enhanced sampler design, we provide a first BLISS architecture for Xilinx Spartan-6 FPGAs that integrates fast FFT/NTT-based polynomial multiplication, sparse multiplication, and a Keccak hash function. Additionally, we compare the CDT with the Bernoulli approach and show that for the particular BLISS-I parameter set the improved CDT approach is faster with lower area consumption. Our core uses 2,431 slices, 7.5 BRAMs, and 6 DSPs and performs a signing operation in 126 μs on average. Verification takes even less with 70 μs.

**Keywords:** Ideal Lattices, Gaussian Sampling, Digital Signatures, FPGA.

## 1 Introduction and Motivation

Virtually all currently used digital signature schemes rely either on the factoring (RSA) or the discrete logarithm problem (DSA/ECDSA). However, with Shor's algorithm [39] sufficiently large quantum computers can solve these problems in polynomial time which potentially puts billions of devices and users at risk. Although powerful quantum computers will certainly not become available soon, significant resources are definitely spent by various organizations to boost their

L. Batina and M. Robshaw (Eds.): CHES 2014, LNCS 8731, pp. 353–370, 2014.

further development [35]. Also motivated by further advances in classical crypt-analysis (e.g., [4,5,20]), it is important to investigate potential alternatives now to have secure constructions and implementations at hand when they are finally needed.

In this work we deal with such a promising alternative, namely the Bimodal Lattice Signature Scheme (BLISS) [12], and specifically address implementation challenges for constrained devices and reconfigurable hardware. First efforts in this direction were made in 2012 by Güneysu et al. [16] (GLP). Their scheme was based on work by Lyubashevsky [26] and tuned for practicability and efficiency in embedded systems. This was achieved by a new signature compression mechanism, a more "aggressive", non-standard hardness assumption, and the decision to use uniform (as in [25]) instead of Gaussian noise to hide the secret key contained in each signature via rejection sampling. While GLP allows high performance on low-cost FPGAs [16] and CPUs [17] it later turned out that the scheme is suboptimal in terms of signature size and its claimed security level compared to BLISS. The main reason for this is that Gaussian noise, which is prevalent in almost all lattice-based constructions, allows more efficient, more secure, and also smaller signatures. However, while other techniques relevant for lattice-based cryptography, like fast polynomial arithmetic on ideal lattices received some attention [1,32,36], it is currently not clear how efficient Gaussian sampling can be done on reconfigurable and embedded hardware for large standard deviations. Results from electrical engineering (e.g., [19,41]) are not directly applicable, as they target continuous Gaussians. Applying these algorithms for the discrete case is not trivial (see, e.g., [8] for a discrete version of the Ziggurat algorithm). First progress was recently made by Roy et al. [37] based on work by Galbraith and Dwarakanath [13] providing results for a Gaussian sampler in lattice-based encryption that requires low resources. We would also like to note that for lattice-based digital signature schemes large tables in performance optimized implementations might imply the impression that Gaussian-noise based schemes are a suboptimal choice on constrained embedded systems. A recent example is a microcontroller implementation of BLISS [7] that requires tables for the Gaussian sampler of roughly 40 to 50 KB on an ATxmega64A3. Other lattice-based signatures with explicit reductions to standard lattice problems [14,24,28] are also inefficient in terms of practical signature and public key sizes (see [3] for an implementation of [28]). Thus, despite the necessity of improving Gaussian sampling techniques (which is one contribution of this work) BLISS seems to be currently the most promising scheme with a signatures length of 5600 bit, equally large public keys, and 128-bit of equivalent symmetric security. There surely is some room for theoretical improvement, as suggested by the new compression ideas developed by Bai and Galbraith [2]; one can hope that all those techniques can be combined to further improve lattice-based signatures.

**Contribution.** One contribution of this work are improved techniques for efficient sampling of Gaussian noise that support parameters required for digital signature schemes such as BLISS and similar constructions. First, we detail how to accelerate the binary search on a cumulative distribution table (CDT) using a shortcut table of intervals (also known as guide table [9, 11]) and develop an optimal data structure that saves roughly half of the table space by exploiting the properties of the Kullback-Leibler divergence. Furthermore, we apply a convolution lemma [29] for discrete Gaussians that results in even smaller tables of less than 2.1 KB for BLISS-I parameters. Based on these techniques we provide an implementation of the BLISS-I parameter set on reconfigurable hardware that is tweaked for performance and offers 128-bit of security. For practical evaluation we compare our improvements for the CDT-based Gaussian sampler to the Bernoulli approach presented in [12]. Our implementation includes an FFT/NTT-based polynomial multiplier (contrary to the schoolbook approach from [16]), more efficient sparse multiplication, and the KECCAK-$f$[1600] hash function to provide the full picture of the performance that can be achieved by employing latest lattice-based signature schemes on reconfigurable hardware. Our implementation on a Xilinx Spartan-6 FPGA supports up to 7958 signatures per second using 7,491 LUTs, 7,033 flip-flops, 6 DSPs, and 7.5 block RAMs and outperforms previous work [16] both in time and area.

In order to allow third-party evaluation of our results, source code, testbenches, and documentation is available on our website[1].

## 2   The Bimodal Lattice Signature Scheme

The most efficient instantiation of the BLISS signature scheme [12] is based on ideal-lattices [27] and operates on polynomials over the ring $\mathcal{R}_q = \mathbb{Z}_q[x]/\langle x^n + 1 \rangle$. For quick reference, the BLISS key generation, signing as well as verification algorithms are given in Figure 1 and implementation relevant parameters as well as achievable signature and key sizes are listed in Table 1. Note that for the remainder of this work, we will focus solely on BLISS-I. The BLISS key generation basically involves uniform sampling of two small and sparse polynomials $\mathbf{f}, \mathbf{g}$, computation of a certain rejection condition ($N_\kappa(\mathbf{S})$), and computation of an inverse. For signature generation two polynomials $\mathbf{y}_1, \mathbf{y}_2$ of length $n$ are sampled from a discrete Gaussian distribution with standard deviation $\sigma$. Note that the computation of $\mathbf{ay}_1$ can still be performed in the FFT-enabled ring $\mathcal{R}_q$ instead of $\mathcal{R}_{2q}$. The result $\mathbf{u}$ is then hashed with the message $\mu$. The output of the hash function is interpreted as sparse polynomial $\mathbf{c}$. The polynomials $\mathbf{y}_{1,2}$ are then used to mask the secret key polynomials $\mathbf{s}_{1,2}$ which are multiplied with the polynomial $\mathbf{c}$ and thus "sign" the hash of the message. In order to prevent any leakage of information on the secret key, rejection sampling is performed and signing might restart. Finally, the signature is compressed and $(\mathbf{z}_1, \mathbf{z}_2^\dagger, \mathbf{c})$ returned. For verification the norms of the signature are first validated, then the input to the hash function is reconstructed and it is checked whether the corresponding hash output matches $\mathbf{c}$ from the signature.

---

[1] See http://www.sha.rub.de/research/projects/lattice/

**Algorithm** KeyGen()

1. Choose $\mathbf{f}, \mathbf{g}$ as uniform polynomials with exactly $d_1 = \lceil \delta_1 n \rceil$ entries in $\{\pm 1\}$ and $d_2 = \lceil \delta_2 n \rceil$ entries in $\{\pm 2\}$
2. $\mathbf{S} = (\mathbf{s}_1, \mathbf{s}_2)^t \leftarrow (\mathbf{f}, 2\mathbf{g} + 1)^t$
3. **if** $N_\kappa(\mathbf{S}) \geq C^2 \cdot 5 \cdot (\lceil \delta_1 n \rceil + 4\lceil \delta_2 n \rceil) \cdot \kappa$ **then restart**
4. $\mathbf{a}_q = (2\mathbf{g} + 1)/\mathbf{f} \bmod q$ (restart if $\mathbf{f}$ is not invertible)
5. **Return**$(pk = \mathbf{A}, sk = \mathbf{S})$ where $\mathbf{A} = (\mathbf{a}_1 = 2\mathbf{a}_q, q - 2) \bmod 2q$

**Alg.** Sign($\mu$,$pk$=**A**,$sk$=**S**)

1. $\mathbf{y}_1, \mathbf{y}_2 \leftarrow D_{\mathbb{Z}^n, \sigma}$
2. $\mathbf{u} = \zeta \cdot \mathbf{a}_1 \cdot \mathbf{y}_1 + \mathbf{y}_2 \bmod 2q$
3. $\mathbf{c} \leftarrow H(\lfloor \mathbf{u} \rceil_d \bmod p, \mu)$
4. Choose a random bit $b$
5. $\mathbf{z}_1 \leftarrow \mathbf{y}_1 + (-1)^b \mathbf{s}_1 \mathbf{c}$
6. $\mathbf{z}_2 \leftarrow \mathbf{y}_2 + (-1)^b \mathbf{s}_2 \mathbf{c}$
7. **Continue** with probability
$$1 \Big/ \left( M \exp\left(-\frac{\|\mathbf{Sc}\|^2}{2\sigma^2}\right) \cosh\left(\frac{\langle \mathbf{z}, \mathbf{Sc} \rangle}{\sigma^2}\right) \right)$$
otherwise **restart**
8. $\mathbf{z}_2^\dagger \leftarrow (\lfloor \mathbf{u} \rceil_d - \lfloor \mathbf{u} - \mathbf{z}_2 \rceil_d) \bmod p$
9. **Return** $(\mathbf{z}_1, \mathbf{z}_2^\dagger, \mathbf{c})$

**Alg.** Verify($\mu$,$pk$=**A**,($\mathbf{z}_1$,$\mathbf{z}_2^\dagger$,$\mathbf{c}$))

1. **if** $\|(\mathbf{z}_1 | 2^d \cdot \mathbf{z}_2^\dagger)\|_2 > B_2$ **then** Reject
2. **if** $\|(\mathbf{z}_1 | 2^d \cdot \mathbf{z}_2^\dagger)\|_\infty > B_\infty$ **then** Reject

3. **Accept** iff $\mathbf{c} = H\big(\lfloor \zeta \cdot \mathbf{a}_1 \cdot \mathbf{z}_1 + \zeta \cdot q \cdot \mathbf{c} \rceil_d + \mathbf{z}_2^\dagger \bmod p, \mu\big)$

**Fig. 1.** The Bimodal Lattice Signature Scheme [12]

# 3  Improving Gaussian Sampling for Lattice-Based Digital Signatures

*Target distribution.* We recall that the centered discrete Gaussian distribution $D_{\mathbb{Z}, \sigma}$ is defined by a weight proportional to $\rho_\sigma(x) = \exp(\frac{-x^2}{2\sigma^2})$ for all integers $x$. Our goal is to efficiently sample from that distribution for a constant value $\sigma \approx 215.73$ as specified in BLISS-I (precisely $\sigma = 254 \cdot \sigma_{bin}$ where $\sigma_{bin} = \sqrt{1/(2\ln 2)}$ is the parameter of the so-called binary-Gaussian; see [12]). This can easily be reduced to sampling from a distribution over $\mathbb{Z}^+$ proportional to $\rho(x)$ for all $x > 0$ and to $\rho(0)/2$ for $x = 0$.

*Overview.* Gaussian sampling using a large cumulative distribution table (CDT) has been shown to be an efficient strategy for the software implementation of BLISS given in [12]. In this section, we further enhance CDT-based Gaussian sampling for use on constrained devices. For simplicity, we explicitly refer to the parameter set BLISS-I although we remark that our enhancements can be transferred to any other parameter set as well. To increase performance, we first analyze and improve the binary search step to reduce the number of comparisons (cf. Section 3.1). Secondly, we decrease the size of the precomputed tables. In Section 3.3 we therefore apply a convolution lemma for discrete Gaussians adapted from [30] that enables the use of a sampler with much smaller standard deviation $\sigma' \approx \sigma/11$, reducing the table size by a factor 11. In Section 3.4 we

Table 1. Parameters proposals from [12]

| Name of the scheme | BLISS-I | BLISS-II | BLISS-III | BLISS-IV |
|---|---|---|---|---|
| Security | 128 bits | 128 bits | 160 bits | 192 bits |
| $(n, q)$ | (512,12289) | (512,12289) | (512,12289) | (512,12289) |
| Secret key densities $\delta_1, \delta_2$ | 0.3 , 0 | 0.3 , 0 | 0.42 , 0.03 | 0.45, 0.06 |
| Gaussian std. dev. $\sigma$ | 215.73 | 107.86 | 250.54 | 271.93 |
| Weight of the challenge $\kappa$ | 23 | 23 | 30 | 39 |
| Verif. thresholds $B_2, B_\infty$ | 12872, 2100 | 11074, 1563 | 10206,1760 | 9901, 1613 |
| Repetition rate | 1.6 | 7.4 | 2.8 | 5.2 |
| Signature size | 5.6kb | 5kb | 6kb | 6.5kb |
| Secret key size | 2kb | 2kb | 3kb | 3kb |
| Public key size | 7kb | 7kb | 7kb | 7kb |

finally reduce the size of the precomputed table further by roughly a factor of two using floating-point representation by introducing an *adaptive mantissa size*. For those last two steps we require the "measure of distance"[2] for a distribution, called Kullback-Leibler divergence [10, 23], that offers tighter proofs than the usual statistical distance (cf. Section 3.2). Kullback-Leibler is a standard notion in information theory and already played a role in cryptography, mostly in the context of symmetric cryptanalysis [6, 42].

### 3.1 Binary Search with Shortcut Intervals

The CDT sampling algorithm uses a table $0 = T[0] \leq T[i] \leq \cdots \leq T[S + 1] = 1$ to sample from a uniform real $r \in [0, 1)$. The output $x$ is the unique index satisfying $T[x] \leq r < T[x + 1]$ and it is obtain via a binary search. Each output $x \in \{0 \ldots S\}$ has a probability $T[x + 1] - T[x]$. For BLISS-I we need a table with $S = 2891 \approx 13.4\sigma$ entries to dismiss only a portion of the tail less than $2^{-128}$. As a result, the naive binary search would require $C \in [\lfloor \log_2 S \rfloor, \lceil \log_2 S \rceil] = [11, 12]$ comparisons on average.

As an improvement we propose to combine the binary search with a hash map based on the first bits of $r$ to narrow down the search interval in a first step (an idea that is not exactly new [9, 11], also known as guide tables). For the given parameters and memory alignment reasons, we choose the first byte of $r$ for this hash map: the unique $v \in \{0 \ldots 255\}$ such that $v/256 \leq r < (v+1)/256$. This table $I$ of intervals has length 256 and each entry $I[v]$ encodes the smallest interval $(a_v, b_v)$ such that $T[a_v] \leq v/256$ and $T[b_v] \geq (v + 1)/256$. With this approach, the search can be directly reduced to the interval $(a_v, b_v)$. By letting $C$ denote the number of comparison on average, we have that $\sum_v \frac{\lfloor \log_2(b_v - a_v) \rfloor}{256} \leq C \leq \sum_v \frac{\lceil \log_2(b_v - a_v) \rceil}{256}$. For this distribution this would give $C \in [1.3, 1.7]$ comparisons on average.

---

[2] Technically, Kullback-Leibler divergence is not a distance; it is not even symmetric.

## 3.2    Preliminaries on the Kullback-Leibler Divergence

We now present the notion of Kullback-Leibler (KL) divergence that is later used to further reduce the table size. Detailed proofs of following lemmata are given in the full version [31].

**Definition 1 (Kullback-Leibler Divergence).** *Let $\mathcal{P}$ and $\mathcal{Q}$ be two distributions over a common countable set $\Omega$, and let $S \subset \Omega$ be the strict support of $\mathcal{P}$ ($\mathcal{P}(i) > 0$ iff $i \in S$). The Kullback-Leibler divergence, noted $D_{KL}$ of $\mathcal{Q}$ from $\mathcal{P}$ is defined as:*

$$D_{KL}(\mathcal{P}\|\mathcal{Q}) = \sum_{i \in S} \ln\left(\frac{\mathcal{P}(i)}{\mathcal{Q}(i)}\right)\mathcal{P}(i)$$

*with the convention that $\ln(x/0) = +\infty$ for any $x > 0$.*

The Kullback-Leibler divergence shares many useful properties with the more usual notion of statistical distance. First, it is additive so that $D_{\mathrm{KL}}(\mathcal{P}_0 \times \mathcal{P}_1 \| \mathcal{Q}_0 \times \mathcal{Q}_1) = D_{\mathrm{KL}}(\mathcal{P}_0 \| \mathcal{Q}_0) + D_{\mathrm{KL}}(\mathcal{P}_1 \| \mathcal{Q}_1)$ and, second, non-increasing under any function $D_{\mathrm{KL}}(f(\mathcal{P})\|f(\mathcal{Q})) \leq D_{\mathrm{KL}}(\mathcal{P}\|\mathcal{Q})$. An important difference though is that it is not symmetric. Choosing parameters so that the theoretical distribution $\mathcal{Q}$ is at KL-divergence about $2^{-128}$ from the actually sampled distribution $\mathcal{P}$, the next lemma will let us conclude the following[3]: if the ideal scheme $\mathcal{S}^{\mathcal{Q}}$ (*i.e.* BLISS with a perfect sampler) has about 128 bits of security, so has the implemented scheme $\mathcal{S}^{\mathcal{P}}$ (*i.e.* BLISS with our imperfect sampler).

**Lemma 1 (Bounding Success Probability Variations).** *Let $\mathcal{E}^{\mathcal{P}}$ be an algorithm making at most $q$ queries to an oracle sampling from a distribution $\mathcal{P}$ and returning a bit. Let $\epsilon \geq 0$, and $\mathcal{Q}$ be a distribution such that $D_{KL}(\mathcal{P}\|\mathcal{Q}) \leq \epsilon$. Let $x$ (resp. $y$) denote the probability that $\mathcal{E}^{\mathcal{P}}$ (resp. $\mathcal{E}^{\mathcal{Q}}$) outputs 1. Then, $|x - y| \leq \sqrt{q\epsilon/2}$.*

In certain cases, the KL-divergence can be as small as the square of the statistical distance. For example, noting $\mathcal{B}_c$ the Bernoulli variable that returns 1 with probability $c$, we have $D_{\mathrm{KL}}(\mathcal{B}_{\frac{1-\epsilon}{2}}\|\mathcal{B}_{\frac{1}{2}}) \approx \epsilon^2/2$. In such a case, one requires $q = O(1/\epsilon^2)$ samples to distinguish those two distribution with constant advantage. Hence, we yield higher security using KL-divergence than statistical distance for which the typical argument would only prove security up to $q = O(1/\epsilon)$ queries. Intuitively, statistical distance is the sum of absolute errors, while KL-divergence is about the sum of squared relative errors.

**Lemma 2 (Kullback-Leibler divergence for bounded relative error).** *Let $\mathcal{P}$ and $\mathcal{Q}$ be two distributions of same countable support. Assume that for any $i \in S$, there exists some $\delta(i) \in (0, 1/4)$ such that we have the relative error bound $|\mathcal{P}(i) - \mathcal{Q}(i)| \leq \delta(i)\mathcal{P}(i)$. Then*

$$D_{KL}(\mathcal{P}\|\mathcal{Q}) \leq 2\sum_{i \in S} \delta(i)^2\mathcal{P}(i).$$

---

[3] Apply the lemma to an attacker with success probability 3/4 against $\mathcal{S}^{\mathcal{P}}$ and number of queries $< 2^{127}$ (amplifying success probability by repeating the attack if necessary), and deduce that it also succeeds against $\mathcal{S}^{\mathcal{Q}}$ with probability at least 1/4.

Using floating-point representation, it seems now possible to halve the storage ensuring a relative precision of 64 bits instead of an absolute precision of 128 bits. Indeed, storing data with slightly more than of relative 64 bits of precision (that is, mantissa of 64 bits in floating-point format) one can reasonably hope to obtain relative errors $\delta(i) \leq 2^{-64}$ resulting in a KL-divergence less than $2^{-128}$. We further exploit this idea in Section 3.4. But first, we will also use KL-divergence to improve the convolution Lemma of Peikert [30] and construct a sampler using convolutions.

## 3.3   Reducing Precomputed Data by Gaussian Convolution

Given that $x_1, x_2$ are variables from continuous Gaussian distributions with variances $\sigma_1^2, \sigma_2^2$, then their combination $x_1 + cx_2$ is Gaussian with variance $\sigma_1^2 + c^2\sigma_2^2$ for any $c$. While this is not generally the case for discrete Gaussians, there exists similar convolution properties under some smoothing condition as proved in [29, 30]. Yet those lemmata were designed with asymptotic security in mind; for practical purpose it is in fact possible to improve the $O(\epsilon)$ statistical distance bound to a $O(\epsilon^2)$ KL-divergence bound. We refer to [30] for the formal definition of the smoothing parameter $\eta$; for our purpose it only matters that $\eta_\epsilon(\mathbb{Z}) \leq \sqrt{\ln(2 + 2/\epsilon)/\pi}$ and thus our adapted lemma allows to decrease the smoothing condition by a factor of about $\sqrt{2}$.

**Lemma 3 (Adapted from Thm. 3.1 from [30]).** *Let* $x_1 \leftarrow D_{\mathbb{Z},\sigma_1}$, $x_2 \leftarrow D_{k\mathbb{Z},\sigma_2}$ *for some positive reals* $\sigma_1, \sigma_2$ *and let* $\sigma_3^{-2} = \sigma_1^{-2} + \sigma_2^{-2}$, *and* $\sigma^2 = \sigma_1^2 + \sigma_2^2$. *For any* $\epsilon \in (0, 1/2)$ *if* $\sigma_1 \geq \eta_\epsilon(\mathbb{Z})/\sqrt{2\pi}$ *and* $\sigma_3 \geq \eta_\epsilon(k\mathbb{Z})/\sqrt{2\pi}$, *then distribution* $\mathcal{P}$ *of* $x_1 + x_2$ *verifies*

$$D_{KL}(\mathcal{P}\|D_{\mathbb{Z},\sigma}) \leq 2\left(1 - \left(\frac{1+\epsilon}{1-\epsilon}\right)^2\right)^2 \approx 32\epsilon^2.$$

*Remark.* The factor $1/\sqrt{2\pi}$ in our version of this lemma is due to the fact that we use the standard deviation $\sigma$ as the parameter of Gaussians and not the renormalized parameter $s = \sqrt{2\pi}\sigma$ often found in the literature.

*Proof.* The proof is similar to the one of [30], with $\Lambda_1 = \mathbb{Z}$, $\Lambda_2 = k\mathbb{Z}$, $\mathbf{c}_1 = \mathbf{c}_2 = \mathbf{0}$; but for the last argument of the proof where we replace statistical distance by KL-divergence. As in [30], we first establish that for any $\bar{x} \in \mathbb{Z}$ one has the following relative error bound

$$\mathbb{P}_{x \leftarrow \mathcal{P}}[x = \bar{x}] \in \left[\left(\frac{1-\epsilon}{1+\epsilon}\right)^2, \left(\frac{1+\epsilon}{1-\epsilon}\right)^2\right] \cdot \mathbb{P}_{x \leftarrow D_{\mathbb{Z},\sigma}}[x = \bar{x}].$$

It remains to conclude using Lemma 2.                                    □

To exploit this lemma, for BLISS-I we set $k = 11$, $\sigma' = \sigma/\sqrt{1 + k^2} \approx 19.53$, and sample $x = x_1 + kx_2'$ for $x_1, x_2' \leftarrow D_{\mathbb{Z},\sigma'}$ (equivalently $k \cdot x_2' = x_2 \leftarrow D_{k\mathbb{Z},k\sigma'}$). The smoothness conditions are verified for $\epsilon = \sqrt{2^{-128}/32}$ and $\eta_\epsilon(\mathbb{Z}) \leq 3.92$.

Due to usage of the much smaller $\sigma'$ instead of $\sigma$ the size of the precomputation table reduces by a factor of about $k = 11$ at the price of sampling twice. However, the running time does not double in practice since the enhancement based on the shortcut intervals reduces the number of necessary comparisons to $C \in [0.22, 0.25]$ on average. For a majority of first bytes $v$ the interval length $b_v - a_v$ is reduced to 1 and $x$ is determined without any comparison.

*Asymptotics cost.* If one considers the asymptotic costs in $\sigma$ our methods allow one to sample using a table size of $\Theta(\sqrt{\sigma})$ rather than $\Theta(\sigma)$ by doubling the computation time. Actually, for much larger $\sigma$ one could use $O(\log \sigma)$ samples of constant standard deviation and thus achieve a table size of $O(1)$ for computational cost in $O(\log \sigma)$.

### 3.4   CDT Sampling with Reduced Table Size

We recall that when doing floating-point error analysis, the relative error of a computed value $v$ is defined as $|v - v_e|/v_e$ where $v_e$ is the exact value that was meant to be computed. Using the table $0 = T[0] \leq T[i] \leq \cdots \leq T[S + 1] = 1$, the output of a CDT sampler follows the distribution $\mathcal{P}$ with $\mathcal{P}(i) = T[i + 1] - T[i]$. When applying the results from KL-divergence obtained above, the relative error of $T[i + 1] - T[i]$ might be significantly larger than the one of $T[i]$. This is particularly true for the tail, where $T[i] \approx 1$ but $\mathcal{P}(i)$ is very small. Intuitively, we would like the smallest probability to come first in the CDT. A simple workaround is to reverse the order of the table so that $1 = T[0] \geq T[i] \geq \cdots \geq T[S + 1] = 0$ with a slight modification of the algorithm so that $\mathcal{P}(i) = T[i] - T[i + 1]$. With this trick, the subtraction only increase the relative error by a factor roughly $\sigma$. Indeed, leaving aside the details relative to discrete Gaussian, for $x \geq 0$ we have

$$\int_{y=x}^{\infty} \rho_s(y)dy \Big/ \rho_s(x) \leq \sigma \quad \text{whereas} \quad \int_{y=0}^{x} \rho_s(y)dy \Big/ \rho_s(x) \xrightarrow[x \to \infty]{} +\infty.$$

The left term is an estimation of the relative-error blow-up induced by the subtraction with the CDT in the reverse order and the right term the same estimation for the CDT in the natural order. We aim to have a variable precision in the table $T[i]$ so that $\delta(i)^2 \mathcal{P}(i)$ is about constant around $2^{-128}/|S|$ as suggested by Lemma 2 while $\delta(i)$ denotes the relative error $\delta(i) = |\mathcal{P}(i) - \mathcal{Q}(i)|/\mathcal{P}(i)$. As a trade-off between optimal variable precision and hardware efficiency, we propose the following data-structure. We define 9 tables $M_0 \ldots M_8$ of bytes for the mantissa with respective lengths $\ell_0 \geq \ell_1 \geq \cdots \geq \ell_8$ and another byte table $E$ for exponents, of length $\ell_0$. The value $T[i]$ is defined as

$$T[i] = 256^{-E[i]} \cdot \sum_{k=0}^{8} 256^{-(k+1)} \cdot M_k[i]$$

where $M_k[i]$ is defined as 0 when the index is out of bound $i \geq \ell_k$. Thus, the value of $T[i]$ is stored with $p(i) = 9 - \min\{k|\ell_k > i\}$ bytes of precisions. More precisely,

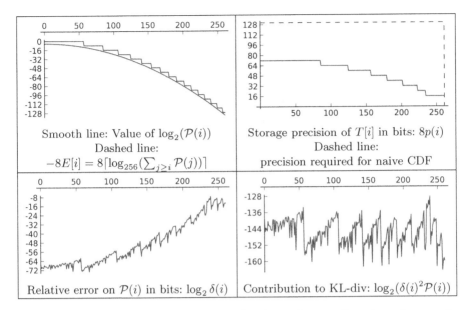

**Fig. 2.** Data of our optimized CDT sampler for a discrete Gaussian of parameter $\sigma' \approx 19.53$

lengths are defined as $[\ell_0, \ldots, \ell_8] = [262, 262, 235, 223, 202, 180, 157, 125, 86]$ so that we store at least two bytes for each entry up to $i < 262$, three bytes up to $i < 213$ and so forth. Note that no actual computation is involved in constructing $T[i]$ following the plain CDT algorithm.

For evaluation, we used the closed formula for KL-divergence and measured $D_{\mathrm{KL}}(\mathcal{P}\|\mathcal{Q}) \leq 2^{-128}$. The storage requirements of this table is computed by $2\ell_0 + \ell_1 + \cdots + \ell_8 \approx 2.1$ KB. The straightforward CDF approach requires each entry up to $i < 262$ to be stored with $128 + \log_2 \sigma$ bits of precisions and thus requires a total of at least 4.4 KB. The storage requirements are graphically depicted by the area under the curves in the top-right quadrant of Figure 2.

# 4    Implementation on Reconfigurable Hardware

In this section we provide details on our implementation of the BLISS-I signature scheme on a Xilinx Spartan-6 FPGA. We include the enhancements from the previous section to achieve a design that is tweaked for high-performance at moderate resource costs. For details on the implementation of the Bernoulli sampler proposed in [12] we refer to the full version [31].

## 4.1    Enhanced CDT Sampling.

Along the lines of the previous section our hardware implementation operates on bytes in order to use the 1024x8-bit mode of operation of the Spartan-6

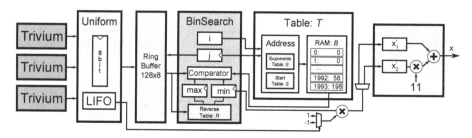

**Fig. 3.** Block diagram of the CDT sampler which generates two samples $x_1', x_2'$ of standard deviation $\sigma' \approx 19.53$ which are combined to a sample $x = x_1' + 11x_2'$ with standard deviation $\sigma = 215.73$. The sampling is performed using binary search on the size optimized Table $T$.

block RAMs. The design of our CDT sampler is depicted in Figure 3 and uses the aforementioned convolution lemma. Thus two samples with $\sigma' \approx 19.53$ are combined into a sample with standard deviation $\sigma \approx 215.73$. The BinSearch component performs a binary search on the table $T$ as described in Section 3.4 for a random byte vector $r$ to find a $c$ such that $T[c] \geq r > T[c+1]$. It accesses $T$ byte-wise and thus $T_j[i] = M_{j-E[i]}[i]$ denotes the entry at index $i \in (0, 261)$ and byte $j$ where $T_j[i] = 0$ when $j - E[i] < 0$ or $i \geq \ell_{j-E[i]}$. When a sampling operation is started in the BinSearch component we set $j = 0$ and initialize the pointer registers min and max with the values stored in the reverse interval table $I[r_0]$ where $r_0$ is the first random byte. The reverse interval table is realized as 256x15-bit single port distributed ROM (6 bits for the minimum and 9 bits for the maximum). The index of the middle element of the search radius is $i = (\texttt{min}+\texttt{max})/2$. In case $T_j[i] > r_j$ we set $(\texttt{min} = i, i = (i+\texttt{max})/2, \texttt{max} = \texttt{max}, j = 0)$. Otherwise, for $T_j[i] < r_j$ we set $(i = (\texttt{min}+i)/2, \texttt{min} = \texttt{min}, \texttt{max} = i, j = 0)$ until $\texttt{max} - \texttt{min} < 2$. In case of $T_j[i] = r_j$ we increase $j = j+1$ and thus compare the next byte. The actual entries of $M_0 \ldots M_8$ are consecutively stored in block memory $B$ and the address is computed as $a = S[j - E[i] + i]$ where we store the start addresses of each byte group in a small additional LUT-based table $S = [0, 262, 524, 759, 982, 1184, 1364, 1521, 1646]$. Some control logic takes care that all invalid/out of bound requests to $S$ and $B$ return a zero.

For random byte generation we use three instantiations of the Trivium stream cipher (each Trivium instantiation outputs one bit per clock cycle) to generate a uniformly random byte every third clock cycle and store spare bits in a LIFO for later use as sign bits. The random values $r_j$ are stored in a 128x8 bit ring buffer realized as simple dual-port distributed RAM. The idea is that the sampler may request a large number of random bytes in the worst-case but usually finishes after one or two comparisons due to the lazy search. As the BinSearch component keeps track of the maximum number of accessed random bytes, it allows the Uniform sampler to refresh only the used $\max(j) + 1$ bytes in the buffer. In case the buffer is empty, we stop the Gaussian sampler until a sufficient amount of randomness becomes available. In order to compute the final sample $x$ we determine sign bits of two samples $x_1', x_2'$ and finally output $x = x_1' + 11x_2'$.

To achieve a high clock frequency, a comparison in the binary search step could not be performed in one cycle due to the excessive number of tables and range checks involved. We therefore allow two cycles per search step which are carefully balanced. For example, we precompute the indices $\mathtt{i}' = (\mathtt{min+i})/2$ and $\mathtt{i}'' = (\mathtt{max+i})/2$ in the cycle prior to a comparison to relax the critical paths. We further merged the block memory $B$ (port A) and the exponent table $E$ (port B) into one 18k block memory and optimized the memory alignment accordingly. Note also that we are still accessing the two ports of the block RAM holding $B$ and $E$ only every two clock cycles which would enable another sampler to operate on the same table using time-multiplexing.

## 4.2   Signing and Verification Architecture

The architecture of our implementation of a high-speed BLISS signing engine is given in Figure 4. Similar to the GLP design [16] we implemented a two stage pipeline where the polynomial multiplication $\mathbf{a}_1\mathbf{y}_1$ runs in parallel to the hashing $H(\lfloor \mathbf{u} \rceil_d, \mu)$ and sparse multiplication $\mathbf{z}_{1,2} = \mathbf{s}_{1,2}\mathbf{c}+\mathbf{y}_{1,2}$[4]. For polynomial multiplication [1,32,36] of $\mathbf{a}_1\mathbf{y}_1$ we rely on a publicly available FFT/NTT-based polynomial multiplier [33] (PolyMul). The public key $\mathbf{a}_1$ is stored already in NTT format so that only one forward and one backward transform is required. The multiplier also instantiates either the Bernoulli or the CDT Gaussian sampler (configurable by a VHDL generic) and an intermediate FIFO for buffering. When a new triple $(\mathbf{a}_1\mathbf{y}_1, \mathbf{y}_1, \mathbf{y}_2)$ is available the data is transferred into the block memories BRAM-U, BRAM-Y1 and BRAM-Y2 and the small polynomial $\mathbf{u} = \zeta\mathbf{a}_1\mathbf{y}_1 + \mathbf{y}_2$ is computed on-the-fly and stored in BRAM-U for later use. The lower order bits $\lfloor \mathbf{u} \rceil_d \bmod p$ of $\mathbf{u}$ are saved in the RAM-U. As random oracle we have chosen the KECCAK-$f[1600]$ hash function for its security and speed in hardware [22,38]. A configurable hardware implementation[5] is provided by the KECCAK project and the mid-range core is parametrized so that the KECCAK state it split into 16 pieces ($Nb = 16$). To simplify control logic and padding we just hash multiples of 1024 bit blocks and rehash in case of a rejection. Storing the state of the hash function after hashing the message (and before hashing $\lfloor \mathbf{u} \rceil_d \bmod p$) would be possible but is not done due to the state size of KECCAK. After hashing the ExtractPos component extracts the $\kappa$ positions of $\mathbf{c}$ which are one from the binary hash output and stores them in the 23x9-bit memory RAM-Pos.

For the computation of $\mathbf{s}_1\mathbf{c}$ and $\mathbf{s}_2\mathbf{c}$ we then exploited that $\mathbf{c}$ has mainly zero coefficients and only $\kappa = 23$ coefficients set to one. Moreover, only $d_1 = \lceil \delta_1 n \rceil = 154$

---

[4] Another option would be a three stage pipeline with an additional buffer between the hashing and sparse multiplication. As a tradeoff this would allows to use a slower and thus more area efficient hash function but also imply a longer delay and require pipeline flushes in case of an accepted signature.

[5] See http://keccak.noekeon.org/mid_range_hw.html for more information on the core.

coefficients in $s_1$ are $\pm 1$ and $s_2$ has $d_1$ entries in $\pm 2$ where the first coefficient is from $\{-1, 1, 3\}$. The simplest and, in this case, also best suited algorithm for sparse polynomial multiplication is the row- or column-wise schoolbook algorithm. While row-wise multiplication would benefit from the sparsity of $s_{1,2}$ and $c$, more memory accesses are necessary to add and store inner products. Since memory that has more than two ports is extremely expensive, this also prevents or at least limits efficient and configurable parallelization. As a consequence, our implementation consists of a configurable number of cores $(C)$ which perform column-wise multiplication to compute $z_1$ and $z_2$, respectively. Each core stores the secret key (either $s_1$ or $s_2$) efficiently in a distributed RAM and accumulates inner products in a small multiply-accumulate unit (MAC). Positions of $c$ are fed simultaneously into the cores. Another advantage of our approach is that we can compute the norms and scalar products for rejection sampling parallel to the sparse multiplication. In Figure 4 a configuration with $C = 2$ is shown for simplicity but our experiments show that $C = 8$ leads to an optimal trade-off between speed and resource consumption. Our verification engine uses only the PolyMul (without a Gaussian sampler) and the Hash component and is thus much more lightweight compared to signing. The polynomial $c$ stored as (unordered) positions is expanded into a 512x1-bit distributed RAM and the input to the hash function is computed in a pipelined manner when PolyMul outputs $a_1y_1$.

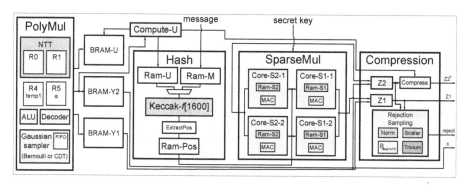

**Fig. 4.** Block diagram of the implemented BLISS-I signing engine

## 5   Results and Comparison

In this section we discuss our results which were obtained post place-and-route (PAR) on a Spartan-6 LX25 (speed grade -3) with Xilinx ISE 14.6.

**Gaussian Sampling.** Detailed results on area consumption and timing of the CDT and Bernoulli Gaussian sampler designs are given in Table 2. The results show that the enhanced CDT sampler consumes less logic resources than the Bernoulli sampler, as described in the full version [31], at the cost of one 18k block memory to store the tables $E$ and $B$. This is a significant improvement in terms of storage size compared to a naive implementation without the application of the Kullback-Leibler divergence and Gaussian convolution. A standard CDT implementation would require at least $\sigma\tau\lambda = 370$ kbits (that is about 23 many 18K block Rams) for the defined parameters matching a standard deviation $\sigma = 215.73$, tailcut $\tau = 13.4$ and precision $\lambda = 128$.

Regarding randomness consumption the CDT sampler needs on average 21 bits for one sample (using two smaller samples and the convolution theorem) which are generated by three instantiations of Trivium. The Bernoulli sampler on the other hand consumes 33 bits on average, generated by two instantiations of Trivium. With respect to the averaged performance, 7.4 and 18.5 cycles are required by the CDT and the Bernoulli sampler to provide one sample, respectively.

As a consequence, by combining the convolution lemma and KL-divergence we were able to maintain the advantage of the CDT, namely high speed and relative simple implementation, but significantly reduced the memory requirements (from $\approx$ 23 18K block RAMs to one 18K block RAM). The convolution lemma works especially well in combination with the reverse tables as the overall table sizes shrink and thus the number of comparisons is reduced. Thus, we do not expect a CTD sampler that samples directly from standard deviation $\sigma$ to be significantly faster. Additionally, larger tables would require more complex address generation which might lower the achievable clock frequency. The Bernoulli approach on the other hand does not seem as suitable for an application of the convolution lemma as the CDT. The reason is that the tables are already very small and thus a reduction would not significantly reduce the area usage.

Previous implementations of Gaussian sampling for lattice-based public key encryption can be found in [34,37]. However, both works target a smaller standard deviation of $\sigma = 3.3$. The work of Roy et al. [37] uses the Knuth-Yao algorithm (see [13] for more details), is very area-efficient (47 slices on a Virtex-5), and consumes few randomness but requires 17 clock cycles for one sample. In [34] Bernoulli sampling is used to optimize simple rejection sampling by using Bernoulli evaluation instead of computation of exp(). However, without usage of the binary Gaussian distribution (see [12]) the rejection rate is high and one sample requires 96 random bits and 144 cycles. This is acceptable for a relatively slow encryption scheme and possible due to the high output rate (one bit per cycle) of the used stream cipher but not a suitable architecture for BLISS. The discrete Ziggurat [8] performs well in software and might also profit from the techniques introduced in this work but does not seem to be a good target for a hardware implementation due to its infrequent rejection sampling operations and its costly requirement on high precision floating point arithmetic.

**BLISS Operations.** Results for the BLISS signing and verification engine and sub-modules can be found in Table 2 including averaged cycle counts for successfully producing a signature. Note that the final slice, LUT, and FF counts of the signing engine cannot directly be computed as the sum of the sub modules due to cross module optimizations, timing optimization, and additional control logic between modules. One signing attempt takes roughly 10k cycles and on average 1.6 trials are necessary using the BLISS-I parameter set. To evaluate the impact of the sampler used in the design, we instantiated two signing engines of which one employs a CDT sampler and the other one two Bernoulli samplers to match the speed of the multiplier. For a similar performance of roughly 8,000 signing operations per second, the signing instance based on the Bernoulli sampler has a significantly higher resource consumption (about 470 extra slices). Due to the two pipeline stages involved, the runtime of both instances is determined by $\max(\text{Cycles}(\texttt{PolyMul}), \text{Cycles}(\texttt{Hash})) + \text{Cycles}(\texttt{SparseMul})$ where the rejection sampling in Compression is performed in parallel. Further design space exploration (e.g., evaluating the impact of a different number of parallel sparse multiplication operations or a faster configuration of KECCAK) always identified the PolyMul component as performance bottleneck or did not provide significant savings in resources for reduced versions. In order to further increase the clock rate it would of course also be possible to instantiate the Gaussian sampler in a separate clock domain. The verification runtime is determined by $\text{Cycles}(\texttt{PolyMul}) + \text{Cycles}(\texttt{Hash})$ as no pipelining is used and PolyMul is slightly faster than for signing as no Gaussian sampling is needed.

**Table 2.** Performance and resource consumption of the full BLISS-I signing engine using the CDT sampler or two parallel Bernoulli samplers (Ber) on the Spartan-6 LX25 for a small 1024 bit message

| Configuration and Operation | Slices/LUT/FF /BRAM/DSP | MHz | Cycles | Operations per second (output) |
|---|---|---|---|---|
| Sign-I (CDT, C=8) | 2,431/7,491/7,033/7.5/6 | 129 | ≈16,210 | ≈7958 (signature) |
| Sign-I (Ber, C=8) | 2,960/9,029/8,562/6.5/8 | 131 | ≈16,210 | ≈8,081 (signature) |
| Ver-I | 1,727/5,275/4,488/4.5/3 | 142 | 9,835 | 14,438 (valid/invalid) |
| CDT sampler | 299/928/1,121/1/0 | 129 | ≈7.4 | ≈17,432,432 (sample) |
| Bernoulli sampler | 416/1,178/1,183/0/1 | 138 | ≈18.5 | ≈7,459,459 (sample) |
| PolyMul (CDT) | 1,138/3,259/3,242/6/1 | 130 | 9,429 | 13,787 ($\mathbf{a} \cdot \mathbf{y}_1$) |
| Hash ($Nb = 16$) | 752/2,461/2,134/0/0 | 149 | 1,931 | 77,162 (**c**) |
| SparseMul ($C = 1$) | 64/162/125/0/0 | 274 | 15,876 | 17,258 ($\mathbf{c} \cdot \mathbf{s}_{1,2}$) |
| SparseMul ($C = 8$) | 308/918/459/0/0 | 267 | 2,436 | 109,605 ($\mathbf{c} \cdot \mathbf{s}_{1,2}$) |
| SparseMul ($C = 16$) | 628/1847/810/0/0 | 254 | 1,476 | 172,086 ($\mathbf{c} \cdot \mathbf{s}_{1,2}$) |
| Compression | 1,230/3,851/3,049/3/0 | 151 | - | parallel to SparseMul |

**Comparison.** In comparison with the GLP implementation from [16], the design of this work achieves higher throughput with a lower number of block RAMs and DSPs. The structural advantage of BLISS is a smaller polynomial modulus (GLP: $q = 8383489$/BLISS-I: $q = 12289$), less iterations necessary for a valid signature (GLP: 7/BLISS-I: 1.6), and a higher security level (GLP: 80 bit/BLISS-I: 128 bit). Furthermore and contrary to [16], we remark that our implementation takes the area costs and timings of a hash function (KECCAK) into account. In summary, our implementation of BLISS is superior to [16] in almost all aspects.

**Table 3.** Signing or verification speed of comparable signature scheme implementations. The GLP implementation was measured on a Spartan-6 device, the B-163 ECDSA one on a Cyclone II and the other implementations were done on Virtex-5.

| Operation | Security | Algorithm | Resources | Ops/s |
|---|---|---|---|---|
| GLP [sign] [16] | 80 | GLP | 7465 LUT/ 8993 FF/ 28 DSP/ 29.5 BRAM18 | 931 |
| GLP [ver] [16] | 80 | GLP | 6225 LUT/ 6663 FF/ 8 DSP/ 15 BRAM18 | 998 |
| ECDSA [sign/ver] [21] | 80 | Full ECDSA; B-163 | 15,879 LE / 8,472 FF/ 36 M4K | 1063/621 |
| RSA [sign] [40] | 103 | RSA-2048; private key | 3237 LS/ 17 DSPs | 89 |
| ECDSA [sign] [15] | 128 | Full ECDSA; secp256r1 | 32299 LUT/FF pairs | 139 |
| ECDSA [ver] [15] | 128 | Full ECDSA; secp256r1 | 32299 LUT/FF pairs | 110 |

In addition to that Glas et al. [15] report a vehicle-to-X communication accelerator based on an ECDSA signature over 256-bit prime fields. With respect to this, our BLISS implementation shows higher performance at less resource cost. An ECDSA implementation on a binary curve for an 80-bit security level on an Altera FPGA is given in [21] and achieves similar speeds and area consumption compared to our work. Other ECC implementations over 256-bit prime or binary fields (e.g., such as [18] on a Xilinx Virtex-4) only implement the point multiplication operation and not the full ECDSA protocol. Finally, a fast RSA-2048 core was presented for Virtex-5 devices in [40] which requires more logic/DSPs and provides significantly lower performance (11.2 ms per operation) than our lattice-based signature instance.

**Acknowledgment.** We express our gratitude to David Xiao and Vadim Lyubashevsky for helpful conversations. We also thank the anonymous CHES'14 reviewers for detailed comments. This research was supported in part by the DARPA PROCEED program, NSF grant CNS-1117936, German Research Foundation (DFG), DFG Research Training Group GRK 1817/1 and the German Federal Ministry of Economics and Technology (Grant 01ME12025 SecMobil). Opinions, findings and conclusions or recommendations expressed in this material are those of the author(s) and do not necessarily reflect the views of DARPA, NSF, DFG, or German Federal Ministry of Economics and Technology.

# References

1. Aysu, A., Patterson, C., Schaumont, P.: Low-cost and area-efficient FPGA implementations of lattice-based cryptography. In: HOST, pp. 81–86. IEEE (2013)
2. Bai, S., Galbraith, S.D.: An improved compression technique for signatures based on learning with errors. In: Benaloh, J. (ed.) CT-RSA 2014. LNCS, vol. 8366, pp. 28–47. Springer, Heidelberg (2014)
3. Bansarkhani, R.E., Buchmann, J.: Improvement and efficient implementation of a lattice-based signature scheme. In: Lange, T., Lauter, K., Lisoněk, P. (eds.) SAC 2013. LNCS, vol. 8282, pp. 48–67. Springer, Heidelberg (2014)
4. Barbulescu, R.: Selecting polynomials for the function field sieve. Cryptology ePrint Archive, Report 2013/200 (2013), http://eprint.iacr.org/2013/200
5. Barbulescu, R., Gaudry, P., Joux, A., Thomé, E.: A heuristic quasi-polynomial algorithm for discrete logarithm in finite fields of small characteristic. In: Nguyen, P.Q., Oswald, E. (eds.) EUROCRYPT 2014. LNCS, vol. 8441, pp. 1–16. Springer, Heidelberg (2014), http://arxiv.org/abs/1306.4244
6. Blondeau, C., Gérard, B.: On the data complexity of statistical attacks against block ciphers (full version). Cryptology ePrint Archive, Report 2009/064 (2009), http://eprint.iacr.org/2009/064
7. Boorghany, A., Jalili, R.: Implementation and comparison of lattice-based identification protocols on smart cards and microcontrollers. Cryptology ePrint Archive, Report 2014/078 (2014), http://eprint.iacr.org/2014/078
8. Buchmann, J., Cabarcas, D., Göpfert, F., Hülsing, A., Weiden, P.: Discrete ziggurat: A time-memory trade-off for sampling from a Gaussian distribution over the integers. In: Lange, T., Lauter, K., Lisoněk, P. (eds.) SAC 2013, vol. 8282, pp. 402–417. Springer, Heidelberg (2014)
9. Chen, H.-C., Asau, Y.: On generating random variates from an empirical distribution. AIIE Transactions 6(2), 163–166 (1974)
10. Cover, T.M., Thomas, J.: Elements of Information Theory. Wiley (1991)
11. Devroye, L.: Non-Uniform Random Variate Generation. Springer-Verlag (1986), http://luc.devroye.org/rnbookindex.html
12. Ducas, L., Durmus, A., Lepoint, T., Lyubashevsky, V.: Lattice signatures and bimodal gaussians. In: Canetti, R., Garay, J.A. (eds.) CRYPTO 2013, Part I. LNCS, vol. 8042, pp. 40–56. Springer, Heidelberg (2013)
13. Dwarakanath, N.C., Galbraith, S.D.: Sampling from discrete Gaussians for lattice-based cryptography on a constrained device. In: Applicable Algebra in Engineering, Communication and Computing, pp. 1–22 (2014)
14. Gentry, C., Peikert, C., Vaikuntanathan, V.: Trapdoors for hard lattices and new cryptographic constructions. In: Ladner, R.E., Dwork, C. (eds.) 40th ACM STOC, Victoria, British Columbia, Canada, May 17-20, pp. 197–206. ACM Press (2008)
15. Glas, B., Sander, O., Stuckert, V., Müller-Glaser, K.D., Becker, J.: Prime field ECDSA signature processing for reconfigurable embedded systems. Int. J. Reconfig. Comp. (2011)
16. Güneysu, T., Lyubashevsky, V., Pöppelmann, T.: Practical lattice-based cryptography: A signature scheme for embedded systems. In: Prouff, E., Schaumont, P. (eds.) CHES 2012. LNCS, vol. 7428, pp. 530–547. Springer, Heidelberg (2012)
17. Güneysu, T., Oder, T., Pöppelmann, T., Schwabe, P.: Software speed records for lattice-based signatures. In: Gaborit, P. (ed.) PQCrypto 2013. LNCS, vol. 7932, pp. 67–82. Springer, Heidelberg (2013)

18. Güneysu, T., Paar, C.: Ultra high performance ECC over NIST primes on commercial fPGAs. In: Oswald, E., Rohatgi, P. (eds.) CHES 2008. LNCS, vol. 5154, pp. 62–78. Springer, Heidelberg (2008)
19. Gutierrez, R., Torres-Carot, V., Valls, J.: Hardware architecture of a Gaussian noise generator based on the inversion method. IEEE Trans. on Circuits and Systems 59-II(8), 501–505 (2012)
20. Joux, A.: A new index calculus algorithm with complexity l(1/4 + o(1)) in very small characteristic. Cryptology ePrint Archive, Report 2013/095 (2013), http://eprint.iacr.org/2013/095
21. Järvinen, T.M.K., Skyttä, J.: Final project report: Cryptoprocessor for elliptic curve digital signature algorithm, ECDSA (2007), http://www.altera.com/literature/dc/2007/in_2007_dig_signature.pdf
22. Jungk, B., Apfelbeck, J.: Area-efficient FPGA implementations of the SHA-3 finalists. In: Athanas, P.M., Becker, J., Cumplido, R. (eds.) ReConFig, pp. 235–241. IEEE Computer Society (2011)
23. Kullback, S., Leibler, R.A.: On information and sufficiency. Ann. Math. Statist. 22(1), 79–86 (1951)
24. Lyubashevsky, V.: Lattice-based identification schemes secure under active attacks. In: Cramer, R. (ed.) PKC 2008. LNCS, vol. 4939, pp. 162–179. Springer, Heidelberg (2008)
25. Lyubashevsky, V.: Fiat-shamir with aborts: Applications to lattice and factoring-based signatures. In: Matsui, M. (ed.) ASIACRYPT 2009. LNCS, vol. 5912, pp. 598–616. Springer, Heidelberg (2009)
26. Lyubashevsky, V.: Lattice signatures without trapdoors. In: Pointcheval, D., Johansson, T. (eds.) EUROCRYPT 2012. LNCS, vol. 7237, pp. 738–755. Springer, Heidelberg (2012)
27. Lyubashevsky, V., Peikert, C., Regev, O.: On ideal lattices and learning with errors over rings. In: Gilbert, H. (ed.) EUROCRYPT 2010. LNCS, vol. 6110, pp. 1–23. Springer, Heidelberg (2010)
28. Micciancio, D., Peikert, C.: Trapdoors for lattices: Simpler, tighter, faster, smaller. In: Pointcheval, D., Johansson, T. (eds.) EUROCRYPT 2012. LNCS, vol. 7237, pp. 700–718. Springer, Heidelberg (2012)
29. Micciancio, D., Peikert, C.: Hardness of SIS and LWE with small parameters. In: Canetti, R., Garay, J.A. (eds.) CRYPTO 2013, Part I. LNCS, vol. 8042, pp. 21–39. Springer, Heidelberg (2013)
30. Peikert, C.: An efficient and parallel gaussian sampler for lattices. In: Rabin, T. (ed.) CRYPTO 2010. LNCS, vol. 6223, pp. 80–97. Springer, Heidelberg (2010)
31. Pöppelmann, T., Ducas, L., Güneysu, T.: Enhanced lattice-based signatures on reconfigurable hardware. IACR Cryptology ePrint Archive, 2014:254 (2014)
32. Pöppelmann, T., Güneysu, T.: Towards efficient arithmetic for lattice-based cryptography on reconfigurable hardware. In: Hevia, A., Neven, G. (eds.) LatinCrypt 2012. LNCS, vol. 7533, pp. 139–158. Springer, Heidelberg (2012)
33. T. Pöppelmann and T. Güneysu. Towards practical lattice-based public-key encryption on reconfigurable hardware. T. Lange, K. Lauter, and P. Lison?ek
34. Pöppelmann, T., Güneysu, T.: Area optimization of lightweight lattice-based encryption on reconfigurable hardware. In: ISCAS (to appear, 2014), http://www.sha.rub.de/media/sh/veroeffentlichungen/2014/03/23/iscas_web_version.pdf
35. Rich, S., Gellman, B.: NSA seeks quantum computer that could crack most codes. The Washington Post (2013), http://wapo.st/19DycJT

36. Roy, S.S., Vercauteren, F., Mentens, N., Chen, D.D., Verbauwhede, I.: Compact hardware implementation of Ring-LWE cryptosystems. IACR Cryptology ePrint Archive, 2013:866 (2013)
37. Roy, S.S., Vercauteren, F., Verbauwhede, I.: High precision discrete Gaussian sampling on FPGAs. In: Lange, T., Lauter, K., Lisoněk, P. (eds.) SAC 2013. LNCS, vol. 8282, pp. 383–401. Springer, Heidelberg (2014)
38. Shahid, R., Sharif, M.U., Rogawski, M., Gaj, K.: Use of embedded FPGA resources in implementations of 14 round 2 SHA-3 candidates. In: Tessier, R. (ed.) FPT, pp. 1–9. IEEE (2011)
39. Shor, P.W.: Algorithms for quantum computation: Discrete logarithms and factoring. In: 35th FOCS, Santa Fe, New Mexico, November 20-22, pp. 124–134. IEEE Computer Society Press (1994)
40. Suzuki, D., Matsumoto, T.: How to maximize the potential of FPGA-based DSPs for modular exponentiation. IEICE Transactions 94-A(1), 211–222 (2011)
41. Thomas, D.B., Luk, W., Leong, P.H.W., Villasenor, J.D.: Gaussian random number generators. ACM Comput. Surv. 39(4) (2007)
42. Vaudenay, S.: Decorrelation: A theory for block cipher security. Journal of Cryptology 16(4), 249–286 (2003)

# Compact Ring-LWE Cryptoprocessor

Sujoy Sinha Roy[1], Frederik Vercauteren[1], Nele Mentens[1],
Donald Donglong Chen[2], and Ingrid Verbauwhede[1]

[1] ESAT/COSIC and iMinds, KU Leuven
Kasteelpark Arenberg 10, B-3001 Leuven-Heverlee, Belgium
{firstname.lastname}@esat.kuleuven.be
[2] Department of Electronic Engineering,
City University of Hong Kong
Tat Chee Avenue, Kowloon, Hong Kong SAR
donald.chen@my.cityu.edu.hk

**Abstract.** In this paper we propose an efficient and compact processor
for a ring-LWE based encryption scheme. We present three optimizations for the Number Theoretic Transform (NTT) used for polynomial
multiplication: we avoid pre-processing in the negative wrapped convolution by merging it with the main algorithm, we reduce the fixed computation cost of the twiddle factors and propose an advanced memory
access scheme. These optimization techniques reduce both the cycle and
memory requirements. Finally, we also propose an optimization of the
ring-LWE encryption system that reduces the number of NTT operations
from five to four resulting in a 20% speed-up. We use these computational optimizations along with several architectural optimizations to
design an instruction-set ring-LWE cryptoprocessor. For dimension 256,
our processor performs encryption/decryption operations in 20/9 $\mu s$ on
a Virtex 6 FPGA and only requires 1349 LUTs, 860 FFs, 1 DSP-MULT
and 2 BRAMs. Similarly for dimension 512, the processor takes 48/21
$\mu s$ for performing encryption/decryption operations and only requires
1536 LUTs, 953 FFs, 1 DSP-MULT and 3 BRAMs. Our processors are
therefore more than three times smaller than the current state of the art
hardware implementations, whilst running somewhat faster.

**Keywords:** Lattice-based cryptography, ring-LWE, Polynomial multiplication, Number Theoretic Transform, Hardware implementation.

## 1 Introduction

Lattice-based cryptography is considered a prime candidate for quantum-secure
public key cryptography due to its wide applicability [27] and its security proofs
that are based on worst-case hardness of well known lattice problems. The *learning with errors* (LWE) problem [26] and its ring variant known as ring-LWE [17]
have been used as a solid foundation for several cryptographic schemes. The
significant progress in the theory of lattice-based cryptography [19,20,25] has
recently been followed by practical implementations [1,7,9,22,23,28].

L. Batina and M. Robshaw (Eds.): CHES 2014, LNCS 8731, pp. 371–391, 2014.
© International Association for Cryptologic Research 2014

The ring-LWE based cryptosystems operate in a polynomial ring $R_q = \mathbb{Z}_q[\mathbf{x}]/\langle f(x)\rangle$, where one typically chooses $f(x) = x^n + 1$ with $n$ a power of two, and $q$ a prime with $q \equiv 1 \bmod 2n$. An implementation thus requires the basic operations in such a ring $R_q$, with multiplication taking up the bulk of the resources both in area and time. An efficient polynomial multiplier architecture therefore is a pre-requisite for the deployment of ring-LWE based cryptography in real world systems.

The most important hardware implementations of polynomial multipliers for the rings $R_q$ are [1,9,22,23]. In [9], a fully parallel butterfly structure is used for the polynomial multiplier resulting in a huge area consumption. For instance, even for medium security, their ring-LWE cryptoprocessor does not fit on the largest FPGA of the Virtex 6 family. In [22], a sequential polynomial multiplier architecture is designed to use the FPGA resources in an efficient way. The multiplier uses a dedicated ROM to store all the twiddle factors which are required during the NTT computation. In [23] the authors integrated the polynomial multiplier [22] in a complete ring-LWE based encryption system and propose several system level optimizations such as a better message encoding scheme and compression technique for the ciphertext. The work [1] tries to reduce the area of the polynomial multiplier by computing the twiddle factors whenever required, but as we will show, this could be improved substantially by re-arranging the loops inside the NTT computation. Furthermore, the paper does not include an implementation of a complete ring-LWE cryptoprocessor.

**Our contributions:** In this paper we present a complete ring-LWE based encryption processor that uses the Number Theoretic Transform (NTT) algorithm for polynomial multiplication. The architecture is designed to have small area and memory requirement, but is also optimized to keep the number of cycles small. In particular, we make the following contributions:

1. During the NTT computation, the intermediate coefficients are multiplied by the twiddle factors that are computed using repeated multiplications. In [22] a pre-computed table (ROM) is used to avoid this fixed computation cost. The more compact implementation in [1] does not use ROM and computes the twiddle factors by performing repeated multiplications. In this paper we reduce the number of multiplications by re-arranging the nested loops in the NTT computation.
2. The implementations [1,22] use negative wrapped convolution to reduce the number of evaluations in both the forward and backward NTT computations. However, the use of the negative wrapped convolution has a pre- and post-computation overhead. In this paper we basically avoid the pre-computation which reduces the cost of the forward NTT.
3. The intermediate coefficients are stored in memory (RAM) during the NTT computation. Access to the RAM is a bottleneck for speeding-up the NTT computation. In the implementations [1,22], FPGA-RAM slices are placed in parallel to avoid this bottleneck. In this paper we propose an efficient memory access scheme which reduces the number of RAM accesses, optimizes

the number of block RAMs and still achieves maximum utilization of the computational blocks.

4. The Knuth-Yao sampler [28] is slow due to the costly bit scanning operation. We reduce the cycle count using fast table lookup operations. We also optimize the area of the Knuth-Yao [28] sampler by reducing the width of the ROM. For the standard deviation 3.33 the area-optimized sampler consumes only 32 slices and is thus more compact and faster than the Bernoulli sampler in [24].

5. The proposed optimization techniques are applied to design a compact architecture for the NTT computation. We also implement pipelines in the architecture targeting high-speed applications. The pipeline technique derives an optimal pipeline depth for the architecture to achieve the fastest computation time.

6. Finally, we optimize one of the most popular ring-LWE encryption schemes by reducing the number of NTT computations from five to four, thereby achieving a nearly 20% reduction in the computation cost.

The above optimizations result in a very compact architecture that is three times smaller than the current state of the art implementation [23] and even runs somewhat faster.

The remainder of the paper is organized as follows: In Section 2 we provide a brief mathematical background on ring-LWE and the NTT. Section 3 contains our optimization techniques of the NTT and Section 4 presents the actual architecture of our optimized NTT algorithm. A pipelined architecture is given in Section 5. In Section 6, we propose an optimization of an existing ring-LWE encryption scheme and propose an efficient architecture for the complete ring-LWE encryption system. Finally, Section 7 reports on the experimental results of this implementation.

# 2    Background

In this section we present a brief mathematical overview of the ring-LWE problem, the encryption scheme we will be optimizing and the NTT.

## 2.1    The LWE and Ring-LWE Problem

The *learning with errors* (LWE) problem is a machine learning problem that is equivalent to worst-case lattice problems as shown by Regev [26] in 2005. Since then, the LWE problem has become popular as a basis for developing quantum secure lattice-based cryptosystems.

The LWE problem is parametrized by a dimension $n \geq 1$, an integer modulus $q \geq 2$ and an error distribution, typically a discrete Gaussian distribution $\mathcal{X}_\sigma$ over the integers with deviation $\sigma$ and mean 0. The probability of sampling an integer $z \in \mathbb{Z}$ in the Gaussian distribution $\mathcal{X}_\sigma$ is given by $\rho_\sigma(z)/\rho_\sigma(\mathbb{Z})$ where $\rho_\sigma(z) = \exp\left(\frac{-z^2}{2\sigma^2}\right)$ and $\rho_\sigma(\mathbb{Z}) = \sum_{z=-\infty}^{+\infty} \rho_\sigma(z)$. Note that some authors use the parameter $s = \sqrt{2\pi}\sigma$ to define the Gaussian distribution or even denote the parameter $s$ by $\sigma$ to add to the confusion.

For a uniformly chosen $\mathbf{s} \in \mathbb{Z}_q^n$, the LWE distribution $A_{s,\mathcal{X}}$ over $\mathbb{Z}_q^n \times \mathbb{Z}_q$ consists of tuples $(\mathbf{a}, t)$ where $\mathbf{a}$ is chosen uniformly from $\mathbb{Z}_q^n$ and $t = \langle \mathbf{a}, \mathbf{s} \rangle + e$ mod $q \in \mathbb{Z}_q$ and $e$ is sampled from the error distribution $\mathcal{X}$. The *search* version of the LWE problem asks to find $\mathbf{s}$ given a polynomial number of pairs $(\mathbf{a}, t)$ sampled from the LWE distribution $A_{s,\mathcal{X}}$. In the *decision* version of the LWE problem, the solver needs to distinguish with non-negligible advantage between a polynomial number of samples drawn from $A_{s,\mathcal{X}}$ and the same number of samples drawn from $\mathbb{Z}_q^n \times \mathbb{Z}_q$. For hardness proofs of the search and decision LWE problems, interested readers are referred to [15].

The initial LWE encryption system in [26] is based on matrix operations which are quite inefficient and result in large key sizes. To achieve computational efficiency and to reduce the key size, an algebraic variant of the LWE called *ring*-LWE [17] uses special structured ideal lattices. Such lattices correspond to ideals in rings $\mathbb{Z}[\mathbf{x}]/\langle f \rangle$, where $f$ is an irreducible polynomial of degree $n$. For efficiency reasons, the ring is often taken as $R_q = \mathbb{Z}_q[\mathbf{x}]/\langle f \rangle$ with $f(x) = x^n + 1$, where $n$ is a power of two and the prime $q$ is taken as $q \equiv 1$ mod $2n$. The ring-LWE distribution on $R_q \times R_q$ consists of tuples $(a, t)$ with $a \in R_q$ chosen uniformly random and $t = as + e \in R_q$, where $s \in R_q$ is a fixed secret element and $e$ has small coefficients sampled from the discrete Gaussian above. The resulting distribution on $R_q$ will also be denoted $\mathcal{X}_\sigma$.

The ring-LWE based encryption scheme that we will use was introduced in the full version of [17] and uses a global polynomial $a \in R_q$. Key generation, encryption and decryption are as follows:

1. $KeyGen(a)$ : Choose two polynomials $r_1, r_2 \in R_q$ from $\mathcal{X}_\sigma$ and compute $p = r_1 - a \cdot r_2 \in R_q$. The public key is $(a, p)$ and the private key is $r_2$. The polynomial $r_1$ is simply noise and is no longer required after key generation.
2. $Enc(a, p, m)$ : The message $m$ is first encoded to $\bar{m} \in R_q$. Three polynomials $e_1, e_2, e_3 \in R_q$ are sampled from $\mathcal{X}_\sigma$. The ciphertext then consists of two polynomials $c_1 = a \cdot e_1 + e_2$ and $c_2 = p \cdot e_1 + e_3 + \bar{m} \in R_q$.
3. $Dec(c_1, c_2, r_2)$ : Compute $m' = c_1 \cdot r_2 + c_2 \in R_q$ and recover the original message $m$ from $m'$ using a decoder.

One of the simplest encoding functions maps a binary message $m$ to the polynomial $\bar{m} \in R_q$ such that its $i$-th coefficient is $(q-1)/2$ iff the $i$-th bit of $m$ is 1 and 0 otherwise. The corresponding decoding function then simply reduces the coefficients $m'_i$ of $m'$ in the interval $(-q/2, q/2]$ and decodes to 1 when $|m'_i| > q/4$ and 0 otherwise.

## 2.2    Parameter Sets

To enable fair comparison with the state of the art [23], we have chosen to instantiate the cryptoprocessor for the same parameter sets $(n, q, s)$ (recall $s = \sqrt{2\pi}\sigma$), namely $P_1 = (256, 7681, 11.32)$ and $P_2 = (512, 12289, 12.18)$. Note that the choice of primes is not optimal for fast modular reduction. To estimate the security level offered by these two parameter sets we follow the security analysis in [16] and [14] which improves upon [15,29]. Apart from the dimension $n$, the hardness of the ring-LWE problem mainly depends on the ratio $q/\sigma$, where clearly the problem becomes easier for larger ratios. Although neither parameter set was analyzed in [16], parameter set $P_1$ is similar to the set $(256, 4093, 8.35)$ from [16] which requires $2^{105}$ seconds to break, or still over $2^{128}$ elementary operations. For paramater set $P_2$ we expect it to offer a high security level consistent with AES-256 (following [9]).

We limit the Gaussian sampler in our implementation to $12\sigma$ to obtain a negligible statistical distance ($< 2^{-90}$) from the true discrete Gaussian distribution. Although one can normally sample the secret $r_2 \in R_q$ also from the distribution $\mathcal{X}_\sigma$, we restrict $r_2$ to have binary coefficients.

## 2.3    The Number Theoretic Transform

There are many efficient algorithms in the literature to perform polynomial multiplication and a survey of fast multiplication algorithms can be found in [2]. In this section we review the Number Theoretic Transform (NTT) which corresponds to a Fast Fourier Transform (FTT) where the roots of unity are taken from a finite ring instead of the complex numbers.

**The FFT and NTT.** Recall that the n-point FFT (with $n = 2^k$) is an efficient method to evaluate a polynomial $a(x) = \sum_{j=0}^{n-1} a_j x^j \in \mathbb{Z}[x]$ in the $n$-th roots of unity $\omega_n^i$ for $i = 0, \ldots, n-1$ where $\omega_n$ denotes a primitive $n$-th root of unity. More precisely, on input the coefficients $[a_0, \ldots, a_{n-1}]$ and $\omega_n$, the FFT computes $FFT([a_j], \omega_n) = [a(\omega_n^0), a(\omega_n^1), \ldots, a(\omega_n^{n-1})]$ in $\theta(n \log n)$ time. Due to the orthogonality relations between the $n$-th roots of unity we can compute the inverse FFT simply as $\frac{1}{n} FFT(\cdot, \omega_n^{-1})$.

The NTT replaces the complex roots of unity by roots of unity in a finite ring $\mathbb{Z}_q$. Since we require elements of order $n$, $q$ is chosen to be a prime with $q \equiv 1 \mod 2n$. Note furthermore that the NTT immediately leads to a fast multiplication algorithm in the ring $S_q = \mathbb{Z}_q[x]/(x^n - 1)$: indeed, given two polynomials $a, b \in S_q$ we can easily compute their (reduced) product $c = a \cdot b \in S_q$ by computing

$$c = NTT_{\omega_n}^{-1}\left(NTT_{\omega_n}(a) * NTT_{\omega_n}(b)\right), \qquad (1)$$

where $*$ denotes point-wise multiplication.

The NTT computation is usually described as recursive, but in practice we use an in-place iterative version taken from [4] that is given in Algorithm 1. For the inverse NTT, an additional scaling of the resulting coefficients by $n^{-1}$ is performed. The factors $\omega$ used in line 8 are called the *twiddle factors*.

**Multiplication in $R_q$.** Recall that we will use $R_q = Z_q[\mathbf{x}]/\langle f \rangle$ with $f = x^n + 1$ and $n = 2^k$. Since $f(x)|x^{2n} - 1$ we could use the $2n$-point NTT to compute

**Algorithm 1:** *Iterative NTT*

---
**Input**: Polynomial $a(x) \in \mathbb{Z}_q[\mathbf{x}]$ of degree $n - 1$ and $n$-th primitive root $\omega_n \in \mathbb{Z}_q$ of unity
**Output**: Polynomial $A(x) \in \mathbb{Z}_q[\mathbf{x}] = \text{NTT}(a)$
1 **begin**
2     $A \leftarrow BitReverse(a)$;
3     **for** $m = 2$ *to* $n$ *by* $m = 2m$ **do**
4        $\omega_m \leftarrow \omega_n^{n/m}$ ;
5        $\omega \leftarrow 1$ ;
6        **for** $j = 0$ *to* $m/2 - 1$ **do**
7           **for** $k = 0$ *to* $n - 1$ *by* $m$ **do**
8              $t \leftarrow \omega \cdot A[k + j + m/2]$ ;
9              $u \leftarrow A[k + j]$ ;
10              $A[k + j] \leftarrow u + t$ ;
11              $A[k + j + m/2] \leftarrow u - t$ ;
12           **end**
13        $\omega \leftarrow \omega \cdot \omega_m$ ;
14     **end**
15   **end**
16 **end**

---

the multiplication in $R_q$ at the expense of three $2n$-point NTT computations and a reduction by trivially embedding the ring $R_q$ into $S_q$, i.e. expanding the coefficient vector of a polynomial $a \in R_q$ by adding $n$ extra zero coefficients. However, we can do much better by exploiting the special relation between the roots of $x^n + 1$ and $x^{2n} - 1$ using a technique known as the *negative wrapped convolution*.

Indeed, using the same evaluation-interpolation strategy used above for the ordinary NTT, we conclude that we can efficiently multiply two polynomials $a, b \in R_q$ if we can quickly evaluate them in the roots of $f$. These roots are simply $\omega_{2n}^{2j+1}$ for $j = 0, \ldots, n - 1$ (since the even exponents give the roots of $x^n - 1$) and as such can be written as $\omega_{2n} \cdot \omega_n^j$. These evaluations can thus be computed efficiently using a *classical* $n$-point NTT (instead of a $2n$-point NTT) on the scaled polynomials $a'(x) = a(\omega_{2n} \cdot x)$ and $b'(x) = a(\omega_{2n} \cdot x)$. The point-wise multiplication gives the evaluations of $c(x) = a(x)b(x) \bmod f(x)$ in the roots of $f$, and the classical inverse $n$-point NTT thus results in the coefficients of the scaled polynomial $c'(x) = c(\omega_{2n} \cdot x)$. To recover the coefficients $c_i$ of $c(x)$, we therefore simply have to compute $c_i = c_i' \cdot \omega_{2n}^{-i}$. Note that the scaling operation by $n^{-1}$ can be combined with the multiplications of $c_i'$ by $\omega_{2n}^{-i}$.

# 3 Optimization of the NTT Computation

In this section we optimize the NTT and compare with the recent hardware implementations of polynomial multipliers [1,22,23]. First, the fixed cost involved in computing the powers of $\omega_n$ is reduced, then the pre-computation overhead in the forward negative-wrapped convolution is optimized, and finally an efficient memory access scheme is proposed that reduces the number of memory accesses during the NTT and also minimizes the number of block RAMs in the hardware architecture.

## 3.1 Optimizing the Fixed Computation Cost

In line 13 of Algorithm 1 the computation of the twiddle factor $\omega \leftarrow \omega \cdot \omega_m$ is performed in the $j$-loop. This computation can be considered as a fixed cost. However in [1,22] the $j$-loop and the $k$-loop are interchanged, such that $\omega$ is updated in the innermost loop which is much more frequent than in Algorithm 1. To avoid the computation of the twiddle factors, in [22] all the twiddle factors are kept in a pre-computed look-up table (ROM) and are accessed whenever required. As the twiddle factors are not computed on-the-fly, the order of the two innermost loops does not result in an additional cost. However in [1] a more compact polynomial multiplier architecture is designed without using any look-up table and the twiddle factors are simply computed on-the-fly during the NTT computation. Hence in [1], the interchanged loops cause substantial additional computational overhead. In this paper our target is to design a very compact polynomial multiplier. Hence we do not use any look-up table for the twiddle factors and follow Algorithm 1 to avoid the extra computation of [1].

## 3.2 Optimizing the Forward NTT Computation Cost

Here we revisit the forward negative-wrapped convolution technique used in [1,22,23]. Recall that the negative-wrapped convolution corresponds to a classical $n$-point NTT on the scaled polynomials $a'(x) = a(\omega_{2n} \cdot x)$ and $b'(x) = (\omega_{2n} \cdot x)$. Instead of first pre-computing these scaled polynomials and then performing a classical NTT, it suffices to note that we can integrate the scaling and the NTT computation. Indeed, it suffices to change the initialization of the twiddle factors in line 5 of Algorithm 1: instead of initializing $\omega$ to 1, we can simply set $\omega = \omega_{2m}$. The rest of the algorithm remains exactly the same, and no pre-computation is necessary. Note that this optimization only applies to the NTT itself and not to the inverse NTT.

## 3.3 Optimizing the Memory Access Scheme

The NTT computation requires memory to store the input and intermediate coefficients. When the number of coefficients is large, RAM is most suitable for hardware implementation [1,22,23]. In the innermost loop (lines 8-to-11) of Algorithm 1, two coefficients $A[k+j]$ and $A[k+j+m/2]$ are first read from memory and then arithmetic operations (one multiplication, one addition and one subtraction) are performed. The new $A[k+j]$ and $A[k+j+m/2]$ are then written back to memory. During one iteration of the innermost loop, the arithmetic circuits are thus used only once, while the memory is read or written twice. This leads to idle cycles in the arithmetic circuits. The polynomial multiplier in [22] uses two parallel memory blocks to provide a continuous flow of coefficients to the arithmetic circuits. However this approach could result in under-utilization of the RAM blocks if the coefficient size is much smaller than the word size (for example in the ring-LWE cryptosystem [17]). In the literature there are many papers on efficient memory management schemes using segmentation and efficient address generation (see [18]) for the classical FFT algorithm. Another well known approach is the constant geometry FFT (or NTT) which always maintains a constant index difference between the processed coefficients [21]. However the constant geometry algorithm is not in-place and hence not suitable for resource constrained platforms. In [1] memory usage is improved by keeping two coefficients $A[k]$ and $B[k]$ of the two input polynomials $A$ and $B$ in the same memory location. We propose a memory access scheme which is designed to minimize the number of block RAM slices and to achieve maximum utilization of computational circuits present in the NTT architecture.

Since the two coefficients $A[k+j]$ and $A[k+j+m/2]$ are processed together in Algorithm 1, we keep the two coefficients as a pair in one memory location.

Let us analyze two consecutive iterations of the $m$-loop (line 3 in Algorithm 1) for $m = m_1$ and $m = m_2$ where $m_2 = 2m_1$. In the $m_1$-loop, for some $j_1$ and $k_1$ (maintaining the loop bounds in Algorithm 1) the coefficients $(A[k_1 + j_1], A[k_1 + j_1 + m_1/2])$ are processed as a pair. Then $k$ increments to $k_1 + m_1$ and the processed coefficient pair is $(A[k_1 + m_1 + j_1], A[k_1 + m_1 + j_1 + m_1/2])$. Now from Algorithm 1 we see that the coefficient $A[k_1 + j_1]$ will again be processed in the $m_2$-loop with coefficient $A[k_1 + j_1 + m_2/2]$. Since $m_2 = 2m_1$, the coefficient $A[k_1 + j_1 + m_2/2]$ is the coefficient $A[k_1 + j_1 + m_1]$ which is updated in the $m_1$-loop for $k = k_1 + m_1$. Hence during the $m_1$-loop if we swap the updated coefficients for $k = k_1$ and $k = k_1 + m_1$ and store $(A[k_1 + j_1], A[k_1 + j_1 + m_1])$ and $(A[k_1 + j_1 + m_1/2], A[k_1 + j_1 + 3m_1/2])$ as the coefficient pairs in memory, then the coefficients in a pair have a difference of $m_2/2$ in their index and thus are ready for the $m_2$-loop. The operations during the two consecutive iterations $k = k_1$ and $k = k_1 + m_1$ during $m = m_1$ are shown in Algorithm 2 in lines 8-15. During the operations $u_1$, $t_1$, $u_2$ and $t_2$ are used as temporary storage registers.

A complete description of the efficient memory access scheme is given in Algorithm 2. In this algorithm for all values of $m < n$, two coefficient pairs are processed in the innermost loop and a swap of the updated coefficients is performed before writing back to memory. For $m = n$, no swap operation is required as this is the final iteration of the $m$-loop. The coefficient pairs generated by Algorithm 2 can be re-arranged easily for another (say inverse) NTT operation by performing address-wise bit-reverse-swap operation. Appendix A describes the memory access scheme using an example.

# 4    The NTT Processor Organization

In this section we present an architecture for performing the forward and backward NTT using the proposed optimization techniques. Our NTT processor (Figure 1) consists of three main components: the arithmetic unit, the memory block and the control-address unit.

**The Memory Block** is implemented as a simple dual port RAM. To accommodate two coefficients, the word size is $2\lceil \log q \rceil$ where $q$ is the prime modulus.

**Algorithm 2**: *Iterative NTT : Memory Efficient Version*

**Input**: Polynomial $a(x) \in \mathbb{Z}_q[\mathbf{x}]$ of degree $n - 1$ and $n$-th primitive root $\omega_n \in \mathbb{Z}_q$ of unity
**Output**: Polynomial $A(x) \in \mathbb{Z}_q[\mathbf{x}] = \text{NTT}(a)$
1 **begin**
2     $A \leftarrow BitReverse(a)$; /* Coefficients are stored in the memory as proper pairs */
3     **for** $m = 2$ *to* $n/2$ *by* $m = 2m$ **do**
4         $\omega_m \leftarrow m$-th primitiveroot(1) ;
5         $\omega \leftarrow squareroot(\omega_m)$ or 1 /* Depending on forward or backward NTT */ ;
6         **for** $j = 0$ *to* $m/2 - 1$ **do**
7             **for** $k = 0$ *to* $n/2 - 1$ *by* $m$ **do**
8                 $(t_1, u_1) \leftarrow (A[k + j + m/2], A[k + j])$ /* From MEMORY[k+j] */ ;
9                 $(t_2, u_2) \leftarrow (A[k + m + j + m/2], A[k + m + j])$ /* MEMORY[k+j+m/2] */ ;
10                 $t_1 \leftarrow \omega \cdot t_1$ ;
11                 $t_2 \leftarrow \omega \cdot t_2$ ;
12                 $(A[k + j + m/2], A[k + j]) \leftarrow (u_1 - t_1, u_1 + t_1)$ ;
13                 $(A[k + m + j + m/2], A[k + m + j]) \leftarrow (u_2 - t_2, u_2 + t_2)$ ;
14                 $MEMORY[k + j] \leftarrow (A[k + j + m], A[k + j])$ ;
15                 $MEMORY[k + j + m/2] \leftarrow (A[k + j + 3m/2], A[k + j + m/2])$ ;
16             **end**
17             $\omega \leftarrow \omega \cdot \omega_n$ ;
18         **end**
19     **end**
20     $m \leftarrow n$ ;
21     $k \leftarrow 0$ ;
22     $\omega \leftarrow squareroot(\omega_m)$ or 1 /* Depending on forward or backward NTT */ ;
23     **for** $j = 0$ *to* $m/2 - 1$ **do**
24         $(t_1, u_1) \leftarrow (A[j + m/2], A[j])$ /* From MEMORY[j] */ ;
25         $t_1 \leftarrow \omega \cdot t_1$ ;
26         $(A[j + m/2], A[j]) \leftarrow (u_1 - t_1, u_1 + t_1)$ ;
27         $MEMORY[j] \leftarrow (A[j + m/2], A[j])$ ;
28         $\omega \leftarrow \omega \cdot \omega_m$ ;
29     **end**
30 **end**

In FPGAs, a RAM can be implemented as a *distributed* or as a *block* RAM. When the amount of data is large, block RAM is the ideal choice.

**The Arithmetic Unit (NTT-ALU)** is designed to support Algorithm 2 along with other operations such as polynomial addition, point-wise multiplication and rearrangement of the coefficients. This NTT-ALU is interfaced with the memory block and the control-address unit. The central part of the NTT-ALU consists of a modular multiplier and addition/subtraction circuits.

Now we describe how the different components of the NTT-ALU are used during the butterfly steps (excluding the last loop for $m = n$). First, the memory location $(k + j)$ is fetched and then the fetched data $(t_1, u_1)$ is stored in the input register pair $(H_1, L_1)$. The same also happens for the memory location $(k + j + m/2)$ in the next cycle. The multiplier computes $\omega \cdot H_1$ and the result is added to or subtracted from $L_1$ using the adder and subtracter circuits to compute $(u_1 + \omega t_1)$ and $(u_1 - \omega t_1)$ respectively. In the next cycle the register pair $(R_1, R_4)$ is updated with $(u_1 - \omega t_1, u_1 + \omega t_1)$. Another clock transition shifts the contents of $(R_1, R_4)$ to $(R_2, R_5)$. In this cycle the pair $(R_1, R_4)$ is updated with $(u_2 - \omega t_2, u_2 + \omega t_2)$ as the computation involving $(u_2, t_2)$ from the location $(k + j + m/2)$ lags by one cycle. Now the memory location $(k + j)$ is updated with the register pair $(R_4, R_5)$ containing $(u_2 + \omega t_2, u_1 + \omega t_1)$.

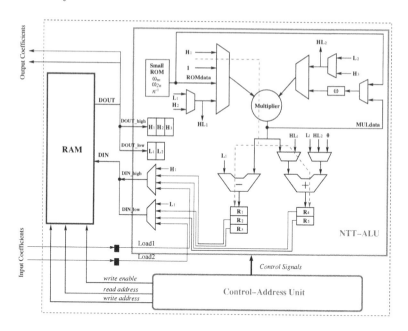

**Fig. 1.** Hardware Architecture for NTT

Finally, in the next cycle the memory location $(k + j + m/2)$ is updated with $(u_2 - \omega t_2, u_1 - \omega t_1)$ using the register pair $(R_2, R_3)$. The execution of the *last* $m$-loop is similar to the intermediate loops, without any data swap between the output registers. The register pair $(R_2, R_5)$ is used for updating the memory locations. In Figure 1, the additional registers $(H_2, H_3$ and $L_2)$ and multiplexers are used for supporting operations such as addition, point-wise multiplication and rearrangement of polynomials. The Small-ROM block contains the fixed values $\omega_m$, $\omega_{2n}$, their inverses and $n^{-1}$. This ROM has depth of order $\log(n)$.

**The Control-and-Address Unit** consists of three counters for $m$, $j$ and $k$ in Algorithm 2 and comparators to check the terminal conditions during the execution of any loop. The read address is computed from $m$, $j$ and $k$ and then delayed using registers to generate the write address. The control-and-address unit also generates the write enable signal for the RAM and the control signals for the NTT-ALU.

## 5  Pipelining the NTT Processor

The maximum frequency of the NTT-ALU is determined by the critical path (red dashed line in Figure 1) that passes through the modular multiplier and the adder (or subtracter) circuits . To increase the operating frequency of the processor, we implement efficient pipelines based on the following two observations.

**Observation 1.** During the execution of any $m$-loop in Algorithm 2, the computations (multiplication, addition and subtraction) involving a coefficient pair have no data dependency on other coefficient pairs. Such a data-flow structure is suitable for pipeline processing as different computations can be pipelined without inserting bubbles in the datapath.

Assume that the modular multiplier has $d_m$ pipeline stages and that the output is latched in a buffer. In the $(d_m + 1)$th cycle after the initialisation of $\omega \cdot t_1$, the buffer is updated with the result $\omega \cdot t_1$. Now we need to compute $u_1 + \omega \cdot t_1$ and $u_1 - \omega \cdot t_1$ using the adder and subtracter circuits. Hence we delay the data $u_1$ by $d_m$ cycles so that it appears as an input to the adder and subtracter circuits in the $(d_m + 1)$th cycle. This delay operation is performed with the help of a shift register $L_1, \ldots, L_{d_m+1}$ as shown in Figure 2.

**Observation 2.** Every increment of $j$ in Algorithm 2 requires a new $\omega$ (line 17). If the multiplier has $d_m$ pipeline stages, then the register-$\omega$ in Figure 1 is updated with the new value of $\omega$ in the $(d_m + 2)$th cycle. Since this new $\omega$ is used by the next butterfly operations, the data dependency results in an interruption in the chain of butterfly operations for $d_m + 1$ cycles. In any $m$-loop, the total number of such *interruption cycles* is $(m/2 - 1) \cdot (d_m + 1)$.

To reduce the number of interruption cycles, we use a small look-up table to store a few twiddle factors. Let the look-up table (red dashed rectangle in

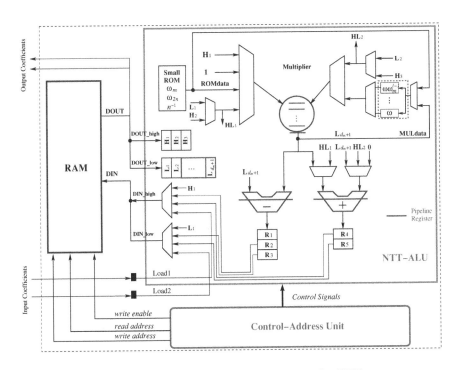

**Fig. 2.** Pipelined Hardware Architecture for NTT

Figure 2) have $l$ registers containing the twiddle factors $(\omega, \ldots \omega \omega_m^{l-1})$. This look-up table is used to provide the twiddle factors during the butterfly operations for say $j = j'$ to $j = j' + l - 1$. The next time $j$ increments, new twiddle factors are required for the butterfly operations. We multiply the look-up table with $\omega_m^l$ to compute the next $l$ twiddle factors $(\omega \omega_m^l, \ldots \omega \omega_m^{2l-1})$. The multiplications are independent of each other and hence can be processed in a pipeline. The butterfly operations are resumed after $\omega \omega_m^l$ is loaded in the look-up table. Thus using a small-look-up table of size $l$ we reduce the number of interruption cycles to $(\frac{m}{2l} - 1) \cdot (d_m + 1)$. In our architecture we use $l = 4$; a larger value of $l$ will reduce the number of interruption cycles, but will cost additional registers.

**Optimal Pipeline Strategy for Speed.** During the execution of any $m$-loop in Algorithm 2, the number of butterfly operations is $n/2$. In the pipelined NTT-ALU, the cycle requirement for the $n/2$ butterfly operations is slightly larger than $n/2$ due to an initial overhead. The state machine jumps to the $\omega$ calculation state $\frac{m}{2l} - 1$ times resulting in $(\frac{m}{2l} - 1) \cdot (d_m + 1)$ interruption cycles. Hence the total number of cycles spent in executing any $m$-loop can be approximated as shown below:

$$Cycles_m \approx \frac{n}{2} + (\frac{m}{2l} - 1) \cdot (d_m + 1)$$

Let us assume that the delay of the critical path with no pipeline stages is $D_{comb}$. When the critical path is split in balanced-delay stages using pipelines, the resulting delay $(D_s)$ can be approximated as $\frac{D_{comb}}{(d_m + d_a)}$, where $d_m$ and $d_a$ are the number of pipeline stages in the modular multiplier and the modular adder (subtracter) respectively. Since the delay of the modular adder is small compared to the modular multiplier, we have $d_a \ll d_m$. Now the computation time for the $m$-loop is approximated as

$$T_m \approx \frac{D_{comb}}{(d_m + d_a)} \left[ \frac{n}{2} + (\frac{m}{2l} - 1) \cdot (d_m + 1) \right] \approx D_s \frac{n}{2} + C_m.$$

Here $C_m$ is constant (assuming $d_a \ll d_m$) for a fixed value of $m$. From the above equation we find that the minimum computation time can be achieved when $D_s$ is minimum. Hence we pipeline the datapath to achieve minimum $D_s$. The DSP based coefficient multiplier is optimally pipelined using the Xilinx IPCore tool, while the modular reduction block is suitably pipelined by placing registers between the cascaded adder and subtracter circuits.

# 6    The Ring-LWE Encryption Scheme

The ring-LWE encryption scheme in [23] optimizes computation cost by keeping the fixed polynomials in the NTT domain. The message encryption and decryption operations require three and two NTT computations respectively. In this paper we reduce the number of NTT operations for decryption from two to *one*. The proposed ring-LWE encryption scheme is described below:

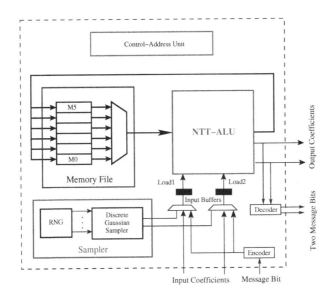

**Fig. 3.** Ring-LWE Cryptoprocessor

1. $KeyGen(a)$ : Choose a polynomial $r_1 \in R_q$ from $\mathcal{X}_\sigma$, choose another polynomial $r_2$ with binary coefficients and then compute $p = r_1 - a \cdot r_2 \in R_q$. The NTT is performed on the three polynomials $a$, $p$ and $r_2$ to generate $\tilde{a}$, $\tilde{p}$ and $\tilde{r_2}$. The public key is $(\tilde{a}, \tilde{p})$ and the private key is $\tilde{r_2}$.
2. $Enc(\tilde{a}, \tilde{p}, m)$: The message $m$ is first encoded to $\bar{m} \in R_q$. Three polynomials $e_1, e_2, e_3 \in R_q$ are sampled from $\mathcal{X}_\sigma$. The ciphertext is then computed as:

$$\tilde{e}_1 \leftarrow NTT(e_1); \quad \tilde{e}_2 \leftarrow NTT(e_2)$$
$$(\tilde{c}_1, \tilde{c}_2) \leftarrow \left(\tilde{a} * \tilde{e}_1 + \tilde{e}_2; \; \tilde{p} * \tilde{e}_1 + NTT(e_3 + \bar{m})\right)$$

3. $Dec(\tilde{c}_1, \tilde{c}_2, \tilde{r}_2)$ : Compute $m'$ as $m' = INTT(\tilde{c}_1 * \tilde{r}_2 + \tilde{c}_2) \in R_q$ and recover the original message $m$ from $m'$ using a decoder.

The scheme requires both encryption and decryption to use a common primitive root of unity.

### 6.1   Hardware Architecture for the Ring-LWE Encryption Scheme

Figure 3 shows a hardware architecture for the ring-LWE encryption system. The basic building blocks used in the architecture are: the memory file, the arithmetic unit, the discrete Gaussian sampler and the control-address generation unit. The arithmetic unit is the NTT-ALU that we described in the previous section. Here we briefly describe the memory file and the discrete Gaussian sampler.

**The Memory File** is designed to support the maximum memory requirement that occurs during the encryption of the message. Six memory blocks $M_0$ to $M_5$ are available in the memory file and are used to store $\bar{a}$, $\bar{p}$, $e_1$, $e_2$, $e_3$ and $\bar{m}$

respectively. The memory blocks have width $2\lceil\log q\rceil$ bits and depth $n/2$. All six memory blocks share a common read and a write address and have a common data-input line, while their data-outputs are selected through a multiplexer. Any of the memory blocks in the memory file can be chosen for read and write operation. Due to the common addressing of the memory blocks, the memory file supports one read and one write operation in every cycle.

**The Discrete Gaussian Sampler** is based on the compact Knuth-Yao sampler [13] architecture proposed in [28] and have sufficiently large precision and tail-bound to satisfy a maximum statistical distance of $2^{-90}$ to a true discrete Gaussian distribution for both $s = 11.32$ and $s = 12.18$. Though the sampler in [28] is very compact it is also quite slow due to sequential scanning of the probability bits. We improve the cycle requirement of the sampler using two look-up tables. The first lookup table directly maps eight parallel random bits into a sample value or an intermediate distance in the 8th column of the probability matrix [28]. A successful look-up operation returns a sample and the sign of the sample is determined by the 9th random bit. If the first look-up operation fails, then another lookup is performed in the next 5 columns to get a sample value or an intermediate distance in the 13th column of the probability matrix. When the second lookup operation fails (probability<0.0016) then bit-scan based Knuth-Yao random walk [28] is started with the initial distance obtained from the second lookup operation.

**The Cycle Count** for the encryption and decryption operations can be minimized in the following way. During the encryption operation, first the three error polynomials $e_1$, $e_2$ and $e_3$ are generated by invoking the discrete Gaussian sampler $3n$ times. Next the encoded message $\bar{m}$ is added to $e_3$ and then three consecutive forward NTT operations are performed on $e_1$, $e_2$ and $(e_3 + \bar{m})$. Finally the ciphertext $\tilde{c}_1$, $\tilde{c}_2$ is obtained using two coefficient-wise multiplications followed by two polynomial additions and two rearrangement operations. The decryption operation requires one coefficient-wise multiplication, one polynomial addition and finally one inverse NTT operation.

During the encryption operation, $3n$ samples are generated to construct the three error polynomials. Our fast Knuth-Yao sampler architecture requires 805 and 1644 cycles for the dimensions 256 and 512 respectively on average to generate the three error polynomials. The polynomial addition and point-wise multiplication operations require $n$ cycles each with a small overhead. The consecutive processing of $I$ forward NTTs share a fixed computation cost $fc_{fwd}$ and require in total $fc_{fwd} + I \times \frac{n}{2}\log(n)$ cycles. Similarly $I$ consecutive inverse NTTs are processed in $fc_{inv} + I \times \frac{n}{2}\log(n) + I \times n$ cycles. One interesting point is that the fixed cost $fc_{inv}$ is larger than $fc_{fwd}$ as it includes the computation of $\omega_{2n}^i/N$ (Section 2.3) for $i = (0\ldots n-1)$. This observation has been used to optimize the overall ring-LWE based encryption scheme in Section 6. The additional $I \times n$ cycles during the inverse NTTs are required to multiply the coefficients by the scaling factors. The rearrangement of polynomial coefficients after an NTT operation requires less than $n$ cycles. From the above cycle counts for each primitive operations, we see that the encryption and decryption operations require total

Table 1. Performance and Comparison

| Implementation Algorithm | Parameters | Device | LUTs/FFs/ DSPs/BRAM18 | Freq (MHz) | Cycles/Time($\mu s$) Encryption | Cycles/Time($\mu s$) Decryption |
|---|---|---|---|---|---|---|
| Our RLWE | (256,7681,11.32) | V6LX75T | 1349/860/1/2 | 313 | 6.3k/20.1 | 2.8k/9.1 |
| Our RLWE | (512,12289,12.18) | | 1536/953/1/3 | 278 | 13.3k/47.9 | 5.8k/21 |
| RLWE [23] | (256,7681,11.32) | V6LX75T | 4549/3624/1/12 | 262 | 6.8k/26.2 | 4.4k/16.8 |
| RLWE | (512,12289,12.18) | V6LX75T | 5595/4760/1/14 | 251 | 13.7k/54.8 | 8.8k/35.4 |
| RLWE-Enc[24] | (256,4096,8.35) | S6LX9 | 317/238/95/1 | 144 | 136k/946 | - |
| RLWE-Dec | | | 112/87/32/1 | 189 | - | 66k/351 |
| ECC[3] | Binary-233 | V5LX85T | 18097/-/5644/0 | 156 | 1.9k/12.3 | 1.9k/12.3 |
| NTRU[12] | NTRU-251 | XCV1600E | 27292/5160/14352/0 | 62.3 | -/1.54 | -/1.41 |

$fc_{fwd} + \frac{3}{2}n \log(n) + 10n$ and $fc_{inv} + \frac{n}{2} \log(n) + 3n$ cycles respectively along with additional overhead. Our ring-LWE architecture has the fixed computation costs $fc_{fwd} = 667$ and $fc_{inv} = 1048$ cycles for $n = 256$; and $fc_{fwd} = 1139$ and $fc_{inv} = 1959$ cycles for $n = 512$.

# 7    Experimental Results

We have implemented the proposed ring-LWE cryptosystem on the Xilinx Virtex 6 FPGA for the parameter sets $(n, q, s) : (256,7681,11.32)$ and $(512,12289,12.18)$. The area and performance results are obtained from the Xilinx ISE12.2 tool after place and route analysis and are shown in Table 1. In the table we also compare our results with other reported hardware implementations of the ring-LWE encryption scheme. The HDL codes of our ring-LWE processors are freely available and the results can be verified by the research community [1].

Our implementations are both fast and small thanks to the proposed computational optimizations and resource efficient design style. The cycle counts shown in the table do not include the cycles for data loading or reading operations. Our Knuth-Yao samplers have less than $2^{-90}$ statistical distances from the corresponding true discrete Gaussian distributions and consume around 164 LUTs and have delay less than $2.5ns$ (with optimization goal for speed). Such a small delay makes the sampler suitable for integration in the pipelined ring-LWE processor under a single clock domain. We use nine parallel true random bit generators [8,6] to generate the random bits for the sampler. The set of true random bit generators consumes 378 LUTs and 9 FFs.

The first hardware implementation of the ring-LWE encryption scheme in [9] uses a heavily parallel architecture to minimize the number of clock cycles for the NTT computation. Due to the many parallel computational blocks, the architecture is very large (0.29 million LUTs and 0.14 million FFs for $n = 256$) and does not even fit on the largest FPGA of the Virtex 6 family. Performance results such as cycle count and frequency are not reported in their paper. The ar-

---

[1] Please contact the first author of the paper for the HDL codes.

chitecture uses a Gaussian distributed array for sampling of the error coefficients up to a tail-bound of $\pm 2s$.

The implementation in [23] is small and fast due to its resource-efficient design style. A high operating frequency is achieved using pipelines in the architecture. The architecture uses a ROM that keeps all the twiddle factors required during the NTT operation. This approach reduces the fixed computation cost $(fc)$ but consumes block RAM slices in FPGAs. Additionally, the parallel RAM blocks in the NTT processor result in a larger memory requirement compared to our design. The discrete Gaussian sampler is based on the inversion sampling method [5] and has a maximum statistical distance of $2^{-22}$ to a true discrete Gaussian distribution. Since the inversion sampling requires many random bits to output a sample value, an AES core is used as a pseudo-random number generator. The AES core itself consumes an additional 803 LUTs and 341 FFs compared to our true random number generator. Another reason behind the larger area consumption of [23] compared to our architecture is due to the fact that the architecture supports different parameter sets at synthesis time. Our ring-LWE processor is also designed to achieve scalability for various parameter sets. In our architecture the control block remains the same; while only the data-width and the modular reduction block changes for different parameter sets. Hence our architecture is also configurable by generating the HDL codes for various parameter sets using a C program.

Although our architecture does not use a dedicated ROM for storing the twiddle factors, it still achieves slightly smaller cycle count and faster computation time compared to [23]. The encryption scheme in [23] computes one forward and two inverse NTTs; while our encryption scheme computes only forward NTTs and hence does not require the $4n$ cycles for the scaling operation. Additionally our negative convolution method is free from the precomputation that takes $n$ cycles in [23]. Hence we save $5n$ cycles in total during the NTT operations in an encryption operation. Since the fixed computation cost $fc_{fwd}$ is smaller than $5n$, we gain in cycle count for the encryption operation. The decryption operation in our case is trivially faster than [23] as only one NTT is performed. We also reduce the area and memory requirement significantly compared to [9,23]. This reduction is achieved by our resource-efficient design decisions such as 1) absence of a dedicated ROM for the twiddle factors, 2) an efficient RAM access and storage scheme, 3) use of one modular multiplier, 4) use of a smaller and faster (low-delay) discrete Gaussian sampler, and finally 5) the resource sharing between different computations.

A very recent paper [24] proposes ring-LWE encryption and decryption architectures targeting small area at the cost of performance. The implementation uses a quadratic-complexity multiplier instead of a complicated NTT based polynomial multiplier. Additionally the special modulus also saves some amount of area as the modular reduction is free of cost. However if we consider a similar quadratic-complexity multiplication based architecture in the dimension $n = 512$, then the cycle requirement will be nearly 40 times compared to our NTT-based ring-LWE processor. Our target was to use FPGA resources more efficiently without affecting the performance and to achieve similar speed as [23]. The paper [24] also designs a compact Bernoulli sampler that consumes 37 slices for the standard deviation 3.33 and is thus smaller in area compared to the Knuth-Yao sampler in [28]. The Bernoulli sampler requires on average 96 random bits and 144 cycles to output a sample. In the contrast the Knuth-Yao sampler [28] requires on average 5 random bits and 17 cycles per sample and is thus faster than the Bernoulli sampler. In this paper we have reduced the area consumption of the Knuth-Yao sampler [28] by reducing the width of the ROM and the scan-register from 32 bits to 12 bits and by simplifying the control unit. These area optimizations do not affect the cycle requirement of the sampler, but result in an area of only 32 slices for the overall sampler. The area optimized Knuth-Yao sampler is both smaller and faster compared to the Bernoulli sampler in [24].

We also compare our results with other cryptosystems such as ECC and NTRU. The ECC processor [3] over the NIST recommended binary field $GF(2^{233})$ requires 12.3 $\mu s$ to compute one scalar multiplication and is faster than our ring-LWE processor. However the ECC processor is designed to achieve high speed and hence consumes very large area compared to our ring-LWE processor. The NTRU scheme [12] is much faster than our ring-LWE processor due to its less complicated arithmetic. However the parameters chosen for the implementation in [12] have security around 64 bits [11]. Though secure parameter sets for the NTRU based encryption have been proposed in [10], no hardware implementation for the secure parameter sets is available in the literature.

# 8 Conclusion

This paper proposed several optimizations for implementing a ring-LWE based encryption system. The first set of optimizations improved the NTT by reducing the computation cost of the twiddle factors, avoiding the pre-computation during the forward NTT, and deriving an efficient memory access scheme that increases the utilization of the arithmetic components and the memory blocks. A further optimization reduced the number of NTTs required in the encryption scheme from five to four. The proposed optimizations are implemented in an efficient cryptoprocessor for the ring-LWE encryption system that not only is three times smaller in area and memory than any other reported implementations, but also even faster. These features make the architecture suitable for resource constrained platforms. Furthermore, the paper investigated architectural acceleration to meet the high speed requirement for real-time applications and proposes an optimal pipeline strategy that results in a very fast computation time whilst using minimum area and memory. Although the paper focuses on implementation of the ring-LWE based encryption system, we finally remark that the proposed optimization techniques for the NTT computation are applicable for other lattice based cryptosystems where similar polynomial multiplications are performed.

**Acknowledgment.** This work was supported by the Research Council KU Leuven: TENSE (GOA/11/007), by iMinds, by the European Union Seventh Framework Programme (FP7/2007-2013) under grant agreement n. 609611 (PRACTICE), by the Flemish Government, FWO G.0550.12N, by the Hercules Foundation AKUL/11/19. The first author is supported by the Erasmus Mundus PhD Scholarship. We are thankful to Bohan Yang and Vladimir Rozic for useful technical discussions related to memory utilisation and random number generation.

# References

1. Aysu, A., Patterson, C., Schaumont, P.: Low-cost and Area-efficient FPGA Implementations of Lattice-based Cryptography. In: HOST, pp. 81–86. IEEE (2013)
2. Bernstein, D.: Fast Multiplication and its Applications. Algorithmic Number Theory 44, 325–384 (2008)
3. Rebeiro, C., Roy, S.S., Mukhopadhyay, D.: Pushing the Limits of High-Speed $GF(2^m)$ Elliptic Curve Scalar Multiplication on FPGAs. In: Prouff, E., Schaumont, P. (eds.) CHES 2012. LNCS, vol. 7428, pp. 494–511. Springer, Heidelberg (2012)
4. Cormen, T., Leiserson, C., Rivest, R.: Introduction To Algorithms, http://staff.ustc.edu.cn/~csli/graduate/algorithms/book6/toc.htm
5. Devroye, L.: Non-Uniform Random Variate Generation. Springer-Verlag, New York (1986)
6. Dichtl, M., Golić, J.D.: High-Speed True Random Number Generation with Logic Gates Only. In: Paillier, P., Verbauwhede, I. (eds.) CHES 2007. LNCS, vol. 4727, pp. 45–62. Springer, Heidelberg (2007)
7. Frederiksen, T.: A Practical Implementation of Regev's LWE-based Cryptosystem (2010), http://daimi.au.dk/jot2re/lwe/resources/
8. Golic, J.D.: New Methods for Digital Generation and Postprocessing of Random Data. IEEE Transactions on Computers 55(10), 1217–1229 (2006)
9. Göttert, N., Feller, T., Schneider, M., Buchmann, J., Huss, S.: On the Design of Hardware Building Blocks for Modern Lattice-Based Encryption Schemes. In: Prouff, E., Schaumont, P. (eds.) CHES 2012. LNCS, vol. 7428, pp. 512–529. Springer, Heidelberg (2012)
10. Hirschhorn, P., Hoffstein, J., Howgrave-graham, N., Whyte, W.: Choosing NTRU-Encrypt parameters in light of combined lattice reduction and MITM approaches. In: Abdalla, M., Pointcheval, D., Fouque, P.-A., Vergnaud, D. (eds.) ACNS 2009. LNCS, vol. 5536, pp. 437–455. Springer, Heidelberg (2009)
11. Howgrave-Graham, N.: A Hybrid Lattice-Reduction and Meet-in-the-Middle Attack Against NTRU. In: Menezes, A. (ed.) CRYPTO 2007. LNCS, vol. 4622, pp. 150–169. Springer, Heidelberg (2007)
12. Kamal, A., Youssef, A.: An FPGA implementation of the NTRUEncrypt cryptosystem. In: 2009 International Conference on Microelectronics (ICM), pp. 209–212 (December 2009)
13. Knuth, D.E., Yao, A.C.: The Complexity of Non-Uniform Random Number Generation. In: Algorithms and Complexity, pp. 357–428 (1976)
14. Lepoint, T., Naehrig, M.: A Comparison of the Homomorphic Encryption Schemes FV and YASHE. IACR Cryptology ePrint Archive, 2014:62 (2014)

15. Lindner, R., Peikert, C.: Better Key Sizes (and Attacks) for LWE-based Encryption. In: Kiayias, A. (ed.) CT-RSA 2011. LNCS, vol. 6558, pp. 319–339. Springer, Heidelberg (2011)
16. Liu, M., Nguyen, P.Q.: Solving BDD by enumeration: An update. In: Dawson, E. (ed.) CT-RSA 2013. LNCS, vol. 7779, pp. 293–309. Springer, Heidelberg (2013)
17. Lyubashevsky, V., Peikert, C., Regev, O.: On Ideal Lattices and Learning with Errors over Rings. In: Gilbert, H. (ed.) EUROCRYPT 2010. LNCS, vol. 6110, pp. 1–23. Springer, Heidelberg (2010)
18. Ma, Y., Wanhammar, L.: A Hardware Efficient Control of Memory Addressing for High-performance FFT Processors. IEEE Transactions on Signal Processing 48(3), 917–921 (2000)
19. Micciancio, D.: Lattices in Cryptography and Cryptanalysis (2002)
20. Nguyên, P.Q., Stern, J.: The Two Faces of Lattices in Cryptology. In: Silverman, J.H. (ed.) CaLC 2001. LNCS, vol. 2146, pp. 146–180. Springer, Heidelberg (2001)
21. Pollard, J.: The Fast Fourier Transform in a Finite Field. Mathematics of Computation 25, 365–374 (1971)
22. Pöppelmann, T., Güneysu, T.: Towards Efficient Arithmetic for Lattice-Based Cryptography on Reconfigurable Hardware. In: Hevia, A., Neven, G. (eds.) LatinCrypt 2012. LNCS, vol. 7533, pp. 139–158. Springer, Heidelberg (2012)
23. Pöppelmann, T., Güneysu, T.: Towards Practical Lattice-Based Public-Key Encryption on Reconfigurable Hardware. In: Lange, T., Lauter, K., Lisoněk, P. (eds.) SAC 2013. LNCS, vol. 8282, pp. 68–85. Springer, Heidelberg (2014)
24. Pöppelmann, T., Güneysu, T.: Area Optimization of Lightweight Lattice-Based Encryption on Reconfigurable Hardware. In: Proc. of the IEEE International Symposium on Circuits and Systems, ISCAS 2014 ( preprint, 2014)
25. Regev, O.: Quantum Computation and Lattice Problems. SIAM J. Comput. 33(3), 738–760 (2004)
26. Regev, O.: On Lattices, Learning with Errors, Random Linear Codes, and Cryptography. In: Proceedings of the Thirty-Seventh Annual ACM Symposium on Theory of Computing, STOC 2005, pp. 84–93. ACM, New York (2005)
27. Regev, O.: Lattice-Based Cryptography. In: Dwork, C. (ed.) CRYPTO 2006. LNCS, vol. 4117, pp. 131–141. Springer, Heidelberg (2006)
28. Sinha Roy, S., Vercauteren, F., Verbauwhede, I.: High Precision Discrete Gaussian Sampling on FPGAs. In: Lange, T., Lauter, K., Lisoněk, P. (eds.) SAC 2013. LNCS, vol. 8282, pp. 383–401. Springer, Heidelberg (2014)
29. van de Pol, J., Smart, N.P.: Estimating key sizes for high dimensional lattice-based systems. In: Stam, M. (ed.) IMACC 2013. LNCS, vol. 8308, pp. 290–303. Springer, Heidelberg (2013)

# Appendix A

Table 2 shows the memory contents during the execution of Algorithm 2 for $n = 16$. The column-heading represents $(m, j, k)$ during the iterations. The end loop in line 19 of Algorithm 2 for $m = 16$ performs no swap and is shown in the table using $\star$ symbol.

# Appendix B

Our ring-LWE cryptoprocessor has one instruction-register, one iteration-register, one read-memory-index-queue and one write-memory-index-queue (Figure 4).

**Table 2.** Memory content during the steps in a 16-point NTT

| Address | Initial | (2,0,0) | (2,0,6) | (4,0,0) | (4,0,4) | (4,1,4) | (8,3,0) | (16,7,0)⋆ |
|---|---|---|---|---|---|---|---|---|
| 0 | $A_1\ A_0$ | $A_2\ A_0$ | $A_2\ A_0$ | $A_4\ A_0$ | $A_4\ A_0$ | $A_4\ A_0$ | $A_8\ A_0$ | $A_8\ A_0$ |
| 1 | $A_3\ A_2$ | $A_3\ A_1$ | $A_3\ A_1$ | | | $A_5\ A_1$ | $A_9\ A_1$ | $A_9\ A_1$ |
| 2 | $A_5\ A_4$ | | $A_6\ A_4$ | $A_6\ A_2$ | $A_6\ A_2$ | $A_6\ A_2$ | $A_{10}\ A_2$ | $A_{10}\ A_2$ |
| 3 | $A_7\ A_6$ | | $A_7\ A_5$ | | | $A_7\ A_3$ | $A_{11}\ A_3$ | $A_{11}\ A_3$ |
| 4 | $A_9\ A_8$ | | $A_{10}\ A_8$ | | $A_{12}\ A_8$ | $A_{12}\ A_8$ | $A_{12}\ A_4$ | $A_{12}\ A_4$ |
| 5 | $A_{11}\ A_{10}$ | | $A_{11}\ A_9$ | | | $A_{13}\ A_9$ | $A_{13}\ A_5$ | $A_{13}\ A_5$ |
| 6 | $A_{13}\ A_{12}$ | | $A_{14}\ A_{12}$ | | $A_{14}\ A_{10}$ | $A_{14}\ A_{10}$ | $A_{14}\ A_6$ | $A_{14}\ A_6$ |
| 7 | $A_{15}\ A_{14}$ | | $A_{15}\ A_{13}$ | | | $A_{15}\ A_{11}$ | $A_{15}\ A_7$ | $A_{15}\ A_7$ |

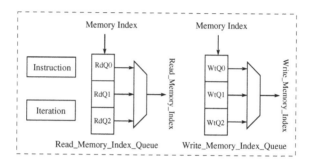

**Fig. 4.** Instruction Execution Hardware

The read and write memory-index-queues are loaded with the memory indexes. Since our ring-LWE cryptoprocessor has six memory blocks $M0$ to $M5$, the indexes are in the range 0 to 5. The instruction is stored in the *Instruction* register and the number ($I$) of consecutive NTT operations is kept in the *Iteration* register. The following instructions are supported by the processor.

1. LOAD : A memory block indexed by $WtQ0$ is loaded with $n$ coefficients. Since two coefficients are processed in a cycle, the instruction takes $n/2 + \epsilon$ cycles.
2. ENCODE-LOAD : A memory block indexed by $WtQ0$ is loaded with an encoded message. The input message bits are first encoded using the encoder and then loaded in the memory block as proper coefficient-pairs. This instruction requires $n + \epsilon$ cycles.
3. GAUSSIAN-LOAD : A memory block indexed by $WtQ0$ is loaded with $n$ samples. The cycle count for this operation depends on the standard deviation and $n$.

4. FNTT/INTT : Is used to perform inplace forward or inverse NTT. The number of consecutive NTTs is stored in the iteration-register and the indexes of the memory blocks are kept in the read-memory-index-queue

5. ADD/CMULT : Two memory blocks indexed by $RdQ0$ and $RdQ1$ are added or coefficient-wise multiplied. The result is stored in the memory block indexed by $WtQ0$. These two instructions require $n + \epsilon$ cycles.

6. REARRANGE : Performs rearrangement of coefficient pairs in a memory block indexed by $RdQ0$. This instruction requires less than $n$ cycles.

7. READ : The contents of a memory block indexed by $RdQ0$ are read. This instruction requires $n/2 + \epsilon$ cycles.

# ICEPOLE: High-Speed, Hardware-Oriented Authenticated Encryption

Paweł Morawiecki[1,2], Kris Gaj[5], Ekawat Homsirikamol[5],
Krystian Matusiewicz[8], Josef Pieprzyk[3,4], Marcin Rogawski[7],
Marian Srebrny[1,2], and Marcin Wójcik[6]

[1] Institute of Computer Science, Polish Academy of Sciences, Poland
[2] Section of Informatics, University of Commerce, Kielce, Poland
[3] Department of Computing, Macquarie University, Australia
[4] Electrical Engineering and Computer Science School,
Science and Engineering Faculty,
Queensland University of Technology, Brisbane, Australia
[5] Cryptographic Engineering Research Group, George Mason University, USA
[6] Cryptography and Information Security Group,
University of Bristol, United Kingdom
[7] Cadence Design Systems, San Jose, USA
[8] Intel, Gdańsk, Poland

**Abstract.** This paper introduces our dedicated authenticated encryption scheme ICEPOLE. ICEPOLE is a high-speed hardware-oriented scheme, suitable for high-throughput network nodes or generally any environment where specialized hardware (such as FPGAs or ASICs) can be used to provide high data processing rates. ICEPOLE-128 (the primary ICEPOLE variant) is very fast. On the modern FPGA device Virtex 6, a basic iterative architecture of ICEPOLE reaches 41 Gbits/s, which is over 10 times faster than the equivalent implementation of AES-128-GCM. The throughput-to-area ratio is also substantially better when compared to AES-128-GCM. We have carefully examined the security of the algorithm through a range of cryptanalytic techniques and our findings indicate that ICEPOLE offers high security level.

**Keywords:** authenticated encryption scheme, authenticated cipher, ICEPOLE.

## 1 Introduction

Protocols such as SSL/TLS [12,16], the backbone of the Internet, are designed to provide data confidentiality and authenticity. Often the underlying algorithms of these protocols realize encryption and authentication separately (e.g., AES in CBC mode for encryption and HMAC-SHA1 for authentication). Although this approach leads to relatively easy security analysis, the performance, due to

L. Batina and M. Robshaw (Eds.): CHES 2014, LNCS 8731, pp. 392–413, 2014.

two separate algorithms, does not meet demands of modern applications. Hence, recently, the symmetric crypto community focuses its attention on dedicated authentication encryption schemes, which aim to provide message encryption and authentication more efficiently. An interest in new efficient and secure solutions is manifested in the recently launched competition called CAESAR [1].

This paper presents our new design of the authenticated encryption scheme called ICEPOLE. It is a family of authenticated ciphers with two parameters: key length (128 or 256 bits) and nonce length (between 0 and 128 bits). Our primary recommendation is ICEPOLE-128 which uses 128-bit key and 128-bit nonce. The claimed security level for the primary variant is 128 bits and it is supported by our extensive cryptanalysis. ICEPOLE is based on the duplex framework introduced by Bertoni et al. in [8]. At the heart of the duplex framework is a permutation and the ICEPOLE permutation is our new design. In particular, inspired by the Keccak non-linear step [7], we introduce a new S-box with good security properties and low implementation cost.

ICEPOLE is a high-speed hardware-oriented scheme, suitable for high-throughput network nodes or more generally any environment where specialized hardware (such as FPGAs or ASICs) can be used to provide high data processing rates. ICEPOLE-128 is very fast. On the modern FPGA device Virtex 6, a basic iterative architecture of ICEPOLE reaches 41 Gbits/s, which is over 10 times faster than the equivalent implementation of AES-128-GCM [23] (one of the most common standards for authenticated encryption). The throughput-to-area ratio is also substantially better than AES-128-GCM results.

The paper is organized as follows. ICEPOLE specification is given in Section 2. Our security analysis is presented in Section 3. Next, Section 4 shows hardware performance on FGPA devices and the comparison with the AES-GCM hardware implementation. Then, software performance is given in Section 5. Finally, in Section 6, we describe all the key decisions with motivation and justification behind them.

## 2  Specification

Our primary recommended parameter set is: 128-bit key and 128-bit nonce. The ICEPOLE variant with these recommended parameters is called ICEPOLE-128. We also define two ICEPOLE variants serving as drop-in replacements for AES-128-GCM and AES-256-GCM. These variants are ICEPOLE-128a (128-bit key, 96-bit nonce) and ICEPOLE-256a (256-bit key, 96-bit nonce). The following specification refers to the primary recommendation ICEPOLE-128. A specification of ICEPOLE-128a and ICEPOLE-256a is nearly the same and the differences are described in Appendix D.

### 2.1  State Organization and Notations

The algorithm works on the 1280-bit state $S$. The state $S$ is organized as the two-dimensional array $S[4][5]$ where each element of the array is a 64-bit word.

When we refer to the particular bit, we introduce the third index: $S[x][y][z]$. The mapping between the bits of vector $v$ and those of $S[x][y][z]$ is $v[64(x+4y)+z] = S[x][y][z]$. (At some points in the algorithm's description we xor the state with a vector so this mapping must be specified.) If the bits of the state share the same $z$ coordinates, they form a *slice*. As $z$ ranges from 0 to 63, there are 64 slices in the state. If the bits of the state share the same $x$ and $z$ coordinates, they form a *row*. It is also convenient to introduce a notation which allows referring to the first $n$ bits of the state. Let $S_{\lfloor n \rfloor}$ denotes the first $n$ bits of the state, namely those bits $S[x][y][z]$ for which $64(x+4y)+z < n$.

We use the following notation: $\oplus$ (bitwise XOR), $\cdot$ (bitwise AND), $\neg$ (negation).

## 2.2    Scheme Overview

ICEPOLE-128 encrypts and authenticates a message with a 128-bit key and a 128-bit nonce. There are 3 phases of the algorithm as shown in Figure 2.2.

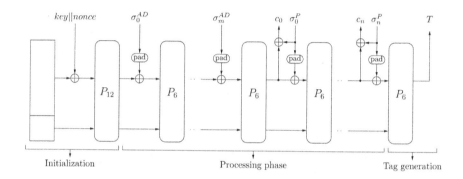

**Fig. 1.** General scheme of ICEPOLE encryption and authentication

At the heart of ICEPOLE there is the 1280-bit permutation denoted by $P$. Let us first describe this permutation.

## 2.3    Permutation P

$P$ is an iterated permutation and a number of rounds is a parameter of the permutation. In the presented algorithm the 6- and 12-round variants (denoted by $P_6$ and $P_{12}$) are used. Each round $R$ consists of five steps labelled by the Greek letters: $\mu$ (mu), $\rho$ (rho), $\pi$ (pi), $\psi$ (psi), $\kappa$ (kappa).

$$R = \kappa \circ \psi \circ \pi \circ \rho \circ \mu$$

Each step updates the state as follows.

**$\mu$:**

In the $\mu$ step bits are mixed through the MDS (Maximum Distance Separable) matrix. Every 20-bit slice is mixed through the matrix given below. Formally, a column vector $(Z_0, Z_1, Z_2, Z_3)$ is multiplied by a constant matrix producing a vector of four 5-bit words.

$$\begin{pmatrix} 2 & 1 & 1 & 1 \\ 1 & 1 & 18 & 2 \\ 1 & 2 & 1 & 18 \\ 1 & 18 & 2 & 1 \end{pmatrix} \begin{pmatrix} Z_0 \\ Z_1 \\ Z_2 \\ Z_3 \end{pmatrix} = \begin{pmatrix} 2Z_0 + Z_1 + Z_2 + Z_3 \\ Z_0 + Z_1 + 18Z_2 + 2Z_3 \\ Z_0 + 2Z_1 + Z_2 + 18Z_3 \\ Z_0 + 18Z_1 + 2Z_2 + Z_3 \end{pmatrix}$$

The operations are done in $GF(2^5)$. Here the multiplication is defined as the multiplication of binary polynomials modulo the irreducible polynomial $x^5 + x^2 + 1$. There are only three distinct terms in the chosen matrix, namely 18, 2, 1 and they correspond to the polynomials $x^4 + x$, $x$, and 1, respectively. The $\mu$ step can be efficiently implemented with simple bitwise equations (see Appendix G).

### $\rho$:

The $\rho$ step is the bitwise rotation applied to each of the twenty 64-bit words of the state. The bitwise rotation moves bit at position $z$ into position $(z + r_{value})$ modulo 64. For each word $r_{value}$ is different.

$$S[x][y] := S[x][y] \lll \text{offsets}[x][y] \qquad \text{for all } (0 \le x \le 3), (0 \le y \le 4)$$

The rotation offsets are given in Appendix A.

### $\pi$:

$\pi$ reorders the words in the state. Words are moved from $S[x][y]$ to $S[x'][y']$ and the new coordinates $(x', y')$ are calculated from the following simple formula.

$$x' := (x + y) \bmod 4$$
$$y' := (((x + y) \bmod 4) + y + 1) \bmod 5$$

### $\psi$:

In the $\psi$ step the ICEPOLE S-box is applied to each of 256 rows of the state. The S-box maps a 5-bit input vector $(M_0, M_1, ..., M_4)$ to a 5-bit output vector $(Z_0, Z_1, ..., Z_4)$. The S-box functionality can be easily described by the following bitwise equation. Operations on the index $k$ are done modulo 5. The bitwise AND operator $\cdot$ is omitted for clarity.

for all $(0 \le k \le 4)$
$$Z_k = M_k \oplus (\neg M_{k+1} M_{k+2}) \oplus (M_0 M_1 M_2 M_3 M_4) \oplus (\neg M_0 \neg M_1 \neg M_2 \neg M_3 \neg M_4)$$

## $\kappa$:

In $\kappa$ the 64-bit constant is xored with $S[0][0]$.

$$S[0][0] := S[0][0] \oplus \text{constant}[\text{numberOfRound}]$$

The constant value for each round is different. The values are given in Appendix B.

### 2.4  Initialization Phase

First, the state is initialized with the 1280-bit pseudorandom constant. The constant was obtained by applying the Keccak-f[1600] permutation (an underlying permutation of the SHA-3 standard) to the all-zero vector and truncating the result to 1280 bits. (The constant is given in Appendix C.)

Once the state is filled with the constant, the 128-bit key $K$ and the 128-bit nonce are introduced into the state. $K_0$ and $K_1$ denote two 64-bit words of the key, $nonce_0$ and $nonce_1$ denote two 64-bit words of the nonce.

$$S[0][0] := S[0][0] \oplus K_0$$
$$S[1][0] := S[1][0] \oplus K_1$$
$$S[2][0] := S[2][0] \oplus nonce_0$$
$$S[3][0] := S[3][0] \oplus nonce_1$$

Then, the $P_{12}$ permutation is run on the state $S$.

$$S := P_{12}(S)$$

### 2.5  Processing Phase

The input data is processed in blocks. First, the associated data blocks $\sigma_i^{AD}$ are processed and next the plaintext blocks $\sigma_i^P$. The plaintext blocks are authenticated and encrypted whereas the associated data blocks are only authenticated.

A block length has to be between 0 (the empty block) and 1024 bits. Each block is padded to be 1026 bits long and the padding rules are as follows. First, every block is appended with the *frame bit*. The frame bit is set to 1 for the last $\sigma^{AD}$ block and all $\sigma_i^P$ except the last one. Otherwise the frame bit is set to 0. Once the frame bit is appended, a given block is padded with a simple rule: append 1 and such a number of 0's which gives 1026-bit block. Thus the padded block has at least two padding bits (the frame bit and 1) and maximally 1026 padding bits (in case of the empty block).

In the processing phase the ciphertext blocks $c_i$ are produced and the state is updated.

**for all** blocks $\sigma_i^{AD}$ {
$\quad \sigma_i^{AD} := pad(\sigma_i^{AD})$
$\quad S_{\lfloor 1026 \rfloor} := S_{\lfloor 1026 \rfloor} \oplus \sigma_i^{AD}$

$$S := P_6(S)$$
$$\}$$

**for all** blocks $\sigma_i^P$ {
$$c_i = S_{\lfloor l \rfloor} \oplus \sigma_i^P \ (l \text{ is a length of } \sigma_i^P)$$
$$\sigma_i^P := pad(\sigma_i^P)$$
$$S_{\lfloor 1026 \rfloor} := S_{\lfloor 1026 \rfloor} \oplus \sigma_i^P$$
$$S := P_6(S)$$
$$\}$$

## 2.6  Tag Generation

When the blocks processing is finished, $P_6$ is run on the state and the 128-bit authentication tag $T$ is derived. ($T_0$ and $T_1$ denote two 64-bit words of $T$.)

$$S := P_6(S)$$
$$T_0 := S[0][0]$$
$$T_1 := S[1][0]$$

## 2.7  Decryption and Verification

Decryption and verification are done basically with the same scheme as for encryption. The only difference is that now the input data are the ciphertext blocks and the associated data blocks. Figure 2.7 shows the scheme. We stress that the same permutation $P$ (and not its inverse) is used for decryption and verification. Once the processing phase is finished, the tag $T$ is generated and verified with the tag received from the sender. If the tags match, the data is authenticated.

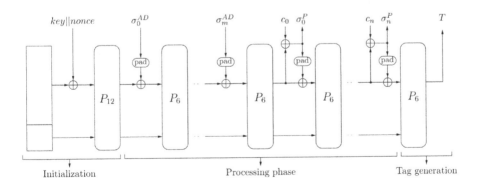

**Fig. 2.** ICEPOLE decryption

# 3  Security Analysis

In 2010, Bertoni et al. introduced the duplex construction [8] which provides the framework for an authenticated encryption scheme. ICEPOLE is based on this construction and thus ICEPOLE general security claims are inherited from it. The duplex construction can be seen as a particular way of using the sponge construction [6]. Similarly, there are two parameters, namely $r$ (bitrate) and $c$ (capacity). The sum of these two parameters makes the state size. Different values for bitrate and capacity give trade-offs between speed and security; a higher bitrate gives a faster construction at the expense of a lower security. For ICEPOLE-128, $r$ is 1026 bits and $c$ is 254 bits. In case of ICEPOLE variants with a 256-bit key, $r$ is 962 bits and $c$ is 318 bits.

In [3], it was proved that the sponge construction is secure against generic attacks with complexity below $2^{c/2}$. However, when a sponge or duplex object is used in conjunction with a secret key, one can prove more refined bounds taking into account the data complexity. In [4] Bertoni et al. proved that if the data complexity is limited to $2^a$ $r$-bit blocks, the keyed mode withstands generic attacks with time complexity up to $2^{c-a}$ calls of the underlying permutation. If $a < c/2$, this results in an increase of the security strength from $c/2$ to $c - a$. This comes in handy particularly for 256-key ICEPOLE variants, where we would like to keep 256 bits of security without expanding the state or introducing any serious changes in the algorithm's specification. By limiting the number of blocks (encrypted under the same key) to $2^{62}$, ICEPOLE-256 stands up to any attack up to $2^{318-62} = 2^{256}$ (unless easier generically). For ICEPOLE-128 the limit (rather purely theoretical) is $2^{126}$ blocks and hence the security level is $254 - 126 = 128$ bits.

In [6] it was shown that the security level can be proven under the assumption that the underlying permutation $P$ has not any exploitable properties (there are no structural distinguishers of the permutation). Therefore the security analysis of ICEPOLE comes down to analysis of the permutation $P$. Below we give our cryptanalysis indicating that $P$ is indeed a secure permutation.

A user of ICEPOLE is required to use a nonce. However, in the case of nonce reuse ICEPOLE provides some intermediate level of robustness. The nonce reuse leads to leaking XOR of plaintexts (via XOR of ciphertexts) and this cannot be avoided in our case. The secret key used with the same nonce also leads to the situation where the adversary can control the XOR differences after the 12-round initialization. But our cryptanalysis (given below) strongly indicates that the 6-round permutation $P$ (run at the processing phase) is secure, in particular against differential and linear cryptanalysis. Therefore we argue that in the case of nonce reuse the key-recovery attack is not possible.

## 3.1  Differential Cryptanalysis

Differential cryptanalysis, introduced by Biham and Shamir [9], has become very powerful technique of modern cryptanalysis. One of the most convincing way of showing the resistance against differential attacks is to provide a lower bound on the weight of any differential characteristics (also called differential trails or paths) over a number of rounds. For example, in the AES the structure of the cipher and its diffusion properties allow to provide such bounds analytically [11]. However for 'bit-oriented constructions (e.g., Keccak or MD6 hash function) it is not possible to derive differential characteristics bounds in a very straightforward and convenient manner. In such cases computer-aided proofs are provided and for ICEPOLE we take this approach.

**Computer Aided Proof**

A brute-force strategy to check all possible characteristics (even for a very small number of rounds) fails. The 1280-bit state is too big, even when exploiting all possible symmetries. Instead of the plain brute-force we used a SAT-solver. A SAT solver is an algorithm, which decides whether a given propositional (Boolean) formula (typically described in the Conjunctive Normal Form) has a satisfying valuation. Generally, to solve a problem: (1) translate the problem to SAT (in such a way that a satisfying valuation represents a solution to the problem); (2) run a favourite SAT solver to find a solution.

First, we focused on the problem of finding the 3-round characteristic with the minimum number of active S-boxes. The problem was encoded as a SAT formula in the Conjunctive Normal Form with the aid of the CryptLogVer toolkit [18]. Crypto-MiniSat2 [25] is able to solve it in a few hours on a desktop PC. The solution, that is the minimum number of active S-boxes for 3 rounds, is 9. Then, we tried to repeat the experiments for 4 rounds, but the problem was too hard for the SAT-solver. However, if we slightly change the problem and ask the solver about a particular number (up to 13) of active S-boxes on the 4-round differential path, the answer is provided by the solver. For 4 rounds there are no paths with 13 or fewer S-boxes. Again, checking a higher number of S-boxes turned out to be infeasible.

If a number of active S-boxes is at least 14 (for 4 rounds) and the highest probability of a difference transition through the S-box is $2^{-2}$ (deduced from the difference distribution table of the S-box, given in Appendix F), then the lowest weight for 4 rounds is $2^{-2*14} = 2^{-28}$. So for 12 rounds a weight equals $2^{-28*3} = 2^{-84}$ and hence data complexity for the attack is $2^{84}$ plaintexts. Please note that this is already a much bigger number than the limitation ($2^{62}$) for ICEPOLE-256 on a number of blocks of plaintexts encrypted under the same key.

We believe that the complexity of differential attack should be much higher than the lower bound of $2^{84}$ plaintexts. The first reason for that is the difference transitions through the S-box with the weight $2^{-2}$ happen very rarely. Out of 337 possible difference transitions only 10 (3%) has the weight $2^{-2}$. Most of the transitions (216) has the weight $2^{-4}$ and the average weight is $2^{3.4}$. The second argument strongly indicating that ICEPOLE is resistant to a differential attack is our experimental results. These gives some more insight into the difference propagation in ICEPOLE. Details are presented in Appendix D.

**Internal Differentials.** The best collision attack against Keccak was obtained through the technique called internal differentials [13]. While in standard differential attacks we consider two different plaintexts, in internal differential attacks only one plaintext is considered, and the statistical evolution of the differences between its parts is followed. In the attack against Keccak two properties were exploited, which led to the successful attack against the round-reduced Keccak. These properties are: very low Hamming weight constants (which helps to keep the state in the desired symmetry) and the fact that the state is initialized with the all-zero vector (which allows to construct the initial difference). For ICEPOLE it is not the case as the state is initialized with the pseudorandom constant and the round constants have much higher Hamming weight. Therefore we conclude it is not possible (or heavily limited) to successfully apply the internal differential technique to our scheme.

### 3.2    Linear Cryptanalysis

Linear cryptanalysis, formally introduced by Matsui [21], has become another powerful tool against modern cryptographic primitives. The main idea is to construct the linear approximation of the algorithm. In many ways this technique resembles differential cryptanalysis. Tracing the evolution of differences has the counterpart in tracing linear masks. Usually the complexity of the attack is also determined by the number of active S-boxes in the trail. One excellent example of exploiting the duality between these two techniques is the analysis of AES provided by its designers.

Although the structure of ICEPOLE does not allow for a straightforward and completely parallel analysis with respect to the two types of attacks, we think that ICEPOLE (and its permutation $P$) should offer very similar security margin against linear and differential cryptanalysis. First indication of it is the examination of the linear profile of the S-box. (The complete profile is given in Appendix H.) The highest bias of the linear approximation of the S-box is $2^{-2}$ and on average the bias is lower as the value of $2^{-2}$ happens rarely. (Note that the highest probability of difference transitions in the S-box is also $2^{-2}$). The complexity of the linear attack is not only determined by the S-box properties but also by a number of active S-boxes on the trail. The $\mu$ step brings diffusion to the algorithm and hence it is the main factor for increasing a number of active S-boxes. The $\mu$ step affects linear and differential trails in the same way. Therefore we conclude that the complexity of the linear attack against ICEPOLE should be comparable with differential analysis and after 5-6 rounds the complexity becomes completely intractable.

### 3.3    SAT-Based (Logic) Cryptanalysis

We encoded the following problem into SAT: an adversary knows a part of the input state, a part of the output state and the goal is to retrieve the unknown part of the input state. For ICEPOLE this problem models two types of attacks. The first type is the key recovery where an unknown part of the state is a secret key. The second type of the attack is the state recovery (in the processing phase) where the attacker tries to recover the unknown capacity part of the state.

To encode the problem into a SAT instance we used the toolkit presented in [18]. We obtained a SAT instance describing a single round of $P$ with roughly 6400 variables and 35300 clauses. In attacks we used CryptoMiniSAT2, a gold medallist from recent SAT competitions [25]. We tried to solve three variants of the problem where 64-, 80-, and 128-bit part of the input state remains unknown. For 2 rounds CryptoMiniSAT2 was able to find the solution in a few seconds on a desktop PC. For 3 rounds only 64-bit variant of the problem was solved (also in a matter of seconds) and for 4 rounds, with 48-hour time limit, CryptoMiniSAT2 was unable to provide any solution. It looks as the hardness of the problem grows super exponentially in a number of rounds and this effect has been also observed in SAT-based attacks on other cryptographic primitives [18,24]. Thus we conclude that ICEPOLE with the 12-round initialization and the 6-round processing phase is secure against the SAT-based attack.

### 3.4 Rotational Cryptanalysis

The technique was formally introduced in [20]. Unlike differential analysis, where the attacker follows the propagation of the xor differences of two plaintexts through the cryptographic system, in rotational analysis, the adversary investigates the propagation of the rotational relations between plaintexts. In [22] rotational cryptanalysis was applied to Keccak and since there are some similarities between ICEPOLE and Keccak, we take a closer look whether that technique could be used against ICEPOLE. In the attack on Keccak two properties were exploited, namely very low Hamming weight constants (which helps keep the states in the desired rotational relation) and the fact that the state is initialized with the all-zero vector (which allows to construct the initial rotational relation). For ICEPOLE it is not the case as the state is initialized with the pseudorandom constant and the round constants have much higher Hamming weight. Therefore we conclude it is not possible (or heavily limited) to apply rotational cryptanalysis to our scheme.

### 3.5 Techniques Exploiting Low Algebraic Degree

There are several cryptanalytic techniques, which exploit a low algebraic degree. These are, for example, the cube attack [14] or the zero-sum distinguisher [2]. An algebraic degree of a single round of $P$ (or its inverse) is 4. Then, after four rounds the algebraic degree is 256, which stops the mentioned attacks from reaching the attack complexity lower than the claimed security level $2^{128}$. Thus ICEPOLE with its 12-round initialization is completely secure against techniques exploiting a low algebraic degree.

## 4   Hardware Performance

A proof-of-concept basic iterative architecture of ICEPOLE-128 was implemented. Figure 4 shows an overview of a datapath design. The presented cryptographic core is capable of performing encryption and decryption, and contains a full padding unit.

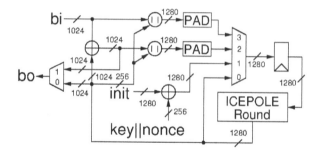

**Fig. 3.** A proof-of-concept single iterative round design for the hardware implementation of ICEPOLE

AES-GCM is used as a basis of our comparison as it is one of the most widely accepted standards for authenticated encryption [23]. The same basic iterative architecture is implemented for a direct comparison. Both implementations use also the same interface and communication protocol in order to reduce any discrepancies between the two designs. Similar to ICEPOLE, AES-GCM contains the full padding unit and supports both encryption and decryption within a single core.

Both cryptographic cores were described using VHDL language and verified against software generated test vectors using ModelSim. The results were generated using ATHENa [17] using two high-performance FPGA families from two major FPGA vendors, Xilinx and Altera. These FPGA families are Xilinx Virtex 6 and Altera Stratix IV, respectively. No dedicated resources, such as Block RAMs or DSP units, were used in either implementation. The comparison between ICEPOLE-128 and AES-128-GCM using a basic iterative architecture is shown in Table 1. The throughput shown in the table is based on the throughput of long messages.

**Table 1.** The comparison between ICEPOLE-128 and AES-128-GCM using an iterative architecture

|  | Xilinx Virtex 6 | | | Altera Stratix IV | | |
|---|---|---|---|---|---|---|
|  | ICEPOLE-128 | AES-128-GCM | ratio | ICEPOLE-128 | AES-128-GCM | ratio |
| throughput (Gbit/s) | 41.364 | 3.539 | 11.7 | 38.779 | 3.612 | 10.7 |
| area (Slices/ALUT) | 1501 | 940 | 1.6 | 4564 | 4025 | 1.13 |
| throughput-to-area | 27.56 | 3.76 | 7.3 | 8.5 | 0.9 | 9.4 |

With the exception of resource utilization, ICEPOLE-128 consistently outperforms AES-128-GCM in terms of the throughput and the throughput-to-area ratio. For Xilinx Virtex 6, with only 60% increases in area, ICEPOLE-128 achieves almost 12 times the speed of AES-128-GCM, and seven times higher the throughput-to-area ratio. For Altera Stratix IV, due to the unique behaviour of Altera Adaptive Look Up Tables (ALUTs), the resource utilization is similar for both algorithms, with ICEPOLE-128 consuming only 13% more area. At the same time, ICEPOLE-128 outperforms AES-128-GCM by a factor of 11 in terms of throughput and a factor of 9 in terms of the throughput-to-area ratio.

We strive to provide the fairest possible comparison with AES-GCM. When we state that the design used is an 'iterative architecture', this means that it takes 10 clock cycles to calculate the AES. Certainly, we selected the multiplier unit that optimizes the unit to meet that latency. This means that we are performing a 128-bit × 128-bit multiplication using at least a 128-bit × 16-bit multiplier to satisfy the 10 clock cycles requirement. For a fair comparison, we selected a 128-bit × 16-bit multiplier because 128-bit × 32-bit or larger multiplier would increase the area unnecessarily.

As ICEPOLE is inspired by the Keccak permutation, it is natural to ask whether our new construction offers better performance over the Keccak permutation. The main reason ICEPOLE permutation is faster than Keccak is that the linear step $\mu$ can be implemented in the single layer of LUTs whereas Keccak $\theta$ needs 2 layers. Hence both area and throughput for this step would be to ICEPOLE advantage. Other steps in permutation are basically equivalent in terms of performance. Our experiments supports this analysis. The experiment was conducted by wrapping ICEPOLE and Keccak permutations with a shift register for I/O. Then the same optimization technique used in our paper was applied to both designs. The improvement in speed is consistent across all device families with the highest performance gain in Altera as much as 20%.

## 5    Software Performance

While the primary focus of the ICEPOLE design is hardware performance, the cipher is also amenable to efficient software implementations. The three steps that require nontrivial implementations are $\mu$, $\rho$ and $\psi$. They all can be easily implemented on platforms supporting 64-bit XORs, logical ANDs and rotations. We measured that a rather straightforward C implementation compiled for speed (with no beyond-C optimization efforts like code vectorization using AVX or intrinsics use) runs for very long messages at about 9 cycles per byte on Intel Ivy Bridge i5-3320M processor. The same implementation runs at about 8 cpb on a Haswell (Intel Xeon E3 1275) machine.

We believe there is still room for possible improvements. A better code optimization (e.g., making sure that the compiler uses the andn a, b instruction on Haswell for $\neg A \cdot B$ extensively used in the step $\psi$) could lead to a better performance than the reported 8 cycles per byte. Additionally, one could think about an AVX-based implementation where the whole state is kept in five YMM registers. Compared to the pure C code this could save time on memory loads and stores but at the expense of the more complex $\mu$ step. For 32-bit platforms, only rotation performance will scale worse than linearly (compared to the straightforward 64-bit version). It is because in such a case the rotations need to be combined from more than two instructions.

# 6 Design Rationale

We have aimed at high-speed, hardware-oriented authenticated encryption scheme, suitable for high-throughput network nodes or any environment where specialized hardware (such as FPGAs or ASICs) can be utilized to provide desired high data processing rates. Our main inspiration comes from the duplex construction with the round-reduced Keccak-f permutation [5]. We have decided to keep the general framework (namely the duplex construction) and design an underlying permutation from scratch.

In the Keccak-f permutation, the linear step $\theta$ brings most of diffusion to the algorithm and is roughly two times slower (when considering the FPGA design) than the non-linear part (a layer of S-boxes). Our general approach to the design of the permutation $P$ has been to make steps more balanced. We have wanted to make the linear part simpler (faster) and improve the properties (diffusion, algebraic degree) of the non-linear part (in comparison to Keccak-f). The challenge has been that a more complex S-box layer should not nullify the gain from introducing a lighter linear part. Our second starting idea was to take into consideration cryptanalysis of Keccak-f and its round-reduced variants. Those findings have determined some of our decisions for ICEPOLE and its $P$ permutation.

## 6.1 Permutation P Steps

Let us first explain design rationale behind the $P$ permutation steps.

$\mu$:

We have aimed at a possibly simple and implementation-friendly linear step. The step does not have to have an efficient inverse as in the duplex construction the permutation is calculated only in one way (both for encryption and decryption). Additionally, we have required that the linear step has very good diffusion properties. In [19] Junod and Vaudenay presented their research on building MDS matrix (known for an excellent diffusion property) under the criteria, which perfectly suit our needs, that is an efficient implementation and neglecting an inverse of the matrix. We have decided to use one of the 'optimal' matrices presented in [19].

The $\mu$ step also helped determine the size and organization of the state. First, we tried to keep the same state organization as in Keccak-f[1600] that is $5 \times 5 \times 64$. However the 'optimal' $5 \times 5$ MDS matrix did not give us a clear advantage (in terms of hardware implementation efficiency) over the linear step presented in Keccak. Hence we have decided to use the smaller $4 \times 4$ matrix, which would operate on four 5-bit vectors. The linear operation based on the chosen matrix can be implemented in just a single layer of LUTs in the modern FPGA devices. Consequently, to let our new linear step be applied naturally, the state has been organized as the two dimensional array $4 \times 5$ of 64-bit words, giving the 1280-bit state.

## $\rho$:

The $\rho$ step is essential to bring diffusion along $z$ axis in the state. Otherwise a given bit would only affect bits from its slice (the bits sharing the same $z$ coordinate). The 20 offsets are calculated from a simple formula $i(i+1)/2$ modulo the word length (64 bits in the case of ICEPOLE). This formula is the same as in the Keccak permutation. A nice feature of this formula is that in the case of shorter word lengths, each word (or nearly each word) has a distinct offset value. This might come in handy when one tries to build ICEPOLE variant with a smaller state, better suited for constrained environments.

## $\pi$:

The $\pi$ step reorders the words in the state. We have introduced this step to bring extra diffusion between the words (which is already provided by $\mu$ and $\psi$). In hardware, $\pi$ and $\rho$ are 'cheap', their computational cost corresponds to wiring. The $\pi$ formula has been chosen for its simplicity.

## $\psi$:

We have aimed at the non-linear step (an S-box), which would have the following properties: good differential and linear profiles, an algebraic degree higher than 3, compact boolean circuit (low implementation cost). We have concluded that the Keccak S-box would not be the best choice mainly for its slow diffusion. Every bit affects only 3 others whereas we need better diffusion to complement $\mu$. Secondly, the Keccak S-box algebraic degree is only 2 and for a small number of rounds techniques exploiting a low algebraic degree might be a threat. Therefore, ideally, we would like to keep good differential and linear profiles of the Keccak S-box and increase its diffusion and the algebraic degree. Our idea to achieve this goal was as follows. If we change the truth table of the Keccak S-box very little, differential and linear profiles should stay much the same (Though it needs to be verified.) Hopefully, a small change would improve diffusion and increase the algebraic degree. In the Keccak S-box the input vector '00000' is mapped onto '00000' and '11111' onto '11111'. If we switch them ('00000' $\Rightarrow$ '11111' and '11111' $\Rightarrow$ '00000'), this seemingly tiny change gives us all we want. Now every output bit depends on all 5 input bits (better diffusion then) and the algebraic degree now equals 4, also the inverse of the new S-box has degree equals 4. The boolean description is still very compact, the equations are given in Section 2. As expected the differential and linear profiles remain very the same, keeping their good properties. The profiles are given in Appendix.

## $\kappa$:

$\kappa$ adds the 64-bit round constant and for each round a constant is different. Without $\kappa$ all rounds of the permutation $P$ would be equal making it subject to attacks exploiting symmetry such as slide attacks [10]. The constants used in

Keccak have very low Hamming weight and this feature was exploited in two cryptanalytic attacks [13,22] against the round-reduced Keccak. These results motivated us to introduce constants with much higher Hamming weight. The constant values are taken as the output of a simple 64-bit maximum-cycle Linear Feedback Shift Register (LFSR). The polynomial representation of LFSR is $x^{64} + x^{63} + x^{61} + x^{60} + 1$. The LFSR state is initialized with the 64-bit vector '0123456789ABCDEF' (hexadecimal format) and then each cycle generates a subsequent constant. Thus $\kappa$ can be implemented as a simple LFSR circuit or a precomputed look-up table.

**Steps order within a Round**

$\mu$ is the step, which provides the best mixing between the unknown part of the state (a secret key $K$) and the remaining part of the state which would be known to the attacker. Hence we have placed $\mu$ as the first step in a round. The order of other steps is arbitrary.

## 6.2   ICEPOLE Parameters and Decisions

ICEPOLE works on the 1280-bit state and the reason for that is explained above in the subsection on the $\mu$ step. ICEPOLE-128 (our primary recommendation) uses the 1024-bit input data block to be more hardware friendly. This value is a power of 2 and allows a more natural I/O operation in hardware as opposed to the slightly bigger size of 1088 bits (which could be also a choice). With 6-round processing phase where a large amount of data must be transferred within a short period, a non-power-of-2 block size can introduce an inefficiency in data transmission when the I/O width is large. Furthermore, with the 1024-bit input data block, a hardware implementation can more efficiently uses its storage, which can be important where aiming for an extremely small design.

Before $P$ is applied, the state is initialized with the pseudorandom 1280-bit constant. This decision has been motivated by cryptanalysis on the round-reduced Keccak where two different techniques [13,22] have exploited the fact the state is initialized with the all-zero maintaining many different symmetries.

The number of rounds in Initialization is 12. This value is based on our differential cryptanalysis shown in Section 3. After Initialization an adversary should not have any control over the differences (when mounting the differential attack). The experiments indicate that 6 rounds are sufficient and we have doubled this value to get a solid security margin.

The number of rounds in Processing Phase is 6. This value is based on our SAT-based cryptanalysis given in Section 3. We were able to recover a small unknown part of the state for 3 rounds. To get a solid security margin we have doubled the number of rounds in Processing Phase to 6.

The frame bit (introduced as a part of the padding) is needed for security analysis of the duplex construction working in the authenticated encryption mode [6, Section 4.1.5]. The chosen padding rule is the simplest sponge-compliant padding [6, Definition 2].

# 7    Conclusion

We have proposed the dedicated authenticated encryption scheme called ICE-POLE. It is very fast on the modern hardware platforms and its hardware performance is substantially better than the AES-GCM. Our software non-optimized implementation, running at 8 cycles per byte, is also a promising result. We performed a security analysis with aid of many cryptanalytic tools and our findings show that ICEPOLE offers solid security margin. Our new permutation $P$ (combining with the sponge construction [6] or other permutation-based modes) could become a building block for a new, high-speed cryptographic primitive such as a hash function or a stream cipher.

**Acknowledgment.** Project was financed by Polish National Science Centre, project DEC-2013/09/D/ST6/03918. Josef Pieprzyk was supported by the ARC grant DP0987734. The work described in this paper has been supported in part by EPSRC grant EP/H001689/1.

# References

1. CAESAR: Competition for Authenticated Encryption: Security, Applicability, and Robustness, http://competitions.cr.yp.to/caesar.html
2. Aumasson, J.P., Meier, W.: Zero-sum distinguishers for reduced Keccak-f and for the core functions of Luffa and Hamsi. Tech. rep., NIST mailing list (2009)
3. Bertoni, G., Daemen, J., Peeters, M., Van Assche, G.: On the Indifferentiability of the Sponge Construction. In: Smart, N.P. (ed.) EUROCRYPT 2008. LNCS, vol. 4965, pp. 181–197. Springer, Heidelberg (2008) http://sponge.noekeon.org/
4. Bertoni, G., Daemen, J., Peeters, M., Assche, G.V.: On the security of the keyed sponge construction. Symmetric Key Encryption Workshop (SKEW) (February 2011)
5. Bertoni, G., Daemen, J., Peeters, M., Assche, G.V.: Permutation-based encryption, authentication and authenticated encryption (July 2012)
6. Bertoni, G., Daemen, J., Peeters, M., Van Assche, G.: Cryptographic sponges, http://sponge.noekeon.org/CSF-0.1.pdf
7. Bertoni, G., Daemen, J., Peeters, M., Van Assche, G.: Keccak sponge function family main document, http://keccak.noekeon.org/Keccak-main-2.1.pdf
8. Bertoni, G., Daemen, J., Peeters, M., Assche, G.V.: Duplexing the sponge: single-pass authenticated encryption and other applications. Cryptology ePrint Archive, Report 2011/499 (2011), http://eprint.iacr.org/
9. Biham, E., Shamir, A.: Differential Cryptanalysis of DES-like Cryptosystems. Journal of Cryptology 4(1), 3–72 (1991)
10. Biryukov, A., Wagner, D.: Slide attacks. In: FSE, pp. 245–259 (1999)
11. Daemen, J., Rijmen, V.: The Design of Rijndael: AES - The Advanced Encryption Standard. Information Security and Cryptography. Springer (2002)
12. Dierks, T., Rescorla, E.: The Transport Layer Security (TLS) Protocol. Tech. rep., Network Working Group (2008)
13. Dinur, I., Dunkelman, O., Shamir, A.: Collision attacks on up to 5 rounds of sha-3 using generalized internal differentials. Cryptology ePrint Archive, Report 2012/672 (2012), http://eprint.iacr.org/

14. Dinur, I., Shamir, A.: Cube attacks on tweakable black box polynomials. In: Joux, A. (ed.) EUROCRYPT 2009. LNCS, vol. 5479, pp. 278–299. Springer, Heidelberg (2009)

15. Duc, A., Guo, J., Peyrin, T., Wei, L.: Unaligned Rebound Attack - Application to Keccak. Cryptology ePrint Archive, Report 2011/420 (2011)

16. Freier, A., Karlton, P., Kocher, P.: The Secure Sockets Layer (SSL) Protocol. Tech. rep., Internet Engineering Task Force, IETF (2011)

17. Gaj, K., Kaps, J.-P., Amirineni, V., Rogawski, M., Homsirikamol, E., Brewster, B.Y.: ATHENa - Automated Tool for Hardware EvaluatioN: Toward Fair and Comprehensive Benchmarking of Cryptographic Hardware Using FPGAs. In: FPL, pp. 414–421 (2010)

18. Homsirikamol, E., Morawiecki, P., Rogawski, M., Srebrny, M.: Security margin evaluation of SHA-3 contest finalists through SAT-based attacks. In: Cortesi, A., Chaki, N., Saeed, K., Wierzchoń, S. (eds.) CISIM 2012. LNCS, vol. 7564, pp. 56–67. Springer, Heidelberg (2012)

19. Junod, P., Vaudenay, S.: Perfect diffusion primitives for block ciphers. In: Handschuh, H., Hasan, M.A. (eds.) SAC 2004. LNCS, vol. 3357, pp. 84–99. Springer, Heidelberg (2004)

20. Khovratovich, D., Nikolić, I.: Rotational cryptanalysis of ARX. In: Hong, S., Iwata, T. (eds.) FSE 2010. LNCS, vol. 6147, pp. 333–346. Springer, Heidelberg (2010)

21. Matsui, M., Yamagishi, A.: A new method for known plaintext attack of FEAL cipher. In: Rueppel, R.A. (ed.) EUROCRYPT 1992. LNCS, vol. 658, pp. 81–91. Springer, Heidelberg (1993)

22. Morawiecki, P., Pieprzyk, J., Srebrny, M.: Rotational cryptanalysis of round-reduced Keccak. In: Moriai, S. (ed.) FSE 2013. LNCS, vol. 8424, pp. 241–262. Springer, Heidelberg (2014)

23. National Institute of Standards and Technology: Recommendations for Block Cipher Modes of Operation: Galois/Counter Mode (GCM) and GMAC. NIST special publication 800-38D (November 2007)

24. Rivest, R., Agre, B., Bailey, D.V., Crutchfield, C., Dodis, Y., Fleming, K.E., Khan, A., Krishnamurthy, J., Lin, Y., Reyzin, L., Shen, E., Sukha, J., Sutherland, D., Tromer, E., Yin, Y.L.: The MD6 hash function, http://groups.csail.mit.edu/cis/md6/

25. Soos, M.: CryptoMiniSat 2.5.0. In: SAT Race competitive event booklet (July 2010), http://www.msoos.org/cryptominisat2

# Appendix

## A

The rotation offsets used in the $\rho$ step are given below.

| | | | |
|---|---|---|---|
| offsets[0][0] := 0 | offsets[0][1] := 36 | offsets[0][2] := 3 | offsets[0][3] := 41 |
| offsets[0][4] := 18 | offsets[1][0] := 1 | offsets[1][1] := 44 | offsets[1][2] := 10 |
| offsets[1][3] := 45 | offsets[1][4] := 2 | offsets[2][0] := 62 | offsets[2][1] := 6 |
| offsets[2][2] := 43 | offsets[2][3] := 15 | offsets[2][4] := 61 | offsets[3][0] := 28 |
| offsets[3][1] := 55 | offsets[3][2] := 25 | offsets[3][3] := 21 | offsets[3][4] := 56 |

## B

The round constants used in the $\kappa$ step are given below. The values are given in hexadecimal using the little-endian format.

constant[0] := 0091A2B3C4D5E6F7
constant[2] := 002468ACF13579BD
constant[4] := 00091A2BFC4D5E6F
constant[6] := 0002468AFF13579B
constant[8] := 000091A2BFC4D5E6
constant[10] := 00002468EFF13579

constant[1] := 0048D159E26AF37B
constant[3] := 00123456F89ABCDE
constant[5] := 00048D15FE26AF37
constant[7] := 000123457F89ABCD
constant[9] := 000048D1DFE26AF3
constant[11] := 00001234F7F89ABC

## C

At the start of Initialization Phase the 1280-bit state is initialized with the pseudorandom constant. The values are given in hexadecimal using the little-endian format.

$S[0][0] := FF97A42D7F8E6FD4$
$S[0][2] := 8C5BDA0CD6192E76$
$S[0][4] := 30935AB7D08FFC64$
$S[1][1] := A9A6E6260D712103$
$S[1][3] := 43B831CD0347C826$
$S[2][0] := 05E5635A21D9AE61$
$S[2][2] := 613670957BC46611$
$S[2][4] := 8C3EE88A1CCF32C8$
$S[3][1] := 1841F924A2C509E4$
$S[3][3] := 75F644E97F30A13B$

$S[0][1] := 90FEE5A0A44647C4$
$S[0][3] := AD30A6F71B19059C$
$S[1][0] := EB5AA93F2317D635$
$S[1][2] := 81A57C16DBCF555F$
$S[1][4] := 01F22F1A11A5569F$
$S[2][1] := 64BEFEF28CC970F2$
$S[2][3] := B87C5A554FD00ECB$
$S[3][0] := 940C7922AE3A2614$
$S[3][2] := 16F53526E70465C2$
$S[3][4] := EAF1FF7B5CECA249$

## D

**ICEPOLE-128a.** We specify ICEPOLE-128a to have a drop-in replacement for AES-128-GCM run with most common parameters, namely a 96-bit nonce and a 128-bit tag. The only differences between ICEPOLE-128 (specified above) and ICEPOLE-128a is that in ICEPOLE-128a a nonce is 96 bits long. The nonce is padded with 32 zeros and introduced into the state in the same way as for ICEPOLE-128.

**ICEPOLE-256a.** We specify ICEPOLE-256a to have a drop-in replacement for AES-256-GCM run with most common parameters, namely a 96-bit nonce and a 128-bit tag. ICEPOLE-256a encrypts data with a 256-bit key, a 96-bit nonce and the data is authenticated with a 128-bit tag. The 96-bit nonce is padded with 32 zeros. A 256-bit key consists of four 64-bit words $K_0 \ldots K_3$ and the padded nonce consists of two 64-bit words. The key and the nonce are introduced into the state as follows.

$$S[0][0] := S[0][0] \oplus K_0$$
$$S[1][0] := S[1][0] \oplus K_1$$
$$S[2][0] := S[2][0] \oplus K_2$$
$$S[3][0] := S[3][0] \oplus K_3$$
$$S[0][1] := S[0][1] \oplus nonce_0$$
$$S[1][1] := S[1][1] \oplus nonce_1$$

The data blocks have the length between 0 and 960 bits and the padded blocks are 962 bits long. For ICEPOLE-256a the number of blocks encrypted under a single key should be less than $2^{62}$. All other parameters and steps of the specification are the same as for ICEPOLE-128.

# E

## Differential Path Search

We were inspired by the work of Duc et al. [15] where the algorithm for differential path search was given for the Keccak permutation. They managed to provide the best differential paths for the round-reduced variants of the permutation. Our permutation shares some key features with the Keccak permutation (in particular how the state is organized and 'bit-oriented' propagation) and hence we think that a similar algorithm may be fruitful also for our analysis.

The goal of the algorithm is to derive differential paths by maintaining the bit difference Hamming weight as low as possible. We note that $\mu$, $\rho$, $\pi$ are all linear mappings (denoted altogether by $\lambda$, while $\psi$ acts as the non-linear S-box. $\kappa$ (adding round constants) does not affect differential analysis in any way. Furthermore, $\rho$ and $\pi$ do not change the number of active bits in a differential path, but change only bit positions. Hence, $\mu$ and $\psi$ are critical when analysing differential paths. Since $\psi$ is followed by $\mu$ in the next round (ignoring $\kappa$), we consider these two mappings together by treating a slice of the state as a unit, and try to find the potential best mapping of the slice through $\psi$ with the following rule.

- Given an input difference of the slice find all possible output differences by looking into the S-box differential profile. Then, among all combinations of possible output differences, choose a combination which would give the state the minimum Hamming weight after an application of $\mu$.

It is not possible to check all possible states as the starting points for a differential path because the state is too big, even if we take advantage of symmetries. We limit the space of starting points to the states with a single active bit. For the 20-bit slice there are 20 such cases. For our permutation (as in the case of the Keccak permutation) a differential path is invariant through position rotation along the $z$ axis so choosing a particular slice does not matter.

We start our search from $b_1$ point, i.e., the state after the linear mappings (denoted by $\lambda$) in the second round, and compute backwards for one round, and a few rounds forwards, as shown below.

$$a_0 \xleftarrow{\lambda^{-1}} b_0 \xleftarrow{\psi^{-1}} a_1 \xleftarrow{\lambda^{-1}} \mathbf{b_1} \xrightarrow{\psi} a_2 \xrightarrow{\lambda} b_2 \xrightarrow{\psi} a_3 \xrightarrow{\lambda} b_3 \dots$$

The forward part is longer than the backward part because the diffusion of $\mu^{-1}$ is better than for $\mu$, so it will be easier to control the bit differences Hamming weight for several rounds forwards (instead of backwards). Table 2 shows probabilities of the best paths we found with the aid of the algorithm.

**Table 2.** Best differential paths results. The third column shows the weights of rounds for a given path.

| rounds | total probability | products |
|--------|-------------------|----------|
| 1 | $2^{-2}$ | $2^{-2}$ |
| 2 | $2^{-10}$ | $2^{-8} \cdot 2^{-2}$ |
| 3 | $2^{-18.4}$ | $2^{-8.4} \cdot 2^{-2} \cdot 2^{-8}$ |
| 4 | $2^{-52.8}$ | $2^{-8.8} \cdot 2^{-2} \cdot 2^{-8} \cdot 2^{-34}$ |
| 5 | $2^{-186.2}$ | $2^{-10.4} \cdot 2^{-2} \cdot 2^{-8} \cdot 2^{-36} \cdot 2^{-129.8}$ |
| 6 | $2^{-555.3}$ | $2^{-10.4} \cdot 2^{-2} \cdot 2^{-8} \cdot 2^{-36} \cdot 2^{-129.8} \cdot 2^{-369}$ |

The weight of the 3-round path matches the bound we provided $(2^{-18})$ very closely. We investigated up to 6 rounds as the complexity of the attack exploiting the 5-round path is already completely intractable.

# F

# G

The $\mu$ step changes the $S$ state according to the following equations.

**for** $(z := 0;\ z < 64;\ z := z + 1)$ {

$S'[0][4][z] := S[0][3][z] \oplus S[1][4][z] \oplus S[2][4][z] \oplus S[3][4][z]$
$S'[0][3][z] := S[0][2][z] \oplus S[1][3][z] \oplus S[2][3][z] \oplus S[3][3][z]$
$S'[0][2][z] := S[0][4][z] \oplus S[0][1][z] \oplus S[1][2][z] \oplus S[2][2][z] \oplus S[3][2][z]$
$S'[0][1][z] := S[0][0][z] \oplus S[1][1][z] \oplus S[2][1][z] \oplus S[3][1][z]$
$S'[0][0][z] := S[0][4][z] \oplus S[1][0][z] \oplus S[2][0][z] \oplus S[3][0][z]$

$S'[1][4][z] := S[0][4][z] \oplus S[1][4][z] \oplus S[2][0][z] \oplus S[3][3][z]$
$S'[1][3][z] := S[0][3][z] \oplus S[1][3][z] \oplus S[2][4][z] \oplus S[3][2][z]$
$S'[1][2][z] := S[0][2][z] \oplus S[1][2][z] \oplus S[2][3][z] \oplus S[3][4][z] \oplus S[3][1][z]$
$S'[1][1][z] := S[0][1][z] \oplus S[1][1][z] \oplus S[2][2][z] \oplus S[2][0][z] \oplus S[3][0][z]$
$S'[1][0][z] := S[0][0][z] \oplus S[1][0][z] \oplus S[2][1][z] \oplus S[3][4][z]$

**Table 3.** The difference distribution table of the S-box. Input and output differences are given in the hexadecimal format. Each element of the table represents the number of occurrences of the corresponding output difference $\Delta OUT$ given the input difference $\Delta IN$. For clarity '-' denotes 0.

| $\Delta OUT$ / $\Delta IN$ | 00 | 01 | 02 | 03 | 04 | 05 | 06 | 07 | 08 | 09 | 0a | 0b | 0c | 0d | 0e | 0f | 10 | 11 | 12 | 13 | 14 | 15 | 16 | 17 | 18 | 19 | 1a | 1b | 1c | 1d | 1e | 1f |
|---|---|---|---|---|---|---|---|---|---|---|---|---|---|---|---|---|---|---|---|---|---|---|---|---|---|---|---|---|---|---|---|---|
| 00 | 32 | - | - | - | - | - | - | - | - | - | - | - | - | - | - | - | - | - | - | - | - | - | - | - | - | - | - | - | - | - | - | - |
| 01 | - | 8 | - | - | - | - | - | - | - | 6 | - | - | - | - | 2 | - | - | 6 | - | - | - | - | 2 | - | - | 8 | - | - | - | - | - | - |
| 02 | - | - | 8 | 6 | - | - | - | - | - | - | - | - | 2 | - | - | - | 6 | 8 | - | - | - | - | - | - | - | - | 2 | - | - | - | - | - |
| 03 | - | - | 2 | 4 | - | - | - | - | - | 4 | 2 | - | - | - | - | - | - | 4 | 4 | 2 | - | - | - | - | - | 4 | 4 | - | 2 | - | - | - |
| 04 | - | - | - | - | 8 | 6 | 6 | 8 | - | - | - | - | - | - | - | - | - | - | - | - | - | - | - | - | - | 2 | 2 | - | - | - | - | - |
| 05 | - | - | - | - | 4 | - | 4 | - | 2 | - | - | - | 2 | - | 4 | - | - | - | - | 2 | - | 4 | - | 2 | - | - | - | - | 4 | - | 4 | - |
| 06 | - | - | - | - | 2 | 4 | 4 | 4 | - | 2 | - | - | - | - | - | - | - | - | 4 | 4 | 2 | 4 | - | - | - | 2 | - | - | - | - | - | - |
| 07 | - | - | - | - | 2 | - | 2 | 2 | - | - | - | 2 | 2 | 2 | - | 2 | - | - | - | 2 | 2 | 2 | 2 | - | - | 2 | - | 2 | 2 | 2 | 2 | - |
| 08 | - | - | - | - | - | - | - | 8 | - | 6 | - | 6 | - | 8 | - | - | - | - | 2 | - | 2 | - | - | - | - | - | - | - | - | - | - | - |
| 09 | - | 4 | 2 | 2 | - | - | - | - | - | - | - | - | 4 | - | 4 | - | 4 | - | 4 | - | - | - | - | - | - | - | - | 2 | 2 | - | 4 | - |
| 0a | - | - | - | - | - | - | 2 | 4 | - | - | 4 | 4 | - | - | 2 | 2 | - | - | - | - | - | - | - | 2 | - | - | 4 | 4 | - | - | 4 | - |
| 0b | - | 2 | 4 | - | - | - | - | - | - | - | - | - | - | 6 | 4 | - | - | - | - | - | - | - | - | - | - | - | - | 4 | 6 | - | - | - |
| 0c | - | - | - | - | - | - | - | 2 | 4 | 4 | 4 | 4 | 2 | 4 | 4 | - | - | 2 | - | - | - | - | 2 | - | - | - | - | - | - | - | - | - |
| 0d | - | - | - | - | 2 | - | 6 | - | 4 | - | 4 | - | - | - | - | - | - | - | 4 | - | 4 | - | 2 | - | - | - | - | - | - | - | - | - |
| 0e | - | 2 | - | - | - | - | - | 2 | 2 | - | 2 | 2 | 2 | 2 | 2 | - | - | - | - | - | 2 | - | - | 2 | 2 | 2 | 2 | 2 | 2 | 2 | - | 2 |
| 0f | - | - | - | - | 2 | 2 | 2 | - | 2 | 2 | 2 | - | - | - | - | - | - | - | 4 | 2 | 2 | 2 | 4 | 2 | 2 | 2 | - | - | - | - | - | - |
| 10 | - | - | - | - | - | - | 2 | - | - | 2 | - | - | - | - | 8 | - | - | 6 | - | - | 6 | - | - | - | 8 | - | - | - | - | - | - | - |
| 11 | - | 2 | - | - | 4 | - | - | - | 4 | 2 | - | - | 4 | - | - | - | 4 | - | - | 2 | - | - | 4 | - | - | - | - | 4 | 2 | - | - | - |
| 12 | - | - | 4 | 4 | 2 | - | 2 | 4 | - | - | - | - | - | - | - | - | - | - | - | - | - | 2 | 4 | 2 | - | - | 4 | 4 | - | - | - | - |
| 13 | - | - | 2 | 2 | - | - | 2 | 2 | 2 | - | 2 | 2 | - | 2 | 2 | 2 | - | - | - | 2 | - | - | 2 | - | - | 2 | 2 | - | 2 | 2 | - | - |
| 14 | - | 2 | - | - | - | - | - | - | - | - | - | - | 2 | - | 4 | 2 | - | - | - | 4 | 4 | 4 | 4 | - | - | - | - | - | 2 | 4 | - | - |
| 15 | - | 4 | - | - | - | - | - | 2 | - | 4 | - | - | - | - | - | 6 | 2 | - | - | - | - | - | 4 | - | 6 | - | - | - | 4 | - | - | - |
| 16 | - | - | 2 | 6 | 4 | 4 | - | - | - | - | - | - | - | - | - | - | - | - | - | - | - | - | 4 | 4 | 2 | 6 | - | - | 4 | - | - | - |
| 17 | - | - | 2 | 2 | 2 | 2 | - | - | - | 4 | 2 | 4 | 2 | - | - | - | - | 2 | - | - | 2 | - | - | 2 | 2 | 2 | 2 | - | 2 | 2 | 2 | - |
| 18 | - | - | - | - | 2 | - | - | - | - | - | - | - | - | 2 | 2 | - | 4 | - | 4 | - | 4 | - | 4 | - | 2 | - | 4 | - | 4 | - | - | - |
| 19 | - | 2 | - | 2 | 2 | 2 | - | 2 | - | - | - | 2 | - | 2 | - | 2 | - | 2 | - | 2 | 2 | 2 | - | 2 | - | - | - | - | 2 | - | 2 | - |
| 1a | - | - | - | - | - | - | - | 2 | - | - | 4 | 6 | - | - | 4 | 4 | - | 2 | 4 | - | - | 6 | - | - | - | - | - | - | - | - | - | - |
| 1b | - | 2 | 2 | - | - | 4 | 4 | - | - | 2 | 2 | - | - | 2 | 2 | - | - | 2 | 2 | - | - | 2 | 2 | - | - | - | - | - | - | 2 | 2 | - |
| 1c | - | - | 2 | - | - | - | - | - | - | - | 2 | - | - | 2 | 2 | 2 | 2 | - | 2 | 2 | 2 | 2 | 2 | 2 | 2 | 2 | - | 2 | 2 | - | - | - |
| 1d | - | 2 | - | 4 | - | 2 | - | 2 | - | 2 | - | - | - | 2 | 2 | - | 4 | - | 2 | - | 2 | - | 2 | - | 2 | - | 2 | - | - | 2 | - | - |
| 1e | - | - | - | - | - | - | - | 2 | 4 | 2 | 2 | 2 | 2 | - | 2 | 2 | 4 | 2 | 2 | 2 | 2 | - | 2 | - | 2 | - | - | - | - | - | - | - |
| 1f | - | 2 | 2 | - | 2 | - | - | 2 | 2 | - | - | 2 | - | 2 | 2 | - | 2 | - | - | 2 | - | 2 | 2 | - | - | 2 | 2 | - | 2 | - | - | 2 |

$$S'[2][4][z] := S[0][4][z] \oplus S[1][3][z] \oplus S[2][4][z] \oplus S[3][0][z]$$
$$S'[2][3][z] := S[0][3][z] \oplus S[1][2][z] \oplus S[2][3][z] \oplus S[3][4][z]$$
$$S'[2][2][z] := S[0][2][z] \oplus S[1][4][z] \oplus S[1][1][z] \oplus S[2][2][z] \oplus S[3][3][z]$$
$$S'[2][1][z] := S[0][1][z] \oplus S[1][0][z] \oplus S[2][1][z] \oplus S[3][2][z] \oplus S[3][0][z]$$
$$S'[2][0][z] := S[0][0][z] \oplus S[1][4][z] \oplus S[2][0][z] \oplus S[3][1][z]$$

$$S'[3][4][z] := S[0][4][z] \oplus S[1][0][z] \oplus S[2][3][z] \oplus S[3][4][z]$$
$$S'[3][3][z] := S[0][3][z] \oplus S[1][4][z] \oplus S[2][2][z] \oplus S[3][3][z]$$
$$S'[3][2][z] := S[0][2][z] \oplus S[1][3][z] \oplus S[2][4][z] \oplus S[2][1][z] \oplus S[3][2][z]$$
$$S'[3][1][z] := S[0][1][z] \oplus S[1][2][z] \oplus S[1][0][z] \oplus S[2][0][z] \oplus S[3][1][z]$$
$$S'[3][0][z] := S[0][0][z] \oplus S[1][1][z] \oplus S[2][4][z] \oplus S[3][0][z]$$
$$\}$$
$$S := S'$$

# H

**Table 4.** The linear profile of the S-box. Input and output masks are given in the hexadecimal format. Each element in the table is the number of mismatches between the linear equation represented by the input mask $IN$ and the linear equation represented by the output mask $OUT$. Dividing an element value by 16 gives the probability that the corresponding equations are not equal.

| OUT IN | 00 | 01 | 02 | 03 | 04 | 05 | 06 | 07 | 08 | 09 | 0a | 0b | 0c | 0d | 0e | 0f | 10 | 11 | 12 | 13 | 14 | 15 | 16 | 17 | 18 | 19 | 1a | 1b | 1c | 1d | 1e | 1f |
|---|---|---|---|---|---|---|---|---|---|---|---|---|---|---|---|---|---|---|---|---|---|---|---|---|---|---|---|---|---|---|---|---|
| 00 | 0 | 16 | 16 | 16 | 16 | 16 | 16 | 16 | 16 | 16 | 16 | 16 | 16 | 16 | 16 | 16 | 16 | 16 | 16 | 16 | 16 | 16 | 16 | 16 | 16 | 16 | 16 | 16 | 16 | 16 | 16 | 16 |
| 01 | 16 | 10 | 18 | 24 | 18 | 12 | 16 | 14 | 18 | 16 | 16 | 18 | 16 | 22 | 18 | 20 | 18 | 16 | 16 | 18 | 16 | 14 | 18 | 12 | 16 | 18 | 18 | 16 | 18 | 12 | 16 | 14 |
| 02 | 16 | 18 | 10 | 16 | 18 | 16 | 24 | 18 | 18 | 16 | 12 | 14 | 16 | 18 | 14 | 12 | 18 | 16 | 16 | 18 | 16 | 18 | 18 | 16 | 16 | 18 | 22 | 12 | 18 | 16 | 20 | 14 |
| 03 | 16 | 24 | 16 | 16 | 16 | 12 | 16 | 20 | 16 | 16 | 12 | 12 | 16 | 20 | 12 | 16 | 16 | 16 | 16 | 16 | 12 | 16 | 12 | 16 | 16 | 12 | 20 | 16 | 12 | 12 | 16 | 16 |
| 04 | 16 | 18 | 18 | 16 | 10 | 16 | 16 | 18 | 18 | 16 | 16 | 18 | 24 | 18 | 18 | 16 | 18 | 16 | 16 | 18 | 12 | 22 | 14 | 12 | 16 | 18 | 18 | 16 | 14 | 20 | 12 | 14 |
| 05 | 16 | 8 | 16 | 8 | 16 | 12 | 16 | 20 | 16 | 16 | 16 | 12 | 12 | 16 | 16 | 20 | 12 | 16 | 16 | 16 | 12 | 12 | 12 | 20 | 16 | 16 | 20 | 12 | 12 | 12 | 16 | 16 |
| 06 | 16 | 16 | 24 | 16 | 16 | 16 | 16 | 16 | 16 | 16 | 12 | 12 | 16 | 20 | 16 | 12 | 16 | 16 | 16 | 20 | 16 | 12 | 16 | 16 | 16 | 16 | 16 | 20 | 16 | 12 | 16 | 16 |
| 07 | 16 | 10 | 18 | 16 | 18 | 20 | 16 | 22 | 18 | 16 | 12 | 14 | 16 | 14 | 14 | 16 | 18 | 16 | 16 | 18 | 12 | 18 | 22 | 16 | 16 | 18 | 14 | 20 | 18 | 12 | 16 | 14 |
| 08 | 16 | 18 | 18 | 16 | 18 | 16 | 16 | 18 | 10 | 12 | 16 | 22 | 16 | 14 | 18 | 12 | 18 | 16 | 16 | 18 | 18 | 18 | 16 | 24 | 14 | 18 | 20 | 18 | 12 | 16 | 16 | 14 |
| 09 | 16 | 16 | 16 | 16 | 16 | 20 | 16 | 20 | 8 | 12 | 16 | 20 | 16 | 16 | 16 | 16 | 16 | 16 | 16 | 12 | 16 | 12 | 8 | 20 | 16 | 12 | 16 | 16 | 16 | 16 | 16 | 16 |
| 0a | 16 | 16 | 8 | 16 | 16 | 16 | 8 | 16 | 16 | 20 | 12 | 16 | 16 | 12 | 16 | 20 | 16 | 16 | 16 | 16 | 16 | 16 | 16 | 16 | 12 | 16 | 12 | 8 | 20 | 16 | 12 | 16 |
| 0b | 16 | 18 | 18 | 8 | 18 | 20 | 16 | 14 | 18 | 20 | 12 | 18 | 16 | 18 | 22 | 20 | 18 | 16 | 16 | 18 | 16 | 14 | 18 | 12 | 16 | 14 | 14 | 16 | 18 | 16 | 20 | 14 |
| 0c | 16 | 16 | 16 | 16 | 24 | 16 | 16 | 16 | 16 | 16 | 12 | 12 | 16 | 16 | 16 | 16 | 16 | 20 | 16 | 12 | 16 | 16 | 16 | 12 | 16 | 12 | 16 | 12 | 20 | 16 | 12 | 14 |
| 0d | 16 | 18 | 18 | 16 | 18 | 20 | 16 | 14 | 18 | 12 | 16 | 14 | 8 | 18 | 18 | 16 | 18 | 16 | 16 | 18 | 20 | 18 | 14 | 16 | 16 | 22 | 18 | 20 | 14 | 20 | 12 | 14 |
| 0e | 16 | 18 | 10 | 16 | 18 | 16 | 16 | 18 | 18 | 12 | 20 | 18 | 16 | 22 | 22 | 16 | 18 | 16 | 16 | 18 | 12 | 14 | 14 | 16 | 16 | 20 | 16 | 16 | 20 | 20 | 16 | 22 |
| 0f | 16 | 16 | 12 | 16 | 12 | 16 | 12 | 16 | 16 | 12 | 16 | 16 | 12 | 20 | 16 | 16 | 16 | 12 | 20 | 16 | 16 | 20 | 12 | 16 | 16 | 16 | 16 | 16 | 16 | 16 | 16 | 16 |
| 10 | 16 | 18 | 18 | 16 | 18 | 16 | 16 | 18 | 18 | 16 | 16 | 18 | 16 | 18 | 18 | 16 | 10 | 24 | 12 | 14 | 16 | 18 | 22 | 20 | 16 | 18 | 14 | 12 | 18 | 16 | 12 | 14 |
| 11 | 16 | 16 | 16 | 16 | 16 | 12 | 16 | 12 | 16 | 16 | 16 | 16 | 16 | 16 | 12 | 24 | 16 | 12 | 20 | 16 | 12 | 20 | 16 | 16 | 16 | 16 | 16 | 16 | 16 | 16 | 16 | 16 |
| 12 | 16 | 16 | 16 | 16 | 16 | 16 | 16 | 16 | 16 | 20 | 12 | 16 | 16 | 20 | 12 | 8 | 8 | 12 | 20 | 16 | 16 | 20 | 12 | 16 | 16 | 16 | 16 | 16 | 16 | 16 | 16 | 16 |
| 13 | 16 | 18 | 18 | 16 | 16 | 16 | 8 | 16 | 16 | 16 | 16 | 8 | 16 | 16 | 16 | 16 | 20 | 20 | 12 | 20 | 16 | 16 | 16 | 12 | 12 | 20 | 12 | 16 | 16 | 16 | 16 | 16 |
| 14 | 16 | 16 | 16 | 16 | 8 | 16 | 16 | 16 | 16 | 16 | 8 | 16 | 16 | 16 | 16 | 16 | 20 | 20 | 12 | 20 | 16 | 16 | 16 | 12 | 12 | 20 | 12 | 16 | 16 | 16 | 16 | 16 |
| 15 | 16 | 18 | 18 | 16 | 18 | 12 | 16 | 22 | 18 | 16 | 16 | 18 | 16 | 14 | 18 | 20 | 18 | 8 | 20 | 14 | 18 | 16 | 16 | 18 | 18 | 16 | 22 | 20 | 20 | 14 | 16 | 16 |
| 16 | 16 | 18 | 18 | 16 | 18 | 16 | 8 | 18 | 18 | 16 | 18 | 16 | 20 | 14 | 16 | 18 | 14 | 12 | 18 | 16 | 18 | 20 | 14 | 20 | 16 | 14 | 16 | 16 | 16 | 22 | 20 | 14 |
| 17 | 16 | 16 | 16 | 16 | 16 | 20 | 16 | 12 | 16 | 16 | 12 | 20 | 16 | 20 | 12 | 16 | 16 | 8 | 12 | 12 | 16 | 16 | 20 | 16 | 16 | 16 | 20 | 16 | 12 | 16 | 12 | 16 |
| 18 | 16 | 16 | 16 | 16 | 16 | 16 | 16 | 16 | 16 | 24 | 12 | 16 | 20 | 16 | 12 | 16 | 16 | 12 | 16 | 16 | 12 | 16 | 16 | 16 | 18 | 18 | 16 | 18 | 16 | 20 | 16 | 22 |
| 19 | 16 | 18 | 18 | 16 | 18 | 12 | 16 | 14 | 10 | 20 | 16 | 14 | 16 | 18 | 18 | 16 | 18 | 16 | 12 | 14 | 16 | 22 | 14 | 16 | 16 | 22 | 14 | 16 | 18 | 16 | 20 | 22 |
| 1a | 16 | 18 | 18 | 16 | 18 | 16 | 16 | 18 | 18 | 16 | 16 | 18 | 16 | 14 | 14 | 16 | 18 | 20 | 16 | 16 | 8 | 12 | 16 | 20 | 16 | 16 | 16 | 16 | 16 | 16 | 16 | 16 |
| 1b | 16 | 18 | 18 | 16 | 16 | 16 | 12 | 16 | 12 | 12 | 16 | 16 | 20 | 12 | 16 | 16 | 20 | 12 | 16 | 20 | 20 | 16 | 8 | 12 | 16 | 20 | 16 | 16 | 16 | 16 | 16 | 16 |
| 1c | 16 | 18 | 18 | 16 | 10 | 16 | 16 | 18 | 18 | 12 | 16 | 14 | 16 | 14 | 18 | 20 | 18 | 16 | 12 | 14 | 20 | 14 | 16 | 16 | 12 | 12 | 20 | 16 | 12 | 20 | 16 | 16 |
| 1d | 16 | 16 | 16 | 16 | 12 | 16 | 12 | 16 | 12 | 16 | 20 | 16 | 16 | 20 | 16 | 16 | 16 | 12 | 12 | 16 | 16 | 12 | 16 | 12 | 20 | 16 | 12 | 20 | 16 | 16 | 16 | 16 |
| 1e | 16 | 16 | 16 | 16 | 16 | 16 | 8 | 16 | 16 | 12 | 12 | 16 | 16 | 20 | 12 | 16 | 16 | 16 | 12 | 20 | 20 | 16 | 16 | 16 | 12 | 12 | 12 | 16 | 20 | 16 | 20 | 16 |
| 1f | 16 | 18 | 18 | 16 | 18 | 20 | 16 | 14 | 18 | 20 | 20 | 18 | 16 | 18 | 14 | 12 | 18 | 16 | 20 | 14 | 20 | 18 | 18 | 12 | 16 | 14 | 18 | 12 | 14 | 12 | 12 | 22 |

# FPGA Implementations of SPRING
## And Their Countermeasures against Side-Channel Attacks

Hai Brenner[1], Lubos Gaspar[2], Gaëtan Leurent[3],
Alon Rosen[1], and François-Xavier Standaert[2]

[1] Interdisciplinary Center, Herzliya, Israel
[2] ICTEAM/ELEN/Crypto Group, Université catholique de Louvain, Belgium
[3] Inria, EPI SECRET, Rocquencourt, France

**Abstract.** SPRING is a family of pseudo-random functions that aims to combine the guarantees of security reductions with good performance on a variety of platforms. Preliminary software implementations for small-parameter instantiations of SPRING were proposed at FSE 2014, and have been demonstrated to reach throughputs within small factors of those of AES. In this paper, we complement these results and investigate the hardware design space of these types of primitives.

Our first (pragmatic) contribution is the first FPGA implementation of SPRING in a counter-like mode. We show that the "rounded product" operations in our design can be computed efficiently, reaching throughputs in the hundreds of megabits/second range within only 4% of the resources of a modern (Xilinx Virtex-6) reconfigurable device. Our second (more prospective) contribution is to discuss the properties of SPRING hardware implementations for side-channel resistance. We show that a part of the design can be very efficiently masked (with linear overhead), while another part implies quadratic overhead due to non-linear operations (similarly to what is usually observed, e.g., for block ciphers). Yet, we argue that for this second part of the design, resistance against "simple power analysis" may be sufficient to obtain concrete implementation security. We suggest ways to reach this goal very efficiently, via shuffling. We believe that such hybrid implementations, where each part of the design is protected with adequate solutions, is a promising topic for further investigation.

## 1 Introduction

The quest for secure and efficiently implemented primitives is an ongoing process in cryptography. In the symmetric setting, recent research has led to the development of many standard and lightweight block ciphers. As recently surveyed during the "Crypto for 2020" workshop, current design approaches have been quite successful in optimizing these primitives for various performance metrics, which has led to their deployment in numerous applications [29,31]. Yet, and although the problem of symmetric encryption may sound solved, at least two important (apparently unrelated) problems remain open.

First, from a theoretical point-of-view, there is still a large gap between the formalism used to argue about security in symmetric cryptography (mainly based

L. Batina and M. Robshaw (Eds.): CHES 2014, LNCS 8731, pp. 414–432, 2014.

on cryptanalysis) and the one in asymmetric cryptography (which widely relies on security reductions). While we do not wish to make statements about which approach should currently be privileged and for what application, we believe that any attempt at closing the gap between these two approaches is interesting, since there seems to be no contradiction between implementation efficiency and security reductions from well-understood problems. Note that closing such a gap can naturally benefit both from better security analysis tools for already deployed constructions (as followed by the recent line of research about key alternating ciphers [2,5,6,17,18]) and from "provably secure" constructions leading to efficient implementations, as we pursue in this paper.

Secondly, although block ciphers that perform well on various types of platforms are now mainstream, the problem of securing their implementations against physical (e.g. side-channel) attacks is still quite open. Indeed, the performance overhead caused by standard countermeasures against such attacks (like masking [11,14,27,28] or shuffling [15,33]) are still significant, and the physical assumptions for these countermeasures to provide the expected security improvements are sometimes hard to achieve. (See for example the discussions in [8,22,25].)

Interestingly, and despite looking disconnected, these two problems share a number of (intuitive) similarities, and progresses with respect to one of them could be a source of improvement for the other one. The main reason for this intuition is that one of the main elements that makes asymmetric cryptographic primitives easier to prove by reduction is their more elaborated mathematical structure. But mathematical structure (in particular, certain types of homomorphisms) is exactly what sometimes makes the protection of asymmetric implementations easier, at least from a conceptual point of view [7,16]. As a result, one can generally expect that, as the physical security level of implementations increases, the performance gap between symmetric and asymmetric primitives vanishes. Two recent examples illustrate this hope, namely the masked implementation of the Lapin protocol in [10] and the leakage-resilient MAC in [23]. Unfortunately, both works have some limitations. In the first case, the execution of Lapin requires randomness that seem difficult to protect against side-channel attacks (and was excluded from the physical security analysis so far). In the second case, the MAC relies on quite expensive pairing operations which implies (constant but significant) overhead that dominate the implementation cost in current technologies.

In this paper, we follow this line of work and investigate the implementation properties of a recent Pseudo-Random Function (PRF) candidate called SPRING [3,4]. Based on the "Learning with Rounding" assumption, it enjoys (*i*) compared to the pairings in [23], having underlying operations that can be implemented quite efficiently in software, and (*ii*) compared to Lapin, the advantages of a being deterministic. Besides, and as a PRF, SPRING also corresponds to a stronger and more generic primitive (potentially exploitable for encryption, authentication and hashing). Our contributions are twofold.

We start by describing and evaluating the hardware performance of SPRING within modern FPGAs. For this purpose, we take advantage of its BCH variant described at FSE 2014 and exploit a couple of optimizations, that essentially turn our architecture into a combination of a subset-sum, some Fast Fourier Transforms (FFTs), a rounding step and a BCH code. We show that these operations combine nicely and produce overall performance that is sufficient for a wide range of applications – though still substantially lower than that of AES.

Next, and as part of our motivation relates to physically protected implementation, we also study the extent to which countermeasures against side-channel attacks can be efficiently implemented for SPRING, leading to contrasted conclusions. First, we show that the subset-sum part of our architecture can be masked just as efficiently as Lapin (i.e., independently for each share, with linear overhead). Unfortunately (and quite naturally for a PRF candidate), the rest of its operations are non-linear with respect to the masking scheme, and imply more significant overhead. In this context, we investigate two possible solutions. On the one hand, we estimate the cost of a fully masked implementation, for which the performance is (asymptotically) similar to that of AES. On the other hand, we analyze the cost of a hybrid architecture, where only part of the design is masked and the rest is protected with other means (shuffling, typically). We informally argue about the relevance of this proposal in two directions. First, we observe that standard Differential Power Analysis (DPA) is not possible after the subset-sum operation, because the intermediate computation depends on all the key bits from this point on (so it cannot be enumerated anymore). Secondly, we observe that unmasking before the rounding step will be (theoretically) secure if the leakage function is "rounding" the intermediate values in an appropriate way. In both cases, these arguments suggest that security against Simple Power Analysis (SPA) are sufficient for this part of the design, and we evaluate the cost of a candidate implementation based on this principle.

Overall, our results confirm that SPRING is an interesting family of PRFs for general applications. We also believe that the hybrid countermeasure strategy, that we suggest, is a promising alternative to a secure and efficient implementation, and it leads to interesting open problems. To some extent, it can be viewed as an instantiation of the fresh re-keying scheme in [24], which also combines a DPA-secure linear part with a SPA-secure non-linear one (so connections with such schemes would be interesting to formalize). They also question the families of rounding functions that lead to side-channel resistant PRFs with partial masking, and whether these functions can be implemented physically by a leakage function (possibly as an engineering constraint).

The rest of the paper is structured as follows. Section 2 contains the specifications of SPRING, Section 3 describes its FPGA implementation, and Section 4 discusses its side-channel resistance.

# 2   SPRING Specifications

## 2.1   The SPRING Family of Pseudo-random Functions

One of the main constructions in [4] is a class of PRF candidates called SPRING which is short for "subset-product with rounding over a **ring**." Let $n$ be a power of two, and let $R$ denote the polynomial ring $R := \mathbb{Z}[X]/(X^n+1)$, which is known as the $2n$th *cyclotomic ring*.[1] For a positive integer $q$, let $R_q$ denote the quotient ring:

$$R_q := R/qR = \mathbb{Z}_q[X]/(X^n + 1),$$

i.e., the ring of polynomials in $X$ with coefficients in $\mathbb{Z}_q$, where addition and multiplication are modulo both $X^n + 1$ and $q$. (For ring elements $r(X)$ in $R$ or $R_q$, the indeterminate $X$ is usually suppressed.) Let $R_q^*$ denote the multiplicative group of units (invertible elements) in $R_q$.

For a positive integer $k$, the SPRING family is the set of functions $F_{a,s}$ : $\{0,1\}^k \to \{0,1\}^m$ indexed by a unit $a \in R_q^*$ and a vector $\boldsymbol{s} = (s_1, \ldots, s_k) \in (R_q^*)^k$ of units. The function is defined as the "rounded subset-product":

$$F_{\boldsymbol{s}}(x_1, \ldots, x_k) := S\left( a \cdot \prod_{i=1}^{k} s_i^{x_i} \right), \tag{1}$$

where $S \colon R_q \to \{0,1\}^m$ for some $m \leq n$ is an appropriate "rounding" function. For example, BPR considers the floor rounding function that maps each of its input's $n$ coefficients to $\mathbb{Z}_2 = \{0,1\}$, depending on whether the coefficient (in its canonical form in $\mathbb{Z}_{257}$) is smaller than $q/2$ or not.

It is proved in [4] that when $a$ and $s_i$ are drawn from appropriate distributions, and $q$ is sufficiently large, the above function family is a secure PRF family, assuming that the "ring learning with errors" (ring-LWE) problem [20] is hard in $R_q$.

## 2.2 Implementation Details: Our Chosen Construction

In the following we describe an optimized FPGA implementation of the SPRING PRF family based on the parameters suggested in [3]. These parameters offer high levels of concrete security against known classes of attacks, and lead to efficient implementations. A discussion and more thorough theoretical analysis of these parameters can be found in [3]. Note that this choice is just one of the possible instantiations of the SPRING family. We use it as a case study to show our hardware implementation and side-channel resistance techniques and to evaluate performance. We also suggest ways to secure the computation from leakage of the key by methods of masking (which seem to match the homomorphic characteristics in the subset-sum part of the SPRING PRF quite elegantly) and alternative countermeasures.

Aiming to design practical functions, the SPRING family can be instantiated with relatively small moduli $q$, rather than the large ones required by the theoretical security reductions in [4]. This allows following the same basic construction paradigm as in [4], while taking advantage of the fast integer arithmetic operations. In this paper we follow suit the parameters chosen in [3]:

---

[1] It is the $2n$th cyclotomic ring because the complex roots of $X^n + 1$ are all the $2n$th primitive roots of unity. The BPR functions can be defined over other cyclotomic rings as well, but in this work we restrict to powers of two for simplicity and efficiency.

$$n = 128, \quad q = 257, \quad k = 64,$$

which yields attractive performance, and allows for a comfortable margin of security. The choice of modulus $q = 257$ is akin to the one made in SWIFFT, for a practical instantiation of a theoretically sound lattice-based collision-resistant hash function [19]. Also as in SWIFFT, our implementations build on Fast Fourier Transform-like algorithms modulo $q = 257$.

Choosing an odd modulus $q = 257$ admits very fast subset-product computations in $R_q^*$ using Fast Fourier Transform-type techniques (as mentioned above). However, because $q$ is odd, any rounding function $\lfloor \cdot \rceil \colon R_q \to R_2$, applied to individual coefficients separately, has bias $1/q$ on each of the output bits. Since $q$ is rather small, such a bias is easily noticeable. This poses no problem at all if SPRING is used for authentication schemes. Nevertheless, it clearly renders the function insecure as a PRF.

To reduce bias, a post-processing step $G$ is implemented by using dual BCH error-correcting code: $S(b_1, \ldots, b_n) = G(\lfloor b_1, \ldots, b_n \rceil)$, where $\lfloor \cdot \rceil$ is applied pointwise. $G$ multiplies the 128-dimensional, $1/q$-biased bit vector by the $64 \times 128$ generator matrix of a binary (extended) BCH error-correcting code with parameters $[n, m, d] = [128, 64, 22]$, yielding a syndrome with respect to the dual code. This simple and very fast "deterministic extraction" procedure (proposed in [1]) reduces the bias exponentially in the distance $d = 22$ of the code, and yields a 64-dimensional vector that is $2^{-145}$-far from uniform (when applied to a 128-dimensional bit vector of independent $1/q$-biased bits). However, this comes at the cost of outputting $m = 64$ bits instead of $n = 128$, as determined by the rate $m/n$ of the code.

In terms of implementation, generator matrices of BCH codes over $GF(2)$ are preferable, since the rows of the matrix are cyclic shifts of a single row, which facilitates fast and simple implementation. Note that $n$ is a power of 2, and any BCH code over $GF(2)$ is of length $2^t - 1$ for some integer $t$. To make the matrix compatible with an $n$ that is a power of two, the extended-BCH code can be used. This extended code is obtained in a standard way by appending a parity bit to the codewords, and it increases the code distance $d$ by one. Finally note that for these chosen parameters $n = 128, m = 64$, the BCH code with parameters $[127, 64, 21]$ and its extension with parameters $[128, 64, 22]$ have the largest known minimum distance for these specific rates. For more theoretical details regarding the bias after applying $G$, we refer the reader to [3].

## 2.3   Implementation Details: Fast Subset-Product in $R_q$

The core of the SPRING algorithm is the subset-product calculation expressed by Equation 1. Direct multiplication of polynomials of degree $n$ is quite expensive, but the computation can be efficient using properties of the carefully chosen ring $R_{257}$. Following [3], the Chinese Remainder decomposition of this ring as $R_q \cong \mathbb{Z}_q^n$ given in [19] is used. More precisely, a polynomial in $R_{257}$ is uniquely determined by its evaluation on the $n$-th primitive roots of unity. Denote this isomorphism by $\mathcal{F}$:

$$\mathcal{F} : R_{257} \to \mathbb{Z}_{257}^n, \quad b \mapsto (b(\omega^{2i+1}))_{i=0}^{n-1},$$

where $\omega$ denotes a $2n$-th primitive root of unity. In particular, the multiplicative group of units $R_q^*$ is the set of polynomials whose $\mathcal{F}$ coefficients are all non-zero. This gives the following negacyclic convolution theorem:

$$\mathcal{F}(a \cdot b) = \mathcal{F}(a) \odot \mathcal{F}(b) \tag{2}$$

where $\cdot$ denotes the polynomial product in $R_{257}$, and $\odot$ is the point-wise multiplication of coefficients in $\mathbb{Z}_{257}$.

Moreover, $\mathcal{F}$ and its inverse can be efficiently implemented using an FFT-like algorithm. More precisely, an FFT of size $n$ over the finite field $\mathbb{Z}_{257}$ evaluates a polynomial at all the $n$-th roots of unity: FFT $: b \mapsto (b(\omega^{2i}))_{i=0}^{n-1}$ (we use $\omega^2$ as a primitive $n$-th root of unity). If we first multiply the coefficient of $b$ by powers of $\omega$, we have:

$$b(\omega^{2i+1}) = b'(\omega^{2i}), \qquad \text{where } b_i' = b_i \cdot \omega^i.$$
$$\mathcal{F}(b) = \text{FFT}(b'),$$

Finally, the subset-product of SPRING can be written as:

$$a \cdot \prod_{i=1}^{k} s_i^{x_i} = \mathcal{F}^{-1}\left(\mathcal{F}(a) \odot \mathcal{F}(s_1^{x_1}) \odot \cdots \odot \mathcal{F}(s_k^{x_k})\right). \tag{3}$$

The value of the bit $x_i$ determines whether polynomial $s_i$ is involved in the subset-product multiplication: $s_i^{x_i}$ is either $s_i$ or 1. In practice, indices with $x_i = 0$ are just removed from the product. Using the convolution theorem, the polynomial subset-product is computed by multiplying the $\mathcal{F}$ evaluations point-wise and transforming the result back by $\mathcal{F}^{-1}$. The $\mathcal{F}$ evaluations can be computed just once beforehand, and stored instead of the polynomials. Applying $\mathcal{F}$ on the $a$ and $s_i$, we obtain these sequences:

$$\mathcal{F}(a_0, a_1, \ldots, a_{n-1}) = [A_0, A_1, \ldots, A_{n-1}],$$
$$\mathcal{F}(s_{i,0}, s_{i,1}, \ldots, s_{i,n-1}) = [S_{i,0}, S_{i,1}, \ldots, S_{i,n-1}], \qquad \forall i \in \{1, \ldots, k\}.$$

We can further simplify the implementation by storing only the discrete logs of the sequences $A$ and $S_i$ using a suitable generator element $G$ (we have chosen $G = 3$). We denote those sequences as $\widehat{A}$ and $\widehat{S_i}$, and the exponentiation as $\mathcal{E}$:

$$[A_0, A_1, \ldots, A_{n-1}] = \mathcal{E}(\widehat{A}) = \left[G^{\widehat{A_0}}, G^{\widehat{A_1}}, \ldots, G^{\widehat{A_{n-1}}}\right],$$
$$[S_{i,0}, S_{i,1}, \ldots, S_{i,n-1}] = \mathcal{E}(\widehat{S_i}) = \left[G^{\widehat{S_{i,0}}}, G^{\widehat{S_{i,1}}}, \ldots, G^{\widehat{S_{i,n-1}}}\right], \qquad \forall i \in \{1, \ldots, k\}.$$

Note the entries $A_j$ and $S_{i,j}$ are all non-zero because $a$ and the $s_i$'s are units in $R_{257}$. If the key is stored in this form, the subset-product in SPRING can be computed very efficiently:

$$a \cdot \prod_{i=1}^{k} s_i^{x_i} = \mathcal{F}^{-1}\left(\mathcal{E}\left(\widehat{A} + \sum_{x_i=1} \widehat{S}_i\right)\right), \qquad (4)$$

where the addition is a point-wise modulo 256.

## 2.4   Implementation Details: Counter and Gray-Code Mode

As in [3], we focus on implementing SPRING in a counter-like (CTR) mode. This mode uses Gray code, which is a simple way of ordering the strings in $\{0,1\}^k$ so that successive strings differ in only one position. Then, when running SPRING in counter mode, we store the value $\widehat{B} = \widehat{A} + \sum_{x_i=1} \widehat{S}_i$ and we update this additive state by adding or removing a secret key elements $\widehat{S}_i$. Thus, much of the work across consecutive evaluations is amortized.

More precisely, $\widehat{B}$ is initialized to zero (the Gray code starts with $0^k$). For each iteration, if the next input $x'$ flips the $i$th bit of $x$, then the old subset-product is updated to $\widehat{B}' = \widehat{B} + \widehat{S}_i$ if $x_i = 0$, otherwise $\widehat{B}' = \widehat{B} - \widehat{S}_i$.

## 2.5   Operations in SPRING

Thanks to those optimizations, the SPRING evaluations in CRT mode are now reduced to a few simple operations. In the following description, steps 1–3 compute the subset product $b := a \prod_{i=1}^{n} s_i^{x_i}$, and steps 4–5 perform the rounding function $S(b)$:

1. Update the additive state $\widehat{B}$: $\widehat{B} \leftarrow \widehat{B} \pm \widehat{A}_i$, where $i$ is the flipped bit in the Gray counter
2. Compute the polynomial evaluation of $b$ as $B = [G^{\widehat{B_0}}, G^{\widehat{B_1}}, \ldots, G^{\widehat{B_{n-1}}}]$
3. Interpolate the product by computing $\mathcal{F}^{-1}(B)$
   - Compute $b' = \text{FFT}^{-1}(B)$
   - Deduce $b$ with $b_i = b'_i \cdot \omega^{-i}$
4. Round the coefficient of $b$
5. Apply the BCH code

# 3   FPGA Implementation

In this section we discuss our design choices for unprotected SPRING-BCH (later just SPRING). We present a SPRING co-processor implementation and report its area and timing performance.

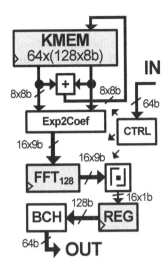

**Fig. 1.** Spring hardware implemenation

## 3.1    General Architecture

Our implementation is depicted in Fig. 1. All arithmetic operations in SPRING are computed modulo $q = 257$ except for the arithmetic operations on exponents which are calculated modulo $q - 1 = 256$. The secret key polynomial FFT coefficients $\widehat{A}$ and $\widehat{S}_i$ (in discrete log form) are stored in true dual port memory KMEM. Each KMEM channel can output 8 exponents (8-bit words) in parallel.

The subset-sum unit (that we detail next) computes addition/subtraction of two polynomials on 8 exponents in parallel, and the results are stored in KMEM. Subsequently, 16 exponents are read from KMEM using both channels and transformed to 9-bit words (representing polynomial evaluations) using table lookups (denoted by Exp2Coef). Next these data are partially processed by the FFT unit (that we also detail next) and stored in its internal registers. This way, in only 8 clock cycles all 128 evaluations are transformed to the polynomial coefficients and stored in the FFT register. When the $\mathrm{FFT}_{128}$ is completed, the resulting 9-bit coefficients are rounded point-wise in 16-coefficient chunks. The floor rounding function replaces each 9 coefficient bits by 1 bit as follows: if a coefficient value is in the range of 0 to 128 the resulting bit equals 0; if a value is in the range of 129 to 256 the resulting bit equals 1. In each clock cycle, 16 rounded 1-bit coefficients are stored in the output data register REG. When all 128 bits are present in REG, they are compressed by the BCH unit to output 64 bits.

## 3.2    Calculation of Subset-Product

We follow the description of Section 2.3 to implement the subset-product as a subset-sum of exponents, followed by an exponentiation, and the $\mathcal{F}^{-1}$ transform.

We store the coefficient sequences $\widehat{A}$ and $\widehat{S}_i$ in RAM during FPGA configuration. Thus, only the point-wise subset-sum, exponentiation with $G$ (using lookup tables) and $\mathcal{F}^{-1}$ operations have to be implemented in hardware. Unlike direct coefficient representation using 9-bit words, the range of exponents is between 0 and 255, thus the exponents are represented using only 8-bit words. Interestingly, the subset-sum of such exponents involves reduction by 256 instead of 257, which is implemented by simply ignoring the most significant bit (carry) generated by the addition. Moreover, the FFT$^{-1}$ differs from FFT by multiplication with the constant $n^{-1}$ which is included in KMEM's initialization data. This way, the FFT$^{-1}$ unit can be replaced by a more simple FFT unit.

### 3.3   Fast Fourier Transform

The FFT on 128 coefficients[2] in parallel is relatively expensive to implement. Instead, we decompose such an FFT unit to smaller FFT blocks. The FFT$_{128}$ decomposition is illustrated in the left side of Fig. 2, where the input sequence of 128 coefficients is organized in a $2 \times 64$ (row-major) matrix processed in 16-coefficient chunks. After transposing this matrix, an FFT$_{64}$ is computed on both columns. The results of the two FFT$_{64}$ blocks are multiplied by powers of a suitable primitive root of unity $\omega$ (we have selected $\omega = 139$), i.e. $\omega^{i \cdot j}$ for $0 \leq i < 64$ and $0 \leq j < 2$. Note, that first 64 powers (with $j = 0$) of $\omega$ are equal to 1, thus no multiplication is required. Although, multiplication with $\omega$ powers is part of the FFT$_{128}$ computation, it is placed inside the FFT$_{64}$ block for convenience. Next, an FFT$_2$ is computed on each row. Finally, the column-major matrix is transposed back to a row-major one and the resulting matrix represents the result of the FFT$_{128}$ transform. Note that the transposition steps are not shown in Fig. 2, because they are either implemented as a wire crossings (for free in hardware) or they are pre-computed during KMEM initialization.

**FFT$_{64}$.** In order to simplify the implementation, an FFT$_{64}$ block is decomposed even further (see Fig. 2), by organizing the 64 input coefficients in an $8 \times 8$ square matrix. Subsequently, the matrix is transposed (part of KMEM initialization), FFT$_8$ is computed on all 8 rows sequentially, and the result is multiplied by powers of a suitable primitive root of unity $\Omega = \omega^2$ (for $\omega = 139$ we have selected $\Omega = 139^2 \bmod 257 = 46$), i.e. $\Omega^{i \cdot j}$ for $0 \leq i < 8$ and $0 \leq j < 8$. The multiplication results form a new matrix that is stored in the FFT register. Subsequently, this matrix is transposed and stored back in the register. Eventually, FFT$_8$ operations (described next) are performed on all 8 rows sequentially. Their result is multiplied with $\omega$ powers (as part of the FFT$_{128}$ computation) and stored back in the FFT register.

**FFT$_8$.** The basic building block of FFT$_{64}$ is FFT$_8$, which is implemented with combinatorial logic only. FFT$_8$ is composed of three layers of four FFT$_2$ butter-

---

[2] Actually, the input to FFT$^{-1}$ is the polynomial *evaluations* and the output is the *coefficients*, but we refer to both as coefficients for simplicity.

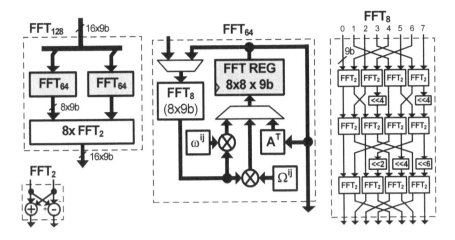

**Fig. 2.** Decomposition of Fast Fourier Transform operating with 128 coefficients

flies, and multiplications by powers of a root of unity. Each butterfly performs one addition and one subtraction. The root of unity $\omega^{16} = 4$ is chosen so that all those constants are powers of two, and can be implemented as shift, as illustrated in Fig. 2. Although the implementation of addition and subtraction is straightforward, the multiplication with a constant could be relatively expensive in $\mathbb{Z}_{257}$. However, $q = 257$ is a Fermat prime number $F_3 = 2^{2^3} + 1 = 257$, thus several interesting properties of arithmetic modulo Fermat numbers can be used to significantly simplify the implementation. Following the description by H. Nussbaumer [26], we introduced an encoding of each 9-bit coefficient $c$ to $C$ as follows:

$$C = (256 - c) \bmod 257. \tag{5}$$

This encoding reduces multiplications inside $\mathrm{FFT}_8$ into simple bit rotations around the 9-bit word, with complementation of the overflowing bits.

### 3.4 Cost and Performance Evaluation

We have synthesized our SPRING co-processor using Xilinx ISE 12.4 for Xilinx Virtex-6 XC6VLX240T FPGAs. The implementation results are summarized in Table 1. KMEM was organized in two 36 kb true dual-port RAMs. As expected, $\mathrm{FFT}_{128}$ occupies 76% of the SPRING area. Inside $\mathrm{FFT}_{128}$, two blocks of $\Omega^{i\cdot j}$ constant multipliers and one block of $\omega^{i\cdot j}$ constant multipliers utilizes most of the resources (roughly 69% of the $\mathrm{FFT}_{128}$). Since these blocks are combinatorial, they are implemented using lookup tables. The two $\mathrm{FFT}_8$ blocks constitute 17% of $\mathrm{FFT}_{128}$. Next, the two FFT registers storing 1152 bits of the *FFT* state occupy roughly 9% of the $\mathrm{FFT}_{128}$ unit. This optimization was achieved using the distributed RAM strategy (only slices are used, no dedicated BRAMs).

Table 1. Resource usage of the SPRING implementation

| Units | Slices | BRAM(36kb) |
|---|---|---|
| KMEM | 0 | 2 |
| Subset-sum | 16 | 0 |
| Exp2Coef | 128 | 0 |
| $FFT_{128}$ total | 1258 | 0 |
| $\rightarrow$ 2x $FFT_8$ | 210 | 0 |
| $\rightarrow$ 2x FFT REG + transpose | 110 | 0 |
| $\rightarrow$ 2x Mult. $\Omega^{i \cdot j}$ | 496 | 0 |
| $\rightarrow$ 1x Mult. $\omega^{i \cdot j}$ | 378 | 0 |
| $\rightarrow$ 8x $FFT_2$ | 64 | 0 |
| Rounding + REG | 32 | 0 |
| BCH | 189 | 0 |
| Control logic | 27 | 0 |
| SPRING - Total | 1650 | 2 |

Other SPRING parts are relatively small. In total, SPRING occupies 1650 slices which is only 4% of the available FPGA resources.

As far as speed performance is concerned, SPRING was designed to operate without idle states in the Gray counter mode. Computation starts by sequentially reading rows of 16 exponents from KMEM. These row exponents are first converted to coefficients, each half of them being processed by one of the two $FFT_8$ blocks, then multiplied with corresponding powers of $\Omega$, and stored in the two FFT registers. All these operations together are executed in only one clock cycle. Subsequently, the same operations are performed on the other 7 rows. Together, all 8 rows are processed in only 8 clock cycles. Next, both FFT registers are transposed in 12 clock cycles. The new 8 rows are processed by the two $FFT_8$ blocks, multiplied with corresponding powers of $\omega$ and stored back to the two FFT registers in 8 clock cycles. In the subsequent 8 clock cycles, 8 parallel $FFT_2$'s are computed on 8 rows. Then, all 9-bit coefficients are rounded to 1-bit coefficients and stored in the 128-bit register. The SPRING output is finally obtained by post-processing the combinatorial BCH unit on this register data. In parallel with the last 28 cycles, a new subset-sum is calculated. Since the subset-sum calculation requires 32 clock cycles, 4 extra clock cycles are necessary. This way, one SPRING execution with subset-sum pre-calculation requires 40 clock cycles. Such a result illustrates the usual trade-off between generic software and specialized hardware. In particular, it outperforms the FSE 2014 software implementation on Intel Core i7 Ivy Bridge (392 clock cycles per one encryption) by an approximate factor 10.

Besides, the maximum operating clock frequency for the selected FPGA device was estimated at 91.7 MHz. This seemed to be a good trade-off between speed and implementation size[3]. Assuming this clock frequency and continuous Gray counter mode operation, 2.3 million encryptions can be carried out in 1 second, which corresponds to a 140 megabits/second throughput.

For illustration purposes, we reported the performances of SPRING and a couple of representative algorithms in Table 2. While not directly comparable, they provide insights about the implementation cost of other recent primitives based on the Learning with Errors problem (yet, used for different purposes such as authentication or public-key encryption) and the AES Rijndael (which although based on totally different assumptions, aims at a similar goal as SPRING, namely PRP). As expected, the performance gap between our SPRING design and AES ones is slightly larger than in a software context, essentially because there are more computation units to implement here. Yet, the cost vs. performance trade-off obtained (in the hundreds of megabits/second range for a few %'s of the FPGA resources) is already sufficient for a wide range of applications.

Table 2. Comparison of different algorithms implemented on a Virtex 6 FPGA

| Alg. | Type | Dapath | LUT | FF | BRAM | DSP | $F_{max}$[1] | Cycles |
|------|------|--------|-----|-----|------|-----|-----------|--------|
| SPRING | PRF | 128/144b | 7292 | 294 | 2x 36k | 0 | 91.7 | 40 |
| Lapin [10] | auth. | 128b | 742 | 140 | 6x 36k | 0 | 140.3 | 1332 |
| Comp-LWE [30] | PKE | N/A | 1879 | 1142 | 3x 18k | 1 | 250.0 | 13287 [2] |
| AES-LUT [9] | PRP | 128b | 933 | 399 | 10x 18k | 0 | 674.0 | 11 |
| AES-COMB [9] | PRP | 128b | 2335 | 535 | 0 | 0 | 218.6 | 11 |
| AES-COMB [9] | PRP | 32b | 467 | 976 | 0 | 0 | 315.1 | 58 |

[1] Maximum frequency is denoted in MHz.
[2] Number of clock cycles for encryption only.

## 4    Towards Side-Channel Resistance

We now move to the second part of our investigation, and discuss two possible approaches to side-channel resistance for hardware implementations of SPRING. The first one takes advantage of standard solutions for masking (a.k.a. secret sharing). As we detail next, it implies more significant overhead for certain parts of the computation than others. Motivated by this observation, we then suggest an alternative approach, where only one part of the implementation is masked, and the other one is shuffled. We show that this alternative is very efficient; we argue about its relevance and suggest open problems based on it.

---

[3] The clock frequency could indeed be higher if the long combinatorial paths were split by pipelining. However, this would result in a substantially larger implementation and latency.

## 4.1    Fully Masked Design

In this first subsection, we show how to secure the computation of SPRING from leakage of key by means of masking. For this purpose, the key is initially split into random-looking shares that are refreshed before each execution, and the computation is made on each of the shares separately. We next refer to the parts of the hardware which handle the computations on specific shares as *parties*. Let $d$ denote the number of parties. The main intuition behind masking is that no information on the original key can be obtained from the computation of less than $d$ parties.

We start by sketching the different steps of a masked SPRING computation.

1. A synchronization step is required to refresh the key shares that are stored in discrete-log (of FFT evaluations) format. For this purpose, a usual strategy is to add a random sharing of zero to the $d$ additive shares stored in memory.
2. The parties compute their subset-sum locally by using only their share, or they update the subset-sum according to the Gray code counter.
3. The parties change their additive shares of the subset-sum to multiplicative shares of the corresponding subset-product by locally using the Exp2Coef lookup table.
4. A second synchronization step converts the parties' current multiplicative shares into additive shares of the same value. We refer to this unit as MM2AM.
5. The parties locally use the FFT unit on their shares of the computation.
6. A last synchronization step is used for the rounding. The parties now have additive shares of the polynomial subset-product in Equation 1. They compute XOR shares of the rounding bit of the coefficients.
7. The parties apply the (linear) binary BCH transformation on their shares locally.
8. Finally, the parties now have XOR shares of the SPRING evaluation. These bits are XORed to obtain the output.

We now describe the whole secure masked computation more extensively.

The process starts with a standard refreshing of the pre-shared key, which is stored as discrete logs of outputs of the FFT procedure on the polynomials $a, s$. As a result, the parties get numbers whose sum modulo 256 corresponds to an original discrete log in the key. As the first step of the SPRING computation is merely a subset-sum of the key (or an update of it according to the Gray-code counter), each of the parties can compute this subset-sum locally and independently. This unit for each of the parties is identical to the corresponding one in the unprotected SPRING implementation. After this computation, each of the parties has an additive share of the subset-sum (modulo 256).

The next unit in the original computation is the Exp2Coef lookup table. This table is used for putting the discrete logs in $\mathbb{Z}_{256}$ into the exponent to get FFT outputs in $\mathbb{Z}_{257}^*$. We apply exactly the same lookup table locally in the computation of each of the parties in parallel. After passing the subset-sum results in the Exp2Coef lookup table, the parties hold point-wise multiplicative shares (modulo 257) of the corresponding subset-product.

Following, the original SPRING evaluation performs the FFT unit. Notice that it is an additively-linear operation, but currently the parties hold multiplicative masking shares of the computation. We apply a synchronization step to convert the multiplicative shares back to additive ones. The unit responsible for this step is denoted by MM2AM.

For this purpose, we use the technique suggested by Ghodosi et al. in [13].[4] This procedure is applied for each entry independently. The MM2AM unit gets in advance random bits and uses them to generate $d^2$ random-looking numbers in $\mathbb{Z}_{257}^*$, such that:

$$\sum_{j=0}^{d-1} \prod_{i=0}^{d-1} \alpha_{i,j} = 1 \qquad (\text{mod } 257).$$

This is easily obtained because we achieve a random number in $\mathbb{Z}_{257}^*$ by adding 1 to an 8-bit random number, and because we can randomize $d^2 - 1$ numbers and compute $r_{0,0}$ so the equation holds. For each $0 \le i < d$, the MM2AM unit provides party $i$ with the numbers $\{\alpha_{i,j}\}_{j=0,\ldots,d-1}$ as auxiliary information. This information is independent from the shares so it can be achieved before the computation reaches the Exp2Coef step. Once the parties get the multiplicative shares $\{m_i\}_{i=0,\ldots,d-1}$ of the subset-product, each party $i$ sends the value $m_i \cdot \alpha_{i,j}$ to party $j$. Next, each party $j$ computes the multiplication $c_j = \prod_{i=0}^{d-1} m_i \cdot \alpha_{i,j}$ (mod 257) as its additive share of the entry. Note that:

$$\sum_{j=0}^{d-1} c_j = \sum_{j=0}^{d-1} \left( \prod_{i=0}^{d-1} m_i \right) \cdot \left( \prod_{i=0}^{d-1} \alpha_{i,j} \right),$$

$$= \left( \prod_{i=0}^{d-1} m_i \right) \cdot \left( \sum_{j=0}^{d-1} \prod_{i=0}^{d-1} \alpha_{i,j} \right),$$

$$= \prod_{i=0}^{d-1} m_i \qquad (\text{mod } 257).$$

Therefore, the parties now have additive masking shares of this step of the computation. Taking advantage of these additive shares, the implementation can perform the (linear) FFT units locally and in parallel. They are identical to the corresponding units in the original unprotected SPRING implementation.

As a result, the parties have additive shares of the polynomial subset-product. It therefore remains to compute the rounding function. We use a masked rounding unit for this purpose, such that its output for each party is a XOR random share of the actual rounding value. We describe the computation of rounding on

---

[4] Other techniques for share conversion exist. The side-channel literature usually refers to [12] for such a task, but the algorithms in this reference are quite sequential. We focus on the approach suggested in [13] which seems easier to parallelize and simpler in our hardware context.

a single coefficient. This process is repeated for all $n$ coefficients of the subset-product. The unit deals in advance random shifts $\{t_i\}_{i=0,...,d-1} \in \mathbb{Z}_{257}^d$ to the parties. Each party is also provided with a pre-generated random-looking table $TAB_i \in \{0,1\}^{257}$. For each $i \geq 1$ the table is merely a random bit array of size 257. The table of party 0 satisfies:

$$TAB_0[v] = \bigoplus_{i=1}^{d-1} TAB_i[v] \oplus \left[ v - \sum_{i=0}^{d-1} t_i \right] \pmod{257} \qquad \forall v \in \mathbb{Z}_{257}, \qquad (6)$$

where $\oplus$ is the XOR operator in $\mathbb{Z}_2$.

Let $v_i$ be the additive share of a single coefficient $v$ kept by party $i$, as computed by the FFT unit. Party $i$ shares $v_i + t_i$ with all the other parties. Next, all parties compute the sum $\sum(v_i + t_i) = v + \sum t_i$, and use $b_i = TAB[v + \sum t_i]$ as their share of the coefficient's rounding output. We note that $\bigoplus_{i=0}^{d-1} b_i$ is indeed the rounded bit of $v$ due to generation of the tables described in Equation 6.

Eventually, as BCH is a linear transformation of the rounding output, the parties compute their shares locally and independently again, using an identical instance of this unit for each party. As a result, all parties have a XOR-share of the PRF evaluation.

**Implementation and Cost Estimation:** The implementation of the fully masked SPRING is depicted in Fig. 3. It operates with $d$ shares in parallel. Essentially, its datapath is composed of $d$ (modified) datapaths of the unprotected SPRING, where mask refreshing, mask conversion (MM2AM) and masked rounding are added. In order to preserve the same timing as the unprotected SPRING version, random masks are added to the KMEM outputs on-the-fly and the MM2AM and masked rounding units are implemented with combinatorial logic.

The cost estimation of these three new units is summarized in Tab. 3. As can be observed, the impact of mask refreshing is negligible. Moreover, its size increases linearly with the number of shares. The other two units are more expensive. For example, in case of a two-share implementation, the mask conversion MM2AM requires 527 slices, whereas masked rounding requires 1321 slices. Furthermore, the size of MM2AM increases quadratically $d$. This is caused by a substantial increase of the number of multiplications performed inside MM2AM. Interestingly, the masked rounding does not utilize expensive multiplications, and so its size increases linearly with d.

Note that Tab. 3 illustrates the costs to protect one 8-bit sensitive exponent or one 9-bit entry (either a polynomial evaluation before the $FFT^{-1}$ step or a polynomial coefficient after this step). However, the implementation illustrated in Fig. 3 operates on $16d$ exponents/coefficients in parallel. Thus, if implemented, these units would increase SPRING size substantially (just as generally observed for masked implementations of block ciphers).

## 4.2   Partially Masked Design

In view of the previous estimations, it appears that certain parts of the SPRING design (namely, until the FFT computation) are very easy to mask, while the

**Table 3.** Estimated costs of basic operations (dependent on $d$) necessary for mask refreshing, $d$-share multipl. to additive masking conv. and masked rounding of one 9-bit entry.

| | Basic operations | | | | | Random | Total # of slices | | | |
|---|---|---|---|---|---|---|---|---|---|---|
| | ADD | MUL | INV | MUX2 | XOR | bits. | $d=2$ | $d=3$ | $d=4$ | $d=5$ |
| Msk. refresh | $d-2$ | 0 | 0 | 0 | 0 | $8(d-1)$ | 3 | 5 | 6 | 7 |
| MM2AM[13] | $d-2$ | $3d^2-2d$ | $d$ | 0 | 0 | $8(d^2-1)$ | 527 | 1353 | 2551 | 4121 |
| Msk. round | $3d-2$ | 0 | 0 | $256d$ | $d-1$ | $266d-257$ | 1321 | 1409 | 1473 | 1894 |

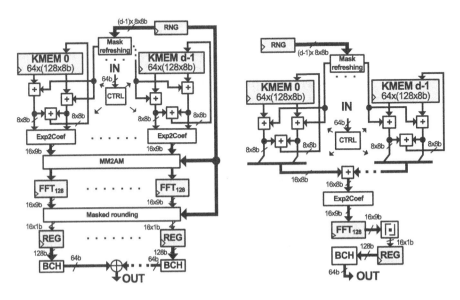

**Fig. 3.** Fully masked implementation    **Fig. 4.** Partially masked implementation

remaining ones imply the usual (quadratic) overhead of non-linear operations. In this context, an appealing solution from the performance point of view would be to unmask the implementation just before these non-linear steps, as illustrated in Fig. 4. Quite naturally, this raises the question whether the partially masked design becomes insecure at this point. We conclude this paper with two simple arguments in favor of such a hybrid strategy.

First, observe that the standard DPA attacks (defined in [21]), that are at the core of most physical security evaluation procedures nowadays, are inherently limited to the exploitation of the leakages corresponding to operations that can be predicted (i.e., that depend on an enumerable part of the key). In the case of SPRING, such operations only appear at the beginning of the encryption, since diffusion is complete after the subset-sum computation. As a result, it could be sufficient to protect this part of the implementation against DPA, and the remaining ones against (single-trace) SPA. (As mentioned in the introduction, such an idea is reminiscent of fresh re-keying schemes[24].) Interestingly, several cheaper solutions exist for this purpose.

For example, shuffling is a usual countermeasure against SPA. In the case of SPRING, our implementation operates on polynomials of 128 coefficients/exponents, but only 16 are processed in parallel (one row). Therefore, 8 consecutive calculations (per row) are necessary to process the full 128 coefficient/exponent state. Since they are computed independently, these operations can be directly executed according to a random 8-permutation. It represents a total of $8! = 40320$ execution permutations which, combined with the high (algorithmic) noise of our hardware design, should prevent SPA.

Concretely, the eight entry rows are easily shuffled by being read from KMEM in a random order. This involves only small changes in the control logic. Hence its impact on the SPRING implementation size is negligible. The only parts that need modification are the matrix transpose and FFT-REG inside each $FFT_{64}$. However, this modification only increases the size of both by 24 slices. Furthermore, shuffling can be preserved up to the REG unit, where the rows have to be stored in a correct position. This operation de-shuffles the state for free.

As can be observed, shuffling presents a very powerful cost-efficient countermeasure. For this reason, we have decided to implement this approach in the masked SPRING implementation. Moreover, only the linear part of SPRING (i.e. subset-sum) is protected by the masking countermeasure. This way, linear increase of the number of shares is reflected in the linear increase of implementation size.

To conclude, let us also observe that, depending on the leakage function, unmasking the last part of the design could simply be secure as such. For example, imagine a leakage function that would "round" the intermediate values, just as required by the SPRING specifications. Then, having unmasked data after the FFT computations would not be a problem at all. Quite naturally, actual leakage functions do not round as proposed in [3,4]. Yet, they usually compress the input range to some extent (e.g. with a Hamming weight function). Furthermore, technology-level countermeasures such as dual-rail logic styles can generally be used to modify the shape of the leakage functions [32]. As a result, it is an interesting open problem to find whether there is a common ground for protected implementation of rounded operations, between theoretical requirements and practical engineering constraints.

**Acknowledgements.** This work has been funded in part by the ERC project 280141 (acronym CRASH) and in part by the Belgian Cybercrime Center of Excellence for Training Research and Education (B-CCENTRE). F.-X. Standaert is an associate researcher of the Belgian Fund for Scientific Research (FNRS-F.R.S.). Research supported by the ERC under the EU's Seventh Framework Programme (FP/2007-2013) ERC Grant Agreement n. 307952.

# References

1. Alberini, G., Rosen, A.: Efficient Rounding Procedures of Biased Samples. Manuscript (2013)

2. Andreeva, E., Bogdanov, A., Dodis, Y., Mennink, B., Steinberger, J.P.: On the Indifferentiability of Key-Alternating Ciphers. In: Canetti, R., Garay, J.A. (eds.) CRYPTO 2013, Part I. LNCS, vol. 8042, pp. 531–550. Springer, Heidelberg (2013)
3. Banerjee, A., Brenner, H., Leurent, G., Peikert, C., Rosen, A.: SPRING: Fast Pseudorandom Functions from Rounded Ring Products. In: FSE 2014, London, UK. LNCS (to appear, March 2014)
4. Banerjee, A., Peikert, C., Rosen, A.: Pseudorandom Functions and Lattices. In: Pointcheval, D., Johansson, T. (eds.) EUROCRYPT 2012. LNCS, vol. 7237, pp. 719–737. Springer, Heidelberg (2012)
5. Bogdanov, A., Knudsen, L.R., Leander, G., Standaert, F.-X., Steinberger, J., Tischhauser, E.: Key-Alternating Ciphers in a Provable Setting: Encryption Using a Small Number of Public Permutations. In: Pointcheval, D., Johansson, T. (eds.) EUROCRYPT 2012. LNCS, vol. 7237, pp. 45–62. Springer, Heidelberg (2012)
6. Chen, S., Steinberger, J.P.: Tight security bounds for key-alternating ciphers. IACR Cryptology ePrint Archive 2013, 222 (2013)
7. Coron, J.S.: Resistance against Differential Power Analysis for Elliptic Curve Cryptosystems. In: Koç, Ç.K., Paar, C. (eds.) CHES 1999. LNCS, vol. 1717, pp. 292–302. Springer, Heidelberg (1999)
8. Coron, J.S., Giraud, C., Prouff, E., Renner, S., Rivain, M., Vadnala, P.K.: Conversion of Security Proofs from One Leakage Model to Another: A New Issue. In: Schindler, W., Huss, S.A. (eds.) COSADE 2012. LNCS, vol. 7275, pp. 69–81. Springer, Heidelberg (2012)
9. Crypto group, UCL, Louvain-la-Neuve, Belgium
10. Gaspar, L., Leurent, G., Standaert, F.X.: Hardware Implementation and Side-Channel Analysis of Lapin. In: Benaloh, J. (ed.) CT-RSA 2014. LNCS, vol. 8366, pp. 206–226. Springer, Heidelberg (2014)
11. Genelle, L., Prouff, E., Quisquater, M.: Thwarting Higher-Order Side Channel Analysis with Additive and Multiplicative Maskings. In: Preneel, B., Takagi, T. (eds.) CHES 2011. LNCS, vol. 6917, pp. 240–255. Springer, Heidelberg (2011)
12. Genelle, L., Prouff, E., Quisquater, M.: Thwarting higher-order side channel analysis with additive and multiplicative maskings. In: Preneel, B., Takagi, T. (eds.) CHES 2011. LNCS, vol. 6917, pp. 240–255. Springer, Heidelberg (2011)
13. Ghodosi, H., Pieprzyk, J., Steinfeld, R.: Multi-party computation with conversion of secret sharing. Designs, Codes and Cryptography 62(3), 259–272 (2012), http://www1.spms.ntu.edu.sg/~ccrg/documents/MPC_SS-sing-2011.pdf (February 2014)
14. Grosso, V., Standaert, F.X., Faust, S.: Masking vs. Multiparty Computation: How Large Is the Gap for AES? In: Bertoni, G., Coron, J.-S. (eds.) CHES 2013. LNCS, vol. 8086, pp. 400–416. Springer, Heidelberg (2013)
15. Herbst, C., Oswald, E., Mangard, S.: An AES Smart Card Implementation Resistant to Power Analysis Attacks. In: Zhou, J., Yung, M., Bao, F. (eds.) ACNS 2006. LNCS, vol. 3989, pp. 239–252. Springer, Heidelberg (2006)
16. Joye, M., Yen, S.M.: The Montgomery Powering Ladder. In: Kaliski Jr., B.S., Koç, Ç.K., Paar, C. (eds.) CHES 2002. LNCS, vol. 2523, pp. 291–302. Springer, Heidelberg (2003)
17. Lampe, R., Patarin, J., Seurin, Y.: An Asymptotically Tight Security Analysis of the Iterated Even-Mansour Cipher [34], pp. 278–295
18. Lampe, R., Seurin, Y.: How to Construct an Ideal Cipher from a Small Set of Public Permutations. In: Sako, K., Sarkar, P. (eds.) ASIACRYPT 2013, Part I. LNCS, vol. 8269, pp. 444–463. Springer, Heidelberg (2013)

19. Lyubashevsky, V., Micciancio, D., Peikert, C., Rosen, A.: SWIFFT: A Modest Proposal for FFT Hashing. In: Nyberg, K. (ed.) FSE 2008. LNCS, vol. 5086, pp. 54–72. Springer, Heidelberg (2008)

20. Lyubashevsky, V., Peikert, C., Regev, O.: On Ideal Lattices and Learning with Errors over Rings. In: Gilbert, H. (ed.) EUROCRYPT 2010. LNCS, vol. 6110, pp. 1–23. Springer, Heidelberg (2010)

21. Mangard, S., Oswald, E., Standaert, F.X.: One for all - all for one: unifying standard differential power analysis attacks. IET Information Security 5(2), 100–110 (2011)

22. Mangard, S., Popp, T., Gammel, B.M.: Side-Channel Leakage of Masked CMOS Gates. In: Menezes, A. (ed.) CT-RSA 2005. LNCS, vol. 3376, pp. 351–365. Springer, Heidelberg (2005)

23. Martin, D., Oswald, E., Stam, M.: A Leakage Resilient MAC. IACR Cryptology eprint Archive 2013, 292 (2013)

24. Medwed, M., Standaert, F.X., Großschädl, J., Regazzoni, F.: Fresh Re-keying: Security against Side-Channel and Fault Attacks for Low-Cost Devices. In: Bernstein, D.J., Lange, T. (eds.) AFRICACRYPT 2010. LNCS, vol. 6055, pp. 279–296. Springer, Heidelberg (2010)

25. Moradi, A., Mischke, O.: How Far Should Theory Be from Practice? - Evaluation of a Countermeasure. In: Prouff, E., Schaumont, P. (eds.) CHES 2012. LNCS, vol. 7428, pp. 92–106. Springer, Heidelberg (2012)

26. Nussbaumer, H.J.: Fast Fourier transform and convolution algorithms. Springer (1982)

27. Rivain, M., Prouff, E.: Provably Secure Higher-Order Masking of AES. In: Mangard, S., Standaert, F.-X. (eds.) CHES 2010. LNCS, vol. 6225, pp. 413–427. Springer, Heidelberg (2010)

28. Roche, T., Prouff, E.: Higher-order glitch free implementation of the AES using Secure Multi-Party Computation protocols - Extended version. J. Cryptographic Engineering 2(2), 111–127 (2012)

29. Rombouts, P.: Lightweight Cryptography: Mission Accomplished. Crypto for 2020 – ECRYPT-II Final Event, Tenerife, Spain (January 2013)

30. Roy, S.S., Vercauteren, F., Mentens, N., Chen, D.D., Verbauwhede, I.: Compact Ring-LWE based Cryptoprocessor. Cryptology eprint Archive, Report 2013/866 (2013), http://eprint.iacr.org/

31. Standaert, F.X.: Future Challenges for Lightweight Cryptography. Crypto for 2020 – ECRYPT-II Final Event, Tenerife, Spain (January 2013)

32. Tiri, K., Verbauwhede, I.: Securing Encryption Algorithms against DPA at the Logic Level: Next Generation Smart Card Technology. In: Walter, C.D., Koç, Ç.K., Paar, C. (eds.) CHES 2003. LNCS, vol. 2779, pp. 125–136. Springer, Heidelberg (2003)

33. Veyrat-Charvillon, N., Medwed, M., Kerckhof, S., Standaert, F.X.: Shuffling against Side-Channel Attacks: A Comprehensive Study with Cautionary Note [34], pp. 740–757

34. Wang, X., Sako, K. (eds.): ASIACRYPT 2012. LNCS, vol. 7658. Springer, Heidelberg (2012)

# FOAM: Searching for Hardware-Optimal SPN Structures and Components with a Fair Comparison

Khoongming Khoo[1], Thomas Peyrin[2], Axel Y. Poschmann[3], and Huihui Yap[1]

[1] DSO National Laboratories, 20 Science Park Drive, Singapore 118230
{kkhoongm,yhuihui}@dso.org.sg
[2] SPMS, Nanyang Technological University, Singapore
thomas.peyrin@ntu.edu.sg
[3] NXP Semiconductors
axel.poschmann@gmail.com

**Abstract.** In this article, we propose a new comparison metric, the *figure of adversarial merit* (FOAM), which combines the inherent security provided by cryptographic structures and components with their implementation properties. To the best of our knowledge, this is the first such metric proposed to ensure a fairer comparison of cryptographic designs. We then apply this new metric to meaningful use cases by studying Substitution-Permutation Network permutations that are suited for hardware implementations, and we provide new results on hardware-friendly cryptographic building blocks. For practical reasons, we considered linear and differential attacks and we restricted ourselves to fully serial and round-based implementations. We explore several design strategies, from the geometry of the internal state to the size of the S-box, the field size of the diffusion layer or even the irreducible polynomial defining the finite field. We finally test all possible strategies to provide designers an exhaustive approach in building hardware-friendly cryptographic primitives (according to area or FOAM metrics), also introducing a model for predicting the hardware performance of round-based or serial-based implementations. In particular, we exhibit new diffusion matrices (circulant or serial) that are surprisingly more efficient than the current best known, such as the ones used in AES, LED and PHOTON.

**Keywords:** SPN, lightweight cryptography, figure of adversarial merit, diffusion matrices.

## 1 Introduction

RFID is a rising technology that is likely to be widely deployed in everyday life, leading to new security challenges. Significant advances in this area have already been obtained. In particular, many lightweight block ciphers [8,10,15,19] have recently been proposed, and designing such ciphers is not an easy task as showed by the numerous candidates that eventually got broken. Moreover, it is interesting to note that in most privacy-preserving RFID protocols proposed [1,16,17]

L. Batina and M. Robshaw (Eds.): CHES 2014, LNCS 8731, pp. 433–450, 2014.

a hash function is required, and since a hash function can be easily built from a block cipher (for example with the Davies-Meyer mode) or a permutation (for example with the sponge construction [7]), a crucial question for the researchers is how to design a hardware efficient permutation.

Hardware efficiency can have very different meanings depending on the utilization scenario targeted by the designer. For example, a classical metric is to estimate the minimum silicon area required by the primitive to perform the cryptographic operations. This, of course, depends on the parameters of the function itself (the area is highly dependent on the amount of memory required) and most lightweight block ciphers have a rather small block size of 64 bits. It is to be noted that the area is usually not directly linked to the security of a primitive, as adding extra rounds will have an impact on the throughput of the implementation, but only a very limited one concerning the area (we assumed that the function has no weakness that is independent of the number of rounds). Area and other metrics such as throughput, latency or power dissipation can be traded-off for one another, making the comparison between different primitives difficult. In the direction of fairer comparisons of hardware implementations of cryptographic primitives, Bogdanov et al. [9] introduced the efficiency metric throughput/area in order to take in account these tradeoffs. However, the possibility of trading off throughput for power was not taken in account and Badel et al. [2] proposed instead a figure of merit, defined as FOM = throughput/area$^2$. However, as of today, no metric takes in account the inherent security of a building block, therefore making it hard to compare for example two diffusion matrices that have different area footprint and different branch number.

The construction of good diffusion matrices has always been an important research topic in cryptography, equally important as the search for good confusion functions. The AES [13] for example uses a $4 \times 4$ matrix with elements in $GF(2^8)$. This matrix is Maximum Distance Separable (MDS), which means that it has a branch number of 5, optimal for a $4 \times 4$ matrix. However, this security feature comes at a cost that computations in $GF(2^8)$ might not be the best choice for some hardware purposes, even though special care has been taken by the designers to choose a circulant matrix instantiated with lightweight coefficients of low Hamming weight. Recently, Guo et al. [14,15] described a new type of diffusion matrix, so-called serial, that trades more clock cycles in the execution for a smaller area. This idea was later extended to the use of linear Feistel-like structures or Linear Feedback Shift Registers (LFSR) to build the diffusion matrix [18,20]. On the opposite side, PRESENT [8] uses a simple bit permutation layer, the real diffusion coming in fact directly from the S-box application. The advantage being that a bit permutation layer is basically free in a hardware implementation. Now, one may ask the following question: what is better when the goal is to maximize some hardware metric, a very weak diffusion matrix with a low area footprint, or a strong diffusion matrix but requiring more silicon?

More generally, many different trade-offs exist when building an AES-like Substitution-Permutation Network (SPN) primitive, such as the general geometry (number of lines and columns), what size of S-box, what type of matrix,

with what branch number, in what finite field, with which irreducible polynomial, etc. When a cryptographer would like to design a permutation with a
specific hardware efficiency metric in mind, it is not trivial for him to make the
best construction choices directly. Since implementing many different trade-offs
is very time consuming, he will have to rely on his own intuition when picking
the basic building blocks and choosing the general structure of the primitive,
therefore accepting that his final design might not be optimal.

**Our Contributions.** In this article, we study the problem of designing hardware efficient permutations for lightweight symmetric key cryptography purposes, and we propose new promising diffusion matrices as building blocks. We
first explain in Section 2 the family of functions that we will study, namely AES-
like SPN permutations, and we describe a new generalized diffusion layer (i.e.
the ShiftRows function in AES), that allows a provable optimal diffusion even
for non-square internal state matrices. Then, we introduce in Section 3 a new
metric, the *figure of adversarial merit* (FOAM), that for the first time takes into
account the inherent security provided by the primitive. We then explain in Section 4 the various SPN design tradeoffs that we will consider for our comparisons,
such as the geometry of the SPN, the S-box size, the type of matrix (circulant
or serial), the field size for the diffusion or even the irreducible polynomial. The
goal being that the designer only has to input the type of implementation (round
and/or serial) and the size of the permutation he would like to build, and he
can directly get the SPN structure and its internal components that are the best
suited for him. We study in Section 5 the security of the AES-like SPN permutations by only taking in account simple linear/differential attacks. In Section 6,
we present formulas for estimating various parts of the ASIC implementations.
We chose to focus our work on designing permutations only since many cryptographic primitives can be built from them. Therefore, we will not cover other
components such as key schedule for a block cipher, or message expansion for
a hash function. Moreover, due to the obviously vast amount of implementation trade-offs, we restricted ourselves to the two most important cases: fully
serialized and round-based.

Finally, the results obtained by our analysis are given in Section 7, with the
best diffusion matrices and SPN parameters we could find for many different
scenarios. Notably, we show that the diffusion matrices of ciphers such as AES,
LED or PHOTON are not the best possible choices. For example, in the case of
AES encryption, a circulant matrix with coefficients (0x01,0x01,0x04,0x8d) would
have been, surprisingly, a better choice in terms of implementation while keeping
the same MDS security.

# 2    Generic SPN with Generalized Optimal Diffusion

In this section, we describe the family of AES-like SPN functions. Our scope is
classical, but we propose a new generalized diffusion layer that allows an optimal
diffusion even for non-square internal state matrices.

436 K. Khoo et al.

## 2.1 Extended AES-like Permutations

An $n$-bit AES-like SPN permutation transforms an $r \times c$ array of $s$-bit cells ($n = r \times c \times s$). During one round, each cell is first transformed by an $s$-bit S-box (similar to the AES SubBytes operation). Then each $r$-cell column is transformed by an $r \times r$ diffusion matrix (similar to the AES MixColumns operation), followed by an optimal diffusion[1] which permutes the $c$ cells of each row to provide further mixing (similar to the AES ShiftRows operation). Finally, an $(r \times c)$-cell constant is xored to complete a round transformation (in block-cipher design, this phase is a subkey addition, but we will not consider key-schedules here). In AES, we have a square array $r = c = 4$ and cell size $s = 8$-bit. The diffusion matrix is usually defined over the finite field $GF(2^s)$ because of the $s$-bit cell size. Sometimes, we might actually use a smaller subfield of size $GF(2^i)$, $i$ divides $s$, in order to define the diffusion matrix. This framework captures many known ciphers such as AES, PRESENT, LED, etc.

A cell is called differentially (resp. linearly) active if its value (resp. mask value) is non-zero in a differential (resp. linear) attack. The differential branch number of a diffusion matrix is the minimum number of differentially active input and output cells (among all non-zero inputs). The notion of linear branch number is similar, except that we consider the transpose of the diffusion matrix instead. From this point onwards, we will not distinguish between differential and linear branch number unless necessary. That is, when we say a matrix has branch number $B$, both its differential and linear branch numbers are equal to $B$. The maximum branch number for an $r$ by $r$ diffusion matrix is $r + 1$, and a matrix which achieves this optimal branch number is called MDS. If the diffusion matrix has branch number $r$, then it is called almost-MDS.

## 2.2 The Generalized Optimal Diffusion

In this section, we generalize the concept of optimal diffusion [13] for non-square state array. This has been done already when $r < c$ with a security bound equivalent to the case where $r = c$ (square array) [13]. When $r > c$ and $c$ divides $r$, a simple generalization has been proposed in [11] where a 4-round security bound is proven when the diffusion matrix is MDS. In this section, we propose a generalized optimal diffusion for the case $r > c$ where $c$ may not divide $r$ and the diffusion matrix may not be MDS, i.e. for all branch number $B \leq r + 1$.

An example of optimal diffusion is the ShiftRows operation of AES which helps to diffuse the effect of the AES SubBytes and MixColumns operation over 32-bit to the whole 128-bit block. The AES ShiftRows transforms a $4 \times 4$ byte-array by rotating row $r$ to the left by $r$ bytes, for $r = 0, 1, 2, 3$. Due to ShiftRows, each byte of an input column is mapped to a different output column. This is captured by the concept of optimal diffusion (another example is SQUARE cipher [12]'s ArrayTranspose map).

---

[1] Note that here, without loss of generality, we apply the permutation operations from right-to-left, i.e. SC (SubCells) is first applied, followed by MC (MixColumn) and then the optimal diffusion.

**Definition 1.** *For an r-by-r cell-array, the optimal diffusion map is a cell-permutation that maps each cell of an input column to a different output column.*

However, the optimal diffusion only applies for $r \times c$ cell array where $r \leq c$. When $r > c$, there are not enough output columns $c$ to map each of the $r$ cells of an input column. Thus, we extend a new concept from [11] called Generalized Optimal Diffusion (GOD) for $r \times c$ cell-array when $r > c$, which we describe below[2]. Our strategy is to distribute the cells of an input column as uniformly as possible to each output column.

**Definition 2.** *For an $r \times c$ cell-array, a generalized optimal diffusion is a cell-permutation such that looking at any r-cell column:*

1. *$\lceil r/c \rceil$ input cells are mapped to each of $(r \mod c)$ output columns.*
2. *$\lfloor r/c \rfloor$ input cells are mapped to each of $c - (r \mod c)$ output columns.*

*Example 1.* Consider $r = 5$, $c = 3$. For each input column of 5 cells, $\lceil 5/3 \rceil = 2$ input cells are mapped to each of $(5 \mod 3) = 2$ columns. $\lfloor 5/3 \rfloor = 1$ input cell is mapped to $3 - (5 \mod 3) = 1$ column. One example is given by the transform of the following arrays:

$$\begin{pmatrix} a_1 & b_1 & c_1 \\ a_2 & b_2 & c_2 \\ a_3 & b_3 & c_3 \\ a_4 & b_4 & c_4 \\ a_5 & b_5 & c_5 \end{pmatrix} \text{ maps to } \begin{pmatrix} a_1 & b_1 & c_1 \\ a_2 & b_2 & c_2 \\ c_3 & a_3 & b_3 \\ c_4 & a_4 & b_4 \\ b_5 & c_5 & a_5 \end{pmatrix}$$

**Theorem 1.** *Consider a 4-round AES-like SPN as follows (omitting the constant addition since it has no effect on our reasoning):*

$$\text{GOD} \circ \text{MC} \circ \text{SC} \circ \text{GOD} \circ \text{MC} \circ \text{SC} \circ \text{GOD} \circ \text{MC} \circ \text{SC} \circ \text{GOD} \circ \text{MC} \circ \text{SC},$$

*where*

1. SubCells *is a nonlinear substitution layer with $r \times c$ s-bit S-boxes acting in parallel.*
2. MixColumns *is a layer of c parallel* MixColumn *transforms each mapping $r$ cells to $r$ cells with branch number $B$, i.e.* MixColumns$(x_1, \ldots, x_c) = ($MixColumn$(x_1), \ldots, $MixColumn$(x_c))$*, each $x_i$ corresponding to a column of $r$ cells.*
3. GOD *(generalized optimal diffusion) is as defined above which distributes the $r$ cells of an input column almost uniformly to $c$ output columns.*

*Then the number of active S-boxes over 1 and 2 rounds are at least 1 and B respectively. For 4 rounds it is at least $B \times B'$ where $B' = \max\{2; x + y\}$ and:*

$$\begin{cases} y = \min\{2 \times (r \mod c)); \lfloor B/\lceil r/c \rceil \rfloor\} \\ x = \quad \lceil (B - \lceil r/c \rceil \times y)/\lfloor r/c \rfloor \rceil \end{cases}$$

---

[2] The Generalized Optimal Diffusion (GOD) defined in [11] applies only when $r$ is a multiple $c$. Here, we define GOD for any $r > c$.

We provide the proof of this theorem in the full version of this paper. We note that it is tight in the sense that it naturally provides a 4 round path that corresponds to a "luckiest" scenario for the attacker, which involves the minimum number of active Super-Sboxes (the $(c \times s)$-bit S-boxes composed of two SubCells layers surrounding one MixColumns).

Let us look at an application example of Theorem 1 to derive the number of active S-boxes of an AES-like SPN structure, which cannot be deduced by the known results of [11,13]. Consider an SPN structure with state size 24-cell, the diffusion matrices being an $8 \times 8$ matrix with branch number 7, i.e. $r = 8$, $c = 3$ and $B = 7$. By Theorem 1, we have $y = 2$ and $x = 1$, therefore $B' = \max\{2; x + y\} = 3$ and there are $B \times B' = 7 \times 3 = 21$ active S-boxes guaranteed over 4 rounds of this 24-cell SPN structure.

# 3    FOAM: Figure of Adversarial Merit

As explained in the introduction, the various trade-offs inherent in any design of a cryptographic primitive make a fair and consistent comparison of software and hardware implementations thereof a challenging task. For hardware implementations exist a few metrics, like the *Area-Time (AT) product*, which multiplies the area in *Gate Equivalents* (GE) occupied by the design with the number of clock cycles required (the smaller the number, the more efficient is the design). Closely related is the *hardware efficiency* [9], which divides the throughput at a given frequency by the area (hence the greater the number, the better the design). In order to also address the area-power trade-off, [2] proposed a new *Figure of Merit (FOM)*: throughput divided by the area squared. The latter two metrics are frequency dependent, which can complicate comparisons.

We propose a new metric called Figure of Adversarial Merit (FOAM) in order to resolve the aforementioned shortcomings. It is defined as

$$FOAM(x) = \frac{1}{S(x) \times A^2}$$

where $S(x)$ and $A$ are basically equivalent to special definitions of speed and area, respectively. More precisely, $S(x)$ denotes the speed of the cipher based on the number of rounds required to achieve a certain security $x$ against some set of attacks (in this article, we will later restrict ourselves to simple differential/linear attacks). For a round-based permutation, it is defined as $S(x) = p(x) \times t$ where $p(x)$ represents the number of rounds required to achieve security $x$, and $t$ the number of clock cycles to perform one round. Moreover, for SPN-based primitives, we decompose the area requirements $A$ into six parts: the intermediate state memory cost $C_{mem}$, the S-boxes implementation cost $C_{sbox}$, the diffusion matrix implementation cost $C_{diff}$, the constant addition $C_{cst}$, the control logic cost $C_{log}$, and the IO logic cost $C_{io}$:

$$FOAM(x) = \frac{1}{S(x) \times A^2} = \frac{1}{p(x) \times t \times (C_{mem} + C_{sbox} + C_{diff} + C_{cst} + C_{log} + C_{io})^2}$$

This FOAM metric will be useful to compare different design strategies, different building blocks (such as diffusion matrices) with a simple value computation.

Even better, we would like to roughly compare all these possible design trade-offs without having the hassle to implement all of them: in Section 6 we present formulas to estimate these six subparts of the area cost and the number $t$ of clock cycles required to perform one round. The value $p(x)$ can be deduced by the number of active S-boxes proven in Theorem 1 and the S-box cryptographic properties (see Section 5). Note that in the rest of the paper, we consider that the security aimed by the designer is equal to the permutation size, i.e. we are aiming at a security of $2^n$ computations (thus $p(x) = p(2^n)$).

# 4  Trade-Offs Considered

We explain all the various trade-offs we consider when building an AES-like SPN permutation. The goal being that a designer specifies a permutation bitsize $n$, the metric he would like to maximize (area, FOAM), the degree up to which serial or round-based implementations are important, and he directly obtains the best parameters to build his permutation.

**The S-box.**  One of the first choice of the designer is the size of the S-box, and we will consider two possible trade-offs: $s = 4$ and $s = 8$. Note that, for simplicity, we will consider that the S-box chosen has perfect differential and linear properties relative to its size (one could further extend the trade-offs to non-optimal but smaller S-boxes, but the search space being very broad we leave this as an open problem).

**The Geometry of the Internal State.**  When building an AES-like SPN permutation, one can consider several internal state geometries (the values $r$ and $c$). The classical case is a square state, like for AES. However, depending on the diffusion matrices available, it might be worth considering more line-shaped or column-shaped designs.

**Diffusion Matrix Field Size.**  The designer can choose the field size $2^i$ in which the matrix computations will take place. The classical case, like in AES, being that the field size for the diffusion matrix is the same as the S-box. However, depending on the diffusion matrices available, it might be worth considering designs with thinner diffusion layers but repeated several times. For example, in the case of AES, instead of the MixColumns matrix one could use a $4 \times 4$ diffusion matrix on $GF(2^4)$ applied two times (one time on the 4 MSB and one time on the 4 LSB of the 8-bit cells in the AES column). Overall, we will cover a scope from binary matrices (in GF(2)) up to matrices on the same field size as the S-box (in $GF(2^s)$).

**Irreducible Polynomial for the Diffusion Matrix Field.**  Once the field size $2^i$ is fixed, the designer can choose the irreducible polynomial defining the field. For $i = 1$ and $i = 2$ only a single polynomial exists, while for $i = 4$ at most 3 choices are possible ($\alpha^4 + \alpha + 1$, $\alpha^4 + \alpha^3 + 1$ and $\alpha^4 + \alpha^3 + \alpha^2 + \alpha + 1$). For the $i = 8$ case, many polynomials are possible (this was already observed by [3]), thus in order to focus the search space we will only consider the irreducible polynomial used in AES ($\alpha^8 + \alpha^4 + \alpha^3 + \alpha + 1$) and in WHIRLPOOL hash function [5] ($\alpha^8 + \alpha^4 + \alpha^3 + \alpha^2 + 1$).

**Type of Diffusion Matrix.** The designer can choose what type of matrix he will implement, the two main hardware-friendly types being circulant or serial. In the circulant case, the designer picks $r$ coefficients $Z = (Z_0, \ldots, Z_{r-1})$ and the matrix $Z$ is defined as

$$
\begin{pmatrix}
Z_0 & Z_1 & Z_2 & . & . & . & Z_{r-2} & Z_{r-1} \\
Z_{r-1} & Z_0 & Z_1 & . & . & . & Z_{r-3} & Z_{r-2} \\
Z_{r-2} & Z_{r-1} & Z_0 & . & . & . & Z_{r-4} & Z_{r-3} \\
. & . & . & . & . & . & . & . \\
. & . & . & . & . & . & . & . \\
Z_1 & Z_2 & Z_3 & . & . & . & Z_{r-1} & Z_0
\end{pmatrix}
$$

In the serial case, the designer picks $r$ coefficients $Z = (Z_0, \ldots, Z_{r-1})$ and the matrix $Z$ is defined as

$$
\begin{pmatrix}
0 & 1 & 0 & 0 & . & . & 0 & 0 \\
0 & 0 & 1 & 0 & . & . & 0 & 0 \\
0 & 0 & 0 & 1 & . & . & 0 & 0 \\
. & . & . & . & . & . & . & . \\
. & . & . & . & . & . & . & . \\
0 & 0 & 0 & 0 & . & . & 0 & 1 \\
Z_0 & Z_1 & Z_2 & . & . & . & Z_{r-2} & Z_{r-1}
\end{pmatrix}^r
$$

The matrix therefore takes $r$ operations to be computed.

**Branch Number of the Diffusion Matrix.** In general, implementing a matrix with very good diffusion property will cost more area and/or cycles than a weak one. For example, the AES matrix has ideal MDS diffusion property, but certainly requires more area to implement than a simple binary matrix with weaker properties. Since the former is bigger but stronger and the latter is smaller and weaker, it is not clear which alternative will lead to the best FOAM. Therefore, the designer can choose between a wide range of possibilities concerning the branch number $B$ of the diffusion matrix, from $B = 3$ to $B = r+1$ (MDS).

## 5   Security Assessment of AES-like Primitives

The FOAM metric takes into account the security of the permutation with regards to simple differential/linear attacks. We would like to evaluate this security for the AES-like SPN permutations we are considering. Theorem 1 gives us the minimal number of active S-boxes for a given number of rounds[3], and knowing the S-box cryptographic properties we can compute the maximum differential and linear characteristic probabilities of our generic SPN ciphers easily. In other words, we can easily compute the number of rounds $p(x) = p(2^n)$ required to achieve the aimed security $2^n$.

As stated before, for simplicity, in the rest of this article we will consider that the S-boxes have perfect differential and linear properties: for a 4-bit S-box the maximum differential and linear characteristic probabilities are $2^{-2}$ (e.g. PRESENT S-box), while for a 8-bit S-box the maximum differential and linear characteristic probabilities are $2^{-6}$ (e.g. AES S-box). One can extend the trade-off by considering other S-boxes, that might require a smaller area, but will have worse security properties.

Reusing the example from Section 2.2, from Theorem 1, there are at least 21 active S-boxes over 4 rounds of this SPN permutation. Suppose that 8-bit S-boxes are of maximum differential and linear probabilities $2^{-6}$. Then the maximum differential and linear characteristic probabilities over four rounds are upper-bounded by $(2^{-6})^{21} = 2^{-126}$.

We are aware that other attacks rather than simple differential/linear might exist. However, our goal here is not to fully specify a permutation, but to compare many trade-offs and design strategies that will lead to good hardware performances. Therefore, we emphasize that the number of rounds $p(x)$ is not the number of rounds that should be chosen by a designer. This number should be carefully chosen after thorough cryptanalysis work on the entire primitive. Yet, we believe that this simple differential/linear criterion is a quite accurate way to compare the security of AES-like SPN permutations.

# 6  Implementations in ASIC

In this section, we introduce some notation before we present formulas to estimate serialized and round-based implementations (we restricted ourselves to these two important practical cases due to the obviously vast amount of implementation trade-offs). Please note that all estimates have to be seen as *lower bounds*, as we use scan flip-flops, and consider neither reset nor I/O requirements, which can significantly impact the area count in practice. We argue that those requirements –though very important in practice– are highly application specific, and will be the same for any permutation for a given target application scenario. Thus for a fair comparison of permutation constructions we will not consider them. In practice, a higher throughout can be achieved by using pipelining techniques to reduce the critical path at the cost of additional area.

---

[3] We note that the number of active S-boxes given by Theorem 1 is tight if the number of rounds is not equal to 3 modulo 4 (even in that case the theorem gives a very close estimation). This does not mean that the maximum differential and linear characteristic probabilities computed are tight, since it is unknown how many active S-boxes can use the maximum differential and linear characteristic probabilities at the same time (this remains an open problem).

As this design goal is, again, highly application specific and FOAM is designed to be frequency independent, we have not considered it in our analysis.

We have estimated all serial architectures with the single optimization goal of minimal area in mind. In practice, some design decisions will most likely use another trade-off point more in favor of smaller time and larger area. To reflect this, we have estimated all round-based architectures optimized for maximum FOAM.

The table below provides an overview over the hardware building blocks we used, their notation and typical area requirements for a UMC 180 nm technology.[4]

| Notation | Description | GE | Notation | Description | GE |
|----------|-------------|-----|----------|-------------|-----|
| $DFF$ | 1-input flip-flop | 4.67 | $XOR$ | 2-input exclusive Or | 2.67 |
| $SFF$ | 2-input flip-flop | 6 | $SB4$ | 4 x 4 S-box (PRESENT) | 22 |
| $MUX$ | 2-input multiplexer | 2.33 | $SB8$ | 8 x 8 S-box (AES) | 233 |

We give in Table 1 the estimates for the various parts of the ASIC implementations. The details on how these formulas were obtained will be provided in the full version of this paper.

**Table 1.** Estimates for various parts of the ASIC implementations. ( $i$ denotes the exponent for the field $GF(2^i)$; $a_r$, $a_c$ and $a_p$ denote the counters for rows, columns and rounds respectively; $cg$ and $oc$ denote clock gating and other combinational logic respectively; $b$ denotes the area requirement for the finite state machine.)

| | Serial architectures | Round-based architectures |
|---|---|---|
| $C_{mem}$ | $s \cdot \left( r - \lfloor \frac{i}{s} \rfloor \right) \cdot SFF + \lfloor \frac{i}{s} \rfloor s \cdot DFF$ , $c = 1$ <br> $2 \cdot s \cdot r \cdot SFF + s \cdot r \cdot (c-2) \cdot DFF$ , $c \geq 2$ | $s \cdot r \cdot c \cdot SFF$ |
| $C_{sbox}$ | $SB4$ , $s = 4$ <br> $SB8$ , $s = 8$ | $r \cdot c \cdot SB4$ , $s = 4$ <br> $r \cdot c \cdot SB8$ , $s = 8$ |
| $C_{diff}$ | $A \cdot XOR$ , for serial mat. <br> $A \cdot XOR + (s \cdot r - i) \cdot DFF + i \cdot MUX$ , for circulant mat. | $A \cdot r \cdot c \cdot \frac{s}{i} \cdot XOR$ |
| $C_{cst}$ | $s \cdot XOR$ | $s \cdot r \cdot c \cdot XOR$ |
| $C_{log}$ | $a_r + a_p + SFF \cdot 2 + oc$ , $c = 1$ <br> $a_r + a_c + a_p + b + cg + oc$ , $c \geq 2$ | $a_p + b$ |
| $C_{io}$ | $s \cdot MUX$ | $0$ |
| $t$ | $r \cdot c + (c-1) + (\frac{s}{i} \cdot r + 1 - \lfloor \frac{i}{s} \rfloor) \cdot c$ , $c \geq 2$ serial mat. <br> $r \cdot c + (c-1) + (2 \cdot \frac{s}{i} \cdot r) \cdot c$ , $c \geq 2$ circulant mat. <br> $r \cdot c + \frac{s}{i} \cdot r$ , $c = 1$ serial mat. <br> $r \cdot c + (2 \cdot \frac{s}{i} \cdot r - 1)$ , $c = 1$ circulant mat. | $1$ |

---

[4] This is just *one example* for a technology and the area of the building blocks can be easily adapted for other technologies.

# 7  Results and New Diffusion Matrices

In this section we provide the results of our framework, as well as new diffusion matrices that are very interesting for hardware implementations. As explained in Section 4, the designer's input is the permutation bitsize $n$, the metric he would like to maximize (area or FOAM), and the degree up to which serial or round-based implementations are important. To illustrate our method, we focused on the case where the designer would like to build a 64-bit permutation (which is a typical state size for a lightweight block cipher). For the implementation types, we focused on three scenarios: only serial implementation is important, only round-based implementation is important, serial and round-based implementations are equally important for the designer. Further, we only considered encryption.

Before describing our results, we first explain how we found good diffusion matrices (circulant and serial), which outperform known ones from the AES, LED ciphers and the PHOTON hash function.

## 7.1  Lightweight Coefficients

Consider the AES matrix, a circulant matrix with coefficients (0x01, 0x01, 0x02, 0x03) over $GF(2^8)$ defined by the irreducible polynomial $\alpha^8 + \alpha^4 + \alpha^3 + \alpha + 1$. The matrix appears to be very lightweight due to the low Hamming weight of its entries. But surprisingly, we found an even lighter circulant matrix over the same field with coefficients[5] (0x01,0x01,0x04,0x8d). We now explain why this is so.

We first illustrate how to compute the number of XORs required to implement a multiplication by a finite field element $x$, by using $GF(2^8)$ defined by $\alpha^8 + \alpha^4 + \alpha^3 + \alpha + 1$ as an example. Let $x = x_7 \cdot \alpha^7 + x_6 \cdot \alpha^6 + \cdots x_1 \cdot \alpha + x_0 = (x_7, x_6, \cdots, x_1, x_0)$. For ease of explanation, we employ hexadecimal encoding: $(x_7, x_6, x_5, x_4, x_3, x_2, x_1, x_0)$ can be encoded as a tuple of hexadecimal numbers (0x80, 0x40, 0x20, 0x10, 0x08, 0x04, 0x02, 0x01). Then, the multiplication of 0x04 is represented as:

$$0x04 \cdot x = (x_5, x_4, x_3 + x_7, x_2 + x_6 + x_7, x_1 + x_6, x_0 + x_7, x_6 + x_7, x_6)$$
$$= (0x20, 0x10, 0x88, 0xc4, 0x42, 0x81, 0xc0, 0x40).$$

We see that the number of XORs required for the multiplication of 0x04 by $x$ is 6. Now we can compute

$$0x8d \cdot x = (\alpha^7 + \alpha^3 + \alpha^2 + 1) \cdot x$$
$$= \big(0xb1, 0x58, 0x2c, 0x96, 0xfa, 0x4c, 0xa6, 0x62\big) \oplus \big(0x10, 0x88, 0xc4, 0x62, 0xa1, 0xc0, 0x60, 0x20\big)$$
$$\oplus \big(0x20, 0x10, 0x88, 0xc4, 0x42, 0x81, 0xc0, 0x40\big) \oplus \big(0x80, 0x40, 0x20, 0x10, 0x08, 0x04, 0x02, 0x01\big)$$
$$= (0x01, 0x80, 0x40, 0x20, 0x11, 0x09, 0x04, 0x03)$$
$$= (x_0, x_7, x_6, x_5, x_0 + x_4, x_0 + x_3, x_2, x_0 + x_1)$$

---

[5] We use the binary representation to represent finite field elements. E.g., 0x8d is 10001101 in binary, which corresponds to the finite field element $\alpha^7 + \alpha^3 + \alpha^2 + 1$ in $GF(2^8)$.

Due to the *'cancellation of XORs'*, we see that multiplication of $x$ by 0x8d requires only 3 XORs. In a similar fashion, the multiplication of $x$ by 0x02 and 0x03 requires 3 and 11 XORs respectively.

Hence we are able to come up with the XOR count table for any finite field. Table 2 of Appendix A shows the XOR count for $GF(2^4)$ defined by $\alpha^4 + \alpha + 1$. The tables for $GF(2^4)$ and $GF(2^8)$ defined by different irreducible polynomials are provided in the full version of this paper.

Now we explain how to use the tables to calculate $A$ the number of XORs required to implement a row of a matrix. Denote a given row of an $r \times r$ matrix by $(x_1, x_2, \cdots x_r)$ over a finite field $GF(2^i)$. Let $\gamma_j$ be the XOR count(e.g. Table 2 of Appendix A for $i = 4$) corresponding to the field element $x_j$. Then $A$ is equal to $(\gamma_1 + \cdots + \gamma_r) + (z - 1) \cdot i$, where $z$ is the number of non-zero elements in the row. We give some examples: row (0x1,0x1,0x4,0x9) uses $(0 + 0 + 2 + 1) + 3 \times 4 = 15$ XORs to implement over $GF(2^4)$; the AES matrix uses $(0 + 0 + 3 + 11) + 3 \times 8 = 38$ XORs to implement per row over $GF(2^8)$. Similarly, the circulant matrix with coefficients (0x01,0x01,0x04,0x8d) uses 33 XORs to implement per row over $GF(2^8)$, and is thus lighter than the AES matrix.

## 7.2   Subfield Construction

In this section, we describe the subfield construction[6] which allows us to outperform the AES matrix even more than the optimal matrix found in Section 7.1. As computed in the previous subsection, the MDS circulant matrix $circ(0\text{x}1, 0\text{x}1, 0\text{x}4, 0\text{x}9)$ over $GF(2^4)$ defined by $\alpha^4 + \alpha + 1$ requires 15 XORs to implement per row. Using the method of [11, Section 3.3], we can form a circulant MDS matrix over $GF(2^8)$ by using two parallel copies of $Q = circ(0\text{x}1, 0\text{x}1, 0\text{x}4, 0\text{x}9)$ over $GF(2^4)$. The matrix is formed by writing each byte $q_j$ as a concatenation of two nibbles $q_j = (q_j^L || q_j^R)$. Then the MDS multiplication is computed on each half $(u_1^L, u_2^L, u_3^L, u_4^L) = Q \cdot (q_1^L, q_2^L, q_3^L, q_4^L)$ and $(u_1^R, u_2^R, u_3^R, u_4^R) = Q \cdot (q_1^R, q_2^R, q_3^R, q_4^R)$ over $GF(2^4)$. The result is concatenated to form four output bytes $(u_1, u_2, u_3, u_4)$ where $u_j = (u_j^L || u_j^R)$. This matrix needs just $15 \times 2 = 30$ XORs to implement per row. In comparison, the lightest MDS circulant matrix $circ(0\text{x}01, 0\text{x}01, 0\text{x}04, 0\text{x}8d)$ over $GF(2^8)$ defined by $\alpha^8 + \alpha^4 + \alpha^3 + \alpha + 1$ requires more XORs (33 XORs per row).

Further, we can serialize the above multiplication to do the left half followed by the right half, in which case only 15 XORs are needed to implement one row of the MDS matrix over $GF(2^8)$. Another advantage of subfield construction is exemplified by the SPN-Hash construction [11]. Instead of finding an $8 \times 8$ serial MDS matrix over $GF(2^8)$ exhaustively, two parallel copies of the PHOTON $8 \times 8$ serial MDS matrix over $GF(2^4)$ were concatenated to form the $8 \times 8$ serial MDS matrix over $GF(2^8)$ for SPN-Hash.

---

[6] This idea of subfield construction was used in the SHA3 submission ECHO [6] and later in WHIRLWIND [4] and SPN-Hash [11].

We can generalize this method to form a diffusion matrix with branch number $B$ over $GF(2^s)$ from $s/i$ copies of a diffusion matrix of the same branch number over a subfield $GF(2^i)$, where $i$ divides $s$.

### 7.3   Good Matrices

We search for optimal low-weight $r \times r$ circulant and serial matrices of different branch numbers (3 to $r + 1$) over the finite fields $GF(2)$, $GF(2^2)$, $GF(2^4)$ and $GF(2^8)$, and list them in Table 3 of Appendix A. Using the construction of Section 7.2, we can form diffusion matrices to transform nibbles and bytes from these subfields.

The optimal matrices are found by exhaustively checking the branch number of all matrices and choosing the one with the least number of XORs according to the method explained in Section 7.1. To check the branch number of matrix $Q$, we concatenate it with the identity matrix $I_r$ to form $(I_r|Q)$, the generating matrix of the corresponding linear code, and use the MAGMA software to find the distance[7]. For branch number $B$, we check that both $Q$ and its transpose $Q^t$ has branch number $B$.

The matrices are optimal in the sense that they need minimal number of XORs to implement. In the events of a tie between two matrices, possibly over different finite field representations, we just list one of them. For example, the circulant matrices $circ$(0x01,0x01,0x04,0x8d) over $GF(2^8)$ defined by $\alpha^8 + \alpha^4 + \alpha^3 + \alpha + 1$ and $circ$(0x01,0x01,0x04,0x8e) over $GF(2^8)$ defined by $\alpha^8 + \alpha^4 + \alpha^3 + \alpha^2 + 1$ both outperforms the AES matrix by using 33 XORs to implement one row, so we just list the latter. We use "-" when no circulant matrix with branch number $B$ exists (verified by exhaustive search or coding theory bounds). For example, it can be verified that $8 \times 8$ circulant MDS matrix does not exist in the finite field $GF(2^4)$. However, we could not find the optimal $8 \times 8$ circulant MDS matrix over $GF(2^8)$. Because the search space is too big to exhaust, we just list the WHIRLPOOL matrix which is MDS and low weight.

We use "*" to denote that we have not found the serial matrix with branch number $B$ at this point of time due to the huge search space. For instance, as the search space is too big to exhaust, we could not find a $8 \times 8$ serial MDS matrix over $GF(2^8)$. In this case, we can employ the method of subfield construction (described in Section 7.2), i.e. use two parallel copies of the $8 \times 8$ MDS serial matrix with last row (0x2,0xd,0x2,0x4,0x3,0xd,0x5,0x2) (refer to second row of $8 \times 8$ subtable of Table 3) over $GF(2^4)$ to obtain the desired matrix over $GF(2^8)$.

### 7.4   Application: FOAM Comparison for 64-bit SPN Structures

In this section, we compare the FOAM metric for 64-bit SPN Structures. Table 4 in Appendix A gives the results for a SPN structure based on 4-bit PRESENT S-box with circulant matrices or serial matrices. Due to space constraints, we will

---

[7] We are aware that better techniques than naive exhaustive search might be used here. However, such improvements are not the goal of this article and we leave them as potential future work.

provide the results for a SPN structure based on 8-bit AES S-box with circulant matrices or serial matrices in the full version of this paper. The diffusion matrices are based on the optimal matrices found in Section 7.3. To compute $p(2^{64})$, the number of rounds to achieve differential/linear probability $\leq 2^{-64}$, we use the fact that the differential/linear probability of the PRESENT S-box is $2^{-2}$ and that of the AES S-box is $2^{-6}$. Then we lower bound the number of active S-boxes by concatenating 4-round bounds with $B \times B'$ active S-boxes from Theorem 1, 2-round bounds with $B$ active S-boxes and 1-round bound which involves only 1 active S-box. We also write down $t$, the time to compute one round for serialized implementation (the time $t$ for round based implementation is the constant 1, so it is not presented).

We compute the FOAM for round-based and serialized implementation based on the formula found in Section 6. We also present the FOAM for half-half implementation, where we take the average, i.e. equal weighting, of the round-based and serialized FOAM. This corresponds to implementations which are good for both scenarios. However, this represents just one example, as the weighting of the scenarios is clearly a designer's choice. The structure with the best area and FOAMs are in bold.

We see that for designing 64-bit SPN:

1. For minimal area the geometry is the most important criterion, while the choice of the field of the MDS matrix is of less importance. The geometry should be chosen, such that $c$ is maximized, and consequently, many internal columns can be realized with 1-input flip-flops. A serial matrix is favorable over a circulant matrix and in general smaller fields allow to save a few GE, but come at a high timing overhead.

2. **PRESENT S-box**
   - When Circulant Matrices are used with PRESENT S-box in Table 4 from Appendix A, the $4 \times 4$ almost-MDS circulant matrix $circ(0x1, 0x1, 0x1, 0x0)$ over $GF(2^4)$ gives the best FOAM for round-based, serial and half-half implementations.
   - When Serial Matrices are used with PRESENT S-box in Table 4 from Appendix A, the $4 \times 4$ almost-MDS serial matrix with last row (0x1, 0x0, 0x2, 0x1) over $GF(2^4)$ defined by $\alpha^4 + \alpha + 1$ gives the best FOAM for round-based, serial and half-half implementations.

3. **AES S-box**
   - From our results for AES S-box (provided in the full version of the paper), when Circulant Matrices are used with AES S-box, two parallel copies of the $4 \times 4$ MDS matrix $circ(0x1, 0x1, 0x4, 0x9)$ over $GF(2^4)$ defined by $\alpha^4 + \alpha + 1$ gives the best FOAM for round-based implementation. The $4 \times 4$ MDS matrix $circ(0x01, 0x01, 0x04, 0x8e)$ over $GF(2^8)$ defined by $\alpha^8 + \alpha^4 + \alpha^3 + \alpha^2 + 1$ gives the best FOAM for serial and half-half implementations.
   - When Serial Matrices are used with AES S-box, two parallel copies of the $4 \times 4$ MDS serial matrix with last row (0x2, 0x1, 0x1, 0x4) over $GF(2^4)$ defined by $\alpha^4 + \alpha + 1$ gives the best FOAM for round-based

implementation. The $8 \times 8$ serial matrix (having branch number 6) with last row (0x01, 0x01, 0x00, 0x00, 0x01, 0x01, 0x02, 0x00) over $GF(2^8)$ defined by $\alpha^8 + \alpha^4 + \alpha^3 + \alpha + 1$ gives the best FOAM for serial and half-half implementations and is also very competitive for round-based FOAMs. It is thus a very interesting choice for many different applications.

4. Structures based on PRESENT S-box have higher FOAM for round-based and half-half implementations than those based on AES S-box. On the other hand, structures based on AES S-box have higher FOAM for serial implementation than PRESENT S-box, because they need significantly less rounds.

5. For structures using both types of S-boxes, $4 \times 4$ matrices have higher FOAM than $2 \times 2$ and $8 \times 8$ matrices.

6. Based on the above observations, we do not always go for the matrix with the best branch number: for PRESENT S-box in Table 4 from Appendix A, we use almost-MDS $4 \times 4$ matrix which gives better trade-offs and a higher FOAM than MDS matrix. Moreover, we found that when AES S-box is used with $8 \times 8$ matrices, we go for the one with branch number 6 instead of the optimal 9.

# References

1. Avoine, G., Oechslin, P.: A Scalable and Provably Secure Hash-Based RFID Protocol. In: PerCom Workshops, pp. 110–114. IEEE Computer Society (2005)
2. Badel, S., Dağtekin, N., Nakahara Jr., J., Ouafi, K., Reffé, N., Sepehrdad, P., Sušil, P., Vaudenay, S.: ARMADILLO: A Multi-purpose Cryptographic Primitive Dedicated to Hardware. In: Mangard, S., Standaert, F.-X. (eds.) CHES 2010. LNCS, vol. 6225, pp. 398–412. Springer, Heidelberg (2010)
3. Barkan, E., Biham, E.: In How Many Ways Can You Write Rijndael? In: Zheng, Y. (ed.) ASIACRYPT 2002. LNCS, vol. 2501, pp. 160–175. Springer, Heidelberg (2002)
4. Barreto, P.S.L.M., Nikov, V., Nikova, S., Rijmen, V., Tischhauser, E.: Whirlwind: a new cryptographic hash function. Des. Codes Cryptography 56(2-3), 141–162 (2010)
5. Barreto, P.S.L.M., Rijmen, V.: Whirlpool. In: Encyclopedia of Cryptography and Security, 2nd edn., pp. 1384–1385 (2011)
6. Benadjila, R., Billet, O., Gilbert, H., Macario-Rat, G., Peyrin, T., Robshaw, M., Seurin, Y.: SHA-3 Proposal: ECHO. Submission to NIST (2008)
7. Bertoni, G., Daemen, J., Peeters, M., Assche, G.V.: Sponge functions. In: Ecrypt Hash Workshop 2007 (May 2007)
8. Bogdanov, A., Knudsen, L.R., Leander, G., Paar, C., Poschmann, A., Robshaw, M.J.B., Seurin, Y., Vikkelsoe, C.: PRESENT: An Ultra-Lightweight Block Cipher. In: Paillier, P., Verbauwhede, I. (eds.) CHES 2007. LNCS, vol. 4727, pp. 450–466. Springer, Heidelberg (2007), http://lightweightcrypto.org/present/
9. Bogdanov, A., Leander, G., Paar, C., Poschmann, A., Robshaw, M.J.B., Seurin, Y.: Hash Functions and RFID Tags: Mind the Gap. In: Oswald, E., Rohatgi, P. (eds.) CHES 2008. LNCS, vol. 5154, pp. 283–299. Springer, Heidelberg (2008)
10. De Cannière, C., Dunkelman, O., Knežević, M.: KATAN and KTANTAN — A Family of Small and Efficient Hardware-Oriented Block Ciphers. In: Clavier, C., Gaj, K. (eds.) CHES 2009. LNCS, vol. 5747, pp. 272–288. Springer, Heidelberg (2009)

11. Choy, J., Yap, H., Khoo, K., Guo, J., Peyrin, T., Poschmann, A., Tan, C.H.: SPN-Hash: Improving the Provable Resistance against Differential Collision Attacks. In: Mitrokotsa, A., Vaudenay, S. (eds.) AFRICACRYPT 2012. LNCS, vol. 7374, pp. 270–286. Springer, Heidelberg (2012)
12. Daemen, J., Knudsen, L.R., Rijmen, V.: The Block Cipher SQUARE. In: Biham, E. (ed.) FSE 1997. LNCS, vol. 1267, pp. 149–165. Springer, Heidelberg (1997)
13. Daemen, J., Rijmen, V.: The Design of Rijndael: AES - The Advanced Encryption Standard. Springer, Heidelberg (2002)
14. Guo, J., Peyrin, T., Poschmann, A.: The PHOTON Family of Lightweight Hash Functions. In: Rogaway, P. (ed.) CRYPTO 2011. LNCS, vol. 6841, pp. 222–239. Springer, Heidelberg (2011)
15. Guo, J., Peyrin, T., Poschmann, A., Robshaw, M.: The LED Block Cipher. In: Preneel, B., Takagi, T. (eds.) CHES 2011. LNCS, vol. 6917, pp. 326–341. Springer, Heidelberg (2011)
16. Henrici, D., Götze, J., Müller, P.: A Hash-based Pseudonymization Infrastructure for RFID Systems. In: SecPerU, pp. 22–27 (2006)
17. Lee, S.M., Hwang, Y.J., Lee, D.-H., Lim, J.-I.: Efficient Authentication for Low-Cost RFID Systems. In: Gervasi, O., Gavrilova, M.L., Kumar, V., Laganá, A., Lee, H.P., Mun, Y., Taniar, D., Tan, C.J.K. (eds.) ICCSA 2005. LNCS, vol. 3480, pp. 619–627. Springer, Heidelberg (2005)
18. Sajadieh, M., Dakhilalian, M., Mala, H., Sepehrdad, P.: Recursive Diffusion Layers for Block Ciphers and Hash Functions. In: Canteaut, A. (ed.) FSE 2012. LNCS, vol. 7549, pp. 385–401. Springer, Heidelberg (2012)
19. Shibutani, K., Isobe, T., Hiwatari, H., Mitsuda, A., Akishita, T., Shirai, T.: *Piccolo*: An Ultra-Lightweight Blockcipher. In: Preneel, B., Takagi, T. (eds.) CHES 2011. LNCS, vol. 6917, pp. 342–357. Springer, Heidelberg (2011)
20. Wu, S., Wang, M., Wu, W.: Recursive Diffusion Layers for (Lightweight) Block Ciphers and Hash Functions. In: Knudsen, L.R., Wu, H. (eds.) SAC 2012. LNCS, vol. 7707, pp. 355–371. Springer, Heidelberg (2013)

# A    Tables

Table 2. XORs required to implement a multiplication by $x$ over $GF(2^4)$

| $x$ (hexadecimal representation) | 0 | 1 | 2 | 3 | 4 | 5 | 6 | 7 | 8 | 9 | a | b | c | d | e | f |
|---|---|---|---|---|---|---|---|---|---|---|---|---|---|---|---|---|
| $\alpha^4 + \alpha + 1$ | | 0 | 0 | 1 | 5 | 2 | 6 | 5 | 9 | 3 | 1 | 8 | 6 | 5 | 3 | 8 | 6 |

**Table 3.** Good Circulant Matrices of Size $2 \times 2$, $4 \times 4$ and $8 \times 8$ $B$ denotes the branch number; The "First Row" and the "Last Row" column (in hexadecimal) represents the first row of the circulant matrix and the last row of the serial matrix (as described in Section 4) respectively; $A$ denotes the number of XOR gates needed to implement one row of the circulant matrix and the last row of the serial matrix respectively.

**$2 \times 2$**

| Finite Field | $B$ | Circulant matrices | | Serial matrices | |
|---|---|---|---|---|---|
| | | First Row | $A$ | Last Row | $A$ |
| $GF(2^8)$, $\alpha^8 + \alpha^4 + \alpha^3 + \alpha^2 + 1$ | 3 | 1,2 | 11 | 1,2 | 11 |
| $GF(2^4)$, $\alpha^4 + \alpha + 1$ | 3 | 1,2 | 5 | 1,2 | 5 |
| $GF(2^2)$, $\alpha^2 + \alpha + 1$ | 3 | 1,2 | 3 | 1,2 | 3 |
| $GF(2)$ | 3 | - | - | - | - |

**$4 \times 4$**

| Finite Field | $B$ | Circulant matrices | | Serial matrices | |
|---|---|---|---|---|---|
| | | First Row | $A$ | Last Row | $A$ |
| $GF(2^8)$, $\alpha^8 + \alpha^4 + \alpha^3 + \alpha^2 + 1$ | 5 | 1,1,4,8e | 33 | 1,2,1,4 | 33 |
| | 4 | 1,1,1,0 | 16 | 1,0,2,1 | 19 |
| | 3 | 1,0,0,2 | 11 | 1,0,0,1 | 8 |
| $GF(2^4)$, $\alpha^4 + \alpha + 1$ | 5 | 1,1,4,9 | 15 | 2,1,1,4 | 15 |
| | 4 | 1,1,1,0 | 8 | 1,0,2,1 | 9 |
| | 3 | 1,0,0,2 | 5 | 1,0,0,1 | 4 |
| $GF(2^2)$, $\alpha^2 + \alpha + 1$ | 5 | - | - | - | - |
| | 4 | 1,1,1,0 | 4 | 1,0,2,1 | 5 |
| | 3 | 1,0,0,2 | 3 | 1,0,0,1 | 2 |
| $GF(2)$ | 5 | - | - | - | - |
| | 4 | 1,1,1,0 | 2 | - | - |
| | 3 | - | - | 1,0,0,1 | 1 |

**$8 \times 8$**

| Finite Field | $B$ | Circulant matrices | | Serial matrices | |
|---|---|---|---|---|---|
| | | First Row | $A$ | Last Row | $A$ |
| $GF(2^8)$, $\alpha^8 + \alpha^4 + \alpha^3 + \alpha^2 + 1$ | 9 | 1,1,4,1,8,5,2,9 | 105 | * | * |
| | 8 | 1,0,1,1,2,2,1,8e | 57 | 1,1,2,0,1,8d,2,1 | 57 |
| | 7 | 1,0,0,1,1,1,2,8e | 46 | 1,1,2,1,0,0,1,8d | 46 |
| | 6 | 1,0,0,0,1,1,1,2 | 35 | 1,1,0,0,1,1,2,0 | 35 |
| | 5 | 1,0,0,0,0,1,1,2 | 27 | 1,0,0,1,1,1,0,0 | 24 |
| | 4 | 1,0,0,0,0,0,1,1 | 16 | 1,0,0,0,0,1,1,0 | 16 |
| | 3 | 1,0,0,0,0,0,0,2 | 11 | 1,0,0,0,0,0,1,0 | 8 |
| $GF(2^4)$, $\alpha^4 + \alpha + 1$ | 9 | - | - | 2,d,2,4,3,d,5,2 | 50 |
| | 8 | 1,0,1,1,2,9,2,1 | 27 | * | * |
| | 7 | 1,0,0,1,1,1,2,9 | 22 | 1,0,2,1,1,1,2,0 | 22 |
| | 6 | 1,0,0,0,1,1,1,2 | 17 | 1,1,0,0,1,1,2,0 | 17 |
| | 5 | 1,0,0,0,0,1,1,2 | 13 | 1,0,0,1,1,1,0,0 | 12 |
| | 4 | 1,0,0,0,0,0,1,1 | 8 | 1,0,0,0,0,1,1,0 | 8 |
| | 3 | 1,0,0,0,0,0,0,2 | 5 | 1,0,0,0,0,0,1,0 | 4 |
| $GF(2^2)$, $\alpha^2 + \alpha + 1$ | 9 - 8 | - | - | 2,1,0,3,1,2,0,1 | 13 |
| | 7 | - | - | 1,0,0,1,1,1,0,2 | 9 |
| | 6 | 1,0,0,0,1,1,1,2 | 9 | 1,0,0,1,1,1,0,0 | 6 |
| | 5 | 1,0,0,0,0,1,1,2 | 7 | 1,0,0,0,0,1,1,0 | 4 |
| | 4 | 1,0,0,0,0,0,1,1 | 4 | 1,0,0,0,0,0,1,0 | |
| | 3 | 1,0,0,0,0,0,0,2 | 3 | 1,0,0,0,0,0,1,0 | 2 |
| $GF(2)$ | 9 - 6 | - | - | 1,0,0,1,1,1,0,0 | 3 |
| | 5 | | | 1,0,0,0,0,1,1,0 | 2 |
| | 4 | 1,0,0,0,0,0,1,1 | 2 | 1,0,0,0,0,0,1,0 | |
| | 3 | - | - | 1,0,0,0,0,0,1,0 | 1 |

**Table 4.** FOAM for 64-bit SPN based on 4-bit PRESENT S-box and Circulant Matrices or Serial Matrices

| Finite Field | $r$ | $c$ | $B$ | $p(2^{64})$ | $t$ | Area (GE) rd based | Area (GE) serial | FOAM $\times 10^{-9}$ rd based | FOAM $\times 10^{-9}$ serial | FOAM $\times 10^{-9}$ half-half |
|---|---|---|---|---|---|---|---|---|---|---|
| Circulant Matrices | | | | | | | | | | |
| $GF(2^4)$ | 2 | 8 | 3 | 16 | 55 | 1156 | 541 | 46.76 | 3.88 | 25.32 |
| $GF(2^2)$ | 2 | 8 | 3 | 16 | 87 | 1199 | **540** | 43.48 | 2.46 | 22.97 |
| $GF(2^4)$ | 4 | 4 | 5 | 8 | | 1579 | 652 | 50.16 | 5.77 | 27.96 |
| | 4 | 4 | 4 | 8 | 51 | 1280 | 633 | **76.34** | **6.12** | **41.23** |
| | 4 | 4 | 3 | 16 | | 1156 | 630 | 46.76 | 3.09 | 24.92 |
| $GF(2^2)$ | 4 | 4 | 4 | 8 | 83 | 1280 | 627 | 76.34 | 3.83 | 40.08 |
| | 4 | 4 | 3 | 16 | | 1199 | 629 | 43.48 | 1.90 | 22.69 |
| $GF(2)$ | 4 | 4 | 4 | | 147 | 1280 | 624 | 76.34 | 2.18 | 39.26 |
| $GF(2^4)$ | 8 | 2 | 8 | 8 | | 2091 | 873 | 28.58 | 3.35 | 15.96 |
| | 8 | 2 | 7 | 10 | | 1882 | 864 | 28.22 | 2.73 | 15.48 |
| | 8 | 2 | 6 | 12 | 49 | 1669 | 851 | 29.92 | 2.35 | 16.14 |
| | 8 | 2 | 5 | 14 | | 1498 | 840 | 31.83 | 2.07 | 16.95 |
| | 8 | 2 | 4 | 16 | | 1284 | 827 | 37.89 | 1.87 | 19.88 |
| | 8 | 2 | 3 | 22 | | 1161 | 823 | 33.73 | 1.37 | 17.55 |
| $GF(2^2)$ | 8 | 2 | 6 | 12 | | 1712 | 834 | 28.45 | 1.48 | 14.96 |
| | 8 | 2 | 5 | 14 | 81 | 1541 | 829 | 30.09 | 1.28 | 15.69 |
| | 8 | 2 | 4 | 16 | | 1284 | 821 | 37.89 | 1.15 | 19.52 |
| | 8 | 2 | 3 | 22 | | 1204 | 823 | 31.38 | 0.83 | 16.10 |
| $GF(2)$ | 8 | 2 | 4 | 16 | 145 | 1284 | 818 | 37.89 | 0.64 | 19.27 |
| Serial Matrices | | | | | | | | | | |
| $GF(2^4)$ | 2 | 8 | 3 | 16 | 39 | 1156 | 513 | 46.76 | 6.09 | 26.42 |
| $GF(2^2)$ | 2 | 8 | 3 | 16 | 63 | 1199 | **508** | 43.48 | 3.85 | 23.67 |
| $GF(2^4)$ | 4 | 4 | 5 | 8 | | 1579 | 586 | 50.16 | 10.39 | 30.27 |
| | 4 | 4 | 4 | 8 | 35 | 1322 | 570 | **71.48** | **10.99** | **41.23** |
| | 4 | 4 | 3 | 16 | | 1113 | 561 | 50.41 | 5.66 | 28.04 |
| $GF(2^2)$ | 4 | 4 | 4 | 8 | 55 | 1365 | 559 | 67.08 | 7.26 | 37.17 |
| | 4 | 4 | 3 | 16 | | 1113 | 556 | 50.41 | 3.67 | 27.04 |
| $GF(2)$ | 4 | 4 | 3 | 16 | 87 | 1113 | 553 | 50.41 | 2.35 | 26.38 |
| $GF(2^4)$ | 8 | 2 | 9 | 6 | | 3074 | 794 | 17.64 | 8.01 | 12.82 |
| | 8 | 2 | 7 | 10 | | 1882 | 724 | 28.22 | 5.78 | 17.00 |
| | 8 | 2 | 6 | 12 | 33 | 1669 | 711 | 29.92 | 5.00 | 17.46 |
| | 8 | 2 | 5 | 14 | | 1455 | 697 | 33.73 | 4.45 | 19.09 |
| | 8 | 2 | 4 | 16 | | 1284 | 687 | 37.89 | 4.02 | 20.95 |
| | 8 | 2 | 3 | 22 | | 1118 | 681 | 36.36 | 2.97 | 19.67 |
| $GF(2^2)$ | 8 | 2 | 7 | 10 | | 2053 | 700 | 23.72 | 4.00 | 13.86 |
| | 8 | 2 | 6 | 12 | | 1712 | 689 | 28.45 | 3.44 | 15.94 |
| | 8 | 2 | 5 | 14 | 51 | 1455 | 681 | 33.73 | 3.02 | 18.37 |
| | 8 | 2 | 4 | 16 | | 1284 | 676 | 37.89 | 2.68 | 20.29 |
| | 8 | 2 | 3 | 22 | | 1118 | 675 | 36.36 | 1.95 | 19.16 |
| $GF(2)$ | 8 | 2 | 5 | 14 | | 1455 | 673 | 33.73 | 1.90 | 17.81 |
| | 8 | 2 | 4 | 16 | 83 | 1284 | 671 | 37.89 | 1.67 | 19.78 |
| | 8 | 2 | 3 | 22 | | 1118 | 673 | 36.36 | 1.21 | 18.78 |

# Secure Lightweight Entity Authentication with Strong PUFs: Mission Impossible?

Jeroen Delvaux[1,2], Dawu Gu[2], Dries Schellekens[1], and Ingrid Verbauwhede[1]

[1] ESAT/COSIC and iMinds, KU Leuven,
Kasteelpark Arenberg 10, B-3001 Leuven-Heverlee, Belgium
{jeroen.delvaux,dries.schellekens,ingrid.verbauwhede}@esat.kuleuven.be
[2] CSE/LoCCS, Shanghai Jiao Tong University,
800 Dongchuan Road, Shanghai 200240, China
dwgu@sjtu.edu.cn

**Abstract.** Physically unclonable functions (PUFs) exploit the unavoidable manufacturing variations of an integrated circuit (IC). Their input-output behavior serves as a unique IC 'fingerprint'. Therefore, they have been envisioned as an IC authentication mechanism, in particular for the subclass of so-called strong PUFs. The protocol proposals are typically accompanied with two PUF promises: lightweight and an increased resistance against physical attacks. In this work, we review eight prominent proposals in chronological order: from the original strong PUF proposal to the more complicated converse and slender PUF proposals. The novelty of our work is threefold. First, we employ a unified notation and framework for ease of understanding. Second, we initiate direct comparison between protocols, which has been neglected in each of the proposals. Third, we reveal numerous security and practicality issues. To such an extent, that we cannot support the use of any proposal in its current form. All proposals aim to compensate the lack of cryptographic properties of the strong PUF. However, proper compensation seems to oppose the lightweight objective.

**Keywords:** physically unclonable function, entity authentication, lightweight.

## 1 Introduction

In this work, we consider a common authentication scenario with two parties: a **low-cost resource-constrained token** and a **resource-rich server**. Practical instantiations could be the following: RFID, smart cards and a wireless sensor network. One-way or possibly mutual entity authentication is the objective. The server has secure computing and storage at its disposal. Providing security is a major challenge however, given the requirements at the token side. Tokens typically store a secret key in non-volatile memory (NVM), using a mature technology such as EEPROM and its successor Flash, battery-backed SRAM or fuses. Cryptographic primitives import the key and perform an authentication protocol. Today's problems are as follows. First, implementing cryptographic

L. Batina and M. Robshaw (Eds.): CHES 2014, LNCS 8731, pp. 451–475, 2014.

primitives in a resource-constrained manner is rather challenging. Second, an attacker can gain physical access to the integrated circuit (IC) of a token. NVM has proven to be vulnerable to physical attacks [22]: the secret is stored permanently in a robust electrical manner. Third, most NVM technologies oppose the low-cost objective. EEPROM/Flash requires floating gate transistors, resulting in additional manufacturing steps with respect to a regular CMOS design flow. Battery-backed SRAM requires a battery. Circuitry to protect the NVM contents (e.g. a mesh of sensing wires) tends to be expensive.

**Physically Unclonable Functions** (PUFs) offer a promising alternative. Essentially, they are binary functions, with their input-output behavior determined by IC manufacturing variations. Therefore, they can be understood as a unique IC 'fingerprint', analogous to human biometrics. They might alleviate the aforementioned problems. Many PUFs allow for an implementation which is both resource-constrained and CMOS compatible. Furthermore, the secret is hidden in the physical structure of an IC, which is a much less readable format. Invasive attacks might easily destroy this secret, as an additional advantage. Several PUF-based protocols have been proposed, in particular for the subclass of so-called strong PUFs. We review the most prominent proposals: controlled PUFs [4–6], Öztürk et al. [17], Hammouri et al. [8], logically reconfigurable PUFs [11], reverse fuzzy extractors (FEs) [24], slender PUFs [16, 20] and the converse protocol [12]. The novelty of our work is threefold. First, we employ a unified notation and framework for ease of understanding. Second, we initiate direct comparison between protocols, which has been neglected in each of the proposals. Third, we reveal numerous security and practicality issues. To such an extent, that we cannot support the use of any proposal in its current form.

The remainder of this paper is organized as follows. Section 2 introduces notation and preliminaries. Section 3 describes and analyzes the strong PUF protocols. Section 4 provides an overview of the protocol issues. Section 5 concludes the work. We operate at protocol level, considering PUFs as a black box. The low-level protocol of Hammouri et al. [8] is therefore largely discussed in Appendix B, preceded by a discussion of PUF internals in Appendix A.

## 2    Preliminaries

### 2.1    Notation

Binary vectors are denoted with a bold lowercase character, e.g. $c \in \{0,1\}^{1 \times m}$. All vectors are row vectors. Their elements are selected with an index $i \geq 1$ between round brackets, e.g. $c(1)$. The null vector is denoted as $\mathbf{0}$. Binary matrices are denoted with a single bold uppercase character, e.g. $\boldsymbol{H}$. Operations are the following: addition modulo 2 (XOR), e.g. $x \oplus c$, multiplication modulo 2, e.g. $e \cdot \boldsymbol{H}^T$, concatenation, e.g. $x \| c$, and bit inversion, e.g. $\bar{r}$. Variable assignment is denoted with an arrow, e.g. $d \leftarrow d - 1$. Functions are printed in *italic*, with their input arguments between round brackets, e.g. Hamming weight $HW(\boldsymbol{r})$ and Hamming distance $HD(\boldsymbol{r_1}, \boldsymbol{r_2})$.

## 2.2   Physically Unclonable Functions: Black Box Description

The $m$-bit input and $n$-bit output of a PUF are referred to as challenge $c$ and response $r$ respectively. Unfortunately for cryptographic purposes, the behavior of the challenge-response pairs (CRPs) does not correspond with a random oracle. First, the **response bits are not perfectly reproducible**: noise and various environmental perturbations (supply voltage, temperature, etc.) result in non-determinism. The reproducibility (error rate) differs per response bit. Second, the response bits are **non-uniformly distributed**: bias and correlations are present. The latter might enable so-called modeling attacks. One tries to construct a predictive model of the PUF, given a limited set of training CRPs. Machine learning algorithms have proven to be successful [21].

PUFs are often subdivided in two classes, according to their number of CRPs. **Weak PUFs** offer few CRPs: their total content ($2^{m+n}$ bits) is of main interest. Architectures typically consist of an array of identically laid-out cells (or units), each producing one response bit. E.g. the SRAM PUF [9] and the ring oscillator PUF[1] [23] are both very popular. The total bit-content scales roughly linear with the required IC area. Although there might be some spatial correlation or a general trend among cells, a predictive model is typically of no concern. The response bits are mostly employed to generate a secret key, to be stored in volatile memory, in contrast to NVM. Post-processing logic, typically a fuzzy extractor (FE) [3], is required to ensure a reproducible and uniformly distributed key.

**Strong PUFs** offer an enormous number of CRPs, often scaling exponentially with the required IC area. They might greatly exceed the need for secret key generation and have been promoted primarily as lightweight authentication primitives. Architectures are typically able to provide a large challenge (e.g. $m = 128$), but only a very small response, mostly $n = 1$. CRPs are highly correlated, making modeling attacks a major threat. The most famous example is the arbiter PUF [13], described in appendix A. The definition of strong PUFs has shifted over the years. The original more specific notion in [7] assumes a large response space in addition to strong cryptographic properties: resistance against modeling and tamper evidence. Although more relevant than ever, we stick to the more practical recent notion.

## 2.3   Secure Sketch

The non-determinism of a PUF causes the regenerated instance of a response $r$ to be slightly different: $\widetilde{r} = r \oplus e$, with $HW(e)$ small. Secure sketches [3] are a useful reconstruction tool, as defined by a two-step procedure. First, public helper data is generated: $p = Gen(r)$. Second, reproduction is performed: $r = Rep(\widetilde{r}, p)$. Helper data $p$ unavoidably leaks some information about $r$, although this entropy loss is supposed to be limited. Despite the rather generic definition, two

---

[1] We consider the most usable read-out modes which avoid correlations, e.g. pairing neighboring oscillators.

constructions dominate the implementation landscape, as specified below. Both the code-offset and syndrome construction employ a binary $[n, k, t]$ block code $\mathcal{C}$, with $t$ the error-correcting capability. The latter construction requires a linear block code, as it employs the parity check matrix $\boldsymbol{H} \in \{0, 1\}^{(n-k) \times n}$. Successful reconstruction is guaranteed for both constructions, given $HW(\boldsymbol{e}) \leq t$. Information leakage is limited to $n - k$ bits. The hardware footprint is asymmetric: $Gen$ is better suited for resource-constrained devices than $Rep$ [24].

|  | $Gen$ | $Rep$ |  | $Gen$ | $Rep$ |
|---|---|---|---|---|---|
| code-offset | Random $\boldsymbol{w} \in \mathcal{C}$ $\boldsymbol{p} \leftarrow \boldsymbol{r} \oplus \boldsymbol{w}$ | $\widetilde{\boldsymbol{w}} \leftarrow \widetilde{\boldsymbol{r}} \oplus \boldsymbol{p} = \boldsymbol{w} \oplus \boldsymbol{e}$ Error-correct $\widetilde{\boldsymbol{w}}$ to $\boldsymbol{w}$ $\boldsymbol{r} \leftarrow \boldsymbol{p} \oplus \boldsymbol{w}$ | syndrome | $\boldsymbol{p} \leftarrow \boldsymbol{r} \cdot \boldsymbol{H}^T$ | $\boldsymbol{s} \leftarrow \widetilde{\boldsymbol{r}} \cdot \boldsymbol{H}^T \oplus \boldsymbol{p} = \boldsymbol{e} \cdot \boldsymbol{H}^T$ Determine $\boldsymbol{e}$ $\boldsymbol{r} \leftarrow \widetilde{\boldsymbol{r}} \oplus \boldsymbol{e}$ |

# 3  Lightweight Authentication with Strong PUFs

We analyze all strong PUF authentication schemes in chronological order. One can read the protocol discussions in arbitrary order, although we highly recommend to read Sections 3.1 and 3.2 first. All schemes employ two phases. The first phase is a one-time enrollment in a secure environment, following IC manufacturing. The server then obtains some information about the PUF, CRPs or even a predictive model via machine learning, to establish a shared secret. The destruction of one-time interfaces might permanently restrict the PUF access afterwards. The second phase is in-the-field deployment, where tokens are vulnerable to physical attacks. Token and server then authenticate over an insecure communication channel. In general: challenge $\boldsymbol{c}$ and response $\boldsymbol{r}$ are required to be of sufficient length, e.g. $m = n = 128$, to counteract brute-force attacks and random guessing.

## 3.1  Reference

For proper assessment, we define two reference authentication methods. Reference I employs a token with a secret key $\boldsymbol{k}$ programmed in NVM, as represented by Figure 1(a). Additional cryptographic logic performs the authentication. For ease of comparison, we opt for a hash function, hereby limiting ourselves to token authenticity only. The server checks whether a token can compute $\boldsymbol{a} \leftarrow Hash(\boldsymbol{k}, \boldsymbol{n})$, with $\boldsymbol{n}$ a random nonce. Reference II employs PUF technology, potentially providing more physical security at a lower manufacturing cost. We employ a weak PUF[2] to generate a secret key, as represented by Figure 1(b). The reproducibility and non-uniformity issue are resolved in a sequential manner, using a FE. A secure sketch first ensures reproducibility. $Gen$ is executed only once during enrollment. Public helper data $\boldsymbol{p}$ is stored by the server, or alternatively at the token side in insecure (off-chip) NVM. A hash function performs entropy compression, hereby compensating the non-uniformity of

---

[2] Logic for generating challenges is implicitly present and might be as simple as reading out the full cell array.

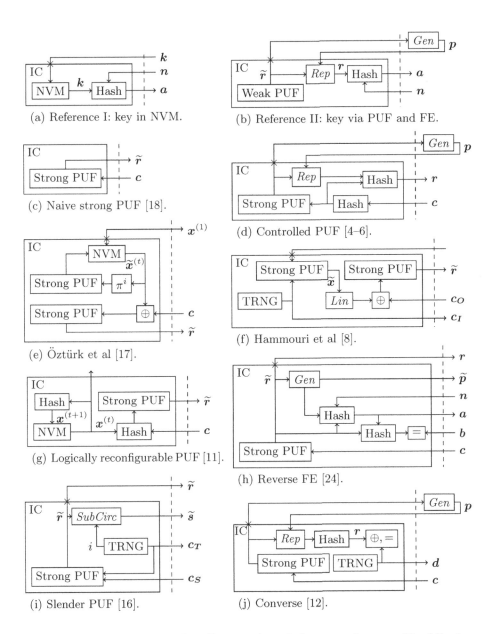

(a) Reference I: key in NVM.

(b) Reference II: key via PUF and FE.

(c) Naive strong PUF [18].

(d) Controlled PUF [4–6].

(e) Öztürk et al [17].

(f) Hammouri et al [8].

(g) Logically reconfigurable PUF [11].

(h) Reverse FE [24].

(i) Slender PUF [16].

(j) Converse [12].

**Fig. 1.** Token representation for all protocols and the two references. The following IC logic is not drawn: expansion of the strong PUF responses, intermediary registers (volatile) and control. A dashed line represent the interface with the server. One-time interfaces destructed after enrollment are marked by the symbol ×.

$r$, in addition to the entropy loss caused by the helper data. One could generate a key as $k \leftarrow Hash(r)$. We perform an optimization by merging this step with the authentication hash: $a \leftarrow Hash(r, n)$.

## 3.2 Naive Authentication

The most simple authentication method employs an unprotected strong PUF only [18], as shown in Figure 1(c). Figure 2 represents the corresponding protocol. The server collects a database of $d$ arbitrary CRPs during enrollment. We assume the use of a true random number generator (TRNG). A genuine token should be able to reproduce the response for each challenge in the server database. Only an approximate match is required, taking PUF non-determinism into account: Hamming distance threshold $\epsilon$ implements this. To avoid token impersonation via replay, CRPs are discarded after use, limiting the number of authentications to $d$. Choosing e.g. $m = 128$, an attacker cannot gather and tabulate all CRPs and clone a token as such. Choosing e.g. $n = 128$, randomly guessing $r$ is extremely unlikely to succeed.

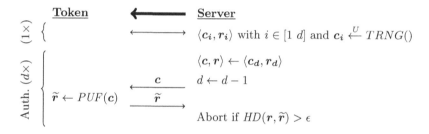

**Fig. 2.** Naive authentication protocol. The thick arrow points from verifier to prover.

**Modeling Attacks.** Strong PUFs are too fragile for unprotected exposure, as demonstrated by a history of machine learning attacks [21]. A predictive PUF model would enable token impersonation. So far, no architecture can claim to be practical, well-validated and robust against modeling. Stated otherwise: no architecture does satisfy the original strong PUF definition given in [7], as has been observed by others (e.g. [14]). Two fundamental problems undermine the optimism for a breakthrough. First, strong PUFs extract their enormous amount of bits from a limited IC area only, hereby using a limited amount of circuit elements. A highly correlated structure is the unavoidable consequence. The arbiter PUF model in appendix A.2 provides some insights in this matter. Second, the more entangled and diffusing the structure of the PUF, the more robust against modeling, but the less reproducible the response as it accumulates more contributions from local noise sources. Appendix A.3 provides some insights in this matter.

**Limited Response Space.** In practice, strong PUFs provide a small response only, often $n = 1$. Replicating the PUF circuit is a simple but unfortunately very expensive solution. The lightweight approach is to evaluate a list of $n$ challenges, hereby concatenating the response bits. Various methods can be employed to generate such a list. The server could generate the list, requiring no additional IC logic, but resulting in a large communication overhead [8]. A small pseudorandom number generator (PRNG), such as a linear feedback shift register (LFSR), is often employed [8, 16, 19, 20, 24]. Challenge $\boldsymbol{c}$ is then used as a seed value: $\widetilde{\boldsymbol{r}} \leftarrow PUF(PRNG(\boldsymbol{c}))$. A variety of counter-based solutions can be applied as well [11]. Most protocol proposals in the remainder of this work suggest a particular response expansion method. We make abstraction of this, except when there is a related security problem.

### 3.3 Controlled PUFs

Controlled PUFs [4–6] provide reinforcement against modeling via a cryptographic hash function (one-way). Two instances, preceding and succeeding the PUF respectively, are shown in Figure 1(d). Figure 3 represents the corresponding protocol[3]. The preceding instance eliminates the chosen-challenge advantage of an attacker. The succeeding instance hides exploitable correlations due to the PUF structure. The latter hash seems to provide full protection by itself, but requires the use of a secure sketch: its avalanche effect would trigger on a single bit flip. CRPs stored by the server are accompanied by helper data.

| | Token | | Server |
|---|---|---|---|
| $(1\times)$ | | $\longleftarrow$ <br> $\longleftrightarrow$ | $\langle \boldsymbol{c_i}, \boldsymbol{r_i}, \boldsymbol{p_i} \rangle$ with $i \in [1\ d]$ <br> and $\boldsymbol{c_i} \overset{U}{\leftarrow} TRNG()$ |
| Auth. $(d\times)$ | | | $\langle \boldsymbol{c}, \boldsymbol{r}', \boldsymbol{p} \rangle \leftarrow \langle \boldsymbol{c_d}, \boldsymbol{r_d}, \boldsymbol{p_d} \rangle$ <br> $d \leftarrow d - 1$ |
| | | $\xleftarrow{\boldsymbol{c},\, \boldsymbol{p}}$ | |
| | $\boldsymbol{r} \leftarrow Hash(Rep(PUF(Hash(\boldsymbol{c})), \boldsymbol{p}), Hash(\boldsymbol{c}))$ | $\xrightarrow{\boldsymbol{r}}$ | |
| | | | Abort if $\boldsymbol{r} \neq \boldsymbol{r}'$ |

**Fig. 3.** Authentication with controlled PUFs

**Inferior to Reference II.** The proposal seems to be inferior to reference II. First, the PUF is required to have an enormous instead of modest input-output space. This is inherently more demanding, even if one would extend reference II with a few challenge bits to enable the use of multiple keys. Second, server storage requirements scale linearly with the number of authentications, in contrast to constant-size.

[3] Controlled PUFs were proposed in a wider context than CRP-based token authentication only.

## 3.4  Öztürk et al.

Öztürk et al. [17] employ two easy-to-model PUFs, as shown in Figure 1(e). Figure 4 represents the corresponding protocol. The outer PUF is assumed to possess a large response space, without defining challenge expansion logic however: it equips the token with CRP behavior. To prevent its modeling by an attacker, an internal secret $\widetilde{x}$ is XORed within the challenge path. A feedback loop, containing a (repeated) permutation and an inner PUF with a single response bit, is employed to update $\widetilde{x}$ continuously. During enrollment, the server has both read and write access to $\widetilde{x}$ via a one-time interface. This allows the server to construct models for either PUF, followed by an initialization of $\widetilde{x}$. The server has to keep track of $\widetilde{x}$, which is referred to as synchronization. The non-determinism of the inner PUF makes this non-trivial. One assumes an excellent match between the responses of the inner PUF and its model. At most one bit of $\widetilde{x}$ is assumed to be affected, in the seldom case of occurrence. An authentication failure (violation of $\epsilon$) provides an indication thereof. One proposes a simple recovery procedure at the server side: bits of $x'$ are successively flipped until the authentication succeeds.

| Token | | Server |
|---|---|---|
| $(1\times)$ Read/write-secure NVM: $\widetilde{x}^{(t)}$ | $\longleftarrow\longrightarrow$ | Train models $\widetilde{PUF}_I$ and $\widetilde{PUF}_O$ |
| | | $\widetilde{x}^{(1)} = x'^{(1)} \overset{U}{\leftarrow} TRNG()$ |
| Auth. $(\infty)$ $\forall i: \widetilde{x}^{(t+1)}(i) \leftarrow PUF_I(\pi^i(\widetilde{x}^{(t)}))$ | $\overset{c}{\longleftarrow}$ | $c \overset{U}{\leftarrow} TRNG()$ |
| $\widetilde{r} \leftarrow PUF_O(\widetilde{x}^{(t+1)} \oplus c)$ | $\overset{\widetilde{r}}{\longrightarrow}$ | |
| | | $\forall i: x'^{(t+1)}(i) \leftarrow \widetilde{PUF}_I(\pi^i(x'^{(t)}))$ |
| | | $r' \leftarrow \widetilde{PUF}_O(x'^{(t+1)} \oplus c)$ |
| | | Abort if $HD(\widetilde{r}, r') > \epsilon$ |

**Fig. 4.** Authentication protocol of Öztürk et al

**Issues Regarding $\widetilde{x}$.** There are several issues related to the use of $\widetilde{x}$. First, it implicates the need for secure reprogrammable NVM, hereby undermining the advantages of PUFs. Either read or write access would enable an attacker to model the system, as during enrollment. Second, the synchronization effort is too optimistic. PUFs and their models typically have a $1 - 10\%$ error rate. The server faces a continuous synchronization effort, not necessarily limited to a single error. Third, it enables denial-of-service attacks. An attacker can collect an (unknown) large number of CRPs, desynchronizing $\widetilde{x}$ and $x'$. Propagation of errors across authentications makes the recovery effort rapidly infeasible.

**Feedback Loop Comments.** The permutation has to be chosen carefully. Repetition is bound to occur, as determined by the order $k$: $\pi^k = \pi$. This would implicate $\widetilde{x}$ to have identical bits, opposing its presumed non-uniformity.

A simple simulation confirms the significance for 64-bit vectors. The estimated probability of a randomly chosen permutation to have $k \le 63$ equals $\approx 9\%$. Furthermore, the need for the inner PUF is questionable. First, its non-determinism poses a limit on the complexity of the feedback loop, and hence the modeling resistance of the overall system. Second, the outer PUF and the initialization of $\tilde{x}$ already induce IC-specific behavior. Using a cryptographic hash function as feedback would resolve all foregoing comments. The resulting system would then be remarkably similar to a later proposal: logically reconfigurable PUFs [12].

### 3.5   Hammouri et al.

Hammouri et al. [8] employ again two strong PUFs, as shown in Figure 1(f). As before, both PUFs are modeled during enrollment. The outer PUF is an arbiter PUF. The inner PUF is a custom architecture based on the arbiter PUF. *Lin* largely compensates the non-linearity of the outer arbiter PUF. Figure 5 represents the authentication protocol. The proposal is non-generic, in comparison with all other protocols: correct functioning strongly depends on internal PUF details. We consider this a bad practice. Only a brief summary of the issues is provided here: we refer to Appendix B for the low-level argumentation.

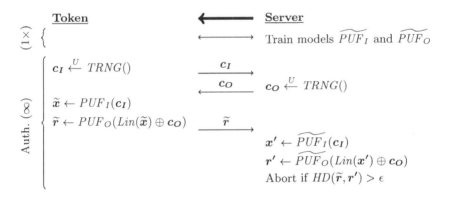

**Fig. 5.** Authentication protocol of Hammouri et al

**Unusual Inner PUF, Prone to Modeling Deficiencies.** The inner PUF is a rather unusual extension of the arbiter PUF. The ability to construct a model, under the given procedure, is strongly layout-dependent and hence prone to deficiencies.

**Unusual Modeling Procedure: Contradictive and Overcomplicated.** Reading out $\tilde{x}$, the response of the inner PUF, via a one-time interface would have made the enrollment easy. This would allow to model both PUFs separately. However, one designed a rather complicated procedure to model the inner PUF via the response of the outer PUF. For this purpose, one did introduce a function *Lin* to linearize the outer arbiter PUF. This is rather contradictive as it degrades the overall modeling resistance. Furthermore, the enrollment might be problematic for a significant fraction of the fabricated tokens, depending on the IC-specific behavior of the outer PUF.

**Non-functional: Error Propagation.** We believe the proposal to be non-functional: non-determinism of the inner PUF is strongly amplified, leading to a persistent authentication failure. A minor modification could resolve this issue.

### 3.6 Logically Reconfigurable PUF

Logically reconfigurable PUFs [11] were proposed in order to make tokens recyclable, hereby reducing electronic waste. An internal state $x$ is therefore mixed into the challenge path, as shown in Figure 1(e). Read access to $x$ is allowed, although not required. There is no direct write access, although one can perform an update: $x^{(t+1)} \leftarrow Hash(x^{(t)})$. Figure 6 represents the authentication protocol.

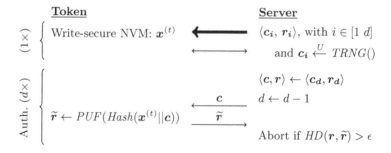

**Fig. 6.** Authentication protocol for logically reconfigurable PUFs

**Exacting PUF Requirements.** The proposal does not aim to prevent PUF modeling attacks, despite providing forward/backward security proofs with respect to $x$. Therefore, the practical value of the proposal is rather limited: the protocol cannot be instantiated due to lack of an appropriate strong PUF.

**Issues Related to NVM.** The proposal requires reprogrammable write-secure NVM, which is not free of issues. First, it undermines a main advantages of PUFs: low-cost manufacturing. Second, it enables denial-of-service attacks. An attacker can update $x$ one or more times, invalidating the CRP database of the server. The proposal does not describe an authentication mechanism for the reconfiguration.

## 3.7 Reverse Fuzzy Extractor

The reverse FE proposal [24] provides mutual authentication, in contrast to previous work. The term 'reverse' highlights that $Gen$ and not $Rep$ is implemented as token hardware, as shown in Figure 1(h). As such, one does benefit of the lightweight potential of $Gen$. Figure 7 represents the protocol[4]. One raises the concern of repeated helper data exposure: an attacker might collect helper data $\{\widetilde{p}_1, \widetilde{p}_2, \ldots\}$ for the same challenge $c$. Therefore, one does recommend the syndrome construction, as there is provably no additional leakage with respect to the traditional $n - k$ entropy loss. One author proposed a modified protocol in [14]. A reversal of authentication checks is stated to be the main difference, although there are two other fundamental changes as clarified hereafter.

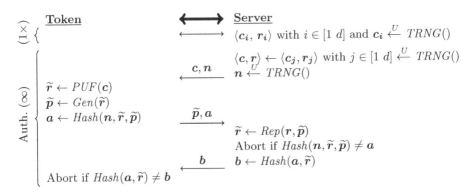

**Fig. 7.** Reverse FE protocol (token identifier omitted)

**PUF Non-determinism.** Non-determinism is essential to avoid replay attacks. For tokens, one does reuse the PUF for this purpose, hereby avoiding the need for a TRNG. A lower bound for the PUF non-determinism is imposed, in order to avoid server impersonation. However, this seems to be a very delicate balancing exercise in practice, opposing more conventional design efforts to stabilize PUFs. The need for environmental robustness (perturbations of outside temperature, supply voltage, etc.) magnifies this opposition. An attacker might immerse the IC in an extremely stable environment, hereby minimizing the PUF error rate. For genuine use however, one might have to provide correctness despite large perturbations, corresponding to the maximum error rate. The modified protocol proposal [14] does not discuss the foregoing contradiction, although its use of a token TRNG provides a resolution.

**PRNG Exploitation.** The proof-of-concept implementation expands the 1-bit response of an arbiter PUF via a PRNG: $\widetilde{r} \leftarrow PUF(LFSR(c))$. Due to

---

[4] The use of a token identifier (public, could be stored in insecure NVM) is omitted for simplicity, as it seems to have no impact on security. The server has been maintained as protocol initiator.

code size limitations, $\tilde{r}$ is subdivided in non-overlapping sections: a set of helper data vectors, of length $n - k$ each, is transferred rather than a single $\tilde{p}$. One employs 7 sections with $k = 21$, aiming at a security level of $128 < 7 \cdot 21$ bit. The proposal does not provide an explicit warning to refuse fixed points of the LFSR, e.g. $c = 0$. This would have been appropriate in order to avoid a trivial server impersonation attack. Fixed points will result in either $\tilde{r} = 0$ or $\tilde{r} = \overline{0}$, assuming stability for one particular response bit. An attacker could hence then guess $b$ with success probability $1/2$. A token impersonation threat, which is far less obvious, is described next.

First consider the unrealistic but desired case of a perfectly deterministic PUF. Consider an arbitrary response section, denoted as $r$. Helper data leakage can be understood via an underdetermined system of linear equations $H \cdot r^T = p^T$, having $n - k$ equations for $n$ unknowns. Consider a challenge $c_1$ leading to an expanded response $r_1 = (r_1\ r_2 \ldots r_n)$. One could easily construct a challenge $c_2$ leading to a response $r_2 = (r_2\ r_3 \ldots r_{n+1})$, given the use of an LFSR. Repeating the former mechanism, we can construct challenges $c_3$, $c_4$, ..., $c_q$, with $r_q = (r_q\ r_{q+1} \ldots r_{q+n-1})$. An attacker collects all data in a single system of equations:

$$A \cdot (r_1\ r_2 \ldots r_{q+n-1})^T = \begin{pmatrix} p_1^T \\ p_2^T \\ \vdots \\ p_q^T \end{pmatrix} \quad \text{with } A = \begin{pmatrix} H & 0^T & \ldots & 0^T \\ 0^T & H & \cdots & 0^T \\ \vdots & \vdots & \ddots & \vdots \\ 0^T & 0^T & \cdots & H \end{pmatrix}.$$

Equation dependencies have to be considered. We performed experiments where $A$ is transformed to reduced row echelon form (*rref*). A distinction between cyclic and non-cyclic codes seems to be crucial, as illustrated in Figure 8. In the latter case, $q$ can be small and an attacker is quasi able to solve the system. The persistence of few unknowns is only a minor inconvenience. In the former case, the number of unknowns remains $k$. However, a repeated machine learning attack can be performed instead, for large $q$, exploiting the introduction of sections. Arbiter PUFs can be modeled with only a few thousand CRPs, so consider e.g. $q = 10000$, including both training and verification data. The correct combination of unknowns (only $2^k = 2^{21}$ possibilities) would result in the observable event of a high modeling accuracy.

We now consider a PUF which is not perfectly deterministic. To minimize this inconvenience, an attacker could ensure the IC's environment to be very stable. Code parameters, which are normally chosen in order to maintain robustness against a variety of environmental perturbations (supply voltage, outside temperature, etc.), become relatively relaxed then. Subsequently, we consider a transformation $H^\star = T \cdot H$, which selects linear combinations of the rows of $H$. The transformation is chosen so that the rows of $H^\star$ do have a low Hamming weight, making it feasible to incorporate a limited set of stable bits only. One could develop a variety of algorithms in order to find a suitable transformation.

**Suboptimal.** Even with $d = 1$, the protocol still allows for an unlimited number of authentications. Token impersonation via replay has already been prevented

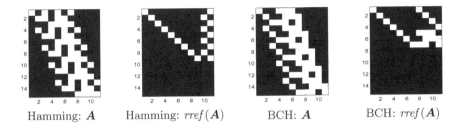

Hamming: $A$      Hamming: $rref(A)$      BCH: $A$      BCH: $rref(A)$

**Fig. 8.** PRNG exploitation for the reverse fuzzy extractor: illustration for non-cyclic Hamming and cyclic BCH codes, with $[n = 7, k = 4, t = 1]$ and $q = 5$. Black and white represent 0 and 1 respectively.

by the use of nonce $n$. This observation could result in numerous protocol simplifications, as has been acknowledged in [24]. However, one does not state clearly that there would a simplification for the PUF as well: the enormous input-output space is no more required, even a weak PUF could be employed. Despite all the former, one still promotes the use of $d > 1$, arguing that it offers an increased side channel resistance. We argue that this countermeasure might not outweigh the missed advantages and that there might be numerous more rewarding countermeasures. The modified protocol proposal [14] does not discuss the foregoing efficiency matter, although it uses $d = 1$, hereby providing a weak PUF (with implicit challenge) as an example.

### 3.8   Slender PUF

The slender PUF proposal [16] includes three countermeasures against modeling, while avoiding the need for cryptographic primitives, as clear from Figure 1(i). First, one requires a strong PUF with a high resistance. A model is constructed during enrollment via auxiliary one-time interfaces. One employs a variant of the XOR arbiter PUF for this purpose (see appendix A.3). Second, the exposure of $\tilde{r}$ is limited to random substrings $\tilde{s}$, hereby obfuscating the CRP link. The corresponding procedure $SubCirc$ treats the bits in a circular manner. Third, server and token both contribute to the challenge via their respective nonces $c_S$ and $c_T$, counteracting chosen-challenge attacks. Figure 9 represents the protocol.

A protocol extension has been proposed in [20]. One presents a fourth countermeasure against modeling. Substring $\tilde{s}$ is padded with random bits before transmission, again in a circular manner: $SubCirc(\tilde{s}_P, j) \leftarrow \tilde{s}$ with $\tilde{s}_P \in \{0, 1\}^{1 \times n_P} \xleftarrow{U} TRNG()$ and $j \in [1 \ n_P] \xleftarrow{U} TRNG()$. Furthermore, the optional establishment of a session key is introduced, via concatenation of secret indices $i$ and $j$. A repeated execution of the protocol is required to obtain a key of sufficient length.

**PRNG Exploitation.** The protocol employs a PRNG to expand the PUF response space: $\tilde{r} \leftarrow PUF(PRNG(c_S, c_T))$. However, the PRNG construction of the proof-of-concept implementation might allow for token impersonation:

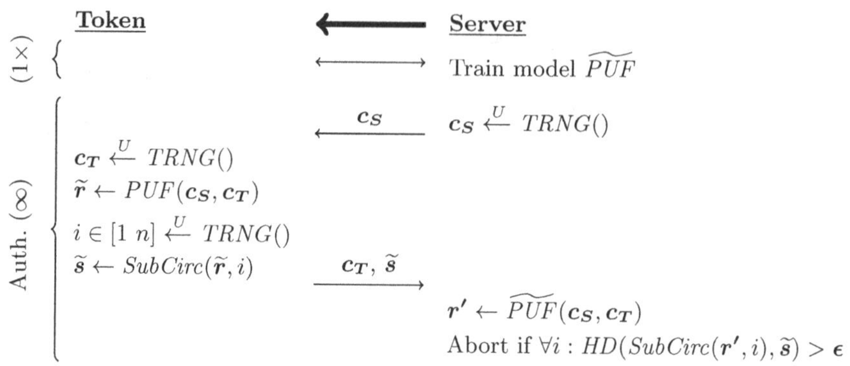

$$\text{(1×)} \left\{ \begin{array}{c} \text{\underline{Token}} \quad\quad\quad \longleftarrow\!\!\!\!\!\longrightarrow \quad\quad \text{Server} \\ \text{Train model } \widetilde{PUF} \end{array} \right.$$

**Fig. 9.** Slender PUF protocol

$PRNG(c_S, c_T) = LFSR(c_S) \oplus LFSR(c_T)$. We assume an identical feedback polynomial for both LFSRs, which is the most intuitive assumption[5]. A malicious token might then return $c_T \leftarrow c_S$, resulting in an expanded list of challenges all equal to $\mathbf{0}$. The server's PUF model outputs either $r' = \mathbf{0}$ or $r' = \overline{\mathbf{0}}$. So provided a substring $\widetilde{s} = \mathbf{0}$ (or $\widetilde{s}_P = \mathbf{0}$), authentication does succeed with a probability $1/2$. Via replay, one could increase the probability to 1. Eavesdropping on a single genuine protocol execution is required: $c_S^{(1)}$, $c_T^{(1)}$ and $\widetilde{s}^{(1)}$. The malicious prover gets authenticated with the following: $c_T^{(2)} \leftarrow c_S^{(2)} \oplus c_S^{(1)} \oplus c_P^{(1)}$ and $\widetilde{s}^{(2)} \leftarrow \widetilde{s}^{(1)}$. One can easily replay old sessions keys as well. We stress that careful PRNG redesign can resolve all of the former.

**Exacting PUF Requirements.** The PUF requirements are rather exacting and partly opposing. On one hand, the PUF should be easy-to model, requiring a highly correlated structure. On the other hand, CRP correlations enable statistical attacks, due to the lack of cryptographic primitives. Such attacks exploit the knowledge of a function $P(r_u = r_v) = f(c_u, c_v)$ for a certain strong PUF architecture. CRPs with $|P(r_u = r_v) - 1/2| > 0$ are correlated and hence exploitable. One might be able to retrieve indices $i$ (and $j$) as such[6], circumventing the SubCirc countermeasure and hence restoring the CRP link. Although the proposed PUF seems to offer this delicate balance (see Appendix A.4), it

---

[5] The proof-of-concept implementation employs 128-bit LFSRs, with $c_S$ and $c_T$ as the initial states, without specifying feedback polynomials. Furthermore, FPGA implementation results (Table III in [16] and Table 8 in [20]) strongly suggest the use of identical feedback polynomials.

[6] The slender PUF protocol has a direct predecessor: the pattern matching key generator [19], which serves as an alternative for a conventional fuzzy extractor [3]. CRP correlation attacks are equally dangerous for this construction and might lead to key-recovery. However, the risk has not been analyzed as thoroughly as in [16]. Furthermore, another statistical attack of fundamentally different nature has recently been published [2].

comes at a price: several one-time interfaces[7], high response non-determinism and a limited modeling accuracy. Furthermore, the user's control regarding the challenge list should be highly restricted: statistical attacks are very powerful if an attacker has a (partial) chosen-challenge advantage. The PRNG-TRNG construction should accomplish this goal.

### 3.9   Converse Authentication

Figures 1(j) and 10 represent the converse authentication protocol [12]. The authentication is one-way, in a less conventional setting where tokens verify the server. The difference vector (XOR) between two responses is denoted as $d$. The restriction $d \neq 0$ prevents an attacker from impersonating the server, choosing $\{c_i = c_j, p_i = p_j\}$. Optionally, one can extend the protocol with the establishment of a session key $k \leftarrow Hash(r_i \| r_j)$. The attacker capabilities are restricted: invasive analysis of the prover IC is assumed to be impossible. Furthermore, one assumes an eavesdropping attacker, trying to impersonate the server given a log of genuine authentication transcripts.

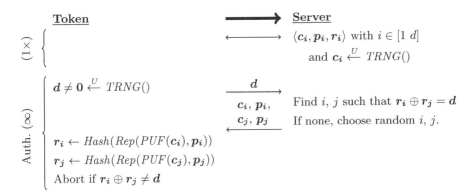

**Fig. 10.** Converse authentication protocol

**Attacker Overly Restricted.** The attacker capabilities are unclear and overly restricted to be practical. First, restricting invasion would automatically extend to physical attacks in general. Furthermore, this greatly reduces the need for PUFs, with respect to the traditional approach of storing a key in NVM. It is also not clear whether an attacker is allowed to freely query the server, as exploited hereafter. We argue that this should be possible, as the protocol is initiated by the token.

**Scalability Issues.** The probability of success for a randomly guessing attacker would be $1/2^n$, when trying to impersonate the server. In certain sense,

---

[7] Chains are modeled separately via machine learning, before XORing takes place.

the server faces a similar probability, posing an upper limit on $n$ for practicality reasons. Successful authentication of the server relies on the availability of a given $d$ within its database. A scalable method to (construct and) search within a database was not discussed and seems far from obvious. Assume a cumbersome trial and error procedure as a search method: a pairwise selection has a probability of $1/2^n$ to be usable. Memory requirements are mild compared to the search workload, as there are $\frac{d(d-1)}{2}$ pairwise selections, although still enormous in comparison to all other proposals. A database of size $d = 2^{25}$ is mentioned to be realistic. A major threat for server impersonation is the following. An attacker might query the server and construct a personal database: $\langle d_i, c_{i1}, p_{i1}, c_{i2}, p_{i2} \rangle$. Authentication will succeed, although a session key cannot be retrieved if present.

**Predecessor Issues.** Although the protocol is in essence identical to a direct predecessor [1], it is not described in terms of modifications. Nevertheless, a few issues have (quietly) been resolved. We observe five modifications. First, *Rep* is acknowledged to require helper data. Second, one introduces the restriction $d \neq 0$. However, this event occurs so seldom that an explicit check could be regarded as overhead. Third, $d$ is generated by a TRNG instead of a PRNG. To avoid replay, the latter construction would require secure NVM, hereby undermining the advantages of PUFs. Fourth, the protocol is initiated by a token instead of the server. Unfortunately, this enables exhaustion of the server database as described before. Fifth, PUF responses are reinforced by a cryptographic hash function. In its absence, we see a direct opportunity for prover impersonation in the occasional case that $HW(d) < t$. Consider an arbitrary response $r = Rep(PUF(c), p)$. For both secure sketch constructions, an attacker might be able to produce a given $d$:

Code-offset construction: $r \oplus d = Rep(PUF(c), p \oplus d)$.
Syndrome construction:   $r \oplus d = Rep(PUF(c), p \oplus d \cdot H^T)$.

## 4    Overview and Discussion

Tables 1 and 2 provide an overview of Section 3. We do not support the use of any strong PUF proposal in its current form, given the numerous amount of issues. However, we do not object the use of both weak PUF protocols: reference II and the modified reverse FE proposal [14]. We now discuss the strong PUF issues.

Two proposals rely on **reprogrammable NVM**: Öztürk et al. [17] and logically reconfigurable PUFs. Their respective assumptions of R/W- and W-security undermine a major benefit of PUF technology: an increased resistance against physical attacks. Furthermore, the need for reprogramming undermines a second potential benefit: low-cost manufacturing, as CMOS-compatible fuses cannot be used. Finally, updating the NVM state was identified as a denial-of-service attack for both proposals.

**Table 1.** For all protocols: token hardware (left), the authenticity provided (middle) and the secret stored by the server (right)

| | Weak PUF | Strong PUF¹ | NVM | TRNG | Gen | Rep | Hash | 1× interface | Other | Token auth. | Server auth. | #Auth. | CRPs | Model | Key |
|---|---|---|---|---|---|---|---|---|---|---|---|---|---|---|---|
| Reference I | × | × | ✓ | × | × | × | ✓ | ✓ | × | ✓ | × | ∞ | × | × | ✓ |
| Reference II | ✓ | × | × | × | × | ✓ | ✓ | ✓ | × | ✓ | × | ∞ | × | × | ✓ |
| Naive | × | ✓ | × | × | × | × | × | × | × | ✓ | × | $d$ | ✓ | × | × |
| Controlled | × | ✓ | × | × | × | ✓ | ✓ | ✓ | × | ✓ | × | $d$ | ✓ | × | × |
| Öztürk et al. | × | ✓² | ✓⁶ | × | × | × | × | ✓ | ✓ | ✓ | × | ∞ | × | ✓ | × |
| Hammouri et al. | × | ✓² | × | ✓ | × | × | × | ✓ | ✓ | ✓ | × | ∞ | × | ✓ | × |
| Reconfiguration | × | ✓³ | ✓⁶ | × | × | × | ✓ | × | ✓ | ✓ | × | $d$ | ✓ | × | × |
| Reverse FE | × | ✓⁴ | × | × | ✓ | × | ✓ | ✓ | ✓ | ✓ | ✓ | ∞ | ✓ | × | × |
| Slender | × | ✓⁵ | × | ✓ | × | × | × | ✓ | ✓ | ✓ | × | ∞ | × | ✓ | × |
| Converse | × | ✓ | × | ✓ | × | ✓ | ✓ | ✓ | ✓ | × | ✓ | ∞ | ✓ | × | × |

¹ Including response expansion.   ⁴ Non-determinism lower bound.
² Easy-to-model.   ⁵ Both easy- and hard-to-model.
³ Robust against modeling.   ⁶ Reprogrammable.

**Table 2.** Issues revealed in this work. Implementation-dependent issues are printed in *italic*.

| Protocol | Issues |
|---|---|
| Controlled | - Inferior to reference II. |
| Öztürk et al. [17] | - NVM undermines the advantages of PUFs.<br>- Synchronization effort is presented too optimistic.<br>- Denial-of-service attack.<br>- *Choice of permutation requires care: avoid low orders.* |
| Hammouri et al. [8] | - Unusual inner PUF, prone to modeling deficiencies.<br>- Non-functional: internal error propagation.<br>- Unusual modeling procedure: contradictive and overcomplicated. |
| Reconfiguration | - Unrealistic PUF requirement: robust against modeling.<br>- NVM undermines the advantages of PUFs.<br>- Denial-of-service attack. |
| Reverse FE | - Exacting PUF requirements to counteract replay attacks.<br>- *PRNG exploitation, leading to token/server impersonation.*<br>- No need for strong PUF. |
| Slender PUF | - *PRNG exploitation, leading to token impersonation.*<br>- Exacting PUF requirements to counteract statistical attacks. |
| Converse | - Attacker model too restricted.<br>- Scalability issues, leading to server impersonation.<br>- Predecessor issues. |

**PUF responses are not perfectly reproducible.** Protocols employ two approaches to overcome this issue: error correction and error tolerance. Unfortunately, two proposals struggle with the latter approach. PUF non-determinism is greatly underestimated in Öztürk et al. [17]: the protocol synchronization effort is presented too optimistic. We believe the proposal of Hammouri et al [8]. to be non-functional because of internal error propagation.

In practice, **strong PUFs do have a small output space.** There are various methods to resolve this issue, all imposing a certain efficiency burden. However, the protocol proposals have very little attention for this topic. Even though system security is not necessarily unaffected. We specified attacks for the proof-of-concept implementations of the reverse FE and slender PUF proposal, both exploiting the challenge expansion PRNG.

In practice, **strong PUFs are insecure against modeling.** Two proposals are therefore too demanding: logically reconfigurable PUFs and the slender PUF protocol. Although the latter offers some countermeasures, there is an opposing requirement for the PUF to be easy-to-model, leading to a delicate balancing exercise. In general, proposals not reinforced by a cryptographic hash function are much more likely to be vulnerable.

Several proposals rely on a **secure TRNG.** Tampering with its randomness opens new perspectives for a physical attack. Its use seems unavoidable however if server authentication is a must, as for the converse protocol, to avoid replay attacks. The reverse FE proposal extracts its non-determinism from the PUF instead, which has been identified as a delicate balancing exercise. Two protocols without server authentication employ their TRNG as a modeling countermeasure: Hammouri et al. [8] and the slender PUF protocol.

All proposals aim to provide lightweight entity authentication, which addresses a highly relevant need. However, in many use cases, there will be accompanying security requests: message confidentiality and integrity, privacy, etc. We did not consider **protocol extensibility** in this work, although it might be of interest when designing a new protocol. References I and II, which employ a secret key, might benefit from a huge amount of scientific literature. Like-minded, the establishment of a session key has been proposed as an extension for the converse and slender PUF proposals.

# 5    Conclusion

Various protocols utilize a strong PUF to provide lightweight entity authentication. We described the most prominent proposals using a unified notation, hereby creating a first overview and initializing direct comparison as well. We defined two reference authentication methods, to identify the misuse of PUFs. Our analysis revealed numerous security and practicality issues. Therefore, we do not recommend the use of any strong PUF proposal in its current form. Most proposals aim to compensate the lack of cryptographic properties of the strong PUF. However, proper compensation seems to be in conflict with the lightweight objective. More fundamental physical research is required, aiming to create a truly strong PUF with great cryptographic properties. If not, we are inclined to recommend conventional PUF-based key generation as a more promising alternative. The observations and lessons learned in this work can facilitate future protocol design.

**Acknowledgment.** The authors greatly appreciate the support received. The European Commission through the ICT programme under contract FP7-ICT-2011-317930 HINT. The Research Council of KU Leuven: GOA TENSE (GOA/11/007), the Flemish Government through FWO G.0550.12N and the Hercules Foundation AKUL/11/19. The national major development program for fundamental research of China (973 Plan) under grant no. 2013CB338004. Jeroen Delvaux is funded by IWT-Flanders grant no. 121552. The authors would like to thank Anthony Van Herrewege (KU Leuven, ESAT/COSIC) for his valuable comments.

# References

1. Das, A., Kocabaş, Ü., Sadeghi, A.-R., Verbauwhede, I.: PUF-based secure test wrapper design for cryptographic SoC testing. In: Design, Automation & Test in Europe, DATE 2012, pp. 866–869 (March 2012)
2. Delvaux, J., Verbauwhede, I.: Attacking PUF-Based Pattern Matching Key Generators via Helper Data Manipulation. In: Benaloh, J. (ed.) CT-RSA 2014. LNCS, vol. 8366, pp. 106–131. Springer, Heidelberg (2014)
3. Dodis, Y., Ostrovsky, R., Reyzin, L., Smith, A.: Fuzzy Extractors: How to Generate Strong Keys from Biometrics and Other Noisy Data. SIAM J. Comput. 38(1), 97–139 (2008)
4. Gassend, B., Clarke, D.E., van Dijk, M., Devadas, S.: Silicon physical random functions. In: ACM Conference on Computer and Communications Security, CCS 2002, pp. 148–160 (November 2002)
5. Gassend, B., Clarke, D.E., van Dijk, M., Devadas, S.: Controlled Physical Random Functions. In: Annual Computer Security Applications Conference, ACSAC 2002, pp. 149–160 (December 2002)
6. Gassend, B., van Dijk, M., Clarke, D.E., Torlak, E., Devadas, S., Tuyls, P.: Controlled physical random functions and applications. ACM Trans. Inf. Syst. Secur. 10(4) (2008)
7. Guajardo, J., Kumar, S.S., Schrijen, G.-J., Tuyls, P.: FPGA Intrinsic PUFs and Their Use for IP Protection. In: Paillier, P., Verbauwhede, I. (eds.) CHES 2007. LNCS, vol. 4727, pp. 63–80. Springer, Heidelberg (2007)
8. Hammouri, G., Öztürk, E., Sunar, B.: A tamper-proof and lightweight authentication scheme. Journal Pervasive and Mobile Computing 6(4) (2008)
9. Holcomb, D.E., Burleson, W.P., Fu, K.: Power-Up SRAM State as an Identifying Fingerprint and Source of True Random Numbers. IEEE Trans. Computers 58(9) (2009)
10. Hospodar, G., Maes, R., Verbauwhede, I.: Machine Learning Attacks on 65nm Arbiter PUFs: Accurate Modeling poses strict Bounds on Usability. In: IEEE Workshop on Information Forensics and Security (WIFS) 2012, pp. 37–42 (December 2012)

11. Katzenbeisser, S., Kocabaş, Ü., van der Leest, V., Sadeghi, A.-R., Schrijen, G.-J., Schröder, H., Wachsmann, C.: Recyclable PUFs: Logically Reconfigurable PUFs. In: Preneel, B., Takagi, T. (eds.) CHES 2011. LNCS, vol. 6917, pp. 374–389. Springer, Heidelberg (2011)
12. Kocabaş, Ü., Peter, A., Katzenbeisser, S., Sadeghi, A.-R.: Converse PUF-Based Authentication. In: Katzenbeisser, S., Weippl, E., Camp, L.J., Volkamer, M., Reiter, M., Zhang, X. (eds.) Trust 2012. LNCS, vol. 7344, pp. 142–158. Springer, Heidelberg (2012)
13. Lee, J.W., Lim, D., Gassend, B., Suh, G.E., van Dijk, M., Devadas, S.: A technique to build a secret key in integrated circuits for identification and authentication applications. In: 2004 Symposium on VLSI Circuits, pp. 176–179 (June 2004)
14. Maes, R.: Physically Unclonable Functions: Constructions, Properies and Applications. PhD Thesis, KU Leuven (August 2012)
15. Majzoobi, M., Koushanfar, F., Potkonjak, M.: Testing techniques for hardware security. In: IEEE International Test Conference (ITC), pp. 1–10 (October 2008)
16. Majzoobi, M., Rostami, M., Koushanfar, F., Wallach, D.S., Devadas, S.: Slender PUF Protocol: A Lightweight, Robust, and Secure Authentication by Substring Matching. In: IEEE Symposium on Security and Privacy (SP), pp. 33–44 (May 2012)
17. Öztürk, E., Hammouri, G., Sunar, B.: Towards Robust Low Cost Authentication for Pervasive Devices. In: IEEE Conference on Pervasive Computing and Communications, PerCom (March 2008)
18. Pappu, R.: Physical One-Way Functions. PhD Thesis, MIT, ch. 9 (2001)
19. Paral, Z., Devadas, S.: Reliable and Efficient PUF-Based Key Generation Using Pattern Matching. In: Hardware-Oriented Security and Trust, HOST 2011, pp. 128–133 (June 2011)
20. Rostami, M., Majzoobi, M., Koushanfar, F., Wallach, D.S., Devadas, S.: Robust and Reverse-Engineering Resilient PUF Authentication and Key-Exchange by Substring Matching. IEEE Transactions on Emerging Topics in Computing, 13 (2014)
21. Rührmair, U., Sehnke, F., Sölter, J., Dror, G., Devadas, S., Schmidhuber, J.: Modeling attacks on physical unclonable functions. In: ACM Conference on Computer and Communications Security, CCS 2010, pp. 237–249 (October 2010)
22. Skorobogatov, S.: Semi-invasive attacks - a new approach to hardware security analysis, University of Cambridge, Computer Laboratory (April 2005)
23. Suh, G.E., Devadas, S.: Physical unclonable functions for device authentication and secret key generation. In: Design Automation Conference, DAC 2007, pp. 9–14 (June 2007)
24. Van Herrewege, A., Katzenbeisser, S., Maes, R., Peeters, R., Sadeghi, A.-R., Verbauwhede, I., Wachsmann, C.: Reverse Fuzzy Extractors: Enabling Lightweight Mutual Authentication for PUF-Enabled RFIDs. In: Keromytis, A.D. (ed.) FC 2012. LNCS, vol. 7397, pp. 374–389. Springer, Heidelberg (2012)

# A    Arbiter PUF

## A.1    Architecture

Arbiter PUFs [13] quantify manufacturing variability via the propagation delay of logic gates and interconnect. The high-level functionality is represented by Figure

11(a). A rising edge propagates through two paths with identically designed delays, as imposed by layout symmetry. Because of nanoscale manufacturing variations however, there is a delay difference $\Delta t$ between both paths. An arbiter decides which path 'wins' the race ($\Delta t \lesssim 0$) and generates a response bit $r$.

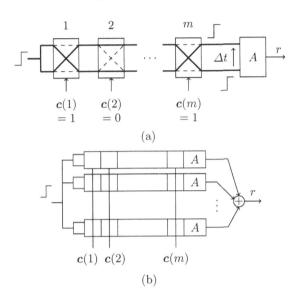

**Fig. 11.** Arbiter PUF (a) and its XOR variant (b)

The two paths are constructed from a series of $m$ switching elements. The latter are typically implemented with a pair of 2-to-1 multiplexers. Challenge bits determine for each stage whether path segments are crossed or uncrossed. Each stage has a unique contribution to $\Delta t$, depending on its challenge bit. Challenge vector $c$ determines the time difference $\Delta t$ and hence the response bit $r$. The number of CRPs equals $2^m$. The response reproducibility differs per CRP: the smaller $|\Delta t|$, the easier to flip side because of various physical perturbations.

### A.2   Vulnerability to Modeling Attacks

Arbiter PUFs show additive linear behavior, which makes them vulnerable to modeling attacks. A decomposition in individual delay elements is given in Figure 12. Both intra- and inter-switch delays contribute to $\Delta t$, as represented by white and gray/black squares respectively. We incorporate the latter in their preceding switches, without loss of generality, to facilitate the derivation of a delay model. In the end, delay elements are important as far as they generate delay differences between both paths. Therefore, each stage can be described by two delay parameters only: one for each challenge bit state, as illustrated in Figure 13. The delay difference at the input of stage $i$ flips in sign for the crossed configuration and is incremented with $\delta t_i^1$ or $\delta t_i^0$ for crossed and uncrossed configurations respectively.

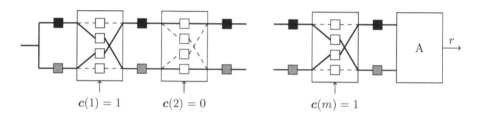

$$c(1) = 1 \qquad c(2) = 0 \qquad c(m) = 1$$

**Fig. 12.** Arbiter PUF decomposed in individual delay elements, represented by small squares which are prone to manufacturing variability. The interconnecting lines have zero delay.

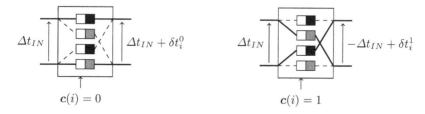

$$c(i) = 0 \qquad\qquad c(i) = 1$$

**Fig. 13.** Delay behavior of an arbiter stage

The impact of a $\delta t$ on $\Delta t$ is incremental or decremental for an even and odd number of subsequent crossed stages respectively. By lumping together the $\delta t$'s of neighboring stages, one can model the whole arbiter PUF with $m + 1$ independent parameters only (and not $2m$). A formal expression for $\Delta t = \gamma \tau^T$ is shown below. Vector $\gamma \in \{\pm 1\}^{1 \times (m+1)}$ is a transformation of challenge vector $c$. Vector $\tau \in \mathbb{R}^{1 \times (m+1)}$ contains the lumped stage delays. The more linear a system, the easier to learn its behavior. By using $\gamma$ instead of $c$ as ML input, a great deal of non-linearity is avoided. The non-linear threshold operation $\Delta t \lessgtr 0$ remains however. Only 5000 CRPs were demonstrated to be sufficient to model non-simulated 64-stage arbiter PUFs with an accuracy of about 97% [10].

$$\tau = \frac{1}{2} \begin{pmatrix} \delta t_0 & \delta t_1^0 - \delta t_1^1 \\ \delta t_1^0 + \delta t_1^1 & + \ \delta t_2^0 - \delta t_2^1 \\ & \vdots \\ \delta t_{m-1}^0 + \delta t_{m-1}^1 & + \ \delta t_m^0 - \delta t_m^1 \\ \delta t_m^0 + \delta t_m^1 & \end{pmatrix}^T \text{ and } \gamma = \begin{pmatrix} 1 - 2(c(1) \oplus \ldots \oplus c(m)) \\ 1 - 2(c(2) \oplus \ldots \oplus c(m)) \\ \vdots \\ 1 - 2c(m) \\ 1 \end{pmatrix}^T .$$

### A.3   XOR Variant

Several variants of the arbiter PUF increase the resistance against ML. They introduce various forms of non-linearity for this purpose. We only consider the XOR variant. The response bits of multiple arbiter chains are XORed to produce a single response bit, as shown in Figure 11(b). All chains have the same challenge as input. The more chains, the more resistance against ML: the required number of CRPs and the computation time both increase rapidly [21]. However, the reproducibility of $r$ decreases with the number of chains as well: each additional chain injects non-determinism into the overall system. A practical limit on the ML resistance is hence imposed. Modifications to the architecture can improve former trade-off [15]: e.g. a permutation of the challenge bits across chains, as employed for the slender PUF protocol [16,20].

## A.4   CRP Correlations: Enabling Statistical Attacks

Machine learning attacks exploit CRP correlations in a implicit manner. Statistical attacks benefit from their explicit exploitation, hereby assuming the knowledge of a function $P(r_1 = r_2) = f(c_1, c_2)$. Such functions have already been determined via simulations [15]. We are the first to derive an analytical model, as demonstrated for the the arbiter PUF and its XOR variant in Figure 14. Modified architectures can converge to the ideal curve $f = 1/2$ more rapidly. Let $\mathcal{N}(\mu, \sigma)$ denote a normal distribution with mean $\mu$ and standard deviation $\sigma$. Let $\phi(x, \sigma)$ and $\Phi(x, \sigma)$ denote the probability density function and cumulative distribution function respectively, assuming $\mu = 0$. We assume all $\delta t$'s to have a distribution $\mathcal{N}(0, \sigma_1)$, which is a common and well-validated practice in previous work. Although not fully correct[8], we then assume the elements of $\tau$ to have a distribution $\mathcal{N}(0, 2\sigma_1)$. We introduce the variable $h = HD(\gamma_1, \gamma_2)$.

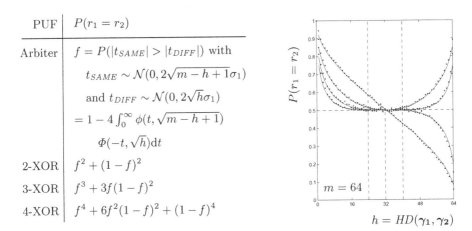

| PUF | $P(r_1 = r_2)$ |
|---|---|
| Arbiter | $f = P(\|t_{SAME}\| > \|t_{DIFF}\|)$ with $t_{SAME} \sim \mathcal{N}(0, 2\sqrt{m - h + 1}\sigma_1)$ and $t_{DIFF} \sim \mathcal{N}(0, 2\sqrt{h}\sigma_1)$ $= 1 - 4 \int_0^\infty \phi(t, \sqrt{m - h + 1})$ $\Phi(-t, \sqrt{h})dt$ |
| 2-XOR | $f^2 + (1 - f)^2$ |
| 3-XOR | $f^3 + 3f(1 - f)^2$ |
| 4-XOR | $f^4 + 6f^2(1 - f)^2 + (1 - f)^4$ |

**Fig. 14.** Correlations for the arbiter PUF and its XOR variant. Dots represent simulations results. The mathematical model, drawn continuously although of discrete nature, matches reasonably well. Vertical dashed lines enclose 99% of the data for randomly chosen challenges. The more chains being XORed, the better one approximates the ideal behavior $f = 1/2$, but the larger the response non-determinism.

---

[8] We neglect dependencies within $\tau$ and we also ignore the different form of $\tau(1)$ and $\tau(m + 1)$

# B    Hammouri et al. [8]

## B.1    Unusual Inner PUF, Prone to Modeling Deficiencies

The inner PUF is a custom architecture based on the arbiter PUF. One proposes a rather unusual extension of the challenge space. Out of two individual chains, one aims to construct a single reconfigurable chain. For each stage, one out of two switching elements is selected, hereby introducing a second challenge $s$. The proposal ignores the need to describe the reconfiguration logic: Figure 15 (right) provides a generic schematic, including both intra- and inter-switch delays. Via reconfiguration, one aims to provide a large response space. One does evaluate $c_I$ for a fixed list of configurations vectors $\{s_1, s_2, \ldots\}$, hereby concatenating the response bits. The configuration vectors are generated by a PRNG, having $s_1$ as initial state. Note that one could have provided a large response space with a regular arbiter PUF as well, given the use of a PRNG.

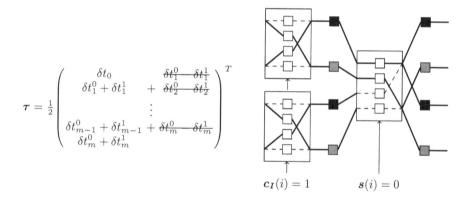

$$\tau = \frac{1}{2} \begin{pmatrix} \delta t_0 & \delta t_1^0 - \delta t_1^1 \\ \delta t_1^0 + \delta t_1^1 & + \delta t_2^0 - \delta t_2^1 \\ & \vdots \\ \delta t_{m-1}^0 + \delta t_{m-1}^1 & + \delta t_m^0 - \delta t_m^1 \\ \delta t_m^0 + \delta t_m^1 \end{pmatrix}^T$$

$$c_I(i) = 1 \qquad s(i) = 0$$

**Fig. 15.** Reconfigurable stage of the inner PUF

The architecture is required to be easy-to-model: the server has to construct a model during enrollment. The overall structure is additive, as for a regular arbiter PUF, and therefore we expect modeling to be feasible. Although one could have derived a generic (but complicated) delay model, possibly leading to an efficient modeling method, the authors propose a shortcut. The overall delay model is supposed to be separable in terms of the individual chains. One does construct a model $\tau_U$ for the upper chain, applying $s = 0$. Similar, one obtains a model $\tau_L$ for the lower chain, applying $s = \overline{0}$. The overall model $\tau(s)$ selects elements from both vectors: $\tau(i) = s(i)\tau_L(i) + \overline{s(i)}\tau_U(i)$. The variability of intra-stage delays is being neglected, justified by placing the stages far apart in the circuit lay-out. An approximating delay model for upper/lower chain is derived as well, as shown in Figure 15 (left).

Although it might be possible to make all the former workable (there is no proof-of-concept implementation), the approach is strongly layout-dependent and prone to modeling deficiencies. Apart from being area consuming: positioning stages far apart might not be sufficient to justify separability. Intra- and inter-stage variations originate from CMOS transistors and metal interconnect respectively. We highly doubt that the former would be per se negligible with respect to the latter. It is possible though to enhance separability: upsizing transistors of the switches, inserting minimum-sized inverter chains in between switches, etc. Furthermore, one should distinguish the metal interconnect before and after the stage selection logic, as shown in Figure 15 (right). Variability of the latter would undermine the separability. We stress that all these complications could have been avoided easily, e.g. by using a regular arbiter PUF.

## B.2    Unusual Modeling Procedure: Contradictive and Overcomplicated

Reading out $\widetilde{x}$, the response of the inner PUF, via a one-time interface would have made the enrollment easy. This would allow to model both PUFs separately. However, one designed a rather complicated procedure to model the inner PUF via the response of the outer arbiter PUF. The latter has a single bit response: during authentication, a list of challenges $c_O/c_I$ is transferred between token and server to expand its response space. One does introduce a function $Lin$, compensating the non-linearity of the arbiter PUF, apart from the final thresholding step: $\Delta t$ is a linear function of $Lin(\widetilde{x})$. This transformation is relatively simple, as shown below. We note that this is rather contradictive: it degrades the overall modeling resistance. Fixing $c_O = 0$, one obtains a system $\widetilde{r} \leftarrow PUF_O(Lin(\widetilde{x}))$. Error propagation from $\widetilde{x}$ to $\widetilde{r}$ is very limited then. An error in bit $\widetilde{x}(i)$ would flip the sign of $\gamma(i)$ only, corresponding to $h = 1$ in Figure 14. During enrollment, one can force the PRNG to maintain either $0$ or $\overline{0}$ as its state, allowing to model the upper and lower chain separately. This requires some sort of destructive interface, similar to our proposal to read out $\widetilde{x}$ directly. Depending on $c_I$, $\widetilde{x}$ will be either $0$ or $\overline{0}$, apart from potential noisiness, hereby maximizing $h$. As a consequence, one can distinguish either case, as $\widetilde{r}$ is very likely to flip. This enables modeling of the inner PUF. Although some IC samples might be problematic: the pair $\widetilde{x} = 0/\overline{0}$ occasionally result in $\Delta t \approx 0$, maintaining $\widetilde{r}$ in a noisy state.

$$
Lin(\widetilde{x}) = \begin{pmatrix} \widetilde{x}(1) \oplus \widetilde{x}(2) \\ \widetilde{x}(2) \oplus \widetilde{x}(3) \\ \vdots \\ \widetilde{x}(m-1) \oplus \widetilde{x}(m) \\ \widetilde{x}(m) \end{pmatrix}^{T}.
$$

## B.3    Non-functional: Error Propagation

We believe the proposal to be non-functional: non-determinism of the inner PUF is strongly amplified, leading to a persistent authentication failure. The minimization of $h$ does not hold for the system $\widetilde{r} \leftarrow \widetilde{PUF_O(Lin(\widetilde{x})} \oplus c_O)$, in the general case that $c_O \neq 0$. A single error in $\widetilde{x}$ will flip the sign of $\widetilde{r}$ with a probability close to $1/2$. This could have been avoided by implementing the system $\widetilde{r} \leftarrow PUF_O(Lin(\widetilde{x} \oplus c_O))$ instead.

# Efficient Power and Timing Side Channels
## for Physical Unclonable Functions

Ulrich Rührmair[1,*], Xiaolin Xu[1,*], Jan Sölter[3], Ahmed Mahmoud[1],
Mehrdad Majzoobi[4], Farinaz Koushanfar[4], and Wayne Burleson[2]

[1] Technische Universität München, 80333 München, Germany
[2] University of Massachusetts Amherst, Amherst, MA 01003, USA
[3] Freie Universität Berlin, 14195 Berlin, Germany
[4] Rice University, Houston, TX 77005, USA
ruehrmair@in.tum.de, xiaolinx@umass.edu, jan_soelter@yahoo.com
ahmed.mahmoud@tum.de, m.majzoobi@gmail.com
fkl@rice.edu, burleson@umass.edu

**Abstract.** One part of the original PUF promise was their improved resilience
against physical attack methods, such as cloning, invasive techniques, and arguably also side channels. In recent years, however, a number of effective physical attacks on PUFs have been developed [17,18,20,8,2]. This paper continues
this line of research, and introduces the first power and timing side channels (SCs)
on PUFs, more specifically on Arbiter PUF variants. Concretely, we attack so-
called XOR Arbiter PUFs and Lightweight PUFs, which prior to our work were
considered the most secure members of the Arbiter PUF family [28,30]. We show
that both architectures can be tackled *with polynomial complexity* by a combined
SC and machine learning approach.

Our strategy is demonstrated in silicon on FPGAs, where we attack the above
two architectures for up to 16 XORs and 512 bits. For comparison, in earlier
works XOR-based Arbiter PUF designs with only up to 5 or 6 XORs and 64 or
128 bits had been tackled successfully. Designs with 8 XORs and 512 bits had
been explicitly recommended as secure for practical use [28,30].

Together with recent modeling attacks [28,30], our work shows that unless
suitable design countermeasures are put in place, no remaining member of the
Arbiter PUF family resists all currently known attacks. Our work thus motivates
research on countermeasures in Arbiter PUFs, or on the development of entirely
new Strong PUF designs with improved resilience.

**Keywords:** Physical unclonable functions (PUFs), side-channel attacks, power
side channel, timing side channel, modeling attacks, machine learning, hardware
security.

## 1 Introduction

One part of the original PUF promise was their improved resilience against many classical attack forms, in particular physical attacks. This included cloning, invasive techniques, and arguably also side channels (SC). Regarding the latter, recall that Strong

---

* These two authors contributed equally.

L. Batina and M. Robshaw (Eds.): CHES 2014, LNCS 8731, pp. 476–492, 2014.

PUF based identification schemes [22] do not require a standard key that is processed bit by bit, a fact that arguably led to hopes about improved SC resilience within the community.

Recent years have put these assumptions to the test, but sometimes with a negative outcome. Let us start with non-physical attacks: Firstly, machine learning (ML) based modeling attacks have proven a more efficient threat than originally assumed. When the first of these attacks were put forward in 2004 [9], it was supposed that they could be thwarted by adding simple non-linear elements to Arbiter PUF designs, for example XOR gates or feed-forward loops. However, by improved ML algorithms, Rührmair et al. in 2010 and 2013 [28,30] also tackled XOR-based Arbiter PUFs up to 64 or 128 bits and 5 XORs, and Feed-Forward Arbiter PUFs up to essentially arbitrary sizes. As a second, non-physical attack form, PUF protocol attacks have been devised in recent years. Since they are not in the focus of this work, we refer interested readers to the literature on this topic [26,25].

Also dedicated physical attacks on PUFs have been devised lately. For example, the physical unclonability of PUFs, one of their core properties, has been investigated more closely. It is obvious that complex three-dimensional objects like PUFs cannot be cloned atom by atom by current fabrication technology. Generating a *perfect clone* thus to date is infeasible. However, *functional clones* are easier to construct, i.e., PUFs that merely agree with the original in their challenge-response behavior. In a breakthrough effort, Helfmeier et al. [8] in 2013 were indeed able to functionally clone SRAM PUFs by tuning the power-up states of SRAM cells. Soon after, invasive attacks on SRAM PUFs have been presented by Nedospasov et al. [20] in 2013. The authors apply semi-invasive, single-trace, backside readout of logic states to to obtain the responses of SRAM PUFs. This compromises any secret keys that would be derived from these responses.

Around the same time, first side-channel attacks on PUFs have been investigated. In 2011, Merli et al. [17] demonstrated SC attacks on the error correcting (EC) module of PUFs. Their attack is indirect in the sense that it does not target the PUF itself, but a specific EC module of the PUF, working only for certain modules. Furthermore, Merli et al. reported electromagnetic analyses on ring oscillator PUFs in two consecutive works in 2011 and 2013 [18,19]. Also in 2013, Delvaux et al. [2] exploited the instabilities of Arbiter PUF responses as side channel, implementing an idea originally suggested by Rührmair et al. in [28]. While the work of Delvaux et al. is quite fascinating due to the fact that it does not use any machine learning algorithms, it must be said that it performs slightly worse than pure machine-learning based modeling *without* side channels [28,30,2].

We continue this line of research, and introduce in this paper the first power and timing side channel attacks on PUFs. Our approach constitutes one of the first physical attacks on Strong PUFs [24,27,29] that can *notably increase* attack performance in comparison with existing, non-physical methods, specifically with pure modeling attacks [28,30].

In greater detail, we devise power and timing SCs for XOR Arbiter PUFs and Lightweight PUFs that provide the adversary with information about the *cumulative* number of zeros and ones in the outputs of the $k$ parallel Arbiter PUFs before the XOR gate. We then adapt existing machine learning (ML) techniques to efficiently exploit this information. This "hybrid" attack form can tackle XOR Arbiter PUFs and Lightweight PUFs with a *polynomial complexity* in their number of XORs, bitlengths, and number of required CRPs, while pure modeling attacks on these two PUFs have *exponential complexity* [28,30]. We provide a full proof of concept on FPGAs, attacking XOR Arbiter PUFs and Lightweight PUFs for up to 16 XORs and 512 bits. Comparably large sizes of these two PUFs had hence never been realized before in silicon; in earlier works, already XOR Arbiter PUFs with 8 XORs and 512 bits had been explicitly suggested as secure [28,30].

*Organization of this Paper* Section 2 provides the necessary background and methodology. Sections 3 and 4 describe the design and implementation of our power and timing side channels, respectively. Section 5 details our adaptation of logistic regression to incorporate SC information. Section 6 lists silicon results on FPGA implementations and provides an asymptotic peformance analysis. We conclude the paper in Section 7.

# 2   Background, Methodology, and Definitions

*Background on XOR Arbiter PUFs and Lightweight PUFs.* Together with SRAM PUFs, the Arbiter PUF family [7,31] is arguably the best studied PUF design, and also the most popular implementation of so-called "Strong PUFs" [24,27]. Nevertheless, a large number of its members have been attacked successfully by so-called modeling attacks in recent works [28,30]. The currently *only* remaining Arbiter PUF variants which partly resist modeling, since they cause exponential modeling efforts (i.e., exponential training times of the ML algorithm), were so-called XOR Arbiter PUFs [9,31] and Lightweight PUFs [11].

In an XOR Arbiter PUF, $k$ Arbiter PUFs are used in parallel, and the same, multi-bit challenge is applied to all of them. The final, one-bit response is defined as the XOR of all the parallel $k$ outputs [9,31]. In a Lightweight PUF [11,28], again $k$ Arbiter PUFs are used in parallel, but different challenges $C^1, \ldots, C^k$ are applied to them, all of which are generated by some "input mapping" from a single, global challenge $C$ (see [11] for the details of the mapping). The $k$ outputs of the single Arbiter PUFs are used (without error correction) as input to a postprocessing function, which XORs subsets of them together in order to produce an $m$-bit output string (see again [11] for details). From a machine learning and modeling perspective, the optimal bit security is achieved if *all* of the $k$ outputs are XORed to produce a *single bit output* [28,30]. Therefore earlier works [28,30] focused exactly on this case and on this special architecture of the Lightweight PUF, and so do we in this paper. If nothing else, this evaluates the maximally achievable bit security in a Lightweight PUF architecture. Using the same Lightweight PUF variant as [28,30] also allows a fair comparison with our results.

*FPGA Implementations.* We implemented the above XOR Arbiter PUFs and Lightweight PUFs on Xilinx Spartan-6 FPGAs. In order to balance FPGA routing asymmetries, a lookup table (LUT) based programmable delay line (PDL) has been implemented [13,10,15]. This is the standard approach for realizing Arbiter PUFs on

FPGAs, and ensures a balanced output between zeros and ones in each single Arbiter PUF. For each CRP, majority voting over five repeated measurements of the response to the same challenge was performed in order to determine the final response. The challenges were generated by an n-bit maximal-length linear feedback shift register (LFSR) with polynomial $f = 1 + x^1 + x^3 + x^4 + x^{64}$.

*Machine Learning Definitions and Computational Resources.* Following [28,30], we use the following definitions throughout the paper: The prediction error $\epsilon$ is the ratio of incorrect responses of the trained ML algorithm when evaluated on the test set. The prediction rate is $1 - \epsilon$. For all ML experiments throughout this paper, each test set consisted of 10,000 randomly chosen CRPs. The term $N_{CRP}$ (or simply *"CRPs"*) denotes the number of CRPs employed in an attack, i.e., the size of the training set. We used an Intel Xeon X5650 processor at 2.67GHz with 48 GB of RAM in all of our ML experiments, having a value of a few thousand Euros. All computation times (= "training times") are calculated for one core of one processor of this hardware.

# 3 Power Side Channels on XOR-Based Arbiter PUFs

## 3.1 Basic Idea of the Power Side Channel

Currently known pure modeling attacks on XOR-based Arbiter PUFs require training times of the ML algorithm that are exponential in the number of XORs [28,30]. This makes it difficult to tackle XOR-based Arbiter PUFs with more than five or six single parallel Arbiter PUFs, and with bitlengths longer than 128, by pure modeling attacks [28,30]. XOR-based Arbiter PUF architectures are therefore the currently most secure designs from the Arbiter PUF family. Our side-channel attacks now take a novel route: They gain additional information from the physical implementation of XOR-based Arbiter PUFs, and use this information to improve the ML computation times (i.e., training times) from exponential to polynomial.

One straightforward power side channel is to apply power (i.e., current) tracing to determine the transition from zero to one of the latches (i.e., the arbiter elements) in the single Arbiter PUFs. The power tracing is based on measuring the amount of current drawn from the supply voltage during any latch transition to one. We implemented a first SPICE simulation to validate this approach, and to verify the power consumption of an arbiter circuit with different loading outputs. Only one latch (i.e., arbiter circuit) is used in the simulation, but with three different outputs loading scenarios (i.e., floating output, output connected to one gate, and output connected to four gates). Figure 1 illustrates the results, and shows the different amount of current drawn for the three different output loading scenarios. The reason for having different values for the different loadings is that an additional amount of charges is required to charge the capacitance of each gate. Hence, the amount of drawn charges, which is the integration of the current curve, is linearly proportional with the number of loading gates. Taking this phenomenon into consideration, the amount of charges normally drawn in case of a floating load should be subtracted.

In XOR-based architectures with $k$ parallel single Arbiter PUFs, the current that is drawn *in sum* and *altogether* in principle tells the (cumulative) number of latches that

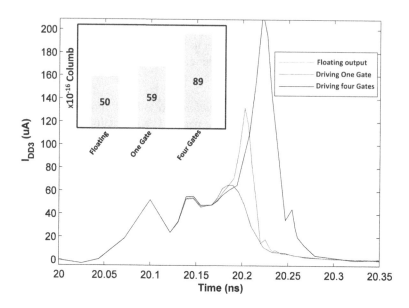

**Fig. 1.** The power tracking side-channel analysis for a latch that had a transition to 1, with different driving loads, in SPICE simulation. The inset is the amount of drawn charges, which is calculated from the area under each curve. The amount of charges is linearly proportional with the number of gates. The amount of charges normally drawn for a floating load should be subtracted.

are zero, and the (cumulative) number that are equal to one. Please note, however, that it does *not* tell us *which* of the $k$ parallel Arbiter PUFs had *which* output. If it did, CRPs from every single Arbiter PUF could be collected, and every single Arbiter PUF could be machine learned separately. As this is not possible, a more complicated strategy is required, in particular a way to exploit the cumulative number of zeros and ones beneficially in the ML process, as detailed in Section 5. But before we move on to the details of the ML process, we discuss the exact implementation of the side channels in this and the next section.

## 3.2   Practical Implementation of the Power Side Channel

**Measurement Noise.** To further validate the practicality of our power SC, we had to move beyond the simplifications of SPICE simulations, most notably the absence of supply and measurement noise and real process variations. We extracted the power trace of 30 sub-response patterns from Lightweight PUFs on FPGA (see Figure 2). However, we found that the 30 power traces are difficult to be differentiated from each other (as are their power consumptions). In other words, in practical implementations, a straightforward identification of the desired power side channel information from the measured power (current) traces appears infeasible.

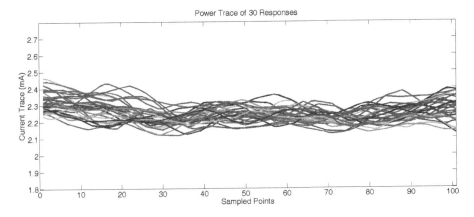

**Fig. 2.** Power trace of 30 different sub-responses, collected from FPGA, illustrating the difficulty of differentiating them from each other

There are two reasons for this problem:

1. In real silicon Arbiter and Lightweight PUFs, the final XOR function usually consumes no more than 5% silicon resource of the whole design. Thus, it is difficult to extract the power consumption of XOR function, which consumes much less power compared with the whole circuits;

2. Unlike a simulated PUF, measuring real silicon PUF circuit is always impacted by the noise from supply voltage and measurement, which plays a negative role in extracting the desired power information.

To overcome this problem and maintain the feasibility of our power side channel, we developed a new, statistical signal processing strategy.

Our main objective is to extract the subtle power consumption of XOR gates and transform it into a recognizable format, which is correlated with the cumulative number of one or zero sub-responses. Even though the extra power consumed by active XOR gates is not directly extractable, it does really affect the whole power consumption. Thus, it should change the probability distribution functions (PDF) of the measured power leakage, if it can extract the probability distribution of leaked power information, the cumulative of one sub-responses can be inferred. For this purpose, we apply a "challenge-dependent responses estimation" method to calculate the PDF of every power trace collection.

The "challenge-dependent responses estimation" is implemented by comparing the power trace just before and after the generation of response to distinguish subtle changes. In the experiment, we measure the power trace of a single PUF response for totally $m$ times, and record all of them in parallel. If denoting the generation time of the $ith$ PUF response $R_i$ as $t_i$, we can then filter out the two adjacent sections of power trace (length of which is $T_i^{before}$ and $T_i^{after}$) just before and after time $t_i$. Assume that $T_i^{before} = T_i^{after}$, then we divide each time slice into $n$ parts with the collected power trace (current trace) data. Based on the divided current trace data, we can calculate the power consumption of each $n$ part before and after the generation of response $R_i$.

By denoting power consumption of all the $2*n$ parts of the $ith$ PUF response under the $lth$ measurement (totally $m$ measurements are did as described above, thus, $l \in (1...m)$) as $P_{lij}^{before}$ and $P_{lij}^{after}$ respectively ($j \in (1...n)$), two matrices including the power consumption information of the $i_{th}$ response are obtained as:

$$M_i^{before} = \begin{pmatrix} P_{11}^{before} & P_{12}^{before} & P_{13}^{before} & ... & P_{1n}^{before} \\ P_{21}^{before} & P_{22}^{before} & P_{23}^{before} & ... & P_{2n}^{before} \\ ... & ... & ... & ... & ... \\ P_{m1}^{before} & P_{m2}^{before} & P_{m3}^{before} & ... & P_{mn}^{before} \end{pmatrix} \tag{1}$$

$$M_i^{after} = \begin{pmatrix} P_{11}^{after} & P_{12}^{after} & P_{13}^{after} & ... & P_{1n}^{after} \\ P_{21}^{after} & P_{22}^{after} & P_{23}^{after} & ... & P_{2n}^{after} \\ ... & ... & ... & ... & ... \\ P_{m1}^{after} & P_{m2}^{after} & P_{m3}^{after} & ... & P_{mn}^{after} \end{pmatrix} \tag{2}$$

Based on the power trace processing above, we now denote the power information of a single PUF response with two matrix: $M_i^{before}$ and $M_i^{after}$. Assuming that we totally collect $K$ response bits, then the power consumption matrix for all responses can be described as (for brevity, "$b$" means before and "$a$" means after):

$$M^{before/after} = \left( M_1^{b/a} \ M_2^{b/a} \ M_3^{b/a} \ ... \ M_K^{b/a} \right) \tag{3}$$

Due to the existence of environmental and measurement noise, the $m$ parallel segmentations of measured power trace (such as $P_{11}^{before}, P_{21}^{before} ... P_{m1}^{before}$ in Equation 1, and $P_{11}^{after}, P_{21}^{after} ... P_{m1}^{after}$ in Equation 2) consumption would build $n$ PDF respectively. Since we divide power trace slice into 2 parts (before and after), thus totally $2*n$ PDF are generated for each response. As we discussed, though there is no directly leaked power information that we can extract for the XOR function, it impacts the probability distribution of the whole power trace. To convert the PDF information into the cumulative number of one and zero responses, we applied histograms method to describe the PDF, and then implement basic calculus computation to get the cumulative distribution function (CDF):

$$C_j^{before/after}(x) = \sum_{x_j<x} PDF(X=x_j) = \sum_{x_j<x} p(x_j) \tag{4}$$
$$j \in (1..n)$$

Based on Equation.4, the original leaked power information can be transformed as CDF. To filter out the difference between two power trace segments: before and after time $t_i$, and erase the impact of environmental and measurement noise, we then calculate the mean-squared-error (MSE) following Equation 5:

$$MSE_j = E[(C_j^{before}(x) - C_j^{after}(x)^2], \ j \in (1..n) \tag{5}$$

then, all of the $n$ MSEs are summed up for a final sub-response estimation: $E_i$, which reflects and amplifies the impact of active XOR gates on leaked power:

$$E_i = \sum_{j=1}^{n} MSE_j, \ j \in (1..n) \tag{6}$$

With the proposed "challenge-dependent responses estimation" method, the power trace of different challenge-dependent responses patterns are transformed into an estimated value: "$E_i$". Thus, we can deduce the pattern of CRPs and integrate them within our proposed ML attacks.

**Determining the Generation time of PUF Response.** In the previous paragraph, we applied the "challenge-dependent responses estimation" method to extract the power side channel information of active XOR gates, assuming that we know the generation time of the $ith$ PUF response $R_i$ as $t_i$. However, one additional problem is that in practice, $t_i$ is not a direct known parameter. In this last paragraph, we will now detail how we overcame this final problem.

If we randomly set a $t_{i\_random}$ as the generation time of response $R_i$, the power information of a certain PUF response $R_i$ can be described as:

$$P_i = P_{i\_noise}^{before} + P_{i\_oc}^{before} + P_{i\_XOR}^{before} + P_{i\_noise}^{after} + P_{i\_oc}^{after} + P_{i\_XOR}^{after}, \qquad (7)$$

where $P_{i\_noise}^{b/a}$ denotes the environmental and measurement noise (as before, "$b$" abbreviates before and "$a$" after $t_{i\_random}$ here), $P_{i\_oc}^{b/a}$ stands for the power consumption of "other circuitry", again before and after $t_{i\_random}$, while $P_{i\_XOR}^{b/a}$ denotes the similar power information of XOR functional circuitry. Since based on the measurement, we can roughly tell the range of a PUF response generation time, we would have several choices of $t_{i\_random}$. To determine the exact generation time of each PUF responses, we move the $t_{i\_random}$ in the approximate time range, then we will get different power side channel informative patterns.

Since the PUF circuitry are measured for multiple times, and under the same environment, we can assume that for each response, we will have:

$$P_{i\_noise}^{before} \approx P_{i\_noise}^{after} \ and \ P_{i\_oc}^{before} \approx P_{i\_oc}^{after} \qquad (8)$$

thus, if we measure the power trace of a single PUF response for multiple times, we get:

$$\sum P_{i\_noise}^{before} - \sum P_{i\_noise}^{after} \approx 0 \ and \ \sum P_{i\_oc}^{before} - \sum P_{i\_oc}^{after} \approx 0 \qquad (9)$$

Based on this algorithm, it is clear that only when $t_i$ is set as the correct generation time, the $E_i$ in Equation 6 is maximized.

# 4   Timing Side Channels on XOR-Based Arbiter PUFs

As with our power side channel, the objective of the timing side channel is providing additional information about the individual response bits (i.e., PUF output bits) even though the response bits are XOR'ed together for providing the output. Assume that $k$ response bits $\{r_1, \ldots, r_k\}$ are XOR'ed to form a single output bit $b_{out}$. (Note that a k-input XOR shall consist of several stages of smaller XOR gates. For the sake of demonstration, assume that the delay of the response bit $r_i$, denoted by $t_{r_i}$ follows a certain order, say $t_{r_1} \le t_{r_2} \cdots \le t_{r_{k-1}} \le t_{r_k}$). Our timing side-channel approach is based on a delay measurement circuit, which can be used to characterize the delay length of different patterns of $k$ response bits $\{r_1, \ldots, r_k\}$.

## 4.1   Timing Characterization Method

Every ASIC manufactured chip undergoes a set of structural and functional tests which measure/ evaluate the IC's physical and logical properties respectively. Measuring the delay of certain combinational paths in the circuit is a part of standard structural testing. Since the internal combinational paths are typically inaccessible, the timings are indirectly inferred from the FF outputs using clock sweeping. The FF values can be set using a testing scan-chain while all the FFs are connected to the global chip clock. The pertinent chip is referred to as Circuit Under Test (CUT). The frequency of this clock is swept in a continuous monotonic fashion from a high to low value while the path under measurement is toggled using the logic at the input FF. When the frequency is higher than the path delay, the output FF does not have enough time to settle which is called a "fail". Once the frequency approaches the path delay, the output FF sets to the correct value (from the initial reset dictated by the scan chain) which is the "pass" state. The frequency at which this transition occurs denotes the path delay and this overall testing method is called pass/fail timing test.

On our FPGA testbed, the pass/fail timing tests have to be implemented by reconfiguration. We adopt the measurement circuitry from [14,15] that is demonstrated in Figure 3. Note that because of the timing uncertainty around the FF metastability point, the toggle between the pass/fail states appears with a certain property. Thus, error density estimation followed by smoothing methods are used for inferring the exact toggle point from a set of stochastic measurements.

To estimate the probability of error at a certain clock frequency, an error histogram accumulator is realized using two counters. The first one is an error counter whose value increments by one each time an error occurs. The second one counts the clock cycles; after $2^N$ clock cycles, this counter clears (resets) the error counter and then restarts again, where $N$ is the binary counters' size. The error counter value is stored in the memory one clock cycle before it is reset. Now, the stored number of fails normalized to $N$ would yield the error probability value for each target frequency.

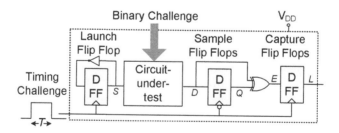

**Fig. 3.** The timing signature extraction circuit

Next, we linearly and continually sweep the input clock frequency: in $T_{sweep}$ seconds from $f_i = \frac{1}{2T_i}$ to $f_t = \frac{1}{2T_t}$, where $T_t < t_p < T_i$. For each frequency sweep, a separate set of registers count the number of clock pulses. We use this counter as an accurate timer which records the frequency of the timing errors. This counter value is retrieved every time the content of the error counter is written into memory. The system described above can be configured and utilized for extracting the delays of any CUT implemented on FPGA. We use this adaptation of pass/fail timing test to measure the delay between the FF storing the challenge input, to the output of the PUF which shall be stored in an output register. To prevent attacks, this output is measured after XORing the arbiter values. Note that the scanning for extracting delay values could also be performed in parallel to reduce the characterization time [14,15].

## 4.2   Characterization Accuracy

The resolution of the delay measurement, i.e., the measured delay's accuracy, is a function of a few factors: (i) the clock noise and skew, (ii) the sweeping frequency resolution, and (iii) the number of pulses at each frequency. The output of the characterization circuit is a binary zero/one (pass/fail) value. A real-valued output can be measured by repeating several (same width) clock pulses to the circuitry and accumulating the number of ones at the output. The resulting value, when normalized, shows the probability at which the timing errors occur for each input clock's pulse width. The more the input clock pulse is repeated, a higher sampling resolution and accuracy can be achieved.

For now assume that the clock pulse (of width $T$) is sent to the CUT for $M$ times. Because of clock skew and phase noise, the characterization circuitry receives a clock pulse with width $T_{eff} = T + T_j$, where $T_j$ is the additive jitter. Suppose that $T_j$ is a random variable with a zero mean and symmetric distribution around its mean. The output probability is a continuous and smooth function of $T_{eff}$; thus, approximating the probability by averaging shall be an asymptotically unbiased estimator as $M \to \infty$. Lastly, the minimum measurable timing is a function of the maximum clock speed at which the FFs can be run (maximum clock frequency). During a linear frequency sweep, a longer sweep time increases both items (ii) and (iii) and thus the characterization accuracy.

## 4.3   Parameter Extraction

Thus far, we have described a system that measures the probability of timing errors for various clock pulse widths. The error probability can be fully represented by a set of few parameters; the parameters are directly related to the CUT delay and FF setup and hold times. It can be shown that the probability of timing errors shall be written as the sum of shifted Gaussian CDFs [14,15]. The central limit theorem can determine the Gaussian nature of the error probabilities which can be explained by Equation 10 showing the parameterized error probability function.

$$f_{\mathbf{D},\Sigma}(t) = 1 + 0.5 \sum_{i=1}^{|\Sigma|-1} -1^{\lceil i/2 \rceil} \left[ Q(\frac{t - d_i}{\sigma_i}) \right] \tag{10}$$

where $Q(x) = \frac{1}{\sqrt{2\pi}} \int_x^\infty \exp\left(-\frac{u^2}{2}\right)$ and $d_{i+1} > d_i$. To estimate the timing parameters, $f$ is fit to the set of measured data points $(t_i, e_i)$, where $e_i$ is the error value recorded when the pulse width is $t_i$.

## 4.4  Side Channel Timing Analysis of XOR'ed Outputs

The pass/fail timing measurement above is able to estimate the delay of the overall PUF path (after XOR'ing). As we sweep the clock, we eventually get to a stable regime, i.e., the regime where the overall output does not change any more. However, before getting to this stable regime, there are clock periods for which only a few XOR inputs (i.e., response bits) change. Sweeping the clock frequency could yield the information about the approximate timing of the XOR inputs: every time one of the inputs to the XOR network, i.e., an arbiter output, changes, there will be a toggle. Even though it is not possible to distinguish the response bit that has changed, it is possible to estimate the number of flipping XOR inputs with a good probability. This number shall be vague if the timings of two or more response bits coincide. Since the probability of such a coincidence is rather low, in most instances clock sweeping shall yield an approximation of the number of flipped XOR inputs, i.e., the cumulative number of zeros and ones among the single Arbiter PUF responses $r_1, \ldots, r_k$.

## 5  Adapting Machine Learning Algorithms to Side Channel Information

The question how (and if at all) SC information on the cumulative number of zeros and ones can be efficiently exploited in PUF modeling turned out to be highly non-trivial. Eventually, we found a gradient based optimization similar to the logistic regression (LR) algorithm of [28,30]. The following treatment assumes some familiarity with this algorithm and with the work in [28,30].

Let $r_i(C) \in \{0, 1\}$ be the output of the $i^{\text{th}}$ Arbiter PUF within a $k$-XOR Arbiter PUF (or within a Lightweight PUF with $k$ parallel Arbiter PUFs) to a challenge $C$. The side-channel information then yields the number $n$ of individual Arbiter PUFs with output one: $n = \sum_i r_i(C)$. It lies in contrast to the general setting of binary outputs in LR on an interval scale. Therefore, instead of optimizing the binary class probabilities [28,30], we rely on minimizing the squared error between a side-channel model $f(w, C)$ and the actual outputs $n$:

$$l(\mathcal{M}, w) = \sum_{(C, t) \in \mathcal{M}} (f(w, C) - n)^2.$$

The corresponding gradient

$$\nabla l(\mathcal{M}, w) = \sum_{(C, r) \in \mathcal{M}} 2 \left( f(w) - n \right) \nabla f(w) \tag{11}$$

is highly similar to the gradient in LR. We again applied the RProp update scheme (as in [28,30]) to find a solution $\hat{w}$ with minimal error $l$.

Assuming the standard linear additive delay model [9,6,28,30], one obtains the following model of the side-channel information:

$$f(w, C) = \sum_i \Theta(w_i^T \Phi_i).$$

Note that the model only depends on the direction, but not on the length $\|w_i\|$ of the weight vectors. That is, any two solutions $w_i$ and $\alpha w_i, \alpha \in \mathbb{R}^+$ are equivalent. Therefore we might substitute the Heaviside function by the differentiable logistic sigmoid $\sigma(x) = (1 + e^{-x})^{-1}$ to enable gradient based optimization. This is a reasonable substitution as $\lim_{\|w\| \to \infty} \sigma(w^T \Phi) = \Theta(w^T \Phi)$ and, as noted above, a valid solution is unaffected by scaling of $w$.

As this substitution makes the model differentiable, we obtain the following gradient to insert in Equation 11:

$$\nabla f(w_j) = \sigma(w_j^T \Phi_j)(1 - \sigma(w_j^T \Phi_j))\Phi_j. \tag{12}$$

This gradient of an individual Arbiter PUF's weight vector $w_j$ depends only on the value of the weight vector itself, being in strong contrast to the case without side-channel information [28,30]. The decoupling of individual Arbiter PUF updates thus drastically simplifies the ML problem, provided that side-channel information is available.

In addition to the above new regression, we applied a two step optimization methodology: First we optimized the PUF model based on the above process and gradient, using the side-channel information, until a fraction of $f = 0.95$ percent of the final XOR Arbiter output was correctly reproduced. Secondly, we further refined and optimized the model with the "standard" LR algorithm applied in [28,30] for 1000 iterations. This led to very low error rates around 2% or below. For all experiments, we used hundred times more CRPs than free parameters in the model, i.e.,

$$N_{CRP} \approx 100 \times \text{bitlength} \times \text{no. of XORs}.$$

Note that the above equation merely describes a linear CRP consumption in the problem parameters. This is in stark contrast to the exponentially growing complexities of pure ML attacks on XOR Arbiter and Lightweight PUFs [28,30].

While our approach in the first step of the above methodology mostly converged to the global minimum, in a few cases it got stuck (i.e., the performance after 5000 iterations was worse than 5% remaining missclassifications). In this case, we restarted the algorithm with a different random initialization of $w$.

## 6    Results and Asymptotic Performance Analysis

We applied our adapted ML methods (see Section 5) to CRP data and SC information gathered from FPGAs (see Sections 2, 3, and 4), both for power and timing SCs. The results are presented in Tables 1 and 2. The attacks perform extremely efficiently, as we were able to successfully attack XOR Arbiter PUFs and Lightweight PUFs for up to 16 XORs and for bitlengths of up to 512 (timing SCs) and 128 (power SCs). No implementations of comparable sizes of these two PUFs in silicon had ever been considered or reported before. Furthermore, pure modeling attacks thus far had only been able to tackle the two PUFs for up 5 or 6 XORs and bitlength 64 [28,30]. Both facts illustrate the impact and reach of our new method.

Tables 1 and 2 already indicate that the CRP requirments and computation times grow very mildly, with the same holding for the prediction errors. In order to quantify

**Table 1.** Effectiveness of *timing* side-channel attacks on the XOR Arbiter PUF and Lightweight PUF (LW PUF), all carried out on FPGA implementations

| No. of XORs | Bit Length | CRPs ($\times 10^3$) | Prediction Rate XOR Arb. PUF | Training Time XOR Arb. PUF | Predict. Rate LW PUF | Training Time LW PUF |
|---|---|---|---|---|---|---|
| 8 | 64 | 26 | 98.5% | 2 min | 98.5% | 1 min |
|  | 128 | 51.6 | 97.5% | 12 min | 98.2% | 9 min |
|  | 256 | 103 | 97.7% | 1:35 hrs | 97.8% | 1:00 hrs |
|  | 512 | 205 | 97.4% | 16:50 hrs | 97.5% | 3:30 hrs |
| 12 | 64 | 39 | 98.1% | 16.5 min | 98.5% | 2 min |
|  | 128 | 77.4 | 97.4% | 38.5 min | 97.9% | 24.1 min |
|  | 256 | 154.5 | 97.1% | 3.8 hrs | 97.3% | 1.75 hrs |
|  | 512 | 308 | 96.92% | 56.25 hrs | 97.11% | 9.55 hrs |
| 16 | 64 | 52 | 98% | 37 min | 98% | 7 min |
|  | 128 | 103.2 | 97.5% | 2 hrs | 97.5% | 51.7 min |
|  | 256 | 206 | 97.3% | 15.1 hrs | 96.9% | 4.8 hrs |
|  | 512 | 410 | 96.5% | 102 hrs | 96.7% | 20.2 hrs |

**Table 2.** Effectiveness of *power* side-channel attacks on the XOR Arbiter PUF and Lightweight PUF (LW PUF), all carried out on FPGA implementations

| No. of XORs | Bit Length | CRPs ($\times 10^3$) | Prediction Rate XOR Arb. PUF | Training Time XOR Arb. PUF | Predict. Rate LW PUF | Training Time LW PUF |
|---|---|---|---|---|---|---|
| 8 | 64 | 26 | 98.1% | 3 min | 98.4% | 1.25 min |
|  | 128 | 51.6 | 98% | 13 min | 98.1% | 9.25 min |
| 12 | 64 | 39 | 98.3% | 11 min | 98.2% | 3.5 min |
|  | 128 | 77.4 | 97.3% | 47 min | 97.8% | 25 min |
| 16 | 64 | 52 | 98% | 38 min | 98% | 6.5 min |
|  | 128 | 103.2 | 97.5% | 2:28 hrs | 97.5% | 46.5 min |

this with yet more data points, we conducted comprehensive ML experiments on simulated CRPs and simulated SC data. The CRPs were generated by the linear additive delay model (LADM), similarly as in earlier ML experiments [28,30]. We executed these simulated attacks on XOR Arbiter PUFs and Lightweight PUFs for 2, 3, ..., 16 XORs, and with 64, 128, 256 and 512 bits. This means that we treated $2 \cdot 15 \cdot 4 = 120$ different architectures in sum, investing hundreds of hours of computation time. The generated data points are shown in Figure 4, and fully confirm the suspected mild, actually cubic growth. For those cases where we also had silicon data for comparison (see Tables 1 and 2), the silicon and the simulated attacks performed very similarly, confirming both earlier conjectures [6,28,30] on the validity of the additive linear delay model, as well as the accuracy of our side-channel measurements. The empirically estimated computational complexity of our attacks is hence $O(n^3)$, or, in other words, low-degree polynomial, in the problem size. Furthermore, as indicated already in Section 5, the number of used/required CRPs is merely linear in the same parameter.

Two important aspect should not go unnoticed. Firstly, our power side channel is more noisy than the timing side channel. This had the effect that we could only handle

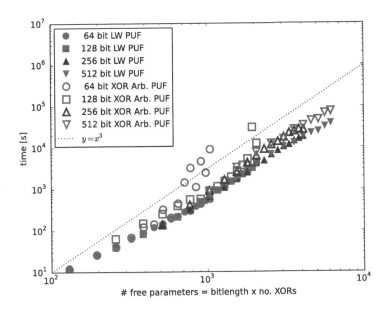

**Fig. 4.** The training times for our ML-algorithm on Lightweight PUFs (LW PUFs) and XOR Arbiter PUFs on a logarithmic scale. They show that the computational complexity regarding training times is cubic, i.e., $O(x^3)$.

bit lengths of up to 128 by use of the power SC. Improved, less noisy versions seem possible, but also non-trivial, and are left to future work.

Secondly, in the presence of side-channel information, our ML algorithms perform slightly faster on Lightweight PUFs than on XOR Arbiter PUF. Without side channels, the converse effect has been observed [28,30]. Intuitively, the challenge input mapping of the Lightweight PUF creates a more diverse and stable information basis for the ML algorithm, which leads to faster convergence. A full, rigorous mathematical analysis of this effect will be conducted in future work.

# 7    Summary and Conclusions

In this paper, we introduced and implemented the first power and timing side channels (SCs) on PUFs, more precisely on XOR Arbiter PUFs and Lightweight PUFs. These two PUF designs were chosen by us due to their particular relevance: The Arbiter PUF family is arguably the most studied electrical Strong PUF design, and said two PUFs are the most secure representatives of this family according to recent work [28,30]. Our two SCs consisted of (i) power tracing of the arbiter element (i.e., the latch) in Arbiter PUFs, and (ii) marking different response patterns with corresponding timing signatures. Both SCs tell us the *cumulative* number of zeros and ones in the outputs of the $k$ parallel Arbiter PUFs within XOR-based Arbiter PUF variants, such as the XOR Arbiter PUF or the Lightweight PUF. One main obstacle in exploiting the above SCs efficiently was that the attacker does not learn *which* of the single Arbiter PUF outputs is zero or one. This makes the cumulative information worthless at first sight. However, we were able to devise adapted, tailor-made ML algorithms, which can exploit the information very efficiently.

We carried out a full silicon proof of concept on FPGAs, attacking the two above PUFs for up to 16 XORs and bitlengths of 512 bits (by timing SCs) and 128 bits (by power SCs). Their smaller noise levels made timing SCs the yet more efficient tool, even though improved future versions of the power side channels seem possible. Interestingly, XOR-based Arbiter PUF variants had never even been *implemented* (left alone attacked) for comparable sizes in the literature, since already versions with 8 XORs and 512 bits had been recommended as practically secure against known attacks in earlier works [28,30]. This may illustrate the relevance and strength of our results. A close asymptotic analysis on simulated CRP data furthemore showed that our attacks have only *cubic complexity*. This is a drastic improvement over the exponential complexity of state-of-the-art, pure modeling attacks [28,30].

Our methods are the first physical attacks on Strong PUFs, i.e., on PUFs with many CRPs, that can notably increase attack performance. Overall, they imply that *as long as no suitable design countermeasures are put in place*, no currently existing architecture from the Arbiter PUF family can withstand all known attacks: "Standard" Arbiter PUFs as well as Feed-Forward Arbiter PUFs have been attacked by pure modeling attacks with polynomial complexity [28,30]; and XOR-based variants such as the XOR Arbiter PUF and the Lightweight PUF are susceptible to the methods presented in this paper, which have polynomial complexity, too.

We did not explicitly deal with design countermeasures in this paper for space reasons. However, one conceivable strategy against power SCs could consist of using two symmetric, inverted output signals with two latches. This construction could neutralize and balance power consumption, regardless of the PUF's output. Interestingly, this could even be used to detect and stabilize output errors in Arbiter PUF variants, even though we did not follow this route in in this paper. Countermeasure against our timing SCs would probably have to focus on the construction of an isochronous hardware. Implementing such strategies is left to future, follow-up works.

We believe that the PUF attacks presented in this and other papers should be interpreted in a balanced fashion. None of them "kills" the field in its entirety. In our opinion, they are part of a natural consolidation process in the PUF area, similar to the consolidation that classical security primitives have undergone already some time ago. The occurence of this process could be seen as indication that the field is becoming increasingly mature. One typical byproduct is the insight that certain aspects are not as simple as originally believed, which may be disappointing at first sight. Overall, however, a sound consolidation will be beneficial to the field, eventually creating more research opportunities than it destroys. This paper could be seen as one (of many) steps within this process.

**Acknowledgements.** The work at the University of Massachusetts Amherst was supported in part by SRC task 1836.074, US NSF grants 0923313 and 0964641, and US DHHS grant 90TR0003/01. The work at Rice University was supported in part by NSF

CCF-1116858:SHR:Small, NSF CNS-1059416:CI-ADDO-NEW: Trust-Hub, and ONR ONR N00014-11-1-0885 grants.

# References

1. Bishop, C.M., Nasrabadi, N.M.: Pattern recognition and machine learning. Springer, New York (2006)
2. Delvaux, J., Verbauwhede, I.: Side channel modeling attacks on 65nm arbiter PUFs exploiting CMOS device noise. In: HOST (2013)
3. Delvaux, J., Verbauwhede, I.: Attacking PUF-Based Pattern Matching Key Generators via Helper Data Manipulation. IACR Cryptology ePrint Archive, Report 2013/566
4. Delvaux, J., Verbauwhede, I.: Key-recovery Attacks on Various RO PUF Constructions via Helper Data Manipulation. IACR Cryptology ePrint Archive, Report 2013/610
5. Delvaux, J., Verbauwhede, I.: Fault Injection Modeling Attacks on 65nm Arbiter and RO Sum PUFs via Environmental Changes. IACR Cryptology ePrint Archive, Report 2013/619
6. Devadas, S.: Physical unclonable functions and secure processors. In: Clavier, C., Gaj, K. (eds.) CHES 2009. LNCS, vol. 5747, pp. 65–65. Springer, Heidelberg (2009)
7. Gassend, B., Clarke, D., van Dijk, M., Devadas, S.: Silicon physical random functions. In: ACM Conference on Computer and Communications Security, pp. 148–160 (2002)
8. Helfmeier, C., Nedospasov, D., Boit, C., Seifert, J.-P.: Cloning Physically Unclonable Functions. In: HOST 2013 (2013)
9. Lim, D.: Extracting Secret Keys from Integrated Circuits. MSc Thesis, MIT (2004)
10. Majzoobi, M., Koushanfar, F., Devadas, S.: FPGA PUF using programmable delay lines. In: IEEE Workshop Information Forensics and Security, WIFS (2010)
11. Majzoobi, M., Koushanfar, F., Potkonjak, M.: Lightweight Secure PUFs. In: ICCAD, pp. 607–673 (2008)
12. Majzoobi, M., Koushanfar, F., Potkonjak, M.: Testing techniques for hardware security. In: Proceedings of the International Test Conference (ITC), pp. 1–10 (2008)
13. Majzoobi, M., Koushanfar, F., Potkonjak, M.: Techniques for Design and Implementation of Secure Reconfigurable PUFs. ACM Trans. Reconfigurable Technology and Systems 2(1) (2009)
14. Majzoobi, M., Dyer, E., Elnably, A., Koushanfar, F.: Rapid FPGA Characterization using Clock Synthesis and Signal Sparsity. In: International Test Conference (ITC), pp. 1–10 (2010)
15. Majzoobi, M., Koushanfar, F.: Time-Bounded Authentication of FPGAs. IEEE Transactions on Information Forensics and Security (TIFS) 6(3), 1123–1135 (2011)
16. Rostami, M., Majzoobi, M., Koushanfar, F., Wallach, D., Devadas, S.: Robust and Reverse-Engineering Resilient PUF Authentication and Key-Exchange by Substring Matching. IEEE Transactions on Emerging Topics in Computing (2014)
17. Merli, D., Schuster, D., Stumpf, F., Sigl, G.: Side-Channel Analysis of PUFs and Fuzzy Extractors. In: McCune, J.M., Balacheff, B., Perrig, A., Sadeghi, A.-R., Sasse, A., Beres, Y. (eds.) Trust 2011. LNCS, vol. 6740, pp. 33–47. Springer, Heidelberg (2011)
18. Merli, D., Schuster, D., Stumpf, F., Sigl, G.: Semi-invasive EM attack on FPGA RO PUFs and countermeasures. In: ACM Workshop on Embedded Systems Security, WESS 2011 (2011)
19. Merli, D., Heyszl, J., Heinz, B., Schuster, D., Stumpf, F., Sigl, G.: Localized electromagnetic analysis of RO PUFs. In: HOST 2013 (2013)
20. Nedospasov, D., Helfmeier, C., Seifert, J.-P., Boit, C.: Invasive PUF Analysis. In: Fault Diagnonsis and Tolerance in Cryptography, FDTC 2013 (2013)

21. Pappu, R.: Physical One-Way Functions. PhD Thesis, Massachusetts Institute of Technology (2001)

22. Pappu, R., Recht, B., Taylor, J., Gershenfeld, N.: Physical One-Way Functions. Science 297, 2026–2030 (2002)

23. Riedmiller, M., Braun, H.: A direct adaptive method for faster backpropagation learning: The RPROP algorithm. In: IEEE International Conference on Neural Networks, pp. 586–591 (1993)

24. Rührmair, U., Devadas, S., Koushanfar, F.: Security based on Physical Unclonability and Disorder. In: Tehranipoor, M., Wang, C. (eds.) Introduction to Hardware Security and Trust, Springer, Heidelberg (2011)

25. Rührmair, U., van Dijk, M.: Practical security analysis of PUF-based two-player protocols. In: Prouff, E., Schaumont, P. (eds.) CHES 2012. LNCS, vol. 7428, pp. 251–267. Springer, Heidelberg (2012)

26. Rührmair, U., van Dijk, M.: PUFs in Security Protocols: Attack Models and Security Evaluations. In: IEEE Symposium on Security and Privacy, Oakland 2013 (2013)

27. Rührmair, U., Holcomb, D.E.: PUFs at a glance. In: DATE 2014, pp. 1–6 (2014)

28. Rührmair, U., Sehnke, F., Sölter, J., Dror, G., Devadas, S., Schmidhuber, J.: Modeling Attacks on Physical Unclonable Functions. In: ACM Conference on Computer and Communications Security (2010)

29. Rührmair, U., Sölter, J., Sehnke, F.: On the Foundations of Physical Unclonable Functions. Cryptology e-Print Archive (June 2009)

30. Rührmair, U., Sölter, J., Sehnke, F., Xu, X., Mahmoud, A., Stoyanova, V., Dror, G., Schmidhuber, J., Burleson, W., Devadas, S.: PUF Modeling Attacks on Simulated and Silicon Data. IEEE Transactions on Information Forensics and Security, IEEE T-IFS (2013)

31. Edward Suh, G.: Physical Unclonable Functions for Device Authentication and Secret Key Generation. In: DAC 2007, pp. 9–14 (2007)

# Physical Characterization of Arbiter PUFs

Shahin Tajik[1], Enrico Dietz[2], Sven Frohmann[2], Jean-Pierre Seifert[1],
Dmitry Nedospasov[1], Clemens Helfmeier[3],
Christian Boit[3], and Helmar Dittrich[2]

[1] Security in Telecommunications, Technische Universität Berlin, Germany
{shahin,jpseifert,dmitry}@sec.t-labs.tu-berlin.de
[2] Teraherz Spectroscopy, Technische Universität Berlin, Germany
{dietz,sf}@physik.tu-berlin.de
[3] Semiconductor Devices, Technische Universität Berlin, Germany
{clemens.helfmeier,christian.boit}@tu-berlin.de

**Abstract.** As intended by its name, Physically Unclonable Functions
(PUFs) are considered as an ultimate solution to deal with insecure
storage, hardware counterfeiting, and many other security problems.
However, many different successful attacks have already revealed vulnerabilities of certain digital intrinsic PUFs. Although settling-state-based
PUFs, such as SRAM PUFs, can be physically cloned by semi-invasive
and fully-invasive attacks, successful attacks on timing-based PUFs were
so far limited to modeling attacks. Such modeling requires a large subset of challenge-response-pairs (CRP) to successfully model the targeted
PUF. In order to provide a final security answer, this paper proves that
all arbiter-based (i.e. controlled and XOR-enhanced) PUFs can be completely and linearly characterized by means of photonic emission analysis. Our experimental setup is capable of measuring *every* PUF-internal
delay with a resolution of 6 picoseconds. Due to this resolution we indeed require only the theoretical minimum number of linear independent
equations (i.e. physical measurements) to directly solve the underlying
inhomogeneous linear system. Moreover, we neither require to know the
actual PUF challenges nor the corresponding PUF responses for our
physical delay extraction. On top of that devastating result, we are also
able to further simplify our setup for easier physical measurement handling. We present our practical results for a real arbiter PUF implementation on a Complex Programmable Logic Device (CPLD) from Altera
manufactured in a 180 nanometer process.

**Keywords:** Arbiter PUF, photonic emission analysis, backside, physical
characterization.

## 1 Introduction

Physically Unclonable Functions (PUFs) offer a promising solution for future
security problems [9]. PUFs can be utilized as the basis for many security applications, such as encryption [13,29] and hardware fingerprinting [26,33]. Although there are different PUF classifications in the literature regarding their

L. Batina and M. Robshaw (Eds.): CHES 2014, LNCS 8731, pp. 493–509, 2014.

characteristics, they can generally be categorized in two distinct classes of PUFs: settling-state-based PUFs and timing-based PUFs [15]. The former is based on bistable circuits such as SRAMs, while the latter is based on intrinsic differences in timing of a set of symmetric circuit paths.

Although *unclonability* and *unpredictability* are the main PUF requirements [3,22], previous work in the literature has shown how different PUFs can be attacked and cloned. Settling-state-based PUFs such as SRAM PUFs can be characterized and cloned physically by semi-invasive and fully invasive attacks [10,20]. Timing-based PUFs such as Arbiter PUFs are vulnerable to machine-learning attacks, which make it possible to emulate the PUF response [12,24]. However, machine-learning attacks require a large number of challenge-response pairs (CRP) to predict the response with high probability. Any non-linearity in the PUF response can negatively impact the effectiveness of machine-learning techniques [13,32]. As a result substantially more CRPs together with extra side channel information are required to model the PUF response successfully [16]. However, in a real attack scenario, the intrinsic PUF response may be unavailable to the attacker [8,14]. Moreover, trying a large set of CRPs may also be infeasible due to other countermeasures implemented on modern secure devices [23].

This work demonstrates that arbiter PUFs and more generally, timing-based PUFs can be characterized by high-resolution temporal photonic emission analysis from the chip's backside. This approach does not need any readout of PUF response nor does it require a substantial number of challenges to characterize the PUF. Our methodology is based on measuring the time difference between enabling the PUF and photon emission at the output of the last stage. For our Proof-of-concept (PoC), we have implemented an arbiter PUF on a Complex Programmable Logic Device (CPLD). The delay between the input of the PUF and the output of photodetector can be measured with an overall resolution of approximately 6 picoseconds by a Time-to-Digital Converter (TDC). As a result, the PUF response is determined by comparing the measured delays on both PUF chains. Furthermore, in our methodology, the required challenges for the physical characterization of the PUF increase linearly with PUF length. Finally, based on a mathematical approach we find the minimum number of necessary challenge combinations, which are required to characterize the PUF. Using this methodology it also possible to characterize controlled PUFs [8], where the challenge is inaccessible to the attacker. As compared to other characterization techniques, such as machine learning, this methodology greatly reduces the amount of measurements that are necessary to characterize the intrinsic PUF behavior. The main contributions of this paper are as follows:

**Physical Characterization of Timing-Based PUFs.** We present the first physical characterization attack on timing-based PUFs with the help of photonic emission analysis. This approach is capable of physically characterizing the intrinsic behavior of the circuit by measuring the delays within the circuit with a high degree of accuracy. In the case of an arbiter PUF this consists of measuring the intrinsic delays of each individual stage of the circuit. As compared to other heuristic methodologies which require a substantially greater number of measurements than individual PUF stages, our methodology requires just two measurements per PUF stage.

**Low-Cost Measurement Setup for Measuring the Delay with the Resolution of 6 ps.** We introduce an efficient and cost-effective experimental setup with a substantial temporal resolution. The setup is capable of performing temporal measurements with an approximate time resolution of 6 ps. The time resolution of the setup allows for the exact characterization of the intrinsic delays of each individual stage of the PUF. Moreover, the setup provides sufficient time resolution for modern process nodes.

**Practical Evaluation against a Proof-of-Concept Arbiter PUF Implementation.** The PoC implementation was realized on a common programmable logic platform. To extract the device's intrinsic behavior, we performed dynamic semi-invasive backside analysis of the photonic emissions of the device. Because the analysis techniques are semi-invasive the integrity of the device's intrinsic response is not changedpre.

**Mathematical Approach for Measurement Optimization.** In order to physically characterize the PUF, we propose a measurement technique to minimize the number of challenges that are necessary for a PUF characterization. Furthermore, we provide a mathematical approach for minimizing the effort of measurement for arbiter PUFs in general. Combined, these techniques greatly reduce the number of measurements and measurement locations that are necessary for PUF characterization.

The rest of this paper is organized as follows: Section 2 presents background information on the delay-based PUFs and photonic emission in CMOS technology. Moreover, the programmable logic architecture is explained and the related work is reviewed. In Section 3, the utilized experimental setup is presented. Section 4 introduces the mathematical approach for the optimized measurement. Section 5 demonstrates the practical results, where we were able to measure the small delay differences. In Section 6, we present additional considerations about our methodology. Finally in Section 7, we conclude the paper.

# 2    Background

## 2.1    Arbiter-Based PUF

Due to manufacturing variations, there are small random delay differences on symmetrical electrical paths on a chip. The entropy of the delays is sufficient to ensure a unique PUF response for each individual device instance. Arbiter and Ring-oscillator PUFs are two examples of timing-based PUFs [15]. Arbiter PUFs utilize the intrinsic timing differences of two symmetrically designed paths to a single bit of the response at the output of the circuit [12]. It consists of multiple connected stages and an arbiter at the end of the chain, see Figure 1. Each stage consists of two outputs and three inputs, a single bit of the challenge and the two outputs from the previous stage. The inputs of the first stage are connected

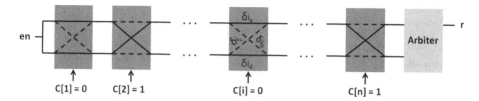

**Fig. 1.** Arbiter PUF

to a common enable signal. The outputs of the last stage are connected to a so-called arbiter, which determines which signal arrived first. Based on this result, the arbiter generates a single bit known as the response. Although the nominal delays of direct paths and crossed paths are equal ($\delta_{i_a} = \delta_{i_d}$ and $\delta_{i_b} = \delta_{i_c}$), due to the intrinsic delays of the circuit, different challenges produce different results. The differences between two identical device instances will be sufficient to differentiate the unique responses of the devices.

## 2.2   Photonic Emission in CMOS

Individual logic gates are implemented on the Complementary Metal Oxide Semiconductor (CMOS) Integrated Circuits (ICs) by a set of connected p-type and n-type Metal Oxide Semiconductor (MOS) transistors. In a static state, where no transistor devices are switching, there is at least one transistor in the off region between the supplied power (VDD) and ground (GND). Therefore, the current consumption of the gate is minimal. However, during a switching event a substantial current passes through the circuit. As a result, the transistors enter an operating region known as *saturation* for a short period of time. During saturation, the kinetic energy of accelerated hot carriers can be released via photon emission [4]. n-type transistors emit significantly more photons as compared to p-type transistors, due to the higher mobility of electrons than holes. Hence, only photons emitted by n-type transistor can be observed in general. The emission rate of the transistors is proportional to the switching frequency of the circuit. However, raising the supply voltage also increases the amount of photons emitted by the device exponentially.

Due to multiple interconnect layers on the frontside of modern IC designs, the optical path is obstructed [23]. Therefore, it is almost impossible to observe photonic emissions from the frontside. However, photonic emissions can be observed from the IC backside as well. Although, silicon substrate is highly absorptive for wavelengths shorter than the bandgap energy, the silicon substrate is transparent to near infrared (NIR) emissions. Hence, any NIR photons emitted by the device will pass through the silicon substrate and can be observed from the IC backside.

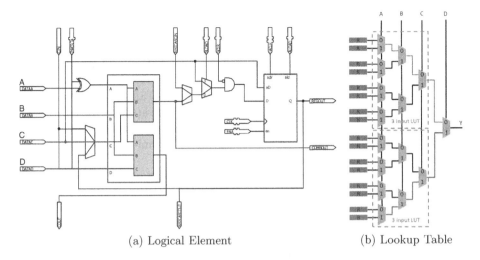

(a) Logical Element                                         (b) Lookup Table

**Fig. 2.** (a)Architecture of a Logical Element in an Altera MAX V CPLD: A configurable 4-input combinatorial circuit (blue). Additionally each LE consists of multiple control inputs as well as global signals such as clock and enable [2]. (b)The LUT is realized by multiple multiplexers, which are controlled by the data inputs. The output of the LUT is loaded from the existing SRAM cells inside the LUT. In our PUF design, each signal path is connected to one of the LUT's inputs (input A). The challenge signal is connected to all other three inputs (B, C and D) in order to limit the routing only to two paths inside the LUT.

### 2.3   Programmable Logic Architecture

PUFs can be realized in different types of hardware implementations. Timing-based PUFs can also be implemented on a programmable logic device, i.e. FPGAs and CPLDs. The architecture of modern CPLDs and FPGAs is very similar and the architectures of any given vendor share many commonalities. The primary architectural differences of modern CPLDs and FPGAs are logical size, the complexity of the routing network and the hard macros available to the design. Moreover, CPLDs generally store the configuration within the same device package, whereas FPGAs generally require external memory for storing the device configuration. Programmable logic devices consist of an array of configurable Logic Elements (LEs), see Figure 2. The configuration determines the logical behavior of each individual LE. The LEs themselves are commonly realized using so called Look-Up-Tables (LUTs) in which the output values are stored for a particular input combination. Combinatorial logic of a particular design can be entirely realized using LUTs. The Altera Max V architecture utilized in this work utilizes two 3-input LUTs to realize a 4-input LE, see Figure 2(a). Each LE also provides an additional configurable register with multiple control inputs and an output for realizing sequential logic. LEs are organized into groups of ten which form so called Logical Array Blocks (LABs). In addition to global routing resources, each LAB provides additional routing to each LE within the LAB.

## 2.4   Related Work

In recent years, many different attacks on PUFs have been proposed. Settling-state based PUFs, such as SRAM PUFs, can be physically cloned by semi-invasive attacks [10]. The authors of this work demonstrated how SRAM PUF responses can be characterized by a Focused Ion Beam (FIB) circuit edit. More-over, SRAM PUFs are also vulnerable to fully-invasive attacks, due to lack of tamper detection mechanism [20]. It was also shown that timing-based PUFs, such as Ring-oscillator PUFs, are also vulnerable to semi-invasive electromag-netic (EM) side channel attacks [18].

However, to this date, arbiter PUFs are only the target of mathematical mod-eling attacks. Modeling attacks require a subset of CRPs to build a model on that and predict the PUF response for all possible challenges [12]. One of the first utilized modeling techniques was linear programming to model the timing-based PUF [21]. Machine-learning tools such as Logistic Regression (LR) can also be utilized to model the arbiter PUF successfully [24]. The modeling attacks becomes more difficult by introducing non-linearities to the PUF delays and re-sponses. Two example of non-linear PUFs are Feed-forward arbiter PUFs [13] and XOR-PUFs [32]. However, it has been shown that Feed-forward PUFs are vulnerable to evolutionary algorithm [25]. Moreover, a modeling attack based on higher number of CRPs and power side channel information can be applied successfully to XOR-arbiter PUFs [16]. Other modeling techniques include solv-ing integer equations utilize the CMOS noise as a side channel information or environmental changes as a fault injection technique to model the timing-based PUFs [6,5].

Photonic emission analysis is introduced as a new side channel attack to ana-lyze security applications on the chip such as cryptographic ciphers [7]. In order to bypass the multiple interconnect layers on the frontside of the chip, photonic emission analysis and photonic fault injection attacks can be conducted from the backside [31,30]. It has been shown that chips, such as microcontrollers, can be functionally analyzed by their optical emissions during runtime [19]. Sim-ple Photonic Emission Analysis (SPEA) is another approach that can recover the full AES secret key by monitoring access to S-Box [28]. Furthermore, the full AES secret key can be recovered by a similar approach called Differential Photonic Emission Analysis [11].

# 3   Experimental Setup

## 3.1   Measurement Setup

The experimental setup, shown schematically in Figure 3, is an optimized in-frared microscope equipped with a scientific Si-CCD camera and an InGaAs avalanche diode as detectors for spatial and temporal analysis [27]. The Si-CCD is a back illuminated deep depletion type featuring high quantum efficiency in the NIR region. To minimize dark current it is cooled down to $-70\,^{\circ}\mathrm{C}$, which

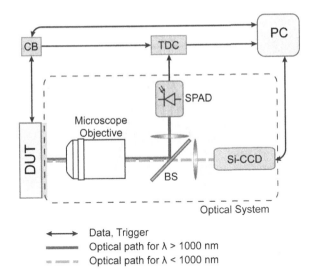

Fig. 3. Controlling the DUT with the CB and capturing emitted photons from the DUT by SI-CCD camera and InGaAs-SPAD

allows long exposure times to accumulate enough photons from the weak hot carrier emission. Due to the long integration time of several seconds and the limited readout speed of the CCD sensor, it is used for spatial analyses only. The temporal analysis of the photonic emission requires a very fast infrared detector. Therefore a free-running InGaAs avalanche detector in Geiger Mode (SPAD) is used to detect single photons. Its sensitivity covers a wavelength range between 1 to 1.6 $\mu$m with peak quantum efficiency of 20%. Thermoelectrical cooling reduces the dark count rate below 2 kHz.

The Device under Test (DUT), is controlled by a computer via a control box (CB), which provides the enable signal for the PUF and a time reference signal for the time to digital converter (TDC). Photons emitted from the DUT are collected by the microscope objective (NA = 0.45) and divided into two optical paths by a short-pass beam splitter (BS). Short-wave photons below 1 $\mu$m are transmitted to the Si-CCD camera while the long-wave photons are reflected onto the InGaAs-SPAD. This configuration allows capturing images with the CCD and time resolved measurements with the SPAD simultaneously. An incoming photon from the DUT causes the avalanche breakdown of the SPAD and the resulting electrical pulse is registered by the TDC. The FPGA-based TDC time tags each occurring event with a resolution of 81 picoseconds. This way both the enable signal of the PUF chain and the detected photons from the chain's output transistor are time tagged allowing a direct calculation of the their delay. Due to jitter in the response time of the SPAD and electrical jitter in the CB and TDC the overall time uncertainty for a single photonic event is 190 ps rms. An accumulation of multiple photonic events is used to improve the time

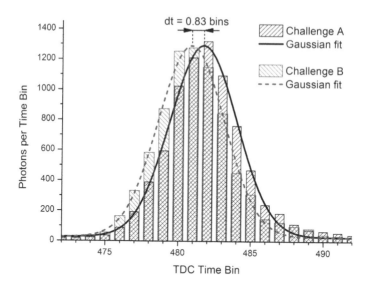

**Fig. 4.** Timing difference of two different challenges at the output of last stage. The time bin width is 81 ps

resolution by calculating the centroid of the Gaussian-like distribution of the delay time histogram, see Figure 4. This super-resolution technique enhances the time resolution significantly beyond the 81 ps granularity of the TDC and allows measurements of very small shifts in the delay time. Experiments showed that the accuracy of our current setup is limited by drifts in the electronics to 6 ps rms. Apart from the custom made holding of the DUT to a 3-dimensional moving stage and electronics to control and communicate with the CPLD, the setup consists of commercially available components. As the focus of the setup is on time resolved measurements, it can be realized for about 30000 Euros.

## 3.2    Device under Test

In this work, Altera MAX V CPLD devices (part number 5M80ZT100C5N) were utilized for the physical experiments [1]. A backside reflectance image of the CPLD shows the presence of 240 LEs on the device, see Figure 6. However, this device allows the use of 80 Logic Elements (LE) in total. The device contains 24 Logic Array Blocks (LAB) with 10 LEs each. The non-volatile memory and additional infrastructure logic is located on the upper half in Figure 6, I/O pads are clearly visible on the perimeter of the device. The devices were decapsulated using the Ultratec ASAP-1 mechanical polishing machine exposing the backside. The bulk silicon material of the devices was thinned down significantly. The silicon surface was polished to expose a surface suitable for optical imaging.

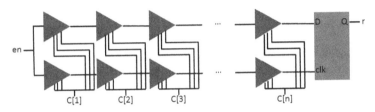

**Fig. 5.** Implementation of arbiter PUF by two independent buffers chains

To further improve the surface quality and optical properties of the devices, an anti reflective coating (ARC) was applied to the devices. Finally, the devices were soldered onto a custom printed circuit board (PCB) to allow capturing of images from the exposed backside of the device while maintaining full electrical connectivity.

### 3.3    PUF Implementation on CPLD

One possibility for implementing arbiter PUFs is to utilize digital multiplexers. In this case, each PUF stage requires two multiplexers. As each multiplexer is realized by a LUT, two inputs out of four available inputs of LUT are utilized, see Figure 2(b). Based on *don't-care* inputs, the output of multiplexer can be loaded from different SRAM cells inside the LUT and take different routes to the output. This fact leads to different propagation delays, and consequently, delay imbalances for the two PUF routes. Therefore, due to routing constraints in a LUT of CPLD, we have implemented the stages by two independent LUTs as in [17], see Figure 5. To validate our concept, the design consists of an 8-bit arbiter PUF on the CPLD. Each stage is placed manually in an individual LAB on the CPLD to make the PUF chains symmetric. Due to very little delay differences between two chains, the arbiter can sample a meta-stable signal. Moreover, due to asymmetric length of data and clock lines, the delay between the outputs of the last stage and the inputs of the arbiter cannot be designed symmetrically. Hence, instead of using an arbiter, we readout the response by measuring the overall delays of both chains with the help of photonic emission analysis.

## 4    Measurement Approach

For completeness we present in this section two approaches to solve the underlying linear system of arbiter PUFs — first, the slightly more elaborate approach for MUX-based PUFs although it is unnecessary for our PoC implementation. Second, the related but simpler approach for our delay-based PUF implementation.

## 4.1   Optimized Measurement for Ordinary MUX-Based PUF Characterization

In a MUX-based arbiter PUF, each stage consists of four different propagation delays: two direct path delays and two switching path delays, see Figure 1. In order to completely characterize an $n$-stage arbiter PUF, all propagation delays of each stage have to be known, hence, 4n delays must be characterized in total. One conceivable way would be to naively measure all 4 propagation delays at all $n$ stages individually by moving the optical setup *over* both inputs and both outputs of each stage, and simply try both challenge states. However, this technique would require the movement of the chip and adjusting the focus for each movement. However, this process could be automated as well, but our measurement setup lacked this capability. As our setup has a very high spatial resolution, a precise aperture movement would be very time consuming, but eventually yield the $4n$ arbiter delays. While practically certainly feasible and also theoretically optimal, we can do much better in terms of physical measurement efforts. A more intelligent solution will simply try to measure the overall propagation delays of each PUF chain at the outputs of the very last stage for sufficiently many selected challenge combinations. As the overall delay at the outputs of the last stage is the sum of all $n$ delays in each stage, cf. additive linear model due to [13,13], every measurement has to consider for every chosen challenge the complete propagation time of two distinct but possible paths — the upper output (D input to sampling flip-flop) and the lower output (C input to sampling flip-flop). If we denote by $r_i$ the resulting overall time of an individual challenge measurement, we conclude that we get an inhomogeneous system of linear equations

$$\mathbf{C} \cdot \boldsymbol{\delta} = \mathbf{r}$$

for our $4n$ unknowns $\delta_{i_a}, \delta_{i_b}, \delta_{i_c}$, and $\delta_{i_d}$ and the challenge matrix $\mathbf{C}$ with entries from $\{0,1\}$ which encode the different valid paths through the arbiter chain. We call a path $\mathbf{c}_i \in \{0,1\}^{4n}$ *valid* if its respective challenge setting within $\mathbf{C}$ allows a full signal propagation of length $n$, i.e., until its very end. By induction the following is easy to see.

**Proposition 1.** *For an arbiter PUF of length $n \geq 1$ let $\mathbf{C}$ be the $(2^{n+1}) \times (4n)$ matrix consisting of all valid paths through the respective arbiter chain. Then* $\mathrm{rk}(\mathbf{C}) = 2n + 2$.

Seeing now that we have only $2n + 2$ linear independent equations in $\mathbf{C}$, we need to generate the remaining $2(n-1)$ linear independent equations to completely solve our system in another way. Thus, we are forced to consider also partial valid paths instead of full propagation paths. Let $\mathbf{c}_i \in \{0,1\}^{4n}$ be a valid path; for integers $1 \leq u, v \leq n$ a vector of the form

$$(0, \ldots, 0, c_{4u}, c_{4u+1}, c_{4u+2}, c_{4u+3}, \ldots, c_{4v}, c_{4v+1}, c_{4v+2}, c_{4v+3}, 0, \ldots, 0) \in \{0,1\}^{4n}$$

will be called a *partial valid* path.

*Note 1.* For a partial valid path we will measure its signal time only from the inputs of arbiter stage $u$ until its output at stage $v$ and deliberately denote this partial time simply also by $r_i$.

Including such partial measurements $r_i$ (i.e. including measurements within the arbiter chain) and their corresponding paths $\mathbf{c}_i$ we also get by induction.

**Proposition 2.** *For an arbiter PUF of length $n \geq 1$ and its $2n + 2$ valid paths (corresponding to the linear independent row vectors) there exist $2(n-1)$ appropriate partial valid paths such that their combined challenge matrix $\mathbf{C}$ has full rank $4n$.*

This Proposition implies that we only need $2(n-1)$ partial measurements which we classify with respect to $u$ and $v$ into three classes:

1. $u = 1$ and $1 \leq v < n$: Measurement begins at the inputs of the first stage and ends in the middle of the chain.
2. $1 < u, v < n$: Measurement starts at some inputs in the middle of the chain and also ends in the middle of the chain.
3. $1 < u \leq n$ and $v = n$: Measurement starts at the inputs in the middle of the arbiter chain and and ends after the last stage.

In order to keep the previously discussed physical measurement efforts minimal, it is therefore obvious to generate the missing linear independent equations out of group 1 or 3 — dependent on varying setup advantages. This completes our description of an optimized measurement for a classical MUX-based PUF with $n$ stages.

## 4.2   Simplified Measurement for Delay-Based PUFs

As we already pointed out in Section 2.1, we have $\delta_{i_a} = \delta_{i_d}$, and $\delta_{i_b} = \delta_{i_c}$ for their respective buffers. Moreover, as the two paths, i.e., the upper and the lower path are not crossing at all, in other words they are disjoint, we can consider them completely separately, see Figure 5. Towards this, let us consider the upper path and simply denote its $n$ unknown delays by $\delta_1, \ldots, \delta_n$. I.e., setting the respective $i^{\text{th}}$ challenge bit to 1 adds the delay $\delta_i$ to the overall complete signal propagation time which will be denoted by $r_j$ for the $j^{\text{th}}$ measurement from the first input until the last output — just through all $n$ stages. If we now define the distinguished variable $\Delta_{n+1}$ as the overall complete signal propagation time for setting all $n$ challenge bits to 0 we get the (already solved) linear system

$$\begin{pmatrix} 1 & 0 & \cdots & 0 & 0 \\ 0 & 1 & \cdots & 0 & 0 \\ \vdots & & \ddots & & \vdots \\ 0 & 0 & \cdots & 1 & 0 \\ 0 & 0 & \cdots & 0 & 1 \end{pmatrix} \cdot \begin{pmatrix} \Delta_1 \\ \Delta_2 \\ \vdots \\ \Delta_n \\ \Delta_{n+1} \end{pmatrix} = \begin{pmatrix} r_1 \\ r_2 \\ \vdots \\ r_n \\ r_{n+1} \end{pmatrix}$$

for which we simply require the measurements $r_i$, $i = 1, \ldots, n + 1$. The lower path can be handled in an analog way, say $\mathbf{C}' \cdot \boldsymbol{\Delta}' = \mathbf{r}'$. Moreover, using the unit vectors $\mathbf{e}_i \in \{0, 1\}^{n+1}$, $i = 1, \ldots, n + 1$, we find that we get from

$$\mathbf{e}_i \cdot \boldsymbol{\Delta} - \mathbf{e}_{n+1} \cdot \boldsymbol{\Delta} = r_i - r_{n+1}, \quad \text{and}$$

$$\mathbf{e}_i \cdot \boldsymbol{\Delta}' - \mathbf{e}_{n+1} \cdot \boldsymbol{\Delta}' = r_i' - r_{n+1}'$$

the two individual buffer delays $\delta_i$ and $\delta_i'$ of stage $i$ incurred by setting the $i^{\text{th}}$ challenge bit to 1. We thus conclude that we need only $2n + 2$ "full path" measurements to completely characterize a delay-based PUF with $n$ stages.

## 5  Results

We have chosen the challenge 00000000 as the reference challenge for our measurements. In order to measure the effect of each challenge bit, we have tried the challenge combinations with hamming distance one to see the effect of each challenge bit individually. The enable signal was switched with a frequency of 4 MHz and the chip was supplied with 2.2 V. The optical emission of the PUF circuit reveals the position of each stage, see Figure 6. Moreover, the inputs and output of each stage for measurement can also be found on this emission image. In case of controlled PUFs, where no electrical access to challenges is available [8], comparing the optical emission of the PUF stages can also reveal the state of individual challenge bits. By changing each challenge bit, the emission pattern of each LE is changed, and therefore, the challenge can be read without any electrical access to it, see Figure 7. Therefore, the equations provided in Section 4 can still be used to characterize the PUF by finding challenges with hamming distance one from each other. We repeated the measurement 50 million cycles to capture enough number of photons for analysis. The reference challenge also has been measured multiple times during our experiments to compare the consistency of measurements. The measurement results of 8 challenge combinations compared to the reference challenge can be found in Figure 8. Positive timing difference means that the delay is decreased in comparison to reference challenge and vice versa. It can be seen that flipping the challenge bit from 0 to 1, makes in most cases both upper and lower chains faster. Moreover, the timing differences between both chains can also be found in the table. Based on the overall delay difference of two chains, the response can be predicted. In this case, if the timing difference between two chains is positive, the response is 1, otherwise the response is 0.

According to the measured values, we can predict the behavior of both chains for all other challenge combinations based on the linear additive model of the arbiter PUF. To prove the applicability of this model, we predicted theoretically the overall delay of both chains for a set of arbitrary challenge combinations, and then measured the timings in practice. For instance, the calculated timing difference between both chains for the challenge 00000111 is the sum of measured differences of challenges 00000001, 00000010 and 00000100, which is 195 ps.

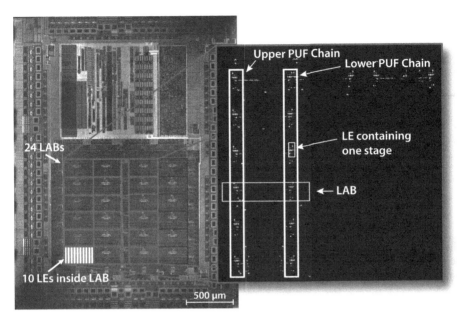

**Fig. 6.** The backside reflectance image acquired using a laser scan microscope (left). Inside the framed area, all programmable logic cells are located. The grid corresponds to the placement of 4 by 6 LABs with additional routing infrastructure in-between. Within each LAB, 10 LEs are located (only a single LAB is shown containing the LEs). Optical emission of the 8-bit arbiter PUF on the CPLD (right). Each stage is realized by two LEs in a LAB in parallel.

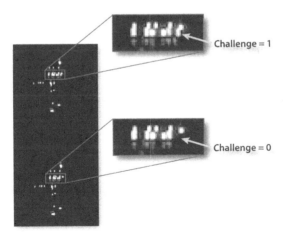

**Fig. 7.** Reading challenge bit from the emission image of each LE

The measured value is 199 ps, with 4 ps deviation from the predicted value. However, the response can be clearly predicted as logical 1 due to large positive difference. Another example shows that by applying a set of challenges, such as

| | | | | | | | | | | | | | | | | |
|---|---|---|---|---|---|---|---|---|---|---|---|---|---|---|---|---|
| **Challenge** | 1 0 0 0 0 0 0 0 | 0 1 0 0 0 0 0 0 | 0 0 1 0 0 0 0 0 | 0 0 0 1 0 0 0 0 | 0 0 0 0 1 0 0 0 | 0 0 0 0 0 1 0 0 | 0 0 0 0 0 0 1 0 | 0 0 0 0 0 0 0 1 | 1 1 1 0 0 0 0 0 | 1 0 1 0 0 1 0 0 | 1 0 1 0 1 0 1 0 | 0 0 0 0 0 1 1 1 | 0 1 0 1 0 1 0 1 | 0 0 0 0 1 1 1 1 | 0 1 1 0 0 1 1 1 | 1 1 1 1 1 1 1 1 |
| measured Δt in ps — chain u | 43 | 79 | 48 | 63 | 29 | 76 | 39 | 76 | 174 | 179 | 181 | 127 | 313 | 217 | 356 | 510 |
| measured Δt in ps — chain l | 33 | -106 | 45 | 74 | 45 | 91 | 59 | 74 | -20 | 185 | 208 | 156 | 143 | 237 | 190 | 368 |
| measured Δt in ps — diff. | 10 | 185 | 3 | -11 | -16 | -14 | -20 | 3 | 195 | -6 | -27 | -29 | 170 | -20 | 166 | 141 |
| measured response | 1 | 1 | 1 | 0 | 0 | 0 | 0 | 1 | 1 | 0 | 0 | 0 | 1 | 0 | 1 | 1 |
| calculated Δt in ps — chain u | | | | | | | | | 170 | 167 | 159 | 115 | 295 | 192 | 319 | 453 |
| calculated Δt in ps — chain l | | | | | | | | | -28 | 168 | 182 | 150 | 132 | 224 | 162 | 314 |
| calculated Δt in ps — diff. | | | | | | | | | 199 | -1 | -23 | -35 | 162 | -32 | 157 | 140 |
| calculated response | | | | | | | | | 1 | 0 | 0 | 0 | 1 | 0 | 1 | 1 |

**Fig. 8.** Measurement results of challenge combinations with hamming distance one (the 8 combinations from the left). Measurement results of set of arbitrary challenge combination (the last 8 combinations from the right). The reference challenge is 00000000.

00100101, the timing difference between two chains will be quite small both in calculation and measurement. Hence, these combinations can drive the arbiter into a metastable condition, and the response will not be consistent. It can also be seen in the results that although the PUF is implemented symmetrically on the hardware, a set of challenge bits can have much more effect on the delay of the chain than others. For example, when the second challenge bit is flipped, large delay difference on the lower chain is observed. As it can be seen in Figure 8, by applying the challenge 10101010, four challenge bits are flipped from the reference challenge. Although the flipping effect of 4th, 6th and 8th bits are comparable to each other, the 2nd bit has much more effect that make the response prediction much easier. These *dominant* stages have more influence on the response than other stages, and make the response prediction easier. Therefore, finding these stages can potentially turn out a threat for arbiter PUFs.

## 6   Discussion

In order to obtain spatial orientation of the PUF circuit by the CCD detector, the chip has to be thinned. Thinning the silicon substrate from the backside of the chip can destruct the PUF. However, the InGaAs SAPD is still able to detect photons without thinning the substrate. Therefore, only one IC sample has to be thinned, if we want to apply the same approach on multiple IC samples. While our proof of concept implementation utilized a CPLD, the results are directly applicable to all classes of arbiter PUFs realized in CMOS. All CMOS devices are vulnerable to photonic emission analysis, as the transistors emit photons during switching. Therefore, the same measurement methodology can be applied to all platforms, such as FPGAs or Application Specific Integrated Circuits (ASICs).

Although our experiment was conducted with an 8-bit arbiter PUF, the same delay measurement technique can be applied to arbiter PUFs with higher number of stages. In comparison to machine learning attacks, our methodology requires far less challenges to predict the response. Furthermore, no response is required to physically characterize the PUF. Logistic regression classification model requires 2555 and 18050 CRPs for a response prediction rate of 99% for an 64-bit and 128-bit Arbiter PUF, respectively [24]. Our approach requires only the measurement of 65 challenges for 64-bit and 129 challenges for 128-bit. Moreover, XOR-arbiter PUFs with 9 parallel 64 and 128 stages are modeled with 200000 and 500000 CRPs, receptively, plus the power side channel information for a 95% response prediction rate [16]. In this case, our methodology requires only $9 \times 65$ and $9 \times 129$ challenges for 64-bit and 128-bit arbiter PUF, respectively. This shows that the number of required challenges in our approach increases only linearly with the increase of number of stages. Furthermore, having XOR at the end of multiple chains has no impact on the linearity of our approach. However, trying the same challenge more than one million times to capture enough photons by the detector, is the disadvantage of this methodology. Besides, our attack requires direct physical access to the DUT, while it may not be required by modeling attacks.

Measuring the effect of each challenge takes approximately 12.5 seconds by supplying the chip with 2.2 V and enabling the PUF input with 4MHz frequency. Supplying the chip with 1.8 V, for example, reduces the number of emitted photons by a factor of 3, and the measurement time increases consequently by a factor of 3. However, we can increase the frequency to 100MHz to increase the number of emitted photons and to reduce the measurement time. Furthermore, immersion objectives or objective lenses with larger numerical aperture can be utilized to reduce the measurement time for each challenge to under 1s. Our physical characterization of an arbiter PUF can also find the dominant stages in the chain. Measuring a set of dominant stages can make the response prediction much easier. Therefore, this technique can help to improve the PUF behavior by designing and constructing more balanced routes and stages.

# 7   Conclusion

In this work, we demonstrated how photonic emission analysis from the backside of the chip can help us to physically characterize arbiter PUF. The experimental results with minimum number of measurements have shown that the arbiter PUF can be effectively characterized. The comparison between our approach and modeling techniques has shown that our methodology requires far less challenges than modeling attacks. Furthermore, our technique does not require any PUF response. Although we carried out our experiments on a CPLD PUF implementation, the same methodology can be applied to other hardware implementations. As a result, it is revealed that the timing-based PUFs, specifically arbiter PUFs, are vulnerable to photonic emission analysis.

**Acknowledgements.** The authors would like to acknowledge the support of the German Federal Ministry of Education and Research in the project PhotonFX and the Helmholtz Research School on Security Technologies.

# References

1. Altera: MAX V Device Handbook. Altera Corporation, San Jose (2011)
2. Altera: Quartus II Web Edition Software (2013),
   http://www.altera.com/products/software/
   quartus-ii/web-edition/qts-we-index.html
3. Armknecht, F., Maes, R., Sadeghi, A., Standaert, O.X., Wachsmann, C.: A Formalization of the Security Features of Physical Functions. In: 2011 IEEE Symposium on Security and Privacy (SP), pp. 397–412. IEEE (2011)
4. Boit, C.: Fundamentals of Photon Emission (PEM) in Silicon – Electroluminescence for Analysis of Electronic Circuit and Device Functionality. In: Microelectronics Failure Analysis: Desk Reference, p. 356. ASM International (2004)
5. Delvaux, J., Verbauwhede, I.: Fault Injection Modeling Attacks on 65nm Arbiter and RO Sum Pufs via Environmental changes. Tech. rep., Cryptology ePrint Archive: Report 2013/619 (2013), https://eprint.iacr.org/2013/619
6. Delvaux, J., Verbauwhede, I.: Side Channel Modeling Attacks on 65nm Arbiter PUFs Exploiting CMOS Device Noise. In: 2013 IEEE International Symposium on Hardware-Oriented Security and Trust (HOST), pp. 137–142. IEEE (2013)
7. Ferrigno, J., Hlaváč, M.: When AES Blinks: Introducing Optical Side Channel. Information Security, IET 2(3), 94–98 (2008),
   http://dx.doi.org/10.1049/iet-ifs:20080038
8. Gassend, B., Clarke, D., Van Dijk, M., Devadas, S.: Controlled Physical Random Functions. In: Proceedings of the 18th Annual Computer Security Applications Conference 2002, pp. 149–160. IEEE (2002)
9. Gassend, B., Clarke, D., Van Dijk, M., Devadas, S.: Silicon Physical Random Functions. In: Proceedings of the 9th ACM Conference on Computer and Communications Security, pp. 148–160. ACM (2002)
10. Helfmeier, C., Boit, C., Nedospasov, D., Seifert, J.P.: Cloning Physically Unclonable Functions. In: 2013 IEEE International Symposium on Hardware-Oriented Security and Trust (HOST), pp. 1–6. IEEE (2013)
11. Krämer, J., Nedospasov, D., Schlösser, A., Seifert, J.-P.: Differential Photonic Emission Analysis. In: Prouff, E. (ed.) COSADE 2013. LNCS, vol. 7864, pp. 1–16. Springer, Heidelberg (2013)
12. Lee, J.W., Lim, D., Gassend, B., Suh, G.E., Van Dijk, M., Devadas, S.: A Technique to Build a Secret Key in Integrated Circuits for Identification and Authentication Applications. In: 2004 Symposium on VLSI Circuits, Digest of Technical Papers, pp. 176–179. IEEE (2004)
13. Lim, D., Lee, J.W., Gassend, B., Suh, G.E., Van Dijk, M., Devadas, S.: Extracting Secret Keys from Integrated Circuits. IEEE Transactions on Very Large Scale Integration (VLSI) Systems 13(10), 1200–1205 (2005)
14. Maes, R., Van Herrewege, A., Verbauwhede, I.: PUFKY: A Fully Functional PUF-Based Cryptographic Key Generator. In: Prouff, E., Schaumont, P. (eds.) CHES 2012. LNCS, vol. 7428, pp. 302–319. Springer, Heidelberg (2012)
15. Maes, R., Verbauwhede, I.: Physically Unclonable Functions: A Study on the State of the Art and Future Research Directions. In: Towards Hardware-Intrinsic Security, pp. 3–37. Springer (2010)

16. Mahmoud, A., Rührmair, U., Majzoobi, M., Koushanfar, F.: Combined Modeling and Side Channel Attacks on Strong PUFs. Tech. rep., Cryptology ePrint Archive: Report 2013/632 (2013), https://eprint.iacr.org/2013/632
17. Majzoobi, M., Koushanfar, F., Devadas, S.: FPGA PUF using Programmable Delay Lines. In: 2010 IEEE International Workshop on Information Forensics and Security (WIFS), pp. 1–6. IEEE (2010)
18. Merli, D., Schuster, D., Stumpf, F., Sigl, G.: Semi-invasive EM Attack on FPGA RO PUFs and Countermeasures. In: Proceedings of the Workshop on Embedded Systems Security, p. 2. ACM (2011)
19. Nedospasov, D., Schlösser, A., Seifert, J.P., Orlic, S.: Functional Integrated Circuit Analysis. In: 2012 IEEE International Symposium on Hardware-Oriented Security and Trust (HOST), pp. 102–107 (2012)
20. Nedospasov, D., Seifert, J.P., Helfmeier, C., Boit, C.: Invasive PUF Analysis. In: 2013 Workshop on Fault Diagnosis and Tolerance in Cryptography (FDTC), pp. 30–38. IEEE (2013)
21. Oztiirk, E., Hammouri, G., Sunar, B.: Towards Robust Low Cost Authentication for Pervasive Devices. In: Sixth Annual IEEE International Conference on Pervasive Computing and Communications, PerCom 2008, pp. 170–178. IEEE (2008)
22. Parusiński, M., Shariati, S., Kamel, D., Xavier-Standaert, F.: Strong PUFs and their (Physical) Unpredictability: A Case Study with Power PUFs. In: Proceedings of the Workshop on Embedded Systems Security, p. 5. ACM (2013)
23. Rankl, W., Effing, W.: Smart Card Handbook, 4th edn. Wiley (2010)
24. Rührmair, U., Sehnke, F., Sölter, J., Dror, G., Devadas, S., Schmidhuber, J.: Modeling Attacks on Physical Unclonable Functions. In: Proceedings of the 17th ACM Conference on Computer and Communications Security, pp. 237–249. ACM (2010)
25. Rührmair, U., Sölter, J., Sehnke, F.: On the Foundations of Physical Unclonable Functions. IACR Cryptology ePrint Archive 2009, 277 (2009)
26. Sadeghi, A.R., Visconti, I., Wachsmann, C.: Enhancing RFID Security and Privacy by Physically Unclonable Functions. Springer, Heidelberg (2010)
27. Schlösser, A., Dietz, E., Frohmann, S., Orlic, S.: Highly Resolved Spatial and Temporal Photoemission Analysis of Integrated Circuits. Measurement Science and Technology 24(3), 035102 (2013)
28. Schlösser, A., Nedospasov, D., Krämer, J., Orlic, S., Seifert, J.-P.: Simple Photonic Emission Analysis of AES. In: Prouff, E., Schaumont, P. (eds.) CHES 2012. LNCS, vol. 7428, pp. 41–57. Springer, Heidelberg (2012)
29. Škorić, B., Tuyls, P., Ophey, W.: Robust Key Extraction from Physical Uncloneable Functions. In: Ioannidis, J., Keromytis, A.D., Yung, M. (eds.) ACNS 2005. LNCS, vol. 3531, pp. 407–422. Springer, Heidelberg (2005)
30. Skorobogatov, S.: Optical Fault Masking Attacks. In: 2010 Workshop on Fault Diagnosis and Tolerance in Cryptography (FDTC), pp. 23–29. IEEE (2010)
31. Skorobogatov, S.P., Anderson, R.J.: Optical Fault Induction Attacks. In: Kaliski Jr., B.S., Koç, Ç.K., Paar, C. (eds.) CHES 2002. LNCS, vol. 2523, pp. 2–12. Springer, Heidelberg (2003)
32. Suh, G.E., Devadas, S.: Physical Unclonable Functions for Device Authentication and Secret Key Generation. In: Proceedings of the 44th Annual Design Automation Conference, pp. 9–14. ACM (2007)
33. Tuyls, P., Batina, L.: RFID-tags for anti-counterfeiting. In: Pointcheval, D. (ed.) CT-RSA 2006. LNCS, vol. 3860, pp. 115–131. Springer, Heidelberg (2006)

# Bitline PUF: Building Native Challenge-Response PUF Capability into Any SRAM

Daniel E. Holcomb and Kevin Fu

University of Michigan, Ann Arbor MI 48109, USA
{danholcomb,kevinfu}@umich.edu

**Abstract.** Physical Unclonable Functions (PUFs) are specialized circuits with applications including key generation and challenge-response authentication. PUF properties such as low cost and resistance to invasive attacks make PUFs well-suited to embedded devices. Yet, given how infrequently the specialized capabilities of a PUF may be needed, the silicon area dedicated to it is largely idle. This inefficient resource usage is at odds with the cost minimization objective of embedded devices. Motivated by this inefficiency, we propose the Bitline PUF – a novel PUF that uses modified wordline drivers together with SRAM circuitry to enable challenge-response authentication. The number of challenges that can be applied to the Bitline PUF grows exponentially with the number of SRAM rows, and these challenges can be applied at any time without power cycling. This paper presents in detail the workings of the Bitline PUF, and shows that it achieves high throughput, low latency, and uniqueness across instances. Circuit simulations indicate that the Bitline PUF responses have a nominal bit-error-rate (BER) of 0.023 at 1.2 V supply and 27°C, and that BER does not exceed 0.076 when supply voltage is varied from 1.1 V to 1.3 V, or when temperature is varied from 0°C to 80°C. Because the Bitline PUF leverages existing SRAM circuitry, its area overhead is only a single flip-flop and two logic gates per row of SRAM. The combination of high performance and low cost makes the Bitline PUF a promising candidate for commercial adoption and future research.

**Keywords:** VLSI, SRAM, PUFs, Strong PUFs.

## 1 Introduction

An emerging alternative to classical cryptography in embedded systems is the use of physical unclonable functions (PUFs). PUFs use random manufacturing variations constructively, either to generate cryptographic keys, or to implement physical hash functions for challenge-response authentication [32]. The secret key style of PUF is sometimes called a weak PUF, and PUFs capable of challenge-response hashing are sometimes called strong PUFs [7]. We adopt the weak versus strong naming convention for this paper, and further clarify that strong

L. Batina and M. Robshaw (Eds.): CHES 2014, LNCS 8731, pp. 510–526, 2014.

PUF here denotes a circuit that natively provides physical challenge-response hashing, to distinguish it from a weak PUF that is used to key a classical hash function to provide the logical equivalent of a strong PUF.

In this paper we present a novel strong PUF termed the Bitline PUF. The Bitline PUF leverages the storage cells and support circuitry of SRAM to save area cost, and achieves high throughput by using individual SRAM columns as parallel PUFs instances. The main contributions of this paper are as follows:

- We present the first strong PUF that creates responses from contention between cells in pre-existing circuitry.
- We show that adding a small amount of circuitry to SRAM creates a new strong PUF based on bitline contention.
- We present in detail the operation of the Bitline PUF and analyze its throughput, latency.
- We evaluate using circuit simulation the uniqueness, reliability, power consumption, and susceptibility to modeling attacks of the Bitline PUF.

## 2  Static Random-Access Memory

Static Random-Access Memory (SRAM) is a ubiquitous building block of integrated circuits that is found in caches, register files, and buffers. Single VLSI circuits commonly contain millions of bits of SRAM storage. Each bit of SRAM is typically implemented by a single 6-transistor cell (Fig. 1a). An SRAM cell has two stable states, and in each stable state node $A$ or $B$ is pulled high through transistor $p_1$ or $p_2$ while the other is pulled low through $n_1$ or $n_2$. The cell is read and written using complementary bitlines $(BL)$ and $(BLB)$ through two access transistors $n_3$ and $n_4$. The two access transistors of a cell are controlled by a single wordline.

The SRAM cells in a memory are arranged in a matrix of rows and columns (Fig. 1b). SRAM cells in the same column share common bitlines and hence only one cell per column is accessed at any time. SRAM cells in the same row share a wordline but have independent bitlines and are therefore read and written in parallel as data words. Each SRAM column uses support circuitry to read and write its cells. A cell is written by setting one bitline high and the other low and then asserting the wordline to transfer the bitline values to the cell.

An evaluation of the Bitline PUF is similar to an SRAM read operation, and hence a detailed explanation of the SRAM read operation is given here as background. The support circuitry for a read operation comprises precharge logic at the top of each column and a sense amplifier at the bottom (Fig. 1c). Fig. 2a shows the timing of the control signals $(PRE, WL,$ and $RE)$ for a read operation and shows overlaid bitline waveforms from reading cells with different process variations. During an SRAM read operation, both bitlines are first charged and equalized by the precharge circuit at the top of the column. Next, the precharge signal $(PRE)$ goes high to end the precharge phase and the wordline $(WL)$ for a single row is asserted. The wordline connects a cell to the precharged bitlines and

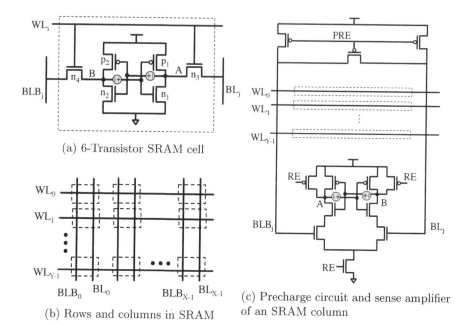

(a) 6-Transistor SRAM cell

(b) Rows and columns in SRAM

(c) Precharge circuit and sense amplifier of an SRAM column

**Fig. 1.** SRAM cells are arranged in a matrix of rows and columns. SRAM rows share wordlines, and columns share bitlines. Each column uses a precharge circuit and a sense amplifier to perform read operations. Note that the circuitry used for writing values to cells is not depicted.

depending on the state of the cell, transistor $n_1$ or $n_2$ will begin to discharge one of the bitlines through the corresponding access transistor. The discharge rate of the bitline varies depending on the random variation of the transistor that is discharging it [8]. A fixed time after the wordline is asserted, a read-enable signal ($RE$) is asserted to activate the sense amplifier. The sense amplifier detects the difference in voltage across the two bitlines and generates from it a digital 0 or 1 value. The digital value in the sense amplifier is the final result of the SRAM read operation, and can be sent out of the SRAM.

# 3    System Description of Proposed Bitline PUF

The proposed Bitline PUF is a novel PUF formulation that borrows much of its circuitry from SRAM. The operation of the Bitline PUF can be viewed as an attempt to read multiple cells in a column at the same time, creating contention that is resolved according to process variation. A challenge is applied to the PUF by pre-loading chosen values into the cells, and choosing the wordlines to concurrently activate. The PUF response is simply the value that the SRAM produces from a read operation when the challenge condition is applied. The Bitline PUF requires additional circuitry to enable the concurrent activation of

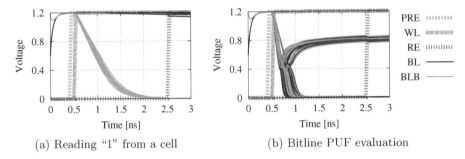

(a) Reading "1" from a cell            (b) Bitline PUF evaluation

**Fig. 2.** SRAM read operation and bitline PUF evaluation use the same control signal timing. The precharge signal (PRE) is asserted to stop charging the bitlines, and the wordline (WL) is asserted to begin the discharging of the bitline. The read enable signal (RE) is asserted 2 ns later to activate the sense amplifier that detects the voltage difference between the two bitlines. The thin lines (BL and BLB) are overlaid plots of the bitline voltages from 30 different trials; only one bitline discharges in the read operation, but in the PUF evaluation both bitlines initially discharge and then stabilize with one high and one low.

multiple wordlines because the capability of activating multiple wordlines has no use in SRAM's traditional tasks of reading, writing, and storing data.

Let the challenge applied to a Bitline PUF be $C : \{c_0, c_1, \ldots, c_{Y-1}\}$, where $Y$ is the number of rows in the SRAM. Each element $c_i$ of the challenge corresponds to SRAM row $i$ as follows, and we say that any row is *active* in a challenge if its corresponding challenge element ($c_i$) is either 0 or 1.

- if $c_i = 0$, then row $i$ is loaded with 0s and $WL_i$ is on during evaluation.
- if $c_i = 1$, then row $i$ is loaded with 1s and $WL_i$ is on during evaluation.
- if $c_i = 2$, then row $i$ is loaded with 0s and $WL_i$ is off during evaluation
- if $c_i = 3$, then row $i$ is loaded with 1s and $WL_i$ is off during evaluation

A single SRAM column constitutes a Bitline PUF with a 1-bit response, and Bitline PUFs are therefore inherently parallel because a challenge is applied concurrently to many SRAM columns. Let a 1-bit PUF at column $i$ be denoted $P_i$, and its response to challenge $C$ be denoted $P_i(C)$. Let an $X$-column Bitline PUF be denoted $P_{0:X-1}$ and its response be $P_{0:X-1}(C) = \{P_0(C), P_1(C), \ldots, P_{X-1}(C)\}$. Note that for simplicity the same challenge is applied to all columns of the SRAM PUF[1]. Therefore, a Bitline PUF with $Y$ rows and $X$ columns has $4^Y$ possible challenges and $2^X$ possible responses.

---

[1] Different challenges can be applied to different columns provided that the challenges agree on which rows are active. This can be particularly useful in the case of inactive rows that retain pre-existing data through a challenge.

## 3.1  Challenge-Response Operation

The sequence of events necessary to operate the Bitline PUF is shown in Fig. 3. The first two phases set up the desired challenge by loading values into SRAM cells and enabling the appropriate wordlines. The final phase evaluates the PUF response by reading the value produced when the challenge is applied. The Bitline PUF evaluation is destructive with respect to active rows only. It is therefore possible to use only some rows of SRAM as part of a Bitline PUF evaluation while others rows are being used as storage. The three phases of operation are described in the following paragraphs.

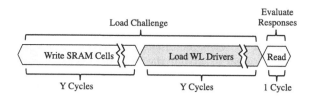

**Fig. 3.** Sequence of operations for evaluating the PUF response to a challenge

**Write Values into SRAM Cells.** The values loaded into the SRAM cells of active rows will determine which transistors will ultimately be used to discharge the bitlines during the evaluation of the PUF response. To load a specific challenge, the cells of each row $i$ are written with the value specified by $c_i$. The SRAM cells, as in other write operations, are written one row at a time, so the time to write all $Y$ rows is $Y$ cycles.

**Load Wordline Drivers Using Accumulators.** The proposed SRAM PUF requires augmentation to the wordline control circuitry so that multiple wordlines can be concurrently enabled during PUF evaluation. In a typical SRAM, an externally supplied $\log_2(Y)$-bit address is decoded to select exactly one of the $Y$ rows for reading; the selected row then uses a clocked driver to set its wordline high at the appropriate time during the clock cycle. The proposed PUF requires multiple wordlines to be concurrently enabled, and this can be accomplished by having at the input of each wordline driver a flip-flop (Fig. 4) that accumulates wordline activation signals. At the start of the second phase of Fig. 3, the accumulator of every wordline is reset. In each of the subsequent $Y$ cycles, a $\log_2(Y)$-bit select signal sets high the flip-flop of one active wordline. Once all flip-flops are appropriately loaded, an evaluation signal passes the loaded values to the wordline drivers, so that multiple wordlines are asserted in the same cycle during the PUF evaluation. One wordline accumulator per SRAM row is the only additional circuitry required to create bitline PUFs from an SRAM.

**Evaluate Responses.** Evaluating the PUF response is identical to an SRAM read operation, except that multiple wordlines are asserted. For each column,

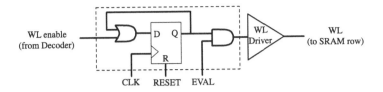

**Fig. 4.** The wordline accumulator circuit enables sequential loading and concurrent activation of wordlines

the cells at any active row will discharge one of the two complementary bitlines, and considering that different cells in the column will discharge each bitline, this causes both bitlines of a column to be discharged during the evaluation. The discharging of bitlines for a variety of challenges are shown in Fig. 2b. While both bitlines initially discharge, there is no stable state in which both bitlines are fully discharged due to the cross-coupled inverters in the active SRAM cells. Contention thus ensues until a stable state is reached with one bitline charged and the other fully discharged. Note that the charged bitline in the stable state does not charge all the way to $V_{dd}$, but only charges to $V_{dd} - V_{th}$ because it is being pulled high by SRAM cells through an NMOS access transistor that causes a voltage drop of $V_{th}$. If the bitlines reach a stable state in the time between the assertion of the wordline and the assertion of the read enable (RE) signal, then the sense amplifier unambiguously detects the large differential voltage of $\pm(V_{dd} - V_{th})$ across the bitlines, and generates a digital output as in a normal SRAM read operation. This output is the response to the applied challenge.

### 3.2 Performance

The three phases of Bitline PUF operation (Fig. 3) define its latency and through-put. All cells are written in $Y$ cycles, all wordline accumulators are loaded in $Y$ additional cycles, and all $X$ columns are evaluated in parallel during a single cycle. Therefore, the latency to obtain an $X$-bit response is $2Y + 1$ cycles and the response throughput is $\frac{X}{2Y+1}$. For a 256-column by 256-row SRAM with a 5ns cycle time, this corresponds to a latency of 2.6 $\mu$s and a response throughput of 99.8 Mbps.

## 4 Methodology

The results in this paper are obtained from circuit simulation using the Ngspice simulator (Rev 25). On account of the long runtimes of large SPICE simulations, the columns of the simulated bitline PUFs have only 16 rows, whereas a real SRAM would typically have hundreds of rows.

### 4.1 Transistor Models and Sizing

Transistor and interconnect models are from the freely-available Predictive Technology Model (PTM). More specifically, the transistor models are BSIM4 PTM

**Table 1.** Transistor sizes and process variation. The transistor sizes used within SRAM cells are adopted from Nii *et al.* [23], and threshold voltage variation depends on transistor size (Eq. 1).

| | | Sizing | | Process Variation | | | |
|---|---|---|---|---|---|---|---|
| | | W [nm] | L [nm] | vth0 [mV] | | lint [nm] | |
| | | | | $\mu$ | $\sigma$ | $\mu$ | $\sigma$ |
| SRAM cell | n1,n2 | 200 | 90 | 397 | 13.4 | 7.5 | 3 |
| | n3,n4 | 140 | 90 | 397 | 16.0 | 7.5 | 3 |
| | p1,p2 | 140 | 90 | -339 | 16.0 | 7.5 | 3 |
| Sense Amp | NMOS | 1000 | 90 | 397 | 6.0 | 7.5 | 3 |
| & Precharge | PMOS | 1000 | 90 | -339 | 6.0 | 7.5 | 3 |

models for a 90 nm process [29]. Transistor sizes are shown in Tab. 1; the six transistors in the SRAM cell are sized to match the design of Nii *et al.* [23], and the transistors in the sense amplifier and precharge circuits are upsized.

### 4.2   Bitline Model

To better represent a real design, the 16 SRAM rows simulated are modeled as being distributed over a typical-length bitline. In this way, the 16 rows can be considered as existing among many others within a realistic-sized SRAM. Keeping with the work of Nii *et al.* [23], we assume for bitline modeling an SRAM with 520 rows and a cell height of 0.72 $\mu m$, for a total length of 374.4 $\mu m$ per bitline. According to the PTM interconnect calculator [30], a 374.4 $\mu m$ local interconnect in 90 nm technology has a total resistance of 183.04 $\Omega$ and capacitance of 69.67 fC. The resistance and capacitance is distributed such that the bitlines between each of pair of adjacent rows is implemented by a wire model with an 11.44 $\Omega$ resistance between two capacitors of 2.17 fC each.

### 4.3   Process Variation

To model process variations from fabrication, random parameter variation is applied to every transistor of each PUF instance. The transistor parameters determining threshold voltage and length are replaced by normally distributed $\mathcal{N}(\mu, \sigma^2)$ random variables. Table 1 shows the mean and standard deviation for each such parameter.

Random dopant fluctuation is represented in transistor parameter vth0. The mean value for threshold voltage is the default value in the transistor model, and the standard deviation depends on transistor geometry according to Eq. 1 [27]; larger devices have less threshold variation than the small devices in the SRAM cells. We use a value of 1.8 $mV\mu m$ for $A_{VT}$ [31].

$$\sigma_{VT} = \frac{A_{VT}}{\sqrt{WL}} \qquad (1)$$

Variations in effective transistor length are represented by changes to parameter `lint`[2]. The nominal value of `lint` is 7.5 nm and its standard deviation is set to 3 nm based on the observation that effective transistor length has a $3\sigma$ value that is 10% of overall transistor length [1]

### 4.4   Modeling Noise

Thermal noise is modeled in SPICE by transient random voltage sources. As represented by small grey circles in Fig. 1a and Fig. 1c, noise sources are added between the cross-coupled state nodes of SRAM cells [34] and sense amplifiers. The magnitude of thermal noise at each node depends on the node capacitance (Eq. 2). The standard deviation of noise for each SRAM cell node is set to 4.5mV, and for each sense amplifier node is 1.7 mV[3].

$$\sigma_{NOISE} = \sqrt{\frac{k_B T}{C}} \qquad (2)$$

## 5   Evaluation

The simulation methodology explained in the previous section is used for experimental evaluation of the Bitline PUF. Uniqueness of responses, and reliability with respect to temperature and supply voltage variation are evaluated. Finally, power consumption and susceptibility to modeling attacks are considered. These experimental results indicate that the Bitline PUF is promising as a reliable and unique strong PUF.[4]

### 5.1   Unbiased Challenges to Elicit Unique Responses

The mixture of $c_i$ values in each challenge can bias PUFs toward producing 0-responses or 1-responses, but ideal challenges should produce either response with equal probability across a population. From a circuit perspective, ideal challenges should discharge both bitlines with equal strength to increase the sensitivity of response to process variations. For a symmetric SRAM cell, where only variation differentiates $n_1$ and $p_1$ from $n_2$ and $p_2$, the two complementary bitlines discharge with equal strength when the same number of NMOS transistors (i.e, $n_1$ or $n_2$ of each active cell) are discharging each one. The challenges that cause this situation are those having an equal number of $c_i = 0$ and $c_i = 1$ values, along with some unspecified mixture of inactive rows with $c_i = 2$ or $c_i = 3$; challenges satisfying this condition are therefore denoted as "unbiased".

---

[2] `lint`, standing for internal length, represents the difference between nominal and effective transistor length

[3] Ngspice source `vxx a an dc 0 trrandom (2 100p 0 1.7m 0)`

[4] All software used in experiments is freely available, and the source code for all experiments in this paper is provided online at
`https://spqr.eecs.umich.edu/papers/Holcomb-bitline-CHES2014.zip`

The heat map of Fig. 5a confirms that unbiased challenges are the ones most likely to elicit different responses from different PUF instances. For each of the 64 squares in the plot, 1000 randomly generated challenges with the specified number of 0s and 1s are created. Each of the challenges is applied to two randomly selected PUF instances to check whether the responses differ. For the unbiased challenges, along the diagonal of Fig. 5a, the responses of the two PUFs differ in roughly half of all trials. For challenges that are slightly biased (i.e. close to the diagonal), the PUFs sometimes produce differing responses. For challenges that are highly biased (e.g. at the upper left and bottom right corners of Fig 5a), all PUF instances produce the same response.

The number of unbiased challenges having exactly $k$ challenge values with $c_i = 0$ and $k$ with $c_i = 1$ is given by $n'_k(Y)$ (Eq. 3). The number of total unbiased challenges with any number of $c_i = 0$ and $c_i = 1$ values is given by $n(Y)$ (Eq. 4). The number of unbiased challenges is exponential in the number of rows $Y$ (i.e. the challenge size). Therefore, an adversary cannot hope to mimic a PUF by simply recording all challenge-response pairs, and must instead resort to predicting responses using a parametric model [17,33] (see Sec. 5.4).

$$n'_k(Y) = \binom{Y}{k} * \binom{Y-k}{k} \tag{3}$$

$$n(Y) = \sum_{k=1\ldots\frac{Y}{2}} n'_k(Y) \tag{4}$$

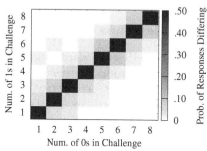
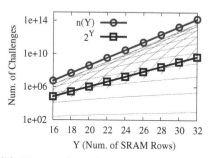

(a) Challenges with an equal number of 0 and 1 values are termed unbiased

(b) The number of unbiased challenges is exponential in the number of SRAM rows

**Fig. 5.** Challenges with equal numbers of 0 and 1 values are most likely to produce different responses across PUF instances. We refer to these challenges as unbiased. The number of unbiased challenges grows exponentially in the number of SRAM rows; this is depicted at right where $Y$ is the number of rows and $n(Y)$ (Eq. 4) is the number of unbiased challenges. The thin lines at right depict $n'_k(Y)$ (Eq. 3), the number of unbiased challenges with exactly $k$ 0s and $k$ 1s, for all values of $k$.

## 5.2   Within-Class and Between-Class Hamming Distances

A single PUF should always respond to the same challenge similarly, and two PUF instances should never respond to the same unbiased challenges similarly. For a challenge $C$, a comparison of two responses from the same PUF is denoted "within-class", and a comparison of responses from two different PUFs is denoted "between-class." Hamming distance (Eq. 5) is used to quantify the similarity of responses in each between-class or within-class comparison. Within-class distances are a measure of unreliability, and between-class distances are a measure of uniqueness.

Within-class and between-class Hamming distances are evaluated experimentally on 32-column bitline PUFs. For each of 200 random unbiased challenges, 5 PUF instances are generated and the challenge is applied 6 times to each. Within-class distances are obtained by comparing the responses of the same PUF to the same challenge, and between-class distances are obtained by comparing the response of different PUFs to the same challenge. The separability of within-class and between-class Hamming distances (Fig. 6) implies that responses are unique across Bitline PUF instances. The average within-class Hamming distance is 0.75 for a 32-bit response, and the average between-class distance is 16.01.

$$\mathrm{HD}(P_{0:X-1}, P'_{0:X-1}, C) = \sum_{i=0...X-1} P_i(C) \oplus P'_i(C) \tag{5}$$

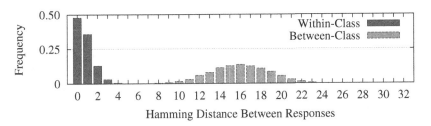

**Fig. 6.** Within-class and between-class Hamming distances for 32-bit PUF responses. The separation between the distributions shows uniqueness of instances.

## 5.3   Sensitivity to Supply Voltage and Temperature Variations

A PUF response should not be highly sensitive to changes in supply voltage or temperature, as this would restrict its useful application to tightly controlled environments. PUF responses at the nominal operating conditions of 1.2 V supply and 27°C are compared against a variety of temperatures from 0°C to 80°C and supply voltages from 1.1 V to 1.3 V (Fig. 7). For each comparison 10,000 random PUF instances are created. For each instance, a randomly chosen unbiased challenge is applied to the PUF at both conditions; the BER is the fraction of these 10,000 trials in which the two responses differ. While changing supply voltage

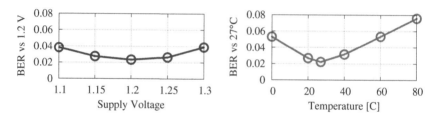

**Fig. 7.** Bit error rate of responses when one is collected at nominal conditions of 1.2 V and 27°C, and the second at a different supply voltage or temperature.

or temperature does increase the BER of responses, at all tested conditions the BER remains less than 0.076.

## 5.4   Modeling Attacks

The Bitline PUF is susceptible to modeling attacks if the challenge-response pairs (CRPs) can be observed, and therefore care must be taken to avoid or obfuscate the CRPs of the Bitline PUF. Otherwise, an adversary can use a parametric model to predict the PUF response to any challenge [17,33], without needing a dictionary of all possible challenge response pairs.

We demonstrate a modeling attack on bitline PUFs using support vector machine (SVM) classification. The task of the SVM classifier is, after training on some number of observed CRPs, to correctly predict responses to new challenges. To use SVM classification, each CRP is converted to a pair $(x, y) \,|\, x \in \{0, 1\}^{4Y}, y \in \{-1, +1\}$ where $Y$ is the number of rows in the PUF and the number of values in the challenge. In the pair $(x, y)$, $x$ represents the challenge and is determined according to Eq. 6, while $y$ represents the response of the PUF to the challenge. Note that for SVM classification, negative responses are entered as the value -1 instead of 0.

$$
x_{4i:4i+3} = \begin{cases} 1,0,0,0 & \text{if } c_i == 0 \\ 0,1,0,0 & \text{if } c_i == 1 \\ 0,0,1,0 & \text{if } c_i == 2 \\ 0,0,0,1 & \text{if } c_i == 3 \end{cases} \tag{6}
$$

Fig. 8 shows the prediction accuracy of SVM classification using the tool $SVM^{light}$ [13], applied to three different bitline PUF instances. For each PUF instance, 1000 CRPs are collected and cross-validation is used to examine how the prediction accuracy varies with the size of the training set. After 500 CRPs are observed, responses can be predicted with approximately 90% accuracy. While for clarity only three PUFs are plotted in Fig. 8, these three results are typical of observed prediction accuracy trends for bitline PUFs.

Parametric models exist for many PUFs including the arbiter PUF [17,33]. Yet, the practical usefulness of PUFs with parametric models is not diminished

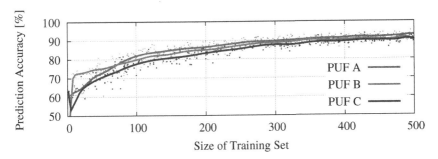

**Fig. 8.** Modeling attacks are possible if the challenge-response pairs of bitline PUFs are not protected. The data points in the plot are cross-validation results for prediction accuracy using support vector machine classification, and the curves are fit lines for the results.

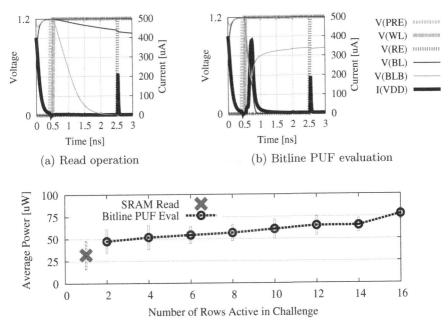

(a) Read operation

(b) Bitline PUF evaluation

(c) Average power versus number of active rows. Error bars mark the standard deviation over 100 trials.

**Fig. 9.** While a bitline PUF is metastable, there exists a current path from supply to ground through active SRAM cells. The average power of a bitline PUF evaluation therefore exceeds that of an SRAM read operation, and increases with the number of active cells in a challenge.

because modeling resistance can be assured through obfuscating or preventing access to the PUF responses [36]. The Bitline PUF is uniquely suited to protection via access control because it uses ordinary SRAM, and as such can employ SRAM access protection mechanisms including ARM TrustZone [2].

## 5.5    Power Consumption

The power consumption of a bitline PUF evaluation is higher than that of a standard SRAM read operation. More specifically, a bitline PUF draws significant current during metastability when the bitline potentials are approximately equal. During metastability, all of the cells that are active in the challenge are drawing current, either through $p_1$ and $n_2$, or else through $p_2$ and $n_1$.

Fig. 9a shows a normal SRAM read operation and its current draw; the most significant instantaneous currents are consumed when the bitlines are precharged, and when the sense amplifier turns on. During a bitline PUF evaluation (Fig. 9b), an additional third current spike is observed during metastability. The power consumed by a bitline PUF evaluation depends on the size of this current spike. When more cells are active, there is a potential for larger instantaneous current and therefore higher power. Fig. 9c shows that average power increases with the number of rows that are active in a challenge.

# 6    Related Work

Strong PUFs are marked by the ability to map challenges to responses according to a function determined by random physical variations. The first such PUF was based on optical scattering [26], but the practicality of strong PUFs increased with the invention of silicon PUFs that can be integrated in VLSI circuits. The first and best-known silicon PUFs are delay-based PUFs [6] including the arbiter PUF [16] and variants thereof [21,18].

The Bitline PUF shares many similarities with two particular strong PUFs – the bistable ring PUF [5] and a low power current-based PUF [20]. The similarity to the bistable ring PUF is the use of controllable electrical contention that resolves to one of two states according to variation. The similarity to the current-based PUF is the use of a sense amplifier to detect a differential signal from a controllable set of variation-sensitive elements; the significant difference is that the Bitline PUF uses pre-existing variation-sensitive elements (SRAM cells) and sense amplifiers.

Weak PUFs do not perform challenge-response hashing, but instead function as physically obfuscated keys. Weak PUFs can either use special purpose variation-sensitive circuits or clever ways of detecting variations in existing circuits. Examples of custom-circuit weak PUFs include designs based on variations in drain currents [19], stabilization of cross-coupled devices [35], stabilization of cross-coupled devices in the presence of delay variations [22], and the skewed tendencies of sense amplifiers [3]. Examples of weak PUFs utilizing variations in existing circuitry include ones based on clock skew [14,37] and random flash memory latencies [28].

Several prior works have proposed PUFs based on ordinary or slightly modified SRAM. A common mechanism used by SRAM PUFs is the uniqueness of power-up state [11,7]. The reliability of SRAM power-up state PUFs can be enhanced by detecting and using only cells with large mismatch [10], or by electrically biasing cells to reinforce inherent tendencies [4]. Aside from power-up state, a PUF can be created from ordinary SRAM using unique minimum data retention voltage signatures [12] or failure signatures from attempted writes at low voltages [38]. PUF mechanisms in modified SRAM arrays include unique signatures based on error locations under varied wordline duty cycles [15], and the resolution of SRAM cells under a non-standard metastable write [24]. The significant difference between the Bitline PUF and prior SRAM-based PUFs is that the Bitline PUF generates responses based on mismatch across the cells within a column, instead of just mismatch within a single SRAM cell.

# 7 Future work

As this work is the first to propose the Bitline PUF, there are many interesting directions that warrant future research. The reliability of Bitline PUF responses with respect to circuit aging should be considered, as well as its susceptibility to cloning attacks [25,9]. For SRAM with asymmetric cells or timing mismatch in the wordline drivers, unbiased challenges may not be those with an equal number of 0 and 1 values, and future work can consider the problem of finding challenges to maximize the uniqueness of responses in these cases. Finally, we will look to fabricate an SRAM with the wordline accumulator circuits that are required for bitline PUF operation, and use data from this implementation to further evaluate the Bitline PUF.

# 8 Conclusion

This work presents a new PUF design termed the Bitline PUF. The Bitline PUF is a low cost solution that shares most of its circuitry with SRAM, and is created by adding two logic gates and a flip-flop to the wordline driver of each SRAM row to enable challenge-response hashing. The Bitline PUF, applied to a SRAM of typical size, has a response latency of 2.6 $\mu s$ and response throughput of 99.8 Mbps. Circuit simulation indicates that responses produced by the Bitline PUF in 90 nm technology have a nominal bit error rate of 0.023, and that the bit error rate does not exceed 0.076 for any supply voltage between 1.1 V and 1.3 V, or temperature between 0°C and 80°C.

**Acknowledgment.** This work was supported in part by C-FAR, one of six centers of STARnet, a Semiconductor Research Corporation program sponsored by MARCO and DARPA, and by NSF CNS-1331652. Any opinions, findings, conclusions, and recommendations expressed in these materials are those of the authors and do not necessarily reflect the views of the sponsors.

# References

1. Anis, M., Aburahma, M.H.: Leakage Current Variability in Nanometer Technologies. In: 2005 Proceedings of the Fifth International Workshop on System-on-Chip for Real-Time Applications, pp. 60–63 (2005)

2. ARM Limited. ARM Security Technology: Building a secure system using trust-zone technology,
   http://infocenter.arm.com/help/topic/com.arm.doc.prd29-genc-009492c/
   PRD29-GENC-009492C_trustzone_security_whitepaper.pdf
   (last Viewed June 13, 2014)
3. Bhargava, M., Cakir, C., Mai, K.: Attack Resistant Sense Amplifier Based PUFs (SA-PUF) with Deterministic and Controllable Reliability of PUF Responses. In: 2010 IEEE International Symposium on Hardware-Oriented Security and Trust, HOST (2010)
4. Bhargava, M., Cakir, C., Mai, K.: Reliability Enhancement of bi-stable PUFs in 65nm Bulk CMOS. In: 2012 IEEE International Symposium on Hardware-Oriented Security and Trust (HOST), pp. 25–30 (2012)
5. Chen, Q., Csaba, G., Lugli, P., Schlichtmann, U., Rührmair, U.: The Bistable Ring PUF: A New Architecture for Strong Physical Unclonable Functions. In: 2011 IEEE International Symposium on Hardware-Oriented Security and Trust (HOST), pp. 134–141 (2011)
6. Gassend, B., Clarke, D., Van Dijk, M.: Silicon Physical Random Functions. In: Proceedings of the 9th ACM Conference on Computer and Communications Security, pp. 148–160 (2002)
7. Guajardo, J., Kumar, S.S., Schrijen, G.-J., Tuyls, P.: FPGA Intrinsic PUFs and Their use for IP Protection. In: Paillier, P., Verbauwhede, I. (eds.) CHES 2007. LNCS, vol. 4727, pp. 63–80. Springer, Heidelberg (2007)
8. Heald, R., Wang, P.: Variability in Sub-100nm SRAM Designs. In: IEEE/ACM International Conference on Computer Aided Design, ICCAD-2004, pp. 347–352 (2004)
9. Helfmeier, C., Boit, C., Nedospasov, D., Seifert, J.P.: Cloning Physically Unclonable Functions. In: 2013 IEEE International Symposium on Hardware-Oriented Security and Trust (HOST), pp. 1–6 (2013)
10. Hofer, M., Boehm, C.: An Alternative to Error Correction for SRAM-like PUFs. In: Mangard, S., Standaert, F.-X. (eds.) CHES 2010. LNCS, vol. 6225, pp. 335–350. Springer, Heidelberg (2010)
11. Holcomb, D.E., Burleson, W.P., Fu, K.: Power-up SRAM State as an Identifying Fingerprint and Source of True Random Numbers. IEEE Transactions on Computers (2009)
12. Holcomb, D.E., Rahmati, A., Salajegheh, M., Burleson, W.P., Fu, K.: DRV-Fingerprinting: Using Data Retention Voltage of SRAM Cells for Chip Identification. In: Hoepman, J.-H., Verbauwhede, I. (eds.) RFIDSec 2012. LNCS, vol. 7739, pp. 165–179. Springer, Heidelberg (2013)
13. Joachims, T.: Making Large-Scale SVM Learning Practical. In: Schölkopf, B., Burges, C., Smola, A. (eds.) Advances in Kernel Methods - Support Vector Learning, pp. 169–184. MIT Press, Cambridge (1999)
14. Kohno, T., Broido, A., Claffy, K.: Remote Physical Device Fingerprinting. In: 2005 IEEE Symposium on Security and Privacy, pp. 211–225 (2005)
15. Krishna, A.R., Narasimhan, S., Wang, X., Bhunia, S.: MECCA: A Robust Low-overhead PUF Using Embedded Memory Array. In: Preneel, B., Takagi, T. (eds.) CHES 2011. LNCS, vol. 6917, pp. 407–420. Springer, Heidelberg (2011)
16. Lee, J.W., Lim, D., Gassend, B., Suh, G.E., Van Dijk, M., Devadas, S.: A Technique to Build a Secret Key in Integrated Circuits for Identification and Authentication Applications. In: 2004 Symposium on VLSI Circuits, 2004. Digest of Technical Papers, pp. 176–179 (2004)

17. Lim, D.: Extracting Secret Keys from Integrated Circuits. MS thesis, Massachusetts Institute of Technology (May 2004)
18. Lin, L., Holcomb, D.E., Krishnappa, D.K., Shabadi, P., Burleson, W.P.: Low-power Sub-threshold Design of Secure Physical Unclonable Functions. In: ISLPED 2010: Proceedings of the 16th ACM/IEEE International Symposium on Low Power Electronics and Design (August 2010)
19. Lofstrom, K., Daasch, W.: IC Identification Circuit Using Device Mismatch. In: International Solid State Circuits Conference, pp. 372–373 (2000)
20. Majzoobi, M., Ghiaasi, G., Koushanfar, F., Nassif, S.R.: Ultra-low Power Current-based PUF. In: 2011 IEEE International Symposium on Circuits and Systems (ISCAS), pp. 2071–2074 (2011)
21. Majzoobi, M., Koushanfar, F., Potkonjak, M.: Lightweight Secure PUFs. In: IEEE/ACM International Conference on Computer-Aided Design, ICCAD 2008, pp. 670–673 (2008)
22. Mathew, S.K., Satpathy, S.K., Anders, M.A., Kaul, H., Hsu, S.K., Agarwal, A., Chen, G.K., Parker, R.J., Krishnamurthy, R.K., De, V.: A 0.19pJ/b PVT-variation-Tolerant Hybrid Physically Unclonable Function Circuit for 100% Stable Secure Key Generation in 22nm CMOS. In: 2014 IEEE International Solid-State Circuits Conference Digest of Technical Papers (ISSCC), pp. 278–279 (2014)
23. Nii, K., Tsukamoto, Y., Yoshizawa, T., Imaoka, S., Yamagami, Y., Suzuki, T., Shibayama, A., Makino, H., Iwade, S.: A 90-nm Low-power 32-kB Embedded SRAM with Gate Leakage Suppression Circuit for Mobile Applications. IEEE Journal of Solid-State Circuits 39(4), 684–693 (2004)
24. Okumura, S., Yoshimoto, S., Kawaguchi, H., Yoshimoto, M.: A 128-bit Chip Identification Generating Scheme Exploiting SRAM Bitcells with Failure Rate of $4.45*10^{-19}$. In: Proceedings of the 37th European Solid-State Circuits Conference, pp. 527–530 (2011)
25. Oren, Y., Sadeghi, A.-R., Wachsmann, C.: On the Effectiveness of the Remanence Decay Side-channel to Clone Memory-based PUFs. In: Bertoni, G., Coron, J.-S. (eds.) CHES 2013. LNCS, vol. 8086, pp. 107–125. Springer, Heidelberg (2013)
26. Pappu, R., Recht, B., Taylor, J.: Physical One-Way Functions. Science (2002)
27. Pelgrom, M.J.M., Duinmaijer, A.C.J., Welbers, A.P.G.: Matching Properties of MOS Transistors. IEEE Journal of Solid-State Circuits 24(5), 1433–1439 (1989)
28. Prabhu, P., Akel, A., Grupp, L.M., Yu, W.-K.S., Suh, G.E., Kan, E., Swanson, S.: Extracting Device Fingerprints from Flash Memory by Exploiting Physical Variations. In: McCune, J.M., Balacheff, B., Perrig, A., Sadeghi, A.-R., Sasse, A., Beres, Y. (eds.) Trust 2011. LNCS, vol. 6740, pp. 188–201. Springer, Heidelberg (2011)
29. Predictive Technology Model. 90nm NMOS and PMOS BSIM4 Models, http://ptm.asu.edu/modelcard/2006/90nm_bulk.pm (last Viewed June 13, 2014)
30. Predictive Technology Model. Interconnect, http://ptm.asu.edu/interconnect.html (last Viewed June 13, 2014)
31. Qazi, M., Tikekar, M., Dolecek, L., Shah, D., Chandrakasan, A.: Loop Flattening & Spherical Sampling: Highly Efficient Model Reduction Techniques for SRAM Yield Analysis. In: DATE 2010: Proceedings of the Conference on Design, Automation and Test in Europe (March 2010)
32. Rührmair, U., Holcomb, D.E.: PUFs at a Glance. In: DATE 2014: Proceedings of the Conference on Design, Automation and Test in Europe (March 2014)

33. Rührmair, U., Sehnke, F., Sölter, J., Dror, G., Devadas, S., Schmidhuber, J.: Modeling Attacks on Physical Unclonable Functions. In: CCS 2010: Proceedings of the 17th ACM Conference on Computer and Communications Security (2010)
34. Seevinck, E., List, F.J., Lohstroh, J.: Static-noise Margin Analysis of MOS SRAM cells. IEEE Journal of Solid-State Circuits 22(5), 748–754 (1987)
35. Su, Y., Holleman, J., Otis, B.: A 1.6 pj/bit 96% Stable chip-ID Generating Circuit Using Process Variations. In: International Solid State Circuits Conference, pp. 406–407 (2007)
36. Suh, G.E., Devadas, S.: Physical Unclonable Functions for Device Authentication and Secret Key Generation. In: DAC 2007: Proceedings of the 44th Annual Design Automation Conference (2007)
37. Yao, Y., Kim, M., Li, J., Markov, I.L., Koushanfar, F.: ClockPUF: Physical Unclonable Functions Based on Clock Networks. In: DATE 2013: Proceedings of the Conference on Design, Automation and Test in Europe, pp. 422–427 (2013)
38. Zheng, Y., Hashemian, M.S., Bhunia, S.: RESP: A Robust Physical Unclonable Function Retrofitted into Embedded SRAM Array. In: DAC 2013: Proceedings of the 50th Annual Design Automation Conference (2013)

# Embedded Evaluation of Randomness in Oscillator Based Elementary TRNG

Viktor Fischer[1] and David Lubicz[2,3]

[1] Laboratoire Hubert Curien, Université Jean Monnet, Université de Lyon,
F-42000 Saint-Etienne, France
[2] DGA-Maîtrise de l'information, BP 7419, F-35174 Bruz, France
[3] Intitut de Mathématiques de Rennes, Université de Rennes 1, Campus de Beaulieu,
F-35042 Rennes, France

**Abstract.** Jittery clock signals produced in oscillators, particularly in ring oscillators are commonly used as a source of randomness in true random number generators (TRNG). The robustness of the generators, and hence their security, is closely linked to the entropy of the generated bit stream, which depends on the size of the jitter. Known jitter size can be used as an input parameter in a stochastic model for the estimation of entropy. Good entropy management can guarantee the security of the generator. We propose a simple precise method for measuring jitter that can be easily embedded in logic devices. It can be used to calibrate an oscillator based TRNG and/or for assessment of the entropy rate while the TRNG is in operation. The method was thoroughly evaluated in simulations and hardware tests and we show that despite its simplicity and small area requirements, it enables the jitter to be measured with an error of less than 5 %.

**Keywords:** hardware random number generators, ring oscillators, jitter model, entropy, statistical tests.

## 1 Introduction

Random numbers play a crucial role in modern cryptography: they are used as confidential keys, initialization vectors, padding values, and also as random masks in side-channel attack countermeasures. Since the era of Kerckhoff, cryptographic algorithms have been designed to be secure so that even if their principle is known by adversaries, useful information cannot be accessed without knowledge of the secret key. The security of modern cryptographic systems using approved cryptographic algorithms is thus based on the confidentiality of the cryptographic keys generated in random number generators. If the secret key is compromised, the whole cryptographic system may be compromised.

This is why random number generators have attracted the attention of researchers, especially in last two decades. Nevertheless, designing a good true random number generator (TRNG) that can be easily implemented in logic devices is still a challenge, mainly because digital integrated circuits offer only a

L. Batina and M. Robshaw (Eds.): CHES 2014, LNCS 8731, pp. 527–543, 2014.

limited choice of sources of randomness, such as clock jitter [14], metastability [19], oscillatory metastability [18], write collisions in dual-port RAMs [7] or random initialization of a bi-stable circuit [16]. Furthermore, most of these sources are very sensitive to variations in environmental conditions. This makes even a seamlessly good TRNG vulnerable to attacks [12].

Although some published designs were said to be provably secure, it turned out that they cannot resist some active attacks [2]. Instead of relying on the robustness of the proposed principles, designers should thus propose efficient, on-line tests that are capable of rapidly detecting any deviation from normal behavior. Unfortunately, high quality standard statistical tests [13] are too slow and too expensive.

The aim of this paper is to provide a simple efficient way to evaluate the source of randomness directly in the device and to estimate on-line the entropy of the generated signal in a dedicated and consequently efficient and rapid statistical test.

Very few methods of the embedded measurement of the clock jitter as a source of randomness were published up to now. Moreover, they are complex and not aimed for cryptography [20] or they cannot distinguish the jitter coming from the thermal noise from that coming from the flicker noise that is known to be autocorrelated [17].

*Our contribution*

1. We propose an original, simple, precise method of jitter measurement that can be implemented inside logic devices.
2. We demonstrate that together with a suitable statistical model (e. g. [1]), the measured jitter can be used to estimate entropy at the output of the generator.
3. We show that the proposed entropy estimator can serve as a basis for a rapid on-line dedicated statistical test, that is perfectly adapted to the generator's principle. This approach complies with recent recommendations for evaluation of TRNGs [10].

*Organization of the paper:* in Section 2, we discuss basic security requirements for random number generators in cryptography. In Section 3, we describe an elementary oscillator-based random number generator and its characteristics. Section 4 is dedicated to the new randomness evaluation method, which is then evaluated by simulations in Section 5. In Section 6 we describe the implementation of the method in hardware. We discuss our results in Section 7 and in Section 8 we draw some conclusions.

# 2    Security Requirements on RNGs in Cryptography

Security of a TRNG design must be thoroughly evaluated [5]. Namely, two security requirements must be fulfilled:

- *The statistical quality of generated numbers* guarantees that attacks can only succeed by using an exhaustive search for the secret.
- *Unpredictability* means that even knowing the last generator's output, no other output can be predicted with non-negligible probability in a forward or backward direction.

While the statistical quality of the generated numbers is relatively easy to verify, evaluating unpredictability is not straightforward, since it cannot be measured or tested. The entropy (and thus unpredictability) can only be estimated using a *stochastic model*.

A perfect generator should be *robust against environmental fluctuations, aging and attacks*. In practice, perfect and permanent robustness against attacks and manipulations cannot be reached. Even a generator that is robust to all known attacks may be vulnerable to new attacks in the future. The only way to ensure long term resistance against attacks is to *execute permanently dedicated on-line tests* able to detect, quickly and reliably, even temporary reduction of the entropy rate. Embedded tests must be based on existing stochastic model having, as an input parameter, the size of the physical phenomenon that is used as a source of entropy (e. g. the clock jitter).

We can conclude that permanent evaluation of the entropy contents of the raw binary signal, which is the main objective of this paper, will ensure all security requirements are respected.

# 3 Elementary Oscillator-Based Random Number Generator

In this section, we present a structure called an elementary oscillator-based TRNG (EO TRNG). This structure is useful for several reasons: (1) it is simple enough so that a comprehensive and relatively simple statistical model can be created (see [1]); (2) it can be used as a basic building block for almost an entire class of oscillator-based TRNGs; (3) it can be used as a construction element for a scalable TRNG.

## 3.1 Definition of the Elementary Oscillator-Based TRNG

An elementary oscillator-based TRNG is composed of two oscillators, $Osc_i$ for $i = 1, 2$. The output of one oscillator is used to determine the instants of sampling the output of the second one in a sampling unit, e. g. a synchronous D flip-flop (see Figure 1). The frequency of the sampling oscillator is divided by $K_D$. The division factor $K_D$ makes it possible to determine the time interval needed to accumulate the phase jitter to a sufficient extent, to ensure a suitable entropy rate in the TRNG output bit stream. In the rest of the paper, we suppose that $Osc_1$ is the oscillator generating the sampled signal and that oscillator $Osc_2$ generates the sampling clock signal.

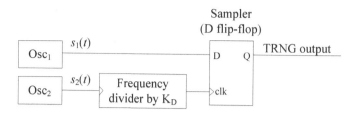

**Fig. 1.** *Structure of an oscillator-based elementary TRNG*

For $i = 1, 2$, the output signal of $Osc_i$ is given by a periodic function of time $t$ that takes the form

$$s_i(t) = f(\omega_i(t + \xi_i(t))),\tag{1}$$

where $f$ can generally be any real valued function with period 1. In our case, we suppose that we are dealing with TRNG implementation in logic devices and therefore for $\alpha \in [0, 1)$, we define $f_\alpha$ as a specific real valued 1-periodic function such that $f_\alpha(x) = 1$ for all $0 < x < \alpha$ and $f_\alpha(x) = 0$ for $\alpha < x < 1$, and $f_\alpha(0) = f_\alpha(\alpha) = 1/2$. We use $f_\alpha$ as a convenient model for the digital clock signal produced by a clock generator and in particular by a ring oscillator. Note that the clock edge is not necessarily in the middle of the interval $[0, 1)$, since oscillators can often have imbalanced half periods. We do not consider amplitude fluctuations in our model since their contribution to phase jitter is negligible in clock signal generation as explained in [11, p. 134].

In practice, we accept that the frequencies of both signals $s_i(t)$, $i = 1, 2$, fluctuate. Therefore, $\omega_i$ is the *mean frequency* of the signal $s_i(t)$, $(\omega_i(t + \xi_i(t)))$ is the *phase* of the oscillator and the function $\xi_i(t)$ represents the *absolute phase drift*. Similarly, $T_i = 1/\omega_i$ is the mean period of $s_i(t)$. The parameter $\zeta = \omega_1/\omega_2$ is the *relative mean frequency* of the elementary TRNG.

As we mainly deal with the relative phase between $Osc_1$ and $Osc_2$, we make the simplifying assumption that $Osc_1$ is a perfectly stable oscillator and that all the phase drift of the elementary TRNG comes from $Osc_2$, so that we have $\xi_1 = 0$ and we would like to characterize the phase jitter $\xi_2 = \xi$.

As shown in [1], the evolution of the phase can be modeled by an *ergodic stationary Markov process* $\Phi(t)$: for any time $t, t_0$, such that $t \geq t_0$, the phase $\Phi(t)$ determined by the initial value $\Phi(t_0) = x_0$ follows a probability distribution depending only on $\Delta t = t - t_0$ with mean $\xi(t_0) + \mu(\Delta t)$ and variance $V(\Delta t)$ where $V, \mu$ are real valued functions. In the following, we only consider a realization $\xi(t)$ of $\Phi(t)$ and use the stationarity of the process to compute probabilities, which are independent of the time of the realization. For instance, as $\mathbb{P}\{\Phi(t_0 + \Delta t) - x_0 \leq x | \Phi(t_0) = x_0\}$ is independent of $t_0$, this probability can be computed by taking the probability over $t_0$ of the realization: $\mathbb{P}_{t_0}\{\xi(t_0 + \Delta t) - \xi(t_0) \leq x\}$.

As $s_2(t) = f_\alpha(\omega_2(t + \xi(t)))$ where $\omega_2$ is the mean frequency of $s_2$, we deduce that $\mu(\Delta t) = \omega_2 \Delta t$. Thus, if the Markov process is Gaussian (i.e. $\frac{d}{dx}\mathbb{P}\{\Phi(t) \leq x | \Phi(t_0) = x_0\}$ is a Gaussian distribution), it is completely determined by $V(\Delta t)$.

The random walk component of the phase jitter is produced by noise sources which affect each transition *independently*. This component is described by a Gaussian probability distribution of variance $\sigma_0^2 \Delta t$.

Other noise sources, such as the $1/f^\beta$ noises, where $0 < \beta < 2$, also contribute to phase jitter. Unfortunately, they are usually autocorrelated. Moreover, because their variance depends quadratically on the jitter accumulation time interval, after longer accumulation, they dominate the jitter coming from the thermal noise. For this reason, the accumulation time should be as short as possible, but long enough to obtain a measurable jitter. In practice, both uncorrelated and correlated noise sources exist and a typical log-log plot of $V(\Delta t)$ versus the measurement delay $\Delta t$ can be used to separate regions with slope 1 and 2 as explained in [8].

# 4   Randomness Evaluation Method

In this section, we present a kind of Monte Carlo method to recover the probability density function $\frac{d}{dx}\mathbb{P}\{\Phi(t) \le x | \Phi(t_0) = x_0\}$ of the jitter accumulated during time interval $\Delta t$ from knowledge of an output bit sequence of an elementary oscillator-based TRNG depicted in Figure 1 with $K_D = 1$ so that the mean frequency of the sampling signal is $\omega_2$. For $n \in \mathbb{N}^*$, let $(t_j)_{j \in \{1,...,n\}}$ be the time sequence and $(b_j)_{j \in \{1,...,n\}})$ be the output bit sequence corresponding to the rising edges of $Osc_2$ as depicted in Fig. 2. Recall that the sampled signal is $s_1(t) = f_\alpha(\omega_1 t)$ for $\alpha \in [0,1)$ and that by definition $t_j = jT_2 - \xi(t_j)$.

Next, we introduce a notation of $\epsilon$-uniformity that we use in the remainder of the paper. It uses the modulo operation on real numbers illustrated in Fig. 2: for all $x \in \mathbb{R}$ and $T \in \mathbb{R}$, let $x \mod T = x - \max\{i \in \mathbb{Z} | x - iT \ge 0\}T$.

**Fig. 2.** *Relation between the sampling process and function* $f_\alpha(\cdot)$

Let $J$ be a subset of $\{1, \ldots, n\}$ and $\epsilon > 0$, we say that the distribution of samples $\{(jT_2 - \xi(t_j)) \mod T_1\}_{j \in J}$ is $\epsilon$-uniform if for all $[a, b] \subset [0, T_1]$, we have:

$$\left| \frac{\#\{j \in J | (jT_2 - \xi(t_j)) \mod T_1 \in [a, b]\}}{\#J} - \frac{b - a}{T_1} \right| < \epsilon.$$

In other words, the number of samples in interval $[a, b]$ inside the translated period $T_1$, over the number of samples in subset $J$ is $\epsilon$-close to the size of interval $[a, b]$ over period $T_1$. With this definition, we can state the following fact:

**Fact 1** *Let $N \in \mathbb{N}$ and for $i \in \{1, \ldots, n - N + 1\}$, we set $S_i = \{i, \ldots, i + N - 1\}$. Let $\epsilon > 0$ be such that for all $i \in \{1, \ldots, n - N + 1\}$ the distribution of samples $\{(jT_2 - \xi(t_j)) \mod T_1\}_{j \in S_i}$ is $\epsilon$-uniform. Let $N \in \mathbb{N}$ be small enough so that the differences between successive values $\delta(j) = \xi(t_{j+M}) - \xi(t_j)$ are negligible (in other words, the value of $\delta(j)$ is almost constant, but sufficiently big) when $j$ runs across all the elements of $S_i$ for a fixed $i \in \{1, \ldots, n - N - M + 1\}$. For $i_0 \in \{1, \ldots, n - N - M + 1\}$, we define*

$$\mathbb{P}_{S_{i_0}}\{b_j \neq b_{j+M}\} = \frac{\#\{j \in S_{i_0} | b_j \neq b_{j+M}\}}{\#S_{i_0}}.$$

*We see that if $(MT_2 + \xi(t_{i_0}) - \xi(t_{i_0+M})) \mod T_1 \leq \min(\alpha T_1, (1 - \alpha)T_1)$, then*

$$\left| \mathbb{P}_{S_{i_0}}\{b_j \neq b_{j+M}\} - \left( \frac{2(MT_2 + \xi(t_{i_0}) - \xi(t_{i_0+M}))}{T_1} \mod 1 \right) \right| < \epsilon,$$

*if $(MT_2 + \xi(t_{i_0}) - \xi(t_{i_0+M})) \mod T_1 \geq \max(\alpha T_1, (1 - \alpha)T_1)$, then*

$$\left| \mathbb{P}_{S_{i_0}}\{b_j \neq b_{j+M}\} + \left( \frac{2(MT_2 + \xi(t_{i_0}) - \xi(t_{i_0+M}))}{T_1} \mod 1 \right) \right| < \epsilon,$$

*otherwise*

$$\left| \mathbb{P}_{S_{i_0}}\{b_j \neq b_{j+M}\} - 2\min(\alpha, 1 - \alpha) \right| < \epsilon.$$

Proof of Fact 1 is given in Appendix A. It can be observed that for given values $M$, $T_1$, and $T_2$, the variance of the phase difference between samples at distance $M$ (of the accumulated jitter we want to measure) is proportional to the variance of number of different samples in the given set of samples over the total number of samples in this set.

In the following, we present a very interesting application of Fact 1 that is able to recover the distribution of the phase jitter accumulated over a given number $M$ of periods of $Osc_2$. We make $M$ big enough so that the jitter accumulated during $MT_2$ is not negligible and $N$ small enough so that the phase jitter can be considered as almost constant in the time period $NT_2$. Then Fact 1 signifies that it is possible to recover a good approximation of $(2(MT_2 + \xi(t_{i_0}) - \xi(t_{i_0+M}))/T_1)$ mod 1 or $-(2(MT_2 + \xi(t_{i_0}) - \xi(t_{i_0+M}))/T_1)$ mod 1 by computing $\mathbb{P}_{S_{i_0}}\{b_j \neq b_{j+M}\}$. More precisely, if we denote $\mathscr{C}$ the set of convergents of the continued fraction decomposition of $T_2/T_1$ (see [9] for the definition of the convergents of continued fraction decomposition) a careful analysis shows that in Fact 1, we can take $\epsilon = 1/\kappa$ where $\kappa = max\{q < N | p/q \in \mathscr{C}\}$. In practice, we have $\epsilon \approx 1/N$. If we make $M$ small enough so that the standard deviation of the distribution of the jitter accumulated during $MT_2$ is small compared to $\min(\alpha T_1, (1-\alpha)T_1)$, the values of samples $(-MT_2 - \xi(t_{i_0}) + \xi(t_{i_0+M}))/T_1$ mod $1/2$ or $(MT_2 + \xi(t_{i_0}) - \xi(t_{i_0+M}))/T_1$ mod $1/2$ follow the probability density function $\frac{d}{dx}\mathbb{P}\{\Phi(MT_2) \leq x | \Phi(0) = x_0\}$ up to a translation. If we denote $V(t)$ the variance of the probability distribution $\mathbb{P}\{\Phi(t) \leq x | \Phi(0) = x_0\}$, we obtain Algorithm 1 to compute $V(MT_2)$.

It can be seen that Altorithm 1 is very simple: for computing the variance, it is necessary to count $K$-times, in successive $N$ couples of bits, the number of

**input** : The output sequence $[b_1, \ldots, b_n]$ of an elementary TRNG with $K_D = 1$, $K$, $M$ and $N$ integers.

**output**: $V_0 = 4V/T_1^2$ where $V$ is the variance of the jitter accumulated during $MT_2$.

**for** $i = 0, \ldots, K$ **do**
$\quad S_i \leftarrow [Ni + 1, \ldots, Ni + N]$;
$\quad c[i] = \mathbb{P}_S(b_j \neq b_{j+M})$;
**end**

$V_0 \leftarrow \frac{1}{K} \sum_{i=0}^{K} c[i]^2 - \left( \frac{1}{K} \sum_{i=0}^{K} c[i] \right)^2$;

**return** $V_0$;

**Algorithm 1:** *Algorithm for computing the variance $V$ of the jitter*

couples having different bit values. The distance between the two bits in each couple is $M$. In practice, $K \sim 10000$, $N \sim 100$ and $M > N$, we let $M$ vary between 200 and 1600.

It should be noted that $\mathbb{P}_{S_{i_0}}\{b_j \neq b_{j+M}\}$ may not return an approximation of $(2(MT_2 + \xi(t_{i_0}) - \xi(t_{i_0+M}))/T_1)$ mod 1 or $(-2(MT_2 + \xi(t_{i_0}) - \xi(t_{i_0+M}))/T_1)$ mod 1 if $(MT_2 + \xi(t_{i_0}) - \xi(t_{i_0+M}))/T_1$ mod 1 $\in [\min(\alpha, 1 - \alpha), \max(\alpha, 1 - \alpha)]$ but, as in practice $|\alpha - 1/2|$ is always small, these occurrences are rare and easy to detect.

# 5    Evaluation of the Method by Simulations

We evaluated the principle of the jitter measurement by simulations. In order to maintain coherence with later hardware simulations, we used VHDL package *rng.pkg* [15] for generating jittery clock signals. Using this package, we dynamically modified the timing of the two signals by adding a Gaussian jitter with zero mean and known standard deviation to each generated half period. The obtained clocks were used to generate a bitstream according to Fig. 1. The obtained bitstream file was then used as an input in mathematical evaluations. The objective of the simulations was to recover the jitter size that was indeed introduced to generated clocks, independently from the frequency ratio.

First, the mean clock period of the sampled oscillator $Osc_1$ was $T_1 = 8\,923$ ps and that of the sampling oscillator $Osc_2$ was $T_2 = 8\,803$ ps. For $i = 1, 2$, the output clock signal of $Osc_i$ was given by $f_i = f_{1/2}(1/T_i(t + \xi_i(t)))$, where $\xi_i$ is the random walk phase drift such that $\frac{d}{dx}\mathbb{P}\{\xi_i(t + \Delta t) \leq x | \xi_i(t)\}$ follows a Gaussian distribution of mean 0 and variance $\sigma_i^2 \Delta t/T_i$. It is satisfactorily approximated by oscillator $Osc_1$ with a fixed period and oscillator $Osc_2$ with a relative jitter $\xi(t)$ such that $\frac{d}{dx}\mathbb{P}\{\xi(t + \Delta t) \leq x | \xi(t)\}$ is a Gaussian distribution $G_{\Delta t}(x)$ with mean 0 and variance $\sigma_{T_2}^2 \Delta t/T_1 \simeq 2\sigma_c^2 \Delta t/T_1$ (see [1, Appendix C] for justification).

For $\sigma_c = 10$ ps, 15 ps, and 20 ps, we generated EO TRNG output bit sequences using the *rng.pkg* package. Next, using Algorithm 1, we computed the variance $V(M)$ of $G(MT_2)$ as a function of $M$ and we plotted the graphs of $V(M)$ as a function of $M$ for three above mentioned sizes of injected jitter (see left panel in Fig. 3 for $\sigma_c = 10$ ps). Similar results were obtained for different frequency ratios.

The variance was satisfactorily approximated by a linear function with slope $a$. We then compared the size of the injected jitter $(\sigma_c/T_1)$ with that obtained from the slope $(\sqrt{a}/2)$. The results presented in the right panel in Fig. 3 show that we were able to recover expected noise parameters with good precision – the error was less than 5 %.

Note that our simulation does not take the $1/f$ noises into account, because there are no generators of such noises generating sufficiently long sequences available right now. Also note, that global noises need not be included: because of the use of the differential measurement principle – two ring oscillators implemented in the same device – impact of the global noise sources is eliminated (see [6] for more details).

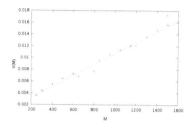

| Injected jitter | Calculated slope | $\sigma_c/T_1$ | $\sqrt{a}/2$ | Error percentage |
|---|---|---|---|---|
| $\sigma_c$ | $a$ | | | |
| 10 ps | 9.299909 $10^{-6}$ | 0.00156 | 0.00152 | 2 % |
| 15 ps | 2.03211 $10^{-5}$ | 0.00234 | 0.00225 | 3 % |
| 20 ps | 2.03211 $10^{-5}$ | 0.00312 | 0.00297 | 5 % |

**Fig. 3.** Simulation results, left panel: $V(M)$ as a function of $M$ (jitter with $\sigma_c = 10$ ps was injected); right panel: error percentage for three sizes of the jitter – 10 ps, 15 ps, and 20 ps

# 6    Hardware Implementation of the Embedded Jitter Measurement

The jitter variance measurement was implemented in hardware according to Algorithm 1. It is presented in two blocks. The first block (see Fig. 4) computes $K$ successive values $c_i = Nc[i]$ by comparing the output values of the first and the last stage of an $(M+1)$-stage shift register and counting unequal bits during $N$ periods of $s_2(t)$.

The lower panel in Fig. 4 shows waveforms for the relative mean frequency $\zeta = T_2/T_1 = 10/7$ and given initial phase $\xi_0$. The sampler output features a repetitive pattern (in bold), depending on $\zeta$ and $\xi_0$. Two cases are depicted: in one, the distance between samples is $M = 6$ and in the other, $M = 3$. Since $\zeta$ and $\xi_0$ are constant, the pattern remains the same, but the XOR gate output differs. In fourteen ($N = 14$) clock periods $T_2$, we see 12 different bits in the first case and 8 in the second. According to Fact 1, for jitter-free clocks, these values will remain constant in all successive blocks of $N$ bits, but in the presence of the jitter, their variance will be proportional to the variance of the jitter.

A compromise must be found when determining the distance $(M)$ between samples: for short distances, the accumulated jitter is too small and the precision

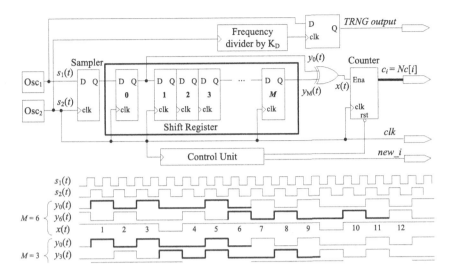

**Fig. 4.** *Structure of the block aimed at counting successive values $c_i = Nc[i] = N\mathbb{P}_S(b_j \neq b_{j+M})$ and two waveform examples for $M = 6$ (top panel) and $M = 3$ (bottom panel)*

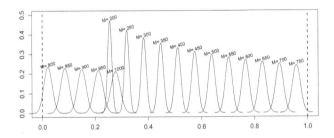

**Fig. 5.** *Example of distribution of values $c[i]$ between 0 and 1 (dashed vertical lines), for different values of $M$ in steps of 50*

is thus reduced; for long distances, two phenomena can occur: 1) the proportion of the flicker noise can become dominant or 2) accumulated jitter can become too big.

One important fact must be considered: since the relative mean frequency and phase cannot be controlled (oscillators are free running), the mean number of unequal samples can be any value from interval $[0, N]$, depending on $\zeta = \omega_1/\omega_2$ and distance $M$. If the mean value is close to the border values of this interval, some measurements may fall outside the interval and cause a measurement error (see curves for $M=750$ and 800 in Fig. 5). Of course, this error could be corrected by translating the period $T_1$. However, this would require some additional computations. It is consequently more practical to ensure that the standard deviation of the accumulated jitter is much smaller than period $T_1$ and the mean values of $c[i]$ are sufficiently far from the interval borders. Distance $M$, whose values $c[i]$ do not fulfill the last condition should not be used for variance computation. The practical setup of the distance $M$ will be discussed later.

The second block computes the relative variance $4V/T_1^2$ from $K$ values $c[i]$ according to Algorithm 1 (see Fig. 6). The implementation of the block is quite straightforward. It uses two accumulators, two multipliers connected as squaring units and one subtractor. If the $K$ value is chosen so that it is a power of two, division by $K$ and $K^2$ can be implemented at no cost by shifting the result $\log_2 K$ and $2\log_2 K$ positions to the right, respectively.

Notice also, that this second computing block is used once per $N$ periods $T_2$ and can thus be easily shared by several EO TRNGs without loss of performance.

Both blocks were implemented in VHDL as parameterized modules depending on parameters $\{NDE1, NDE2, M, N, \text{ and } K\}$. The two oscillators were implemented as NDE1- and NDE2-element ring oscillators. Parameters $M$, $N$, and $K$ represent the distance between samples, the length of measurement and the number of measurements, respectively.

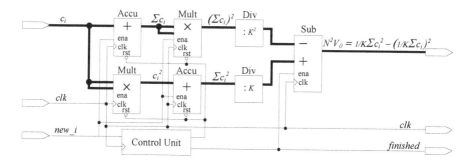

**Fig. 6.** *Structure of the block aimed at computing variance $V_0$ using $K$ successive values* $c[i] = \mathbb{P}_S(b_j \neq b_{j+M})$

## 6.1   Hardware Implementation Results

We tested the jitter measurement method in two different hardware configurations: 1) EO TRNG, jitter measurement and data interface (USB) were implemented in the same device; 2) the EO TRNG core in Fig. 1 was implemented in one FPGA and the jitter measurement and data interface were implemented in another. The aim of these two implementations was to observe the impact of the jitter measurement circuitry on the generator.

The first hardware configuration was implemented using an evaluation board dedicated to TRNG designs, featuring Altera Cyclone III FPGA and low noise linear power supplies (because of blind review, we will give the reference for the card only in the final version of the paper). As mentioned above, the elementary oscillator based TRNG is negligibly small. Its size is determined essentially by the number of delay elements of the two ring oscillators.

The size of the jitter measurement circuitry is determined by parameters $M$, $N$, and $K$. Practical experiments showed that the shift register should have between 200 and 500 stages (we recall that the depth of the shift register is linked to parameter $M$, which determines the jitter accumulation time). For less than 200 stages, the accumulated jitter variance only differed by a few bits and the precision was not sufficient (see Fig. 7). For bigger register sizes, the unwanted jitter coming from the correlated flicker noise became non negligible. According to Fact 1 and the simulation results presented in Section 5, to increase the precision of the measurement, the value of parameter $N$ (number of samples used for computing mean values $c[i]$ from Algorithm 1) should be less than that of $M$. For this reason, we selected the $N$ value to be around 150 and $M$ between 250 and 450. For easy division by $K$, its value was set at 8192. The value $V_0 = 4V/T_1^2$ was then computed according to Algorithm 1 using 32-bit arithmetic operations and sent to PC via USB interface for further analysis. In the given configuration, the EO TRNG including jitter measurement circuitry occupied 301 logic cells (LEs), maximum 450 memory bits, plus one DSP block 9x9 and four DSP blocks 18x18.

Results of the jitter measurement in the first hardware configuration implemented in Altera Cyclone III FPGA for $M$ varying between 250 and 1200, $N \sim 120$ and $K = 8192$ are depicted in Fig. 7. The left panel of the figure shows, that the variance increases linearly for $250 < M < 450$. This interval corresponds to accumulation times, during which the thermal noise dominates. The right graph in Fig. 7 is a zoom on this zone. From the dependence of the variance on $M$ (the slope) and the period $T_1 = 7.81$ ns, we were able to compute the jitter size $\sigma = 5.01$ ps per period $T_1$.

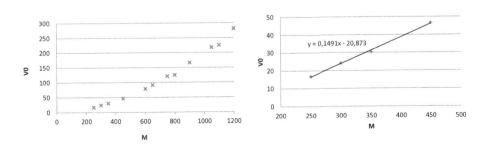

**Fig. 7.** *Results of the jitter measurement in hardware*

The same measurement method was applied in the second hardware configuration, in which EO TRNG was implemented in a separate FPGA and the jitter measurement circuitry and data interface were implemented in the same evaluation board as the first configuration described above (Cyclone III FPGA). Both FPGAs were interconnected via the LVDS (low voltage differential signaling) interface for the transmission of two signals: the reference clock and the EO TRNG sampler output signal.

It is important to underline that because the TRNG signal was output after the sampler, the FPGA input/output circuitry did not have any impact on the jitter measurement, as is the case when standard jitter measurement methods are used to measure the jitter of outputs of the two rings using external equipment (e.g. oscilloscope).

The result of this second experiment was that the jitter standard deviation was $\sigma = 4.9$ ps per period $T_1 = 7.69$ ns. This is a negligible change from the jitter of 5.01 ps in the previous experiment. This means that the jitter measurement can be embedded in the same device as the EO TRNG.

# 7  Discussion on Entropy Management Using Embedded Jitter Measurement

During the jitter evaluation described in the previous section, we calculated jitter from the slope of the variance depending on $M$. This method was useful to determine the interval in which variance depends linearly on the accumulation time. However, for implementation inside the device, this would require additional circuitry (to compute the slope and variance from the slope) to be implemented inside the device. Fortunately, knowing that the dependence in the selected interval is linear, it is sufficient to permanently measure just one point of the curve, i.e. just one value $V_0 = 4V/T_1^2$. We measured the jitter at $M = 300$. The measured standard deviation was $\sigma_0 = 2\sqrt{V}/T_1 = 5.01$ ps.

As explained in Sec. 6, for practical reasons, the variance should not be computed for values $M$, whose mean values $c[i]$ are close to zero or one. These values are not known in advance since oscillators are free running. If the jitter is sufficiently small compared to the $T_1$ period, which is always true for small accumulation times, these cases are rare, but unavoidable. For this reason, the shift register has several outputs around stage 300 and we selected one of the outputs, for which the computed values $c[i]$ were close to 0.5. This means the computation of their variance is free of errors.

Knowing the size of the jitter, we were able to manage the EO TRNG entropy: by entering the known jitter size in the model presented in [1], we computed the value of frequency divider $K_D$, to ensure that the entropy per bit is higher than $H_{min} = 0.997$, as required by AIS 31 [10]. The formula is derived from [1] and it gives $K_D$ as an expression of $\sigma_c$, $T_1$, $T_2$ and $H_{min}$.

$$K_D = \frac{-\ln\left(\frac{\pi}{2}\sqrt{(1 - H_{min})\ln(2)}\right)}{2\pi^2 \frac{T_2}{T_1} \frac{\sigma_c^2}{T_1^2}} \tag{2}$$

For $T_1 = 8.9$ ns, $T_2 = 8.7$ ns, $\sigma_c = 5.01$ ps and $H_{min} = 0.997$, we got $K_D \approx 430\,000$.

In this context, the role of the proposed jitter measurement circuitry is different: the continuous jitter measurement can be used as an on-line test, which should guarantee that the jitter never falls under the value that was used for entropy estimation and management (in our case, $\sigma = 5.01$ ps per period $T_1$ and $K_D = 430\,000$).

As mentioned above, the jitter measurement circuitry we proposed can be used in conjunction with a suitable stochastic model as a dedicated statistical test. In comparison with standard statistical tests, this test is performed closer to the source of randomness and can thus more accurately and more rapidly detect incorrect behavior of the generator.

For example, the tests FIPS 140-1 included in the AIS 31 RNG evaluation methodology require $20\,000$ input bits. Note that in our case, to obtain $20\,000$ bits at the generator output, we would need $K_D = 430\,000$ times more bits at the sampler output, i.e. at least $8.6 \cdot 10^9$ bits. However, in order to perform our dedicated test, which is better adapted to the detection of specific TRNG weaknesses (reduction in the jitter from the thermal noise or locking of the rings [3]), we only need $N \cdot K$ bits (around $1 \cdot 10^6$ sampler output bits). The dedicated test is thus more than $8\,600$ times faster and still very efficient. Our experiments showed that FIPS 140-1 tests were far less restrictive – the RNG output passed these tests for $K_D$ as low as $100\,000$, probably because of the flicker noise.

As an example, we demonstrate the efficiency of the proposed test during a temperature attack on real hardware in Appendix B.

# 8    Conclusion

In this paper, we presented an original, simple and precise method of jitter measurement that can be implemented inside logic devices. We demonstrated that in conjunction with a suitable statistical model, the measured jitter can be used to estimate entropy at the output of the generator. We also showed that the proposed entropy estimator can be used to build a rapid dedicated on-line statistical test that is perfectly adapted to the generator's principle. This approach complies with recent recommendations for TRNG evaluation [10] and ensures a high level of security by rapidly detecting all deviations from correct behavior.

Since the EO TRNG is the basic construction element of many oscillator based TRNGs including those based on self-timed rings [4], the proposed principle can be widely applied. However, in order to prevent attacks like those described in [12] and [2] (locking of rings), the jitter needs to be evaluated for all ring oscillators exploited in the generator. If necessary, the variance computation circuitry, as well as shift registers and counters of unequal samples, can be shared by all the rings in time.

# References

1. Baudet, M., Lubicz, D., Micolod, J., Tassiaux, A.: On the security of oscillator-based random number generators. Journal of Cryptology 24, 398–425 (2011)
2. Bayon, P., Bossuet, L., Aubert, A., Fischer, V., Poucheret, F., Robisson, B., Maurine, P.: Contactless Electromagnetic Active Attack on Ring Oscillator Based True Random Number Generator. In: Schindler, W., Huss, S.A. (eds.) COSADE 2012. LNCS, vol. 7275, pp. 151–166. Springer, Heidelberg (2012)
3. Bochard, N., Bernard, F., Fischer, V., Valtchanov, B.: True-Randomness and Pseudorandomness in Ring Oscillator-Based True RandomNumber Generators. International Journal of Reconfigurable Computing, Article ID 879281, p. 13 (2010)
4. Cherkaoui, A., Fischer, V., Fesquet, L., Aubert, A.: A Very High Speed True Random Number Generator with Entropy Assessment. In: Bertoni, G., Coron, J.-S. (eds.) CHES 2013. LNCS, vol. 8086, pp. 179–196. Springer, Heidelberg (2013)
5. Fischer, V.: A Closer Look at Security in Random Number Generators Design. In: Schindler, W., Huss, S.A. (eds.) COSADE 2012. LNCS, vol. 7275, pp. 167–182. Springer, Heidelberg (2012)
6. Fischer, V., Bernard, F., Bochard, N., Varchola, M.: Enhancing Security of Ring Oscillator-based RNG Implemented in FPGA. In: Proceedings of Field Programmable Logic and Applications – FPLA 2008 (2008)
7. Guneysu, T.: True random number generation in block memories of reconfigurable devices. In: Zhao, K., Bian, J., Zhou, Q. (eds.) Field-Programmable Technology – FPT 2010, pp. 200–207. IEEE Press (2010)
8. Hajimiri, A., Limotyrakis, S., Lee, T.: Jitter and phase noise in ring oscillators. IEEE Journal of Solid-State Circuits 34(6), 790–804 (1999)
9. Ya Khinchin, A.: Continued fractions. The University of Chicago Press, Chicago, Ill.-London (1964)
10. Killmann, W., Schindler, W.: A proposal for: Functionality classes for random number generators, version 2.0. Technical report, Bundesamt fur Sicherheit in der Informationstechnik (BSI), Bonn (September 2011) (accessed: March 01, 2014)
11. Maichen, W.: Digital Timing Measurements: From Scopes and Probes to Timing and Jitter. In: Frontiers in Electronic Testing. Springer, Heidelberg (2010)
12. Markettos, A.T., Moore, S.W.: The Frequency Injection Attack on Ring-Oscillator-Based True Random Number Generators. In: Clavier, C., Gaj, K. (eds.) CHES 2009. LNCS, vol. 5747, pp. 317–331. Springer, Heidelberg (2009)
13. NIST SP800-22 rev. 1. A statistical test suite for random and pseudo-random number generators for cryptographic applications (August. 2008), http://csrc.nist.gov/CryptoToolkit/tkrng.html
14. Sunar, B., Martin, W.J., Stinson, D.R.: A Provably Secure True Random Number Generator with Built-In Tolerance to Active Attacks. IEEE Transactions on Computers, 109–119 (2007)
15. Swaminathan, G.: Random number generators (RNG) VHDL package (1992), http://www.ittc.ku.edu/EECS/EECS_546/magic/files/vlsi/vhdl/random.pkg (accessed: March 01, 2014)
16. Taylor, G., Cox, G.: Behind Intels New Random-Number Generator (2011), http://spectrum.ieee.org/computing/hardware/ behind-intels-new-randomnumber-generator/0 (accessed: March 01, 2014)
17. Valtchanov, B., Aubert, A., Bernard, F., Fischer, V.: Modeling and observing the jitter in ring oscillators implemented in FPGAs. In: 11th IEEE Workshop on Design and Diagnostics of Electronic Circuits and Systems (DDECS 2008), pp. 1–6 (2008)

18. Varchola, M., Drutarovsky, M.: New High Entropy Element for FPGA Based True Random Number Generators. In: Mangard, S., Standaert, F.-X. (eds.) CHES 2010. LNCS, vol. 6225, pp. 351–365. Springer, Heidelberg (2010)
19. Vasyltsov, I., Hambardzumyan, E., Kim, Y.-S., Karpinskyy, B.: Fast Digital TRNG Based on Metastable Ring Oscillator. In: Oswald, E., Rohatgi, P. (eds.) CHES 2008. LNCS, vol. 5154, pp. 164–180. Springer, Heidelberg (2008)
20. Xueqing, W., Eisenstadt, W.R., Fox, R.M.: Embedded jitter measurement of high-speed i/o signals (2007)

# Appendix

## A    Proof of Fact 1

In this section, we use the following notations: for interval $I$ and $t \in \mathbb{R}$, $I + t$ is the interval $\{x + t | x \in I\}$. If $I, J$ are intervals, $I + J$ is the interval $\cup_{t \in J} I + t$. We consider intervals that are invariant under translation by $T \in \mathbb{R}$. Thus, if $I \subset \mathbb{R}$ is an interval, we let $I_T = \cup_{n \in \mathbb{Z}}(I + nT)$. For instance, $[0, 1)_2 = \cup_{i \in \mathbb{Z}}[2i, 2i + 1)$. If $I = [x, y]$ is an interval, by convention, we set $I = \emptyset$ if $x > y$, and we have the obvious extension for open or semi-open intervals.

*Proof.* We suppose that $\alpha \leq (1 - \alpha)$, if necessary by changing $f_\alpha$ by $1 - f_\alpha$. For $j \in \{1, \ldots, n\}$, we let $\tau_j = jT_2 - \xi(t_j) \mod T_1$. By definition, for all $j \in \{1, \ldots, n - M\}$, $b_j = f_\alpha(\omega_1(jT_2 - \xi(t_j)))$ and $b_{j+M} = f_\alpha(\omega_1((j + M)T_2 - \xi(t_{j+M})))$. As $f_\alpha$ is 1-periodic, we have $b_j \neq b_{j+M}$ if and only if the cardinality of the intersection of the interval $[\tau_j, \tau_{j+M}]_{T_1} = [0, (MT_2 + \xi(t_j) - \xi(t_{j+M})) \mod T_1]_{T_1} + ((jT_2 - \xi(t_j)) \mod T_1)$ with the set $\{0, \alpha T_1\}$ is equal to 1 (see Figure 8).

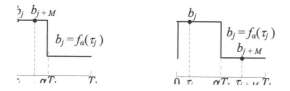

**Fig. 8.** *Keeping the notations of the proof of Fact 1, we have $b_j = b_{j+M} = 1$ (left) and $b_j = 1 \neq b_{j+M} = 0$ (right)*

Let $i_0 \in \{1, \ldots, n - N - M + 1\}$, using the hypothesis that $\delta(j) = \xi(t_{j+M}) - \xi(t_j)$ is almost a constant equal to $\delta(i_0)$ when $j$ runs across all the values of $\{i_0, \ldots, i_0 + N - 1\}$, we deduce that $\mathbb{P}_{S_{i_0}}\{b_j \neq b_{j+M}\}$ is given by

$$P = \mathbb{P}_X\{\#(([0, (MT_2 + \xi(t_{i_0}) - \xi(t_{i_0+M})) \mod T_1]_{T_1} + X) \cap \{0, \alpha T_1\}) = 1\},$$

where $X$ is a random variable, which follows the same distribution in the interval $[0, T_1]$ as the sample $\{(jT_2 - \xi(t_j)) \mod T_1\}_{j \in S_{i_0}}$ . Let $\ell = (MT_2 + \xi(i_0) - \xi(i_0 + M)) \mod T_1$. Suppose that $\ell \leq \alpha T_1$, then the set of $x \in [0, T_1]$ such that $\#([x, x + \ell]_{T_1} \cap \{0, \alpha T_1\}) = 1$ is $([-\ell, 0]_{T_1} \cup [\alpha T_1 - \ell, \alpha T_1]_{T_1}) \cap [0, T_1]$. The size of the last interval is $2\ell$. The case $\ell \geq (1 - \alpha)T_1$ comes down to the preceding case by replacing $\ell$ by $T_1 - \ell$ and computing the complementary event. We obtain the size of $x \in [0, T_1]$ such that $\#([x, x + \ell]_{T_1} \cap \{0, \alpha T_1\}) = 1$ is $2(T_1 - \ell)$. On the other hand, if $\alpha T_1 \leq \ell \leq (1 - \alpha)T_1$, the set of $x \in [0, T_1]$ such that $\#([x, x + \ell]_{T_1} \cap \{0, \alpha T_1\}) = 1$ is $([-\ell, \alpha T_1 - \ell]_{T_1} \cup [0, \alpha T_1]_{T_1}) \cap [0, T_1]$, the size of which is $2\alpha T_1$.

Finally, by assuming that the distribution of $X$ is $\epsilon$-uniform in the interval $[0, T_1]$, we find that if $\ell \leq \alpha T_1$ then $|P - \frac{2\ell}{T_1}| < \epsilon$, if $\ell \geq (1 - \alpha)T_1$ then $|P - 2 + \frac{2\ell}{T_1}| < \epsilon$, and otherwise $|P - 2\alpha| < \epsilon$. This concludes the proof.

# B    Experiments on Detection of Attacks Using the Proposed Dedicated Test

The studied elementary oscillator based TRNG can be attacked by reducing the jitter, e. g. by decreasing the temperature and thus the thermal noise causing the jitter. We evaluated reaction of the proposed dedicated test on this attack.

In our experiments, we modified the temperature of the generator and we observed the size of the measured jitter and compared it with the pre-computed threshold in the dedicated test. The temperature was rapidly reduced to $-20\,°C$ and left to rise back to $21\,°C$. We repeated this cycle several times. The results of the jitter measurement in one experiment are depicted in Fig. 9.

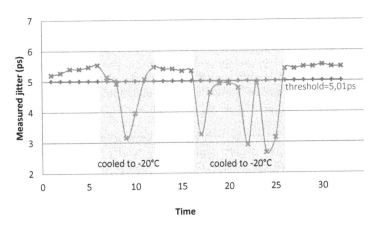

**Fig. 9.** *Evolution of the temperature attack in time*

We see that as expected, the test was able to detect the jitter reduction coming from the temperature decrease and activate the alarm.

# Entropy Evaluation for Oscillator-Based True Random Number Generators

Yuan Ma*, Jingqiang Lin**, Tianyu Chen, Changwei Xu,
Zongbin Liu, and Jiwu Jing

Data Assurance and Communication Security Research Center,
Chinese Academy of Sciences, Beijing, China
State Key Laboratory of Information Security,
Institute of Information Engineering, Chinese Academy of Sciences, Beijing, China
{yma,linjq,tychen,xuchangwei,zbliu,jing}@is.ac.cn

**Abstract.** True random number generators (TRNGs) are crucial to the implementations of cryptographic algorithms and protocols. The quality of randomness directly influences the security of cryptographic systems. Oscillator-based sampling is popular in the design of TRNGs due to its nice properties of elegant structure and high speed. However, the credibility of randomness generated from high-speed oscillator-based TRNGs, especially ring oscillator-based (RO-based) ones, is still in controversy. This is mainly because pseudo-randomness is hardly distinguished from true randomness and RO-based TRNGs are susceptible to external perturbations. In this paper, we present a stochastic model to evaluate the entropy of oscillator-based TRNGs, and then deduce the requirement of design parameters (including the sampling interval) for sufficient entropy per random bit, i.e., to ensure true randomness. Furthermore, we design a jitter measuring circuit to verify the theory, and the theoretical results are confirmed by both the simulation and practical experiments. Finally, we apply the stochastic model to analyze the effect of deterministic perturbations, and demonstrate that the randomness of RO-based TRNGs (under deterministic perturbations) can be overestimated and predicting the "random" bits could be possible.

**Keywords:** True random number generators, ring oscillators, sufficient entropy, perturbation, stochastic model.

## 1 Introduction

True random number generators are employed in many cryptographic applications such as key generation, digital signature and key exchange, and their

* The authors were partially supported by the National 973 Program of China under award No. 2013CB338001. Yuan Ma, Jingqiang Lin, Tianyu Chen and Jiwu Jing were also partially supported by the National 973 Program of China under award No. 2014CB340603.
** Corresponding author.

L. Batina and M. Robshaw (Eds.): CHES 2014, LNCS 8731, pp. 544–561, 2014.
© International Association for Cryptologic Research 2014

security is crucial for cryptographic systems. The oscillator-based TRNG has been widely employed due to its nice properties of elegant structure and high speed. In oscillator-based TRNGs, a fast oscillator signal is sampled by a slow one which is generated by another oscillator or an external crystal oscillator, and the timing jitter in the signals is the entropy (randomness) source.

Randomness evaluation is important for both the design and the use of TRNGs. In general, there are two methods for randomness evaluation: black-box statistical tests and white-box stochastic models. The existing statistical tests, such as FIPS 140-2 [11], NIST 800-22 [16] and Diehard [14] measure the balance and independence of random bits through various test items. However, passing these statistical tests can only be considered as a necessary condition for true randomness (as deterministic sequences with good statistical properties can also pass these tests). Therefore, it seems extremely difficult to test the true randomness only from the outputting sequences of TRNGs. For this reason, it is necessary to evaluate TRNGs from stochastic models, which are directly related to the entropy of TRNGs.

In addition, from the white-box stochastic models, it is feasible to derive the requirements for the design parameters of TRNGs. In oscillator-based TRNGs, one of the most important parameters is the sampling interval, which determines the generation speed of TRNGs. To model oscillator-based TRNGs, Killmann and Schindler [12] used a common stochastic model, where the flipping times are independent and identically distributed (i.i.d.), and provided a tight lower bound for the entropy of the TRNG. Yet, the model is not able to provide a precise entropy, or the probabilities of outputting certain bit patterns. Using a phase-oriented approach, Baudet et al. [2] provided a more comprehensive model and calculated the precise entropy for RO-based TRNGs. The model also allowed for computing the maximal bias on a short vector and recovering the main stochastic parameters of a TRNG. Amaki et al. [1] proposed a stochastic behavior model using Markov state transition matrix to calculate the state probability vector. Some other related works for TRNG modeling are presented in [15,5,3].

Another issue for modeling the stochastic behavior of RO-based TRNGs is deterministic perturbations. In general, the perturbations can be generated from an unstable switching power, or another oscillator inside the chip. They can even be injected by attackers [13]. The effect of deterministic perturbations has been discussed in the literature. The process of injecting deterministic perturbations is simulated in [4], and the authors observe that the engagement of perturbations makes it easier to pass statistical tests due to the joining of pseudo-randomness. The improvement of statistical properties was also investigated by the theory and the experiment in [1]. Baudet et al. [2] presented a differential measurement method to acquire non-deterministic jitter, and concluded that the deterministic perturbations do not undermine the randomness of a TRNG by itself, but can lead to a dangerous overestimation of randomness jitter. In addition, the effect of deterministic perturbations on the inherent randomness was discussed in [13,7].

In this paper, by improving the stochastic model in [12], we propose a more precise and comprehensive stochastic model for evaluating the entropy of oscillator-based (more precisely, RO-based) TRNGs, and theoretically give the required parameters for sufficient entropy per bit. In order to verify the theory, we design a novel jitter measuring circuit by employing an internal measuring method. The theoretical results are verified with both simulation and practical experiments. Meanwhile, the consistencies with the previous models are also investigated. Furthermore, we apply the model to analyze and explain the effect of deterministic perturbations. We demonstrate that the randomness of RO-based TRNGs under deterministic perturbations can be overestimated, and it could be possible to predict the "random" bits.

In summary, we make the following contributions.

- We propose a new modeling method for stochastic behaviors to evaluate the entropy of oscillator-based TRNGs, and deduce recommended design parameters for sufficient entropy.
- We design a novel jitter measuring circuit by employing an internal measuring method to verify the theory, which is crucial and helpful in acquiring the design parameters of the TRNGs.
- We perform a comprehensive study on the effect of deterministic perturbations, and point out that deterministic perturbations make it possible to predict the generated random sequences, though the sequences under the effect are easier to pass statistical tests.

The rest of the paper is organized as follows. In Section 2, we present the stochastic model for oscillator-based TRNGs. In order to verify the theory, we design a novel jitter measuring circuit for experimental verification, and discuss the modeling assumption in Section 3. In Section 4, we verify the theoretical results and give the requirement of parameters. We analyze the effect of deterministic perturbations in Section 5. In Section 6, we conclude the paper.

## 2  Stochastic Model

A typical example of oscillator-based TRNG is shown in Figure 1. A stable slow clock signal samples an unstable fast oscillator signal to generate random bits. As the sampling interval increases, the jitter of the fast oscillator signal are accumulating. The foundation of generating random bits is the unpredictability of the number of fast signal periods (more precisely, half-periods) in the duration of a single slow signal period.

**Definitions.** The important notations in oscillator-based TRNGs are shown in Figure 2, where the half-periods $X_k$ is the time interval between two flopping times. In this paper, we assume that $X_k$ are i.i.d., and the reason is discussed in Section 3.4. The mean and variance of half-periods are denoted as $\mu$ and $\sigma^2$, respectively, i.e. $\mu = E(X_k)$ and $\sigma^2 = \text{Var}(X_k)$. The sampling time with the equal interval $s$ are represented as $s_0, s_1, ..., s_i$, i.e. $s_i = is$. The waiting time $W_i$ denotes the timing distance of $s_i$ to the following closest edge.

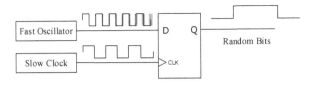

**Fig. 1.** Oscillator-based TRNG

**Fig. 2.** Definitions of oscillator-based TRNGs

The number of edges within $(s_{i-1}, s_i]$ is denoted by $R_i$, then the $i$th sampling bit $B_i$ is represented as $B_i = (B_{i-1} + R_i) \bmod 2$.

Note that the operation of adding $R_i$ with $B_{i-1}$ can be treated as a type of post-processing, which is not considered in this paper; the operation causes no impact on the information entropy, thus we take $B_i = R_i \bmod 2$ in the remainder for convenience.

### 2.1   Preliminary Analysis of the Stochastic Model

We briefly summarize some important results from [12] on probability calculation of sampling bits, which is the base of our work.

Let $R_i = \min\{k \mid T_k > s\}$, where $T_k = X_1 + X_2 + ... + X_k$, meaning $R_i$ is the first increasing $k$ ensuring that $T_k$ is larger than $s$. The probability

$$\text{Prob}(R_i = k + 1) = \text{Prob}(T_k \leq s) - \text{Prob}(T_{k+1} \leq s). \tag{1}$$

The distribution of $T_k$ is derived from the central-limit theorem (CLT), so it is deduced that

$$\text{Prob}(\frac{T_k - k\mu}{\sigma\sqrt{k}} \leq x) \to \Phi(x), k \to \infty, \tag{2}$$

where $\Phi(x) = \int_{-\infty}^{x} e^{-t^2/2} dt / \sqrt{2\pi}$ denotes the cumulative distribution function of the standard normal distribution $N(0, 1)$. Then we have

$$\text{Prob}(R_i = k + 1) = \text{Prob}(T_k \leq s) - \text{Prob}(T_{k+1} \leq s) \tag{3}$$

$$\approx \Phi((v - k) \cdot \frac{\mu}{\sigma\sqrt{k}}) - \Phi((v - k - 1) \cdot \frac{\mu}{\sigma\sqrt{k+1}}),$$

where $v = s/\mu$ represents the frequency ratio. Then the probability distribution of sampling bit $B_i$ is

$$\mathrm{Prob}(B_i = b_i) = \mathrm{Prob}(R_i \bmod 2 = b_i) \qquad (4)$$
$$= \sum_{j=1}^{\infty} \mathrm{Prob}(R_i = 2j - b_i) \; for \; b_i \in \{0,1\}.$$

## 2.2   Improved Model for RO-Based TRNGs

In oscillator-based TRNGs, especially in RO-based TRNGs, the amount of jitter is very small [6], i.e., $\sigma/\mu \ll 1$. The possible values of $k$ are restricted in a small interval zone near the mean $v$. In addition, as the fast oscillator signal is dozens of times faster than the slow clock, $v$ is not a small value. Therefore, it is reasonable to assume that $\sqrt{k} \approx \sqrt{k+1} \approx \sqrt{v}$.

Setting $q = \sigma\sqrt{v}/\mu$ as the quality factor which is used to evaluate the quality of TRNGs, we have

$$\mathrm{Prob}(R_i = k + 1) \approx \Phi((v - k) \cdot \frac{\mu}{\sigma\sqrt{k}}) - \Phi((v - k - 1) \cdot \frac{\mu}{\sigma\sqrt{k+1}})$$
$$\approx \Phi(\frac{v - k}{q}) - \Phi(\frac{v - k - 1}{q}). \qquad (5)$$

For the probability of $B_i = 1$, we have

$$\mathrm{Prob}(B_i = 1) = \sum_{j=1}^{\infty} \mathrm{Prob}(R_i = 2j - 1) \approx \sum_{j=1}^{\infty}(\Phi(\frac{v - 2j}{q}) - \Phi(\frac{v - 2j - 1}{q})),$$

which can be described as the sum of the interleaved column areas below the normal distribution curve in Figure 3.

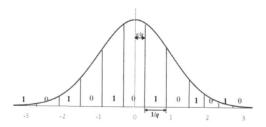

**Fig. 3.** The probability distribution ofthe sampling bit ($W_i = 0$)

In Figure 3, $W_i$ is set to 0 for convenience. The area between the normal distribution curve and $x$ axis (equaling to 1) is divided at $1/q$ interval, and the area of each column corresponds to the probability of $R_i$ equaling to each $k$. The larger $q$ is, the finer the column is divided, which means that the areas of

'0' and '1' are closer. Another observation is that, besides $q$, the value of $r$ also affects the bias of the sampling bit. Variable $r$ is the fractional part of $v$, i.e., $r = v \bmod 1$. The dividing position is determined by $r/q$, as shown in Figure 3. Obviously, when $W_i = 0$ and $r = 0$, the areas of probabilities '0' and '1' are equal regardless of $q$. The most unbiased case is $r = 0.5$ when $W_i = 0$, where the distance between probabilities '0' and '1' becomes largest compared to the other cases with the same $q$. Therefore, a robust TRNG design should have sufficient entropy even in the worst (most unbiased) case.

**The Probability Distribution of the Waiting Time.** In consecutive sampling, two adjacent sampling processes are dependent as the waiting time $W_i$ generated by the $i$th sampling affects the $(i + 1)$th one. Referring to renewal theory, the probability of $W_i$ is

$$P_W(y) = \text{Prob}(W_i \leq y) = \frac{1}{\mu} \int_0^y (1 - P_X(u))du, \qquad (6)$$

where $P_X(\cdot)$ denotes the cumulative distribution function of half-periods $X_i$. Furthermore, because $\sigma \ll \mu$, $P_W(y)$ is approximated to

$$P_W(y) \approx \begin{cases} \dfrac{1}{\mu} \displaystyle\int_0^y 1 du = \dfrac{y}{\mu}, & 0 \leq y \leq \mu; \\[4mm] 1, & y > \mu \end{cases} \qquad (7)$$

which can be treated as the uniform distribution on the interval $[0, \mu]$.

**Sampling Process Approximation.** Inspired by Equations (5) and (7), we approximate the consecutive sampling described in Figure 1 to the following process - a slow signal with jitter sampling a fast stable signal.

– The fast oscillator signal is stable.
– The slow oscillator signal which sampling the fast signal is unstable with jitter. The periods follow $(v\mu, v\sigma^2)$ normal distribution.

Easy to verify that the probability distributions for $R_i$ and $W_i$ under the model are corresponding with Equations (5) and (7), respectively. Therefore, the approximated model is equivalent to the original one under the assumption of small jitter. In fact, the approximated process is also a common type in oscillator-based TRNGs. The stochastic behavior of the approximated process is easier to model, so we use it as an improved model to calculate and evaluate the entropy of TRNGs.

### 2.3    Entropy Calculation

The improved model for consecutive sampling is described in Figure 4. For normalization, we define $W_i'$ as the ratio of the $W_i$ to the mean $\mu$. We calculate the probability of $B_{i+1} = b_{i+1}$ under the condition of $W_i' = w_i'$,

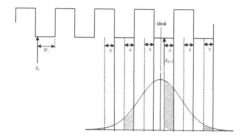

**Fig. 4.** The new model for entropy calculation

$$\text{Prob}(b_{i+1}|w_i') = \sum_{i=-\infty}^{+\infty} (\Phi(\frac{2i+1-c_i}{q}) - \Phi(\frac{2i-c_i}{q})) \tag{8}$$
$$:= J_{i+1}(w_i')$$
$$(c_i = (v - w_i' - (1 - b_{i+1})) \bmod 2).$$

From Figure 4, we have

$$\text{Prob}(W_{i+1}' \le x, b_{i+1}|w_i') = \sum_{i=-\infty}^{+\infty} (\Phi(\frac{2i+1-c_i}{q}) - \Phi(\frac{2i-c_i+1-x}{q}))$$
$$:= F_{i+1}(x, w_i'),$$

which is the area of the shaded part in Figure 4.

By defining $G_i(x) := \text{Prob}(W_i' \le x|b_i, \dots, b_1)$, we have the conditional probability of sampling bits

$$\text{Prob}(b_{i+1}|b_i, \dots, b_1) = \int_0^1 J_{i+1}(x)G_i(dx) := K(b_{i+1}). \tag{9}$$

Due to the uncertainty of the initial sampling position, we assume the distribution of $W_0'$ is also uniformed in $(0, 1)$. Therefore,

$$G_1(x) = \text{Prob}(W_1' \le x|b_1) = \int_0^1 \text{Prob}(W_1' \le x|b_1, w_0')dw_0' = \int_0^1 \frac{F_1(x, w_0')}{J_1(w_0')}dw_0'.$$

Then, using the property of the Markov process

$$\text{Prob}(b_{i+1}|w_i', b_i, w_{i-1}', \dots) = \text{Prob}(b_{i+1}|w_i'),$$

we calculate the following $G_i(x)$:

$$G_i(x) = \int_0^1 \frac{F_i(x, w_{i-1}')}{K(b_i)}G_{i-1}(dy).$$

Then we get the $n$-bit probability distribution for certain bit patterns

$$p(\boldsymbol{b}) = \mathrm{Prob}(b_n, \ldots, b_1) = \prod_{i=1}^{n} K(b_i), \tag{10}$$

and the $n$-bit entropy

$$H_n = \sum_{\boldsymbol{b} \in \{0,1\}^n} -p(\boldsymbol{b}) \log p(\boldsymbol{b}). \tag{11}$$

# 3   Experiment Design for Model Verification

In this section, using an internal measuring method we design an improved jitter measurement circuit to verify the stochastic model. The advantage of the circuit is that it is able to acquire the approximated quality factor while the sampling bits are generated, which is useful to verify the stochastic model.

## 3.1   Dual-Counter Measurement Circuit

The ring oscillator is formed by a set of inverters that are chained into a ring, while the number of the inverters must be an odd number. A typical RO structure in FPGAs is shown in Figure 5, where these inverters are implemented by Look-Up Tables (LUTs) in FPGAs. The ideal period of the oscillator signal is represented as $2X$, where $X$ is the delay of all the RO components, i.e., the half-period.

**Fig. 5.** Ring oscillator

In order to measure the jitter more accurately, we improve the internal measurement circuit [18]. In contrast to the only one positive or negative edge counter used in [18], two voltage-crossing counters are utilized in our measurement method, as shown in Figure 6. Besides improving the sensitivity to jitter accumulation, this method helps us directly obtain the sampling bits from the counting results. The counting process is the (delayed) renewal process, so the variance with the interval of $s$ is represented as $s(\sigma^2/\mu^3) + o(s) = q^2 + o(s)$, where $o(s) \to 0$ when $s \to \infty$. Therefore, by calculating the standard variance of the counting results, we can acquire the approximated quality factor $q$. It should be noticed that, when the interval is not large enough, $q$ is overestimated, since $o(s)$ cannot be ignored under the interval.

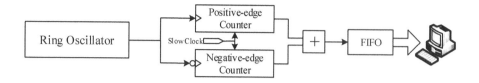

**Fig. 6.** Dual-counter measurement circuit

In the improved measuring method, two counters are employed to measure the number of positive edges and negative edges in the duration of a single slow clock period, respectively. Then, the two counter results are added to form the outputting values. After each count finishes, the counters should be cleared to start the next count. The clear signal is generated through the clear circuit which is driven by both the ring oscillator signal and the slow clock. The counting process of the positive-edge counter with the sampling interval of $s$ is depicted in Figure 7. Between the two adjacent counts, the clear signal lasts accurately one period of the oscillator signal by using the clear circuit. If the oscillator frequency is too high to clear the counters within one cycle, the number becomes two or three.

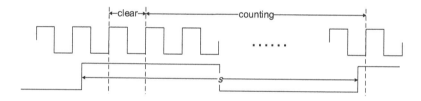

**Fig. 7.** The counting process (positive edge)

Consecutive sampling is adopted in the measurement, and the sampling type is useful to simplify the counting process, because we just need to do the counting collection only once for the longer sampling intervals of $ms$, rather than do $m$ times. After getting numbers of count results in the duration of $s$, we can sum the $m$ non-overlapping results to obtain the number of edges in the duration of $ms$, then we can figure out the quality factor under the interval of $ms$ by calculating the standard variance of these sums. Although the clear mechanism makes all sums smaller than the real values by $m - 1$, it has no impact on calculating the variances of these values.

## 3.2 Jitter Measurement

We implement the circuit with 3-inverter RO on Xilinx Virtex-5 FPGA. The RO frequency is about 484 MHz, and the slow clock is a 5 MHz crystal oscillator signal, and the circuit output is the number of RO edges within the duration of

$s = 200\ ns$. Having numbers of outputting values in the interval $s$, we can figure out the number of edges within the sampling interval $ms$ by $m$-time accumulating. For the sampling interval $ms$, we can calculate the standard deviation $\sigma_{ms}$ of the accumulation results. From the renewal theory under i.i.d. assumption, $\sigma_m = \sqrt{ms}(\sigma/\mu^{3/2}) = \sqrt{m}\sigma_1$, $s \to \infty$, where $\sigma_m$ denotes the standard variance under the interval of $ms$.

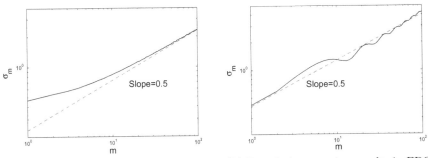

(a) Simulation results with white noises    (b) Practical measuring results in FPGA

**Fig. 8.** The measuring results with ideal vs. practical noises

The simulation and practical results for the measurement method at logarithmic coordinates are shown in Figure 8, whose $x$-axis is $m$ and $y$-axis is standard deviation $\sigma_m$. In Figure 8(a), with $m$ increasing, the slope of the standard deviation curve is approaching to 0.5, which is consistent with the theory. As mentioned, if $ms$ is not large enough, meaning the accumulated jitter is small, the measuring result is larger than the real value. Fortunately, we observe that the overhead will be no more than 10% when the measuring standard deviation is larger than 0.8, so these results are available.

Surprisingly, the practical measuring result is quite different, as shown in Figure 8(b). We find the existence of deterministic (sinusoidal) perturbations which make the $\sigma_m$ curve form a wavy pattern of rising. In addition, when the sampling interval $ms$ is large (about $m > 50$), we also observe the existence of correlated noise, under which the standard variance increases faster and the slope becomes larger than 0.5.

### 3.3    Filtering Deterministic Jitter

Deterministic perturbations make an overhead for the estimation of random jitter. In order to filter deterministic jitter, a measurement method using dual oscillators was presented in [8]. The method is based on the fact that the effect of deterministic perturbations is global. We use a 15-inverter RO signal as the slow clock to filter the perturbations and measure the random jitter of fast oscillator signal. In contrast to the clock measuring result, the RO measuring result does

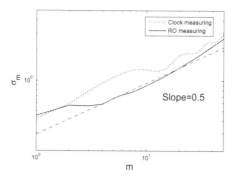

**Fig. 9.** RO measuring result

not display an obvious wavy pattern of rising, as shown in Figure 9. Therefore, we obtain the data $R_i$ without the perturbations, which are the experimental data base for verifying the theory.

### 3.4 Discussion for Modeling Assumption

In our stochastic model, we assume that the jitter or the noises are i.i.d., but the correlation is observed in the experiment when the sampling interval is long. According to [10], correlated noise (such as $1/f$ noise) is embodied at low frequency in oscillators, while the noise at high frequency is white (or independent). The correlated noise was also observed in [19] which suggested that the sampling frequency should be fast enough to avoid the influence of correlated noise. In our proposed TRNG model, the focused sampling interval is $m < 12$ (see Section 4.2) where the accumulated jitter is insufficient or almost sufficient, so the effect of correlated noise is weak in this region. Therefore, for simplicity, we do not involve the modeling for correlated noises or jitter in the stochastic model of the TRNG.

Correlated noise makes the jitter and the counting results have long-term dependence, which also affects sampling bits, so it shall be noted that the effect of correlated noise (especially mixed with white noise) on sampling bits in RO-based TRNG is actually an open problem due to the complexity and variety of correlated noise. As a preliminary analysis, we do not observe the correlation inherited in the sampling bits under correlated noise when accumulated independent jitter is sufficient (see Figure 10).

## 4    Entropy Evaluation

In this section, using the formula of entropy calculation, we deduce the requirement of RO-based TRNGs parameters for sufficient entropy per bit. The results are verified by experiments, and the comparison with other work is also presented.

## 4.1 Parameters for Sufficient Entropy

In consecutive sampling, $H_n$ can be derived from Equation (11). The bit-rate entropy is denoted as $H = H_n/n$. According to the experimental result in [12], the threshold value of bit-rate entropy is chosen as 0.9999, i.e., $H$ should be larger than 0.9999 to achieve sufficient security. We calculate the bit-rate entropy in term of $q$ for various $r$ from 0 to 0.5 using Matlab numerical calculation (shown in Figure 11). The required $q$ values for different $r$ to achieve sufficient entropy (0.9999) are listed in the second row of Table 1.

In contrast to the example of $W_i = 0$ in Figure 3, the consecutive sampling has the worst balance at $r = 0$, because the waiting time $W_i$ has a uniform distribution in consecutive sampling. In the case of $r = 0$, when $q$ is larger than 0.9264, the bit-rate entropy is sufficient. On the contrary, the generator with $r = 0.5$ is easiest to acquire sufficient entropy, and the required $q$ is only 0.6511. Given the parameters $\sigma$ and $\mu$ of the fast oscillator signal , we can figure out the required sampling interval for sufficient entropy.

Table 1. The required $q$ to achieve sufficient entropy for different $r$

| $r$ / Req. $q$ | $r=0$ | $r=0.1$ (0.9) | $r=0.2$ (0.8) | $r=0.3$ (0.7) | $r=0.4$ (0.6) | $r=0.5$ | Remark |
|---|---|---|---|---|---|---|---|
| Theory | 0.9264 | 0.9209 | 0.9029 | 0.8673 | 0.7895 | 0.6511 | $H > 0.9999$ |
| Sim. Measured | 0.9778 | 0.9392 | 0.9198 | 0.8759 | 0.7928 | 0.7002 | passing FIPS 140-2 |

## 4.2 Experimental Verification

In order to verify the parameter requirement, we use the statistical tests FIPS 140-2 [11] to test the sampling bits, including monobit test, poker test, runs test and longest run test. We record the required $q$ values for the sampling bits passing all items of FIPS 140-2, and compare them with the theoretical ones.

**Matlab Simulation.** We first use Matlab simulation to verify the theoretical results, as the environment can be ideal as expected. In the simulation, the half-periods of the fast oscillator signal are set to $(1.125, 0.017^2)$ i.i.d. normal distribution. Using the measuring method under a preset sampling interval, we can get the counting results, whose standard variance and LSBs can be treated as $q$ and sampling bits, respectively. With the sampling interval increasing, the passing point for each $r$ can be observed, as shown in the third row of Table 1. As we mentioned in Figure 8, the measured $q$ values are a little larger than the real values when $m$ is small. Therefore, the simulation results approximately match with the theory in Table 1, especially in the aspect of variation tendency. The difference between these two results is because that the criteria of the theoretical entropy and FIPS 140-2 are not completely consistent.

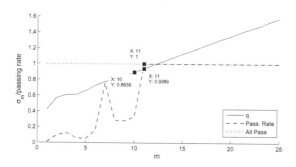

**Fig. 10.** Results of measured $q$ and FIPS 140-2 tests in FPGA

**Practical Experiment.** We also implement the measurement circuit in the FPGA platform. The measuring and test results are shown in Figure 10, where the passing rate means the ratio of the number of passed test items to the number of all items. We observe that the passing point lies in the interval $q \in [0.8936, 0.9389]$, which nearly corresponds with the simulation and theory. However, it seems infeasible to measure the right $r$ at this point to do a further verification, since a tiny measuring error will make the measured $r$ totally different in such a high frequency of the fast oscillator signal. In addition, it should also be noticed that correlated noise makes an overestimation for thermal jitter, especially when $m$ is large. One can employ the method presented in [9] to measure the thermal noise contribution to the jitter.

### 4.3   Comparison with Previous Work

For the entropy evaluation of oscillator-based TRNGs, a tight lower bound was provided in [12], and the bit-rate entropy was calculated in [2] by using a phase-oriented method. The main results of [12] and [2] are presented as Equations (12) and (13), respectively.

$$H(B_i|B_{i-1}, \ldots, B_1) \geq H(B_i|W_{i-1}) \approx \int_0^s H(R^{(s-u)} \mod 2)P_W(du) \quad (12)$$

$$H_n \approx n - \frac{32(n-1)}{\pi^4 \ln(2)} \cos^2(\pi r)e^{-\pi^2 q^2} \quad (13)$$

In Equation (12), $R^{(s-u)}$ represents the number of crossing edges in the duration of $(s - u)$, and the variables in Equation (13) have been converted for the correspondence of definitions.[1] Our estimated bit-rate entropy is larger than the lower bound of [12] as expected, and is almost identical to the result of [2] at the worse cases ($r = 0,\ 0.1,\ 0.2$), as shown in Figure 11.

---

[1] The quality factor $Q$ defined in [2] equals to $q^2/4$.

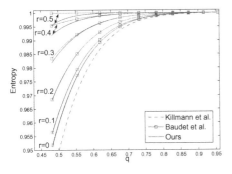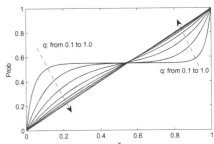

**Fig. 11.** Comparison result for entropy estimation

**Fig. 12.** Prob($W_i \leq x|b_i$) for different $q$ at $r = 0$

However, there are some inconsistencies in the comparison of our result with [2] when $r \geq 0.3$, especially at $r = 0.5$. According to Equation (13), $H_n$ approximately equals to $n$ when $r = 0.5$, meaning that the bit-rate entropy $H$ achieves the maximum value 1. That is to say, so long as the sampling interval $s$ satisfies that $(s \mod \mu)/\mu = r = 0.5$ in consecutive sampling, the bit-rate entropy is close to 1 regardless of $q$. Nonetheless, the conclusion is not confirmed in both our theory and simulation experiment. In our opinion, $r = 0.5$ can only guarantee the balance of sampling bits[2], rather than the independence. Therefore, when $r = 0.5$ the generated sequences can pass the statistical tests once the independence of sampling bits is satisfied. That is why the generators with $r = 0.5$ are easier to acquire sufficient entropy. Obviously, when $q$ is small, the correlation of sampling bits cannot be eliminated, thus the $n$-bit entropy cannot approximately equal to $n$. The sampling correlation is further illustrated via the following independence condition.

### 4.4   Independence Condition

The sampling correlation is derived from the transfer of the waiting time $W_i$ which affects the $(i + 1)$th sampling result. Therefore, the independence of sampling bits should satisfy

$$\forall b_i \in \{0, 1\}, \mathrm{Prob}(W_i \leq x|b_i) = \mathrm{Prob}(W_i \leq x) = \frac{x}{\mu}.$$

For various $q$ values at $r = 0$, the conditional probability distributions $\mathrm{Prob}(W_i \leq x|b_i)$ are shown in Figure 12, where the curves from outside to inside correspond to the $q$ values from 0.1 to 1 at 0.1 interval. Note that $r$ does not make the conditional distribution become uniform easier, but only affects the cross position of these probability curves. Therefore, we only present the result of $r = 0$. When

---

[2] The balance holds only when $W_i$ is uniformly distributed, which just requires a very small $q$ (about 0.1).

$q$ is less than 0.5, the probability distribution is non-uniform, meaning that the correlation still exists. Until $q$ is approximately larger than 0.6, the distribution becomes uniform and the correlation is almost eliminated, which is consistent with the calculation results in Table 1. In addition, the experimental result in the next section also confirms the independence condition.

## 5   The Effect of Deterministic Perturbations

In this section, we show that the deterministic perturbations make the sampling bits appear to be more "random" and easier to pass statistical tests. More importantly, we point out that the seemingly random sequence actually has a vulnerability which makes it possible to predict the sequence.

### 5.1   The Effect on the Statistical Test

In order to analyze the effect on the statistical test, we carry out the measurement and FIPS 140-2 statistical tests with deterministic jitter. Under deterministic perturbations, the TRNG is easier to pass the test, as shown in Figure 13, where the passing position is $m = 9$ and the other is $m = 11$.

It is interesting that the passing rate of RO sampling has an abrupt rise at $m = 7$, which is precisely the position of the crest of the perturbations, meaning that the sampling sequence suddenly becomes more "random". The reason is that the deterministic jitter is not completely filtered out by the dual-oscillator method, since the perturbation effects on the two oscillators cannot be exactly identical, though they have been placed as close as possible. Moreover, the observation validates the fact that injecting deterministic jitter does improve the randomness of outputting sequences. However, note that the deterministic perturbation in our experiment is slight and balanced. Once the perturbation becomes strong, it will reduce the amount of inherent independent jitter; once it becomes biased, it will degrade the quality of sampling bits.

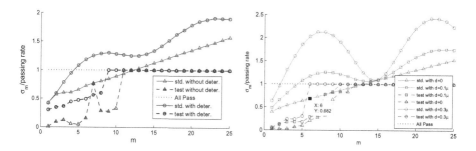

**Fig. 13.** Measuring results with and without deterministic perturbations

**Fig. 14.** Simulation results with varying deterministic jitter

## 5.2    The Bound for the Randomness Improvement

Increasing the amplitude makes it easier to pass the statistical tests. However, when we keep increasing the amplitude more than $0.3\mu$, the passing position does not move up any more, as shown in Figure 14. The final position stops at $m = 6$, and the current standard deviation caused by random jitter is 0.682, which is consistent with the independence condition. Therefore, we can infer that the engagement of deterministic perturbations causes little impact on the correlation of sampling bits but improves the balance of sampling sequences. With the deterministic jitter increasing, the sequences can pass the statistical test when the dependence condition holds.

However, though the balance is achieved for sampling sequences, for each sampling bit the balance is insufficient, because the jitter accumulation for each sampling has not been enough. This causes some security problems, such as predicting the sampling bits.

## 5.3    Predicting the "Random" Bits

The deterministic perturbation is assumed as sinusoidal signal $D(t) = A\sin(\frac{2\pi t}{T_D} + \phi_0)$. The half-period after perturbing becomes $X'_i = \int_{T_i}^{T_{i+1}}(1 + D(t))dt$. we have the following reasonable physical assumptions for deterministic perturbations [2]: $T_D >> \mu$ (slow variations of $D(t)$) and $X'_i \approx X_i$ (small deterministic jitter). Therefore, it is easy to deduce that the uniform distribution in $[0, \mu]$ still approximately holds for the new waiting time. Furthermore, compared with the sampling interval $s$ in the model without perturbations, the mean of the new $i$th interval is equivalent to $s - d_i$ to apply the model in Section 2, where $d_i = \int_{s_{i-1}}^{s_i} D(t)dt$. As we mentioned, it is useful to improve the balance of the whole sequence, however, the impact is very limited on a given sampling bit, which allows us to predict the seemingly random bits. The probability of the $i$th bit equaling to $b_i$ can be derived from the total probability formula $\text{Prob}(b_i) = \int_0^1 \text{Prob}(b_i|w_i)P_W(du)$, where $\text{Prob}(b_i|w_i)$ can be calculated from Equation (8) using the modified sampling interval $s - d_i$.

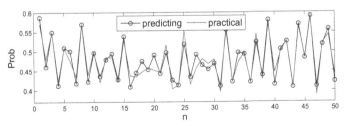

**Fig. 15.** The comparison of predicting and practical probabilities

Therefore, if precisely knowing the mean $\mu$, standard variance $\sigma$, and the behaviors of deterministic jitter, one can precisely compute the probabilities of sample bits in advance. We perform a prediction simulation, and compare the predicting probabilities with the practical ones in Figure 15. The practical probabilities come from the statistics of 1000 simulation samples that can pass FIPS 140-2. It is shown that the two sets of probabilities are consistent with each other in most sampling bits. Using the predicting results, one can optimize brute-force attacks to significantly reduce the breaking complexity. In practical terms, the more precise parameters of TRNGs one knows, the more effective attacks one can perform.

Though the TRNG output can pass the statistical tests under the perturbations, with environmental factors (such as supply voltage) changing, the frequency and amplitude of the perturbation might change to the values that no longer help to improve the "randomness" (e.g. the frequency changes to the multiples of the sampling frequency). Therefore, one way to guarantee the security of under-perturbation TRNGs is to keep the entropy sufficiency in each sampling bit, i.e. the $q$ should be large enough. As $d_i \ll s$, the requirement for $q$ value is approximately identical to that without deterministic perturbations at the worst case $r = 0$.

# 6    Conclusion and Future Work

In this paper, we propose an improved modeling method for oscillator-based TRNGs, and deduce the requirement for the parameters of security TRNGs. In order to verify the theory, we design an improved measuring circuit for acquiring the TRNG parameters. The measuring circuit can also be integrated into hardware for online tests and inner tests of the TRNGs. Furthermore, we apply the stochastic model to analyze the TRNGs with deterministic perturbations. We investigate the positive effect of perturbations on the statistical tests, and also provide the bound for the randomness improvement. By performing a simulated attack, we demonstrate that predicting the random bits could be possible. In future work, we will further analyze the accuracy of the measuring method and extend our stochastic model to the multiple-RO structures [17], especially for those injection-locked oscillators.

**Acknowledgements.** The authors would like to acknowledge the contribution of Dr. Wei Gao from Tsinghua University. We also thank the anonymous reviewers for their invaluable suggestions and comments to improve the quality of this paper.

# References

1. Amaki, T., Hashimoto, M., Mitsuyama, Y., Onoye, T.: A worst-case-aware design methodology for noise-tolerant oscillator-based true random number generator with stochastic behavior modeling. IEEE Transactions on Information Forensics and Security 8(8), 1331–1342 (2013)

2. Baudet, M., Lubicz, D., Micolod, J., Tassiaux, A.: On the security of oscillator-based random number generators. J. Cryptology 24(2), 398–425 (2011)

3. Bernard, F., Fischer, V., Valtchanov, B.: Mathematical model of physical RNGs based on coherent sampling. Tatra Mountains Mathematical Publications 45(1), 1–14 (2010)

4. Bochard, N., Bernard, F., Fischer, V., Valtchanov, B.: True-randomness and pseudo-randomness in ring oscillator-based true random number generators. Int. J. Reconfig. Comp. 2010 (2010)

5. Bucci, M., Germani, L., Luzzi, R., Trifiletti, A., Varanonuovo, M.: A high-speed oscillator-based truly random number source for cryptographic applications on a smart card IC. IEEE Transactions on Computers 52(4), 403–409 (2003)

6. Coppock, W.R., Philbrook, C.R.: A mathematical and physical analysis of circuit jitter with application to cryptographic random bit generation. Major qualifying project report, Worcester Polytechnic Institute (2005)

7. Dichtl, M., Golić, J.D.: High-speed true random number generation with logic gates only. In: Paillier, P., Verbauwhede, I. (eds.) CHES 2007. LNCS, vol. 4727, pp. 45–62. Springer, Heidelberg (2007)

8. Fischer, V., Bernard, F., Bochard, N., Varchola, M.: Enhancing security of ring oscillator-based trng implemented in FPGA. In: FPL, pp. 245–250 (2008)

9. Haddad, P., Teglia, Y., Bernard, F., Fischer, V.: On the assumption of mutual independence of jitter realizations in P-TRNG stochastic models. In: IEEE Design, Automation and Test in Europe Conference and Exhibition (DATE), pp. 1–6 (2014)

10. Hajimiri, A., Limotyrakis, S., Lee, T.H.: Jitter and phase noise in ring oscillators. IEEE Journal of Solid-State Circurts 34(6) (1999)

11. Information Technology Laboratory: FIPS 140-2: Security Requirement For Cryptographic Modules (2011)

12. Killmann, W., Schindler, W.: A design for a physical RNG with robust entropy estimators. In: Oswald, E., Rohatgi, P. (eds.) CHES 2008. LNCS, vol. 5154, pp. 146–163. Springer, Heidelberg (2008)

13. Markettos, A.T., Moore, S.W.: The frequency injection attack on ring-oscillator-based true random number generators. In: Clavier, C., Gaj, K. (eds.) CHES 2009. LNCS, vol. 5747, pp. 317–331. Springer, Heidelberg (2009)

14. Marsaglia, G.: Diehard Battery of Tests of Randomness, http://www.stat.fsu.edu/pub/diehard/

15. Petrie, C., Connelly, J.: A noise-based IC random number generator for applications in cryptography. IEEE Transactions on Circuits and Systems I: Fundamental Theory and Applications 47(5), 615–621 (2000)

16. Rukhin, A., et al.: A statistical test suite for random and pseudorandom number generators for cryptographic applications. NIST Special Publication 800–22, http://csrc.nist.gov/publications/nistpubs/ 800-22-rev1a/SP800-22rev1a.pdf

17. Sunar, B., Martin, W.J., Stinson, D.R.: A provably secure true random number generator with built-in tolerance to active attacks. IEEE Transactions on Computers 56(1), 109–119 (2007)

18. Valtchanov, B., Aubert, A., Bernard, F., Fischer, V.: Modeling and observing the jitter in ring oscillators implemented in FPGAs. In: DDECS, pp. 158–163 (2008)

19. Valtchanov, B., Fischer, V., Aubert, A., Bernard, F.: Characterization of randomness sources in ring oscillator-based true random number generators in FPGAs. In: DDECS, pp. 48–53 (2010)

# Side-Channel Leakage through Static Power

## Should We Care about in Practice?

Amir Moradi

Horst Görtz Institute for IT Security, Ruhr University Bochum, Germany
amir.moradi@rub.de

**Abstract.** By shrinking the technology *static* power consumption of CMOS circuits is becoming a major concern. In this paper, we present the first practical results of exploiting *static* power consumption of FPGA-based cryptographic devices in order to mount a key-recovery side-channel attack. The experiments represented here are based on three Xilinx FPGAs built on 65 nm, 45 nm, and 28 nm process technologies. By means of a sophisticated measurement setup and methodology we demonstrate an exploitable information leakage through *static* power of the underlying FPGAs. The current work highlights the feasibility of side-channel analysis attacks by *static* power that have been known for years but have not been performed and investigated in practice yet. This is a starting point for further research investigations, and may have a significant impact on the efficiency of DPA countermeasures in the near future.

## 1 Introduction

After the introduction of execution time [15] in scientific literature as the first practical side channel to recover the secret key of implementations of cryptographic algorithms, other side-channel analysis approaches have been introduced one after each other. For example, power consumption [16], electromagnetic emanation [2,10,21], acoustic [11], optical emission [9], and temperature [14] are amongst those which have been brought to the attention of scientific communities. However, due to their efficiency, low-cost, and simplicity power consumption and electromagnetic emanation side channels have been widely investigated and applied in academia as well as in industry more then the others.

During the golden years of side-channel analysis when academia showed interest in the field, researchers have put much effort in exploring and analyzing the theoretical and practical aspects of side-channel analysis. Not all, but most of the activities in this area have been done based on the principles of CMOS circuits, i.e., focusing on the main power consumption factor of the circuits, namely *dynamic* power consumption. Therefore, the attacks and analysis schemes as well as countermeasure techniques introduced to the community are mainly based on the dynamic power consumption of the underlying circuit. However, during the last years by shrinking the technology the VLSI community reported the dependency of *static* power consumption of a CMOS circuit to its internals (see [13,17]). Moreover, interesting results are shown in [3] and [4], where an

L. Batina and M. Robshaw (Eds.): CHES 2014, LNCS 8731, pp. 562–579, 2014.

attack using static power is called *Leakage Power Analysis* (LPA). There even exist a few works proposing related countermeasures (see [5,27]). This issue, which has been denoted mainly based on the simulation results, was not taken as a serious threat by the side-channel community.

The main reason behind disregarding this information leakage source is due to the very small scale of the signal amplitude (of static power consumption) which cannot be easily measured in practice by means of the currently available facilities and equipments. Indeed, the belief of the community – which is not much far away from reality – is that the information available through the dynamic power consumption channel is much more and much easier to detect compared to that of the static power.

This article demonstrates the first practical results of a side-channel analysis using information leakage through static power consumption. All the experiments shown here are based on Xilinx FPGAs. In order to make the analyses more comprehensive three FPGA families (Virtex-5, Spartan-6, Kintex-7) with three different process technologies, namely 65 nm, 45 nm, and 28 nm, are considered in the experiments.

We first illustrate the measurement setup and the methodology used to exploit the static power of the considered platforms. This includes a couple of engineering adjustments and tricks which make the desired measurement possible. Our experiments start with investigation of dependency of static power to the content of basic elements of FPGA internals, e.g., registers, LUTs, and connections (i.e., routings done by the switch boxes). By means of these experiments we elaborate on a clear dependency between the static power and each of the aforementioned resources for all the targeted platforms. We extend our experiments toward a crypto device by evaluating the static power of an exemplary circuit containing an 8-bit key addition followed by an AES S-box. We demonstrate how to make use of its static power to recover the 8-bit secret key. One step further, we examine a masked AES S-box, and show how to apply a second-order attack through static power consumption. As the final step a complete implementation of an AES encryption engine equipped with both masking and shuffling is considered. We demonstrate in which circumstances an attack using static power can overcome the protection provided by the aforementioned countermeasures.

## 2    Methodology

Three Side-channel Attack Standard Evaluation Boards (SASEBO) [1]

- SASEBO-GII, with *Target* FPGA as a Virtex-5 (65 nm),
- SAKURA-G, with *Target* FPGA as a Spartan-6 (45 nm),
- SAKURA-X, with *Target* FPGA as a Kintex-7 (28 nm)

are the platforms considered in our experiments. On each board there exists another FPGA (so-called *Control*) responsible to communicate with *Target* as well as with the PC via UART. We have developed a dedicated framework (designs for both *Control* and *Target*) for each of the platforms to fulfill the requirements

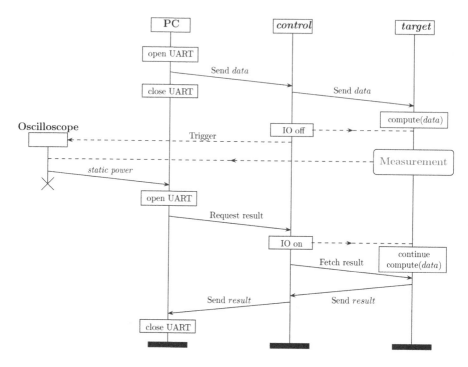

**Fig. 1.** Procedure of a single measurement of static power consumption

we explain in details below. *Target* is in contact only with *Control*, and all its input signals including the clock signal are provided by *Control*.

## 2.1 Communication

The procedure which is followed to measure static power consumption of a design embedded on *Target* is depicted by graphics in Fig. 1.

1. The PC opens the UART communication channel and sends *data* to *Control*. Right after that, the PC closes the UART channel.
2. *Control* communicates with *Target* and sends the corresponding *data*. Right after finishing the desired operations on *Target*, *Control* switches off all the IO pins including the clock of *Target*.
3. *Control* issues a trigger signal to the oscilloscope. After that, the static power consumption of *Target* can be measured (explained later).
4. The PC opens the UART channel and requests *Control* to send the result back.
5. *Control* switches on the IO signals, drives the *Target* clock, and fetches the result of the desired computation done by *Target*.
6. *Control* sends the fetched result to the PC via UART, and the PC closes the UART channel right after the reception.

Our experiments show that the IO signal values have a significant effect on the amount of static power consumption. Therefore, as stated in the above procedure, the output signals of *Target* as well as of *Control* which drive the inputs of *Target* must be at a constant state (e.g., all at LO) during the measurement. Further, noise of the UART channel, which is realized by a USB module (FTDI chip[1]) on SASEBO platforms, also hugely affects the static power. So, keeping the UART channel closed during the measurement is inevitable.

## 2.2    Measurement

The measurement point provided by the SASEBO boards is the heads of a resistor placed in the Vdd path of *Target* internal core. According to the SASEBO quick start guides [1], a usual way to measure the voltage drop over this shunt resistor is to monitor the voltage of the *Target* Vdd pins. It should be noted that setting the coupling of the corresponding oscilloscope channel to AC, which might be beneficial to reduce the measurement noise when measuring dynamic power, cannot be used in our case. It is because the AC coupling is a kind of a high-pass filter which stops the DC part of the signal. However, we are interested to measure the DC shift of the power consumption signal to be able to monitor the static power. Therefore, keeping the DC coupling of the corresponding oscilloscope channel is a must.

Another issue regarding the measurement is due to the small-scale shunt resistor. The resistor originally embedded on the SASEBO boards is $1\,\Omega$ for SASEBO-GII (Virtex-5) and SAKURA-G (Spartan-6) and $10\,\mathrm{m}\Omega$ for SAKURA-X (Kintex-7). Since we are planing to measure the current passing through this resistor by monitoring its voltage, the magnitude and type of this resistor significantly affect our measurement accuracy. Therefore, we replaced the shunt resistor of all the platforms by a certain type $1.0\,\Omega$ resistor with low temperature coefficient. So, we use the same shunt resistor in all our experiments. Further, due to the voltage drop by the shunt resistor we modified the boards[2] to supply a certain voltage thereby driving exactly $1.0\,\mathrm{V}$ at *Target* internal core Vdd pins. This way, *Target* of all our platforms are supplied by the same voltage magnitude.

We should mention that amplifiers like ZFL-1000LN+ from Mini-Circuits[3] or PA303 from Langer EMV-Technik[4], which are common components used for enhancing measurement of small-scale dynamic power signals, cannot be equipped in our setup. That is because these amplifiers have a high-pass filter at their input removing the DC shift of the incoming signal. The same holds for the amplifier originally embedded on SAKURA-G (Spartan-6). Instead, we have used a LeCroy AP 033 differential probe which includes a ×10 internal amplifier and does not cause the aforementioned problem. By means of the differential probe and a LeCroy HRO66Zi WaveRunner 12-bit oscilloscope we monitored

---

[1] Future Technology Devices International Ltd. http://www.ftdichip.com/
[2] By adjusting the potentiometer of the corresponding voltage regulator.
[3] http://www.minicircuits.com/
[4] http://www.langer-emv.de/

the voltage drop by the shunt resistor. Since the differential probes consist in active components, they usually introduce higher noise to the resulting signal compared to common coaxial-cable passive probes.

Each measurement is performed by sampling the amplified signal (output of the differential probe) with the highest vertical accuracy ($200\,\mu V/\text{div}$ in our setup), at a sampling rate of $1\,GS/s$ and bandwidth limit of $20\,MHz$. A long trace with a length of $10\,ms$ containing $10\,M$ sample points is measured, and its average is computed by the oscilloscope. In contrast to a dynamic power measurement, where a trace over time is collected, a singular value (the afore-mentioned averaged value) is the result of a static power measurement. This procedure (see Fig. 1) can be repeated to collect the magnitude of static power consumption for different *data* values.

## 3   Preliminary Studies

According to the VLSI theory and the simulation results [13,17] *leakage current* (directly proportional to static power) of a CMOS gate depends on the content of its output as well as its inputs. In the following – by means of a couple of case studies – we try to investigate the effect of the FPGA internals on the amount of the chip's leakage current.

### 3.1   Registers

As the simplest case study we consider the registers as of fundamental elements available in any FPGA. We first considered *Target* of SASEBO-GII (Virtex-5) and made a design consisting of several registers. All registers are configured as FDCPE, i.e., "D Flip-Flop with Clock Enable and Asynchronous Preset and Clear" (see [25]). As shown by Fig. 2(a), CE (clock enable) is always '1', and D (register input) is connected to '0'. So, by a positive edge at CLK (clock) the register stores '0'. Further, since the register is configured as "with Asynchronous Preset and Clear", the register stores '1' by seeing HI level ('1') at the PRE (preset) signal. CLK and PRE of all registers are connected together and are handled by *Control*. Therefore, *Control* can change the content of the registers by handling these two signals. More precisely, when signals (CLK, PRE) change from (0,0) to (1,0) or to (0,1) the registers save '0' or '1' respectively. Also changing the signals back to (0,0) does not alter the registers content. This indeed helps us to switch off the IO signals without affecting the internals when measuring leakage current as explained in Section 2.

We have implemented $14\,400$ instances[5] of the above explained register, and controlled the placement process to place them in desired locations[6]. An impor-tant issue is regarding the Q(out) signal of the registers. These signals are not

---

[5] Half of the available registers in Virtex-5 LX50.

[6] The placement of the registers does not affect the result of this experiment, but the manual placement is done to keep its consistency with the next experiments as explained later.

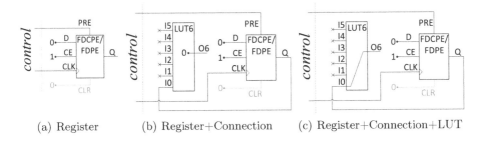

(a) Register          (b) Register+Connection       (c) Register+Connection+LUT

**Fig. 2.** Design of basic elements of the preliminary case studies

connected to anywhere. This gives us the chance to examine only the effect of the register contents on static power. In order to avoid optimization and trimming the unconnected resources by the synthesizer tools, we explicitly forced the tools to keep these signals[7] thereby preventing the registers to be trimmed.

In the measurement phase, the leakage current of two cases is to be measured: *i*) when all the registers contain '0' and *ii*) when all the registers contain '1'. As stated before, during both measurements the environmental situation like the IO signals – of both *Target* and *Control* – must be the same, and the difference between these two cases must only be the content of the registers. We followed the procedure explained in Section 2 for each case separately to obtain two singular values as amounts of corresponding leakage current. Repeating this process 1000 times (done in 17 minutes) led to two curves shown by Fig. 3(a).

As shown by the graphics, the dependency of the leakage current to the registers' content is clear. Although the leakage currents greatly vary over time, their difference (of two cases) is relatively constant. We realized that the reason behind this remarkable variation is temperature inconstancy. The chip temperature as well as room temperature significantly affects the leakage current measurements[8]. Since the temperature of the equipped differential probe steadily increases after power up, it also has a huge impact on the measured leakage current. In order to diminish these issues we employed a thermobox to isolate the platform and the differential probe from environmental temperature variations. This makes the situation better, but does not completely solve the problem.

By repeating the same experiment with the same number of registers on two other platforms, SAKURA-G (Spartan-6) and SAKURA-X (Kintex-7)[9], we obtained the leakage current curves shown by Fig. 3. Dependency between static power and the registers' content is obviously shown, but comparing these three results brings some interesting conclusions:

---

[7] By KEEP and SAVE NET FLAG constraints (see [23]).

[8] As an interesting experience, approaching human body ($\sim 37°C$) to the FPGA chip causes the leakage current to rapidly change.

[9] FDCPE instances are replaced by FDPE "D Flip-Flop with Clock Enable and Asynchronous Preset" as FDCPE does not exist in Spartan-6 and Kintex-7 libraries (see [24] and [26]).

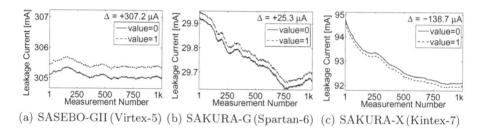

(a) SASEBO-GII (Virtex-5)   (b) SAKURA-G (Spartan-6)   (c) SAKURA-X (Kintex-7)

**Fig. 3.** Measured leakage current of 14 400 registers on all three platforms

- In case of SASEBO-GII (Virtex-5) and SAKURA-G (Spartan-6), when the content of the registers is '1', the leakage current is higher compared to when the registers stored '0'. This polarity is reversed in case of SAKURA-X (Kintex-7). Since the underlying FPGAs are from different families with different technologies, and the details of each process technology are not publicly available, we cannot comment on this behavior.
- Leakage current of SASEBO-GII (Virtex-5 65 nm) ∼ 300 mA is much higher than that of other platforms with lower process technology. Also it does not decrease by shrinking the technology as ∼ 30 mA for SAKURA-G (Spartan-6 45 nm) and ∼ 90 mA for SAKURA-X (Kintex-7 28 nm). Note that we supplied all three FPGAs with the same internal core voltage (1.0 V).
- Moreover, the part of the leakage current related to the registers' content is not higher for smaller process technologies. 307 μA, 25 μA, and 138 μA respectively for the 65 nm, 45 nm, and 28 nm chips. It means that side-channel vulnerability of these circuits through static power does not necessarily increase by shrinking the technology. In our experiments, the difference between leakage current of two cases (registers = '1' or '0') of SASEBO-GII (Virtex-5 65 nm) is the highest compared to that of the others.

## 3.2   Connections

The FPGA internal connections are realized by programmable switch boxes which play an important role regarding the amount of (dynamic) power consumed by a design. The number of switch boxes, which exist in the routing of a signal, significantly affects its delay as well as the energy consumed when it toggles. The more switch boxes a signal passes, the higher is its toggles' power consumption. Accordingly, the amount of leakage current of a switch box, which is made by CMOS circuits, should be affected by the value of the signal. In order to examine this issue we have developed the next experiment. As shown in Fig. 2(b), in the same way as in the last experiment a register is employed. The output of the register is given to a look-up table (LUT6) whose

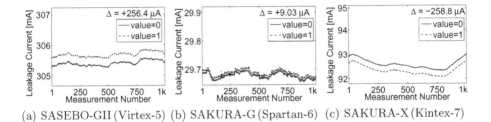

(a) SASEBO-GII (Virtex-5)  (b) SAKURA-G (Spartan-6)  (c) SAKURA-X (Kintex-7)

**Fig. 4.** Measured leakage current of 14 400 registers + connections on all three platforms

output – regardless of its inputs – is always '0'. This gives us the opportunity to exclude the effect of the LUT6 output toggles in our investigations. However, having the LUT6 in the design is mandatory; otherwise the signal routing (switch box connection) will not be realized.

In order to limit the number of switch boxes involved in each signal routing, the register and the connected LUT6 instance are forced to be placed at the same slice by manual placement. In order to make the connection the register output must be routed to the CLB[10]-dedicated switch box and come back to the same slice to be connected to the LUT6 input (see Fig. 12). It indeed makes a loop going out of and coming back to the slice[11]. It also guarantees that only one switch box is involved in each signal routing. Similar to the last experiment, we developed a design as *Target* with 14 400 instances of these elements. The same placement as that of the last experiment is done here to keep the consistency of the two experiments. Further, we provided appropriate constraints to avoid trimming the registers and the LUT6 instances since the LUT6 output is connected to nowhere.

After developing this design on all our platforms we measured the corresponding leakage current 1000 times for each of the cases of the registers' content. The results of the measurements are shown by Fig. 4. By comparing the results of the last and the current experiments on SASEBO-GII (Virtex-5) (Fig. 3(a) and Fig. 4(a)), it becomes clear that the difference between leakage current of two cases of the registers' content is smaller when the connections are added to the design. It can be concluded that the polarity of the dependency of leakage current to the value of the connected signals is the inverse of that to the registers' content. The same behavior is seen for the second platform SAKURA-G (Spartan-6); compare Fig. 3(b) and Fig. 4(b). However, the last platform SAKURA-X (Kintex-7) behaves differently (see Fig. 3(c) and Fig. 4(c)). Introducing the connections to the design increases the difference between the measured leakage currents. It means that the effect of the value of the connected signals on leakage current has the same polarity as that of the register's content.

---

[10] Configurable Logic Block: containing two slices in Virtex-5, Spartan-6, and Kintex-7 families. Each slice consists of four LUT6 and at least four registers.

[11] Note that an opposite connection which connects a LUT6 output to a register input at the same slice does not necessarily leave the slice and pass a switch box.

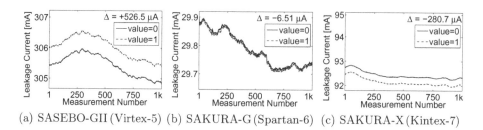

(a) SASEBO-GII (Virtex-5)  (b) SAKURA-G (Spartan-6)  (c) SAKURA-X (Kintex-7)

**Fig. 5.** Measured leakage current of 14 400 registers + connections + LUTs on all three platforms

As stated before, since these FPGAs are developed under different technologies, these observed dissimilar behaviors cannot be easily justified. It is worth to mention that these results stand for a couple of connections made around a slice then repeated several times for other slices. Based on these results we cannot conclude about the effect of every connection made by switch boxes in an FPGA.

### 3.3 Look-Up Tables

As the last experiment with FPGA fundamental elements, we examine the effect of the look-up table's (LUT) output value on leakage current. As shown by Fig. 2(c), compared to the last experiment we only changed the configuration of the LUT6 to make its output always the same as its first input, i.e., the register output. In this design when the register output toggles, the value of the routed signal (connection) as well as the value of the LUT6 output changes. This way, sum of the effect of all these three elements on leakage current is observed in this experiment. Repeating the last experiment with the slightly modified designs (only changing the LUT6 configurations) led to the results shown in Fig. 5. It should be noted that everything including the number of elements (14 400), placement, and routing are the same as that of the experiment expressed in Section 3.2.

Comparing the results of this experiment with that of two previous ones it can be concluded that the LUT6 output value has a considerable impact on leakage current in case of SASEBO-GII (Virtex-5). The same influence with a smaller factor can be seen on the other platforms. The polarity of this dependency – similar to the previous experiments – is different from one platform to another.

**Table 1.** Dependency of leakage current to basic FPGA internal elements

| Platform | FPGA | Technology | Register | | | Connection | | | LUT | | |
|---|---|---|---|---|---|---|---|---|---|---|---|
| | | | μA | % | ↕ | μA | % | ↕ | μA | % | ↕ |
| SASEBO-GII | Virtex-5 | 65 nm | 307.20 | 49 | ↑ | 50.80 | 8 | ↓ | 270.10 | 43 | ↑ |
| SAKURA-G | Spartan-6 | 45 nm | 25.30 | 44 | ↑ | 9.03 | 29 | ↓ | 6.51 | 27 | ↓ |
| SAKURA-X | Kintex-7 | 28 nm | 138.70 | 49 | ↓ | 120.10 | 43 | ↓ | 21.90 | 8 | ↓ |

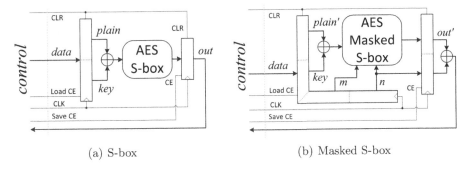

(a) S-box                    (b) Masked S-box

**Fig. 6.** Design of exemplary circuits

To sum up the result of the experiments expressed so far Table 1 presents the amount and polarity of dependency of leakage current to the targeted fundamental elements on all our three platforms.

### 3.4    AES S-box

Up to now all the presented case studies were based on many registers, connections, and LUTs having the same value. In order to move toward a crypto device, and examine whether a side-channel attack is possible we developed the fourth case study as an 8-bit key XOR followed by an AES S-box. For the S-box circuit we took the very small design of [7]. A diagram of the circuit is shown by Fig. 6(a). Two 8-bit registers supply the inputs of the key addition and the S-box, and one register is responsible to save the S-box output. All the registers are handled by *Control*.

As shown in previous experiments, the dominant term affecting leakage current is temperature variations. Therefore, to exploit the amount of leakage current relevant to the processed data we should continuously measure the leakage current of a deterministic state of the underlying device, e.g., RESET after power up. In case of our exemplary AES S-box design, forcing the device to RESET state is done by handling the CLR signal which causes all three registers to clear their content. Therefore, to diminish the effect of temperature we followed the below procedure:

1. *Control* forces *Target* to RESET state by setting CLR signal.
2. The procedure of Fig. 1 is followed to measure leakage current as $l_{\mathrm{RESET}}$.
3. $data = (plain, key)$ as input is provided by *Control* for *Target*.
4. Again based on the procedure of Fig. 1 leakage current as $l_{data}$ is measured when the S-box output is ready to be saved in the register.
5. The amount of leakage current related to $data$ is reported as $(l_{data} - l_{\mathrm{RESET}})$.

Therefore, for each given $data$ the measurement process should be performed twice to obtain a singular value as relevant leakage current. Apparently the delay between these two measurements should be kept as small as possible.

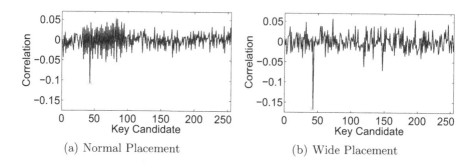

(a) Normal Placement                    (b) Wide Placement

**Fig. 7.** CPA attack using HW of the S-box output on leakage current of the design of Fig. 6(a) implemented on SAKURA-X (Kintex-7), 10 000 measurements

For the rest of the experiments we focus on the third platform SAKURA-X (Kintex-7). After implementing the aforementioned design on *Target*, we kept the 8-bit *key* constant and performed the procedure explained above 10 000 times with random 8-bit *plain* values. This way we obtained 10 000 measurements of leakage current related to the known *plain* values. In sum, whole of the measurement process took around 2.5 hours. Similar to when applied on dynamic power traces, a power analysis attack can now be mounted using the collected measurements of leakage current. Several techniques like DPA [16], CPA [6], and MIA [12] can be used to examine whether the selected *key* value can be extracted. An obvious difference to when they are applied on dynamic power traces is the absence of time domain since each measured static power (leakage current) is a singular value.

We have tried the aforementioned power analysis techniques with different hypothetical models. The result of a CPA attack with Hamming weight (HW) model (S-box output) is shown in Fig. 7(a). The efficiency of the attack is obvious, but it is strongly affected by the placement and routing strategy of *Target*. A different placement and routing causes a different number and types of connections to be used to realize the design. As shown by the presented experiments, this directly affects the amount of leakage current related to the value of the connected signals. For example, forcing the S-box output register to be placed far away from the S-box combinatorial circuit causes the corresponding connections to be very long passing many switch boxes. This has a huge impact on the attack (CPA-HW) efficiency as shown in Fig. 7(b). As a short notice, since the internal connections (signal routings) are amongst the dominant factors affecting leakage current of an FPGA, in contrast to what is reported in [17] for a simulated ASIC, HW model might be not necessarily a suitable model in case of FPGAs.

### 3.5   Masked AES S-box

Now an interesting question is whether a higher-order attack is possible through static leakage when the implementation is equipped with a masking

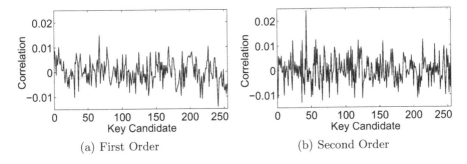

(a) First Order                        (b) Second Order

**Fig. 8.** CPA attack using HW of the S-box output on leakage current of the design of Fig. 6(b) implemented on SAKURA-X (Kintex-7), 50 000 measurements

countermeasure. So, another exemplary design as shown in Fig. 6(b) is taken into account. The masked AES S-box is taken from the very compact design of [8] which realizes first-order Boolean masking. For each given *plain* value, two 8-bit values $m$ and $n$ as input and output masks are randomly selected. *data* as $(plain', key, m, n)$ is composed and sent to *Target* by *Control*, where *plain'* denotes *plain* $\oplus$ $m$ (masked input). When the input registers have stored *data*, the masked S-box output as $S(plain \oplus key) \oplus n$ is ready to be saved in the output register. Similar to the last experiment, we took SAKURA-X (Kintex-7) as the platform and performed the leakage current measurements according to the procedure explained in Section 3.4. During all 50 000 measurements (taken in 12 hours) *plain* as well as $m$ and $n$ were selected randomly while the *key* value was kept constant.

The first-order leakage of the underlying masked S-box design through dynamic power is known (see [18]). We have also tried to mount a *correlation collision attack* [18] to examine its first-order leakage through leakage current (see Appendix). Nevertheless, as shown by Fig. 8(a) CPA attacks using common models (S-box output HW) are ineffective to recover the secret. However, a second-order attack is expected to be efficient. So, the collected leakage current values are made mean free and then squared. Afterwards, the same CPA attack, indeed a zero-offset second-order attack [22], is performed whose result is depicted by Fig. 8(b). It clearly shows that the same principles of higher-order attacks are valid in case of leakage current. The main difference is due to having only univariate measurements in this case.

## 4   Realistic Scenario

After performing quite exhaustive preliminary experiments, it is now time to examine under which conditions a crypto device can be attacked through its static power. We have developed a full AES-128 encryption engine with a 32-bit width datapath, where at each clock cycle a column is processed as four S-boxes or one MixCoulmns. Figure 13 shows an overview of the design, as can be seen both masking and shuffling are employed. The masking scheme is

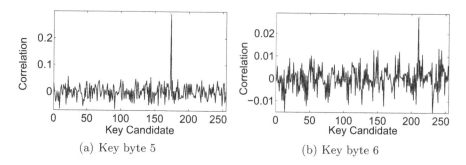

(a) Key byte 5                                    (b) Key byte 6

**Fig. 9.** AES-128 encryption engine, PRNG off, CPA attack results with S-box output HW model, 100 000 measurements

first-order Boolean, and the underlying masked S-box is the same as the one used in Section 3.5. The shuffling is realized by randomly selecting the order of processing the columns (Sel_Col signal). Moreover, during the computation of SubBytes the four instances of the S-box circuit are randomly assigned to the given column (Instance Shuffling signal). Within loading the plaintext, key, and masks the initial masking as well as AddRoundKey are performed. Then, the SubBytes operation is performed in 4 clock cycles. Afterwards, it takes 4 clock cycles to finish MixColumns and AddRoundKey at the same time. During this period the S-box instances are used by KeySchedule. The "Mask Correction" unit also changes the masks after each MixColumns and prepares the round output to be again masked by input mask $m$. Clearly at the "Final Round" MixColumns is not operated, and the mask of the S-box output is removed after the last AddRoundKey and before saving them back to the state register.

**PRNG Off.** The design is implemented on SAKURA-X (Kintex-7), and for the first try the PRNG which generates random values for input and output masks $m$ and $n$ as well as for shuffling (Sel_Col and Instance Shuffling) is switched off. As stated before, for leakage current measurements we require a deterministic state, e.g., RESET, to continuously measure its relevant leakage current. Since in the underlying FPGAs the content of the registers after power up is deterministic (specified as '0' or '1' by the bitstream), we continuously power down and up the *Target* FPGA in order to obtain $l_{\mathrm{RESET}}$ for each *data*-dependent leakage current measurement. After supplying a new *data* by *Control*, *Target* is kept running till end of the SubBytes operation of the first cipher round, i.e., 4 clock cycles after starting the encryption. As stated before, at this time instance all IO signals provided by *Control* including CLK go LO; then the leakage current of *Target* is measured. It should be noted that for each relative leakage current measurement *Target* is powered down and up again to obtain a new $l_{\mathrm{RESET}}$. In this setting we repeated the leakage current measurements 100 000 times when supplying the inputs by random 128-bit plaintexts and a constant 128-bit key.

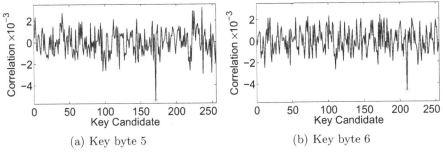

(a) Key byte 5                                    (b) Key byte 6

**Fig. 10.** AES-128 encryption engine, PRNG on, second-order CPA attack results with S-box output HW model, 1 000 000 measurements

A similar attack as before, CPA by HW of the S-box output, might be able to recover the secrets. During the attack we noticed that four key bytes can be detected much easier than the others. When the leakage current is being measured, one column of the SubBytes result stored in the state registers is available at the MixColumns circuit's input. The key bytes related to this column are discovered easier compared to that of other columns which are only available at the column-selecting multiplexer. Figure 9 shows the result of the attack targeting two different key bytes. Indeed, this result shows the same concept as attack using dynamic power. The leakage solely related to the registers' content is not easily detectable, but when they drive a considerably large combinatorial circuit, e.g., an AES S-box, the data-dependent leakage is much more exploitable. This is in fact the reason behind the high efficiency of Hamming distance (HD) model when attacking a hardware design through its dynamic power.

**PRNG On.** As the last experiment we repeated the previous procedure while the PRNG is switched on and provides uniformly distributed values. The PRNG is embedded on *Control*, seeded by the PC after each power up, and all required random values are sent to *Target* before starting the encryption. Therefore, reseting *Target* to obtain $l_{\text{RESET}}$ does not affect the distribution of the random numbers provided by *Control*. This time we performed 1 000 000 leakage current measurements which took 10.7 days. As shown in Section 3.5, we can mount a second-order attack. In this case when the leakage current is measured, a randomly selected column (by Sel_Col) appears at the MixColumns input. Therefore, all key bytes can be recovered relatively with the same effort. The results of the second-order CPA with HW model on two key bytes are shown in Fig. 10. In short, the attack succeeds even when both masking and shuffling are applied.

# 5   Conclusions

In this work we have presented the first practical results of using static power to mount a successful side-channel attack. All the results illustrated are based on three FPGAs and a couple of exemplary circuits. Note that it cannot be concluded that any implementation on any FPGA can be broken by means of its static power. The results we observed and the conclusions we gave may not hold for another FPGA family or for an ASIC platform. In addition, there are a couple of important facts which should be noted:

- The main power-consuming components in FPGAs are connections (signal routings). This is not true for ASIC platforms, and wires should not significantly affect the chip leakage current. In this case the registers' content and gates' output should be the main leakage sources.
- Although we have used a specific measurement setup, a dedicated setup to amplify the DC signals as well as to reduce the noise by low-pass filters should be developed for further analyses.
- By means of e.g., a climate chamber a constant temperature should be maintained during the static power measurements.
- The measurements of static power are more time consuming compared to that of dynamic power.
- Due to the very small amplitude of the signal as well as high noise, Signal to Noise Ratio (SNR) in this case is much smaller than that of dynamic power. Therefore, many measurements are required to mount a successful attack.
- Similar to the case of using dynamic power, knowing the design architecture of the device under attack in some cases is essential for a successful key-recover attack. It is more critical to know at which time instance (which clock cycle) the IO should be off to measure the static power.

The current study shows that the attacks using static power are practical, but – using the current facilities and known measurement setup – they are still less efficient than the attacks using dynamic power. Moreover, in case of static power attacks the adversary model is quite strong as he/she ideally needs to control the clock signal. So, many other attacks, e.g., fault injection attacks, are potentially possible.

We should highlight that the results demonstrated here are preliminary, and there are many more issues to be discovered in practice. If it is confirmed by practice for ASIC platforms or micro-controllers (of course by a sophisticated measurement setup) the masking schemes might be in danger. The leakage is always univariate in case of static power, and the leakage of different shares of a shared secret are always added and can be seen through the device static power. Therefore, the designs like [20] as a univariate-resistance approach will be vulnerable through static power (e.g., using higher-order moments) similar to only-first-order-resistant approaches like [19].

# References

1. Side-channel Attack Standard Evaluation Board (SASEBO). Further information are available via, http://www.morita-tech.co.jp/SAKURA/en/index.html
2. Agrawal, D., Archambeault, B., Rao, J.R., Rohatgi, P.: The EM side-channel(s). In: Kaliski Jr., B.S., Koç, Ç.K., Paar, C. (eds.) CHES 2002. LNCS, vol. 2523, pp. 29–45. Springer, Heidelberg (2003)

3. Alioto, M., Giancane, L., Scotti, G., Trifiletti, A.: Leakage Power Analysis attacks: Well-defined procedure and first experimental results. In: Microelectronics 2009, pp. 46–49. IEEE (2009)
4. Alioto, M., Giancane, L., Scotti, G., Trifiletti, A.: Leakage Power Analysis Attacks: A Novel Class of Attacks to Nanometer Cryptographic Circuits. IEEE Trans. on Circuits and Systems 57-I(2), 355–367 (2010)
5. Basel Halak, A.Y., Murphy, J.: Power Balanced Circuits for Leakage-Power-Attacks Resilient Design. Cryptology ePrint Archive, Report 2013/048 (2013), http://eprint.iacr.org/
6. Brier, E., Clavier, C., Olivier, F.: Correlation Power Analysis with a Leakage Model. In: Joye, M., Quisquater, J.-J. (eds.) CHES 2004. LNCS, vol. 3156, pp. 16–29. Springer, Heidelberg (2004)
7. Canright, D.: A Very Compact S-Box for AES. In: Rao, J.R., Sunar, B. (eds.) CHES 2005. LNCS, vol. 3659, pp. 441–455. Springer, Heidelberg (2005), http://faculty.nps.edu/drcanrig/pub/index.html
8. Canright, D., Batina, L.: A Very Compact "Perfectly Masked" S-Box for AES. In: Bellovin, S.M., Gennaro, R., Keromytis, A.D., Yung, M. (eds.) ACNS 2008. LNCS, vol. 5037, pp. 446–459. Springer, Heidelberg (2008), the corrected version at Cryptology ePrint Archive, Report 2009/011, http://eprint.iacr.org/
9. Ferrigno, J., Hlaváč, M.: When AES blinks: introducing optical side channel. IET Information Security 2(3), 94–98 (2008)
10. Gandolfi, K., Mourtel, C., Olivier, F.: Electromagnetic Analysis: Concrete Results. In: Koç, Ç.K., Naccache, D., Paar, C. (eds.) CHES 2001. LNCS, vol. 2162, pp. 251–261. Springer, Heidelberg (2001)
11. Genkin, D., Shamir, A., Tromer, E.: RSA Key Extraction via Low-Bandwidth Acoustic Cryptanalysis. Cryptology ePrint Archive, Report 2013/857 (2013), http://eprint.iacr.org/
12. Gierlichs, B., Batina, L., Tuyls, P., Preneel, B.: Mutual Information Analysis. In: Oswald, E., Rohatgi, P. (eds.) CHES 2008. LNCS, vol. 5154, pp. 426–442. Springer, Heidelberg (2008)
13. Giorgetti, J., Scotti, G., Simonetti, A., Trifiletti, A.: Analysis of data dependence of leakage current in CMOS cryptographic hardware. In: ACM Great Lakes Symposium on VLSI, pp. 78–83. ACM (2007)
14. Hutter, M., Schmidt, J.-M.: The Temperature Side Channel and Heating Fault Attacks. In: Francillon, A., Rohatgi, P. (eds.) CARDIS 2013. LNCS, vol. 8419, Springer, Heidelberg (2014)
15. Kocher, P.C.: Timing Attacks on Implementations of Diffie-Hellman, RSA, DSS, and Other Systems. In: Koblitz, N. (ed.) CRYPTO 1996. LNCS, vol. 1109, pp. 104–113. Springer, Heidelberg (1996)
16. Kocher, P.C., Jaffe, J., Jun, B.: Differential Power Analysis. In: Wiener, M. (ed.) CRYPTO 1999. LNCS, vol. 1666, pp. 388–397. Springer, Heidelberg (1999)
17. Lin, L., Burleson, W.: Leakage-based differential power analysis (LDPA) on sub-90nm CMOS cryptosystems. In: ISCAS 2008, pp. 252–255. IEEE (2008)
18. Moradi, A., Mischke, O., Eisenbarth, T.: Correlation-Enhanced Power Analysis Collision Attack. In: Mangard, S., Standaert, F.-X. (eds.) CHES 2010. LNCS, vol. 6225, pp. 125–139. Springer, Heidelberg (2010)
19. Nikova, S., Rijmen, V., Schläffer, M.: Secure Hardware Implementation of Nonlinear Functions in the Presence of Glitches. J. Cryptology 24(2), 292–321 (2011)
20. Prouff, E., Roche, T.: Higher-Order Glitches Free Implementation of the AES Using Secure Multi-party Computation Protocols. In: Preneel, B., Takagi, T. (eds.) CHES 2011. LNCS, vol. 6917, pp. 63–78. Springer, Heidelberg (2011)

21. Quisquater, J.-J., Samyde, D.: ElectroMagnetic Analysis (EMA): Measures and Counter-Measures for Smart Cards. In: Attali, S., Jensen, T. (eds.) E-smart 2001. LNCS, vol. 2140, pp. 200–210. Springer, Heidelberg (2001)
22. Waddle, J., Wagner, D.: Towards Efficient Second-Order Power Analysis. In: Joye, M., Quisquater, J.-J. (eds.) CHES 2004. LNCS, vol. 3156, pp. 1–15. Springer, Heidelberg (2004)
23. Xilinx. Constraints Guide (2008),
    http://www.xilinx.com/itp/xilinx10/books/docs/cgd/cgd.pdf
24. Xilinx. Spartan-6 Libraries Guide for HDL Designs (April 2012),
    http://www.xilinx.com/support/documentation/
    sw_manuals/xilinx14_1/spartan6_hdl.pdf
25. Xilinx. Virtex-5 Libraries Guide for HDL Designs (April 2012),
    http://www.xilinx.com/support/documentation/
    sw_manuals/xilinx14_1/virtex5_hdl.pdf
26. Xilinx. Xilinx 7 Series FPGA Libraries Guide for HDL Designs (April 2012),
    http://www.xilinx.com/support/documentation/
    sw_manuals/xilinx14_1/7series_hdl.pdf
27. Zhu, N., Zhou, Y., Liu, H.: Counteracting leakage power analysis attack using random ring oscillators. In: Sensor Network Security Technology and Privacy Communication System 2013, pp. 74–77. IEEE (2013)

# Appendix

## First-Order Leakage of the Masked S-box

In order to examine the first-order leakage of the masked AES S-box of Fig. 6(b), we collected two sets of 50 000 leakage current measurements with two different 8-bit *key* values. Similar to that of [18] we estimated the mean of these two sets based on the value of *plain* and obtained two 256-element mean vectors. Permuting one of the mean vectors based on the guessed $\Delta key$ and correlating with another mean vector led to the result shown by Fig. 11. Indeed it confirms that the same concept as first-order leakage of the employed masked S-box is valid in case of leakage current as the attack can recover the linear difference between two selected *key* values.

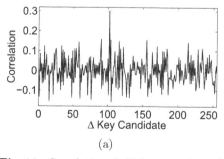
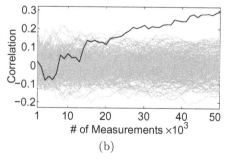

(a)    (b)

**Fig. 11.** Correlation Collision attack on leakage current of the masked AES S-box design of Fig. 6(b) implemented on SAKURA-X (Kintex-7), (a) using 50 000 measurements, (b) over number of measurements

# Supporting Figures

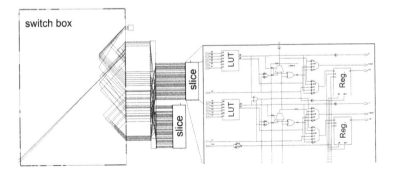

**Fig. 12.** Virtex-5 internal architecture, CLB (two slices) and its dedicated switch box

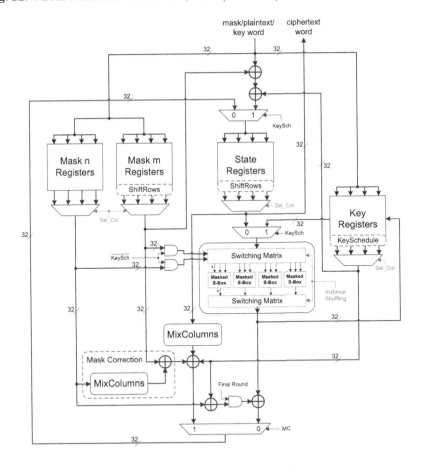

**Fig. 13.** Architecture of the masked shuffled AES encryption engine

# Gate-Level Masking under a Path-Based Leakage Metric

Andrew J. Leiserson, Mark E. Marson, and Megan A. Wachs

Cryptography Research, Inc.
425 Market Street, 11th Floor, San Francisco, CA 94105, USA
{andy,mark,megan}@cryptography.com

**Abstract.** Masking is a popular countermeasure against differential power analysis (DPA) and other side-channel attacks. When designing integrated circuits to resist DPA, masking at the logic gate level has the benefit that it can be implemented without consideration of the high-level function of the circuit. However, the phenomena of *glitches* and *early propagation* reduce the effectiveness of many gate-level masking schemes. In this paper we present a new technique for gate-level masking that is free of glitches and early propagation, yet requires only cell-level "don't touch" constraints. Our technique, which we call *LUT-Masked Dual-rail with Precharge Logic* (LMDPL), can therefore be implemented in a typical FPGA or standard cell ASIC design flow. LMDPL does not require routing constraints, nor sequencing of the evaluation of individual gates with enables, registers, or latches. We verify our techniques with an AES implementation on an FPGA. Our implementation shows no significant leaks in evaluations using up to 200 million traces.

**Keywords:** DPA, Side-Channel Analysis, Masked Logic, Dual-Rail Precharge Logic, Glitches, Early Propagation, AES, S-box.

## 1 Introduction

Many devices leak information through side channels such as power consumption or radiated electromagnetic energy. Side channel analysis techniques such as differential power analysis (DPA) [11] can recover information about secrets manipulated in a cryptographic device. Given enough measurements, these techniques may enable an attacker to recover a portion, or the entirety, of a secret key intended to be kept secure within a cryptographic device.

Masking countermeasures [4] seek to prevent DPA attacks by making the electrical activity in a device independent of secret values being operated upon. This is done by dividing the secret into multiple shares. The shares can be combined to recover the original secret, but each share is random when considered individually. Thus, operations may be performed on the shares without leaking information about the secret. For example, given a secret value $k$ in some group $G$, a first-order additive masking uses a mask $m$ chosen randomly from $G$, and divides $k$ into the shares $m$ and $m + k$. Each of these shares is, when considered individually, independent of $k$.

L. Batina and M. Robshaw (Eds.): CHES 2014, LNCS 8731, pp. 580–597, 2014.

Gate-level masking strategies attempt to construct masked versions of the elemental Boolean functions (AND, OR, etc.). For example, two common masked versions of a two-input Boolean function $f : a, b \rightarrow q$ are:

$$g(a \oplus m_a, b \oplus m_b, m_a, m_b, m_q) = f(a, b) \oplus m_q \tag{1}$$

$$h(a \oplus m, b \oplus m, m) = f(a, b) \oplus m \tag{2}$$

The masked function $g$ uses two independent mask bits for the inputs, and produces an output masked with a third mask that is independent of the input masks. The function $h$ uses a common mask bit that is reused for both of the inputs and the output.

Suppose we can construct a masked gate that can compute Boolean functions without leaking the unmasked values of the secret data $a$, $b$, and $q$. Then, more complex functions can be constructed from those masked gates, ideally in the same manner that any circuit can be constructed out of standard logic gates. Alternatively, given an implementation of some cryptographic circuit constructed using standard Boolean gates, the masked gates could perhaps be swapped for the standard gates to yield a masked implementation of the circuit. Our goal is to create such a masked gate.

## 1.1 Previous Work

Masking countermeasures have been studied extensively. We focus here on techniques that are most relevant to hardware implementations. Trichina et al. made an early proposal for a masked AND gate using four ANDs and four XORs [28]. Subsequent study found that direct implementation of masked operations in hardware may leak information through extraneous signal transitions known as *glitches*, due to the multitude of paths through the circuit [7, 13].

This led to the proposal of masked dual-rail with precharge logic (MDPL) [22]. MDPL avoids glitches through the use of precharged, monotonic, dual-rail logic, with each signal **x** encoded as a complementary pair $(x, \overline{x})$. The authors observe that the $h$ version of a masked AND gate can be implemented as:

$$q_m = \mathrm{MAJ}(a_m, b_m, m)$$

$$\overline{q_m} = \mathrm{MAJ}(\overline{a_m}, \overline{b_m}, \overline{m}) \tag{3}$$

However, it was later shown that MDPL circuits exhibited significant first-order leakage due to *early propagation* [12, 21, 26]. Improved MDPL (iMDPL) addresses early propagation, but requires use of latches to control the moment at which gates evaluate [21].

In addition to the above issues, MDPL and other maskings of the form $h$ described in Eq. 2 may not provide adequate resistance against attacks that examine leakage distributions [6, 8, 24, 29]. Another technique that can be used to attack protected implementations is the *collision-correlation attack* [17]. This is a powerful technique for exploiting complex leakages such as those arising from incompletely masked combinational logic [14, 15].

The maskings shown in Eqs. 1 and 2 divide a secret into two shares. It is also possible to utilize more than two shares. Techniques from the field of multi-party computation may be used to perform computations without ever operating on all the shares simultaneously, thus ensuring immunity from glitch-related leakage [23]. However, a *memory effect* was identified, in which leakages from a computation can persist in a circuit for a period of time after the computation occurs. This phenomenon can impact the security of schemes thought to be immune to univariate attacks [16].

The technique of Prouff and Roche [23] performs shared multiplications in $GF(2^8)$. In contrast, *threshold implementations* instead use bitwise shares. The product of the values $x = x_1 + x_2 + x_3$ and $y = y_1 + y_2 + y_3$ is a collection of $x_i y_j$ terms, which can be allocated to output shares such that no single output share contains sufficent information to leak the secret. Thus, threshold implementations also address the problem of glitches [2, 18, 19, 20].

Of the foregoing techniques, threshold implementations offer the greatest promise for strong masking of arbitrary circuits, but doing so still requires insertion of additional registers in some cases. In this work, we offer a strategy for general gate-level masking that does not require additional registers.

## 1.2   Roadmap

The paper is organized as follows. First, we briefly describe the idea of path-based leakage assessment. Next, we introduce LUT-Masked Dual-rail with Precharge Logic (LMDPL), a masking technique that is leak-free under a path-based leakage metric. Finally, we present some experimental results obtained from FPGA implementations of an LMDPL AES core.

# 2   Path-Based Leakage Assessment

Many previous countermeasures have been justified with arguments that the settled final values of each circuit node in each clock cycle are independent of secret data. However, such analyses cannot identify ways in which the transient electrical behavior may correlate with secret data. In practice, designs constructed without consideration of transient electrical behavior have remained vulnerable to side-channel attacks.

Most contemporary semiconductor devices are implemented using complementary metal-oxide-semiconductor (CMOS) or closely related technology. In CMOS technology, when a logic gate changes state, the parasitic capacitance at the inputs of downstream gates must be either charged or discharged. Ignoring quasi-static operating conditions such as supply voltage and temperature, the time it takes to (dis)charge the inputs of downstream gates still depends on many factors. The factors can include the number of inputs of a gate that are switching, the transition time (slew rate) at the switching inputs, and the logic state (voltage) present at non-switching inputs. When considering whether the electrical activity is independent of a secret, these effects should be considered cumulatively for the entire propagation path. For example, in a two-share scheme, if the output transition of an early gate exhibits a slight delay depending on the value of one share, and this output propagates to a gate at which the activity depends on the other share, the combination of these two effects may make the electrical activity at the downstream gate correlated with the unmasked secret.

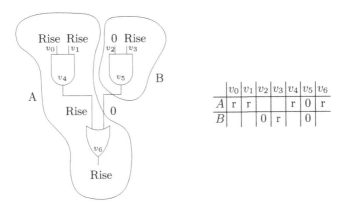

**Fig. 1.** Two activity images, A and B, for a simple circuit

To investigate whether masked logic styles leak due to this type of electrical effect, we have developed a technique that we call *activity image analysis*. Due to space constraints we include only a brief description of the technique here. Activity image analysis determines whether electrical activity at upstream and downstream gates can combine to leak a secret by considering the switching events at adjacent gates jointly, rather than separately. The idea is illustrated in Fig. 1. A circuit is leak-free under an activity image metric if, for each activity image, observation of that image does not correlate with any secret value. This is a significantly stronger condition than balancing the distribution of final gate output values.

Activity image analysis is more comprehensive than toggle simulation analysis, which analyzes a single extracted model of propagation time through gates and wires, and applies to a single combination of operating conditions. Similar to structural clock domain crossing checks, activity image analysis examines the logical structure of the circuit and provides an assurance that is robust to timing variation. We also believe activity images can be helpful in detecting early propagation, but have no formal proof.

Appendix A shows an activity image analysis of iMDPL. Residual leakage in an iMDPL implementation due to circuit effects was also examined in [14]. Based on the results we have obtained from activity image analysis, we question whether mapping a single-rail circuit to a dual-rail circuit (as done e.g. in [5]) is an effective technique for producing first-order masked implementations.

# 3    LUT-Masked Dual Rail Logic

In this section, we introduce LMDPL, explain its usage, and then describe how we implemented AES using LMDPL.

## 3.1    The LMDPL Non-linear Gate

It is well-known that linear functions are amenable to being computed on a shared representation of their argument, while non-linear functions pose substantial difficulty. Consequently, our efforts focused on identifying a way of computing non-linear functions in masked logic while satisfying the activity image leakage metric. We arrived at the dual-rail table lookup structure shown in Fig. 2. In our schematics, wires shown crossing at a right angle are not electrically joined, whereas wires shown meeting at a tee are electrically joined.

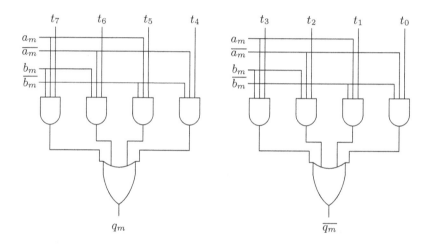

**Fig. 2.** LMDPL Non-linear Gate

The LMDPL non-linear gate is intended to be used with a masking in the form of Eq. 1. Secret inputs $a$ and $b$ are converted to masked representation by obtaining two random mask values $m_a$ and $m_b$, and computing

$$a_m = a \oplus m_a$$
$$b_m = b \oplus m_b \tag{4}$$

The values $m_a$ and $m_b$ constitute one share (the "mask share"), and $a_m$ and $b_m$ constitute the other share (the "masked data share"). In dual-rail logic, each logical value is represented by a complementary pair of signals, only one of which may be active at any time. The masked data values $a_m$ and $b_m$ are input in dual-rail encoding at the left of Fig. 2. The eight $t_i$ inputs at the top of the figure provide the values of a lookup table. By supplying the appropriate lookup table corresponding to the desired function $f$ and the mask values $m_a$, $m_b$, and $m_q$, the LMDPL gate produces a pair of complementary outputs that are a dual-rail encoding of $q_m$. We will return to the computation of the lookup table values in Section 3.2. Although the LMDPL non-linear gate may be used to implement an arbitrary two-input function, more compact alternatives are available for linear functions.

The structure shown in Fig. 2 is important. If EDA tools are permitted to freely restructure the logic, the gate will no longer pass a path-based leakage assessment. Fortunately, it is not difficult to instruct common EDA tools to preserve certain cell instantiations with a mechanism known as a *don't touch* constraint. Limited restructuring of the gate is acceptable. For example, ASIC implementations may prefer the NAND/NAND structure obtained by applying De Morgan's Law. We suggest some strategies for implementing LMDPL with common tools in Appendix B

Between each evaluation, the circuit must be precharged by driving both signals in each masked data pair to zero. Zeros on the four masked data inputs will propagate to the outputs, hence a precharge applied at the masked data inputs of a collection of LMDPL gates will propagate to the final outputs. During the evaluation of the gate, a transition away from zero on an output requires a non-zero value to have arrived on one of the component signals of each dual-rail input pair. Thus, the LMDPL gate does not exhibit early propagation.

LMDPL avoids glitches through the use of monotonic gates, in the same manner as the original MDPL. In the course of any evaluation, each of the $q_m$ and $\overline{q_m}$ outputs will transition at most once.

On any evaluation, exactly one of the AND gates in the LMDPL non-linear gate will produce a rising transition at the output. Even after fixing any or all of the unmasked data values, each of the eight AND gates has an equal probability of being the active gate upon each evaluation, depending upon the mask values. This effect is similar to Baddam et al.'s path switching countermeasure [1].

## 3.2   Implementing LMDPL

A simple circuit constructed using LMDPL is illustrated in Fig. 3. The circuit has three inputs, $x$, $y$, and $z$, and one output, $w$. The top portion of the figure operates on the mask share, and the bottom portion of the figure operates on the masked data share. The lookup tables $t_i$ for the LMDPL gates are passed from the mask share to the masked data share through registers. There are two non-linear gates, so the mask share takes two fresh mask bits from the RNG. Each of the mask share logic and masked data share logic is constructed by making modifications to the original circuit. The mask share retains linear elements, ties the output of each non-linear element to an RNG bit, and instantiates a "Table Gen" component for each non-linear element. The masked data share replaces the linear elements with corresponding dual-rail versions, and replaces the non-linear elements with instances of the LMDPL non-linear gate.

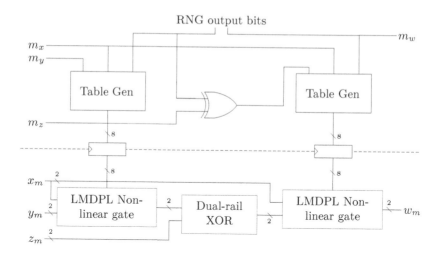

RNG output bits

**Fig. 3.** A simple circuit using LMDPL

The "Table Gen" components compute the $t_i$ values for each non-linear gate in the manner typical of masked lookup tables. A function $f : \mathrm{GF}(2) \times \mathrm{GF}(2) \to \mathrm{GF}(2)$ is assigned to each table generator according to the original circuit. Each table generator accepts input masks $m_a$ and $m_b$ and an output mask $m_q$, which vary for each evaluation, and computes a varying table for each evaluation by the following formula.

Let $\mathbf{m} = (m_b, m_a)$ and $\mathbf{i} = (i_1, i_0)$ with $i_0, i_1 \in \{0, 1\}$. Then,

$$t_{4+2i_1+i_0} = f(\mathbf{i} \oplus \mathbf{m}) \oplus m_q = f(i_1 \oplus m_b, i_0 \oplus m_a) \oplus m_q$$
$$t_{2i_1+i_0} = t_{4+2i_1+i_0} \oplus 1 \tag{5}$$

The non-linear function implemented by the LMDPL gate will commonly be a logical AND: $f(a, b) = a \cdot b$. The operation of the table generation logic for this case is shown in Table 1.

### 3.3    Implementing Linear Functions

Circuits typically also include gates that are linear (or affine) under boolean masking. When implementing linear gates, it is not necessary to consider the masking, so LMDPL is compatible with the linear gates from non-masked dual-rail logic styles such as WDDL [27]. We review briefly how to implement NOT and XOR gates.

A NOT gate can be implemented without any transistors, simply by swapping the complementary dual-rail signals. That is, $\mathbf{q} = \mathrm{NOT}(\mathbf{a})$ is implemented by:

$$q = \overline{a}$$
$$\overline{q} = a \tag{6}$$

**Table 1.** Computation of the $t_i$ for $f(a, b) = a \cdot b$

| $m_q$ | $m_b$ | $m_a$ | $t_7$ | $t_6$ | $t_5$ | $t_4$ | $t_3$ | $t_2$ | $t_1$ | $t_0$ |
|---|---|---|---|---|---|---|---|---|---|---|
| 0 | 0 | 0 | 1 | 0 | 0 | 0 | 0 | 1 | 1 | 1 |
| 0 | 0 | 1 | 0 | 1 | 0 | 0 | 1 | 0 | 1 | 1 |
| 0 | 1 | 0 | 0 | 0 | 1 | 0 | 1 | 1 | 0 | 1 |
| 0 | 1 | 1 | 0 | 0 | 0 | 1 | 1 | 1 | 1 | 0 |
| 1 | 0 | 0 | 0 | 1 | 1 | 1 | 1 | 0 | 0 | 0 |
| 1 | 0 | 1 | 1 | 0 | 1 | 1 | 0 | 1 | 0 | 0 |
| 1 | 1 | 0 | 1 | 1 | 0 | 1 | 0 | 0 | 1 | 0 |
| 1 | 1 | 1 | 1 | 1 | 1 | 0 | 0 | 0 | 0 | 1 |

XOR gates should be implemented as monotonic logic (i.e., constructed out of AND and OR gates) to ensure the logic remains glitch-free and to correctly propagate the precharge state. An XOR gate $\mathbf{q} = \mathrm{XOR}(\mathbf{a}, \mathbf{b})$ can be implemented as follows:

$$q = \overline{a} \cdot b + a \cdot \overline{b}$$
$$\overline{q} = \overline{a} \cdot \overline{b} + a \cdot b \qquad (7)$$

### 3.4  AES Implementation

To test the effectiveness of LMDPL, we developed an implementation of AES. The overall architecture of the AES implementation is shown in Fig. 4. The design computes a complete round transformation in parallel, and thus has 16 S-boxes. We favor simplicity and use a clock-based approach for the precharge, driving inputs to the LMDPL logic to zero in alternate cycles. Recall that sophisticated masking techniques are required only for non-linear operations, and the only non-linear operation in AES is the $\mathrm{GF}(2^8)$ inversion within SubBytes. We implement only the inversion in LMDPL, and implement the remainder of the round transformation (including the linear portions of SubBytes) in ordinary logic. The sequence of operation is:

0. Initially, the LMDPL inversion logic is precharged.
1. In cycle 1 of a cipher operation, ordinary logic performs AddRoundKey and converts bytewise to the subfield basis used for inversion. The LMDPL logic is still precharged.
2. In cycle 2, the LMDPL logic computes bytewise inversion in $\mathrm{GF}(2^8)$.
3. In cycle 3, ordinary logic converts bytewise to the standard AES basis, applies the SubBytes affine transformation, performs ShiftRows, MixColumns, and AddRoundKey, and then converts bytewise back to the subfield basis. Also in cycle 3, the LMDPL logic is precharged.
4. In subsequent even cycles, the LMDPL logic is active.
5. In subsequent odd cycles, the ordinary logic is active, and the LMDPL logic is precharged.

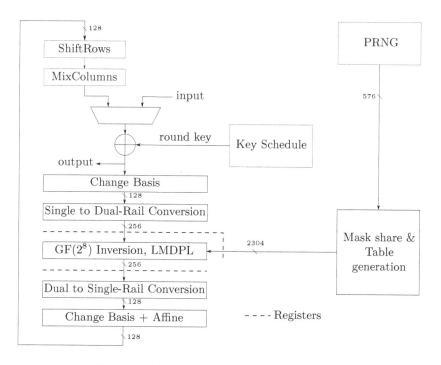

**Fig. 4.** Architecture of the AES implementation

Fig. 4 emphasizes the masked data share logic. The mask share logic (not shown in detail) mirrors the masked data share logic, with the table generation implemented according to Fig. 3, and without the need for registers surrounding the $GF(2^8)$ inversion.

The $GF(2^8)$ inversion uses the $GF(((2^2)^2)^2)$ normal basis identified in [3]. This implementation requires 36 bit-multiplications in $GF(2)$. Some additional detail on our implementation of the inversion is provided in Appendix B.

The mask share (the $t_i$) would ideally be kept in the Hamming-weight-balanced 8-bit encoding to minimize leakages usable by second-order attacks. However, this is quite expensive. At some cost in resistance to second-order attacks, we generate and register only half of the table. The complementary half is obtained by inversion. In some cases, registers with complementary outputs could be used.

For purposes of comparison, we synthesized an ASIC version of our LMDPL AES core using Synopsys Design Compiler 2013.03-SP2. Table 2 compares our implementation with several others reported in the literature. Note that the threshold implementations [2, 18] have the advantage that the S-box can be pipelined, meaning the overall throughput is one S-box evaluation per clock rather than 1/latency. However, this benefit disappears in fully parallel implementations, as it is necessary to obtain the previous round's SubBytes output and apply the remaining transformations of an AES round before the next

**Table 2.** Comparison of implementations. Area reported both as count of Virtex 5 LUTs and as NAND2-normalized ASIC area ("Gate Equivalents"). Area does not include PRNG. LMDPL S-box area includes pre- and post-inversion data registers, single/dual rail conversion, table generation, table registers, and basis converters implemented in single-rail logic.

| | Random bits per S-box | S-box latency | Parallel AES | | Per S-box | |
|---|---|---|---|---|---|---|
| | | | LUTs | GE | LUTs | GE |
| [16] | 8 | 132 | 21,328 | | 1,387 | |
| [18] | 48 | 5 | | | | 4,244 |
| [2] | 44 | 3 | | | | 3,003 |
| This work | 36 | 2 | 8,538 | 59,311 | 447 | 2,825 |

SubBytes input is ready. Also, note that although it requires fewer random bits per S-box, the parallel AES presented in this work requires more random bits in per-clock terms (576/2) compared to the threshold implementations with 8-bit datapaths (44/3 and 48/5). As was the case for the threshold implementations, we have provided ASIC area figures for comparison, while presenting evaluation results from an FPGA.

# 4 Experimental Results

This section presents assessments of DPA resistance on two designs incorporating LMDPL. Each design is described in Verilog, and implemented for Xilinx Virtex-5 FPGA using Synplify Pro 2009.03 and Xilinx ISE 13.2.

## 4.1 Evaluation Methodology

To evaluate the information leakage in different designs, we used the test vector leakage assessment (TVLA) methodology proposed by Goodwill et al. [9]. The TVLA methodology is designed to measure information leakage and provide an objective score. It specifies test vectors and uses Welch's t-test to measure the significance in the difference of means of two distributions. One of the tests in the methodology is known as the "fixed versus random" (FVR) test. In this test, the measurements are collected as the device operates repeatedly using fixed input data and randomly varying input data. (The fixed and random input vectors are randomly interleaved.) Welch's t-test is then used to score the differences between the two sets of measurements. We follow [9] and use $|t| < 4.5$ as the criteria for a passing result.

The fixed versus random evaluation technique does not target specific leaks. Rather, it measures aggregate information leakage at each point in time during the cryptographic operation. It is extremely powerful and can often find potential vulnerabilities with fewer traces than needed to identify specific leakages. In particular, for designs where the parallelism exceeds the portion of the key that can be guessed by a DPA attack, a leak identified by the FVR test is stronger than that which would actually be available to an attacker who cannot guess the entire key at once. Nevertheless, a failure of the FVR test does represent some correlation with secret intermediates, and the goal of masking is to eliminate such correlations.

Another characteristic of the FVR test is that false positives may arise due to the plaintext and ciphertext being fixed. The dilemma is similar to the need in conventional DPA attacks to select an intermediate separated from the plaintext or ciphertext by a non-linear function. We avoided the problem of input and output leaks by splitting the input into separate mask and masked data shares prior to transfer to the device under test (DUT), and likewise retrieving mask and masked data shares from the DUT before combining. We refer to this scheme as *externally applied masking* and the more conventional scheme where the DUT divides the data into shares as *internally applied masking*.

We also perform a variant of a collision correlation attack [17]. Our simulated collision correlation (SCC) attack operates by dividing the pool of traces into two equal-size groups and computing for each group the 256 means corresponding to the possible values of the S-box input. Then, for each of 256 possible "guesses" of a linear key byte distance, the means in one group are permuted according to the guess, and the correlation computed between the two sets of means. The unpermuted case represents the "correct" guess. To select points for this attack, we used one-way analysis of variance (ANOVA) to identify points with the strongest dependency on the S-box input value.

Our evaluation setup uses a Sasebo-GII board and a Signatec PX14400A PCI-E card for data acquisition. The signal is taken from the $1\,\Omega$ supply-side sense resistor on the Sasebo-GII and connected through a Mini-Circuits BLK-89-S+ DC blocker, a Mini-Circuits BLP-150+ LPF, and a Mini-Circuits ZFL-1000+ amplifier before driving the input of the Signatec card, which has a sample rate of 400 MS/s and 14 bits of resolution.

The design operates at 24 MHz. Our evaluation harness performs 2,000 consecutive AES operations with data obtained from and stored to buffers on the FPGA. The design provides a trigger signal concurrent with the start of the first AES operation. This signal is used as an external trigger for the Signatec card. To ensure that the 400 MS/s sample rate does not impact the alignment quality when analyzing our traces, we use a technique similar to that of [10] to achieve sub-sample alignment resolution.

## 4.2    Results from a Single S-box Design

Prior to presenting results from the full AES implementation, we present results from a simplified design. The simplified design maintains the 128-bit parallel datapath of the full AES implementation, but replaces 15 of the 16 S-boxes with passthroughs. We chose this approach, rather than a true 8-bit datapath AES, to focus on leakage from the LMDPL S-box as opposed to leakage from registers.

We first disabled the mask generator and collected waveforms from 10,000 encryptions. For each encryption, we chose with even probability between the fixed plaintext and a random plaintext. Fig. 5 shows several analyses of these

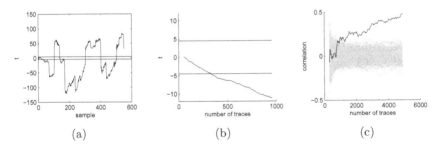

**Fig. 5.** Single S-box design, masking disabled. (a) sample-wise $t$ statistic on 10,000 traces, (b) sample 71 $t$ statistic vs. number of traces, (c) SCC attack using sample 71

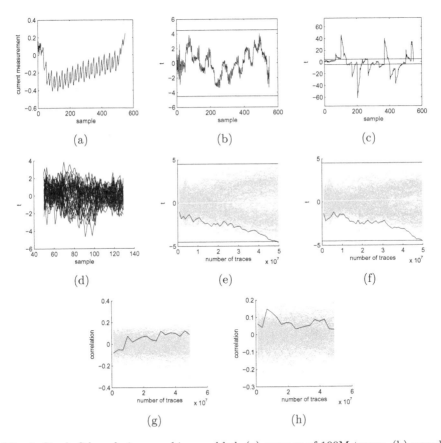

**Fig. 6.** Single S-box design, masking enabled. (a) average of 100M traces, (b) sample-wise FVR $t$ statistic, (c) sample-wise 2nd-order FVR $t$ statistic, (d) overlay of 2nd-order $t$ for each of the 36 S-box non-linear gate outputs, (e) $t$ for each of 256 possible key guesses, bit 25 sample 92, (f) $t$ for each of 256 possible key guesses, bit 25 sample 99, (g) first-order SCC using sample 86, and (h) second-order SCC using sample 86.

traces. A sample-wise plot of the $t$ statistic (a) immediately indicates that the design is leaking. We selected sample 71, the point in the first round with the greatest $|t|$ value, for further analysis. For this design, slightly over 300 traces are needed before the $|t| > 4.5$ threshold is reached for sample 71 (b). We then performed a SCC attack at sample 71. For this evaluation, between 1,000 and 1,500 traces are needed before the correct guess becomes dominant (c).

We next enabled the mask generator and collected 100,000,000 traces, again choosing evenly between a fixed plaintext or a random plaintext for each encryption. Fig. 6 presents analysis of these traces. With the masking enabled, the $t$ statistic does not exceed the $|t| > 4.5$ threshold with 100M traces (b), demonstrating that the first-order masking is effective. However, the design exhibits second-order leakage, as can be seen by using the $t$ statistic to compare the squared residuals between the two groups (c).

We used the 50,000,000 random traces out of the same data set to develop an attack exploiting the second-order leakage. We sorted the traces based on the output from each of the 36 non-linear gates in the S-box. The difference in variance due to the value of a single bit is smaller than the difference that arises when the entire plaintext is fixed, but it it still detectable. We examined all 36 candidates (d) and selected for the attack the bit and time sample combinations with the largest $|t|$. The first candidate, bit 25 at sample 92, does not result in selection of the correct key guess with 50 million traces (e). The second candidate, bit 25 at sample 99, does result in the selection of the correct key guess with 50 million traces (f). First- and second-order versions of our SCC attack on this design were not successful (g,h).

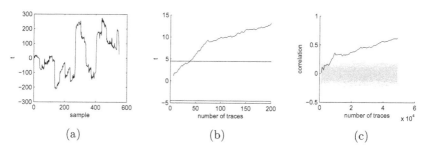

(a)                    (b)                    (c)

**Fig. 7.** Parallel design, masking disabled. (a) sample-wise FVR $t$ statistic on 100,000 traces, (b) sample 441 FVR $t$ statistic vs. number of traces, (c) SCC attack using sample 71

### 4.3   Results from a Parallel Design

One possible strategy to improve upon the resistance of the single S-box implementation would be to incorporate higher-order masking. However, in low-noise environments, the security benefit of higher-order masking is limited [25]. With this in mind, we explored the resistance of an AES-256 implementation performing SubBytes on the entire round state in parallel.

We again measured the design with masking disabled as a baseline. For the parallel design we collected 100,000 traces. For each trace, we chose randomly between the fixed plaintext or a random plaintext. Fig. 7 shows our analysis of these traces. Fig. 7(a) is a plot of the FVR $t$ statistic versus the sample index, and as with the corresponding plot for the serial implementation, provides immediate evidence that the design is leaking. Fig. 7(b) plots the $t$ statistic between the fixed and random traces at sample 441 (the sample with the largest absolute $t$ value), and shows that less than 50 traces are needed before the $|t| > 4.5$ threshold is reached. Finally, Fig. 7(c) shows the results of our SCC attack at sample 71. The correct key guess becomes dominant after about 10,000 traces.

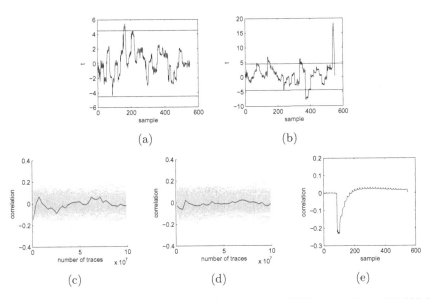

**Fig. 8.** Parallel design, masking enabled. (a) sample-wise FVR $t$ statistic on 200,000,000 traces, (b) sample-wise 2nd-order FVR $t$ statistic on 200,000,000 traces, (c) first-order SCC attack at sample 87, (d) second-order SCC attack at sample 87, (e) CPA vs. round1-round2 mask Hamming distance

Finally, we enabled the mask generator in our parallel design and collected 200,000,000 traces. Fig. 8 shows our results. The first-order FVR $t$ has only marginally exceeded the $|t| > 4.5$ threshold with 200,000,000 traces. In contrast with the serial implementation, where the second-order $t$ statistic reached significantly larger values than the first-order $t$, the second-order $t$ for the parallel implementation reaches only slightly larger values than the first-order $t$. The spike at the end of the second-order analysis in Fig. 8(b) is due to the final masked output, and mask, being manipulated at the end of the calculation, and does not represent a leak of sensitive information. We performed the SCC attack on this design, and it was not successful (c,d).

Fig. 8(e) is shown to demonstrate a technique that we use to investigate the behavior of our designs and to verify that our data collection is correct. The masked implementation used for evaluation allows re-seeding of the PRNG with an externally-supplied per-encryption seed. This allows us to compute the values of circuit intermediates that are a function of the mask, which would normally not be predictable by an attacker. The figure shows the correlation between the current measurement and the Hamming distance between the round one and round two masks. Because the mask values for successive rounds overwrite each other in the mask share logic, a strong correlation is expected and is indeed present. We additionally note that the memory effect [16] is clearly visible here. The register update occurs at the time of the initial downward spike around sample 83. A strong correlation exists for around 50 samples (3 clock cycles) after the register update, and a weak correlation persists throughout the encryption.

## 5    Conclusion

In this work, we propose the use of a path-based model for the leakage from combinational circuits. Unlike traditional methods that focus on the settled values of circuit nodes, activity image analysis considers ways that data-dependent behavior can accumulate as transitions propagate through combinational logic.

We also present LMDPL, a new technique for gate-level masking. LMDPL compares competitively or favorably with previous techniques on multiple metrics. Furthermore, LMDPL does not require routing constraints, and does not require that sequential elements or enable signals be used to delay the propagation of signals through the circuit.

## References

1. Baddam, K., Zwolinski, M.: Path switching: a technique to tolerate dual rail routing imbalances. Des. Autom. Embed. Syst. 12(3), 207–220 (2008)
2. Bilgin, B., Gierlichs, B., Nikova, S., Nikov, V., Rijmen, V.: A More Efficient AES Threshold Implementation. Cryptology ePrint Archive, Report (2013), http://eprint.iacr.org/2013/697
3. Canright, D.: A Very Compact S-Box for AES. In: Rao, J.R., Sunar, B. (eds.) CHES 2005. LNCS, vol. 3659, pp. 441–455. Springer, Heidelberg (2005)
4. Chari, S., Jutla, C.S., Rao, J.R., Rohatgi, P.: Towards Sound Approaches to Counteract Power-Analysis Attacks. In: Wiener, M. (ed.) CRYPTO 1999. LNCS, vol. 1666, pp. 398–412. Springer, Heidelberg (1999)
5. Chen, Z., Haider, S., Schaumont, P.: Side-Channel Leakage in Masked Circuits Caused by Higher-Order Circuit Effects. In: Park, J.H., Chen, H.-H., Atiquzzaman, M., Lee, C., Kim, T.-h., Yeo, S.-S. (eds.) ISA 2009. LNCS, vol. 5576, pp. 327–336. Springer, Heidelberg (2009)

6. De Mulder, E., Gierlichs, B., Preneel, B., Verbauwhede, I.: Practical DPA attacks on MDPL. In: First IEEE International Workshop on Information Forensics and Security, WIFS 2009, pp. 191–195 (2009)
7. Fischer, W., Gammel, B.M.: Masking at Gate Level in the Presence of Glitches. In: Rao, J.R., Sunar, B. (eds.) CHES 2005. LNCS, vol. 3659, pp. 187–200. Springer, Heidelberg (2005)
8. Gierlichs, B.: DPA-Resistance Without Routing Constraints? In: Paillier, P., Verbauwhede, I. (eds.) CHES 2007. LNCS, vol. 4727, pp. 107–120. Springer, Heidelberg (2007)
9. Goodwill, G., Jun, B., Jaffe, J., Rohatgi, P.: A testing methodology for sidechannel resistance validation. In: Non-Invasive Attack Testing Workshop, Nara (2011), http://csrc.nist.gov/news_events/non-invasive-attack-testingworkshop/papers/08_Goodwill.pdf
10. Homma, N., Nagashima, S., Imai, Y., Aoki, T., Satoh, A.: High-Resolution Side-Channel Attack Using Phase-Based Waveform Matching. In: Goubin, L., Matsui, M. (eds.) CHES 2006. LNCS, vol. 4249, pp. 187–200. Springer, Heidelberg (2006)
11. Kocher, P., Jaffe, J., Jun, B.: Differential Power Analysis. In: Wiener, M. (ed.) CRYPTO 1999. LNCS, vol. 1666, pp. 388–397. Springer, Heidelberg (1999)
12. Kulikowski, K., Karpovsky, M., Taubin, A.: Power attacks on secure hardware based on early propagation of data. In: 12th IEEE International On-Line Testing Symposium, pp. 131–138. IEEE Computer Society Press, Los Alamitos (2006)
13. Mangard, S., Pramstaller, N., Oswald, E.: Successfully Attacking Masked AES Hardware Implementations. In: Rao, J.R., Sunar, B. (eds.) CHES 2005. LNCS, vol. 3659, pp. 157–171. Springer, Heidelberg (2005)
14. Moradi, A., Kirschbaum, M., Eisenbarth, T., Paar, C.: Masked Dual-Rail Precharge Logic Encounters State-of-the-Art Power Analysis Methods. IEEE Transactions on Very Large Scale Integration (VLSI) Systems 20(9), 1578–1589 (2012)
15. Moradi, A., Mischke, O.: How Far Should Theory Be from Practice? In: Prouff, E., Schaumont, P. (eds.) CHES 2012. LNCS, vol. 7428, pp. 92–106. Springer, Heidelberg (2012)
16. Moradi, A., Mischke, O.: On the Simplicity of Converting Leakages from Multivariate to Univariate. In: Bertoni, G., Coron, J.-S. (eds.) CHES 2013. LNCS, vol. 8086, pp. 1–20. Springer, Heidelberg (2013)
17. Moradi, A., Mischke, O., Eisenbarth, T.: Correlation-Enhanced Power Analysis Collision Attack. In: Mangard, S., Standaert, F.-X. (eds.) CHES 2010. LNCS, vol. 6225, pp. 125–139. Springer, Heidelberg (2010)
18. Moradi, A., Poschmann, A., Ling, S., Paar, C., Wang, H.: Pushing the Limits: A Very Compact and a Threshold Implementation of AES. In: Paterson, K.G. (ed.) EUROCRYPT 2011. LNCS, vol. 6632, pp. 69–88. Springer, Heidelberg (2011)
19. Nikova, S., Rechberger, C., Rijmen, V.: Threshold Implementations Against Side-Channel Attacks and Glitches. In: Ning, P., Qing, S., Li, N. (eds.) ICICS 2006. LNCS, vol. 4307, pp. 529–545. Springer, Heidelberg (2006)
20. Nikova, S., Rijmen, V., Schläffer, M.: Secure Hardware Implementation of Nonlinear Functions in the Presence of Glitches. Journal of Cryptology 24(2), 292–321 (2010)
21. Popp, T., Kirschbaum, M., Zefferer, T., Mangard, S.: Evaluation of the Masked Logic Style MDPL on a Prototype Chip. In: Paillier, P., Verbauwhede, I. (eds.) CHES 2007. LNCS, vol. 4727, pp. 81–94. Springer, Heidelberg (2007)
22. Popp, T., Mangard, S.: Masked Dual-Rail Pre-charge Logic: DPA-Resistance Without Routing Constraints. In: Rao, J.R., Sunar, B. (eds.) CHES 2005. LNCS, vol. 3659, pp. 172–186. Springer, Heidelberg (2005)

23. Prouff, E., Roche, T.: Higher-Order Glitches Free Implementation of the AES Using Secure Multi-party Computation Protocols. In: Preneel, B., Takagi, T. (eds.) CHES 2011. LNCS, vol. 6917, pp. 63–78. Springer, Heidelberg (2011)
24. Schaumont, P., Tiri, K.: Masking and Dual-Rail Logic Don't Add Up. In: Paillier, P., Verbauwhede, I. (eds.) CHES 2007. LNCS, vol. 4727, pp. 95–106. Springer, Heidelberg (2007)
25. Standaert, F.-X., Veyrat-Charvillon, N., Oswald, E., Gierlichs, B., Medwed, M., Kasper, M., Mangard, S.: The World Is Not Enough: Another Look on Second-Order DPA. In: Abe, M. (ed.) ASIACRYPT 2010. LNCS, vol. 6477, pp. 112–129. Springer, Heidelberg (2010)
26. Suzuki, D., Saeki, M.: Security Evaluation of DPA Countermeasures Using Dual-Rail Pre-charge Logic Style. In: Goubin, L., Matsui, M. (eds.) CHES 2006. LNCS, vol. 4249, pp. 255–269. Springer, Heidelberg (2006)
27. Tiri, K., Verbauwhede, I.: A logic level design methodology for a secure DPA resistant ASIC or FPGA implementation. In: DATE 2004, vol. 1, pp. 246–251. IEEE Computer Society Press, Los Alamitos (2004)
28. Trichina, E., Korkishko, T., Lee, K.-H.: Small Size, Low Power, Side Channel-Immune AES Coprocessor: Design and Synthesis Results. In: Dobbertin, H., Rijmen, V., Sowa, A. (eds.) AES 2005. LNCS, vol. 3373, pp. 113–127. Springer, Heidelberg (2005)
29. Ye, X., Eisenbarth, T.: On the Vulnerability of Low Entropy Masking Schemes. In: Francillon, A., Rohatgi, P. (eds.) CARDIS 2013. LNCS, vol. 8419, pp. 44–60. Springer, Heidelberg (2014)

# A    Activity Image Analysis Example

Table 3 presents an activity image analysis of iMDPL in tabular form. Each row describes one activity image. Columns to the left of the double line represent states observed at the output of each gate in the circuit. The columns to the right of the double line are labeled with a value $x^*$ of the secret $x = x_m \oplus m$, and entries in those columns report the count of observations of that row's activity image when $x$ takes the value $x^*$. In this example there are eight possible inputs to the circuit, corresponding to the two possible values for each of $x_m$, $y_m$, and $m$. Evaluation of a circuit for a given input may exhibit multiple activity images.

We define a circuit to be balanced under the activity image metric if, for any value $x^*$ that the secret $x$ may take, the conditional probability that $x = x^*$, given that some particular activity image was observed, is the same as the unconditional probability that $x = x^*$. In other words, the observation counts in each row of the table must have the same proportion as the global probabilities of the associated $x^*$ values. In the case of iMDPL, $\Pr\{x = 0\} = \Pr\{x = 1\} = 0.5$, so the requirement is that the counts in each row be equal. The iMDPL circuit is not balanced, as the observation counts are different in 6 of the 10 rows. The same analysis for the LMDPL circuit (omitted for space reasons) shows that it is balanced under this metric.

**Table 3.** iMDPL AND, assuming AND/OR decomposition

$$a0 = x_m \cdot y_m \qquad a1 = x_m \cdot m \qquad a2 = y_m \cdot m \qquad q_m = a0 + a1 + a2 \qquad (8)$$

| $x_m$ | $y_m$ | $m$ | a0 | a1 | a2 | $q_m$ | $x^* = 0$ | $x^* = 1$ |
|---|---|---|---|---|---|---|---|---|
| 0 | r |  |  |  | 0 |  | 1 | 1 |
| r | 0 |  |  |  | 0 |  | 1 | 1 |
| r | r | 0 | 0 | r | r |  | 0 | 1 |
| 0 | r |  |  | 0 |  |  | 0 | 2 |
| 0 | r |  | 0 |  |  |  | 1 | 1 |
| r |  | 0 |  | 0 |  |  | 0 | 2 |
| r |  | r | 0 | r | 0 | r | 1 | 0 |
| r | 0 |  | 0 |  |  |  | 1 | 1 |
| r | r |  | r | 0 | 0 | r | 0 | 1 |
| r | r | r | r | r | r | r | 1 | 0 |

# B  Details on Implementing AES with LMDPL

As discussed in Section 3.1, LMDPL requires the structure of the non-linear gate be preserved with don't touch constraints (sometimes called "keep" constraints). For an ASIC design, library cells implementing the elemental functions may be instantiated in the HDL description, and a don't touch attribute applied to the instantiations. A common and simple way to do this is to use a distinguishing prefix in the instance names, and use a wildcard pattern to identify for the tool the cells not to touch. For either an ASIC or an FPGA, the elemental functions (AND/OR/NAND) used in the gate may be placed in a dedicated module, and a hierarchy-preserving attribute or directive applied to that module.

For the Virtex 5 FPGA, hierarchy preservation attributes limited the amount of packing the place and route tools would perform. We obtained better results by applying net preservation directives to the interface of the modules implementing the elemental functions, or to the interface of the module implementing the LMDPL gate. For example, preserving the interface of the dual-rail XOR (a 4-input, 2-output function) allows it to be packed in a single dual-output LUT. Similarly, appropriate constraints enable the eight AND gates of the non-linear gate to be packed pairwise into four dual-output LUTs.

Our AES implementation incorporates an optimized inversion circuit, which uses functions other than AND for some of the 36 non-linear gates. We created a Liberty-format library description containing cells of unit area implementing the XOR and XNOR functions, and cells of ten units area implementing each of the non-linear two-input boolean functions. We then used Synopsys Design Compiler to map the normal-basis $GF(2^8)$ inversion onto this library. The netlist from Design Compiler contained 37 non-linear gates rather than the expected 36, however, inspection revealed that two of the non-linear gates could be combined with minor rearrangement of neighboring XORs to achieve a 36-gate implementation. This optimized circuit was used as the basis for translation to LMDPL mask and masked data share implementations.

# Early Propagation and Imbalanced Routing, How to Diminish in FPGAs

Amir Moradi[1] and Vincent Immler[2,*]

[1] Horst Görtz Institute for IT Security, Ruhr University Bochum, Germany
[2] Fraunhofer Research Institution for Applied and Integrated Security (AISEC),
Munich, Germany
amir.moradi@rub.de, vincent.immler@aisec.fraunhofer.de

**Abstract.** This work deals with DPA-resistant logic styles, i.e., cell-level countermeasures against power analysis attacks that are known as a serious threat to cryptographic devices. Early propagation and imbalanced routings are amongst the well-known issues of such countermeasures, that – if not considered during the design process – can cause the underlying cryptographic device to be vulnerable to certain attacks. Although most of the DPA-resistant logic styles target an ASIC design process, there are a few attempts to apply them in an FPGA platform. This is due to the missing freedom in FPGA design tools required to deal with the aforementioned problems. Our contribution in this work is to provide solutions for both early propagation and imbalanced routings considering a modern Xilinx FPGA as the target platform. Foremost, based on the WDDL concept we design a new FPGA-based logic style without early propagation in both precharge and evaluation phases. Additionally, with respect to the limited routing resources within an FPGA we develop a customized router to find the best appropriate dual-rail routes for a given dual-rail circuit. Based on practical experiments on a Virtex-5 FPGA our evaluations verify the efficiency of each of our proposed approaches. They significantly improve the resistance of the design compared to cases not benefiting from our schemes.

## 1 Introduction

Counteracting state-of-the-art power analysis attacks (so called DPA [13]) is a must for cryptographic devices which may fall into the hands of malicious users, who can control over the device in a hostile environment. Up to now several DPA countermeasures at different levels of abstraction have been proposed. Many try to provide resistance by manipulating the underlying cryptographic algorithm in order to randomize its intermediate values, i.e., masking at the algorithmic level, e.g., [24,25]. Some introduce noise, e.g., [7,17] or randomize either the program flow or the order of the operations, i.e., shuffling, e.g., [10,17]. A couple

---

* The majority of the work was performed while Vincent Immler was with Ruhr University Bochum.

L. Batina and M. Robshaw (Eds.): CHES 2014, LNCS 8731, pp. 598–615, 2014.

of other schemes try to solve the problem from scratch, i.e., avoiding the dependency of the power consumption of the circuit to the processed data. These countermeasures at the cell level, called DPA-resistant logic styles, aim at equalizing the power consumption of a cryptographic device regardless of any input, intermediate, or output value.

After a proper evaluation [30] it was discovered that most of the proposed logic styles, such as WDDL [32] and MDPL [27], suffer from the early propagation effect. This phenomena, also called data-dependent time-of-evaluation, refers to the cases where a gate fires (evaluates) its output at different time instances depending on the value of its input. It becomes more problematic when several of such gates are cascaded to realize a combinatorial circuit. So, it causes the power consumption pattern of the circuit to have a clear dependency to its input value.

Moreover, most of the known logic styles face a common difficulty, i.e., routing imbalances. Equal power consumption, which is expected to be achieved by Dual-Rail Precharge (DRP) logic, needs a proper balance between the capacitances of each dual-rail signal. Otherwise, transitions of TRUE and FALSE lines of a dual-rail signal require different amounts of energy, which can be explored by a DPA attack. Therefore, some place-and-route methods such as [6,33] have been proposed to diminish the load imbalances of complementary signals in an ASIC design process. Although iMDPL [26], which solves the early propagation effect of MDPL, was designed to relax the necessity of balanced routings, still has exploitable leakages due to imbalanced routing of the dual-rail mask signal [20].

**State-of-the-Art.** Even though most of the proposed logic styles target an ASIC platform, at the early stage of their development some have been evaluated using FPGAs. Since the FPGA design tools miss the flexibility required for balanced routing, most of the efforts in this direction led to *duplication* schemes. They follow the idea of dual-rail concept without precharging the signals. This indeed leads to making a dual copy of a fully placed-and-routed circuit which – in theory – should consume the complement amount of energy that the original counterpart does. However, the problem arising by this scheme is due to non-dual glitches happening in original and dual part of the circuit, that causes the design to be vulnerable to the state-of-the-art attacks.

In this direction we can refer to [11], where – in addition to the dual of the circuit – precharge registers are inserted to the design. As the authors also showed, their design can be broken because of glitches. In another work [8] a specific configuration for FPGA Look-Up-Tables (LUT) is used to make the delay of the gates constant. Two global signals connected to all LUTs are also used to handle the precharge and evaluation of the gates. After developing the circuit by this configuration, the dual part of the circuit is inserted to the design. Unfortunately their design still has glitches when the combinatorial circuit has two or more logic depth.

As another example we should refer to DWDDL [36] which applies the duplication on a circuit realized by a kind of WDDL. There exists other works which make use of the duplication on the circuits built by FPGA Block RAMs (BRAM). For example, the authors of [34] introduced a precharge signal for each BRAM address in order to provide precharge and evaluation phases in this context. By certain inappropriate assumptions, e.g., ignoring the leakage associated to glitches occurring at the LUTs' output as long as they do not leave the slice, they developed a design methodology.

In the work of [28] the authors tried to realize WDDL on an Altera Stratix-II FPGA. They used DES as the target algorithm and have examined two different place-and-route (PAR) strategies as 1) the TRUE and FALSE signals of each gate are placed and routed as close as possible, and 2) all TRUE signals are placed close together (the same for all FALSE signals). The drawbacks of their work are 1) no attempt to avoid early propagation, and 2) no control over the delay between the rails of dual-rail signals.

In another work [15] a triple-rail logic has been designed for a Xilinx Spartan-3 FPGA. In order to avoid early propagation in both precharge and evaluation phases they utilized a generalized form of Muller C-element (the main element of asynchronous logic designs [22]). Although the goal of preventing early propagation is fulfilled, the number of toggles happening at internal signals is not balanced, i.e., they are different depending on the gate inputs' value. It is because 6 LUTs are used to build a triple-rail gate, and the toggles of output of these 6 LUTs are not balanced for all input cases. Therefore, it most likely leads to different power consumption patterns detectable by a DPA attack.

Other works e.g., BCDL [23] employed a global precharge signal, which must be connected to all gates. The gates do not evaluate their output till the global precharge goes e.g., LOW thereby preventing early propagation in both phases. But at the start of the precharge phase all gates simultaneously precharge their output leading to a much higher power consumption peak compared to the evaluation phase. Based on an Altera Stratix-II FPGA each BCDL gate is realized by two 5-input LUTs, but they have not taken care about the routing of dual-rail signals.

In a follow-up work [3] the global precharge of BCDL is removed and following the WDDL concept each gate is actualized by two 4-input LUTs. The style, which is called DPL_noEE, prevents the early propagation in the evaluation phase, but nothing is considered to deal with the start of the precharge phase. Similar to the case of BCDL, a Stratix-II FPGA has been used for practical evaluation of an AES encryption module under DPL_noEE scheme. According to the claims of the authors, the leakage could be reduced to half while no restrictions have been put into the placement and routing processes.

**Our Contribution.** In this work we first re-iterate the definition of *early propagation* and address the cases in the literature where this concept in the *precharge phase* has been mixed with the concept of *data-dependent time-of-precharge*. As an example we focus on DPL_noEE [3] and demonstrate that preventing early propagation in the evaluation phase might be not enough to reduce the associated leakage.

In the second part of this article we aim at designing a variant of WDDL for FPGA platforms without early propagation in both phases. With the help of the asynchronous design concept we achieve an architecture which follows the WDDL definitions, but its time-of-evaluation as well as its time-of-precharge is independent of the processed values. More importantly it propagates the evaluation wave (resp. the precharge wave) only when all inputs are evaluated (resp. precharged).

However, the imbalanced routings caused by uncontrolled FPGA design tools (placer and router) makes the power consumption of the circuit to be still related to its input value. Therefore, the next contribution of this article deals with balanced dual-rail routing in FPGAs. By means of a sophisticated routing algorithm as well as information we extract about the route delays, we are able to route the dual-rail signals with minimum imbalances. As a target design and platform we selected an AES S-box to be realized on a Xilinx Virtex-5 FPGA. Our experimental results show that both (more) balanced routings and avoiding early propagation significantly reduce the amount of leakage extractable by a power analysis attack.

## 2   WDDL and Early Propagation

Wave Dynamic Differential Logic (WDDL) was developed to avoid the necessity of a full-custom design tool. Similar to other precharge logic styles every gate operates in two phases, i.e., precharge and evaluation, which are controlled by the clock signal. However, as shown by Fig. 1(a) the signals are converted to dual-rail precharge form prior to the WDDL circuit, and the clock signal is not routed to the WDDL logic cells. Figure 1(a) shows the concept and the design of a WDDL AND/NAND gate. These gates can straightforwardly be actualized by FPGA LUTs, but the concept which is followed by DPL_noEE [3] is shown in Fig. 1(b). The idea is to prevent the evaluation as long as the inputs are not complete[1].

In order to deal with early propagation issue we first assume that though the delay of different dual rails are not the same, the delay of TRUE and FALSE signals of each dual rail are the same. In other words,

$$\text{Delay}(A_t) = \text{Delay}(A_f) > \text{Delay}(B_t) = \text{Delay}(B_f).$$

Figure 2 depicts the timing diagram of three different cases of the inputs for both WDDL and DPL_noEE AND/NAND gates. By comparing cases 1 and 3 ($\Delta te_1$ vs. $\Delta te_3$) we can conclude that the start of the evaluation phase of the WDDL gate depends on its input values. This issue, which is addressed in [30], is known as data-dependent time-of-evaluation. Examining cases 1 and 2 ($\Delta tp_1$ vs. $\Delta tp_2$) also shows the dependency of the start of the precharge phase to the gate input, which is referred as data-dependent time-of-precharge.

---

[1] Note that here we showed a simplified view of DPL_noEE, the authors of [3] considered both '0' and '1' as the precharge value of the gates in their design.

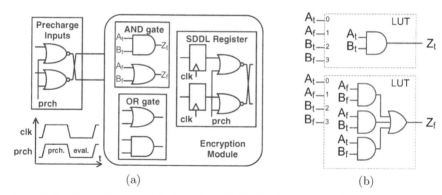

(a)                                    (b)

**Fig. 1.** (a) WDDL concept (taken from [32]), (b) DPL_noEE AND/NAND gate

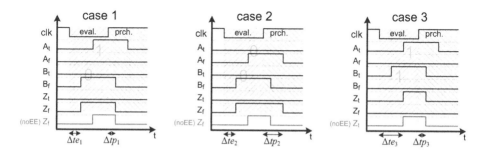

**Fig. 2.** Timing diagram of three input cases, WDDL and DPL_noEE AND/NAND gates

The situation for DPL_noEE is different as its time-of-evaluation is data independent. It also instantly goes to the precharge phase once one of its inputs goes to precharge. Although its time-of-precharge does not depend on its input value, it fits to the definition of *early propagation in precharge phase*. We should refer to [26], where it is stated as "According to our analysis, DRSL does not completely avoid an early propagation effect in the precharge phase". From this perspective DPL_noEE and DRSL [5] have the same specification. Both have data-independent time-of-evaluation and time-of-precharge, and both do not avoid early propagation in the precharge phase. On the contrary, the precharge phase of each iMDPL [26] gate starts when all its inputs are in precharge. Here the question is how critical it is to not avoid early propagation in precharge phase while it is data independent?

To answer this question we should highlight two points:

– In this setting – considering a combinatorial circuit, e.g., an AES S-box, made by several gates – the propagation of the precharge wave is faster than that of the evaluation wave. This results in a difference between the power consumption patterns of the evaluation and precharge phases as the dynamic

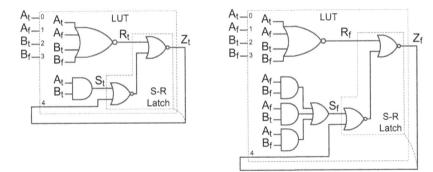

Fig. 3. AWDDL AND/NAND gate[2]

power consumption peak in the precharge phase is expected to be higher. The same is observed when a global precharge signal is used as in SABL [31].
– All the statements given above about the data independence of time-of-evaluation as well as of time-of-precharge are valid as long as the first assumption $\mathsf{Delay}(A_t) = \mathsf{Delay}(A_f)$ (resp. $\mathsf{Delay}(B_t) = \mathsf{Delay}(B_f)$) holds. If the routings are imbalanced and this assumption is not valid, both time-of-evaluation and time-of-precharge would be data dependent.

Therefore, in this setting we expect that the leakage in the precharge phase is more easily detectable compared to that in the evaluation phase since slight routing imbalances still would exist in practice. We deal with this issue in Section 4 when we demonstrate the corresponding practical results.

### 2.1 Avoiding Early Propagation in Both Phases

Our goal here is to develop a design similar to DPL_noEE but without early propagation in the precharge phase. So, we consider an asynchronous design for each WDDL gate. Following standard asynchronous design schemes one can make the flow table for the desired gate behavior, and realize it using e.g., S-R approach, where S-R latches are utilized. Figure 3 shows an exemplary design of our desired WDDL AND gate, which we call Asynchronous WDDL (AWDDL). Note that this design is only suitable for the FPGA platforms to realize the gate outputs by LUTs. It cannot be considered as an ASIC solution due to the unbalanced number of toggles happening on the internal signals. Since we use a modern Xilinx FPGA as the target platform, every gate is realized by two hard-coded LUT6 instances, i.e., to provide $Z_t$ and $Z_f$. Furthermore, every LUT output should be routed to its input, i.e., an external loop around every LUT is essential. Since the 6-input LUTs are the currently biggest LUT available in

---

[2] The mapping of the input and output signals to the LUT6 instances is of highly importance. Having the *Xilinx Libraries Guide for HDL Designs* [35] in mind, input I5 of the LUT6_2 should be connected to '1' thereby utilizing only O6 as the gate output. The LUT must be configured in a way that O5 always provides '0'.

FPGA architectures, unfortunately our proposed scheme cannot be extended to consider one more dual-rail mask input signal to realize a kind of iMDPL cell [26].

With respect to the asynchronous design concept and the S-R latches our design of AWDDL guarantees no early propagation in both precharge and evaluation phases. Due to the lack of space we omit presenting the figures for other AWDDL gates. However, the formulas for the set and reset signals $(S, R)$ of the conceptual S-R latch of 2-input gates are listed below. Similar to WDDL, the inverted gate is realized by swapping the dual-rail output signals. Below, $+$ stands for the logical OR operation.

$$\text{all gates}: \quad R_t = R_f = \overline{A_t + A_f + B_t + B_f}$$

$$\text{AND}: \begin{cases} S_t = A_t\,B_t \\ S_f = A_f\,B_f + A_f\,B_t + A_t\,B_f \end{cases}$$

$$\text{OR}: \begin{cases} S_t = A_t\,B_t + A_t\,B_f + A_f\,B_t \\ S_f = A_f\,B_f \end{cases}$$

$$\text{XOR}: \begin{cases} S_t = A_t\,B_f + A_f\,B_t \\ S_f = A_t\,B_t + A_f\,B_f \end{cases}$$

We should emphasize that we are aware of the problem of single-rail WDDL register cells mentioned in [19]. Our contribution focuses on the combinatorial part of the logic style, and as stated in [19], the master-slave register cells must be used to prevent the leakage of the registers.

## 3   Dual-Rail Routing

The problem of dual-rail routing is a challenge to perfectly balance the capacitance of both rails of a signal. Otherwise, transitions on these signals need a different amount of energy, which may make it possible to distinguish on which rail the transition happens. On the other hand, the capacitive imbalance causes the delay of the rails to be different. Then, the arrival time of a dual-rail input signal of a gate depends on its value. Since a gate without early propagation in both phases, e.g., our AWDDL, fires (resp. precharge) the output when all input signals arrived (resp. precharged), the time of evaluation (resp. precharge) of the gate will still depend on its inputs' value. This propagates through the whole combinatorial circuit, and makes the power consumption patterns different depending on the circuit input value.

Before we focus on our dual-rail routing approach, we should emphasize that, as stated in [32], a WDDL circuit – without an inversion – can be implemented using a divided approach, where first a network of TRUE signals, i.e., $Z_t$ output of all gates, are placed and routed. Then, the dual of the same network with the same routing is copied to make the FALSE signals. However, this approach is not applicable in case of our proposed AWDDL since each TRUE and FALSE part of every gate requires to have both TRUE and FALSE rails of all input signals. For

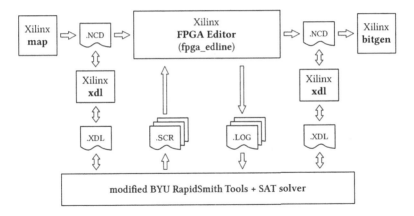

**Fig. 4.** Illustration of the custom workflow to process designs containing dual-rails requiring balanced routing

the same reason we cannot make use of the approach presented in [9] because their scheme is also based on complete separation of TRUE and FALSE networks. Therefore, we need to develop a mechanism capable of routing dual-rail signals as balanced as possible. While it is unlikely to achieve a perfectly balanced routing due to the given structure of the FPGA, it is likely to reduce the leakage compared to the default routing of the FPGA standard tools. We tried to achieve this by developing a customized router which is presented hereafter.

### 3.1 Customized Router

As stated before, our target is a Xilinx Virtex-5 FPGA; therefore, we could make use of the RapidSmith library [14]. In order to route balanced dual-rails we implemented a customized local router. It utilizes the Xilinx Design Language (XDL) and is based on a custom workflow as depicted in Fig. 4. Up to the end of mapping, the design is processed by the default Xilinx ISE tools. Note that for the case of Virtex-5 map performs the placement as well. The only modifications we made up to this step are i) to put all elements requiring balanced routing into a closed group which is area constrained, ii) to keep the input PIN positions of the LUTs realizing the AWDDL gates locked, and iii) to put LUTs of each AWDDL gate into the same slice using the LUTs (A, B) or (C, D) for $(Z_t, Z_f)$ respectively.

After mapping, the intermediate file is processed by our customized router. The first step is to extract all dual-rail connections (source, destination) from the given data structure. This is done by using a simple naming scheme to detect corresponding nets within the XDL file. The next step is to find a set of possible routings for each of the dual-rail connections. To do so, for each possible output of a LUT (e.g., A and AMUX), all possible exit nodes of the adjacent switch box are used once to find a possible route. This idea is illustrated in Fig. 5. The routing itself for each of these candidates uses a maze router with a priority

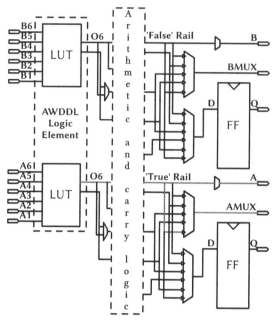 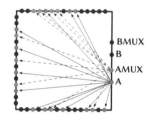

(a) Each pair of LUTs hold a single AWDDL logic element. Hence, a maximum of two AWDDL gates per slice is possible.

(b) A simplified representation of a switch box. Blue and red dots represent PIPs that may be used as exit node.

**Fig. 5.** Basic idea how to create multiple routing candidates

queuing, favoring those nodes with the least Manhattan distance. This process is executed for both connections of a dual-rail to finally make a set of possible routings for each of the dual-rail connections.

Since extracting the capacitance of each route is not feasible, we had to consider other metrics to give priorities to the different routings. They include:

- the signal delays, extracted using the command line tool `fpga_edline` (due to the phenomena expressed above),
- the number of switch boxes the signal passes (due to their significant role in amount of dynamic energy consumption),
- the number of Programmable Interconnect Points (PIP), i.e., internal connections of the switch boxes, and
- the type of the wire, e.g., `long`, `pent`, and `double`.

For each of the routing possibilities, the above mentioned properties are extracted. Properties not dependent on the delay are easily extracted by their XDL representation. The delay of each single route must be extracted using a script file (`.scr`) that controls `fpga_edline`. An example for a script is given below:

```
open design ncdfileName.ncf pcffileName.pcf
setattr main edit-mode Read-Only
setattr main auto_load_delays true
select netName
delay
exit
exit³
```

The result of running this script is a log file (.log) that contains the delay information of every route within that net. It is therefore required to parse the log files and extract the only valid delay for the route made (see Fig. 4). Note that for each single route the corresponding NCD file must be generated. Then, the above script and process should be run to extract the associated delay.

Here we make the restrictions. Based on the extracted information (as explained above) we restrict the dual-rail routes based on a threshold for delay of each route, for the difference between delay of the rails, for the number of switch boxes each route passes, for the number of PIPs, and etc. As the last step, as given below, the output is converted into a Boolean satisfiability (SAT) problem to select a conflict-free routing. If the problem is satisfiable, the conflict-free setting is put together and written to a new XDL file. All the previously routed nets are then locked, while the remaining unrouted nets are auto-routed using `fpga_edline`.

### 3.2  Representing Routing as SAT

Let $n$ denote the number of dual-rail connections that the router should make. We first make a collection $\mathbb{S} = \{S^1, S^2, \ldots, S^n\}$, where $S^{i \in \{1, \ldots, n\}}$ represents a set of possible routing candidates $\{s_1^i, s_2^i, \ldots, s_{n_i}^i\}$ for the dual-rail connection $i$.

Accordingly we define Boolean variables $x_j^i$ indicating whether the dual-route $s_j^i$ is selected. Clearly, one must select exactly one candidate $s_j^i$ from each set $S^i$ to achieve a complete routing. This requirement can be encoded using the following formula [12]:

$$\text{AtLeastOne}(S^i) = \bigvee_{j=1}^{n} x_j^i,$$

$$\text{AtMostOne}(S^i) = \bigwedge_{j=1}^{n-1} \bigwedge_{k=j+1}^{n} (\neg x_j^i \vee \neg x_k^i),$$

$$\text{ExactlyOne}(S^i) = \text{AtLeastOne}(S^i) \wedge \text{AtMostOne}(S^i).$$

Therefore, $\text{ExactlyOne}(S^i) = \text{TRUE}$ for $\forall\, i \in \{1, \ldots, n\}$ are added as clauses to the SAT.

Another issue is related to the loop which must be made at every LUT. As stated in Section 2.1, the output of the LUT must be presented as one of its

---

[3] Using the exit command twice is required to properly exit the command-driven mode in addition to gracefully terminate the tool.

inputs to realize the internal S-R latch. For simplicity and consistency we tried to make the same loop at every LUT which is used as AWDDL gate. To achieve this we define collection $\mathbb{S}^{\star} = \{S^{\star 1}, S^{\star 2}, \ldots, S^{\star l}\}$, where $l$ denotes the number of possible dual-rail loop routings, and $S^{\star i \in \{1,\ldots,l\}}$ a set of the same dual-rail loop routing for all AWDDL gates of the design, i.e., $\{s_1^{\star i}, \ldots, s_m^{\star i}\}$, where $m$ stands for the number of AWDDL gates in the design. Therefore, only one of these sets amongst collection $\mathbb{S}^{\star}$ must be selected. Accordingly we define Boolean variables $x_j^{\star i}$ due to the selection of the routing $s_j^{\star i}$. Moreover, a set of $l$ commander-variables $C = \{c_1, \ldots, c_l\}$ are defined indicating the selection of $S^{\star 1}, \ldots, S^{\star l}$.

In order to consider the commander-variables into the SAT, one needs to include ExactlyOne($C$) = TRUE to make sure that only one loop set is selected. Moreover, the following formula must be also considered to prevent a selection of a mixture of different loop sets:

$$\text{AllFalse}(S^{\star i}) = c_i \vee \bigwedge_{j=1}^{m} \neg x_j^{\star i} \quad \text{AllTrue}(S^{\star i}) = \neg c_i \vee \bigwedge_{j=1}^{m} x_j^{\star i}.$$

Therefore, AllFalse($S^{\star i}$) = TRUE and AllTrue($S^{\star i}$) = TRUE for $\forall i \in \{1, \ldots, l\}$ are added to the SAT.

We should emphasize that two slices are connected to the same switch box, and we use either (A, B) or (C, D) LUTs to realize each AWDDL gate. Since the loop routing possibilities of these cases are different, we have to consider four different $\mathbb{S}^{\star}$ collections (and four different commander-variable set $C$ respectively) to cover all these cases.

However, the above illustrated expressions do not reflect possible routing conflicts yet. The conflicts must also be encoded by doing a pairwise comparison of all possible routing candidates, and the corresponding clauses must be added to the SAT. Suppose that $x_j^i$ and $x_{j'}^{i'}$ are corresponding Boolean variables of two conflicting routings $s_j^i$ and $s_{j'}^{i' \neq i}$. So, $\neg x_j^i \vee \neg x_{j'}^{i'}$ = TRUE must be added to the SAT. This should be done for all possible pairwise conflicting routings (extracted by means of RapidSmith) including those which can be between collections $\mathbb{S}$ and $\mathbb{S}^{\star}$. This encoding can be realized in $\mathcal{O}(n^2)$. It should be noted that if the SAT solver fails to find a conflict-free solution, the restrictions – explained at the end of Section 3.1 – to make collections $\mathbb{S}$ and $\mathbb{S}^{\star}$ should be relaxed and the process should be repeated.

The runtime of the whole process is determined by the slow file conversion (Xilinx ISE tools) from NCD to XDL and vice-versa. This step needs to be executed for each delay extraction and though being massively parallelized using 16 cores (siblings), still takes around 6 hours for a design including $m = 122$ AWDDL gates and 8 additional LUTs for the single-to-dual rail conversion, where $n = 606$ dual-rail connections should be made. In contrast, SAT encoding typically requires about 20 minutes and solving less than a minute using CryptoMiniSat 2.9.4 [1].

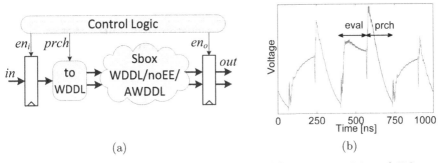

(a)                                    (b)

**Fig. 6.** (a) The exemplary design block diagram, (b) Superimposition of 256 mean traces of the WDDL design

## 4 Practical Investigations

In order to examine the effectiveness of our proposed schemes we made an exemplary design which in addition to surrounding and control logics consists in an AES S-box. We have taken the area-optimized S-box by Canright [4], and manually instantiated all the logic by 2-input AWDDL gates (in sum 122). A block diagram of the design is shown by Fig. 6(a). The Virtex-5 FPGA (XC5VLX50) of the side-channel evaluation platform SASEBO-GII [2], on which our target design is embedded, receives an input byte from the PC (via a controlling FPGA) and stores it into the input register by controlling $en_i$ signal. At a certain clock cycle, the control logic disables $prch$ signal, and the "to WDDL" conversion unit (the same scheme shown in the left part of Fig. 1(a)) propagates the dual-rail input to the AWDDL AES S-box thereby initializing the evaluation phase. In the next half of the clock cycle the control logic enables $prch$ signal and the precharge phase is started. In a common WDDL circuit $en_o$ should be active at the start of the precharge phase in order to store the output of the combinatorial circuit (here the AES S-box). However, since we aim at evaluating only the leakage associated to the combinatorial circuit, we must exclude the leakage of the output register (see [19]). Therefore, the control logic does not enable $en_o$ signal and the register does not store the S-box output[4]. During these two (evaluation and precharge) phases the power consumption of the Virtex-5 FPGA is measured using a LeCroy WaveRunner HRO 66Zi oscilloscope at the sampling rate of 1GS/s while the design runs at a clock frequency of 3 MHz.

At the first step, we defined an area in the target FPGA for the placement of AWDDL gates, and as stated before we constrained the placer to assign two LUTs of the same slice to each AWDDL gate. At this stage we did not apply our customized router and used the default ISE routing tools. For the sake of similarity and fair comparison, we made also a WDDL and DPL_noEE compatible version of the fully placed-and-routed AWDDL design. This has been done by editing the XDL file (of the AWDDL design) and only modifying the

---

[4] In order to check the correct functionality of the circuit, $en_o$ signal becomes active by the control logic in another clock cycle which is not covered by the measured power traces.

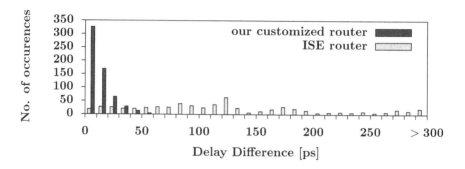

**Fig. 7.** Histogram of the delay difference of all dual-rail routes of AWDDL designs

content of the LUTs[5]. So, the placement and routing of all these three designs are the same allowing for a fair comparison. As the fourth design we used our customized router in order to route the AWDDL design while its placement has not been altered.

In sum we evaluated four design profiles as:

1. WDDL AES S-box routed by ISE,
2. DPL_noEE AES S-box, the same placement and routing as profile 1,
3. AWDDL AES S-box, the same placement and routing as profile 1,
4. AWDDL AES S-box, the same placement as profile 1, but routed by our customized router.

As listed in Section 3.1, we have considered many different criteria to make routing collections $\mathbb{S}$ and $\mathbb{S}^*$. The best result is achieved by considering a delay difference below 60 ps, the realization of identical feedback loops, and by considering minimum number of switch boxes and PIPs in each route. It should also be mentioned that we used the same wire type for both rails of a signal and prohibited to use **long** wires.

In order to compare the result of our routing with that of ISE, we provided two histograms illustrating the difference between the delay of each dual-rail signal in the AWDDL S-box circuit. Although it is not possible to find dual-rail routes with zero delay difference for all 606 dual-rail connections, the histograms shown in Fig. 7 indicate the effectiveness of our approach. Nevertheless, it is worth to mention that the average and the worst delay difference in case of our router are 11.7 ps and 58 ps respectively. These numbers are incomparable to those obtained by the ISE router as 125 ps and 520 ps respectively.

To evaluate and fairly compare the side-channel leakage of our target designs we applied the information theoretic (IT) analysis of [29] as it has been used for the same purpose e.g., in [16]. So, we collected 512,000 traces for each target design, i.e., 2000 traces for each S-box input value. By estimating the mean and

---

[5] Although it is possible to realize each WDDL as well as DPL_noEE gate by a 5-to-2 LUT, we made the two 6-to-1 LUT version to keep it as similar as the AWDDL one and to follow the same design architecture given in [3].

variance of the traces for each S-box input we obtained 256 Gaussian distributions at each sample point (256 mean traces of the WDDL design are shown by Fig. 6(b) where evaluation and precharge phases are marked). It allows us to estimate the probability distribution of the leakages essential in the IT analysis. Here we should emphasize two points:

- There is no source of randomness in our exemplary designs, and electrical noise – well modeled by Gaussian [17] – is the only noise source in our measured traces. Therefore, ignoring the higher statistical moments in probability estimations – as in Gaussian – does not cause any information loss.
- The AES S-box circuit operates in precharge-evaluation mode, and in contrast to a CMOS combinatorial circuit its leakage does not depend on two consecutive inputs (input transitions). Therefore, our selection of estimating the probabilities based on the S-box input is a valid choice (the same is given in [16]).

Performing the IT analysis using the mean and variance traces of each of our target designs led to the mutual information curves presented by Fig. 8. As expected, the WDDL design – due to its data-dependent time-of-evaluation and time-of-precharge – has the highest leakage. Interestingly the DPL_noEE and the AWDDL designs have relatively the same amount of leakage in evaluation phase as they operate the same in this phase. However, DPL_noEE has a higher leakage in the precharge phase. It indeed confirms our claim in Section 2 that due to the early propagation of DPL_noEE in the precharge phase, in presence of imbalanced routings its leakage should be more easily detectable compared to that in the evaluation phase.

A comparison between the result of the AWDDL designs (routed by ISE vs. routed by our customized router) clearly shows the effectiveness of our developed router to reduce the information leakage. We should stress again that except the LUTs' configuration all details and specification of the first three designs are the same, that allowed us to fairly compare these logic styles. The same holds for the two AWDDL designs which only differ in the routing of the AES S-box circuit.

Independent of the attack strategy, IT analysis captures the amount of information available to the worst-case adversary. In order to quantify the data complexity (the number of required traces) of attacks on our target designs, we performed first-order profiling moments-correlating DPA [21]. Indeed, for each design profile we used a set of 100,000 profiling traces to estimate first-order moments, and made use of them as power models to perform a CPA attack on another set of 100,000 traces. The corresponding results are shown by Fig. 9. Thanks to the metric feature of moments-correlating DPA, we can directly conclude the following ratios between the data complexity of the attack on different profiles:

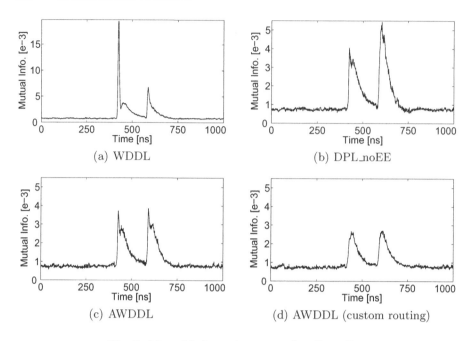

(a) WDDL

(b) DPL_noEE

(c) AWDDL

(d) AWDDL (custom routing)

**Fig. 8.** Mutual information curves for all profiles

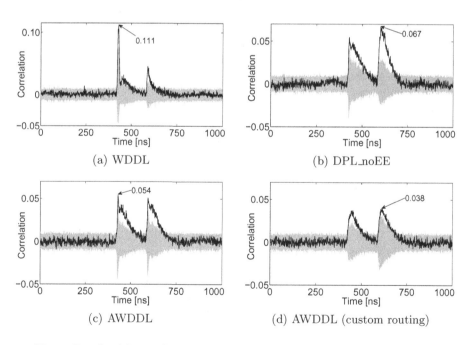

(a) WDDL

(b) DPL_noEE

(c) AWDDL

(d) AWDDL (custom routing)

**Fig. 9.** Result of first-order profiling moments-correlating DPA on all profiles

- DPL_noEE versus WDDL: $\left(\frac{0.111}{0.067}\right)^2 = 2.7$,
- AWDDL versus DPL_noEE: $\left(\frac{0.067}{0.054}\right)^2 = 1.5$,
- AWDDL (custom routing) versus AWDDL: $\left(\frac{0.054}{0.038}\right)^2 = 2.0$.

As a side note, though the leakage extractable from our AWDDL design is mitigated, it is not a perfect solution to prevent a key-recovery attack. Therefore – as it is well known – DPA-resistant logic styles, e.g., AWDDL, should be combined with other countermeasure such as algorithmic masking which usually cannot prevent DPA attacks when implemented in hardware [18].

## 5  Conclusions

In this work we have shown how to design WDDL gates for FPGA platforms with independent time-of-evaluation and time-of-precharge. This, achieved by realizing a latch inside every LUT by means of a feedback loop, could guarantee the disappearance of early propagation in both evaluation and precharge phases. Our practical investigations confirm that by using our designed AWDDL style the level of security improves when compared to classical WDDL or to its main competitor DPL_noEE of [3]. However, routing imbalances still impose a threat to the security of dual-rail precharge logic. Therefore, as the second contribution of this work we developed a customized tool to reduce this imbalance by selecting the most similar routes for the signals of a dual-rail connection. This approach, whose effectiveness has been demonstrated using our proposed logic style, could also be applied to similar logic styles or other applications requiring balanced routes, e.g., TRNGs and PUFs. It is noteworthy to mention that applying our customized router does not cause any area overhead. In fact, it only changes the way the routing resources (PIPs) are configured.

The only available source for delay of the signal routes is the ISE tool. Therefore, the effectiveness of a customized router relies on the conformity of ISE reports and the underlying FPGA chip. Due to the process variation as well as publicly unknown architecture of the FPGAs these numbers might be different from chip to chip or (even slightly) different to reality. Hence, as a future work, we plan to develop a mechanism to practically examine the differential delay as well as the power consumption of the dual-rail routings based on the target FPGA chip, where the design is supposed to be realized.

**Acknowledgment.** The authors would like to thank Ali Ahari, from Sharif University of Technology (Tehran, Iran), for useful discussions on routing features of RapidSmith.

# References

1. CryptoMiniSat. Available as download here,
   https://gforge.inria.fr/frs/?group_id=1992
2. Side-channel Attack Standard Evaluation Board (SASEBO). Further information
   are available via, http://www.morita-tech.co.jp/SASEBO/en/index.html
3. Bhasin, S., Guilley, S., Flament, F., Selmane, N., Danger, J.-L.: Countering early
   evaluation: an approach towards robust dual-rail precharge logic. In: WESS 2010,
   p. 6. ACM (2010)
4. Canright, D.: A Very Compact S-Box for AES. In: Rao, J.R., Sunar, B. (eds.)
   CHES 2005. LNCS, vol. 3659, pp. 441–455. Springer, Heidelberg (2005)
5. Chen, Z., Zhou, Y.: Dual-Rail Random Switching Logic: A Countermeasure to Reduce Side Channel Leakage. In: Goubin, L., Matsui, M. (eds.) CHES 2006. LNCS,
   vol. 4249, pp. 242–254. Springer, Heidelberg (2006)
6. Guilley, S., Hoogvorst, P., Mathieu, Y., Pacalet, R.: The "Backend Duplication"
   Method. In: Rao, J.R., Sunar, B. (eds.) CHES 2005. LNCS, vol. 3659, pp. 383–397.
   Springer, Heidelberg (2005)
7. Güneysu, T., Moradi, A.: Generic Side-Channel Countermeasures for Reconfigurable Devices. In: Preneel, B., Takagi, T. (eds.) CHES 2011. LNCS, vol. 6917,
   pp. 33–48. Springer, Heidelberg (2011)
8. He, W., de la Torre, E., Riesgo, T.: A Precharge-Absorbed DPL Logic for Reducing Early Propagation Effects on FPGA Implementations. In: ReConFig 2011,
   pp. 217–222. IEEE Computer Society (2011)
9. He, W., Otero, A., de la Torre, E., Riesgo, T.: Automatic generation of identical
   routing pairs for FPGA implemented DPL logic. In: ReConFig 2012, pp. 1–6. IEEE
   (2012)
10. Herbst, C., Oswald, E., Mangard, S.: An AES Smart Card Implementation Resis-
    tant to Power Analysis Attacks. In: Zhou, J., Yung, M., Bao, F. (eds.) ACNS 2006.
    LNCS, vol. 3989, pp. 239–252. Springer, Heidelberg (2006)
11. Kaps, J.-P., Velegalati, R.: DPA Resistant AES on FPGA Using Partial DDL. In:
    FCCM 2010, pp. 273–280. IEEE Computer Society (2010)
12. Klieber, W., Kwon, G.: Efficient CNF Encoding for Selecting 1 from N Objects.
    In: Workshop on Constraints in Formal Verification - CFV (2007)
13. Kocher, P.C., Jaffe, J., Jun, B.: Differential Power Analysis. In: Wiener, M. (ed.)
    CRYPTO 1999. LNCS, vol. 1666, pp. 388–397. Springer, Heidelberg (1999)
14. Lavin, C., Padilla, M., Lamprecht, J., Lundrigan, P., Nelson, B., Hutchings, B.,
    Wirthlin, M.: RapidSmith – A Library for Low-level Manipulation of Partially
    Placed-and-Routed FPGA Designs. Technical report, Brigham Young University
    (September 2012)
15. Lomné, V., Maurine, P., Torres, L., Robert, M., Soares, R., Calazans, N.: Evalua-
    tion on FPGA of triple rail logic robustness against DPA and DEMA. In: DATE
    2009, pp. 634–639. IEEE (2009)
16. Macé, F., Standaert, F.-X., Quisquater, J.-J.: Information Theoretic Evaluation of
    Side-Channel Resistant Logic Styles. In: Paillier, P., Verbauwhede, I. (eds.) CHES
    2007. LNCS, vol. 4727, pp. 427–442. Springer, Heidelberg (2007)
17. Mangard, S., Oswald, E., Popp, T.: Power Analysis Attacks: Revealing the Secrets
    of Smart Cards. Springer (2007)
18. Mangard, S., Pramstaller, N., Oswald, E.: Successfully Attacking Masked AES
    Hardware Implementations. In: Rao, J.R., Sunar, B. (eds.) CHES 2005. LNCS,
    vol. 3659, pp. 157–171. Springer, Heidelberg (2005)

19. Moradi, A., Eisenbarth, T., Poschmann, A., Paar, C.: Power Analysis of Single-Rail Storage Elements as Used in MDPL. In: Lee, D., Hong, S. (eds.) ICISC 2009. LNCS, vol. 5984, pp. 146–160. Springer, Heidelberg (2010)

20. Moradi, A., Kirschbaum, M., Eisenbarth, T., Paar, C.: Masked Dual-Rail Precharge Logic Encounters State-of-the-Art Power Analysis Methods. IEEE Trans. VLSI Syst. 20(9), 1578–1589 (2012)

21. Moradi, A., Standaert, F.-X.: Moments-Correlating DPA. Cryptology ePrint Archive, Report 2014/409 (2014), http://eprint.iacr.org/

22. Muller, D.E., Bartky, W.S.: A Theory of Asynchronous Circuits. Report no. 78 at University of Illinois at Urbana-Champaign. Dept. of Computer Science (1959)

23. Nassar, M., Bhasin, S., Danger, J.-L., Duc, G., Guilley, S.: BCDL: A high speed balanced DPL for FPGA with global precharge and no early evaluation. In: DATE 2010, pp. 849–854. IEEE (2010)

24. Nikova, S., Rijmen, V., Schläffer, M.: Secure Hardware Implementation of Nonlinear Functions in the Presence of Glitches. J. Cryptology 24(2), 292–321 (2011)

25. Oswald, E., Mangard, S., Pramstaller, N., Rijmen, V.: A Side-Channel Analysis Resistant Description of the AES S-Box. In: Gilbert, H., Handschuh, H. (eds.) FSE 2005. LNCS, vol. 3557, pp. 413–423. Springer, Heidelberg (2005)

26. Popp, T., Kirschbaum, M., Zefferer, T., Mangard, S.: Evaluation of the Masked Logic Style MDPL on a Prototype Chip. In: Paillier, P., Verbauwhede, I. (eds.) CHES 2007. LNCS, vol. 4727, pp. 81–94. Springer, Heidelberg (2007)

27. Popp, T., Mangard, S.: Masked Dual-Rail Pre-charge Logic: DPA-Resistance Without Routing Constraints. In: Rao, J.R., Sunar, B. (eds.) CHES 2005. LNCS, vol. 3659, pp. 172–186. Springer, Heidelberg (2005)

28. Sauvage, L., Nassar, M., Guilley, S., Flament, F., Danger, J.-L., Mathieu, Y.: DPL on Stratix II FPGA: What to Expect? In: ReConFig 2009, pp. 243–248. IEEE Computer Society (2009)

29. Standaert, F.-X., Malkin, T., Yung, M.: A Unified Framework for the Analysis of Side-Channel Key Recovery Attacks. In: Joux, A. (ed.) EUROCRYPT 2009. LNCS, vol. 5479, pp. 443–461. Springer, Heidelberg (2009)

30. Suzuki, D., Saeki, M.: Security Evaluation of DPA Countermeasures Using Dual-Rail Pre-charge Logic Style. In: Goubin, L., Matsui, M. (eds.) CHES 2006. LNCS, vol. 4249, pp. 255–269. Springer, Heidelberg (2006)

31. Tiri, K., Akmal, M., Verbauwhede, I.: A dynamic and differential CMOS logic with signal independent power consumption to withstand differential power analysis on smart cards. In: Solid-State Circuits Conference - ESSCIRC 2002, pp. 403–406 (2002)

32. Tiri, K., Verbauwhede, I.: A Logic Level Design Methodology for a Secure DPA Resistant ASIC or FPGA Implementation. In: DATE 2004, pp. 246–251. IEEE Computer Society (2004)

33. Tiri, K., Verbauwhede, I.: Place and Route for Secure Standard Cell Design. In: CARDIS 2004, pp. 143–158. Kluwer (2004)

34. Velegalati, R., Kaps, J.-P.: Techniques to enable the use of Block RAMs on FPGAS with Dynamic and Differential Logic. In: ICECS 2010, pp. 1244–1247. IEEE (2010)

35. Xilinx. Virtex-5 Libraries Guide for HDL Designs. Available via (April 2012), http://www.xilinx.com/support/documentation/sw_manuals/xilinx14_1/virtex5_hdl.pdf

36. Yu, P., Schaumont, P.: Secure FPGA circuits using controlled placement and routing. In: CODES+ISSS 2007, pp. 45–50. ACM (2007)

# Author Index